Richard Ollard was born and broug[...] [...] Dragon School, Oxford, he won a s[...] in Classics, winning an Exhibition to New College, Oxford. After three years' war service he read History and was appointed a Lecturer in History and English at the Royal Naval College, Greenwich. Since 1960 he has been an editor at Collins, the publishers. His other books are *The Escape of Charles II* (1966) and *Man of War: Sir Robert Holmes and the Restoration Navy* (1969). Richard Ollard is married and has three children.

PEPYS

a biography by Richard Ollard

Pan Books London and Sydney

First published in Great Britain 1974 by Hodder and Stoughton
This edition published 1977 by Pan Books Ltd, Cavaye Place,
London SW10 9PG
© Richard Ollard 1974
ISBN 0 330 25010 8
Printed and bound in Great Britain by
Richard Clay (The Chaucer Press) Ltd, Bungay, Suffolk

TO PETER AND CHRISTOPHER

Acknowledgments

The debts incurred in writing this book are many. For permission to quote from manuscripts in their possession I wish to thank the Master and Fellows of Magdalene College, Cambridge, the Curators of the Bodleian Library, the Warden and Fellows of All Souls College, Oxford, the Marquess of Bath, and the Trustees of the National Maritime Museum. To the librarians and archivists who have made this material available to me I wish to record my gratitude. Those who have been fortunate enough to work in Duke Humfrey will know that the magic of the room is matched by the speed, efficiency and helpfulness of its staff. Without the privileges that the London Library extends to its members, writing this book would have been impossible.

For information and advice as to pictures I am particularly grateful to Sir Oliver Millar, the Keeper of the Queen's Pictures, Mr. David Piper, Director of the Ashmolean and to Mr. E. H. H. Archibald of the National Maritime Museum. I should also like to thank Messrs. Bell & Sons for their kind permission to reproduce the two maps of London in Pepys's time drawn by the late T. F. Reddaway for their new edition of the Diary.

Pepys is a subject of such extraordinary variety and richness that it would be difficult for me to express how and why in writing and thinking about him I have felt myself indebted to particular teachers, authors, scholars, friends (so often the four capacities are combined). To drop the names of the well-known, to call the roll of men whose memory lives chiefly in the minds of their pupils, would be either presumptuous or inept. No disclosure of such liabilities could be complete, yet to say nothing would have been ungrateful.

Associated with the institutions I have mentioned are people who have made research more than usually pleasurable. At Magdalene the Master and Mr. Richard Martineau both of whom taught me at school have been kindness itself: in the Pepys Library Dr. Robert Latham, Mr. Derek Pepys Whiteley and the late Dr. R. W. Ladborough have made every visit seem too short. To Dr. Latham indeed, a Pepysian scholar unrivalled in eminence as in generosity, I owe a large debt. To Professor Christopher Lloyd who read my typescript and improved it by his criticism I am most grateful.

There are debts too of a more obvious kind. Where would any student of Pepys be without the scholarship of the late J. R. Tanner, or without the transcriptions of Professor Matthews and the late Edwin Chappell? To the publications of the Navy Records Society as to the *Mariner's Mirror*, the journal of the Society for Nautical Research, anyone who writes on the seventeenth-century navy will be under many obligations. If I do not list the general works on the period it is not because I have not many reasons to be grateful to them. But there are several excellent bibliographies and I can see no purpose in listing all the works I have read.

Contents

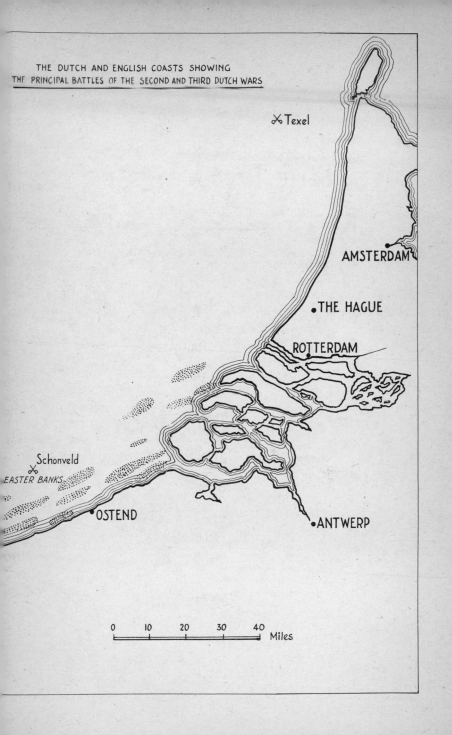

THE DUTCH AND ENGLISH COASTS SHOWING
THE PRINCIPAL BATTLES OF THE SECOND AND THIRD DUTCH WARS

⚔ Texel

• AMSTERDAM

• THE HAGUE

• ROTTERDAM

Schonveld
⚔
EASTER BANKS

• OSTEND

• ANTWERP

0   10   20   30   40
|——|——|——|——|——| Miles

Line Drawings

A Note on Dates and References

All dates given in this book follow the accepted compromise between the old and the new style, i.e. the year begins on January 1st, not March 25th, but the month date goes by the English calendar, then ten days behind that in general use abroad.

In citing references I have been more eclectic. Where my source is obvious from the context, easily accessible in print and precisely identifiable by use of an index, e.g. an entry in the Diary describing the Fire of London, I have not cited it. But where these conditions are not satisfied, e.g. an expression of opinion or emotion lacking any particular (and thus identifiable) application, I have. Unpublished sources are, of course, cited in full. I have further assumed that anyone in search of an authority will be acquainted with the printed materials, all admirably edited and indexed, of which I have given the short title in the left-hand column of the list given on pages 343–4.

Lastly, the facts and incidents of Pepys's career up to the end of his official career in the spring of 1689 are so amply documented in Sir Arthur Bryant's three volumes, *The Man in the Making* (1933), *The Years of Peril* (1935) and *The Saviour of the Navy* (1938) that it seems pointless to duplicate the clear and thorough scholarly apparatus there provided. Incorporating not only the fruits of the author's own researches, but the notes that Wheatley and, after him, Tanner, the doyen of Pepysian scholars, had each collected towards a biography, its signposts to the mass of material that confronts the student are invaluable. If I have here and there corrected a slip, I have kept in mind M. de Turenne's maxim: 'He that has made no mistakes has made little war.'

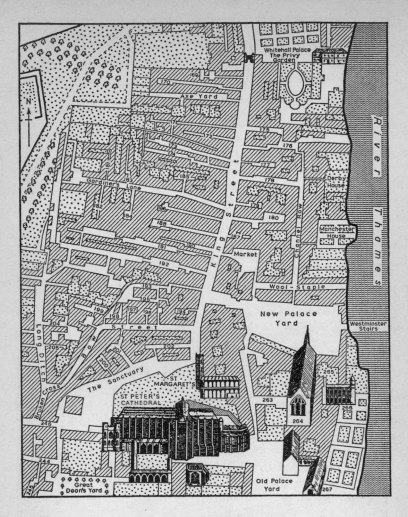

Westminster: Axe Yard and King Street.
Map prepared by the late Professor T. F. Reddaway from R. Morden and P. Lea, 'A Prospect of London and Westminster', 1682. Reproduced by permission of Bell & Sons.

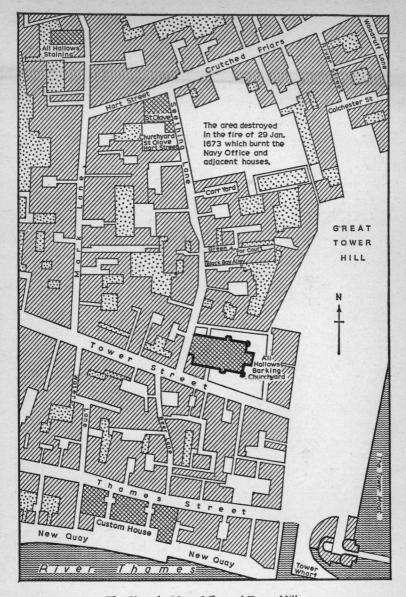

The City: the Navy Office and Tower Hill.
Map prepared by the late Professor T. F. Reddaway from J. Ogilby and W. Morgan,
'A Large and Accurate Map of the City of London', 1677. Reproduced by permission of
Bell & Sons.

I

Beginnings

———

To attempt a life of Samuel Pepys is to defy a prudent limitation of ends to means. Several lifetimes would not suffice to master all the evidence that could reasonably be described as relevant. And Pepys's mind is so many-sided, his curiosity so rich, his achievements so substantial and so far-reaching, his friendships so wide and so tenacious, his tastes so various, his appetites so keen, his own consciousness so present to his mind, so searchingly investigated and so carefully recorded, that a biographer who felt himself competent to the task would himself be something of a prodigy. But books must have readers as well as writers; and the reader who wants a life of this astonishing man may, like Pepys's contemporary, Andrew Marvell, not have world enough and time for the coyness of too nice a conscience.

It is the secret of Pepys's fascination that one never gets to the end of him. The contrasts, not to say contradictions, of his character, emotions, tastes, opinions, conduct and circumstances challenge our understanding. Partly, no doubt, they can be explained by his extraordinary capacity for absorbing experience and making it nourish the consciousness that neither age nor disease could blunt or blur. Spiritually and mentally his arteries never hardened; the process of growing up did not, as with most people, end with the coming of middle age. His ear for the music of life always kept him in time; he could make a harmony of the trials and infirmities of old age as he had of the hot idleness of youth and the rush-hour traffic of middle age.

Partly the sturdy intellectual honesty of the diarist who wanted to see himself as he really was forced him to recognise the complexity of questions that most men in most ages never so much as ask themselves. But when all is said and done it is the very extent of our knowledge that shows us the range of our ignorance. We know more about Pepys than about any other individual Englishman of his time, far more than we know about Charles II or Clarendon, Sir Isaac Newton or Sir Christopher Wren, James II or Shaftesbury, to name but a few of the eminent contemporaries to whom he was more or less well known. Luckily for us he was one of the most observant and articulate men who ever lived; and by further good fortune his life covered the most exciting and eventful period of English history. And though he is that history's most vivid single witness (the account in the Diary of the Fire of London alone is one of the masterpieces of reporting in our language) he was by no means a spectator standing apart from the life of his time. He was at different times a Member of Parliament, a Fellow and President of the Royal Society, and, for nearly all his working life, both a confidential servant of men who were making policy and an expert government official. The Royal Navy owes more to him, is more his handiwork, than that of any other possible claimant from King Alfred downward. The passion for professionalism, the insistence on administrative discipline that his work for the navy exemplified in itself exerted a powerful creative influence on the civil service. Sea power and efficient bureaucracy were the means that had enabled the Dutch to overhaul and surpass the imperial predominance of the Spaniards and the Portuguese. In Pepys's early manhood England had challenged (he thought rashly) the Dutch title to the world championship. If it were to be made good, the same simple formula was required. Pepys more than any man of his time supplied it. In the words of J. R. Tanner, the great scholar, who has put all students of Pepys in his debt, he was 'one of the best officials England ever had'.[1]

It is easy to underestimate the historical importance of Pepys. We are too familiar with the randy bewigged figure whose name, as a symbol of a slightly *risqué* conviviality, has been appropriated by this wine-shipper or that restaurant. An irresistible air of bedroom farce clings to him, partly deriving from the candour of the Diary, partly from the bawdiness of Restoration comedy that gives so much life and colour to our picture of the age. As Mr. Tattle scampers across the stage, baulked of the seduction of Miss Prue by an unwelcome intrusion, we are reminded of the furtive and futile lecheries so vivaciously recorded by Pepys and for the moment identify the great civil servant with a character described by his creator as a half-witted Beau. It is not that we need to believe that great men have no sex life, a feat of historical credulity possible to few: it is that greatness seems incompatible with consciously making an ass of oneself. And yet Pepys was — and did.

To have written the Diary clearly sets him apart from the ordinary run of humanity which it reflects and judges with such piercing discernment. Most men can brace themselves to the shock of self-knowledge provided that they can look away again quickly. Moral and intellectual courage of a high order is required for the sustained, relentless, clinical examination of the private world of thoughts and emotions as well as the half public one of actions and words. Why did Pepys keep his Diary? Did he know in his heart of hearts that it would become one of the great books of our language? Perhaps he did. But there is no evidence of it. Indeed as J. H. Plumb has pointed out so accomplished a writer would not have plunged his reader into a stream of consciousness that rapidly becomes a whirlpool, as persons, places, allusions are dashed in his face with hardly a word of explanation. Was his principal motive religious and moral? Pepys was a Puritan by upbringing and, in the opinion of so great a scholar as J. R. Tanner, always remained a Puritan at heart. Puritans set great store by the keeping of diaries as a systematic form of self-examination. Or was his ultimate purpose aesthetic, the artist's need to impose some order on the untidiness of experience? Certainly this was among his deepest springs of action. Was it accountancy on the grand scale, the apotheosis of those close reckonings in which he took such evident delight? Very possibly. Was it scientific curiosity, an attempt to establish the fundamentals of psychology by the study of the phenomena readiest to hand — namely himself? Such a motive would not be inappropriate to a Fellow and a future President of the Royal Society. Other reasons could be plausibly advanced. As Robert Latham, the greatest Pepys scholar of our day, has written in his introduction to his definitive edition of the diary:

> After all is said, the origins of so deeply personal a document must themselves be personal. One origin is certainly the vanity which is so clearly marked a feature of Pepys's character. Another, equally certainly, is his love of life. The diary is a by-product of his energetic pursuit of happiness. The process of recording had the effect, as he soon found out, of heightening and extending his enjoyment.

It would be surprising if there were an obvious explanation of anything so extraordinary as the Diary. Everyone who reads it and who goes on to find out more about its writer will form his own opinion. This in itself suggests something of the multiplicity of the man, the multiplicity that characterises a classic in which generations of readers catch echoes of sounds that they have heard when no one else was about. Variety, richness, depth: without these qualities no book could have lasted as long as Pepys's has. But how did they get there? Where do they come from? Not, surely, from that devious, shrewd Mr. Worldly Wiseman who is busily totting up his accounts or deceiving his wife in some liaison which by no stretching of language could be called romantic. Shallow, mean and monotonous would, at first sight, more aptly describe the preoccupation of the greedy, pushful, jealous little bureaucrat it reveals. True – as far as it goes. But Pepys possessed to a high degree the power of empathy, of entering into a mind or a milieu very different from his own and, as he did so, changing the colour and the tone of his mentality with the naturalness of a chameleon. Except that unlike the chameleon he was in some way changed and enriched by his experience. Rather, like Ulysses, he was a part of all that he had met. The combination of passionate curiosity about other people with an equally passionate interest in himself reminds one of Boswell. So does the tendency, most marked in early life, but still clearly discernible in old age, to set up a model of taste and conduct. 'Be Lord Kames!' Boswell's frenzied self-adjuration was carrying things too far. Pepys was at once too cautious and too self-reliant to tell himself to 'be' Sir William Coventry or, later in life, to 'be' John Evelyn. The phrase of the Psalmist 'when I awake up after thy likeness I shall be satisfied with it' comes nearer the mark.

If Pepys was in some respects like Boswell, in more important ones he resembled Dr. Johnson, notably in tenacity, decisiveness and independence of mind. The Diary and Boswell's *Life of Johnson* both owe to their method of composition an immediacy that transcends time. To both of them, with the necessary substitution, might be applied Stendhal's judgment of Cellini's autobiography: 'C'est le livre qu'il faut lire avant tout si l'on veut deviner le caractère italien.' The similarities of the two men, their moral seriousness, their political scepticism, their love of learning, their hatred of cant, their capacity for and need of affection, their kindness, are profound. Their differences are magnified or distorted by the fact that the close-ups we possess of each of them belong to opposite ends of their manhood. Johnson was fifty-four when Boswell met him and began that series of studies on which the great portrait is based. Had Pepys chosen that moment in life at which to begin his diary we should have had a self-portrait of the President of the Royal Society and Secretary of the Admiralty, Deputy Lieutenant for Huntingdonshire and Master of

Trinity House, a Member of Parliament and a great patron of learning
and the arts — a very different person from the young man whom we first
see dining at home in the garret off the remains of the turkey on January
1st, 1660. And had Boswell by some inspired tinkering with the time
machine been enabled to meet Johnson at the corresponding period of
life several years before his own birth he would have found a much more
Bohemian and dissolute character than the monumental figure who
squashed him flat in the back room of Davies's shop that May afternoon
in 1763. This is not to deny the contrasts in temperament and talent that
would have been marked at any stage in life. It is an attempt, crude but
necessary, to put the Diary and its author into some kind of perspective,
without falsifying the stature of either. The Diary is a great work, as
literature, as history, as a psychological document and as a key to what has
been known as the English character in an age of national cultures perhaps soon to become extinct. It is thus almost impossible to exaggerate
its value and its importance. But Pepys's closest friends and most whole-
hearted admirers would have been dumbfounded if they had been told
that posterity would think of him as a diarist. They would not have been
surprised that his name should still be as familiar as that of his great
contemporaries Newton and Wren. But as a diarist! None of them even
knew that he kept one. They did know him as a man of extraordinary
parts and of outstanding achievements. It is almost as though we should
be told that Sir Winston Churchill will be remembered by his countrymen for a series of philosophical arguments unearthed among the
Chartwell papers a century after his death.

The two facts, that Pepys wrote a diary and that its publication in a
mutilated and bowdlerised version in 1825, a hundred and twenty years
after his death made his name immortal, are common knowledge. Two
other facts, that the Diary covers only nine years of a lifespan of seventy
and that it was written in shorthand under the strictest secrecy, are perhaps less widely known or at least less often remembered. Yet to a proper
understanding of the man they are not less important. Historically the
Diary has been the making of Pepys; in real life the Diary was of his
making. It is this paradox that helps one to allow for the magnetic pull
into anachronism exerted by so highly charged a work.

Samuel Pepys was born on February 23rd, 1633, the fifth child of
eleven children born to John Pepys and his wife Margaret in the house in
Salisbury Court, under the shadow of St. Bride's, between Fleet Street
and the river, where his father carried on his business as a tailor. Like so
many families with legal and commercial connections the Pepyses defy
any rigid social classification. Among the kinsmen of his name John Pepys

numbered two or three landed gentry, two lawyers, one of whom rose to be Chief Justice of Ireland, a doctor, a don and a number of tradesmen and artisans. It was the kind of family, commoner in our time than that of our grandfathers, that ranged over the whole spectrum of class and profession. It traced its origins to the fenland countries of Cambridge and Huntingdon in which its nuclei were still clustered. The first Pepys to emerge from the collective anonymity of villeinage did so as a reeve, as we should say a farm manager or agent, to the abbey of Crowland, a position in which he was succeeded by others of his name. By the time of the Reformation the most successful members of the family were on the fringe of the landed class. An advantageous marriage in Elizabeth's reign was followed under James I by a further coup: Paulina Pepys, John's aunt, married Sir Sydney Mountagu, brother of the Lord Treasurer whom Charles I was to create Earl of Manchester. The lands, preferment and connections of the Mountagu family made them one of the richest and most influential in the kingdom. Nowhere was this more evident than in Huntingdonshire, where the great estates of Kimbolton and Hinchingbrooke had recently passed into their hands, or in the University of Cambridge which eagerly sought the patronage of such powerful neighbours. The prospects that opened before the Pepys family were hopeful.

John Pepys, the diarist's father, was not however well placed to exploit them. At the time of his aunt's awe-inspiring marriage in 1618 he was still serving his apprenticeship as a tailor. In 1626 he himself contracted a marriage whose motive, whatever it was, can hardly have been social advantage. Margaret Kight, Samuel's mother, was the sister of a butcher. The glittering alliance with the Mountagus did not seem to be shedding much radiance over Salisbury Court. In fact the fruits were reserved for Samuel to gather.

What were his immediate family like? The Diary depicts his mother as querulous, quarrelsome and feeble-minded. Granted she was by then old and often ill. But her son was a compassionate man and would have made allowances for her that we do not need to do for him. As for his father, Mrs. Heath in her valuable and perceptive *The Letters of Samuel Pepys and his Family Circle* prints enough letters from him to justify her estimate of him as 'a father never quite equal to the occasion, always demanding or receiving some type of aid'.[2] Nonetheless the courtesy, kindness and patience which his son showed him in his old age seems as much the product of natural affection as of filial duty. This at least suggests the possibility that John Pepys within the limits of a humourless and apprehensive nature had been a good father.

Of his ten brothers and sisters only three survived infancy. His elder
brother and sister both died when he was seven. Did he miss having someone older to play with or did he find his promotion to the status of eldest
child exciting and enriching? We do not know. In fact we know very little
indeed about his childhood and that little all from stray references in the
Diary, prompted usually by some topographical reminder. A Sunday
excursion takes him to the village of Kingsland, near Hackney, where he
and his younger brother Tom were put out to nurse and where he remembers shooting with his bow and arrow in the fields. Prevented by violent
weather from taking a boat he has to walk back from Deptford to London
and finds himself passing through Horsleydown where he has not been
since as a very small boy he went to inquire after his father, overdue and
feared lost on a return passage from Holland. Another Sunday excursion
to Islington prompts the memory of his father treating the family to
cakes and ale at the King's Head there. And so on. There is no comment;
no glimpse of character. An attenuated aura of placidity seems to hang for
an instant over these recollections before they themselves dissolve in the
strong consciousness of the present moment. So far as the indications go
it would appear that Pepys's childhood was not unhappy.

His schooldays have left a sharper impress on his Diary. A single
reference to 'one that went to school with me at Huntingdon' is the only
evidence of his attendance at Huntingdon Grammar School, whose most
distinguished old boy, Oliver Cromwell, retained Pepys's admiration in
days when he could not publicly avow it. Probably Pepys was at the school
during 1644–5: perhaps a little earlier. And probably he lived with his
uncle Robert at Brampton, a small property a mile to the south-west which
he and his father were to inherit. What is certain is that somewhere about
1646 he had returned to London and entered St. Paul's school where he
remained until he went to Cambridge in 1650. St. Paul's in his time was
a stronghold of Puritanism and classical learning. The High Master who
set the tone of the place is not mentioned by Pepys but his successor,
the then Sur Master, Samuel Cromleholme, clearly stimulated his intelligent and high-spirited pupil. A fine scholar and a collector of books
(the destruction of his library in the Great Fire of 1666 is said to have
brought on a decline) is it fanciful to see in him the first of many models
on which Pepys formed himself? He evidently kept up with him after
coming down from the University because he is still in touch with him
during the period of the Diary. Even when he sees him the worse for drink
in a tavern in the autumn of 1662 he prefaces his criticism of this indiscreet behaviour with the words 'though I honour the man and he doth
declare abundance of learning and worth'. Two and a half years later

this has become: 'Lord! to see how ridiculous a conceited pedagogue he is, though a learned man, he being so dogmatical in all he do and says. But among other discourse we fell to the old discourse of Paule's Schoole.' From the angle at which the graph of this relationship descends its peak it must have been a high one. The value that Pepys continued to set on the Latin and the Greek that he learned there is a measure of the teaching when he was a boy and Cromleholme was in his prime.

Like all good schools it endowed friendships. The Diary preserves the memory of half a dozen old Paulines whom its author still recalled with pleasure. Only one, Richard Cumberland, remained a friend for life and Cumberland's charming dedication of a learned work dates their friendship from their undergraduate days at Magdalene, Cambridge. Pepys left St. Paul's in 1650 with an Exhibition towards the cost of a University education. Cambridge was the obvious choice for someone of his connections, and Trinity Hall which numbered among its Fellows a first cousin of his father's seemed the obvious college. It had the additional recommendation of being in Dr. Latham's words 'very much a lawyer's college' and the law like the church, was a career open, or at least ajar, to the talents. Indeed in the revolutionary period of the 1650s when the whole form and constitution of the church was the subject of fierce political controversy the attractions of the law for a clever and ambitious young man must have been far superior. It was only six weeks since the Archbishop of Canterbury had been publicly executed. No Lord Chief Justice had suffered such a fate: and everywhere one looked, in politics, in administration, in diplomacy, the lawyers were riding high. Dr. John Pepys of Trinity Hall was himself a lawyer. When his young cousin's name was entered on the college books in June 1650 it would have been rational to predict a legal career.

But some other current was running beneath the surface. In October he was entered at Magdalene, came into residence there the following March and was elected to a scholarship a month later. Whatever the reason for the change, no association could have been happier for him or turned out more fortunately for posterity. Of all the scenes of Pepys's life, his college is the one that we can most nearly share with him. He himself saw the city of his childhood and schooldays destroyed by fire: the Whitehall and Westminster of his young manhood are changed out of all recognition: the house at Clapham where he ended his days is long since demolished: only the houses in Buckingham Street which he knew as York Buildings retain much of their original appearance although they have been in effect re-sited by the embanking of the river. But to pass into the front court at Magdalene is to see much of what Pepys would have seen when he came up as a freshman in the spring of 1651. And through the far passage is the library that enshrines him.

We know so little about Pepys's early life and education that it is unsafe to assert any reason for this happy change of plan. One possible explanation is a change of regime at Magdalene. Dr. Edward Rainbowe, the Royalist master who had brought himself to swallow the Solemn League and Covenant refused to sign the positive Engagement to support the Commonwealth government that was now required of all office-holders. He was replaced on August 31st, 1650 by one of Pepys's neighbours in Salisbury Court, a certain John Sadler who had forsaken a promising academic career at Emmanuel for a chancery practice in Lincoln's Inn. Sadler was a rising star in 1650. Only the year before he had been appointed Town Clerk of London and had been offered by Cromwell himself the lucrative post of Chief Justice of Munster. What more natural than that the new Master who continued to live and work principally in London should extend his patronage to a neighbour's son on the threshold of a Cambridge career, particularly as the boy was intelligent, lively and well affected to the Government? The dates fit: in June Pepys is entered at Trinity Hall; in August Sadler becomes Master of Magdalene; in October Pepys is entered there.

On the other hand it is possible that it may derive from the first unseen connection of his career with that of his rich and rising cousin Edward Mountagu whose patronage was to be the foundation of his fortunes. There are two clues, one very slender; Mountagu's chaplain was a Magdalene man: the other, obscure, but substantial, is Pepys's tutor, Samuel Morland, who was made a baronet at the Restoration.

Sir Samuel Morland's experiments in matrimony and the natural sciences, usually unsuccessful, sometimes disastrous and always expensive, bring him at frequent intervals into Pepys's Diary and correspondence. He personified to a high degree the bewildering versatility of his age, achieving considerable reputation as a mathematician and as a diplomatist, as a latinist and as an inventor, as a cryptographer and as a double agent working for Charles II in Thurloe's secret service. His skill in hydrostatics and hydraulics was such that both Charles II and Louis XIV employed him in the devising of those elaborate ornamental waterworks that to their eye so appropriately expressed the magnificence of kingship. He has undoubted claims to a place in the pedigree both of the computer and of the steam engine. He invented the speaking-trumpet and published a collection of documents concerning the history of the Waldensians. At the time when Pepys became his pupil, he had been a Fellow for less than eighteen months and must have been among the most talented dons of his time.

How and when Morland first came into contact with Mountagu is
not known. But that it must have been round about the time of
Pepys's entry to Magdalene is shown by a secret report on Mountagu's
political complexion that Morland wrote for Clarendon and Charles
II in the summer of 1659 when the tide was beginning to run for a
restoration of the monarchy. He prefaced it by claiming to have been
'acquainted most intimately with the man for at least these seven or eight
years'.[3]

Mountagu, a young Cromwellian colonel whose attachment to the
person and family of the Protector was stronger than any positive ideological commitment, had been living at Hinchingbrooke since the execution of the King in January 1649. Coming of a naturally Royalist
family he had been drawn to the Parliamentary side not only by the mag-
netism of Cromwell but by the moderation, tolerance and general good
sense of the family into whom he had married, a refreshing contrast to
the sour shut-in conservatism of his own father. Old Sir Sydney Mountagu
had been a Puritan Royalist whose perceptions and sympathies had not
mellowed or softened since their formation in the reign of Queen
Elizabeth.* A generous nature could hardly fail to react against them.
Equally it might be repelled by the exultation with which Pepys as a
schoolboy greeted the execution of Charles I. Did the cousins meet while
Pepys was at Cambridge? We do not know. In any case they must have
met very soon after, as Mountagu returned to public life in the Barebones
Parliament of 1653 and Pepys was acting as his secretary and man of
business in London certainly by late 1655 and probably earlier. Both men
evidently were shrewd enough to recognise congruities under different
surfaces – the clever undergraduate fluent in fashionable views and the
young man who had learned to keep his head and hold his tongue in the
harder school of war and revolution.

What did Pepys do at Cambridge? The award of two college scholar-
ships suggests that he must have done *some* work. But the only certain fact
of his university career is that he was admonished in the presence of all
the Fellows of the college then resident for being scandalously overseen in
drink. This evidence that pleasure and conviviality were never too far
away is supported by the few scattered references to his undergraduate
days that come to mind. A day's outing to Aristotle's Well one hot day in
summer was remembered twenty-five years later not, it is true, for its own
sake but because it marked a turning-point in the agonising disease of the
stone from which Pepys had suffered from his earliest childhood:

* His views on pre-marital sexual relations as quoted by his son (D. 7 Oct. 1660)
cannot be criticised for excessive liberality.

I remember not my life without the pain of the stone in the kidneys (even to the making of bloody water upon any extraordinary motion) till I was about 20 years of age, when upon drinking an extraordinary quantity of conduit water out of Aristotle's well near Cambridge (where some scholars of us were for refreshment in a hot summer's day walked), the weight of the said water carried after some day's pain the stone out of the kidneys more sensibly through the ureter into the bladder, from which moment I lived under a constant succession of fits of stone in the bladder till I was about 26 years of age when the pain growing insupportable I was delivered both of it and the stone by cutting and continued free from both (by God's blessing) to this day, more than what may be imputed to it of the aptness which I still retain to cold and wind and the pain attending the same in those parts.'[4]

How much of the mature Pepys is in that immense sentence winding its way through the easy open country of his mind. The exactness, the thoroughness, the judicial matter-of-factness: the intellectual manliness that refuses to disguise what is unpleasant or to indulge in self-pity over what is painful. And amidst all this careful historical documentation, scientific description and rational analysis there is the parenthesis irresistible to the artist 'where some scholars of us were, for refreshment on a hot summer's day walked'. In one stroke the divisions of time are cancelled. We can almost catch the talk of a group of young men drifting along in the sunshine as though the world belonged to them. The very structure of the clause with the word 'walked' pushed to the end renders the oppressiveness and lassitude of cloudless, windless heat. Pepys's mind when he wrote it was on a comprehensive assessment of his general physical condition at the age of forty-five, but he could allow his inner eye to bring before him a sudden brilliant image of his Cambridge days without losing the thread of his argument.

The artist in Pepys lies at the root of his nature. A passion for perception and a passion for imposing order on everything he perceived run through and through his life. He was an aesthete, if not after Walter Pater's own heart at least after his famous formula:

Every moment some form grows perfect in hand or face; some tone on the hills or the sea is choicer than the rest; some mood of passion or insight or intellectual excitement is irresistibly real and attractive to us— for that moment only. Not the fruit of experience, but experience itself, is the end. A counted number of pulses only is given to us of a variegated, dramatic life. How may we see in them all that is to be seen in them by the finest senses? How shall we pass most swiftly from point to point, and be present always at the focus where the greatest number of vital forces unite in their purest energy?

To burn always with this hard, gemlike flame, to maintain this ecstasy, is success in life.

The fineness of Pepys's senses might be questioned in the light of Pater's own standards but no one could deny the power, duration and range of his appetite for experience. By the time he is writing the Diary all the arts matter to him. And to some his responses are so highly developed that he has to take measures to prevent them from taking charge of his life. Plays, books, pictures, buildings elicit, generally, a reaction that is unself-consciously aesthetic. Pepys even seems surprised at this recognition of himself in the mirror — 'a strange slavery that I stand in to beauty, that I value nothing near it'.[5] The immediate context of this reflection was his susceptibility to pretty women. All the more appropriately, for in the most famous expression in the Diary of his deepest aesthetic response to his favourite art, music, he makes this identification explicit:

But that which did please me beyond anything in the whole world was the wind-musique when the angel comes down [he had been to a per-formance of Massinger and Dekker's *The Virgin Martyr*] which is so sweet that it ravished me, and indeed, in a word, did wrap up my soul, so that it made me really sick, just as I have formerly been when in love with my wife; that neither then, nor all the evening, going home and at home, I was able to think of anything, but remained all night trans-ported, so as I could not believe that ever any musick hath that real command over the soul of a man as this did upon me . . .[6]

'Musique is the thing of the world I love most.'[7] These words or their paraphrase run through the Diary. As there was so little in the world that Pepys did not love, the depth and ardour of his passion could find no stronger expression. It created his tenderest friendships; it hurt and healed his marriage. It was the only art in which he combined the four functions of patron, critic, executant and creator. It is impossible to doubt that he would have recognised his own profoundest perceptions in Pater's famous dictum: 'All art constantly aspires towards the condition of music.'

All of which makes it as certain as anything can be in the absence of explicit evidence that part of what Cambridge had to offer was the development, perhaps the formation, of his musical character. Probably the study of the subject and the learning of an instrument had no place in his academic curriculum. But music was a conspicuous feature of the

life and leisure of cultivated society in seventeenth-century England; and
two undergraduates who were up in Pepys's time, one at Trinity, one at
St. John's, provide specific evidence that music teaching was available in
Cambridge.[8] Singing and playing must have claimed much of his time:[9]
he was musical, he was pleasure-loving, he was young: it was not in
character for him to reject the advice given in an ode of Horace that he
must have construed as a boy at St. Paul's: *carpe diem:* make the most of
the present.

But what had the University to offer in its regular degree courses?
What was the particular intellectual and moral aura of the early 1650s?
What did one read? Who were the leading figures who might influence
an intelligent and impressionable undergraduate? Had ten years of civil
war and revolution culminating in a military regime reduced academic
life to the repetition of safe opinions and the avoidance of anything that
might prove controversial? The surprising fact is that both Universities
in this uneasy and uncertain period were confident, lively, stimulating
and, to an astonishing degree, tolerant of dissenting views and even
generous to political opponents. At Cambridge this civilised temper
perhaps owed something to the leading school of divines, the so-called
Cambridge Platonists, who were about as unlike the popular representation of Puritans as it was possible to be. 'Nothing spoils human nature
more than false zeal. The good nature of an heathen is more God-like
than the furious zeal of a Christian.' 'Men have an itch rather to make
religion than to use it.' 'Whosoever scornfully uses any other man dis-
parages himself.' To these aphorisms[10] of Benjamin Whichcote, Provost of
Kings' and Vice-Chancellor of the University, it is difficult to attach the
familiar labels of intolerant, humourless, gloomy, sour or self-satisfied.
Reason, common sense and courtesy are the great virtues, never more
needed than in periods where everything is to be put to rights, that
Whichcote and his friends and pupils brought to the religious contro-
versies of their time. Pepys was no theologian and not much of a philosopher: but his own precept and practice as an administrator was to
correspond exactly to the detachment, intellectual good manners and
absence of bigotry exemplified by the then Master of St. John's, himself a
strong puritan, who in elections to fellowships '. . . was determined to
choose none but scholars, adding very wisely, they may deceive me in their
godliness, they cannot in their scholarship'.[11] The tone and colour of an
institution often influence people in ways that they do not themselves
recognise and perhaps could not identify. Pepys probably learned from
Cambridge more than we can know.

The formal instruction offered at both Universities was still in essence the scholasticism of the Middle Ages. That is, by and large the limits and possibilities of knowledge and the means of apprehending it were what all the universities of Europe had for centuries taken them to be. The methods of teaching employed were, naturally enough, also medieval. The undergraduate attended lectures which he was often expected to take down, in their entirety – a practice known as 'diting'. No wonder that shorthand systems were much in demand among the more enterprising. Shelton's *Tachygraphy*, the system Pepys has immortalised by writing his Diary in it, was in such demand at Cambridge that the University Press had published three editions by the time he came into residence at Magdalene. The principal subject of the lectures was formal logic; the structure of rational argument and the technique of its application. But the most characteristic and effective academic exercise was the disputation, a gladiatorial display of logical virtuosity in which one had to prove and another disprove the truth of a given proposition. A disputation could be in varying degrees public or private; it might be a very grand affair but its everyday use was for the tutor, acting as part referee, part drill-sergeant, to put a group of pupils through the paces he had taught them. It was an educational device that must have been congenial to a person, like Pepys, of quick intellectual reflexes and of an aggressively competitive nature. As Father Costello points out in his admirable survey of the whole system. 'Such exercises in sharp and exact statement lie behind much seventeenth-century prose.'[12] The characteristic fault, noted by several contemporaries, was that it disposed the mind towards a tiresome plausibility in argument which we call sophistry and the spirit towards an instinctive contradictiousness which our ancestors thought ill-bred. No doubt this was even more conspicuous when, as in the seventeenth century, a university education generally coincided with adolescence rather than with young manhood. Pepys, who went to the University at the comparatively advanced age of eighteen, was perhaps less immature; but the vices and virtues of his intellectual training are discernible in the diarist.

Perhaps the most radical and pointed criticism of the scope and technique of Cambridge education had been delivered only two years before Pepys came into residence by a writer of his own generation:

I could never yet make so bad an Idea of a true university, as that it should serve for no nobler end than to nurture a few raw striplings come out of some miserable country school with a few shreds of Latin that is as immusical to a polite ear as the gruntling of a sow or the noise of a saw can be to one that is acquainted with the laws of harmony? . . .
Again I have ever expected from a university that though all men

cannot learn all things, yet they should be able to teach all things to all men . . . We have hardly professors for the three principal faculties, and these but lazily read — and carelessly followed. Where have we anything to do with Chimistry which hath snatcht the Keyes of Nature from the other sects of philosophy by her multiplied experiences? Where any manual demonstrations of Mathematical theorems or instruments? . . . Where an examination of all the old tenets? . . . Where is there a solemn disquisition into history? A nice and severe calculation and amendment of the epochs of time? Where a survey of antiquities and learned descants upon them? Where a ready and generous teaching of the tongues? Free from pedantisme and the impertinencies that that kind of learning hath been pestered with?[13]

It is almost word for word what the Victorian Royal Commissions were to say about the universities and Public Schools two centuries later. It is also a very fair statement of the views that Pepys himself was to hold in later life.

What books he read, what authors he admired, what general stock of culture he brought back with him to London, we can only infer from the later days of the Diary. Presumably one could not be Morland's pupil without acquiring some inkling of the new experimental philosophy, some awareness of a new wind blowing from an unknown quarter. Clearly Pepys kept up and probably extended his reading of the Latin classics. Perhaps he formed that taste for plays, poetry and history that is so strongly developed in the Diary. We know that he began to write a romance which ten years later he came across in clearing out old papers: 'Reading it over to-night I liked it very well, and wondered a little at it myself at my vein at that time when I wrote it, doubting that I cannot do so well now if I would try.'[14]

There is nothing that suggests the anxieties or discomforts of the scholarship boy with his way to make in the world. Sir Thomas More remembered all his life the cold and hunger of his Oxford days and Dr. Johnson still felt the sting of humiliation when he told Boswell of the poverty that had blighted his time as an undergraduate. Not so with Pepys. All is spacious, sunlit, contented, tranquil. If there is silence it requires no explanation. From the first Cambridge was associated with happiness and when he revisited the place, as he often did, he found it there. Without advantages of birth or wealth, in the middle of a period of war and uncertainty, Pepys had made the most of his time at the University. It is the first instance of that genius for adapting himself to the positive possibilities of any situation: a genius that reflects the light striking the moving surface of his life.

2

Early life in London

When Pepys left Cambridge for the great world in the spring of 1654, Cromwell's regime had achieved an authority at home and abroad such as had not been known since the days of Queen Elizabeth. The Protectorate, as his dictatorship was styled, might be a constitutional dead end: but it was every inch as solid as it looked, and it provided its subjects with humane and sensible government. Abroad the transformation was even more astonishing. On the morrow of a long and exhausting civil war England had challenged the most formidable naval power in the world and had in a series of hard-fought, close-run battles won a complete and decisive victory. The early Stuart navy had been too decrepit and ineffective even to protect the channel coast from Barbary pirates, much less to maintain national sovereignty in home waters against the fleet of a European state. But Warwick's vigorous and professional handling of the navy in the Civil War had shown what a versatile instrument of policy had been rusting unused. In the early 1650s while Pepys was up at Cambridge its fullest potentialities were demonstrated in Blake's brilliant victories at the Kentish Knock and off Portland and in Monck's crowning success at the Gabbard.

The First Dutch War established the foundations of that permanent professional navy of which Pepys was to be the master-builder. The sound of the guns carried on the wind from those terrible tearing actions off the mouth of the Thames conveyed no overtones of personal significance to the unmilitary aesthete. It would be a very different matter in the year '66 when the distant thunder of the Four Days Battle brought anxious thoughts to the rising official of the Navy Board as he walked in Greenwich Park. But though Pepys had no reason as an undergraduate to identify himself with the navy, his keen interest in history and in contemporary politics must have made him alive to the importance and to the novelty of what was happening. Fifty years before he was born the defeat of the Spanish Armada had shown that England could at a moment of supreme danger muster naval forces that could meet and repel an all-out attack by the greatest power in Europe. Besides that, it had confirmed that England could not be excluded from the oceans and the wealth that beckoned across them. This was a sufficiently remarkable achievement for a small country that had come comparatively late to the opening of the world but it was by no means equivalent to an aggressive assertion of naval supremacy. It was essentially a defensive victory. Even though Drake and Hawkins had achieved dazzling offensive successes against the Spaniards, it was no small part of their success that they had dared to take the offensive at all against an opponent so much bigger and stronger than themselves. And even Drake and Hawkins never succeeded in capturing the *flota*, the annual Treasure Convoy, as did the Dutch, or would have sought a set battle against the Spanish fleet. The forces they disposed of, the administration that manned and equipped and provisioned their ships, were simply not conceived on this scale. The navy of the Tudors was much more like a seaborne feudal levy, untrained, undisciplined, unintegrated, than like the specialised professional forces of a modern state. It was not expected to keep the sea for more than a very few weeks at a time, and that only when the country was either launching or expecting an invasion. It was an emergency service whose only wholetime officers were clerks or technicians, men who could look after ships and guns and stores and who could see that there were enough of them in the right place at the right time. All the men and most of the ships would be provided by commandeering the vessels and pressing the men of the merchant marine, reinforcing them with soldiers and other landsmen and entrusting the command to someone of conspicuous military talent and experience who had acquired the habit of being obeyed.

Fundamentally this was the feudal system, the system by which an agrarian society organised itself for defence, transposed from land to sea. It bore the marks of the society that produced it in that it was hierarchical, static and defensive. It would not have suited Attila or Louix XIV or Napoleon or Theodore Roosevelt because it excluded the concept of expansion. It was designed to enable people to hold on to what they had got. It made no allowance for technical developments in the art of war which might require specialised knowledge or training. This was no doubt adequate for the hand-to-hand butchery of medieval sea-fights but in the sixteenth century the coming of the great gun following on the improvement of the sail and rigging plan that dates from fifty years earlier offered opportunities of sophisticated tactics that were not to be fully exploited until Pepys's time. As is well known the Armada Fight was the first major sea action whose tactics were determined by the great gun. What is sometimes forgotten is that no ship on either side was sunk or even badly damaged by the incessant cannonading. The new weapon was still at an experimental stage.

What prevented further and rapid development was precisely the character of the navy as an expedient only to be resorted to in the direst peril. No English monarch except in extreme necessity was going to spend the huge sums necessary to fit out and victual ships and pay the officers and men aboard them. Charles I's Ship Money Fleets which might appear to contradict this, in reality confirm it. Had the sailors been properly fed and clothed and paid, had the officers commanded well-found ships, the Royal Navy would not have embraced the Parliamentary cause with the alacrity and the warmth that it did. The aspect of sea-power that interested Charles I, the greatest connoisseur of the fine arts in English history, was the visual. How beautiful a man-of-war can be may still be judged from the painting of the *Sovereign of the Seas*, the hundred-gun ship that Peter Pett built for him. Pepys spoke of her with particular admiration as 'a most noble ship' when he first saw her in 1661. But, as with the policy her name symbolised, performance did not match appearance. She played little part in the Civil War and next to none in the Dutch Wars. The number of men she required to work and fight her was out of proportion to her effectiveness. Her design, it is true, anticipated to an astonishing degree the ultimate potentialities of the sailing ship as an instrument of war. The function of a warship is however to fight in the battles of her own time. A superb military extravagance, she survived as a monument to the amateur in an age that encouraged professionalism.

Nowhere was this more true than in the great naval struggle with the Dutch. The victories that resounded through Europe while Pepys was a young man at Magdalene were won by superior professional skill, not by luck, or dash, or courage though these are of course as essential to success in war as oxygen is to human life. What Blake, the great admiral of the Commonwealth, did was to refine the natural courage and aptitude of his captains and crews by the scientific application of the lessons that he had learned from his experience of handling ships and fighting battles. As Clarendon the great Royalist historian pronounced: 'He was the first that infused that proportion of courage into the seamen, by making them see by experience what mighty things they could do if they were resolved; and taught them to fight in fire as well as upon water; and though he hath been very well imitated and followed, he was the first that drew the copy of naval courage, and bold and resolute achievement.' Blake's courage indeed deserves all that Clarendon says: but Clarendon knew more about brave men than he did about naval warfare as his somewhat airy, off-hand treatment of Blake's contribution reveals: 'He . . . was the first man that declined the old track and made it manifest that the science might be attained in less time than was imagined, and despised those rules which had long been in practice to keep his ship and his men out of danger . . .' There was more to it than that as J. R. Powell has demonstrated in his studies of a commander whom Nelson acknowledged as his superior.[1]

The transformation of the navy as a fighting force could not have been achieved without some corresponding changes in its administration. Here the moving spirit, certainly during the critical period of the Dutch War, was Sir Henry Vane. Pepys, who diligently collected all he could find about his predecessors in the Navy Office and at the Admiralty, must have known in later life how crucial Vane's part was. He may well have been struck by some remarkable parallels to his own career and to his own methods and policies. Yet he says surprisingly little about him, even in the privacy of his Diary at the very moment in May 1662 when he is searching through Vane's naval papers to find some shreds of plausibility for the judicial murder of a man whom the King considered 'too dangerous to let live'. Vane had come to his position of chief naval executive at the height of a major war by a route very different from that of the tailor's son. Rich and well-connected, Governor of Massachusetts at the age of twenty-three, appointed Joint Treasurer of the Navy in 1639 ironically enough by court favour, Vane served on the Parliamentary committees of the navy or the Admiralty or both from the outbreak of the Civil War. But it was not until the end of 1652 that the appointment of a small Admiralty Commission with powers to run the naval war gave Vane his chance.

Suddenly the creaking machinery of administration changes its note to that low purposeful hum that we associate with Lord Barham or with Pepys himself. Everything is to be done and everything will be done. Letters and instructions pour smoothly from the office when they are needed even if it is a Saturday or the hours are small. A drunken captain is replaced, powder and provisions are punctually dispatched, money is sent down to pay the seamen, conferences are arranged with the

Commanders-in-Chief: yet all this urgent work does not prevent the commission from initiating wide-ranging reforms to cover wages and prize-money, the care of the sick and wounded, and the codification of naval law. The overcoming of an immediate difficulty is not seized on as a pretext for postponing action on larger and more complicated issues. Rather it acts as a spur on an administrative instinct which has been roused to its fullest, clearest consciousness. *L'appétit vient en mangeant.*

There is a parallel even more striking. One of Pepys's supreme achievements, the Act of 1677 for the building of thirty new ships, was foreshadowed in the approval by Parliament in September 1652 for a construction programme of exactly the same size. Unlike Pepys's Act, Vane's was never carried out. In April 1653 Cromwell expelled the Rump and drove Vane out of public life.[2] Here again the mature Pepys, twice dismissed from control of naval affairs through a sudden shift in political power, might see a paradigm of his own experience.

Pepys, like everyone else, was much struck nine years later by the courage Vane showed on the scaffold. When the trial was read aloud to him he found it 'a very excellent thing, worth reading and him to have been a very wise man'. Why then does he say comparatively little about him, especially as a naval administrator?

Personal partisanship certainly must be taken into account. Two of his senior colleagues when he was first appointed to the Navy Office had been advanced and befriended by Vane. And in the two first and most serious attempts ro ruin him the attack was led by men who had had a hand in running the navy during the interregnum and challenged Pepys with the record of their own performance. It thus became a matter of self-preservation to establish the superiority of Restoration practice over that of the Commonwealth. Besides the personal there was also the political. Vane was a revolutionary. Unlike Cromwell, he had thought out his political position and was ready, in Cromwell's favourite description of doctrinaire republicanism, to put all things into blood and confusion. Like most Englishmen then and since Pepys preferred Cromwell's pragmatic approach. In the period between the death of the Protector in September 1658 and the Restoration of Charles II in May 1660 Vane had been a prominent and active promoter of daring constitutional schemes and desperate political coalitions. Pepys was by then a member of the political nation, even though a humble and junior one. Vane's political aspirations, empty though they proved, might therefore in Pepys's eyes have told against a fair acknowledgment of his work for the navy.

But this silent evolution of the service in which Pepys was to make his career did not yet concern him directly. The consequences, both immediate and distant, of England's sudden rising from the waves as a first-class naval power can hardly be over-estimated. In the short term it made Cromwell unshakable at home and abroad: in the long term it shaped so much of English life and policy and had such diverse and far-reaching effects on so many other countries as to overwhelm any attempt at concise statement. Pepys as a young man of intense curiosity about the world he lived in must certainly have been conscious of the enhanced power of government and of the military and diplomatic standing England now enjoyed among the great powers. It seems unlikely that even so intelligent a young man would perceive the underlying relation between cause and effect. Certainly we have no evidence that he did; and we know that his entry into the Navy Office some six years after he had come down from the University was not the fulfilment of some long-cherished ambition but the direct consequence of his employment as secretary to his cousin Edward Mountagu.

Mountagu, as has been briefly indicated, was the man who launched Pepys on his public career. He and his concerns run through the years of the Diary and provide the only direct evidence of Pepys's early manhood in London. Nothing whatever is known of what Pepys did from the time that he left Cambridge in the spring of 1654 until some references in Mountagu's letters and papers show that he was acting as a kind of resident steward — secretary would be almost too grand a word — to his cousin. He was expected to see that the maids behaved themselves, to make and receive payments on behalf of his master, to carry out any necessary errand and to keep an eye on things generally. The earliest evidence of this not very exalted or exacting employment dates from December 1655 but it seems likely that the arrangement really began when Pepys came down from the University. Answering a House of Commons Committee some years later Pepys described himself as Mountagu's secretary at this period, but such a context is the last one in which he could be expected to descend to personal particulars, especially if too detailed a reply might expose him to the sneers and the malice of his enemies. The truth is that Pepys, when we first glimpse him through a few fugitive references in accounts and letters, is a rather idle, perhaps somewhat disgruntled, inmate of the housekeeper's room who knows that his talents and education have fitted him for a higher place in society. If he was idle, it was not from choice. Like the vast majority of gifted people in an economically undeveloped society he knew the frustration of under-employment. Can anything else explain the exultant hedonism with which throughout his long official career he flung himself on work, any work, however tedious in itself? Only the active pursuit of pleasure could rival its attraction.

The transition from futility to fulfilment was made possible by Pepys's relationship to Mountagu, a figure whose importance to the subject of this biography can hardly be exaggerated. His mere existence shaped the strategy of Pepys's career. Had they never met the fact that he was what he was would still have influenced the life of his cousin, just as the existence of a fleet that may never see action or a bomb that may never be dropped may affect profoundly the direction of policy and the course of affairs. Mountagu's golden gift of reticence has concealed from posterity as it did from the less perceptive of his contemporaries how great a part he played in the peaceful transition – so easy and inevitable at three hundred years distance, so perilous then – from Cromwell to Charles II. What other politician of the first rank – a member of the Council of State under Oliver, Commander-in-Chief, ambassador and privy councillor under Charles II – was trusted and respected, even, it seems, liked by these dissimilar and by no means undiscerning masters? Sir Anthony Ashley Cooper, Earl of Shaftesbury, Mountagu's brother-in-law and a much more brilliant politician, held positions of at least equivalent importance under both but was distrusted and in the end defeated alike by Protector and King. Monck who shared with Mountagu the credit and rewards of the Restoration was a through-and-through military professional who served both regimes faithfully without displaying the least spark of interest in the politics of either. There were, of course, there always are, a host of smooth, sleek ingratiators who did well out of both the Protectorate and the Restoration, just as there were a number of able and conscientious public servants who, like Monck, were ready to work for any government that seemed to offer stability. But Mountagu occupies a unique position; a politician more of the Tudor than the Stuart type, guarded but daring, resolute but pliant, a man who could take an initiative but could not enunciate a principle.

In 1654 when Pepys came down from Cambridge Mountagu was already in the inner circle of government as a member of Oliver's Council of State, the fifteen-man executive whose wide powers were wholly independent of Parliament. In August he was made a Treasury Commissioner. As such he led for the Government in the crucial debates – crucial, that is, for the first Protectorate Parliament – on the financial provision for the navy and the constitutional control of the militia. Both debates took place about the turn of the year and both resulted in Government defeats. The open forum was not Mountagu's chosen field. This did not, in the event, matter much because Cromwell turned out the Parliament and retained the minister. Employed in a bewildering variety of Government business, Mountagu was finally selected by Oliver for the all-important assignment

of understudying Blake, whose health had long been failing, in command
of the fleet. Late in 1655 he was made a Commissioner of the Admiralty
and early in 1656 he was appointed a General-at-Sea.

There is to our ears something agreeably informal and amateurish
about this rank, held, from first to last, only by seven men. And so, in a
sense, there was. One thinks of Monck delighting the sailors with his
landsman's orders of 'wheel to the right' when he wanted the fleet to
go about on the starboard tack. Of the seven only one, Sir William Penn,
was a professional seaman. Yet a list of seven naval commanders that
includes Blake and Popham, Deane and Monck, Penn and Mountagu has
a ratio of success in action not easily equalled at any period in our history.
This is the flavour of the age that Pepys was young in: and nowhere was it
more pronounced than in the navy. Suddenly about the middle of the
seventeenth century the clouds parted to reveal limitless prospects. It
was not only in the furnace of politics and war, and not only Cromwell who

> . . . cast the kingdoms old
> Into another Mould.

Ideas and institutions that had been rigid for generations were melting
into a miraculous pliancy. In science, in scholarship, in finance, in public
administration, new techniques and fresh insights were transforming
familiar views and discovering new horizons. The men who in the next
decade would form the Royal Society were already active in the University
of Oxford. The spirit of the age was expressed by its greatest poet:

> 'The World was all before them'.

It is difficult for the sceptic of the twentieth century, hag-ridden by the
horrors of pollution and over-population, to conceive the optimism and
self-confidence of men who had in general seen far more of violence and
disease and starvation than most of us. Nothing explains Cromwell or
Blake or Wren or Newton: but their careers and achievements, and those
of many other brilliantly gifted contemporaries, both gave to and drew
from the age that saw them flower. Without this awareness of enlarged
possibilities neither Mountagu nor Pepys could have climbed as high as
they did.

Mountagu, it seems, had matured young. To defy one's father at the
age of seventeen in the choice of a wife and at the same time to range
oneself on the opposite side in a civil war was no easy course for a young
man bred up to succeed to the family estates. It was either recklessness
or uncommon strength of character and independence of judgment.
Everything about Mountagu's career shows that he was not reckless. And

both the wife and the political allegiance proved well chosen indeed. So did the early, and steady, adherence to Cromwell.[3] Mountagu's withdrawal from politics over the trial and execution of the King confirmed that he had a mind of his own. His return showed his acceptance of the Commonwealth and, subsequently, of the Protectorate. Loyalty and decisiveness are useful qualities in a commander. So is tact. To share the command of a fleet with the towering figure of Blake and not to be either an irritant or a nonentity must have required a good deal. Yet in spite of attempts to make mischief, especially on the part of the Royalists, it seems clear from Blake's letters that he found Mountagu a valuable colleague. That Cromwell was satisfied with his choice is evident from his continuing to employ him until his own death in September 1658.

Mountagu's prolonged absences at sea inevitably increased the scope and importance of the business which he had to entrust to his confidential servants. Almost as soon as Mountagu steps on to his quarterdeck Pepys makes his earliest appearance in the Government offices that were to be his terrain for thirty years. At first he simply signs receipts or makes payments on behalf of his master. But he is so interested, so observant, so incurably sociable that he is soon beginning to be a useful source of political information. He still does the shopping and sends off parcels but he is rapidly becoming in fact the secretary that he has claimed to be all along. Somewhere about this time – certainly before Cromwell's death – Pepys also acquires a part-time job as a secretary to that formidable civil servant and diplomat George Downing, at that time employed in the Exchequer. This does not mean that he has done with his humbler domestic duties but he has at last embarked on his true career.

Not before time, since he had, most imprudently, married the fifteen-year-old daughter of a Huguenot expatriate. The wedding took place on December 1st, 1655, but perhaps owing to the extreme youth of the bride they did not begin to live together as man and wife until October 10th, 1656. That, anyhow, was the anniversary that Pepys, a great keeper of anniversaries, habitually celebrated as his wedding night.

Pepys's marriage, alone among his many and much canvassed sexual encounters, is undeniably romantic. Little as we know about their life together until the Diary opens, there is even then a strong tide of passion still running. Pepys married Elizabeth St. Michel because he found her captivating. No other explanation is thinkable. Judged by all the criteria of prudence, social, financial, professional, political, it was crazy. And these were precisely the criteria which Pepys systematically applied to the conduct of life, his own just as much as other people's. She was penniless and he had not got a proper job, not the most hopeful basis for marriage in any age. But this was just the beginning. She was half a foreigner, and, worse still, had acquired what education she had in a convent in Paris. In Puritan England it would be difficult to imagine more disadvantageous antecedents. True, her father had loudly renounced the Romish Church for himself and his children, and had lost a considerable inheritance in France by so doing. But, laudable as this might be in general, did it not show in this particular case a certain irresponsibility about property? Would one choose to be connected with people who acted in this head-strong way? Might one not oneself all too soon find that the cost of these grand gestures fell largely on the family of the man who made them? And it was not as though Pepys had not enough family commitments already. There were two younger brothers to be educated and given a start in life; a sister of disagreeable temper and no personal attraction to be provided for; the parents whose business this was were at best ineffective, at worst querulous and quarrelsome; little was to be expected, and with advancing years, much was to be feared from that quarter. To add anything to this formidable burden was rash. To add the St. Michels was besotted.

Pepys, we may be sure, realised all this. There can be few figures whose acuteness and objectivity a biographer would be more foolish to underrate. It is a measure of his passion for Elizabeth that he could contemplate, and having contemplated accept, the bizarre encumbrances of her father Alexander Le Marchant, Sieur de St. Michel, and her brother Balthazar, the 'brother Balty' who erupts so vigorously in the Diary and in Pepys's letters. But what to a contemporary eye would have been even more elo-quent proof of a high, romantic emotion is that he should have allowed himself to be impelled into marriage by the mere fact of having fallen in love. Such behaviour was not unknown among the aristocracy and the landed gentry who could afford to please themselves, though even there it was unusual. Marriage, with all that flowed from it, the transmission and amalgamation of property, the network of local and political alliances known comprehensively as 'interest', the connections that might accelerate or retard promotion, was a professional and economic option of crucial importance. To throw it away because one had lost one's heart to a girl would for someone of Pepys's class have been thought as eccentric as for a London bank clerk to buy a house in Switzerland because he had fallen in love with the landscape. A house, in the best-known modern definition, is a machine for living in: it must, even more obviously, be within one's means and within reach of one's work. So, in the seventeenth century, it was with marriage. A wife, to sustain Le Corbusier's bleak metaphor, was part of one's social and economic plant.

Viewed in this light Elizabeth Pepys might appear a questionable investment. And, since our knowledge of her derives almost entirely from her husband's diary, this is the impression that sometimes comes uppermost. But only sometimes. Much more often we catch echoes of shared anxieties and pleasures, of furious quarrels caused by her muddle or his meanness, of reconciliations which, since he was generally the aggressor, show her essentially affectionate and generous nature, above all of talk, without which any marriage is insipid. All this belongs to the Diary period when the marriage was already of several years standing. Of the first years all we know is that they started their life together in one room in Mountagu's lodging in Whitehall and that at some point during the first two years the marriage broke down and Elizabeth went to live with friends at Charing Cross. Perhaps the root of the trouble was sexual. All we *know* is that whatever it was it did not last long and that Pepys hated to be reminded of it. He was certainly a jealous husband and latterly an unfaithful one. Had there been infidelities before the Diary opens? We know too from the Diary that Elizabeth suffered from a gynaecological complaint that prolonged her menstrual periods. No doubt there were difficulties. But the significant fact is that both Pepys and his wife enjoyed recalling their early life together.[4]

Whatever Mountagu may have thought of his cousin's prudence he countenanced the marriage by providing the young couple with a lodging and a livelihood. He himself had married young, younger than Pepys, and against his father's wishes. But he had married into a family whose political connections helped him in the earliest stages of his career and had chosen a wife who had perfect manners, perfect sense and inexhaustible good nature. Even Pepys who at one time or another finds fault with nearly everyone never speaks of her with anything but admiration and affection. In any case the difference in rank and wealth between the two men makes Pepys's action, even supposing Elizabeth's qualities the equal of Lady Jem's,* much the more daring.

More immediately alarming than the consequences of an imprudent marriage was the state of his health. All his life he was troubled by pain or discomfort in his bowel and bladder, caused, as he correctly diagnosed, by the formation of stones in the kidney. All his life these and other symptoms were excited or intensified by cold weather and humidity. In the long, comprehensive and lucid minute on the state of his health which he drafted at the age of forty-five,[5] he summarises, classifies and explains his ailments with an objectivity that eschews self-pity and yet conveys the unmistakable personality of the patient. From the passage already quoted

* Short for Jemimah; the affectionate term by which Pepys usually refers to her in the Diary.

on page 27 we have seen that the chronic condition — 'I remember not my life without the pain of the stone' — was aggravated about the age of twenty and grew steadily worse until at the age of twenty-six its severity had become unendurable. Pepys prepared to face the ordeal by surgery, hazardous and terrifying as it was, that offered the only chance of ending present agony.

The chances of success in even the simplest surgical operation were inevitably slender in an age that was ignorant of sepsis. The certainty of pain, of extreme and prolonged pain in an operation such as lithotomy, from which there were no anaesthetics to give total or even partial relief, made most men recoil. Even those whose stoicism was equal to contemplating such a prospect could hardly be expected to undergo the actual experience in silence or without a struggle. The first essential of a surgeon's equipment was a length of stout cord with which the patient could be trussed to the operating table, or, as in the lithotomies that John Evelyn witnessed in Paris, to a high chair. Evelyn was appalled by what he saw: yet twenty years later when his own brother was advised that only a lithotomy could save his life, he had no hesitation in urging him to have the operation, and supported his arguments by bringing Pepys round to show him the stone extracted from his own body. Unhappily even these persuasions were unavailing.[6]

Dark though the prospect must have been there were glimmers of light. Lithotomy was one of the few branches of surgery that could report a recent advance in technique: and Thomas Hollier the leading surgeon at St. Thomas's Hospital had achieved a notable reputation for successful cutting for the stone. How Pepys prepared himself for what he certainly regarded as one of the most solemn and decisive occasions of his life we do not know, but from his subsequent commemoration of it it seems probable that he prepared himself for death. The house of his cousin, Jane Turner, wife to a lawyer, was larger and better suited to the surgeon's requirements than that of his parents. No doubt, too, the Turners would be less emotionally exhausting to the patient. Here on March 26th, 1658, Pepys underwent the operation with a success for which he never failed to give thanks. Whatever criticisms may be made of him he cannot ever be accused of undervaluing the gift of life. In a few weeks he was again attending to his business and enjoying better health than he had ever known. Sometime in August he and Elizabeth set up house for the first time in Axe Yard, not far from the present Admiralty building, and engaged a maid. Tuning up was finished: the overture was about to begin.

3

On the eve

———

The pursuit of pleasure and the love of life take in Pepys an added brightness from his conscious and articulate recognition of their importance to him, indeed as he thought to every rational man.

> The truth is, I do indulge myself a little the more pleasure, knowing that this is the proper age of my life to do it, and out of my observation that most men that do thrive in the world do forget to take pleasure during the time that they are getting their estate but reserve that till they have got one, and then it is too late for them to enjoy it with any pleasure.[1]

Such a perception can only have been intensified by the prolonged contemplation of death and the experience of extreme pain and fear from which he was now happily delivered. The world that received him back, his spirits disburdened, his health full and free, his appetites sharpened by denial, would in any case have appeared inexhaustibly fascinating. In the event reality was to exceed every expectation. For a young man of Pepys's social, political and intellectual tastes and powers of observation to find himself in London in the summer of 1658 connected with men such as Mountagu and Downing who were at the heart of things was to have drawn a high prize in the lottery of life.

The only certainty of England's political future at that point in time was that it could not be dull. Cromwell's adventurous foreign policy had raised the standing of his Government both at home and abroad. But the financial underpinning of a military regime was bound to produce political and constitutional problems. Sooner or later a Parliament of sorts would have to be called again. What would happen then was anybody's guess. In spite of doing his best to pack his parliaments with docile and well-affected persons Cromwell had three times failed to attain this objective. The nation was, as he realised better than some of his critics, far too fiercely divided in politics and religion to make government by consent a feasible proposition. The Royalists, the Republicans and the Levellers had all shown themselves more or less irreconcilable. And besides these rational, or at least intelligible, forms of political opposition there were yet higher and more thrilling peaks from which to look down on the kingdoms of the world, such as those scaled by the Fifth Monarchy men who believed that direct rule by the Ancient of Days was about to replace more conventional forms of government and who wished, like millenarians in all ages, to quicken the dawdling steps of history. On past form Cromwell should have been able to hold all these forces at bay. Only that spring he had sent his last Parliament packing without subjecting his regime to any visible strain. Rather the foreign observers best qualified to judge such as the French ambassador thought the Protectorate stronger than ever. So did Clarendon, the best informed and most objective of the Royalist exiles who advised Charles II. But Cromwell was beginning to feel his years. Two bereavements in the happy and affectionate family of which he was the centre drained his reserves. In August he was seriously ill. On September 3rd, the anniversary of his famous victories at Dunbar and Worcester, he was dead.

Suddenly political questions that had long been kept shut were unfastened and swinging in the wind. Were the Stuarts going to come in again? To judge by the pathetic failure of every Royalist rising, the latest still fresh in people's minds, it did not seem likely. Were the Republican Old Guard, men like Sir Henry Vane, at last to enter into the inheritance that Cromwell had denied them? Would they make common cause with the Fifth Monarchy men and light a real revolutionary bonfire? Would the Long Parliament return either as that final fragment of the original body popularly termed the Rump or in the somewhat larger edition that Colonel Pride had purged? Would the army endeavour to perpetuate themselves as the arbiters of political power which they evidently were when they lent their weight to Cromwell's dying wish that he might be succeeded by his amiable but ineffective son Richard? To a serious follower of politics such as Pepys these were all possibilities exciting beyond expression: and every scrap of evidence suggests that he discussed them with fascinated interest in the taverns and the new coffee houses where so much of his time was spent.

Where, politically, did he himself stand? It seems clear from the Diary that his sympathies lay with the Presbyterian party, that body of Parliament men and common lawyers who had originally taken arms against the King because they resented the policy of Strafford and the pretensions of Laud and the high-churchmen and saw in them the danger signals of absolute monarchy, perhaps even, under the influence of Queen Henrietta Maria, of Popery itself. But all that belonged to the 1630s and 40s. The surviving leaders of the Presbyterian party, men like Fairfax and Holles, had for years been Royalists in all but name. The execution of the King and the proclaiming of a Commonwealth had seemed to them as great a violation of the legality they had fought for as anything the Stuarts might have had in mind. Like all opposition movements their political existence was largely parasitic on the issue they wished to prevent. Once Charles I and Laud and Strafford were beneath the horizon they had no cause to which opinion might be rallied. Even the distinguishing mark of religious opinion from which they took their name became much eroded. Pepys himself had certainly begun to attend the Prayer Book services, still officially banned, that were all but openly conducted in private houses by clergymen ejected from their livings. Not that forms of worship or government were the kind of things for which Pepys would ever have risked martyrdom or even serious inconvenience. To his way of thinking these were matters of taste and preference, like food or clothes. One might have very pronounced likes and dislikes but at a pinch anything was better than starving or shivering.

It might be objected that Pepys's lively horror of revolutionary ideologues such as Vane or Milton flaws this perfect detachment. But it might equally be held to confirm it. If keeping still is the only way to stop the boat from turning turtle the principle operates independently of what course is being steered. Had Vane seized and established power it is hard to imagine Pepys conspiring against the regime. Yet it would be wrong to infer from this obedience to the powers that be either personal or intellectual timidity. We know that Pepys attended and enjoyed the meetings of the Rota Club where in the winter of 1659–60 the highest speculative intelligences controverted and criticised the fundamentals of politics. 'The discourses in this kind were the most ingeniose, and smart, that ever I heard or expect to heare, and bandied with great eagernesse: the arguments in the Parliament house were but flatt to it,' wrote the young

John Aubrey, a fellow member who shared Pepys's addiction to rational discourse.[2]

The pace of events outran speculation. Richard Cromwell succeeded peaceably enough to his father's position and in January 1659 summoned the Parliament that his father had been preparing to hold. But the slack rein on which he rode both alarmed the army leaders and invited them to unseat him. Richard and his Parliament were turned out by a bloodless coup d'état and the army officers, bankrupt as always of political initiative, recalled the Rump early in May. Whatever else that precious remnant of the much purged Parliament elected in 1640 may have lacked it was not spirit. Before the summer was out these fifty-odd veterans had shown that they meant to obtain political control over the Generals who had brought them back. Since this was precisely the same course of action of which Richard's Parliament had been suspected earlier in the year the Generals might reasonably be expected to react in the same way. The Rump promptly cashiered Lambert and Desborough, the two most vigorous army leaders, and vested the command in Fleetwood, the most senior but the least decisive of the Generals, assisted by six commissioners of a strongly Republican complexion. Lambert replied to his dismissal by marching his troops into Westminster and refusing the Rumpers admission to their house. The army was back where it came in.

This was in October. During the summer Lambert had crushed with contemptuous ease the Royalist rising led by Sir George Booth, a rich Cheshire landowner, on which so many hopes had been pinned. Charles II who had been eagerly waiting at Calais now set off for the Pyrenees where, on an island in the Bidassoa, Velazquez and others were setting the scene for one of the great diplomatic congresses of the century that was to negotiate the peace treaty between France and Spain. Cromwell had used the war between the two super-powers to advance his interests in Europe and the New World. Charles hoped to use the peace to secure diplomatic and perhaps military support for his restoration. In the event he obtained nothing. The autumn of 1659 was rock bottom for the Royalists. Hitherto however black the immediate prospect the King could always comfort himself with the thought that Cromwell was not immortal and could pull himself, as émigrés do, out of the pit of despair by the bootstraps of secret reports that his partisans were preparing for the great day. The great day had come and gone: the Royalist rising had fizzled out before it had even caught alight: and the powers of Europe were composing themselves for a period of slumber indifferent to the fate of the King of England.

But it was not only the Royalists who were facing a brick wall. So were the army. What were they to do next? How were they going to raise the money to pay the troops? The only known machinery for taxation needed a Parliamentary driving wheel to set it going. And on what possible basis could a Parliament of any kind be reconstituted by the men who had followed up the dissolution of Richard Cromwell's Parliament by ejecting the Rump? So incompetent were the Generals to answer these conundrums, so universal the dislike of military rule, that by Christmas time the Rump had returned to Westminster and to a nominal assertion of authority. The needle of history seemed to be caught in a scratched record.

Meanwhile the best hope of meeting the short-term demand for cash lay in the city. Merchants and financiers could always provide funds if the inducement offered was sufficient. For the immediate future the need to preserve the city itself from pillage by a large army mutinous from want of pay was a powerful incentive. But in the long run the citizens who were to be called on to act as the Government's bankers would want to have some say in the making of policy and the conduct of affairs. Hence at the point at which Pepys's Diary opens political interest centred on the recent elections to the Common Council of the city of London. These had shown a decisive swing away from both the army and the Rump and had strengthened the demand, voiced ever louder, for a new Parliament.

On the Scottish border George Monck, the General Officer Commanding, was edging his well-found, well-disciplined army closer to England. He had made no secret of his disapproval of army *coups* and of his belief that a soldier's function was to serve the legally constituted civil government. Facing him on the English side lay the troops of John Lambert, the General who had dominated events first by defeating the Royalist rising and then by turning out the Rump, to which he was still unreconciled. In mid-December Lawson, the left-wing Admiral in command of the fleet, had declared for the Rump and had brought his ships up the river to Gravesend. This was the situation when on January 1st, 1660, Pepys began his Diary and, unknown to him, Monck crossed the border at Coldstream. English history's supreme shorthand writer was ready and waiting.

This account of public events sheds no light on the activities of Pepys's two masters, Downing and Mountagu. In this it faithfully represents their own adept concealment of manoeuvres whose object would have been lost by publicity. Downing in particular was uniquely well placed to forecast the winner of every political race and to reinsure himself against unpleasant consequences. Besides his place in the Exchequer he was also English ambassador at The Hague under each successive Government and, as if that was not enough, a veteran of Secretary Thurloe's secret service.

Like Thurloe he therefore knew enough to be sure of powerful friends under any regime. There was nothing to be gained by early and steadfast adherence to any party. Downing could afford to wait and see.

Mountagu, however, was in a much more exposed position. He had identified himself with the house of Cromwell and had avowed his opposition to both the Republicans and the Royalists. The fall of Richard was a severe shock: he could expect nothing from the Rump and a great deal less from any Government headed by men like Vane or Hesilrige. Had he been in England he would have done his best to prevent the door being opened to such firebrands. But in the spring of 1659 as General-at-Sea he had been sent with a powerful fleet to the Baltic. The Swedes and the Danes having at last signed a treaty in 1658 were at each others' throats again and the Dutch, our great maritime rivals, were backing the Danes. To preserve the balance of power in a part of Europe that had a virtual monopoly of masts, spars, pitch, tar and other naval stores was a paramount English interest. Opposed in everything else both Dutch and English wanted a diplomatic settlement rather than a resumption of hostilities. The conduct of such negotiations backed by the presence of a fleet was all in the day's work for a seventeenth-century admiral. Mountagu was within sight of a satisfactory settlement when a frigate arrived with news of Richard's overthrow.

It was a situation that called for coolness of judgment, calmness of manner, complete self-reliance and an exact sense of timing. Everyone knew that the Commander-in-Chief was no friend to Republicanism, the Good Old Cause, whose star was now ascendant. Everyone knew that the exiled Stuarts would go all out to enlist his support now that his loyalty to the Cromwells was no longer an obstacle. Everyone knew that the new Government in London would watch his every move, would surround him with military and diplomatic nominees of their own, would eavesdrop on him, intercept his correspondence, would leave him unsupported while he was abroad, and would at the first opportunity dismiss him summarily from all his appointments. Certainly Pepys knew all this: he even came out to the Sound to bring and take back confidential correspondence and, no doubt, to report to his master on what was being done and said at home. Yet even from so trusted and discerning a servant Mountagu kept inviolate the secrecy of his actions and intentions. A year later when everything was over Pepys confesses his astonishment at hearing from Mountagu's own lips that he had been in correspondence with the King at this very time — 'and I do from this raise an opinion of him to be one of the most secret men in the world, which I was not so convinced of before.'[3]

Pepys was right to be astonished: and those who have smiled at his innocence betray a want of insight. Not only did the Government suspect Mountagu of negotiating with the Stuarts, they sent three commissioners over to keep an eye on him. Not only did one of the commissioners share these suspicions, he was actually present when Mountagu was approached by a Royalist agent ashore one day in Copenhagen. Not only did he report his findings, he openly charged the Commander-in-Chief in the presence of a number of senior officers and diplomats both English and foreign. Not only did he charge him, it was all perfectly true. The whole performance was a triumph of the straight face. When at the end of August 1659 Mountagu brought the fleet home against the wishes of the commissioners and without orders from the Government, the suspicious coincidence of Sir George Booth's abortive rising would have embarrassed or flustered any but a master of impenetrable bluff. But Mountagu carried it off. He lost all his military commands: he was superseded as General-at-Sea; he had already been deprived of his regiment; but he kept his head.

> Much suspected by me
> Nothing proved can be.

The lines that the young Elizabeth scratched on the window-pane epitomise the technique of political survival so successfully practised by Pepys's patron.

The excitement and uncertainty of that autumn were part of what Pepys and his contemporaries knew as London. To us the affairs of the nation are as present in Westmorland or Cornwall as within a stone's throw of the palace of Westminster. Either in London or out of it we can choose whether to contemplate or to ignore the public issues of the day. But what is a matter of choice for us was a matter of geography for our ancestors. In English history not all the world was a stage: only London. The disproportion in wealth and population between the city and the next largest town was so huge as to constitute a difference in kind not in degree. The tension of affairs could be felt there as nowhere else, and felt the more keenly by contrast with the immemorial calm of a countryside that changed only with the seasons. Only in London could Pepys's most characteristic qualities, restlessness, curiosity, competitiveness, multiplicity of consciousness, have grown to the height they did. In his lifetime London was never quiet for long. The sinking of the barometer in 1641, the storm of civil war, the unpredictable yawings that followed the death of Cromwell, the plague, the fire, the Dutch fleet coming up the Medway, the Popish plot, the attempt to exclude James Duke of York from the succession, the punitive reaction that followed, the Glorious Revolution

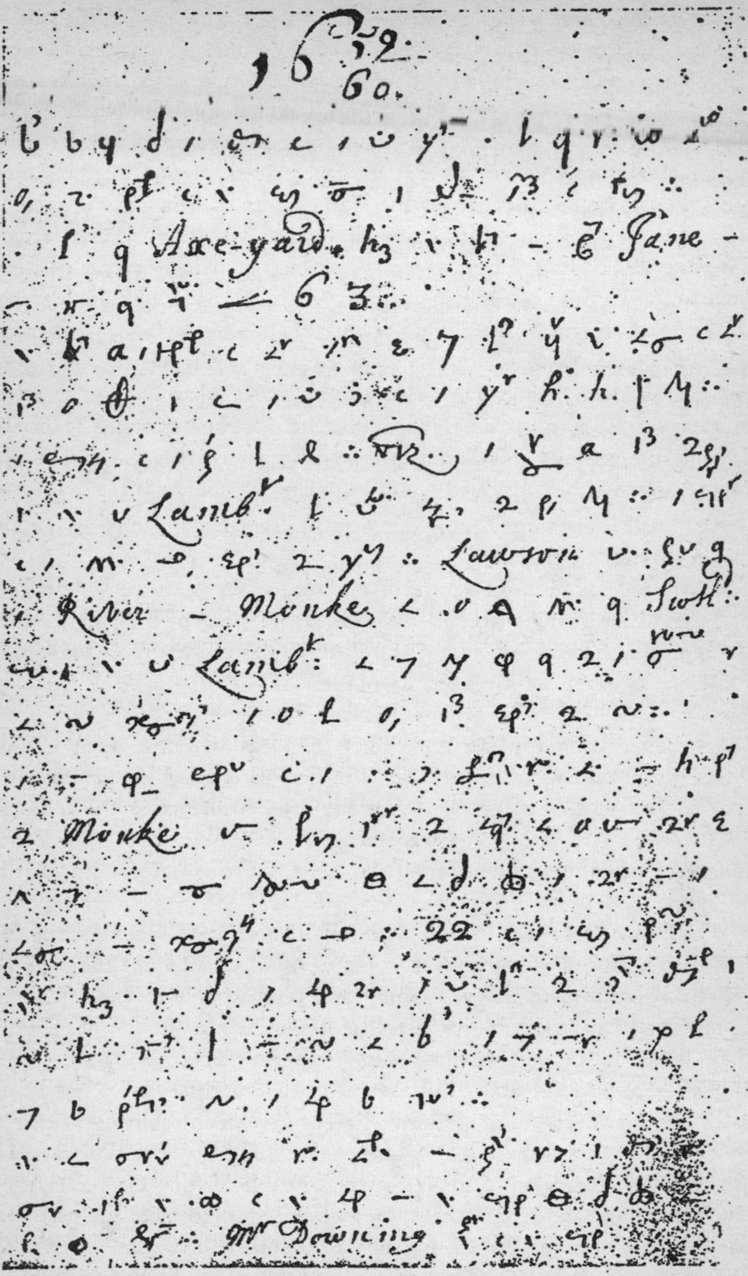
1659
60
Axe-yard
Jane
Lamb
Lawson
River
Monke
Lamb
Monke
Mr Downing

The opening page of the Diary. See page 52.

that turned out James and ended Pepys's own career, the louring of
Jacobite conspiracy that more than once darkened a dignified retirement
with the shadow of arrest, this is a record of experience by no means confined to the tranquil and the serene. Pepys, the supreme observer of his
age, saw it as turbulent and uncertain. He was a Londoner looking at
London.

It is there that he comes before us in his own introduction to the opening entry of the Diary, begun on January 1st, 1660, just as the renewed
momentum of events promised an exciting and perhaps decisive turn in
the affairs of state. With a masterpiece, the reader in his eagerness to see
what all the world says is so wonderful is apt to flash past the opening
phrases. Much can be learned from their content, their manner and above
all the order in which Pepys, most systematic of men, arranged them.

> Blessed be God, at the end of the last year I was in very good health,
> without any sense of my old pain but upon taking of cold.
> I live in Axe-yard, having my wife and servant Jane, and no more in
> family than us three.
> My wife after the absence of her terms for seven weeks, gave me
> hopes of her being with child, but on the last day of the year she hath
> them again. The condition of the State was thus. *Viz.* the Rump, after
> being disturbed by my Lord Lambert . . .

So matter-of-factly, like the screech of a sash-window being thrown
open, begins one of the greatest texts in our history and in our literature.
The subject of this biography turns his head to us across the centuries
and addresses us as though we were only across the room. Not to be moved
is to be deficient in humanity. All the easier not to notice exactly what he
is saying.

The Diary opens (and closes) with the invocation of God. A man who
had been born and brought up in the time of Charles I and Cromwell had
had his bellyful of theology. Is this just a conventional gabble, like grace
in an Oxford college, or does it tell us something about the place taken
by religion in Pepys's view of things? Both. Pepys's religion, unlike
almost everything else about him, seems dry and uninteresting, but it was
not unreal, still less unimportant. Except for an intermittently uneasy
consciousness of sin there seems to have been little specifically Christian
about it: no perception of the beauty and simplicity that George Herbert
had found and expressed: no outgoing of the heart towards the person of
Christ: no love or forgiveness for man as a brother for whom Christ died.
This is not at all to say that Pepys was lacking in compassion or bene-

volence, but that he practised these virtues either from impulse or from
general principles of a moral and religious, but not noticeably Christian,
nature. Moral principle and religious observance lay at the heart of
Pepys's understanding and conduct of life. To argue that he was a hypocrite
because he was unchaste or that he was an unbeliever because he was
worldly is to take up a position that would have been thought extreme in
a Victorian academy for young ladies.

God, then, came first. But hard on his heels came health, the overwhelming preoccupation of the inward-turning mind. Writing about a
country clergyman of Pepys's time who also kept a diary, a modern
scholar comments on the '. . . high incidence of physical distress arising
from the many incurable diseases of pre-industrial society. Only a reading
of the actual diary will bring home to the reader the constant almost
obsessional discussion of pain and sickness.'[4] The same concern is abundantly evident throughout the Diary we are considering. No doubt it is
true that twentieth-century medicine could have saved Pepys much pain
and more anxiety: but to believe that improvements in drugs and surgery
will ever stop humanity from droning on about its ailments is to close
one's mind to what all too often one would have wished to close one's ears.
Pepys's ills were far from imaginary but they did leave him with a sometimes too exalted sense of the duty he owed to his bladder and his colon.

After health came social statistics – a word that only a dozen years later
was to make its début on the linguistic stage.[5] And after social statistics
comes his wife Elizabeth and *her* state of health. The vagaries of her
gynaecological disorder had given them hopes of children but these had
been dashed. (Almost certainly the knife that had relieved Pepys of his
stone had cut off his posterity.)

These matters established and for the time being disposed of we are
free for a tour of the political horizon after which we return to the point
from which we started, the circumstances of the diarist himself:

> My own private condition very handsome; and esteemed rich, but
> indeed very poor, besides my goods of my house and my office, which
> at present is somewhat uncertain. Mr. Downing master of my office.

Pepys has drawn a quick sketch-map of his world that significantly
omits all mention of its most conspicuous feature: Edward Mountagu.
That he, not Downing, was the true centre of hope and interest, of activity
and reward, is clear from the lightest skimming of the first few entries in
the Diary. But in the New Year of 1660 he was lying doggo at Hinchingbrooke. So successfully had he effaced himself that even his most

intelligent and sharp-eyed servant had for the moment forgotten his existence. Such a withdrawal was certainly easier in the days before the car and the
telephone but even then its completeness was sometimes deceptive. Pepys
and others kept Mountagu informed of what was reported in London.
Early in January it was known that Monck had crossed the border at
Coldstream and that Lambert's army was melting away. A month later
Pepys watched him march past Whitehall at the head of his troops and
recorded his impression of a well-found, well-disciplined military force.
What was Monck going to do with it? All the signs were that he would
support the Rump who regarded him as their rescuer from the military
satraps like Lambert and Desborough and their defender against the
resurgent royalism that had taken so dangerous a hold in the City. On
February 9th he was sent there to arrest some of those who had challenged
the Rump's authority and, as Pepys heard, 'clapped up many of the
Common Council'. To teach the City a lesson the Rump further ordered
him to destroy the posts and chains and gates and portcullises by which the
Corporation asserted its ancient freedom and privileges. This Monck
began to do; and the next day, to quote Pepys, 'The city look mighty
blank and cannot tell what in the world to do.' Pepys himself solved this
problem by lying in bed and going late to his office where he spent what
remained of the morning reading a Spanish guidebook to Rome.

> At noon I walked in the Hall [i.e. Westminster Hall] where I heard
> the news of a letter from Monke, who was now gone into the City
> again . . . and it was very strange how the countenance of men in the
> Hall was all changed with joy in half an hour's time. So I went up to
> the Lobby, where I saw the Speaker reading of the letter; and after it
> was read, Sir A. Haslerig came out very angry; and Billing* standing at
> the door, took him by the arm and cried, 'Thou man, will thy beast
> carry thee no longer? thou must fall.'

Pepys's eye had caught the tide at the instant of turning. He went on
to make the approach of the Restoration his own stretch of history. Ever
since the Diary was first published in 1825 it has coloured and shaped the
view of those few weeks like the sun coming up on a winter morning.

> And endeed I saw many people give the soldiers drink and money,
> and all along in the streets cried 'God bless them' and extraordinary

---

* The Quaker who with some of his congregation had been roughly handled by Monck's
soldiers on the day of their arrival in London. It was an apt indeed epigrammatic summing
up of the situation, but one does see why people often found the Quakers exasperating.

good words. Hence . . . to the Star tavern . . . where we drank and I
wrote a letter to my Lord from thence. In Cheapside there was a great
many bonefires, and Bow bells and all the bells in all the churches
as we went home were a ringing. Hence we went homewards it being
about 10 a-clock. But the common joy that was everywhere to be seen!
The number of bonefires, there being fourteen between St. Dunstan's
and Temple-bar. And at Strand bridge I could at one view tell 31 fires.
In King-streete, seven or eight; and all along burning and roasting and
drinking for rumps — there being rumps tied upon sticks and carried
up and down. The buchers at the maypole in the Strand rang a peal
with their knives when they were going to sacrifice their rump . . .
Indeed it was past imagination, both the greatness and the suddenness
of it. At one end of the street, you would think there was a whole lane
of fire, and so hot we were fain to keep still on the further side merely
for heat.[6]

No wonder the young Macaulay was entranced: no wonder that this
passage is quoted at length in the most detailed and technical account of
the restoration by a modern scholar who can certainly not be criticised
for leaning towards the lush or the picturesque.[7] Mountagu was well-
served by his London correspondent.

There were other letters reaching Hinchingbrooke, secret from Pepys
and all the world beside. Mountagu was in indirect touch with the Stuarts
through one of his kinsmen.[8] Within three weeks of Monck's letter to the
Speaker telling him to admit the secluded members and setting a date in
May for a dissolution and fresh elections, Mountagu had been restored
to the colonelcy of his regiment, joined with Monck in the supreme command of the fleet as General-at-Sea, appointed a Commissioner of the
Admiralty and elected to the Council of State. His coyness towards the
King's advances vanished, though his discretion remained impenetrable. It
was reported that he would try to bring back not Charles II but Richard
Cromwell. Clarendon analysing the news across the channel did not believe
it for a moment. Pepys who was closer to the scene of action seems to have
felt less confidence in his own powers of prediction. In the first brief private conversation on politics that he records after Mountagu's return to
London in the first week of March: 'He told me he feared there was a
new design hatching, as if Monke had a mind to get into the saddle.' He
at last showed his hand, or part of it three days later, on March 6th,
that ever-to-be-remembered day on which Mountagu 'called me by myself
to go along with him into the garden, where he asked me how things
were with me', and went on to invite Pepys to go to sea with him as his

confidential secretary and promised to support him in any application for a permanent post in the Government service.

'He told me also that he did believe the King would come in.' That this opinion was conveyed in no ringing tones of royalist fervour may be gathered from the expanded version of these remarks which Pepys found room for later on in his entry for the same momentous day:

> My Lord told me that there was great endeavours to bring in the Protector again; but he told me too, that he did believe it would not last long if he were brought in; no, nor the King neither (though he seems to think that he will come in), unless he carry himself very soberly and well.

It is all very cool, detached, pragmatic. Pepys did not guess that the speaker had, like Monck himself, called in his hedging bets and staked everything on the Stuarts. In any case Mountagu had committed himself unequivocally on a far more interesting question: the future of Samuel Pepys; '. . . and in discourse thereupon my wife and I lay awake an hour or two in our bed.'

Between Monck's *coup de théâtre* and Mountagu's return to London Pepys had paid a brief and bibulous visit to Cambridge to see his brother John settled in at Christ's. The sudden change in the political wind provided an opportunity of combining a private jaunt with a business journey since Hinchingbrooke was only a short ride from Cambridge. Indeed Mountagu's father-in-law, one of the members now readmitted to his place in Parliament, told Pepys on February 21st that his master ought to be sent for at once. On the next day James Pearse, a surgeon whose unusual abilities and connections were to make him into a lifelong friend and colleague, suggested that they should ride down together as he had to rejoin his regiment then stationed at Cambridge. Pepys gladly agreed and they set out early on the 24th 'the day and way very foul'.

Love of travel was a passion that grew stronger as the means of satisfying it grew less. The eagerness with which Pepys in old age planned, directed and vicariously followed the European tour of his stolid nephew John Jackson is part affectionate solicitude, part wistfulness for chances gone beyond recall, but mainly the random avidity of the addict. In young manhood even the mud and the rain of a February day could not quench the exhilaration. At Puckeridge they were very merry over a fried loin of mutton: and when both the day and their horses were spent some six miles short of Cambridge they passed an agreeable evening at an inn playing cards while supper was prepared. Early next morning the two friends parted but by a strange reversal of roles, Pearse went to Hinchingbrooke, 'to speak with my Lord before his going to London', while Pepys went straight to Cambridge to join his brother and his father who was staying at an inn in Petty Cury. Why did Pearse go to call on Mountagu? Does the ease with which he and his pretty wife moved in the circles of the Restoration court and the official appointments subsequently showered on him – Surgeon-General of the Fleet, Surgeon to the Duke of York – afford a clue? We do not know. But it is odd. And it is odd, too, that Pepys, with his way still to make in the world, should join his father and brother for an incessantly convivial weekend before reporting on the latest developments to his patron. Two or three years later he would have treated anyone guilty of such a frivolous misordering of priorities to a severe and ponderous lecture. In the spring of 1660 he had hardly begun the transition from the indolence and self-indulgence of under-employment to the brisk bustle of the rising executive, from uncertainty of his social position and professional future to the confident self-importance of the administrative Prometheus born to bring order and system into the Chaos and Old Night of the Navy Office.

Perhaps Cambridge, for ever associated in his mind with enjoyment and good fellowship, exerted a sympathetic attraction. Certainly no opportunity of either was neglected in a whirl that leaves even the reader of the Diary feeling a little fuddled. Party succeeded party in tavern and college, most notably in Magdalene where Pepys was sumptuously entertained by those very members of the governing body who had previously reproved his alcoholic excesses. There was one faintly ominous moment on the Sunday afternoon when he was called away from a comfortable fireside in Christ's by a message that Pearse was waiting for him at his inn 'who told us that he had lost his Journy, for my Lord was gone from Hinchingbrooke to London on Thursday last, at which I was a little put to a stand'. But only a little. Another drink restored the situation and the rest of the day was spent in heroic tippling.

Not that this seems to have blunted any of Pepys's usual faculties. He records the frequency with which the King's health was drunk; he is amused by the alacrity with which the grave and reverend signiors of his own college liquidated their Puritanism; he buys a book or two; he makes advances to the chambermaid. He rises without apparent discomfort at four o'clock on the Monday morning to ride back to London, breaking the journey at Saffron Walden to see round Audley End. His metabolism was clearly adjusted to hard drinking. In view of what lay before him it was perhaps as well that it should be so.

4

Restoration

Pepys arrived back in London on the Tuesday to find all the shops shut and one of the militia regiments in arms. A day of public thanksgiving for the return of Parliament had been ordered. Riding straight to St. Paul's he left a travelling companion to hold his horse while he went in to hear the preacher and to pick up the latest news. Only then did he return home to his wife and a change of clothes before going to pay his respects to Mountagu, who was most affable. A week later, as has been mentioned, Mountagu declared his readiness to underwrite Pepys's career and invited him to come aboard his flagship as his confidential secretary.

It was the prospect of the silken ladder lowered from the parapets of officialdom that excited Pepys. Next morning he heard of a legal opening in Westminster; and then it seemed there might be something falling vacant in the Exchequer. Pearse the surgeon reappeared with his Cheshire Cat-like ubiquity and 'gave me great encouragement to go to sea with my Lord'. And later that afternoon Pepys met his father, hotfoot from Cambridge, or rather from Brampton, the near-by village where his childless brother Robert, the diarist's uncle, had a small estate. This he had declared his intention of bequeathing to Samuel, no idle statement as according to Pepys *père* 'his leg [was] very dangerous and he doth believe he cannot continue in that condition long'. What was a life on the ocean wave compared to landed proprietorship and a snug place in the civil service? If things went on at this rate the future was assured.

Next day there were disturbing reports of the officers turning nasty and refusing to let in Charles Stuart. Monck asserted his authority and the rumbling died away. Still it was a warning. Pepys resolved to accept the sea secretaryship, the more readily because he had been told how easily he could make money by pocketing the wages of the servants to which the position would entitle him.[1] Two problems flowed from the decision: what to do about the clerkship in Downing's office, which was a personal, not an official position, and what was to happen to Elizabeth while her husband was at sea. The first was easily settled by providing a substitute and the second with rather more anxiety by arranging that she should go to live in the household of a senior Exchequer colleague near Iver.

Elizabeth was very much upset at this sudden disruption of their life together. She was much more dependent on him than he was on her. In what was still a man's world, she had no money, little education and no evident talents or interests to occupy her when she was on her own. Separation, for her, meant suspended animation, which it certainly did not for him. Even her youth and her beauty weighed against her because her husband, as mindful of his own proclivities as of her lack of sophistication, would prescribe a rural seclusion that he would never have tolerated for himself. It is characteristic of Pepys's view of their relationship that he should consult first Mountagu, who suggested the plan, and then his own father, who approved it, before saying a word to his wife. No wonder she was often pettish; and, treated as a child, behaved like one.

Pepys himself, still now in the springtime of their marriage, may have felt a stirring of sympathy, perhaps even a twinge of guilt. At any rate he does not censure her or confide to his Diary the exasperation he found it ever harder to check at such natural distress. But there is no disguising the fact that he was a selfish husband. As Dr. Latham has pointed out, *his* birthday is impressively celebrated in the Diary but *hers* is not even mentioned. There is a strong tincture of *A Doll's House* about the marriage. Cheerful and companionable as he was, Pepys could never take naturally to the idea of partnership or equality.

He was himself both agitated and exulting at the prospect opening before him. Hard drinker as he was at this stage of his life, he began to drink even harder, until sleepless nights and other symptoms warned him to take care. But once the decisions had been taken and accepted, his equilibrium was soon restored. Even a ride down to Iver in lashing rain with a nasty cold on the chest seems to have revived his spirits. And the news that his rival John Creed who had been Mountagu's secretary at the Sound was now to be made Deputy Treasurer of the Fleet acted as a powerful stimulant on his competitive nature. Creed was a man to be watched. He and his brother Richard, who had been Secretary to the great Blake,[2] had naval connections and experience far superior to Pepys's. Probably their social standing was higher too, since Creed was considered a suitable match for Mountagu's niece, herself the daughter of an important and well-connected Parliamentarian. For several years Pepys hob-nobbed with Creed without ever really liking him, fascinated by his cynicism and envying his craftiness. From start to finish he is seen as a competitor, and a dangerous one, in the great race of life. To have supplanted him in the secretaryship was one up to Pepys. There was no doubt about that, least of all in Creed's mind, as Pepys himself had heard at the Navy Office. But did this new appointment put the score level again? It was the kind of question that keyed Pepys up to his keenest and most alert.

What with packing his traps for sea, settling Elizabeth's departure, closing the house, making his will, briefing himself for his new responsibilities and (sweetest of all) engaging a boy and a clerk, supernumerary no doubt, to the shipborne servants whose wages were to be their sole *raison d'être*, Pepys had little time for jealousy or anxiety. In any case the shower of small bribes that had already begun to patter on him whispered delicious intimations of what might be in store. He was wined and dined and flattered and solicited. Best of all, Mountagu continued to distinguish him by marks of particular respect. Bad weather and floods delayed embarkation but at last on March 23rd Pepys and the rest of the Admiral's personal staff went abroad the *Swiftsure* lying at anchor in the river. 'As soon as my Lord on board, the guns went off bravely from the Ships; and a little while after comes the Vice-Admirall Lawson and seemed very respectful to my Lord, and so did the rest of the Commanders of the frigates that were thereabouts.' This was a great point gained. Mountagu had begun his naval career by superseding Lawson, a brave and popular commander, whose advanced Republican views had rendered him suspect to Cromwell and to Blake. Again only a few months earlier it had been Lawson's initiative in bringing the fleet into the river in support of the Rump that had checked the army leaders. Lawson's hold on the loyalty of his officers and men was undoubted. Why should he be content a second time to be passed over in favour of an officer whose professional qualifications were much inferior to his own and whose political inclinations were certainly not towards the left? If we knew the answer to that question we could perhaps explain why English political history has been so much less disastrous than anybody else's.

Pepys was very pleased with the cabin allotted to him. Any discomfort was more than compensated for by the fact that it was 'the best that any had that belonged to my Lord'. Indeed he could hardly believe the deference shown to him. In the great cabin at formal meals he took precedence over everyone except the Captain. And even the Captain went out of his way to distinguish the secretary with unheard-of marks of civility. He came to drink a bottle of wine with Pepys in his cabin to celebrate the hallowed anniversary of his lithotomy, staying till eleven o'clock at night 'which is a kindness he doth not usually do to the greatest officer in the ship'. A few days later after the Admiral had transferred his flag to his old ship the *Naseby* 'the Captain would by all means have me up to his cabin; and there treated me huge nobly, giving me a barrel of pickled oysters, and opened another for me, and a bottle of wine, which was a very great favour'. No wonder Pepys was charmed by the hospitality and comradeship of naval life. Even a day or two's seasickness when the fleet moved down to the mouth of the Thames hardly spoiled the fun — 'every day bringing me a fresh sense of the great pleasure of my present life'.

He got through a great deal of work, attacking it with the vigour, method and thoroughness that he was to apply throughout his professional life and increasingly to his personal affairs and intellectual pursuits. He records for the first time his pleasure in having cleared his mind by the efficient discharge of business. He had, at last, been given a job that took some doing and had found that he could do it easily. To the discovery of his own powers was added the approval of his superiors, the deference, the compliments, even the substantial *douceurs* of important people, and the infinite agreeableness of living in a well-mannered society. There were only two flaws in the perfection of existence: separation from Elizabeth and (occasional) reunion with Creed. Even these were only passing clouds. Creed had come aboard the *Swiftsure* the day after Pepys 'and dined very boldly with my Lord', but mercifully there was not an empty bed left on board. When the Admiral shifted into the *Naseby* Creed, not to be caught the same way twice, had had his things sent aboard beforehand but to Pepys's glee Mountagu's personal steward resented Creed's high-handedness and had him sent ashore.

The incessant comings and goings aboard the flagship made up both the business and the pleasure of life. Sailors are sociable people and the hospitality of the State's ships seems to have been worthy of the standards subsequently maintained by the Royal Navy. A large fleet at anchor keeps its boats' crews busy. Pepys dined on successive days with Lawson in the *London* and with Captain Clarke in the *Speaker*. Invitations such as these were a distinction indeed. And not a day went by but Lawson or Stayner, Mountagu's old colleague now appointed Rear-Admiral, or some of the senior captains came over for a conference and stayed for a meal and a private talk with the Admiral at which Pepys was often invited to remain. Some of the captains were suspected of dangerously Republican sympathies and were sent off out of harm's way to escort a convoy to the Straits. It was a situation that demanded the closest possible personal contact between the Commander-in-Chief and his captains. A division in the fleet would expose the country to incalculable risks. Whatever they did they must do together. And as the country waited for the new Parliament to meet it was overwhelmingly clear that a Stuart Restoration was the direction in which everything was moving. Even before Pepys left London the exultant inscription on the empty niche of Charles I's statue at the Royal Exchange *Exit tyrannus, regum ultimus . . .* had been painted out by a man who came with a ladder and a brush during working hours when the floor was buzzing with merchants and jobbers. Not only had no one questioned the man's authority but 'there was a great bonefire made in the Exchange and people cried out "God bless King Charles the Second"'. Ever since the fleet had moved down the river there had been a stream of Royalist agents and sympathisers coming aboard for passes or even for orders for passage in State's ships.

To spend one's days talking on terms of equality with the captains who had won the great victories of the Commonwealth against the Dutch and the Spaniards or receiving the respectful addresses of rich and important Royalists in need of a passport or a passage was to pass from the cinders of everyday life to the pumpkin coach and the glass slippers of fairyland. Pacing the quarterdeck under the stars with Captain Cuttance it was pleasant to be instructed in nautical terminology. And with all the bustle of business and the courtesies of social life there was still plenty of time for music and plenty of people, including Mountagu himself, who shared Pepys's enjoyment of it.

Those happy spring days aboard the *Naseby* breathe in the Diary the freshness of the season, the sharp tang of the sea air, above all the delight in being alive that makes Pepys like Falstaff a favourite in every age. They also introduce us to a number of the principal characters in his life. One of the very first to put in an appearance was Pearse the surgeon. Like Pepys he combined to an uncommon degree astuteness in promoting his own career with a conscientiousness in discharging his duty. He was to be one of that select circle, Sir John Narbrough the Admiral was another, of professional colleagues whom Pepys both respected and liked. All these men belonged to what was virtually a new social category — the expert permanently employed in Government service. It was appropriate that some of them should meet aboard the ship that was to be freighted with the new age.

Next day three figures from a past that was by no means dead and buried came over the side of the *Naseby*. Colonel George Thomson, the veteran whose wooden leg had taken him from the battlefield to the Parliamentary Commission of the Admiralty and Navy, was to infuriate Pepys by his pertinacious criticism of the Navy Board in the Second Dutch War. William Penn, who accompanied him, was to be even more of a menace. With Mountagu and Monck he was the only survivor of the seven Generals-at-Sea, and as a sea officer he outclassed them both. Neither, after all, could handle a ship, much less a fleet, without professional assistance. Penn could. It was Penn whose tactical brilliance had earned Blake's highest praise at the battle of the Kentish Knock, Penn whose bold initiative had rescued the great Admiral from a very tight corner at Portland. Worse still from the point of view of a competitor such as Mountagu he had long been suspected of Royalist sympathies and had been left unemployed for several years. Once the Restoration was assured he was a much more formidable rival than Lawson. How much Pepys feared his superiority is evident from the abuse heaped on him in the Diary during the years that they were colleagues at the Navy Office. The last of the trio Robert Blackborne held the post of Secretary to the Admiralty Committee and had an awkward, shy nephew, Will Hewer, who was to grow up into Pepys's right-hand man and closest friend.

Two days later appeared the bizarre figure who was to put Pepys's strong sense of family obligation to its longest and severest trial — Elizabeth's brother Balty. If Balthasar St. Michel had not existed only Dickens could have invented him. The character revealed in his letters to Pepys has much of the roseate irresponsibility of Mr. Micawber, much of the unctuous craftiness of Uriah Heep, but remains, like all the highest flights of imagination, unique and unmistakable. Strutting, protesting, wheedling, cadging, whining, once or twice, when the mask drops, snarling, Balty is always voluble, always larger than life, always, somehow, sham, as if his troubled spirit recognised that it had been classified under the wrong category. On this his first appearance as in so many subsequent ones he was in search of a job that would not depreciate his social pretensions. As his understandably irritated brother-in-law was to write when these applications were repeated a few weeks later, 'I perceive he stands upon a place for a gentleman that may not stain his family; when God help him, he wants bread.' Pepys who had only just got a toe-hold himself was embarrassed. What might not Balty do or say? What would the senior officers who had treated him so civilly think of him for bringing so strange a relation on board? And how was he to get rid of him without offending Elizabeth? Balty wanted to stay aboard the flagship as a Reformado, that is a supernumerary officer without regular duties, a terrifying prospect. The only hope of relief was an appeal to Mountagu who had, at dinner, shown his usual courtesy to his secretary's uninvited guest. Mountagu promised a letter recommending him as a Reformado to a Captain whom, a few days later, he confessed to disliking. Pepys breathed again and sent Balty early to bed in a cabin whose regular occupant was sleeping ashore.

Two days later the flagship sailed out of the river to join the fleet in the Downs. The weather turned rough and Pepys felt squeamish. But walking on deck and eating and drinking soon put him right. He was much pleased by his first sight of the French coast and perhaps even more by seeing Balty safely off the ship on his way to Deal and back to London with fifteen shillings for Elizabeth. It was now early April and the spring flowers of Royalist revival scented every breeze from shore. Mountagu was chosen M.P. for Weymouth and was offered the honour of representing the University of Cambridge. Even the news that Lambert had escaped from the Tower on April 10th, presumably to head a last stand against the restoration of the monarchy, hardly signified. The tide that Pepys had seen turn only a few weeks earlier was running now in overwhelming strength. By the 18th he had concluded 'that it is evident now that the Generall and Council do resolve to make way for the King's coming. And it is now clear that either the Fanatiques must now be undone, or the Gentry and citizens throughout England and clergy must fall, in spite of their Militia and army, which is not at all possible I think.' Events proved him right. On the 24th he heard that Lambert had been taken in Northamptonshire. The last guttering flame had been snuffed out.

On May Day the King was proclaimed in London amid scenes of rapture such as the Stuarts especially inspire in those separated from them by space or time. Two days later Pepys at the Council of War aboard the flagship read the King's letter to the assembled commanders who accepted the Restoration with markedly less enthusiasm than the sailors who were subsequently mustered on the quarterdeck to hear the same message. Perhaps the seamen recognised a welcome opportunity for plenty of free drink where their officers saw a threat to their own employment. Pepys anyhow enjoyed himself being rowed from ship to ship while the men cheered and the bullets hissed overhead from the flagship firing her salute. The days that followed were an ambrosial foretaste of the joys that Pepys was to find in an official career. Work was always at high pressure, letters to be drafted, orders to be sent off, commissions to be made out, either on the spot or against a tight deadline. And when work had been dispatched, social life succeeded at the same brisk pace. Oysters and wine and barrels of ale, songs and music and half-tipsy horseplay, ninepins and gossip and wearing a new fine cloth suit, here was every pleasure life could afford except the company of women and the enchantment of the stage. Most delectable of all was the consciousness of being on the inside: to be shown private letters from the King and the Duke of York, to hear Mountagu's private opinion of Monck 'but a thick-skulled fellow' and to know which of the important people around one were on the way up and which on the way down. And to be paid for all this, paid to enjoy oneself; surely the world had nothing more to offer except to prolong and to extend this state of affairs.

On May 12th the flagship weighed anchor, bound for The Hague where she was to embark the King and his brothers for England. On passage the tailors and painters set about changing the flags and other emblems from those of the Commonwealth to those of Charles II. Two royalists who came aboard from another ship told Pepys that his old employer Downing was in bad odour with the court and had been sent home in disgrace. This, as Pepys soon found out, was a mistaken report, but they had more accurate news of his old tutor at Magdalene, Samuel Morland, who had been knighted by the King that every week for his activities as a double agent in Thurloe's intelligence service.

On the 14th Pepys on waking looked out of the scuttle and saw the Dutch coast close to. In spite of the big sea that was tumbling the boats and soaking their occupants he was one of the first to obtain leave to go ashore in the afternoon. The weather was filthy: the landscape nothing but sand-dunes: and supper – for ten – consisted of a salad and two or three mutton bones. A traveller less resolved to admire might have growled: but Pepys was delighted with the neatness of the town, the civility of its inhabitants, the prettiness of the women. Returning on board next day he found that his old tutor, now Sir Samuel, had put in an appearance but had been treated with contempt by Mountagu and the other senior officers. Neither he nor Downing, soon, like him, to be knighted and to appear aboard the flagship, could even in that far from censorious age expect to be thought of as men of honour. It was one thing to change sides: public life could not go on if people did not. It was quite another to betray one's friends.

Preparations for the reception of the royal party were accelerated by the arrival of Peter Pett, the Commissioner of Chatham Dockyard, that rich administrative fief over which his dynasty had held sway since the time of

James I. Pepys and he were to wrestle many a fall without either securing a lock on the other. But for the moment all eyes were turned towards the King and his brother James, Duke of York, newly appointed Lord High Admiral.

Pepys, who had gone ashore with Mountagu's young son Edward, was introduced into the royal presence by the agency of a convivial royal chaplain whom he had met in an inn. He kissed the hands of both brothers and records his first impression: 'the King seems to be a very sober man'. The Chancellor, Hyde, later Earl of Clarendon, although in bed with the gout 'spoke very merrily to the child and me'. The merriment seems to have communicated itself to Pepys who, casting responsibility to the winds, spent the next three days in an alcoholic whirl of sightseeing and party-going, during the course of which he twice lost the child committed to his care. It was fortunate that Holland was the most orderly and civilised country in Europe even if the pubs were full of 'Duch boores eating of fish [in] a boorish manner'. Indeed it was the boy's zest for seeing the country that caused these anxious separations. On the first occasion he accompanied a party to Delft, where Pepys pursued him and met him on the road. On the second he disappeared, leaving no message, so that Pepys, looking out of a picture dealer's shop at The Hague next day was not a little relieved to see his young charge among a crowd of passengers landing on the quay at which the Leiden boat had just made fast. Twice was enough. Pepys made sure of his child-minding arrangements that evening before going out with friends in search of nocturnal sport.

What did the young Pepys, already an inveterate book-buyer and soon to be a patron of artists and a collector of prints, make of his first visit to the Holland of Rembrandt and Ruisdael, of Steen and Van der Velde, the centre not only of living artists but of the fine art trade as it had long been of publishing and bookselling? He bought two or three books 'for the love of the binding', he went to picture dealers and visited famous rooms in famous houses where famous paintings were hanging, but he does not describe them or name the painters. On his visit to Delft he is much struck with the realism of a sea-battle carved on Van Tromp's monument but says nothing of the paintings of Vermeer. What really takes his fancy are the echoes artfully achieved in various great houses which he tests by singing or playing the flageolet: or the *faits divers* with which guides have regaled tourists from the dawn of the industry, such as the story of the lady whose stinginess was punished by a pregnancy terminating in the birth of 365 children. Pepys's artistic taste like his genius was an addition to, not a substitute for, the curiosity and suscepti-bility of everyman. Appetite preceded and subsequently accompanied discrimination: he was *gourmand* before he was *gourmet*. And at all stages of his life he was a chameleon. Had he been travelling with John Evelyn, whom he had not yet met, we should have a very different story. His company on this occasion, apart from Master Edward Mountagu and Will Howe, the steward from Hinchingbrooke, consisted of shipmates ashore, chance encounters in inns, odd acquaintances from Cambridge or London who were heading the goldrush for jobs under the new Government. Conducted tours, hearty jokes, tippling and titillation filled a round of pleasure which Pepys could enjoy to the utmost.

Blearily he scrambled back aboard the *Naseby* with a hangover such that he slept the clock round 'and rising to piss, mistook the sun-rising for the sun-setting on Sunday night'. He therefore returned to bed and slept for a further five hours until woken by the Captain's boy with a present of four barrels of Breton oysters, sent by another captain who desired his favour. Luckily there was a lull in the work to be done, since Mountagu thought it tactful to defer all to the new Lord High Admiral, who was expected on board directly. On May 22nd late in the forenoon James and his brother the young Duke of Gloucester were received with a general salute. After they had been shown over the ship 'upon the Quarter Deck table under the awning the Duke of Yorke and my Lord, Mr Coventree and I spent an houre at allotting to every ship their service in their return to England'.

One day, says a Latin quotation familiar to Pepys, contains the whole of life. That hour on the quarter-deck contains the best part of his. Here joined together for the first time in the conduct of naval affairs were the men who through nearly thirty years constituted the directing intelligence of the service, planning, administering, commanding. With these three Pepys was to rise and, at last, with James, the sole survivor, to fall. Their opinion was the constellation by which he shaped the course of his life. All of them were by social and political position so far superior to Pepys that his relationship to them, even when he had long been accepted as an intimate and indispensable colleague, could never be hurt by the violent competitiveness of his nature. James, as a royal duke and later king, belonged to a species still generally accorded more divinity than it claimed: even Pepys after years of day-to-day contact with the royal family still recorded his amazement at the King's being a man like other men. Such a divinity was, as in the ancient world, perfectly compatible with lechery, frivolity and idleness. But Coventry and Mountagu, aristocrats who were at home in court or camp, were in Pepys's mind always mortals, even if mortals of a higher order. As such they could properly be taken as models in habits, manners, opinions and taste. And it was William Coventry, in this inconspicuous entry dwarfed by James's height and Mountagu's bulk, who was to have far the deepest influence on Pepys's mind and character.

The principals are completed by the entrance of the King, amid the huzzas of the whole cast. The *Naseby*, now renamed the *Royal Charles*, weighed anchor and sailed on a fresh breeze for England. The pleasant weather encouraged the King in two favourite activities that his courtiers were to find penitential: walking up and down (he was a tall man and walked fast) and telling the story of his adventures as a hunted man after the battle of Worcester. Pepys was entranced. He loved a good story (and it is one of the best in English history); he had too the yearning for first-hand evidence that turns a man into a historian, an activity to which both Coventry and Evelyn were later to urge him and which he recognised to 'sort mightily with my genius'. Twenty years later he took down in shorthand the full account that the King dictated to him while at New-market for the races. This he supplemented with other narratives of those who took part, some of whom he further questioned about discrepancies and gaps in the various sources to which he had access. So the grave and reverend Pepys of the Kneller portrait and the Cavalier medallion sustains the curiosity and imaginative sympathy of his younger self.

So the voyage passed, a Watteau-esque voyage to Cythera, the decks paced by persons of honour, the weather glorious, the conversation smart. On May 25th, two days after setting sail, the King landed at Dover amidst scenes of rejoicing that defeat even Pepys's vivid powers of description. From there he went on to Canterbury and London while Pepys and Moun-tagu returned to their ship: 'My Lord almost transported with joy that he hath done all this without any the least blur and obstruccion in the world that would give an offence to any, and with the great Honour that he thought it would be to him.'

And well he might be. As a Commander-in-Chief, as a politician, as a courtier and *chef de protocol* in an age that took these minutiae with maniac seriousness, he had not put a foot wrong. After so long a winning run it was time to cash the chips. Pepys, too, by the terms of that memorable conversation in the garden, stood to collect a share of the winnings. Even before the King had left, largesse had been distributed on no contemptible scale. One way and another Pepys had managed to put by as much in the two months of his secretaryship as he had in the preceding five or six years. But what both he and his patron wanted, at different levels, was office. Discussing the future in the Admiral's cabin Mountagu was re-assuring: 'We must have a little patience and we will rise together. In the meantime I will do you all the good Jobbs I can.' It all looked hopeful. And on the very day that the King landed the Duke of York had spoken to Pepys by name and had promised his future favour.

It was thus natural that Pepys should see in the rewarding of his patron some indication of what might be in store for him. By the first post Mountagu received an earldom: by the second the far rarer honour of the Garter. What might not be had for the asking if only master and man were at Whitehall? But Mountagu was a serving officer and could not leave his post until ordered. At last after dinner on June 7th the longed for summons arrived. Early the next morning Pepys took horse at Deal, dined at Canterbury and went round the Cathedral, resumed his journey by Sittingbourne and Chatham and Rochester to Gravesend, dismounting hot and tired, but not too tired to kiss 'a good handsome wench, . . . the first that I have seen a great while', nor to stay up late drinking huge quantities of beer with a naval captain. Next morning the whole party travelled to London in six boats. Although it was a Saturday and about midday when they disembarked at the Temple stairs, Pepys spent the whole of the afternoon and evening in attendance on Mountagu, accompanying him to Whitehall to wait upon the King. He slept at his father's house still not having seen Elizabeth from whom he had been parted for nearly three months. In the morning he again went first to Mountagu's lodging and after that to church. Only when he returned to his father's house for dinner was he reunited with his wife. In the afternoon they went for a walk by themselves in the grounds of Lincoln's Inn. For all the public boisterousness and the drinking of loyal toasts, for all the gallantry which Pepys records in his Diary after each visit to Court, the Restoration was for him a time of tension. A great opportunity might offer itself at any moment and might, if he were not vigilant to seize it, slip away never to recur.

That Mountagu's star was still rising no one could doubt. Within a week he was given one of the most important and supposedly one of the most lucrative household offices, the Mastership of the Great Wardrobe. The post carried with it a large house and a large establishment: besides these there would be contracts for clothes, robes of state, hangings and such like that could yield handsome fees and commissions. Even during the first few days back in London people were constantly pressing sums into Pepys's hand either to secure his recommendation to Mountagu's favour or to repay him for having forwarded their business when he was Admiral's secretary at sea. How was this happy state of affairs to be put on a permanent footing? This is the thought that hammers through the June entries in the Diary, drowning the raptures of reunion with Elizabeth (though he did find the night she went to Buckinghamshire to collect her things 'very lonely') and confining to one terse phrase the heartfelt relief of returning home to their little house in Axe Yard.

In fact Mountagu could hardly have acted quicker or more effectively. On the 18th he told Pepys 'that he did look after the place of the Clerk of the Acts for me'. Pepys makes no comment. Yet it was one of the four senior posts in the administration of the navy, and probably the only one to which a young man who was neither an expert nor an aristocrat could aspire. On the 23rd he told him that he had obtained the promise of the place 'at which I was glad'. Indeed from that moment it dominated his consciousness. On the 25th he asked and received William Coventry's promise of assistance. On the same day he had a civil meeting with a Mr. Turner of the Navy Office who was a rival candidate for the job. Later in the day he heard that Monck had his eye on the place for a nominee of his own and had asked Mountagu to give way. Mountagu refused in crisp terms. Next day a merchant offered Pepys £500 to withdraw his candidature. Pepys prayed for divine guidance. On the following day Mountagu and Pepys went to see the Duke of York who as Lord High Admiral ordered William Coventry 'to despatch my business of the Acts, in which place everybody gives me joy as if I were already in it, which God send'. (Presumably he had advised against accepting the £500.) On the 29th Pepys secured his warrant for the place from the Duke of York – the first obstacle in the bureaucratic assault course. But that same afternoon a friend in the Admiralty told him 'that Mr Barlow my Predecessor, Clerk of the Acts, is yet alive and coming up to town to look after his place – which made my heart sad a little'. And well it might. But the imperturbable Mountagu informed of this the same evening told Pepys to make sure of his patent – the final stage in the administrative process initiated by the warrant – 'and he would do all that could be done to keep him out'.

How Pepys struggled over the nightmarish barriers erected by the capricious and extortionate freeholders in public administration, that happy band of licensed highwaymen whom he most ardently wished to join, has been so well told by Sir Arthur Bryant and can be so fully reconstructed from the Diary itself that no further account is necessary. Offstage the infirm but inexorable steps of old Barlow totter menacingly nearer while the distraught Pepys rushes up and down Chancery Lane to find an engrossing clerk, pulls every string to have his warrant turned into a bill and the bill into a patent, until, after a fortnight of frenzy, punctuated by hard bargaining with his rivals and consoled by reports of Barlow's age, ill-health and disinclination to resume the life of a civil servant, the patent is, on July 13th, signed and sealed by the Lord

Chancellor himself. It only remained to negotiate a financial arrangement with Barlow in exchange for his renouncing all future claims. This was easily and amicably achieved. Barlow turned out to be a nice old man who obligingly died five years later without having caused any further trouble. Pepys was in.

5

The Navy Board

Only a few weeks before his appointment Pepys had known very little about the Navy Office. He had, as he records, seriously considered accepting a lump sum of a few hundred pounds to abandon his pursuit of the Clerkship there. Yet the pride with which Pepys presented his wife with the patent certifying his appointment and the joy with which she received it still glow in the Diary. Why had he warmed so suddenly to what was to be his life's work? What was the Navy Office? Who were its other members and what was its standing in the hierarchy of Government? What was the pay? What were the opportunities of supplementing it by open or furtive corruption?

Pepys did not yet know the full answers to these questions on July 13th, 1660, the date of his patent, but he knew quite enough to justify his enthusiasm. He had, in the first place, discovered that the Navy Office in Seething Lane, north-west of the Tower of London, contained handsome private houses for its four Principal Officers of whom the Clerk of the Acts was one. A man who lived in such a house maintained at the public charge would belong to a different world from that of Axe Yard. And evidently a Government department which accommodated its chief servants in such grandeur must be a very important department indeed. This had been confirmed by experience only the previous week. Pepys had been approached by a man who wanted to buy a place as one of his assistants. Assistant clerks in Government offices made their living by charging private individuals fees for the transaction of public business. The cost of a place was thus an excellent indicator of the level of activity. Pepys named £100, a very large sum in such a context. On the same day he had discovered that the salaries of all the Principal Officers were to be substantially increased. The Clerk of the Acts went up from £182 p.a. to £350. The others, the Surveyor, the Comptroller and the Treasurer, already higher were raised in the same generous proportion. Indeed the Treasurership at £2,000 p.a. became one of the best-paid posts in the public service. And like their assistants these senior officials stood to make even larger sums out of the glorified system of tips that traditionally stimulated the discharge of their functions.

Were these functions really proportionate to their rewards? Surely old Barlow even in his palmiest days had never cut much of a figure in the service of his country? True. But the navy Barlow had known was the old navy of the Tudors, dwindling by his time into the decrepitude of James I and Charles I. The navy Pepys was heir to was the large, modern, well-found force that had, arguably, won the Civil War for the Parliament and had, beyond any possible dispute, taught the proudest nations of Europe to treat Cromwell with respect. If such a fleet was to be kept in being the Navy Office would be the largest spending department of all. And everything pointed to that intention. Sandwich (as Pepys's patron Mountagu had now become) was an aggressive partisan of overseas expansion. Monck believed in foreign war as the sovereign remedy for disunity at home. The city wanted a strong navy to protect its growing merchant fleet from the piracy of the North African ports and to check the lawlessness of the European powers. There was even a more hawkish element that wanted the Dutch dealt with once and for all. The new navy was beginning to look indispensable.

The Navy Board as an administrative institution was both old and new. Old in that it could show a pedigree of continuing existence from Henry VIII to the Civil War and could plausibly trace an even more distant ancestry to the medieval Clerk of the King's Ships. New in that Charles II in reconstituting the Board after the twenty years of Parliamentary and Protectoral interlopers known as Navy Commissioners had improved not only the pay but the status and the calibre of its members. Pepys, though he would never have admitted it once he had shaken down into his clerkship, had joined a strong team.

The Treasurer, Sir George Carteret, was one of the best qualified men ever to have held that office. After long and varied service as a sea-officer he had joined the board as Comptroller five years before the outbreak of the Civil War. During the war he had reconquered his native island of Jersey for the King and had used it as a base for a privateering fleet which he organised and commanded with notable success. Such was the skill and resolution with which he defended the place when all else was lost that it was not until December 1651, more than three years after the end of the Second Civil War, that Blake at last compelled him to capitulate. Both Charles II and Clarendon had been sheltered by him when every man's hand was against them so that in the shifting sands of the Court no man's position was more firmly founded than his. Such a combination of proved efficiency as a sea-officer, as a naval administrator and as an independent Commander would have been remarkable enough without the special access to the King and the Chancellor that his past services had won him. It was reinforced by a passion for hard work that made little allowance for the susceptibilities of colleagues and none, as even his enemies admitted, for his own ease and pleasure.

The Comptroller, Sir Robert Slyngsbie, was another old Cavalier of high professional competence. Born into the navy (his father had been Comptroller) his sea service was even longer than Carteret's, but unlike Carteret he knew how to enjoy himself. Pepys found him the most congenial of his colleagues and was much distressed by his premature death in the autumn of 1661. Both the old Royalist and the young clerk wanted to institute radical reform in the navy and both chose a historical and comparative approach. Slyngsbie's *Discourse upon the past and present state of his Majesty's navy* states briefly and well many of the criticisms and proposals that Pepys was to spend the better part of his life in pressing. Their natures had marked affinities, including the vanity proper to an author. Turning over the sheets of the *Discourse* Pepys recorded in the Diary that 'he doth seem to have too good an opinion of them himself'. Slyngsbie's successor, Sir John Mennes, who had an even longer record of command at sea, was something of a man of letters and good company over a bottle of wine. But of his work he had no grasp at all.

The Surveyor of the Navy, Sir William Batten, was an old seaman of a very different type. Carteret, Slyngsbie and Mennes had been made sea officers as Gentlemen, Batten as a Tarpaulin. This distinction, differently phrased and variously interpreted, can be discerned at every stage of naval history from the remotest beginnings to the days of Queen Victoria. Its explanation lies in the fact that sailing a ship and fighting a battle are two different sorts of activity for which English society could supply two different sorts of men. Sailing was a skilled trade: fighting, or at any rate leading men into battle, was supposed to be the function of the aristocracy. In the Middle Ages when the art of sea warfare consisted in grappling the enemy ship and fighting it out hand to hand the military facts bore some crude relation to this social analysis. The seamen manoeuvred the ship alongside and the soldiers did the rest. But even then the division of labour was not quite so neatly defined. The sailors could hardly stand aside as neutrals or non-combatants since horrid experience taught them that the vanquished, unless rich enough to be worth a personal ransom, would all be butchered in cold blood. From its origins, then, the distinction was easier to maintain in theory than in practice. With the coming of the great gun and the almost coincident development in sail-plans and rigging, even the theoretical basis was largely knocked away. A naval ship became a special kind of ship designed exclusively for fighting other ships (by means of guns carried on her broadside) and the art of handling her became a skill of its own, drawing on but distinct from the arts of the navigator, the seaman, the gunner and the soldier. We can see this through the long perspective of hindsight. Pepys and a few others had the penetration and the insight to grasp it against the received ideas of their time. The Gentlemen versus the Tarpaulins was an antithesis that was to occupy his mind one way and another for most of his official life. It is a topic which must be enlarged later in this book. But though it has burst in unannounced in the person of Sir William Batten it must not be allowed to obscure him.

Batten, as Pepys never tires of making clear, was not a gentleman. But in knowledge of ships and in experience of sailing them in peace and war, above all in the variety, duration and extent of his experience of command he outranged even such formidable competitors as Carteret and Slyngsbie. And beyond that he was easily at home in territory where they could not follow. Batten had been bred to the sea. His father had been a master, that title, far older than captain, which designated the officer responsible for navigation and sailing.

'Very well, sir, very well. You have done your duty by making this remonstrance. Now pray let me do mine by laying me alongside the French admiral.' Hawke's reply* to his master who had demurred at taking the fleet among the reefs and shoals of Quiberon Bay in the fading light of a November afternoon with a gale rising from seaward is the classic definition of responsibility between the military caste (admiral, captain and lieutenant) and the civilian (master, boatswain and mate).

* Hawke's latest biographer (R. F. Mackay, *Admiral Hawke*, Oxford: Clarendon Press, 1965) concludes that the story is apocryphal. Accepting his arguments, I have therefore not felt obliged to follow either of the two variants he prints, since there can be no authority for a remark that was never made. The historicity of the incident is of course irrelevant to the point it illustrates.

Batten knew everything a seaman knew: and he had himself made the transition to military status by obtaining letters of marque, that is legal protection for privateering, when in command of a whaler. The extent of his success must be judged by his appointment in 1638 as Surveyor of the Navy against hot competition from a number of well-placed courtiers. It was confirmed by Warwick's retention of him as Vice-Admiral of the Parliamentary fleet throughout the Civil War. When in 1648 he was replaced by Colonel Rainborough half the ships revolted and sailed over to Holland to join the Royalists in exile. Here Batten had joined them with a privateer, reputed the fastest sailer of her day, in which he owned a substantial share. The true-blue Royalists however neither liked nor trusted him. There were mutters about taking bribes from the London merchants to let their ships go free instead of carrying them into continental ports as prize-of-war. It was remembered that Batten's squadron had forced the Queen to take cover in a ditch after he had chased her into Bridlington Bay and had opened fire on the military cargo she had landed for her husband's army. Compromised with both sides Batten took advantage of an amnesty to return to England, restoring his fine frigate to the Commonwealth in exchange for his freedom as a private citizen.

The hard life aboard a whaler or a man of war had by no means blunted Batten's appreciation of the comforts and pleasures of life. Pepys, who was often censured by himself and others for his love of luxury, speaks of his living 'like a prince' at his country house at Walthamstow. He was certainly a very rich man, avaricious and corrupt even by the unexacting standards of his day. His meanness in defrauding the seamen of what little pitiable provision had been made for them against sickness and poverty is odious in an old sailor.[1] But he had been brought up in a hard school that left compassion and justice to those who could afford them.

The Treasurer, the Comptroller, the Surveyor and the Clerk:* these are the historic four Principal Officers of the navy. But Charles II's board was strengthened by Commissioners whose authority was no less and whose influence was greater than that of the traditional quartet. During the years that Pepys was learning the business of the office it was dominated by two men of very different backgrounds and very different professional abilities, Sir William Penn and Sir William Coventry. Both men have, briefly, appeared in this biography: both will be familiar to all who have read the Diary: Coventry as the pattern of a brilliant and well-bred public servant, high-minded, witty, informed, lucid and incisive, Penn as the almost direct antithesis, low, crafty, lumpish and

* 'Of the Acts' simply means that he recorded what was done at the Board: what we should now call a Secretary.

absurd. If the portrait of Coventry is a little heightened by hero worship that of Penn hardly reaches the level of caricature. It seems odd that Pepys's vision, as revealed to us in the Diary, is so distorted. It is even odder, on a close reading, that Coventry, the shrewd superintelligence on whom no one could impose, should give no sign of being aware how worthless and wicked Penn was. Pepys of course is writing a diary, not giving sworn evidence before the bar of history. He can there purge his mind of fear and jealousy, he can let his prejudices rip, he can abandon himself to the delights of unreason without hurting himself or anybody else.

But it is the function of reason, if it can, to unravel the irrational. Why did Pepys come to hold such violent opinions about Penn who, on the clear evidence of the Diary itself, went out of his way to make himself agreeable to a junior whose cocksure and aggressive behaviour must often have been trying? Penn's whole record shows him to have been a firm disciplinarian but an easygoing, perhaps too easygoing, colleague. If he had been a little sharper to the valetudinarian Venables with whom he had been joined in command of the expedition against Hispaniola both his own career and Cromwell's imperial policy might have benefited. If he had been less self-effacing the credit for the great English victory off Lowestoft in 1665 would have been given to him rather than to the Duke of York. But Pepys, as the years went by, became bitterer and bitterer, his scurrility verging at times on the hysterical. What lies behind this?

Jealousy. Rivalry. Or rather a double rivalry. Pepys was a member of the Navy Board because Lord Sandwich had put him there. But both Penn and Coventry represented a grave threat to Sandwich's naval influence. Sandwich's claim to power and office and all that went with it was that he was a Cromwellian General-at-Sea who had seen the light in 1659. But Penn was an infinitely more distinguished naval commander, also an ex-General-at-Sea, who, it was generally believed, had seen the light a lot earlier. Penn was therefore a potential rival to Sandwich, and thus at one remove to Pepys. In addition as a colleague at the same board, as a neighbour in a Navy Office house, sharing the Navy Office garden and the Navy Office pew at St. Olave's Hart Street, he was a direct competitor: a competitor for power, for patronage, for perquisites. And a competitor, a dangerously well-equipped competitor, for the good opinion of William Coventry.

For Coventry too was no friend of Sandwich's. He had fought for the King in the Civil War: he was detested by Clarendon, the great minister with whom Sandwich had close political relations: and, worst of all, he was the steady advocate of the personal and professional merits of Sir

William Penn. Pepys's relations with Coventry, the burgeoning love of
one born administrator for another, the ardent courtship, the bliss of
requited professional respect, nourished his genius. But Penn, blackened
in the pages on which Coventry glistens, is no less important to the understanding of Pepys.

Penn, like Batten under whose command he had served at sea during
the Civil War, was a tarpaulin inasmuch as he was a seaman born and
bred. The son of a Bristol merchant who traded to the Mediterranean
in his own ships, he belonged like Blake to a class that would have been
reckoned certainly superior to Batten's and perhaps to Pepys's. As a fighting sailor and a fleet commander his record was unrivalled. As a young
captain in the Civil War he had matched seamanship with the military
qualities of boldness and initiative in the conduct of combined operations
in Ireland. His share in Blake's great victories over the Dutch has already
been indicated. And the credit for snatching the valuable prize of
Jamaica from the fiasco of the expedition against Hispaniola belonged to
him. Carteret, Slyngsbie and Batten were veteran sea officers as well as
naval administrators but none of them had commanded a squadron in a
fleet action or knew what the Dutch meant when they attributed the
English victories in the recent war to their tactics of fighting in line.
Penn was the only man who had and did and could do it again.

These considerations were clear to the King and to the Duke of York
both of whom have been allowed by their harshest critics to be outstanding
judges of naval affairs. They must also have been clear to Pepys. Yet to
run the eye over the index entries under Penn, Sir William, in Wheatley's
edition of the Diary is to see accusations of knavery, deceit, cheating and
cowardice leaping from the page. Pepys could not bear a rival. Even in
his Diary where he opens his mind and scrutinises his conscience with a
candour that hurt his self-esteem, the antennae retract. The shell clamps
shut at the approach of a possible competitor. It is a reflex anterior to any
intellectual process, an animal instinct of fear and self-preservation. The
acute powers of analysis, the detachment, the observation that make Pepys's
mind perpetually refreshing are drowned under a dark rushing torrent of
cheapness and silliness and plain untruth. Can he really have believed, as he
implies as late as 1667, that Penn's whole career from first to last was maintained by bribing a clerk at the Navy Board who was junior to them both?
It is difficult to escape the conclusion that when Pepys is agitated by
jealousy he can convince himself of anything. He lets his will cook accounts
that only the mind can audit.

The Navy Board that Pepys attended for the first time at the beginning
of July 1660 was a body of men much older, tougher, and in every point

THE NAVY BOARD 79

except native genius more formidable than himself. Yet it is characteristic that he never for an instant seems to have felt out of his depth. What these grizzled veterans thought of their soft rather overdressed young colleague can, to some extent, be informed from the Diary. All of them except perhaps Carteret understood the proper use of conviviality. Olyngobie was from the first the easiest and most congenial, but there are other cheerful scenes in the early months of the new board's existence in which the unsteady figures of the young clerk and the two old Parliamentarian commanders can be discerned giving that support that the one ought to have of the other as they return from an evening's tippling. But as day by day they take decisions, award contracts, grant requests, make appointments, the occasions of conflict multiply. At first Pepys hardly knows enough to have a point of view. He watches, he listens, he records. But not for long. Soon, indeed, the very Navy Board itself is too narrow a compass for the full exercise of his administrative talent. The project outlined over dinner by the Lord Chamberlain's secretary 'for all us Secretaries to join together and get money by bringing all business into our hands'[2] might appear over-ambitious but it had the root of the matter in it. Within a month of his appointment to the Navy Board Pepys received the additional favour of a Clerkship at the Privy Council. Clerks took it in turn to do a month's duty at the Privy Seal Office, a mere administrative tollgate that yielded quick and easy money. Delightful as this was it offered no scope for the exercise of intelligence or curiosity. After a couple of years Pepys gratefully abandoned it (for various reasons it had anyhow become less profitable). But in 1665 he added two new provinces to his administrative empire: the Treasurership of the Tangier Commission and the Surveyorship of the navy's victualling. Each of these by itself would have been enough for a man of energy and professional skill. To combine them with the work of the Navy Board at the very moment when the country had embarked on a war with the greatest naval power in Europe is a dumbfounding display of self-confidence and of appetite for business.

The distinction between the work of the Navy Board and the duties of the Lord High Admiral corresponds pretty well to that between Tarpaulin and Gentleman. It was the Navy Board's business to provide the ships and everything that was needed to sail them, spars, masts, cordage, sails, flags, anchors, and the whole range of ships' stores together with the experts who knew how to use them, master, boatswain, carpenter, cook, gunner and purser. It was left to the Lord High Admiral to recruit, appoint and promote the officers, to issue instructions as to tactics and discipline and to advise the Government on the use of the navy as an instrument of policy. It was difficult for a Lord High Admiral even for so lordly and high a fighting admiral as James, Duke of York, to discharge so many and such complicated functions, which is why the office has since his time been almost continuously delegated to a Commission of Lords of the Admiralty. But before that was done it was natural that he should lean very heavily on the exceptionally strong Navy Board that his brother had appointed, and therefore natural that a Navy Board officer should become familiar with what was strictly Admiralty business. And since the Duke's secretary, Sir William Coventry, was also a member of the Navy Board it was inevitable that Pepys should form the habit of looking at a proposed course of action as a man informed by the views of experts and by the practice of the department rather than limited by them.

Pepys soon came to have still grander visions of naval administration. Even if, some day, he were to control both the Admiralty and the Navy Board there were matters still more essential to sea-power that would lie outside his authority. Where were the men to come from? Who was to be responsible for feeding them? Or taking care of them if they were wounded or fell ill? What about the guns and powder and shot? And where was the money to pay for all this? This last question remained unanswered. Public finance was unsophisticated: public honour was not exemplary. Experience taught that if people were left unpaid they would in time die. Those who like Pepys could not bear untidiness and preferred to be honest were disturbed by this state of affairs and, intermittently, cogitated possible remedies.

The question of pay was the root of the question of manning. Men were unwilling to serve, and this in an age when unemployment was always high and starvation never remote, because they had good reason to believe that they would be cheated of their wages. The provision of funds was for the King and Parliament to settle. Part of Pepys's job at the Navy Office was to brief his Parliamentary colleagues — Coventry, Carteret, Penn and Batten were all M.P.s — when they were trying to obtain more money from the House or to defend themselves from uncomfortable inquiries as to what they had done with what had already been granted. But financially the main concern of the office was in making payments, or, more often, failing to make them. When a ship was to be paid off one or more of the Board had to be present. When there was no money, or not enough, to pay the seamen's wages, tickets were issued which were in theory redeemable in cash at the Navy Office. Brokers bought up the tickets at a heavy discount and, knowing their way about, made large profits. Starving seamen who knew their rights and nothing else sometimes besieged the office or attacked the prosperous-looking officials. Of those requiring payment the seamen were only one class, and in some ways the easiest to manage. They could as a last resort be kept at sea. The workmen in the dockyards could not be conjured away so painlessly. And the merchants who supplied the timber and the hemp, the tar and the sail-cloth, were reluctant to supply goods on credit until their past accounts had been settled. Round the neck of Charles II's navy hung the huge debt incurred under the Commonwealth.

Manning was a problem for which the Navy Board shared responsibility with a number of other bodies, local government officials for instance, or even more the sea officers in the ships. But the other questions raised two or three pages back did not, in July 1660, come within the purview of the Navy Office at all. Guns and powder and shot were the responsibility of the Ordnance Board. Feeding the seamen was the province of the Victualler. Looking after the wounded was nobody's business, once a man had been discharged from his ship. To all these matters Pepys was, with varying success, to address himself. From the first day of his connection with the navy the searching, generalising scientific bent of his mind disposed him to acquire information pell-mell, to elicit principles of efficiency and to embody these in a scheme of administrative reform. The wide-ranging curiosity, the need to impose order and the instinct for business run through and through Pepys from young manhood to old age. Like Luther he could no other. 'Would to God,' he wrote to Coventry on August 22nd, 1662, 'you could for a while spare two after-noons a week for generall debates; . . . Contracts . . . ye many old Rates to be enquired into, Tickets. . . . regulating ye slopsellers practices with forty more scandalous errors . . .'[3]

Coventry was in all these matters his ally and his pattern. Of the three men who dominated his life Sandwich raised him, Coventry formed him and Evelyn refined him. It was the cutting edge of Coventry's mind, the wit, the clarity, the force that captivated Pepys and that still retains the power to delight. What a colleague to find on a committee, incapable apparently of being dull, devious, timid or obtuse. How accurately and gracefully he says what he has to say and how perfectly the swift unstudied beauty of his hand conveys the character of the writer. That he talked as well as he wrote, the Diary abundantly confirms: 'very good discourse . . . most excellent discourse . . . in short I find him the most ingenuous person I ever found in my life'.[4] And as a man of business in Pepys's considered judgment: 'the best Minister of State the King hath'[5] leaves nothing more to be said. That Coventry also thought highly of Pepys we are left in no doubt. His words as reported by Sandwich 'that I was indeed the life of this office'[6] are happily chosen: and ten years later Coventry wrote to his nephew who had just succeeded to his own old post of Secretary to the Lord High Admiral 'you may receive more help and learn more of the Navy affairs from him than from any man living'. Pepys was so pleased by this compliment that he began to copy the letter that contains it in his own hand.[7]

Coventry did not join the Navy Board until Pepys had been there for two years. But from the first as Secretary to the Lord High Admiral he bulked large in the affairs of the navy. Alone of all the senior officials he had a policy and the qualities needed both to articulate it and to carry it out. He believed that England must have a large permanent navy and that she could afford it if only she would abandon slapdash methods of administration and finance. In support of such a policy he was willing to forego the handsome sums that officials such as he received by way of presents for each appointment they made. The sale of places, as it was called, was corrupt in principle and corrupted the service by example. Since he could not in the event induce his colleagues to abolish the practice he did in fact accept and profit by it. But of the sincerity of his desire to end it as of his personal honour there seems no doubt. Like Evelyn but unlike Sandwich he was against graft.

All this strongly appealed to Pepys. His mind recognised the force of Coventry's arguments; his conscience, well developed by his Puritan upbringing, swelled within him; his passion for order pressed him forward. But there were inhibitions. Bribes, presents, call them what you will, are pleasant things to an impecunious young man with an appetite for enjoyment. Deliberate dishonesty such as charging for goods that had never been supplied or claiming pay and allowances for people who had never existed was one thing. But when an officer whom one had helped to advance — on grounds of merit naturally — showed his appreciation by a gift of money or plate was there anything wrong in accepting it? Or put the case that a merchant had tendered for better quality masts beneath the going rate, should the King be denied the advantage of a contract with him just because the generous fellow had presented the Clerk of the Acts with forty gold pieces in a glove? Readers of the Diary will recognise the tune. Even in moral questions Pepys instinctively favoured a commercial approach. He was, in most cases, ready to do a deal. Treachery, disloyalty, cringing were unthinkable. But everything else was relative and therefore up to a point negotiable.

One enriching influence of Pepys's work at the Navy Board was that it brought him into close and regular contact with the great London merchants. Determined to know his job thoroughly he soon started investigating the markets and methods of production and supply of the principal commodities needed by the navy. Hob-nobbing with hemp importers, mast contractors, canvas merchants and the like he learned the price structure of half a dozen trades. He also made some profitable contacts and some true friends. These, perhaps, were the men with whom he was most at home: cultivated citizens of the world, citizens not aristocrats, men who carried their urbanity even into their country retirements. It is hardly too much to say that Pepys saw in them the highest type of civilisation, a dislike of force, a tolerance, a range of curiosity and a well-proportioned, high-minded worldliness that answered to his own most characteristic aspirations. Such were the Houblon family, Flemish refugees with extensive interests in the Mediterranean trade, and such was Thomas Hill, the music-loving Lisbon merchant whose portrait hangs in the Pepys Library.

Sir William Coventry however held firm views about merchants. Pepys hankered after injecting brisk and businesslike habits into the unsystematic and discursive transactions of his colleagues. But Coventry would have none of it. When in November 1664 it was decided to strengthen the Navy Board by the appointment of another Commissioner the choice lay between Lord Brouncker, the mathematician and first President of the Royal Society, and Sir William Rider, the great hemp merchant. In a letter to Pepys telling him that Brouncker had been chosen Coventry wrote:

> My Lord Brunkard is a very ingenious and honest person and I hope may bee usefull. Sir William Rider is able but a Merchant, and if the Merchants come in to rob the office of its reputation I am sure they shall take the burthen of it alsoe, and I will content myselfe to act as some others of my fellowes, for I never expect reputation by acting there, after a Merchant hath soe donne there.[8]

It would be easy to find other indications of the low opinion that he held of what his age called merchants and ours calls businessmen. He thought their reputation for efficiency overvalued: 'the laziness of the merchant' he affirmed to Pepys was the principal reason for our poor performance in competing with the Dutch. He had been brought up as a member of a noble family in the service of Charles I and could hardly divest himself of the standards and prejudices of his time and place. And he reinforced these with a strictness over money that Pepys found uncomfortably fastidious.[9] Coventry heightened and extended Pepys's ideas both of public service and of the aristocracy whose justification was supposed to lie in undertaking it. Coventry's tastes, appetites and affinities were, at first sight, far less congenial than Sandwich's. Though a man of the world he lacked the avidity for easy money and obvious pleasures that Pepys shared with his patron. On the other hand he touched chords in Pepys that Sandwich could never reach. He was witty; he was well-read; he enjoyed argument and preferred his ideas clear, sharp-edged and un-ambiguous; he took a pride in doing whatever he did as well as it could be done; he had style.

So vivid a figure could not but make enemies. It is safe to assume that the merchants liked him as little as he liked them. Clarendon and Sandwich recognised him as an enemy; Sir George Carteret, who soon ratified his political allegiance by marrying his son to Sandwich's daughter, resented him; cunning old professionals like Batten and pompous old fuddlers like Sir John Mennes saw him as a threat. For all his brilliant gifts and for all his high position, Secretary to the Duke, a prominent figure in the House of Commons, he was not so safe and so prudent an investment for an ambitious follower as Sandwich was. But it is the argument of this book that Pepys's deepest springs of action were artistic. 'An artist,' wrote Jane Austen, 'cannot do anything slovenly.' It was this divine dis-content with the serviceable second-best that recognised in Coventry the master it had been looking for.

6

Style of life

In Restoration England, as in most unindustrialised societies, obverse sides of life, the public and the private, work and play, interpenetrated each other. The shape of the day will not fit a twentieth-century pattern. Office hours, for instance, seem irregular and idiosyncratic. Even so relentlessly methodical a man as Pepys was surprisingly free from the servitude of the clock. Indeed he did not acquire a watch until the spring of 1665 and, like the Chinese on their introduction to clockwork, was rather fascinated by its potentialities as a toy than awed by its power to dismember the continuity of existence. Pepys's readiness to take the afternoon off to go to a theatre, or, should the weather prove irresistible, to embark with his wife and her maid on an expedition on the river, seems by twentieth-century standards irresponsible. After one or two narrow squeaks with authority, particularly as personified by Sir William Coventry, Pepys eventually begins to think so too. But he recognised this as a change in himself, in his way of looking at life, more precisely in his calculations as to how to extract the maximum of enjoyment from it: 'My mind, I hope, is set to fallow my business again, for I find that two days neglect of business doth give me more discontent in mind than ten times the pleasure thereof can repair again, be it what it will.'[1]

Adaptable as he was, the transition from semi-menial under-employment to a chief place in one of the busiest and most important Government offices required time for adjustment.

This was true in private and domestic matters as well as in habits of work. Indeed as has been suggested the two went together more closely in those days than in ours. Company and tastes which were perfectly acceptable in one of Sir George Downing's clerks or in a member of Sandwich's household would not do in a Principal Officer of the Navy Board. The move from Axe Yard, Westminster to Seething Lane in the City marked an end and a beginning socially and intellectually, even if the dividing line was not so immediately discernible as in the comforts and graces of life. Which leads straight to what the poet has called:

> That topic all absorbing, as it was,
> Is now and ever shall be, to us – CLASS.

What did Pepys think about it? How did he react to its manifestations? Was he a snob?

In a sense, and that not a snobbish one, Pepys remained all his life a tailor's son. He was for ever trying on new clothes and seeing how he looked in them. Fashions and materials and styles and novelties fascinated him. No one can read far in the Diary without recognising his passion for clothes and his knowledge of them. 'This day I put on first my fine cloth suit'[2] made of a cloak that had been overtaken by an unfortunate accident when first worn the preceding year. 'This morning came home my fine Camlott cloak with gold buttons – and a silk suit; which cost me much money and I pray God to make [me] be able to pay for it.'[3] Four days later his brother Tom, who had joined his father in the shop, brought round 'my Jackanapes coat with silver buttons'. And Elizabeth's taste in dress was scrutinised with no sentimentally indulgent eye. No wonder that in one of their sharpest quarrels when he taunted her with having brought him no dowry she replied by calling him 'prick louse', a pointed allusion to the needles from which he had sprung.[4] But it is the metaphorical rather than the literal application that perhaps yields some insight into the questions of snobbery and class. Pepys put on the clothes of recognised and approved types – the man of fashion, the man of informed and fastidious taste, the man of affairs. To look the part required, in each case, an air and an attitude that must be studied by imitation. Hence the crucial importance of such models as Sandwich, Coventry or Evelyn. Hence, too, the readiness to pick up hints from colleagues whom his jealousy led him to despise or dislike such as the rich and exquisite Mr. Povy or the shrewd and knowing Creed. Pepys was too much of a realist not to see how society worked. But, strangely for so impressionable a man, he was too little of a romantic to be swept off his feet by the glamour of aristocracy, just as he was never taken in by the mumbo-jumbo of nationalism. Measured against Dr. Johnson, himself neither a snob nor a flag-waver, Pepys is cooler and more detached. The poet in Johnson was stirred by the idea of ancient loyalty: 'I am quite feudal, sir'[5]; and his views on the natural superiority of England to the constituent nations of the auld alliance are too well known to bear re-stating. Pepys, on the other hand, spent his best energies in resisting aristocratic pretensions unsupported by professionalism 'the commanders, the gentlemen that could never be brought to order, but undid all'.[6] And of his objectivity towards his compatriots this is but one of many examples:

> The nature of the English is generally to be self-lovers, and thinking everything of their own the best, viz. our beef, beer, women, horses, soldiers, religion, laws, etc., and from the same principles are over-valuers of our ships.[7]

Pepys accepted the class structure of society as he accepted the nation state. But he appears to have been unmoved by the mythology with which some have felt it necessary to invest them. That he loved, as he undoubtedly did, being taken up by the great is no argument that he took them at their own valuation.

If Pepys did not romanticise the facts of the social system it was not because he had a soul above such considerations. Almost as soon as he has established himself in his new situation he begins to feel ashamed of the low connections and boorish behaviour of his own family and to criticise Elizabeth for not running the house in an appropriate style. But there were, as he recognised with unflinching self-knowledge, aspects of his own conduct that called for some alteration. Chief among these was drink. Conviviality, as we have seen, was not second but first nature to Pepys. As a hard-up young clerk he and his fellows used to meet for a weekly club at a tavern in Pall Mall. His diary shows what use he could make, on still very slender means, of the opportunities offered by a visit to Cambridge or a spell afloat. Now that he was master of an assured income and in a good way to make a great deal more he could afford to drink as hard as he liked. His colleagues at the Navy Board were for the most part glad of an excuse to ply the bottle. And the host of people who came into the office, merchants seeking contracts or settlement of unpaid bills, petitioners for places and pensions, boatswains and gunners in search of a sea billet, found it easier to press their causes by adjourning them to a wine house. Drunkenness was not generally regarded as disgraceful. The Court, the City companies and the world of fashion made it hard to do so. But beastly habits exact a price in health, efficiency and dignity, three topics on which

Pepys was, all his life, acutely sensitive. Dignity was affronted when he was, to quote his own expression, too foxed to read family prayers 'for fear of being perceived by my servants in what case I was'. Efficiency suffered through headaches, lassitude, indisposition: even, so his surgeon Hollier suggested, to the extent of impairing his memory. But the gravest threat to health that Pepys saw was to his sight. The first of many references in the Diary explicitly identifies this cause: 'I was much troubled in my eyes, by reason of the healths I have this day been forced to drink.'[8]

The diagnosis, as Pepys himself later came to realise, was wrong. But this did not reduce its urgency as a motive to action. And action was, in Pepys's view, at once the test and purpose of moral and intellectual consciousness. He would certainly have shared Dr. Johnson's contempt for professions of generosity or sympathy unaccompanied by practical effort. 'They *pay* you by *feeling*.' He had recognised alcoholism as an unacceptable risk and he set about taking measures against it in the same way as he would have tackled some abuse in the methods by which boatswains accounted for their stores. He pressed all sides of his nature into the service: the residual Puritanism of his upbringing, the fiercely competitive ambition and the passion for good order; he said his prayers and took solemn vows; finally, as J. R. Tanner happily puts it, he hit upon 'the ingenious idea of enlisting a lesser vice to destroy a greater. Pepys was careful about money and he attached money penalties to the breaches of his vow, thus fining himself into sobriety.'[9]

With what distaste the aristocrat averts his gaze, with what audible superiority the Marxist sniffs at this deplorable triumph of middle-class morality. The conception and the execution are so characteristically bourgeois; the readiness to do a deal (even with one's lower nature), the reluctance to rely solely on principle, so inescapably English. And what aggravates the offence to such *bien pensants* is that Pepys actually managed to extract pleasure from the process of discipling himself in this low, commercial fashion: 'I drank but two glasses of wine this day, and yet it makes my head ake all night, and indisposed me all the next day – of which I am glad.'[10]

Boozing had been overcome but drinking remained a pleasure. How could it be otherwise to a man who took nothing for granted? He enjoys the cup of cider or the bottle of beer that refresh his frequent walks between the dockyards at Deptford and Woolwich just as, even when cold and tired, he enjoys the weather. 'And I walked with a Lanthorn, weary as I was, to Greenwich; but it was a fine walk, it being a hard frost.'[11] Wine he bought with care and drank with discrimination. The cork, without which wine cannot achieve the subtleties that come from bottle age,

only began to come into use about the time of his death so that his taste
lies on the medieval side of that dividing line. Writing in 1677 when his
mature habits had long been formed he sums them up thus:

> . . . I never drink to excess and seldom or not at all but at meals and
> thereto at dinner principally now, but then I drink liberally (with a
> temperance still) and for the most part of the wines that are reckoned
> strong, viz – Greek, Italian, Spanish and Portuguese and at the small
> Bordeaux claret.
>
> The thin French wine, flying presently into my head, occasioning
> a moisture . . . I rarely meddle with any of these sorts where any other
> coarser or stronger wine can be had.[12]

The same taste is evident in the purchases mentioned in the Diary,
especially in the cellar inventoried with some pride on July 7th, 1665,
claret, canary, sack, tent,* Malaga and white wine. Haut Brion, the only
claret at this period to bear the name of the estate on which it was made,
is, on another occasion, particularly commended: 'a sort of French wine,
called Ho Bryan, that hath a good and most particular taste that I never
met with'. Pepys kept his wine in cask and was duly impressed by the
novelty and splendour of Povy's cellar management: '. . . where upon
several shelves there stood bottles of all sorts of wine, new and old, with
labells pasted upon each bottle, and in that order and plenty as I never saw
books in a bookseller's shop.'[13] As he grew richer Pepys provided better
and better wine for his guests, reaching the heights at a dinner given for
Sandwich and the Earl of Peterborough, together with two or three
important members of the House of Commons on January 23rd, 1669:

> . . . dinner was brought up, one dish after another, but a dish at a
> time, but all so good; but above all things the variety of wines, and
> excellent of their kind, I had for them, and all in so good order that
> they were mightily pleased and myself full of content at it; and indeed
> it was, of a dinner of about six or eight dishes, as noble as any man need
> to have I think; at least all was done in the noblest manner that ever I
> had any, and I have rarely seen in my life better anywhere else, even
> at the Court . . .

Such a passage, drowsy with good living, hardly suggests the angry
upbraiding of Elizabeth for her inadequacies as a hostess, the pitiless
scrutiny of her kitchen accounts ('and there find 7s. wanting – which did
occasion a very high falling out between us'), the basting of maids with

---

* tinto. Dark-coloured Spanish red wine.

broom-handles and the other unedifying scenes through which the pair of
them had passed on their pilgrimage. But it does sound a note, deeply
characteristic of its author, of disgust at grossness, even of disapproval at
elevating eating and drinking into topics of polite conversation. Dining
with the Lieutenant of the Tower and the distinguished soldier and colonial
administrator Colonel Norwood he remarks on the 'strange pleasure they
seem to take in their wine and meat, and discourse of it with the curiosity
and joy that methinks was below men of worth'.[14] The judgment gains in
authority from being passed on men whose birth and breeding were better
than his own.

Food and drink, as any casual reading of the Diary shows, were in the
first place direct and primary pleasures like sunshine or starlight. Their
secondary importance was of two kinds. First as an indicator of social
position; a hashed pullet, a roast sirloin of beef and a jowl of ling are
delightful in themselves but even more for the cachet they confer. Second
as a social emollient: 'strange it is, to see how a good dinner and feasting
reconciles everybody'.[15] Such pre-eminently was the function of the great
banquets given by the Brethren of Trinity House, or by the Clothworkers'
Company to both of which Pepys was admitted during his years at the
Navy Office.

These years are the centre of Pepys's life, personally, professionally and
intellectually. Professionally he entered the office as a barely known young
hanger-on of Lord Sandwich — 'Chance, without merit, brought me in' —
and left it as unquestionably the ablest naval· administrator of his time.
Personally and intellectually the transformation is less dramatic, but still
considerable. Some aspects of his character, and those among the most
likeable, remain unchanged. His loyalty to, and care for, his generally
tiresome and sometimes embarrassing relations does not falter. Privately
he finds their oafishness, their stupidity, their discourtesy and their
unreliability harder to bear as he strives to root out the lurking remnant
of such qualities from his own manners and conduct. But he does not
make them feel this. He may decline an invitation from one of his
mother's poor connections 'where I should have been, but my pride
would not suffer me';[16] he may find his cousins the Joyces, his uncles and
aunts Wight and Fenner disgusting in their habits and tedious in their
table-talk. He says so so often and so vehemently that it is easy to believe
that he had good reason. But what is distinctive about this familiar reaction
to sudden social and professional success is that Pepys recognises it as a
shortcoming of his own at least as much as of theirs. 'But I do condemn
myself mightily for my pride and contempt of my aunt and kindred
that are not so high as myself, that I have not seen her all this while, nor

invited her all this while.'[17] Even more remarkable is the kindliness and indulgence of so irritable and exacting a man towards his brother-in-law, Balty. Balty, like Captain Grimes, is of the immortals. Across the centuries he distils an aura of dud cheques and ingratiating fecklessness. Pepys had already perceived that Balty looked at jobs in the light of his own social pretensions rather than as a means of earning a living. By January 1664 he had concluded that he was idle. Yet after Balty's only recorded effort at self-help, a year's service in the Dutch army, Pepys obtained him an appointment in Albemarle's troop of the Life Guard under the command of the fashionable and exquisite Sir Philip Howard.* In March 1666 he sent him to sea as a muster-master, an official appointed by the Navy Board to check the corrupt practices of the Captains and Pursers. Both posts entailed considerable risks for Pepys. Albemarle was no friend of his: and the one quality for which Pepys and Coventry admired him was 'that he never would receive an excuse if the thing was not done; listening to no reason for it, be it good or bad'.[18] And to employ one's brother-in-law to keep an eye on the muster books was to lay oneself open to the counter-charges of an unscrupulous or resentful sea officer.

Pepys's own family, his father, mother, sister and his two brothers, had cause to bless his good fortune. All of them were generously helped when they needed money; all of them found the time and trouble of the busiest bureaucrat in England always at their disposal; all of them were treated with a kindness and consideration that must sometimes have been heroic. Only between him and his father was there strong affection:

> . . . it joys my very heart to think that I should have his picture so well done – who, besides that he is my father, and a man that loves me and hath ever done so – is also at this day one of the most careful and innocent men in the world.[19]

His mother was sliding into senility. At her death in March 1667 Pepys was evidently moved, but this was the re-emergence of a stream that had long run underground. His feelings for his brothers and sister were less tender. Tom, who was only a year his junior, seems to have aroused little affection and much anxiety. When their father retired to the small estate at Brampton which Samuel inherited on the death of his Uncle Robert in 1661, Tom was left to run the tailor's shop. Samuel doubted if he had either the intelligence or the industry needed and set about finding him a wife whose dowry would at least provide some working capital. Three

* The style in which he discharged his military duties (D. 21 Nov. 66) might have commended itself to the Duke of Dorset in *Zuleika Dobson*.

times he came near success but Tom cannot have been much of a help –
indeed one of the young ladies declined on the grounds of the imperfection
in his speech. Was there perhaps some congenital or glandular disorder?
By the autumn of 1663 the business was on the rocks. In the winter Tom
fell ill and died the following March.

The sequence of entries in which Pepys records his reactions to his
brother's deathbed is one of the most remarkable in the Diary. When
first told that his brother is 'deadly ill' he is shocked. But when he hears
that it is venereal disease he is horrified. It is only fear of what people may
say that induces him to visit the dying man, whom he finds delirious
though capable of recognising him. Talking to the housemaid he finds that
his brother is deep in debt: and, as if humiliation were not already complete, she hints strongly at homosexual relations with a neighbour in Fleet
Lane. 'So that upon the whole I do find he is, whether he lives or dies, a
ruined man. And what trouble will befall me by it I know not.'

On his next visit the same piercing candour reveals an entirely different
yet equally real facet of the diarist. 'He talks no sense two words together
now. And I confess it made me weep to see that he should not be able
when I asked him, to say who I was.' But, looking in later in the day it is
the extent of Tom's debts that dominates his brother's thoughts. Next
day, however, a second opinion pooh-poohs the diagnosis of venereal
disease, upon which Pepys sends for a barrel of oysters 'and we were very
merry'. After dinner he visited the patient, who was still delirious, and
conducted with the doctor an examination that satisfied them both that
Tom was free from all taint of the pox. He was by then very near death so
that when Pepys 'began to tell him something of his condition, and asked
him whither he thought he should go' the spiritual curiosity seems as
ghoulish as the physical. Yet when the death rattle began Pepys could not
bear to see him die. Returning a quarter of an hour later he fell into paroxysms of grief. When at last he and Elizabeth went up to bed, 'I lay
close to my wife, being full of disorder and grief for my brother that I
could not sleep nor wake with satisfaction.'

A few days later Tom was buried with six biscuits a-piece and abundance of burnt claret for the mourners (120 were invited but nearer 150
turned up) followed by an even more magnificent spread for the family.

. . . being too merry for so late a sad work; but Lord to see how the
world makes nothing of the memory of a man an hour after he is dead.
And endeed, I must blame myself; for though at the sight of him, dead
and dying, I had real grief for a while, while he was in my sight, yet
presently after and ever since, I have had very little grief endeed for him.

The self-revelation is as profound as the understanding. The egocentric and the unfeeling are shot through with touches of compassion and flashes of insight into the depths and shallows of the human heart. The mind has been cleared of cant.

Tom left behind him a number of debts (which Samuel had to pay), an illegitimate daughter (towards whose fostering further expense was to be incurred) and a pile of letters. Among these were several from the youngest brother John which referred to Samuel in most offensive terms. Worse, there was clear evidence of collusion between the two brothers to deceive their benefactor and some suggestion that their father might have guilty knowledge though himself innocent of any malicious intention. Two days after the funeral Samuel called both father and brother into his study and read the letters aloud. His father's evident contrition and his brother's obstinate churlishness confirmed his reading of their characters. His brother was stupid as well as underhand. In the anger of the moment Pepys swore not to let him have any more money and vowed to remember his ingratitude to his dying day.

John had seemed the one member of the family who might, in a modest way, fit himself to share in his brother's success. Like Samuel he had been educated at St. Paul's and Cambridge (scholar of Christ's: and there was even talk of a fellowship) but in spite of his brother's encouragement and assistance he wasted his time. The coolness that followed Tom's death did not last long. Two years later when he decided to take orders Samuel gave him money, brought him a smart clerical outfit, and tried to find him a benefice. In 1670 when these hopes had been abandoned he was made, through Samuel's wire-pulling, Clerk of Trinity House and in 1673, by the same agency, joint Clerk of the Acts at the Navy Office. He was still holding both these positions on his death in 1677. By then his elder brother had long come to regard him as to some extent competent and trustworthy;[20] but of affection or sympathy there appears no trace.

The last of Pepys's immediate family, his sister Paulina, played a much greater part during the years of his rise to wealth and position. Not that she can have been anything but a handicap to the pursuit of either. The unattractiveness of her person and the disagreeableness of her temper are palpable across the centuries. Right through the Diary period Pepys busies himself with negotiations for her marriage, ultimately going as high as five or six hundred pounds in the dowry he was prepared to provide for her. At last in the spring of 1668 she was married to a Huntingdonshire neighbour, 'Mr. Jackson, who is a plain young man, handsome enough for Pall, one of no education nor discourse, but of few words, and one altogether that I think will please me well enough'. His taciturnity remained his only recommendation. But in fathering two sons, one of whom, John, survived to be the hope of Pepys's old age, he contributed more than the rest of the family put together to the happiness of their benefactor.

Pall, her brother thought, was improved by marriage; and in her widowhood when Pepys was the victim of a political conspiracy that might have cost him his life she proved staunch and true. But in the Diary she rarely if ever appears in an admirable light. Almost as soon as the Pepyses were settled in to their handsome new house they decided to kill two birds with one stone by taking on Pall as a servant. She arrived in January 1661 and her brother showed her her place in the household by pointedly not inviting her to sit down at table. In spite or, perhaps, because of, hints of this kind Pall became insufferably proud and idle. By the end of July it was clear that she would have to go. Early in September she was packed off to Brampton to live with her parents, 'crying exceedingly'.

This attempt to harness family obligation to domestic convenience was not repeated. In January 1663 Elizabeth was in want of a lady's maid and suggested that Pall might be better suited to this than to housework. Pepys was very pleased indeed with his wife for proposing her but even though he groaned at good wages going outside the family he could not bear the prospect. Only once again did he think of mixing the two worlds of servants and relations. In January 1667 after so many disappointments a marriage had been arranged for Pall, but the bridegroom upset it all by dying. Growing desperate, Pepys offered her to his most valued secretary, Will Hewer, who pleaded a preference for bachelorhood. It is doubtful if anything could have deepened or strengthened the bond that formed of itself between the two men. Marriage with Pall might have blighted its growth.

Servants were one of the principal causes of friction between the Pepyses. Elizabeth had neither the temperament nor the experience to manage them. How, indeed, could she be expected to possess either, married so young and brought up so oddly? Pepys, who had been a kind of servant himself, understood matters better and became, in his official capacity at least, the object of loyalty, even devotion, to most of those who worked for him. Elizabeth, uncertain of herself, oscillated between over-familiarity and sudden bouts of petulant assertiveness. At least that is the impression conveyed by the Diary, our only source but hardly a disinterested one.

Pepys does not disguise his own irritability nor the cowardly violence he sometimes used against people who could not hit back. He kicks the cook and is mortified by being caught in the act by Sir Willian Penn's footboy. He bastes his maid and even, on one occasion, locked 'our little girle' into the cellar for the night. Boys, naturally, were treated much more roughly. One in particular Wayneman Birch was several times thrashed so energetically that Pepys complained of exhaustion and an aching arm. Such harshness long remained the rule. In the next century Dr. Johnson, kind and tender-hearted as he was, believed firmly in the moral and intellectual benefits of the rod. Even in the nineteenth century Dr. Keate the great headmaster of Eton who raised the standard of scholarship and introduced debating societies into the school once flogged eighty boys in a day and stood astonished at his own moderation. There were men in Pepys's time, John Aubrey was one, and before, such as the Ferrars at Little Gidding, who thought such proceedings uncivilised or unchristian. By the end of his life Pepys might well have agreed with them. Even when he was punishing poor Wayneman, whom both he and Elizabeth liked best of all their boys in spite of his naughtiness, he had his doubts: 'I am afeared it will make the boy never the better'.[21] After boxing Will Hewer's ears in annoyance at being contradicted, Pepys records a sense of shame or is it a sense of impropriety? The words '. . . which I never did before, and so was afterwards a little troubled at it'[22] bear either interpretation. From the start Hewer was in any case partly an apprentice to the business of the Navy Office, in which he rapidly became Pepys's right-hand man, and partly a domestic. Probably Hewer, unlike Wayneman, belonged by a narrow margin to a class of people that one did not knock about. He was the nephew of Robert Blackborne who had been secretary to the Admiralty under Cromwell and was to become secretary to the East India Company, an important and useful man to know. Had anyone dared to box Pepys's ears when he began life as a servant to Mountagu? It is difficult to imagine such an outrage.

If master and mistress sometimes applied a discipline that seems to us ferocious or unreasonable they also admitted their servants to a degree of equality that the polite servants of succeeding centuries would have thought rustic. Pepys loved horseplay and so, when she was in health, did Elizabeth. The round games and frolics of Twelfth Night were enjoyed by the whole household: the summer parties of pleasure by coach, or on the river often included Elizabeth's maid or Will Hewer; and one of the first recommendations to any post in their domestic service was musical ability. The new house gave Pepys opportunities of singing in the garden or on the leads which he was anxious to enhance with a soprano or an alto to balance his bass. There were, too, other qualifications; youth, charm and beauty. But these inviting vistas deserve the opening not the closing of a chapter.

7

Licence and morality

Those who see in Pepys a forerunner if not an exponent of the view, seminal to modern advertising, that sex will cure us from all ills in this world and the next are under a misapprehension. Sex as such was not a concept or even a word with which he was familiar, except in the narrow sense of physiological gender. The deity venerated by D. H. Lawrence and to which chantries of strange dedication are still served was unknown to him; and, on the evidence, if known, would have been abhorrent.

It seems important to state this point, if only to disentangle it from two others cardinal to any understanding of the man: first that he was lecherous and second that his opinions and attitudes, his philosophy if that is not too pretentious an expression, anticipate to a remarkable degree the kind of questions that perplex us. Both are true: but neither has the slightest connection with the other. Still less is it possible to infer from them any mystical or even giggling enthusiasm for sex *per se*. On the contrary:

. . . Sir J. Mennes and Mr Batten both say that buggery is now almost grown as common among our gallants as in Italy, and that the very pages of the town begin to complain of their masters for it. But blessed be God, I do not to this day know what is the meaning of this sin, nor which is the agent nor which the patient.[1]

It is difficult to discern here so much as the glimmer of approaching dawn. Taken with his reaction to the insinuations about his brother Tom the passage hardly suggests that its author held any view of the sexual urge as a liberating force or of the sexual act as a fulfilment of the personality.

In all these matters Pepys was both in theory and in practice thoroughly conventional. He believed firmly in marital fidelity and lost, as he himself admits, all sense of proportion when he began to imagine without a shred of evidence that Elizabeth was having an affair with her dancing master. So far from regarding his own infidelities as a matter of pride he records them in the Diary in an absurd macaronic jumble of languages that would hardly have deceived Elizabeth had she *per impossibile* mastered his shorthand and broken the lock under which he kept those dangerous volumes. The only gaze from which he was disguising them was his own.

Except for one or two letters written by other people all the surviving evidence on this aspect of Pepys's life comes from the Diary. It is difficult for anyone who is not either an exhibitionist by temperament or a clinician by training to be candid, still less objective about a subject so private and so sensitive. Nothing can staunch the flow of sexual reminiscence: but in all reminiscences the varnish of a lifetime's self-satisfaction is apt to produce effects that seem, somehow, too good to be true. Fresh, direct, undoctored evidence given at the time with a real attempt at truthfulness is rare. It is hard for a man, particularly a vain, fastidious and conventional man, not to suppress matter necessarily known only to himself that exposes him to derision or contempt. The *soi-disant* successful sexual athlete has a compelling motive to tell all: so does the professional breast-beater. But Pepys was too sensitive, too subtle and too clear-headed to be open to such inducements. No topic in the Diary reveals its author in so unheroic a light: and that is the true measure of the heroism required for so unswerving a pursuit of truth.

Pepys's self-revelation on the subject epitomises the Protean quality that makes him slip for ever through fingers stretched to catch him. He boxes the compass of humanity, so that almost every reading of him is true. Even the too familiar representation of the naughty, bottom-pinching bounder of musical comedy can be adequately documented. But so can many other interpretations. Where so much, most of it apparently irreconcilable, can be maintained, it is perhaps best to start with what every reader of the Diary must have observed, namely appetite. Its crudest manifestations are so often described that some have thought Pepys's sexuality exceptional. But what is the exception and what the rule and on what evidence can we arrive at either? Sir D'Arcy Power, the surgeon, suggests that both Pepys's kidney condition and the post-operative consequences

of his lithotomy combined to excite his sexual desires.[2] Whatever the
explanation the fact is explicit. And simply by contrast with the general
reticence on this subject Pepys, at first, may appear to some highly sexed.
There seems no evidence that he himself thought so. What he did notice
in himself was a diffused romantic feeling towards the opposite sex as a
whole (women, not a woman) akin to that which Sterne elaborates in *A
Sentimental Journey*.

In the physical satisfaction of his appetite it is the cautious and calculating side of his nature that rules all. So far as we know Pepys never attempted
an affair with anyone who came near to his own station in society, let
alone with those above him. Servants, shopgirls, barmaids, prostitutes;
there is a chilling prudence about the choice. And yet there was sometimes
a real tenderness, particularly in his relations with the young girls who
came to live in the house as companion to Elizabeth. The fact of their
femininity, their innocence, their simplicity and sweetness of nature
enchanted him. Perhaps they roused sleeping affection for the children
that he had once wanted but had reconciled himself to not having.
Gosnell, Ashwell, Mercer and last, most poignant of all, Deb Willett
touched emotions very different from those which the diarist records
in his transactions with the shifty and unprepossessing ladies he was
accustomed to pick up in Westminster Hall. And different from
either was the long liaison between Pepys and the pretty wife of a
subordinate, which throws light on so many contrasting aspects of his
character.

On a wet afternoon in July 1663 Pepys ended a not very strenuous day
by having himself rowed down to Deptford:

> . . . and there mustered the yard, purposely (God forgive me) to find out
> Bagwell, a carpenter whose wife is a pretty woman, that I might have
> some occasion of knowing him and forcing her to come to the office
> again – which I did so luckily, that going thence, he and his wife did of
> themselfs meet me in the way, to thank me for my old kindness; but
> I spoke little to her, but shall give occasion for her coming to me . . .[3]

What the old kindness was we do not know. Bagwell was at that moment
carpenter of the *Dolphin*,[4] a fifth-rate captured from the French,[5] so that
it is possible that Pepys had in some way helped to obtain the place. But
the conscious use of official position and an official pretext, the admission
even if only conventional, of guilt, and the frank intention to deceive
leave no room for speculation. Whatever heats of passion might follow
this is a fairly cold-blooded opening.

A week later Pepys was again down the river visiting the yards when the Bagwells saw him:

> ... and they would have me into their little house: which I was willing enough to, and did salute his wife. They had got wine for me and I perceive live prettily; and I believe the woman a virtuous modest woman.
>
> Her husband walked through to Redriffe [Rotherhithe] with me, telling me things that I asked of in the yard; and so by water home, it being likely to rain again to-night, which God forbid.[6]

Pepys, it appears, was touched by the friendliness of the young warrant officer, by the care taken to offer generous hospitality, and by the knowledgeable enthusiasm of a young man who wanted to succeed in his career. At any rate the divine aid was only invoked to improve the weather, which suggests a more temperate and decent state of mind. Indeed he seems to have taken no further initiative in the matter. But on an evil day some six months later Mrs. Bagwell sought him out at the office to ask his help in finding a new appointment for her husband. Pepys chucked her under the chin 'but could not find in my heart to offer anything uncivil to her, she being I believe a very modest woman'.[7] Another three months passed without any sign of the Bagwells but on May 31st

> ... a great while alone in my office, nobody near, with Bagwell's wife of Deptford; but the woman seems so modest that I durst not offer any courtship to her, though I had it in mind when I brought her into me. But am resolved to do her husband a courtesy for I think he is a man that deserves very well.

But early in October Bagwell's professional merits were still unrecognised. On the 3rd Pepys met Mrs. Bagwell at the office:

> and there kissed her only. She rebuked me for doing it; saying that did I do so much to many bodies else, it would be a stain to me. But I do not see but she takes it well enough; though in the main, I believe she is very honest.

A turning-point seems to have been reached on October 20th when

> ... I to my office, where I took in with me Bagwell's wife; and there I caressed her and find her every day more and more coming, with good words and promises of getting her husband a place, which I will do.

Easily enough, one would have thought, with a full-scale war against the
Dutch on the point of breaking out. But on November 3rd he made an
assignation with her in Moorfields:

> . . . and there into a drinking house – and all alone eat and drank
> together. I did there caress her; but although I did make some offer,
> did not receive any compliance from her in what was bad, but very
> modestly she denied me; which I was glad to see and shall value her the
> better for it – and I hope never tempt her to any evil any more.

These resolutions proved infirm. Twelve days later he seduced her in the
same unromantic surroundings to her evident distress and his great
pleasure. Just before Christmas he went to great trouble to repeat the
performance and was vexed when she resisted him. However the next
day, December 20th, he found a pretext to visit Deptford yard and:

> . . . walked, without being observed, with Bagwell home to his house
> and there was very kindly used, and the poor people did get a dinner
> for me in their fashion – of which I also eat very well. After dinner I
> found occasion of sending him abroad; and then alone avec elle je
> tentoy a faire ce que je voudrais, et contre sa force je la faisoy, bien
> que pas a mon contentment.

And so, both trust and hospitality betrayed, he took leave and walked
home.

The affair, for want of a better word, went on for two or three years.
A month later Pepys was shaking his head over female virtue:

> . . . and there I had her company toute l'apres dîner and had mon plein
> plaisir of elle – but strange to see how a woman, notwithstanding her
> greatest pretences of love a son mari and religion may be vaincue.[8]

Smugness greased the slipway of routine: routine led to boredom:
boredom to distaste: and distaste to active repulsion. Eighteen months
later Pepys arranged to spend the night at the little house in Deptford.

> . . . but though I did intend para aver demorado con ella toda la night,
> yet when I had done ce que je voudrais, I did hate both ella and la
> cosa; and taking occasion from the uncertainty of su marido's return
> esta noche, did me levar; and so away home late . . .[9]

None the less Pepys still continued to avail himself of her services for another six months. He had at the beginning of the war obtained a better post for Bagwell — carpenter of the *Providence*, a fourth-rate — and as it drew towards its close he had him appointed to a new third-rate building at Harwich. He continued to watch over his career with a headmasterly sententiousness, in the circumstances more than usually revolting. Twelve years later in a long letter announcing his promotion from the *Resolution*, a third-rate, to the *Royal Prince*, a first-rate fitting out at Bristol he urges:

> . . . the study of the Art of ship-building as well as the Common prac-
> tices which as your friend I would advise you to apply some of your present
> leisure to, the King being one that understands it soe well as makes it
> unsafe for any shipwright to approach him that is not a Master of the
> Theory of the Trade, as well as of the ordinary labour of it.[10]

Four years later still, when himself out of office and only two years beyond the Tower and the threat of execution, he wrote to Lord Brouncker, his old colleague at the Navy Board, to solicit a dockyard appointment for Bagwell.[11] Restored to power he was not able to reward his protégé as soon as he desired and wrote him a firm, perhaps rather too magisterial letter, explaining that Mrs. Bagwell's constant visits to the office would in no way promote the end in view.[12] Finally as the curtain fell on his own official career after the Revolution of 1688 and the scene-shifters were jostling round him, one of his last acts was to recommend Bagwell for a vacancy in Chatham Dockyard.[13]

How deeply the whole story bears the impress of Pepys. And how sharp and distinct are the contrasting flavours of his personality. Like the Impressionists he disdains the neutral tints. The actor-narrator provides insights of his own that could support a Marxist indictment of bourgeois exploitation, a Christian exposition of sin, and the more cynical view that morality consists in what one can get away with. But for all its univer-sality of application it does draw lines of perspective in which class domi-nates the scene. Pepys sometimes desires Mrs. Bagwell, sometimes pities her, sometimes despises her. There is no suggestion of love or tenderness, no talk of standing in strange slavery to beauty, no comparison to the enchantments of music, no hint, however distant, of romance. These higher feelings were inspired by women of a higher class. Lady Castlemaine, for instance, or even the Queen, Catherine of Braganza, were the objects of Pepys's cerebral lust, issuing sometimes in dreams of ecstasy. The wives and daughters of colleagues and friends frequently elicit a response, part aesthetic, part sexual, that corresponds more closely to the ideas of Plato than to the actuality of Mrs. Bagwell. The nearer Pepys approaches to particularity, the lower burns the flame of romance. A shop girl seen in passing could retain her status as part of the feminine ideal and inspire feelings generally reserved for her social betters.[14]

To all this must be added a touch of the *voyeur*. He feels a vicarious thrill at seeing two 'gallants' dragging a pretty girl out of her stall on Ludgate Hill with the evident intention of raping her: and the cavortings of the King and his mistresses sometimes excite these susceptibilities. More often, it is true, they provoke an outburst on Charles II's frivolity or a denunciation of the wrath to come upon a nation that has forgotten its purer traditions.

For Pepys found no difficulty in combining a self-indulgence that he never pretends to condone with a strong moral and social code which he never hesitates to proclaim. On this account he has often been accused of hypocrisy. He might more justly be admired for integrity in refusing to deny principles he believed to be right simply because he did not live up to them. Certainly he was prepared to take extraordinary risks in maintaining the proprieties, whereas in defying them he was notably timid.

The most striking example of his boldness is the famous episode of what Pepys called 'my great letter of reproof'. The story, astonishing enough in itself, becomes even more amazing when it is remembered that it took place at almost exactly the same time as Pepys was making the opening moves in the Bagwell campaign.

Early in 1663 Sandwich who had been in poor health through most of the winter fell very ill. On his recovery in the spring he took lodgings in Chelsea, then a pretty village on the Thames, where he remained for several months to recruit his strength. At the beginning of August Pepys heard from his old fellow-servant Will Howe that their master had become infatuated with the daughter of the house in which he was staying and was behaving in the most indiscreet and scandalous manner. The story was soon corroborated by the other senior members of Sandwich's household, Moore and Creed, and heightened by the lurid account given by Ned Pickering, a young kinsman of his patron for whom Pepys usually had little time.

. . . he telling me the whole business of my Lord's folly with this Mrs Becke at Chelsy, of all which I am ashamed to see my Lord so grossly play the beast and fool, to the flinging off of all Honour, friends, servants and every thing and person that is good, and only will have his private lust undisturbed with this common whore – his sitting up night after night alone, suffering nobody to come to them, and all the day too – casting off Pickering, basely reproaching him with his small estate which is yet a good one; and other poor courses to obtain privacy beneath his Honour – with his carrying her abroad and playing on his lute under her window, and forty other poor sordid things; which I am grieved to hear, but believe it to be to no good purpose for me to meddle with it; but let him go on til God Almighty and his own conscience and thoughts of his Lady and family do it.[15]

Pepys was always quick to prefer the colourful to the humdrum. Provided the story were good enough he was ready to suspend his critical faculties. Whether Sandwich, that portly, cool, reserved figure, was likely to behave in a way that suggests the undergraduate Pepys he did not stop to wonder. He had had, at this point, no opportunity of meeting the lady and judging for himself whether Howe's description of her 'a woman of a very bad fame and very impudent' or Moore's 'a common Strumpett' in any way fitted the facts. Sandwich he considered 'a man amorous enough' – had he not attempted Elizabeth's virtue? – and it was not surprising that he 'now begins to allow himself the liberty that he sees everyone else at Court takes'. But he had already, as the passage quoted makes clear, considered and rejected the course of speaking to his patron for his own good.

A few days after this conversation both families adjourned to Huntingdonshire, Pepys to view his property at Brampton and Sandwich to enjoy the beauties of Hinchingbrooke in early autumn. For the first time Pepys derived pleasure instead of vexation from his inheritance. Riding with Elizabeth in his own woods and gathering nuts he thought himself a lucky man. She looked well on a horse and conscious of being, for once, admired and approved of was excellent company. On Sunday the two families met at church, walking back afterwards to Hinchingbrooke where a large party sat down to a noble dinner. Before the meal Sandwich took his guests round the garden, distinguishing his dependent by asking his opinion, in front of all the company, as to the re-designing of a wall that closed the perspective of the walks. Soothed by such characteristically beautiful manners, relaxed by fresh air and exercise, happy and contented in body and estate, away from the wrangles of the Navy Board and the irritations of a busy life, Pepys let his anxieties fall away. Whatever anyone might say there was no denying, once one was among them, that the Sandwiches were a most affectionate and united family. Official duties called Pepys back to London immediately but Sandwich spent another four or five weeks in the tranquillity of the country. When the two men met again in London at the end of October Pepys's mind was full of a host of other things – the effectiveness of the Emperor in resisting the

Turk, the results of his interminable litigation with his co-heirs, the need to get more money and the imperative necessity of spending it. Sandwich, helpful as always, undertook to see about getting Pepys a place on the Fishery Commission, another of those opportunities of being paid for doing nothing which in those days relieved the hard-pressed servant of Government. So matters went on until, on November 9th, just when Pepys's new periwig had so transformed his appearance that the Duke of York declared that he did not recognise him, up bobbed Pearse the surgeon. Did Pepys know anything of Sandwich's being out of favour with the King? His absence from court was the subject of much adverse comment. To judge from the moral diatribe which Pearse at once launched into, the Court would have seemed an admirable place to stay away from — 'nobody looking after business but every man his lust and gain'. But the alarm bells were ringing in Pepys's mind. If Sandwich lost the royal favour his dependents could expect short shrift. As Pearse turned to go, up came Creed and Ned Pickering. They dined together at the King's Head where Pickering's criticism of Sandwich shocked and disgusted Pepys by its extravagance.

For two days he did nothing, but on the 12th, dining with Moore, they talked of nothing but Sandwich's absence from court, its incalculable consequences and its scandalous cause. At last Pepys resolved on immediate action. He took a coach to Sandwich's lodgings, determined to have it out man to man. He was met by Will Howe who went over the same ground in long, lugubrious detail. After some time Sandwich appeared. Pepys began 'to fall in discourse with him, but my heart did misgive me that my Lord would not take it well, and then found him not in a humour to talk; and so after a few ordinary words, my Lord not talking in that manner as he uses to do, I took leave . . .' Rejoining Howe he told him that he thought it would be better done in writing, a decision which Howe applauded.

Was it chance that made Sandwich, usually so approachable, discourage his cousin from plunging into some topic about which he was evidently agitated? Men do not survive in the politics of civil war and revolution unless equipped with antennae. If Pepys's emotions had not been roused, his own skill in handling people would surely have enabled him to read the signal then made to him. But he bustled on. By the 16th he had drafted, not without pain, his letter of reproof. On the 17th he read it over to Moore who received it with rhapsodies and offered to send a duplicate signed by himself, a proposal which Pepys still retained enough sense to refuse. On the 18th he had it personally delivered by Will Hewer with orders not to stay for an answer.

Why had Pepys acted in this reckless if heroic manner? If he himself was not only planning the seduction of Mrs. Bagwell but habitually deceiving his wife with his doxies in Westminster, why should not Sandwich 'a man amorous enough' partake also of pleasure that flattered their sovereign by imitation? Even had they been equals it would have been in a high degree presumptuous to issue such a warning. To write on such a matter to a man far above one in social position, wealth and political power was to defy the rules of prudence and the deference to social order that Pepys held all but sacred. Strangest of all he had rushed into this course on the hearsay of Howe, Moore, Creed and Pickering, all of whom, in his heart, he either distrusted or despised. He had not so such as set eyes on the lady whose feral attractions were wreaking such havoc. When he did, several months afterwards, he found her charming, intelligent and well-bred, the exact opposite of what she had been represented 'one that hath not one good feature in her face and yet is a fine lady'. With a lame show of bluffing it out he concludes 'and I dare warrant him she hath brains enough to entangle him'.[16] Why did he persist in taking so grave a risk on such frivolous evidence?

A number of reasons might be given. Certainly Sandwich seemed to be withdrawing from public life – Pearse the surgeon had emphasised this. And Pepys as one who was both professionally and financially involved in Sandwich's affairs knew that he was heavily in debt. It was essential to bring him back into the game if all was not to be lost. But why should Sandwich, hitherto so adroit a performer, have abandoned the field? A woman. Of course it must be a woman. Look at the King. Look at the Duke of York. Look at – but without multiplying examples beyond necessity, the report from Chelsea explained everything.

This pragmatic explanation of Pepys's conduct is possibly true as far as it goes. But it does not go nearly far enough. Pepys was shocked by what he heard, shocked socially and morally. Peers of the realm ought not to misbehave in a notorious manner. And morally an action was not less wrong because it was common. Behind these feelings lay other springs of action. Pepys was a busybody by instinct. Both by taste and education he had in him much of the teacher and of the lawyer. Naval administration, as his bulging files still show, was to give both faculties almost unlimited scope. To show someone what they ought to do and how they ought to do it and to analyse a case were among his greatest pleasures and commonest duties. These aptitudes were not happily applied to the moral and caution-ary instruction of one's patron. One further element may here have played its part – vanity. Pepys fancied himself – and with reason – both as a letter writer and as a man who could draw up a brief. The urgency, the concern and the distress of 'my great letter of reproof' are palpable. It conveys exactly what its author intended. Was it not too well written to throw away?

Sandwich's reception of it mystified and alarmed Pepys. No thunderbolt flashed from the sky; but equally there was no invitation to intimate discussion. Pepys had been expecting anger or gratitude: embarrassment seems not to have occurred to him as a possible reaction. Agonised inquiries of those about his patron, Moore and Howe, were met with comforting reassurance that the letter 'hath wrought well upon him', the phrase Pepys habitually employs to describe the effects of purgatives. After four days of suspense the two men met on Sunday morning as Sandwich was preparing to go to chapel at Whitehall. Sandwich was firm and brisk but not unkind: since Pepys had reported these allegations he must disclose his sources. Pepys broke down and wept. As soon as Sandwich had obtained the information he wanted he closed the subject and 'begun to talk very cheerfully of other things, and I walked with him to Whitehall and we discussed of the pictures in the gallery'. Pepys was so upset that he missed the whole drift of the sermon and was only brought to present-mindedness by the anthem composed by one of the choirboys. It was some months before he felt the same ease in Sandwich's company as he had before. Indeed was it ever quite the same ease? The impassive surface of Sandwich's nature disconcerted Pepys's vivacity. But within the month Sandwich had had him put on the Fishery Commission.

At first sight these two episodes seem to illustrate two opposing sides of Pepys's approach to these matters at this stage of his life. And so, in many ways, they do. In the first he is selfish and calculating; in the second wildly rash. In the one he plays the lecher, in the other he champions what Mr. Doolittle would dismiss as middle-class morality. What imposes the unity of his personality on these evident contrasts is that unlike the generality of mankind he is rash in defence of respectability and staid in pursuing his amours. It is, further, perfectly clear from the account of his relations with Mrs. Bagwell that he felt ashamed of himself. Perhaps the contradictions are more superficial than profound.

8

Taste and curiosity

The years at the Navy Office saw the flowering of that universal curiosity
that Pepys himself recognised as indivisible from his consciousness. 'But
I, as I am in all things curious . . .' 'A liberall genius, as I take my own
to be, towards all studies and pleasures.'[1] So deeply did he admire this
faculty in himself that he devoted the better part of a Sunday to trying to
celebrate it in verse before abandoning the attempt. But the judgment hit
the mark even if the lines fell short. The work of the office itself opened
fresh vistas of practical and theoretical study. He began, naturally, by
mastering day-to-day technicalities, who did what, how much things cost,
by what standards they were judged or measured. Such questions touched
on a host of specialised skills whose practitioners could not always give a
lucid or coherent account of their mastery — 'their knowledge lying in their
hands confusedly' as Pepys himself brilliantly expressed it in a survey of
the leading shipwrights of the 1680s. Pepys's hands, like ours, acquired
their knowledge by turning the pages of books.

Not that he disdained or even underrated the educative value of apprenticeship. On the contrary his greatest single achievement, the professionalis-
ing of the naval officer, rested on this foundation. In his own life a true
passion for learning the job always got the better of vanity and self-
importance, qualities which were at no stage negligible. He was never too
proud to begin at the beginning or to take instruction from a man of
simple qualifications. When he had been two years in the office, calculating

wages, measuring tonnage and striking bargains of many kinds, he engaged a mathematics master to teach him the multiplication table.

The arrangements with old Barlow had been reached partly through the agency of Sir William Petty, whom Pepys had seen at Harrington's Rota Club, and John Graunt, who was deputed to receive Barlow's share of the salary. Graunt's *Observations on the Bills of Mortality*, edited by Petty and published in 1662, is still on Pepys's shelves at Cambridge. A pioneer work of social statistics it is the foundation both of life insurance and of scientific demography. These were the kind of people and the kind of questions that fascinated Pepys. Petty became a lifelong friend whose views on religion or plans for constructing a double-bottomed vessel Pepys carefully preserved among his own papers. In the breadth of his curiosity as in his good nature and in his unblushing readiness after greatly enriching himself as a Government servant to utter piteous cries of destitution, he has obvious affinities with Pepys. But in originality and intellectual power he outclassed him. Anatomist, physician, land-surveyor, naval architect and above all political economist Petty personifies the age of the Royal Society to which he was elected on its foundation. No doubt his scepticism and his humour delighted Pepys. Aubrey tells us that 'He can be an excellent Droll (if he haz a mind to it) and will preach *extempore* incomparably, either the Presbyterian way, Independent, Cappucin frier, or Jesuite.'[2] But it was in his insistence on numeracy and his determination to quantify that he made his impact on the minds of his time. No one else argued so tirelessly for statistics as the prerequisite for policy. Did Pepys, consciously or unconsciously, learn this lesson from him? It certainly characterised his own administrative practice.

John Evelyn, that other great virtuoso whose influence on Pepys can hardly be overestimated, did not enter his life until after the outbreak of war in 1665. It is strange that Pepys should owe his election as a Fellow of the Royal Society not to his close friends Petty or Evelyn but to Thomas Povy, a man whom he first envied or despised and seems, ultimately, to have hated.[3] The elegance of his cellar management has already been described. Elegance, indeed, was Povy's long suit. His house in Lincoln's Inn Fields was 'beset with delicate pictures'; his stable contained 'some most delicate horses, and the very racks painted, and mangers, with a neat leaden painted cistern and the walls done with Dutch tiles like my chimnies'.[4] Dazzled by this splendour, irritated by Povy's incompetence as a colleague in Government service, jealous of the rich appointments, that, for no discernible merit, had been showered on him, Pepys reluctantly admired his taste, even, on occasion, enjoying his company. But it was the possessions not the man that formed a model:

... his room floored above with woods of several colours, like, but above the best Cabinet-work I ever saw – his grotto and vault, with his bottles of wine and a well therein to keep them cool – his furniture of all sorts – his bath at the top of his house – good pictures and his manner of eating and drinking, doth surpass all that ever I did see of one man in all my life.[5]

Like Povy, Pepys was already, in a much humbler way, a collector of books and engravings and a patron of artists. But it was music and the theatre that, at this period of his life, provided his keenest aesthetic excitement. Music, the thing he loved best in the world, had always been with him. But the theatre was a new pleasure, one of the indisputable advantages of the Restoration. Pepys went to a play with the uninhibited expectation of pleasure that owed a great deal to the novelty of the experience. By the end of the Diary he is becoming more critical or more jaded. In the years before the war he is forced to take the same measures of self-discipline against playgoing, fines and vows, as against drinking. That the plays he saw fired his imagination and held him rapt we cannot doubt. But what it was he saw in them, why for instance, he admired Massinger's *The Bondman* to such an extravagant degree, why he thought *Romeo and Juliet* 'the worse I ever heard in my life' or considered *A Midsummer Night's Dream* insipid and ridiculous, or why he should be moved by *Hamlet* and *Othello* (which he none the less rated below a trivial and forgotten comedy translated from the Spanish) are all questions that must puzzle more than they enlighten.

That Pepys's taste was unsure, that it leaned towards the conventional, his literary judgments strongly suggest. If one enjoys Fuller's racy and entertaining *Church History of Britain* how could one endure repeated readings of Bacon's sententious *Faber Fortunae*, which at this period was Pepys's favourite piece of prose? He read widely, prose and poetry, Spanish and French and Latin, history and law, plays and books of travel. If we can discover no unifying principle in his opinions and cannot understand why he should like some books or dislike others, it is at least manifest that he thought about what he read and made up his own mind about its merit. Twice he bought Butler's *Hudibras* because everyone else told him how amusing it was and twice he yawned and threw it away. For this, as for his Shakespearian judgments, he has been generally patronised by later writers. Sir Sidney Lee[6] confidently attributes it to his being a bone-headed businessman with no imagination, an explanation perhaps more baffling than the phenomena to be explained. To convict him of crass materialism because he was perceptive enough to identify an uncomfortable seat as prejudicing him against a play, or, conversely, the appearance of a pretty and favourite actress as predisposing him to enjoyment seems perverse. It would be impossible to make out a case for the originality or the inherent interest of his taste. As in every other department of life he unashamedly enjoyed much that was commonplace.

The Diary years are years of appetite, not digestion. A taste would form, an outline would harden. But it would come through the multiplicity of life. Like a child in a toy department at Christmas, Pepys's eye was for ever absorbing him in some new prospect of delight. And like a child he continued to notice what other men of his age generally take for granted. What Londoner has ever extracted more pleasure from the weather or found more to enjoy in the routine journeys entailed in the day's work? '. . . and there it begun to be calme and the stars to shine', '. . . a most fine bright moonshine night and a great frost' – the language is suddenly lyrical, with no changing of gear from a matter-of-fact account of, it may be, some dubious commercial transaction or an ugly scene with Elizabeth. As in childhood all experience comes in through the same front door. Pepys understood the use of a tradesman's entrance as well as any man. His filing system, his personal and official accounts, his determination to master all relevant knowledge from the multiplication table to the best methods of measuring and storing masts attest a mind whose power to specialise and subdivide would be approved by an industrial consultant. What raises a mentality in its component parts so often commonplace to the level of genius is a capacity to keep this intellectual gadgetry in its proper place. Pepys does not anticipate his own responses. Ordinary things, a pot of beer, a walk through a dockyard, a night journey on the river, are apprehended as though they were being offered fresh on the first day of creation, instead of for the hundredth time in a busy life.

This applied equally to ideas as to the impressions of the senses. Sermons, books, tavern gossip, professional interchanges and the conversation of learned men tumble pell-mell into the Diary. Sometimes a quick and summary judgment is passed but more often the idea is examined, squeezed between finger and thumb, and put aside without comment or commitment. Except in practical affairs Pepys liked to defer judgment. Predisposed to a rational explanation of phenomena he by no means closed his mind to the mysterious or the magical. Even in a matter of such concern as his health he could write, 'But am at a great loss to know whether it [his unusually good state of health] be my Hare's foote, or taking every morning a Pill of Turpentine, or my having left off the wearing of a gowne.'[7] Three weeks later, within a fortnight of his election to the Royal Society, these doubts were refined

. . . Mr Batten in Westminster hall . . . showed me my mistake, that my hares-foot hath not the joint to it, and assures me he never had his chollque since he carried it about him. And it is a strange thing how fancy works, for I no sooner almost handled his foot but my belly begin to be loose and to break wind; and whereas I was in some pain yesterday and tother day, and in fear of more to-day, I became very well, and so continue.[8]

If detachment and empiricism characterised his view of nature, what, in that highly theological age, of his religion? So far as he dared he maintained the same stance. To eschew the dangers of Popery to the right or Fanaticism to the left came easily to him. So did regularity of attendance at public worship. Some churches – St. Dionis Backchurch in particular – offered an exceptionally fine range of female beauty in the congregation. Others – notably Captain Cooke and his choirmen at the Chapel Royal – maintained a high musical standard. All offered sermons, good, bad or indifferent, whose texts Pepys usually misremembered but whose arguments, if properly thought out, he would listen to in the spirit of a tutor appraising an undergraduate's weekly essay. Yet little as religion interested him his easy conformity had its limits. During the Diary years he never received the sacrament, an omission that could have caused him trouble if any malicious person had made use of the fact. Indeed when, many years later, he was accused of being a secret Roman Catholic both he and his parish priest at St. Olave's swore that he had been a regular communicant during this period. Although he had, to his mother's sorrow, accepted the restored liturgy of the Church of England, he had not yet come under the influence of that learned circle of High Churchmen and Non-Jurors to whom he was drawn after the Revolution of 1688. Sympathising with the Presbyterians and detesting the bishops he occupied the conventional position of the educated non-partisan. He seems to have been faintly shocked, or was he merely surprised at finding Sandwich '. . . plainly to be a Scepticke in all things of religion and to make no great matter of anything therein'.[9] Agnosticism was by and large congenial to his own temperament. But atheism, especially if publicly professed, he found offensive. Interested in and tolerant of other people's religion he is one of the first Englishmen to have left on record a description of a visit to the synagogue of the recently readmitted Sephardic Jews and he frequently attended Mass in the Queen's Chapel.

It was against the grain of his nature to isolate abstract questions. Religion, like politics, much more often presented itself to his mind in the form 'who whom'. Religion, in its public manifestations, was indeed an

GRANA
ANGELICA:
OR,

The rare and singular Vertues and Uses of those Angelick and innocent PILS, discovered and left to posteritie, by Doctor Patrick Anderson, late Physician of Edinburgh.

Mongst the most eminent Physicians of this age, the late famous Doctor ANDERSON is most deservedly to be esteemed; for he spared no Travel nor Study, that he might be serviceable to the Diseased of his Country; and returning from his Travels, with a mind fully enriched, amongst other things, he brought from thence this inestimable Jewel; whose Vertues and Uses are these.

For the pain of the Stomach.

For diseases of the Head.

For the diseases of the Belly.

Against Worms.

For the natural Infirmity of Women.

For Stomach, eyes, dropsy, Swelling, Plurisy, Cholick, Dropsie.

For the Gravel, Scurvy, and Palsie.

Against Catarrhes and Defluxions in the Joynts. The way of taking them.

For children, and old men.

I. They extreamly comfort and strengthen the Stomach; they restore the lost appetite, they purge Choler and Melancholy; but chiefly Phlegm and waterish matter: they cleanse the same of all putrid, gross and thick humors; they comfort the bowels, open obstructions, and disperse all the pain of these places.

II. They strengthen the head and all the senses, but chiefly that of hearing and sight, whose weakness and pain they remove; they help the giddiness thereof and the Megrim; and as they comfort and purge the Stomach, so they do the like both to Head and Heart, and have this excellent faculty, that being mixed with other Physick, they correct its malignity, and make it unhurtful to the Stomach, and are therefore to be preserved to all other gentle and easie Medicines.

III. They are wonderfully helpful to all diseases of the womb, and all other maladies belonging to women, that proceed from coldness by chance or constitution: for they safely and easily purge and empty the Belly, without pain or grippings, and carry out by their proper passages, all those vicious humors and other dregs that are stopped on a woman after her delivery; and they much help barrenness that proceedeth from uncleaness of the Womb, and cleanse women from their white-flux, and so fitteth and enableth them for conception. Also they may be taken by women with child, for yielding them ease in their bellies gently, without any hazard of miscarrying at all, one every night before Supper.

IV. They kill and choak all worms that are bred in the Womba of Children, big-bellied women that are bound in the belly, and of men, yea not any body, that frequently use these Pills, can breed worms at all.

V. And if in women with child the belly be bound, which often happeneth, you must have a special care that in the time of her birth, the great Guts, being examined with excrements, do not overcharge her paine in travell; to avoid which, it is my counsel, that in such cases, you have already ready in your Cabinet Case of these Pils...

VII. They hinder likewise the procreation of many diseases, and the corruption of the food; and wonderfully defend the body against surfeits in eating or drinking, which most frequently after sleep beget outrage and crude humors, and so are a sovereign help for the gravel, Scurvey, Cholick, and Dropsie, and green sickness and Palsie, one every day.

VIII. If the head, subject to defluxions, keepeth intelligence with a moist and fuming Stomach, and threatneth the joynts with a deluge; these Angelick grains will so stop their Screens, that famous Physician hath promised they shall be free from the Gout, and all other diseases of the Joynts, who shall use these Pils frequently and familiarly...

IX. You may use of them at your pleasure, whether late or early, or at any hour of the day, before meat or after meat, or in the time of feeding; but being taken in time of Supper, they defend the head (as we have said) from those vapours and fumes that ascend to it in the night. They are familiarly taken in time of need, without trouble to the Body, and not any hindrance of your business. The Dose is Seven, Nine or Eleven, and that three or four times a month, as necessity or the temper of the Body shall require. They give not many stools, neither do they worke violently nor sad only...

X. They are of so easie and innocent operation, that they may be given to children and decrepit old men, and that most securely: and to delicate persons who are not much imployed in labour, and others that cannot away with other purgatives, may easily swallow down these. They are an enemie to most diseases, and have much friendship to the subject Secrat of the bodie, and is of so wholsome and general use, and so much both known and approved in this Nation...

XI. We suppose there be few or none in this Kingdom, but knows of the use and excellency of Doctor Andersons Angelical pils, who perhaps are ignorant of the dangerous abuse and counterfeiting of them by sundry unskilled women...

And all the Boxes are sealed with her Name and Arms, K. A.

These Pils are to be sold by *Katharine Anderson*, Daughter to the late Dr. *Patrick Anderson*, at her house in *Edinburgh*, on the south-side of the street, in *Sir John Smiths* Close, over against the head of the Land-Market: And they are to be sold by Mrs. *Reddess* at her house in *Kings-street Westminster*, at the signe of the Cradle; and no where else at *London*.

Printed in the Year, 1677.

Handbills for quacks and patent medicines.

In the *Strand* near the Middle *Exchange* in *Salisbury* Street, at the Second House on the Right hand where a Barber's Pole hangs out, Liveth *John Butler*, An Expert Operator and Oculist.

You may find him there from Seven in the Morning till Twelve, And then he goes into *Sweeting's* Alley, to that which was *Joseph's* Coffee-House, now called the *Flanders* Coffee-House, next Door to the Sign of the Horse-Shoe near the *Royal Exchange*, there he stayes till Four of the Clock, who (by Gods Blessing) Cureth the Distempers following, (*Viz.*)

He Cureth Blindness by Couching of Cataracts, He taketh Specks off the Eyes, and Cureth Defluxions of Rheums in the Eyes; He hath singular good Skill and Knowledg in Curing of Deafness, when the Party comes to him, he will tell them the cause of their Deafness, whether the Deafness be Internal or External, or whether curable or no. He Cureth Noises, Singing or Buzzing in the Ears; He cureth Bursten Bellies, he cureth Ulcerated Legs, and Itch in any part of the Body; He hath an Excellent Art in drawing forth of Corns out of the Feet and Toes with the whole substance in length and similitude of a Clove, and drawing no blood, nor putting the Party to any pain at all: And by the Operation of a Plaister to kill them, that no other Corns will ever come again in the same places.

He is none of those which you call by that Vulgar name Corn-Cutters, could he perform it no better than such persons, he would scorn to set it forth in Print. For every Corn he draweth in his Chamber is Six pence; if any person sends for him to their dwelling places, he expects Twelve pence. If any person doth conjecture that other Corns will come again in the same places, upon Consideration he will admit of a Years trial and take nothing for the present; And if other Corns do come again in the same places within the Year, then he will expect nothing.

Alderman *Rugg* dwelling in St. *Albans* in *Hertfordshire*, he was very Lame with Corns, he had Five and Fifty Corns taken out 26 years ago by this Professor, and never any other Corns came again in the same places.

Capt. *Body* dwelling in *London*-Street in *Ratcliff*, had Thirty Corns taken out Three years ago, and never any come since; he was so troubled with them, that he was forc'd to Ride up and down to do his business; but now goes very well without any pain.

Mr. *Morgan* a Herald-Painter in *Threadneedle*-Street near the *Royal Exchange*, he was much troubled with Corns, I took them out Two Years ago, And he was never troubled with any Corns since that time.

Mr. *Peck* now dwelling in *Noble*-Street, he had Fourteen Corns taken out by the Professor hereof Four and Twenty Years ago, and was never troubled with any Corns since.

He can give Testimonies of some Hundreds of Persons more that he hath Cured of the Particulars abovesaid, since his coming to *London*, which will be too Tedious to Insert here. He cureth many other Distempers not here mentioned.

This Oculist has a Large House and Shop wherein he now dwells, known by the Sign of the *BELL* in *Pye-Corner* near *Smithfield*, which he is willing to Sell, Lett, or Exchange for another of the like Value in or near the City.

If any Person please to send for him, they are desired to leave a Note at his Chamber.

These handbills, preserved by Pepys, are among his papers in the Bodleian.

aspect of politics. The great Catholic question which was to play such a destructive part in Pepys's later career first forced itself on him in the person of Elizabeth. But whatever he may have feared or suspected she did not avow her Catholicism until the Diary was nearing its end; when, indeed, their marriage had been undermined by estrangement and deception.

In the early years at the Navy Office Pepys made at least spasmodic efforts to share with his wife the enchantments offered by the great fair of the world. He took her with him to the theatre. He engaged a music master for her so that she might join in his keenest pleasure. He even — advanced test of matrimony — enjoyed teaching her the mathematics. He arranged drawing lessons for her and was surprised and impressed by her pictures '. . . which now she is come to do very finely, to my great satisfaction, beyond what I could ever look for'.[10] They often read to each other; and even more often Pepys records his pleasure in his wife's conversation. From the evidence of the Diary, indeed the only source on this topic, it was not the widening of Pepys's intellectual and artistic horizons that loosened the ties between them. Elizabeth's formal education, like her antecedents, left, no doubt, much to be desired. Left to herself she would, it seems, have preferred playing blind-man's-buff with the maids to hearing about the methods of limiting population practised in East Prussia or the million other subjects on which Pepys was ready to absorb information. But she consistently shows in the Diary an attractive and unselfish readiness to enter into her husband's interests and to offer him her untutored natural abilities and tastes to shape and direct.

'What would you give, my lad, to know about the Argonauts?'
'Sir,' (said the boy) 'I would give what I have.'
Johnson was much pleased with his answer, and we gave him a double fare.

Is there an exchange in the whole of English literature that states a purer ideal of education or a more eloquent profession of the trust implied? Elizabeth was ready to make such a profession good. She was generous, her husband mean.

The benevolence that makes the letters of the ageing Pepys so delightful was, like his sobriety, not achieved without a struggle. The Pepys of the Diary is in many ways mean and even harsh. If he was generous to his own family he was stingy to his wife. Lady Sandwich, whose kindness and good sense he admired, felt at last impelled to speak to him about it:

Among other things, my Lady did mightily urge me to lay out money upon my wife, which I perceived was a little more earnest than ordinary; and so I seemed to be pleased with it and do resolve to bestow a lace upon her.[11]

Elizabeth was told to make a selection and then to leave the final choice to Lady Sandwich. Two days later:

> . . . I find my Lady hath agreed upon a Lace for my wife, of £6, which I seemed much glad of that it was no more, though in my mind I think it too much, and I pray God keep me so to order myself and my wife's expenses that no inconvenience in purse or honour fallow this my prodigality.

Was it so very prodigal for a man who was making money hand-over-fist and spending it freely enough on the things that pleased or amused him? The conclusive answer may be found two years later when Pepys had been spending an evening over his accounts:

> . . . and to my great sorrow, find myself £43 worse than I was the last month; which was then £760 and now is but £717. But it hath chiefly arisen from my layings-out in clothes for myself and wife — viz., for her, about £12; and for myself £55 or thereabouts . . .[12]

Lady Sandwich, least interfering of women, had evident reason for her action. Only when he was very rich — worth over £2,000 besides his Brampton estate — did he give Elizabeth a diamond ring ' — valued at about £10 — the first thing of that nature I did ever give her'.[13] 'Valued' it will be noticed: even then Pepys had not bought it for her: it was a present to him for helping a man to a purser's berth.

It would be easy to multiply instances; but there are aspects of his behaviour to her which, if not so cold-bloodedly selfish, are scarcely less repulsive. That he should nag and bully over her running of the house was to be expected. The idea that it was hers as much as his clearly never entered his mind. But the physical and psychological violence that he resorted to sometimes made him ashamed. It was cowardly to pull her nose and make her cry. It was disgraceful to black her eye in bed. But it was perhaps more odious to damage in childish spite the workbasket he had given her as a present; and unforgivable to snatch his old love-letters out of her desk and tear them up in front of her.

And yet it was not that he was not in love with her: '. . . sad for want of my wife, whom I love with all my heart, though of late she hath given me some troubled thoughts'.[14] When it seemed that a minor operation on her might be necessary he could not bear the idea of witnessing it.[15] And the jealousy that he himself recognised as making 'a very hell in my mind'[16] perhaps drew something from his love. Mainly it was nourished by his selfishness, his competitiveness, his egocentricity. And it was these as yet untamed forces that estranged him from the wife whom he loved and who loved him. As in the spring of 1660 when he went to sea with Mountagu she still had no power, no resources, no friends. Her *raison d'être* was to please him. She could make herself disagreeable, but that was all. He held all the cards; money, freedom, social opportunity, and played them for himself. Increasingly this meant that the world he lived in grew apart from hers. Sometimes the fact could soothe a qualm of conscience, if cited as evidence of her inadequacy to the position he had won: '. . . the indiscretion of a wife that brings me nothing almost (besides a comely person) but only trouble and discontent.'[17] Sometimes he recognised that the inequality was of his own making. Children, the natural corrective of his egoism and her boredom, were denied them. Signs of winter were appearing in his most intimate affection at a time when his intellectual and aesthetic responses were at their spring.

9

A very rising man

Even when every allowance is made for the inextricable confusion of business and pleasure that was natural to the seventeenth century and seems so odd in the twentieth, it still takes an effort to realise that while Pepys was experiencing life with a multiplicity of consciousness that takes the breath away he was also establishing himself as the most brilliant new arrival in the most important department of government. 'Chance without merit brought me in' he remarked to his friend Thomas Hill on November 1st 1665. But as early as August 1662 Coventry had described him to Sandwich as 'the life of this office ... So that on all hands by God's blessing I find myself a very rising man.' Less than three years after that Albemarle, a gruff and severe critic at the best of times, told Pepys to his face '... that I was the right hand of the Navy here ... so that he should not know what could be done without me — at which I was [from him] not a little proud.[1] It was even more telling from its timing. War had been declared on the Dutch and the first fleet action could not be more than a few weeks, perhaps only days, away. No one knew better than Albemarle, a professional of forty years' standing, that battles are won by proper preparation, or at least cannot be won without it.

Had Pepys devoted himself single-mindedly to naval administration it would still have been an astonishing achievement to have won such an opinion from such a man at such a moment less than five years after entering the office as a novice. But even in that part of his life which, as it whirls past us, we can plausibly identify as naval or, more broadly, concerned with Government business, it is by no means the good of the service or the interest of the state that is his sole preoccupation. The opportunities for enriching oneself in the Government service were large. Pepys was poor, extravagant and greedy. The charm and vivacity of his personality have combined with the immensity of his public service to melt the sternest judicial glare that has been turned on his early career as Clerk of the Acts. Except, perhaps, the coldly penetrating gaze of Pepys himself. 'We do nothing in this office like people able to carry on a war. We must be put out or other people put in.'[2] Yet, so rapidly do the facets of Pepys's mind spin round, in the same short entry, a bare half-dozen lines away, he justifies to himself a monumental piece of corruption over the Tangier victualling contract: ' – for which God be praised. For I can with a safe conscience say that I have therein saved the King £5,000 per annum, and yet got myself a hope of £300 per annum without the least wrong to the King.' God be praised indeed: but as the gentlest of judges has written of this very transaction in his authoritative book on Navy Board contracts, 'This, of course, is nonsense.'[3]

What makes the contemplation of Pepys, either in general or in detail, so dizzying is that the interlocking circles of his nature revolve too fast for the eye to distinguish a clear and individual movement. It is like watching an electric egg-whisk. Pepys is the life of the office, the right hand of the navy. Coventry says so, Albemarle confirms it. But Pepys is also corrupt. He is, further, a factious and disloyal colleague – witness a hundred entries in the Diary, notably those concerning Sir William Penn. But, as we shall see, he is also a tenaciously loyal colleague – witness his lifelong relationship with Hewer – and the man who time and again defends the office when it is under attack. He is a demon for efficiency and reform: yet no one watches more closely or understands more profoundly the dynastic nature of the Navy Office – witness Sir George Carteret's allying himself by marrying a son to one of Sandwich's daughters and a daughter to a (supposed) illegitimate son of Prince Rupert, that alarming, uncompromising, unpredictable figure. Sandwich and Coventry, Penn and Batten, Monck and Rupert, the King and the Duke, patrons, colleagues, politicians, admirals, princes, all these forces are constantly in a state of flux, constantly acting on each other, and yet must be severally and collectively held in equilibrium to promote the career of Samuel Pepys. So viewed, and that is how the Diary views it, this looks a full-time job. But not at all. There is the theatre, books, music, lust, social pleasures and social obligations, all the hundred and one themes already touched on, whirring round at full speed without, apparently, ever getting in each other's way.

At least so full a life must surely have required a high degree of organisation. In the sense of reducing matters to order, of imposing form on chaos, of keeping records, accounts, files, minutes, even a diary, this is evidently true of Pepys. But it is far from true of the way in which he organised his day. Regularity of hours was not his habit. If he wanted to finish some major undertaking, a paper on the method of measuring masts or mustering stores, a letter to the Duke on the general administration of the navy or to Sir William Coventry on pursery and victualling, he would work from four to five o'clock in the morning till midnight for several consecutive days. On the other hand the office hours that he kept during the winter of 1662 for example sort oddly with Coventry's description, unquestionably correct, of the rising man. On November 26th a hangover kept him in bed till near midday and he did not visit the office till summoned there in the late afternoon. On the 28th it was again afternoon before he attended the office and on the next day he did not get up until his colleagues sent word that the Duke of York required their presence at Whitehall that afternoon. Apart from this brief interview the day's official labours seem to have consisted of a very fine dinner at Sir William Coventry's lodging and a visit to the theatre with Sir William Penn. This agreeable course of life persisted into December until on the 14th the diarist himself remarks on it: 'All the morning at home, lying abed with my wife till 11 a-clock — such a habitt we have got this winter of lying long abed.' Pepys was no sluggard but he was not, as so many of his successors are, a slave of the clock.

It will be remembered that one of Pepys's first concerns was to master the nuts and bolts of his job. In particular he set himself to learn his way about those commodity markets in which the navy was a large buyer. Masts, canvas, timber, iron, hemp, tar and the whole range of ships' stores were his immediate preoccupation. The artist in administration had to master his medium. It was intolerable to be ignorant of that which could be learnt by taking pains. No entry in the Diary is more characteristic than the comment on the signing and sealing of the contract for the building of the mole at Tangier: 'a thing I did with a very ill will, because a thing which I did not at all understand, nor any or few of the whole board.'[4] Muddle enraged him: and to the man of business no muddle is more exasperating than the lazy confusion of what can be known with what cannot. The mole at Tangier to which his colleagues so lightheartedly put their names that afternoon was, as Pepys's sure instinct warned him, a gigantic undertaking, demanding the closest scrutiny and assessment. Not until we reach our own age has any English government in time of peace committed so vast a proportion of the nation's expenditure to so ambitious and so fruitless a project. To construct an artificial harbour in deep tidal water exposed to the violent storms of the Atlantic and to the frequent and fierce gales from the Levant on a part of the African coast, twelve hundred miles from the nearest English port, that was dominated by a wild and warlike Moorish tribe was an amazing venture by the standards of the seventeenth century. Simply as a piece of engineering the mole was the greatest work ever undertaken by Englishmen. And the cost proved, before long, far beyond the resources of a pre-industrial economy. Pepys could not have known this: but he understood at once that a decision involving huge sums and incalculable consequence was being taken casually and carelessly. And this offended him.

But the artist was, if the deepest, only one of his parts. The opportunist was another. If the government had however rashly committed itself to pouring out hundreds of thousands on Tangier, it was not in Pepys's character to watch the gold flow by without seeing what could be done to divert some of it in his own direction. He had been appointed a Commissioner in November 1662 and finding 'Tangier one of the best flowers in my garden' drove a bargain with the elegant but futile Povy to succeed him as Treasurer of the Commission in the spring of 1665. Even splitting fifty-fifty with Povy he made money hand-over-fist, much of it, as is clear from the Diary, by the corrupt practices he denounced in others.

The same easy transitions may be observed in his Navy Office negotiations. He sets out to master the commodity markets because he wants to know, he must know, he cannot bear to be at the mercy of other people when industry could make him his own master. He hob-nobs with Captain Cocke, the hemp contractor, with Sir William Warren, the great importer of masts. He knows the going rate and he investigates the possibility of alternative sources of supply. He is not too proud to go to school to shipwrights, ropemakers, boatswains and such people. His blood boils when he learns the tricks put upon the King by dishonest contractors and connived at by his colleagues. And yet when Cocke offers him a rake-off he jumps at it. When Warren provides him with arguments to convince the board of the superior value his masts offer to those of his rival, Wood, who is hand-in-glove with Sir William Batten it is difficult not to feel that best argument of all was the £100 in a bag handed over in the Sun tavern on September 16th, 1664. All through the Diary period Pepys is using the technical and commercial knowledge he has acquired to line his own pockets.

Was he then insincere in professing a desire to root out corruption and to see that the King was given value for money? Was his enthusiasm for the reforms propounded by Slyngsbie and Coventry a pretence? There seems no reason to think so. Pepys was often hypocritical, notably in his holier-than-thou headshakings over the shiftiness of his colleagues, but he is rarely cynical. On the other hand his admirers have perhaps been in more of a hurry than Pepys was to establish his reputation as a public servant of fearless probity. That was what he became; it was not the point from which he started.

The chameleon quality which made, and makes, Pepys so companionable exacts its price. The company of shrewd and thrusting dealers like Cocke and Warren teaches other lessons besides the quayside costs of Milan hemp or the different methods of sawing Eastland timber. Not that all the people Pepys did business with were city magnates. Some were country gentlemen like Colonel Bullen Reymes of Waddon in Dorset, a Royalist who had been brought up in the service of the first Duke of Buckingham. Reymes, like Cocke, was an M.P. and had connections at court: it was his brother-in-law who had sheltered Charles II at Trent when he was on the run after the battle of Worcester in 1651. A widower, he had, after the Restoration, entered into a partnership as much personal as commercial with a remarkable woman who was wife to the Puritan mayor of Weymouth. Mrs. Pley and Reymes were important suppliers both of West Country and Breton sailcloth. There were two other career women whom Pepys evidently respected for their commercial talents. Mrs. Russell, the tallow chandler, seems to have been unremarkable beyond the fact that she was a woman in business. Mrs. Bland, another sailcloth supplier, emigrated with her husband to Tangier where they quarrelled fiercely with the military governor. Their son emigrated to America and took part in one of the earliest attempts at revolution. He was captured, sentenced and executed. Mrs. Bland's last letter to Pepys, a bitter, fearless denunciation of the whole system of government brought her to the attention of the Attorney-General.[5]

In spite of Sir William Coventry's disapproval the commercial and the official worlds interpenetrated each other. Bullen Reymes, for instance, was sent out as a special emissary to report on the state of affairs at Tangier after the Governor and a large part of the forces under his command had been cut to pieces by the Moors.[6] Both he and Captain Cocke were joined with John Evelyn in the Commission for the Sick and Wounded set up just before the outbreak of the Second Dutch War. The Houblons, too, with their network of trading connections in Spain and the Western Mediterranean were invaluable sources of intelligence and could often keep a useful eye on the activities of captains who thought themselves far enough away from Admiralty surveillance to do pretty well as they liked.

Altogether these connections with the merchants who supplied the navy or who, like the Houblons, needed its protection against the Arab pirates of North Africa were among the most enjoyable as well as the most instructive aspects of life as Clerk of the Acts. The people involved were diverse; they were all experts; they were all quick-witted; they were all citizens of the world. As has already been pointed out they were often men of high civilisation. But they had yet greater charms than these. None of them was a colleague. None could ever be a rival. All were, in some degree, suitors for Pepys's favours. A rejected suitor might, of course, turn nasty and tell Batten or Penn things that were either untrue or embarrassing. Most of them had the sense not to prejudice happier relations by such proceedings. And all of them understood that an official had to live.

Besides increasing his practical knowledge Pepys also set himself to learn something of the arts and sciences material to his profession. Hydrography, navigation, naval architecture, naval history and maritime law found a place in his intellectual curriculum which they retained to the end of his life; indeed beyond, for these subjects are nobly represented in the library that is his chosen monument. The study of naval architecture led to one of the longest and most fruitful of Pepys's long and fruitful professional relationships. Anthony Deane, assistant shipwright at Woolwich, taught Pepys enough to hold his own against the experienced sea officers on the board and supplied him with drawings, still preserved in his library, that were much admired by John Evelyn, one of the greatest connoisseurs of the century. In return Pepys was a zealous promoter of Deane's career. In October 1664 when war was imminent he secured his appointment as Master Shipwright at Harwich. The ships he built there won him a European reputation. Louis XIV and Colbert courted him: at the end of the century his son went to Russia to superintend the shipyards of Peter the Great. But eminent as he might become, he was the protégé, Pepys the patron. Strong paternal admonition characterised such a relationship

. . . I will not dissemble with you because I love you. I am wholly dissatisfied in your proceedings about Mr Browne and Mr Wheeler . . . Mr Deane, I do bear you still good respect, and (though it may be you do not now think that worth keeping) I should be glad to have reason to continue it to you. But, upon my word, I have not spared to tell the Board my opinion about this business, as you will shortly see by a letter we have wrote to Commissioner Taylor. Wherein I have been very free concerning you, and shall be more so if ever I meet with the like occasion.[7]

This letter was written after Deane had established himself at Harwich
and was within a few years of a knighthood and a large fortune. Perhaps the
vehemence and openness of Pepys's communications with his subordinates,
so very different from Sandwich's well-bred reserve, made friendship
easy. Certainly Deane's attachment never weakened in fair weather or in
foul.

The same is true of the closest of all Pepys's associations, that with
Will Hewer. Pepys's intolerance of deviation in the matter of dress led
to correction that did not always stop at words. Hewer's habit of wearing
his hat in the house affronted Pepys. His wearing his cloak 'flung over his
shoulder like a Ruffian' enraged him. It was Hewer's 'slight answer' on
this occasion that provoked Pepys to box his ears. Worse followed two
months later when Pepys who had waited up for Hewer at the office till
late at night found that he had gone straight home from the job he had
been doing at Deptford and was 'at ease in his study'. Pepys lost his temper and hit him. He then stayed up even later 'chiding him' and at last,
after midnight, stalked off, convinced that Hewer 'hath got a taste of
liberty since he came to me that he will not leave' and threatening to find
a replacement for him. Hewer's mildness in the face of such treatment is
the more remarkable in that he was evidently a young man of means.
When in 1663 he left Pepys's house to live in lodgings of his own Pepys
was much impressed by their splendour. It is characteristic of them both
that Hewer should present, and Pepys send back, 'a locket of dyamonds
worth about £40' to Elizabeth, 'out of his gratitude for my kindness and
hers to him'. 'It becomes me more to refuse it than to let her accept it.'
Of that kindness, and of the fierce loyalty that went with it, there can be
no doubt. Early in 1662 Penn had advised Pepys to get rid of Hewer
because Sir George Carteret believed that he was passing on confidential
information to his uncle Robert Blackborne. It took some pluck to disregard such a hint from such a quarter.

Gradually Hewer took the place of the son that Pepys could not have. In
his will Pepys acknowledged 'his more than filial affection and tenderness
expressed to me through all the occurrences of my life for forty years
past'. Other relationships were briefly contemplated and, happily, dismissed. Hewer as we have seen declined Pall's hand out of a general disinclination to matrimony. Pepys's lurid jealousy tried once or twice to
imagine him carrying on an adulterous intrigue with Elizabeth but collapsed at the effort. On the contrary when Pepys's infidelities at last
threatened the marriage with disaster it was Hewer who did more than
anyone else to save it. How close their professional relationship was is
early apparent. Pepys trusted Hewer absolutely. Hewer knew and used the

system of shorthand in which minutes of confidential matters were better kept.

Pepys was not always so fortunate or so perceptive in his choice of assistants. An example of some interest because it involved a head-on collision with a sea officer of some standing comes to mind in the person of Richard Cooper, whom he employed to teach him mathematics. The two men had first met in the spring of 1660 aboard the *Naseby*; Cooper was master's mate, that is assistant navigator, junior enough to be approachable and expert enough to be worth learning from. He was serving in the same capacity aboard the *Royal James* when Pepys ran across him again in July 1662. Impressed by his ability and prudently reflecting that he was unlikely to ask much in the way of a fee Pepys promptly engaged him. The lessons were a success. By the beginning of August the syllabus had apparently been extended to include mechanics[8] and Pepys was able to reward his tutor by having him appointed master of a fourth-rate under orders for a voyage to the Straits and Tangier. By the end of September she had sailed.

But she was back before the swallows, bringing trouble with her. Early in March Pepys met her Captain fresh from sea who told him:

> strange stories of the faults of Cooper, his master, put in by me; which I do not believe but am sorry to hear, and must take some course to have him removed, though I believe that the Captain is proud and the fellow is not supple enough to him.[9]

Both these judgments were to receive abundant confirmation. Meanwhile Pepys lost no time in writing to Cooper urging him to make a clean breast at once as the only means by which his patron could defend him from injustice:

> You are said to be a Mutinere, a man ignorant in your duty that have several times endangered the shipp and very often been drunk . . . you know wherein you are justly accused, wherein not . . .[10]

To strengthen his flank with an impartial expert Pepys also wrote to the Commissioner at Chatham, where the ship was lying, asking his opinion of Cooper's fitness for his post. Commissioner Pett replied that Cooper though of a weak brain and 'sometimes disguised with drink' might be continued in his appointment provided that he chose a competent master's mate. This was hardly what was wanted to beat off an attack from so formidable a figure as Robert Holmes, the Captain who had made the complaint. Holmes's record both as a young cavalry officer in the Civil War and as Rupert's right-hand man in the semi-piratical cruise to Portugal, the Mediterranean, West Africa and the West Indies that had followed it was evidence enough that here was no tame conventional spirit. In any case Pepys already knew Holmes and had been rather frightened by his open cynicism. No wonder that his first reaction had been to accept Cooper's dismissal as a foregone conclusion, even though to save the Board's honour and his own reputation within it some show of resistance would have to be made.

In the event it was very much more than a show. At a full meeting of the Navy Board on the afternoon of Saturday, March 21st:

> Captain Holmes being called in, he began his high complaint against his Master, Cooper, and would have him forthwith discharged – which I opposed, not in his defence but for the justice of proceeding, not to condemn a man unheard. Upon [which] we fell from one word to another that we came to very high Termes, such as troubled me, though all and the worse I ever said was that was insolently and illmannerdly spoken – which he told me it was well it was here that I said it. But all the officers, Sir G. Carteret, Sir J. Mennes, Sir W. Batten and Sir W. Penn cried shame of it. At last he parted, and we resolved to bring the dispute between him and his Master to a trial next week – wherein I shall not at all concern myself in defence of anything that is unhandsome on the Maister's part, nor willingly suffer him to have any wrong. So we rose and I to my office troubled, though sensible that all the officers are of opinion that he hath carried himself very much unbecoming him.

This was an age when duelling was common: even more common, where a man of rank considered his dignity impugned by a social inferior, was naked violence. The solidarity of one's colleagues at the Navy Board was no doubt consoling but it would not be much comfort if one was set on by a gang of thugs or was to find oneself at the point of a sword with Holmes's thin-lipped face behind it. Pepys spent a thoroughly uncomfortable weekend. On the Monday duty took him, in spite of trepidation, to Whitehall and a meeting of the Tangier Committee. At last in the evening where he least expected it he ran into Holmes on Sandwich's doorstep. Holmes made as if to go away. Pepys would not have it and himself offered to go. In this exchange of civilities and the conversation that ensued Holmes 'did as good as desire excuse for the high words that did pass in his heat the other day, which I was willing enough to close with'. That is easily believed. What is interesting is that Pepys should have allowed his strong sense of propriety, of what was owing both to the dignity of his own position and to the conduct of official business, to overcome his prudence, not to say his timidity. And what of Holmes? Why did he not teach that soft and self-important young Clerk of the Acts a lesson? For all his amoral professions he never lacked loyalty or courage and may have respected Pepys for an unlooked-for display of both. He was, too, himself a highly efficient and professional officer, qualities again that he could have seen reflected in Pepys. Or it may have been a simple calculation. For a sea officer to assault or even to challenge a member of the Navy Board might risk a scandal even in that loose and bullying age.[11]

The next day saw the end of the matter. At the board:

> . . . among other things, had Cooper's business tried against Captain Holmes. But I find Cooper a fudling, troublesome fellow, though a good artist [i.e. mathematician]; and so am content to have him turned out of his place. Nor did I see reason to say one word against it, though I know what they did against him was with great envy and pride.[12]

The proud and envious 'They' of this passage must refer to Pepys's colleagues on the board. But, as in the Great Caucus Race, everyone has won so everyone must have prizes. Holmes has got rid of an incompetent master. Pepys has successfully maintained the principles or at least the procedures of elementary justice. Cooper may have been fudling and troublesome; he may have been the object of envy and pride; but at least he was not condemned without being heard.

But who was right, in the matter of professional judgment? Was Cooper as Holmes maintained a drunken neurotic, unfit to be trusted with the safety of a man of war? Or was he 'a good artist' as Pepys continued to insist? Three years later towards the end of the Four Days Battle, one of the fiercest of all the fierce sea-fights with the Dutch, the *Royal Prince*, flagship of the White squadron, ran aground on the Galloper sand where the Dutch captured and burnt her, taking Sir George Ayscue, back to Holland as a prisoner. This is the only occasion in the history of the Royal Navy that a flagship has been captured and her admiral made prisoner. The master responsible for the navigation and pilotage was Richard Cooper.[13]

This conflict with Holmes foreshadows much in Pepys's own career. And not only in Pepys's. Here in embryo is the division between the frocks and the brass that grew to such alarming proportions in the First World War. Pepys himself would have seen it as an early confrontation with one of the gentlemen captains whose arrogance and indiscipline undid all. Again it could be interpreted as an incident of political gang warfare. Cooper as well as Pepys were Sandwich's men; Holmes was Prince Rupert's. A case could be made out for all three views, none of which are mutually exclusive. But what is illuminating about the facts is that Pepys's judgment seems to have been hasty and unwise. And what a difference the affair reveals between the England of Cromwell and that of Charles II. One can hardly imagine one of the Protector's civil servants quaking about his business in the expectation of physical violence from a serving officer. The lesson was not lost on Pepys.

From his appointment to the Navy Office in the summer of 1660 to the outbreak of war with the Dutch in the spring of 1665 Pepys was laying the foundations of achievement, talking, listening, reading, learning, measuring men and mastering detail. If he had fallen a victim to the plague that made its appearance late in 1664 what would have been his record as a naval administrator? Hundreds of letters would confirm the evidence of the Diary that he had shown himself a man of system, order and business-like habits. He had realised to the full the ambition he had set before himself in his official dealings. '. . . that . . . which I labour most to merit by – I mean the easiness, civility and dispatch which I pretend to give to all that have occasion of applications to my Office.'[14] He had prepared important state papers on victualling and on the pursery; he had criticised estimates and schemes for remodelling the finances of the navy; but solid achievement, so far, had been limited to standardising the stationery in official use at Woolwich Dockyard.[15]

He had made a reputation. He was known to all the people who mattered. The King knew him.[16] The Duke of York saw him day in day out. His secretary Coventry was among his warmest admirers. Clarendon, the Lord Chancellor knew him. So did Lord Ashley, who as Earl of Shaftesbury was to do all he could to destroy him. The men behind the scenes, Sir Philip Warwick who ran the Treasury, Sir George Downing, who managed Anglo-Dutch relations and much else besides, the City men, the Royal Society men, all knew Pepys. 'How little merit doth prevail in the world, but only favour' he had argued in the conversation with his friend Hill, quoted at the beginning of this chapter. But he went on to draw confidence from his own diligence: 'living as I do among so many lazy people, that the diligent man becomes necessary, that they cannot do anything without him.'

10

The right hand of the navy

If mastery of the multiplication table was a rare achievement in seventeenth-century England, calculation of the Mystical Number in the Book of Daniel and the Revelation of St John was commonplace. The object of these exercises was to predict the end of the world: and the year 1666, compounded as it was of 1000, a hot favourite for Doom in its day, and the magical number 666, was widely recommended as a solution of the problem. If it was not to prove the Time of the End, in spite of the promising adjuncts of War, Pestilence and Fire, it was at least the year of destiny for Samuel Pepys. By its close he had shown indisputable mastery of the business of the Navy Office which he had often been left to manage on his own, and this under the stress of war conducted by a government that was neither experienced nor strong. He had also made himself a rich man. The war with the Dutch that he had feared, opposed and bewailed had established him.

The immediate cause of the war was the attack on the West African possessions of the Dutch East India Company mounted by a naval force under the command of Pepys's recent adversary Robert Holmes.[1] Technically the naval vessels that fired on the Dutch forts were rented to the Royal African Company, a body in which the King, the Duke of York, Prince Rupert and many of their servants (but not Pepys) had some financial interest. Thus some thin disguise could be put on what was nakedly a

challenge to the Dutch. Holmes had interpreted his instructions, in themselves aggressive enough, with characteristic brio. To satisfy the decencies
of international life he was sent to the Tower on his return. But the Dutch
ambassador reported, quite correctly, that this was mere deception. Sir
George Downing at The Hague, the thrusters among the city men, the
younger politicians and courtiers who resented the power of the old Royalists and its personification in Clarendon, were all hot for war. Captain
Cocke hemp merchant, Cavalier member of Parliament and a director of the
Royal African Company, put the matter succinctly when he told Pepys,
'. . . that the trade of the world is too little for us two, therefore one must
down'.

Cocke like many of his contemporaries took it for granted that the
volume of world trade was static, from which it followed that a nation
could increase its share only by wresting something from someone else.
This robust view of the commercial process was supported by the political
wisdom of non-partisan patriots such as Monck who saw in fighting the
foreigner the surest way to unify the nation and to submerge the memories
of civil war. Whether the King favoured this policy is at least doubtful:
but his brother, as Lord High Admiral, was naturally enthusiastic for a
war that was bound to be ninety per cent naval and perhaps to offer him
the chance of a place in history beside Henry V or the Black Prince.
Coventry, both as his secretary and as a leader of the anti-Clarendonians,
was, at this stage of the game, also in favour of the war.

Pepys's opposition was emphatic and consistent. All through the spring
and summer of 1664 the Diary records nothing but dread and foreboding
at the general desire for war. Largely this was the sober judgment of an
expert who knew the true state of naval affairs reacting against a fatuous
national conceit. But partly it derived from the fact of Sandwich's being
out of things, a condition that Coventry was anxious to perpetuate. If he
succeeded, Pepys's position would be difficult indeed. Sandwich's power
was based on the navy. If he were to be excluded from command in a major
war, he, and perhaps Pepys with him, would be left high and dry. Hence
from Pepys's point of view the necessity of reinsuring with Coventry,
whom in any case he liked and admired. Personally no less than pro-
fesionally he found himself in a most delicate situation, especially when
Coventry commissioned him to sound out Sandwich's readiness to command a squadron of twelve ships that was being fitted out in the summer
of 1664. Was not so minor a post beneath the dignity of a General-at-Sea?
Coventry hoped he would think so as then he would be out of play when
the real game began. Sandwich told Pepys that he was ready to serve in
that or any other sea command that might be offered. Coventry and the

Duke of York received this coolly. In the event of war the Duke wanted to command the fleet himself; and how, with three Generals-at-Sea, Sandwich, Penn and Albemarle, still active, not to mention Prince Rupert, was the conduct of operations against the first naval power of the world to be entrusted to a man who had seen no service at sea? The King, it seems, found the solution that satisfied everybody. His brother was to have the command of the fleet, with Penn at his elbow in the unique appointment of Great Captain Commander. Sandwich was to be Rear-Admiral of the Fleet and to command the Blue Squadron, Rupert was to have the White, and Albemarle, the elder statesman of war, was to remain ashore to give the King and Council the benefit of his advice. Pepys always admired Charles's judgment in naval affairs of which this is a good instance.

For Pepys the advantages of this arrangement were nicely counterbalanced. It removed the horrid prospect of a collision between Sandwich and Coventry. But the immense prestige acquired by Sir William Penn drove Pepys into paroxysms of jealousy. Even before the war broke out the regard paid by the Duke to Penn's experience against the Dutch could, Pepys was sure, only be explained '. . . by some strong obligations he hath laid upon Mr Coventry, for Mr Coventry must needs know that he is a man of very mean parts, but only a bred seaman.'[2] And the elevation of Prince Rupert was even worse. Pepys had seen him as a colleague on the Tangier Committee where he had not been impressed. 'Prince Robert [Rupert] doth nothing but swear and laugh a little, with an oath or two, and that's all he doth.'[3]

That the Diary alone provides good evidence of Rupert's remarkable range as scientist and artist makes no matter. Antipathy probably, fear certainly, inspire a vision of an overbearing brute of a cavalryman that is difficult to reconcile with what we know of the most intellectual of the later Stuarts. Perhaps his manner gave offence. It is clear that both Clarendon and Pepys disliked and resented him. Rupert for his part was not the man to conceal his conviction that his past services and professional talents were much superior to Sandwich's.

War was declared on February 22nd, 1665. A month later the Commander-in-Chief went aboard his flagship, accompanied by Coventry, Penn, and a host of lesser lights. Courtiers wished themselves on to captains of their acquaintance as volunteers so that the official world of London and Westminster was suddenly emptier. The size of the pond had not changed but there were noticeably fewer fish. The balance of power at the Navy Board tilted sharply in Pepys's favour. For who else could be applied to if men or stores were urgently needed at Plymouth or Dover or Chatham or Harwich? Penn and Coventry were with the fleet, Carteret, as a Privy Councillor and Vice-Chamberlain of the House-hold, was often required to attend the King. To answer questions and get things done the only people to apply to were Batten, Pepys, Mennes and Lord Brouncker. Brouncker, an eminent mathematician, was a good man of business when he could spare the time from his commitments as President of the Royal Society and from his domestic obligations to an ugly mistress in Covent Garden. Coventry had summed the matter up in his usual inimitable manner when Pepys had gone to call on him as he was packing for sea:

> He tells me the weight of despatch will lie most upon me. And told me freely his mind touching Sir W. Batten and Sir J. Mennes — the latter of whom, he most aptly said, was like a lapwing; that all he did was to keep a flutter to keep others from the nest that they would find.[4]

It was at this period that Albemarle paid Pepys the great compliment already mentioned. Batten was his superior in standing and in experience but he was beginning to feel his years. At the outbreak of war he was seriously ill and not expected to live. He did in fact recover and survive till a few months after the peace but at critical moments he was often absent from the office through ill-health.

So almost before he was aware of it Pepys found himself running a naval war of unprecedented proportions. The fleet with which the Duke of York sailed from the Gunfleet in April 1665 was the largest that England had ever sent out. Penn's son who had been with his father till the landsmen were ordered ashore counted 103 men of war besides fire ships and ketches, a figure substantially confirmed by Will Hewer from Harwich a few days later. Even if we accept the slightly lower estimate of modern scholars[5] it was still by the standards of those days enormous. And manning, victualling, paying and supplying it were a challenge worthy of administrative genius. In theory not all these tasks should have fallen on the Navy Board. In practice they did. If the fleet had run out of beer, if the victualling ships were still taking on stores in the river when they should have been at sea, it was Pepys not Gauden the victualler who threatened, pestered, ordered and went in person to see that his orders were obeyed. Pepys cut through red-tape. Organisations naturally engender a prejudice in favour of obstruction. To get anything out of them the prerequisite is to find a heretic prejudiced in favour of action. Once such people have been identified the channels of business change course towards them. By this process Pepys soon became what Albemarle called him.

The Diary for the opening months of the war records the range and tempo of Pepys's activity. But for the sheer mass of detail, marshalled by an exact and lawyerlike intelligence, the best evidence is the Letterbook of his official correspondence now in the National Maritime Museum. A business letter from Pepys must often have sounded to the recipient like the opening speech of prosecuting counsel, recapitulating all the facts and circumstances of the case to be tried. The charge that subordinates or colleagues found themselves most frequently accused of was failure to observe the proper routine:

I returne you the enclosed bill for Knees* (though signed) that you may certify them (as the Duke commands) to be agreed by contract. By which omission I wonder you should so often put us upon a necessity either of delaying satisfaction to merchants (as now in this case of Mr Castle's) or of passing their bills unjustifiably. Pray let it be completed as it should be and sent hither by the messenger tomorrow and at the same time let me know the reason of our not receiving the whole parcell (of which he complaines) it being a commodity which wee should unwillingly spare any at this time . . .

The two senior shipwrights at Deptford perhaps thought that they knew more about buying knee timber than Pepys did. Their answer appears to have been disrespectful; perhaps even ribald, for the very next day an even more orotund and circumstantial letter of reproof was directed at them:

I am sorry you should thinke soe slight an answer as that I received from you this morning should satisfie me being (I thinke) not used to ask questions to so little purpose. But since you have so mistaken me let me rectify it by observing to you that I doe not think you can imagine that the Principal Officers turned over every knee but in general did very well like of their appearance . . .

But let me tell you either they were very good and worth our money, or the contrary. If the former, then at a time of such use for them as this, why should we not have the whole quantity . . .? If the latter, why should we not know in what manner they are found so defective as that of 80 loades you should receive but 47 or if (as you say) you had nothing to do with the quality of them, how come you to except against any of them?[6]

---

* Crooked pieces of timber used to connect the deck-beams with the sides of a vessel.

And so, inexorably, on, referring them to an earlier letter to the merchant of which they had been sent a copy. How were unlettered shipwrights to stand against the method of argument taught at the Universities? This technique was better reserved for inferiors or perhaps equals. Employed against men like Prince Rupert or the Duke of Albemarle it could be counterproductive.

Fitting out a fleet created shortage in everything the Navy Office existed to provide — rope, masts, plank, tar, sailcloth, flags and, above all, seamen. Stockpiling against emergencies was impossible because Charles II's Government never had enough money to pay off its creditors, let alone finance forward buying. Pepys who never tired of demonstrating the obvious proves in letter after letter and memorandum after memorandum that the Government inflated the prices of all its purchases by its known inability to pay up. Shortage of ready money is the shortage most often mentioned by Pepys since it made his job more and more difficult as the war went on. But at the outset it was shortage of goods that was most serious. Demand had mopped up supply. Hence the importance he attached to the safe arrival of the Hamburg convoy with its cargo of masts, spars, pitch, tar and shiptimber. Its capture by the Dutch on May 20th was a heavy blow.

'Up betimes to the Duke of Albemarle about money to be got for the Navy, or else we must shut up shop.'[7] The war had not been going for two months when that entry was written. Always, for the rest of the war, Pepys was saying that this was the end; that things just could not go on like this; that men were starving in the dockyards for want of pay; that widows and discharged seamen were dying in the street. Always he was securing the last parcel of Milan hemp, even at an astronomical price; his dockyard commissioner was cajoling a blacksmith who had not been paid for twenty months into repairing one last anchor before dowsing the fire of his forge for good. Sometimes the reader is reminded of the early silent films in which hero or heroine is forever hanging on by the eyebrows while the cliff-top slowly crumbles. Was the abyss into which the Clerk of the Acts was gazing real, or a figure of speech employed to get results?

Pepys's reports of men unpaid, of workmen starving, of small tradesmen ruined, of widows and children thrown on the world have every appearance of truth and are supported by much other evidence. Probably, too, he was not exaggerating when he warned that certain essential stores were in dangerously short supply. But simply on the facts that the war went on, that ships did, somehow, get repaired, that the sails, masts and spars so abundantly destroyed in action were replaced, it seems that

Pepys underestimated the resilience and the sheer power of survival that so often goes with poverty. Like most of us Pepys had never known hunger and hardship, had never depended on his will to keep him alive when his reason told him that statistically he might as well lie down and die. It is this quality that constantly compels the admiration of everyone who studies the past. And again how are we to reconcile those heartfelt cries about the total absence of cash with the ecstatic reckonings of the diarist's huge personal gains? On December 31st, 1665, after only ten months of war he could write, 'I have raised my estate from £1300 in this year to £4,400'. He was not counting in cowrie shells. And what of his friends who supplied the navy on a large scale, Cocke and Warren and the rest? They seem to have commanded large funds with which to sweeten the conclusion of Navy Board contracts. There was more money about than Pepys sometimes cares to admit: and insiders like himself were well placed to catch it. The public finances of Caroline England were like some antiquated system of domestic water supply subjected to constant airlocks. A monitory gurgling and shuddering in the pipes told the initiated when the taps might be expected to emit. It is characteristic of Pepys that he used his expertise in financial plumbing not only to enrich himself but to promote efficiency and to honour public obligations. It was Batten, not Pepys, who was Treasurer of the Chatham Chest, that pioneer scheme of contributory social insurance for seamen initiated by Sir John Hawkins. But it was Pepys, not Batten, who saw to it that the administrators of the Chest were notified when a ship was to be paid. The deductions from the seamen's wages were, as things stood, the only source of its income; and consequently the only source of pensions for the disabled. Pepys was among the first to recognise the inadequacy and to press Coventry for its improvement.[8]

In the sharpening necessities of war Pepys's immediate financial concern was obtaining money. But he never forgot that public servants are accountable down to the last penny and that some day he would have to answer to some tribunal, the Treasury, the Council or a Parliamentary Committee, that might well be hostile. It was, obviously, extremely difficult to keep proper accounts in the press and confusion of war. Writing to Sir Philip Warwick, an old Royalist whose grasp of Treasury affairs Pepys wholeheartedly admired, he prefaced his accounts for the first six months of the war as follows:

. . . But many difficulties concur to make it impracticable to state the last six months expense in the method and with the positiveness I have heretofore done it. For in the unavoidable confusion we have for some time been in, 'tis not possible to take a right muster of ye men where Commanders are never bounded as to number nor (through the sickness [i.e. the plague], death, insufficiency and other necessities of altering their number for supplying other ships or prizes) are capable of ascertaining their complement three days together. This makes the computing of wages, victuals, wear and tear (the three great articles of our expense) noe more to be perfected than by estimate . . .[9]

A sympathetic and intelligent colleague was one thing: a Day of Reckoning was another. Yet Pepys, for all his apprehensions as to the course and outcome of the war, doubled, trebled and even tried to quadruple his administrative stake. A month after war had been declared he negotiated his appointment to the treasurership of Tangier in succession to Povy. In November he became Surveyor-General of the Victualling, in itself a vast commitment. And even before the war had started Pepys had joined the other Principal Officers in an application to be made Commissioners of Prize. On Coventry's advice (the letter giving it is endorsed in Pepys's own hand 'His advice to mee most friendlily touching the Prize Office'[10]) this was not pursued. But for a man who expected the war to end in humiliation and who knew better than anyone else how vulnerable were those charged with its administration this was boldness indeed.

> He either fears his fate too much
> Or his deserts are small
> That puts it not unto the touch
> To win or lose it all.

Again it would be misleading to represent Pepys simply as a daring administrator who had done his sums and knew his stuff. Like Winston Churchill he was often fascinated by the details of material problems and clearly enjoyed fresh challenges to his ingenuity. One of the first shortages complained of was the absence of wadding for the guns. Pepys at once consulted Mr. Myngs, the shoemaker, father of one of the bravest and most humane commanders of the Restoration navy. Pepys thought that the leather shavings might be bound up and used for this purpose, but Myngs père '. . . feares (the common shavings being but very small snips) wee shall finde but few fitt for our turne'. Undeterred Pepys inquires what might be thought of using tobacco stalks and follows the letter up with a consignment of them together with some twine.[11]

And besides finding men, money and supplies, besides the meeting of unexpected demands and the solving of problems that no one had foreseen, there was endless opportunity for making, or at least influencing, appointments. One of the roles in which Pepys perhaps fancied himself was that of the righteous magistrate, rewarding merit and punishing failure. To advance a promising young carpenter like Bagwell was a pleasure in itself, irrespective of others incidental to it. So, too, with an outstanding naval architect like Deane. And the provision of parsons and surgeons diversified the strictly naval aspect of the business. Already from the weeks he had spent in the fleet as Sandwich's secretary he had acquired a useful knowledge of the personal reputation of most of the leading officers. Now that he was exchanging letters almost every day with Coventry he was building up an index of sea officers that would help him to shape the profession and to frame its rules.

But as the professional tempo grew, so did the private. The different parts of his personality move at a uniform velocity, maintaining a rhythmic balance that is his triumph in the art of life. His official business increases, and vastly; his private transactions soar. Yet it is at this period that his intellectual life expands with his election to the Royal Society; that assignations with Mrs. Bagwell, musical evenings with Hill the merchant, buying books, buying clothes, sauntering, gossiping, arguing, flirting, every pleasure in the Pepysian calendar, are pursued more and more avidly. Intensified activity is matched by intensified observation and intensified self-awareness. The more he does the more there is to notice and to analyse. He observes (how few do!) that as he grows richer he grows stingier.[12] And the scenes of London in the plague and the fire are stated with the directness and the poignancy of a Breughel.

The plague elicits perhaps the first example of that steady persevering courage, unexpected in so volatile and timid a man, that was one of the very few virtues or vices to escape the attention of its possessor. 'You, sir, took your turn at the sword: I must not grudge to take mine at the pestilence.' These words with which Pepys answered Coventry's solicitude for his safety are the only evidence of conscious pride in his physical courage. Confessions of fear, candid admissions of cowardice, are common in the Diary. Pepys exemplifies Dr. Johnson's dictum that every man thinks meanly of himself for not having been a soldier or a sailor. Coventry had fought in the Civil War and was serving with the fleet while the London Bills of Mortality climbed into the hundreds and the thousands. In July Pepys moved his wife to lodgings in Woolwich. In August the Navy Board were assigned quarters in the magnificent but still unfinished King's Pavilion at Greenwich, the building that now forms the right-hand side of the Grand Square viewed from the river. But neither wife nor colleagues could stop Pepys from continuing to live and work in Seething Lane. He was never an easy man to stop.

'Pleased with the danger when the waves ran high.' Was there an element of this in Pepys? His conduct over the Great Letter of Reproof might be adduced in support. Certainly be admitted to a touch of ghoulishness, making sure of a good place at a public execution and enjoying a pleasurable shudder at the horrors of the plague-pits:

. . . so I went forth and walked toward Moorefields to see (God forgive my presumption) whether I could see any dead Corps going to the grave; but as God would have it, did not. But Lord, how everybody's looks and discourse in the street is of death and nothing else, and few people going up and down, that the town is like a place distressed — and forsaken.[13]

A few days later in a letter to one of Sandwich's daughters he refines and extends the description:

. . . I having stayed in the city till above 7400 died in one week, and of them above 6000 of the plague, and little noise heard day nor night but tolling of bells; till I could walk Lumber Street [Lombard Street] and not meet twenty persons from one end to the other, and not fifty upon the Exchange; till whole families (ten and twelve together) have been swept away; till my very physician, Dr Burnet, who undertook to secure me against any infection (having survived the month of his own being shut up) died himself of the plague; till the nights (though much lengthened) are grown too short to conceal the burials of those that died the day before, people being thereby constrained to borrow daylight for that service; lastly, till I could find neither meat nor drink safe, the butcheries being everywhere visited, my brewer's house shut up, and my baker with his whole family dead of the plague.[14]

Such perfection of phrasing makes one forget that Pepys was in London to run a war, not simply to write one of the greatest books in our language. In spite of his apprehensions, the first fleet action of the war resulted in an English victory. After two fruitless cruises off the Dutch coast the English fleet was at anchor in Southwold Bay — Sole Bay as it was then called — when the combined fleets of the United Provinces were reported in sight in the afternoon of May 31st. The English at once stood out towards them and for two days kept as close as they could get to the enemy who had the wind of them. On the third day the wind began to shift, enabling the English to close. Very early in the morning of June 3rd the two fleets engaged some forty miles south-east of Lowestoft, both somewhat out of the intended formation of line ahead. Like almost every action against the Dutch, the battle was hard-fought and bloody. Rupert's White or Van squadron took the brunt at first, but in the later stages Sandwich's flagship found herself knocking it out for two hours with four or five large ships of the line including Obdam's *Eendracht*, the flagship of the combined Dutch fleet. He was joined by the Duke of York in the *Royal Charles* at about four in the afternoon, and almost immediately the *Eendracht* blew up. The Dutch who had been getting the worst of it thereupon fled, closely pursued by their enemy. Total victory might well have been achieved, but during the night a courtier aboard the flagship, pretending the authority of the Duke, ordered the captain to shorten sail. As a result the Dutch reached safety without further loss.

Not that their losses had been light; seventeen ships sunk or captured, three admirals killed, and about five thousand casualties against the English loss of one ship, two admirals, and about eight hundred casualties. So complete a victory ought to have been more decisive. Pepys, like everyone else, did not learn about this scandalous misconduct until long after the event. It was to cost him and his colleagues at the Navy Board a high price in suspicion and mistrust. At the time however his mood seems to have veered from detachment, verging on irresponsibility, to euphoria. On the day on which news of the Dutch sighting reached London Pepys had only spent the morning at the office, going on to the Exchange at noon to do some business before returning home for his dinner. He then put on his 'new silk Camelott sute – the best that ever I wore in my life' and went off to a very splendid funeral in the City where the press of people was so great that even a silk suit was too hot; unless it was a plain silk suit which, struck by the thought, he briefly left the entertainment to order. When the festivities were at last over he took a coach to Westminster Hall,

> where I took the fairest flower and by coach to Tothill fields for the ayre, till it was dark. I light, and in with the fairest flower to eat a cake, and there did do as much as was safe with my flower, and that was enough on my part.

By the time he had taken the girl back and got home himself (twice changing coaches to prevent recognition) the hour must have been late. Yet it is only as he goes to bed that he records the certain news that the two fleets were in sight of each other.

The next entry opens, 'Lay, troubled in mind, abed a good while, thinking of . . .' Of what? The impending battle on which so much lay at stake, for the country, for the Navy Office and for Pepys himself?

Not a bit of it. It was 'my Tanger and victualling business' that pre-occupied him. It is only late in the afternoon, after a morning spent chiefly in flirtation, that the imminence of a fleet action is again mentioned. The following day the sound of the guns, heard clearly on the river and roundabout, filled Pepys with concern for the safety of 'Lord Sandwich and Mr Coventry after his Royal Highness'. The order of the names, no less than the saving clause, reveals Pepys's instinct for harmonising the natural with the formal even in so intimate a record. The next two days brought confused and uncertain reports of the Dutch in full retreat. Some thought this a tactical ruse; and Pepys himself was so sceptical of an English success that on the 6th he derided Batten's dispatch from Harwich announcing a victory for its clumsiness of expression. On the 7th there was still no news. It was so oppressively hot that the whole household, Elizabeth, the maids, the boy and even Will Hewer, rose at two o'clock in the morning 'to refresh themselves on the water to Gravesend'. Pepys had to stay behind to clear Sir George Carteret's accounts, a process that was completed by a hilarious dinner at the Dolphin tavern where Sir George was host to his colleagues. The day grew hotter; so hot indeed that Pepys abandoned his office for the river and the cool walks of Spring Garden. There was still no news, even though he waited up till midnight for the return of his wife and family. The heat persisted, matching its oppressiveness to the apprehension Pepys felt at having seen that afternoon two or three houses nailed up in Drury Lane 'marked with a red cross upon the doors, and "Lord have mercy on us" writ there'. It was the first evidence he had seen of the silent, invisible invader.

A short night was disturbed by flashes of lightning and one great shower of rain. At five in the morning Elizabeth came in and lay down on the bed, too tired to undress. Pepys spent the morning in the office and dined at home, again alone as the rest of the household were at a family party. He had an appointment that afternoon to meet some of the leading bankers at the Lord Treasurer's house with the object of wheedling a loan out of them. It was there, early on the afternoon of the 8th that '. . . I met with the great news, at last newly come . . . from the Duke of Yorke, that we have totally routed the Dutch. That the Duke himself, the Prince, my Lord Sandwich* and Mr Coventry are all well. Which did put me into such a joy, that I forgot almost all other thoughts.'

The news was confirmed by the Duke of Albemarle 'like a man out of himself with content' at the Cockpit, and, most reassuring of all, by a letter in Mr Coventry's own hand. The Diary becomes ecstatic. 'A great

---

* Pepys here gives the flag officers in order of squadronal command, not of personal concern.

victory, never known in the world. They are all fled . . . my heart full of Joy.' How full may be gauged by the fact that he distributed four shillings in largesse to the boys in the street and, after a visit of congratulation to Lady Penn, actually brought himself to write 'and good service endeed is said to have been done by him'. Raising money from the stoniest banker was easier than allowing any merit to Sir William Penn. When Pepys went to bed that night his heat was 'at great rest and quiet, saving that the consideration of the victory is too great for me presently to comprehend'.

Even at the moment of great events Pepys is at least as much interested in his own reactions as in the events that call them forth. This is the inspiration of his historical sense and of his genius as a reporter. His mind, sceptical, critical and informed, had been prepared for disaster and had to find room for triumph. As we have seen the triumph was not, as things turned out, proportionate to the victory. It was thus easy for Pepys to revert to the mood in which he had originally viewed the war and to which he remained constant. But in terms of his own personal affiliations the battle of Lowestoft had achieved all and more that he could have hoped for. Sandwich, by all accounts, had seen some of the hottest fighting and had shown the coolness, tactical sense and will to win required of a commander. Coventry shared in the honour won by his master the Duke of York as Commander-in-Chief and, together with Penn, had won for the administrators some of the glory usually reserved for the sea officers. All Pepys's patrons, actual and potential, Sandwich, Coventry and the Duke of York, had done more than well and, best of all, not at each other's expense. True some of Pepys's enemies and rivals had done well too: Sir William Penn, Prince Rupert and his formidable follower Robert Holmes. But even here fortune was unexpectedly favourable. Penn made no attempt to exploit the credit, so obviously his, for the successful handling of a huge fleet largely inexperienced in fighting a formal battle. Prince Rupert was still in bad health, was sometimes confined to his cabin and might have to come ashore. And Holmes had thrown up his commission in a rage at not being given, as Rupert wished, the Rear-Admiral's flag vacant by Sansum's death in action.[15] Even the casualties turned to the advancement of Sandwich. Lawson, his old rival from pre-Restoration times, died of wounds he had received. And the slaughter, by one piece of chain shot, of three court favourites standing beside the Duke of York — 'their blood and brains flying in the Duke's face' — lent powerful support to those, the King among them, who thought that the succession to the throne should not be exposed to such risks. If the Duke were to be relieved, if the Prince was unwell, Sandwich, as the senior flag officer, would have strong claims to command in chief.

Sandwich himself was too wary to take anything for granted. He met the congratulations of his cousin by pointing out that his name was hardly mentioned in the official account of the victory in spite of the fact that he had been in action for longer than any other flag officer and had had more men killed in his ship than any other commander except Jeremy Smith in the *Mary*. Success at sea must be made good by strengthening his position at Court. He therefore proposed that Pepys should open negotiations for a marriage between his daughter, Lady Jemimah and Sir George Carteret's eldest son Philip. No commission could have given greater pleasure. To combine busybodying and amorous intrigue with innocence, indeed with a virtuous sense of doing one's duty; to play the parts of man of the world, of confidential servant, of go-between, of humorous observer all in the same aristocratic comedy – what could any actor ask more? The ineptitude of the young principals for love scenes of any kind provided Pepys with endless material for the type of joke he most enjoyed.

Fortunately for Sandwich, both Coventry and the Duke of York seem to have regarded Prince Rupert's succession to the command as the danger to be avoided at all costs. Sandwich told Pepys how they had all three joined in laughing at Rupert behind his back; and Coventry, reunited to his adoring colleague, after the first exchange of endearments was careful to report 'how my Lord Sandwich, both in his counsels and personal service, hath done most honourably and serviceably'. For one brief moment Sandwich, the champion of sea-borne empire, the prime mover in the acquisition of Tangier (had not he and Oliver aspired to the capture of Gibraltar?), the protagonist of the blue-water school, was in alliance with Coventry who had not yet found his true position as a kind of seventeenth-century forerunner of John Bright, bent on reducing military expenditure and avoiding commitments overseas. It was an alliance on which everything smiled. Coventry was knighted and made a Privy Counsellor. Sandwich was given the command of the fleet with Penn, readier to serve his country than to urge his own claims, as his Vice-Admiral. The Duke of York was sent to the north to guard against a Dutch landing, Albemarle remained in London, Rupert, who had angrily rejected proposals of a joint command, was left without employment. Their turn would come soon enough: and so would that of the Captains who had been knighted and given flags for their performance in the opening battle, Spragge, Tiddeman, Jordan, Allin, Myngs, Harman and Jeremy Smith. Meanwhile there was news of rich Dutch convoys inward bound from the Indies and the Eastern Mediterranean. Early in July Sandwich and Penn were at sea with sixty ships to intercept them.

11

Pepys, Sandwich and Coventry: the height of the War, 1666

The perfect coalition of Pepys's interests and loyalties had hardly been achieved before it began to disintegrate. Sandwich, that shrewd, wary watcher of steps, was suddenly guilty of two careless misjudgments that might easily have ruined him. The first was in a field of war and diplomacy peculiarly his own. The Dutch merchantmen that he was out to catch were returning northabout round Scotland, intending to make use of the neutral harbours of Scandinavia for shelter. Through our ambassador in Copenhagen it was proposed that Denmark should, when the ships were safe in harbour, denounce her treaty with Holland, join the English in seizing the ships and split the proceeds. The ambassador, according to Sandwich, gave him to understand that 'the king of Denmark was ready to declare his treaties broken with the Hollander but would be glad to take an advantageous time to say it'.[1] Without any written agreement, without any further intelligence that the King had communicated his intentions to his commanders on the spot, Sandwich at the end of July detached a squadron under Sir Thomas Tiddeman to attack the two convoys that were known to be sheltering in Bergen. The result was unrelieved disaster. The Danish governor had no instructions to permit this invasion of his country's neutrality. When Tiddeman attacked the Dutch ships the Danish forts opened fire on the English who after some hours were forced to retire. Damage and casualties were severe – Sandwich's son was among those killed – and the Dutch had hardly suffered at all. The blame lay fair and square on the Commander-in-Chief.

The fillip to Dutch recovery was angrily recognised in London. It was immediately and immensely increased by the safe return home of the great De Ruyter, commanding the small escort force that Sandwich's fleet could have eaten for breakfast if only it had come up with it. A much stronger Dutch force then put to sea to bring home the Bergen ships. Irresponsibility and ineptitude had thrown away the fruits of the great victory in June.

Action, successful action, was imperative if Sandwich and those who depended on him were not to be swept away. The fleet had had to come in again, partly to make good the damage suffered but mainly to replenish the victuals that, throughout the year, consistently fell short of both the quantity and quality contracted for. At the end of August the fleet sailed with fifteen days' supply of beer and ten weeks' dry provisions. Five days out Sandwich's frigates sighted seven or eight strange sail about 100 miles north-north-west of the Texel. The English gave chase and, in the laconic words of Sandwich's journal: 'In the evening we took them, viz. 2 great East Indiamen and 4 men of war; 1300 prisoners. The *Hector* of ours sunk by a shot or his lee ports neglected; the Captain and near 80 men drowned.'

Six days later even closer to the Dutch coast another fifteen sail were sighted and chased. Four large warships were taken with nearly a thousand prisoners and half a dozen or so smaller merchant ships including two West Indiamen. Four days afterwards on September 13th Sandwich brought his prizes into the Nore. The year's campaign was over.

In the fortnight that the fleet had been at sea Pepys's effervescence had lost some of its sparkle. The Bills of Mortality were beginning to shake his nerve. In the office there was no money and no prospect of any. Huge sums were already owing to the seamen and to the merchants who supplied the navy. There had already been a strike among the shipwrights and carpenters in Woolwich Dockyard. The Government was tired: '. . . the King is nor hath been of late very well, but quite out of humour and, as some think, in a consumption and weary of everything.'[2] The well-informed like Pepys and Evelyn and Captain Cocke were

> . . . full of discourse of the neglect of our masters, the great officers of state, about all business, and especially that of money – having now some thousands prisoners kept to no purpose, at a great charge, and no money provided almost for the doing of it. We fell to talk largely of the want of some persons understanding to look after business, but

all goes to wrack. 'For', says Captain Cocke, 'My Lord Treasurer he minds his ease and lets things go how they will; if he can have his £8000 per annum and a game at Lombre, he is well. My Lord Chancellor, he minds getting of money and nothing else; and my Lord Ashly will rob the devil and the Alter but he will get money if it be to be got.' But that that put us into this great melancholy was news brought to-day, which Captain Cocke reports as a certain truth, that all the Dutch fleet, men-of-war and merchant East India ships, are got every one in from Bergen the 3rd of this month, Sunday last – which will make us all ridiculous. The fleet came home with shame to require great deal of money, which is not to be had – to discharge many men, that must get the plague then or continue at greater charge on shipboard. Nothing done by them to encourage the Parliament to give money – nor the Kingdom able to spare any money if they would, at this time of the plague. So that as things look at present, the whole state must come to Ruine. Full of these melancholy thoughts, to bed – where though I lay the saftest that I ever did in my life, with a down bed . . . yet I slept very ill, chiefly through the thoughts of my Lord Sandwiches concernment in all this ill-success at sea.[3]

Pepys did not, as it happens, share Cocke's opinion of the three politicians in question, but Cocke's words convey perfectly the mood and temper of the moment.

The depression of the dark hour lent brilliance to the dawn. Leaving Cocke's comfortable house at Greenwich Pepys walked over to spend Sunday with his wife at her lodgings in Woolwich. He found her overcome at alarming news of her father's health and had to tell her that it might be the plague as he had noticed that the house was shut up. But just before he left to return to Greenwich an express letter arrived from William Coventry, enclosing Sandwich's report of his first success on September 3rd.

'This news doth so overjoy me, that I know what to say enough to express it.' Arriving at Cocke's he found not only Evelyn, his fellow guest of the previous night, but his colleagues Mennes and Brouncker.

. . . the receipt of this news did put us all into such an extasy of joy, that it inspired into Sir J. Mennes and Mr Eveling such a spirit of mirth that in all my life I never met with so merry a two hours as our company this night was . . . it being one of the times of my life wherein I was the fullest of true sense of joy.

Against all expectation Sandwich's colours were first past the post. Dazed with delight his backers had barely time to cheer the winner into the unsaddling enclosure before it was known that an objection had been laid. A pay-off there was to be; but not in the sense that Pepys had looked for.

The immense wealth of the Dutch prizes – Pepys estimated their value at between £350,000 and £400,000 – had proved too tempting. When a ship was taken custom allowed the seamen, but not their officers, the plunder of all goods lying between decks. They were expressly prohibited from 'breaking bulk', that is, opening the holds and rummaging the cargo. The sale of ship and cargo and the division of the proceeds among those entitled to a share was the function of the Prize Court and the Prize Commissioners. The money so obtained was, right up to Victorian times, easily the most lucrative reward to which an officer and even more a Commander-in-Chief could look forward. Pay was a mere appetiser in comparison.

Hardly had the ships come into the river before it was known that Sandwich, in collusion with some of his subordinate flag officers but in direct opposition to others, had himself broken bulk, and had even trans-shipped some of the goods aboard a vessel bound for King's Lynn so that they could travel easily and cheaply up the Ouse to Hinchingbrooke. So flagrant a breach of the rules was too good an opportunity for his enemies to miss. Monck had been biding his time. Coventry seized on the dis-respect shown to the Duke of York as Lord High Admiral in this open defiance of instruction and precedent. In next to no time there was talk of an impeachment.

Sandwich was saved by the King. Charles was not yet ready to throw over the Clarendonians. And to throw to the wolves of the House of Commons one whom he had himself honoured and promoted would certainly bring back unfortunate memories of his father. But though he could save him, he was not going to take any chances. In a remarkably short space of time Sandwich was sent out of the country as Ambassador to Madrid. This postponed the inevitable inquiry into his conduct over the Prize Goods until his return to England three years later.

From Pepys's point of view the balance of power at the Navy Office that had been achieved at the outbreak of war was now in ruins. He im-mediately set to work to construct another, based this time on Coventry's improved position and his own undeniable success. But first of all he had to extricate himself from the scandal. Like his patron he had himself acted with less than his usual circumspection but he had not so far to fall – yet. And he certainly showed more agility in scrambling back to safety when no one was looking. His involvement began on September 18th, the day that he and Cocke went aboard Sandwich's flagship at the Nore. At Cocke's suggestion Pepys borrowed £500 from Will Howe, Deputy Treasurer of the fleet, to buy 'above £1000 – worth of goods, Mace, Nutmeggs, Cynamon and Cloves' on behalf of themselves and Lord Brouncker. Ten days later Cocke arrived unannounced at Pepys's temporary office in the King's Pavilion at Greenwich with the first wagon load. The office seemed the obvious place to store the goods: 'but then the thoughts of its being the King's house altered our resolution, and so put them at his friend's'. Pepys had already scented trouble. After another ten days two more wagons rolled up, hotly pursued by two customs officers who attempted to seize the goods while Pepys was stowing them in the lodgings of the office messenger. By now it was clear that unwelcome publicity could not be avoided. Indeed the next convoy of wagons was arrested in the street by Greenwich Church. Pepys was summoned by an agitated servant of Cocke's; angry words were exchanged; a crowd collected; the game was up. Pepys wrote urgently to warn his master, adding:

> . . . And further, my Lord Brouncker has wrote me word that the King and Duke do disown their order or allowance in the case. Whence this arises, your Lordshipp can best tell upon the place, but I pray God there be no foule meaning towards your Lordshipp in it.[4]

Sandwich was apparently nettled by this solicitude. In a stiff letter Pepys was told:

> The King hath confirmed it, and given me order to distribute these very proportions to the flag-officers, so that you are to own the possession of them with confidence; and if anybody have taken security from them upon seizure, remand the security in my name, and return their answer. Carry it high; and own nothing of baseness or dishonour, but rather intimate that I know who have done me indignities. Thank my Lord Brouncker and Sir John Minnes for civilities and tell them I expect no less in reality, for I have befriended them; and that I shall very ungratefully hear of news of base examinations, upon any action of mine.[5]

For all his bold words Sandwich had been sufficiently perturbed to hurry to Oxford where the King and Court had gone to avoid the plague and where the new session of Parliament was opening. Even this venture was unlucky since the Dutch chose the moment of his absence from his post of duty to put to sea for a final cruise off the mouth of the Thames. Albemarle in London threatened to take the fleet to sea himself, but as there were barely half a dozen ships in any sort of readiness there was in fact nothing any one could do. Nonetheless it helped the anti-Sandwich movement. Too late, in the last week of October, the Commander-in-Chief rejoined his ship. During the preceding days when he had been in Oxford Coventry had been active in carrying the First Reading of a bill to make it felony to break bulk. That the Dutch fleet should be riding in English home waters while the English admiral was ashore defending his own dubious transactions could hardly help his reputation.

Sandwich was technically right and Pepys's informant Brouncker wrong on the point of the King's having granted a post-dated authority to the division of the prize goods among the flag officers. But Pepys had read the signs that Sandwich, strumming his guitar in the great cabin of the *James*, had missed. Bluff and threats, 'Carry it high . . . tell them I expect no less . . .' would not answer. Retreat was the only sound tactic. On September 27th Cocke had offered Pepys £500 clear profit in exchange for his share. Pepys stood out for £600. The ominous weeks that followed brought down his price and on November 13th he was glad to settle for the original offer. On November 22nd Sandwich hauled down his flag. The bad weather that had kept the Dutch from doing any serious mischief had at last driven them back to the shelter of their home ports. But the storm that was brewing over the prize goods looked ever blacker. On December 6th Pepys was not less surprised than delighted to hear of his patron's appointment as Ambassador to Spain. It was his habit on the last day of the year to survey in his diary the general and personal course of events in an annual stocktaking and casting up of accounts. In spite of his personal prosperity the year had been bad. There had been the plague; the war had not gone well. But to neither of these does Pepys give pride of place:

> The great evil of this year and the only one endeed, is the fall of My Lord of Sandwich whose mistake about the Prizes hath undone him, I believe, as to interest at Court; though sent (for a little palliateing it) Imbassador into Spayne . . . and endeed, his miscarriage about the prize-goods is not to be excused, to suffer a company of rogues to go away with ten times as much as himself, and the blame of all to be deservedly laid upon him.

That conclusion epitomises Pepys's view of embezzlement and corruption. Sandwich had acted wrongly, he admits: but, far worse, he had acted stupidly and obtained no adequate *quid pro quo*. Worst of all he appeared to have forfeited his credit with the King and Duke.

Pepys by contrast had enlarged both his fortune and his reputation. Quietly disembarrassing himself of the prize goods (and making a handsome profit in the process) he had diagnosed in the malfunctions of the victualling system the main cause of England's failure at sea and, after a careful analysis of the symptoms, now proposed a remedy. There were two ways of victualling the navy, by contract or by direct supply, victualling 'on account' as it was called, in which the Government undertook the whole business through its own officials. In Cromwell's war with the Dutch, the obvious precedent to consult in any difficulty, the navy had been victualled on account. This had worked well under a strong Government but the changes and uncertainties of the eighteen months between Cromwell's death and Charles II's Restoration produced chaos and complaint. The King had therefore reverted to the earlier practice and had granted the contract to a merchant, Denis Gauden, whose brother John was the ghost-writer of the record-breaking best-seller of Royalist propaganda, Εἰκὼν βασιλική, the Pourtraicture of His Sacred Majestie in His Solitudes and Sufferings. This work, which purported to record the meditations of Charles I during his last days, ran into forty-seven editions and, at the Restoration, won its author in rapid succession the Bishoprics of Exeter and Worcester. He had, however, set his heart on the see of Winchester, in which diocese his brother Denis had built him a house of suitably prelatical proportions at Clapham, which Pepys visited and described in his diary on July 25th, 1663, and which, as Will Hewer's guest, was to be the home of his old age. But Bishop Gauden died in the autumn of 1662, of rage, it was believed, at not being preferred to Winchester. The ultimate rewards of authorship reaped by his brother were to consist in the profits of supplying substandard groceries to sailors.

Not that Pepys, who in any case did not have to live on purser's issue, contended that Gauden was profiteering. Indeed the first grounds on which he had criticised the system in a letter to Sir George Carteret in August[6] was that Gauden's services were too valuable for the state to expect from one man in a time of plague. Simple prudence demanded that the one responsibility that could accurately be described as vital should be shared among at least three or four competent persons. To prove that there was no personal animosity or censure implicit in this suggestion he at first proposed that Gauden should take his own sons into partnership. But as he examined the returns from the ports and compared them with the accounts and requisitions from the ships it became plainer to him that the discrepancies between what the Victualler claimed to have delivered and what the Purser, often supported by his Captain, admitted to receiving could only be cleared up by an administrator who would be, preferably, beholden to neither. In October when the prize goods scandal was at its height he wrote a long letter to Monck proposing that a surveyor of victualling should be appointed to each port, charged with the duty of sending to a Surveyor-General in London a weekly report of all victualling transactions together with a statement of what provisions were, at the time of writing, available on the spot. This would not only go far to prevent fraud. It would, much more important, let the central government know what the real position was. And that would be the first step towards a remedy for the random, unpredictable returning to port of a famished or parched fleet whose business ought to have kept it at sea. Efficient victualling was not only essential to the proper deployment of sea-power. It was, on the longer term, the master key to discipline and, above all, manning. Starvation was a standing incitement to desertion. As Pepys himself wrote towards the end of his official life in one of his most familiar aphorisms:

> Englishmen, and more especially seamen, love their bellies above anything else, and therefore it must always be remembered in the management of the victualling of the Navy that to make any abatement from them in the quantity or agreeableness of the victuals is to discourage and provoke them in the tenderest point, and will sooner render them disgusted with the King's service than any one other hardship that can be put upon them.[7]

Within a week of sending the letter Pepys heard both formally and informally that it had been warmly approved by the King and the Duke and their principal advisers. On the 19th he wrote to Coventry proposing himself for the position of Surveyor-General. The letter was opened in Coventry's absence by the Duke of York who at once indicated his support. On the 27th over dinner Albemarle offered him the post and he accepted it. The salary was £300 a year but Gauden supplemented it by a further £500, thus making nonsense of one of Pepys's main arguments for instituting the arrangement.[8] The other, one might have thought, had already been knocked endways by combining the job in the person of the Clerk of the Acts and the Treasurer of Tangier.

Pepys valued the appointment the more from the terms in which, according to Albemarle Coventry had proposed him: 'the most obliging that ever I could expect from any man and more – it saying me to be the fittest man in England . . .' Gratifying as this must have been, the

announcement a few weeks later that next year's fleet was to be under
the joint command of Prince Rupert and the Duke of Albemarle must
have taken a little gilt off the gingerbread. In spite of Albemarle's present
cordiality Pepys feared, disliked and distrusted him. And Prince Rupert
was never a man that Pepys would have chosen to serve. Sure enough they
had the temerity to ruffle his administrative feathers.

> . . . We are not [they wrote to the King on August 29th 1666]
> supplied with provisions according to the necessity of your affairs,
> notwithstanding the repeated importunities we have used . . . and that
> when we send up our demands instead of having them answered, we
> have accounts sent us, which are prepared by Mr Pepys of what hath
> been supplied for the fleet, whereas that will not satisfy the needs of
> the ships except we could find them also here in specie.'9

Throughout the campaign of 1666 Coventry remained ashore, in ever
closer collaboration with Pepys. As their admiration and value for each
other increased so did their common hostility and contempt towards the
joint Commanders-in-Chief. By the end of the summer correspondence
was acrid. And when Rupert presented his report to the House of Commons at the end of the war he complained of:

> . . . the intolerable neglect in supplying provisions during the whole
> summer's expedition, notwithstanding the extraordinary and frequent
> importunity of our letters which were for the most part directed to
> Sir William Coventry . . . and to the Commissioners of the Navy . . .'10

Strong words. But by then the whole Navy Office was under heavy attack
as Pepys had always known it one day would be.

The year began badly with a declaration of war from France and Denmark. If, as seemed likely, the French fleet then based on Toulon were to
leave the Mediterranean and join forces with the Dutch, the English
would have heavy odds against them. As it was, the Dutch fleet of 1666
was slightly superior in ships and guns to that commanded by Rupert
and Monck. Any further tilting of the balance would be extremely
dangerous. Consequently when the French fleet sailed out of the Strait of
Gibraltar on May 8th English nerves were stretched for reports of movements in the western approaches to the channel. At the end of May just
when the Dutch were ready to sail and the English were sending their
fleet down to the anchorages in the mouth of the river, exactly such a
report was received. Instantly the decision was taken to divide the fleet.
Rupert was sent to the westward with twenty ships to pick up reinforce-

ments at Plymouth and find the French. Monck was left with about
sixty ships of the line to act as he thought best against De Ruyter with
eighty-four. Almost as soon as Rupert had sailed on May 29th it was
known that the Dutch fleet had put to sea. Immediate orders were sent
to recall him but these did not reach him until June 1st when he was off
St. Helen's. The decision to divide the fleet, hotly debated then and since,
at once imposed on Albemarle another not less fiercely contested, whether
to keep the fleet in safety until Rupert had rejoined or to fight the Dutch
with a far inferior force.

His decision to fight was so much in character that his enemies and
critics, Pepys among the bitterest and best-informed of them, have never
allowed him a rational defence. Yet as Dr. Anderson has pertinently
inquired[11] what would have happened to Rupert and his twenty ships if
Monck had withdrawn to the safety of the Thames and left the channel to
De Ruyter? Once the decision to divide the fleet had been taken the risk of
fighting on disadvantageous terms had to be accepted.

The Battle of the Four Days, initiated by Monck bearing down with
some fifty-five ships on De Ruyter's eighty-four on the morning of June 1st
ranks with Dunkirk and the Armada Fight as one of the longest, fiercest
and most desperate actions ever fought in home waters. The punishment
taken by the English fleet was terrible: the damage inflicted on the Dutch
comparatively slight. On the second day Monck's losses meant that he
was fighting at odds of two to one and on the third he had been forced
back towards the Thames when late in the afternoon Rupert's squadron
was sighted coming up channel on a light south-easterly breeze. At a council
of war held that evening it was agreed that Rupert's fresh force should
lead the attack on the following day. The fury of the final engagement
fought, at last, on more or less equal terms was unabated. But though it
was the Dutch who in the end broke off the action no huzzas could disguise the fact that the English had suffered a costly defeat. Recriminations
began at once and quickly grew more envenomed. Albemarle blamed the
cowardice of his captains. 'I assure you I never fought with worse officers
than now in my life, for not above twenty of them behaved themselves
like men.' Rupert blamed Coventry for sending his recall by express post
and not by special messenger. But the most powerful lobby of naval
experts, Coventry, Pepys, Sir William Penn, Sir John Harman, Pearse
the surgeon (who as usual was present at the battle) united in blaming
Albemarle for fighting once the fleet had been divided. And as soon as it
became known that the original report that the French fleet had been
sighted was false a hubbub of accusation broke out whose confusion and
ferocity were worthy of the battle itself.

Pepys's own reactions to a series of events that seemed, repeatedly, to graze the edge of disaster was calmer and more tranquil than the alarms recorded in the Diary for 1665. Partly this may have been because he was in better form. The entries for 1666 overflow with high spirits and conscious enjoyment. The plague if not gone was evidently going. He had brought back his wife to Seething Lane in the autumn. He was making a lot of money and winning golden opinions. His sexual partners were submissive and his wife unsuspicious. He was conscious, as perhaps never before, of power, position, independence and appetite. 'I must now stand upon my own legs' he had written in the aftermath of Sandwich's fall; and he had proved that he could do it.

The news, dated eleven o'clock on June 1st and received on June 2nd, that action was imminent 'put us at the board into a tosse'. Within a few minutes Pepys was called away from the table to organise food and transport for 200 soldiers who were to be sent as urgent reinforcements to the fleet. Finding ships to carry them took him down to Greenwich and there in the park he 'could hear the guns from the Fleete most plainly. . . . All our hope now is that Prince Rupert with his fleet is coming back and will be with the fleet this noon . . .' Subsequent cross-checking of times and narratives led him to doubt it might have been thunder. But the tension of the moment touches his reader across the centuries as does his observation of the shouts and kisses with which the soldiers, now mostly drunk, parted from their wives and sweethearts as they sailed on the afternoon tide. The next day, Whitsunday, brought a mixture of reports including a letter from Harman in the *Henry*, aboard which Balty was serving as muster-master, telling a fearful tale of fire and slaughter. Pepys sighed for the dangers his brother-in-law was undergoing, but pursued a round of pleasure that included two morning services at Westminster (St. Margaret's and the Abbey), a particularly rewarding visit to one of his Westminster Hall ladies, and a jaunt to Hyde Park by coach in the company of Creed. Creed and Pepys shook their heads over the probable outcome, spared a thought for the nation and agreed how lucky it was that Sandwich was not involved. Pepys's patriotism was never a lush, romantic growth.

On the 4th the longed-for news of Rupert's junction with Albemarle was brought by a young officer well-known to Pepys 'all muffled up and his face as black as the chimney and covered with dirt, pitch and tar, and powder, and muffled with durty clouts and his right eye stopped with Okum'. Together with other wounded he had been put ashore at Harwich at two in the morning and had ridden through the night. Relief at the avoidance of disaster for a time encouraged optimism, but as the damage and casualties became known Pepys eagerly substantiated his hostility to the two commanders. The courage and leadership that could inspire men to go out and fight a much stronger enemy who had already mauled them not once but twice and even three times seems to have passed him by. Yet he knew very well that these things mattered. Among the killed was Sir Christopher Myngs, whose funeral Pepys and Coventry attended as a mark of respect to a flag officer. The unforgettable testimony to the affection and loyalty that he had inspired in his men, recorded in the Diary on that occasion, touches the naval profession with the sublime.

About a Dozen able, lusty, proper men came to the coach-side with tears in their eyes, and one of them, that spoke for the rest, begun and says to Sir W. Coventry — 'We are here a Dozen of us that have long known and loved and served our dead commander, Sir Chr. Mings, and have now done the last office of laying him in the ground. We would be glad we had any other to offer after him, and in revenge of him — all we have is our lives. If you will please to get his Royal Highness to give us a Fireshipp among us all, here is a Dozen of us, out of all which choose you one to be commander, and the rest of us, whoever he is, will serve him, and, if possible, do that that shall show our memory of our dead commander and our revenge.' Sir W. Coventry was herewith much moved (as well as I, who could hardly abstain from weeping) and took their names; and so parted, telling me that he would move his Royal Highness as in a thing very extraordinary.
. . . .

But Pepys passes straight from admitting his emotion to the reflection that Myngs will be quite forgotten in a short time because he died before he had taken the opportunity of enriching himself. And with that he sneaks off to Mrs. Bagwell, secure in the knowledge that her husband, if not killed or wounded, must be safely aboard his ship.

Monck and Rupert might complain of the administrative system that kept them hammering the table with demands for men and beer and victuals when they should have been free to concentrate on fighting the enemy: Pepys and Coventry might sneer at the admirals as a pair of fire-eating old blockheads, ignorant of everything involved in running a navy and careless of the new science of sailing-ship tactics. But whatever may be said of the campaign of 1666 the quality of leadership and administration that could take the fleet out to fight and win a major battle six weeks after so searing a defeat proves itself beyond any need of demonstration.

From the moment that the Commanders-in-Chief had ceased to engage the Dutch they turned a brisk fire on to their subordinate officers and civilian colleagues. Almost all their ships were severely damaged and many required a complete refit. 'We desire you with all imaginable expedition to fit a whole suit of masts and yards for the *Royal James*, boltsprit excepted, and such other sails and cordage and such stores expended as Sir Tho. Allen Admiral of the White shall give you an account as wanting in the said ship.'[12] This order dated June 7th is eloquent of the shattered condition of the fleet. Every need was more pressing than every other. Apart from the damage to be made good and the stores to be replaced, the English had been at a disadvantage from a want of fireships and boats, so often the surest method of communication when signalling was still in its infancy. Above all else towered the want of men. Skilled men, carpenters and sailmakers, first to help to fit the ships: but seamen, watermen, even soldiers, to man them as soon as they were ready for sea. Monck and Rupert reckoned they needed at least 3,000 straightaway. The first ships that left dockyard hands were sent out to prey on English merchantmen homeward bound, pressing the prime seamen before they could escape ashore. In spite of constant objections from Sir William Coventry the admirals also kept up a hot press in London. They might tread on powerful and privileged toes but they did get results. Pepys, whose sympathies certainly lay with Coventry and whose humanity was outraged by the operation of so barbarous a system[13], bears them out. At midnight on July 2nd he wrote to Coventry:

My whole time yesterday till midnight and the same time this day till now hath been spent in the businesse of Prest men. We have cleared all places and ye numbers shipped away is about 1000 little more or less. . . . More will be gotten to-morrow and sent away besides Sir Jo: Robinson's* 100 souldiers . . .[14]

Pepys was too good a Government servant and too sensible a man not to see the urgency of the requirements and to do his best to meet them. Yet his neat, orderly fastidiousness was revolted by the hugger-mugger of it all. While the admirals' letters to him are full of agonised demands for every necessity of sea warfare, his own letters to the Lord High Admiral are full of agonised recapitulations of the expense incurred by buying on credit instead of paying in cash. The administrative offence of being in a hurry is gross. Matters reached a climax at the beginning of the second week in July. Three new ships of the line, the *Cambridge*, the *Greenwich*

* Lieut-Governor of the Tower.

and the *Warspight* were all but ready to join the fleet. Monck and Rupert, knowing that the Dutch were off the mouth of the Thames, were fretting to get out. Thanks to the enormous efforts of the past few weeks the bulk of their force was with them at the Nore and could sail on the next tide. When were the new ships coming? At last on July 9th they sent Sir Robert Holmes up the river with a party of seamen from his own division with orders to bring the ships down and further orders to their captains to do what Holmes told them.[15] The reaction of the officials was predictable:

> He [Coventry] spoke contemptibly of Holmes and his Mermidons that came to take down the ships from hence, and have carried them without any necessaries or anything almost, that they will certainly be longer getting them ready than if they had stayed here.[16]

Was Coventry, and by association Pepys, right? We hear the same dispute, conducted in exactly the same tone, as that which still rages over Lord Beaverbrook's tenure of the Ministry of Aircraft Production in the summer and autumn of 1940. It is entirely appropriate that Pepys should figure as the protagonist of a professional civil service against the buccaneering, inspired or reckless who shall say, of the man who thinks that rules were made to be broken.

But the Battle of Britain was a victory and so was the battle, fought on St. James's Day, July 25th, in which these laggard vessels took part. This time numbers were equal and, in spite of Pepys's strictures on the Commanders-in-Chief, the tactics employed come closest of all the battles of that war to the scientific copybook pattern of fighting in line. Pearse the surgeon drew an elaborate plan of its three stages which Pepys preserved among his own papers.[17] The battle ended in the rout of the Dutch van and centre leaving their rear squadron with the whole English fleet to evade or fight. When darkness fell Sir Jeremy Smith commanding the English rear anchored, perhaps too prudently, well off the Dutch coast. The waters were dangerous: his pilot was apprehensive. But the Dutch saw their chance and took it. Morning showed their masts safe behind the sand bars and shoals where no English ship could follow. Once again an English victory had not paid off.

The fierce recriminations that at once broke out among the sea officers foreshadowed the Parliamentary accusations of misconduct which almost everyone involved in the direction of the war would have to face. Sir Robert Holmes who had commanded the rear division of the centre squadron flatly accused Smith of cowardice, subsequently fighting a duel with him and ultimately provoking the King in Council to pronounce on the conduct of the battle. A bad matter was made worse by the fact that Holmes was Prince Rupert's particular favourite and Smith was Monck's. But Pepys, gliding on a euphoric current of easy money and easy success, knew nothing of the rough weather blowing up towards him. He was convinced that the disorder of the Rupert–Monck regime could produce no good – 'no discipline – nothing but swearing and cursing, and everybody doing what they please; and the Generalls, understanding no better, suffer it . . .'[18] But these jeremiads are pitched in a key that Johnson identified in his remark to Boswell: 'When a butcher tells you that *his heart bleeds for his country* he has, in fact, no uneasy feeling'. On the next day Pepys was able to spend the morning 'setting money-matters and other things of mighty moment to rights, to the great content of my mind' and spent the afternoon listening to the royal architect, Hugh May, on the proper principles of laying out gardens. And the day after that is hallowed by the entry, sacred to all who know and love his library:

. . . And then comes Simpson the Joyner, and he and I with great pains contriving presses to put my books up in, they now growing numerous, and lying one upon another on my chairs, I lose the use, to avoid the trouble of removing them when I would open a book.

The guns were heard plain at Whitehall on St. James's Day while the Court were at chapel, celebrating the patronal festival of the Lord High Admiral. But after the distant reverberations died away no news reached London for forty-eight hours, and then only the letter of a Captain who took such good care of himself and his ship that he left the battle almost before it had begun. Not till the 29th when Pepys was in church did an official dispatch addressed to Batten arrive soon after the preacher had mounted the pulpit. Pepys sent it out unopened to Batten's house, stoically sweating out the sermon. In fact the dispatch was about something else but as Pepys pushed his way out the bells were ringing for a victory. Both Pepys and Coventry correctly interpreted its value '. . . but a poor result after the fighting of two so great fleets . . .' Which, as Pepys candidly admits in summarising the months events, was exactly what he wanted:

Mighty well and end this month in content of mind and body – the public matters looking more safe for the present than they did. And we having a victory over the Duch, just such as I could have wished, and as the Kingdom was fit to bear – enough to give us the name of conquerors and to leave us maisters of the sea. But without any such great matters done as should give the Duke of Albemarle any honour at all, or give him cause to rise to his former insolence.

Passages such as this make it absurd to pretend that Pepys, at this period, put the interests of his country above all considerations of faction or party, let alone of crude personal gain.

12

The Dutch in the Medway

———

Hardly a fortnight later Pepys had news of another victorious action, executed by a handful of ships and costing less than a dozen casualties, that inflicted damage estimated at the then staggering figure of a million pounds. Sir Robert Holmes took a few light craft and fireships into the anchorage of the Vlie and burnt well over a hundred (Coventry put it at a hundred and sixty) merchantmen. The ratio of force employed to results obtained was inverse to that of the St. James's Day Fight. Holmes's bonfire, as it was called, was the last, and certainly the most brilliant, action of the campaign. In the following month Monck was recalled from his sea command to lend his strength and solidity to a government dazed and shocked by the Fire of London. The fleet came in early in October to a general feeling of opportunities missed and money thrown away, of divisions and quarrels among the commanders and the civilian administrators, of shock, of exhaustion, of a wide and deep lack of confidence in the policy and purpose and prosecution of the war.

Glummest of all were Pepys and Coventry. The mood of summer had gone with the season. It was so stale a topic of conversation with them that the gentlemen captains had undone all and ruined the discipline of the fleet that the groans of the Diary take this proposition for granted. Yet one may wonder what ideals of discipline and loyalty were cherished by a senior official of the navy who clearly encouraged captains to denigrate their admirals, and admirals to speak to the dishonour of their Commanders-in-Chief.[1] There had already been an alarming scene in cabinet when Pepys, called to attend a meeting on the state of the navy and finding his colleagues silent, gave impromptu a lucid account in the course of which he found himself admiring his own powers of exposition. He had only too good reason. The minute he had finished Prince Rupert jumped up and complained angrily to the King of the aspersions cast on the condition in which he had brought the fleet back to base. Pepys apologised for giving offence but pleaded that he was merely transmitting the reports of the dockyard authorities. Rupert muttered a repetition of his complaint. A long, embarrassed silence followed, ending in the withdrawal of Pepys and his fellow officers, Batten, Mennes and Brouncker. Coventry, as a member of the council, stayed behind and tried to smoothe things down.[2] Pepys, after a twinge of apprehension, felt sufficient confidence in the weight of his evidence and the strength of his position to dismiss the matter from his mind. The contrast between his agitation after the scene with Holmes at the Navy Board and his calmness after Rupert's attack in front of the King and the principal ministers shows how far he had travelled in three and a half years.

The disgust that Pepys and Coventry felt for the indiscipline and favouritism of the courtiers and gentlemen captains, the contempt in which they held the late Commanders-in-Chief, and the galloping financial deficit of the navy all distracted them from bothering about the Dutch and turned their attention more and more to the in-fighting of domestic politics. No one believed in the war any more: diplomatic negotiations were opened in Paris in December. It became increasingly clear that no provision would be made to fit out a fleet for the summer of 1667.

Yet the Government was perfectly well aware that the Dutch were by no means running down their war machine. Intermittently it even initiated defensive measures based on this intelligence, as for instance when a new fort was planned at Sheerness to strengthen the defences of the fleet anchorage in the Medway. The Elizabethans had recognised how vulnerable a position this was and had protected it by a chain across the river at Upnor. In Charles I's time Sir William Monson recommended the strengthening of Upnor Castle and urged that the ships themselves should never be without at least some of their guns and ammunition even when out of commission.[3] All this was half remembered. The King and the Duke went down to inspect the site for the new fort at Sheerness in February 1667. Four weeks later Penn, Spragge, the flag officer in charge and Pett, the Commissioner at Chatham, took a host of officials down to do the same. A month after that an officer was sent down to superintend the construction and no doubt given a few months more something might actually have been done. But the Government had not got its mind on the job. It was thinking about the peace negotiations, about the threatening noises Parliament was already making at being asked to pay the debts of a stupid and unnecessary war, about the possible fall of Clarendon, the personification of traditional Royalism. Even Pepys, recording in the Diary entry for March 23rd Penn's plans for defending the ships laid up in the Medway, notes the necessity with somnolent approval. Indeed, the King and the Duke and Sir William Penn seem to have had the clearest grasp of how serious and urgent the matter was. Coventry and Pepys, for all their self-congratulation and mutual compliments, did in fact little or nothing to forestall the greatest disaster of the war. Coventry had entered the John Bright phase of his career and was bent on cutting down military expenditure. As early as mid-December he and Pepys were sneering at the pride and perversity of Sir Robert Holmes who had objected to the discharge of the officers and men under his command at Chatham.[4] But Holmes knew that bonfires was a game that two could play.

The servants of the Restoration Government, civil and military, were so often obsessed with faction that it was all too easy for them to see the national interest entirely in its light. A course of action became good or bad, wise or foolish, according as it was championed or opposed by particular people. Every subsequent writer has endorsed Pepys's condemnation of the indiscipline of the Gentlemen officers, but his own standards have generally escaped criticism. Largely this may be explained by the brilliance of his record as an administrator and by the profusion of documents that support it. But we should not be blind to the fact that Pepys was every inch as factious as Monck, Rupert, Holmes and the rest of them; nor to the fact that their judgment, acquired in a lifetime devoted to the profession of arms, was sometimes superior to his own. Holmes and the others who had opposed paying off the ships were right: Penn who had pressed for the strengthening of the Medway defences was right: Pepys and Coventry in opposing the one and lending insufficient support to the other had mistaken their priorities. It was to prove an expensive error.

In March negotiations with the Dutch had fixed on Breda as the seat of the Peace Conference. In May the delegates arrived there and at once embarked on the wrangles over precedence and procedure that took up so much of the time and energy devoted to diplomacy in the seventeenth century. In what order were the ambassadors of the powers to enter the room? In what order were their names to be appended to any agreement that they might reach? On such points were careers blasted and treaties brought to nothing. But while the English Government and its representatives gave these matters their best attention they were kept fully informed of the alarming activity in the Dutch naval bases and arsenals. The failure of the King and his ministers to act on the overwhelming intelligence available to them is indefensible. But though Pepys and Coventry constantly deplored the idleness and irresponsibility of their masters they show no sign of having grasped the real danger. Coventry indeed was pressing for the reduction of the already undermanned complements of the fireships in the Thames and Medway as late as May 29th. And on June 3rd, when the Dutch fleet was known to be at sea, he wrote to the Navy Board:

We heare by the letters from Holland that the Dutch fleete are certainly abroad, consisting of about 80 men of warre and neare 20 fireshipps, and although I do not thinke they will make any attempt here in the River, yet it will be fitting that ye command[rs] of the frigatts that are in the Hope be on board to provide against anything may happen.[5]

The Hope is the first great loop made by the river before it straightens out into Gravesend reach. Four days after that letter was written the Dutch fleet was to be anchored in the King's Channel at the mouth of the Thames: forty-eight hours later a squadron had been sent up to deal with the frigates in the Hope. Only a lucky change in wind and tide saved them. Coventry's misjudgment was total.

Pepys, for all the vehemence of his strictures on others, did no better. He had a long talk with Coventry on the morning of June 3rd but their topics were chiefly the preparation of naval accounts and the shortcomings of Sir George Carteret in this particular. As it was Trinity Monday Pepys attended the Trinity House dinner where he found his friend John Evelyn. Evelyn seems to have impressed him for a moment with the gravity of the situation. But the next day the Dutch have faded into the background: the question that presses is whether Pepys can afford to keep a coach. The following day brings another long and delightful conference with Sir William Coventry 'he being a most excellent man, and indeed, with all his business, hath more of his employed upon the good of the service of the Navy than all of us, that makes me ashamed of it'. Coventry provided 'a very good and neat dinner, after the French manner, and good discourse', but no one seems to have touched on the subject of defending the fleet and its principal bases from imminent attack. Nor is it so much as mentioned for the rest of the week until on Saturday Pepys received reliable reports of a Dutch fleet of eighty sail off Harwich and of gunfire heard to the north-east of London on Friday night. But even this was not allowed to disturb the characteristically Pepysian round of Sunday pleasures: a long chat with Coventry, sermon-tasting in Whitehall and Southwark, a visit to the submissive Mrs. Martin of Westminster, rounded off by a long and beautiful evening on the river, alone with an excellent translation of an amusing Spanish book. The Diary communicates no sense of emergency. Pepys went 'as high as Barne Elms, and there took a turn'. The situation of the kingdom might have been as calm and still as the evening itself. When he got home he found his colleagues Penn and Batten returned from their country houses dealing with demands for the immediate provision of fireships for use against the Dutch, now known to be in the King's Channel and hourly expected up higher.

By the morning of Monday the 10th even Coventry's complacency was shaken. The Dutch had reached the Nore. Fireships were now the only hope of defence. The danger signals had been repeatedly disregarded: humiliation was now certain and disaster probable. Batten, Penn and Pepys rushed to St. James's but found the Lord High Admiral already gone from his lodging to hurry reinforcements down to Chatham. Pursuing him across the park to Whitehall they met Coventry, 'who presses all that is possible for fireships'. So back they all tore to Seething Lane where they found Sir Frescheville Holles, a gentleman captain, a friend of Sir Robert Holmes, a courtier, everything that in the ordinary course of life Pepys most feared and detested. Normally too Pepys took great exception at his profanity and deplored the debauchery that his men acquired from the example of their commanding officer. But men like this had their uses in a desperate situation. Holles was ready to command the fireships 'in some exploits he is to do with them on the enemy in the River' and not even Pepys doubted his courage, his dash and his leadership. So down they all went to Deptford to choose the ships and to set men to work. Six ships were quickly chosen, one of them, a Dutch prize, ironically bearing the name *De Ruyter*, the admiral who at that very moment held England's lifeline in his hand. This vessel lay down the river at Grays, so Pepys was sent down to Woolwich to see about fitting her out while Holles went up to the Ordnance Office to obtain materials for fire-raising.[6] The enemy were reported to be already in the lower end of the Hope and to have fired the villages on the Essex side. Pepys, who seems to have regarded his mission as a pretext for a general reconnaissance, broke his journey at Greenwich and extended it beyond Grays to Gravesend where he found the Duke of Albemarle, attended by 'a great many idle lords and gentlemen with their pistols and fooleries'.[7] The place, in Pepys's view, could not have maintained its defence for half an hour. Most of the inhabitants had left in a panic, taking their valuables with them but Pepys found no difficulty in being served with a meal. Fortunately the Dutch had withdrawn down to Sheerness where Albemarle intended to go next day, having first ordered such warships as were at Gravesend to be moored in line with the two blockhouses. 'Which I took then to be a ridiculous thing.' The word 'then' is a rare tribute, paid in writing up the Diary entry, to Albemarle's superior judgment. When it had come to praising Monck and recognising the merits of Sir Frescheville Holles things must have looked black. However Pepys could still appreciate the beauty of the evening. In the boat that bore him up to London he read Boyle's *Hydrostatics* as long as the light lasted and then took a nap. It was one in the morning when he got home and at once sat down to write a report to Coventry.

On the 11th it became clear that the crisis was imminent. Letters from Commissioner Pett at Chatham 'who is in a very fearful stink for fear of the Dutch, and desires help for God and the King and the kingdom's sake' brought news that Sheerness was already in Dutch hands. The Commissioner's state of mind communicated itself to his colleagues who hurried down to Deptford to 'consider of several matters relating to the dispatch of the fireships'. The phrase hardly answers to the urgency of the occasion. Pepys and Batten then went back to the office

and there to our business, hiring some fire-ships, and receiving every hour almost letters from Sir W. Coventry, calling for more fire-ships; and an order from Council to enable us to take any man's ships; and Sir W. Coventry . . . says he do not doubt but that at this time, under an invasion, as he owns it to be, the King may, by law, take any man's goods.'[8]

Pepys was determined, even at so grave an hour in his country's fortunes, to minimise this threat to his own. Acting on a timely tip from Hewer that the paymaster to the navy had some cash in hand he secured £400 in respect of his own salary. And that evening he discussed with Elizabeth the possibility that the Government might abandon the city to its fate. Not that he had any more intention of deserting his post than he had had in the plague or the fire. But a prudent man had to look to his own, especially when the Government was thinking of making free of every man's property.

Wee have been considering of the yet further number of fireshipps which you demand [he wrote to Coventry] . . . but wee thought it convenient to tell you that to take them up by treaty will aske soe much time and the taking of them by violence never a whitt lesse (because of the owners determyning theyr furniture and many other obstructions they will give us) that considering that and the difficulty of manning them wee doe dispayr of having them in any reasonable time, at least soone enough, by many days, to accompany these.[9]

Pepys's cool realism brings Coventry's excited proposal for invoking emergency powers firmly but courteously down to earth. What good will it do? And what use are ships without the means of damaging the enemy, above all without men?

This was the constant, enraged cry of Monck as he ranged tirelessly up and down the estuaries of the Thames and the Medway, trying every expedient, gathering every scrap of material to make some show of defence against a daring and powerful enemy. But where were the men? The ships had been paid off, or the sailors, starved and cheated in the King's service, had deserted. The dockyards had been unpaid so long that at Chatham he found, '. . . scarce twelve of eight hundred men which were then in the king's pay, in his Majesty's yards; and these so distracted with fear that I could have little or no service from them.'[10] The tale of incompetence, corruption, neglect and cowardice culminated in the most humiliating defeat ever suffered by the Royal Navy when the Dutch broke through the chain in Gillingham reach, defied the shore defences, burnt the newest and most powerful units of the fleet and towed away the flagship.

Even before the full extent of the disaster was known Pepys realised that anyone at all responsible for naval policy and administration was in hideous danger. The office might be attacked by an infuriated mob and he and his colleagues lynched. There was no police in seventeenth-century London: he had several times been pursued and threatened with violence by angry sailors demanding their pay: only two years earlier the populace of Amsterdam had reacted to the far less disgraceful defeat off Lowestoft by throwing the Commander-in-Chief into the sea. The precedents for mob vengeance were many and suggestive. Still more probable was the prospect of being made a scapegoat by a Government anxious to save its own skin. The certainty of Parliamentary inquiry receded into the background before these lively terrors.

Pepys faced them with the rational, stoic calm that he kept in reserve for the moments of real danger. His father was staying in the house, a useful circumstance to be framed into the plan of action. On the evening of the 12th, the day that Pepys knew that the Dutch had broken the chain at Gillingham and burned the ships, he called his father and Elizabeth up to her room,

> and shut the door; and told them the sad state of the times how we are like to be all undone; that I do fear some violence will be offered to this office, where all I have in the world is; and resolved upon sending it away — sometimes into the country — sometimes my father to lie in town and have the gold with him . . .

The next day brought confirmation of the disaster and added the alarming news that the King and the Duke of York had been personally supervising the sinking of ships by Barking Creek since four in the morning. A Dutch attack on the city seemed imminent. Pepys at once decided on sending his wife and father into the country. Within two hours they were in a coach with £1,300 in gold in their night-bag. All the money standing to his credit with the various Government departments, notably the Tangier Commission, might be written off but both Pepys and Hewer showed, as might be expected, a superior turn of speed in the run on the banks that had almost exhausted their liquidity. This produced considerable sums which still required safe disposal. About midday Pepys sent away one of his clerks to Huntingdon with a thousand guineas, under the pretext of his carrying an express letter to Sir Jeremy Smith,

> . . . who is, as I hear, with some ships at Newcastle; which I did really send to him, and may, possibly, prove of good use to the King; for it is possible, in the hurry of business, they may not think of it at Court, and the charge of an express is not considerable to the King. So though I intend Gibson no further than to Huntingdon I direct him to send the packet forward.

Even in so pressing an emergency there is time for self-justification. Gibson's mission broke the back of the problem. For the rest Pepys endured the discomfort of wearing a specially made girdle with £300 in gold 'in case I should be surprised'. His two silver flagons were sent to one cousin; his most important private papers 'and my journals which I value much' to another, '. . . that so, being scattered what I have, something might be saved'. Two hundred pounds' worth of silver coin still presented a difficulty. It was impossible to change it for gold: it was too bulky to carry about. Pepys thought of flinging it into the earth closet but was understandably deterred by the problem of retrieval.

All these dispositions had to be made under the cover of an industrious official constant to his duty. 'My business the most of the afternoon is listening to everybody that comes to the office, what news?' There was grave unrest in the city; talk of being betrayed by the Papists and others about the King, reports of attacks on the Lord Chancellor, rumours of French troops massing at Dunkirk for an invasion. The Papists were sure to be at the bottom of it, as, no doubt, they had been the year before in the Fire. The point was at least half established by the recent slighting of Upnor, 'the good old castle built by Queen Elizabeth' and thus an edifice conspicuous for its Protestantism, and clinched by the assertion (untrue, as it happened) that Legge, a protégé of Spragge's recently promoted to command the *Pembroke*, was a Papist.

In these lurid vapourings the silhouette of a scapegoat became gradually discernible. Pett, the Commissioner at Chatham, had got black marks from everybody. He had failed to carry out the Navy Board's repeated instructions to take the *Royal Charles* higher up the river 'and deserves, therefore, to be hanged for not doing it'.[11] He had antagonised Spragge, the senior naval officer in the river, by assuring Albemarle, against Spragge's advice, that the Dutch could be confined to the lower reaches of the Medway by sinking three ships at the Mussel Bank. And he had exasperated Albemarle by proving wrong in this particular and ineffective in every other task assigned him. To the innumerable professional delinquencies of which he was accused was added the report that he had employed scarce dockyard labour in carrying his own possessions to safety when the ships and yards entrusted to his care cried out for every pair of hands. To some of these charges Pett could, in time, produce a convincing answer; and from others he could find shelter in the sheer volume of allegations made against him. No doubt he was very much to blame; but it would be absurd to attribute so vast a failure to the derelictions of one man. Pepys was quick to notice the turn affairs were taking and to see how he might profit by it. On the 14th he comments on the dullness of the letter from Chatham giving the official account composed by Pett and Lord Brouncker of the events of the week and concludes darkly, 'I doubt they will be found to have been but slow men in this business.' On the 15th he hears of 'horrible miscarriages' and of the use of men and boats to carry away private possessions: 'and I hear that Commissioner Pett will be found the first man that began to remove; he is much spoken against, and Brouncker is complained of and reproached for discharging the men of the great ships heretofore.' If Brouncker could be carted for Coventry's policy of paying off the fleet before the war was over and if Pett could be made the scapegoat for everyone else, things were looking up. In any case the clerk Gibson had returned with news of the safe arrival of all the money, except for one or two pieces that fell out of a broken bag. The next day a warrant was issued for committing Pett to the Tower.

Pepys, when he heard of this on the 18th, was for a moment shaken: '. . . which puts me into a fright, lest they may do the same with us as they do with him. This puts me upon hastening what I am doing with my people [i.e. his clerks] and collecting out of my papers our defence.' The historian's insistence on documentation, instinctive to Pepys, provided ammunition for the beleaguered defenders of the Navy Office. The very next afternoon he was ordered to attend the Council bringing with him all his books and papers relating to the Medway. Although the probable reason for this summons was the examination of Pett, there was an unpleasant possibility that the door would open to the dock and not the witness-box. At the preliminary examination before a large and formidable committee of the Council – Albemarle was there, and all the rising stars of the Cabal, Arlington, Ashley, Clifford and Lauderdale – Pett cut a very poor figure. 'He is in his old clothes, and looked most sillily', an impression confirmed by his answers. Hostility slid into derision. Arlington had spiced his questions with the candid aside that if Pett was not guilty the world would think the Council was. Pepys, when called on, gratefully adopted this policy of *sauve qui peut*:

> I all this while showing him no respect, but rather against him for which God forgive me! for I mean no hurt to him, but only find that these Lords are upon their own purgation and it is necessary I should be so in behalf of the office.

The Committee then adjourned briefly, ordering, on Arlington's suggestion, that the minutes of Pett's examination should be given to Pepys, the acknowledged expert, to knock into shape. On his return with his books and papers he still felt apprehensive:

> . . . I thought myself obliged to salute people and to smile, lest they should think I was a prisoner too . . . but my fear was such . . . that at my going in I did think fit to give T. Hater, whom I took with me to wait the event, my closet-key and directions where to find £500 and more in silver and gold . . . in case of any misfortune to me.

Pepys's instinct was sure. He and everyone else who had had a hand in the running of the war might count themselves lucky that the storm of resentment should break on the unhappy Pett. But the weather would not clear for many days thereafter. There were too many scandals to be smoked out, too many old scores to pay, too many trumps left undrawn. It was naïve to imagine that there was enough flesh on Pett to satisfy the robust appetites of faction or that public opinion would accept him as responsible for everything that had gone wrong. Marvell's lines on the subject are among the supreme achievements of English political satire

> Whose counsel first did this mad war beget?
> Who all commands sold through the Navy? *Pett.*
> Who would not follow when the Dutch were beat?
> Who treated out the time at Bergen? *Pett.*
> Who the Dutch fleet with storms disabled met,
> And, rifling prizes, them neglected? *Pett.*
> Who with false news prevented the Gazette,
> The fleet divided, writ for *Rupert? Pett.*
> Who all our seamen cheated of their debt?
> And all our prizes who did swallow? *Pett.*
> Who did advise no navy out to set?
> And who the forts left unprepared? *Pett*
> Who to supply with powder did forget
> *Languard, Sheerness, Gravesend and Upnor? Pett*
> Who all our ships exposed in Chatham net?
> Who should it be but the fanatick *Pett?*
> *Pett,* the sea-architect, in making ships
> Was the first cause of all these naval slips.
> Had he not built, none of these faults had been;
> If no creation, there had been no sin.

Pepys, when he read them noted how sharply they reflected on Sandwich. Satire by its nature must be selective in its targets. Marvell, whose authorship of the poem was a well-kept secret, had a strong partisan interest in naval affairs. Sir Jeremy Smith, Monck's protégé who was given his flag in 1666, was a close personal and political friend. Marvell was to act as executor of his will and Smith exerted considerable local influence in the borough that returned Marvell to Parliament and paid his wages.[12] The wit, the force, the mastery of his poem have dominated the general historiography of the Second Dutch War, have cast the heroes and villains of the piece, just as Dryden's *Absalom and Achitophel* has for the Exclusion Crisis a decade later. The hero of Marvell's interpretation is Smith's patron, Monck. Full credit is given for his activity in the moment of national paralysis when the Dutch were in the river; but nothing is said of what many contemporaries thought the worst mistake of the war, his decision to fight after the fleet had been divided in June 1666. Similarly James, Duke of York's victory off Lowestoft is lost behind criticism of the misconduct that followed; and of Smith's arch-enemy, Holmes, who had inflicted more damage on the enemy at less cost than any other commander, there is no mention. Piercing and brilliant as Marvell's analysis is Pepys was entirely justified in scouting its impartiality.

But at the high tide of danger it was Pett over whom the flood waters surged. Pepys and the others trembled for their defences and listened for the cracking and rending of the dykes. Each day was a day gained and soon it began to appear that the worst was over. The Dutch were still blockading the river and threatening the East Anglian and Northern Channel ports – what was there to stop them? But the peace negotiations were going forward; the populace had not rioted; no other Navy Commissioner had joined Pett in the Tower. By June 19th Elizabeth had returned from Brampton and there was even leisure for speechless rage at her folly in permitting his father to bury the gold in the garden in broad daylight during churchtime on Sunday instead of after dark. There was leisure too for an orgy of theatre-going and for river-parties and excursions to the country. So urbanised has Pepys become that a shepherd met on Epsom Downs appears in the Diary as a romantic even a picturesque figure, half from pastoral poetry, half from the Bible.

In August the Peace Treaty was signed at Breda. All through July it had grown clearer that the Dutch, having strengthened their position by their brilliant raid, had no further interest in prolonging the war, indeed by exposing their returning East India Fleet might lose by doing so. For Pepys, relief that the whole futile business was at last over was balanced by disgust, contempt and anger at the frivolity and incompetence of his masters. He had made so much money and so much reputation that he knew now that he could not be easily overset. The long and intimate association with Sir William Coventry had brought him as close to that detachment and fearless honesty of mind, so very different from the shrewd realism of Sandwich, as it was possible for a man dependent on his service to Charles II's Government to go. On the day that news of the ratification reached London Pepys and Coventry were discussing what had to be done in the navy and agreeing how cordially they had long detested the war. In the course of their talk Pepys suddenly realised that Coventry really believed in and acted on the disinterested impartiality that he preached: 'I perceive he do really make no difference between any man.'[13] It was a recognition that echoed the profoundest quality of Pepys's own mind, instanced in his freedom from national prejudice in comparing the enemy's performance with our own.[14] Nowhere in the Diary is the scorn for Charles II's levity more repeatedly expressed. It was the son of an old Royalist actually imprisoned by the Protector who prompted Pepys's famous observation, 'It is strange how he and everybody do now-a-days reflect upon Oliver, and commend him, what brave things he did and made all the neighbour princes fear him.' And the same man, a courtier and Pepys's colleague on the Tangier commission went on to declare 'that he expects that of necessity this kingdom will fall back again to a commonwealth, and other wise men are of the same mind'.[15] No longer the client of Lord Sandwich or the jealous rival of Sir William Penn, Pepys, for the moment, withdraws to the heights from which in our day the Treasury and the Cabinet secretariat survey the crimes and follies of mankind. He is not a whit dismayed at the ending of his profitable appointment as Surveyor of the Victualling. He even contemplates (though not seriously or for very long) a premature retirement.

The carelessness and mismanagement that had humiliated the nation left the professional administrative interest represented by Pepys and Coventry for the moment in a strong position *vis-à-vis* the courtiers and favourites. But the Quaker whom Pepys saw pass through Westminster Hall, 'naked . . . only very civilly tied about the privities to avoid scandal, and with a chafing-dish of fire and brimstone burning upon his head . . . crying "Repent, Repent"', was only translating into more scriptural language the message that his co-religionist Billing had put with his customary pithiness a week earlier:

'Well,' says he, 'now you will all be called to an account;' meaning the Parliament is drawing near.[16]

13
Fire and brimstone

———

The last year of the war marks a turn in Pepys's private as in his professional life. Perhaps for all his pleasure at bringing his wife home after the plague he had in her absence acquired or developed tastes and connections that, somehow, excluded her. Business brought him into ever more interesting and sophisticated circles. His infidelities increased and Elizabeth herself, it seems, no longer excited his desire. On August 2nd, 1667, he recalls that he has not lain with her for a whole half-year and thinks it possible she may have noticed this. The old simplicities and shared amusements of the marriage are neither so spontaneous nor so frequent. The world of the Diary was changing.

By far the most dramatic transformation was effected by the Fire of London in September 1666. In a few hours the great medieval city that Pepys had known from earliest childhood, his father's house, the school where he had gone as a boy, the physical background of every memory and every impression of his formative years had been effaced. Like Johnson, like Dickens, Pepys was a Londoner to the roots of his being. The pages in which he describes the fire, besides being among the best reporting in our language, are more eloquent of deep emotion than any passage in the Diary except for one or two inspired by music. Every faculty, every sensibility, every power of observation is at once heightened and their perceptions articulated into the wholeness craved by the spirit of the artist. Everything is freshly, sharply, distinctly seen, and yet perfectly, mysteriously, related. Design is imposed on chaos. Comprehension inspires action. The artist and the administrator are at one. The opening passages bring details and individuals to instant life:

> Everybody endeavouring to remove their goods, and flinging into the River or bringing them into lighters that lay off. Poor people staying in their houses as long as till the very fire touched them, and then running into boats or clambering from one pair of stair by the water-side to another. And among other things, the poor pigeons I perceive were loath to leave their houses, but hovered about the windows and balconies till they were some of them burned, their wings, and fell down.[1]

After watching the fire rage from about half-past eight to half-past nine in a boat just above London Bridge, Pepys noticed that no steps were being taken to put it out. He went straight up the river to Whitehall where, as it was a Sunday, he found the King and Duke in chapel. His was the first news the Court had had, so word was sent in to the King who at once came out with his brother to hear what Pepys had to say. They listened with some anxiety and the King accepted Pepys's urgent recommendation of creating fire-breaks by destroying houses that lay in the path of the fire. Armed with royal commands to this effect Pepys sped back to the city in search of the Lord Mayor:

> At last met my Lord Mayor in Canning Streete, like a man spent, with a hankercher about his neck. To the King's message, he cried like a fainting woman, 'Lord, what can I do? I am spent. People will not obey me. I have been pulling down houses. But the fire overtakes us faster than we can do it.' That he needed no more soldiers; and that for himself, he must go and refresh himself having been up all night. So he left me, and I him and walked home – seeing people all almost distracted and no manner of means used to quench the fire.

It was still hardly midday, and warm, brilliant weather. Faced with such obstructive futility, Pepys enjoyed the last cooked meal he was to have for some days and entertained the guests invited to Sunday dinner as well as he could. By the afternoon the King and the Duke had come down in their barge to give personal orders for the pulling down of houses. But now the fire had got a real hold both above and below the bridge and the chance of stopping it had been lost. In the early evening Pepys crossed for coolness to an alehouse at Bankside:

. . . and there stayed until it was dark almost and saw the fire grow; and as it grow darker, appeared more and more, and in Corners and upon steeples and between churches and houses, as far as we could see up the hill of the City, in a most horrid malicious bloody flame, not like the fine flame of an ordinary fire. . . . We stayed till, it being darkish, we saw the fire as only one entire arch of fire from this to the other side the bridge, and in a bow up the hill, for an arch of above a mile long. It made me weep to see it. The churches, houses, and all on fire and flaming at once, and a horrid noise the flames made, and the cracking of houses at their ruine . . .

So far Pepys had done nothing to save his own possessions. Coming home that night he found his clerk, Hayter, with a few of his things salvaged from his house in Fish Street Hill, one of the first places to be engulfed. Pepys gladly gave him shelter but nobody got much sleep as the night was spent in shifting furniture out into the garden, money and strong-boxes down to the cellar, and collecting papers, bags of gold and Exchequer tallies into the office ready for a hurried departure. Pepys's neighbours the Battens had brought in carts from the country. About four in the morning Lady Batten sent over to offer him one. Up came the strong-boxes from the cellar and Pepys accompanied by his plate, the Diary and all his most treasured possessions (the gold only excepted) jolted off to Sir William Rider's house in Bethnal Green. Pushing his way back on foot he joined Elizabeth in transferring everything that was movable on to a lighter lying at the quay above the Tower dock. Such an upheaval provided rich material for the social observer. Looking at other people's goods piled into lighters Pepys noticed that almost one household in three possessed a pair of virginals.

Anxiety for his own goods, anxiety over preserving official papers, snatched meals, snatched sleep, did not blunt his perception or diminish his industry in noting down what he saw. On the Tuesday, when the fire had reached Tower Street he joined Batten in digging a pit in the garden to accommodate Batten's wine (his vineyard at Walthamstow produced, we are told, some notable bottles) and his own papers and Parmesan cheese. Early the next morning he was roused by Elizabeth to find the fire had reached All Hallows' church at the bottom of Seething Lane. It was time to be gone. Taking his bags of gold (£2,350 worth) he embarked for Woolwich with Elizabeth, Will Hewer and Jane the cook. He never expected to see his house again.

But when he came back about seven in the morning he was astonished and delighted to find that the fire had at last suffered a check. The wind had fallen in the night but the real improvement came from Pepys's own suggestion, made to Penn the previous afternoon, that the dockyard hands from Woolwich and Deptford should be sent for to help blow up houses. Penn had acted and the Navy Office had saved itself by its own exertions. From this point Pepys resigns his executive obligations in favour of his descriptive genius. Anyone who wants to know what it was like to be in London during the closing stages of the fire has only to read the Diary. The hot ash burning through the soles of one's shoes, the pathetic groups of people clutching a few fragments of what had been home, jealously kept separate as though their identity depended on it, the melted, buckled, stained glass from a church window, the cellars full of oil still burning after the fire had receded, the desolation of a lunar landscape – how faithfully all this was observed could be confirmed by the many survivors of the Blitz. It was widely believed that so enormous a disaster could not have come about (as in fact it did) simply by accident. The French probably, the Papists certainly, must be at the back of it. Riots were feared and feeling ran high but its eruption was postponed a dozen years to the Popish Plot.

On the Saturday there was leisure to exchange anecdotes of the meanness shown by the rich in rewarding people such as the dockyard men who had often risked life and limb to save their property. In the afternoon Pepys retrieved his Journal from Bethnal Green and much of the Sunday was devoted to writing up the entries for the past week. The next few days saw the gradual return of furniture, valuables, wife, gold and the rest and their re-installation in their proper places. There was so much to do that the unexpected arrival from sea of Brother Balty was greeted with positive pleasure instead of the usual wary apprehension. He apparently made himself useful and returned two days later bringing his own wife to stay. Balty's somewhat shaky career was at this point promising a degree of robustness. As a Muster Master, an officer appointed at Pepys's instigation to check the grosser frauds of captains and pursers. Balty had got on well with his shipmates and, far rarer achievement, had won golden opinions from his brother-in-law. 'I do much wish,' Pepys had written to Prince Rupert's secretary only ten days earlier, 'that the Muster Masters were quickned for we owe to their negligence our Ignorance in the manning of the fleet, having not to this day received Bookes (as we ought) from more than one or two of all the Muster Masters in the fleet.'[2] That Balty was the shining exception is made plain in a Table of Muster Books returned which Pepys constructed at the end of the year.[3] By September 20th, a fortnight after the fire, the house was almost back to normal. Even the books were in their places, except for five particularly valuable ones whose mislaying nagged at their owner (they turned up in the end). Both Balty and his wife were commended for their usefulness, but Elizabeth soon counterbalanced this with tales, all too characteristic, of their selfish and improper behaviour to her father and mother.

Pepys himself was not best placed to cast the first stone, if selfishness or impropriety were in question. The Bagwell affair had now reached a degree of squalor at which even he felt repulsion. Mrs. Martin and the Westminster Hall troupe went regularly through the motions required of them; the servants at Seething Lane were the frequent recipients of their master's attentions. Elizabeth's suspicions and jealousies, so long evaded or repressed, began to break out with disturbing frequency. At first it was the actresses such as Mrs. Knepp or her friend Mrs. Pearse, the surgeon's wife, both long and openly admired by Pepys, that excited accusations and quarrels. In both cases Elizabeth's bitterness was intensified by being left at home, bored and kept short of money, while her husband was not stinting himself or these ladies in pursuit of the gay life. The balance of power within the marriage was beginning to shift. On September 22nd, 1667, Pepys records his annoyance at being obliged to accept his wife's domestic accounts and not being in a position to find fault. 'The truth is I have indulged myself more in pleasure for these last two months than ever I did in my life before, since I come to be a person concerned in business.' Elizabeth had got the better of him at his own game.

It was an unfortunate moment at which to lose ground. Two days later a catspaw of wind ruffling the surface of the Diary presages its fiercest emotional storm.

This evening my wife tells me that W. Batelier [brother to Mary, the linen draper, whom Pepys considered one of the finest women he ever saw] hath been here to-day, and brought with him the pretty girl he speaks of, to come to serve my wife as a woman, out of the school at Bow. My wife says she is extraordinary handsome, and inclines to have her, and I am glad of it – at least, that if we must have one, she should be handsome.

Deb Willett's entrance is characteristic: graceful, unobtrusive, touching the imagination with the serious innocence so irresistible in children. It was this quality that captivated Pepys from the moment he set eyes on her.

While I was busy at the Office, my wife sends for me to come home, and what was it but to see the pretty girl which she is taking to wait

upon her: and though she seems not altogether so great a beauty as she
had before told me, yet indeed she is mighty pretty: and so pretty, that
I find I shall be too much pleased with it, and therefore could be contented as to my judgment, though not to my passion, that she might
not come, lest I may be found too much minding her, to the discontent
of my wife . . . she seems by her discourse, to be grave beyond her big-
ness and age, and exceeding well bred as to her deportment, having
been a scholar in a school at Bow these seven or eight years. To the
office again, my head running on this pretty girl . . .[4]

Deb had hardly been in the house a fortnight before Elizabeth was showing signs of jealousy. Pepys seems to have lacked the energy to control a
situation whose dangers he had recognised from the start. For once the
multiplicity of his consciousness weakened instead of strengthening him.
On the professional side of his life the menacing steps of the Committee
of Inquiry into the miscarriages of the war were drawing closer. On the
family side the problem of marrying off Pall if not solved soon would
lead to others yet more intractable. On the personal side there was his
failure of will in not enforcing self-discipline in matters of money and
pleasure; and worse, far worse and worst of all was the fear of failing
eyesight that runs through the Diary from the end of the war to the poignancy of its closing entry. Pepys felt, for once, self-doubt and loss of
nerve. 'I do plainly see my weakness that I am not a man able to go through
trouble, as other men, but that I should be a miserable man if I should
meet with adversity, which God keep me from.'[5] He underrated himself.

But his original estimate of the risk he was running in falling in love
with Deb was only too accurate. In spite of Elizabeth's acute perception,
or perhaps because of it, he seems to have achieved an unusual restraint
over his passion; and passion it was, tender, strong, at times harrowing,
as unlike the computerised lechery of the Bagwell affair as could be. It was
nearly Christmas before he first kissed her. And he had in the meantime
made notable efforts to resuscitate his marriage.

. . . I bought some Scotch cakes at Wilkinson's in King Street, and
called my wife, and home, and there to supper, talk, and to bed.
Supped upon these cakes, of which I have eat none since we lived at
Westminster.

This affectionate revival of the old days in Axe Yard took place early in
December. A little later another entry remarks on the interruption of
conjugal relations caused by Elizabeth's being ill for two or three days.

And just before Christmas the Diary is full of affectionate distress at the pain she suffers from an abscess on a tooth. But there was too long a tale of selfishness and neglect for the old ease and security to be so easily restored. At the end of December she made a dreadful scene, 'mad as a devil, and nothing but ill words between us all the evening while we sat at cards — W. Hewer and the girl by — even to gross ill words, which I was troubled for . . .', when she heard that her husband had been to the theatre with Mrs. Knepp and Mrs. Pearse. They went to bed without speaking to each other. Next day they made it up. But less than a fortnight later on January 12th there was another searing score-raking row, this time over the question of Pepys *père* coming to live with them after Pall's marriage, an event that against all the odds was now about to take place. Elizabeth could not abide her father-in-law, as her husband was at last forced to recognise. Yet only the day before she had pleased him by offering to have Pall married from their house. There is a ding-dong, over-excited quality about their married life at this time. Hardly a month goes by without Elizabeth turning on Deb or picking a quarrel with her husband. She had, as the Diary shows, better reason than she knew. Beside the liaison with Deb that she yet only suspected, beside the junketings with Mrs. Knepp and Mrs. Pearse that especially enraged her, Pepys still employed the frequent services of Mrs. Martin, had even re-opened the affair with Mrs. Bagwell, and yet prowled the streets eager for fresh adventures. No doubt her suspicions deepened as her tight-fisted husband dangled a coach before her, thought better of it and offered the redecoration of her room in lieu, finally settling on an even more splendid equipage than he had first proposed. Pepys, too, knew that he was playing with fire. He seems to have hoped, not without reason, that the flames would spread to his old passion for Elizabeth. There were expeditions of pleasure, to Oxford, Salisbury, Bath and Bristol. Elizabeth's beauty was, again, much admired. Samuel Cooper, perhaps the greatest artist of the age, took her portrait in miniature.

But returning from their jaunt to the West in the middle of June Pepys was glumly forced to the conclusion that 'my wife hath something in her gizzard, that only waits an opportunity of being provoked to bring up'. Two nights later it came up with a vengeance. In the small hours Elizabeth became hysterical. In the morning she asked for a separation so that she could go and live in France by herself; 'and then all come out, that I loved pleasure and denied her any, and a deal of do; and I find that there have been great fallings out between my father and her, whom, for ever hereafter, I must keep asunder for they cannot possibly agree.' Pepys was mild, pacific, conciliatory. She quietened down. They went to the theatre

together with great pleasure. Only two days after these disturbances
Pepys could write contentedly '. . . dined with my wife and Deb alone,
but merry and in good humour, which is, when all is done, the greatest
felicity of all . . .' But his passion for Deb grew overmastering. On
October 25th Elizabeth, whose irritability must have revealed her suspicions, found them embracing. The fury and recrimination that followed
may easily be imagined and are vividly sketched in the Diary. Elizabeth
certainly showed signs of hysteria, perhaps of mental instability: but it is
difficult to criticise the rationality of her refusal to trust her husband.
Pepys longed above all things for domestic peace and good temper
(enhanced to a psychological necessity by the dangerous mood of politics
and the threat to his sight). Yet he could not bear to part with Deb.
Leave the house she must: abjure her he must: but never to see her again,
so young, so tender, so trusting, was this endurable? To stop Elizabeth's
shrill stormings he would agree to anything: but if he broke his agreement
would he be found out?

There is abundant evidence in the Diary that Pepys was a kind-hearted
man, that he had a strong sense of justice, that he had the rare courage to
face his own shortcomings and the rarer resolve to make them good. But
he had not yet taught himself magnaminity. Thus although he could
sympathise with, or at any rate admit, the justice of Elizabeth's anger
and distress, although he could pity Deb and lament the trouble he had
brought on her, although (in different ways) he really loved both women,
his inveterate egocentricity was the force that told. How unconscious
this was is suggested by Pepys's words after a secret assignation, in direct
breach of his repeated promises: 'I did give her the best council I could,
to have a care of her honour, and to fear God, and suffer no man para
haber to do con her as yo have done.' Deb passes from the Diary and
thus from history[6] with the same well-bred refusal to draw attention to
herself with which she entered it. Unlike Elizabeth, Deb hardly speaks.
She looks, she lowers her eyes to hide a tear, she smiles; at our last glimpse
of her she even winks. Lashed by Elizabeth's tongue she does not answer
back; and Pepys records no word of reproach for the embarrassment and
disgrace he had caused her.

Next to Deb the most attractive role is that of Will Hewer. So
transparent was his affection and loyalty that Elizabeth, overwrought as
she was, had no hesitation in trusting him where she could not trust her
husband. Hewer was charged with the delicate task of preventing his
master from pursuing Deb 'like a jaylour, but yet with great love and to
my great good liking, it being my desire above all things to please my wife
therein.'

With so much good will the marriage would surely have mended. But the male supremacy on which Pepys had traded had gone for good. Elizabeth had seen him abject before her fury and neither would be likely to forget it. And a new danger had been revealed in the terrible flow of emotional lava: Elizabeth had returned to the Roman Catholicism of her upbringing. All this required most careful handling. A month after the great eruption Pepys could write:

> Lay long in bed with pleasure (with my wife), with whom I have now a great deal of content, and my mind is in other things also mightily more at ease, and I do mind my business better than ever and am more at peace, and trust in God I shall ever be so, though I cannot yet get my mind off from thinking now and then of Deb, but I do ever since my promise a while since to my wife pray to God by myself in my chamber every night, and will endeavour to get my wife to do the like with me ere long, but am in much fear of what she lately frighted me with about her being a Catholique . . .

Meanwhile both her and his attention had been thrillingly distracted by the purchase of a coach and all its attendant magnificences: horses, harness, livery for the coachman, painted panels and heaven knows what. Pepys had chosen the vehicle and agreed its price the day before his domestic downfall. But even in the week that followed he found time to think of taking Povy, the supreme arbiter of the elegances of life, to run his eye over it. Povy was aghast. It was badly designed: it was much too heavy: it was out of fashion. Pepys accepted his criticism humbly and gratefully (but does the memory of it help to explain his uncharacteristic bitterness towards Povy in later life?)* and commissioned a new one to be built to his specifications. It was delivered in time, but only just in time, for an outing on May Day 1669, the apotheosis of the married splendour that had taken its rise, also in a coach, when Pepys showed Elizabeth his patent as Clerk of the Acts in the summer of 1660.

> At noon home to dinner and there find my wife extraordinary fine, with her flowered tabby gown that she made two years ago, now laced exceeding pretty: and indeed was fine all over; and mighty earnest to go, though the day was lowering; and she would have me put on my fine suit, which I did. And so anon we went alone through the town with our new liveries of serge, and the horses' manes and tails tied with red ribbons, and the standards there gilt with varnish, and all clean, and

* See p. 34b, Chapter VIII, note 3.

green reines that people did look mightily upon us; and, the truth is, I did not see any coach more pretty, though more gay, than ours, all the day.

So, in the last month of the Diary, in the last few months of Elizabeth's life, the Pepyses sweep past our dazzled eyes at a spanking trot. If the diarist himself had been able to fix a single impression on posterity that would stand as the symbol of how he wished his married life to appear, this would surely have been his choice. But the reality he records was naturally less decorous, less imposing. Deb's banishment by no means soothed Elizabeth's agitation and Pepys himself could not unlearn his old ways all at once. Summing up the position on New Year's Eve he recognises that his domestic tranquillity is precarious and admits his own responsibility:

> . . . the year ends, after some late very great sorrow with my wife by my folly, yet ends, I say, with great mutual peace and content, and likely to last so by my care, who am resolved to enjoy the sweet of it . . .

Yet three days later he annoyed her by haggling over her dress allowance. Next day he not only gave way, but gave her more than she had expected. A week passed, heavy with Elizabeth's unspoken suspicions. She was snappish, he was sulky. On the night of January 12th she refused all entreaties to come to bed, stoking the fire and lighting fresh candles. After some hours Pepys, alarmed, tried again to persuade her, only to be met with furious (but vague) accusations about secret trysts with Deb. 'At last, about one o'clock, she come to my side of the bed, and drew my curtaine open and with the tongs red hot at the ends, made as if she did design to pinch me with them.' Pepys leapt up, and with a few words easily induced her to lay down her arms. But it took another hour of listening and reasoning before she could be got to bed. The even tenor of life for which Pepys yearned seemed to have been broken. Even when he took her to the play his roving eye gave grounds for offence. At last on January 21st when Elizabeth had been 'mighty dogged' and he had been 'mightily troubled' he left her sulking and silent and went to bed 'weeping to myself for grief, which she discerning, come to bed and mighty kind and so with great joy on both sides to sleep'. There were fallings-out after that – and only too good grounds for them on Pepys's own evidence – but the era of red-hot tongs was over.

The marriage was both strained and strengthened by the threat of Parliamentary inquiry that hung over the heads of Pepys and all his colleagues. Strained, because coming home worried, apprehensive and exhausted he was easily irritated by Elizabeth and the more inclined to seek the company of women who would distract and amuse instead of nagging: strengthened, because Elizabeth really did share his joys and sorrows as no one else; and the dangers and triumphs of the post-war period in Pepys's career seemed at the time immense.

The scale and the thoroughness with which the House of Commons was preparing its investigation into the whole conduct of the war could only be alarming to men like Pepys and Coventry. They knew that they had acted in good faith and had set high standards of efficiency and order. But they had had a hand in many pies, some of which hardly did credit to the administrative cuisine. How could it be otherwise? They had to act with colleagues, some of whom were in varying degrees incompetent, dishonest or lazy. They had to carry out orders whether they thought them sensible or no. In either of these broad contexts it would be impossible for any man to appear blameless. And they had made enemies, known and unknown. The courtiers, the gentleman-captains who undid all, would certainly take the opportunity of making mischief. The merchants who had not succeeded in landing profitable contracts, the men who had applied for jobs and had been sent away without them, the officials who had been dismissed for misconduct, the jealous, the resentful, the malicious, all these persons could mount attacks that not even the most agile tactician could forestall. And in Pepys's case, if not in Coventry's, there was a great deal that simply could not be explained away. The huge bribes from Sir William Warren and Captain Cocke, the large sums paid by the Houblons to secure passes for their ships trading to the Mediterranean, the frequent use of naval property for private purposes, the cutting of corners and the breaking of rules that Pepys knew himself to be guilty of cannot have made for ease of mind.

The Committee to inquire into the miscarriages of the war was appointed in October 1667. Signs of a political upheaval had been evident some time before. A month earlier Coventry had astonished Pepys by the news that he was leaving the Duke of York's service. But Pepys, who had been taken by surprise at the King's dismissal of Clarendon a week earlier quickly recognised the connection between the two events. Clarendon was the Duke of York's father-in-law: and Coventry had worked tirelessly for the great minister's downfall. Coventry, who still remained a Navy Commissioner and a member of the Privy Council, insisted to Pepys that he had long been seeking an opportunity of resigning his secretaryship to the Duke. He may well have been speaking the truth; Pepys, always impressed by his open dealing, clearly thought so; in any case the two explanations do not exclude each other. What is certain is that Clarendon's fall opened a breach between the King and his brother the Lord High Admiral at a moment when the Royal Navy needed every hand to work her out of range of the Parliament's batteries.

Pepys was pleased and flattered to hear that he had been considered as Coventry's successor. But he was not, as in the filling of a later vacancy in the same post, in the least hurt or disappointed. He had more than enough to do in fighting the Navy Office's corner without undertaking to defend the strategic conduct of the war. In this as much as ever Coventry was the only ally on whom he could wholly depend. Coventry's advice given on December 3rd, 1667, is the timeless directive for a civil servant charged with drafting a Parliamentary answer:

> He advises me . . . to be as short as I can, and obscure, saving in things fully plain; and that the greatest wisdom in dealing with Parliament in the world is to say little, and let them get out what they can by force.

Coventry turned the same clear, penetrating gaze on the King his master and, on occasion, told him unpalatable truths. No wonder he did not last long: but no wonder that Pepys exclaimed after one of their wide-ranging talks, 'the ability and integrity of Sir William Coventry in all the King's concernments I do and must admire'. As early as December 1667, within a week of Clarendon's exile, Captain Cocke reported that Coventry's impeachment was imminent. The detail and the timing were both far out, but the point was true, as Coventry himself knew well enough when he told Pepys at this very time:

> that the serving a Prince that minds not his business is most unhappy for them that serve him well, and an unhappiness so great that he declares he will never have more to do with a war, under him.

This insight was echoed by the comments in the Diary two days later, December 9th, on the King's carefree disloyalty to the men who had served him and were now under attack.

It was an attack mounted on two Parliamentary fronts: the Committee for Miscarriages already referred to, and the Committee for Accounts, later called the Brooke House Committee from the place assigned for it to sit. The Brooke House Committee was not nominated until December 1667 and did not get into its stride for another two years. Pepys at first approved the expert knowledge and intellectual calibre of its membership but lived, as we shall see, to revise these opinions when he found himself the principal object of its investigations. His Homeric exchanges with it must be postponed to another chapter. But to understand the strain he was under, it is important not to forget its existence. He knew that if and when he escaped with a whole skin from the Committee bent on knowing why the war had gone so badly he would have to face another determined to find out what the Navy Office had done with the unheard-of sums of money that had been voted it.

The Committee for Miscarriages lost no time in getting down to business. Within four days of its appointment Pepys heard that he was to be summoned before it to answer questions about the Medway disaster. But by then it had already ripped off the coverings beneath which one of the most celebrated scandals of the war had been concealed. The fatal order to shorten sail that had allowed the Dutch to escape annihilation after the great victory off Lowestoft in 1665 had been nailed on Henry Brouncker, the courtier brother of Pepys's colleague. Since Pepys himself with all his personal sources of information had not previously established this fact, the Committee had shown an alarming grip. Pepys slept badly, spent a harassing morning preparing the Board's case and hurried straight to the Commons without time for any dinner. As he drove there in Lord Brouncker's coach he and his colleagues anxiously tried to co-ordinate their defence in the immensely complicated business of discharging of seamen by ticket about which they had been severally and collectively accused of malpractices. With a body like a House of Commons Committee one could never be sure that they would stick to one thing at a time. After a short period of waiting Pepys found himself facing his examiners. In the heat of exposition there was no time for nerves; and no need either, since his habitual lucidity and his methodical documentation at once brought every neutral to his side. A chair was brought for his books and papers, and the sun went down and candles were called for before he had finished. He knew he had dominated his audience and watched scornfully while Commissioner Pett and Lord Brouncker mumbled and bumbled. Congratulations flowed in. Cousin Roger, the member for Cambridge, was among the first to tell him how well he had done. He returned to a hearty supper and a contented night's rest.

His colleagues knew that their best hope lay in keeping quiet and letting him do the talking. Walking in the Matted Gallery at Whitehall a few weeks later he and Coventry agreed 'that we that have taken the most pains are called upon to answer for all crimes, while those that, like Sir W. Batten and Sir J. Minnes, did sit and do nothing, do lie still without any trouble.' This last statement was incontestably true of Batten who had

died eight weeks earlier. Towards the end of January 1668 the Committee
for Accounts began to show unwelcome signs of life. Here again Pepys
was to answer for the office. But what really agitated him was the knowledge
that they were going to question him about that unfortunate business of the
prize goods. Worse still they examined him on oath. If they did not get
under his guard, he still felt only a modest satisfaction at his performance.
By the middle of February the double pressure was beginning to tell:

> All the morning till noon getting some things more ready against the
> afternoon for the Committee of Accounts, which did give me great
> trouble, to see how I am forced to dance after them in one place, and
> to answer Committees of Parliament in another.

At any moment cats might leap out of a number of ill-secured bags. Sir
William Warren hinted that the Navy Board's failure to place any recent
orders with him might lead him into unfortunate — and uncharacteristic —
candour about past transactions when these were scrutinised by the Committee. Pepys concluded that he was bluffing: but he noted uneasily a day
or two later

> . . . I do perceive by Sir W. Warren's discourse, that they [the House]
> do all they can possibly to get out of him and others, what presents
> they have made to the Officers of the Navy;* but he tells me that he
> hath denied all, though he knows that he is forsworn as to what
> relates to me.[7]

Even Coventry, whom Pepys met next day, was apprehensive of the
trouble he would find himself in through taking the customary fees for
appointments until his own suggestion of a fixed salary in lieu had at
last been adopted. If Coventry, the most scrupulous public servant of
Pepys's acquaintance, felt cause for alarm, the chances for anyone else
must have looked slender. Coventry identified Sir Frescheville Holles
as the man who was stirring the pot. He had recently been elected to the
House of Commons and had thus found wider scope for the profanity and
mischief that so scandalised Pepys. And yet was he quite so thorough-
paced a villain as he appears on the occasions when he was so impertinent
as to question the wisdom and efficiency of the Navy Board? Only a
month later he entertained Pepys and Lord Brouncker in the officer of
the guard's room at Whitehall in the most friendly manner and performed

---

* 'Officer of the Navy' meant member of the Navy Board. What we call a naval officer
Pepys and his contemporaries called a sea officer.

with great skill on the bagpipes. And a week after that he went out of his way to warn Pepys, whom he met by chance at a play, of an impending move in the Committee for Miscarriages. In any case Holles, high-spirited, dashing, indisciplined, ought, on Pepys's principles, to be no match for the steady systematic professionals like Coventry and himself. More was to be feared from malicious and disgruntled insiders.

Two of these soon disclosed themselves. James Carcasse, a protégé of Lord Brouncker's, had been dismissed from his post in the Ticket Office through Pepys's exposure of his corrupt practices. Seeing a chance of getting his own back he charged Pepys and his colleagues with paying the crew of a privateer which they jointly owned in preference to the sailors of the Royal Navy. The charge appears to have been well-founded. But much more serious mischief was to be feared from the activities of an old Cromwellian sea officer, Valentine Tatnell. Tatnell's career in the Commonwealth navy had not been spectacular. At the Restoration he had been in command of a hired merchantman and, ambitious of better things, had sent Pepys a barrel of oysters. But promotion did not come his way. Instead he was reduced to service with the Press Gang, in which connection there was an ugly story of cheating the widow of a brother officer out of some money due to her. Before that, too, he had been involved in a case of fraud over seamen's tickets, for which he was kept in prison for several months.[8] Tatnell was now reported to be active in promoting charges against both Coventry and Pepys. In late seventeenth-century England once the wound of an accusation had been inflicted it was sure to swarm with maggots of this kind. A decade later in the heyday of the Popish Plot men were to be sent to a horrible death on the evidence of men with an unbroken record of utter rascality.

The crisis was to come early in March. The Commons had appointed Thursday, March 5th, as the day on which the Navy Board was to answer the allegations of sharp practice over the seamen's tickets. As the date drew nearer Pepys became more and more anxious and despondent, relieving his fear and despair by raging at his colleagues for being so little use in their common danger and, surest solvent of all, by immersing himself in the detailed preparation of their defence. The tempo increased. The last Sunday Pepys spent in prolonged conferences with Coventry and Will Hewer, apart from the usual intermission with one of his Westminster women. On the Monday he and his clerks worked till after midnight 'preparing my great answer'. Hewer reported the latest rumour that all the Officers were to be sacked except 'honest Sir John Minnes, who, God knows, is fitter to have been turned out himself than any of us, doing the King more hurt by his dotage and folly than all the rest can do by their knavery, if they have a mind to it.' On the Tuesday he was infuriated by finding that Lord Brouncker was trying to save his own skin at the expense of everyone else and, particularly, of Pepys. Wednesday was cold and wet: even the rich binding of a newly acquired book could give no pleasure. There was nothing for it but to close the doors of the office and work with the clerks until the mind ground to a standstill. Too ill and exhausted to eat any supper, sleep did not come easily: nor, when it came, was it deep or long: 'but then waked, and never in so much trouble in all my life of mind, thinking of the task I have upon me, and upon what dissatisfactory grounds, and what the issue of it may be to me.'

At six o'clock he could stand it no longer and sought comfort from Elizabeth. She soothed him at last by convincing him that a career that involved so much worry was not worth pursuing, once he had cleared himself of the charges now laid against him. The recognition that life was not bounded by the Board on the one side and the Committee on the other was a glimpse of daylight after nightmare. Pepys returned refreshed for a final tussle with his notes. Then at nine o'clock he took a boat up to Westminster with his faithful assistants, Hayter and Hewer. It was the moment of calm before the curtain goes up, before the light goes on, before the trolley squeaks down the corridor to the operating theatre. The adrenal glands took over. Pepys reinforced them with half-a-pint of mulled sack at the Dog and a dram of brandy at Westminster Hall. Between eleven and twelve they were called in, Pepys, Brouncker, Mennes and their newest colleague, Sir Thomas Harvey. Penn as a member of the House was sitting in his place. Pepys saw that 'the whole House was full and full of expectation'. They were not to be disappointed.

Exposition was Pepys's forte. Clarity of mind, method of analysis, organisation of matter: the reasonableness of the civil servant, the authority of the lawyer, more than a touch of the schoolmaster. There are few among the hundreds of official papers that Pepys has left behind which do not show most, if not all, of these his most characteristic attributes. This speech, it is clear, exhibited them in their highest degree. Never again, certainly not when he was a Member of Parliament, was he to dominate the House of Commons with such intoxicating success:

After the Speaker had . . . read the Report of the Committee, I began our defence most acceptably and smoothly, and continued at it without any hesitation or losse, but with full scope, and all my reason free about me, as if it had been at my own table, from that time till past three in the afternoon; and so ended, without any interruption from the Speaker; but we withdrew. And there all my Fellow-Officers, and all the world that was within hearing, did congratulate me, and cry up my speech as the best thing they ever heard; and my Fellow-Officers overjoyed in it.

The salutes of praise reverberated for several days. 'Good-morrow, Mr Pepys, that must be Speaker of the Parliament-house,' was Coventry's greeting when they met next morning. The Solicitor-General thought Pepys 'spoke the best of any man in England'. In the Park the King and the Duke of York came up and congratulated him. Men whose Parliamentary memories went back to Charles I's time were emphatic that it was the best speech that they had ever heard. By common consent it transformed the position of the Navy Board and it confirmed beyond a doubt Pepys's own standing as by far the ablest man in his field. Neither he nor his colleagues were safe yet, but the betting was now on their being so.

14

Recriminations: the Brooke House Committee

The threats to marriage and career had been met, if not mastered: there remained the threat of going blind. Pepys first found his eyes troublesome in the days when he was drinking too much. With sobriety these symptoms disappeared. But the long hours of close work, much of it by candlelight, which the war and his increased commitments imposed soon produced fresh complaints of strain and soreness. By the autumn of 1667 he was seriously alarmed: 'My eyes so bad since last night's straining of them that I am hardly able to see, beside the pain which I have in them.' That winter he went to the leading spectacle-maker of the day, whose advice has been described by a modern authority as 'superlatively bad'.[1] The spring and summer that followed the triumph before the Committee for Miscarriages brought some relief, no doubt because the jaunts to Cambridge and Brampton, to Oxford and the West took him away from his books and papers. But at the end of June, with an answer to prepare for the Brooke House Committee in July, the pain and incapacity were causing him acute anxiety. '. . . I very melancholy under the fear of my eyes being spoiled and not to be recovered: for I am come that I am not able to read out a small letter . . .' Recourse to the spectacle-maker again proved useless. In the middle of July bleeding, the first and last shot in the medical locker of the seventeenth century, was tried. At last in August, in the middle of drafting a 'great letter' to the Duke of York which would (he hoped) reform the administration of the navy at the cost (he feared) of mortally antagonising all his colleagues, he heard of an expedient that really had some effect. This was the paper tube spectacles, to which the addition of a glass – pooh-poohed by Pepys's expert adviser – brought a marked improvement of vision. But it was still summer with enough hours of daylight for even so busy a man as Pepys. The winter brought the glitter of candles and the glare of snow. Both hurt him cruelly. By the spring even strong daylight brought pain and watering of the eyes. On May 8th, 1669, 'now I am not able to bear the light of the windows in my eyes', he changed the place he had occupied during the eight years and more that he had sat at the Navy Board for one on the other side of the table. A week later he applied to the Duke of York for three or four months' leave of absence, 'his sole aim being the relieving of his eyes by such a respite from his present labour'.[2] At the end of the month he wrote his final entry in the Diary, closing it with the coda that echoes in the mind of every reader:

And thus ends all that I doubt I shall ever be able to do with my own eyes in the keeping of my Journal, I being not able to do it any longer, having done now so long as to undo my eyes almost every time that I take a pen in my hand; and, therefore, whatever comes of it, I must forbear: and, therefore, resolve from this time forward, to have it kept by my people in long-hand, and must therefore be contented to set down no more than is fit for them and all the world to know; or, if there be any thing, which cannot be much, now my amours to Deb. are past, and my eyes hindering me in almost all other pleasures, I must endeavour to keep a margin in my book open, to add, here and there, a note in short-hand with my own hand.

And so I betake myself to that course, which is almost as much as to see myself go into my grave: for which, and all the discomforts that will accompany my being blind, the good God prepare me!

The truth of the heart is so poignant and so solemn that it seems almost trivial to remind oneself that Pepys did not go blind: that great as his achievements had been, still greater were to come; that he was to survive into a long and cultivated retirement, corresponding with the leading scholars and scientists of his day and reading, shortly before his death, the opening Books of Clarendon's great *History of the Rebellion*, first given to the world in the reign of the author's granddaughter. The liability to eyestrain remained a nuisance. In the memorandum on the state of his health already referred to, which Pepys drew up in 1677, the limits that it set are precisely defined. Most of them could be overcome by secretarial assistance. To quote his own words:

But when I came to leave off working with my own eyes and fell to the employing clerks, my eyes shortly grew well, and from that time to this never knew any of that pain till [by] the necessity of my employment, which is often indispensable, I am driven often to write and read with my own hand and eyes when pain immediately ensues (as I have already said) and continues longer or shorter as I continue working with them.[3]

In the spring of 1669 Pepys could not know that, any more than he could know that he was suffering from 'hypermetropia with some degree of astigmatism' (the latter a condition that was not identified until the early nineteenth century). There was in fact no danger of his going blind. But this fact by no means disposes of the counter fact that he, after taking the best advice available, thought that there was.

Such an interruption to a man's career must always appear disastrous. In this case it must have been the more bitter (though Pepys does not say so) because he had, quite suddenly, arrived at the summit. The end of the war had left him as one of the leading men, and certainly the best hope, in naval affairs. Then within a few weeks Batten had died, Carteret had exchanged his place with Lord Anglesey, the Deputy Treasurer of Ireland, and Penn was (most unjustly) under a cloud over the Medway disaster. But Sir William Coventry even though no longer (after 1667) a Commissioner of the Navy, no longer (after 1668) Secretary to the Lord High Admiral, was still a Commissioner of the Treasury, still a member of the Privy Council, still, in Pepys's view, the most effective man in the Government. On certain points of naval policy and finance, in particular his contention that the navy could be maintained acceptably on a budget of £200,000 a year, Pepys ventured to differ, even to criticise. But in doing so he showed an unaffected deference, an anxiety to win approval rather than to win an argument, that leaves no room for doubt that he thought of Coventry as his superior not only in age and in rank but in professional knowledge and capacity. And besides Coventry, the noonday sun of Pepys's career, Sandwich, its morning star, was again visible in the heavens. Late in October 1668 Pepys went to call on his old patron who had concluded his mission to Madrid.

With Sandwich and Coventry both in play Pepys could hardly feel himself a principal. And yet in spite of himself he was forced to recognise that he was. Both men had lost the self-confidence, the assurance of their position, which Pepys, for his part, would never have questioned. Rumours that Coventry was on the way out disturbed him late in September, though he could hardly credit them. Yet by December 7th when he walked over to see him, enjoying the first frosty weather of the winter, to both men his dismissal had become far from unthinkable, Pepys 'telling him that, with all these doings, he, I thanked God, stood yet' and Coventry telling Pepys that 'he is represented to the King by his enemies as a melancholy man, and one that is still prophesying ill events, so as the King called him Visionaire . . . whereas others that would please the King do make him believe that all is safe'. Under fire Pepys's loyalty redoubled. Coventry was (on November 27th) 'the man of all the world that I am resolved to preserve an interest in'. When, in the spring of 1669, Coventry, at Buckingham's instigation, is disgraced and sent to the Tower, Pepys visits him every day. Even after his release when he judges, regretfully, that it would be impolitic to be seen with him walking in St. James's Park he still qualifies the decision with words that show his true feeling 'though to serve him I should, I think, stick at nothing'.[4]

The contrast between these feelings and those evoked by Sandwich is conspicuous. At their first meeting on his return from Madrid both men seem to have felt a certain reserve. This hardened at what should have been an intimate discussion on November 9th, when Pepys was in the throes of Elizabeth's first fury over Deb and Sandwich was to appear before the Tangier Committee to give an account of his mission and justify his expenses. Creed and Pepys agreed that he made a poor fist of it 'I fearing that either his mind and judgment are depressed, or that he do it out of his great neglect'. Was Sandwich a depressive? He was certainly not the singleminded, unemotional player of the power game such as the bare outline of his career might suggest. The depths that mystified Pepys open wider as their association lengthens. A fortnight later he found him 'now so reserved, or moped rather, I think, with his own business, that he bids welcome to no man, I think, to his satisfaction.' The patron he had known best and longest had become a stranger.

On personal grounds this was a matter for regret but professionally it had its advantages. When Sandwich proposed the creation of a local paymastership at Tangier and nominated one of his followers for it, the Duke of York at a formal meeting of the Tangier Board deferred the decision until Pepys's views were known. Pepys's description of Sandwich recounting the story to him fixes the last phase of their relationship and opens the chapter of direct royal patronage that was to close only with the Revolution of 1688:

This my Lord Sandwich in great confidence tells me, that he do take very ill from the Duke of York, though nobody knew the meaning of these words but him; and that he did take no notice of them, but bit his lip, being satisfied that the Duke's care of me was as desirable to him as it could be to have Sir Charles Harbord [the man Sandwich had proposed]: and did seem industrious to let me see that he was glad that the Duke of York and he might come to contend who shall be the kindest to me, which I owned as his great love, and so I hope and believe it is, though my Lord did go a little too far in this business to move it so far without consulting me.[5]

Pepys ended this crucial conversation by inviting him to the splendid collation mentioned on page 89, 'he having never yet eat a bit of my bread'. Sandwich's unhesitating acceptance confirmed to the world in the plainest terms what Pepys records more subtly in his Diary. He had dipped his ensign to his ex-servant: and the salute had been gracefully, but none the less confidently, acknowledged.

The head of the department, shrewd, authoritative, self-important, is beginning to cast his shadow over the pages, so near their end, that reveal the devices and desires of a much merer mortal. After the spring of 1669 we can see Pepys only as his contemporaries saw him, as indeed everyone else sees each one of us, from the front he chose to turn to the world. Sometimes, as in letters to old and intimate friends, he is open, easy and communicative. Sometimes in the mass of official correspondence there is a flash of the Cambridge undergraduate, a wink from the *vieux boulevardier* of Restoration London. There is always — how could there not be? — wit, clarity, zest, punch. There is abundant material for portraiture, but there is not the gift of systematic self-revelation. Before the lights of the Diary have dropped behind in the darkness a last look at that incomparable self-portrait in motion may sharpen the blunter perceptions of a biographer.

No man, says Johnson, is a hypocrite in his pleasures. What, at the end of the Diary period, was Pepys's idea of pure enjoyment? On March 2nd, 1669, he records '. . . extraordinary pleasure, as being one of the days and nights of my life spent with the greatest content; and that which I can but hope to repeat again a few times in my whole life.' To anatomise these delights is to see how little Pepys has changed in spite of wealth and success, in spite of the Royal Society and Mr Povy, of the world of the City and the Court. The interesting part of the day began with his coming back from the office at noon, to a family dinner party of eight guests at which the women much outnumbered the men. Socially they

they ranged from the Roger Pepyses (M.P. for Cambridge and a successful lawyer) down to an ex-barrister's clerk. The dinner itself was 'noble' but no hushed gastronomic awe prevented the party from going with a swing: 'mighty merry, and particularly myself pleased with looking on Betty Turner [one of his young cousins], who is mighty pretty.' After the meal people were free to talk to each other *tête-à-tête*, and the host indulged the pleasure of showing off his books, his furniture, his pictures, the setting in which he took such pride. This was followed by a paper game, something on the lines of Consequences, in which Betty's elder sister, The. (short for Theophila) was praised for her wit, though Pepys would have traded some of it for more of Betty's gaiety and good-nature. By now it was beginning to get dark. Musicians arrived – carefully chosen like every other item of the entertainment: two excellent violins and the best theorbo in London. The office had been made ready, candles were lit, the party was strengthened by half a dozen more guests, including two strangers introduced by Will Howe as dancing partners for the young ladies. The fiddles struck up and they danced till two in the morning, breaking off only for a good supper. It was the jigs and country dances that Pepys remembered in writing up the entry. The laughter and high spirits are captured in the Diary as nowhere else. The junketings of Mr. Wardle and the Pickwick Club have the same flavour but the exuberance has got into the description instead of staying in the scene described.

Pleasure had not been displaced by business from its primacy in the Pepysian view of life. Rather business had been subsumed as an important source of active enjoyment. Few men explored a wider range or developed a more conscious and explicit philosophy of the subject. Innocent pleasure has, to twentieth-century ears, a faintly mocking, patronising overtone. There is an implication of naivety, inexperience, lack of self-awareness. Not, one would have thought, the first ideas that come to mind in connection with Pepys. Yet from the rich and varied catalogue of hedonism that could be extracted from the Diary simplicity and innocence easily outshine all other qualities. Weather, music, good-tempered domesticity, a family party such as that just described, are at the end as they were in the beginning the inspiration of its lyricism. Here is the key to Pepys's mind and personality, or if we adopt the bold intellectualism of his own motto *Mens cujusque is est quisque,** to the man himself.

Tributary pleasures were continually added or extended. The books and prints, the fine bindings and the portraits of himself and his wife, pleased not only in and for themselves but as a collection that could be shown to visitors and guests. Pepys had the instincts and gradually

---

* For a translation of this phrase and Pepys's own commentary on it see below, p. 326-7.

acquired the knowledge of a connoisseur. He was feeling too the first tug of an interest that was to grow in strength until it became, in his eyes, a vocation: the urge to write history, or at least, to collect and criticise the materials for so doing. As long ago as June 13th, 1664, Coventry had suggested to Pepys that he should write the history of the First Dutch War, 'which I am glad to hear, it being a thing I much desire, and sorts mightily with my genius, and, if well done, may recommend me much'. The Second Dutch War was upon him before he had gone far in his researches, but he put them to immediate use by drawing comparisons between the performance and expenditure of the navy in the two wars wherever it suited his argument to do so. Soon after the war had ended he was entertaining his clerks to dinner, an occasion he always enjoyed, when he discovered to his great delight that one of them, Richard Gibson, shared his historical enthusiasm: 'he telling me so many good stories relating to the warr and practices of commanders, which I will find a time to recollect: and he will be an admirable help to my writing a history of the Navy, if ever I do.' The saving clause was, sadly, justified in the event. But manuscripts both in his own library at Magdalene and in the Rawlinson collection at the Bodleian bear substantial evidence to the zeal with which he pursued the material for such a study. A year later, on March 12th, 1669, he found, after several attempts, a rich haul of Navy Accounts and Treasurer's patents in the office of Auditor Beale: and three days later he bestows a rare accolade of praise on the Rolls Office for the excellent order in which they kept their records.

In historical research, and even more in forming his collection of engravings, he was later to profit from the guidance of a man whom he already knew and respected, his fellow diarist John Evelyn. Their earliest connections were official. Evelyn had married into the hierarchy of naval officeholders. His father-in-law was the grandson and great-grandson of successive Treasurers of the Navy under Queen Elizabeth. Evelyn himself had been a Commissioner for the Sick and Wounded in the war; and his house and estate at Deptford adjoined the navy yard. As a leading Fellow of the Royal Society he would have been familiar to Pepys even before their occasions brought them together. He was to be the evening star, as Sandwich had been the morning and Coventry the sun at noon. In the spring of 1669 all these luminaries are clearly visible in the Pepysian heavens.

Steadily growing in intimacy was Pepys's friendship with the Houblons, that remarkable family of Flemish origin who combined a cultivated and affectionate domestic life with a business reputation for honesty, judgment and valuable connections overseas. On February 14th, 1668, Pepys records seeing 'old Mr Houblon, whom I never saw before, and all his sons about him, all good merchants'. This was old James Houblon, the father of the London Exchange, whose epitaph Pepys was to compose, commemorating the facts that on his death at the age of ninety his five sons were all flourishing City merchants and that out of a hundred grandchildren seventy survived him. James Houblon the younger was Pepys's closest friend among the brothers. As has been pointed out earlier they represent much that he most valued in the civilisation of his time. Rich, high-minded, liberal, owing nothing to aristocratic or territorial influences, repudiating religious bigotry and the vulgar prejudices of nationalism, making straight in the wilderness of the seventeenth century the pathway for Free Trade and the Idea of Progress, the Houblons, like Pepys himself, seem to

> Show what Everybody might
> Become by simply doing Right.

When at the end of his life Pepys sent his nephew John Jackson on a tour of Europe he drew heavily on Evelyn for advice in the planning of it and on the Houblons for introductions, letters of credit and practical help of every kind. That he consulted Evelyn for his own much less ambitious expedition with Elizabeth in the early autumn of 1669 is, unfortunately, about all we know of a journey which this passionate traveller recalled in old age as one of the most valuable experiences of his life. Evelyn gave him some introductions in Paris, recommended some names to look out for on his visits to the printsellers and, anxious not to overburden his friend – 'Yours is a Running voyage and desultory' – left it at that. Since Pepys was still, even on holiday, the Government's leading naval expert, the tour began with a visit to the principal Dutch naval bases. From the coast Pepys and Elizabeth, accompanied by her brother Balty, made their way through Holland and Flanders to Paris. On their way back they broke the journey at Brussels. The whole expedition lasted, as Pepys himself emphasised thirty years afterwards, 'a bare two months'. Two months for the Holland of Rembrandt, whose etchings are among the glories of the Pepys library, for the Flanders still aglow with the colours of Rubens and Van Dyck, for the Paris where the *Institut* was rising on the left bank, was a thin ration for such an artistic and intellectual appetite. But the rarer talent for enjoyment triumphed over every limitation, up to the tragedy with which this last great party ended. Coming back through Flanders Elizabeth caught a fever. By the time they had got back to London she was very ill. On November 10th, only three weeks after they had landed, she was dead.

Of the distress and of the unselfpitying courage with which it was met, Pepys's silence is eloquent. Fortunately for him there was work, more work, and more work yet that would leave him no leisure for the foreseeable future. The Brooke House Committee had called in the Navy Board to answer the charges of misconduct and corruption that had been so freely bandied about in the humiliation with which the war had ended: and Pepys was, obviously, the only man who could confront so formidable a prosecution. He had in fact already done so by letter before leaving for his holiday in August as far as concerned his own irregularities. But on his return he found waiting for him a paper containing eighteen separate and highly detailed accusations, among which the very charges he had angrily rebutted were once again set out. One of them concerned his own grossly improper conduct in selling flag-material to the Board of which he was a member. As it was certainly true, the challenge could not be refused. Even while Elizabeth was still on her deathbed, he was checking his references, collating his materials and applying to the Brooke House Commissioners themselves for access to the Navy Office Contract Books on which they had founded their charges.[6] The lawyer, the historian and the rhetorician in Pepys all had their work cut out. After Elizabeth's death he must have worked almost without interruption, for by November 25th he had prepared an answer that in length, argumentative force and above all command of intricate detail showed the Commissioners that they would have to fight every inch of the way against an enemy who knew the country blindfold. But before the letter could have achieved its full effect of strengthening the faint-hearted in the administration and cooling the ardour of its critics, the Parliamentary situation suddenly got out of hand. A demand for the report of the Brooke House Commissioners resolved itself into a vote of censure on Sir George Carteret. The Commons suspended him from the House, on which the King at once prorogued them and announced that he himself would hear the charges against Carteret and the Navy Board in the presence of his Council.

This meant in effect that Pepys had to prepare all over again a defence brief for virtually the whole financial and administrative conduct of the war. The original charges would form the spearhead of the attack he would have to meet. But the power of the Commissioners to argue, to question, to raise new topics, to switch the hunt made the whole undertaking more perilous. It was one thing to refute a case stated in black and white with an answer which had itself been pondered, tested in the undisturbed stronghold of a Government office with its superb (because Pepysian) filing system and its posse of clever young clerks. It was another to think on one's feet. Pepys, fortunately and exceptionally, enjoyed both forms of intellectual exercise. But he was too old a hand to rely simply on the quickness of his wits and the readiness of his tongue, much as he valued himself on both. He knew that his real power to annihilate his enemies lay in his unique mastery of the relevant records and statistics: they were his creation, his instrument, on which, given time, he could pick out any tune he chose. The rights and wrongs of any single question could soon lose their sharpness of outline once it could be lured into the forests of administrative detail where he alone knew the paths. The preparation of so gigantic a brief, the organisation of such unwieldy materials into a form in which everything that might be wanted would lie ready to hand turns the imagination faint. It stimulated Pepys to the height of his powers. This time it was all or nothing.

So crucial seemed this official inquiry, in its procedure something like a modern Special Tribunal, that Pepys kept a journal of its proceedings as they affected himself. Although written in the first person it has little else in common with the great Diary so lately closed. It is in long-hand (not his own) and the style, like the matter, is much closer to that of the civil service panjandrum, sure of a respectful and patient audience, so familiar in his letterbooks. It records – unsurprisingly – a series of exchanges in which Pepys invariably gets the better of his opponents: its tone towards the King shows, predictably, none of the freedom and candour of the Diary; and the Commissioners are treated with a weary irritability that perfectly suggests to the reader the amateurishness and malice that may safely be ascribed to all who presume to criticise officials. In all this, as in some of its direct statements, the document is intentionally misleading. Pepys did not think that Charles II had deserved well of his country by his conduct of the war. He did not think, as Sir Arthur Bryant appears to suggest, that Lord Brereton, the Chairman of the Commissioners, was a pompous booby of a country squire. On the contrary he knew him as a founder member of the Council of the Royal Society and a man whose breadth of learning was admired by John Evelyn.[7] Indeed he had greeted the news of his appointment to the Commission with particular approval.[8] On the incapacity of Colonel Thomson, a wooden-legged Cromwellian who played a leading role on the Commission, Sir Arthur enriches the Brooke House Journal with sallies of his own. But what Pepys had written in the Diary on February 14th, 1668, was '. . . Colonel Thomson, one of the Committee of Accounts, who, among the rest, is mighty kind to me, and is likely to mind our business more than any; and I would be glad to have a good understanding with him.' Yet the clear and vivid account given in the first chapter of *Years of Peril* is faithful both to the letter and to the spirit of the Brooke House

Journal, particularly in the half-pitying, half-sneering representation of Thomson as a bumbling old bore intent on proving how much better the First Dutch War had been run when he was a Commissioner of the Admiralty and Navy and Cromwell was in Whitehall.

This goes far to explain why Pepys both at the Committee and in the Journal did all he could to ridicule and discredit him. His real opinion of Thomson has already been cited. He was in Pepys's eyes exceptionally qualified to drive home the question everyone was asking: why did the First Dutch War, fought a dozen years earlier, result in a resounding victory and the Second, in spite of unparalleled Parliamentary votes of money, in defeat? This was saying in public what Pepys and Coventry had been deploring to each other for the past two years. What was on trial at Brooke House was not simply the conduct of Sir George Carteret and his colleagues but the performance of Charles II's government, even the whole Restoration regime. Pepys in his Diary has shown how largely he sympathised with the critics. But the Brooke House Journal is, as he had envisaged, '. . . kept by my people in long-hand, and [I] must be contented to set down no more than is fit for them and all the world to know.'

At Brooke House Pepys is defending himself, and that left him, as we have seen, some awkward corners to turn. He is defending his colleagues, complaining even in this semi-public journal loud and long at how much he does for them and how little they do for him, but he stands or falls with the office. He is the champion, directly and without any intermediary, of the King and the Duke, and carries the Stuart colours. Sandwich and Coventry have been left behind, though not abandoned or even abated in personal loyalty or affection. Like a medieval tenant-in-chief he holds directly of the King. He was to maintain this position unchanged though not uninterrupted for the rest of his public career. To fulfil it a seat in Parliament was almost a necessity. Pepys had expended a good deal of time and ink that summer in an unsuccessful attempt to secure election at Aldeburgh. But that is a trivial and temporary setback. At Brooke House Pepys has established himself as a bulwark of the regime.

Powerful as all these motives were to vindicate himself and to out-argue the opposition there was a yet deeper spring of action. Be the rights and wrongs of the matter what they may, Colonel Thomson by the very nature of his case was advancing himself and the Government he had served in the first war as rivals to Pepys and his masters in the second. A rival was not to be treated with civility; a successful rival was not to be endured.

Pepys's historical collections gave him valuable material for a counterattack. Any reader of the Journal might conclude that he felt nothing but professional contempt for the administration of the navy under the Protectorate. He certainly felt at all stages of his career that he could do better. But except when playing the role of advocate he listened to its survivors with a respect that is the best evidence of his real opinion.

Above all Pepys clearly enjoyed himself at Brooke House. He allowed himself an exuberance, sometimes a loquacity, that tested everybody's patience. He began in fine style by twitting Lord Brereton for not having made in the Commons the full and civil acknowledgment now offered that Pepys had, by his letter, cleared himself of one matter alleged against Sir George Carteret. Pressing the attack briskly he charged the Commissioners with the same economy of truth concerning £514,000 voted by Parliament '. . . to have given occasion to the World's believing that it had been to uses of Pleasure or other Private respects of his Ma^{ty}'s wch it will be very hard now by any meanes to undeceive them in. Of which the King largely expressed his resentment.'[9] To represent Charles in a posture of injured virtue was a bold *coup*.

The hearings lasted from the beginning of January 1670 to the last week in February. The only anxieties that Pepys records are at those moments at which his colleagues took the floor. '. . . soe much trouble as I of long done and must still look for, while yoak'd with persons who every day make worke for futer censure while I am upon ye tenters in their preservation from ye blame done to their failures past.'[10] Watching them swear to their papers on oath he observes 'Sir John Mennes did ye like, though poor man to that day he had not seen one word of it.'[11]

The charges themselves and the arguments they gave rise to covered every major and many minor aspects of naval administration. Pay, victualling, stores: the purchase of masts, plank, timber, sailcloth, flags, and iron for anchors: even on occasion, operational matters such as the provision of convoy. The councillors stifled their yawns while Pepys and Thomson argued long and learnedly as to whether it had or had not been the practice of the navy at any time to measure masts at the butt end instead of at the partners, the point at which mast and deck meet. Thomson accused Pepys of insufficient eagerness in the purchase of English plank: Pepys rhapsodised over English plank, only deploring its absence from the market at the height of the war. Besides plank and timber it had been the King's policy to encourage domestic production of sailcloth, most of which now came from Brittany, and iron, hitherto largely bought in Sweden or Spain. Only masts could not be found in English forests in anything like sufficient size and quantity.

Masts was an embarrassing subject. Commissioner Pett had given sworn evidence of a cheap offer that the Board had rejected. And how did it come about, in the general scarcity of money, that Sir William Warren seemed to have received so much cash on the nail? 'Imprests' was the term used for such payments, nowadays called advances. The Commissioners, by Pepys's account, '. . . proceeded . . . pressing very earnestly ye great value of ye Imprests granted to Sir William Warren and that in a particular beyond what wee were obliged to do by any Contract appearing.'[12] They were getting warm. But Pepys threw them off the scent by defining with elaborate pedantry the different occasions on which Imprests were, or should be, granted, a masterly and successful switch of the argument from the particular to the general. By the time they struggled back to masts Pepys had moved on to the sellers market created by the Swedish king's edict prohibiting felling for the next seven years. Against the fierce competition from Dutch and French buyers England should think herself lucky to have any supplies at all.

Through the pages of the Brooke House Journal Pepys and Colonel Thomson circle the ring, waiting for an opening, clinching, breaking, planting a quick punch. Why was the fleet in the Channel put on short allowance – the lighter diet on which ships were victualled for the Mediterranean and the Indies? First, replies Pepys, there is no evidence that the efficient conduct of the war was in any way impaired on the occasion cited: second that no ship's company complained more than that of the Commanders-in-Chief who were in the best position to judge such questions: third there were such a number of supernumeraries on board: fourth

that ye shipps happned in both yeares to fight presently after there takeing on their victualls soe as to be forced to fling over much Provisions to make roome for Wounded men . . . After all wch I appealed to them . . . what service or designe . . . during the whole warr has suffered any miscarriage by this want of provisions or ye badness thereof; takeing upon mee the makeing some comparison between the management of ye victualling between this and ye former warr wherein soe many Thousands of Tuns and Provisions were Flung overboard, Fleets come in for want, Men Mutinying and ye Contractors, but for ye friendshipp wch ye interest of some of them found, had probably been hanged for it . . . Thomson answered that Gauden [Pepys's colleague in the victualling] was then one of them. I replied that Pride was another . . .[13]

It was a brilliant touch to rake up the hated associations of Pride's Purge; and it was characteristically bold to challenge comparison with the first

war. By the speed of his footwork as much as by his professional assurance Pepys forestalled his opponents 'by letting the world see that . . .
matters in ye Navy have been at least as well or rather much better than in
ye time of usurpation'.[14] On the historical evidence he had collected it
was a perfectly tenable view; certainly it has gained ground from the most
recent publications of modern scholarship. But the proof of the pudding
is in the eating, and Cromwell had won his war outright.

The burden of the charges against the Navy Board was that they had not
obtained value for the country's money. The burden of Pepys's answer is
contained in his own epigrammatic phrase 'the costliness of poverty'.
The necessities of war had to be met at their own pace and pressure, not
at the irregular tempo of the Treasury's disbursements. Credit cost money.
Pepys and Coventry had been saying this to each other from the first day
of the war to the last; and the observation gains nothing from repetition.
But Pepys like Burke,

> . . . too deep for his hearers, still went on refining
> And thought of convincing, while they thought of dining.

The Journal gives us instances of material that Pepys thought too good to
throw away even though by an uncovenanted mercy his audience had
escaped it.

> . . . Thomson replyd that method might be as easily observed in a great
> Action as in a little one and instanced that a defect in Architecture
> might be sooner observed in Pauls as Pancrace.* At which position and
> Instance ye King and ye Board seeming to make mirth of it I thought
> it unnecessary for mee to returne any answer to it though I had an
> Instance in my mind which my Lord Brereton as an Understander of
> musick would have allowed mee for good. viz. if a theorbo is neither
> soe soon putt nor so easily and cheaply kept in tune as a violin or a
> Trump-marine; nor a harp as a Jew's trump . . .[15]

A man who could be so easily pleased with his own ingenuity was over the
sharpness of bereavement.

What Pepys was like when he got the bit between his teeth is perfectly
hit off by Sir Arthur Bryant when he describes his 'interminable oration on
the complicated business of balancing Storekeepers' Accounts'.[16] Like the
Victorian artists Pepys valued detail for its own sake. He fingers it lovingly
and can hardly bear to let it go. To it he even sacrifices the passion for
order that puts his mind in tune. One of the thorniest of questions on

* St Pancras: not the present church which dates from the early nineteenth century.

which the Board collectively and Pepys individually had to acquit themselves was Payment by Ticket. In an age when few seamen were literate and none had bank accounts any system of deferred payment was certain to produce injustice and confusion on a large scale and to offer easy opportunities of fraud and corruption. Here Pepys drew a telling comparison with the practice of the Cromwellian administration which had not even felt able to introduce printed tickets and counterfoils until after the war had ended in 1654. He had tried to maintain peacetime standards but could not feel guilty at falling short of '. . . the preservation of ye nicety of a new Forme in ye Hurry of a warr, in ye management of an infinite number of loose single papers, each conteyning for every single man as many several circumstances to be attended to, if not more, in a warrant for a six months Victuall for a whole shipp.'[17] In expounding the insanities of a system under which most of the men to be paid off were scattered on shore or serving in different ships his style loses its structure as detail after detail, each too important to be omitted, presents itself to his mind:

> . . . Nay, and frequently ships newly fitted forth could not be mann'd but by inviting men on Board with promise of paying them their wages due to them for other shipps, then I say it was impossible for either counterparts to be lookt into or sea books and muster books compar'd whilst nobody could either foresee what shipps these men should belong to, and so neither what counterparts or books should be sent to the pay.[18]

The only remedy yet discovered for these ills was to compound them. As Pepys shrewdly pointed out:

> Great summes of money are yet due to Seamen for service before ye 14 March 1658 wch might have in part been satisfyed if ye shipps kept long uselessly in pay by ye Commissioners of Parliament had been discharged by Tickett . . .[19]

As concerned himself, Pepys was accused of a misdemeanour, of which he was probably guilty, and of a crime which seems in the highest degree improbable. The misdemeanour consisted in diverting money to pay the crew of the *Flying Greyhound*, a privateer. leased to himself, Penn and Batten, in preference to honouring the tickets of men serving in the King's ships.[20] The crime was ticket-broking: buying a man's ticket at a discount and cashing it in full at the Ticket Office. To steal from the starving was not in Pepys's character. Both his Diary and his corres-

pondence throughout the war provide abundant evidence of his detestation
of ticket-broking, of attempts to prevent it by administrative reform,
and even of action against individuals involved in it.[21] The charge rested
on the deposition of James Carcasse, who had been dismissed from the
Ticket Office, at Pepys's instigation, for improper conduct. Lauderdale,
a powerful member of the Council, remembered the name and 'askt what
Carkes this was . . . whether the same that . . . had beene turned out of the
office and that it was a pretious youth.'[22] Pepys denied the charge in the
most vehement and absolute terms, challenging the Commission to produce evidence of a single such case.

> 'How, Mr Pepys [said Lord Brereton], do you defy the whole world
> in this matter?'
> I replied, 'Yes, that I do defy the whole world and my Lord Brereton
> in particular if he would be thought one if it.'[23]

According to Pepys his antagonist was 'strook dumb'. But repeated warn-
ings that the Commissioners had a card up their sleeve seemed to be justified when, just over a week later, Lord Brereton produced a ticket for
£7. 10s. made out to one of the *Lion*'s ships company but inscribed in the
hand of Sir George Carteret's clerk 'Paid to Mr Pepys'. Pepys stuck to his
guns. Whatever the explanation he knew nothing of it. The King publicly endorsed his denial by asking whether it was likely that an official
who had had the handling of such vast sums for so long a period would
have chosen to betray his trust for £7. 10s. The matter was never officially
cleared up. But after the Brooke House hearings had ended Pepys took
it up with Carteret's clerk in a firm, candid letter that could never have
been written by a man with anything to hide. No answer survives, but the
sad history of Carcasse, who ultimately went off his head, suggests an
obvious solution.

By this time both the Council and the Brooke House Commissioners
had had enough of each other; enough, too, even his admirers may dare to
conjecture, of Pepys on the proper method of mustering carpenter's stores
or whether the Treasurer of the Navy had been allowed Exchequer fees in
the reign of Queen Elizabeth. The attack, formidably mounted, had been
beaten off. With the King as judge it could hardly have been a fair fight.
But would the House of Commons have been any fairer? Certainly Pepys
was helped over some exposed ground by the King's covering fire. Still,
the defence had stood up because the Navy Board had, on the whole,
discharged its duties honestly and efficiently and because Pepys knew his
job well enough to demonstrate this convincingly. The core of all the

trouble, and thus the core of the defence, was inadequate public finance. As Pepys put it at one of the last hearings 'the observation itself answers itself when want of money is considered'.[24]

What was becoming daily clearer was that if once the Committee were allowed to adduce further charges beyond those already laid there was no logical stopping-place. Or as Pepys at his most orotund expresses the same point:

> . . . Besides that I observed . . . that they did now not only suppress ye old instances they are satisfy'd in, but bring upon us new ones by surprize contrary not only to all faire proceedings but to our repeated desires by letter . . . and my Lord Brereton's and Colonel Thomson's repeated promises before His Majesty and this Board . . .
>
> W[ch] method of theirs I showed would more over perpetuate ye dispute without any end to be foreseen of it while answers being given to satisfaction shall never be owned, but in lieu thereof a new race of objections shall be started, soe as I plainly told His Majesty my work must bee to get a son and bring him up only to understand this controversy between brook-house and us and that H.M. too should provide for successors to be instructed on his part in ye state of this case, which otherwise would never likely bee understood either as to what thereof had allready been adjusted or what remained further to bee looked after in it.[25]

That Pepys could joke in public about fathering a son shows, if the Brooke House Journal has not already shown, how far he had recovered from the shock of Elizabeth's death. With his sentiments about Brooke House the King heartily agreed. No more hearings were called and the Committee lapsed when Parliament was adjourned. At last Pepys was free from the recriminations of the Second Dutch War.

15

Secretary to the Admiralty

For the ten years between the dismissal of Sir William Coventry in the spring of 1669 and the terrorism of the Popish Plot, Pepys was always in fact and latterly in name the man in charge of the navy. Sir William Penn, cleared of the unjust imputations put on him over the Medway disaster, might have challenged his supremacy. But his health had long been failing. In the summer of 1670 he knew that he was dying. His son's conversion to Quakerism and his committal to Newgate for street preaching in defiance of the Conventicle Act agitated his last few weeks. But suddenly the sea fell smooth: his son, against all the evidence and against the pressure of the bench, was acquitted: the King and the Duke who had wished to raise the Great Captain Commander to the peerage with the title of Baron Weymouth exchanged an honour that the son would have disclaimed for the even greater one of naming the New England state of Sylvania after the family in whom its governorship was made hereditary. Penn, to quote his monument in St. Mary Redcliffe, 'with a Gentle and Even Gale, In much peace, Arrived and Anchored In his Last and best Port'.

To what transports of rage Pepys would have been moved if Penn had been ennobled is, fortunately, a matter for speculation. Certainly he never forgave him the trust and admiration that Coventry and the Duke of York felt for him as a great public servant and a great admiral. This vindictiveness reveals itself in the notes he continued to make of gossip alleging Penn's cowardice or incompetence in action. It reveals itself too in the hostility with which he pursued those sea officers who had been connections or protégés of Penn. Luckily for them the Duke of York did not forget his own loyalties and understood, as Pepys whole-heartedly confirms, the business of a Lord High Admiral. The service career of Sir William Poole, offers the best example of these powerful cross-currents.[1]

In this clean sweep of experienced administrators it seems strange that Pepys was not promoted either to a higher position at the Navy Board or to the personal staff of the Lord High Admiral. That Pepys himself felt this is shown by his efforts to secure the appointment of secretary to the Duke of York when the post fell vacant in the summer of 1672. He applied at once to Coventry, who had himself filled the position with such distinction, for his backing. This would gladly have been forthcoming had not a nephew of Coventry's been nominated before there was even time to write a letter. What could an uncle do? Pepys understood his difficulty and simply asked his good offices with his successful rival. He was rewarded by a letter which described him in such terms that he copied a part of it in his own hand.

> How long [wrote Coventry to his agreeable but scapegrace nephew] your relation to the Navy is like to continue I will not take upon me to prognosticke, but I will with confidence say that while it doth continue you may receive more help and learn more of the Navy affairs from him than from any man living.[2]

This apparently humiliating defeat at the hands of a young courtier who knew nothing of the job soon proved itself a fortunate deliverance. The Third Dutch War, engineered by Charles II in collusion with Louis XIV as the first fruits of their secret treaty, recoiled on its maker. At sea the United Provinces ought to have been easy meat for the combined navies of England and France. Yet the cold-blooded act of villainy with which England opened the war, an unprovoked attack on the Dutch Smyrna convoy as it made its way up channel in the spring of 1672, only achieved disgrace at a bitter cost in casualties. Two months later the great De Ruyter caught the allied fleet napping at Solebay and forced the stronger side into a desperate and bloody battle in which Sandwich, among many, lost his life. Even more disastrous for this experiment in *Realpolitik* was the effect of allied success on land. The French army swept all before them: the Dutch, faced with the subjugation offered as terms of peace, overthrew the great leaders of the Republic and turned to the House of Orange to lead the nation once again in a struggle for national existence against the dominant power in Europe. These events awoke swelling echoes in the hearts of God's Englishmen. Once again a small Protestant nation was confronting the Popish Goliath. Once again the Low Countries, that dagger pointed at the heart of England, felt Goliath's fingers closing round them. The fact that the French squadron had not taken the same hammering as the English at Solebay had already provoked a revulsion of feeling against the alliance. With Charles II's Declaration of Indulgence relaxing the penal laws against Roman Catholics and Dissenters in the spring of 1673, the anti-Catholic, anti-French reaction grew more menacing. Not only was the King forced to withdraw the Declaration but the famous Test Act was passed, excluding all but members of the Church of England from civil or military employment. James as Lord High Admiral was the first and most eminent victim of this law. The Admiralty was put into commission and Pepys was appointed Secretary. Had he obtained the post of James's secretary the year before he might have prejudiced his chances. As events were soon to show he was already tarred with the Papist brush. Had not his wife, hardly the discreetest of women, disclosed dangerous leanings? Was not the man always buying foreign books and pictures, some of which to be sure offended Protestant susceptibility? Had not his curiosity and his love of music taken him more than once to hear mass in the Queen's chapel? The age of the Royal Society was also the age of the Popish Plot.

The promotion was of more external than intrinsic importance. Coventry had, as so often, put the matter in a nutshell in the letter just quoted. Wherever Pepys was, be it Navy Board or Admiralty, there was the nerve centre of naval planning and administration. The division of responsibilities between an Admiralty that supplied and controlled commissioned officers and a Navy Board that supplied and controlled everything else was perfectly sensible in an age when the navy was thought of as something one did not need every day, or even every year. But once the idea of a permanent force had been reluctantly accepted the division became ever more pointless until it was finally abolished in the early nineteenth century. What counted was where business was transacted and where decisions were made. To do the one effectively and to base the other on rational grounds bureaucracy is indispensable. Pepys's animating principle bureaucratised his surroundings just as culture put into a glass of milk transforms it into yogurt. During the five years between the wars when he was still at the Navy Office the Lord High Admiral consulted him or, more exactly, was prodded into action by him on matters well beyond his strict province as Clerk of Acts. Pepys reported on the competence of his colleagues, suggested appointments and re-allocation of duties, drew up estimates, planned new construction, was courted by captains and even admirals. He recruited and trained the men who were to run the navy well into the next century. Some, like Hewer, were too closely identified with him to survive his fall. Others like Sotherne and Burchett did not enjoy an untroubled relationship with him. But they all served their administrative apprenticeship under a great master. Creative, omniscient, efficient and formidable Pepys did not need position and title, much as he might desire them. The plain fact was that there was no doing anything in the navy without him.

The change to the Admiralty in 1673 perhaps did more for that institution than it did for Pepys. The Navy Board had had, as we have seen, snug quarters in the city that had survived not only the overturnings of the Commonwealth and the Restoration but the Great Fire. The Admiralty on the other hand inhered in the person of the Lord High Admiral and one or two secretaries. It had no postal address. Pepys's elevation changed all that. Wherever he was, his files, his clerks, his porters and messengers must be too. His fondness for his home in Seething Lane and the time and money he had spent in its embellishment might have led him to bring the business of the Admiralty there. But there had been a fire early in 1673 that had destroyed most of the old Navy Office and had forced him to take lodgings near by. It is possible that this coincidence had some part in determining the place and the manner in which the control of English sea-power was institutionalised. Certainly the active interest of the King in even the minutiae of maritime affairs, so much deplored by Bishop Burnet, exerted a pull up the Thames and away from the City. Official accommodation was ultimately found at Derby House, on the river between Whitehall Palace and Westminster. Pepys began to date his letters from there in January 1674. In the following year Will Hewer established himself at York Buildings just by Inigo Jones's Watergate (still standing) on the other side of Whitehall Palace. It was into these comfortable mansions that Pepys was received when he was hounded from office. When he came into his own again he stayed on with Hewer and transacted a good deal of Admiralty business from the house, even giving it official status by adorning it with the Royal Arms in the pediment and a carved shield containing the anchor of the Lord High Admiral. This in its turn led to an acrimonious correspondence with his successors under William III who claimed that the house was now a Government office and that Pepys must clear out. He didn't, at least not until it suited him to do so. But the point that the Admiralty was now a great Government department that had its own local habitation next door to the King was established.

The King was now Pepys's immediate superior. He did not openly resume the office of Lord High Admiral, of which his brother's tenure had been circumscribed and sometimes overshadowed by his own proprietary interest, but presided in person at the Commission to whom he had in theory delegated his functions. As Michael Lewis has well written:

'Charles was now not only his own First Lord of the Admiralty. He was much more: he was really his own Lord High Admiral, with all that official's powers and perquisites . . . he had gone back through the centuries and reassumed the Crown's original control.'[3] Thus, although Pepys suffered no sea-change in his translation from Navy Board to Admiralty, he did find the potentialities much greater. He was, as he had been before, in the driver's seat: but the car was a new and improved model.

Following his sovereign's example of centralising control he ordered the Navy Board to report weekly to the Admiralty at eight o'clock each Saturday morning. This to us ungodly hour was that at which the Board of Admiralty itself sat on Mondays, Wednesdays and Fridays.[4] The vast bulk of business was routine, often of a minute and sometimes a homely kind, and whatever was decided took executive shape in a letter from Pepys. September 25th, 1673 offers a good representative example of his day-to-day work at the Board. His first letter was to the Navy Board telling them to discharge two smacks that had been commandeered for intelligence purposes. He then writes to encourage the captain of a fireship and to warn the captain of a privateer against expecting the Admiralty to subsidise him without a clear agreement as to the use of the vessel. The captain of a pink is told that the Navy Board will honour his bill for stores taken in at Yarmouth and that he is to lose no time in getting to sea. The captain of an escort vessel for a convoy bound to the Straits hears that his reasons for coming into port without orders have provisionally been accepted but he is to take care to obey the orders of the Commander-in-Chief of the western squadron. The Governor of Plymouth receives the sympathy of the Board at having the returning Virginia fleet driven back and damaged by storms but he will have to wait till the Straits fleet are in before he can have a convoy for Havre. The senior officer of the escort is told that the King will examine his allegations of cowardice against Captain Cotterell when the Dutch attacked the convoy off the coast of Virginia. Another escort captain has his excuse for delay accepted but is urged to return to his station as soon as possible to protect the expected convoy from the Straits. Anthony Deane, the great naval architect now Commissioner at Portsmouth, is warned that the Captains due to form the Court-Martial on the Captain and officers of the *Reserve* have been wind-bound in the Downs. Deane's opinion is therefore requested as to whether the ship is, under these personal tensions, an efficient fighting unit and whether the Captain is an alcoholic. Pepys rounds off the day by telling the master of one dogger that his ship seems to be doing too much of her sea-time in the Downs, and ordering another to discharge two men he has pressed out of a ship that had the Duke of York's protection for bringing stone from Portland for the public buildings of London.

Some of these raps on the knuckle evidently originate from Pepys himself, without benefit of the Board's assistance. But then as now it is perennially astonishing to what humble and insignificant detail the most august authority will descend. Can the King really have been interested in the choice of a cook or a carpenter for a fifth-rate? Yet Pepys insists that the warrant must have his approval. When Captain Roome Coyle's wife complained to the Board of her husband's ill-treatment and asked for an allotment out of his pay he was ordered to appear before them and answer to the King in person. The Royal Navy had, in those days, some of the characteristics of a family firm. Too many in Pepys's view. The King's control over commissions and appointments often, through a lazy pretence to good nature, favoured the incompetent and the fashionable. His frivolous use of warships, equipped and manned at great expense, to fetch home a present of wine instead of paying the freight charges infuriated Pepys both as an administrator and as an accountant.[5] All this was the more exasperating since Pepys very soon realised and for the rest of his life freely acknowledged that Charles 'best understands the business of the sea of any prince the world ever had'.[6] Why then was he ready to stand with his arms folded, imperturbably watching fools make a hash of naval affairs even to the extent of putting England's sea-power at risk? Pepys could not have kept quiet in his place for any consideration. His itch to regulate and to teach, above all the creative ordering instinct of the artist, would have been too strong. He could diagnose the strange passivity of the King so well hit off in Halifax's character: 'It was resolved generally by others, whom he should have in his Arms, as well as whom he should have in his Councils. Of a Man who was so capable of choosing, he chose as seldom as any Man that ever lived.'[7] But, unlike Halifax, he could not understand it.

The tone of his Admiralty letters, preserved in fourteen folio volumes in the Pepys Library, is sharp and shrewd but not unkindly. He inquires, he reproves, he raps out orders, but he also commends and sympathises. No one understood better the timely use of what he calls 'a letter of civility'. Tact, mastery of detail, energy, promptitude, all the virtues of

a great manager are much in evidence. But beyond and behind this scin-
tillating display of executive talent was a searching, generalising, codifying
intelligence: the omnivorous reader, the Fellow of the Royal Society, the
historian and the aesthete. What was the function of the navy? Did its
organisation correspond to its purposes? Could it do its job better or
cheaper? Who ought to ask these questions and who was qualified to
answer them? Pepys approached the large problems with the same intellectual fearlessness, the same confidence that they would yield to rational
analysis, that he had brought in his early days at the Navy Board to matters
hitherto considered as belonging to the mystery of the shipwright or the
seaman. But even when immersed in the calculations of the commodity
market he had never slipped into a technocrat's view of the service. It
was men first and last that he was judging and assessing.

The navy as it was and the ideas Pepys had of remodelling it demand a
separate chapter. Before embarking on it something must be said of his own
altered circumstances as a rich widower, eminent in the public service and
in the friendship of the most distinguished men of his time. Circumstances is often genteel long-hand for money. Pepys's translation to the
Admiralty put him well above the sordid shifts to which he had resorted
in his earlier days at the Navy Office. His salary rose from £350 to £500,
but that was a trivial improvement. What really brought in the cash – and
hard cash too since it did not come from the public revenue – was the
customary payment of twenty-five shillings for each pass granted to a ship
trading with the Mediterranean. Since the number in any year ran well
into four figures this was a handsome income in itself. Pepys whose estimates of his own financial affairs are conceived in the pessimistic spirit
of a man preparing a valuation for probate admits to a thousand which
would bring in £1,250. The real figure was probably three or four times
as much. And Tangier if no longer the best flower in so thriving a garden
was still blooming. Promotion enabled a man to provide for his connections. Pepys's surviving brother John, the unbeneficed parson whose
spiteful letters had given such offence, was made joint Clerk of the Acts
with Thomas Hayter one of the best and most faithful of Pepys's assistants. Elizabeth's brother Balty, appointed Muster-Master at Deal on the
strength of his performance in the earlier Dutch War added the responsibility of Deputy Commissioner for the Sick and Wounded during the
third one. There is no more eloquent testimony to the effect of knowing
that Pepys had his eye on one than the fact that these two dubious figures
discharged their duties at least satisfactorily. The rest of the family were
settled on the small estate at Brampton.

What of Pepys's domestic arrangements? The comfort and order of his

new quarters may be easily imagined. Although the fire at the Navy Office
had destroyed part of his collection of prints the bulk of his library survived as did the famous presses that the joiner had built to his own
specification. The lady who presided over the household was the young
daughter of a city neighbour, Mary Skinner. That their relationship was
close, tender and enduring is evident from the rest of his life. Why they
did not marry is still a mystery and was, at first, a cause of bitter exchanges
with her family. Had it something to do with the long-standing family
friendship with that dangerous figure John Milton? The sonnet addressed
to Mr. Cyriack Skinner, Mary's uncle, was first published in the 1673
edition of the *Poems** and one of her brothers, Daniel, was the poet's last
amanuensis. Towards the end of 1676 Pepys was horrified to hear that the
young man whom he had recommended to the English ambassador at
Nimwegen was making arrangements with the great Dutch publishing
house of Elzevier to bring out a posthumous edition of some political
and theological writings that Milton had entrusted to him. Sir Joseph
Williamson, a don turned civil servant who was now Secretary of State,
gobbled with fury at the news. Skinner abandoned the project with
the same airy insouciance he had shown in initiating it, cheerfully
handing over the last manifestoes of the great Republican to the King's
agents.

> . . . invocato Deo never had I the least thought of prejudicing either
> King or State, being infinitely loyall to one and mighty zealous for the
> other, all the concerns that ever I had with Milton or his works being
> risen from a foolish yet plausible ambition to learning.[8]

Milton is one of the two contemporary writers of genius – Bunyan is the
other – virtually unrepresented in the Pepys Library.† His name is not
so much as mentioned in the Diary. Some have seized on this as confirming
the shallowness of taste they find in his judgments of books and plays.
'Il restera à la porte du seul poème epique de l'Angleterre; Milton jouait de
l'orgue dans une cathédrale inaccessible.'[9] To those who do not find it
necessary to pity Pepys's sensibility a more obvious explanation suggests
itself: that he found Milton's doctrines pernicious and subversive. To

---

* The even more alarming 'To Mr. Cyriack Skinner upon his blindness', in which
Milton glories in having sacrificed his eyesight 'In libertyes defence', remained unpublished
until 1694.

† Some minor works of Milton and a biography of him appear in the catalogue. *Paradise
Lost*, like *The Pilgrim's Progress*, is conspicuous by its absence. Bunyan is, however, included
in the collection of portraits.

admire or to possess his books might, to a servant of Charles II's Government, seem rash or improper. Pepys had passed his formative years in an age of revolution; he was to prove entirely right if he thought that the nasty political habits then acquired, denunciation, witch-hunts, judicial murder, were likely to reappear.

To marry into the Milton circle might be imprudent. But was it not, by Pepys's standards, sluttish to live openly with a woman? Lord Brouncker, his colleague and neighbour at the Navy Office, is constantly censured in the Diary for this very reason. This is one of the puzzles of Pepys's life — another is why he was never knighted. Certainly Mary Skinner was accepted by close friends like Evelyn as though she were his wife: and Robert Hooke, the brilliant scientist and architect, who was only a slight acquaintance, actually refers to her as Mrs. Pepys in his Diary.[10] The disparity in age made it natural for Pepys to call her as she comforted his deathbed his 'dear child': some of the letters of his last years are written in her hand and her none too literate spelling. She was not, in his eyes or her own, his equal. Perhaps that was one reason why the relationship was so tranquil. In any case Pepys was ripening and mellowing. The course of his life was less combative and more sedate. No man was ever more punctilious in matching his style to his stage in life. Perhaps the bust of Elizabeth, her head turned in laughter towards the Navy Office pew in St. Olave's, offers the best comment on his decision not to marry again.

Her death freed his social life from the embarrassments so often recorded in the Diary. His remaining years at the Navy Office and his establishment at Derby House saw the widening and deepening of friendships begun at Whitehall or at the Royal Society with men like Evelyn, Sir Robert Southwell, Sir William Petty or Sir Christopher Wren, and with the haute bourgeoisie of the City. He was a liveryman of the Clothworkers' Company (Master in 1677); he was elected an Elder Brother of Trinity House in 1672.

His social, professional and intellectual life interpenetrated each other. Evelyn was not only the greatest connoisseur of his time but a man whose political judgment and executive abilities were highly valued. His performance as Commissioner for the Sick and Wounded earned Pepys's respect. The King encouraged him to write the history of the Dutch Wars 'enjoyning me to make it a little keene, for that the Hollanders had very unhandsomely abused him, in their pictures, books & libells etc'.[11] On February 19th, 1671, he records 'this day dined with me Mr Surveyor Dr. Chr: Wren, Mr Pepys, Clerk of the Acts, two extraordinary ingenious, and knowing persons, and other friends; I carried them to see the piece of Carving which I had recommended to the King'.[12] This was by Grinling Gibbons whom Evelyn had discovered copying a Crucifix from a Tintoretto cartoon in a country cottage. Here, surely, is the genesis of Gibbons' magnificent carving of the Eye in Glory, the showpiece of the famous Boardroom at the Admiralty, a room known to Nelson and to Churchill but to which Pepys can have been present only in spirit. There is no telling where Evelyn will crop up. His expert knowledge of dendrology was extremely useful to Pepys in his efforts to plan the future timber supplies of the navy.

Sir William Petty's versatility has already been mentioned. He had begun life as a ship's boy but was forced to abandon the sea because his short-sight made him dangerous as a look-out. His skill as an economist and statistician made his conversation especially valuable to the administration of the largest spending department in government. His plans for building a double-bottom boat, though ultimately unproductive, received much practical encouragement from Pepys. Similarly Sir Robert Southwell, Petty's great friend, mixed the speculative life of the Royal Society with a successful career as a diplomat and civil servant. Both men were the kind of people one met dining at the Houblons. And such men profited in one way and another from their association with Pepys. Southwell for instance found a valuable ally to protect his family's interest in the victualling contract at Kinsale, said to be the most lucrative of the home stations.[13] The Houblons in their turn provided foreign and commercial intelligence besides letting the Secretary of the Admiralty know more about the activities of H.M. ships in the Mediterranean than he could glean from the dispatches and journals of their captains. The real task of the navy as Pepys saw it was to promote and protect English seaborne trade. Claims to the sovereignty of the sea and the right of salute to the flag were doctrines of which he became increasingly sceptical. City merchants, not courtiers, lawyers or politicians, were the people with whom he preferred to discuss naval policy.

The Third Dutch War, during which he attained the Secretaryship, was, by these standards, a misuse of sea-power. Its pretext was an assertion of the sovereignty of the sea so grotesque as to have embarrassed anyone except Charles II who put it forward or Sir George Downing who was sent to The Hague to make sure it became a *casus belli*. John Evelyn condemned it in scathing terms and is one of the many witnesses to Sandwich's double conviction that the war was a disaster and that it would cost him his life. His flagship was burnt to the waterline at Solebay and his body was afterwards found at sea. Pepys was one of the six who attended the coffin carrying the Mountagu bannerols at the state funeral in Westminster Abbey. Solebay was the end of an era in the Restoration navy. It was the last battle at which James, Duke of York commanded in chief 'most pleasant when the great shot are thundering about his ears'. The old flagmen of the earlier war had had their day. Rupert, Harman, Spragge, Kempthorne and Jordan were to serve, some to lose their lives in the murderous battles of 1673 when so little was achieved at so high a cost. But the admirals with whom Pepys was to deal were for the most part men he had first known as Captains and Lieutenants. In the case of Rupert it was perhaps as well. He had growled at Pepys's remarks about the condition of his fleet in 1666. How long would he have been content to be addressed in such firm no-nonsense tones as this?

... And further we do expect to receive from you advice of your haveing sent away the ships for the westerne squadron or others in their roome, the necessity of secureing that coast calling for their dispatch thither, the Virginia fleete being dayly lookt for home.[14]

Pepys knew that he had the whip hand. Charles had never forgiven Rupert for his tiresome insistence on honouring debts instead of relieving his penniless exile with the money he had realised on winding up the affairs of the Royalist navy in 1653.

In November 1673 Pepys was elected M.P. for Castle Rising. The support of the King and the Duke turned the scale with the borough's patron, Lord Howard, later Earl of Norwich and Duke of Norfolk, whom Pepys had already solicited unsuccessfully for an earlier vacancy. Even so the election was contested and the defeated candidate carried the war into the House of Commons, challenging the validity of Pepys's right to sit on the grounds that he was a Papist and that Lord Howard, a known Papist, had used improper influence. The petition was supported by the partisans of Lord Shaftesbury, dismissed from office in the same month as Pepys entered Parliament. Shaftesbury himself, whom Pepys had known as a connection of Sandwich's for twenty years and as a Prize Commissioner in the Second Dutch War, was quoted as having seen an altar and a crucifix in Pepys's house in Seething Lane. Pepys, as might be expected, furiously denied these and similar allegations. A Committee was appointed to investigate. In the strong tide of anti-Catholic emotion then running Pepys was lucky that his old and fearless friend Sir William Coventry was one of its three members. The charges crumbled. Most witnesses flatly denied having laid the information alleged: and even Shaftesbury, turning and twisting with well-bred effrontery, left nothing but a smear. In such times a smear is all that is asked or desired. It was the prorogation

of the House, not the demolition of the evidence, that saved Pepys from
expulsion.

In spite of the brilliant début defending the Navy Office before a
committee of the whole House six years before he entered it as a member,
Pepys was not a conspicuous success in Parliament. In his first encounter
he had been lucky to get away without serious damage. As it was the taint
of Catholicism was already successfully planted on him. And in spite of
Lord Howard's noble patronage the bill he had to foot was immense.
£700. Even that, as it turned out at the next election, did not buy security
of tenure. He had wanted to enter the house as he said in a letter to
Henry Savile, Coventry's nephew who had obtained the secretaryship
Pepys had coveted the year before:

> . . . not so much, I do assure you, out of any ambition, as the just
> consideration of those opportunities it might give me of doing His
> Majesty and Royal Highness better service in the station I am now in:
> having too many instances before me of the prejudices and dis-
> advantages the affairs of the Admiralty and Navy, and the King's
> service in both, have fallen into and with difficulty been afterwards
> delivered from, for want of timely remedy, which a few hands in
> Parliament thoroughly conversant in these affairs, might with ease
> enough have administered.[15]

Give or take a parenthesis, this is to say that a great spending department
ought to have an expert to represent it in the Commons. In this respect
Pepys achieved a good deal, notably in driving through his great naval
construction programme of 1677 'the thirty new ships'. But he was not
by temperament a House of Commons man. He preferred hierarchy to
equality, order to rough-and-tumble, the conversation of learned men to
the upper-cuts of debate. He could triumph as a virtuoso but he had not
always at command the steady nerve and even temper that made a man
like Coventry so effective in the Long Parliament of the Restoration.
Indeed on the negative side his fellow-members were often irritated by
his punditry.

In spite of this Pepys had many of the requirements for success in
Parliamentary politics, a ready tongue, a quick mind, astuteness in judging
people and tact in handling them. What he had not, in any form, was the
instinct of the games player. He despised gambling and was revolted by
the cruel sports of his contemporaries. Politics is a game, however deadly,
however earnest, and perhaps in each age takes some of its colour from the
prevailing idiom of play. The man who would rather prove himself

right than win a point is at a disadvantage. Such, certainly, was Pepys. He knew that he knew more about the navy than anyone else. He had a programme of action and an administrative machine of his own design and building with which to carry it out. In the prime of life, at the height of his powers, he had been given somewhere to stand and he would move the world.

16

Pepys and the sea officers

For posterity Pepys's literary fame rests on a book that none of his contemporaries knew that he had written. For his friends, ironically, it grew on a book he never wrote: but which, according to Evelyn, 'he had for divers years under his hand the History of the Navy, or, *Navalia* (as he call'd it).'[1] Like Lord Acton's *History of Freedom* it remains one of the unexecuted masterpieces of English historiography. The site was laid out, the materials bought (they still form the most important single part of the Pepys Library) but the book was not written. Had it been we should, for a certainty, have had a lucid analysis and an exact definition of what its author conceived the functions of the navy to be. In its absence a clumsier hand must do what it can with the edged tools of his letters, journals, notes and memoranda.

Pepys saw the navy, as he saw many things, in two lights. First in its immediate application, a national force to defend national interests at sea, and second as part of the general scheme of civilisation, that higher and nobler concept that has in different ages been invoked under such different names as Christendom, Reason, Progress or Humanity. The priority of the first, defence against invasion, protection of trade, was of course absolute; but that does not mean that the second was negligible. Exploration and hydrography are two of the most obvious ways in which a navy can serve the general good of mankind. In both of these fields

Pepys was energetic in promoting enterprise and in publishing the results to the world at large. He was aware of the arguments and the mentality that were in the fullness of time to produce the Official Secrets Act and jealous of their encroachment. He noted with approval the self-confidence of the French in publishing the *Neptune François*, a magnificent collection of charts of their own coast, at the very height of a war against the English and the Dutch.[2] The charts of the Straits of Magellan that Sir John Narbrough drew on his voyage to the South Sea in 1669–70 are dedicated to Pepys, whose name was at the same time given to an island in the South Atlantic. Alas for the mutability of things: the island is no longer there; probably it never was; an error in navigation may have invested one of the Falkland Islands with undeserved dignity. As master's mate Narbrough had with him John Wood, assisted by Greenville Collins, both as Captains to leave their names in the history of exploration and hydrography. In 1676 Wood commanded the *Speedwell* in an attempt to discover the North-East passage. Collins sailed with him as master and preserved his notes and observations when she was lost on the coast of Novaya Zemlya. Pepys had devoted much care and time to the preparations for this expedition in which the Royal Society was as much interested as the Royal Navy. There were other considerations too. The *Speedwell*, fortunately for her company who would otherwise have frozen or starved to death, was accompanied by the *Prosperous* pink, freighted with a cargo for trading on the coast of Tartary or Japan. Pepys was one of the eight adventurers, headed by the Duke of York, who had a share in her.

Narbrough's and Wood's voyages are the earliest examples of exploration directly commissioned by the Admiralty and conducted by naval officers in naval ships. Pepys had been instrumental in opening the line that leads to Cook and Scott. Greenville Collins left as his monument the magnificent folio *Great Britain's Coasting Pilot* (1693) that went into edition after edition for a century after its first publication.[3] All three men found Pepys a steady friend to their careers.

It would certainly be in character, with his love of order and his concern for justice, to credit him with a vision of the navy as the upholder of *Pax Britannica*, 'a security for such as pass on the seas upon their lawful occasions'. But the navy with which he had to do was too puny to undertake so vast a responsibility. It could be argued that the Mediterranean policy which he and his patron Sandwich had always championed led in this direction, since it involved maintaining a base and a permanent force to keep the North African pirates from having things all their own way. This was the *raison d'être* of Tangier. After Tangier had been abandoned

Pepys turned to Gibraltar, the original choice of Cromwell and Sandwich. Early in 1686 Jonathan Gauden, the Victualler's son, was sent out there with instructions from Pepys to obtain what base facilities he could, if necessary by bribing the Spanish Governor.[4]

The Barbary ports of North Africa, Algiers and Tripoli within the Straits and Sallee outside them, were the wasps that stung England into sea-power. It had been their intolerable intrusions into the channel, not only seizing ships but dragging off terrified Devon villagers into slavery, that had brought the ship-money fleets of Charles I into being. From there the line to the Commonwealth navy runs straight and true. Cromwell's use of this instrument, 'the brave things he did and made all the neighbour princes fear him', let the genie out of the bottle. A permanent, professional navy, inherently probable since the emergence of the gunned warship in the sixteenth century, had come to stay. In Pepys's words:

> What could the naval strength of this nation be when the Crown had no other force at sea in the case of invasion than the command of what ships and stores it could find from the merchants? And what would that do at this day, whatever it did then? And therein is our policy quite altered, our neighbours being so much stronger than before, and there being quite a different use and service for men-of-war now than there was then, when merchants' vessels and those of war were the same.[5]

The behaviour of the European powers, Spain, France and Holland, rapidly became more reasonable when it was clear that England was able to defend her growing share of sea-borne trade, into the Mediterranean, down the African coast and across the Atlantic, by a professional navy. The Barbary ports had nothing to gain from being reasonable: they lived by piracy and holding poor sailors to ransom. An occasional punitive expedition such as Blake's in 1655 or Narbrough's in 1677 might induce a brief spell of law-abiding conduct, but, like the tribesmen on the North-West Frontier, they did not wish to enter the comity of nations. Thus all through Pepys's time even when England was not at war some naval force, often a sizeable fleet, was usually present in the western Mediterranean.

To maintain a squadron on a foreign station presented problems of finance, supply and manning. But these, to Pepys, were child's play compared with the problem of discipline. What was the use of keeping ships out there if the Captains did not do what they were told and if the Admiralty did not know even where its ships would be? If one had to sum up the difference between Pepys's time at the Navy Office and his years at the Admiralty, in a phrase, one could say that at the first he was always complaining that there was no money and at the second that there was no discipline. And by that he meant the Captains. 'I dread not the men: it is the indiscreet, licentious conversation of the officers which produces all our ills'. St. Vincent's words after the great mutinies of 1797 express Pepys's apprehensions of a century and a quarter earlier. All that the men needed was to be properly fed and paid. The only difficulty there was getting hold of the money. But the officers – there were problems there to occupy Pepys for the whole of his professional life and to reflect on during a long retirement.

The heart of the matter lay in the distinction so often drawn by Pepys himself between the Gentlemen and the Tarpaulins. The Gentlemen, as we have seen, get the rough edge of his tongue: 'the gentlemen captains who undid all . . .' is a theme that approaches monotony. Yet in his *Naval Minutes*, those pithy, darting sentences that condense a lifetime's reflection, it transpires that Pepys's considered criticism of the officer structure is not that it is too aristocratic but that it is not aristocratic enough. Socially the sea is a despised profession:

Have any of our Heralds allowed in express words the seamen for a gentleman? Observe the maliciousness of our English proverb towards the service of the sea, viz. that the sea and the gallows refused nobody. Which is verified too much in our practice of sending none thither but the vicious or poor. And where a merchant or seaman gets an estate, he either out of pride or some other less satisfactory reason seldom brings up a son to his own trade, but advances him in the Law, the Court, the University, or disposes of him some otherwise than to the sea; whereas you shall have lawyers and gownmen of all sorts, soldiers and courtiers, continue their trades from father to son for many generations, seldom assigning any to the sea but in the cases above mentioned. And it was the Rebellion and necessity that made seamen of the King and Duke.[6]

In a comparison of genius he cites the reinforcement of the already formidable battery of game laws 'while how few and imperfect are all that I can find towards the obtaining any discipline or even securing our ordinary trade at sea.'[7] Once the aristocracy could be induced to identify themselves with the navy they would exert their influence and power on its behalf. Pepys was anxious to welcome them in, provided they were serious about their profession. Recommending a Reformado, or supernumerary officer serving as ship's company, to the Captain of the *Reserve* he wrote:

He is ye first that I have interested myself so far for, and I am apt to believe may be ye only one for whom I shall concern myself in that kind: nor should I have done it for him but for ye assurance I have from himself and his friends of his resolucon to betake himself most strictly to ye Duty and labor of a Seaman . . .'[8]

What he did not want and all too often got was '. . . land-commanders . . . pestering and annoying the ships with their hen-coops etc.'[9]

That Pepys himself was without social prejudice seems clear from the impartiality with which he was attacked. He records with amusement that in the Parliamentary furore of the Popish Plot, Colonel Birch, an old Commonwealthsman attacked him for favouring gentlemen and cavaliers at the expense of the old salts who had learned their trade under Blake and Penn.[10] The preference that he and Coventry repeatedly expressed for the old Cromwellian commanders had nothing to do with their social origins: it was a rational, unbiased recognition of their superiority in seamanship, experience and discipline. The same critical eye discerned the limitations of the Tarpaulin considered as a type. Admirable as private captains or as junior flag officers, stout fellows who would knock it out yardarm to yardarm as long as their ships would swim, punctual, obedient and faithful to their duty, were not their very virtues inimical to the intellectual detachment, the originality, the flair that distinguishes the grand chef from the bon ordinaire? It was this perhaps that Pepys had in mind when he wrote of Sandwich, 'The King, Duke and he the most mathematick Admirals England ever had.'[11] What is quite certain is that Pepys believed that a trained mind could master the lore and the skills of the Tarpaulin and the shipwright;[12] like Drake he would have the gentleman to haul and draw with the mariner and the mariner with the gentleman. A professional himself, he did not want to settle for anything less than professionalism in the sea officers.

In his second tenure of the Secretaryship he had in James II a master who was, for all his crudity and want of judgment, straightforward and loyal to his subordinates. Charles II was none of these things. Intelligent, devious, charming, amused at the jokes his courtiers made to his face about his untrustworthiness, he was the last man to stiffen the disciplinary backbone of the service. Pepys in attempting a course that was certain to make him powerful enemies and might at any time be disowned showed courage of a high order. Again, though he makes no parade of it, he knew and prided himself on the risk he was taking. Like Danby he refused to take out the normal political life insurance of a Royal pardon which could be pleaded as a bar to Parliamentary vengeance.[13] Danby had been Joint

Treasurer of the Navy from 1668, subsequently holding the office alone from 1671 till his elevation to the Lord Treasureship in 1673. Pepys respected him as a colleague. There are, particularly at this stage, similarities in their careers and their objectives and both were to be struck down in the Popish Plot. Both men disdained an easy popularity. The language in which Pepys recalled an errant captain to his duty was not that in which the gentry were used to being addressed by the son of a tailor. Indeed given the conventions of military and naval service hitherto prevailing it was inevitable that they should feel resentful and insulted. But it was precisely the conventions that Pepys wanted to change.

The indiscipline of the Captains took many forms. Absence without leave was the speciality of Captain Preistman whom Pepys 'spied . . . at a distance sauntering up and down Covent Garden', when he and his ship ought to have been in Portsmouth. That was on July 9th, 1675. Pepys, double-shotting his guns, found that he had brought his ship into the river without orders, no doubt to facilitate access to the bright lights. On July 19th he fired his broadside. But Captain Preistman was unsinkable. In spite of repeated indiscipline he was given command after command. Although a favourite of both Charles and James he survived the Revolution. Pepys's last sardonic reference to him shows him for five weeks in the company of his own successor as Secretary of the Admiralty taking the waters at Tunbridge Wells, at the height of King William's war.[14]

Loitering in port was even more common, particularly when the port was an agreeable one (Leghorn was a great favourite on the Mediterranean station: and the ships in the West Indies sometimes passed several months without putting to sea). With what glee Pepys must have seized on the dereliction of Penn's kinsman, Sir Richard Rooth, in the *Adventure*. '. . . Of the whole 21 months which he was abroad [May 1675–Jan. 1677] beeing sent particularly to attend to the services of Sally . . . he spent only 4 months on that service, 13 months in port and the rest on other service . . . 43 days in Cadiz when ordered not to spend above 6' etc. etc.[15] The practice variously known as 'freight' or 'good voyages' was, in Pepys's eyes, the most pernicious of all. This was a constructive and highly profitable abuse of a practice permitted, even discreetly encouraged, by the Admiralty down to the beginning of the twentieth century. If a warship was under orders for a particular voyage her captain was entitled to take on board such freight or more often bullion as he thought consistent with maintaining the sea-worthiness and efficiency of his ship. In an age when the sea teemed with pirates and privateers this was a limited form of commerce protection that yielded a useful return:

officially the captain was allowed to charge one per cent of the value of the cargo but the rate was often much higher since this kind of regulation was very difficult to enforce. In the Mediterranean and on more distant stations captains grew adept at concocting excuses for taking their ships on voyages that offered this traffic. 'Good voyages' as they were called were a red rag to Pepys; perhaps it was the use of the word 'good' about which he can hardly control his sarcasm. Their danger lay in dissolving a fleet into so many floating strongrooms plying for private charter. As he found when he went out to Tangier in 1683 it was often impossible to tell where any ship was going to be when.

Indiscipline worked upwards and downwards. Captains disobeyed the orders of their flag officers, sometimes to the extent of refusing action or even shamefully surrendering without a fight. In return the lieutenants either disputed their captain's authority or the officers were split into factions. The patient investigation of these collisions of personality took up an infinity of time. What sort of a service do they reveal? In July 1678 Pepys ordered the convening of a court-martial to 'examine matters in difference' between Captain Roydon of the *Sweepstakes* (a fourth-rate) and his Lieutenant, George Aylmer, 'the said Lieutenant haveing (either with or without cause) absented himself for several months from his shippe'.[16] The proceedings suggest how richly eccentricity could luxuriate aboard a seventeenth-century man of war.

At the end of October 1677 the *Sweepstakes* was at anchor off Kinsale. At one o'clock in the morning her Captain came aboard 'crying a huge storme, calling for the Master, bidding I should be Caled and if I did not Com I should be dragued out. A Rogue! What! Not come and save ye King's ship?' The calmness of the weather contrasted with the excitement of the commanding officer. He continued in this state for several days, abusing his Lieutenant and striking him with his cane. Aylmer therefore applied to the Duke of Ormonde the Lord-Lieutenant at Dublin Castle for permission to come ashore 'by reason of his Captain's usage'. This was granted pending further directions from England. Roydon countered this version of events by asserting that Aylmer was constantly absent from his duty and that he boasted that he had come up from being a footman.

The spiritual state of the vessel appears to have been no happier than the temporal. When the ship had been in Portsmouth the chaplain George Bradford had a run ashore with the Corporal of Marines. While they were drinking and playing cards 'my Corporall found that my Chaplin put the bent on him'. Taxed with this the enraged cleric exploded with, 'God Damn him and sinck him: soe upon that the said Corp. went to leave him, the Chaplin ketching hold of him and called for six canns of beer more and swore by God that he should take part of that beer and pay sheere of the reckning . . .'

In Ireland his conduct was even less edifying:

At Dublin the said Chaplin being drinking and ranting with the Collegeants and having dranck soe much that he took off his clothes and swearing God Damn Him he was a man of warr: soe that the people had much adoe to gett him into the house and afterward did gett from them and leapt over the wall and tore his shirt almost from his back . . .

At Carrickfergus the minister complained to the Captain:

. . . that he could not be at peace for my Chaplin being there a-catterwoolding till twelve or one o'clock in the morning with his wife . . . they coming both together dressing and undressing one another in an Antick manner . . .

Mr. Bradford was dismissed the service and Captain Roydon relieved of his command. Next year when Pepys was a victim of the Popish mania Roydon did his best to get his own back by claiming that he had been dismissed for saying that his Lieutenant was a Papist. It seems most improbable that he was, as he was continuously employed throughout the high tide of anti-Catholic hysteria. And the allegation that he had been a footman* was perhaps Roydon's way of expressing his resentment at Aylmer's having enjoyed the favour of aristocratic patronage.

Out of material such as this Pepys set about constructing a profession. It is perhaps possible to detect in the account given of life aboard the *Sweepstakes* the 'us' and 'them' division in the form characteristic of the late seventeenth century both in Parliament — Court versus Country — and on the stage — the sophisticates of London against the rural booby squires. Captain Roydon, one feels sure, would not have applied to the Duke of Ormonde in Dublin Castle: and if he had the butler would have shown him the door. Divisions in any society outlive their original causes and nourish themselves on fresh issues. At the Restoration a gentleman officer was by definition a cavalier. Thus by an easy progression the Tarpaulins become to some extent identified with the Country party, and the faction fights of politics are domesticated in the navy. The Revolution of 1688 by changing the parties round only strengthened a tradition that was not entirely extinguished until the two world wars of our own century.

* See p. 282.

The same pattern can be discerned in another row that took up the best part of James II's reign (October 1685–January 1688) and has left seventy-six folio pages of documentation among Pepys's papers in the Bodleian.[17] In an altercation with Mr. Trevor, the purser of the *Suffolk*, Captain Vittells, the Master Attendant at Chatham broke a boat-hook over his head. There are sworn statements before magistrates, doctors' certificates, and every conceivable kind of written evidence relevant and irrelevant. But once again there is the smell of faction, social, political and religious. All the standing officers of the yard – Tarpaulins by definition – swear in Vittells's defence that Trevor was always ashore and never did his job, while Trevor throws into the scale certificates of his religious orthodoxy attested by the Dean of Rochester. The fact of the assault was not denied so Pepys and Lord Dartmouth closed the matter by ordering Vittells to pay the purser £50 in five quarterly instalments.

Pepys was no friend to doctrinal inquisitions. He had noted as a young man how easily the fellows of his college conformed to the ideology required of them and he carried out the injunctions of the Test Act without enthusiasm.[18] Neither personal honour nor professional competence, the two things that mattered in a sea officer, could be guaranteed by such methods. If there were to be examinations, let them be professional ones. As to character, aspiring officers should be made to serve a proper apprenticeship and to produce their captain's reports on their behaviour. Above all to encourage literate and orderly habits every officer should be required to keep a journal. This was the three-pronged strategy by which Pepys hoped to eliminate the stubborn inarticulacy of the Tarpaulin and the go-as-you-please dilettantism of the Gentleman, infusing both of them, for good measure, with a tincture of the Royal Society. The great triumph of this policy, the cornerstone, ever since, of the officer structure of the Royal Navy, was the introduction of the examination for the rank of Lieutenant in 1677. Like the introduction of a driving test on the roads or the abolition of purchase in the army this was the kind of measure that people may resist but which they will never dare to rescind. Had Pepys died of a heart attack on the day after it had been accepted he would still tower above any rival as the radical reformer, the remodeller of the naval profession. He had introduced a principle that must sooner or later carry all before it. No newcomer to the service after December 1677 was going to be allowed to hold a Lieutenant's commission, much less a Captain's, who had not satisfied the stringent requirements which Pepys had, at the Admiralty's invitation, defined. A candidate presenting himself for 'a solemn examination' at the Navy Board of 'his ability to judge of and perform the duty of an able seaman and a midshipman and his having attained to a sufficient degree of knowledge in the theory of navigation capacitating him thereto' by three senior officers including a flag officer and a commander of a first- or second-rate had first of all to produce evidence of three years' service at sea, of which one year at least must have been as a midshipman. He had to produce certificates from his commanding officers as to his 'sobriety, diligence, obedience to order and application to the study and practice of the art of navigation' and he must be at least twenty years of age. This last provision was often bent in the next century: Nelson was a captain at the age of twenty and no one thought this anything out of the way: but the rest of this rigorous code was generally observed. In Pepys's time it certainly was: only a few months after its adoption he was rubbing his hands:

. . . I thank God we have not half the throng of those of the bastard breed pressing for employments which we heretofore used to be troubled with, they being conscious of their inability to pass this examination, and know it to be to no purpose now to solicit for employments till they have done it.[19]

The smoothness and speed with which this major reform was carried through illustrates both Pepys's opportunism and his ability to bide his time. The initiation of the policy, so skilfully camouflaged as to conceal its real outlines, can be traced to November 1674. On the 14th of that month Pepys at a Board meeting drew attention to a dangerous anomaly. By custom sixth-rates did not, like larger vessels, carry a master. Since the captain was expected to discharge this function it seemed sensible to lay it down that before a man could be appointed to command a sixth-rate he must produce a certificate of competence from Trinity House. The agenda was huge: Pepys raised the point after they had already been sitting for some time and still had a lot of business to get through. In any case it seemed obvious common sense. Everyone agreed and they sped on to discuss the generous offer of the Genoese Republic to present the King with a galley for Tangier. There the matter rested for close on three years when Pepys raised another dangerous anomaly arising out of the first. What was the form when a man who had previously commanded one of the higher rates (and there enjoyed the services of a master) found himself appointed to a sixth-rate, which did not carry one? In logic should not such an officer submit himself to an examination in seamanship and navigation by the Brethren of Trinity House? The point was not merely academic since Captain Preistman, that ornament to the service, finding himself in this situation had employed a master and had left the Admiralty to pay his wages. The Duke of York was present at this meeting of the Board from membership of which he was disabled by his Catholicism and clearly added his voice to the general support for Pepys's view. Indeed he went further and deplored the inadequate standards in these matters among the 'young gentlemen with pretensions to lieutenancies'. Could not Trinity House examine them while they were about it? Or the Navy Board? Or both? It is hard to believe that Pepys had not planted these questions. Sir John Narbrough's complaints from the Mediterranean of the deficiencies of his lieutenants certainly reinforced them.

Pepys was invited to prepare a draft of the duties of a lieutenant and to propose a suitable method of examination. On December 1st he produced his scheme which was approved except that Rupert and Lord Ossory argued that the duty of an ordinary midshipman was 'a service beneath the quality of a gentleman to go through'. This particular was referred to a special committee consisting of the Principal Officers of the Navy Board and a distinguished list of senior commanders, both Tarpaulins and Gentlemen. A week later they all turned up at the Board meeting and were so emphatic in their repudiation of the social slur detected by Rupert that they delegated Legge, the future Lord Dartmouth, a gentleman of the gentlemen, to digest their reasons. These the Board found

. . . so convincing that not one word was afterwards urged in the opposition . . . saving this question – whether he [Legge] did ever perform one year's midshipmanship before he pretended to the office of lieutenant? To which he answering *No*, but that it had cost him many an aching head and heart since to make up the want of it, that point was unanimously RESOLVED on . . .[20]

Describing the scene Pepys alludes to the attendance of 'several commanders, both gentlemen and others, which distinction I am both ashamed and afflicted to mention, and should be more, but that among other good ends of what I am now doing the removing of that distinction will be one'.[21] This is the note of integrity, not simply in the sense of honesty but in the sense of concerting moral, intellectual and practical concern, that sounds so insistently through Pepys's later life. He has outgrown the sleaziness of the deals with Captain Cocke and Sir William Warren. The standards of Sir William Coventry and John Evelyn have become natural to him.

To those rash enough to offer a bribe for place or promotion the answer was stunned and stunning.[22] Even more strait-laced by the accepted notions of the time was his attitude towards nepotism. To appoint a relation, a friend's son, even a friend's nominee, to a vacancy was perfectly proper. He had brought his brother John into the Navy Office, Balty into his place at Deal, and was ready to do the same kindness for others. All this was common form. What was unusual was his regulation of this practice by the requirements of the service and the idea of justice. His ghost was looking over the shoulder of Lord Fisher when he wrote in the log at Dartmouth, 'Favouritism is the secret of efficiency.'

In October 1676 the Purser of the *Royal Sovereign*, a first-rate, died suddenly. A pursery, in effect a privileged monopoly selling to a captive market, was a plum. Pepys was besieged by applications, including some from his oldest most respected friends. On the 19th Sir William Coventry wrote applying on behalf of his landlord's brother.[23] Living at Minster Lovell he had not been as quick off the mark as everyone else. Only the day before Pepys had written to Elizabeth Pearse, the good-looking wife of his close friend the Surgeon-General to the Navy, declining with tact and gentleness to put forward the claims of their son. His position, he explains, would be impossible since he has at last induced the King and Duke to encourage honesty and good service among the pursers by reserving the top jobs for men who have proved themselves in lesser ones. He has had

> applications from commanders, old clerks of ye Navy and ancient Pursers from whom I have a whole bundle of petitions and recommendations to present H.M. with at his return and such as I must confesse were it for my brother or son I could not justify to myself overbearing in behalf of one that had never knowne any part of ye service abroad which he is pretending to (and which I could wish you would think fit to let Mr James have) and this upon ye first Ship Royal of England where ye Charge of a Purser calls for little less experience than any one office in a Fleet.
>
> 'This Madam, for your satisfaction and for ye doing right to my owne friendship I thought fit for me to observe to you . . .[24].'

The next day he saw the King and the place went to the purser of the *London* who was himself succeeded by a senior clerk in the Navy Office.[25]

The respect paid to truth and propriety as well as to the feelings of others, above all the care taken by an eminent and busy man to make sure that his correspondent who has asked a favour shall understand completely why it must be refused, stand comparison with Dr. Johnson. Neither Coventry nor the Pearses stopped asking him favours. Indeed hardly six

months later Pearse tried, unsuccessfully, to obtain the pursery of the
Royal James for his son. Pepys's interest in the boy and readiness to help
were steady and unaffected. They were, by the same token, realistic as
the following letter[26] shows:

To Mr James Pearse.

Derby House, 27 September 1677

His Majesty's service beginning now to call for the employment of a
muster-master to his ships in the Straits, I have out of my confidence
of your having so improved the time you have already spent in the Navy,
and now at sea, as to have qualified yourself for the well executing
thereof, obtained and herewith send you His Majesty's commission
and instructions for that employment, as one instance of the remembrance I have of and the care I shall always have for you so long as the
respect which I truly bear to my worthy friends your father and mother
shall be accompanied with a just endeavour of sobriety and diligence on
your part to deserve it. For so long as you give me that encouragement,
I shall not only continue your benefit and advancement but take delight
in doing so; but must, on the other hand, be as plain with you in telling
of you that I shall be inquisitive after you, as having heard of some of
your past liberties, though from my willingness to impute them to your
youth I never took notice of them till now; that having provided you
a commission that entitles you to the trust and business of a man, my
kindness to you, as well as justice to myself, will not let me longer
withhold my giving you the same cautions which I would with more
severity give a child of my own (and did to my only brother in the last
day he lived in the Navy)* namely that you do never entertain one
thought of any indulgence from me under any neglects of business,
and much less under any misdoings therein, for I am one that will never
be guilty of contributing to the advancement of any man that will not
be contented to rise by the same steps of diligence and faithfulness
which have (by God's blessing) raised me to this capacity of doing
good offices. And this I the rather choose to observe to you out of the
hopes I have that what my example may want my friend your father
will supply to you, of the fruits of whose cares and labours in the
world you have so largely tasted in your liberal education . . .

To a twentieth-century reader the formality of language gives, at first, a
flavour of pomposity just as the characteristically Pepysian length of the
opening sentence, like a morning mist, hangs for an instant over the clarity

* John Pepys had died in that year.

revealed by the brightness of his irrepressible intelligence. He could not be obscure because he had always used his mind before he began to speak or write. Like Sir Winston Churchill he felt the structure of an English sentence to be a noble thing and used his architectural sense to relieve his central theme with features suggested by the multiplicity of a mind that was never still or empty. Yet, as with Johnson, it is the grand and simple virtues, justice, uprightness, warmth of heart, that this style, at a superficial view so elaborate, expresses so compellingly. The cold folksiness of our now fashionable informality is shown up as a sham.

Patronage, nepotism, influence, 'interest' to use the word most comprehensively employed to denote these things, was bound to affect the career of an officer in a service which did not yet offer continuous employment. As Pepys, and Lord Fisher two and a half centuries later, understood, this could be used to give the outstanding man a great deal more than his fair share of the jobs that were going. Sir John Narbrough and Sir Clowdisley Shovell are often cited with approval as examples of officers who got to the top of the late-seventeenth-century navy through their own unaided merit. Unaided? Both came into the service as the protégés of Myngs, to whom it seems likely they were related. Both came from the same parish in Norfolk. After Myngs' death Narbrough looked after Shovell and gave him his first great opportunity as his lieutenant in the attack on Tripoli. This, as Pepys is at pains to emphasise in his letter to young Pearse, is the proper and intelligent use, indeed one of the obligations, of executive power. Narbrough who perhaps came closest to Pepys's idea of what a sea officer should be was an old and trusted friend of the Pearses and gave James passage in his own ship when he took up his appointment in the Mediterranean.

Until the navy was given enough money to provide its officers with a continuous career there could be no automatic system of seniority. Its absence vexed Pepys with petty personal jockeyings that could yet have serious consequences in the conduct of operations. Suppose a squadron contained a second-rate, commanded by some young sprig of nobility, and a third-rate whose captain knew every part of his job from twenty or thirty years' experience. Which, in the absence or incapacity of their flag officer, should take his place, the 'eldest captain' or 'the greater ship'? Pepys had no doubt that it was right to go for the man. He argued the case one afternoon late in 1683 when, together with Lord Dartmouth and some other captains, he had been dining aboard the *English Tiger* off Tangier as the guest of Captain Preistman. The conversation had already acquired a note of asperity. Preistman and others had been critical to the point of disrespect about the drafting of their instructions. Pepys had countered

with some pointed remarks about commanding officers lying ashore without leave:

> But all ended with his observing that there was wanting in the Navy
> a certain settlement about commands at sea . . . whether the greater
> ship or the older commander. . . . I did tell him that in this we might
> learn of the French, for they were under a rule in it and it was according
> to the seniority of the commander, to which like a fool he found fault
> that we should be thought to learn anything of the French (though I
> showed him we did much and might more) and yet he agreed that
> method was the true rule to go by.

The French had already, as Pepys pointed out to the Duke at Newmarket
in 1680, cut the Gordian knot by keeping 'their commanders and lieutenants constantly in pay'. This is, after all, the fundamental criterion by
which the professional is distinguished from the amateur.

Pepys did not live to see the completion of the officer structure he spent
his best energies in building. To the creative mind such a loss may be of
only minor importance. Certainly Pepys saw deeply enough into what he
was fashioning to apprehend the realities that he could only know in imagination. He was, for instance, alert to the new dangers of the *esprit de corps*
he was seeking to create:

> Observe the impropriety of a court-martial of commanders to judge
> of the ignorance or negligence of a master or pilot, who do not pretend
> or dare take upon them any answerableness for the safe navigating of
> their ships, but are continually putting the King to the charge of
> pilotage, even of the 5th-rates, in or out of the River of Thames
> or over to the coasts of Holland or France, and in case of any mis-
> carrying lay all upon their master; and yet at other times take it ill
> not to be thought great seamen, and presume at a court-martial to
> censure a master or pilot as if themselves were the only judges of
> navigation.[27]

He notes with approval his old clerk Gibson's observation:

> . . . how certainly partial our courts-martial ever are to commanders
> in any matters of difference between them and their under-officers,
> or in cases of miscarriage where it is possible to lay it upon any under-
> officer, instancing at present in Captain Greydon's case for the loss, I
> think, of the *St David*, where the court laid it upon the carpenter, and

after the rising thereof one of the captains were heard to say to Greydon: 'God damme, Jack, we have made shift to bring you off, but by God you must remember to do the like by any of us when it comes to our turn.'[28]

Here expressed in the idiom of the quarter-deck these sentiments are nothing if not professional.

Although the creation (give or take a decade or two) of the regular naval officer was Pepys's most lasting contribution to the service and to the social ethos of England at the height of her power, it was by no means the only or most obvious one. He himself clearly considered the condition and power of the King's ships and the regularity of naval finances during the periods at which he was responsible for them to be his best claims on the gratitude of his country. There was no aspect of naval affairs that he did not in some measure improve or rationalise. In the next chapter something must be said of them.

17

Men and ships

It is a paradox that Pepys, least military of men, should have won his place in history as the architect of a great fighting service. But it is sometimes forgotten that to most civilised men participation in war is a duty not a choice. Pepys hated from the heart cruelty and killing, destructiveness and waste. Where he accepted them, as in watching a public execution, he did so because they seemed the only means of serving a yet higher purpose; justice, order, the preservation of society. He would not have felt anything but horror at witnessing an underworld execution. Similarly although the navy existed to exert armed force Pepys conceived that function as defensive – 'our neighbours being so much stronger than before' – and disapproved of aggression. The reader of the Diary can see how wholeheartedly he detested not only the policy that produced the Dutch Wars but the mentality that underlay it. Anyone who reads through the *Naval Minutes* or the *Tangier Papers*, those distillations of a mind glancing, reflecting, grappling with every aspect of naval theory and practice, will search in vain for traces of jingoism.

His most characteristic and congenial achievements for the navy are thus not necessarily the most conspicuous. The officers who were charged with the maintenance of ships and men in soundness and health, the master, the surgeon, the purser, the parson (though he was not, and is not snow, an officer) all felt their professional standing and qualification scrutinised and improved. The victualling was regulated by a scale that was at least generous in aspiration, if even Pepys could not extirpate the inveterate corruption of this easiest of fields for the swindler. The terms under which men served and the punctuality with which they were paid challenged his sense of justice. A delight in good craftsmanship and proper materials naturally attracted him to the world of the shipwrights and the dockyards. Artist, scientist, administrator and jurist, Pepys found scope for his constructive talents in the non-combatant side of the service.

For the master Pepys won higher esteem by his insistence on a certificate from Trinity House. No doubt this contributed to the steady rise in his pay. But the most characteristic expression of his heightened value was the foundation of the Mathematical School at Christ's Hospital. This was designed specifically as a nursery for navigators. Pepys was the moving spirit in putting forward the idea, in obtaining Government money, in choosing the mathematics master and in making sure that he did what he was paid to do. Not the least part of this achievement was that commemorated in Verrio's painting in the hall of Christ's Hospital, the dignifying of a hitherto base mechanic trade with the panoply of royal patronage. This is the quintessence of Pepys. He knows how to use the political machinery of his time, the social prejudices of his age, the needs of an expanding merchant marine to forward the aims he has at heart: the diffusion of useful knowledge, the opening of a career to the talents, and the provision of a pool of navigators from whom the navy can draw in an emergency. He was appointed a Governor on February 1st, 1676, and the seriousness with which he took his duties is attested by the mass of correspondence still preserved in the Pepys Library.

Pepys's great interest in questions of health and his (rare) experience of successful surgery would have doubtless led him to reconstruct the ramshackle medical services of the navy if he had not, for once, had as colleagues in this department two men whom he admired and trusted, two, indeed, of his closest friends, John Evelyn and James Pearse. For once Pepys seems to have been entirely content to play second fiddle: to Evelyn and his fellow-commissioners for the Sick and Wounded during the wars; to Pearse in providing such medicines, doctors and other services as the poverty, both of the navy and of medical knowledge could supply. Pearse was a professional of Pepysian quality. In the earlier of Charles II's two Dutch Wars it was he who pressed for the commissioning of a hospital ship and, powerfully seconded by William Coventry at sea and John Evelyn ashore, obtained one in 1665 and two in 1666.[1] This is the first time in English naval history that such a vessel is even mentioned, barring one obscure reference in the disastrous expedition against

Hispaniola in 1654 when the troops from General Venables downwards seem to have been in such a miserable state that the description would have fitted almost every vessel in the fleet. Pearse, who throughout the war was styled Surgeon-General of the Fleet, a title that, incredibly, carried no salary or fees, was brought ashore in the summer of 1666 and made Warden of the Company of Barber-Surgeons who maintained such medical services as the fleet enjoyed. He went back to sea for the St. James's Day Fight, following the action in a yacht which left him leisure to observe and record its developments.* His account is in a class by itself. But his energy and administrative skill were even more fruitful ashore. Although he returned to private practice at the end of the war (because his appointment as a naval surgeon was at once terminated) he was at last, in April 1670, established at a retainer of £100 a year in the post of 'Chyrurgeon Generall of H.M. Navy'.

By the time the Third Dutch War broke out in 1672 Pearse had made his preparations. His draught of equipment for a hospital ship includes for the first time the supply of soap at the public charge. Most akin to Pepys was his introduction of a system of printed forms to control and record the medical treatment of the seamen, particularly in securing accommodation and attendance for men discharged to shore, and to prevent embezzlement and fraud. Once again on the outbreak of war the Commission for the Sick and Wounded and Prisoners was reconstituted with John Evelyn as its moving spirit. When it was dissolved in 1674 Pearse as Surgeon-General was specifically directed to take over its duties. He held his appointment until after the Revolution, inspiring in Pepys's great building programme of 1677 the bold requirement of three hospital ships, two for the Channel and one for the Mediterranean. The disasters that overtook Pepys in 1679 might easily have destroyed Pearse, since as personal surgeon to the Duke of York his connection was even more dangerous. He survived but it was not until Pepys came back to the Admiralty in 1684, and most notably when he set up the Special Commission of 1686† that Pearse was able to take his reforming programme a stage further. In the report on his department that he submitted in September 1687 he claimed in words reminiscent of his friend the Secretary to have 'reduced it into such a method that it is not possible for me (or whoever shall succeed me) to wrong his Majesty or injure his subjects'. He was denied the chance of putting it to the test: in 1689 his close personal attachment to both the Stuart brothers cost him his post. His great contribution to an efficient medical service, the raising of the surgeon's rate of pay, a truly Pepysian criterion of professionalism, did not

* See p. 348, note 17.   † See pp. 287–291.

save him from dying in poverty. In 1696 his widow whose beauty had excited Pepys in the days of the Diary asked him to act as trustee in the sale of her house.

But the best provision that could be made to keep men in health was to see that they were properly clothed and fed. Under the captain this responsibility fell upon the purser. This officer was to the old sailing-ship navy what the mother-in-law was to the music-hall. Jokes about his dishonest practices easily outweigh all other types of humour. As so often in government service he was put in a position where he was invited if not actually commanded to make money by sharp practice. 'A purser without professed cheating is a professed loser' Pepys wrote in his Navy Office days. His experience at the Admiralty confirmed this judgment. As the licensed supplier of victuals paid for by the Government and the monopolist of everything else the ship's company might want he was well placed to swindle both of them. Who, except the captain, could tell if he gave the sailors less than the Government had contracted for, or if, still more common, he charged the Government for victualling men who had died, or, perhaps, had never existed? Collusion, between captain and purser, was common. One captain was alleged to have borne his dog on the ship's books under the name of Mr. Bromley.[2] But most of these frauds lacked this touch of bravura: and a very large number were perpetrated against the seamen. It was to remedy this state of affairs that Pepys insisted on the appointment of Muster-Masters. But the only real solution was to raise the standards and the self-respect of pursers and captains by rewarding merit, enforcing discipline and paying the rate for the job.

No one can read far in lower deck autobiography without being disgusted by details of biscuits alive with weevils, mouldy bread, rotten cheese, beer that stank, wine that turned the stomach and water too foul for human consumption. How different it sounds from the Victualling Contract of 1677 for which Pepys was responsible and in which he took such pride:

> . . . Viz. every man to have for his allowance by the day, one pound avoirdupois, of good, cleane, sweet, sound, well bolted with a house[3] cloth, well-baked and well-conditioned wheaten Bisquet, of wch samples are to be brought unto and approved of by the Principall Officers and Commissioner of H.M. Navy . . . once every three months; one Gallon, wine measure, of Beer of such a standard. [Here follows a sentence on the quantity and quality of malt and hops and on the arrangements for judging them, so exact, so specific and so parenthetically qualified that even Pepys could hardly have taken it at a canter]

> . . . Two pounds, avoirdupois of Beef, killed and made up with salt
> in England, of a well-fed Ox not weighing lesse than 5 cwt. . . .

Enough is enough. The wholesome plenty of Pepys's Victualling Contract leaves one feeling that the calorie intake needs watching. Even the lighter diet prescribed for vessels sailing to the warmer climates south of 39°N — figs, currants, rice, olive oil and wine — sounds appetising and abundant. Yet, as Pepys's own Admiralty letters show, reality fell far short. Thorough, resourceful, vigilant, he was all, perhaps rather more than all, that an administrator could be. But he could not, like Moses striking the rock, produce money by rapping people's knuckles. Unpunctual payment meant bad provisions. The contractors had to make a profit to stay in business. When Pepys fell from office in 1679 his successors reversed the system of victualling by contract and returned to the practice of the Commonwealth which had run its own state victualling department. Alone of the changes they introduced this seems to have been an improvement. Pepys himself retained it when he returned to the Admiralty in 1684.

If money dictated what could or could not be done in the matter of food, still more obviously was this the case with pay. Apart from keeping a sharp eye on the Ticket Office and punishing ticket brokers when evidence could be produced against them Pepys could do little. 'The King's wages better than merchantmen's yet his service shunned by reason of bad pay.' As usual it is impossible to better his own summary. The affront to his sense of justice as well as to his passion for good order did not diminish with the passage of time. It led him, as a modern scholar [4] has shown, into disingenuousness in the famous passage so often quoted from his *Memoires*, the *pièce justificative* that he published in 1690.

> . . . not a *Penny* left unpaid to any *Officer, Seaman, Workman, Artificer* or *Merchant*, for any *service* come in, or *commodity* delivered to the use of the *Navy*, either at sea or on shore, within the whole time of this *Commission* where the Party claiming the same was in the way to receive it . . .

The statement is, strictly, true thanks to the qualifying phrase. The Commission to which Pepys refers had been set up in March 1686. During the two and a half years that he had subsequently spent at the Admiralty the arrears of wages due to the seamen had risen to the enormous sum of £85,244, while the arrears due to the merchants and dockyard workmen were in comparison trivial. Safe aboard a man-of-war, especially if bound for the West Indies or the Mediterranean, the Party claiming the same was not indeed in much of a way to receive it. The best of a bad job was all that Pepys could make of paying the seaman; he carried the habit on in arguing his own case.

Unsatisfactory as both naval pay and victualling were there is good ground for thinking that both were, on the whole, better than those prevailing in merchant ships. Pepys certainly believed that they were. His views are powerfully supported by the direct statement of Edward Barlow, whose journal gives the fullest picture we have of the life of a Restoration seaman: 'Their Majesties ships are better victualled than most merchant ships are, and their pay surer . . .'[5] Why, if this were true, were sailors so unwilling to serve in the navy?

One answer is, no doubt, that it is quite impossible to generalise about conditions either in the navy or the merchant service. Barlow's contemporary, Edward Coxere, gives a charming account of transferring from a state ship to a merchantman in the Mediterranean simply because the pay was higher. The captain raised no objection; indeed the only solicitude he felt was for Coxere's safety. 'When I was in the boat the captain called "Edward, have a care!"'[6] Even in the navy itself conditions varied so widely from ship to ship and captain to captain that a clear-cut statement such as Barlow's has to be taken as the evidence of one man's experience, indicative, suggestive, but not definitive.

But on another point, itself almost a sufficient explanation of the navy's unpopularity, there is complete unanimity, and that is impressment. To the modern reader the press gang means grinning sailors armed with clubs and cutlasses dragging poor wretches from the streets and taverns. To men like Barlow and Coxere it meant something more callously unjust and more desperately resented, the boarding of ships inward bound after a voyage of perhaps two or three years and the pressing of men without allowing them to see their wives and children or to collect their wages. Men like Coxere who had actually been imprisoned by the Turks were not exaggerating when they compared, as they sometimes did, the humanity of their countrymen unfavourably with that of the infidel.

Pepys sympathised. Where he could, he secured the release of individuals. When he could, he resisted pressure from captains to be allowed to make up deficient complements by pressing. Seamen, unlike carpenters and sawyers for the dockyard, were in theory only liable to impressment in time of war. Money, of course, would have disposed of the whole problem. But society had established a prescriptive right to claim the seaman's services without paying him and it would take more than Pepys's sense of justice to induce the rich and powerful to abandon so profitable a form of exploitation. Disgraceful as it was, it was not practical politics to abolish it. Pepys therefore tried to contain it by observing such limitations as the law had put upon it and to work for its supersession by campaigning for a navy that would be properly paid and adequately financed. When at the very end of his career his old friend James Pearse 'putt a precedent into my hand' for the pressing of surgeons for the fleet that was going out to meet the Dutch invasion of 1688, Pepys even in that dark hour would not grant a press-warrant until he had examined the matter more thoroughly and discussed it with his friend.[7] Exceptionally in the summer of 1675 when England was at peace in Europe he allowed the ships sent to reinforce Narbrough in the Mediterranean to press after all else had failed.[8] Since the country was in a state of war with Tripoli this was perfectly legal. But much more characteristic is his intervention on behalf of four carpenters and a bricklayer engaged in building a new house for his friend Sir John Bankes at Aylesford, dangerously accessible to the pressing parties from the Medway Towns.[9] Watching from a disgruntled retirement the naval conduct of King William's war Pepys observed that

> more complaints arise, and justly, every day of the irregularities and violences committed in that one particular of the pressing of men, than would by many degrees be consequential to all the power of coercion that needed to be asked of a Parliament for securing the government of the service of the seamen it hath, and making their number more.[10]

Injustice, irregularity and violence are the despised marks of amateurism in administration.

It was perhaps Pepys's sense of the injustice suffered by the seamen that led so hearty an anticlerical to champion the cause and raise the status of the naval chaplain. Like the surgeon the chaplain was subsidised by compulsory deductions from the men's wages — twopence a month for the doctor, fourpence for the parson. All that the Government paid was the wage of an ordinary seaman. In Charles I's time there had been so few takers for employment offered on such wretched terms that the seamen's groats — their monthly fourpences — accumulated into a pile over which courtiers and placemen squabbled at the trough. Even after the Restoration two flag officers, Sir Thomas Allin and Sir William Berkeley, secured grants of £1,000 apiece from this source.[11] Under the Commonwealth the chaplain had risen high. One of them had even challenged the dubious practices of the Pett dynasty in Chatham dockyard and had come off equal. The importance of preaching in the Puritan Revolution raised them, in some cases, almost to the position of a political commissar. This was going too far for Pepys: but he meant to see that the men got value for the money that was spent in their name and that Divine service should, at least, be conducted without indecency.

It was a tall order. That the pranks of the chaplain of H.M.S. *Sweepstakes* did not seem as extraordinary then as they would now is suggested by the terse comment of the Dean of Rochester recommending one of his brethren for a vacant living: 'He has been a sea chaplain for some years and unlike most of them is a sober well-tempered man.'[12] To proceed to Holy Orders was still the obvious step for a young man who had taken a university degree but had no particular prospect of employment. Poverty might drive them to serve as a chaplain, as was the case with the most famous of them, Henry Teonge. His Diary gives perhaps the most vivid picture we have of life aboard a Restoration man-of-war; certainly, reflecting the personality of its author, one of the most cheerful and good-natured. Teonge was a country clergyman with a wife and family to support. He went to sea in 1675 because he could hold his benefice in plurality with a chaplaincy. His naval pay, modest though it was, thus increased his total income. Sensible, kindly, mature and responsible he stands at the opposite end of the parsonical spectrum from Mr. Bradford of the *Sweepstakes*. No sot, he enjoyed to the full the hospitality and sociability of ward-room life and as a man who had often gone hungry he relished the huge quantity and excellent quality of the food provided at the captain's table or ashore by the English consuls and merchants at the ports at which they called. Teonge took his ministry too much for granted to say much about it. He was conscientious in preaching, although it appears that he delivered the same sermon, or at least preached on the same text, for four Sundays out of five (on the fifth there were prayers but no sermon) in the summer of 1676. None the less when, confined to bed with an attack of influenza, he heard that Lord Mordaunt, a rich young volunteer, had per-suaded the captain to let him preach at Sunday prayers he struggled to his feet and prevented it. For an obscure, penniless parson to antagonise a courtier and an aristocrat was a bold act. Teonge may safely be taken as the highest type of man likely to have served as a chaplain in the navy of Charles II. Yet his mental culture, for all that he was a Cambridge graduate and a man of lively mind, would have left Pepys politely pitying. He believed that the marabouts of Tripoli could make fogs to cover their fleet's putting to sea. He thought that Prester John regulated the flooding of the Nile Delta by an elaborate series of sluices and dams for which the Egyptians paid him a kind of water rate.

Pepys was too much of a realist to expect a learned ministry. And his own theological leanings were still vestigially Presbyterian. Were episco-pally ordained ministers essential to the service? For his own part he thought not.[13] Still, on grounds of supporting the established order in church and state, he accepted them. And having accepted them he naturally wished to regulate their appointment 'with respect both to the honour of God Almighty and the preservation of sobriety and good discipline in His Majesty's Fleet'.[14] In 1677, that *annus mirabilis* of the Lieutenants' examination and the Thirty New Ships, he established procedures for notifying requirements to the Bishop of London who would then propose suitable candidates. No chaplain was to be admitted on board who had not produced a certificate from the Bishop as to his piety, learning, conformity and other qualifications. The success of the scheme was limited. Compton, the Bishop of London, was touchy and difficult. Hewer, he said, had been rude to him – an accusation that Pepys politely but firmly declined to credit. The list of ships requiring chaplains had reached him at insufficient notice, and he was riled at Captain Langstone preferring his old chaplain to the candidate suggested. Pepys defended the captain. The King and their Lordships had found the style and orthography of a paper delivered by Compton's candidate 'not over-Clerk-like'.* Courteous up to this point Pepys cannot resist the chance to cut the proud prelate down to size:

. . . And for what concernes myself in ye point wherein yr. Lp. is pleased (in yr. owne right) to observe yr. getting nothing by this employment I beseech you to believe that I who have not in near 20 years service once descended to ye taking of a Fee (though my knowne right) for a Comm[n] or warrant to any-one Lay-Officer in ye Navy neither have nor will ever blemish that costly self-denial of mine by beginning an Imposture on ye Church, towards whose prosperity I shall ever acquit myself as becomes a Dutifull sonn . . .'[15]

A further sign that the right men did not come forward in sufficient numbers may be discerned in Pepys's praiseworthy efforts to make sure that the surplus of seaman's groats should go to the Chatham Chest, not to some greedy official.[16] No doubt if the money had run to it Pepys would himself have devised and conducted a chaplain's examination of his own. How he would have set about it may be seen from the methods he employed in judging the candidates for a chaplaincy at Bridewell. He drew up a table under the following headings and recorded his assessments.[17]

* That this was probably not an isolated instance is suggested by the fact that Mr Bradford of the *Sweepstakes* had been approved by Compton. Rawl. A 181, f. 383.

Prayer: (set or ex tempore)
Text
Appositeness: mostly 'none'
Action, voice, tone and stile: 'Presbyterian' 'ordinary'
                              'stiff and schoolboylike'
Age:
Countenance: 'Tolerable' 'Grave' 'Very Good'
             (this applied to nearly all)
Length: 'Convenient' '5 Quarters' 'An hour'
Within-book (i.e. read): about half the candidates.
Learning: 'Little' 'Much latine' 'none'
Orthodoxness: All were good except two: the first 'Good, saving much
              freewill' and the second 'Not conformable to himselfe,
              inferring from Humane history, ye truth of ye Scripture.'

Statistical analysis is still a fascinating instrument: what must it have
been to a man of Pepys's intellectual appetite when it was brand-new?

But it was the material side of his naval achievement in which Pepys
took the greatest pride and felt the keenest pleasure. The Thirty Ships of
1677 represented the largest building programme England had ever
carried through. The size of them – they were all second- or third-rates –
except the *Britannia* a first – increased the power of the Royal Navy in
relation to its rivals, the French and the Dutch, beyond the mere increase
in units. Into their design and their armament had gone, not only Pepys's
comprehensive knowledge, long experience and power of rationalising
and standardising, but the skill of the marine architects, notable among
them Sir Anthony Deane, whose friend and patron he was. Deane, perhaps,
was the only man who could match his combination of technical knowledge
(in which indeed he far surpassed him), managerial skill and varied experience of naval affairs. He had been a master mariner before he turned to
shipbuilding and was at different times in charge of dockyards, victualling
and storekeeping. An artist whose draughts were admired by Evelyn he
was an extremely capable man of business. Above all he could argue and
discuss, unlike the older type of craftsman so perfectly caught in Pepys's
phrase 'their knowledge lying in their hands confusedly'.

At the same time as Pepys, almost single-handed, won the approval of
a by no means docile House of Commons for the Thirty Ships he secured
the acceptance at the Admiralty Board for his establishment of men and
guns. From that point on a commander would be able to calculate with
exactitude the weight of a broadside that a ship of any given rate could
throw. He would know, too, exactly what type of ordnance each ship

would carry and in what numbers. The scientific or as Pepys would have put it 'Mathematick' approach to naval warfare was gaining ground. In all the achievements of this wonderful year the debt to the example of the French and the Dutch and to the active and informed support of the King is evident and freely acknowledged. Pepys was never too proud to learn.

It was much easier to maintain good discipline and efficient service in the dockyards than in the fleet, partly because they were more directly under the hand and eye of the Admiralty and the Navy Board but most because they offered continuity of service. Although they were not troubled with the pretensions of courtiers they had an entrenched aristocracy of their own which Pepys could neither overawe nor afford to disregard. The great dynasty of Pett at Chatham has already been mentioned. The family of Shish, about whom Pepys generally had some waspish things to say, had established similar but less extensive bailiwicks at Woolwich and Deptford and Sheerness. Deane himself was an important figure in his native town of Harwich, for which he and Pepys were elected to Parliament in the spring of 1679. But the general run of resident commissioners were appointed by Pepys in consultation with the King and Duke strictly on merit. Men such as Colonel Thomas Middleton, who served successively as Commissioner at Portsmouth, and Chatham before becoming Comptroller of the Navy exemplify the standards that Pepys demanded. His correspondence with them is not so much taken up with reproving their delinquencies as with palliating the symptoms of incurable financial paralysis – strikes, absenteeism, desertion arising from unpaid wages, press warrants to obtain the necessary labour – the old, old tale of accounts unsettled and supplies refused familiar from earliest days at the Navy Office. Theft and corruption were still common, unsurprisingly; but they certainly did not run riot.

18

Prisoner of State

To Pepys the strengthening of the fleet that resulted from his efforts was obviously defensive. It would protect our trade: it would preserve a balance of power against the Dutch and the French. To those who distrusted the good faith, the Protestant sympathies and the constitutional intentions of Charles II any accretion of military power under the direct control of the King was deeply disturbing. A lot had happened since those scenes of intoxicated enthusiasm with which the Diary chronicles the Restoration. To a Catholic Queen Mother had been added a Catholic Queen Consort. The year of 1672 had witnessed the disclosure of the alliance with the militantly Catholic Louis XIV and the Declaration of Indulgence which everyone saw as a transparent disguise for suspending the good old penal laws against the Catholics. And then, in the uproar of enraged Protestant reaction, James, Duke of York, heir to the throne, had publicly avowed his conversion to Catholicism. In the very year in which Pepys had pressed through his naval programme the King had been up to his tricks again in Europe, raising troops nominally to assist the Dutch against the French but bringing them back with unwelcome suddenness and failing to disband them with yet more unwelcome delay. From the distance of three centuries we can see that Charles II was too clever a man to attempt a military imposition of Catholic absolutism *à la Française* on the England he knew. But perhaps we forget that to contemporaries he had shown himself too clever by half. We know that the explanation of this last action lies in a bungled diplomatic *coup*: his contemporaries may be forgiven for not perceiving this. Its effect, anyway, was catastrophic.[1] The anti-Catholic hysteria that ran so deep yet lay so near the surface of English political consciousness in the seventeenth century was ready for its most violent eruption. The popular conviction that the Great Fire had been a piece of Catholic sabotage, the smouldering resentment over the French alliance and the Declaration of Indulgence, all the pent-up hatreds and fears of a society that had known revolution and preferred conspiracy to all other theories of politics, formed one vast pile of psychological tinder. Titus Oates was ready with his flame.

In the hideous light of such a conflagration what shadows would be cast by the figure of Pepys? Pepys, who had married a Catholic wife, whose house was known to be full of altars and images and suchlike superstitious bric-à-brac, who had worked in the closest intimacy with the Duke of York, who had devoted his life to increasing the military power of the Crown and in doing so had shown his resentment of Parliamentary control and scrutiny. He had left only a touch or two to be added by the artist in political denunciation.

The attack, when it came, was launched obliquely. Doubly so, for Pepys, who was struck at through a subordinate, was himself to be the means of striking at the Duke of York. It was a classic example of what is now called the Domino Theory: knock over the front rank and the others will collapse in series. From the energy with which Pepys reacted it seems that he thought this tactical appreciation of the situation dangerously sound.

The mass hysteria of the Popish Plot was unleashed by a murder which has remained one of the most famous of unsolved mysteries. The body of Sir Edmund Berry Godfrey, a London magistrate, was found several days after his disappearance in a place and in circumstances that clearly bore no relation to the manner of his death. The sword that transfixed him had been run through his body when it was already cold and stiff; and the evidence of bruising, like the planting of the corpse, suggests in itself the underworld killing that Professor Kenyon in the most recent and authoritative study of the subject accepts as the most probable explanation. What makes further pursuit of the topic futile is, as Professor Kenyon emphasises, our virtually entire ignorance of a seventeenth-century criminal world that was, to say the least, complex and sophisticated. Isolated incidents such as the Popish Plot or Colonel Blood's attempts to kidnap the ex-Lord-Lieutenant of Ireland or to steal the Crown Jewels present a sudden view of a society and a way of life that we can never see steadily or investigate with any system. That the underworld afforded a number of people a long and various career; that its ramifications extended across frontiers and that it was used and sometimes protected by governments and eminent persons could be demonstrated from the history of the plot alone. But beyond that lies darkness, and the endless, pointless gabble of mendacious hearsay. Criminals do not keep records and if they did they would be worthless. Then as now vanity, egocentricity and the hope of easy money were powerful inducements to talk, but are less compelling as credentials.

How Oates, the psychopath who had been bundled out of a naval chaplaincy for homosexuality, exploited Godfrey's murder belongs to the general story of the plot. The flanking attack on Pepys that developed directly from it, so directly as to suggest a co-ordinating intelligence, was led by a straight professional rascal from a milieu to which Pepys was soon to devote his energetic curiosity and talent for research. William Bedloe, sharper, forger and confidence trickster, had swindled his way across Europe before the happy chance of being in his native land at the time of Godfrey's murder put him in the way of the rich rewards open to the informer. Among the innocent men whom he either sold or did his best to sell to the barbarities of execution on a charge of treason were several who had employed or befriended him. The accusation brought against Pepys's clerk, Samuel Atkins, by so cold-blooded a villain was no random lie. He claimed to have seen Atkins by the light of a dark lantern standing over the corpse of Sir Edmund Berry Godfrey in Somerset House two nights after the murder had been committed by a gang in Jesuit pay. The melodramatic irrelevancies bear the hallmark of perjured testimony. People who deal in lies take the bigger the better for their first axiom. The original allegations against Atkins had been made, much less daringly, by a disgraced gentleman captain who had surrendered his ship* to the Algerines without firing a shot. He deposed that Atkins had asked him to recommend a seaman of his acquaintance who would stick at nothing as Pepys had a grudge against Godfrey and wanted some assistance in murdering him. It was on this absurd story that Atkins was arrested.

Pepys at once set to work organising his defence. By the time the trial came on in February 1679 — Godfrey's body had been discovered in

---

* The *Quaker* ketch. This vessel's name, a strange choice for a man-of-war, proved uncomfortably apt. Her next captain was court-martialled and sentenced to death for striking his top-sails to a Spanish ship in the Bay of Biscay. Since the officer, an old tarpaulin of proven courage, was thought to be unhinged by reason of head wounds, he was to be pardoned after being brought before the firing party. Pepys seems to have found nothing objectionable in this cat-and-mouse cruelty.

mid-October and Atkins had been imprisoned at the beginning of November – he had put together an armour-plated alibi for his young assistant covering the whole of the material weekend during which Godfrey was alleged to have been murdered and Atkins had been, so Bedloe asserted, keeping vigil over his body. The total demolition of the prosecution case marked the first check to the mad, evil hunt on which the nation was hallooing. Even so shameless a liar as Bedloe was discomfited and made to mumble that he might have made a mistake. The key witness was Captain Vittells, whose hot temper was to bring him before the judgment of Pepys and Lord Dartmouth in the next reign. At this point Vittells was captain of a small dispatch vessel on which, that Saturday afternoon, Atkins and two young ladies had been his guests. Such was the hospitality that Atkins when rowed home at midnight by two of Vittells's seamen was in no state to keep vigil over anyone with or without a dark lantern. Lord Chief Justice Scroggs, dismissing the case, seized with relief on its convivial aspect. But it had been no laughing matter for Pepys: still less for young Atkins who had been alternately coaxed and threatened to perjure himself and incriminate his employer by men, Shaftesbury and Buckingham in particular, of whom he must have been terrified. Pepys was amazed and heartened by his courage and staunchness: 'For certainly no youth of his wit and straightness of fortune ever withstood such temptations to have been a villain.'[2]

The grotesque case against Atkins suggests very strongly that he was hurriedly brought in as a last-minute substitute for Pepys himself. On the eve of the weekend during which Bedloe claimed to have witnessed Godfrey's murder Pepys had been unexpectedly summoned to Newmarket by the King. So complete and so public an alibi was too much for the most dedicated perjurer to swear away. But no one, certainly not Pepys himself, thought that he was out of danger: or even that if Atkins got off he would be safe. Friends such as Sir Robert Southwell shook their heads and watched for the fatal stroke: '. . . And Mr Pepys, however prepared, must certainly be destroyed.' This was written two months after Atkins' acquittal, when the Parliamentary attack on Pepys and Deane was swelling in fury and when the King was giving ground to an opposition he could not master. What everyone, friend and foe, seems to have left out of account was Pepys's skill and courage in fighting back. Considering how often this had been demonstrated it was a surprising oversight.

The principal agent of the men compassing his destruction was a figure whose universal shadiness beggars description, a certain Colonel John Scott. The military title, mandatory for ruffians with social pretensions in every age of English history, had perhaps a slender technical validity. Scott *may* have talked the Dutch into giving him command of a regiment but the story that says he did ends with his ignominious dismissal at the first whiff of grapeshot. Killing and firearms, even cannon, certainly feature in his *curriculum vitae* but he took great care never to expose himself to the unpleasant risks attendant on the military profession.

Scott entered Pepys's life under one of his many disguised identities. At the height of the hue and cry after Godfrey's murder he had left London for France in a most suspicious and circuitous manner, riding first to Gravesend, doubling on his tracks by disembarking at Margate and then hurrying to Folkestone where he took passage in a fishing smack. All this cloak-and-dagger activity roused the local officials. Pepys was informed and issued immediate orders to the commander in the channel. But by then Scott was safe in Paris. Not, indeed, that he had much to fear from the police work of a century that knew nothing of fingerprints or photographs, had no system of criminal records and no force specifically charged with keeping an eye on professional criminals. Throughout his long career which included murder, rape, bigamy, fraud, theft, desertion and suchlike Scott rarely seems to have encountered the difficulties on crossing a frontier which beset even the most innocent traveller in the twentieth century. He had begun active life in New England, returned to his native Kent, found his way back to New York and from there to the West Indies where he appears actually to have got as far as the scaffold before his gift of the gab came to his rescue. Next it was England again, then Holland (and his alleged Colonelcy) then Flanders and, at the time of the plot, a regular alternation between London and Paris, selling his services to a number of important people in both capitals. Long after the plot he was apparently in London again and one of Pepys's correspondents records a somewhat inconclusive conversation with him in a Norwegian port in 1683. How much of all this is true no one can tell because almost all of it comes either from Scott's own associates, *ipso facto* untrustworthy, or else from sources whose reliability we cannot evaluate. Pepys collected all the material to which Sir Arthur Bryant has faithfully adhered in his full and vigorous portrait of this entirely odious man.[3] Extraordinary it may sound, but there is nothing incredible in the story: In history as in life it seems that Scott's gift is to render improbability no barrier to belief.

His function in the plot was to establish a treasonable connection between Pepys and the French, thus reinforcing the allegations of secret Catholicism for which there was such a dangerous abundance of circumstantial evidence. Pepys had not been to Paris since his one short visit with Elizabeth just before her death, but his closest colleagues Anthony Deane and Will Hewer had been received at the French court and had met the principal naval ministers and officials in 1675 when Deane took over two yachts that he had built for the lake at Versailles. Scott claimed to have conclusive evidence of Deane's having sold the French secret charts of English coasts and harbours for the furtherance of a Popish invasion, a conspiracy of which Pepys had been the mainspring.

Who paid Scott to concoct these stories? A connection with the Duke of Buckingham, whose morality was never fastidious, seems well established. Pepys himself was satisfied that Shaftesbury was deeply involved: certainly his lieutenants in the Commons were, notably William Harbord, brother of Sandwich's young friend and companion in arms who had lost his life at Sole Bay. And it was Harbord who produced the much more damaging evidence of Pepys's ex-butler John James who testified to his old master's secret Romanism. James had been dismissed after he had been found in bed with the housekeeper by Pepys's domestic musician, Cesare Morelli. Morelli had been recommended to Pepys in April 1673 by his friend Thomas Hill, the Lisbon merchant, as having 'a most admirable voyce, and sings rarely to his Theorba, and with great skill'. To his gifts as an executant he added, as his correspondence shows, considerable musicianship. But he neither concealed nor paraded his Roman Catholicism. In Lisbon the Inquisition had apparently found him too lax, perhaps because of his readiness to associate with foreign Protestants. In London Pepys had, in the early stages of the anti-Catholic witch-hunt, attempted to convince him of the errors of the Church of Rome through the agency of his friend James Houblon. Morelli remained unshaken. In obedience to the proclamation banishing all Papists from London he left Derby House for lodgings in Brentford and prepared to go abroad. James was not behindhand in seizing the opportunity for revenging himself at one stroke on both his ex-employer and the foreigner who had cost him his job. The usual rubbish about images, pistols, daggers, crucifixes and the rest was heightened with musical touches of Pepys and Morelli singing mass together (Titus Oates swore that Morelli was a Jesuit) and, later, sauced with allusions to Pepys's wind colic.

The importance of James's evidence lies in its extremely full and circumstantial retractation, recorded on his death-bed in March 1680. Here in a document that cannot be impugned are the names of the men who paid him, Harbord among them, and here are clearly established the links that join feeble creatures like James with real villains like Scott. James had also on his own confession helped to fabricate the third charge with which Pepys was to be brought down if Popery and Paris failed, the piracy of the *Hunter* sloop. During the Third Dutch War Balty, characteristically, and Sir Anthony Deane, who ought to have known better, embarked on the risky speculation of leasing a king's ship, the *Hunter*, and fitting her out as a privateer. The inherent disadvantage of such a venture was that its success depended on an altogether improbable combination of honesty, discretion, legal punctilio and piratical dash in the captain. Pepys had burnt his fingers in the earlier war over his partnership with Batten and Penn in the *Flying Greyhound*. Where two such knowing old hands had found themselves in some awkward situations it was hardly to be expected that Balty would escape embarrassment. The *Hunter's* captain, obtaining French letters of marque, did his hunting against English ships which were no doubt easier prey than those of the enemy. Even at the time Pepys was alarmed:

. . . where (as in your Case) the nearness of relation suffices to make me a partaker in the blame, though never so much a stranger to the guilt or matter of it, as you know to how much trouble to me it did in the late case of the Privateer.[4]

Raked up five years later and spiced with a charge of treason against Sir Anthony Deane brought by one of the *Hunter's* captains it gave harmony and elegance to a case that needed something to disguise the total lack of respectable evidence.

In the state of passion and hysteria induced by the anti-Catholic mania (as it seems to us) of the nation and the patent duplicity of the King it was enough, more than enough, to send Pepys and Deane to the Tower. That was on May 22nd, 1679. After the crescendo of the preceding six months the Tower for all its grim associations perhaps afforded a certain tranquillity. Throughout the autumn the storm that had burst on Godfrey's murder had raged unchecked. Danby, the King's first minister, was only saved from impeachment by the Lords: the Duke of York escaped exclusion from the succession by a hair's breadth: the Queen's banishment was voted by the Commons: the Catholic peers were disabled from taking their seats in the Upper House and six of them were sent to the Tower on a charge of High Treason. The King, in a tight corner, showed a boldness, a skill, even a certain tenacity of principle that might if displayed earlier in a more modest degree have prevented the situation from running away with him. He faced the Commons as long as he dared, steadily refusing to throw over his brother or his Queen or even his minister. When he could hold the line no longer he prorogued Parliament on December 30th and dissolved it by proclamation early in February 1679.

At the General Election of the following month – the first since 1661 –

Pepys was busier in securing the return of other members favourable to the Court than in managing his own campaign. His own constituency of Castle Rising had shown ungrateful signs of listening to the accusations of Popery that had, naturally, been revived against him at so propitious a moment. He thought it wise to reinsure by standing at Portsmouth (where he was infuriated by the failure of Legge, the future Lord Dartmouth, the Governor of the town, to unite the Crown interest behind the candidacy of the Chancellor of the Exchequer) and at Harwich, where, thanks to the local influence of his fellow-candidate Sir Anthony Deane they were elected '. . . with an unanimity and excess of courtesy hardly to be equalled in the case of two (both of Court dependence) within the whole kingdom'. He was not less surprised than touched by the generosity of his old enemy, Sir Robert Holmes, in offering to provide him with a seat in the Isle of Wight. Considering the venom with which he and Coventry had been used to speak of him in the old days of the Diary he had good reason. The Revolution of 1688 and Pepys's exile from public life cast their shadows in the letter he wrote to Legge, reproving him and contrasting his conduct with that of Holmes. Things might have turned out very differently for the Dutch task force in 1688 if Holmes had had command of the fleet and Legge the Governorship of the Isle of Wight.

In spite of being elected almost without expenditure and with only the most fleeting visit to the constituency Pepys's electioneering was a disappointment. Castle Rising did turn on its benefactor as a Papist. Sea officers who ought to have remembered whose bread they ate had supported opposition candidates. Sir John Berry had even applied for leave to go and make mischief of this kind at Dover.[5] Pepys spent an unconscionable amount of time in bringing the full weight of the dockyard interest behind his friend Sir John Bankes at Chatham. He was returned. It would indeed have been a bad day for the political stability on whose growth Professor Plumb has recently concentrated attention if the dockyard towns had turned against the ministerialists. But the results as a whole left the King even weaker than before. Oates and the plot-merchants were riding high in spite of Atkins's acquittal. Danby fell, his life at least saved by Charles's issue of a pardon that he had disdained to ensure for himself. Shaftesbury took his place once more at the Council table. At the beginning of March James, the heir-apparent to the throne, was forced into ignominious exile in the Low Countries.

If Charles could not even protect his own brother, he was powerless to defend Pepys. On April 21st the old Admiralty Commission was dissolved. It had included men like Prince Rupert, by no means friendly to Pepys, who knew enough about the navy to put a spoke in his wheel when they wanted to. But compared to the new Commission which soon asked for and obtained wider powers it had been Paradise. The new Commission's most active members were Pepys's declared enemies and none of them knew anything about naval business. Yet, allegedly to repair this deficiency, he was retained as Secretary. Office on such terms was not worth having. On May 6th in a long and eloquent letter to his old master now in exile he urged the Duke to support his request to the King that he might be relieved of the Secretaryship and appointed, if his expert opinion was thought indispensable, a member of the Commission. He opened his plea by arguing the enfeebled state of his health, particularly of his eyesight 'after almost 20 years continued drudgery in the Navy', but disclosed, unanswerably, its real base in these words:

. . . charged with a new piece of duty, and that not a little one, of informing those who should informe and are to command me, and I remain accountable for all the ill success that should attend my obeying those commands, though possibly differing from my own advice.[6]

James answered with the warmth and loyalty that make him so much more likeable than his more talented brother. But release from an impossible situation was to come too swiftly for any help that he could afford. On April 28th the Commons had appointed a committee under the chairmanship of William Harbord to investigate the miscarriages of the navy. This was the tribunal before which Pepys and Deane were to answer the absurd accusations already described. It was on the strength of them that on May 22nd he was committed to the Tower. But before that the whole of his conduct as a naval official had been attacked with the usual recklessness of political controversy. Every appointment had been corrupt, every contract a swindle, every sympathiser with popery had been favoured. Captain Roydon, late of H.M.S. *Sweepstakes*, took the opportunity of explaining that he had been dismissed for calling his Lieutenant a Papist rather than for the state of his ship disclosed by the Court-Martial. Pepys, although his case needed no such extravagance, answered in kind. Among the papers he prepared for submission to the Committee was a list of the names, salaries and wages of all naval office holders. Prince Rupert, as Vice-Admiral of England and Lieutenant-Admiral of the Narrow Seas, leads off with £469. 5s. 9d. Below him comes the Secretary of the Admiralty, Samuel Pepys esq. The clerk drawing up the schedule had left the salary blank. Pepys in his own hand inserted the word 'Nothing'.[7] In the atmosphere of 1679 objectivity was at a discount.

Yet even then there were men who would not go with wind and tide. Sir William Coventry, not the least formidable Parliamentarian among the critics of the court, spoke up for his old colleague, and cast doubts on the trustworthiness of James the butler. Colonel Norwood, the ex-Deputy Governor of Tangier, whose discussion of gastronomic questions Pepys once thought ill-bred, wrote to him in the Tower with the most heart-warming denunciation of Scott. John Evelyn and James Houblon were among the first and most frequent of his visitors. His friends, his relations, his subordinates all stood by him and, even more gratifyingly, senior sea officers such as Narbrough and Sir John Holmes, brother to Sir Robert, wrote to record their solicitude. After the nightmare of the past few weeks he knew where he was and could begin to plan a counter-offensive.

The core of the enemy position was Paris. So far as it is possible to prove a negative Pepys had already ample evidence that he was *not* a Papist, that Morelli was *not* a Jesuit, or even a priest, that he was not and had not ever been in any way involved in whatever mischief the *Hunter* had got up to during the last Dutch War. But Colonel Scott's allegations might unless they were shown to be false open a short way to the scaffold. Pepys's own direct contacts in Paris were few. But there were friends, close friends, with the best of relations there in every department of life: Houblon with the world of commerce and finance: Southwell with that of government and diplomacy: Evelyn and the Royal Society with the great international world of learning and the arts, a passport sometimes more valuable in highly civilised countries than those issued by politicians. Coventry's nephew, Harry Savile, then serving in the English embassy, was a highly intelligent and valuable source. As an official and an aristocrat with a marked taste for conviviality, a sense of humour and not much use for protocol he was better placed than anyone to initiate inquiries about Scott. Savile at once established that he was a criminal of a particularly unpleasant kind. Pepys pressed the embassy to approach the Marquis de Seignelay, to whom he and Deane were alleged to have sold charts and other information prejudicial to England's security but found it reluctant.* Inquiries such as this could not be prosecuted with the necessary rigour through third parties, however well disposed. Pepys needed a man of his own in Paris.

The obvious choice was Balty. '. . . He being', as Pepys wrote two

---

* Sir Arthur Bryant (*Years of Peril*, 273) seems to attribute this to the deference proper to years and lineage: 'But Pepys was insistent and continued to urge that a direct approach should be made to the old aristocrat.' The Marquis was in fact aged twenty-eight and his father, the great Colbert, was himself the son of a draper.

years later, 'the only person (whome from his relation to me together with his knowledge in the place and Language, his knowne dilligence and perticular affection toward me) I could at that tyme and in soe greate a cause pitch on . ...'[8] Balty was on the point of embarking for Tangier where he had been appointed Muster-Master and surveyor of the victualling. The King granted a double request that the Tangier squadron might sail without him and that he might have leave to go to France. Balty's delight at exchanging a long and uncomfortable voyage to a subordinate position in a dismal colonial outpost for independence and an expense account in Paris may easily be imagined. 'Be also as good a Husband as you can,' wrote Pepys apprehensively from the Tower on June the 19th in the letter of instructions he sent him enclosed in a note to Mr. Brisbane, the Secretary of the Paris embassy, under whose wing Balty was to operate. But Brisbane was soon afterwards recalled and Balty for six glorious months was on his own in Paris. For the last three he even had an assistant, characteristically demanded to support pretensions of Herculean labour, characteristically resented as implying a slur on what had been achieved single-handed. This was Balty's finest hour. Absurd, posturing, melodramatic egotist that he was, there is no denying his energy or his anxiety to maintain his brother-in-law's good opinion. Even his absurdities for once could be turned to account: posturing and melodrama are highly congenial to the criminal mind. Balty, it seems probable, got on much better with the con. men and shysters to whom Scott's trail led than abler men like Hewer or James Houblon would have done. They recognised him as a kindred spirit. Certainly he got results. He found the man at whose house Scott lodged when in Paris, a shady English watchmaker called John Joyne, and succeeded in persuading him to come over to London (expenses paid, naturally) to give evidence about Scott's movements and general character that would have been most unwelcome to the prosecution. Through Joyne he met other and even shiftier members of Scott's circle, Sherwin and Foster. Sherwin, like Joyne, had been associated with Scott in an experimental gun-foundry at Nevers in which both Shaftesbury and Prince Rupert had been involved. Foster had known Scott well in Paris. Both were evidently prepared to reminisce in whatever vein their audience required. But both expected a handsome advance on their memoirs (Foster had, apparently, written a Life of Scott): and both turned coy at the idea of appearing in a court of law. From these, and other such sources, Pepys built up that lurid dossier on Scott's career which is contained in 'my two volumes of Mornamont', still in his Library. Their name is that of an imaginary castle which Scott at one time claimed to possess.

It was Balty's other great virtue that he would do what he was told.

Pepys, first from the Tower, then from the Marshalsea, latterly on bail at Hewer's house in York Buildings, kept up a steady stream of instructions. All Scott's allegations were to be pursued by checking them with the French naval officers or courtiers with whom Pepys and Deane were said to have done business. If they were dead, their widows or secretaries must be traced and statements taken. Since the great proportion of them were bound to be Roman Catholics they would hardly at the height of the Plot be much use in the witness box. But the gradual accumulation of truth might provide new vantage-points from which Scott might be exposed. Information properly authenticated, widely collected and systematically co-ordinated must in the end triumph over error and deceit. If it were not so, the faith of the Royal Society would be in vain.

How strong that faith was Pepys's own calm confidence best shows. Even at the worst of times the tone of his letters is cheerful, rational and humane. He jokes ruefully with the exiled Duke of York at the attempts to make him out a Papist. He quietens the agitation felt by Mary Skinner and his old father at Brampton. He remembers that other people have their troubles and where he can he tries to relieve them. Almost the last letter in the vast book that contains file copies of his private correspondence over the seventeen years up to his imprisonment is one soliciting a place at Christ's Hospital for a boy whose widowed mother has three other children to support.[9] When he wrote it he was already embattled in his last forlorn Parliamentary stand. From the Tower he sent money to Morelli at Brentwood and courteously explained to another friend why he was in no position to lend him £100.[10] The wisdom and tact with which, from afar, he handled Balty whose zeal might so easily and so disastrously have outrun discretion show a steadiness of nerve not to be found in a man of weak convictions. Once again he was fighting a battle whose nature gave full scope to his deepest instincts and highest powers, the lawyer's passion for justice and skill in argument, the historian's concern for fact and curiosity as to motive, the scientific urge to amass evidence and to criticise it, the artist's search for order and meaning. He was fighting not only for his life but for everything that made it worth living. His talents were volunteers in the service.

That the case never came to a trial was in some ways a relief, but it was undoubtedly a disappointment. Forced into a war not of his own choosing Pepys had thrown all he had into a campaign whose brilliant success surely deserved to be crowned with a great victory. But this was denied him. On June 20th when the law term opened the prosecution were not ready to proceed. Pepys and Deane applied successfully to be removed from the Tower, an exclusively political prison, and recommitted to the

Marshalsea where they would be under the rules of the King's Bench. On July 9th they were admitted to bail in £30,000, a huge sum in the seventeenth century. At the end of the vacation Pepys pressed for a hearing. Joyne the watchmaker had come over from Paris to give evidence: Balty had garnered a neat sheaf of attestations from the French officers named by Scott: even the Marquis de Seignelay in response to a direct approach from Pepys confounded the Embassy's scruples and wrote a letter disposing of Scott's nonsense.[11] Sherwin, too, had come over, uninvited and unexpected. A doubtful asset in the witness box, supposing that his repugnance to it could be overcome, he introduced Pepys to other associates of Scott from whose conversation it transpired that Balty's airy claim to have discredited his allegations in an important particular was itself ill-founded. The Pepys who gently chided his brother-in-law's dangerous mistake was very different from the man who had bullied Elizabeth for far less serious delinquencies only ten years earlier:

And therefore by the way pray learne of mee this one Lesson, which on this occasion I have Observed not onely you but others of Our Friends, not to have yet met with, vizt to bee most Slow to beleeve what we most wish should bee true . . .'[12]

But in spite of everything the best that Pepys could obtain was a renewal of bail. When term ended in February 1680 he and Deane were released from bail and on June 30th, in face of the continued silence of the prosecution, they were at last discharged. No doubt he owed his freedom to his own exertions. His enemies had found him a tougher nut to crack than the man they had written off as one 'who had known softness and the pleasures of life'. Next to himself he owed most to the affectionate steadfastness of his closest friends: James Houblon, to whom he wrote at once with the first news of his discharge, and Will Hewer, from whose house he was writing. Immediately he had been bailed from the Marshalsea in July 1679 Pepys had written to Balty:

I am now with Will Hewer at his house, and have receiv'd from him all the care, kindness and faithfulness of a son, on this occasion, for which God reward him, if I cann't.'[13]

Such loyalty cost something to give. Hewer did not then or later share Pepys's imprisonment; not having so far to fall he did not experience the humiliation of sudden, violent and public ejection from power and importance to disgrace and nothingness. He even succeeded in the spring of 1680 to the Treasurership of Tangier which both prudence and necessity prompted Pepys to relinquish. Prudence, both because a rich office is a dangerous possession in a time of political gang warfare and because Tangier by draining public money and providing a billet for Catholic officers might easily have found itself in the eye of the storm: necessity, because a prisoner of state is in no position to discharge public business. None the less Hewer did in his quiet way expose himself to danger in that wild and whirling time. The two most witty and damaging of the pamphlets attacking Pepys specifically couple Hewer's name with that of his master: the first, *Plain Truth or Closet Discourse Betwixt P. and H.*, the second *A Hue and Cry after P. and H.* Both make great play with the high standard of living enjoyed by the two, listing with the lip-smacking gusto of a hungry age the delicacies which James the butler had been accustomed to set out for one of his master's nobler entertainments. They hit, too, at a point where Pepys in the days of the Diary had himself felt misgivings: the magnificence of his coach. It was not so long since the Tudor Parliaments had occupied themselves with sumptuary legislation. How strong was the social prejudice it enshrined a century after Pepys can be seen from Johnson's *obiter dictum* about Garrick's style of life:

> You despise a man for avarice, but do not hate him. Garrick might have been much better attacked for living with more splendour than is suitable to a player.

Both pamphlets employ social jealousy to envenom general and specific charges of corruption. As Sir Arthur Bryant has pointed out[14] *Plain Truth* in particular shows a skill in misrepresenting Pepys's administrative reforms that any propagandist must envy. To take but one example, the line that he had taken (and so carefully explained to Mrs. Pearse) over the vacant pursery of a first-rate is brilliantly traduced into a dodge — attributed to Hewer — for multiplying a single vacancy into five or six and collecting a fee on each. Both men certainly accumulated a great deal more money than could have been saved out of their official salaries but it would be as unfair to deny Pepys's passion for justice, as it would be guileless to accept his 'Nothing' as a true return of his salary. That Hewer accepted Pepys's standards in such matters seems certain from the intimate collaboration of a lifetime. Why did he in fact escape so lightly both at the Plot and at the Revolution? It seems probable that his uncle, Robert Blackborne, who had run the Navy Office under the Protectorate and was now Secretary of the East India Company was a useful relation to have.

To James Houblon Pepys acknowledged in the letter already alluded to '. . . obligations to you and your family, which nothing but the grave shall, or can, or ought to put an end to'. Later he sent him his picture,

. . . in hopes that, when he sees that, it will be out of his power not to recollect his errands on my score to Westminster Hall, his visit to the lions,* his passings over the bridge to the Patten in Southwark, and a thousand other things which, by his good will, he would never come within the hearing of

and goes on to imagine the Houblon children asking 'was Mr Pepys in these clothes, father, when you used to go to the Tower to him?' It is one of the most charming of Pepys's many charming letters, written from Brampton in November 1680.

He had been brought there by the death of his father, whose last months had been cheered by the knowledge that his kind, brilliant son had eluded the malice of his enemies. Some virulent infection had visited the place, carrying off Pall's husband in the summer and her father at the beginning of October. Pall herself had caught it and only narrowly survived. As on an earlier visit Pepys found affairs — and his sister — in a most horrid pickle. But clearing up the estate offered in little the satisfaction now denied him in official activity.

Not that he was now capable of being idle. He had passed the summer supervising his French Protestant clerk, Paul Lorrain, in the great work of copying and arranging the materials that form the two volumes of Mornamont and in pursuing the literary, historical and scientific studies that had been pushed to one side by his indictment. He saw a good deal of John Evelyn; he resumed his attendance at the Royal Society; he collected material for his great history of the sea. He renewed his contacts with Cambridge and, in September, was commanded to attend the King at Newmarket. Here, fresh from his own experience of playing fox to the Parliamentary hounds, he took down in shorthand (later transcribing it into longhand) the King's famous, some yawning courtiers thought too famous, account of his escape after the battle of Worcester in 1651. He was at Newmarket when the news of his father's death called him to Brampton early in October.

Was the King, as he reminisced, contemplating, weighing the chances of another civil war? There was always, as Professor Plumb has recently pointed out, an air of carpet-bagging about Charles II's Court. The great political fever of the Plot was unmistakably moving to its climax. For

* The Tower served, among its many purposes, as London's zoo.

more than a year Charles had parried, sidestepped, given ground with a steadiness of nerve that everyone must admire and a coolness perhaps impossible to a generous nature. When Pepys had been sent to the Tower, Richard Hampden, son of the great John, was moving the introduction of a bill to exclude James Duke of York from the succession. Charles had countered by prorogation and in July, when Pepys was admitted to bail, by dissolution. In the same month Chief Justice Scroggs had dared to doubt the truthfulness of Oates and Bedloe in the trial of Sir George Wakeman, the royal physician, on a charge of attempting to poison the sovereign. The exposure of this seventeenth-century Doctor's Plot might have given pause. But in August the King fell dangerously ill without benefit of medical assistance. James had to be recalled from exile. On his brother's recovery he was sent abroad again but almost at once appointed High Commissioner in Edinburgh. A new Parliament, summoned in October 1679 was immediately prorogued. The King was inching back but he was not yet ready.

For twelve months he went on proroguing, waiting for an opening in foreign affairs, waiting for the tide of the plot to ebb. It was only a shift in the diplomatic scene that, at last, enabled the King to face his Parliament in October 1680. Of the alarming turn that affairs then took Pepys was informed at Brampton through the correspondence of Hewer and James Houblon. The possibility of anti-French coalition that Charles dangled before the Commons was brushed aside. In November the Exclusion Bill passed the Commons who then began to turn their attention to Tangier, that nest of Papists. But on November 15th William Coventry's nephew, Halifax, saved the day for the King and Duke in a Lords' debate that changed our history and enriched our literature. The Exclusion Bill was thrown out. The rage of the Commons inspired one last set piece of vindictive wickedness, the impeachment and execution of the old and harmless Catholic, Lord Stafford. Declining Halifax's compromise schemes of limiting James's powers, they tried direct bargaining. No supplies would be voted for Tangier unless Exclusion were granted. In mid-December Charles, predictably, turned them down: on January 7th the Commons raised their terms: no supplies at all. On January 10th, as they were frenziedly voting that the Fire of London was the work of the Papists, Charles prorogued them. Dissolution followed a few days later.

Pepys was back in London by November 20th. Returning, he had been robbed by highwaymen near Highgate but what was that with the country on the edge of civil war? 'Forty-one is come again' was a terrible refrain to the ears of his generation. The King, however, could see light at the end of the tunnel. Another twist to the European kaleidoscope had opened the probability of fresh subsidies from France. With a light heart he summoned his last Parliament to meet at Oxford in March: with a light heart he dissolved them. The French subsidy was secure. By July Shaftesbury was in the Tower. The Stuart counterattack was to be pressed hard and savagely.

In all this Pepys stood on the sidelines. He was not in office: he had not sat in either of the two Parliaments that had been elected since his fall. His sympathies could not for a moment be in doubt, but his talents were not called on until the reign was nearing its end. The power of the Whigs, as Shaftesbury's party had come to be called, was effectively broken by the summer of 1681, yet Pepys was not re-employed until the summer of 1683. He had plenty to do on his own account and there were plenty of public bodies, Christ's Hospital, Trinity House, the Royal Society, his old college, to whom he could be of service. But admirable and useful as these institutions were, they could manage without him. The navy, it seems, could not. Evidence superabounds that the commissioners of 1679 were wholly incompetent. Pepys had seen and said as much in the few weeks he had worked with them. The Dutch and the French intelligence services rapidly confirmed his judgment to their Governments. Above all, Charles II, one of the foremost naval experts in Europe, in charge of the Government and in day-to-day contact with these amateurs certainly knew. Why, once he was master in his house, did he not replace them? Even Pepys confessed himself amazed.

No king ever did so unaccountable a thing to oblige his people by, as to dissolve a commission of the Admiralty then in his own hand, who best understands the business of the sea of any prince the world ever had, and things never better done, and put it into hands which he knew were wholly ignorant thereof, sporting himself with their ignorance . . .[15]

The final phrase perhaps glimpses the depths of frivolity in a nature otherwise shallow. If there is a better explanation it has yet to be provided.

19

Tangier

The autumn of 1680 took off more than old John Pepys and Pall's husband: it took off Balty, at long last, to assume his deferred appointment in Tangier. By the time he had got as far as the Downs he was already complaining bitterly of the weather, the food, the unfairness of life, the insulting treatment he received from those he considered his inferiors at the Navy Office and of Pepys's failure to make the King sufficiently sensible of his past services. The present appointment was '. . . to my misfortune and ruine . . . (for which ware I not more then comon man I shoold Runn to dispaire).' He had been

> . . . towrne from the Bowells of my sweet litill famely; and from my five small babes whoe cryed after their owne father, at my departure from them, and that to, after all my youth Spent in his Majesty's service in Ever and all dangers and trubles . . . to have at last noe other recompence than to be sent to the Divill for a New yeares gift.

Balty's devotion to family life had not been so touchingly apparent during his time in Paris, except for a suggestion, outrageous to the prudent Pepys, that he should bring home a French tutor for his children. As he recounted the misadventures of his journey, he reflected 'how full of thornes my life hath bine, and that I, and only I of My age Ever had the like measure in this world, from my first Essay in Bloody fights, both at home and a broad, to all the dangerous imployments on shore . . .' This was pitching it a bit strong for his years as Muster-Master at Deal. '. . . (Lord why was I borne) shall I never have rest from fightgs and stormes . . .' Apparently not, if he were to judge from '. . . the slights the world . . . show me dayley at the Navey office &c: beleeving me, most Ignorent in imployments and of less sowle then any other.' 'Sowle' was so obviously Balty's long suit that their imperceptiveness is unforgivable. His brother-in-law could have easily put them right about that. And it was with appeals to his brother-in-law, greased with a fulsomeness and a flattery that would offend a much grosser taste, that this very long letter[1] ends.

Pepys, who had no job himself, who had had his work cut out to secure Balty's reversion to the Tangier post, saw things very differently. At least the man was provided for, out of harm's way and without much opportunity of spending or borrowing money. His wife was under no such inhibitions. Pepys soon settled matters by packing her and the children off to Brampton to live rent-free. But even that did not answer. Ester St. Michel was no Elizabeth. Bombarded with furious injunctions to live within the twenty shillings a week that he reluctantly allowed her, exhorted with the example of Elizabeth's household accounts 'even to a bunch of carrot and a ball of whiteing which I have under her own hand to show you at this day',[2] she won in the end through her invincible incompetence. Still, Brampton, like Tangier, did form an obstacle to extravagance.

Pall had fallen ill again, or perhaps she had never properly recovered, about the time that Balty was arriving in Tangier. She came to London, vacating Brampton for the St. Michels, but was not well enough to look after her children, Samuel and John. The two boys were boarded with a schoolmaster in Huntingdon; Pepys, who was to make each in turn his heir, paid for their maintenance in a cheese-paring style. The bargain price for victualling and clothing people one did not see had become a reflex. Finally Mary Skinner's scapegrace brother Daniel had been sent to the Barbados with a letter of introduction to Will Howe, Sandwich's old steward, now married and settled there. Will Howe found him 'something soft in his Disposition' and disinclined, like so many of Pepys's young protégés, to regular employment. But the letter bearing this news did not begin its homeward journey until June 1681 so that for most of the year Pepys was freer than usual from family concerns.

He made the most of his liberty. His two charming and lively young cousins, Lady Mordaunt and Mrs. Steward, enjoyed the chief share of his

gallantries. For ten years past they with his friend Thomas Hill, the
Lisbon merchant, had formed a quartet expert in all the sighings and
teasings of an *amitié amoureuse*. And the music, which had been by his own
account the only relaxation of the days when he was new-modelling the
navy, took its proper place again as the true passion of his life. Morelli
on Easter Monday 1681 sent him the score of some operas he had trans-
scribed for him and promised the immediate delivery of 'them songs
wich You intend to sing with Mrs Houblon'. There were occasional
commands to attend the court at Newmarket or Windsor. There were
even faint echoes of his past, as when Hewer eagerly told his master that
when something had been 'moved in Counsill relating to salutes, ye King
was pleased to respite the doeing anything therein till they had discoursed
you: this Mr Blathwaite* acquainted me with and desired me to signify
the same to you . . .'3 Was there a chance of a come-back or was Hewer
whistling to keep his master's spirits up? Pepys, whatever his secret hopes,
acted on the principle he had impressed on Balty of being most slow to
believe what he would most wish true. He threw his energies into reviving
the mathematical school at Christ's Hospital which had drifted into torpor
through the appointment of a man who was far too learned to bother himself with elementary teaching. He set out to win prestige for the foundation by arranging that Verrio should be commissioned to paint a grand
scene of the mathematical scholars being received by the King. In the
picture Pepys himself appears in a furred aldermanic gown borrowed from
Sir Thomas Beckford, the great navy contractor. Although it was not
finished until 1685 (and the King is therefore James and not Charles)
Pepys borrowed Beckford's gown in February 1682.4 The heavy, rolling
figure, curiously foreshadowing Reynolds's magnificent portrait of Johnson,
the wide eyes and strong face so much more eloquent than the more
measured statements of other likenesses taken in middle age, may therefore express the frustrations of an uncertain retirement.

To complete retirement Pepys could, no doubt, have reconciled himself.
He had interests enough to fill ten lives: his power of adapting himself to
circumstance was his most marked characteristic. That he should talk
on his visits to Cambridge of the happiness to be found in breaking away
from affairs and devoting the rest of his life to learning was true of his
nature. On August 8th, 1681, at nine o'clock at night one of his friends
there sent off a special messenger to tell him of the sudden death of the
Provost of King's.

---

* William Blathwayt, soon to be Secretary-at-War, like Pepys a prototype of the professional administrator.

. . . the preferment is 7 hundred pounds per annum and I am sure you would be as acceptable a man as the King could present unto it so that if no time be lost I should with all the joy imaginable salute you Provost . . .

Pepys was attracted: he thought his academic qualifications inadequate but owned the '. . . possibility of supplying, by some other way of usefulness to the College, what I should fall short in of knowledge.' But what determined him against standing was his desire not to intrude. He had heard that there was a Fellow of the College already recommended to the King by George Legge, an old pupil.[5] Once again, this time inadvertently, Legge had got in the way.

The loss, if any, was to Cambridge. Pepys's friends there, to judge from his correspondence, were either cranks like Dr. Vincent of Clare Hall or amiable fuddlers like Dr. Peachell, the Master of Magdalene. Dr. Vincent's magpie mind recommended itself to Pepys by a collection of Conjectura Nautica. He valued himself most however on inventions such as

. . . a way of writing which can never be deciphered. It beares the reading, but a very few Minutes, and then its characters vanish . . . by which meanes the writer is secured . . . against Curiosity, sawciness or Accidental discoveries.

Dr. Vincent wondered whether the King or the Duke of York would think it worth a thousand pounds. 'I reckon it to be much more worth to a foreign Prince engaged in wars.' Pepys in a long and courteous letter demonstrated its entire worthlessness.[6] Undeterred Dr. Vincent communicated to him his experiment '. . . of relieving and interrupting the noctilucal flame . . . to find by it ye hour of the night upon a watch'.[7] He had resolved to leave Cambridge.

That happy place has been my abode from seven years of age: & whether my spirits are overcharged or insufficiently nourished by . . . ye *occultus vitae cibus* [the hidden food of life] of ye place I know not: but this I know I must transplant if I will grow any longer . . .

He thought of moving to London or Bury St. Edmunds and there 'setting to work on those two great questions Resistance to a Lawful Prince and Passive Obedience.'[8] None the less Pepys set a real value on his learning and years later granted his request for £25 to buy a rare historical work that was coming up for auction.[9]

The true centre of Pepys's intellectual life was that group of Fellows of the Royal Society, Evelyn, Southwell, Petty, with whom, when they were out of London, he maintained a voluminous correspondence. Even in the depths of the country they retain an urbanity that makes the likes of Dr. Vincent sound provincial:

> I am here among my children which is at least an innocent scene of life, & endeavour to explain to them the difference between right & wrong. My next care is to contend for that health which I lost by sitting many years at ye sackbottle soe that to keepe my selfe in idleness and in motion is a great part of my discipline . . .[10]

Thus Sir Robert Southwell from his country house near Bristol. It is the tone of Pepys's proper circle. People who write like that are too grown-up to play with invisible ink or to occupy themselves with the stale arguments for the Divine Right of Kings. But they are not too superior to enjoy the little things of life. Among the letters of these eminent men Pepys has preserved a quack advertisement ('My Rupture is Cured!') and a letter to Charles II from the King of Bantam 'perfum'd with the musky odoure of sincerity' requesting 'of your love that you would send us by every ship sailing to Bantam Gunpowder and Great Guns and Match and Bullets and wherein to put the powder and match . . .' A well-conditioned mind requires diversion.

The main preoccupation of these years, the use to which the Provostship would have been put, was the research and the assembling of materials for the great history of the sea. Evelyn with characteristic generosity put the treasures of his library and the fruits of his own labours on the Third Dutch War at the disposal of his friend (the books and manuscripts are still in the Pepys Library but Evelyn's own work has, alas, vanished). He warned him eloquently of the hazards of the undertaking:

> . . . 'tis not easily to be imagined the sea and ocean of *papers*, *treaties*, *declarations*, *relations*, *letters* and other pieces, that I have ben faine to saile through, reade over, note, and digest, before I set pen to paper; I confesse to you the fatigue was unsufferable, and for the most part did rather oppresse and confound me than inlighten, so much trash there was to sieft and lay by, and I was obliged to peruse all that came to hand . . .'[11]

And his heart-cry, uttered four months later, echoes in the mind of every practitioner of the craft.

It is not imaginable to such as have not tried, what labour an historian (that would be exact) is condemned to. He must reade all, good and bad, and remove a world of rubbish before he can lay the foundation.[12]

Pepys, apparently, was not a whit discouraged. But the first gleams of return to public life broke, for a moment, through the historical cloudbank. In May 1682 he was invited to accompany the Duke of York on a voyage to Edinburgh and himself to receive the freedom of Newcastle-upon-Tyne. It was not much, but it was something. Unfortunately the expedition was marred by disgrace and disaster. The *Gloucester* in which the Duke was sailing was wrecked in calm clear weather close inshore through the carelessness of the pilot. Inexcusably, nearly all the ship's company were lost though the Duke, his footman, and even his dog, were taken off with an observance of ceremony disgusting even to that age of excessive formality.* The public horror was in many hearts compounded by private grief for the loss of Pepys who was assumed to have accepted the Duke's pressing invitation to join him in the *Gloucester*. Happily he had preferred an ampler berth in one of the escorting yachts. All this agitation supplanted the excitement of travel: his letters tell us little about his only visit to Scotland: like almost every visitor he was nauseated by the abysmal standards of personal hygiene; like almost every visitor for the next hundred years he was much taken with the beauty of Glasgow and, by contrast, says nothing of Edinburgh. He stayed at Berwick, made an expedition to Holy Island, was entertained at Seaton Delaval (the pre-Vanbrugh house), fêted at Newcastle and shocked by the princely state kept by the Bishops of Durham.

Back in London he was rapturously received by the Houblons and the ladies of Winchester Street, Lady Mordaunt and Mrs. Steward. Once the excitement was over the rest of the year passed uneventfully. He was defeated over the appointment of a mathematical master at Christ's Hospital. One learned man simply made way for another learned man. What Pepys had intended as a polytechnic was taken over for a research fellowship. He resigned from the School's Committee. On the domestic front a tolerable quiet reigned. Balty had popped up again in January, returning from Tangier unannounced and without first obtaining leave. His excuse was the non-payment of his salary. Pepys quickly smoothed things over with the officers of the Navy Board, enlisted the good offices of Lord Brouncker and succeeded in getting Balty, lachrymose and loquacious as ever, aboard a vessel bound for Tangier early in March. A silence of

* For this the ubiquitous Legge seems to have been largely responsible. See Pepys's long and circumstantial letter to Hewer, printed in Howarth, 133–6.

fifteen months ensues in the surviving documents broken at the end of
June 1683 with fresh mewlings 'to [his] Deare Though most cruell
Benifactor to clearly thus forg[et] and leave in afflictions, in a hellish
Torred-zone, a Creatur of your Owne makeing, who never yett Dis-
honoured you . . .'13 By the time this letter reached England Pepys was on
his way to answer in person and at once its somewhat theatrical plea for
'. . . Redemption from this hell, this hell of Brimston and fire, and Egipts
plaugues.'

Not that Balty's *cri du cœur* had supplied the initiative. The enormous
expense of the Tangier garrison and the vast capital investment of constructing the mole were probably beyond the resources of any English government of the seventeenth century. They certainly were for a King who had
to rely on French subsidies. The decision, long overdue, was, at last,
taken to liquidate the commitment: to slight the fortifications, blow up
the mole and evacuate the population. It was fitting that Pepys who had
entered public life as the protégé of Mountagu, the champion of the Tangier
policy, who had lined his pockets out of its Treasurership ('one of the
best flowers in my garden'), should assist at its obsequies. Will Hewer,
who had succeeded him in this rewarding horticulture, was also of the
party. It was completed by Henry Sheeres, a versatile military engineer,
the chief constructor of the mole, whom Pepys had once suspected of
designs on Elizabeth's virtue, William Trumbull, a clever young
barrister and Fellow of All Souls with whom Pepys had corresponded on
learned questions, Dr. Thomas Ken, the Canon of Winchester who had
won Charles II's amused respect by refusing to put up Nell Gwynn, and,
in command of the whole expedition, the ever-recurrent George Legge,
now raised to the peerage as Baron Dartmouth.

Tangier was Pepys's second spring. At two days' notice he left London
to join the *Grafton* in Portsmouth harbour. What he was to do was still
hidden from him. But that he was to act once again as a senior (and highly
paid) Government executive in naval business of high importance was
plain beyond doubt. The winter of unemployment was over. For his
biographer too the earth brings forth her increase: Pepys kept a journal of
the whole episode from his setting out from Lambeth on July 30th to his
going on board the *Mountagu* in Tangier Bay on December 1st to take passage for Spain and thence to England. And one other member of the party,
Sir William Trumbull as he had then become, wrote down his own
recollections in the Autobiography he composed some thirty years later.
The *Journal Towards Tangier* is not to be compared either for quality or
extent with the Diary: but it *is* a later work from the same hand. Sir
William Trumbull *was* writing a long time after the events he describes

but he was a highly intelligent and well-informed observer. His autobiography[14] is unsafe in details (e.g. he claims to have embarked on May
9th when the real date was August) but there is an astringency about his
impressions that commands respect. '. . . Sir H. Sheares had written a
book in commendation of Tangier and so was sent with us to confute
every article he had so industriously praised.' French authorities confirm
his assertion that Charles II had done his best to sell Tangier to Louis XIV.
He had, unknown apparently to Trumbull, as a last resort even tried to
raise a bid from the Portuguese. The secrecy that surrounded the whole
affair is indeed understandable. According to Trumbull it was not until
they were off Cape St. Vincent that Dartmouth opened his commission:

> . . . and when he had acquainted Mr Pepys, Sheers and myself with this
> secret we lookt upon one another as those do (at a foolish sport) who
> are equally smutted. But especially ye former [Pepys] who from ye value
> he put upon himself, made him luke upon this as a distrust of him,
> & so an offence equall to sacriledg: However there was no Remedy:
> & so necessity made us (as it does other men) pretty good philosophers.[15]

The picture of Pepys's discomfiture probably owes much to Trumbull's
annoyance three years later when he asked for a man-of-war to carry him
as ambassador to Constantinople. This traditional privilege '. . . of late
yeares upon frivolous reasons (too long to be here mentioned) had been
left off and was deny'd now by positive Mr Pepys.'[16] Certainly Pepys's
Journal shows that Dartmouth had confided in him the whole purpose of
the expedition before they sailed down channel. Trumbull was not let into
the secret for another three weeks. Both men were joined, Trumbull as a
professional lawyer, Pepys as a lay assessor, in a commission to estimate
the value of the property for which compensation might be claimed by the
citizens and to advise Dartmouth on this point in his capacity as
arbitrator. In fact Dartmouth relied on Pepys's judgment and advice over
a far wider range of issues. Perhaps the King foresaw and intended this.

When Pepys received the summons to start at forty-eight hours'
notice, he tidied his desk of correspondence and bought an outfit that suggests a Victorian nanny equipping herself for a visit to an east-coast
watering-place. Galoshes and a sea-gown, plenty of warm underwear
and flannel next to the skin. Nor, as Sir Arthur Bryant points out, did he
neglect the opportunities for reading offered by a long sea-voyage. The
regular intercourse with sea officers would form an ideal background for
serious naval studies: Tangier, the object of the expedition, dictated the
choice of several works on fortification: the proximity of Spain and the

probability of making an expedition there caused him to include a number of the Spanish books in which his library was so rich:[17] for entertainment there was his favourite author Fuller, represented this time by his history of the Crusades, and Butler's *Hudibras*, enjoyed at last: there were, of course, music books and some works of religion. Pepys had been charged with finding a chaplain for Lord Dartmouth and on the advice of his learned cousin by marriage, Dr. Gale, High Master of St. Paul's, selected Dr. Ken, the author of the two beautiful hymns in the Manual for Winchester Scholars which are known to generations of Anglicans as the Morning and the Evening hymn. His fearless moral courage has already been alluded to: besides refusing to countenance Charles II's open infidelities he had earlier, when chaplain at The Hague, reproved the future William III for bullying his wife.

To meet and escort him to Portsmouth Pepys spent the second night of his journey at Winchester, dining next day in hall with Ken who was a Fellow of the College as well as a prebendary of the Cathedral. They reached Portsmouth the same evening. A week later, on Thursday August 9th, they slept for the first time aboard the *Grafton*. Dartmouth came on board next morning and the expedition sailed out of harbour to anchor in St. Helen's. The prevailing westerlies kept them there for nearly ten days, during which Dartmouth revealed the purpose of the voyage to Pepys. The surprise was complete. Most of the time that they were windbound Pepys spent writing letters or being entertained either ashore or aboard their companions. The valetudinarian middle-aged widower ate and drank more discreetly than the young man who had delighted in the naval conviviality of twenty years before. For the rest the only events of interest were the arrival of Colonel Wyndham's yacht, notable as being the only gentleman known to Pepys who sailed purely for pleasure, and seeing a Turk severely whipped and his beard singed for attempting unnatural vice.

When the wind at last came round to the east of south two days' pleasant sailing brought them to anchor in Plymouth Sound. Hewer went ashore to visit relations so Pepys took Trumbull with him to pay two calls on the past. The first to Mount Edgcumbe whose châtelaine was one of his old charges, Lady Anne Mountagu, now wife to Sir Richard Edgcumbe: the second to St. Nicholas island[18] to see Lambert, the last great survivor of the Cromwellian régime. Pepys, perhaps from the force of earlier habit, refers to him as 'my lord Lambert', thus acknowledging the peerage granted by Oliver. The interview, it seems, was unproductive. Lambert was within a few months of his death and had long been ga-ga (fortunately, if such a condition may ever be termed fortunate: it had protected him from Oates's accusations of complicity in the Popish Plot). Trumbull says nothing of it in his autobiography. But the visit is characteristic of Pepys; he could not anchor in sight of the prison that held a great historical figure and not try to see him.

Next day after great comings and goings from shore they sailed for Tangier. For most of the first week the weather was very rough. Pepys was seasick and Hewer prostrated. But on the last day of August both wind and weather came fair. At dinner in the cabin (which Hewer was still too unwell to attend) there was 'a good deal of music and good humour'. In the afternoon Pepys walked the deck with Dartmouth and in the evening he read and discussed a book on the jurisdiction of the Admiralty with Trumbull alone in their cabin. He found him agreeable company though he had been peevish during the rough weather. Life went on in this agreeable manner, enlivened by a good deal of naval gossip when they entertained or were entertained by the captains sailing in company. By September 7th, when they were in the latitude of Finisterre it was warm as well as sunny. Awnings were rigged. At a party to celebrate the anniversary of the King's recovery from illness the gunner got so drunk that he had to be put in the bilboes all night. As they sailed past the mouth of the Tagus Dartmouth formally communicated his instructions to both Pepys and Trumbull. Off Cape St. Vincent Pepys and Ken argued hotly about the existence of spirits. Pepys's attitude, maintained through a long and careful accumulation of evidence for psychical phenomena, was what one might expect of a Fellow of the Royal Society. Ken based his position, interestingly, on the authority of the ancient authors rather than the Bible. On September 13th they opened the straits and came to an anchor in the Bay of Tangier at ten o'clock the following morning.

Relief at being safely arrived was tempered by the discovery that the place was closely besieged by the Moors. This was not at all the kind of thing that Trumbull had bargained for when he weighed up the loss of his vacation business against his fee for service at Tangier. Pepys too was not one of those who instinctively march to the sound of the guns. But his tenacity, as in the days of the plague, easily mastered his qualms. He had come to do a job and he was going to do it. His first reaction to the place and to the sight of the enemy camp is thus neither aesthetic nor self-regarding but professional: 'But Lord! how could ever anybody think this place fit to be kept at this charge, that by its being overlooked by so many hills can never be secured against an enemy.'

Old Tangier hands like Sheeres and some of the captains who had often served on the station looked on this state of affairs as natural. England never came near attaining local superiority during the whole of her tenure

of Tangier. On the contrary total disaster was always a possibility, sometimes advancing but never receding out of sight. The day that Fuzzy
Wuzzy broke a British square had dawned at Tangier two centuries before
Kipling and the Mahdi. In 1664 Lord Teviot, the Governor and
Commander-in-Chief, had been ambushed in a wood near the town and
annihilated with nearly all the officers and the best troops of the garrison.
In the great siege of 1680 only the magnificent leadership of the army
officers under Sir Palmes Fairborne and the presence of a powerful naval
squadron under Admiral Herbert had preserved the town after the outer
forts had fallen. How precarious a toehold Tangier was may be gauged
by the fact that the bones of Teviot's men were still left bleaching in the
wood a few miles outside the walls.

Fairborne had been mortally wounded in the closing stages of the action
in which he had shown the highest military qualities, living just long
enough to hear of the great victory in which the Moors had been driven
back. Sheeres who had served with him throughout the siege and for many
years earlier wrote of him:

> He was a very worthy, able and brave officer, who had made it his
> speciall study to qualify himselfe for his Majesty's service here where
> he had been an officer for neare 18 yeares and I am oblig'd in Justice to
> his memory to avow that (I believe at least) his Majesty hath not a
> subject in his three kingdoms of more proper qualification for this
> post.[19]

His successor who came aboard the *Grafton* shortly after she dropped
anchor was a man of a very different type. Colonel Percy Kirke, immortalised in the name 'Kirke's Lambs' given to his regiment in ironical
tribute to the atrocities with which they were credited after the defeat
of Monmouth's rebellion, was a coarse, drunken brute who commanded a
drunken regiment. Pepys was no prude but the deepest impression he
leaves on the reader of his Journal is disgust at the gross indecency and
lurching sottishness of Kirke and his men. The endless dirty stories of
the Governor's table-talk passed from the distasteful to the unendurable:
and before long Pepys and Ken withdrew from the Government Mess to
dine in each other's company. In Pepys's view Kirke's manners and morals
were reflected in the cruelty and corruption of his administration. There
were ugly stories of soldiers beaten to death with no pretence of legality:
of Jewish refugees returned to the tortures of the Spanish Inquisition
because they could not raise the bribes that Kirke demanded: of rape and
robbery and bullying of the citizens and their wives. Kirke personified

what Pepys called 'the bestiality of this place'. 'Everything,' he wrote, 'runs to corruption here.'

The effect was intensified by the enclosed nature of Tangier society. As an earlier Governor had written '. . . [we] see nothing but Moores and the four ellements and are deprived of all civill and State conversation.'[20] It certainly made itself felt even in the work that Pepys and Trumbull had come to do:

> From Wednesday morning to Thursday morning continually busy till 8 or 9 at night without an interval but only to dinner, and then presently again to receive the claims of people to propriety. But in one word so silly and supine from all of them even the people of most understanding among them, that it is plain there was a habit of disorder and forgetfulness of all method and discipline in [all] they did, even in their own private concernments, taking such evidence for their security as would not be worth sixpence in Westminster Hall . . . So that I think it is impossible for us to give any tolerable report of them, to do either the King right or them, in which Dr Trumbull and I do greatly agree and discourse of it.[21]

Pepys, it is plain, did not like Tangier. Quite apart from the vile tone set by Kirke, the life did not agree with him. The mosquitoes were terrible: the weather, often cold and wet: the women a dowdy lot, except for Lady Mary Kirke, and even she had suffered from living in Tangier. He caught a fearful cold that kept him indoors for most of November. Hardly was he over that before he was 'mightily frightened this morning with my old swimming in my head at my rising'. Perhaps as a prophylactic he adopted the curious specific of washing his feet and thighs in brandy. His health was by no means the only cause for alarm. He much disliked riding outside the walls with Kirke and Lord Dartmouth: the Moors were uncomfortably close, totally unscrupulous and rode like lightning. What if they took it into their heads to seize the Commander-in-Chief and his party? What indeed! And Kirke who had himself once led an embassy to the Emperor of Morocco seems to have encouraged Dartmouth to consider sending Pepys and Trumbull to Fez to negotiate a treaty covering the withdrawal. Dartmouth toyed with the idea for some days but at last, much to Pepys's relief, discarded it. Since he had also been proposing to cheat the Emperor over the amount of gunpowder to be left as the price of an unopposed evacuation it seems probable that had Pepys found himself charged with so unenviable a mission, his biography would have ended at this point. After the detestable Kirke one of the first people Pepys met before going ashore was Balty 'who is mightily altered in his looks, with hard usage as he tells me'. To a degree the alteration must have extended to character since there is no further mention of him, good or bad, during the three months of Pepys's stay. Business and ill-health no doubt restricted the opportunities of social life but the stratification of an imperial outpost perhaps made it difficult for the confidential adviser to the Governor and Commander-in-Chief to hob-nob with the Agent General and Surveyor of the Victualling. The business, unsatisfactory as it was, was soon settled. By October 17th Pepys had estimated the net total payable by the King at £11,243. 17s. 4d. of which only about £7,000 was due to freeholders, the remaining £4,000 odd being in respect of leasehold properties granted by five landlords who had all been either Governors or Deputy Governors. This had, in the inextricable confusion of public and private expenditure, posed the real problem. As Pepys wrote to the local assessor joined with Trumbull and himself, the great bulk of the Commissioner's work was to assess 'stores and workmanship expended upon private Properties att his Majesty's charge'.[22] Even before the work was finished Trumbull was agitating to be sent home, complaining that each day of term lost him ten guineas in fees. Pepys and Dartmouth agreed that his true motive was cowardice. Both were contemptuously glad to see the last of him as he climbed eagerly into the boat of a ship bound for England with letters on October 20th.

In the following two months Pepys's official duties took little of his time. He pursued his general reading and his naval studies with unflagging application: he saw more of the day-to-day life of a fleet than he had done since the Restoration: he talked with an interesting group of senior captains at dinner after dinner in the great cabins, admiring unwillingly the neatness of those ships whose commanders kept the best table. He saw a great deal of Ken and came to know Dartmouth intimately. The days at Tangier, at first sight so remote, constitute an intensive rehearsal for the last act of his official life. Reading his Journal it is difficult to escape the conclusion that this is no effect of historical hindsight. Pepys was amassing detailed, up-to-the-minute information, scrutinising, weighing, planning, with a view to a complete administrative overhaul of the navy: his historical inquiries, serious and deep as they were, were in parenthesis to this immediate purpose. Everything, even his conversations with Ken, was to lead somewhere, to mean something more, in the years that lay ahead. The great second Secretaryship, the Special Commission of the Navy, the Revolution of 1688, the Non-juring circle in which the sturdy Presbyterian of the Diary was to end his days, all cast their shadow over the *Journal Towards Tangier*.

If we are sometimes reminded of the young Clerk of the Acts eagerly questioning, sifting, drawing conclusions, we ought to remember how different a man it was with whom Dartmouth and the rest had to deal. He knew what success was and how little it could count for against personal sorrow or political intrigue. The higher value he put on honesty, courage and independence of judgment is reflected in his attitude to Ken. Not content with having refused to toady to William of Orange and Charles II, who were at least too shrewd not to recognise moral courage when they saw it, Ken had reproved the vices of Tangier and its officers in a sermon that Pepys describes as 'very fine and seasonable but most unsuccessful'. The young Pepys would have been more concerned to be on the winning side: the old Pepys respected and liked Ken the better. Four weeks later he even joined him in 'very high discourse' with Kirke 'about the excessive liberty of swearing and blaspheming we observe here'.

The contrast with Dartmouth is extreme. Although he certainly shared their views and was, after all, Commander-in-Chief he was too frightened of making enemies at home and too sceptical of Charles II's reliability to act on his own judgment. Of that judgment Pepys formed an ever higher opinion. Early in October Dartmouth showed Pepys and Trumbull a draft of his public announcement to the citizens of the intended destruction of Tangier: '. . . wholly taken out [of] my notes that I gave him, but with many good improvements that were really very good and wise and shows him to me to [be] a man of very good understanding and consideration.' Turning, as they often did, from the sterile question of Tangier to the state of the navy, they found a remarkable unanimity as to symptoms, cause and cure. The root of the trouble was indiscipline (Pepys linked this with corruption in one of those self-renewing movements so dear to historical theorists) and the root of that was the Stuart brothers themselves, especially the King. As Pepys himself noted:

> The King's familiarity with commanders and under-officers makes them insolent, presuming upon their access to the King, and frights poor commanders or others their superiors from using their just authority (especially poor tarpaulins) considering what they say of the King's familiarity with those that offend.

Dartmouth, specifically charged by the King to take the opportunity offered by the Tangier voyage of restoring discipline in at least part of the fleet, did not dare: '. . . such is the power of interest and fear of making enemies at home that there is not any one thing that he has durst to rectify . . .' Dartmouth 'notes very soberly that these princes are so much fonder of a penitent sinner than a constant friend, that he prays to God that they may not live to see their friends repent'. Rivalry and political intrigue are foremost in his mind. Will the King back him against his predecessor on the station, Admiral Herbert? He declared to Pepys that there was not room for them both in the service, comparing their case to that of Sir Robert Holmes and Sir Edward Spragge 'when the latter speaking then, as himself do now, said that he was willing to leave it to the King which he would choose, Holmes or him, and that it would spoil his whole service to make use of both'. That was the point, surely. Spragge had gone to the King and spoken out at the risk of his whole career. It was a step of which Dartmouth was temperamentally incapable.

Much as Pepys commended Dartmouth's grasp of naval problems, heartily as he concurred in his pessimistic view of the King's steadfastness, it is doubtful on the very full evidence of the Journal whether he would ever have chosen him to command in chief. For the moment they were allies, united on a common programme of naval reform, each anxious to protect or promote the interest of the other. Dartmouth opened his mind to Pepys to an extent that sometimes recalls the *tête-à-têtes* with Sandwich or Coventry. But it was not the same relationship. Dartmouth, essentially, was the client, hoping that Pepys would give him a good report when they got back to England. It is here, in the winter of 1683–4, that one can find the best evidence for what Pepys must have felt in that crucial winter five years later. The urgency of that crisis left him no time for recording his thoughts and anxieties: the swift and total ruin of his cause made any such retrospect bitter and unprofitable.

Besides the generous rate – £4 a day – at which Pepys was paid, the great attraction of his employment at Tangier was the opportunity of going to Spain. At last in December he and Hewer arrived in Cadiz to stay with Mr. Hodges, a close friend and commercial associate of James Houblon. Pepys had prepared for Spain with the excitement of the born tourist and the system that he brought to everything he did. He knew what he wanted to see and whom he wanted to meet: best of all he brought with him an appetite for new impressions and a delight in observing local peculiarities. No English traveller ever deserved better luck or had worse. His first, his only, continental holiday since Elizabeth's death was ruined by the weather. At Tangier the wind had howled and the rain had beaten down. In Cadiz and Seville it was even fouler. Floods made travel impossible, or nearly so. None the less Pepys forced his way through the elements to some, at least, of his objectives and garnered a small store of those notes on behaviour and appearances that give the Diary its fresh and idiosyncratic quality. Of more particular interest are the notes he took on the Spanish arrangements for training navigators.

The weather was not the only depressing part of his stay in Spain. The drunkenness and indiscipline of English naval officers was especially mortifying in a foreign port. Pepys was eager to be back where he could put his hand to the work he knew. Remorselessly the weather and Dartmouth's indecisiveness combined to prevent his sailing before the beginning of March. After a rough and slow passage Pepys landed at Portsmouth on April 3rd. It had been a longer absence than he had bargained for: 248 days: but at £4 a day that earned him nearly £1,000. He went straight to Whitehall to make his report to the King. Six weeks later, on May 19th, 1684, the incompetent Admiralty Commission was dissolved and Pepys was appointed Secretary for the Affairs of the Admiralty of England at a salary of £2,000 a year. No professional administrator had ever reached so powerful a position in naval affairs; there was no board to deal with — only the King and his brother. No professional administrator, and only a few of the great officers of state, received so enormous a salary. Pepys had done more than make a comeback. He had reached the top.

20

The Second Secretaryship

The Second Secretaryship from May 1684 to February 1689 is the crown and the epitome of Pepys's official career. He ranged over the whole field of naval administration from finance to shipbuilding, from the training and promotion of officers to dockyards and contracts and timber and food. He drew on the earliest lessons he had learnt as Clerk of the Acts: he acted on the up-to-date and comprehensive information accumulated during the past months at Tangier and Cadiz. He allowed his mind to play on the perspectives of naval policy without relaxing his grip on the detailed and the day-to-day. It was the administrative masterpiece for which everything else, even his immense achievements in the two Dutch wars, had been preliminary sketches. It was to form the subject of his only published work, his *Memoires of the Royal Navy*.

As in the past the multiplicity, the scope and pace of his official life stimulated the other sides of his personality. He cultivated the improvement of his library, selling as well as buying. He befriended scholars. He became President of the Royal Society, lending his name to its imprimatur on Newton's *Principia*, the most famous of all books published under its auspices. He became, for a second time, Master of Trinity House. He pursued his studies of naval history. He abated no whit of his interest in psychical research. He obtained from his learned cousin Dr. Gale a transcript of the passage in Tertullian 'touching Tiberius's proposal to the

Roman senate the admitting of Christ for a God'.[1] He corresponded widely on theology (mostly with those, like Petty, who claimed no professional status in the subject) and preserved among his papers a host of notes from his own reading of which this example breathes the *anima Pepysiana*:

> He that makes Reason his guide goes by a Law of God's makeing subject to noe falsifications and misconstructions wch all other guides whether written or others are and must necessarily be.[2]

Are not these the very accents of the Cambridge of his youth? Pepys never let go his past, never lost the curiosity and sense of wonder. A few pages beyond Sir William Petty's paper on liberty of conscience 'written by my desire and given me by himselfe a little before his death' we find a jagged, scorched bit of paper with which the Gunner of the *Coronation* had plugged a hole in his cabin window. It had been struck by lightning. A careful endorsement preserves this circumstance for posterity. The same volume contains information from the happily-named Captain Mudd about dumping rubbish into the Thames at Ratcliff for the purpose of making a causeway.[3] Such universality of appetite in a man who was carrying out a virtual reconstruction of the fleet and reforming, sometimes against dangerous opposition, the rules and customs of the naval profession is amazing.

No cocoon protected the great man from the ordinary rubs of life. The years that he filled with achievement and zest had their share of personal and family troubles. His health was never rude and by the standards of his world he was getting old. At the end of 1686 he suffered severe and prolonged pain from a recurrence of the stone, aggravated by an ulcer and other alarming symptoms. He warned Balty, now making up for the extravagance denied him in Tangier, not to depend on his being well enough to stay in office. Soon afterwards Balty's own wife died in childbirth: 'commissioner St Michell is drowned in tears, and his spirrit sinking under the sence of so heavy a Loss' wrote his assistant in a prose style perhaps influenced by his superior. That meant more nephews and nieces to be settled or, at least, to keep an eye on. Of Pall's boys Samuel was sent out to the West Indies under Narbrough while John went up to Magdalene. Mary Skinner's brother Peter, as plausible as his intellectual brother Daniel, was sent on a Mediterranean cruise under an old and steady Captain. Domestic arrangements too took up time. There was a fire at York Buildings soon after Pepys returned to office. The house escaped, narrowly: but books and papers were so disordered in last-minute attempts at salvage that it took weeks to straighten them out.

Finally Pepys arranged in September 1684 to move the Admiralty Office from Derby House to York Buildings.*

The Secretaryship to which all this bustle was parenthetic is divided into two periods by the Special Commission of 1686, Pepys's last great administrative creation. Much of the first two years was occupied in taking the measure of the problems left by five years mismanagement and in establishing the priorities and the means of dealing with them. The process was interrupted by the death of Charles II early in 1685, at the very moment when Pepys had prepared one of those set-pieces with which he liked to impress his masters at Christmas or New Year. In this case it consisted of a report on the condition of the ships: 'The state of the Royal Navy of England at the Dissolution of the late Commission of the Admiralty, May 1684.' Beautifully bound in black morocco with elaborate tooling, it still graces his library at Cambridge. The tale of neglect, incompetence and decay that it recites is too well known and too well authenticated to detain us. All the terrible rumours that had reached Pepys as a private citizen of how the thirty new ships had been allowed to rot and warp and moulder at their moorings proved exactly true. Within a short time of his return to office the enraged Secretary was gathering 'toad-stools as big as my fists' in the damp, unventilated 'tweendecks of what should have been the most powerful warships afloat. Wooden ships need constant and expert care to counteract the effects of sun and water. The money voted for the great construction programme of 1677 had been thrown away. Already his predecessors, more seasoned in the arts of propaganda than of preserving timber, were putting it about that the fault lay in the original purchases of Eastland plank. It was thus an act of self-defence as well as of methodical administration to assemble all the relevant evidence as to what the state of the fleet was and how it had come about.

The condition revealed in Pepys's report was not merely scandalous: it was alarming. English sea-power was wholly inadequate to the demands of a sudden war with a European power. It could not even teach the Algerines a lesson without cautious weighing of the balance of forces. Once again Barbary pirates were active in the channel. As late as June 1687 two regular packets going over to Holland were captured, one of them with a hundred passengers aboard.[4] The physical reconstruction of the fleet would have to be planned and financed. It was this necessity that issued in the Special Commission of 1686 to which we shall soon return. But there were other necessities in Pepys's view yet more pressing than a lack of ships: the need to re-establish discipline and to restore

* See above, p. 208.

without a moment's delay the professional foundations of the service. Tangier had shown him all too clearly how quickly the jungle of corruption and courtierism surged back over the paths and clearings he had made with so much labour.

What had shocked Pepys most during his spell with Dartmouth's squadron, more even than the dirty stories of the senior officers and the profanities reported of Admiral Herbert, was the lawlessness of a service whose *raison d'être* was law. All the rules that he had instituted were cheerfully flouted: even some of the conventions on which he had built were losing clarity and shape. Of the first the most obvious example was the failure to enforce the regulations laid down for the granting of commissions:

Capt. Dering . . . was not thought fit upon examination to take another voyage. Nevertheless he was soon after made a lieutenant and presently after a captain which he is now.[5]

Of the second the readiest instance was seniority. In the absence of the admiral, who should command? The captain whose commission bore the earliest date or the captain whose ship was rated highest – in Pepysian language, the eldest captain or the greatest ship?* What was quite certain was that it must be one or the other. Yet at Tangier he had found that matters had slipped back towards the general free-for-all that he spent his life in resisting. Admiral Herbert had claimed the right to nominate whom he pleased, even going so far as to leave his own flag flying and his lieutenant as senior officer of the fleet when he himself was ashore.[6] Dartmouth had ruled in favour of the eldest commander:

But here is to be noted the shame that this should be to be looked upon at this time of day a new regulation or rule to set matters right. In this matter that ever was the practice of the Navy in all times.[7]

Pepys exaggerates, as his own notes show, both the certainty and the continuity of the tradition.[8] Its importance in securing professionalism from the encroachments of courtiers and favourites is central.

What happened when these rules and conventions were disregarded, Pepys argues, was that the officer corps degenerated into a greedy and immoral rabble. The Gentlemen versus Tarpaulins issue became even more envenomed when gentility was allowed to consist in mere incompetence, unmitigated by honour or good breeding:

* See above, pp. 231–2.

Sir W. Booth telling me that there are four or five captains which he knows to have been footmen, companions of his own footman, who now reckon themselves among the fine fellows and gentlemen captains of the fleet, it makes me reflect upon it that by the meaning of gentlemen captains, is understood everybody that is not a bred and understanding seaman, and so set up for gentlemen.[9]

The promotion of these 'mean rogues . . . taken out of the streets' Pepys imputes to Herbert's alleged homosexuality. How 'mean' they, in fact, were, how lurid was the love-life of the late Commander-in-Chief of the Mediterranean Fleet are points which would require closer investigation before it would be safe to rest much weight on them. It was then, and long remained, a convenient way of disparaging an officer's social origins to say that he entered the navy as a footman or, by contrast, to heighten his success in his profession by saying that he entered it as a cabin boy. Both, usually, mean exactly the same thing. In almost every walk of life the young man who hoped to rise in the world attached himself in some loose and undefined manner to an already established figure. Pepys himself had done so. Doubtless the courtiers sneered at him for having started life as Lord Sandwich's footman. Captain Roydon of the *Sweepstakes* in the fearful broils with his lieutenant, George Aylmer, already alluded to accused him of having been Lord Arlington's footman. In fact, he had been his page[10] – a very different thing. Sir Clowdisley Shovell has, on the other hand, been admired by successive historians for rising to the top of the service that he had entered as a cabin boy. In fact, as we have seen, he had entered it under the protection of Myngs and Narbrough. The terms used to describe status often tell us more about the prejudice of the writer than about the condition of the man he is writing about. It is perhaps further worth noting that both these officers were on the Tangier station during Pepys's time there: that both were to serve for the rest of their lives, in Shovell's case a long and outstanding career: and that both are severely criticised in the Tangier journal for their frivolity and dereliction of duty. Pepys in office did not permit himself the luxury of the waspishness so often revealed in his private papers. Besides, he had gone out to the Mediterranean to find evidence of the corruption into which the navy had sunk while he was not there to run it. In such cases men are apt to find what they are looking for.

That the service was factious, ill-disciplined and thus inefficient does not admit of a doubt. Behind all the symptoms that Pepys recorded, neglect, amateurism, insubordination, drunkenness and misconduct, lay two conditions that he could treat but which only a miracle could cure:

the system that penalised good discipline and the Stuart brothers who liked it that way. The huge rewards a captain could earn from what Pepys, with furious scorn, called 'Good Voyages' put the service rate of pay into the shade. And it was these, as has been pointed out, that were altogether subversive of good order. Except where a commander was governed by a high sense of duty (and such would almost by definition be 'bred seamen', not court favourites), ships on a foreign station would put to sea or stay in harbour according to the prospect of private gain. For years Pepys, in his earlier tenure of the Secretaryship, had dinned it into the royal heads that they would get better value for money if they raised the officers' wages and forbade 'Good Voyages'. But this serious, prudent approach to the problem was uncongenial to Charles II: and James, though more sympathetic, was too infirm of purpose. Charles, indeed, frankly despised officers who were too scrupulous to make easy money by breaking regulations and told Sir John Berry so to his face.[11]

Charles II quitted the world in that style, so uniquely compounded of panache and obliqueness, that he had lived in it. His deathbed reception into the Roman Catholic Church by the priest who had befriended him when he was on the run after the battle of Worcester thirty-three years earlier was the last and one of the best-kept secrets of a reign in which the right hand rarely knew what the left was doing. Pepys's excitement when the new King confided the story to him and even lent him documents proving his brother's Papist tendencies exceeded anything hitherto stimulated by his historical researches. His two closest friends, John Evelyn and James Houblon, were summoned to dine with him the following Sunday with the irresistible bait: 'I have something to shew you that I may not have againe another time.' After the meal in the privacy of his own room he told them everything and showed them the papers. Evelyn, who had known the late King as well as Pepys and was far better versed in Catholic apologetic, thought them (Charles II's hand was familiar to both), 'so well penn'd as to the discourse, as did by no means seeme to me, to have ben put together by the Late King.'[12] As a political observer no less than as a historian the guest showed a critical power superior to that of his host. Pepys was beside himself with pleasure at being let into so high a secret: Evelyn was saddened by further evidence that the new King was set on a collision course.

Pepys's elation at the beginning of the new reign is indeed understandable. Whatever James II's shortcomings as a king, he was, to a far greater extent than his brother, knowable, predictable and loyal. He and Pepys had shared misfortune and recovery. Both were now riding high. At the coronation Pepys walked in the procession as one of the Barons of

the Cinque Ports, a medieval corporation for which he had neither venera-
tion nor respect, deriding, in his historical notes, their supposed contribution to English sea-power. At the General Election that followed in May
he was returned for both Harwich and Sandwich, choosing to sit for his
old constituency. The complexion of the new House of Commons was
very different from the last Parliament of Charles II. The Court, it seemed,
had everything its own way.

Monmouth's rebellion in the following month provided clinching
evidence. Apart from a few simpletons in the West Country no one rallied
to the Whig banner. In spite of the naval weakness exposed by this landing
of an invading force the Government were never in trouble. It was only
the vindictiveness of Pepys's friend Judge Jeffreys and the brutality of
his old enemy Colonel Kirke after everything was over that roused sympathy for the defeated. Both men certainly expressed the spirit of their
master, who was not, judged by the standards of his day, a humane man.
Even Pepys, who was, clearly approved. Writing to Sir William Poole,
recalled from a lucrative retirement in the Customs at Bristol to command
an armed merchantman during the rebellion, he urges him to drive a hard
bargain with the prisoners sentenced to transportation to Virginia and
the West Indies 'whether to be sold entirely, as blacks are to slavery for
their whole lives, or how long . . .'13

Such mercilessness towards the poor, illiterate dupes of political gam-
blers is repellent. Some have seen in it merely the reflection of a hard age
or of the horror felt by those who have experienced revolution. It runs too
deep in Pepys's nature for such an explanation to be wholly satisfactory.
There is no transaction in his life more disgusting than his sending his
Negro servant out to be sold abroad in 1679. Sir Arthur Bryant's account
solicits the reader's sympathy for Pepys, obliged through loss of office to
cut down his standard of living: 'He was no longer a housekeeper now;
even his black boy had been sold for him by kind Captain Wyborne,
who had taken him off to the Mediterranean in the previous autumn
and brought back instead twenty-five pistoles, transmuted at Cadiz into
chocolate and sherry for Pepys's drinking.'14 One thinks of the care taken
by Johnson to provide for his Negro servant, Francis Barber. That was a
century later. But it is impossible to imagine Evelyn or Ken or Dr. Gale,
to name but a few of Pepys's friends, behaving with such barbarity. There
was a hardness in his nature with which the fineness of his perceptions was
perpetually at war. Unlike James II, when he saw poverty, hunger, suffering he was moved to compassion. The poor sailors and their wives besieg-
ing the Navy Office, real people present to a consciousness amounting to
genius, really touch his heart and his conscience: the lucrative deals by

which money to feed them went into his own pocket could be intellec-
tualised and made abstract. So it is with the victims of Monmouth's
rebellion. So it is, thanks to Captain Wyborne and the remoteness of the
nearest slave-market, with the black servant. So it is in a minor key with
the clerks, James Sotherne, Josiah Burchett and others, who, dismissed
after years of working for him, found repeated apologies and appeals
unanswered. Had he seen them in person, as they and he seem to have
suspected, he might have found inflexibility more difficult. So it is with
his meanness to his Jackson nephews out of sight at Huntingdon and his
generosity once they had entered his circle. If they fell from grace, as the
elder subsequently did by marrying a girl Pepys thought unsuitable,
banishment was the key to punitive action.

James II was altogether without this quickness and intensity of response.
He allowed his nephew, demoralised by failure and exhaustion, to grovel
for mercy before him and then refused it. He expressed his regret at not
being able to be present in person when the Earl of Argyle, the leader of
another unsuccessful rebellion in Scotland, was put to the torture. Yet such
behaviour, hateful as it is, did not spring from a merciless or even an
unkind nature. James's readiness to spare the feelings of a friend, the
warmth and generosity of his loyalty, are too well attested both by his
own actions and by the evidence of men like Bishop Burnet who were
anything but well disposed towards his politics or his religion. It was
his terrible obtuseness, the most unPepysian of all qualities, that undid
him.

How, in three years, the King managed to reverse the popularity and
to alienate the loyalty which he had enjoyed on his accession is only too
well known. What part, if any, did Pepys play in setting the course to
ruin? Essentially, none. Pepys was only a politician to the extent that he
had to be if he were to administer the navy. He would thus support the
Government he served up to and beyond what he might privately think
either wise or expedient. Outside his own department he was not consulted
in the framing of policy: his job was to provide the sea-power necessary
to defence and to diplomacy. He was one of the greatest civil servants that
England has ever had, but he had the misfortune to live before the civil
service had been invented. Thus by adducing his speeches in the Parliaments of Charles and James invariably toeing the Government line, by
citing his approval of James's repressive policy so savagely executed by
Jeffreys and Colonel Kirke, finally by pointing to him in the witness box
at the trial of the Seven Bishops, giving evidence for the Crown in the
most famous of all legal assaults on the liberties of Protestant Englishmen,
it is possible to depict Pepys as an ultra-Tory, perhaps a crypto-Catholic.

Such a view is great nonsense. The only sense in which Pepys, whose whole cast of mind was sceptical and eclectic, could be claimed as a Tory is that in which almost all his contemporaries and every preceding generation were or had been, that is in accepting the authority of government as axiomatic and in looking on opposition, still more on revolution, as wicked. There is nothing in Pepys's life or writings to suggest that he would not have served the dynasty of Oliver Cromwell, once effectively established, with the same loyalty that he gave to the Stuarts. In the case of religion the matter is clearer still. Pepys was a cool, Erastian Protestant, thinking hot-gospellers on the whole ridiculous and priests generally parasitical. His own theology, if that is not too pretentious a term for an attitude of mind rather than a system of ideas, was liberal. Towards the end of his life he came into closer personal sympathy with High Churchmen both of the Non-juring and the Established variety, but whatever the effects of this (and there seem to have been some) the cause would appear to have been the extraordinary learning of these divines (most notably Dr. Hickes) rather than a desire on his part for a more sacramental religion. Of any predilection for Roman Catholicism there is no trace.

How could there be? Pepys for all his long service to the House of Stuart was a born cross-bencher. The battle between Whigs and Tories had cost him severe wounds, but to a mind of his type the whole thing was laughable. In March 1682, when he had been kept for nearly three years powerless at the height of his powers, he wrote to James Houblon from Newmarket:

Sir,
    That I am well got hither and well here, will (I assure myself) give you no disquiet. But how your Whigship will bear my telling you that the Duke of York is so too, and not only so, but plumper, fatter, and all over in better liking than ever I knew him, is a thing that I cannot answer for.
    . . . the King (God be blessed) seems in no point less fortified against mortality than the Duke, but in one particular more; namely that (as much as that signifies) he hath the prayers of the very Whigs for his health, while we Tories are fain to pray, by ourselves, for his brother's . . . [15]

He never wrote in this bantering spirit about anything he took seriously, such as Right and Wrong, scientific evidence, money, or the state of the navy.

It was to this last question that he addressed his full powers. The story of the Special Commission of 1686 has been so well told elsewhere that there is little to add. Pepys himself was the first to tell it in his *Memoires of the Royal Navy*: J. R. Tanner, in his introduction to the *Catalogue of the Pepysian MSS*, was the first scholar to criticise the documents in the Pepys Library of which that book is an extract: Sir Arthur Bryant printed or summarised a great deal more of this material in his *Pepys: The Saviour of the Navy* (1938): more recently Mr. John Ehrman has examined the evidence from a different standpoint in his *The Navy in the War of William III* (1953). All three modern writers agree in accepting the substance of the claims Pepys made in the *Memoires*: indeed in the all-important matter of rebuilding the fleet, without reserve:

> The outstanding work of the Commission, however, lay in this programme of repair. Its success rested upon three distinct achievements. First, the repairs were fully and efficiently carried out; secondly, they did not exceed the original estimate of their cost; and thirdly, they were completed in less than the original estimate of the time required. All these facts were later questioned, but all were finally established by the Parliamentary inquiry of 1691–2, in its elicitation of a defence of their work from Deane and Hewer, the two men principally concerned, and in the detailed acknowledgment of its validity by the Parliamentary Commissioners themselves.
>
> Altogether the Special Commission repaired 69 ships and rebuilt twenty. It also built the three fourth-rates promised, and a hoy and two lighters. By the time it came to a close, only four ships still remained with their repairs not completed, and four more with their repairs not begun. In addition to the work on these 96 ships, a further 29 were repaired which had been at sea when the Commission was inaugurated, and had not been included in the original programme. Pepys's intentions were therefore more than fulfilled in the number of vessels which were tackled.[16]

Pepys's career was crowned by the refashioning of England's sea-power just in time for his patron to lose it. The great war with Louis XIV that followed was often the subject of sardonic comment from Pepys who felt, justly, aggrieved at his treatment: it was the more ironical to know that without his work it could hardly have been fought.

In conception, execution and style the Special Commission was Pepysian through and through. He drafted its terms, he chose its members, he kept, as he said himself, 'my daily eye and hand upon them'. The key appointment was that of Sir Anthony Deane, then at the height of his fame (and fees) as a naval architect. His salary (he had fifteen children to support and wanted £1,000 a year) was the only real difficulty. Neither the King nor the Lord Treasurer wanted to go so high. Pepys outflanked their opposition by producing a list of all the possible alternative candidates that showed all his old fondness for the sharp and cutting phrase. 'A low-spirited, slow and gouty man . . . illiterate and supine to the last degree.' The master-shipwright at Woolwich might stand for all, or almost all. Most, according to Pepys, were drunken, incompetent or senile: the few young men lacked either experience or application. Can they really have been so useless? If so, why had not the veterans been replaced during Pepys's earlier secretaryship? Would they have received the same character if it had been a question of obtaining a pension for them or a grant for one of their widows? When Pepys had set his mind upon some particular end he had no compunction in making free with other people's reputations.

Next to Deane, Will Hewer was the Commissioner on whom Pepys relied most. A strong contingent of sea officers, notable among them Sir John Narbrough and Sir John Berry, combined expert knowledge with personal friendship, both of long standing. The Commission also embraced Resident Commissioners at Portsmouth, Chatham and Deptford, the last of which appointments was bestowed upon Balty. It was a closely knit body.

Its second source of strength was that it combined financial and executive control. The frustration of the Second Dutch War had left its mark. At last Pepys had got his hands on the levers and he was not going to make any mistake. The Commission's terms of reference included its own budget, carefully costed and rigidly adhered to. Very skilfully Pepys retained the Comptroller and Surveyor of the Navy Board that had been responsible for the deplorable state of affairs he was to remedy and charged them with the dire task of presenting their own accounts for the locust years. They were, naturally, outside the Commission. Pepys had spent enough of his administrative life clearing up other people's mess. The Commission was to be positive, executive, in the most literal sense constructive.

In effect it temporarily superseded the Navy Board: the commissioners moved into the houses of the Principal Officers (who were given a house allowance in lieu) and occupied the Board's offices, even adding to them. Its functions were primarily those that the Board had hitherto discharged but it was given a disciplinary brief that derived more from the office of the Lord High Admiral. It was, in a word, to be Pepys put into commission: inquiring, enforcing, reproving, watching, reporting, minuting, buzzing like a gnat in the ears of drowsy officials. From its constitution in April 1686 to its dissolution, its work done, on October 12th, 1688, it provided new, swift channels for the day-to-day administration of the navy as well as giving the service a refit from truck to keel.

Why if the Commission performed such prodigies was it dissolved? Should it not rather have been institutionalised and decent interment given to the old Navy Board? Pepys, highly as he valued its achievement and admired the triumph of his own administrative workmanship, does not seem to have thought so. Historical study and reflection had induced in him, as it does in others, a scepticism towards simple solutions. On April 6th, 1688, in an informal discussion of the navy in general attended only by himself, the King and Godolphin he noted in his own hand

Its science ye most extensive of any.

viz. Comoditys
Trades

Climates	Provisions
Accounts	Shipbuilding
Thrift	Discipline
Seamanship	Winds
Navigation	Tides
Sea-Laws	Seas

Noe one Man qualify'd for all
Nor fitt to bee trusted alone
Therefore ye old Constitution provided for all,
by a Plurality properly qualify'd . . .'[17]

The Special Commission had succeeded brilliantly because it was special, with a limited task, a clear brief, and means proportionate to its ends. It was also a highly personal success, the performance of a lifetime by the maestro conducting players, themselves masters, who had been rehearsing under his baton for a quarter of a century. The magic was in the ingredients, not in the formula. The only long-term solution to the perennial problems of naval mismanagement was, as Pepys constantly reiterates in his *Naval Minutes*, to build up an informed body of opinion among the aristocrats and landed gentry who dominated Parliament. Once they could be induced to send their sons into the service as serious professionals not as dilettanti the old cycle of ignorance and corruption might be broken or, at least, its gyrations become less wild. All this would take time. And a man in his middle fifties with a chronic kidney complaint could not reckon on much of that.

June 10th: 1684.

His Ma:tie Letters Patents for ye Erect=ing the Office of Secry of ye Admiralty of England, & Creating Samuel Pepys Esqr first Secretary therein.

Charles the Second

by the grace of God of England, Scotland, France & Ireland King Defender of the Faith &c: To all to whome these Presents shall come Greeting, Know yee that wee haue thought fitt to Erect, and hereby doe Erect an Office of Secretary to and for the Affaires and Businesse of and Concerning Our Admiralty of England, and wee reposeing especiall Trust and Confidence in ye Experience, Ability, Care and Fidelity of Our Trusty & Welbeloved Samuel Pepys Esqr haue giuen and grant=ed, and by these Presents doe giue and Grant unto the said Samuel Pepys the Office of Secretary of and for the Affaires and Businesse of and Concerning Our Admiralty of England, and him the sayd Samuel Pepys Secretary of and for the Affaires and Businesse of and concerning, Our Admiralty of England Wee doe Create, Make, Ordaine & Constitute by these Presents, to haue, hold, exercise and En=ioy the sayd Office unto the sayd Samuel Pepys during, Our Pleasure, Giuing alloe, and by these Presents granting unto the sayd Samuel Pepys full Power and Authority

to

Patent of Pepys's Secretaryship in the Admiralty from his Day Collection (see page 291). The pen and ink head that embellishes the patent is of Charles II.

At the distance of three centuries the rounding off of a great career with its greatest achievement has an aesthetic rightness doubtless imperceptible to Pepys himself, resentful at his ill-usage and embittered by the preferment of men he thought unworthy. Yet even Pepys may have had, for personal not political reasons, a sense that things were drawing towards their close. We have seen that he warned Balty not to count on his being able to sustain the physical demands of office much longer. Was not the urgency that drove through the Special Commission's three-year programme in two and a half private as much as public? At all costs the machinery of naval administration was to be put into full working order at the earliest possible moment. Expedients that depended on the presence of the master-mechanic must be rejected. It was, surely, Pepys's voice that spoke when Hewer turned down James II's suggestion that the Special Commission might be carried on indefinitely by retaining himself and Sir Anthony Deane as 'Inspectors Marine', 'on the ground that the methods of the navy in accounting are now so clear that only industry and knowledge are needed.'[18] When that answer was given the Glorious Revolution was a bare three weeks away.

The sunset of Pepys's official life displays the whole spectrum of his abilities at their fullest brilliancy. York Buildings combined elegance with efficiency as only an establishment of which Pepys was unchallenged master could do. There was no Elizabeth now to introduce the principle of romantic disorder: no colleagues to obstruct, no patron to be conciliated. A lifetime's love of method and neatness was consummated in the arrangements for transacting business. On his desk lay his Day Collection, exquisitely bound in dark green morocco, containing ready to his hand the regulations and precedents governing pay, pensions, salutes, flags, the rating of ships as to officers and guns together with a complete list of the fleet and its disposition on the day he resumed office. In his pocket he carried a sheet of paper (see the example reproduced on p. 292) neatly folded with notes on each fold of matters to be raised with the King, the Ordnance Board, the Victualling Office, or whoever he might be seeing during the course of that particular day. At longer range and lower priority were his 'Momentalls' (p. 292) and 'Memorandums' a sheet of which endorsed 'Pocket Memorandums to goe before those in my pocket Memorandum Book' may be seen on the next page. The division and arrangement of the matter is a paradigm of his efficiency, of his success, above all of his cast of mind. The left-hand column methodically groups what has to be done under the name of the relevant person or place. But he is never the prisoner of his own system. The right-hand column tumbles out pell-mell all the multifarious pleasures, interests and duties

Memorandums. 91

June 10th: 16..

Admiralty.
List of Books
Bonds
Sr Nicho: Armourer
Books of Fortificacon
Mathem: Paper book &c
Mitrs Cullender
Lady Mordant something
Mr Houblon
His Bond returne
Dr De Moulins
Burialle --- 2:2:6
Brampton
Mr Jolliffe
Katherine
Mourning --- 3:0:0
Advance --- 5:0:0
Trinity-House
Brother Tille --- 4:0:0
Old Pattent & ordr to Copy
My Selfe wanting
Prospective
Reading Desk
A Pincer
Books & Booksellrs
Mathle Paper
Paid Pitts too little
Paid Richard too much

Tostam: Mr Hayter May 27th 16..
Sr Phil: Warwick thank
Sr Robt Howard --- 200:0:0
Mr Gregory answere
Mr Richd Roove for Rich R
Wt my Guilt Cupp
Mr Ethick of Christs Colledge
Mosely Jan: 4th at Burntwood - 15:0
Tower Hill Servants
Hamper of old Books
2d ... in the 6 King John 1205
Dr Bradley by is at least 30
a Day now
Coll: Norwood at Leck-Hampton
Chelsey Delft
Mr Hollier ... 675
Dr Allen
Woodhall Gavllim
Recale Sr Ph Medow's Booke
Mr Sandson at ye Golden Ball
in Hatten Garden
Coll: Phillips & Huelstone
Pay Mr Norwich
Mr Smith Savile --8
Send back to ...
S A D - Mr Forkee
2 H Crowns
Mr Peter Jones Merch: in St Mary Ax
Mr Bovery Merch: in Minchin lane.

Memorandum, Momentalls and Pocket Memorandum.

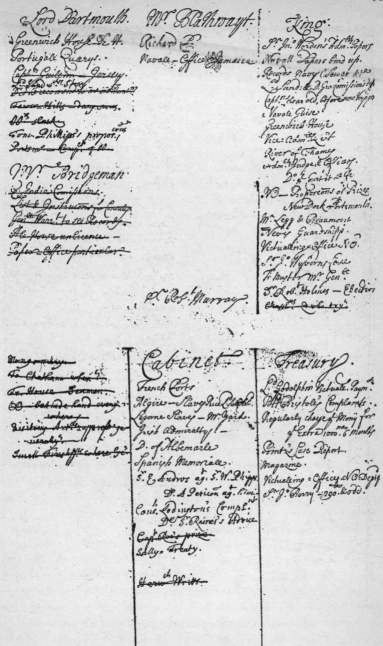

These are described on the preceding page.

of a life in which inertia had no place. Reason, method, exploited to the full, do not for an instant obstruct or inhibit the irrational. It is the hare's foot and the Royal Society transposed to another key. These were but the skirmishers of the great paper army marshalled in his vast filing system ready at a word to spring into action against irregularity or neglect. Whole brigades in full battle order still survive in his own library and among the Rawlinson manuscripts in the Bodleian.

His official correspondence shows that he could still be sharp when the occasion called for it. But the mellowing so long evident has become more pronounced. Sir Robert Holmes, once feared and hated, has become a trusted ally. Sir William Poole, not once but many times the recipient of sulphurous rebukes for idling in port or engaging in 'good' voyages, is told that the Secretary hears excellent reports of his son, now a captain. The letters, always spacious, seem to admit more light and air.

Time was thinning out the friends and associates of early life. Cambridge stood up well with Richard Cumberland, a friendship kept in good repair, and the indestructible Sir Samuel Morland for ever in some scrape over money or matrimony. The period of service with Mountagu had almost faded: Will Howe was in the West Indies, Creed, once Pepys's most formidable rival, seems to have retired into the life of a country gentleman to which his fortunate marriage probably contributed. Of Sandwich's immediate family only his third son, John, Master of Trinity, Cambridge and subsequently Dean of Durham, kept in touch. The years at the Navy Office, too, contribute little. Sir William Warren, fallen at last on hard times, makes one final appearance, 'Majestick though in ruin.' Sir William Coventry, long out of public life though never out of Pepys's admiring affection, died in June 1686 while taking the waters at Tunbridge Wells. In the spring of 1687 a Mr. Dilks was recommended for a lieutenancy: he had been examined by Sir John Narbrough but his sponsor clinches his argument, 'I have nothing more to add on behalfe of this Gentleman but that hee is a relation of Sir William Coventry and then refuse him if you can.' The commission was granted the following month.[19]

At this the peak of his career, powerful, rich, respected, a grave and reverend signior, Pepys was still subject to the capricious influence of favourites and to the pressures and presuppositions of an aristocratic society. To take but a trivial example, when the Duchess of Norfolk (whom Pepys did not know) wanted 'a parcell of pladd' safely transported from Scotland she did not hesitate to ask his good offices.[20] More seriously, in spite of his efforts to ensure that officers should be properly qualified, he hears from Sir John Berry of the Duke of Grafton's proposing to make a lieutenant of a man whom '. . . I was hardly to be brought to signe a Certificatt of his being fitly qualified to be Boatswain of a fourth rate ship: and I am of the same opinion still.'[21] This seems to have been blocked: but in spite of James II's disposition to enforce discipline in general and to support his Admiralty Secretary in particular Pepys could not count on his rules being upheld. What he could do was to make them crystal clear and to fence in, where possible, more of the waste of the manor for others to till when he had gone. The regulations restricting the carriage of freight and bullion dated July 15th, 1686 were framed in stark terms: instant dismissal and incapacitation for future service, all profits to be confiscated to the Chatham Chest. New rates of pay were established and the captain's table allowances codified according to the rate of his ship. Guns, medical stores, prize money, pensions, relief for widows and orphans, the appointment of surgeons, above all the confirmation on April 13th, 1686, of the rules for the admission of volunteers and midshipmen by which Pepys hoped to encourage the gentry to breed their sons to the sea are among the subjects for which he laid down or strengthened an establishment during James's brief reign. In the century that followed these rules were often broken, or lost sight of. But in every case reform or innovation built on his foundations or began where he left off.

To judge from his letters his closest confidant in this last and most creative phase of his administrative life was his great friend James Houblon. It was Houblon who beat down the tapestry man to 25s. 6d. per ell for the walls of York House, a reduction of ten per cent.[22] Houblon who advised on naval intelligence, on the impact of war in the Mediterranean on English trade, on the motives of the Consul at Lisbon in asking for powers to prevent English captains discharging their men there. What the Consul was really after, says Houblon, was the power to compel 'runaways, rebellious and debauched rascals' who 'lye sotting themselves there with all sortes of vice'. The captains would then have to pay off their debts and the Consul would get a rake-off.[23] How sure his understanding and how sound his information may be gauged from this quotation from a letter written to Pepys eighteen months before the Dutch fleet left on the voyage whose landfall opened the Revolution of 1688:

We have from Dutch Land such a clutter of Arming both by sea and Land that makes us poore merchants looke carefully at what may be ye end of it. Glad are we in the meantime to see heer a Disposition for peace and that we shall bee happy in a profitable neutralitie wch wee traders think best for England. I wish ye zelous R. Priesthood & Swordmen thought soe too.[24]

21

James II and the Revolution

James Houblon was not alone among Pepys's friends in taking alarm at James II's policies. Anxiety as to the internal stability of England, still more as to French domination over Europe, was perhaps to be expected from a leading member of a Protestant refugee family: but it was shared to the full by John Evelyn, whose connections and origins were purely Royalist and Tory, and even by the High Churchmen, Hickes and Ken, who became after the Revolution the leaders of the Non-jurors. All these men were close to Pepys. Hickes had been chosen to preach the sermon at his second installation as Master of Trinity House in July 1685; he was to attend him on his deathbed and to conduct his funeral. Evelyn, after Houblon, was his most intimate friend. No one, certainly not Pepys himself, can have had higher expectations of James than he: '. . . there could nothing be more desired, to accomplish our prosperity, but that he were of the national Religion: for certainly such a Prince never had this Nation since it was one.'[1] He took the King's candid profession of Roman Catholicism as evidence of good faith in his solemn promises not to undermine the Church of England. But less than nine months later he was convinced of his mistake: 'All engines being now at worke to bring in popery amaine.'[2]

The immediate provocation of this reflection was James's assault on the Universities. Evelyn, as one of the Commissioners of the Privy Seal, had already refused to seal a patent licensing the King's printer to print Mass Books in defiance of many Acts of Parliament. He was anxious lest the King might again attempt the same short-circuit in order to allow the Master of University College, Oxford, a crypto-Papist who had at last declared himself, to continue to hold his office in spite of the law. He was relieved, personally, that James chose another expedient but his disapproval and his misgivings were no less profound. Flushed with his easy success at University College James moved down the High to Magdalen. In the spring of 1687 the old President of the College died. As soon as the news reached London the King sent his mandate to the Fellows ordering them to elect a young and totally unsuitable Roman Catholic who, even if he had been a member of the established Church, was disqualified for the post under the College statutes. The Fellows however had got wind of this plan and hurriedly elected one of their own number. In the confrontation that followed the King was worsted. Rather than admit defeat he then nominated the Bishop of Oxford, but again the Fellows stood firm. They had elected their President, the Visitor of the College, the Bishop of Winchester, had confirmed him and that was that. On September 5th Pepys's friend and colleague William Blathwayt, who was accompanying the King on his Royal Progress to the West, wrote from Oxford to describe how

> . . . His Majesty being informed that the Fellows of Magdalen College had refused to admitt the Bishop of Oxford to be their President . . . sent for them yesterday after dinner to His Antichamber in Christ Church Colledge where H.M. chid them very much for their disobedience and with much greater appearance of Anger than ever I perceiv'd in H.M. . . .'[3]

The chiding failed of its effect. Either on this or a further occasion James became incoherent with rage and the Fellows were subsequently ejected.*

As a servant of the King Pepys would have felt bound, in public at any rate, to defend his actions. We may doubt if he did so to intimate friends. Evelyn records an earlier instance of Pepys's remaining silent when the King was descanting on the miracles performed in Spain by the *Saludadors*,† one of whom, questioned by Pepys:

---

* An excellent account of the whole affair is to be found in John Carswell, *The Descent on England* (1969).

† Spanish religious enthusiasts who claimed miraculous powers of healing, etc.

. . . ingenuously told him, that, finding he was a more than ordinary
curious person, he would not deceive him, & so acknowledg'd that he
could do none of those feates, realy; but that what they pretended, was
all a cheate. . . . This Mr *Pepys* affirm'd to me; but said he, I did not
conceive it fit, to interrupt his Majestie, who told what they pretended
to do so solemnly.[4]

We have, none the less, to proceed by inference. Pepys was no longer
confiding his private opinions to a diary.

When, however, the King turned his attention from Oxford to
Cambridge Pepys was caught in a conflict of loyalties. Dr. Peachell, his
old friend, had long been Master of Magdalene and was now Vice-
Chancellor. To him fell the dilemma of James's direction, 'to admit one
Alban Francis, a Benedictine Monk, Master of Arts without administering
any oath or oaths to him'.[5] Peachell's first reaction must have been to
consult the College's most distinguished member, who was also his own
friend from undergraduate days and, finally, one of the King's oldest
and most valued advisers. Had the telephone existed this, it may be
suspected, is what Peachell would have done. But *littera scripta manet*: a
letter once written stays written: and if it ask guidance or intervention
the answer accepting or refusing the invitation stays written too. It says
much for Peachell and something for Pepys that he did not take the easy
way out of his difficulties at the expense of involving a friend:

> I could not tell what to do, decline his Majestie's Letter, or his
> Lawes; I could but pray to God to direct, sanctifie, and governe me in
> the wayes of his Lawes; that so through his most mighty Protection,
> both here and ever, I may be preserved in body and soule; then by our
> Chancellor, I indeavoured to obteine his Majestie's release, which
> could not be obteined; I thought it unmannerly to importune his Sacred
> Majestie; and was afraid to straine friends against the graine; and so
> could onely betake myselfe to my owne conscience, and the advice of
> Loyall and prudent men my friends, and after all I was perswaded that
> my Oath as Vice-chancellor founded on the Statutes was against it . . .[6]

Peachell's letter to Pepys from which these quotations are taken opens
with the announcement that his nephew John Jackson has just arrived to
take up residence in the College.

Up to this point Dr. Peachell could hardly have been described as an
impressive figure. Only the redness of his nose and the convivial habits
that caused it have won him a minor immortality in the Diary. Yet

forced to a decision involving at once the painful breach of a lifelong political allegiance and the loss of two much prized positions (he was suspended as Master and deprived of the Vice-Chancellorship) he showed courage and style. A regime that could drive its natural friends into such agonised opposition could not long avoid an explosion.

In the summer of 1688 the fuse was ignited at three points: James's Queen, Mary of Modena, bore him a son who would obviously be brought up in the religion of both his parents; the Seven Bishops, headed by the Primate of all England, were tried (after a brief but electrifying imprisonment) on a charge of seditious libel; and abroad the election of a new archbishop of Cologne was used by Louis XIV to force a confrontation on the rest of Europe. Suddenly the lines were drawn for another gigantic struggle such as had culminated a century earlier in Armada year, with France substituted for Spain, and, unthinkably, England in plausible danger of finding herself on the side of a militant Catholic despotism. James II, naturally, did not see it like this. His own relations with Louis XIV were cool: his nephew and son-in-law William of Orange was Louis's most implacable opponent: and the Pope, whom James was supposed to be reintroducing, was hardly less violent in his determination to resist French aggression. But the King had no one to blame but himself if his subjects were incapable of appreciating these piquant diplomatic paradoxes. And even his own dull political senses told him that something was burning. Peachell was reinstated in his Mastership: President Hough and the ejected Fellows were restored to Magdalen: but by the time these concessions were made full-scale war had broken out on the Continent and William of Orange had staked everything on the great gamble of invading England.

One of the neglected consequences of the Whig interpretation of history so brilliantly defined by Sir Herbert Butterfield is that it has lent a spurious inevitability to the Revolution of 1688, or, more precisely, to the bloodless military success of its achievement. It is hardly possible to exaggerate the daring (to use the most modest and polite term) of William's operational planning. Even in the Second World War, when ships were built of steel and powered by engines, when they could be protected from attack and warned of danger by air-power, radar and a hundred other devices, when the development of meteorology made some sort of weather forecast possible, an assault on the defended coast of a country with a formidable navy and a by no means negligible army at a time of year when daylight was short and rough weather all but certain would have been thought crazy. When ships were built of wood and propelled by wind the risks were far greater. Even if the invasion fleet reached its destination (a far from foregone conclusion) it could be pounded to matchwood in a few hours if a gale were to blow up while the troops were disembarking. And all this takes no account of James's popularity with his soldiers and sailors, of his own record as a courageous and successful commander, of his general aptitude for war. What, too, might be expected of the local population? Public opinion might be distrustful of James, some politicians and some senior officers might have chanced their arm by inviting the Prince of Orange to come over, but violent hostility to a foreign invader is the instinct of ordinary people in every age, particularly in an age that knew from experience that troops lived off the country. It is the measure of William's nerve that none of these daunting elements had been left out of his calculations. One of his most brilliant and original touches was to provide his invading force with plenty of money to pay its way.

That he should have succeeded so completely in so desperate an undertaking may be held to reflect on James as a strategist and tactician and on Pepys as his chief naval executive. Such a judgment owes much to hindsight, and something to Macaulay's indelible picture of James as an infatuated incompetent. Both the King and Pepys had first-hand experience of directing a naval war against the Dutch such as has been available to few men in our history. Both had reflected upon, argued, analysed and examined the whole subject from a number of different standpoints. One feature of these wars can hardly have escaped them: the battle season in the Channel ran from May to July. It was possible for a fleet to keep the sea in August, but even by then the danger of the elements was more to be feared than the violence of the enemy. By September the fleets ought to be in their bases. By October everyone except the standing officers, the ships' caretakers, should have been paid off. The idea of a Channel campaign in November was as unthinkable as a hay-harvest in January.

It was no part of Pepys's business to supply the Government with political and diplomatic intelligence. Sunderland remained Secretary of State and chief architect of James's foreign and domestic policy until the Revolution was open and palpable. Pepys, of course, had his own sources. Apart from the Houblons, his connections as President of the Royal Society with the world of European science furnished him with well-informed correspondents abroad. It was one such, Abraham Hill, Treasurer of the Royal Society, who wrote from Rotterdam on August 19th 'touching ye difficulty of understanding Mr Newton's Booke – & sends with ye Marques de Albevill ye first surpriseing News of ye Dutch Marine preparations'.[7] What was 'surpriseing' was not so much the news of the conspicuous activity in the Dutch bases – this could hardly be concealed and had been common knowledge for months — as the sudden realisation that a major threat, dwarfing the domestic difficulties in which the Government was floundering, had to be met in a matter of weeks, perhaps of days.[8] Both James II and Pepys had been aware that the Dutch were up to no good. A squadron somewhat larger than a normal summer guard but hardly deserving the name of a fleet had been concentrated in the Channel from the end of May, under the command of Sir Roger Strickland, a tactless officer whose exceptional experience and fine fighting record were offset by recusant antecedents and a too close personal link with the King's immediate circle. From the middle of June he was ordered to maintain two frigates cruising off the Goodwin. By the beginning of August Pepys was confident that the number of ships at sea could be reduced 'in one, two or three months at furthest'.[9]

A fortnight later such optimism was no longer possible. On August 16th the 'fleet' was ordered to remain in the Downs and not to proceed to the westward; on the 20th all leave was stopped; on the 21st one of the royal yachts was ordered to reconnoitre the coast of Holland and to report all warship movements. In the week that followed (the week in which Hill's letter arrived) Pepys turned on the heat. Complements were to be brought up to war strength: seven more warships and six fireships were to be fitted out at once and measures taken to prepare eight more fireships and six scouts. At this point James began either to lose interest or to regain confidence: foreign ambassadors reported his daily vacillations: but these did not affect Pepys. Whatever he may privately have thought about the probability of a Dutch invasion in the autumn, he had been given a clear brief to mobilise the fleet. Indeed whatever the Dutch intentions it would be most unwise to allow the balance of effective naval power to tilt any further to their side.

Thanks to the work of the Special Commission the ships were readily available and fit for sea: but storing, victualling and manning were no easier than they had ever been. Rather, with a weak, unpopular and uncertain Government, they were even more difficult. Merchants were reluctant to give credit: seamen decidedly more reluctant to come forward. Strickland's squadron had consisted of seventeen ships of the line (one third-rate, the rest fourths) and nine smaller vessels: to this were to be added in all twenty-one of the line (ten thirds, eleven fourths) and fourteen fireships. In spite of the prodigies performed by Deane and Hewer and even Balty, hardly a ship had joined the fleet before the end of September. October witnessed a steady stream of reinforcements: by the last week of the month, all the ships, except three or four stragglers, had joined.

By that time Strickland was no longer Commander-in-Chief. An

angry exchange with Pepys at the beginning of August over his entitle-
ment to Vice-Admiral's pay during his recent voyage to Portugal hardly
suggests that he was equal to the responsibilities of his present appointment.[10] His subsequent attempt to have mass celebrated aboard his flagship showed even less sense of occasion. The sailors mutinied. On
September 24th he was replaced by Lord Dartmouth, whose experience,
efficiency and popularity with the fleet made him, despite Macaulay's
jibes, a reassuring change. Personally Pepys found him a much better
man to deal with. But would he have chosen him to command at such a
pinch? The news of Narbrough's death in the West Indies, received in
London that July, was a heavy blow, 'not for private friendship's sake
only (tho' that be very great) but for the sake of the King and his Service
in which (without wrong to anybody) I do not think there does survive
one superior, if any one equal (all qualifications considered), to Sir John
Narbrough.'[11] Sir Robert Holmes, a fire-eater feared and hated in the days
of the Diary but now a trusted ally, was gouty and arthritic. Yet only a
year earlier he had actually been appointed to the West Indies command.
His infirmities had proved too much for him and Narbrough had gone in
his stead. None the less he put up a stout-hearted performance as
Governor of the Isle of Wight during the Revolution.

> . . . I am doing all I can to give a stop at Yarmouth and Hurst Castell,
> if I have any helpe from the King they shall not have this island soe
> easily as they may expect. I am in the feild every day, this I write
> before a drumhead, to-morrow I muster 2 hondered dragones that I
> macke out of the mallitia the choice of them . . .[12]

More perhaps than in the frequent and fluent letters of Lord Dartmouth
one catches the ring of a man who means business.

The critical condition of affairs did not deflect Pepys from the ampli-
tude of his high official style. When a sprig of the aristocracy saw fit to be
jocose about so serious a subject as boatswain's stores, the traffic of naval
preparation was held up while a proper rebuke was administered.

> You tell me [wrote Lord Berkeley, commanding the *Mountague*, to
> the Navy Board] you have not power to add to my allowance of junck.*
> This for your honors sake I ought to keep to myself, for should some
> sarcastical people know it, I fear it would be made a mighty jest . . .
> surely you do not think I should eat or sell ye junk, no; but he will
> suffer his boatswain to bobble him.

> * Old rope suitable for use in making fenders, gaskets and such.

The Navy Board's answer, dated two days later, signed by three commissioners of whom Pepys was not one, exists in both rough and fair copies among his papers. Not for much longer would serving officers see the great Secretary coming so characteristically into action, opening up with his secondary armament before letting his big guns speak:

> We have received your Lordships answer of the 17th . . . the stile of which we know how to observe, tho' not to imitate, intending to submit it with all humility to the King to judge of the difference . . . But, my Lord, the King has thought fitt in this and numberless other particulars to limitt us in the dispensing of his stores, and those limitts grounded upon measures not left to us to contrevart, he having paid too deare for the liberty heretofore allowed or taken in that particular. Nor has your Lordship (we feare) computed either the charge or difficulty that would attend the Extraordinary allowance you demand in this so contemptably [word omitted] a Commodity as Junke, should every ship of your rank (and the rest proportionately) have an Extraordinary allowance made it above the proportion established by His Majesty in the adjustment not long since solemnly made . . .[13]

The sentence, still far from its terminal point, uncoils its parentheses, as Pepys for a long moment forgets the Dutch and expounds the theory of efficient and orderly administration, making intellectual mincemeat of his opponent with an orotund gravity proper to a great officer of state and that sharp, no-nonsense tang so natural to himself. It is easy to make fun of Pepys's pomposity. But he lived in an age in which formality and punctilio, in public affairs at least, were carried to great lengths. And how else was a man of humble origins to assert authority against the insolent pretensions of courtiers and aristocrats?

Little enough of that autumn was spent in such congenial activity. James's vacillation and inertia checked the initial spirit of confidence and enterprise in which Dartmouth, most uncharacteristically, had proposed an offensive sweep along the Dutch coast. At the time of his appointment the station of the fleet had been shifted from the Downs to the Nore. Admirable as this sheltered anchorage was for taking on stores and reinforcements it had two grave disadvantages, one psychological the other physical. Its safe riding and its easy accessibility gave captains and officers dangerous opportunities of 'caballing' as their Admiral reported to Pepys with growing uneasiness. And, physically, the east wind that would bring the Dutch out would keep the English in. Towards the end of October, in the face of urgent suggestions from both Pepys and the King to take advantage of the westerly wind and get the fleet clear of the Thames,

Dartmouth moved across to the northern side of the estuary towards Harwich, taking up his station behind the Gunfleet shoal. James, who had fought in these labyrinthine waters, clearly felt the response inadequate but supported his Admiral with a loyalty that cannot have been easy. Dartmouth in a brief phase of euphoria claimed mastery of the situation: 'We are now at sea before the Dutch with all their boasting,' he wrote to the King on October 24th. The Dutch armada, which had in fact sailed a few days earlier, was even then limping, scattered and battered by a fearful gale, back to its home ports. The extent to which the Gunfleet anchorage could be described as 'at sea' was to be defined all too clearly a very few days later when William, in one of the most breathtaking displays of nerve and of leadership in European history, brought the expedition out again to face weather that had already justified his most persistent critics.

To tell the story of the descent on England and to trace the role of the Royal Navy in the Revolution of 1688 lies outside the scope of this book. Both tasks have been admirably executed in works whose titles are echoed in the preceding sentence.[14] But it is over the ground bass of these events that the crescendo of Pepys's official career reaches our ears. It was he, if anyone, who activated the country's defence. James, physically and mentally, was not the man he once had been. Moodiness, indolence, timidity even, are too widely reported of him to be dismissed as malicious, out of character though they are. Dartmouth as Commander-in-Chief of the Fleet was thorough and professional: perhaps sometimes too thorough and professional in his insistence on obtaining for the ships under his command stores and equipment that a more forceful commander would either have commandeered or foregone. The politicians on whom James had relied were in disarray: alienated, discredited or disaffected. The one man who was trying to galvanise the King and the navy into effective action was Pepys, hurrying between Windsor and Westminster, between Westminster and London, keeping the dockyard up to the mark, overseeing the Navy Board (two of whose members, Berry and Booth, had been appointed to commands afloat), hustling the slopsellers, chivvying the victuallers, remonstrating strongly (and with only too much reason) with Dartmouth in his capacity as Chief of the Ordnance Board over the alarming deficiencies in that crucial department. All, and more, that could have been expected of the greatest naval administrator England had ever known was done. All, and more, that could be done by his colleagues Deane and Hewer, brought under his daily eye and hand to concert pitch, was done. But when all was done, it was not enough. Pepys was not cut out to be a Cromwell or a Chatham: he was not a politician, still less a war leader, and did not think of himself as one. In the numbness of purpose, the failure of will, that characterised that nightmare autumn, his sheer thrust came nearest to supplying the resolution that should have been behind him. He deserved a chief of William's temper.

In his Herculean efforts to organise England's naval defence he took one initiative of a wholly political character. When Dartmouth was appointed to supersede the Papist Strickland Pepys was charged, as on the Tangier expedition five years earlier, with finding him a chaplain. Ken, his selection on that earlier occasion, had been one of the Seven Bishops whose successful defiance of the King had just laid his policy in ruins. Even if James could be brought to consider such an appointment a bishop was too venerable an ecclesiastical officer for such a post. But Pepys did the next best thing. In what was clearly a desperate attempt to reconstitute the Tory party of Church and King that James had so fatally divided, he wrote and pressed the job on the red-nosed Dr. Peachell, now happily restored to his Mastership. The fact that Ken had been preferred to a bishopric after holding the same office (*post hoc, propter hoc*) was twice discreetly alluded to. Peachell was startled, if flattered. 'I had a little itch to such a service 30 years agoe, but am now as old againe, and incumbred with businesse and therefore desire 24 Houres to consider & compare.'[15] Next day's Cambridge carrier brought his refusal.[16]

Besides the frantic bustle of mobilising the fleet (as usual the press gangs got hold of people who were legally immune: as usual Balty exceeded his powers, putting himself in the wrong with a short-tempered captain whom he had accused of malingering), besides the unremitting effort to keep the King steady and to get Dartmouth going, Pepys was also conducting an extensive and urgent correspondence over the General Election which the King had called for that autumn. He knew that he and Deane were by no means safe in their old constituency of Harwich. There was a plot to denounce them both as crypto-Catholics on the eve of the poll.[17] Sir Robert Holmes who controlled the Isle of Wight seats was not unhopeful of finding room for him and for Hewer too if need be. But that was reinsurance. Harwich must be fought and if possible won. The vast correspondence with Captain Langley, master of the packet boats and Mayor of Harwich, shows how much time such a campaign consumed. And there were other Admiralty boroughs, Rochester, Portsmouth, Dover, in which Pepys had valuable connections that might be called on by the King's hard-pressed supporters.

Private anxieties, family obligations, calls for help, do not disappear by sympathetic magic from the life of a busy man just because he is at his busiest. Of his Jackson nephews, John, as we have seen, was up at

Cambridge while his elder brother Samuel had just arrived back in late July from a cruise to the West Indies. The smattering of navigation he had picked up was not, as Pepys had evidently hoped, to be put to use in a naval career. Perhaps Pall, his mother, was already ailing. Certainly she died the following autumn and Samuel thereafter managed, not at all satisfactorily, the Brampton estate. What Mary Skinner's brothers were up to we do not know but it was probably mischief. By the following June their mother was imploring Pepys to rescind his decision to have nothing more to do with Peter: 'this Greaceless son of mine . . . o would to God that you had cane'd him, that you had Broken all his Bones Limb from Limb . . .'[18] Sir Samuel Morland, Pepys's first tutor, was still soliciting his old pupil's aid in obtaining a divorce from the coachman's daughter he had married without first verifying his belief that she 'was a very vertuous pious and sweet disposition'd Lady, and an heiress who had 500L per Ann. in Land of inheritance, and 4000L in ready Money . . .'[19] What she had in fact was the pox and a lover. Anyhow Sir Samuel thought that Pepys's constant attendance on the King in these days of crisis would give him an excellent opportunity of putting in a word with the Lord Chancellor. And then there were the usual troubles with servants. Since the offender was in this case black Pepys sent him aboard the ship that had brought Samuel Jackson back from the West Indies to be sold into slavery.[20]

On this buzz of activity fell the thunderclap of William's success. The whole Dutch armada had sailed down the Channel unopposed and had put the troops ashore in Torbay without losing a man. The English fleet, equal more or less in numbers, probably superior in quality, certainly so in striking power since it had no troop convoy to protect and could deny the enemy his bases while having the run of its own, had been windbound, as James and Pepys had warned its Admiral, behind the Gunfleet. Dartmouth, numbed by the magnitude of the disaster, could still hardly credit the fact. That James, his cause ruined by disregard of his repeated advice, could still spare the feelings of a loyal and affectionate servant touches the ignominy of defeat with nobility and pathos.

> . . . 'tis the greatest happynes of my life that yr Ma^ty is sattisfyed with my endeavers tho' they have proved so unlucky hitherto, 'tis strange that such mad proceedings should have such sucess at this time a yeare . . .[21]

William had landed on November 5th.* Dartmouth's letter here quoted

---

* It is worth remembering that England was still using the Old Style in dating: the modern notation would have made it November 15th.

was written on the 11th. Even as he wrote the first desertions from James's army had taken place. By the end of the month the trickle had become a flood, headed by his Commander-in-Chief, his other son-in-law and his nephew. The fleet, when at last it had struggled out to sea, had proved, not surprisingly, unreliable to the point of ineffectiveness. It had hardly got into the Channel before it was separated by violent weather and prevented from re-uniting by an unseasonable calm. Individual captains seized the chance of joining the winning side. Those who remained loyal saw no point in fighting a lost battle. Like the Parliamentary captains at the Restoration they knew that they had the safety of their country in their hands and counted it their first charge.

Pepys, as before in moments of public danger, showed the coolness, the tenacity, the constancy that underpinned the warmth and quickness so much more conspicuous in the everyday conduct of life. As long as James was in business he was in business with him. The sinking of the heart that so experienced and so penetrating an observer must have felt was no excuse for not doing one's job. Reports, requests, entreaties, flowed in from admirals, captains and local commanders at their wit's end what to do or how to do it. Instructions, encouragement, answers at least constructive where possible and rational where not, flowed out. To Dartmouth in particular he showed a magnanimity equal to the King's.

I am yet under some fears of your taking too much to heart your late misfortune . . . pray be fully at ease in this matter, depending upon't that if I knew the least cause for the contrary I would tell you of it. For so upon my faith I would . . . Once more therefore pray be at peace with yourself.[22]

Immediately news of the invasion had reached London James prepared to leave for the west in order to take personal command of the army. On November 17th he had his will solemnly witnessed by the Lord Chancellor, the two Secretaries of State, two Catholic peers and four senior officials of whom Pepys signed first in order of precedence. Early in the afternoon he left for Windsor, the first stage on his journey west. Pepys accompanied him there and secured from him a testimonial of his services to both Charles II and himself and a recommendation to the Lords of the Treasury to do him 'full right' in respect of any sums that might be due to him either as Secretary of the Admiralty or in his past capacity as Treasurer of Tangier. The grand total, according to Pepys's calculations, amounted to £28,007. 2s. 1¼d. It was never paid. Years after his death Hewer, his executor, and Samuel Jackson, his heir, were still keeping up a spirited action with the Treasury.[23] The shade of Pepys, we may be sure, would have approved their refusal to take no for an answer: it would equally have approved the prudent guardianship of public funds that dismissed specious claims from persons already adequately provided for.

After the King's departure Pepys continued as before directing the affairs of the navy, seeking especially to maintain the closest contact with Dartmouth, corresponding with the English consuls in the Mediterranean, gathering intelligence, stiffening morale, maintaining discipline. But the play was over: the stage invaded by the audience: the other actors trooping back in search of parts in the next production. Within ten days the King was back in London a broken man. His health had given way, his army had lost its credibility with the desertion of its general (an act that shocked at least one of William's commanders), there was nothing left in his role but to make an exit. Even this was muffed: and high tragedy closed with the botchings of an under-rehearsed farce. Nervously and physically the King was in no state for so taxing a final scene.

When James, at his second attempt, at last succeeded in leaving the country, it was nearly Christmas. The political uncertainty had already threatened the stability of public order in the capital. Anti-Catholic rioters had burnt down the Spanish embassy and attacked chapels where mass was said. Looting and lynching were in the air. For Pepys who had held high office under the fallen régime and who had great possessions it was a time of anxiety acuter even than the days when the Dutch had been in the Medway. Then, at least, it had been possible to transfer his gold to the safety of Brampton, incompetent though Elizabeth and his father had been over burying it in the garden. In the fire there had been time to take the Diary and other books and papers out to Bethnal Green, even to see to the protection of his wine and Parmesan cheese. But revolutionary anarchy was much more frightening. On December 18th James left Whitehall for Rochester at midday and William arrived at St. James's that afternoon. At least the library, the pictures and the manuscript collections at York Buildings were safe from the mob.

Pepys submitted to the *de facto* Government as became a great public servant, without toadying and without embarrassment. On December 19th he had an audience of the Prince of Orange (as William was styled until, on February 13th, 1689, he and Mary jointly accepted the Crown offered by Parliament). Like his friends and fellow civil servants Blathwayt, Southwell and the rest he was continued in office: but unlike them he found his bitterest political and professional enemies high in the King's favour. Russell and Herbert, the two senior sea officers who had managed the naval side of the Revolution, personified everything that Pepys had spent his life in opposing. They were gentlemen captains of the most formidable type and they knew, as well as Pepys, that there was not room for both themselves and the Secretary in the direction of the service. Besides that there were the strongest personal antipathies: Russell was brother-in-law to Harbord who had done his best to bring Pepys to the block at the time of the Popish Plot; Herbert as Dartmouth's predecessor in command at Tangier had done all he could to harm the men and measures that Pepys from his earliest days as Clerk of the Acts had tried to promote. Both men had often received the sharp letters of inquiry or reproof by which Pepys tried to maintain discipline. No doubt both saw in the Revolution a golden opportunity to be rid of him once and for all. A fighting service, in their eyes, was the proper sphere in which the aristocracy should shine: it had no business with jumped-up bureaucrats.

William, to judge from the men he did retain in office, would perhaps have preferred to keep him; but he had first of all to keep faith with the men who had brought him to the throne. Meanwhile he was at war with France and Pepys's knowledge of the day-to-day state of the fleet as well as his unrivalled grasp of English sea-power made him indispensable to the Government.

What did Pepys think? At first, it seems clear, he recognised that he was at the mercy of Russell, Herbert and the rest. The endorsement of the letter Will Hewer wrote him on the day of his audience with William, 'a letter of great tendernesse at a time of difficulty', even if made after the event speaks a mood of profound resignation. Unlike James, Pepys found light in his darkness. It was no small thing to read these words from a man who had been his closest subordinate and colleague for twenty-eight years.

. . . I know you will chearefully acquiesce in what ever circumstance God-Almighty shall think most propper for you, which I hope may prove more to your satisfaction than you can imagine; you may rest assured that I am wholly yours, and that you shall never want the utmost of my constant, faithfull and personall service, the utmost I can doe being inconsiderable to what your kindness & favour to me has and does oblige me to; And therefore as all I have proceeded from you soe all I have & am, is and shalbe, at your service.[24]

As the days went by he found himself treated with at least the same outward correctness that he had shown to his new masters. Did he begin to hope of holding on? Certainly he made strenuous efforts to secure a seat in the new Parliament at the General Election held in January. As before he was warned of treachery at Harwich and urged to appear in person. Both he and Sir Anthony Deane were defeated and on February 20th he resigned his office. His presence was apparently still necessary for another two days – his last official letter is dated the 22nd – and on March 9th he was ordered to hand over all books and papers belonging to his office to Phineas Bowles, a man of little weight who had been serving as Dartmouth's secretary until chosen as Pepys's successor.

Not, of course, that he was in any true sense Pepys's successor. Herbert and the rest were going to make very sure of that. Both his salary and his status were cut down to a size that declared the uniqueness of Pepys.

22

Retirement

To abandon the practice of a profession in which unrivalled, even un-precedented, mastery has been generally conceded can never be easy. Pepys, as his letters and his *Naval Minutes** show, felt resentment, anger, frustration, cynicism, but never despair. His nature was altogether too positive: he was too interested in justifying himself or in venting the scorn he felt for his successors to have time for self-pity. And in any case there was still more than enough to employ his inexhaustible energies. His books, his pictures, his collections: the Royal Society and the delights of con-versation and correspondence with learned men: his family, his friends, his dependants: above all, the towering literary monument for which through all his working life he had been amassing material, his *Navalia*. Bitter as the first taste might be there was much to be said for retirement. His health would not have stood the pace of executive life much longer: the colleagues he left behind were, almost all, highly uncongenial: the men with whom it had been a pleasure to work, Pearse, Hewer and Deane, left office with him. These were all good reasons for accepting the situa-tion and making the best of it. And Pepys was nothing if not rational. But over and above all this was the quality touched on in the first chapter of this book, the instinct at the heart of his life so perfectly expressed by his friend and contemporary the poet Dryden:

* A collection of notes made during his two periods of retirement and preserved in his library. Published by the N.R.S. in 1926.

From Harmony, from Heavenly Harmony
This Universal Frame began.

No man had a truer ear for the pitch of experience or a more natural sense of its rhythms.

In the savage world of seventeenth-century politics it was not always easy to glide peacefully from Westminster or Whitehall to a bookish retirement. Pepys knew from experience that the first moments out of office are those of intensest danger. It is the opportunity for revenge, for plunder, and for eliminating a rival beyond recall. 'Stone-dead hath no fellow.' The pithy political doctrine of the Earl of Essex, expounded to the young Mr. Hyde as they walked up and down the bowling-green in Piccadilly while Strafford's life hung in the balance and the storm-clouds gathered for the Civil War, was no relic of a picturesque if violent past. Pepys had been a boy of eight when the remark had been made. In the course of his life he had several times witnessed its practical application, most notably in the Popish Plot (of which, with reason, he believed himself to have been an intended victim) and in the subsequent reprisals of the Government. Some of the men who had tried to have him executed had reappeared with William; Harbord, Admiral Russell's brother-in-law, and Major Wildman, whose record in cloak-and-dagger work stretched back over three decades. When Pepys laid down his office he knew with a veteran's certainty that an attack was coming. The only questions would be those of timing, direction and force.

He had in this tactically weak and exposed position two of the veteran's advantages: he knew that attacks, even in intimidatingly superior numbers, do not always succeed; and he knew how to handle his weapons. He had beaten off enemies much stronger than himself by his unrivalled mastery of documentation. The first essential therefore was to prepare a defence of his Secretaryship, to organise his papers so that reinforcements could be rushed to whatever point was chosen for attack. No doubt, as at the time of the Plot, his enemies would try to strike at him through his friends and protégés. He would only be in a position to relieve them if the flag was still flying over his own citadel. This immediate task resulted in his only published book *Memoires . . . of the Royal Navy . . . For Ten Years, Determin'd December 1688* (London, 1690). As its title makes plain this is the classic *pièce justificative* of Pepys's Second Secretaryship and of the Special Commission on which Deane, Hewer and Balty had served. Since its subject-matter has already been discussed in Chapter XX nothing more needs to be said about it here except to reiterate that it succeeded entirely both in its immediate purpose of defeating the formidable Parliamentary attack mounted in 1691–2 and, at a longer perspective, in establishing his own achievement above the tideline of envy and fashion.

As at the time of the Brooke House Committee twenty years earlier Pepys recognised the supreme advantage he enjoyed through mastery of his records. Repeated requests to hand over his Letter Books from his ex-subordinate and ultimate successor, Josiah Burchett, had still met with no success as late as 1700.[1] He had surrendered, not without a tussle, a complete and well-arranged set of official papers (keeping, of course, duplicates for himself) between March and July 1689. But he was not going to part with a scrap of evidence that the strictest interpretation of the law did not oblige him to.[2]

His conduct of the Secretaryship, defended in depth by his filing system, might stand a direct assault. But no one could doubt, and he would have been proud to own, his loyalty to James II. This exposed him for the rest of his life to the suspicions and the occasional interference of the Government. Unlike William's ministers most of whom reinsured themselves by secret correspondence with the Jacobite court Pepys would have scorned to face both ways. Such transparency makes a man vulnerable. It was easy to have him arrested, along with Deane and Hewer, as 'suspected of dangerous and treasonable practices against his Majestye's Government'. All three were taken into custody on May 4th, 1689, and not released until the beginning of July. Pepys was again arrested in June 1690 but on this occasion he was allowed bail after only five days. In October the proceedings against him were dropped and he celebrated the formal restoration of his freedom by inviting his bailors to dinner. All of them, Sir Peter Palavicini, James Houblon, Robert Blackborne and Joseph Martin, were city men with strong connections either with the East India Company or with the Mediterranean. Exactly the men, in short, on whom the traditional Whig interest was founded. So far as is known Pepys suffered no further direct political persecution: but he certainly believed that his correspondence was read; his private papers were, apparently, subject to random seizure and search; and when, as late as 1699, he sent his nephew John Jackson on the Grand Tour he would have so dearly loved to have undertaken himself, the Government kept an eye on Jackson's contacts abroad.[3]

Even after his first arrest Pepys seems not altogether to have abandoned the possibility of a return to public life. Immediately on hearing of the proclamation for a new Parliament in February 1690 he wrote to his old friend Sir Robert Holmes and to the great Tory magnate of the west, Sir Edward Seymour, to solicit a seat. Nothing came of it. Doubtless his second arrest in the following June convinced him that nothing could. It

is however characteristic of his concern for justice and of his strong sense
of duty that he remained ready to expose himself to the snubs, the insolence, even the vindictiveness of his supplanters whenever it seemed that a
man might be penalised for having enjoyed his favour in the past. Such
favour, he had always impressed on its beneficiaries, was absolutely conditional on efficiency and honesty. It was in the logic of his position to
stand up for them against malice and jealousy. As Sir Arthur Bryant has
shown his last days in office were much occupied in the protection both of
old servants and of promising young men whom he did not wish to suffer
through his fall.

In April and May 1689 he exerted himself, without success, to secure
employment for Balty 'after neare 30 Years Service in the Navy, without
Reproach, through many offices of Trust'.[4] Balty's misfortunes were compounded by a total breach with Pepys towards the end of May. The cause,
though unknown, was almost certainly a row over the position occupied
by Mary Skinner.

> I understand [wrote Balty on May 28th] that by the malisious
> inventive ill offices of a female Beast, which you keepe, I am like
> allsoe to lye under your Anger and disgrace (to me more insuportable
> than the former) but I hope, and humbly pray, (though she tould me
> imprudently and arogantly, you scorned to see me) that with your
> Generous Usuall goodness, wisdome, manhood and former kindness
> you will not damn him Unheard whoe shoold Joy to hazard (as in duty
> bound) his dearest Bludd for your Service.'[5]

Pepys would not accept such language from anyone. He never, so far as
we know, wrote or spoke to him again. It seems that he relieved his wants
through an allowance. Balty certainly thanks him for something of the kind
two years later when afflicted 'with Such Sickness and tormenting paines
all over my body, with the adition of the Yellow Jandis and other distempers . . . as but two days agoe, it was thought, I shoold never more
have seene light in this world.'[6] But he rallied, recovering all his stylistic
powers in an appeal for cast-off clothes.

A happier outcome rewarded Pepys's efforts on behalf of his cousin
Charles, master joiner at Chatham Dockyard. On November 10th, 1689,
Charles Pepys wrote in great distress at finding that he was about to be
replaced by his own foreman. Pepys wrote at once to his old friend
Edward Gregory, Commissioner at Chatham, and to Sir John Lowther,
the only member of the new Admiralty Commission whom he respected
and liked, pleading '. . . that as farr as you reasonably may you will require

other crimes to be alledg'd and proved against him (& such I never yet
heard of) besides that of his name and Relationship to your most faithful
and humble servant.'7 Their intervention was prompt and decisive. On
the 23rd Charles Pepys wrote in exultation still vibrant, still breathless,
after three centuries.

Sr
    I had my warrant delivered to me on ye 21st instant of ye ad^{ty} and
I hastened to ye Roy^{ll} navie bord and gat my warrant entred and signed
by 3 Comm^{rs} and so soone as that was done I went to ye River and
tooke a boate that brought me to Graves end and as soon as I came to
Graves end I tooke Coche that brought mee whom [home] in ye
King's yard in Chatham by 3 a Cloke in the morning and at seven a
Cloke I mett ye Comm^r [Pepys's friend, Edward Gregory] & ye Mr
shipwrighte whitche wisht mee mutche joy of my renued warrant thaye
asqued mee how yr honor did and wear glade to hiere yr honor was
well . . .

They were not alone in this: even in his headlong self-concern Charles
Pepys goes on to say how his cousin's ex-clerks in the Admiralty remembered him kindly. Did Pepys, as he read the letter, catch an echo of his
own frantic haste to get a warrant sealed and entered thirty years earlier?
He answered it in one of the last of those many, many letters of a senior
official (though such he was no longer) to a junior in which kindness,
wisdom and justice combine with an irrepressible itch to improve the
occasion.

Cousin Pepys,
    Tis matter of great content to me to find by your letter of ye 23rd
that you are once more settled in yr. Employment. I pray God to give
you Health long to enjoy yr. Benefit & to execute well ye Duty of it;
& very glad I am that in ye Present condicon of Affaires with mee I
have been able to give you any assistance towards the obtaining thereof.
But at ye same time you are not to impute so much of it to me as to
make you forget what you owe to Comm^r Gregory, for without his
timely & hearty appearance at my desire for you by his letter to ye
Navy Board all I did, or could at this time have done on your behalfe
would have signifyed nothing.
    Therefore let me advise you by no means to fail in your dutiful
acknowledgments to him of this happy friendship to you . . . And this I
the rather press you in from ye Error which I find you were fallen into,
when at your last being with me you took ye liberty of complaining so

particularly of ye want of sincerity in those of your seeming Friends at Chatham, as if at ye same time that they were giving you good words they were undermining you behind yr back, in getting yr Employment away for another Man. Whom you meant, I know not. But if yr doubts did reach to ye Comm^r he has given you a very good Proof of yr mistake, worthy to be always remembered by you.

But above all, let me recommend it to you to avoid ye thinking that whatever it is that you owe either to him or me on this occasion, either he or I would have stirred one step for you upon the single Score of yr Relation to me had it not been seconded with ye Opinion we both have of yr Desire, as well as Ability to perform ye Worke of yr Place & that you will not only continue to expresse the same by all ways of Diligence, Sobriety & Faithfulness, but that you will rectify that Lownesse of Spirit & Backwardnesse in appearing in ye Execution of yr Duty, as a Warrant Officer, which (without any other Crime) had, but for ye seasonable kindnesse of Commr Gregory certainly undone you: yr submitting yrself to be imposed upon in yr Office by yr Inferior having given him an Opportunity of carrying away ye credit of all that was done, & you to be lookt upon as a Cypher . . .[8]

The younger generation did not always profit from such exhortation as they should. Pepys's heir, his nephew Samuel Jackson, abandoned the sea officer's career designed for him and was ultimately disinherited in favour of his younger and more docile brother John for marrying a lady whom Pepys thought unsuitable. The young Skinners, Mary's brothers, write with such bland impudence that Pepys was once moved to open his reply with the awe-inspiring form of address 'Young Man'. Even this failed of its effect: although they pass out of his correspondence for a time, Peter reappears, his insouciance untarnished, in a begging letter of delicious cant and flattery written only a few months before the end.[9] A third brother, Corbett, pursued a blameless career in the Excise, in which Pepys ultimately obtained him promotion.[10]

Pepys had enough troubles of his own during this time. Apart from his running battle with the Admiralty over his official correspondence and over the possession of York Buildings, apart from the threat of sudden arrest or seizure of his papers on suspicion of Jacobite plotting, he and Sir Josiah Child the East India Company Director were jointly charged before a Committee of the House of Commons of a high misdemeanour in 'sending the *Phoenix* man of war, to the East Indies, to seiz the ships and goods belonging to the subjects of England.'[11] What had happened was this. The *Phoenix* had been sent out at the end of 1684 to suppress a successful *coup d'état* in the Bombay Presidency led by an ex-Cromwellian officer against the hated rule of the East India Company's governor, Sir John Child (brother of Josiah). On the way out the *Phoenix* caught the *Bristol*, an interloper, that is an English vessel trading in violation of the East India Company's monopoly, in the Mozambique channel. As the *Bristol*'s captain had accidentally shot himself the *Phoenix* put a prize crew aboard and sailed in company for Bombay. Unfortunately the *Bristol* was leaking badly and sank a fortnight later. While she was on the point of foundering the *Phoenix*'s captain looted twenty bales of chintz. After he had arrived at Bombay he had her retrospectively condemned as prize.

These events took place in May and June 1685. Neither Pepys nor anybody else in England knew anything about them until nearly a year later: and the *Phoenix* herself did not enter home waters until August 1687. It was not until 1689 that the owners of the *Bristol* petitioned Parliament for redress against the captain of the *Phoenix* and against those, Sir Josiah Child for the East India Company and Pepys for the Admiralty, who had signed his instructions. Ordinarily such a charge would have been negligible. But in the spring and summer of 1689 Pepys clearly thought it dangerous. The monopolies of the Chartered Companies were identified with the Stuart dynasty. It was easy to represent them as the economic counterpart of political tyranny: it was simple to show that their enforcement was a violation of the liberty of the subject: and how convenient that Mr. Pepys, the lackey of Stuart absolutism, should be caught red-handed at this fell work. The Committee reported on July 18th 'that Mr Pepys by signing the said Instructions . . . [is] guilty of high mis-demeanour . . .' But James Houblon went to see the great lawyer Pollexfen, whose name Pepys put first in his list of its members, and was able to reassure his friend. Pollexfen would remove the sting: 'in ye Report he will cause the word "signed" to be altered and instead of it put "counter-signed."'[12]

In the same month Pepys was ordered to appear before the House of Commons Committee for inquiring into the affairs of Ireland and the fleet. James had landed at Kinsale in March and had ridden in triumph to Dublin. Londonderry, still unrelieved from sea, was at the last gasp of the most famous siege in British history. Why were there only nineteen ships with Herbert in Bantry Bay? But this was Pepys's home ground. He produced at once a complete statement of the strength and disposition of every ship in sea pay as at November 5th (the day William landed), December 18th (the day James left) and on February 20th, his own last day in office.

In spite of his apprehensions Pepys emerged substantially unscathed from the Revolution. He had lost office, but how much longer would age and health have allowed him to hold it? He felt vulnerable and insecure, but could he look back on a single decade of his life in which he had not experienced these unpleasant sensations even more acutely? He did not like losing a large income, but who does? His occasional assertions of poverty, voiced in the plangent tones peculiar to the very rich, are amply contradicted by his style of life, by his eager purchase of books, prints, manuscripts and pictures, by his liberal patronage of scholars, by his benefactions to Christ's Hospital and the University of Oxford, by his hospitality and by his generosity. The long evening of Pepys's life was as rich, as comfortable and, from all the evidence, as happy as his friends could have wished.

At the beginning of his retirement he appears to have considered setting up as a country gentleman. Early in 1690 his old friend Richard Cumberland sent a long and careful description of Walcott House,* not far from Stamford, to Pepys's cousin Dr. Gale. 'I guesse,' he wrote, 'that your Occasion of enquireing about it may bee in behalfe of some purchaser.' Since the letter has come to rest among Pepys's personal papers it seems probable that he was the interested party. But why in that case did he not write to Cumberland direct? His friend had certainly taken pains, covering two sides of a large sheet. 'The house is very beautiful being adorned with a large lanterne as it were on the top . . . Those who are critical about the matter say the house is too large & good for the small estate in land which adjoins it . . . The land about is healthy and most convenient for the pleasure of hunting . . .'[13] Pepys had made a present of his hack to Wynne Houblon in the preceding summer[14] so that this was hardly a temptation.

Wisely such an uprooting was not tried. He remained at York Buildings until the spring of 1700 when, for reasons of health, he paid a long visit to Will Hewer's house at Clapham. In the following spring he settled there for the two years of life that were left to him. He had known the house since it was built by Gauden the victualler and had described it approvingly in his Diary entry for July 25th, 1663. It was so near his friends in London and Westminster, so close to John Evelyn's country house, first at Sayes Court, Deptford and then, after 1694, at Wotton, near Dorking, that he often stayed there even before it became his last home.

York Buildings for the last decade of the century became what another age, another language and another sex would have termed a *salon*. It was a

* Pulled down in the nineteenth century.

centre of the literary, artistic and intellectual life of the capital. Here
dined each week the 'Saturday Academists', a small group of Fellows of
the Royal Society. To the library came scholars, historians, antiquaries
and connoisseurs. Alike in its contents and its methods of arrangement it
expressed the personality that formed it as freshly, as strikingly, as the
Diary which is its most famous possession. As its cataloguer has well
written:

> Were the Diary non-existent, and were no other source of knowledge
> available, a judgment of Pepys's character formed upon a consideration
> of the contents of his library would reveal him to have been a man of
> great breadth of interest and catholicity of taste, an inquisitive scholar
> conversant with more languages than his own, and a person in whom a
> love of order and neatness in detail was paramount[15]

No other collection preserves more perfectly the impress of its maker.
Among the long meditated and carefully drafted instructions embodied
in a codicil to his will Pepys enjoined that except for making good obvious
deficiencies at the time of his death 'thenceforward noe Additions' should
be made. Every volume was to have its individual number, each was to
contain his bookplate and to bear on its outside covers his crest or cypher
stamped in gold, except of course where this would spoil one of the
exquisitely designed and executed bindings in which he took such pleasure.
Everything was catalogued within an inch of its life (the books had been
bought for use, not show) but they were to take their place in his presses
according to their height, not their subject-matter. On this Pepys refined
in his eighth instruction: 'That their placing as to heighth be strictly re-
viewed and where found requiring it more nicely adjusted.' Just as Pepys
himself needed a stool to reach the higher shelves (visible in the illustra-
tion facing p. 209) so the books that were not as tall as their neighbours
were mounted on wooden blocks faced with leather to match their bindings. A work on navigation rubs shoulders with a classical author, a French
historian reposes beside an English poet, a collection of contemporary
pamphlets adjoins a law manual. The extraordinary balance and complexity
of that deceptively clear mind can here be apprehended through sight
and touch. From theology, not so massively represented as in most seventeenth-century libraries, to gay, even licentious poetry (Rochester's
Poems which Pepys at one time thought written 'in a style unfit to mix
with my other books' bear on the spine the slightly shame-faced legend
'Rochester's Life'),[16] from children's books to Atlases, from Economics
to Travel, every category of a well-found library is supplied. And yet the

[handwritten shorthand notes]

May. 31. 2669.

Pepys's Bookplate.

flavour of one man's taste, one man's mind, is not lost in a bland comprehensiveness. It is, naturally, most marked in the special collections, the Navalia and the ballads, distant echoes of summer evenings with Elizabeth and her maid singing catches on the leads of the old Navy Office. The prints, especially the portraits, to which Evelyn's connoisseurship and John Jackson's journeyings were tributary streams, exemplify the fascinated interest in people that is in its turn the root of his own fascination for us.

From Pepys's study was conducted a correspondence that ranged over every field then subject to speculative intelligence or rational inquiry and even opened some — ecology, for example — that belong more to the twentieth century than the seventeenth. The embellishment of the library with a gallery of portraits, the improvement, both by acquisition and by pruning, of the book collection, the cataloguing of the manuscripts and the sorting of a lifetime's accumulation of letters and papers went on continuously. Pepys was assisted in these tasks by two or three clerks, one of whom Paul Lorrain, a Huguenot refugee, took orders, becoming in 1700 prison chaplain at Newgate. For twenty years he earned considerable sums and a minor literary reputation by publishing the authorised confessions of men and women on the point of execution. This grisly output was supplemented by a small work of his own entitled 'The Dying Man's Assistant'. Pepys, characteristically, used his influence with the Archbishop of Canterbury to forward his ordination. But, from his own point of view it was a nuisance, inhibiting '. . . the use I should have to make of him relateing to my books, papers and clerkelike services, other than bare sitting at his deske upon solemne works only.'[17]

For the rest, the household went on much as before. Mary Skinner still presided over a housekeeper, a porter, two footmen, a coachman, a cook, a laundry-maid and a housemaid.[18] Invitations to dinner were accepted with an alacrity that suggests good food and drink, less elaborate perhaps than the gourmandising of younger days and sharper appetites. Dryden is bidden to 'a cold Chicken and a Sallade', Dr. Gale to 'a dish of tripes', Sir James Houblon to 'a piece of mutton' or 'a jole of ling' [best end of cod], and a Baron of the Exchequer to 'a tansey', the lightest of light refreshments.[19] But if grossness was eschewed, so was austerity. John Evelyn, his favourite and most constant guest from Wotton at the end of August 1692, wrote:

Here is wood and water, meadows and mountaines, the Dryads and the Hamadryads; but here's no Mr Pepys, no Dr Gale. Nothing of all the cheere in the parlor that I tast; all's insipid, and all will be so to me 'til I see and injoy you againe . . . *O Fortunate Mr Pepys!* who knows, possesses, and injoyes all that's worth the seeking after. Let me live among your inclinations and I shall be happy.[20]

Deep though the pleasure it gave him, Pepys left this letter unanswered for a fortnight. The reason was that he had gone to ground. The continued suspicions of the Government, the unpredictable searches to which he had been several times subjected had convinced him of the danger he was in by preserving so many of his papers. Until he knew what was lying about for his enemies to pick up he could not be easy. At the end of June he took a house near the Houblons in Epping Forest, put it about that he was spending the summer in the country — and disappeared. In reality he shut himself up in York Buildings, not stirring outside, or even coming downstairs, for the best part of three months. As usual he achieved what he set out to do. But at a certain cost (besides the £30 on the house that had been rented as a blind):

my constant poreing, and sitting so long still in one posture, without any divertings or exercize, haveing for about a month past brought a humour down into one of my leggs, not only to the swelling it to allmost the size of both, but with the giving mee mighty pains, and disabling mee to this day to putt on a shooe on that foot.[21]

Pepys's troubles with the new régime were, in fact, pretty well over. His most dangerous enemy, Admiral Herbert, had been disgraced after the Battle of Beachy Head; Russell, who survived in high command, was perhaps too calculating to indulge the caprice of revenge. Politically there was much less to be feared from men who openly refused to take the oath of allegiance to William and Mary on the grounds that they had already sworn themselves to James — non-jurors as they were called — then from those whose Jacobitism, real or pretended, was secret. Pepys grumbled at paying the double capitation tax imposed on this scruple, but he was never afterwards arrested. If the Secretaryship of the Admiralty was successively in the hands of two clerks with whom he had quarrelled, James Sotherne and Josiah Burchett (the miserable Bowles had not lasted long), there were other clerks such as Richard Gibson who kept their old chief informed and had the sense to avail themselves of his knowledge, his experience and his mastery of official draughtsmanship. When Gibson showed him a copy of a memorial he had drawn up for the King on the state of the navy Pepys noted approvingly that his proposals for victualling the navy were the same as those he had himself offered to Sir William Coventry in his famous New Year letter in 1666. Perhaps this was not altogether surprising since Gibson had, as Pepys acknowledges in the Diary, helped to frame his own ideas on the subject.

His true administrative heir did not, however, come from his most intimate circle of personal assistants but from the system and the tradition that he had shaped. Charles Sergison, who was Clerk of the Acts at the Navy Office from 1690 to 1719, a single-handed tenure of nearly thirty years except for the period 1702–6 when he shared the post with Pepys's old clerk Samuel Atkins, upheld the standards, voiced the very opinions, fought the familiar battles of his great predecessor. He had entered the Navy Office in 1675 as Chief Clerk to Thomas Hayter and Pepys's brother John who were then joined in the Clerkship of the Acts. He continued to serve as Chief Clerk under their successor James Sotherne until, at the beginning of 1690, Sotherne was appointed Secretary of the Admiralty and Sergison stepped into his shoes. How much he had imbibed of the true Pepysian spirit may be gauged from the terms in which, on May 24th, 1699, he and another civilian member of the board pressed William III to release them from office:

. . . we had struggled with many difficulties such as remote and deficient funds, stubborn and refractory officers, insulting superiors, such as rather countenanced than discouraged the loose discipline of the Navy, gratified their own passions and neglected everything else. But nevertheless by our adherence to the ancient rules and methods of the Navy, regularity of our payments and constant diligence and attendance we have overcome them all.[22]

Pepys was never entirely cold-shouldered by the official world he had left. On December 30th, 1689, he received a printed summons to attend the King and Queen on New Year's Day with the 'Mathematicall Boys' of Christ's Hospital. Although endorsed (twice) in his own hand 'went not',[23] his services to that foundation were recognised in April 1699 by the freedom of the City. He protested to Compton, Bishop of London, who asked him to recommend an impoverished cavalier for a clerkship in the Admiralty, that his name would only harm such a cause with Sotherne. Yet he was invited to Trinity House dinners, though no longer one of the Brethren, and from time to time dined with the Navy Board.[24]

Common sense and good feeling triumphed again when he was appointed a member of the Grand Committee for Greenwich Hospital in December 1694. The act of vision that was to transform the decaying Tudor palace of Placentia with its lovelier accretions, the Queen's House and the King's Pavilion, into the supreme composition of English architecture is enhanced by its association with Pepys. Evelyn, the greatest connoisseur of his age and an ex-Commissioner for the Sick and Wounded, was an inevitable choice for a position of control. But it was Pepys that Sir Christopher Wren took with him when he went down to view the site and discuss practicalities in late October or early November, and it was to Pepys that he outlined his first conception of making it the English answer to the Invalides. No one could have received the idea more eagerly. To achieve it, Pepys pointed out, Parliamentary finance was essential. Royal bounty and private charity would never prove adequate to so grand a design.

Once the danger of political persecution had receded, Pepys settled down to the enjoyment of those possessions and inclinations over which Evelyn had rhapsodised. His activity was almost entirely intellectual: his travels few and short: correspondence, conversation and reading made up the business of life. Nothing very much happened to him. He was held up by highwaymen at Michaelmas 1693 while on his way to Chelsea in a coach with Mary Skinner, John Jackson and several ladies. Pepys handed over his valuables without fuss and 'conjured them to be Civil

to the Ladies, and not to Affright them, which they were'.[25] In the
summer of 1694 and again in the spring of 1697 he was dangerously ill.
From time to time his studies were interrupted by domestic broils (his
housekeeper, Mrs. Fane, was so touchy that at last he insisted on her dismissal) or by friends in need. In March and April 1695 he was '. . . concern'd in a most tiresome, vexatious and yet foolish Sollicitation in
Parliament for these last 6 or 7 Weekes, that has not left mee one thought
free till the houre of its Prorogation . . . in behalfe of a friend that is
nearest to my selfe.'[26] The House of Commons was at this time pursuing
allegations of widespread corruption which culminated in the impeachment of Pepys's old ministerial colleague, Danby, now Duke of Leeds.
Among the bodies particularly under attack was the East India Company
with which Will Hewer had always been connected through his uncle
Robert Blackborne and where, after his services were no longer required
by the Admiralty, he had himself found employment, becoming in 1704
Deputy Governor.[27] The opportunity to repay Hewer's staunchness
cannot altogether have come amiss.

But in old age the proportions of experience naturally shift from the
direct to the vicarious. A reflective mind is offered fresh scope both by
the confinements and the liberties of the condition:

> The soul's dark cottage, battered and decayed
> Lets in new light through chinks that time hath made.[28]

Pepys accepted the limitations imposed by age and health with the stoicism
he had always professed and practised. For a man so interested in his
own symptoms he was notably free from hypochondria. The inquiries of
his friends are answered with serene assurances that cannot always have
been easy to give. Even when in the spring of 1700 the wound from his
lithotomy of forty years earlier became dangerously inflamed, necessitating
three further operations and a great deal of pain and discomfort, he
waited till it was all over before alarming his nephew, then on the Grand
Tour, with the news:

> But I have great hopes given mee that what has been since done upon
> the third breach will prove thoroughly effectuall; I being (I thank God)
> once more upon my legs, and though my long lying in bed will cost me
> possibly some time for the removal of my weakness, yet I am in no
> doubt of recovering my first state very soon . . .[29]

It is no mean spirit that rises so gracefully over the temptations to self-
pity.

The freedom conferred by exclusion from affairs was the best of blessings. All his life Pepys had strained to reduce phenomena, physical or psychological, to order because only by that way lay any hope of understanding. By setting down his experience, the totality of it, in a diary he had equipped himself to make sense of it. By preserving everything he could lay hands on in the way of nautical archives, he had equipped himself to reduce the naval universe to a harmonious rationality. The art of the shipwright 'their knowledge lying in their hands confusedly', the cheating of the purser, the economics of sea-power, the correct method of mustering stores, the promotion of hydrography, the virtues of Eastland plank, all the thousand and one topics central or outlying on which Pepys had been amassing material were to be resumed, digested and related in the Navalia which Evelyn awaited with such pleasing awe. And the Diary and the Navalia were but the exemplars of a curiosity that extended to everything it could cognise and of a belief that all phenomena were ultimately capable of rational explanation. He retained the intellectual appetite of a young man: he had spent a great part of his maturity in provisioning for a long voyage. It would not be his fault if he did not touch the happy Isles and see the great Achilles whom he knew.

23

Mens cujusque is est quisque

As a frontispiece to the *Memoires* Pepys printed an engraving of himself with his motto below it. He could not conceal his delight when it came to his ears that the Admiralty, imagining the words to be his own, had been pleased to criticise their sense and style. He wrote to Hewer:

I could be well contented Mr Sotherne were told . . . that whatever reckoning I may make of his learning, I owne too great an esteem for that of my Lord of Pembroke's to think it possible for him to misplace upon me the honour of answering for a sentence soe much above my ambition of fathering, or the authority of any man else to censure but he (if any such there be) that would be thought a Latinist orator and philosopher fit to stand-up with Cicero, whose very words these are in that excellent and most divine chapter his Somnium Scipionis [Scipio's Dream] viz:

Tu vero enitere; et sic habeto, te non esse mortalem, sed corpus hoc. Nec enim is es, quem forma ista declarat; sed *Mens cujusque is est quisque*, non ea figura, quae digito demonstrari potest.

A thought derived to him from Plato, and wrought-upon after him by St Paul.

I am, Your most affectionate servant,

S.P.

No translation can do justice either to the passage or to the phrase that Pepys adopted for his motto, perpetuating its association with his name both by his book-plates and by the inscription on the front of his library. But, as this letter shows, it held so profound a meaning for him that not to translate would be the worse treachery:

Fight the good fight; and always call to mind that it is not you who are mortal, but this body of ours. For your true being is not discerned by perceiving your physical appearance. But 'what a man's mind is, that is what he is', not that individual human shape that we identify through our senses.

For Pepys, the *mens*, the mind, the intellect, reason, was the quality that set man above the beasts that perish and thus, implicit in the phrase if not in logic, his passport to immortality. It was the surest mark of the Divine hand, the thread to follow through the labyrinth in which generations of theologians had imprisoned their victims. In the ten pages of 'Notes from Discourses touching Religion'[1] this theme dwarfs every other. All his life Pepys had looked on atheism with horror. On the other hand there is little suggestion of piety and much to suggest the opposite. A man who goes to church to pinch the bottoms of pretty girls and emerges to pay his weekly visit to his whore can hardly be thought devout. Add to this a cool and sceptical turn of mind, a strong anti-clericalism, an even stronger distaste for religious enthusiasm based on bitter experience of its more frightening manifestations, and it would be plausible to represent Pepys as a sensible, comfortable materialist who conformed to the conventional observances of a religion that had its uses as a social sanction but who privately thought it all great nonsense. To discredit such an interpretation it is enough to read the letter quoted at the beginning of this chapter. There is no mistaking the language of the heart. And the circle in which Pepys passed the last decades of his life, Evelyn, James Houblon, Dr. Gale, Sir William Petty, were men who shared in differing degrees both his belief in God and his learned, critical, often irreverent, scepticism towards ecclesiastical pretensions.

To Pepys and to Petty, in particular, scepticism was a religious obligation. How else was the mass of superstition, hypocrisy, cant, ignorance and plain muddle to be cleared away? Was not this the essence of what the Royal Society was doing in the natural sciences? God had created the world and all that was in it. Religion, rightly understood, imposed on the *mens* the duty of making sense of everything, because every rational explanation of phenomena would uncover another sentence of the divine palimpsest. That is why the recovery and preservation of medieval manuscripts was pursued with the same zest as inquiry into hydrostatics or economics or the laws of chance or demography or the second sight. Knowledge, like God himself, was indivisible. What Pepys had done in the navy he would, had he but world enough and time, have done to the whole of life. Chance, as he truly remarked, brought him into the navy. But whatever he had done he would have instilled order and method, at first because he loved beauty but at last because he loved truth. Next door to Pepys's notes already referred to is a manuscript dialogue on Liberty of Conscience endorsed in Pepys's own hand: '1687. Sir Wm Petty's Paper written at my desire & given mee by himselfe a little before his Death.' Like the notes that precede it its tone is of candid inquiry, never of assertion or dogmatism. Both men (and this is true also of Pepys's other religious mentor, Dr. Gale) are entirely free from sectarianism: indeed in comparing the character and effects of Protestantism and Roman Catholicism they are more alive to the shortcomings of their own persuasion. Pepys even goes so far as to speculate whether a religious minority may not be a good thing in itself: 'It is said that we should live more carefully had we Catholicks amongst us then we doe now. As ye French Protestants were said to doe.'

If some choice souls have been disconcerted by the lack of the numinous in Pepys's religion, they have perhaps overlooked its seriousness and solidity. The cast of his mind was practical, workmanlike, matter-of-fact. The question 'Which, if any, is the true Church' was intellectually analogous to 'What price ought the Navy Board to pay for tallow.'

> It is urged by some that ye present quarrell about Religion has sprung only from ye Priests, those on the Protestant side only beating downe ye Markett and pretending to serve ye people in a cheaper, not better, forme of worship than those of Rome; whereas ye latter are as obstinate in keeping up their price as ye others are concern'd to keep themselves in ye present Employment and power they have gott themselves into, tho' at a lower rate.

This is the tone in which Pepys and his friends talked. They were not sneering at religion any more than people discussing the motives and policies of a Communist Government are deriding Marxism. Any institutionalised system of ideas creates a network of interests. A few pages later Pepys notes:

> D[r] G[ale] observes that places and business of proffitt are not dis-

posed of & managed with grosser methods & Degrees of Coruption in the meanest & worst Societyes of Mankind than in ye Universityes.

It was precisely because he loved learning and adored his University that Gale, Fellow of Trinity, Cambridge, Regius Professor of Greek, High Master of St. Paul's, Fellow of the Royal Society and one of the most eminent scholars of his age, used such language. The universities were then, and long remained, closed clerical corporations. To him, as to Pepys, the offence of the clergy was double: their laziness and greed, bad in themselves, usurped the main resources available for the pursuit of knowledge: 'ye entered not in yourselves and them that were entering in ye hindered.'

It was therefore an essentially religious spirit that sustained the vigorous curiosity of the aging Pepys as it had animated the founders of the Royal Society.[2] Into the Notes touching Religion crowd questions and statements that foreshadow the preoccupations of the next two and a half centuries. 'When all is done reason must govern all since our very faith must be a reasonable faith.' 'Q. how farr mankind may be said to be made up of Different speecies, and where ye Brute ends & Man begins with the consequences thereof.' The age of Pope and the age of Darwin flash into focus. 'Consult Sir Wm Petty about ye N^o of Men in ye World etc.' We are in our own age of anxiety. And there is more than a hint of the modern school of linguistic philosophy in:

> Sir Wm Petty's saying . . . that much ye greatest part of all humane understanding is lost by our discoursing and writeing of matters non-sensically, that is in words subject to more sences than one, to ye rendering disputations Infinite upon every Proposition that can be made in any Science whether divinity, Law etc.

Sometimes it seems that Pepys and his circle anticipated every intellectual attitude familiar to our world. When the Reverend Jeremiah Wells writes to him about a book entitled, 'Men Before Adam' we begin to wonder whether we are in the seventeenth century or the nineteenth. Neither archaeology nor natural science contributed to the arguments of this particular work which was based on internal criticism of the Bible.[3] But more often we recognise ideas and methods of a striking modernity. Dr. Goade's weather forecasts (based on astrology) are tested against observation. For January 27th the guarded prediction 'Curious briske winds & Frosty' was a pale reflection of observed reality: 'M[orning]: blak frost, with some drops of rain, a hard gale. A[fternoon]: more wind likely to snow.'[4] Pepys's historical researches suggest the idea of constructing a comparative price index: 'Confer with Sir James Houblon, Mr Neale, Master of the Mint, etc. about the different par of our moneys compared with common commodities in different ages.'[5] The impact of Graunt and Petty's brilliant work on population statistics can be felt in half a dozen of his fields of interest: history, geography, economics, even, as we have seen, theology. The experiments in weighing and measuring on which Newton and Boyle and Hooke were rearing the topless towers of modern physics were beyond Pepys's competence but not beyond his intuition. Charles II and Samuel Butler might guffaw at the Royal Society:

> To measure wind and weigh the air,
> And turn a circle to a square;
> To make a powder of the sun,
> - By which all doctors should b'undone;
> To find the north-west passage out,
> Although the farthest way about.[6]

Pepys had early recognised mensuration for a tool as diverse in its application and as revolutionary in its results as the wheel. His own mathematical limitations were not allowed to inhibit the play of mind. In November and December 1693 the project for raising money by a national lottery occasioned a long correspondence with Newton on the mathematical probabilities of dicing.[7] In the autumn of 1698 Dr. John Wallis, the Savilian Professor of Geometry at Oxford answered a letter of inquiry with a long disquisition on the mathematical expression of the relation of notes in music.[8] Wallis, like Pepys's old tutor Samuel Morland, had won early and brilliant success in the intelligence service by his skill as a cryptographer. Even in his learned retirement the Government of William III employed him to decipher the intercepted correspondence of the Jacobites.

But Wallis and mathematics were by no means the only connections that Pepys had formed with the University of Oxford. Through his interest in medieval manuscripts and through his friendship with Dr. Hickes, the master-builder of English historical scholarship, he had been drawn into an Oxonian circle, of whom Dr. Charlett, the Master of University College, was the busiest, most self-important and Humphrey Wanley the most learned and distinguished. The extraordinary story of this apparently incompatible group of combative individualists who nevertheless worked in complete harmony has been brilliantly told in

Professor David Douglas's *English Scholars*. Through Hickes and Charlett
Pepys met and befriended the rising scholars, Wanley, the greatest of
English palaeographers, Tanner, whose manuscript collections have
enriched the Bodleian, and Gibson, to whose edition of Camden's
Britannia Pepys contributed 'the account of the Arsenals for the Royal
Navy in Kent with the additions to Portsmouth and Harwich so far as
they relate to the Royal Navy.'[9] Through Evelyn he also met and helped
forward the young Richard Bentley, greatest of English classical scholars
and most tyrannical of Masters of Trinity. All these circles intersected.
Evelyn was himself an antiquary of great erudition: Bentley was a Fellow
of the Royal Society, as was Dr. Gale, who again combined classical and
patristic scholarship with medieval studies. The cross-fertilisation of
intellectual disciplines was never more fruitful than among the friends of
Pepys.

To a heartening extent the spirit of inquiry transcended the divisions of
politics and churchmanship. Apart from old friends in the city like the
Houblons Pepys was on good terms with John Locke, the official philosopher of Whiggism, and with Lord Somers, its most skilful tactician. More
surprising still, his friend Hickes who defied the Government in his
inflexible refusal to take the oaths and whose loyalty to James II had been
subjected to the agonising trial of a brother's execution, extended the same
courtesy and respect to fellow scholars who conformed as to his non-
juring associates. Alone among Pepys's learned correspondents Dr.
Thomas Smith, the Cottonian librarian seems to have been something of
a bigot.[10]

The new scholarship, like the new science, could only grow from the
publishing of results and the pooling of knowledge. In January 1693,
Pepys in exchanging general information with Dr. Plot, the Professor of
Chemistry at Oxford best known for his history of Staffordshire, sketched
the idea of a National Bibliography.[11] Two years later he was writing
to Evelyn in praise of the great survey of the manuscripts in English and
Irish libraries that finally issued from the Oxford University Press in
1697:

> . . . I mean, the reducing into less room what poor mankind is now to
> turn-over soe many cumbersome, jejune, and not seldom unintelligible
> volumes for, and when that's done, not have 5, perhaps not one
> year, to reckon upon of his whole life for the sedate applying and
> enjoying those sorry pittances of seeming knowledge that he possibly
> has been 50 in collecting. What a debt were this to lay upon man-
> kind![12]

Pepys, perhaps out of modesty, had declined an editorial invitation to contribute the catalogue of his own collection. Evelyn told him, what he must have known, how important it was 'for the very greate variety of the choycest subjects, no where else to be found in England'.[13] The Anthony Roll the most beautiful and the most valuable naval document of Henry VIII's time presented to Pepys by Charles II in 1680 alone would prove his case. Was it, perhaps, caution? As Edward Browne was to write in a letter to Dr. Gale preserved among Pepys's papers:

> I do not very well like the printing of our English Mss. at Oxford; 'tis a dangerous thing, and may prove of fatal consequence to us some time or other, as the University of Heydelburg found to their cost, after they had set the Pope a longing for their Mss. upon their publishing a copy of 'em . . . I and you will make a good use of this book of Mss., Dr Gale, but there be those who will not.

To some extent Pepys had anticipated these disadvantages in his letter to Dr. Charlett of August 4th, 1694, where it is not theft so much as 'the unreasonable Importunitys (and Interruptions too, where a Man is his owne only Library-Keeper)' that he fears.[14] None the less he complied: no less than 120 of his manuscripts are listed in the second volume.

The many-sidedness of Pepys at an age when most men are grassing over what they no longer have the energy to cultivate has still to be remembered. His scientific and scholarly pursuits did not distract him from the arts. He collected prints as avidly as ever. He was the patron and friend of Kneller and, in the last year of his life, commissioned him to paint the magnificent portrait of Dr. Wallis which he presented to the University of Oxford. If his musical evenings were more sedate and less frequent than in the days of the Diary, they were eagerly attended by men of taste. On May 30th, 1698, Evelyn records dining 'at Mr Pepyss, where I heard that rare Voice, Mr Pate, who was lately come from Italy, reputed the most excellent singer England ever had: he sang indeede many rare Italian Recitatives, &c: & several compositions of the last Mr Pursal, esteemed the best composer of any Englishman hitherto.' His great valediction to the art is contained in the letter he wrote to Dr. Charlett on November 5th, 1700. Charlett had asked him to comment on a proposed scheme for educating the nobility and gentry. Pepys in reply confines himself to two omissions, music and drawing. This studied passage complements the spontaneity of what he had written in the Diary a generation earlier:

> Musick, a science peculiarly productive of a pleasure that no state of life, publick or private, secular or sacred; no difference of age or season; no temper of mind or condition of health exempt from present anguish; nor, lastly, distinction of quality, renders either improper, untimely or unentertaining.[15]

The modes are different, the theme the same.

A few weeks later Evelyn again dined with Pepys to meet another Englishman whose supremacy was even less disputable. William Dampier who had, as Evelyn remarks, 'ben a famous Buccaneere', had published the year before his A New Voyage Round the World. 'He brought a map, of his observations of the Course of the winds in the South Sea, & assured us that the Maps hithertoo extant, were all false as to the Pacific-sea . . .' Dampier's claims, which led to his being granted a captain's commission in the Royal Navy and the command of a fifth-rate for a further voyage of exploration, were in no way exaggerated. As his most recent biographer has written 'He was the only explorer of any note during that century. He alone could provide descriptions of the flora and fauna of unknown parts of the world. He worked out the wind system of the southern hemisphere. He illustrated his journal with drawings of exotic plants and fruits and described the habits of strange beasts and savages.'[16]

The charm of Pepys's company and conversation is evident from every source. ''Tis never any drudgery to wait on Mr Pepys,' wrote Humphrey Wanley, a scholar more apt to offend than to compliment, 'whose conversation, I think, is more nearly akin to what we are taught to hope for in Heaven, than that of anybody else I know.'[17] The increase of his learning did not make him pedantic. To the end of his life his curiosity was as readily stirred by the things that interest the unlearned as by the questions propounded by savants. Ghost stories and anecdotes of second sight found in him an absorbed if critical listener. The supernatural had on occasion obtruded itself on his official consciousness as when on April 11th, 1672, the Commissioner at Harwich reported that:

> . . . on Munday night last about 10 of ye clocke at night [the Merlin yacht] being at anchor in above 10 fathom water, on a sudden the yacht fell into a shivering and trembling; in soemuch that som thought she had strucke; a souldier and a seaman being upon the Decke the Souldier cryes out they shoot cross barre shot. The Sprit fell from the Mast and all ye Iron rings were broken in small pieces.[18]

Fortunately such visitations were rare. Another correspondent credited Pepys with first-hand psychic experience:

> Sir a gentlewoman of my Acquaintance, tould mee shee had it for a great certainty from the family of the Montagues, that as you were one night playing late upon some Musicall instrument (together with your friends) there Sudainly appeared a Humane feminine Shape and Vanished. And after that sometime, walking in the Studdie, you Espied the Appearing person Demanded of her if at such time shee were not in Such a place. Shee answered no But shee Dream'd shee was and Heard Excellent musick.[19]

Pepys evidently knew the story from another source since he endorsed the letter 'about the Vision appearing (to Mr Mallard) at his playing by night on the viall'.

In the middle of the Revolution of 1688 James Houblon sent his friend an account of the apparition at Cork of a murder victim to the Protestant (and English) maid-servant of one of his Protestant business associates. The 'specter' showed the maid where to dig for his bones which were found the next morning to the excitement of all.[20] It seems improbable that Pepys was much impressed: certainly there is no sign that he followed the story up.

A few years earlier on passage to Tangier, Pepys had been 'very hot' in opposing Dr. Ken's belief in the existence of spirits. His investigation of the matter in his retirement led him to qualify this opinion, or rather to admit the existence of phenomena that could not in the present state of knowledge be satisfactorily explained. The two very long letters that weighed with him, one from Lord Reay and the other from Hickes, deal entirely with manifestations of the second sight in Scotland, especially in the Highlands, and Islands. Hickes had been chaplain to the Duke of Lauderdale when he was High Commissioner of Scotland in the late 1670s. It is clear from Hickes's letter that the Duke, a highly educated man of the world, unromantic to the point of cynicism, accepted absolutely the evidence for second sight and even witchcraft that Hickes was in two minds about. In this he agreed with educated Scottish opinion: 'I never met with any learned man, either among their divines or lawyers, who doubted of the thing.'[21] Pepys himself reserved his position: '. . . as to the business of the second sight, I little expected to have been ever brought so near to a conviction of the reality of it as by your Lordship's and the Lord Tarbutt's authoritys I must already own myself to be,' he wrote to Lord Reay.[22] To compare Pepys's critical assessment of such evidence with that of his slightly older contemporary John Aubrey is to turn from modern science to folk lore. Yet both men, and their many common friends in the Royal Society, would have valued both the older and the newer approach.

The last case in which Pepys took an interest was that of his old friend, Dr. Gale, who died in his Deanery at York in the spring of 1702. A month or two later before any successor had been installed the Vicar Choral who was reading the Second Lesson at Evensong saw in the Dean's stall a robed dignitary constructed on the ample lines of its late familiar occupant. On leaving the lectern the vicar bowed. The figure made no acknowledgment. Small wonder, since it was that of a canon residentiary who had cut it too fine to get into his own stall and had slipped into the Dean's. The vicar, however, construed its embarrassed immobility as evidence of its being Dean Gale's ghost: or at any rate thought it a story worth telling after drinking too much at a Lord Mayor's banquet. The Dean's son, Roger, exploded it in answer to Pepys's inquiry, 'to a person that had rather hear truth than strange storys'.[23]

The correspondence that most perfectly unfolds the mind and temper of the post-official Pepys is that with Evelyn. The letters range easily over all that is doing in the learned world: the praiseworthy efforts of the Virtuosi of Oxford in gathering and printing manuscripts, the progress and careers of the young scholars they were encouraging, the meetings of the Royal Society, the travels abroad of their young friends and relations. At any moment they turn aside to raise a point of scholarship or connoisseurship, to relate a piece of gossip, to discuss (pungently and never at length) the political situation or the conduct of the war. Men of learning and men of the world, they touch every note except flippancy or self-pity. The reader of this book will be tediously familiar with Pepys's ailments; a glance down the relevant column of Dr. Esmond de Beer's index to his magisterial edition of Evelyn's Diary reveals a scarcely less dismaying clinical history. Both men make the most of what is left to them: both urge the other on. 'Why don't you give us a part or two?' Evelyn wrote when the Navalia had still, by the end of 1696, failed to appear. 'Time flies a pace, my friend. 'Tis evening with us; do not expect perfection on this side of life. If it be the very best, as I am sure it is, nothing can be better; no man out-throws you.'[24] Posterity may regret that this excellent advice was not taken. But Pepys, perhaps, had had enough of ambition, though he could never be idle. Writing from Clapham in August 1700 he tells Evelyn that his doctor has forbidden him to bring his books ' "What then," will you say too, "are you a doing?" Why truely nothing that will bear nameing, and yet am not (I think) idle; for who can that has so much (of past and to come) to think on as I have? And thinking, I take it, is working.'[25] Death, never far from their thoughts, is serenely accepted. Evelyn, whose piety was deep and lifelong looked forward to their arrival:

> in those regions of peace and love and lasting friendships, and where those whose refined and exalted nature makes capable of the sublimest mysterys, and aspire after experimental knowledge (truely so called), shall be filled; and there without danger tast of the Fruite of the Tree (which cost our unhapy parents so deare); shall meete with no prohibition of what is desierable, no serpent to deceive, none to be deceived. This is, Sir, the state of that *Royal Society* above, and of those who shall be the worthy members of it.

Pepys acclaimed a Beatific Vision so congenial to his own.

> What then should I have to say to the whole of that glorious matter that was so enclosed in your last? Why truly, neither more nor lesse than that it looks to me like a seraphick *How d'ye* from one already entred into the regions you talk of in it, and who has sent me this for a *viaticum* towards my speeding thither after him.[26]

The letter had begun with this sentence:

> *Dover-Streete* at the topp and *J. Evelyn* at the bottom had alone been a sight equal in the pleasure of it to all I have had before me in my 2 or 3 months by-work of sorting and binding together my nephew's Roman marketings . . .

John Jackson had returned in August 1701 from a two years Grand Tour, planned, financed and followed by his uncle with far greater zest and far acuter perceptions than those of the traveller himself. The account of the tour given by J. R. Tanner in his introduction to the *Correspondence* is too long to quote and too happy to mangle. Perhaps it was Tanner's years as a College Tutor that enabled him to hit off exactly the staid, worthy, complacent dullness of the young man and to contrast it, by implication, with the glittering sprightliness of the old one.

Evelyn supplied the inspiration of the journey. Pepys never tires of telling his friend how he towers above his contemporaries by having added a European to an English education. John Jackson was to receive the benefits of which Pepys felt the lack and which he constantly recommended to friends like Dr. Gale who had sons to bring up. The details of the route, the arrangements for letters of introduction and the provision of foreign exchange were seen to by the Houblons. Besides the chief aims of civilising John Jackson and acquiring books, prints and manuscripts an important subsidiary objective was to witness the opening of the Jubilee Year of 1700 in St. Peter's. Leaving London on October 13th, 1699, Jackson was in time to see the deputy appointed by the Pope open the Holy Door on Christmas Eve. The Pope's illness raised hopes that he might be in Rome for a papal election. Captain Hatton, dining with Pepys, commissioned Jackson to obtain a form book for the big race, 'a Historicall List of the Names, Countrys, Ages, Characters & Interests of all ye Praesent Cardinalls; in order to ye employing Conjectures touching ye Choice to bee made . . .'27 Pepys had earlier passed on a request from 'my Lord Clarendon who you know is a great saladist and curious' that his nephew should dust his letters with Roman lettuce-seed.

To get from London to Rome Jackson had ridden in one October day to New Shoreham, where contrary winds kept him the best part of a week. To his complaints of boredom and low company Pepys pointed out that he was better off waiting ashore than 'beating it to noe purpose at sea'. Landing at Honfleur after a hair-raising voyage in which an alcoholic master ran aground three times, Jackson and his servant passed by way of Rouen to Paris and on to Lyon and Geneva. His aptitude for the delights of travel may be gauged by his writing from Lyon: 'I must not omitt observing to you that I have not yet mett with a dropp of good wine; even in Burgundy itselfe it was hardly tolerable.' From Geneva he crossed the Mont Cenis to Turin and found, at last, in Genoa a town he actually enjoyed. 'But the difficultys wee found in getting away very much allayed this passion of mine.' He had hoped to get a felucca to Leghorn but had to follow the coast road instead. In Rome he conscientiously did what was expected of him: saw the sights, listened, rather glumly, to the singing in the Sistine chapel, obtained both an audience of the Pope (who had rallied a little) and, after much difficulty, transcripts of Henry VIII's letters in the Vatican Library. He obediently sanded his letters with lettuce-seed, he avoided living with English people so as to improve his Italian, and lolloped docilely through the hoops that his enthusiastic ringmaster set up for him by every post.

Naples he disapproved on moral grounds; at Venice he was indisposed. Only on his way back to Genoa to take ship for Provence and Spain was he moved to delight by the intensive culture of the Po valley, attributing it (wrongly) to the natural fertility of the land instead of the remarkable irrigation begun in the twelfth century. In the Midi he visited Montpellier and found 'no manner of amusement or conversation, but dangerous, very dangerous play among the ladys of quality, and idle chatt and ramping among the grisettes'. Spain was expensive but Houblon's trading partner Sir William Hodges entertained him so long and so handsomely that a useful economy was effected. Anticipating this possibility Pepys had specifically warned his nephew to establish himself in lodgings 'that you may be actually fixt therein before you appear to him, that so you may go to him only as a traveller, recommended to him (as before) for moneys and advice as such, without the least appearance, either of designing him other trouble, or drawing on Sir James Houblon or myself any further obligations for the same.' When he heard from Hodges (not from Jackson) that he was not only established as a guest in his house but had let him go to all sorts of trouble to arrange an extended tour in Spain 'a most formal and elaborate tour that I never heard undertaken in Spaine by any private gentleman that was not led to it either by being in the train of some Embassador or by business as a merchant or otherwise' he was very angry. The affectionate curiosity of his side of the correspondence suddenly merges into the tone, half menace, half reproof, that that peccant sea-officers knew so well. Poor Jackson! He had tried to follow Pepys's instructions but Hodges, the Old Wardle of Cadiz, would not take no for an answer. Pepys accepted the situation, grudgingly at first but soon lost sight of his resentment in his anxiety that his nephew should see a bull-fight. All in all Spain was a success: certainly it shone by contrast with Portugal from which country Jackson at last took ship for home.

Throughout the tour Pepys not only told him what to see and do but took great care to form his manners. He must not cadge from Sir William Hodges: he had been very remiss in not writing to thank the Houblons for all the trouble they have taken on his behalf: besides writing himself, 'You should furnish mee with something to say to those friends of ours who have endeavoured to oblige us by theyr recommendatory letters on your behalfe; whatever the fruite of them may have really proved to you.' Pepys cannot have learned his own charming manners from his father and mother. He had acquired them by living on intimate terms with the Mountagu family and as the friend of such men as Sir William Coventry and John Evelyn. For all the affectionate pride he took in his nephew's acquirements – a pride nowhere more evident than in the care taken by his closest friends to say how gifted, how cultivated Mr. Jackson was – he was too much of a realist to credit him with his own powers of observing and assimilating. And Jackson seems to have been well fitted for the part assigned to him. It was the only family relationship that has left no trace of any quarrel.

Pepys's natural tenderness of heart checked by the early frosts of selfishness and competition flowered abundantly in age. Affection so freely given was generously returned. The staunchness of Hewer, the gentleness of Mary Skinner, the simplicity of John Jackson upheld him when the dark days came. In October 1700 Sir James Houblon died, 'one of the longest as well as most approved friends till now left mee in the world'. Dr. Gale, disappointed a second time of the Mastership of Trinity, died in his hated northern Deanery in April 1702. Evelyn, frail and a good twelve years older than Pepys, was the only survivor of his intimate circle. Ill health was closing in. It must have meant much at such a time to receive the offer of an old married servant to leave her own home and help nurse him if need be.[28] To the end he retained his intellectual curiosity. Only a few months before his death he asked John Houghton, the political economist, to send him his notes on population, national income and the avoidance of war. 'Honoured Sir,' replied Houghton, 'if these cogitations shall pass muster, and find a place among the meanest of your Collections, I will not despare but that once in a thousand years it may come among statesmen to be considered whether there may not be a better way for one kingdome to humble another than by killing the people.'[29] The honour paid to Pepys's spirit of rational humanity was richly deserved.

In his last, most golden season, Pepys did not turn inward. If he devoted the bulk of his time to perfecting his collections, arranging and re-arranging them, to the satisfaction of intellectual and artistic tastes and to the cultivation of his many friendships, he did not neglect his duty to his neighbour. His papers include schemes for redeeming the English captives at Algiers, for improving and extending the naval welfare system of the Chatham Chest.[30] He was a benefactor to Christ's Hospital and to the French Church at the Savoy.[31] He was ready to give practical help to refugees from religious persecution.[32] Quite simply he was a good man. When after much pain and discomfort it was clear that he was dying it was of other people, not himself, that he thought. His last letter was an appeal to Sir George Rooke, Commander-in-Chief and Admiralty Commissioner, on behalf of Balty, still without any relief after all his years of service. The letter immediately preceding it written by John Jackson at Pepys's dictation answers a French refugee's request that a grandchild be nominated to a place at Christ's Hospital. Its courtesy, its care and its constructiveness would be notable even from a man who was not on his deathbed.

Whether Pepys saw Balty and was reconciled to him we do not know. Evelyn, himself barely recovered from a broken shin that had taken a long

time to heal, called to say good-bye on May 14th, 'which much affected
me'. John Jackson, Mary Skinner, and Hewer were in constant attendance
and Hickes gave him the Last Sacraments. Jackson's account of his
uncle's affection and tranquillity while in great physical distress is very
moving.[33] Hickes who conducted the funeral as well as attending the
deathbed, wrote to their common friend Charlett:

> The greatness of his behaviour, in his long and sharp tryall before
> his death, was in every respect answerable to his great life; and I believe
> no man ever went out of this world with greater contempt of it, or a
> more lively faith in every thing that was revealed of the world to come.
> I administered the Holy Sacrament twice in his illness to him, and
> had administered it a third time, but for a sudden fit of illness that
> happened at the appointed time of administering of it. Twice I gave
> him the absolution of the Church, which he desired, and received with
> all reverence and comfort; and I never attended any sick or dying person
> that dyed with so much Christian greatnesse of mind, or a more lively
> sense of immortality, or so much fortitude and patience, in so long and
> sharp a tryall, or greater resignation to the will, which he most devoutly
> acknowledged to be the wisdom of God; and I doubt not but he is now
> a very blessed spirit, according to his motto, *Mens cujusque is est
> quisque.*[34]

So circumstantial an account from a scholar of such integrity leaves
nothing more to be said about Pepys's final position on matters of religion.
He died early in the morning of May 26th, 1703. John Jackson, obedient,
we may be sure, to some earlier injunction, noted that it was exactly
'47 minutes past 3 . . . by his gold watch'.

His best epitaph was written, fittingly, in a diary. For all their
familiarity, Evelyn's words will bear repetition:

> This [day] dyed Mr Sam. Pepys, a very worthy, Industrious &
> curious person, none in England exceeding him in the knowledge of
> the Navy, in which he had passed thro all the most considerable
> Offices . . . all which he performed with greate Integrity: when
> K: James the 2d went out of England he layed down his Office, &
> would serve no more . . .
> [He] was universaly beloved, Hospitable, Generous, Learned in many
> things, skill'd in Musick, a very greate Cherisher of Learned men, of
> whom he had the Conversation . . .
> Mr Pepys had ben for neere 40 years, so my particular Friend, that

he now sent me Compleat Mourning: desiring me to be one to hold up the Pall at his magnificent Obsequies; but my present Indisposition hindred me from doing him this last Office.

On June 4th he was laid beside Elizabeth in front of the altar at St Olave's. The funeral took place in the evening, a practice then common in the fashionable world to symbolise the ending of a day. Elizabeth's bust looked down on a gathering representative of almost every stage and facet of her husband's career. Balty was there, supported by one of his daughters. The second Earl of Sandwich and his brother the Dean of Durham sat next to them. A host of Pepys relations and connections echo the pages of the Diary. His doctors, his banker, his book-binder, his lawyer: the Clapham household, the Hewer clan, the President and many of the Fellows of the Royal Society, the Dean of Christ Church and the Master of Trinity, even the venerable Dr. Wallis swell the crowd. The Board of Admiralty were there in force and both the Archbishop of Canterbury and the Bishop of London, though it was the non-juror Hickes who took the service. As in his life, so at the commendation of his soul to God there was room for the people who had loved and served him as well as for the famous and the talented.

Notes

ABBREVIATED TITLES

Mr. Pepys   J. R. Tanner, *Mr. Pepys* (1925).

Pepysiana   *Pepysiana*, Vol. X of H. B. Wheatley's edition of the Diary (1899).

More Pepysiana   W. H. Whitear, *More Pepysiana* (1927).

Costello   W. T. Costello, S.J., *The Scholastic Curriculum at early seventeenth-century Cambridge* (Harvard, 1958).

Ehrman   John Ehrman, *The Navy in the War of William III* (C.U.P., 1953).

Mullinger   J. Bass Mullinger, *The University of Cambridge*, Vol. III (Cambridge, 1911).

Ogg   David Ogg, *England in the Reign of Charles II*, 2 vols. (Oxford, 2nd ed. 1956).

Penn, *Memorials*   Granville Penn, *Memorials of Sir William Penn*, 2 vols. (1833).

Sandwich, *Journal*   *Journal of the First Earl of Sandwich*, ed. R. C. Anderson (N.R.S., 1928).

Cat. Pepysian MSS.   *A Descriptive Catalogue of the Naval Manuscripts in the Pepysian Library at Magdalene College, Cambridge*, ed. J. R. Tanner, 4 vols. (N.R.S., 1903–23).

Naval Minutes   *Samuel Pepys's Naval Minutes*, ed. J. R. Tanner (N.R.S., 1926).

Tangier Papers   *The Tangier Papers of Samuel Pepys*, ed. Edwin Chappell (N.R.S., 1935).

Correspondence   *Private Correspondence and Miscellaneous Papers of Samuel Pepys 1679. 1703 in the possession of J. Pepys Cockerell*, ed. J. R. Tanner, 2 vols (1926).

Further Correspondence   *Further Correspondence of Samuel Pepys 1662–1679*, ed. J. R. Tanner (1929).

Shorthand Letters	*Shorthand Letters of Samuel Pepys*, transcribed and edited by Edwin Chappell (C.U.P., 1933).
Howarth	*Letters and the Second Diary of Samuel Pepys*, ed. R. G. Howarth (1932).
H.T.H.	*The Letters of Samuel Pepys and his Family Circle*, ed. Helen Truesdell Heath (O.U.P., 1955).
D.	Pepys's Diary.

At the moment of going to press the definitive edition of R. C. Latham and W. Matthews has reached December 31st, 1667. For entries after that date I have used Wheatley's edition. For the convenience of the reader all references to the Diary are given by date of entry.

ABBREVIATIONS

Adm.	Admiralty Library.
C.S.P. Dom.	*Calendar of State Papers, Domestic.*
D.N.B.	*Dictionary of National Biography.*
E.H.R.	*English Historical Review.*
LBK	Letterbook in National Maritime Museum Pressmark LBK/8.
M.M.	*Mariners Mirror.*
N.M.M.	National Maritime Museum.
N.R.S.	Navy Records Society.
P.L.	Pepys Library.
Rawl.	Rawlinson MSS. in the Bodleian Library.

NOTES

CHAPTER I

1 Cat. Pepysian MSS., i, 4.

2 *Loc. cit.*, p. xx.

3 F. R. Harris, *Edward Mountagu, 1st Earl of Sandwich* (London, 1912), i, 137.

4 Rawl. MS. A.185, printed in A. Bryant, *Years of Peril*, 410–11.

5 D. 6 Sept. 64.

6 D. 27 Feb. 68.

7 D. 30 July 66.

8 W. T. Costello, S.J., *The Scholastic Curriculum at early seventeenth-century Cambridge* (Harvard U.P., 1958), 142.

9 This conjecture is supported by D. 26 June 62, '. . . comes Mr Nicholson, my old fellow-student at Magdalene, and we played three or four things upon the violin and basse . . .'

10 G. P. H. Pawson, *The Cambridge Platonists* (London, 1930), 19 ff.

11 Quot. *D.N.B.* article on Anthony Tuckney.

12 Costello, *op. cit.*, 48.

13 John Hall, *An Humble Motion to the Parliament of England concerning the Advancement of Learning and Reformation of the Universities* (London, 1649), quoted by Mullinger, iii, 372–3. Spelling and punctuation here modernised.

14 D. 30 Jan. 64.

CHAPTER II

1 Clarendon, *Rebellion*, xv, 57. J. R. Powell, *The Letters of Robert Blake* (N.R.S., 1937), *Robert Blake, General-at-Sea* (1972).

2 On all this see Violet A. Rowe, *Sir Henry Vane the Younger* (1970), a most valuable and original biography.

3 Professor Aylmer has recently pointed out (*History*, lvi, June 1971, pp. 186–7) that Mountagu was a member of the Army Committee that voted a large advance of money to Cromwell in continuance of his military pay in May 1647 when his membership of Parliament should have disqualified him from holding any military appointment.

4 D. 25 Feb. 67.

5 Rawl. MS. A.185, ff. 206–13, printed in A. Bryant, *Years of Peril*, 405–13.

6 *The Diary of John Evelyn*, ed. E. S. de Beer (O.U.P., 6 vols., 1955 and O.S.A., 1 vol., 1959). 3 May 50 (description of lithotomies at La Charité in Paris) and 10 June 69 (Pepys's visit to Richard Evelyn. This is the first mention of Pepys in Evelyn's Diary: Evelyn first appears in Pepys's Diary on 9 Sept. 65).

CHAPTER III

1 D. 10 Mar. 66.

2 Quot. Anthony Powell, *John Aubrey and His Friends* (London, 1948), 93.

3 D. 7 Nov. 60.

4 Alan Macfarlane, *The Family Life of Ralph Josselin* (C.U.P., 1970), 170.

5 In the title of a work published in 1672, *Microscopium statisticum quo status imperii Romano-Germanici repraesentatur*, cited by Roger Mols S.J. in *Fontana Economic History of Europe*, ii, 35.

6 D. 11 Feb. 60.

7 Godfrey Davis, *The Restoration of Charles II 1658–1660* (1955), 283.

8 David Underdown, *Royalist Conspiracy in England 1649–1660* (Yale, 1960), 310–11. For Mountagu's conduct at the Sound (p. 50) see Harris, *op. cit.*, i, 143 ff.

CHAPTER IV

1 D. 8–9 Mar. 60.

2 D., ed. Latham and Matthews, i, 86, n. 2. J. R. Powell (ed.), *The Letters of Robert Blake* (1937), *passim*.

3 Nearly six years later Pepys learned that it was Turner. D. 30 Jan. 66.

CHAPTER V

1 He appears to have helped himself to £500. D. 4 Apr. 68; *Further Correspondence*, 188–9.

2 D. 5 July 60.

3 N.M.M., LBK/8, f. 20.

4 D. 8–9 Aug. 62.

5 D. 14 June 67.

6 D. 20 Aug. 62.

7 Rawl. MS. A.174, f. 239.

8 *Ibid.*, f. 482.

9 D. 7 June 62.

CHAPTER VI

1 D. 30 Sept. 62.

3 D. 29 Apr. 60.

3 D. 1 July 60.
4 D. 2 May 63.
5 R. W. Chapman (ed.), *Journal of a Tour to the Hebrides* (O.U.P., 1970), 246.
6 D. 8 Dec. 67.
7 *Naval Minutes*, 2.
8 D. 25 Apr. 62.
9 J. R. Tanner, *Mr. Pepys*, p. 98.
10 D. 31 July 62.
11 D. 26 Nov. 65.
12 'The Present Ill State of my Health', Rawl. MS. A.185, ff. 206–13, printed in A. Bryant, *Years of Peril*, 412.
13 D. 19 Jan. 63.
14 D. 9 Feb. 66.
15 D. 9 Nov. 65.
16 D. 21 June 66.
17 D. 5 Sept. 64.
18 D. 12 July 66.
19 D. 13 June 66.
20 H.T.H., pp. xxi–xxii.
21 D. 24 Apr. 63.
22 D. 8 June 62.

CHAPTER VII

1 D. 1 July 63.
2 'The Medical History of Mr. and Mrs. Samuel Pepys' in *Pepys Club: Occasional Papers*, i, 86.
3 D. 9 July 63.
4 *Further Correspondence*, 91.
5 Cat. Pepysian MSS., i, 274–5.
6 D. 17 July 63.
7 D. 27 Feb. 64.
8 D. 23 Jan. 65.
9 D. 12 Sept. 66.
10 P.L. 2853, Adty. Letters, vi, 428–9.
11 Bryant, *Years of Peril*, 372.
12 Bryant, *Saviour of the Navy*, 166.
13 *Ibid.*, 386.
14 E.g. D. 6 Sept. 64.
15 D. 9 Sept. 63.
16 D. 14 June 64.

CHAPTER VIII

1 D. 30 Sept. 61; 3 Nov. 61.
2 *Brief Lives*, ed. Lawson Dick, 240.
3 For envy and contempt see the Diary *passim*; for hatred see, e.g., Rawl. MS. A.185 ff. 13–26.
4 D. 19 Jan. 63.
5 D. 29 May 64.

6 'Pepys and Shakespeare' (especially p. 18) in *Pepys Club: Occasional Papers*, ii.

7 D. 31 Dec. 64.

8 D. 20 Jan. 65.

9 D. 15 July 60.

10 D. 29 July 65.

11 D. 9 Nov. 61.

12 D. 31 Oct. 63.

13 D. 14 Aug. 65.

14 D. 15 June 63.

15 D. 17 Nov. 63.

16 D. 26 May 63.

17 D. 4 Feb. 65.

CHAPTER IX

1 D. 24 Apr. 65.

2 D. 10 Sept. 64.

3 Bernard Pool, *Navy Board Contracts 1660–1832* (1966), 38.

4 D. 30 Mar. 63.

5 Chappell, *Shorthand Letters*, pp. 29–30 and Kaufman, *Conscientious Cavalier: Colonel Bullen Reymes M.P., F.R.S.* (1962), *passim*.

6 Kaufman, *op. cit.*, 191–8. Curiously there is no reference to this mission in Miss E. M. G. Routh's excellent book on Tangier.

7 *Further Correspondence*, 122–3, 8 Mar. 66.

8 This seems the inescapable inference from D. 30 July and 7 Aug.

9 D. 6 Mar. 63.

10 LBK, ff. 46–7, 7 Mar. 63.

11 For Holmes in general and this incident in particular see the author's *Man of War* (London, 1969).

12 D. 24 Mar. 63.

13 Rawl. MS. A. 195 f. 53^v.

14 *Further Correspondence*, 290.

15 *Ibid.*, 2.

16 D. 28 Apr. 65.

CHAPTER X

1 It is perhaps still necessary to repeat that Holmes did *not*, as stated in the *D.N.B.*, capture New Amsterdam and rename it New York. For the history of this *canard* see the author's *Man of War*, 209.

2 D. 10 Oct. 64.

3 D. 3 June 64.

4 D. 4 Nov. 64.

5 Ogg, i, 285 puts it at 98.

6 LBK, f. 149, 24 and 25 Jan. 65.

7 D. 7 Apr. 65.

8 E.g. LBK, ff. 305, 323, 332 and, especially, the postscript of 28 Dec. 65, f. 335.

9 LBK, f. 248, 8 Oct. 65.

10 Rawl. MS. A. 174, f. 468.

11 LBK, ff. 176, 182.

12 D. 21 Sept. 64.

13 D. 30 Aug. 65.

14 Howarth, 24–5.

15 Sandwich, *Journal*, 234.

CHAPTER XI

1 Sandwich, *Journal*, 248.

2 D. 7 Sept. 65.

3 D. 9 Sept. 65.

4 Chappell, *Shorthand Letters*, 61.

5 Penn, *Memorials*, ii, 365.

6 *Further Correspondence*, 51.

7 *Naval Minutes*, 250.

8 Cat. Pepysian MSS., i, 154.

9 *The Rupert and Monck Letter Book 1666*, ed. J. R. Powell and E. K. Timings (N.R.S., 1969), 142.

10 *Ibid.*, 287.

11 In his introduction to the *Journals of Sir Thomas Allin*, vol. ii (N.R.S., 1940), where the best and fairest account of the question is to be found.

12 *The Rupert and Monck Letter Book*, 57.

13 See, e.g., D. 1 July 66.

14 LBK, f. 389.

15 *The Rupert and Monck Letter Book*, 94.

16 D. 12 July 66.

17 Reproduced in *The Rupert and Monck Letter Book* and in *Man of War*. On the authorship of the draft see my note in *M.M.*, 57, 215. For the best description of the battle see Dr. R. C. Anderson's introduction to vol. ii of *The Journals of Sir Thomas Allin*, xxvii ff.

18 D. 21 July 66.

CHAPTER XII

1 For examples of both (on consecutive days) see D. 28 and 29 Oct. 66.

2 D. 7 Oct. 66.

3 See on all this P. G. Rogers, *The Dutch in the Medway* (1970) and A. W. Tedder, *The Navy of the Restoration* (Cambridge, 1916).

4 D. 16 Dec. 66.

5 Quot. Rogers, *op. cit.*, 75.

6 Coventry MSS. xcvii, f. 69.

7 D. 10 June 67.

8 D. 11 June 67.

9 Coventry MSS. xcvii, f. 75, 11 June 67.

10 Monck's report quot. Rogers, 87.

11 D. 13 June 67.

12 For this connection see Marvell, *Poems and Letters*, 2 vols. ed Margoliouth (Oxford, 1927), *passim*.

13 D. 9 July 67.

14 E.g. 29 July 67.

15 D. 12 July and 9 Aug. 67.

16 D. 22 July 67.

CHAPTER XIII

1 D. 2 Sept. 66.

2 LBK, f. 404, 25 Aug. 66.

3 *Ibid.*, f. 435.

4 D. 27 Sept. 67.

5 D. 9 Nov. 67.

6 The Deborah Egmont from whom Sir Arthur Bryant prints a letter to Pepys dated 30 January 1689 (*Saviour of the Navy*, Appendix E, p. 400) was not the same person as Deb. Willett. See the author's note in the *T.L.S.* 15 Feb. 1974, p. 164.

7 D. 25 Feb. 68.

8 Coventry Papers, xcvii, f. 111.

CHAPTER XIV

1 D'Arcy Power, 'Why Samuel Pepys Discontinued his Diary', in *Occasional Papers*, i, 63–77.

2 *Further Correspondence*, 239.

3 Bryant, *Years of Peril*, 406–7.

4 D. 31 Mar. 69.

5 D. 18 Jan. 69.

6 N.M.M., LBK, f. 632. For a fuller discussion of the charges in their relation to Pepys see Pool, *Navy Board Contracts*; Bryant, *Years of Peril*; and J. R. Tanner, *Further Correspondence*.

7 *Diary of John Evelyn*, ed. de Beer, iii, 232.

8 D. 12 Dec. 67.

9 P.L. 2874 (the sixth volume of Pepys's Miscellanies which contains the Brooke House Journal), ff. 388–90. In future references this document will be cited as J.

10 J., 393.

11 J., 396.

12 J., 413.

13 J., 480–5.

14 J., 427.

15 J., 425.

16 Bryant, *Years of Peril*, 32.

17 J., 469.

18 J., 477.

19 J., 497.

20 D. 1 Mar. 68.

21 E.g. LBK, f. 423.

22 J., 471.

23 J., 473.

24 J., 496.

25 J., 501.

CHAPTER XV

1 For Pepys's unsleeping vigilance towards this officer's misdemeanours see Tanner, Cat. Pepysian MSS., *passim*, but especially iv, lxix–lxx. For his relation to Penn see Penn, *Memorials*, ii, 559–60. James's confidence in him may be judged by his bringing him out of retirement to command an armed merchantman in the Bristol Channel during Monmouth's Rebellion. P.L. 2858, ff. 209–10.

2 Rawl. MS. A.174, f. 239.

3 Michael Lewis, *The Navy of Britain* (1948), 362.

4 Later reduced to one or two meetings a week. See on all this J. R. Tanner's introduction to Cat. Pepysian MSS. i–iv, *passim*.

5 See, e.g., LBK, f. 760, 6 Jan. 77.

6 *Naval Minutes*, 71.

7 *Works of George Savile, Marquess of Halifax*, ed. Raleigh (Oxford, 1912), 193.

8 Howarth, 64.

9 Quot. Tanner, *Mr. Pepys*, 118n.; from Lucas-Dubreton, *Petite Vie de Samuel Pepys, Londinien* (Paris, 1923).

10 On 15 Dec. 76, *Diary of Robert Hooke* (1672–80), ed. Robinson and Adams (1935), 262.

11 *Diary*, ed. de Beer, iii, 559.

12 *Ibid.*, 570.

13 Cat. Pepysian MSS., iv, 542.

14 P.L. 2849, Adty. Letters, ii, 130, 11 Sept. 73.

15 *Further Correspondence*, 272–3, quot. B. M. Ranft, 'The Political Career of Samuel Pepys', *Journal of Modern History*, xxiv, No. 4, 368–75, who corrects Tanner's conjecture as to the addressee of this letter.

CHAPTER XVI

1 *Diary*, ed. de Beer, v, 538.

2 *Naval Minutes*, 316.

3 See on all this Stuart Mountfield, 'Captain Greenville Collins and Mr. Pepys', *M.M.*, Vol. 56, No. 1., 85–97.

4 Letter Book of J. Gauden, Adm. MS. *passim*, but notably f. 45.

5 *Naval Minutes*, 176–7.

6 *Ibid.*, 62.

7 *Ibid.*, 300.

8 LBK, f. 737, 8 May 76.

9 *Naval Minutes*, 26.

10 *Samuel Pepys and the Royal Navy*, 70.

11 *Naval Minutes*, 418.

12 *Ibid.*, 158.

13 *Ibid.*, 187–8. Although Pepys here specifically names Danby as one who *had* taken out a pardon this was in fact a last-minute expedient of the King's. See Andrew Browning, *Danby* (Glasgow, 1951), i, 317n.

14 Cat. Pepysian MSS., i, 196; iii, 92 and *Naval Minutes*, 322. See also Chappell's article on this officer, *M.M.* (1934), 115–19.

15 Rawl. MS. A.185, f. 110. For the excesses of Captain Ashby in the *Rose* on the same service see *ibid.*, f. 299.

16 For all this see Rawl. MS. A.181, f. 210 and ff. 340–83 where the Captain's name is usually spelled Roydon. Pepys in his Register of Sea Officers spells it Royden. See further pp. 253 and 282.

17 Rawl. MS. A.177, ff. 1–76.

18 *Ibid.*, A.181, ff. 130–93.

19 Cat. Pepysian MSS., i, 202–5.

20 *Ibid.*, iv, 535–6, 543–4.

21 Quot. *ibid.*, i, 203.

22 See examples cited in *Years of Peril*, 134–5.
23 Rawl. MS. A.185, f. 281.
24 LBK, ff. 753–4.
25 Cat. Pepysian MSS., iii, 298.
26 *Further Correspondence*, 310.
27 *Naval Minutes*, 146.
28 *Ibid.*, 323.

CHAPTER XVII

1 For all this see J. J. Keevil, *Medicine and the Navy*, ii, *passim*, but especially 84 ff. and 131–47.
2 Cat. Pepysian MSS., iv, 135.
3 J. R. Tanner reads 'horse cloth'. The MS. is P.L. 2867, f. 416.
4 John Ehrman, *The Navy in the War of William III*, 239–40.
5 Quot. Lloyd, *The British Seaman* (1968), 107.
6 E. Coxere, *Adventures by Sea*, ed. Meyerstein (1945), 71.
7 P.L. 2862, Adty. Letters, xv, f. 226.
8 Cat. Pepysian MSS., iii, 68.
9 LBK, f. 772 and Adty. Letters, vi, f. 116.
10 *Naval Minutes*, 268.
11 Smith, *The Navy and its Chaplains in the Days of Sail* (Toronto, 1961), 21.
12 *Ibid.*, 22.
13 C.S.P. Dom. 28 Nov. 65. Pepys here supports the application for chaplain's pay from an unordained member of the ship's company who had supplied this function in the *Coast* frigate.
14 Cat. Pepysian MSS., i, 205. See also Adty. Letters, x, ff. 353–4.
15 LBK, ff. 816–18.
16 Michael Lewis, *England Sea Officers* (1939), 264.
17 Rawl. MS. A.185, ff. 265–6.

CHAPTER XVIII

1 See on all this John Kenyon, *The Popish Plot* (1972), *passim*.
2 Quot. Bryant, *Years of Peril*, as epigraph to his chapter 'The Trial of Atkins' which gives much the fullest and best account available.
3 *Years of Peril*, 203–9.
4 H.T.H., 36.
5 LBK, f. 885.
6 Howarth, 80.
7 Rawl. MS. A.181, f. 197.
8 H.T.H., 176.
9 LBK, f. 893, 29 Apr. 79.
10 Howarth, 83, 86.
11 *Years of Peril*, 284.
12 H.T.H., 115.
13 *Ibid.*, 74.
14 *Years of Peril*, 279 ff.
15 *Naval Minutes*, 71–2.

CHAPTER XIX

1 24 Sept. 1680; H.T.H., 164–8.
2 H.T.H., 188.
3 Rawl. MS. A. 183, f. 140.
4 Howarth, 126.
5 *Ibid.*, 115–18.
6 *Ibid.*, 145–8.
7 Rawl. MS. A. 178, f. 235
8 *Ibid.*, f. 120.
9 *Ibid.*, A. 179, ff. 24, 30.
10 Ibid., A. 178, f. 34. Sir Arthur Bryant reads 'inkbottle'.
11 Howarth, 120.
12 *Ibid.*, 129.
13 H.T.H., 204–5.
14 All Souls MS., 317.
15 *Ibid.*, f. 10.
16 *Ibid.*, f. 52.
17 See on this Sir Stephen Gaselee's paper on 'The Spanish Books in the Library of Samuel Pepys', *Pepys Club: Occasional Papers*, ii, 117 ff.
18 *Tangier Papers*, 7, where the editor has guessed 'Sir Nicholas Acland' for a difficult reading.
19 Quot. Routh, *Tangier*, 196.
20 Quot. Routh, *Tangier*, 280.
21 *Tangier Papers*, 25–6.
22 Rawl. MS. A. 196 (2 foliations: (1) f. 102; (2) f. 105).

CHAPTER XX

1 Rawl. MS. A. 171, 1 f. 203.
2 *Ibid.*, f. 217.
3 *Ibid.*, 102, 274–5, 287.
4 *Ibid.*, A. 189, f. 125.
5 *Tangier Papers*, 119.
6 *Ibid.*, 122.
7 *Ibid.*, 191.
8 As late as December 1688, in the last weeks of his official life, Pepys was forced to admit that the question was 'Not yet settl'd'. Rawl. MS. A. 186 ff. 29 v, 30.
9 *Tangier Papers*, 121.
10 Rawl. MS. A. 190, f. 236.
11 *Tangier Papers*, 182.
12 *Diary*, ed. de Beer, iv, 477.
13 Quot. Bryant, *Saviour of the Navy*, 124.
14 *Years of Peril*, 336.
15 Howarth, 127–8.
16 Ehrman, 206–7.
17 Rawl. MS. A. 170, f. 217.
18 Cat. Pepysian MSS., i, 90.
19 Rawl. MS. A. 189, f. 146; Cat. Pepysian MSS., i, 345.
20 *Ibid.*, f. 107.

21 *Ibid.*, f. 199.
22 Rawl. MS. A.179, ff. 5 A & B. Sir Arthur Bryant has read '25 per cent' for 25*s*. 6*d*.
23 *Ibid.*, ff. 102–3.
24 *Ibid.*, f. 5B.

CHAPTER XXI

1 *Diary*, 19 Sept. 85.
2 *Ibid.*, 5 May 86.
3 Rawl. MS. A.189, f. 21.
4 *Diary*, 16 Sept. 85.
5 Howarth, 177.
6 *Ibid.*
7 Rawl. MS. A. 186, f. 89. Sir Arthur Bryant (*Saviour of the Navy*, 263) has confused the writer with Pepys's old tutor at Magdalene, Joseph Hill. Abraham was the eldest brother of Thomas, the Lisbon merchant.
8 This was surely the letter whose arrival is so dramatically described by Macaulay (iii, 1105): 'It is said that, when the King had read it, the blood left his cheeks, and he remained some time speechless.' Macaulay and the authorities he cites appear to have misdated it by a month: hence the cautious scepticism of Ehrman, *op. cit.*, 214 n. 6 as to its existence.
9 Quot. Tanner, *E.H.R.* (1893), 'The Naval Preparation of James II in 1688', 272–3.
10 Rawl. MS. A.186, f. 288 ff.
11 Pepys to Captain Smith of the *Falcon*, quot. Bryant, *Saviour of the Navy*, 258.
12 Rawl. MS. A.179, f. 44. For Holmes in general see the author's *Man of War*.
13 *Ibid.*, A.186, ff. 227–9, 308–9.
14 John Carswell, *The Descent on England* (1969) and E. B. Powley, *The English Navy in the Revolution of 1688* (1928).
15 Howarth, 194–5.
16 Rawl. MS. A.179, f. 107.
17 *Ibid.*, f. 179.
18 Howarth, 200–1.
19 *Ibid.*, 175–6, 192.
20 Bryant, *Saviour of the Navy*, 270.
21 Rawl. MS. A.186, f. 396. Dartmouth to James II (holograph) 11 Nov. 88.
22 Quot. Bryant, *Saviour of the Navy*, 305.
23 As late as 1712–14, see N.M.M. MSS. AGC/XX.
24 Howarth, 198.

CHAPTER XXII

1 *Correspondence*, i, 354.
2 See on all this Ehrman, 283 ff., and the same author's article in *M.M.*, Vol. 34, No. 4, 255–70.
3 *Correspondence*, i, 57, 60; *Mr. Pepys*, 270.
4 H.T.H., 224–6.
5 *Ibid.*, 223.
6 *Ibid.*, 229.
7 Rawl. MS. A.170, f. 124.
8 *Ibid.*, f. 26 and 26ᵛ.
9 *Correspondence*, ii, 290–1.

10 *Ibid.*, ii, 156, 188, 190. In his introduction (i, xxxvii) J. R. Tanner inexplicably overlooks Daniel, the most interesting of the three, and debits Mary with only two brothers.

11 Rawl. MS. A.170, ff. 147–69.

12 *Ibid.*, f. 169 and f. 161.

13 *Ibid.*, f. 11.

14 Howarth, 189.

15 F. Sidgwick, *A Descriptive Catalogue of the Library of Samuel Pepys* (1914), Part II, pp. i–ii.

16 *Occasional Papers*, ii, 62.

17 *Correspondence*, i, 200.

18 *Mr. Pepys*, 272.

19 Howarth, 281; *Correspondence*, i, 61; i, 36; i, 137.

20 *Correspondence*, i, 59.

21 *Ibid.*, i, 61.

22 *Sergison Papers*, ed. Merriman (N.R.S., 1950), 6. Sergison probably owed his entry to the office to his being a cousin of Will Hewer's. Smith, *Life, Journals and Correspondence of Samuel Pepys* (1841), ii, 120.

23 Rawl. MS. A.170, f. 100.

24 *Naval Minutes*, 389.

25 *Pepysiana*, 46.

26 Howarth, 257.

27 *Occasional Papers*, ii, 73.

28 These lines first appear in the fifth edition of Waller's *Poems* (1686): Pepys possessed a copy, still in his library, of the fourth (1682).

29 Howarth, 296.

CHAPTER XXIII

1 Rawl. MS. A.171, f. 217 ff.

2 See on this R. K. Merton, *Science, Technology and Society in Seventeenth Century England* (1938: re-issued Harper Torchbooks 1970), esp. pp. 113–14.

3 Rawl. MS. A.183, f. 1.

4 *Ibid.*, A.178, f. 25.

5 *Naval Minutes*, 297.

6 Quot. Marjorie Hope Nicolson, *Pepys's Diary and the New Science* (Charlottesville, Va., 1965), 139.

7 *Correspondence*, i, 72–94.

8 *Ibid.*, i, 155–65.

9 Quot. Douglas, *English Scholars* (1939), 335.

10 E.g. Howarth, 344–6.

11 *Naval Minutes*, 282.

12 *Correspondence*, i, 97. The work in question was *Catalogi librorum manuscriptorum Angliae et Hiberniae in unum collecti* (1697).

13 *Correspondence*, i, 103.

14 *Ibid.*, i, 141; Howarth, 243–6.

15 *Correspondence*, ii, 109.

16 Evelyn, *Diary*, v, 295; Christopher Lloyd, *William Dampier* (1966), 13.

17 Howarth, 331.

18 Rawl. MS. A.174, f. 394.

19 Howarth, 52–3.

20 Rawl. MS. A.186, ff. 110–11.

21 *Correspondence*, i, 367–76.

22 *Ibid.*, i, 241.

23 *Ibid.*, ii, 304–5.

24 *Ibid.*, i, 134–5.

25 *Ibid.*, ii, 35.

26 *Ibid.*, ii, 238–41.

27 N.M.M. MSS. 52/056. In *Correspondence*, where all unattributed quotations referring to Jackson's tour may be found, this letter is printed from a copy.

28 *Correspondence*, ii, 302.

29 *Ibid.*, ii, 263–5.

30 Rawl. MS. A.171, ff. 61^v–62^v.

31 *Occasional Papers*, ii, 66.

32 For the case of Dégalénière, see *Correspondence passim*. An earlier instance may be found in LBK/797.

33 *Correspondence*, ii, 312–14.

34 *Diary*, ed. Wheatley, Vol. i, lii.

Chronology

1633	23 Feb.	Pepys born in Salisbury Court off Fleet Street.
	3 Mar.	Baptised in St. Bride's Church.
c. 1644		At Huntingdon Grammar School.
c. 1646–50		At St. Paul's School.
1650	21 June	Entered on the books of Trinity Hall, Cambridge.
	1 Oct.	Transferred to Magdalene College.
1651	Mar.	Began residence at Cambridge.
1654	Mar.	Took his B.A.
?1654		Employed as some kind of steward to his cousin Edward Mountagu in London. The date at which this arrangement began is not known.
1655	1 Dec.	Married Elizabeth St. Michel.
1656	10 Oct.	Began to live with her as man and wife.
?1656		Employed part-time as a clerk to George Downing in the Exchequer. Again the beginnings of this cannot be accurately dated but it was certainly before Cromwell's death in September 1658.
1658	26 Mar.	Cut for the stone.
	c. Aug.	Set up house in Axe Yard, Westminster.
1659	May	Sent out briefly with letters to Mountagu in the Baltic. Becomes one of his master's principal London correspondents.
1660	1 Jan.	Begins the Diary.
	Mar.	Joins the Fleet as secretary to Mountagu, General at Sea charged with bringing over Charles II from Holland.
	25 May	Witnesses the King's landing at Dover.

	28 June	Resigns Exchequer clerkship.
	29 June	Appointed Clerk of the Acts.
	17 July	Moves to Navy Office house in Seething Lane.
	23 July	Sworn in as Clerk of the Privy Seal.
	24 Sept.	Sworn in as a J.P.
1661	July	Death of uncle Robert Pepys.
		Pepys visits Brampton which he has inherited from him.
1662	15 Feb.	Admitted a Younger Brother of Trinity House.
	17 Aug.	Resigns Clerkship of Privy Seal.
	Nov.	Appointed to the Tangier Commission.
1664	15 Mar.	Death of his brother Tom.
1665	15 Feb.	Elected a Fellow of the Royal Society.
	22 Feb.	Second Dutch War breaks out.
	20 Mar.	Appointed Treasurer for Tangier.
	5 July	Moves his household (but not himself) to Woolwich to avoid the plague.
	27 Oct.	Appointed Surveyor-General of the Victualling.
	Sept.–Dec.	Prize Goods Scandal. Sandwich disgraced and sent as Ambassador to Madrid.
1666	7 Jan.	Brought his household back to London.
	1–4 June	The Four Days Battle.
	25 July	St. James's Day Fight.
	2 Sept.	Fire of London breaks out.
1667	25 Mar.	Death of his mother.
	June	The Dutch in the Medway. Pepys withdraws his gold and sends it with Elizabeth and his father to Brampton for safety.
	28 July	Resigns Surveyorship of Victualling.
	31 July	End of the War.
	Oct.	Visits Brampton to dig up his buried treasure.
	22 Oct.	Defends the Navy Office before Parliamentary Committee.
1668	27 Feb.	Marriage of his sister Paulina to John Jackson.
	5 Mar.	Defends the Navy Office before the House of Commons.
	May–June	Jaunts to Cambridge and to Oxford and the West.
	25 Oct.	Elizabeth discovers his relations with Deb.
1669	Spring	Increasingly troubled with his eyes.
	31 May	Closes the Diary in fear of blindness.
	June–Oct.	Obtains leave for a tour to Holland, France and Flanders at the end of which Elizabeth is taken ill.
	10 Nov.	Death of Elizabeth.
1670	Jan.–Feb.	Brooke House Committee.
	30 Mar.	His brother John appointed Clerk to Trinity House.
1672	24 Jan.	Pepys admitted an Elder Brother of Trinity House.
	Mar.	Outbreak of Third Dutch War.
	7 June	Death of Sandwich at Battle of Solebay.
1673	29 Jan.	Fire at Navy Office in Seething Lane. Pepys moves to Winchester Street.
	Mar.	Test Act excludes Roman Catholics from office.

	June	Duke of York in consequence forced to resign as Lord High Admiral. Pepys appointed Secretary of the Admiralty. Succeeded as Clerk of the Acts by his brother John and his clerk Thomas Hayter.
	Oct.	Elected M.P. for Castle Rising. Attempt to unseat him for alleged Roman Catholicism.
1674	Feb.	End of Third Dutch War.
		Moved from Winchester Street to Admiralty Office at Derby House.
1676	1 Feb.	Appointed a Governor of Christ's Hospital.
	22 May	Elected Master of Trinity House.
1677	Spring	Death of his brother John.
	8 Aug.	Elected Master of the Clothworkers Company.
1679	Feb.	His clerk Samuel Atkins acquitted of murdering Sir Edmund Berry Godfrey.
	Mar.	Elected M.P. for Harwich in first Parliament of 1679.
	Apr.	Dissolution of Admiralty Commission and appointment of a new Board hostile to Pepys.
	May	Fall of Pepys. Resigns Secretaryship of Admiralty, Treasurership of Tangier (in which Hewer succeeds him) and is sent to the Tower.
	July	Released on bail: goes to live with Hewer at York Buildings, near the Watergate.
1680	Feb.	Relieved of bail.
	June	Proceedings abandoned.
	?Aug.–Sept.	Death of his brother-in-law John Jackson.
	Oct.	Death of his father.
1682	Spring	Visits Edinburgh and Newcastle in attendance on Duke of York.
1683	30 July	Leaves London to accompany Dartmouth on expedition to Tangier as his Secretary.
	Dec.	Leaves Tangier to travel in Spain.
1684	Mar.	Returns to England.
	June	Re-appointed Secretary to the Admiralty.
	30 Nov.	Elected President of the Royal Society.
1685	Feb.	Death of Charles II.
	Apr.	Pepys elected M.P. for Harwich.
		Walked in James II's coronation procession as a Baron of the Cinque Ports.
		Appointed a Deputy Lieutenant for Huntingdonshire.
	July	Master of Trinity House for second time.
1686	Mar.	Special Commission begins to sit.
1688	Oct.	Special Commission dissolved.
	Nov.	William of Orange lands at Torbay.
	Dec.	James II flees to France.
1689	Jan.	Pepys defeated at Harwich in elections for the Convention Parliament.

	20 Feb.	Resigns Secretaryship of the Admiralty.
	May–July	Imprisoned in the Gatehouse.
	Aug.	Resigns the Trinity House.
1690	June	Again imprisoned in the Gatehouse.
	Dec.	Published his *Memoires of the Royal Navy 1679–88.*
1693	Sept.	Robbed by highwaymen while driving to Chelsea.
1694	Aug.	Recovering from a serious illness.
1697	Apr.	Again seriously ill.
1699	Oct.	Pepys's nephew John Jackson sets out on his Grand Tour.
1700	?May	Visits Hewer's house at Clapham to recover his health.
	?Dec.	Returns to York Buildings.
1701	?June	Final retirement to Clapham.
	Aug.	Return of John Jackson from the Grand Tour.
1702	Sept.	Presents portrait of Dr. Wallis to the University of Oxford.
	Oct.	Receives the thanks of the University.
1703	26 May	Death of Pepys at Clapham.
	4 June	Burial in St. Olave's, Hart Street.

INDEX

A GUIDE TO OLD ENGLISH

FOURTH EDITION REVISED
WITH PROSE AND VERSE TEXTS
AND GLOSSARY

Bruce Mitchell

Fellow of St Edmund Hall, Oxford

Fred C. Robinson

Douglas Tracy Smith Professor of English,
Yale University

BASIL BLACKWELL

A Guide to Old English © Bruce Mitchell 1964, 1968
A Guide to Old English revised with Texts and Glossary
© Bruce Mitchell and Fred C. Robinson 1982
*A Guide to Old English Revised with Prose and Verse Texts and
Glossary* © Bruce Mitchell and Fred C. Robinson 1986

First edition 1964
Second edition 1968
Reprinted 1971, 1975, 1978, 1981
Revised (3rd) edition with texts and glossary 1982
Reprinted with corrections 1983, 1984 (twice)
Revised (4th) edition with prose and verse texts and glossary 1986

Basil Blackwell Ltd
108 Cowley Road, Oxford OX4 1JF, UK

Basil Blackwell Inc.
432 Park Avenue South, Suite 1503
New York, NY 10016, USA

British Library Cataloguing in Publication Data
Mitchell, Bruce, *1920–*
    A guide to old English. – 4th ed.
    1. Anglo-Saxon language – Grammar
    I. Title   II. Robinson, Fred C.
    429'.5   PE131

    ISBN 0–631–13624–X
    ISBN 0–631–13625–8 Pbk

Typeset by Joshua Associates Limited, Oxford
Printed and bound in Great Britain by Billing & Sons Ltd, Worcester

In Memoriam
DONOVAN F. MITCHELL

'Everyman, I'll go with thee
    And be thy *Guide*.'
And if you don't learn Old English,
    Then Devil take your hide.

Foreword to the Fourth Edition

The *Guide* aims at making easier the initial steps in the learning of Old English. It is intended for beginners and will, it is hoped, prove especially useful to those wishing to acquire a reading knowledge of the language. But potential specialists in philology should find it a help in their preliminary studies of the essential grammar. The *Guide* can be used by students working with or without a teacher; for the latter, a section on 'How to Use this Guide' has been provided.

In general, the *Guide* devotes more space than is usual to the simple explanation of difficult points and to ways of reducing rote learning and of solving problems which arise for the reader of Old English texts. Part One is divided into seven chapters – Preliminary Remarks on the Language, a simple treatment of Orthography and Pronunciation, Inflexions, Word Formation, Syntax (where stress is laid on the important differences between Old and Modern English), a brief Introduction to Anglo-Saxon Studies in which language and literature, history, and archaeology, are discussed, and a highly selective Bibliography for the beginner. Part Two consists of Texts (with notes), and Glossary. Phonology is not treated in a separate section, but is integrated with the grammar, important sound-changes being treated briefly when they provide the accepted explanation of apparent irregularities in inflexion. Those seeking more information on sound-changes and their relation to accidence are recommended in the first place to the work by R. F. S. Hamer cited in §9 Note. But the *Guide* aims at being self-contained, as far as it goes. Chapter 6, An Introduction to Anglo-Saxon Studies, is, like the rest of the book, addressed to the beginner. Its aim is to give in short compass basic facts and background information which will illuminate the prose and verse texts and stimulate the student to pursue paths of interest. This accounts for the mention of some works which to the expert may seem 'popular' or 'out of date', e.g. Jessup's *Anglo-Saxon Jewellery* (§220), with its four colour plates and forty monochrome plates, and Fisher's *Introduction to Anglo-Saxon Architecture and Sculpture* (§220), with over one hundred monochrome plates. The books on metalwork by Wilson and by Hinton, on architecture by Taylor and Taylor, and on sculpture by Cramp and by Bailey – all cited in §258 – are more up to date and offer more detailed information. But in the interests of the beginner, we have retained the simpler books, just as we have provided a Glossary instead of referring him or her to one of the dictionaries.

The prose texts are arranged in order of increasing difficulty. The first three selections are normalized throughout, and palatal *ċ* and *ġ* are distinguished from velar *c* and *g*. The fourth selection is not normalized, but a few peculiarities have been removed to ease transition to the unnormalized texts in the remainder of the readings. The Glossary is extremely detailed, with heavy parsing of words recorded. Similarly, the notes are full, and cross-references to the grammatical explanations in the *Guide* are frequent. So full an apparatus may seem at times to encumber the student with more help than is necessary, but our intention is to make it possible for the student to begin reading Old English from the outset, without obliging the teacher to take up particular topics in the grammar in a particular sequence before assigning texts for translation. Although individual teachers and readers are thus freed to cover the fundamentals of the language in whatever sequence suits their taste, we do think that the order of topics laid out on pages 3 to 5 is recommended both by logic and by our own experience.

The prose and verse texts selected are on the whole those which have traditionally been offered to beginning students to read. We have resisted the temptation to substitute novel selections for the familiar ones: such passages as King Alfred's Preface, the story of Cædmon, the conversion of Edwin, and Cynewulf and Cyneheard, have been chosen by generations of teachers and scholars as the appropriate introductory texts precisely because these are the essential ones for the proper orientation of beginners towards both the literature and culture of Anglo-Saxon England. Replacement of any or all of these with different selections might give the veteran teacher a refreshing change from the canon, but it would also deprive beginning students of important reference points in their initial study of Old English literature.

Bruce Mitchell's original obligations are recorded in the Forewords to the first and second editions. Thanks are now due to Sarah Ogilvie-Thomson and Roy Michael Liuzza. We should emphasize that in the poetic texts, as in the prose texts, we make no claim to originality in our emendations and interpretations. Rather we have tried to select what seemed to us the best scholarly view on each point, and usually this has been the view that enjoys a majority consensus among editors and scholars. We have made no effort to name the scholars who originated and have subscribed to the interpretations selected, for this, it seemed to us, would have cluttered the commentary without serving the student's needs. We make wholesale and grateful acknowledgement here to the Old English scholarly tradition on which we have drawn in preparing this book.

BRUCE MITCHELL
FRED C. ROBINSON

4 July 1986

Contents

Abbreviations and Symbols

LANGUAGES AND DIALECTS

Gmc.	Germanic	nWS	non-West-Saxon
IE	Indo-European	OE	Old English
Lat.	Latin	OHG	Old High German
ME	Middle English	WS	West-Saxon
MnE	Modern English		

Before the name of a language or dialect

e = Early   l = Late   Pr = Primitive

GRAMMATICAL TERMS

acc.	accusative	nom.	nominative
adj.	adjective	pass.	passive
adv.	adverb	p.d.	see §100
conj.	conjunction	pers.	person
cons.	consonant	pl.	plural
dat.	dative	poss.	possessive
dem.	demonstrative	prep.	preposition
fem.	feminine	pres.	present
gen.	genitive	pret.	preterite
imp.	imperative	pret.-pres.	preterite-present
ind.	indicative	pron.	pronoun
inf.	infinitive	ptc.	participle
infl.	inflected	sg.	singular
inst.	instrumental	st.	strong
masc.	masculine	subj.	subjunctive
neut.	neuter	wk.	weak

's' may be added where appropriate to form a plural.

SYMBOLS

>	became
<	came from
*	This precedes a form which is not recorded. Usually it is a form which probably once existed and which scholars reconstruct to explain the stages in sound-changes; see §103.3.

Sometimes it is a form which certainly never existed but which is invented to show that one sound-change preceded another. An example is *ċierfan* in §100, note.

¯ over a letter denotes a long vowel or diphthong.

˘ over a letter denotes a short vowel or diphthong.

⏑̄ means 'short and long', e.g. *ē̆* in §100.

– ⏑ in §41 denote a long and short syllable respectively.

´ ` × denote respectively a syllable carrying full, secondary, or no, stress.

How to Use this Guide

This section is particularly addressed to those of you who are working without a teacher. We hope that when you have finished with this book you will not disagree too strongly – as far as elementary Old English grammar is concerned, at any rate – with the pithy observations made by Dr Johnson to Boswell in 1766:

> People have now-a-days, said he, got a strange opinion that everything should be taught by lectures. Now, I cannot see that lectures can do so much good as reading the books from which the lectures are taken. I know nothing that can be best taught by lectures, except where experiments are to be shown. You may teach chemistry by lectures. – You might teach making of shoes by lectures!

THE IMPORTANCE OF READING AND PARSING

The ability to recognize forms in the texts you are reading and an awareness of the basic structure of Old English are far more important than a parrot knowledge of the paradigms. Hence, from the beginning, you must get into the habit of analysing and thoroughly understanding each form you meet in your texts. Here you will find 'parsing' a great help. Since this word is taboo in many places, it had better be explained if it is to be used here.

All it means, of course, is recognizing what part of speech the word is – noun, pronoun, adjective, verb, and so on – and what particular form the word has in your sentence. If you are uncertain about the meaning of the parts of speech listed below or of other terms such as 'article', 'infinitive', or 'participle', you are advised to consult A. J. Thomson and A. V. Martinet *A Practical English Grammar* (3rd ed., Oxford, 1980, or 4th ed., Oxford, 1986) or David Crystal *A Dictionary of Linguistics and Phonetics* (2nd ed., Basil Blackwell, 1985).

The information needed when parsing Old English words is:

Noun: Meaning, gender, number, case, and the reason for the case, e.g. accusative because it is object, genitive denoting possession, or dative of the indirect object.

Pronoun: Same as for noun. Here you need to know the noun to which the pronoun refers. (If it is a relative pronoun, see §162.)

Adjective: Same as for noun. Sometimes, of course, an adjective is used with a noun, sometimes it is used alone, either as a complement or where a noun is more usual, e.g. 'The good often die before their time'.

Verb: If you have the infinitive, you merely need the meaning. Otherwise you need to work out the person, number, tense, and mood, and then deduce the infinitive. Unless you are familiar with the verb, you will have to do all this before you can find its meaning. For hints on how to do it, see §134.

Adverbs and interjections (a name given to words like 'Oh!', 'Alas!', and 'Lo!') will give little trouble. It is important to notice the case of a word governed by a preposition, for a difference in case sometimes indicates a difference in meaning; see §§213–214. Conjunctions are a greater source of difficulty. Lists of them are given in §§168, 171, and 184, and references to discussions on them are set out in 'Understanding the Syntax' below.

Note

The importance of gender varies. Sometimes it is obvious, sometimes it is of no real importance. But at times it provides a vital clue. Thus in *Hē ġehīerþ þās word and þā wyrcð*, *þās* and *þā* could be acc. sg. fem. or acc. pl. Only the fact that *word* is neuter will tell us that we must translate 'He hears these words and does them'.

LENGTH MARKS

Long vowels have been marked (¯) throughout,with the exception noted below. A knowledge of the length of vowels (or 'quantity', as it is called) is essential for proficiency in reading, for accuracy in translation (compare *god* 'god' with *gōd* 'good'), for the understanding of OE metre, and for the serious study of phonology. Hence, when you learn the inflexions, you will need to remember both the form of the word and the length of its vowels. Long vowels are marked in the Texts and you should take advantage of this by noting carefully those which occur in both familiar and unfamiliar words.

But since the length-marks are not shown in the Old English manuscripts, many editions of prose and verse texts do not show them. Examples are the standard editions of the Anglo-Saxon Chronicle and of the Homilies of Ælfric and Wulfstan, the texts published by Methuen (in their Old English Library) and by the Early English Text Society, and *The Anglo-Saxon Poetic Records* (published by Columbia University Press) which contain all the extant poetry. You will have to use one or more of these works fairly early in your career. In the hope that you will find the transition to such texts easier if you have already seen short passages in the form in which they appear in these works, we have not regularized the spelling (see §3) or marked vowel-length in the illustrative quotations in chapters 5 and 6. Most of the passages quoted are taken from texts which appear in Part Two. You can use these passages by writing them out, marking in the length-marks yourself, and then comparing them with the correct version. You can check individual words in the Glossary. But you will find it more interesting if you track down the context of the longer prose passages and those in verse with the help of the references in the Glossary. By so doing, you will improve your knowledge of vowel quantity and widen your acquaintance with OE literature.

LEARNING THE INFLEXIONS

Those who want to test their knowledge of the paradigms and to try their hand at translating into Old English (a very useful way of learning the language, especially important since no-one speaks it today) will find A. S. Cook *Exercises in Old English* (Ginn, 1895) a useful book. There are second-hand copies about. *An English—Anglo-Saxon Vocabulary*, compiled by W. W. Skeat and printed for private distribution only by the Cambridge University Press in 1879, was reprinted in 1976 by J. D. Pickles of Cambridge, England.

We suggest that those coming to this book without any knowledge of Old English learn the inflexions in the order set out below. But remember that texts must be read and an understanding of the syntax acquired at the same time. Hints on how to do this are given later in this section.

1   Read §§1–4.

2   Now work through §§5–9. Make sure that you can recognize the new letters æ, þ, and ð, and practise reading aloud the Practice Sentences (Text 1), following generally the natural stress of MnE.

3   Now read §§10–12.

4   The next step is to learn the paradigms in A below, in the order in which they are set out there.

5   (*a*) When you have learnt the pronouns, nouns, and adjectives, in A, you can see whether §§77–81 help or hinder you. Experience on this point differs.

(*b*) When you have learnt the verbs in A, you should read §§131–134.

6   You can now turn to the paradigms referred to in B below. B contains what may be called the 'derived paradigms', i.e. those which can be derived from the paradigms set out in A when certain sound-changes are understood. The sound-changes are presented in the hope that they will make your work easier, not as an end in themselves. Thus, if you meet a word *hwatum* in your reading, you will not be able to find out its meaning unless you know that it comes from an adjective *hwæt* 'active, bold'. You will know this only if you have read §70.

7   The paradigms in C are important ones of fairly frequent occurrence

which need not be learnt all at once. When you come across one of them in your reading, you can consult the relevant section. In this way, you will absorb them as need arises.

8 Because of the dialectal variations and inconsistencies in spelling noted in §§2–3, there are many ways of spelling even some of the most common words in the language; for examples, see the word *se* in the Glossary. If all the possible forms of this and other words were given in the paradigms in chapter 3, you would not see the wood for the trees. So those less common variants which occur in the texts will be found as cross-references in the Glossary.

A Key Paradigms

These paradigms must be known thoroughly. At this stage, concentrate on them alone; disregard anything else in these sections.

1   The pronouns set out in §§15–21. Note particularly §19. (The dual forms in §21 may be passed over at first.)
2   *Nama* (§22) and, after reading §§63–64, *tila* (§65).
3   Now read §§26–32.
4   *Stān* (§33), *scip/word* (§34), and *ġiefu/lār* (§§47–48).
5   The strong declension of the adjectives (§§66–67).
6   Now read §§14, 87–89, and 115.
7   *Fremman* (§§116–117) and *lufian* (§§124–125).
8   *Habban* (§126), *bēon* (§127), and *weorþan* (Appendix A.3 (*b*)).
9   The principal parts of the strong verbs (§§90–95).
10 The conjugation of strong verbs (§§110–113).

B Derived Paradigms

The paradigms in this group may be derived from those in A as follows:

1   From *nama*, those in §§23–25.
2   From *stān*, *scip*, or *ġiefu*, those in §§35–44, 48–51, and 52–60. See now §13.
3   From *tila* and *til*, those in §§68–73.
4   From *fremman*, those in §§116–123.
5   From *lufian*, those in §§124–125.
6   From §§90–95, those in §§96–109.
7   From §§110–113, those in §114.

Note
Some nouns which often go like *stān*, *scip*, or *ġiefu*, once belonged to other declensions. As a result, they sometimes have unusual forms which may cause you difficulty

in your reading. It might be just as well if you learnt to recognize these fairly early in your career. They include: *čild* (§34), *hæleþ* and *mōnaþ* (§44), some nouns in *-e* (§§45–46), the feminine nouns discussed in §§49 and 51, the relationship nouns (§60), and the *u* nouns (§§61–62).

C Other Paradigms

1 Other Strong Nouns (§§45–46 and 61–62).
2 Comparison of Adjectives (§§74–76).
3 Numerals (§§82–86).
4 Verbs
    (*a*) Class 3 weak verbs (§126).
    (*b*) *Dōn* and *gān* (§128).
    (*c*) *Willan* (§§129 and 211).
    (*d*) Preterite-present verbs (§§130 and 206–210).
5 Adverbs (§135).

LEARNING THE VOCABULARY

Many OE words are easily recognizable from their MnE counterparts, though sometimes the meaning may be different; see §4 and look up the word 'lewd' in the Oxford English Dictionary.

Other words differ in spelling and pronunciation as a result of changes in ME and MnE. The short vowels *e, i, o, u,* have remained relatively constant (see §7). But the long vowels and the diphthongs have sometimes changed considerably. Words with a long vowel in OE sometimes appear in MnE with the vowel doubled, e.g. *fēt* (masc. pl.) 'feet' and *dōm* (masc.) 'doom'. Sometimes, they have *-e* at the end, e.g. *līf* (neut.) 'life' and (with, in addition, one of the differences discussed below) *hām* (masc.) 'home' and *hūs* (neut.) 'house'.

Correspondences like the last two are more difficult to spot. Yet a knowledge of them is easily acquired and will save you much hard work. Thus, if you know that OE *ā* often appears in MnE as *oa*, you will not need to use the Glossary to discover that *bār* (masc.) means 'boar', *bāt* (fem. or masc.) 'boat', *brād* 'broad', and *hār* 'hoar(y)'. Words like *āc* (fem.) 'oak', *hlāf* (masc.) 'loaf', and *hlāfas* (masc. pl.) 'loaves', will not present much more difficulty.

The table which follows will help you to recognize more of these correspondences. But it is not complete and the correspondences do not always apply. Thus OE *hāt* is MnE 'hot' and you may find it interesting to look up in a glossary or dictionary the four OE words spelt *ār* and see what has happened to them.

OE spelling	MnE spelling	Vowels	Consonants
fæt (neut.)	vat	æ = a	f = v
rǣdan	read	ǣ = ea	
dǣd (fem.)	deed	ǣ = ee	
hāliġ	holy	ā = o	
hām (masc.)	home	ā = o.e	
āc (fem.)	oak	ā = oa	c = k
hlāf (masc.)	loaf		hl = l
ecg (fem.)	edge		cg = dge
dēman	deem	ē = ee	
frēosan	freeze		s = z
ċild (neut.)	child		ċ = ch
miht (fem.)	might		h = gh
scip (neut.)	ship		sc = sh
līf (neut.)	life	ī = i.e	
ġiellan	yell	ie = e	ġ = y
ġiefan	give	ie = i	ġ = g
dōm (masc.)	doom	ō = oo	
hūs (neut.)	house	ū = ou.e	
nū	now	ū = ow	
synn (fem.)	sin	y = i	

See §253 for a book which may help you to learn the vocabulary.

The principles on which words were formed in OE are set out in §§136–138. Once you understand these, you will be able to deduce the meaning of some new words by their similarity to words you already know; see §136. For correspondences in endings, see §138.

UNDERSTANDING THE SYNTAX

The fundamental differences between the syntax of Old English and that of Modern English are set out in §§139–153. These, and §§182–183, should be studied as soon as you can read simple sentences with some degree of fluency and before you pass on to the connected passages of Old English recommended below. Other sections which should be read fairly soon are §§154–155, 157–158, and 160 (noun clauses and their conjunctions), §162 (relative pronouns), §§166–167 and §§169–170 (conjunctions introducing adverb clauses), §189 note, and §§195–199 (the uses of the tenses and the syntax of the resolved verb forms).

The remaining parts of the syntax should be used for reference when the need arises; note especially the topics mentioned in §§141–142 and the lists of conjunctions in §§168, 171, and 184. When you begin to feel some confidence, you can try the exercise in §172.

If at first you find these sections too long and complicated, you are advised to use one of the books cited in §256.

TEXTS TO READ

Part Two of this book starts with a selection of prose texts for beginners, the texts being carefully coordinated with the explanations in the grammar sections. After you have worked your way through these, you will be ready for the poems, which are similarly annotated. This combination of texts should provide a foundation from which you can advance to *Beowulf* and to the prose and verse texts available in Methuen's Old English Library and the Manchester Series.

READING THE TEXTS

Before beginning to read the texts you should do two things: first, study carefully the introduction to the Glossary, and second, familiarize yourself with the function words and word-patterns listed in §§168 and 171. While reading the texts, you should make careful use not only of the Glossary, but also of the Index of Words.

WES þU HAL

It now remains for us to wish you success – and pleasure – in your studies. In 991, before the battle of Maldon, Byrhtnoth called across the cold waters of the river to his Danish foes:

> Nu eow is gerymed;   gað riccne to us,
> guman to guþe;   god ana wat
> hwa þære wælstowe   wealdan mote.
> (*The Battle of Maldon*, ll. 93–95)

This can be paraphrased

> 'Now the way is clear for you; O warriors,
> hasten to the battle; God alone knows
> how things will turn out'.

It is our hope and wish that *your* efforts will prosper – *Wel þe þæs geweorces!*

Part One

I

Preliminary Remarks on the Language

§1 Professor Campbell defines Old English as 'the vernacular Germanic language of Great Britain as it is recorded in manuscripts and inscriptions dating from before about 1100'. It is one of the Germanic group of the Indo-European family of languages. Those who are unfamiliar with this concept should read about it in one of the histories of the English language cited in the Bibliography.

§2 There are four dialects distinguishable in the extant monuments – Northumbrian, Mercian, Kentish, West-Saxon. The differences are apparent in the spelling; otherwise, of course, we should not know about them. After 900 West-Saxon was increasingly used as a standard written language. It is for this reason that, initially at any rate, you learn West-Saxon. But even here the spelling conventions were never as rigidly observed as they are in Great Britain or America today, where compositors, typists, and writers, in different parts of the country use the same spelling, no matter how different their pronunciations may be.

§3 Most OE primers therefore attempt to make things easier for the beginner by 'normalizing', i.e. regularizing, the spelling by eliminating all forms not belonging to the West-Saxon dialect. But difficulty arises because two stages can be distinguished – early West-Saxon (eWS), which is the language of the time of King Alfred (c. 900), and late West-Saxon (lWS), which is seen in the works of Ælfric (c. 1000). Professor Davis, in revising Sweet's *Anglo-Saxon Primer*, followed Sweet and used eWS as his basis. Quirk and Wrenn's *Old English Grammer*, however, normalizes on the basis of Ælfric's lWS. For the beginner, the most important difference is that eWS *ie* and *īe* appear in lWS texts as *y* and *ȳ*; this accounts for such differences as Sweet *ieldra, hīeran*, but Q. & W. *yldra, hȳran*. Another is that *ea* and *ēa* may be spelt *e* and *ē* in lWS (and sometimes in eWS) texts, e.g. *seah* and *scēap*, but *seh* and *scēp*. Since the other differences will scarcely trouble you and since there are some disadvantages in the use of lWS, the paradigms are given here in their eWS forms and the sound laws are discussed with eWS as the basis. Any important variations likely to cause difficulty – apart from those mentioned here – will be noted. Full lists of all dialectal variants will be found in the appropriate section of Campbell's *Old English Grammar*.

In the sections on syntax, the spelling of a standard edition has generally been followed, though occasionally an unusual form has been silently regularized. This should ease the transition to non-normalized texts.

Similarly, in the prose texts provided for reading, we have moved from totally normalized to non-normalized texts. We have not normalized the poems.

§4 As has been explained in the Foreword, this book, after a brief discussion of orthography and pronunciation, deals with accidence, word formation, and syntax (including word-order), and attempts simple explanations of those sound-changes which will help you to learn the inflexions. Other sound-changes, the metre of poetry, and semantics, are not discussed. It is important, however, to remember that many common words have changed their meaning. *Sellan* means 'to give', not just 'to give in exchange for money, to sell'. *Eorl* cannot always be translated 'earl' and *dēor* and *fugol* mean, not 'deer' and 'fowl', but 'any (wild) animal' and 'any bird' respectively. It is also important to note that, while Old English literature was written and/or transmitted by Christians, the Christian poetry was largely written in an originally pagan vocabulary which embodied the values of the heroic code. However, it does not follow that the poetry is rich in pagan elements. You will find that words like *lof* in *The Seafarer* and *wyrd* in *The Wanderer* have acquired Christian connotations. On this point, see further §§218 and 236–246. The Bibliography contains references to useful introductory discussions on all the topics not discussed in this book.

Orthography and Pronunciation

I ORTHOGRAPHY

§5   As a glance at the facsimile of the OE manuscript on page 254 will show, the letters used by Anglo-Saxon scribes were sometimes very like and sometimes very unlike those used today, both in shape and function. Printers of Anglo-Saxon texts generally use the equivalent modern letter form. Hence the sounds [f] and [v] are both represented by *f*, and the sounds [s] and [z] by *s* because the distinctions were less significant in OE; on these and other differences in representing the consonants, see §9. On the value of *y*, which represents a vowel now lost, see §7.

The following symbols are not in use today: æ (ash), which represents the vowel in MnE 'hat', þ (thorn) and ð (eth or, as the Anglo-Saxons appear to have called it, *ðæt*), both of which represent MnE *th* as in 'cloth' and in 'clothe'. Capital ð is written Ð. To make the learning of paradigms as simple as possible, þ has been used throughout chapter 3.

The early texts of the Methuen Old English Library used the runic 'wynn' ƿ instead of *w* and the OE letter ᵹ for *g*. In the latest volumes, these have been discarded.

As is customary, the punctuation in quotations and selections from OE is modern. But see the Note on the Punctuation of Old English Poetry which follows selection 18 in Part Two.

II STRESS

§6   The stress usually falls on the first syllable, as in MnE, e.g. mórgen 'morning'. The prefix *ge-* is always unaccented; hence *gebídan* 'await'. Two main difficulties occur:

1   Prepositional prefixes, e.g. *for-*, *ofer-*, can be either accented (usually in nouns or adjectives, e.g. *fórwyrd* 'ruin') or unaccented (usually in verbs, e.g. *forwíernan* 'refúse').

2   Compound words in which both elements retain their full meaning, e.g. *sǽ-weall* 'sea-wall', have a secondary stress on the root syllable of the second element. There is some dispute about three-syllabled words with a long first syllable (see §26). Some say that *bindende* 'binding' and *timbrode*

'built' have a pattern like MnE 'árchàngĕls', not like 'hástĭlў'. But not every-one agrees.

III VOWELS

§7   Short vowels must be distinguished from long vowels, which are marked (¯) in this book (except as noted on pp. 2–3). Approximate pro-nunciations of OE vowels for those working without a teacher are given as far as possible in terms of Received Standard English.

a	as the first vowel in 'aha'
ā	as the second vowel in 'aha'
æ	as in 'mat'
ǣ	as in 'has'[1]
e	as in 'bet'
ē	approx. as in 'hate', but a pure vowel [cf. German *See*]
i	as in 'tin'
ī	as in 'seen'
o	as in 'cough'
ō	approx. as in 'so', but a pure vowel [cf. German *so*]
u	as in 'pull' [NOT 'hut']
ū	as in 'cool'
y	as *i*, with lips in a whistling position [French *tu*]
ȳ	as *ī*, with lips in a whistling position [French *ruse*]

Vowels in unstressed syllables should be pronounced clearly. Failure to distinguish gen. sg. *eorles* from nom. acc. pl. *eorlas* is characteristic of ME, not of OE.

IV DIPHTHONGS

§8   If you are not sure of the distinction between vowels and diphthongs, you should consult a simple manual of phonetics. It is important to realize that OE words such as *heall*, *hēold*, *hielt*, which contain diphthongs, are just as much monosyllables as MnE 'meat' and 'field' (in which two letters represent one vowel) or MnE 'fine' and 'base', which contain diphthongs. The OE diphthongs, with approximate pronunciations, are

$$ea = æ + a$$
$$ēa = ǣ + a$$
$$eo = e + o$$

---

[1] If you experiment, you will notice that the vowel in 'has' is longer than that in 'mat', though MnE [æ] is frequently described as a 'short vowel'.

$$\bar{e}o = \bar{e} + o$$
$$ie = i + e^1$$
$$\bar{i}e = \bar{i} + e$$

A short diphthong is equal in length to a short vowel, a long diphthong to a long vowel. But remember that, like the MnE word 'I', they are diphthongs, not two distinct vowels such as we get in the *ea* of 'Leander'.

V CONSONANTS

§9 All consonants must be pronounced, e.g. *c* in *cnapa*, *g* in *gnæt*, *h* in *hlāf*, *r* in *þær*, and *w* in *wrītan* and *trēow*.

Double consonants must be pronounced. Thus *biden* and *biddan* differ as MnE 'bidden' and 'bad debt'.

Most of the consonants are pronounced in the same way as in MnE. The main exceptions are set out below.

The letters *s*, *f*, *þ*, and *ð*, are pronounced voiced, i.e. like MnE *z*, *v*, and *th* in 'clothe', between vowels or other voiced sounds, e.g. *rīsan*, *hlāfas*, *paþas*, and *hēafdes*. In other positions, including the beginning and end of words, they are voiceless, i.e. like MnE *s*, *f*, and *th* in 'cloth', e.g. *sittan*, *hlāf*, *pæþ*, and *oft*. This accounts for the different sounds in MnE 'path' but 'paths', 'loaf' but 'loaves', and the like. Initial *ġe-* does not cause voicing; *findan* and its past ptc. *ġe-funden* both have the sound *f*.

The differences described in the preceding paragraph are due to the fact that the pairs *f* and *v*, *s* and *z*, and voiceless and voiced *þ* 'th', were merely variants ('allophones') in OE and not sounds of different significance ('phonemes'). This means that, whereas in MnE speech the distinctions between 'fat' and 'vat', 'sink' and 'zinc', and 'loath' and 'loathe', depend on whether we use a voiceless or voiced sound, both OE *fæt* 'fat' and OE *fæt* 'vat' could be pronounced with initial *f* or *v*, according to dialect.

At the beginning of a word ('initially') before a vowel, *h* is pronounced as in MnE 'hound'. Otherwise it is like German *ch* in *ich* [ç] or *ach* [x], according to the front or back quality of the neighbouring vowel. It can be pronounced like *ch* in Scots *loch*.

Before *a*, *o*, *u*, and *y*, *c* is pronounced *k* and *g* is pronounced as in MnE 'good'. Before *e* and *i*, *c* is usually pronounced like *ch* in MnE 'child' and *g* like *y* in MnE 'yet'. In Part One, the latter are printed *ċ* and *ġ* respectively, except in the examples quoted in chapters 5 and 6.

---

[1] The original pronunciation of *ie* and *īe* is not known with any certainty. It is simplest and most convenient for our purposes to assume that they represented diphthongs as explained above. But by King Alfred's time *ie* was pronounced as a simple vowel (monophthong), probably a vowel somewhere between *i* and *e*; *ie* is often replaced by *i* or *y*, and unstressed *i* is often replaced by *ie*, as in *hiene* for *hine*. Probably *īe* had a similar sound.

After or between back vowels, *g* is pronounced [ɣ], like the *g* sometimes heard in dialectal German *sagen*. Those without a teacher can pronounce it as *w* in words like *dragan* and *boga*.

The combinations *sc* and *cg* are usually pronounced like MnE *sh* and *dge* respectively. Thus *scip* 'ship' and *ecg* 'edge' are pronounced the same in both OE and MnE.

Note

A more detailed account of the pronunciation of Old English will be found in §§9–19 of *Old English Sound Changes for Beginners* by R. F. S. Hamer (Basil Blackwell, 1967).

3

Inflexions

INTRODUCTION

§10 Following (as most primers do) the conventional terminology, we distinguish in Old English the following parts of speech: nouns, adjectives, pronouns (including articles), verbs, adverbs, prepositions, conjunctions, and interjections.

§11 Like most inflected languages, OE distinguishes number, case, and gender, in nouns, pronouns, and adjectives. The numbers are singular and plural; a dual is found in the 1st and 2nd pers. pron. where, e.g. *wit* means 'we two', *ġit* 'you (ye) two'. The main cases are nominative, accusative, genitive, and dative, but in certain parts of the adjective and pronoun declensions an instrumental occurs; where it does not, the dative does its work. If you are unfamiliar with the concept of 'case', you are recommended to consult the sections listed under that word in the Index of Subjects.

§12 There are three genders – masculine, feminine, and neuter. Gender sometimes agrees with sex, e.g. *se mann* (masc.) 'the man', *sēo sweostor* (fem.) 'the sister', or with lack of it, e.g. *þæt scip* (neut.) 'the ship'. This is often called 'natural gender'. But grammatical gender is often opposed to sex, e.g. (with persons) *se wīfmann* (masc.) 'the woman', *þæt wīf* (neut.) 'the woman', and (with inanimate objects) *se stān* (masc.) 'the stone', *sēo ġiefu* (fem.) 'the gift'. These opposing tendencies, which contribute to the later disappearance of grammatical gender in English, sometimes produce 'lack of concord'; see §187.2. Compounds follow the gender of the second element; hence *þæt wīf* (neut.) + *se mann* (masc.) = *se wīfmann* (masc.).

§13 Generally, the gender of nouns must be learnt. The form of the demonstrative is the main clue (see §§16–17). The following nom. sg. endings, however, are significant:

Weak Masc. : *-a*
Strong Masc.: *-dōm*, *-els*, agent nouns in *-end* and *-ere*, *-hād*, concrete nouns in *-ing* and *-ling*, *-scipe*
Strong Fem. : *-nes(s)*, abstract nouns in *-ing/ung*, *-rǣden*, *-þo/þu*
Strong Neut.: *-lāc*

Notoriously ambiguous is the ending *-e*; see §77. On these endings, see further §§136–138.

§14 Verbs. The differences between strong and weak verbs and the system of conjugating the OE verb are described in §§87–89. New developments, many of them important for MnE, are outlined in §§199–203.

I PRONOUNS

§15 You are now ready to learn your first paradigms. The demonstrative *se* serves as a definite article. Both *se* 'that' and *þes* 'this' can be used with nouns, e.g. *se mann* 'the man', or as pronouns, e.g. *hē sorgaþ ymb þā* 'he is concerned about those (them)'.

§16 *se* 'the, that'

	Singular			Plural
	Masc.	Neut.	Fem.	All genders
Nom.	sě	þæt	sēo, sīo	þā
Acc.	þone	þæt	þā	þā
Gen.	þæs	þæs	þære	þāra, þæra
Dat.	þæm, þām	þæm, þām	þære	þæm, þām
Inst.	þȳ, þon	þȳ, þon		

§17 *þes* 'this'

	Singular			Plural
	Masc.	Neut.	Fem.	All genders
Nom.	þes	þis	þēos	þās
Acc.	þisne	þis	þās	þās
Gen.	þisses	þisses	þisse	þissa
Dat.	þissum	þissum	þisse	þissum
Inst.	þȳs	þȳs		

§18 3rd Pers. Pron.

	Singular			Plural
	Masc.	Neut.	Fem.	All genders
Nom.	hē 'he'	hit 'it'	hēo, hīo 'she'	hīe, hī 'they'
Acc.	hine	hit	hīe, hī	hīe, hī
Gen.	his	his	hire	hira, hiera, heora, hiora
Dat.	him	him	hire	him

§19 The following similarities in these declensions may be noted:

1 neut. sg. gen. dat. inst. are the same as the corresponding masc. forms;
2 nom. and acc. neut. sg. are the same;
3 gen. and dat. fem. sg. are the same;

4 pl. is the same for all genders;

5 acc. fem. sg. is the same as nom. and acc. pl.

Note too the way in which the masc. and neut. sg., while agreeing with one another except in the nom. and acc., differ markedly in inflexion from the fem.

§20 *Hwā* is interrogative 'who?' or indefinite 'anyone, someone'. It is not a relative pronoun in OE; see §159.

	Masc. and Fem.	*Neut.*
Nom.	hwā	hwæt
Acc.	hwone	hwæt
Gen.	hwæs	hwæs
Dat.	hwǣm, hwām	hwǣm, hwām
Inst.	hwȳ	hwȳ, hwon

Note the similarities between *hwā* and *se*. The main difference, of course, is that the masc. and fem. of *hwā* are the same. This is easily understandable if we think of what *hwā* means.

§21 1st and 2nd Pers. Prons.

	Singular	*Dual*	*Plural*
Nom.	iċ 'I'	wit 'we two'	wē 'we'
Acc.	mē, meċ	unc	ūs
Gen.	mīn	uncer	ūre
Dat.	mē	unc	ūs

	Singular	*Dual*	*Plural*
Nom.	þū 'thou'	ġit 'you two'	ġē 'ye, you'
Acc.	þē, þeċ	inc	ēow
Gen.	þīn	incer	ēower
Dat.	þē	inc	ēow

The easiest way to learn these is to compare them with their MnE equivalents (the main differences are in pronunciation) and with one another.

II NOUNS AND SOUND-CHANGES RELEVANT TO THEM

Weak Nouns

§22 The basic paradigm of the weak or *-an* nouns is *nama* 'name', the weak masc. noun:

	Singular	*Plural*
Nom.	nama	naman
Acc.	naman	naman
Gen.	naman	namena
Dat.	naman	namum

Notes

1 Any noun with the nom. sg. ending -*a* is weak masc.
2 All other cases have the ending -*an* except gen. pl. -*ena* and dat. pl. -*um*.

Once *nama* is known, the rest follows quite simply without learning further paradigms.

§23 The weak fem. noun *sunne* 'sun' is declined exactly as *nama* apart from the nom. sg.

§24 The weak neut. noun *ēage* 'eye' is declined exactly as *nama* except that, as in all neut. nouns, the nom. and acc. sg. are the same.

§25 Nouns with a nom. sg. ending in a long vowel or diphthong form their oblique cases by adding the consonant of the inflexional ending. So *ġefēa* (masc.) 'joy' has oblique cases *ġefēa/n* except for gen. pl. *ġefēa/na* and dat. pl. *ġefēa/m*.

Some Technical Terms

§26 You now need to know some phonological terms. 'Short vowel' as in MnE 'hit' and 'long vowel' as in the second syllable in MnE 'machine' will present no difficulty. The word *wer* 'man' has a short vowel and is a short syllable. The word *stān* 'stone' has a long vowel and is a long syllable. Such words as *cniht* 'young man' and *cræft* 'strength' have a short vowel. But, since the short vowel is followed by *two* consonants, the syllable is long; cf. the rules of Latin prosody. To summarize, we have

short-stemmed monosyllables[1]	*wer, bæc, feoh*
long-stemmed monosyllables	*stān, cniht, crēap*
short-stemmed dissyllables	*miċel, yfel*
long-stemmed dissyllables	*ēþel, engel*

Forms like *metodes* and *bysiġe* are called 'trisyllabic' and the *o* or *i* is sometimes called the 'medial vowel'.

§27 It is also important to distinguish open and closed syllables. An open syllable ends in a vowel, e.g. *hē* 'he'; a closed syllable ends in a consonant, e.g. *stān* 'stone'. This is clear enough. But difficulty arises with dissyllables. You must take on trust that the gen. sg. *stānes* is divided *stā/nes* (cf. MnE 'stone' but 'sto/ning'), while the infinitive *limpan* divides *lim/pan* (cf. MnE 'limb pad'). So we have

open syllables	*hē*	*stā/nes*
closed syllables	*stān*	*lim/pan*

§28 'Sometimes', it has been observed, 'things may be made darker by definition.' This must not deter us from attempting to define high and low

---

[1] The 'stem' of a word may be defined as that portion to which the inflexional ending is added, e.g. *scip* + -*es* = gen. sg. *scipes*. The stem of words ending in a vowel can usually be found by dropping the final vowel. So *ende* has stem *end*- + -*es* = gen. sg. *endes*.

vowels and back and front vowels. The adjectives 'high, low, back, front' all refer to the position in the mouth occupied by some part of the tongue. The tip of the tongue is not usually important; here it is assumed to be near or touching the lower front teeth. We are concerned with the movement of that part of the tongue which is highest when we pronounce a particular vowel.

§29   What follows is a conventionalized diagram showing the parts of the mouth in which the vowels are pronounced.

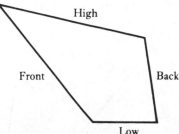

In the front vowels, the 'front' of the tongue is raised towards the hard palate. In the back vowels, the 'back' of the tongue is raised towards the soft palate. To understand this, you may well need the help of a tutor and of a book on the phonetics of your own 'accent' of English. But you can try the following experiment, observing with the aid of a mirror the movements of jaw, lips, and tongue:

1   Practise individually the sounds you have learnt for the OE vowels *i, e, æ, a, o, u*.

2   Sing them in a rough scale in the order given in 1, with the tip of the tongue near or touching the lower front teeth.

§30   Observe:

1   with *i, e, æ,*

    (*a*) a gradual lowering of the jaw;

    (*b*) a gradual lowering of the (front of the) tongue;

    (*c*) the roughly natural position of the lips, i.e. neither unduly spread out nor rounded;

    (*d*) a general feeling that the sounds are being made in the front of the mouth.

2   With the transition from *æ* to *a* a backward and slightly downward movement of the tongue.

3   with *a, o, u,*

    (*a*) progressive raising of the jaw and of the (back of the) tongue;

    (*b*) the way in which the lips become more rounded, i.e. form a progressively smaller circle;

    (*c*) the general feeling of 'backness'.

§31   From this, it should be clear why *i, e, æ*, are called front vowels and *a*, *o*, *u*, back vowels. Another way of feeling the difference is to pronounce the diphthongs made up of *i* + *u*, *e* + *o*, and *æ* + *a*, for if you do this you will feel the backward movement of the tongue. (The two latter sounds will be close to the OE diphthongs *eo* and *ea* respectively.) But you will not feel a great downward movement; roughly speaking, *i* and *u* are pronounced with the highest part of the tongue about the same height in the mouth. Similarly with *e* and *o* and with *æ* and *a*. Now, if you draw the vowel diagram again and try to plot these vowels as you pronounce them, you will get something like this:

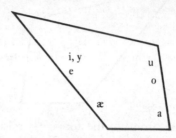

Since we can distinguish *i*, *u*, as high vowels and *æ*, *a*, as low vowels, we can now describe *i* as a high front vowel, *a* as a low back vowel, and so on.

§32 Of course, this is far from being a scientific description of the vowel sounds and you will need to consult a book on phonetics if you wish to learn more. Its incompleteness is illustrated by the fact that OE possesses another high front vowel *y* which (unlike the high front vowel *i*) has lip rounding. (If you try to pronounce the second vowel in 'machine' and to whistle at the same time, you will get a rather strained and tense *ȳ*.) But this outline will suffice for our present purposes.

Strong Nouns like *stān* (masc.) and *scip* (neut.)

§33 Here we can take the masc. and neut. nouns together and deal with the fem. separately; cf. §19. The basic paradigm is the masc. *stān*:

	Singular	*Plural*
Nom.	stān	stānas
Acc.	stān	stānas
Gen.	stānes	stāna
Dat.	stāne	stānum

Notes

1 nom. and acc. sg. the same;

2 nom. and acc. pl. the same – the characteristic strong masc. *-as* which gives the MnE 's' plural;

3 gen. pl. in *-a*;

4 dat. pl. in *-um*.

§34   In the neut. we find

	Singular	*Plural*	*Singular*	*Plural*
Nom.	scip	scipu	word	word
Acc.	scip	scipu	word	word
Gen.	scipes	scipa	wordes	worda
Dat.	scipe	scipum	worde	wordum

These differ from *stān* and from one another only in the nom. and acc. pl. where the short-stemmed *scip* has *scipu* while the long-stemmed *word* remains unchanged; for this absence of *-u*, cf. *ġiefu/lār* (§48) and *sunu/hand* (§61).

Ċild 'child' may follow *word* or may add *r* before the pl. endings – *ċildru, ċildra, ċildrum*; hence MnE 'children', with final *n* from the weak declension. *Ǣġ* 'egg' has nom. acc. pl. *ǣġru*.

§35   Many nouns are exactly like *stān* (e.g. *āþ* 'oath', *dōm* 'judgement', *wer* 'man'), like *scip* (e.g. *god* 'god', *hof* 'dwelling'), or like *word* (e.g. *hūs* 'house', *wīf* 'woman'). But some differ in that, while THEY HAVE PERFECTLY NORMAL ENDINGS like those of *stān*, *scip*, or *word*, THEY SHOW SOME ABNORMALITY IN THE STEM (see §26, note) as the result of certain 'sound-changes' or 'sound-laws'. These 'sound-laws' are not laws in the same sense as the law of gravity is one. People who jump off cliffs always have fallen and (as far as we know) will continue to fall, irrespective of what language they spoke or speak. But each language undergoes different changes at different periods. And the 'sound-laws' in which these changes are summed up are the result of observation by later scholars. Sometimes one of these 'laws' appears not to operate. This, however, is usually because something in a particular word or form prevented it. In such cases, another 'sound-law' was deduced to explain the exception. Thus the sound which was Gmc. *a* usually turns up in OE as *æ*. But in the nouns discussed in §36 we sometimes find *æ*, sometimes *a*. It was as a result of observing such differences that famous scholars first deduced the sound-changes. We can follow in their steps by examining the full paradigms of two nouns, noting the similarities and dissimilarities between them and regular nouns of the same declension, and so deducing the sound-changes necessary to explain the forms we have.

§36   These nouns are *dæġ* (masc.) 'day' and *fæt* (neut.) 'vessel':

	Singular	*Plural*	*Singular*	*Plural*
Nom.	dæġ	dagas	fæt	fatu
Acc.	dæġ	dagas	fæt	fatu
Gen.	dæġes	daga	fætes	fata
Dat.	dæġe	dagum	fæte	fatum

Observe:

1   that their endings are the same as in *stān* and *scip* respectively;
2   that they are short-stemmed monosyllables;

3 that the stem vowel of the nom. sg. is *æ*;

4 that both have *æ* throughout sg., *a* throughout pl.;

5 that where they have *a*, the ending is, or begins with, a back vowel;

6 that where they have *æ*, there is either no ending or an ending which is, or begins with, a front vowel.

Hence we can deduce that *æ* is found in a closed syllable (*dæġ*) or in an open syllable + a front vowel (*dæġes*), but appears as *a* in an open syllable + a back vowel (*dagas*). A simple rule is that these monosyllabic nouns have *æ* in the sg. stem, *a* in the pl. stem.

§37 Long-stemmed monosyllables ending in a vowel or diphthong + *h* take the endings of *stān* or *scip* but show absorption of *h* when it occurs between two vowels. Subsequently the unaccented vowel is also absorbed. Thus the gen. sg. of *scōh* (masc.) 'shoe' is **scōhes* > **scōes* > *scōs*. The paradigm is

Singular: *nom.* scōh, *acc.* scōh, *gen.* scōs, *dat.* scō
Plural: *nom.* scōs, *acc.* scōs, *gen.* scōna (§38), *dat.* scōm

§38 The same thing happens in short-stemmed monosyllables ending in a vowel or diphthong + *h*. But even without the *h* and the vowel, these words appear to have taken roughly the same time to pronounce. (A little experimenting will convince you that this is reasonable.) Hence the stressed vowel or diphthong is lengthened. So we get (these are the recorded forms)

eoh (masc.) 'horse', but gen. sg. *ēos*
feoh (neut.) 'money', but gen. sg. *fēos*, dat. sg. *fēo*

Theoretically, the gen. pl. of *feoh* should be **fēo* < **feoha*, but *fēona*, with the weak ending *-ena*, occurs – doubtless because *fēo* was ambiguous. So also *scōna* (§37).

§39 Loss of *h* with lengthening of the stem vowel or diphthong occurs between *r* or *l* and a vowel in monosyllabic nouns like *mearh* (masc.) 'horse' and *wealh* (masc.) 'foreigner'. The endings are those of *stān*.

	Singular	*Plural*	*Singular*	*Plural*
Nom.	mearh	mēaras	wealh	wēalas
Acc.	mearh	mēaras	wealh	wēalas
Gen.	mēares	mēara	wēales	wēala
Dat.	mēare	mēarum	wēale	wēalum

Note
Here the diphthong of the first syllable has been shown lengthened (as in *fēos*), so that the first syllable of *mēares* is the same length as *mearh*. But metrical and place-name evidence shows that forms with a short diphthong, e.g. *meares*, also occurred under the influence of the short sound in *mearh*; in these, the whole word is the metrical equivalent of *mearh*.

§40 The forms of *bearo*, *-u* (masc.) 'grove' and *searo*, *-u* (neut.) 'device' are

	Singular	*Plural*	*Singular*	*Plural*
Nom.	bearo	bearwas	searo	searo
Acc.	bearo	bearwas	searo	searo
Gen.	bearwes	bearwa	searwes	searwa
Dat.	bearwe	bearwum	searwe	searwum

Thus they add the endings of *stān* and *word* respectively to the stems which before vowels become *bearw-* and *searw-* respectively; cf. §71.

§41 We turn now to dissyllabic nouns which take the endings of *stān*, *scip*, or *word*.

Compounds like *ġewrit* 'writing' and *ġebed* 'prayer' (both neut.), where the stress falls on the second syllable, follow *scip*.

Dissyllabic nouns which are compounds of two nouns, or of an adjective or adverb and a noun, have the second element declined, but not the first, e.g. *hron-fisc* (masc.) 'whale', *hēah-clif* (neut.) 'high cliff', and *in-gang* (masc.) 'entrance'.

Other dissyllables with their stress on the first syllable may follow one of four patterns:

		Masc.	*Neut.*
(*a*)	⏑́ –	*cyning* 'king'	*færeld* (also masc.) 'journey'
(*b*)	–́ –	*Hengest* 'Hengest'	*īsern* 'iron'
(*c*)	–́ ⏑	*engel* 'angel'	*hēafod* 'head'
(*d*)	⏑́ ⏑	*metod* 'creator'	*werod* 'troop'

Types (*a*) and (*b*) are quite regular and follow *stān* or *word* without any variations of stem or ending.

§42 Type (*c*) – long-stemmed dissyllables – add the endings of *stān* or *scip*. But they lose the medial vowel when an ending is added:

	Singular	*Plural*	*Singular*	*Plural*
Nom.	engel	englas	hēafod	hēafdu
Acc.	engel	englas	hēafod	hēafdu
Gen.	engles	engla	hēafdes	hēafda
Dat.	engle	englum	hēafde	hēafdum

Note

This loss of the medial vowel occurs only when an inflexional ending beginning with a vowel is added or (to put it another way) when this medial vowel is in an open syllable. Thus *engel* and *hēafod* have dat. pl. *englum* (NOT **enge/lum* – medial *e* is in an open syllable) and *hēafdum* (NOT **hēafo/dum* – *o* is in an open syllable). Since all the endings of *stān* and *scip* begin with a vowel, the simple statement made above suffices here. But the qualification is important for adjectives; see §68.

§43   Nouns of type (*d*) – short-stemmed dissyllables – are

	Singular	Plural	Singular	Plural
Nom.	metod	metodas	werod	werod
Acc.	metod	metodas	werod	werod
Gen.	metodes	metoda	werodes	weroda
Dat.	metode	metodum	werode	werodum

The masc. nouns therefore follow *stān* exactly. The neut. nouns remain unchanged in the nom. and acc. pl.; in other words, they are like *word*, not *scip*.

§44   But, as Dr. Johnson wisely observed, 'it may be reasonably imagined that what is so much in the power of men as language will very often be capriciously conducted'. For analogy often interferes with the historically-correct forms given in §§42–43. A child learning to speak English today hears those around him forming past tenses of verbs by adding the sound *t*, e.g. 'baked', or *d*, e.g. 'sighed'. So quite naturally he says 'I maked a mud-pie today' or 'I buyed a hat in the shop today'. Thus the process of analogy can produce forms not accepted by most speakers of English today. But since we now have pretty strict notions of 'correctness', we tend to say to children 'No dear, I made a mud-pie' or 'I bought a hat', thereby helping to preserve the now-accepted form.

But many such variant forms are recorded in Old English texts. Alongside the regular nom. and acc. pls. *hēafdu* and *werod*, we find *hēafod*, *hēafodu*, and *weredu*.

Similarly, the process of analogy and earlier differences in some of the words themselves cause type (*d*) nouns ending in *l*, *r*, *m*, or *n*, to appear sometimes with no medial vowel in oblique cases. Thus *fugol* (masc.) 'bird' appears, like *engel*, without the medial vowel, and *wæter* may have gen. sg. *wæteres* or *wætres*, and nom. and acc. pl. *wæter*, *wætru*, or *wæteru*.

Hæleþ (masc.) 'man' and *mōnaþ* (masc.) 'month' may have nom. and acc. pl. the same or may add *-as*.

Masculine and Neuter Nouns in *-e*

§45   Masc. nouns in *-e* are always strong, for weak masc. nouns have nom. sg. in *-a*. Neut. nouns in *-e* can be strong or weak (see §24). Historically speaking, strong nouns in *-e* belong either to a sub-class of the *stān/scip* declension or to another declension. As a general rule, it is safe to say that they drop the *-e* of the nom. sg. and add the endings of *stān* or *scip* as appropriate. Examples are

1   masc.: *ende* 'end', *here* 'army', *wine* 'friend', *stede* 'place';
2   neut.: *wīte* 'punishment', *rīce* 'kingdom', *spere* 'spear'.

The long-stemmed neuters, being dissyllabic in nom. sg., remain dissyllabic in the nom. acc. pl. *wītu*, *rīcu*.

§46   Words like *wine* and *stede* may have nom. and acc. pl. *wine* and *stede*.
A few masc. nouns have only the *-e* form in the nom. and acc. pl.; they
include names of people, e.g. *Seaxe* 'Saxons' and *Dene* 'Danes', and the
common nouns *ielde* 'men' and *lēode* 'people'.

Other forms you need to be able to recognize in your reading are

1   nom. acc. pl. *rīċiu* alongside *rīċu* 'kingdoms';
2   forms with *-(i)ġ(e)-*, e.g. nom. acc. pl. *her(i)ġ(e)as* alongside *heras*
'armies'.

Strong Feminine Nouns

§47   The basic paradigm is *ġiefu* 'gift':

	Singular	Plural
Nom.	ġiefu	ġiefa, -e
Acc.	ġiefe	ġiefa, -e
Gen.	ġiefe	ġiefa, -ena
Dat.	ġiefe	ġiefum

Note the following endings:

1   *-e* in acc. gen. and dat. sg.;
2   alternative nom. acc. pls. *-a*, *-e*;
3   weak *-ena* in gen. pl. alongside *-a*;
4   dat. pl. in *-um*.

§48   The long-stemmed monosyllable *lār* 'teaching' is identical except
for nom. sg.; for absence of *-u* cf. *scipu/word* (§34) and *sunu/hand* (§61).

	Singular	Plural
Nom.	lār	lāra, -e
Acc.	lāre	lāra, -e
Gen.	lāre	lāra, -ena
Dat.	lāre	lārum

§49   Some fem. monosyllables with long front vowels, e.g. *cwēn* 'queen',
originally had nom. and acc. sg. the same and *-e* in nom. acc. pl. Later most
of them (by a perfectly natural confusion) sometimes followed *lār*. But it is
important to note that *brȳd* 'bride', *cwēn* 'queen', *dǣd* 'deed', etc. may be
acc. as well as nom. sg. in your texts, and that all the long-stemmed fem.
monosyllables may have *-a* or *-e* in nom. acc. pl.

§50   Long-stemmed dissyllables, e.g. *sāwol* 'soul' and *ċeaster* 'city', take
the endings of *lār*, but (like *engel* and *hēafod* in §42) lose the medial vowel in
trisyllabic forms.

§51   Some abstract nouns ending in *-þu* and *-u(-o)* can remain
unchanged in the oblique cases (i.e. any case other than the nom.), e.g.
iermþu 'poverty' and *ieldu* 'age'.

i-Mutation

§52　A sound-change which affects certain nouns and verbs must now be explained. The vowel *i* and the related consonant written in phonetic script [j] and pronounced as the first consonant in MnE 'yes' are high front sounds. When in OE one of these followed a stressed syllable, the vowel of that stressed syllable was subject to what is called '*i*-mutation'.[1] In simple terms, the organs of speech and the mind of the speaker got ready for the high front sound too soon and in the process

the low front vowels were dragged up or 'raised'

and the back vowels were pulled forward or 'fronted'.

The *i* or [j] is usually lost but may appear in OE as *e* or *i*.

§53　This change can be explained (unscientifically) in terms of the diagram in §31 as follows:

1　The low front vowels *æ* and *e* move up one place.

2　The back vowels *a* and *o* are pushed straight forward to the corresponding front position.

3　*u* keeps its lip-rounding and goes forward to the rounded *y* described in §32.

The sections which follow give a Table of Correspondences in which the unmutated vowel (as it appears in OE) is shown on the left, and the OE mutated equivalent on the right.

Table of Correspondences

§54　The low front vowels are raised; only the short ones are affected.

$$\breve{æ} \quad : \quad \breve{e}$$
$$\breve{e} \quad : \quad \breve{i}$$

Note

i is not affected because it cannot go any higher.

§55　The back vowels are fronted; both short and long are affected here.

$$\breve{a} \quad : \quad \breve{æ}$$
$$\breve{o} \quad : \quad \breve{e}$$
$$\breve{u} \quad : \quad \breve{y}^{2}$$

But　　　$\breve{a}$ + m, n　　:　　$\breve{e}$ + m, n

§56　The diphthongs *ea* and *eo* (short and long) are affected.

$$\breve{e}a \quad : \quad \breve{i}e$$
$$\breve{e}o \quad : \quad \breve{i}e$$

[1] Unstressed vowels are sometimes affected. But this need not concern us here.

[2] Both $\breve{o}$ and $\breve{u}$ were fully rounded – $\breve{o}$ to $\breve{æ}$ and $\breve{u}$ to $\breve{y}$. But $\breve{æ}$ was usually unrounded to $\breve{e}$.

§57 Thirteen sounds are therefore affected – 2 front vowels, 7 back vowels (including *ă* in two ways), and 4 diphthongs. You should cull your own examples. A very good way to find some is to look at the strong verbs and to compare the stem vowel of the infinitive with the stem vowel of the 2nd and 3rd pers. sg. pres. ind.; see §112.1 and Appendix A. In most of them you will find the non-mutated vowel in the infinitive and its mutated equivalent in the 2nd and 3rd pers. sg. pres. ind. The *i* which caused *i*-mutation in these two forms has either disappeared or become *e*. For further effects of *i*-mutation, see Appendix B, pp. 159–60 below.

Nouns affected by *i*-Mutation

§58 Typical paradigms for those masc. and fem. nouns affected by *i*-mutation are *mann* (masc.) 'man' and *bōc* (fem.) 'book':

	Singular	Plural	Singular	Plural
Nom.	mann	menn	bōc	bēċ
Acc.	mann	menn	bōc	bēċ
Gen.	mannes	manna	bēċ, bōce	bōca
Dat.	menn	mannum	bēċ	bōcum

Notes

1 nom. and acc. sg. the same;

2 gen. sg. masc. like *stān*;

3 gen. and dat. pl. regular;

4 the mutated equivalent of the vowel of the nom. sg. appears in the dat. sg. and nom. and acc. pl. (with no inflexional ending);

5 the gen. sg. with the mutated vowel in the fem. nouns. This should not cause difficulty because the gen. and dat. sg. fem. are usually the same. *Bōce* arises by analogy with *lāre*.

Most of the masc. examples can be recognized by thinking of the MnE plural of the corresponding word, e.g. 'foot' (*fōt*), 'man' (*mann*), 'tooth' (*tōþ*). Most of the fem. nouns have become regular in MnE, e.g. 'book' (*bōc*), 'oak' (*āc*), 'goat' (*gāt*), but a few survive, e.g. 'goose' (*gōs*), 'louse' (*lūs*), 'mouse' (*mūs*).

§59 The nouns *frēond* 'friend' and *fēond* 'enemy', which are formed from pres. ptcs. of verbs, can follow *stān* or can have *īe* in dat. sg. and nom. and acc. pl.; cf. *mann*.

§60 Nouns ending in *-r* which denote relationship are: *fæder* 'father' and *brōþor* 'brother' (both masc.), *mōdor* 'mother', *dohtor* 'daughter', and *sweostor* 'sister' (all fem.). It is difficult to systematize these nouns, for many analogical variations exist, but the following observations may help:

1 All are regular in the gen. and dat. pl., ending in *-a* and *-um* respectively and losing the medial vowel if long-stemmed (§42).

2　All can have the nominative singular form in all remaining cases except for

(*a*) *fæder* which takes *-as* in nom. acc. pl.;

(*b*) *brōþor*, *mōdor*, *dohtor*, which may show *i*-mutation in dat. sg., viz. *brēþer*, *mēder*, *dehter*. These forms may also occur in gen. sg., by analogy with fem. nouns such as *lār* (§48), in which gen. and dat. sg. are the same.

u-Nouns

§61　A few masc. and fem. nouns belong to the *u*-declension. They may be short-stemmed dissyllables with final *-u*, e.g. *sunu* (masc.) 'son' and *duru* (fem.) 'door', or long-stemmed monosyllables, e.g. *feld* (masc.) 'field' and *hand* (fem.) 'hand'; for the absence of *-u* in the latter cf. *scipu/word* and *ġiefu/lār*. Typical paradigms are *sunu* (masc.) and *hand* (fem.):

	Singular	*Plural*	*Singular*	*Plural*
Nom.	sunu	suna	hand	handa
Acc.	sunu	suna	hand	handa
Gen.	suna	suna	handa	handa
Dat.	suna	sunum	handa	handum

Notes

1　Nom. and acc. sg. are the same.

2　All other cases end in *-a* except of course the dat. pl. *-um*.

Other nouns which belong here are *wudu* 'wood', *ford* 'ford', and *weald* 'forest' – all masc.

§62　Masc. nouns like *feld* and fem. nouns like *duru/hand* are all to some extent influenced by *stān* and *ġiefu/lār* respectively and so hover uneasily between two declensions; hence gen. sg. *feldes* and the like. But the most important point to note here is that the ending *-a* is sometimes a dat. sg. in the texts, e.g. *felda*, *forda*, *wealda*.

III　ADJECTIVES

Introduction

§63　Most adjectives can be declined strong or weak. Important exceptions are *ōþer* and the poss. adjs. *mīn*, *þīn*, etc., which are declined strong, and comparatives, which end in *-a* in nom. sg. masc., e.g. *blindra* 'blinder', and are declined weak.

On participles, see §111.

§64 Which form of the adjective is used depends, not on the type of noun with which it is used, but on how it is used. The strong form is used when the adj. stands alone, e.g. 'The man is old' *se mann is eald*, or just with a noun, e.g. 'old men' *ealde menn*. The weak form appears when the adj. follows a dem., e.g. 'that old man' *se ealda mann*, or a poss. adj., e.g. 'my old friend' *mīn ealda frēond*. You can remember that the strong forms stand alone, while the weak forms need the support of a dem. or poss. pron.

Weak Declension

§65 The paradigm is *tila* 'good':

	Singular			Plural
	Masc.	*Neut.*	*Fem.*	*All genders*
Nom.	tila	tile	tile	tilan
Acc.	tilan	tile	tilan	tilan
Gen.	tilan	tilan	tilan	tilra, -ena
Dat.	tilan	tilan	tilan	tilum

The long-stemmed *gōda* 'good' is declined exactly the same. Here the endings are identical with those of the weak noun of the same gender with one addition – the strong form of gen. pl. *tilra* is generally preferred to *-ena*, except in eWS. The dat. pl. *-um* is frequently replaced by *-an* in WS texts and in lWS *-an* is found in the gen. pl. too. Stem changes in the weak declension of the adjectives follow the rules set out in §§68–73.

Strong Declension

§66 The paradigm is *til* 'good', which has a separate inst. form in the masc. and neut. sg.:

	Singular		
	Masc.	*Neut.*	*Fem.*
Nom.	til	til	tilu
Acc.	til*ne*	til	tile
Gen.	tiles	tiles	til*re*
Dat.	til*um*	til*um*	til*re*
Inst.	tile	tile	

	Plural		
	Masc.	*Neut.*	*Fem.*
Nom.	tile	tilu	tile, -a
Acc.	tile	tilu	tile, -a
Gen.	til*ra*	til*ra*	til*ra*
Dat.	tilum	tilum	tilum

Notes

1   Nom. and acc. pl. masc. end in -*e*, e.g. *cwice eorlas* 'living noblemen'; the ending
-*as* belongs to the nouns only.

2   All the other endings are familiar. Those italicized have already been met in
the pronouns (§§16–18). The remainder are endings found in *stān*, *scip*, and *giefu*,
respectively.

§67   The long-stemmed monosyllable *gōd* 'good' varies only in the nom.
sg. fem. *gōd* as against *tilu* (cf. *lār/giefu*) and in the nom. and acc. neut. pl. *gōd*
as against *tilu* (cf. *word/scipu*).

Stem Changes in Adjectives

§68   Long-stemmed dissyllables such as *hālig* add the weak or strong
endings given above as appropriate. The medial vowel is not lost before
endings beginning with a consonant, i.e. in closed syllables – hence *hālig̈/ne*,
hālig̈/re, *hālig̈/ra*.

When the ending begins with a vowel, the medial vowel sometimes disappears; cf. the nouns *engel* and *hēafod* (§42) and *sāwol* (§50). Thus *hālig* has
gen. sg. masc. strong *hālg̈es*. But analogical variations are common, and we
find *hāligan* alongside *hālgan*, *hālig̈es* alongside *hālg̈es*, and so on.

In the nom. sg. fem. and nom./acc. pl. neut. *hālig* (cf. *lār/word*), *hāligu* (cf.
giefu/scipu), and *hālgu* (with loss of vowel) are all found.

§69   Short-stemmed dissyllabic adjectives show forms with no medial
vowel more frequently than the corresponding nouns (§§43–44). Thus *micel*
'great' may have acc. sg. fem. *micele* or *micle*, while *monig̈* 'many' and *yfel* 'evil'
have dat. pl. *monigum* or *mongum* and gen. sg. masc. *yfeles* or *yfles*, respectively.

§70   Short-stemmed monosyllabic adjectives with the stem-vowel *æ*
follow *glæd* 'glad', here declined strong:

	Singular		
	Masc.	Neut.	Fem.
Nom.	glæd	glæd	gladu
Acc.	glædne	glæd	glade
Gen.	glades	glades	glædre
Dat.	gladum	gladum	glædre
Inst.	glade	glade	

	Plural		
	Masc.	Neut.	Fem.
Nom.	glade	gladu	glade
Acc.	glade	gladu	glade
Gen.	glædra	glædra	glædra
Dat.	gladum	gladum	gladum

Here *æ/a* fluctuation occurs. As in the nouns (§36), we find *æ* in a closed syllable, i.e. in the simple form *glæd* and when an ending beginning with a consonant is added, e.g. *glæd/ne*. In open syllables, however, the adjectives have *a* irrespective of whether a front or back vowel follows, e.g. *gla/des, gla/dum*. This is the result of analogy.

§71 Adjectives like *ġearo, -u* 'ready' take the endings of *gōd*. Hence in the strong declension, they remain unchanged in the nom. sg. all genders, acc. sg. neut., and nom. and acc. pl. Before consonants, the stem is *ġearo-* – hence *ġearone, ġearore, ġearora*, but before vowels it is *ġearw-* – hence *ġearwes, ġearwum*; cf. §40. Write out the paradigm. Then see A. Campbell *O.E. Grammar*, §649.

§72 Adjectives such as *hēah* 'high' and *fāh* 'hostile' usually lose their final *h* and contract where possible; cf. §§37 and 38. *Hēah* may have acc. sg. masc. strong *hēanne* or *hēane*.

§73 Adjectives in *-e*, e.g. *blīþe*, behave like the corresponding nouns (§45). Hence they drop the *-e* and add the endings of *til*.

Comparison of Adjectives

§74 Most adjectives add the endings *-ra, -ost* to the stem. Thus we find *lēof* 'dear', *lēofra* 'dearer', *lēofost* 'dearest'. Similarly *glæd* 'glad', *glædra* 'gladder', but *gladost* 'gladdest' (see §70). The comparative is declined weak, the superlative strong or weak (see §64).

§75 Some adjectives, however, add the endings *-ra, -est*, and show an *i*-mutated vowel in the stem, e.g.

eald 'old'	ieldra	ieldest
ġeong 'young'	ġingra	ġingest
lang 'long'	lengra	lengest
strang 'strong'	strengra	strengest
hēah 'high'	hīerra	hīehst

§76 Irregular are:

lȳtel 'little'	læssa	læst
miċel 'great'	māra	mæst
yfel 'bad'	wiersa	wierst
gōd 'good'	betera, sēlra	betst, sēlest

These, of course, can be compared with their MnE equivalents.

IV OBSERVATIONS ON NOUN, ADJECTIVE, AND PRONOUN DECLENSIONS

§77 The weak declension of nouns and adjectives, with *-an* throughout except in a few easily remembered places (see §§22–25), presents little difficulty. The weak masc. noun can always be recognized by -*a* in nom. sg. However, -*e* of the weak fem. and neut. is also found in strong masc. and neut. nouns. But a noun with final -*e* in nom. sg. cannot be strong fem.

§78   Nouns with their nom. sg. ending in a consonant are strong, but can be any gender. See again §13.

§79   In the strong nouns and the strong declension of the adj., the characteristic endings should be noted. The gen. pl. of the noun is -*a*, of the adj. -*ra*. But the weak ending -*ena* is found in nouns like *feoh/fēona* and *ġiefu/ ġiefa* or *ġiefena*, and in the adj. The endings -*ne* (acc. sg. masc.) and -*re* (gen. and dat. sg. fem.) are found in adjs. (strong forms) and prons.

§80   Certain similarities may be noted in the declension of strong nouns, the strong form of the adj., and the dem. and pers. prons. (less 1st and 2nd pers.; on these, see §21). These are

1   neut. sg. nom. and acc. are always the same;
2   nom. and acc. sg. of masc. NOUNS are always the same;
3   nom. and acc. pl. are always the same;
4   gen. and dat. fem. sg. are always the same (with the reservations made in §§58 and 60);
5   within the same declension
   (*a*) masc. and neut. gen. sg. are the same;
   (*b*) masc. and neut. dat. sg. are the same;
   (*c*) masc. and neut. inst. sg. are the same.

§81   A possible source of confusion is the fact that in prons. and adjs., the acc. fem. sg. is the same as nom. and acc. pl., e.g. *þā/þā, þās/þās, hīe/hīe, cwice/ cwice*. This last form *cwice* is properly the masc. pl. But in later texts, it is often used for all genders.

V   NUMERALS

§82   The numerals from 1 to 10 are

	Cardinal	Ordinal
1	ān	forma
2	twēġen	ōþer
3	þrīe	þridda
4	fēower	fēorþa
5	fīf	fīfta
6	siex	siexta
7	seofon	seofoþa
8	eahta	eahtoþa
9	nigon	nigoþa
10	tīen	tēoþa

§83 When declined strong, *ān* means 'one'; when declined weak *āna*, it usually means 'alone'.

Ordinals are declined weak, except *ōþer* which is always strong.

§84 *Twēġen* 'two' and *bēġen* 'both' are declined alike. In the nom. and acc. they have

Masc.		*Neut.*		*Fem.*	
twēġen		twā, tū		twā	
bēġen		bā, bū		bā	

The gen. and dat. are the same for all genders:

twēġra, twēġ(e)a; bēġra, bēġ(e)a
twǣm; bǣm

§85 In the nom. and acc. of *þrīe* 'three' we find

Masc.	þrīe	*Neut.*	þrēo	*Fem.*	þrēo

The gen. and dat. are *þrēora, þrim*.

§86 A knowledge of the remaining numerals is not essential at first. The meaning of many is obvious, e.g. *twēntiġ, þrītiġ, fēowertiġ, fiftiġ*, and those which occur in your texts will be glossed. Full lists will be found in any of the standard grammars. Roman numerals are often used.

VI STRONG VERBS AND SOUND-CHANGES RELEVANT TO THEM

Introduction

§87 Like MnE, OE has two types of verbs – weak and strong. The weak verb forms its preterite and past participle by adding a dental suffix, the strong verb by changing its stem vowel; cf. MnE 'laugh, laughed' and 'judge, judged' with MnE 'sing, sang, sung'. The strong verbs are nearly all survivals from OE; new verbs when made up or borrowed today join the weak conjugation. Thus the strong verb 'drive, drove, driven' survives from OE. When in the thirteenth century 'strive' was borrowed from the French, it followed the pattern of 'drive' because the two infinitives rhymed; hence we get MnE 'strive, strove, striven'. But we conjugate the comparatively new verb 'jive', not 'jive, jove, jiven', but 'jive, jived', i.e. as a weak verb.

§88 Such patterns as 'drive, drove, driven' and 'jive, jived' are called the 'principal parts' of the verbs. It is essential for you to know the principal parts of the Old English verbs. This is important because, if you do not know the patterns which the various verbs display in their principal parts, you will be unable to find out their meaning. You will be in the same position as a foreign student of English looking up 'drove (verb)' in his dictionary. For he can only find out what it means by knowing that it is the preterite of 'drive'.

§89   Both weak and strong verbs in OE distinguish

1   two tenses – present and preterite;

2   indicative, subjunctive, and imperative, moods, in addition to two infinitives – one without *to*, and one (the inflected infinitive) with *to* – and two participles, the present and the past (or second);

3   two numbers – singular and plural. The dual is found only in the 1st and 2nd person pronouns and is used with plural verb forms;

4   three persons, but only in the singular of the present and preterite indicative. All plurals and the singular of the subjunctives are the same throughout;

5   one voice only – the active. One true passive form survives from an earlier stage of the language, viz. *hātte* 'is called, was called'.

On the syntax of these forms and on the beginnings of new methods of expressing verbal relationships, see §§195 ff.

Principal Parts of the Strong Verbs

§90   These verbs show a change of vowel in the stressed syllable in the principal parts. This is known as 'gradation' and the vowels which change – e.g. *ī, ō, i* in 'drive, drove, driven' – are known as the 'gradation' series. The origin of these is to be found in the shifting stress of the original IE language (which later became fixed, usually on the first syllable, in OE). We can see how the pronunciation of a vowel can change according to the amount of stress the syllable carries if we compare the pronunciation of the following three versions of the same MnE sentence:

> Cán he do it?
> Can hé do it?
> Can he dó it?

In the first, the vowel of 'can' has its full value; in the second, a reduced value; and in the third, it has almost disappeared and has what is sometimes called 'zero' value. Such variations in IE may well have been perpetuated when the stress became fixed.

§91   No MnE strong verb has more than three vowels in its gradation series; some, e.g. 'bind, bound, bound', have only two. But in OE, four parts of the verb may be distinguished by different vowels – the infinitive, two preterites, and the past participle, e.g. *crēopan* 'creep', *crēap, crupon, cropen*. But (for various reasons) the same vowel may occur more than once in the same verb. So we find, with three different vowels, *bindan* 'bind', *band, bundon, bunden*, and, with two only, *faran* 'go', *fōr, fōron, faren*.

§92   Many primers show five vowels for the strong verbs, viz. inf. (*crēopan*), 3rd sg. pres. ind. (*crīepþ*), pret. sg. or 1st pret. (*crēap*), pret. pl. or 2nd pret. (*crupon*), past ptc. (*cropen*). The 3rd sg. pres. ind. is not part of the gradation series; its stem vowel is the *i*-mutated equivalent of the vowel of the inf. and can be deduced from that vowel; see §57. So, when we learn a strong verb, we need to remember four vowels – those of the inf., two preterites, and the past ptc. There are in OE seven different 'classes' of verbs, each with a different gradation series. Each type can be recognized by its 'uniform' in the same way as football teams can be distinguished one from the other. So, in addition to the vowels, we need to know the 'uniform' or recognition symbol which will enable us to tell the class to which a verb belongs.

§93   Verbs characteristic of these classes are

Class	Inf.	1st Pret.	2nd Pret.	Past Ptc.
I	scīnan 'shine'	scān	scinon	scinen
II	crēopan 'creep'	crēap	crupon	cropen
	brūcan 'enjoy'	brēac	brucon	brocen
III	breġdan 'pull'	bræġd	brugdon	brogden
IV	beran 'bear'	bær	bǣron	boren
V	tredan 'tread'	træd	trǣdon	treden
VI	faran 'go'	fōr	fōron	faren
VII	(*a*) healdan 'hold'	hēold	hēoldon	healden
	(*b*) hātan 'command'	hēt	hēton	hāten

Roman numerals are here used for the classes of strong verbs, arabic numerals for those of the weak verbs. Thus *scīnan* I 'shine' and *lufian* 2 'love' tell us both the type and class of verb. Class VII verbs are sometimes called 'reduplicating' (abbreviation 'rd.').

§94   From a study of these and the lists of strong verbs set out in Appendix A, the following gradation series will emerge:

Class	Recognition Symbol	Inf.	1st Pret.	2nd Pret.	Past Ptc.
I	*ī* + one cons.	ī	ā	i	i
II	*ēo* + one cons. *ū* + one cons.	ēo ū	ēa	u	o
III	See §102				
IV	*e* + one cons.[1]	e	æ	ǣ	o
V	*e* + one cons.[2]	e	æ	ǣ	e
VI	*a* + one cons.[3]	a	ō	ō	a
VII	See §104				

§95   The gradation series of verbs in classes I and II are quite regular. Class III presents special difficulties because the stem vowels of most verbs are affected by one of several sound laws. For purposes of explanation, we

---

[1] Usually a liquid (*l, r*). But note *brecan* 'break'. On the verbs with nasals, see §103.2.
[2] Usually a stop (*p, t, c, d, g*) or spirant (*f, þ, s*).
[3] *Standan* 'stand', with *-n-* in inf. and past ptc., belongs here.

can take the verb *breġdan* 'pull' as the basic paradigm in terms of which all the other verbs can be explained. *Breġdan* shows the following pattern:

III	*e* + TWO CONS.	e	æ	u	o

A few other verbs, e.g. *streġdan* 'strew', *berstan* 'burst', *þerscan* 'thresh',[1] show the same vowel pattern. But the remainder fall into four groups which are represented by the verbs *weorpan* 'throw'/*feohtan* 'fight', *helpan* 'help', *ġieldan* 'pay', and *drincan* 'drink'. To understand the variations in these verbs, we have to know something about certain sound-changes.

Breaking

§96 The first of these is the diphthongization of a front vowel when it is followed by a consonant or group of consonants produced in the back of the mouth. When moving from a front vowel to a back consonant, the organs of speech do NOT perform the equivalent of the quick march, in which one foot is lifted cleanly from the ground and put down again 30 inches or so further on. They glide more or less smoothly from one position to another, as your feet do when you are dancing a waltz. You can see the result of this process in an exaggerated form if you imagine that you have fallen overboard from a ship and are calling out 'Help'. If you call out loudly and long (you had better do this in a desert place!), you will find that the vowel of the word 'Help' is 'broken' as you glide from the front position of *e* to the back position of *lþ*. If you spell it as you are pronouncing it, you will write something like 'Heulp'. Try the same experiment with words like 'bell', 'fell', 'tell'. You will probably find that a 'glide' develops between the short front vowel *e* and the following *l*. A similar process took place in OE. It is called 'breaking'.

§97 For our purposes, its most important effects are

1 before *h, h* + cons., *r* + cons.[2]

ă > ĕa
ĕ > ĕo

In terms of the diagram in §31, the organs of speech glide back to the back vowel nearest in height to the front vowel from which they started. (See §8, where we assume that the symbol *ea* is pronounced *æa*.)

2 before *l* (here made in the back of the throat) + cons.

ă > ĕa

But ĕ is not usually affected before *l*. We can call this 'limited breaking'; it occurs before *l*, with which the word 'limited' begins!

---

[1] *Berstan* and *þerscan* were originally *brestan and *þrescan, with two medial consonants. But the *r* 'changed places'. This change, known as 'metathesis', is not uncommon; cf. OE *brid* with MnE 'bird'.

[2] Here *r* was probably made with the tip of the tongue curved back.

Note

ĕ does break before *lh*. See §133.2 for an example.

3   before *h* and *h* + cons.

ī > īo > very often ēo

§98   We can now return to the verbs of class III where the basic gradation series is *e, æ, u, o* (§95). If we examine *weorpan* and *feohtan*, we find

weorpan	wearp	wurpon	worpen
feohtan	feaht	fuhton	fohten

Here the medial cons. groups *-rp-* and *-ht-* cause *e* and *æ* to break but do not affect the back vowels *u* and *o*. Hence we get as the gradation series, NOT *e, æ, u, o*, but *eo, ea, u, o*.

§99   In *helpan*, however, the medial group *-lp-* produces only limited breaking and so we get

helpan	healp	hulpon	holpen

where only the 1st pret. *ea* differs from the basic series of *bregdan*, the *e* of the infinitive remaining unchanged.

Influence of Initial *ġ, sc, ċ*

§100   The results of the next sound-change to affect the verbs of class III are seen most commonly in the WS dialect, with which we are mainly concerned. Here the initial palatal consonants *ġ, sc,* and *ċ,* caused the following front vowels *ē* and *æ* to become *ĭe* and *ĕa* respectively. The effect may be produced by an emphatic pronunciation of these consonants, which will produce a glide between the consonant and vowel. A modern parallel may be found in the prolonged 'Yes' in the sentence 'Well, yes, I suppose so' used when one gives hesitating assent or grudging permission; we might spell our pronunciation something like 'Yies'. This change is sometimes called 'palatal diphthongization' (p.d. for short). It is because of it that we find the inf. *ġieldan*. For further examples, see §103.1.

Note

The pret. *ġeald* could be the result of breaking or of p.d. But such forms as *ċeorfan*, which show *eo < e* as the result of breaking, suggest that breaking took place before p.d.; if it had not, we should have had **ċierfan* by p.d. P.d. can take place in such forms as *ġieldan* because *e* did not break before *-ld-* and hence remained until p.d. took place.

Influence of Nasals

§101   The last sound-change which affects verbs of class III is found in verbs in which the first of the two medial consonants is a nasal *m* or *n*. In these circumstances, *i* appears instead of *e*, *a* instead of *æ*, and *u* instead of *o*. So we get

drincan   dranc   druncon   druncen

with *i, a* (sometimes *o*; see §103.2), *u, u* instead of *e, æ, u, o*.

Summary of the Strong Verbs of Class III

§102   The following table summarizes class III verbs. Each of series (*b*)–(*e*) is to be explained by the appropriate sound-change operating on series (*a*). See also §§116 and 133.5.

Sound-Change	*Symbol*	*Example*	*Gradation Series*			
(*a*)						
Basic Series	*e* + 2 cons.	*breġdan*	e	æ	u	o
(*b*)						
Breaking before						
r + cons.	*eo* + *r* + cons.	*weorpan*				
h + cons.	*eo* + *h* + cons.	*feohtan*	eo	ea	u	o
(*c*)						
Limited breaking before						
l + cons.	*e* + *l* + cons.	*helpan*	e	ea	u	o
(*d*)						
Palatal diphthongization	palatal + *ie* + 2 cons.	*ġieldan*	ie	ea	u	o
(*e*)						
Nasal	*i* + nasal + cons.	*drincan*	i	a	u	u

The Effects of Sound-Changes on other Strong Verbs

§103   Some of these sound-changes affect verbs of other classes.

   1   P.d. is seen in:
      Class IV *scieran* 'cut', which has *ie, ea, ēa, o* instead of *e, æ, ǣ, o*;
      Class V *ġiefan* 'give' with *ie, ea ēa, ie*, instead of *e, æ, ǣ, e*,
and in the class VI infinitive *scieppan* 'create'.
   2   Nasals influence class IV *niman* 'take' with *i, a/o, ā/ō* (fluctuation

between *a* and *o* is not uncommon before nasals) and *u* instead of *e, æ, ǣ, o*. On *niman* and *cuman* 'come' see also §109.

3   Breaking before *h* with subsequent loss of *h* between a diphthong and a vowel (see §§37–38) affects the infinitives of the contracted verbs of classes I, V, and VI. The stages can be set out thus:

    I   *wrīhan > *wrēohan > wrēon 'cover'
    V   *sehan   > *seohan   > sēon 'see'
    VI *slahan > *slæhan[1] > *sleahan > slēan 'strike'

4   The infinitives of contracted verbs of class II are affected by loss of *h* only, e.g.

    *tēohan > tēon 'draw'

5   The contracted verbs of class VII – *fōn* 'take' and *hōn* 'hang' – have a complicated phonology; detailed explanation would be out of place here. But see §108.

6   On the principal parts of contracted verbs, see §§107–108. On 3rd sg. pres. ind. of contracted verbs, see §114. On the 'weak presents' of classes V–VII, see §116.

Strong Verbs of Class VII

§104   Strong verbs of class VII show the following characteristics:

1   the same stem vowel in inf. and past ptc. (except *wēpan*);
2   the same stem vowel in 1st and 2nd pret. – either *ēo* or *ē*. On this basis the two sub-classes (*a*) and (*b*) are distinguished.

Important verbs here are: *cnāwan* 'know', *feallan* 'fall', *weaxan* 'grow' (all VII(*a*)), and *drǣdan* 'fear' and *lǣtan* 'let' (both VII(*b*)). It is worth noting that none of them can be mistaken for strong verbs of any other class, for the stem vowels of the inf. are different. But see further §§131–134.

Grimm's Law and Verner's Law

§105   Certain consonant changes which distinguish the Gmc. languages from the other IE languages were first formulated by the German philologist Grimm (of the Fairy Tales) and hence are known as Grimm's Law. But the fact that the expected consonant did not always appear in the Gmc. languages puzzled philologists until the Danish grammarian Karl Verner explained that the differences depended on the position of the stress in the original IE form of the word.

§106   Grimm's Law accounts (*inter alia*) for the variations between Latin (which in the examples cited keeps the IE consonant) and OE seen in such pairs as

---

[1] This variation must be taken on trust. (Those interested can compare §§35–36.)

Lat.	*piscis*	OE	*fisc*	(*p/f*)
Lat.	*frater*	OE	*brōþor*	(*t/þ*)
Lat.	*genus*	OE	*cynn*	(*g/c*)
Lat.	*dentem*	OE	*tōþ*	(*d/t*)

But, if *fisc* corresponds to *piscis* and *brōþor* to *frāter*, we should expect **fæþer* alongside *pǎter*. But we have *fæder*. Verner explained exceptions like this.

We can see the sort of thing which happened if we compare MnE 'éxcellent' and 'ábsolute' on the one hand with MnE 'exám.' and 'absólve' on the other. In the first pair, the stress falls on the first syllable and the consonants which follow are voiceless; we could spell the words 'eks-' and 'aps-'. In the second pair, the stress is on the second syllable, the consonants are voiced, and the words could be spelt 'egz-' and 'abz-'. Similar variations, said Verner, arose in Pr. Gmc. because of similar differences. Greek φράτηρ = Latin *frāter* was stressed on the first syllable. Hence in its Pr. Gmc. equivalent the medial *t* developed regularly by Grimm's Law to voiceless *þ* (cf. MnE 'cloth') in Pr. OE.[1] But Greek πατήρ = Latin *pǎter* was stressed on the second syllable. So in Pr. Gmc. the voiceless *þ* which arose from the *t* by Grimm's Law was voiced to the sound in MnE 'clothe'. This voiced sound subsequently became *d*.

§107 Many standard histories of the English language explain these two Laws in detail; for us their most important effect is seen in the OE strong verbs, where Verner's Law accounts for certain variations in the medial consonant. Thus in class I we find

snīþan snāþ snidon sniden

Here the *þ* of the inf. and 1st pret. is the consonant we should expect by Grimm's Law. The *d* of the 2nd pret. and past ptc. is the Verner's Law form. Similarly we find

II ċēosan ċēas curon coren

and in contracted verbs (which originally had *h* in the inf.; see §§103.3 and 103.4)

I wrēon wrāh wrigon wrigen
V sēon seah sāwon sewen

In these strong verbs, the Verner's Law forms occur in the 2nd pret. and the past ptc., while the inf. and 1st pret. are regular. This is historically 'correct'; we see from the verbs marked † in Appendix A that by Verner's Law TH in the inf. and 1st pret. is LIKELY to be replaced by D in the 2nd pret. and past ptc., S by R, and (mostly in contracted verbs) H by G, W, or (in *hōn* and *fōn*: see below) by NG.[2]

---

[1] Its voicing (§9) comes later; see A. Campbell *Old English Grammar*, §444.

[2] Verner's Law forms are also seen in such related pairs as *ċēosan* 'choose'/*cyre* 'choice' and *rīsan* 'rise'/*ræran* 'raise'. See §136.

§108   The word 'LIKELY' is emphasized because the Verner's Law forms sometimes occur where historically they should not. Thus the principal parts of the contracted verbs of class VII are

hōn	hēng	hēngon	hangen
fōn	fēng	fēngon	fangen

Here the Verner's Law *ng* is extended into the 1st pret.; the same may be true of the *g* in

VI	slēan	slōg	slōgon	slæǧen[1]

Sometimes, on the other hand, the Verner's Law forms are completely eliminated, as in *mīþan* I 'conceal' and *rīsan* I 'rise'; this has happened to all Verner's Law forms in MnE except 'was/were'. This process of systematizing or regularizing by the elimination of odd forms is sometimes called 'levelling'. But, as we see from verbs like *scrīþan*, with past ptc. *scriden* or *scripen*, its results are often capricious because it is not conducted consciously and logically.

§109   These and other levellings which occur in OE can be seen as the first signs of two great changes which overtook the strong verbs as English developed through the centuries. First, we today distinguish fewer classes of strong verbs. For example, the verbs of class V have gone over to class IV. Thus, while OE *specan, tredan, wefan*, have *e* in their past ptcs., MnE 'speak', 'tread', 'weave', have *o*; cf. *beran* IV. Second, while in OE the stem vowels of the 1st and 2nd prets. are different except in classes VI and VII, they are today the same (again except in 'was/were'). The beginnings of this process are seen in *cuman* IV 'come' and *etan* V 'eat', where the vowel of the 2nd pret. is found in the 1st pret. too. The marked confusion of forms in *niman* IV 'take' also results from this levelling. Perhaps you can work out for yourself why *findan* has a 1st pret. *funde*.

Conjugation of the Strong Verb

§110   Our wanderings through what have been called 'the dusty deserts of barren philology' lead us now to the conjugation of the strong verb, here exemplified by *singan* III. Points which must be carefully noted when conjugating these and all strong verbs are set out below; on the uses of the tenses and moods, see §§195–198 and 173–179.

§111   *Singan* 'sing' is conjugated

		Present Indicative	*Preterite Indicative*
Sg.	1	singe	sang
	2	singest	sunge
	3	singeþ	sang
Pl.		singaþ	sungon

[1] But *slōh* does occur, and ME forms suggest that the *g* in *slōg* may be merely a spelling variant of *h*.

	Present Subjunctive	Preterite Subjunctive
Sg.	singe	sunge
Pl.	singen	sungen

Before a 1st or 2nd pers. pron., the plural endings can be reduced to -*e*, e.g. *wē singaþ* but *singe wē*.

Imp. Sg.	sing	*Pl.*	singaþ
Inf.	singan	*Infl. Inf.*	tō singenne
Pres. Ptc.	singende	*Past Ptc.*	(ġe-)sungen

Participles may be declined like adjectives. Strong and weak forms occur, as appropriate.

§112   In the present tense, note:

1   The stem vowel of the inf. appears throughout except in 2nd and 3rd pers. sg. pres. ind., where its *i*-mutated equivalent is found if there is one. Hence *sing(e)st, sing(e)þ* but (< *bēodan*) *bīetst, bīett*.

2   The common WS reduction in these forms whereby the *e* of the endings -*est* and -*eþ* disappears. If this leaves a combination which is difficult to pronounce, it is simplified. So from *bīdan* 'wait for', we get *bīdeþ* > **bīdþ* > **bītþ* > *bītt*. (Try this simple phonetic process for yourself.) Similarly, *bīteþ* from *bītan* 'bite' is also reduced to *bītt*. Hence theoretically *se mann bītt þæt wīf* could mean 'the man is waiting for the woman' or 'the man is biting the woman'.[1] But, in the absence of newspaper reporters in Anglo-Saxon times, this ambiguity does not cause practical difficulty. The most important consequences for you are that 2nd pers. sg. pres. ind. ending in -*tst* and 3rd pers. sg. pres. ind. ending in -*tt* may be from verbs with -*tan* (e.g. *bītan*), -*dan* (e.g. *bīdan*), or -*ddan* (e.g. *biddan*). Since -*sest* and -*seþ* both become -*st, cīest* may be either 2nd or 3rd pers.[2]

3   The endings of the imp. – sg. NIL, pl. -*aþ*.

4   The imp. pl. is the same as the pres. ind. pl.

5   The subj. endings sg. -*e* and pl. -*en*, which also occur in the pret.

6   The pres. subj. sg. is the same as the 1st pers. sg. pres. ind.

§113   In the preterite tense, note:

1   The so-called pret. sg. occurs in TWO PLACES ONLY – 1st and 3rd sg. pret. ind. Hence it is better called the 1st pret.

2   The vowel of pret. pl. (better called the 2nd pret.) is found in all other places in the pret. Hence *þu sunge* may be either pret. ind. or pret. subj.

3   In actual practice, a similar ambiguity exists throughout the pret. pl. Many primers and grammars show -*on* as the ind. ending and -*en* as the subj. ending. But (generally speaking) this distinction does not hold in the manuscripts. This is because the process which led to the reduction of all

---

[1] *Bīdan* 'wait for' can take gen. or acc.   [2] See further, Appendix A.

the inflexional endings to -*e*, -*es*, -*en*, and so on, in ME had already begun in OE. MnE, with its fixed spelling system, still spells differently the second syllables of 'pukka', 'beggar', 'baker', 'actor', and (in some places) 'honour', all of which are pronounced the same by many speakers in Great Britain, and by some in other countries. But in OE the spelling system tended to be more phonetic and we often find scribes writing down in the manuscripts forms which represent the pronunciation they actually used and not the forms which are shown in the grammars. As a result, you may find in your reading pret. pl. forms ending, not only in -*on* and -*en*, but also in -*æn*, -*an*, and -*un*. Any of these may be ind. or subj. Hence the only places in the pret. of the strong verbs where ind. and subj. are clearly distinguished are the two places where the ind. has the 1st pret. form; see 1 above.

4   The variations in the medial cons. caused by Verner's Law; see §§107–108.

§114   Two groups of strong verbs present special difficulties in the present tense. The first – those in classes V and VI with weak presents – are discussed in §116. The others are the contracted verbs, exemplified here by *sēon* V 'see'. Only the present tense is given, for in the pret. it follows the rules given above.

		Present Indicative			*Present Subjunctive*
Sg.	1	sēo			sēo
	2	si(e)hst			sēo
	3	si(e)hþ			sēo
Pl.		sēoþ			sēon
Imp. Sg.		seoh	*Pl.*		sēoþ
Inf.		sēon	*Infl. Inf.*		tō sēonne
Pres. Ptc.		sēonde			

Note
We have already seen in §103.3 that *sēon* is a form produced by breaking and loss of *h*. The whole of the pres. tense except 2nd and 3rd sg. pres. ind. (forms which always require special attention in both strong and weak verbs) is affected by these two sound-changes, e.g.
1st sg. pres. ind. **iċ sehe* > **iċ seohe* > **iċ sēoe* > *iċ sēo*
and so on for the other forms. But the 2nd and 3rd sg. pres. ind. are different. The vowel changes are the result of *i*-mutation; see §112.1. But *h* occurs in these forms because the *e* of the ending disappeared (see §112.2) before the *h* could be lost between vowels. Because the *h* did not disappear, the vowels remained short; cf. the imp. sg. *seoh*.

You may care to note that the pres. subj. sg. is the same as the 1st pers. sg. pres. ind. (*sēo*) and that the subj. pl. and the inf. are the same (*sēon*). This is true of all contracted verbs.

VII WEAK VERBS AND SOUND-CHANGES RELEVANT TO THEM

Introduction

§115 There are three classes of weak verbs in OE. As in MnE, these verbs form their pret. and their past ptc. by the addition of a dental suffix. Normally the stem vowel is the same throughout; for exceptions, see §§122–123 and 126. As will become apparent, the inflexional endings of the strong and weak verbs have much in common.

Class 1

§116 Class 1 of the weak verbs is divided into two sub-classes:

(*a*) exemplified by *fremman* 'do' and *nerian* 'save';
(*b*) exemplified by *hīeran* 'hear'.

Present Indicative

	(*a*)	(*a*)	(*b*)
Sg. 1	fremme	nerie	hīere
2	fremest	nerest	hīerst
3	fremeþ	nereþ	hīerþ
Pl.	fremmaþ	neriaþ	hīeraþ

Imperative

	(*a*)	(*a*)	(*b*)
Sg.	freme	nere	hīer
Pl.	fremmaþ	neriaþ	hīeraþ

Present Subjunctive

	(*a*)	(*a*)	(*b*)
Sg.	fremme	nerie	hīere
Pl.	fremmen	nerien	hīeren

Preterite Indicative

	(*a*)	(*a*)	(*b*)
Sg. 1	fremede	nerede	hīerde
2	fremedest	neredest	hīerdest
3	fremede	nerede	hīerde
Pl.	fremedon	neredon	hīerdon

Preterite Subjunctive

	(*a*)	(*a*)	(*b*)
Sg.	fremede	nerede	hīerde
Pl.	fremeden	nereden	hīerden
Inf.	fremman	nerian	hīeran
Infl. Inf.	tō fremmenne	tō nerienne	tō hīerenne
Pres. Ptc.	fremmende	neriende	hīerende
Past Ptc.	(ġe-)fremed	(ġe-)nered	(ġe-)hīered

Participles may be declined like adjectives.

Like *fremman* are most verbs with short vowel + a double consonant, e.g. *cnyssan* 'knock'. The strong verbs of classes V and VI such as *biddan* 'pray' and *hebban* 'lift' are like *fremman* THROUGHOUT THE PRESENT.[1]

Like *nerian* are nearly all verbs ending in *-rian* (for exceptions, see §132.1). The class VI strong verb *swerian* is like *nerian* THROUGHOUT THE PRESENT.

Like *hieran* are verbs with a long vowel + a single consonant, e.g. *dēman* 'judge', and verbs with a short vowel + two consonants not the same, e.g. *sendan* 'send'. A few verbs of the same pattern as *fremman*, but with a different history, also belong here; they include *fyllan* 'fill'. The strong verb *wēpan* (class VII(*a*)) is like *hieran* THROUGHOUT THE PRESENT. Its past ptc. is *wōpen*.

As is shown in §117, all the verbs of this class have an *i*-mutated vowel throughout the stem except those discussed in §§122–123.

§117 A glance at the conjugation of these three verbs will show that *fremman* sometimes loses an *m*, *nerian* its *i*, and that (compared with *fremman* and *nerian*) *hieran* sometimes loses an *e* in the inflexional endings. These 'losses' (an unhistorical name, as we shall see below) occur in the following places:

1 2nd and 3rd sg. pres. ind.;
2 imp. sg.;
3 throughout the pret. The pret. stems of these three verbs are respectively *fremed-* (with one *m*), *nered-* (with no *i*), and *hierd-* (with no *e*);
4 in the past ptc., except that *hieran* usually has *hiered*.

Note
These variations can be explained briefly as follows. The infinitive of *fremman* was once **framjan*.[2] The *j* – a high front sound – operated like *i* and caused *i*-mutation of *a*, which before *m* became *e*. But *j* had another property denied to *i*; in short-stemmed words it caused lengthening or doubling of any cons. (except *r*) which preceded it, and then disappeared. So **framjan* > *fremman*. In **nærjan* the *j* merely caused *i*-mutation and remained as *i*; hence *nerian*.

But in the places where *fremman* 'loses' an *m*, the inflexional ending originally began with *i*. So e.g., the 3rd sg. pres. ind. of **framjan* was **framjiþ*. Here the *j* was absorbed into the *i* before it could cause doubling; so we get **framiþ*. The *i* caused *i*-mutation and then became *e*, giving *fremeþ*. Similarly **nærjiþ* > **næriþ* > *nereþ*. Similarly, absence of *j* in the pret. gave *fremede* and *nerede*. In *hieran* and the other verbs of sub-class (*b*), the details and the results are different, and can be taken on trust for the time being.

[1] The only verbs with double medial cons. which are strong throughout belong to class III (e.g. *swimman, winnan*) and to class VII (e.g. *bannan, feallan*). Verbs whose infinitives rhyme with any of these four are always strong. See further §133.5.
[2] *j* here and elsewhere is the sound written [j] in phonetic script and pronounced something like MnE *y* in 'year'. It is a high front sound which can be made by saying *i* and then closing the gap between the tongue and the hard palate.

§118 Once these variations are understood, we can observe certain similarities in the inflexional endings of the weak verbs of class 1 and those of the strong verbs. These are

1   The pres. ind. endings of the weak verbs are the same as the endings of the strong verbs. The *-est* and *-eþ* of the 2nd and 3rd sg. pres. ind. are subject to the same reductions as occurred in these forms in the strong verbs (§112.2). However, the weak verbs generally show more unreduced forms than the strong verbs.

2   The pres. and pret. subj. endings are the same in both weak and strong verbs.

3   The pres. subj. sg. is the same as the 1st pers. sg. pres. ind.

4   The endings of the pret. pl. ind. are the same.

5   The endings of the imp. pl., the pres. ptc., and the infs. respectively are the same.

6   The imp. pl. is the same as the pres. ind. pl.

§119 Important differences are seen in

1   the imp. sgs. *freme* and *nere*, where the strong verbs have no final *-e*; cf. *hīer* (see §117.2);

2   the pret. ind. sg., where the endings are *-e*, *-est*, *-e*.

§120 As in the strong verbs, the pret. pl. endings *-on* and *-en* are ambiguous; see §113.3. In lWS the 2nd sg. ending *-est* is often extended to the subj. Hence the pret. ind. and subj. can no longer be distinguished in the weak verbs.

§121 Certain simplifications occur in the pret. and the past ptc.:

1   If in forming the pret. a double consonant followed another consonant, it was simplified. Hence *sendan* has pret. *sende*, not **sendde*.

2   A ptc. such as *sended* may be simplified to *send*.

3   After voiceless sounds (e.g. *p*, *s*, *t*) the dental suffix becomes *t*, e.g. *mētan* 'meet' has *mētte*; cf. MnE 'judged' with 'crept'.

4   **-cd-* appears as *-ht-*. Hence *tǽċan* 'teach' has pret. *tǽhte*, past ptc. (*ġe-*)*tǽht*.

§122 In MnE we have some weak verbs which change their stem vowel in the pret. and the past ptc. as well as adding the dental suffix. They include 'sell/sold', 'tell/told', 'seek/sought', 'buy/bought', 'bring/brought', and 'think/thought', which were weak verbs of class 1 in OE and had the same irregularity even then. There were more of them in OE, for some have disappeared, e.g. *reċċan* 'tell', and some have become regular weak verbs, e.g. *streċċan* 'stretch'.[1] It is simplest just to learn these in the first instance. The most important ones are

---

[1] As you will see from §121.4, the verb *tǽċan* 'teach' usually has the same vowel throughout in WS, but *tāhte*, *tāht*, do occur.

Inf.	Pret. Sg.	Past Ptc.
sēċan 'seek'	sōhte	sōht
sellan 'give'	sealde	seald
cwellan 'kill'	cwealde	cweald
þenċan 'think'	þōhte	þōht
brenġan 'bring'	brōhte	brōht
þynċan 'seem'	þūhte	þūht
bycgan 'buy'	bohte	boht
wyrċan 'work'	worhte	worht

§123   The irregularity of these verbs is due to the fact that there was no *i* in the pret. or the past ptc. to cause *i*-mutation. Hence, while their present tenses have an *i*-mutated vowel like all the other verbs of this class, the vowel of the pret. and past ptc. is unmutated. This can be seen clearly by comparing *sēċan* (< *sōkjan*) with *sōhte/sōht*. However, the parallels in most verbs are obscured by other sound-changes which affected the vowel of the pret. and past ptc. They are

1   Breaking, e.g. *cwellan/cwealde*. Here the *æ* which once occurred throughout has been *i*-mutated to *e* in the pres. and broken to *ea* by the *ld* in the pret.

2   Loss of *n* before *h* with lengthening of the preceding vowel so that the word takes the same time to pronounce. This accounts for *þenċan/þōhte*, *þynċan/þūhte*, and *brenġan/brōhte*. Note that the strong inf. *bringan* usually replaces *brenġan*.

3   A change by which Gmc. *u* under certain conditions became OE *o*. This accounts for the variations in *bycgan/bohte* and *wyrċan/worhte*, where an original *u* has been *i*-mutated to *y* in the pres. and has changed to *o* in the pret.

4   On the derivation of weak verbs of class 1, see Appendix B.

Class 2

§124   The weak verbs of class 2 present few problems. The traditional paradigm is *lufian* 'love'. The long-stemmed *lōcian* 'look' has exactly the same endings.

		Present Indicative	Preterite Indicative
Sg.	1	lufie	lufode
	2	lufast	lufodest
	3	lufaþ	lufode
Pl.		lufiaþ	lufodon
		Present Subjunctive	Preterite Subjunctive
Sg.		lufie	lufode
Pl.		lufien	lufoden

Imp. Sg.	lufa	*Pl.*	lufiaþ
Inf.	lufian	*Infl. Inf.*	tō lufienne
Pres. Ptc.	lufiende	*Past Ptc.*	(ġe-)lufod

All weak verbs of class 2 end in *-ian*. However, most verbs ending in *-rian* belong, not to class 2, but to class 1(*a*) following *nerian*. But *andswarian* 'answer', *gadrian* 'gather', *timbrian* 'build', and one or two other verbs in *-rian*, usually follow *lufian*.

§125   Points to note in the conjugation of *lufian* are

1   The *i* disappears in the 2nd and 3rd sg. pres. ind., the imp. sg., all forms of the pret., and the past ptc. These are exactly the same places where *fremman* 'loses' its *m*, *nerian* its *i*, and *hīeran* its *e*.

2   The *-a* in 2nd and 3rd sg. pres. ind. *lufast*, *lufaþ*, and in imp. sg. *lufa*. So far the verb ending *-aþ* has always signified imp. or pres. ind. pl. In these verbs, *-aþ* is sg., *-iaþ* pl. Beware of this when reading your texts.

3   The *-od* in the pret. stem *lufod-* and in the past ptc. *lufod* where *fremman* has *-ed*.

Apart from these differences, the weak verbs of classes 1 and 2 are conjugated the same.

Class 3

§126   Class 3 contains four weak verbs – *habban* 'have', *libban* 'live', *secgan* 'say', and *hycgan* 'think'. These are conjugated:

Present Indicative

Sg. 1	hæbbe	libbe	secge	hycge
2	hæfst	leofast	sæġst	hyġst
	hafast	lifast	seġ(e)st	hogast
3	hæfþ	leofaþ	sæġþ	hyġþ
	hafaþ	lifaþ	seġ(e)þ	hogaþ
Pl.	habbaþ	libbaþ	secgaþ	hycgaþ
Imp. Sg.	hafa	leofa	sæġe	hyġe, hoga
Pret. Ind. Sg.	hæfde	lifde	sæġde	hogde

With these parts, you can construct the rest of these verbs for yourself, following the conjugation of *fremman* and the rules set out in §118.

To help you with the pres. ind. sg. and imp. sg., see §117.

VIII ANOMALOUS VERBS

Bēon

§127   *Bēon* 'be' has forms from different stems.

Indicative	Pres.		Pres.	Pret.
Sg. 1	eom		bēo	wæs
2	eart		bist	wǣre
3	is		biþ	wæs
Pl.	sind(on), sint		bēoþ	wǣron
Imp. Sg.	bēo, wes	*Pl.*	bēoþ, wesaþ	
Pres. Subj. Sg.	bēo	*Pl.*	bēon	
	sīe		sīen	
Pret. Subj. Sg.	wǣre	*Pl.*	wǣren	

On the distinction in meaning between *eom* and *bēo*, see §196.

Dōn and gān

§128   *Dōn* 'do' and *gān* 'go' have

Present Indicative

Sg. 1	dō	gā
2	dēst	gǣst
3	dēþ	gǣþ
Pl.	dōþ	gāþ
Imp. Sg.	dō	gā
Pret. Ind. Sg.	dyde	ēode
Past Ptc.	ġedōn	ġegān

Note

i-mutation in 2nd and 3rd pers. sg. pres. ind.

The remaining forms can be constructed with the help of §118.

Willan

§129   *Willan* 'wish, will' has

	Present Indicative	*Present Subjunctive*
Sg. 1	wille	wille
2	wilt	wille
3	wil(l)e	wille
Pl.	willaþ	willen
Pret.	wolde	

Preterite-Present Verbs

§130 Some very common verbs have a strong past tense with a present meaning (cf. Lat. *novi* 'I know') and a new weak past tense. Thus *wāt* 'I know, he knows' *witon* 'they know' belongs to class I; cf. *scān, scinon*. Its new past tense is sg. *wiste* pl. *wiston*. Such verbs are called preterite-present verbs. The most important ones are

Meaning	Pres. Ind. Sg. 1, 3	2	Pres. Ind. Pl.	Pret. Sg.
'possess'	āh	āhst, āht	āgon	āhte
'grant'	ann	—	unnon	ūþe
'can, know how to'	cann	canst	cunnon	cūþe
'avail, be of use'	dēah	—	dugon	dohte
'dare'	dearr	dearst	durron	dorste
'remember'	ġeman	ġemanst	ġemunon	ġemunde
'be able'	mæġ	meaht	magon	mihte, meahte
'be allowed to, may'	mōt	mōst	mōton	mōste
'be obliged to'	sceal	scealt	sculon	sceolde
'need'	þearf	þearft	þurfon	þorfte
'know'	wāt	wāst	witon	wiste

IX IS A VERB STRONG OR WEAK? TO WHICH CLASS DOES IT BELONG?

§131 If we assume that you can recognize on sight the strong contracted verbs, the four weak verbs of class 3 (§126), and the verbs discussed in §§127–130, the system set out below will enable you to answer the questions at the head of this section.

Verbs in *-ian*

§132 1 Verbs in *-rian* are class 1 weak.
Exceptions:

(*a*) *swerian* 'swear' (class VI strong with a weak present);
(*b*) *andswarian* 'answer' and a few other verbs which can follow *lufian* 'love'; see §124.

2 All other verbs in *-ian* are class 2 weak.

Verbs in *-an*

§133 These are either strong or class 1 weak. You will find that the recognition symbols for the strong verbs set out in §94 are almost always reliable. Thus if a verb ending in *-an* has *ī* + one cons. in the infinitive, it is probably class I strong. If it has *ū* + one cons., it is probably class II strong. And so on. Exceptions include

1   The strong verbs of classes V, VI, and VII (*wēpan* 'weep'), with weak presents. These too should be recognized on sight.

2   *Fēolan* 'press on' looks like class II strong, but belongs to class III, as the 1st pret. *fealh* shows. (*Felhan > *feolhan by breaking (§97.2) > *fēolan* by loss of *h* + lengthening; see §38.)

3   A verb with *ǣ* + one cons. may be either strong or weak; *lǣtan* 'let' is class VII strong, *lǣdan* 'lead' is class 1 weak.

4   For weak verbs with *ī* and *ēo*, see Appendix A.1 and 2.

5   Verbs with a short vowel + a double cons. are mostly weak class 1, e.g. *fremman*. The recognition symbols of the strong verbs of class III will enable us to distinguish *swimman* 'swim' and *winnan* 'fight' as class III strong; note *i* before the nasals compared witth the *e* of *fremman*. *Bannan* 'summon', *spannan* 'span', *feallan* 'fall', and *weallan* 'boil', are class VII strong. On *bringan*, see §123.2. On *hringan* and *ǥeþingan*, see Appendix A.3.

§134   When you are reading Old English, your problem will often be to find the infinitive from which a certain verb form is derived. Let us take *bītt*, *stæl*, and *budon*, as examples.

For *bītt*, we note *-ī-* and *-tt*. Together these suggest the syncopated 3rd sg. pres. ind. of a verb of class I. The ending *-tt* we know to be a reduction of *-teþ* or *-deþ*. This gives us two possibilities – *bītan* 'bite' or *bīdan* 'await'. The context should determine which we have. In a text which does not mark long vowels, *bitt* could also be from *biddan* V 'ask'.

For *stæl* we note *-æ-*. This suggests the 1st pret. of class IV or V. Hence the inf. is *stelan* 'steal'. The medial *l* decides for class IV.

Budon is perhaps more difficult. Is it strong or (since it ends in *-don*) weak? If it is strong, the medial *u* and the single cons. suggest class II. Therefore the inf. could be *bēodan* or *būdan. The glossary decides for *bēodan* 'command'. If it were a weak pret., the inf. would be *buan*. This would not fit *būan* 'dwell' with pret. pl. *būdon* unless the text did not mark long vowels. If this were the case, the context would again decide.

The verbs discussed in §122 present a problem, but you will soon become familiar with their preterites.

X   ADVERBS

Formation

§135   Characteristic endings of adverbs are *-e* (e.g. *hraþe* 'quickly'), *-līce* (e.g. *hrædlīce* 'quickly'), and *-unga* (e.g. *eallunga* 'entirely'). The ending *-an* usually means 'from', e.g. *norþ* 'north, northwards' but *norþan* 'from the north'.

The gen. and dat. can be used adverbially; see §§190 and 191.

The negative adverb is *ne*. For its use, see §184.4.

Comparison

Adverbs are normally compared by adding *-or, -ost*, e.g. *oft* 'often' *oftor oftost*, and (dropping the *-e* of the positive) *swiþe* 'greatly' *swiþor swiþost*.

Some have an *i*-mutated vowel in the comparative and superlative, e.g. *lange* 'long' *leng lengest* and *feorr* 'far' *fierr fierrest*.

A knowledge of the equivalent OE adjectives and MnE adverbs will enable you to recognize in reading the irregular comparatives and superlatives of the adverbs *wel* 'well', *yfle* 'evilly', *micle* 'much', and *lȳt* 'little'.

4

Word Formation

INTRODUCTION

§136 Old English acquired new words in three ways – by borrowing from other languages (see §234), by making compounds of two words already existing in the language, e.g. *sǣ-weall* 'sea-wall', and by adding affixes to existing words to change their function or meaning, e.g. *blōd* (neut.) 'blood' but *blōd-iġ* 'bloody, blood-stained', and *bēodan* 'command' but *for-bēodan* 'forbid'. A knowledge of these last two methods and of the formative elements used will help you to deduce the meaning of many words which may at first sight seem unfamiliar.

It is also important to realize that parts of speech were not interchangeable in OE as they often are in MnE. Thus the OE noun *drinc* has a corresponding verb *drincan* whereas today 'drink' is both a noun and a verb. Similarly the OE adjective *open* and the verb *openian* are both represented by MnE 'open'. Such correspondences are fairly obvious. But others are more difficult to spot because they are obscured by sound-changes. You may be able to deduce for yourself the change which causes the variations in the following pairs: *scrūd* (neut.) 'clothing' *scrȳdan* 'clothe'; *dōm* (masc.) 'judgement' *dēma* (masc.) 'a judge'; *hāl* 'whole, in good health' *hǣlan* 'heal, make whole'. If you cannot, see §§52–57 and Appendix B. Other groups of related words have different vowels from the same gradation series (see §90), e.g. *beran* 'carry', *bǣr* (fem.) 'bier', and the ending *-bora* (masc.) 'bearer, carrier', which often occurs in compounds such as *sweord-bora* 'sword-bearer'. Both these sound-changes and Verner's Law (§§105–108) obscure the relationship between *ċēosan* 'choose' and *cyre* (masc.) 'choice', where *y* is an *i*-mutation of *u*.

Notes

1 On the gender and declension of nouns formed by compounding or by the addition of suffixes or endings, see §§12, 13, and 41.

2 The work by Madden and Magoun mentioned in §253 adopts a 'packaging principle' by which parent words, their immediate derivatives, and those related by *i*-mutation and gradation, are grouped together. This makes for ease of learning, and is one of the reasons why the book is so useful.

COMPOUNDING

§137 The process of forming new words or compounds by joining together two separate words which already exist was common in OE. Some of the possible arrangements are exemplified below.

Nouns can be formed by combining

1 Noun and noun, e.g. *hell-waran* (masc. pl.) 'inhabitants of hell', *niht-waco* (fem.) 'night-watch', *scip-rāp* (masc.) 'ship-rope', *storm-sǣ* (masc. or fem.) 'stormy sea';

2 Adjective and noun, e.g. *eall-wealda* (masc.) 'ruler of all', *hēah-clif* (neut.) 'high cliff', *hēah-ġerēfa* (masc.) 'high reeve, chief officer', *wīd-sǣ* (masc. or fem.) '(open) sea';

3 Adverb and noun, e.g. *ǣr-dæġ* (masc.) 'early day, first dawn', *eft-sīþ* (masc.) 'return', *inn-faru* (fem.) 'expedition', *inn-gang* (masc.) 'entrance'.

Adjectives are found consisting of

1 Noun and adjective, e.g. *ælmes-ġeorn* 'alms-eager, generous, charitable', *ār-weorþ* 'honour-worthy, venerable', *dōm-ġeorn* 'eager for glory', *mere-wēriġ* 'sea-weary';

2 Adjective and adjective, e.g. *hēah-þungen* 'of high rank', *hrēow-ċeariġ* 'sad' (lit. 'sad-anxious'), *wīd-cūþ* 'widely known', *wīs-hycgende* 'wise-thinking';

3 Adverb and adjective, e.g. *ǣr-gōd* 'very good', *forþ-ġeorn* 'forth-eager, eager to advance', *wel-þungen* 'well-thriven, excellent', *wel-willende* 'well-wishing, benevolent';

4 Adjective and noun, e.g. *blanden-feax* 'having mixed hair, gray-haired', *blīþe-mōd* 'of kindly mind, friendly', *hrēowiġ-mōd* 'gloomy-minded, sad', *salu-pād* 'dark-coated'.

In all these words the first element is uninflected; cf. *folc-lagu* (fem.) 'law of the people, public law' with *Godes* (gen.) *lagu* 'God's law' and *wīn-druncen* 'wine-drunk' with *bēore* (dat.) *druncen* 'drunk with beer'. But compounds do occur with an inflected first element, e.g. *Engla-lond* 'land of the Angles, England' (but cf. *Frēs-lond* 'Frisian land, Frisia') and *eġes-full* 'full of terror, terrible, wonderful' (but cf. *synn-full* 'sinful').

Note
Compounds of three elements are sometimes found, e.g. *wulf-hēafod-trēo* (neut.) 'wolf-head-tree, gallows, cross'.

Today, when we are faced with a new object or idea, we often express it by a compound made up of foreign or of native elements, e.g. 'tele-gram' and 'astro-naut', but 'one-up-man-ship' and 'fall-out'. But OE often 'translated' foreign words. Sometimes the elements of a foreign word were represented by OE equivalents, e.g. *god-spel* (neut.) 'good news', based on *evangelium*, for 'gospel',[1] *þrī-nes* (fem.) representing *Trini-tas* 'The Trinity', and Ælfric's grammatical terms *fore-set-nes* (fem.) for Lat. *prae-positio* 'preposition' and *betwux-āleġed-nes* (fem.) 'between-laid-ness' for Lat. *inter-jectio* 'interjection'. Sometimes the word was analysed into its concepts and these were rendered into English, e.g. two words for 'Pharisees' – *sundor-halgan* (masc. pl.) 'apart-holies' and *ǣ-lārēowas* (masc. pl.) 'law-teachers'. That these processes are no longer natural for speakers of English can be seen in two ways. First, many native compounds such as *tungol-cræft* (masc.) 'star-craft' for 'astronomy' and *lār-hūs* (neut.) 'lore-house' for 'school' have disappeared from the language. Secondly, proposed replacements like the sixteenth-century 'hundreder' for 'centurion' or the nineteenth-century 'folk-wain' for 'bus' seem to us ridiculous, whereas to Germans *Fernsprecher* 'far-speaker' for our Greek-derived 'telephone' is not unnatural, though they do, of course, use *Telephon*.

To help provide the many synonyms beginning with different letters which were essential for the *scop* (poet) working in the alliterative measure, the Anglo-Saxon poets made great use of compounds. Of special interest is the kenning, a sort of condensed metaphor in which (a) is compared to (b) without (a) or the point of the comparison being made explicit; thus one might say of the camel 'The desert-ship lurched on'. So the sea is *hwæl-weġ* (masc.) 'whale-way', a ship *ȳþ-hengest* (masc.) 'wave-horse', and a minstrel *hleahtor-smiþ* (masc.) 'laughter-smith'.

We find too that many set phrases inherited from the days when the poetry was composed orally survive in the lettered poetry. These 'oral-formulae' are set metrical combinations which could be varied according to the needs of alliteration. Thus the phrase 'on, over, across the sea' can be expressed by one of the prepositions *on, ofer, ġeond*, followed by the appropriate case of one of the following words: *bæþ-weġ* 'bath-way', *flōd-weġ* 'flood-way', *flot-weġ* 'sea-way', *hwæl-weġ* 'whale-way' (all masc.), *hran-rād* 'whale-road', *swan-rād* 'swan-road', and *seġl-rād* 'sail-road' (all fem.). References to further discussions on these points will be found in §§265–266.

THE ADDITION OF AFFIXES

§138   These can be divided into prefixes – elements placed at the beginning of words to qualify their meaning – and suffixes. The effect of many which survive today is obvious; we may cite the prefix *mis-* as in *mis-dǣd* (fem.) 'misdeed', prepositions or adverbs used as prefixes, e.g. *ofer-mæġen* (neut.) 'superior force' and *ūt-gān* 'go out', adjectives ending in *-full*, *-isċ*,

---

[1] You should look up the noun 'gospel' in O.E.D. to find out why *godspel* has *ō* when the OE equivalent of 'good' is *gōd*.

and *-lēas*, e.g. *synn-full* 'sinful', *ċild-isċ* 'childish', and *feoh-lēas* 'moneyless, destitute', and nouns ending in *-dōm, -ere, -scipe* (all masc.) and *-nes, -nis, -nys* (fem.), e.g. *wīs-dōm* 'wisdom', *fisc-ere* 'fisherman', *frēond-scipe* 'friendship', and *beorht-nes* 'brightness'. Others which occur frequently but are not so easily recognizable are set out below.

Prefixes

ā- 1 Sometimes it means 'away', as in *ā-fȳsan* 'drive forth'.

2 But sometimes it seems to have no effect on the meaning, e.g. *ā-galan* 'sing'.

ǣġ- It generalizes prons. and advs., e.g. *ǣġ-hwā* 'everyone' and *ǣġ-hwǣr* 'everywhere'.

be- 1 In some words *be-* is the same as the prep. 'about', e.g. *be-gān* 'surround' and *be-rīdan* 'ride round, surround'.

2 Sometimes it is a deprivative, e.g. *be-dǣlan* 'deprive' and *be-hēafdian* 'behead'.

3 It can make an intransitive verb transitive, e.g. *be-þenċan* 'think about' and *be-wēpan* 'bewail'.

for- It is an intensifier, e.g. *for-bærnan* 'burn up, consume', *for-lorenness* (fem.) 'perdition', and *for-heard* 'very hard'.

ġe- 1 In some nouns it has the sense of 'together', e.g. *ġe-fēra* (masc.) 'companion' and *ġe-brōþru* (masc. pl.) 'brothers'.

2 In verbs, it sometimes has a perfective sense, e.g. *ġe-āscian* 'find out' and *ġe-winnan* 'get by fighting, win'; hence its frequent use in past ptcs.

on-, an- 1 In verbs like *on-bindan* 'unbind' and *on-lūcan* 'unlock', it has a negative sense.

2 Sometimes it means 'against', as in *on-rǣs* (masc.) 'attack'.

or- 1 This is a deprivative in *or-mōd* 'without courage, despairing' and *or-sorg* 'without care, careless'.

2 It can also mean 'early, original, primaeval' (cf. *or* (neut.) 'beginning, origin'), e.g. *or-eald* 'of great age', *or-ieldu* (fem.) 'extreme old age', and *or-þanc* (masc.) 'inborn thought, ingenuity, skill'.

tō- 1 Sometimes it is the same as the prep. *tō*, e.g. *tō-cyme* (masc.) 'arrival' and *tō-weard* (prep.) 'towards'.

2 But with verbs it frequently means separation, e.g. *tō-drīfan* (trans.) 'drive apart, disperse, scatter' and *tō-faran* (intrans.) 'go apart, disperse'.

un- 1 This is sometimes a negative prefix, e.g. *un-friþ* (masc.) 'un-peace, war' and *un-hold* 'unfriendly'.

2 Sometimes it is pejorative, as in *un-ġiefu* (fem.) 'evil gift' and *un-weder* (neut.) 'bad weather'.

wan-   This is a deprivative or negative prefix, e.g. *wan-hāl* 'not
               hale, ill' and *wan-hoga* (masc.) 'thoughtless man'.

wiþ-   Its primary sense in compounds is 'against', e.g. *wiþ-cēosan*
               'reject', *wiþ-cweþan* 'reply, contradict', *wiþ-drīfan* 'repel', and
               wiþ-feohtend (masc.) 'enemy, opponent, rebel'.

ymb-   This means 'around', e.g. *ymb-gang* (masc.) 'circuit, cir-
               cumference' and *ymb-lǣdan* 'lead round'.

Suffixes

Nouns

-aþ, -oþ   This forms masc. nouns, e.g. *herg-aþ* 'plundering' and *fisc-oþ*
               'fishing'.

-end   This equals '-er', as in *Hǣl-end* (masc.) 'Healer, Saviour' and
               wīg-end (masc.) 'fighter, warrior'. It derives from the pres.
               ptc. ending *-ende*.

-hād   This introduces masc. nouns and equals MnE '-hood', as in
               cild-hād 'childhood' and *woruld-hād* 'secular life'.

-ing   1 In masc. nouns it means 'son of', e.g. *Ælfred Æþelwulf-ing*
               'Alfred son of Æthelwulf', or 'associated with', e.g. *earm-ing*
               'wretch' and *hōr-ing* 'adulterer, fornicator'.
               2 In fem. nouns, it equals *-ung*; see below.

-mǣl   1 The noun *mǣl* (neut.) 'measure, fixed time' appears in
               compound nouns, e.g. *fōt-mǣl* (neut.) 'foot's length, foot' and
               (with the dat. pl. used adverbially; see §191.3) *floc-mǣlum* 'in
               (armed) bands' and *gēar-mǣlum* 'year by year'.
               2 In the sense 'mark, sign', it appears in compound nouns,
               e.g. *fȳr-mǣl* (neut.) 'fire-mark', and also in compound adjec-
               tives; see below.

-rǣden   This forms fem. abstract nouns, e.g. *hierd-rǣden* 'guardian-
               ship, care, guard'.

-þ(o), -þ(u) This is used to form fem. abstract nouns, e.g. *fǣh-þ(o)*
               'hostility' and *ierm-þ(u)* 'misery, poverty'. Note that *geogoþ*
               'youth' is fem.

-ung, -ing   This is found in fem. abstract nouns formed from verbs, e.g.
               bod-ung 'preaching' and *rǣd-ing* 'reading'.

Adjectives

-en   1 This is the ending of past ptcs. of strong verbs.
               2 It is also found in adjectives with an *i*-mutated vowel in
               the stem, e.g. *ǣttr-en* 'poisonous' and *gyld-en* 'golden'.

-iġ	This equals MnE '-y', as in *cræft-iġ* 'powerful, mighty' and *hāl-iġ* 'holy'.
-liċ	This, originally the same word as *līċ* (neut.) 'body', equals MnE '-ly, -like', e.g. *heofon-liċ* 'heavenly' and *ċild-liċ* 'child-like, childish'.
-mǣl	This element, listed above under Nouns, also occurs in compound adjectives, e.g. *grǣg-mǣl* 'of a grey colour', *hring-mǣl* 'ring-marked, ornamented with a ring', and *wunden-mǣl* 'with curved markings'.
-sum	This occurs in words like *wynn-sum* 'delightful, pleasant' (cf. 'winsome') and *hīer-sum* 'hear-some, obedient'.

Adverbs

See §135.

Verbs

-an	The most common infinitive ending for strong and weak verbs. (For the *-an* in class 1 weak verbs, which was originally **-jan*, see Appendix B.)
-ian	The infinitive ending for class 2 weak verbs. Verbs borrowed from Latin are usually conjugated according to this class, e.g. *declinian* 'decline' < *declināre* and *predician* 'preach' < *praedicāre*.
-rian	See §132.1.
-sian	This is the infinitive ending of a subclass of weak 2 verbs formed from adjectives and nouns, e.g. *clǣnsian* 'cleanse' and *rīcsian* 'be powerful, reign'.
-ettan	This infinitive ending is used to form a subclass of weak 1 verbs from adjectives and nouns, e.g. *lāþ-ettan* 'hate, loathe', *līc-ettan* 'pretend', and *sār-ettan* 'lament'.
-lǣċan	This infinitive ending is also used to form a subclass of weak 1 verbs from adjectives and nouns, e.g. *ġe-ān-lǣċan* 'unite' and *ġe-þwǣr-lǣċan* 'consent'.

5

Syntax

INTRODUCTION

§139 Syntax has been described as the study of 'the traffic rules of language'. If this is so, you are offered here only a simplified Anglo-Saxon highway code, designed to deal with constructions likely to worry the beginner. OE syntax is recognizably English; in some passages the word-order at least is almost without exception that of MnE. At other times, we seem to be wrestling with a foreign language. Some of the difficulties arise from idiosyncrasies due to the Germanic ancestry of OE. Another reason, which obtains mostly in the early writings when OE prose was in a formative state, is that Alfred and his companions were struggling to develop the language as a vehicle for the expression of complicated narrative and abstract thought. They achieved no little success, but had their failures too. The breathless but vigorous account of the Battle of Ashdown (the annal for 871 in the Parker MS of the Anglo-Saxon Chronicle), which sweeps us along on a surging current of simple sentences joined by *ond*, is not untypical of the early efforts of prose writers who were not translating from Latin. There is only one complex sentence in the whole piece (the last but one). That the writer gets into trouble with it is symptomatic; cf. the account of the sea-battle of 897 in the same manuscript, where what has happened is not particularly clear on first reading. This inability to cope with complicated ideas is more apparent in the translated texts, where the influence of the Latin periodic structure often produces stilted prose, as in the story of Orpheus and Eurydice in King Alfred's translation of Boethius. Even Alfred's original prose is sometimes twisted in the same way, e.g. the sentences discussed in §172. Perhaps Latin, being the language of the Church, the language from which many works were translated, and the only model available, was accorded a status denied to it (or to any other original) today.

§140 Another source of difficulty becomes apparent from a study of the major differences between OE and MnE. It is sometimes said that OE is the period of full inflexions, ME the period of levelled inflexions (all with the vowel *e*, e.g. *-e, -es, -en*, as opposed to the endings of OE with their different vowels), and MnE the period of no inflexions. This statement points to the vital truth that MnE depends on word-order and prepositions to make distinctions which in an inflected language are made by the case endings. However, it needs qualification. That there are still a few inflexions in MnE is of little importance. But it might be less misleading to say that OE is a 'half-inflected' language. Firstly, it has only four cases and remnants of a fifth left of the eight cases postulated for the original IE language. Secondly, as has been pointed out in §189 note, there is often no distinction in form between nominative and accusative. Hence word-order is often the only thing which enables us to tell which is subject and which is object; consider *Enoch gestrynde Irad and Irad gestrynde Mauiahel* (and so on) 'E. begat I. and I begat M.' (cf. *Caesarem interfecit Brutus*) and *Hi hæfdon þa ofergan Eastengle and Eastsexe* 'They had then conquered the East Anglians and the East Saxons'. These and many similar examples support the view that the Anglo-Saxons already had the feeling that the subject came first. If we did not have evidence for this, we should have to hesitate instead of automatically following the modern rule and taking *Oswold and Ealdwold* as the subject in the following lines from *Maldon*, for the order object, subject, verb, is possible in OE (see §147):

> Oswold and Ealdwold   ealle hwile,
> begen þa gebroþru,   beornas trymedon

'O. and E., the two brothers, all the time encouraged the warriors'. (More is said in §147 on the triumph of the order 'subject verb'.) Thirdly, prepositions followed by an oblique case are often used to express relationships which could be expressed by case alone; cf. *ond þa geascode he þone cyning lytle werode . . . on Merantune* 'and then he discovered the king [to be] at Merton with a small band (inst. case alone)' with *eode he in mid ane his preosta* 'he went in with one of his priests (*mid* + inst. case)'. All these things suggest a language in a state of transition. The implications of this for the future development of English are mentioned briefly in §231; here we are concerned with it as another source of difficulty.

§141 Important differences between OE and MnE are found in the following:

> the position of the negative (§§144.1 and 184.4);
> the use of the infinitives (§205);
> the uses of moods and tenses of the verb (§§195 ff.);
> the resolved tenses[1] and the function of the participles therein (§§199 ff.);
> the meaning of 'modal' auxiliaries (§§206 ff.);
> agreement (§187);
> the meaning and use of prepositions (§§213–214).

§142 Features found in OE, but not in MnE, include

> strong and weak forms of the adjective (§§63 and 64);
> some special uses of cases (§§188–192);

---

[1] This term is explained in §199.

some special uses of articles, pronouns, and numerals (§§193–194);

the use of a single verb form where MnE would use a resolved tense or mood (§195).

idiomatic absence of the subject (§193.7).

But the main difficulty of OE syntax lies, not in these differences, but in the word-order of the simple sentence or clause, and in the syntax of the subordinate clauses. These fundamental topics are accordingly treated first; if any of the points mentioned in this or the preceding section cause immediate difficulty, see the Contents and read the appropriate section. The order of clauses within the complex sentence is very similar to that of MnE, and will cause little difficulty.

I WORD-ORDER[1]

§143 If we take subject and verb as the fundamental elements of a sentence, we shall find that the following arrangements are common in OE prose:

S.V., where the verb immediately follows the subject;

S. . . . V., where other elements of the sentence come between subject and verb;

V.S., where the subject follows the verb.

The same orders are also found in the poetry. But, like their successors, the Anglo-Saxon poets used the language much more freely than the prose writers did. Hence the comments made below apply to the prose only. But the word-order in the poetry will not cause you much difficulty if you understand what follows.

§144 As in MnE, the order S.V. can occur in both principal and subordinate clauses, e.g. *he hæfde an swiðe ænlic wif* 'he had a most excellent wife' and *þe getimbrode his hus ofer sand* 'who built his house on sand'. Therefore it cannot tell us whether a clause is principal or subordinate, except in the circumstances discussed in §§150 ff. It is also found after *ond* 'and' and *ac* 'but', e.g. *ond his lic liþ æt Winburnan* 'and his body lies at W.'.

There are naturally variations of this order. Some are found in both OE and MnE. Thus an adverb precedes the verb in *Se Hælend ða het þa ðeningmen afyllan six stænene fatu mid hluttrum wætere* 'The Saviour then ordered the servants to fill six stone vessels with pure water'. The indirect object precedes the direct object in *Romane gesealdon Gaiuse Iuliuse seofon legan* 'The Romans gave Gaius Julius seven legions', but follows it in *ac he forgeaf eorðlice ðing mannum* 'but he gave earthly things to men'.

[1] In these sections, the following abbreviations are used: S. (subject), V. (verb), O. (object), Adv. (adverb or adv. phrase). A MnE sentence such as 'Do you sing?' is characterized by v. (auxiliary verb) S.V. Round brackets indicate that the feature in question is optional.

Arrangements not found in MnE are

1   The position of the negative *ne* 'not' immediately before the verb. This is the rule in all three OE word-orders; see §184.4.

2   The placing of a pronoun O., which would be unstressed, between S. and V. when a noun O., which would carry some stress, would follow V. Thus *we hie ondredon* 'we feared them' is an idiomatic variation of the order S.V. rather than an example of S. . . . V.

3   The possibility that an infinitive or a participle may have final position, e.g. *he ne meahte ongemong oðrum monnum bion* 'he could not be among other men' and *Eastengle hæfdon Ælfrede cyninge aþas geseald* 'The East Angles had given King Alfred oaths'. On the order S.V. in non-dependent questions, see §160.

§145   The order S. . . . V. is most common in subordinate clauses, e.g. *se micla here, þe we gefyrn ymbe spræcon* 'the great army which we spoke about before' and *gif hie ænigne feld secan wolden* 'if they wished to seek any open country', and after *ond* 'and' and *ac* 'but', e.g. *Ac ic þa sona eft me selfum andwyrde* 'But again I immediately answered myself'. But it also occurs in principal clauses, e.g. *Ða reðan Iudei wedende þone halgan stændon* 'The cruel Jews in their rage stoned the saint' and *Stephanus soðlice gebigedum cneowum Drihten bæd* . . . 'Stephen however on bended knees besought the Lord . . .'. Hence the order S. . . . V. does not certify that a clause is subordinate. With this order, the verb need not have final position, but may be followed by an adverbial extension, e.g. *ær he acenned wæs of Marian* . . . 'before He was born of Mary' and . . . *þæt hi wel wyrðe beoð þære deoflican ehtnysse. . . .* 'that they will be very worthy of devilish persecution'. On this order in non-dependent questions, see §160.

§146   The order V.S. occurs in MnE in questions with the verbs 'to have' and 'to be', e.g. 'Have you the book?' and 'Are you there?', and in a few other set phrases or constructions, e.g. 'said he', 'Long live the King!', 'be he alive or be he dead', and 'Had I but plenty of money, I would be in Bermuda'. It must not be confused with the normal interrogative word-order of MnE, which is v.S.V., e.g. 'Have you found him?', 'Is he coming?', and 'Do you see him?' In OE the order V.S. is found in

1   Positive non-dependent questions either with or without interrogative words, e.g. *Hwær eart þu nu, gefera?* 'Where are you now, comrade?' and *Gehyrst þu, sælida?* 'Do you hear, sailor?'

2   Negative non-dependent questions, e.g. *ne seowe þu god sæd on þinum æcere?* 'Did you not sow good seed in your field?'

3   Positive statements, e.g. *Wæs he Osrices sunu* 'He was Osric's son' and *Hæfde se cyning his fierd on tu tonumen* 'The king had divided his army in two'.

4   Negative statements, e.g. *Ne com se here* 'The army did not come'.

5   In subordinate clauses of concession and condition, e.g. *swelte ic, libbe ic* 'live I, die I', i.e. 'whether I live or die'.

6   In principal clauses introduced by certain adverbs; cf. MnE 'Then came the dawn'. On the value of this word-order for distinguishing principal from subordinate clauses, see §§150 ff.

Notes

1   The orders described in 3 and 4 above are NOT necessarily emphatic.

2   In *Matthew* 20: 13, we read: *Eala þu freond, ne do ic þe nænne teonan: hu, ne come þu to me to wyrcenne wið anum peninge?* 'Friend, I do thee no wrong; lo, didst thou not come to me to work for one penny?' Here exactly the same word-order is used first in a statement (order 4 above) and then in a question (order 2 above).

§147   Other word-orders may, of course, occur. Some which are used for emphasis are also found in MnE, e.g. *Gesælige hi wurdon geborene* ... 'Blessed they were born', *Micelne geleafan he hæfde* ... 'Great faith he had', and (with a MnE preposition replacing the OE dative case) *þam acennedan Cyninge we bringað gold* ... 'To the newborn King we bring gold' and *Gode ælmihtigum sie ðonc* 'To God Almighty be thanks'. But the order O.V.S. found in *deman gedafenað setl* 'a seat is the proper place for a judge' would be impossible today because, in a MnE sentence of the pattern 'Man flees dog', what precedes the verb must be the subject. Consider what happens to the meaning of the spoken sentence if the word-order is altered. 'Dog flees man', 'Fleas dog man', and even 'Fleas man dog', all mean something different. The absence of endings and the interchangeability of MnE parts of speech have left word-order the only guide and the absolute master. The gradual triumph of this order S.V.O. is one of the most important syntactical developments in English. Its beginnings can be seen in OE. Thus in *Matthew* 7: 24 *ælc þæra þe þas min word gehyrð and þa wyrcð, bið gelic þæm wisan were, se his hus ofer stan getimbrode*, the two subordinate clauses have S. ... V. But in *Matthew* 7: 26 *And ælc þæra þe gehyrð þas min word, and þa ne wyrcð, se bið gelic þam dysigan men, þe getimbrode his hus ofer sandceosel*, they both have S.V. This suggests that any difference there may have been between these orders was disappearing. Again, the old preference for V.S. after an adverb (compare modern German) is at times conquered by the new preference for S.V., e.g. *Her cuomon twegen aldormenn* 'In this year two chiefs came' but *Her Hengest 7 Æsc fuhton wiþ Brettas*[1] 'In this year H. and A. fought against the Britons'. Of course, in OE, where the distinction between the nominative and accusative is not always preserved, freedom sometimes lead to ambiguity, e.g. *Ðas seofon hi gecuron* ..., where only the context tells us that *hī* is the subject. In MnE 'these seven they chose' is unambiguous because of 'they' and because, while the order O.S.V. is possible, the order S.O.V. is not.

---

[1] 7 is a common MS abbreviation for *ond* which is often reproduced by editors.

II SENTENCE STRUCTURE

Three difficulties in sentence structure must now be discussed.

Recapitulation and Anticipation

§148 The first is this. In their attempts to explain complicated ideas, Anglo-Saxon writers often had recourse to a device similar to that used by some modern politician who has the desire but not the ability to be an orator, viz. the device of pausing in mid-sentence and starting afresh with a pronoun or some group of words which sums up what has gone before. A simple example will be found in Alfred's Preface to the translation of the *Cura Pastoralis*. Alfred, having written (or dictated) *Ure ieldran, ða ðe ðas stowa ær hioldon* 'Our ancestors who previously occupied these places' pauses as it were for thought and then goes on *hie lufodon wisdom* 'they loved wisdom', where *hīe* sums up what has gone before and enables him to control the sentence. Compare with this the orator's gesture-accompanied 'all these things' with which he attempts to regain control of a sentence which has run away from him. Other examples of recapitulatory pronouns will be found in *7 þæt unstille hweol ðe Ixion wæs to gebunden, Leuita cyning, for his scylde, ðæt oðstod for his hearpunga. 7 Tantalus se cyning ðe on ðisse worulde ungemetlice gifre wæs, 7 him ðær ðæt ilce yfel filgde ðære gifernesse, he gestilde* 'And the ever-moving wheel to which Ixion, King of the Lapithae, was bound for his sin, [that] stood still for his (Orpheus's) harping. And King Tantalus, who in this world was greedy beyond measure and whom that same sin of greed followed there, [he] had rest'. More complicated examples will be found in *hergode he his rice, þone ilcan ende þe Æþered his cumpæder healdan sceolde* 'He (Hæsten) ravaged his (Alfred's) kingdom, that same province which Æthered, his son's godfather, had the duty of holding', where *his rīce* is qualified by the rest of the sentence, and in the second passage discussed in §172.

The common use of a pronoun to anticipate a noun clause may be compared with this. A simple example is

> þa þæt Offan mæg ærest onfunde,
> þæt se eorl nolde yrhðo geþolian

lit. 'Then the kinsman of Offa first learned that thing (the first *þæt*), that the leader would not tolerate slackness'. We have perhaps all had this experience at the hand of some leader, but MnE would dispense with the tautologic *þæt* in giving it expression. In *þæs ic gewilnige and gewysce mid mode, þæt ic ana ne belife æfter minum leofum þegnum* lit. 'That thing I desire and wish in my mind, that I should not remain alone after my beloved thanes', the pronoun *þæs* anticipates the following *þæt* clause. It is in the genitive after the verbs *gewilnian* and *gewyscan*. The pronoun *hit* is sometimes found similarly used, e.g.

> þæt is micel wundor
> þæt hit ece God   æfre wolde
> þeoden þolian,   þæt wurde þegn swa monig
> forlædd be þam lygenum. . . .

Here the first *þæt* is in apposition with the *þæt* clause in l.2 while *hit* anticipates the *þæt* clause in l.3: lit. 'That is a great wonder that eternal God the Lord would ever permit it, that so many a thane should be deceived by those lies'. Dependent questions may be similarly anticipated, e.g. *Men þa þæs wundrodon, hu þa weargas hangodon* lit. 'Men then wondered at that, how the criminals hung' (where *þæs* is genitive after *wundrodon*) and

> Hycgað his ealle,
> hu ge hi beswicen

lit. 'All [of you] take thought about it, how you may deceive them' (where *his* is genitive after *hycgað*).

Note

It is possible that in the sentence 'He said that he was ill', 'that' was originally a demonstrative – 'He said that: he was ill' – which gradually became a part of the noun clause. If so, the introduction of the second *þæt* or of *hit* illustrates clearly the difficulty our ancestors seem to have had in collecting and expressing complicated thoughts.

The Splitting of Heavy Groups

§149   The second thing which sometimes helps to make OE seem a foreign language is a tendency to split up heavy groups. Thus we say today 'The President and his wife are going to Washington'. But the more common OE arrangement was 'The President is going to Washington, and his wife'. Examples of this tendency are common. We find

1   A divided subject in *eower mod is awend, and eower andwlita* 'your mind and your countenance are changed'. Note here the word-order S.V. and the singular verb; cf. MnE 'Tom was there and Jack and Bill and all the boys'.

2   A divided object in *þa he þone cniht agef 7 þæt wif* 'when he returned the child and the woman'.

3   A divided genitive group in *Inwæres broþur 7 Healfdenes* 'the brother of I. and H.'.

4   Divided phrases in *þa þe in Norþhymbrum bugeað ond on East Englum* 'those who dwell in Northumbria and East Anglia'.

5   Separation of adjectives governing the same noun in *þæt hi næfre ær swa clæne gold, ne swa read ne gesawon* 'that they never before saw such pure, red gold'.

But such groups are not always divided, e.g. *Her Hengest 7 Horsa fuhton wiþ Wyrtgeorne þam cyninge* 'In this year, H. and H. fought against King W.'.

Correlation

§150 The third thing which makes us feel that OE is a foreign language is its marked fondness for correlation. This may have its origin in, and so be a more sophisticated manifestation of, the same feeling of insecurity in the face of the complicated sentence which produced the awkward repetitions already discussed. But it later becomes a very important stylistic device which such an outstanding writer as Ælfric exploited to the full. Consider the following sentence from his Homily on the Passion of St. Stephen: *þider ðe Stephanus forestop, mid Saules stanum oftorfod, þider folgode Paulus, gefultumod þurh Stephanes gebedu* 'Where Stephen went in front, stoned by the stones of Saul, there Paul followed, helped by the prayers of Stephen'. Note:

1 that both the principal and subordinate clause contain the same elements;

2 the word-order S.V. in the subordinate clause *þider ðe Stephanus forestop* and V.S. in the principal clause *þider folgode Paulus*. This is regular OE (see §151) but produces a chiasmus;

3 that the word-order 'prepositional phrase + participle' in the first clause is reversed in the second. Again, both are good OE, but the change produces another chiasmus;

4 the change from *Saules* to *Paulus* – a sermon in itself.

It is (we can say) certain beyond all doubt that Ælfric was influenced by Latin prose style; it is hard to see how it could have been otherwise. But it is equally important to realize that this powerful and moving sentence – parallel yet doubly chiastic and with the effective contrast between Saul and Paul – contains nothing which is not 'good Old English'. It follows therefore that we must avoid the tendency (often found in critics of Milton's *Paradise Lost*) to rush around slapping the label 'Latinism' on anything which deviates in the slightest from our preconceived notions of the norms of ordinary speech.

§151 Much of the difficulty with correlative pairs arises from the fact that (with a few exceptions such as *gif...þonne* 'if... then') the conjunction and the adverb have the same form, e.g. *þa* can mean both 'when' and 'then'. For the interrogatives (with the possible exception of *hwonne* 'when, until') were not used to introduce adjective or adverb clauses in OE; see §159 n. 2. Sometimes the indeclinable particle *þe* is added to the conjunction, e.g. in the passage discussed in §150 *þider ðe* means 'whither' and *þider* 'thither'. But this is by no means the rule. Sometimes the context helps, e.g. we can safely translate *þa se cyng þæt hierde, þa wende he hine west* as 'When the king heard that, then he turned (reflexive) west'. But the word-order is an even more useful and reliable guide, for it may be taken as a pretty safe rule for prose that, when one of two correlative *þa* clauses has the word-order V.S., it must be the principal clause and *þa* must mean 'then'. The temporal clause introduced by *þa* 'when' may have the order S. ... V., e.g. *þa he on lichoman wæs* 'when he was in the flesh', or S.V., e.g. *þa þunor ofslog XXIIII heora fodrera* 'when thunder killed twenty-four of their foragers'. The adverb *þā* may be repeated within the subordinate clause, e.g. *þa he þæt þa sumre tide dyde* 'when he did that on one particular occasion', where it need not of course be translated. Doubled *þā*, as in *ða þa seo boc com to us* 'when the book came to us' and *þa þa Dunstan geong man wæs* 'when Dunstan was a young man' usually introduces a subordinate clause, as the word-order in these examples testifies. Ælfric is very fond of this device.

§152 Other correlative pairs with which we can use word-order to determine which of the clauses is principal are

> *þonne . . . þonne* 'when . . . then'
> *þær . . . þær* 'where . . . there'
> *þider . . . þider* 'whither . . . thither'

On the distinction between *þā* and *þonne*, see §168, s.v. *þonne*.

Note
Correlative pairs to which this rule does not regularly apply include: *ær . . . ær, nū . . . nū, siþþan . . . siþþan, swā . . . swā, þanon . . . þanon, þēah . . . þēah*; on these, see §168. *þēah . . . hwæþre* 'though . . . yet' and *gif . . . þonne* 'if . . . then' present no problems. It should also be noted that the word-order S.V. often occurs after adverbs other than those discussed above; see §147 for an example after *Hēr*, and note *nu todæg hi underfengon Stephanum* 'now today they received Stephen' and *On deaðe he wæs gesett . . .* 'he was placed in death . . .'. S.V. seems to be more common in such sentences when the subject is an unstressed pronoun, as in the last two examples, but often occurs with a noun subject, as in the example in §147. Compare §144.2.

Exceptions to the rule do exist. But you should view with suspicion any you meet, for the punctuation of some modern editions is sometimes at fault. Remember, however, that the rule does not apply to the poetry and that correlation is not essential, e.g.

> þa he þa wið þone here þær wæst abisgod wæs, 7 þa hergas wæron þa gegaderode begen to Sceobyrig on Eastseaxum, 7 þær geweorc worhtun, foron begen ætgædere up be Temese

'When he was occupied against the army there in the west, and the [other] Danish armies were assembled at Shoebury in Essex, and had made a fortress there, they both went together up along the Thames'.

§153 The value of this rule can be demonstrated from the following complicated passage in the Old English version of Bede's account of the poet Cædmon (selection 9, paragraph 2):

> Ond he for þon oft in gebeorscipe, þonne þær wæs blisse intinga gedemed, þæt heo ealle sceolden þurh endebyrdnesse be hearpan singan, þonne he geseah þa hearpan him nealecan, þonne aras he for scome from

þæm symble ond ham eode to his huse. þa he þæt þa sumre tide dyde, þæt he forlet þæt hus þæs gebeorscipes ond ut wæs gongende to neata scipene, þara heord him wæs þære neahte beboden, þa he ða þær in gelimplicre tide his leomu on reste gesette ond onslepte, þa stod him sum mon æt þurh swefn ond hine halette ond grette ond hine be his noman nemnde.

We can begin by underlining the verbs in the second sentence: *dyde, forlēt... ond ūt wæs gongende, wæs... beboden, gesette ond onslēpte, stōd... ond... hālette... ond grētte... ond nemnde*. Now the corresponding conjunctions for these five verbs or groups of verbs are *þā... þā, þæt, þāra, þā... ðā*, and *þā. þæt* introduces a noun clause (§155) and *þāra* an adjective clause (§162). From our word-order rule, we know that '*þā* subject *þā*' introduces a subordinate clause, '*þā* V.S.' a principal clause. Hence the last *þā* means 'then', the syntax of the sentence is clear, and we can translate fairly literally: 'When he did that on one particular occasion, namely left the feast-hall and went out to the stall of the cattle, the care of which had been entrusted to him for that night [and] when in due time he stretched his limbs on the bed there and fell asleep, then a certain man appeared to him in a dream and saluted him and greeted him and called upon him by name'.

Similarly, in the first sentence, we have three *þonne* clauses, viz. *þonne þær wæs..., þonne hē geseah... þonne ārās hē...*. The rule instantly tells us that the last is the principal clause 'then he arose ...'.

III NOUN CLAUSES

Introduction

§154 This heading traditionally comprehends dependent statements, desires (commands, wishes, etc.), questions, and exclamations. The OE patterns conform very closely to those of MnE, apart from the use of *þæt* and *hit* to anticipate a noun clause (see §148).

Dependent Statements and Desires

§155 Dependent statements are introduced by *þæt*, e.g. *ða ðohte he ðæt he wolde gesecan helle godu* 'then he thought that he would seek the gods of hell', or *þætte* (= *þæt þe*), e.g. *ic wene ðætte noht monige begiondan Humbre næren* 'I believe that there were not many beyond the Humber'. *þæt(te)* is sometimes repeated, as in the second sentence discussed in §172, and is sometimes not expressed, e.g. *Swa ic wat he minne hige cuðe* 'So I know he perceived my intention'.

Dependent desires are also introduced by *þæt*, e.g. *bæd þæt hyra randas rihte heoldon* 'requested that they should hold their shields properly', or *þætte*.

þæt clauses are, however, more common in OE than their equivalent in MnE, for they are often found where we should use an accusative and infinitive (as in the last example, where we should say 'requested them to hold their shields properly') or some other construction.

§156 The verb of the *þæt* clause may be indicative or subjunctive. Two questions arise – first, 'What is the significance of the two moods?' and second 'When must the subjunctive be represented in translation?' The first is usually answered in some such way as this:

The *indicative* is used when the content of the noun clause is presented as a fact, as certain, as true, or as a result which has actually followed or will follow.

When the *subjunctive* occurs, some mental attitude towards the content of the noun clause is usually implied; one of the following ideas may be present – condition, desire, obligation, supposition, perplexity, doubt, uncertainty, or unreality.

There is some truth in this. Thus the subjunctive is the natural mood in dependent desires, e.g. *ic ðe bebiode ðæt ðu do* . . . 'I command that you do . . .'. But the indicative sometimes occurs after verbs of commanding, compelling, and the like, e.g. *he bebead Tituse his suna þæt he towearp þæt templ* and *and ðurh ðine halige miht tunglu genedest þæt hi ðe to herað*. Here the indicative emphasizes that the action desired actually took place; hence the translations might read 'Titus carried out his father's command and destroyed the temple' and 'through your holy power you compel the stars to worship you'. These and similar clauses could be called result clauses or noun clauses with the indicative showing that the event actually took place. But 'a rose by any other name . . .'.

Similarly, in dependent statements, the indicative shows that the speaker is certain of the factuality of what he says and is vouching for its truth, e.g. *ic wat þæt þu eart heard mann* 'I know that you are a hard man', . . . *ðe cyðan . . . ðæt me com swiðe oft on gemynd* . . . 'to make known to you that it has often come into my mind . . .', and *þonne wite he þæt God gesceop to mæran engle þone þe nu is deofol* 'let him know therefore that God created as a great angel the creature who is now the devil'. But the subjunctive appears when no certainty is implied about a happening in the future, e.g. *Hit wæs gewitegod þæt he on ðære byrig Bethleem acenned wurde* 'It was prophesied that He should be born in the city of Bethlehem', when the truth of another's statement is not vouched for, e.g. *Be þæm Theuhaleon wæs gecweden . . . þæt he wære moncynnes tydriend, swa swa Noe wæs* 'About that Deucalion it was said that he was the father of mankind, as Noah was', or when it is denied, e.g. *Nu cwædon gedwolmen þæt deofol gesceope sume gesceafta, ac hi leogað* 'Now heretics said that some creations were the work of the devil but they lie'. This distinction between the indicative and the subjunctive is seen clearly in *Ne sæde þæt halige godspel þæt se rica reafere wære, ac wæs uncystig and modegode on his welum* 'The holy gospel did not say that the rich man was a robber, but that he was mean and exulted in his wealth'.

However, the rule does not tell the whole truth. The indicative does not always state a fact, e.g. *And gif hit gelimpþ þæt he hit fint* 'And if it happens that he finds it', nor does the subjunctive always imply uncertainty, doubt, or the like, e.g. *Mine gebroðra, uton we geoffrian urum Drihtne gold, þæt we andettan þæt he soð Cyning sy, and æghwær rixige* 'My brothers, let us offer our Lord gold, that we may confess that He is [the] true King and rules everywhere'; they all believe this. Again, in *Se wisa Augustinus . . . smeade hwi se halga cyðere Stephanus cwæde þæt he gesawe mannes bearn standan æt Godes swyðran* 'The wise Augustine . . . enquired why the holy martyr Stephen said that he saw the Son of Man standing at God's right hand', the subjunctive *gesāwe* does not mean that Augustine is casting doubt on Stephen's statement; it is probably due in part to the 'attraction' of the subjunctive form *cwǣde* and in part to the influence of the verb *cweðan* itself. For, when introducing a dependent statement, *cweðan* prefers the subjunctive, *cyðan* the indicative. This may reflect some original difference in meaning such as 'I (think and) give it as my opinion' as against a more objective 'I (know and) make it known'. Perhaps originally *cweðan* always had the subjunctive and *cyðan* the indicative, and perhaps this situation would have continued if language were always a strictly logical activity in which verbs of thinking took the subjunctive and verbs of knowing the indicative. But it is not. We tend to say 'I think he may come' and 'I know he will come'. But 'I know he may be here in ten minutes, but I can't wait' and 'I think that he is without doubt the cleverest boy in the school' show that no hard and fast rules can be laid down. Each situation must be judged on its merits.

Hence we may say that, while the rule set out above often works, fluctuation between the subjunctive and the indicative in OE noun clauses is often of little significance. It is just as dangerous to place too much reliance on the presence of a subjunctive in OE as it would be to draw firm conclusions about a modern speaker's attitude from the fact that he started his sentence with 'I know that . . .' rather than 'I think that . . .'.

So the answer to our second question 'When must the subjunctive be represented in translation?' can only be something indefinite like 'When the situation demands it'. It is, for example, unnecessary to bring out the fact that a verb of denying or supposing is followed by a subjunctive referring to some past act, for the verb 'to deny' or 'to suppose' is in itself enough to give a modern reader the necessary information. The subjunctive which will be most frequently represented in MnE is that in which some doubt or uncertainty arises over an action which, at the time of speaking, is still in the future. Such a subjunctive, of course, occurs most commonly in dependent desires.

Dependent Questions

§157   Questions fall into two main divisions – those in which the questioner seeks new information, e.g. *Hwær eart þu?* 'Where are you?' and *Hwy stande ge ealne dæg idele?* 'Why do you stand all day idle?', and those in which he asks his hearer to choose between alternatives expressed or implied in the question, e.g. *'Wilt þu we gað and gadriað hie?' Đa cwæð he: 'Nese' '* "Do you wish us to go and gather them?" And he answered "No".' [But he could have answered 'Yes'.] Rhetorical questions may, of course, be of either type.

§158 Those questions which seek new information present little difficulty. The dependent question will include the interrogative word of the non-dependent question. This may be a pronoun (e.g. *hwā* 'who' and *hwæt* 'what'), an adjective (e.g. *hwelć* 'which, what sort of'), or an adverb (e.g. *hū* 'how' and *hwær* 'where'). Other common adverbs are *hwider* 'whither', *hwanon* 'whence', *hwonne* 'when' (see §159 n. 2), *hwȳ* and *hwæt* 'why', and combinations of a preposition + an oblique case of *hwæt*, e.g. *tō hwæs* 'whither', *for hwon* and *for hwȳ* 'why'. These questions may be anticipated by a demonstrative or personal pronoun; see §148.

Note

Some of these interrogative words can also be used indefinitely, e.g. *hwā* can mean 'someone, anyone' and *hwær* 'somewhere, anywhere'.

§159 In MnE many of these interrogative words can also be used as relative pronouns, e.g. 'The man who ...', 'The place where ...', and so on. This use seems to stem (in part at least) from OE sentences of the type 'I know you, what you are' and 'Consider the lilies of the field, how they flourish', in which the main verb has as objects both a noun (or pronoun) and a clause containing a dependent question. A convenient OE example is

> ond ic hean þonan
> wod wintercearig   ofer waþema gebind,
> sohte sele dreorig   sinces bryttan,
> hwær ic feor oþþe neah   findan meahte
> þone þe in meoduhealle   min mine wisse

'and I, miserable, with winter in my heart, made my way thence over the frozen expanse of the waves, sadly seeking the hall of a giver of treasure, [sadly seeking] far and near where I might find one who would show regard for me in the mead-hall'.

Here the two objects of *sōhte* are *sele* and the *hwær* clause.

Note 1

The first object of *sōhte* is *sinces bryttan* if the attractive compound *seledrēorig* 'sad for a hall' is accepted. But the fact that this interpretation is possible emphasizes that the *hwær* clause is interrogative, not adjective. It could not qualify *bryttan*.

Similarly in

> Ne meahte hire Iudas . . .
> sweotole gecyþan   be ðam sigebeame
> on hwylcne se hælend   ahafen wære

hwylcne is strictly an interrogative introducing a noun clause, object of *gecyþan*, and the literal sense is 'Nor could Judas . . . tell her beyond doubt about the victorious tree, [tell her] on which tree the Saviour was raised up'.[1] It is easy to see how such juxtaposition of noun and interrogative would lead to the use of the interrogative as a relative. But this stage has not been reached in OE.

Note 2

Hwonne 'when, until' is perhaps furthest advanced of all the OE interrogatives on the way to becoming a word which could introduce adverb and adjective clauses. Those who are interested may care to look at the ways in which *hwonne* is used in the following examples: *Andreas* l. 136 (noun clause); *Riddle* 31 l. 13 (adjective clause); *Genesis* l. 2603 (adverb clause of time 'when'); *Genesis* l. 1028 (adverb clause of time 'whenever'); and *Andreas* l. 400 (adverb clause of time 'until'). I have put in brackets the interpretation which seems to offer the most convenient translation. But careful consideration will show that an Anglo-Saxon might have regarded all these as noun clauses – if he ever thought about it.

§160   Non-dependent questions inviting a choice between alternatives can be asked in two ways in OE:

1   by the word-order V.S. (as in MnE) – for examples see §§146.1 and 146.2;

2   with *hwæþer* (*þe*) and the word-order S. . . . V., e.g. *Hwæþer þe þin eage manful is?* 'Is your eye evil?', or S.V., e.g. *Hwæðer ic mote lybban oðþæt ic hine geseo?* 'May I live until I see him?'

As in MnE, dependent questions of this type are normally introduced by an interrogative word – either *hwæþer* 'whether', e.g. *Lætaþ þæt we geseon hwæðer Elias cume* 'Let us see whether E. comes', or *ġif* 'if', e.g. *frægn gif him wære niht getæse* 'asked if the night had been pleasant to him'. An occasional example like 'He asked was anybody there' occurs (e.g. *Elene* ll. 157 ff.); in these the original word-order is retained but the tense has been changed.

In the examples cited above, the alternative 'or not' is implied. But it is occasionally expressed, e.g. *Anra gehwylc wat gif he beswuncgen wæs oððe na*

---

[1] The OE relative construction occurs in

> . . . ond geflitu ræran
> be ðam sigebeame   on þam soðcyning
> ahangen wæs . . .

'to stir up controversy about the victorious tree on which the true King was crucified . . .'. Note the difference in mood – *wære* above but *wæs* here.

'Each man knows whether he was beaten, or not'. An unusual example of the type of question under discussion here occurs in *Genesis* ll. 531 ff., where the conjunctions are *þēah . . . þe* 'whether . . . or'.

The remarks made about mood in dependent statements also apply in general to dependent questions.

The Accusative and Infinitive

§161 This construction, well known in Latin, e.g. *Solon furere se simulavit* 'Solon pretended to be mad', and in MnE, e.g. 'I know him to be dead', is also an OE idiom. The subject accusative may be expressed, as in

> Het þa hyssa hwæne   hors forlætan,
> feor afysan,   and forð gangan

'He then ordered each of the warriors to release his horse [and] drive it away, and to go forth', but is often left unexpressed, as in *ond ðe cyðan hate* lit. 'I order [someone] to make known to you . . .', and *he het hie hon on heam gealgum* lit. 'he ordered [someone] to hang them on the high gallows' (where *hīe* is the object of *hōn*). In the last two examples, the subject accusative is not expressed, either because everybody knows or because nobody cares who is to perform the action. In these, it is very convenient to translate the infinitives *cyðan* and *hōn* as if they were passive – 'I order you to be told' (or '. . . that you be told . . .') and 'he ordered them to be hanged'. Much time has been spent in idle controversy over the question whether these infinitives were actually passive; what is important is that, when the subject accusative of the accusative and infinitive is not expressed, the active infinitive can usually be *translated* as a passive.

IV ADJECTIVE CLAUSES

Definite Adjective Clauses

§162 Definite adjective clauses are those which refer to one particular antecedent, e.g. 'This is the man *who did it*' as opposed to indefinite clauses whose antecedent is unspecified, e.g. '*Whoever did it* will be caught'. As in Latin, the relative pronoun agrees with its antecedent (expressed or implied) in number and gender, but takes its case from the adjective clause. There are various ways of expressing it in OE.

1 The indeclinable particle *þe* is very common when the relative is the subject, e.g. *Ic geseah þa englas þe eower gymdon* 'I saw the angels who took care of you', *ælc þæra þe ðas min word gehyrð* 'each of those who hears these my words', and *swa swa hit gewunelic is þæm ðe on wuda gað oft* 'as is customary among those who frequently go in the wood'. It occurs fairly often when the

relative is the object, e.g. *her onginneð seo boc þe man Orosius nemneð* 'here begins the book which one calls Orosius'. It very occasionally functions as a relative in the genitive or dative. Examples are *of ðæm mere ðe Truso standeð in staðe* 'from the sea on whose shore Truso stands' and *oð ðone dæg þe hi hine forbærnað* 'until the day on which they burn him'.

2   In these last two examples, however, the case of the relative pronoun is not immediately clear because *þe* is indeclinable. So the appropriate case of the third person pronoun was sometimes added. Thus there is no ambiguity in *Eadig bið se wer, þe his tohopa bið to Drihtne* 'Blessed is the man whose hope is in the Lord' or in

þæt se mon ne wat
þe him on foldan   fægrost limpeð

'The man for whom it goes very pleasantly on the earth does not know that'.

Note

This combination sometimes occurs when the relative is nominative, e.g. *Paris Psalter* 67 l. 4 (*þe hē*) and, with first person pronouns, *Riddle* 12 l. 14 (*þe ïc*) and *Christ* l. 25 (*þe wē*). With the second person pronoun the regular combination is *þū þe* or *ġē þe*; see *The Review of English Studies* 15 (1964), 135–137.

3   The appropriate case of the demonstrative *se, sēo, þæt* is often used as a relative, e.g. *se hearpere, ðæs nama wæs Orfeus, hæfde an wif, seo wæs haten Eurydice* 'the harper, whose name was Orpheus, had a wife who was called Eurydice', *eall þæt ic geman* 'all that I remember', and *fif Moyses boca, ðam seo godcunde æ awriten is* 'five (of the) books of Moses in which the divine law is written'. Here there is no ambiguity about case and number, but we cannot always be sure whether the pronoun is demonstrative or relative.

4   But there is no ambiguity for us in sentences like ... *and wæs se soþa Scyppend, seþe ana is God, forsewen* '... and the true Creator, who alone is God, was rejected', in which both antecedent and relative have the same case, for *þe* certifies that we have a relative pronoun and *se* tells us its case. This can be called the *seþe* relative. Again, there is no ambiguity for us in sentences like *þa com he on morgenne to þam tungerefan, se þe his ealdormon wæs* 'Then he came in the morning to the steward, who was his superior' and *þystre genip, þam þe se þeoden self sceop nihte naman* 'the cloud of darkness, for which the Lord Himself made the name "night" ', for the presence of the particle *þe* after *se* and *þām* makes it clear that we have to do with a relative pronoun, while *se* and *þām* tell us its case. This pattern, in which the *se* element has the case required by the adjective clause only, can be called the *'seþe* relative. In both these patterns, although the elements are written sometimes together, sometimes separately, by the scribes, the *se* element tells us the case of the relative pronoun.

Note
In the nominative, these combinations can mean 'he who' or 'the one who' or 'whoever'; cf. §164.

5　So far, then, we can say that the OE relatives are the indeclinable particle *þe*, to which the personal pronoun can be added to remove ambiguities of case, and the demonstrative pronoun *se, sēo, þæt* in the case required by the *adjective* clause, either alone or followed by the indeclinable particle *þe* to make clear that we have a relative and not a demonstrative pronoun.

§163　The comments which follow may be useful when you have mastered §162.

1　Another example of the *'seþe* type like those in §162.4 is

> Se wæs Hroþgare　　hæleþa leofost
> rice randwiga,　　þone ðe heo on ræste abreat

'He whom she (the monster) killed in his resting-place was the most beloved of heroes to Hrothgar, a mighty shield-warrior'. But a word of warning is necessary here, because you are likely to meet sentences which seem to contain this combination, but do not. Thus in *gedo grenne finul XXX nihta on ænne croccan þone þe sie gepicod utan* 'put green fennel for thirty nights into a jar which is covered with pitch on the outside' and in

> syððan hie gefricgeað　　frean userne
> ealdorleasne,　　þone ðe ær geheold
> wið hettendum　　hord ond rice

'when they learn our lord to be dead, he who in the past guarded our treasure and kingdom against enemies', *þone þe* is not an accusative relative, for *þone* has the case of the *principal* clause agreeing with its antecedent. Formally, *þone* belongs to the principal clause and we can therefore say that the relative in these examples is *þe*. But they differ from the second and third sentences quoted in §162.1 (where the demonstrative is the only antecedent) in that there is already an antecedent and the demonstrative is therefore superfluous. In earlier times *þone* was no doubt stressed in such sentences – 'our lord ... that one ... he'. But there may be some truth in the view that in our sentences *þone* belonged rhythmically to the adjective clause and was felt as part of the relative; hence we can (if we wish) distinguish the relative in which the demonstrative has the case of the principal clause but is not the antecedent, as the *se'þe* relative. There is no real difficulty in the pattern seen in the *ðā ðe* clause in example B in §172, where the two clauses require different cases (acc./nom.) but where *ðā* can be either nominative or accusative. But you should be on the alert for examples of what I have called the *se'þe* type.

Notes

1   Examples in which real ambiguity occurs are rare. But there is one in *Beowulf* ll. 2291–93:

> Swa mæg unfæge   eaðe gedigan
> wean and wræcsið   se ðe Wealdendes
> hyldo gehealdeþ.

If the relative pronoun is *se'þe*, *hyldo* (indeclinable feminine) is the subject of the adjective clause, *ðe* is accusative, and the translation would read 'So may an undoomed man whom the favour of the Almighty protects easily survive both woe and banishment'. If the relative pronoun is *seþe*, it is nominative, *hyldo* is accusative, and the translation would read 'So may an undoomed man who retains the favour of the Almighty . . .'.

2   Sometimes, when the relative pronoun is in a case other than the nominative, the personal pronoun follows a relative of the *se'þe* type. This enables us to tell immediately the case of the relative pronoun, e.g.

> se biþ leofast   londbuendum
> se þe him God syleð   gumena rice

'that one is most beloved by land-dwellers to whom God gives the kingdom of men' and *se, se þe him ær geþuhte þæt him nan sæ wiþhabban ne mehte þæt he hine mid scipum afyllan ne mehte, eft wæs biddende anes lytles troges æt anum earman men, þæt he mehte his feorh generian* 'he to whom it once had seemed that no sea was so great (lit. could stop him) that he could not fill it with ships, finally asked a wretched man for one little boat so that he could save his life'. See also *Dream of the Rood* ll. 85–6.

2   A not uncommon idiom is found in the sentence about Tantalus quoted in §148. The antecedent *Tantulus* is followed by two adjective clauses joined by *ond*. In the first, *ðe . . . gifre wæs*, the relative pronoun is nominative. The second is *him . . . ðære gifernesse*. Here the relative pronoun is [*þe*] *him* 'whom'. But it is idiomatic not to repeat the *þe*; *him* warns us of the change of case from nominative to dative.

Another idiom is found in

> Nis nu cwicra nan
> þe ic him modsefan   minne durre
> sweotule asecgan.

Here the antecedent is *nān cwicra*. The relative pronoun is *þe him*. *Ic* is the subject of the adjective clause. So we have 'There is no one alive to whom I dare reveal my thoughts'. When the relative pronoun is *þe* + personal pronoun and another pronoun is the subject of the adjective clause, the latter comes between the two elements of the relative. So *þe ic him*.

3   The indeclinable relative *þe* always precedes any preposition which governs it; see the sentence about Ixion quoted in §148.

4   The adjective clause need not immediately follow the antecedent.

5   *þæt* often combines antecedent and relative pronoun. It must then be translated 'what', e.g. *he hæfde ðeah geforþod þæt he his frean gehet* 'he had, however, done what he promised his lord'. This survived into eMnE, e.g. in the Authorized Version *John* 13: 27 'That thou doest, do quickly'. In

> Gode þancode
> mihtigan Drihtne,   þæs se man gespræc,

þæs is genitive after *þancode* and we might expect *þe*: 'thanked God for that which the man spoke'. But this is probably an example of *þæt* 'what' – 'thanked God, the mighty Lord, for what the man spoke'.

6   In MnE the difficulty of combining an adjective clause and a verb of saying or thinking often produces a 'grammatical error', e.g. 'This is the man whom they thought would revolutionize the teaching of English' where we should have '. . . who, they thought, . . .'. The same problem arises in OE and often results in what seems to us a somewhat incoherent arrangement, e.g. *Ða eode he furður oð he gemette ða graman gydena ðe folcisce men hatað Parcas, ða hi secgað ðæt on nanum men nyton nane are, ac ælcum men wrecen be his gewyrhtum; þa hi secgað ðæt walden ælces mannes wyrde* 'Then he went on further until he met the terrible goddesses whom the people of that land call the Parcae, who (they say) show no mercy to any man, but punish each man according to his deserts; these (they say) control each man's fate'. A result acceptable in MnE can be obtained in these examples by omitting the *ðæt*. Sometimes, however, the subject is expressed twice, e.g. *in þære cirican seo cwen gewunade hire gebiddan, þe we ær cwædon þæt heo Cristen wære*. Here we need to omit *þæt hēo* to get the sense: 'in that church the queen who, we said formerly, was Christian, was wont to say her prayers'. But even this is clumsy and needs polishing.

7   Attempts have been made to lay down the rules which governed the use of the various relative pronouns in OE. They have not succeeded, largely because the vital clue of intonation is denied to us.

Indefinite Adjective Clauses

§164   The relative pronouns used in definite adjective clauses also appear in the indefinite ones, e.g.

> þa wæs eaðfynde   þe him elles hwær
> gerumlicor   ræste sohte

'Then it was easy to find whoever (= the man who) sought a bed elsewhere, further away',

> heold hyne syðþan
> fyr ond fæstor ,   se þæm feonde ætwand

'whoever escaped the enemy thereafter kept himself further away and in greater safety', *sægde se þe cuþe* . . . 'he who knew said . . .' (the *seþe* relative; see §162.4), and *Se þe gewemð Godes tempel, God hine fordeð* 'Whoever defiles God's temple, God will destroy him' (the *'seþe* relative; see again §162.4).

As has already been noted, the interrogatives *hwā* 'who', *hwǣr* 'where', and the like, are not used alone in OE as relatives; see §159. But they are used in the indefinite relatives *swā hwā swā* 'whoever', *swā hwæt swā* 'whatever', *swā hwær swā* 'wherever', and so on. One example will suffice – *swa hwa swa þe genyt þusend stapa, ga mid him oðre twa þusend* 'whoever compels thee [to go] one mile, go with him two'.

Mood

§165 The adjective clause usually has its verb in the indicative, even when it is in dependent speech. But the subjunctive may occur in the following situations:

1 When the principal clause contains an imperative or a subjunctive expressing a wish, e.g. *Matthew* 5: 42 *syle þam ðe þe bidde* Authorized Version 'Give to him that asketh thee'. However, the fact that the indicative is found in such circumstances, e.g. *Matthew* 19: 21 *becyp eall þæt þu ahst* Authorized Version 'sell that thou hast', shows that the mood varies with the speaker's attitude and not with any automatic 'law of symmetry'. In the first example, there is uncertainty because the asker is as yet unknown and indeed may not exist; we could translate 'Give to anyone who may ask'. In the second, the young man's possessions exist and are known to him. For, as the story tells us, 'he went away sorrowful, for he had great possessions'.

2 When the principal clause contains a negative, e.g. the second sentence discussed in §163.2. But this again is no automatic rule. The subjunctive is found only when the content of the adjective clause is put forward as unreal; in the example, there is no such person in existence nor probably could there be. But in *Beowulf* ll. 1465–7

> Huru ne gemunde   mago Ecglafes
> eafoþes cræftig,   þæt he ær gespræc
> wine druncen

'However, the son of Ecglaf, powerful in his might, did not remember what he had said before, when drunk with wine', Unferth (*mago Ecgláfes*) actually had spoken the words, but he did not now remember them; the poet could have said that he had forgotten them. In this example, the *ne* negates merely the verb of the principal clause, not the whole idea which follows; hence the indicative in the adjective clause.

3 When the principal clause contains a rhetorical question, e.g.

> Hwa is on eorðan   nu unlærdra
> þe ne wundrige   wolcna færeldes . . . ?

'Who is there on earth among the unlearned who does not wonder at the motion of the clouds . . . ?' The answer demanded is, of course, 'No-one'. Such examples are exactly parallel to those discussed in 2 above, for the poet could easily have said 'There is no-one on earth . . .'.

4 When a limiting adjective clause[1] has as antecedent a genitive depending on a superlative, e.g.

Niwe flodas   Noe oferlað,

. . .

þone deopestan   drencefloda
þara ðe gewurde   on woruldrice.

Here the poet is saying that Noah sailed over the deepest deluge that could ever be or have been. Similar examples occur in *Beowulf* ll. 2129 ff., *Genesis* ll. 626 ff., and *Daniel* ll. 691 ff. In these the subjunctive is used to imply that all the possible examples of floods, griefs, women, and cities, respectively are being considered – those which the writer knows about, those which have happened without his knowledge, and those which may yet happen. That the 'superlative + genitive' does not automatically cause the subjunctive is shown by examples like

. . . ond hi þa gesette   on þone selestan
foldan sceata,   þone fira bearn
nemnað neorxnawong . . .

'and then he placed them in the best regions of the earth, which the sons of men call Paradise', where the non-limiting adjective clause has the indicative.

V ADVERB CLAUSES

Introduction

§166 The conventional classification will serve us here. It distinguishes eight types – place, time, purpose, result, cause, comparison, concession, condition. On the whole, you will find that these clauses are fundamentally very similar to their counterparts in MnE. The main differences to be noted are:

1 the conjunctions themselves;
2 the methods of correlation, linked with
3 the word-order within the clauses. On these two points, see §§150–153;
4 a more frequent use of the subjunctive mood. Sometimes it is used by rule and is of little significance for us, sometimes it makes an important distinction. On this, see §§173–180.

§§167–171 contain a discussion of the conjunctions and alphabetical lists

---

[1] In the sentence 'The soldiers who (that) were tired lay down' the adjective clause does not merely describe the soldiers; it limits the action of lying down to a particular group – those who were tired. Hence it is a 'limiting' clause. But in 'The soldiers, who were tired, lay down' the adjective clause merely tells us something more about all the soldiers. Hence it is 'non-limiting'.

of non-prepositional and prepositional formulae with their main uses. §§173–180 discuss each type of clause in turn, outlining briefly the conjunctions and moods used in them and any other points of special interest.

§167   If we adopt a purely formal classification, we can detect in MnE at least five types of conjunction. Consider the following series of clauses:

1   Christ died, *that* we may live.
2   Christ died, *so that* we may live.
3   *So* boldly did Christ speak, *that* all men listened.
4
5
6   Christ died, *to the end that* we may live.
7   *To this end* Christ died, *that* we may live.

In OE, we can find comparable examples to these and can fill in the missing items 4 and 5:

1   ... *he biþ geseald hæþnum mannum þæt hie hine bysmrian* '... he will be given to heathen men that they may mock him'.

2   *Hæfde se cyning his fierd on tu tonumen, swa þæt hie wæron simle healfe æt ham, healfe ute* 'The king had divided his army into two, so that at any one time half were at home, half in the field'.

3   *He ... swa anræd þurhwunode þæt he nolde abugan to bismorfullum leahtrum* 'he ... remained so resolute that he was unwilling to turn aside to shameful sins'.

4   ... *ond ðæs ðe ðu gearo forwite hwam ðu gemiltsige, ic eom Apollonius, se Tyrisca ealdormann* '... and, so that you may know who is receiving your mercy, I am Apollonius, Prince of Tyre'.

Note: This use of *ðæs ðe* is a rare one, but it is included to complete the series.

5   *Ic wat þæt nan nis þæs welig þæt he sumes eacan ne þyrfe* 'I know that there is no man so wealthy that he does not need more of something'.

6   *And ic hyne nyste, ac ic com and fullode on wætere, to þam þæt he wære geswutelod on Israhela folce* 'And I knew him not, but I came and baptized [him] in water, to the end that he might be manifested to the people of Israel'.

7   [the Heavenly King] *þe to ði com on middangeard þæt he of eallum ðeodum his gecorenan gegaderode* ... '[the Heavenly King] who to this end came into the world that he might gather his chosen from all nations'.

So we find

	MnE	OE
1	'that'	*þæt*
2	'so that'	*swā þæt*
3	'so ... that'	*swā ... þæt*

4		þæs þe
5		þæs ... þæt
6	'to the end that'	tō þām þæt
7	'to this end ... that'	tō þī ... þæt

On the variations *þe/þæt* in 4 and 5 and *þām/þī* in 6 and 7, see §169.

We can therefore speak of prepositional conjunctions (6 and 7) and non-prepositional conjunctions (1–5). We can speak of simple conjunctions (1), grouped conjunctions (2, 4, and 6), and divided conjunctions (3, 5, and 7). MnE has no exact equivalent for types 4 and 5. Their real force cannot be brought out literally today because *þæs* is the genitive of *þæt* used adverbially and we no longer have a genitive of 'that' to use in this way. So we must translate them either 'so that' and 'so ... that', which brings out the adverbial force only, or 'to the end that' and 'to the end ... that', which brings out the adverbial force and at the same time demonstrates the important truth that a good many functions of the OE cases have been taken over by MnE prepositions. Other examples of this type in OE include:

(*a*) *þȳ ... þȳ* (the instrumental of *þæt*) in comparisons, the ancestor of MnE '*the* more, *the* merrier' (lit. 'by that much ... by that much');

(*b*) *þā hwīle þe* 'while'; where we have an accusative of duration of time turned into a conjunction by the addition of the indeclinable particle *þe*;

(*c*) *þȳ læs (þe)* MnE 'lest'. On the use of *þe* in (*b*) and (*c*), see §169.

For practical purposes, the best grouping is a twofold one – non-prepositional conjunctions, simple, grouped and divided (i.e. items 1–5), and prepositional conjunctions or formulae, grouped and divided (items 6–7). The following sections contain separate alphabetical lists of the most important OE conjunctions in these two groups, with any comments necessary on their use. Examples are often given from poems you are likely to read.

Non-Prepositional Conjunctions

§168 (Note: The list mentions any adverbial and prepositional uses of the conjunctions discussed and any pronominal forms with which they may be confused.)

ǣr

  1 Prep. 'before'. As prep. it also introduces prep. conjs. of time; see §171.
  2 Adv. 'formerly'. Often a sign of the pluperfect; see §197.4.
  3 Temporal conj. 'before'. Often takes the subj. But this need not be brought out in translation.

būtan, būton

  1 Prep. 'without'.
  2 Conj. 'except that, but' + ind.
  3 Conj. 'unless, if not' + subj.

ġif

1 Conj. 'if, whether' introducing dependent questions.

2 Conj. 'if' introducing conditional clauses.

hwonne

Conj. 'when'. Originally an interrogative introducing questions, it shades into a temporal conj. 'when, until'; see §159 n. 2.

nefne, nemne, nymþe

The Anglian equivalent of *būton*; you will meet it mostly in the poetry, e.g. *Beowulf* l. 1552.

nō ðȳ ǣr

Adv. 'none the sooner, yet . . . not, not yet'.

nū

1 Adv. 'now'.

2 Conj. 'now that, because', often combining the ideas of time and cause; it takes the ind. and is not used when a false reason is given. It usually refers to a state in the present, e.g. (with present tense) *Maldon* l. 222 and (with preterite tense to be translated as perfect) *Maldon* l. 250. In the latter example, the state in the present is the result of an action completed in the past.

oð

1 Prep. 'until, up to' of time or place. As a prep. it also introduces prep. conjs. of time; see §171.

2 Conj. 'until' marking temporal and/or local limit.

sam . . . sam

'Whether . . . or' in concessive clauses.

siþþan

1 Adv. 'after'.

2 Conj. meaning

(*a*) *ex quo* 'since'.

(*b*) *postquam* 'after'.

(*c*) sometimes 'when, as soon as'.

swā

1 Adv. 'so, thus'. It usually refers back, but may anticipate what is to come.

2 Conj. alone and in combination. The following main uses can be distinguished:

(*a*) In indefinite combinations

in adjective clauses; see §164.

in clauses of place, e.g. *swā hwǣr swā* 'wherever' and *swā wīde swā* 'as widely as'.

in clauses of time, e.g. *swā hraþe swā* 'as quickly as', *swā lange swā* 'as long as', *swā oft swā* 'as often as', and (*swā*) *sōna swā* 'as soon as'.

(*b*) With the superlative

e.g. *swa ðu oftost mæge* 'as often as you can' and *swa hie selest mihton* 'as well as they could'.

(*c*) In clauses of comparison

swā 'as'.

swā swā 'as, just as'.

swā . . . swā 'so . . . as, as . . . so'.

swā . . . swā swā 'so . . . as'.

(*d*) Other uses

swā + subj. often means 'as if', e.g. *Wanderer* l. 96.

swā can sometimes be translated 'as far as', e.g. *Elene* l. 971, or 'wherever', e.g. *Andreas* l. 1582.

swā can sometimes be translated 'because'.

swā sometimes means 'so that'.

Frequently it is 'a rather characterless connective, shading into concession, result, or manner, as the case may be, and, with the negative, corresponding to Modern English "without", "not being" ' (Burnham), e.g. *Hi fuhton fif dagas, swa hyra nan ne feol* 'They fought for five days without any of them falling'.

For *swā . . . swā* 'either . . . or', see §184.3.

With a comparative, *swā . . . swā* means 'the . . . the', e.g. *swa norðor swa smælre* 'the further north, the narrower'.

Note

swā is sometimes translated as a relative pronoun. This is misleading; see *The Review of English Studies* 15 (1964), 140.

swā þæt

Conj. 'so that' introducing result clauses. No unambiguous examples of purpose clauses after *swā þæt* have been noted. But the distinction is often a very fine one, e.g. *swa þæt he mehte ægþerne geræcan*, which might mean either 'was able to reach' or 'might reach'; see §§120 and 207.

swā . . . þæt

Conj. 'so . . . that'. Like its MnE equivalent, it usually introduces result clauses.

swelce, swilce, swylce

1   It can be a form of the pron. *swelc* 'such, such a one, such as, which'.

2   Conj. 'such as', e.g. *Beowulf* l. 757, where it would be *swylcne* if it were the pronoun. In *Dream of the Rood* l. 92 *swylce swā* may be translated 'just as'.

Frequently we can not tell whether we have 1 or 2, e.g. *Seafarer* l. 83. This does not matter.

3   Adv. 'likewise, also'.

4   Conj. 'as if' with subj. or without verb, e.g. *swelce to gamenes* 'as if in fun'.

5   Conj. 'because'.

þā

1   Acc. sg. fem. and nom. acc. pl. of *se*.

2   Adv. 'then'.

3   Conj. 'when'. Used only with pret. ind. of a single completed act in the past. For further explanation, see under *þonne*.

4   *þā . . . furþum* = Lat. *cum . . . primum* 'as soon as', e.g. *Beowulf* l. 465.

5   In *Maldon* l. 5 (quoted in §148) *þā . . . ǣrest* may mean 'as soon as'.

þā hwīle þe

Conj. 'as long as, while' (lit. 'during that time in which', i.e. acc. of duration of time + particle *þe*). It is found only eight times in the poetry, where *þenden* (an older word) is preferred for metrical reasons. *The Battle of Maldon* contains four of these eight examples.

þanon

1   Adv. 'thence'.

2   Conj. 'whence'.

þǣr

1   Adv. of place 'there'. Sometimes it can be translated 'then'.

2   With *wæs*, equals MnE 'there was . . .', e.g. *Beowulf* l. 2105.

3   Conj. 'where', alone, doubled *þǣr þǣr*, or correlative *þǣr . . . þǣr*. (Sometimes it can be translated 'when' or 'because'.)

4   Conj. 'whither, to the place where', e.g. *Dream of the Rood* l. 139.

5   Conj. 'wherever', e.g. *Beowulf* l. 1394.

6   Conj. 'if', especially with pret. subj. of type 3 conditions (§179), e.g. *Beowulf* l. 2730.

7   Introducing a wish with subj. 'if only', e.g. *Metres of Boethius* 8 l. 39.

þæs

Gen. sg. neut. of *þæt* used as an adv.

1   of time 'from that, after'.

2   of extent or comparison 'to that extent, so'; see under *þæs* (*þe*), *þæs . . . þe*, *þæs . . . þæt*.

þæs (*þe*)

1   Gen. sg. masc. or neut. of the relative pronoun; see §162.

2   Conj. of time 'when, after, since', sometimes shading into 'because'.

3   Comparative conj. 'as'.

4   After verbs like *þancian*, see §163.5.

þæs . . . þæt

Conj. 'so . . . that' introducing consecutive clauses, e.g. *Beowulf* ll. 1366–7 and *Seafarer* ll. 39 ff. *þæs . . . þæt* is commoner in the poetry; prose writers prefer *swā . . . þæt*.

Notes

1   The subject for the *þæt* clause in *Beowulf* l. 1367 is absent. Some take *þæt* as rel. pron. 'who'; this would be an early example of the use of *þæt* without regard to gender. Such absence of a subject is, however, idiomatic; see §193.7 and *Christ* ll. 241 ff. where *þæs . . . þæs* is followed by *þe* in what may be an adjective or a consecutive clause. *Metres of Boethius* 28 contains examples of *þæt* and *þe* in clauses which seem the same. It is dangerous to say dogmatically that the former are consecutive clauses with unexpressed subjects, the latter adjective clauses. But this may have been the original situation.

2   In *Seafarer* ll. 39 ff. *þæs . . . þæs* . . . is paralleled by *tō þæs* (3 times); see §171.

þæs . . . þe
See *þæs . . . þæt*.

þæt

1   Neut. dem. and rel. pron. 'that, which, what'; see §§162 and 163.5.
2   Conj. introducing noun clauses; see §155.
3   Conj. 'so that' introducing:
(*a*) clauses of purpose with subj.
(*b*) clauses of result with ind. After verbs of motion, it can be translated 'until'.
(*c*) with ambiguous verb forms, clauses which may be either purpose or result. Often the context makes clear which it is.
4   Conj. introducing some local and temporal clauses where its use is idiomatic, as in MnE, e.g. *Beowulf* l. 1362 and *Maldon* l. 105.

þe

1   In texts which do not mark long vowels, *þe* = *þē* can be a spelling for *þȳ*.
2   Indeclinable rel. pron.; see §162.
3   Subordinating particle turning an adv. into a conj.; see §169.
4   *þēah . . . þe* in *Genesis* ll. 531–2 = 'whether . . . or'.
5   Conj. of time 'when', e.g. *Beowulf* l. 1000. This is not a common use.
6   Sometimes a comparative conj. 'as'; *Maldon* l. 190 is a possible example.

þēah, þēh

1   Adv. 'yet, however'.
2   Alone, or with *þe*, concessive conj. 'although', nearly always with the subj.
3   On *Genesis* l. 531 see s.v. *þe* 4.

þenden

1   Adv. 'meanwhile'.
2   Temporal conj. 'as long as, while'. See *þā hwīle þe* above.

þider

   1   Adv. of place 'thither'.

   2   Conj. of place 'whither'.

þon mā þe

Conj. 'more than', a rare alternative to a comparative + *þonne* in negative sentences. Its literal meaning is *mā* 'more' *þon* (inst. of *þæt* expressing comparison) 'than this' *þe* 'namely' (see §169).

þonne

   1   Adv. of time 'then', frequently correlative with *gif*.

   2   Conj. of time 'when':

      (*a*) with preterite tense, frequentative 'whenever'.

      The difference between *þā* and *þonne* in the past is made clear by a study of the second paragraph of Bede's account of the poet Cædmon, which is quoted in §153. *þā* is used only of a single completed act in the past; note *þa he þæt sumre tide dyde* 'when he did that on one particular occasion'. *þonne* is frequentative 'whenever'; note *oft . . . þonne* 'often . . . whenever'. Cf. Modern German *als* and *wenn*.

      (*b*) in the present and future 'whenever' in both senses:

         (i) of a single act to be performed at some unknown time, e.g. *Beowulf* l. 3106.

         (ii) 'whenever' frequentative of repeated acts, e.g. *Riddle* 7 l. 1.

      As in MnE, the distinction is not always clear; cf. 'I'll see him whenever he comes' with *Beowulf* l. 23.

   3   Comparative conj. 'than':

      (*a*) with full clause following, e.g. *Maldon* l. 195.

      (*b*) with contracted clause following, e.g. *Beowulf* l. 469.

      (*c*) sometimes = 'than that' when two clauses are compared, e.g. *Maldon* ll. 31–33.

þȳ

   1   Inst. of *þæt* in the combination *þȳ . . . þȳ* (lit. 'by that much . . . by that much') MnE 'the . . . the', e.g. *Maldon* ll. 312–13.

   2   Alone, or in the combination *þȳ þe*, 'because', e.g. *Genesis* l. 2626 and *Daniel* l. 85.

þȳ lǣs (þe)

Conj. 'lest' introducing negative clauses of purpose, almost always with the subj.

Prepositional Conjunctions

§169   Basically these consist of a preposition + an oblique case of *þæt* (+ *þæt* or *þe*).

Note

The case used depends on the preposition. Thus, since *for* governs the dat. or inst., we find in the manuscripts *for þæm, for þam, for þan, for þon, for þy, for þi* – all variant spellings of the dat. or inst. (*ð* may appear instead of *þ* in any of these spellings.) The formulae are sometimes written together, e.g. *forþon*. In the discussions which follow, one particular form of the prepositional formula (such as *for þæm*) includes all these variant spellings unless the contrary is specifically stated. *To* sometimes governs the gen. instead of the dat. or inst.; so we find *to þæs* in addition to *to þæm* etc.

These conjunctions probably grew out of an originally adverbial use of a prepositional phrase such as occurs in *ond for ðon ic ðe bebiode ðæt ðu* . . . 'and for that (= 'therefore') I command you that you . . .' and in *for þan wearð her on felda folc totwæmed* . . . 'because of that the army here in the field was divided . . .'. Such phrases were then used as conjunctions by the addition of *þe* or *þæt* to indicate the new function, e.g. . . . *ond he hi him eft ageaf, for þæm þe hiora wæs oþer his godsunu* . . . 'and he afterwards returned them to him, because one of them was his godson . . .'. Here *þe* warns us that the combination is a conjunction. We can call *þe* (if we wish) a subordinating particle. This is the general function of *þe* and its use as a relative pronoun is probably a special adaptation; see §162. We can perhaps get nearest to its original force by translating it as 'namely'. So, in the example above, we have 'and he afterwards returned them to him, for that [reason], namely, one of them was his godson'.

These formulae can be used in two ways. Thus *for þæm* sometimes refers *back* to a reason already given as in the second example above – '[Some fled.] Therefore the army was divided'. Here it is equivalent to MnE 'therefore'. But sometimes it refers *forward* to a reason yet to be given, as in the third example above, where the *þe* warns us not to relax because something – the reason – is still to come, and so tells us that *for þæm* means 'because' and not 'therefore'.

Sometimes *þæt* is used instead of *þe*, e.g. *forþan þæt he wolde Godes hyrde forlætan* 'because he wished to desert God's flock'. This use of *þæt* becomes more common as we move from OE to ME and still survives in Chaucer's metrically useful 'if that', 'when that', and the like.

So far we have distinguished *for þæm* adverb 'therefore' from *for þæm þe* conjunction 'because'. But this distinction was not long preserved by the Anglo-Saxons. They could distinguish adverb and conjunction by the context, word-order, and intonation, just as we can distinguish the use of 'who' in 'The man who did that is a fool' from its use in 'The soldiers, who were tired, lay down'. So they sometimes dispensed with the subordinating particle and used the formula as a conjunction without *þe* or *þæt*, e.g. *Wuton agifan ðæm esne his wif, forðæm he hi hæfð geearnad mid his hearpunga* 'let us give the man back his wife, because he has earned her with his harping'.

Like other adverbs and conjunctions such as *þā* (see §§150 ff.), prepositional conjunctions may be used correlatively. Examples are *forðæm we habbað nu ægðer forlæten ge ðone welan ge ðone wisdom forðæmðe we noldon to ðæm spore mid ure mode onlutan* 'and for that reason we have now lost both the wealth and the wisdom, because we would not bend to the track with our minds', and, without *þe* in the conjunction, *For þon nis me þæs þearf. . . to sec-genne, for þon hit longsum is, ond eac monegum cuð* 'For this reason, there is no need for me . . . to speak of it, because it is long and also known to many'.

So now we have

> *for þæm* adv. 'therefore'
> *for þæm þe* conj. 'because'
> *for þæm* conj. 'because'

and the correlative combination *for þæm . . . for þæm* (*þe*), 'for this reason . . . because'.

One further variation needs to be recorded. We have already seen that conjunctions can be divided. An OE example of a divided prepositional conjunction is *þa comon for ðy on weg ðe ðara oðerra scipu asæton* lit. 'those (men) got for that away, namely, the ships of the others had gone aground' and so 'those escaped because the others' ships were aground'. The causal conjunction is *for ðy . . . ðe*, divided by *on weg*.

§170 Since all these arrangements are possible with the prepositional conjunctions, it follows that, when in your reading you meet *for þæm* or some such combination, it may be

1   an adverb used alone;
2   a conjunction used alone;
3   an adverb used correlatively with a prepositional conjunction;
4   the first part of a divided prepositional conjunction. If it is this, you will need to find the following *þe* or *þæt*.

The combination *for þæm þe* is almost always a conjunction. But sometimes MnE 'for' will be a better translation than 'because'.

§171 The remarks made in §170 about *for þæm* and *for þæm þe* apply to all the prepositional conjunctions set out in the list which follows. It contains all that you are likely to meet. You should note, however, that these combinations may occur 'in their own right' and may not be true prepositional conjunctions. Thus *mid þæm þæt* does not mean 'while' or 'when' in *ealles swiþost mid þæm þæt manige þara selestena cynges þegna forðferdon*; we must translate 'most of all by the fact that (lit. 'with that, namely') many of the king's best thanes died'.

æfter + dat., inst.
    Adv. and conj. 'after'.

Note
æfter is never used alone in OE as a conj. But it does occur as an adv.

ǣr + dat., inst.
  Adv. and conj. 'before'.

Note
ǣr is used alone as a conj. and adv.; see §168.

betweox + dat., inst.
  Conj.'while'.
for + dat., inst.
  See §§169–170 above. *For* alone as a conj. is late.
mid + dat., inst.
  Conj. 'while, when'.
oþ + acc.
  Conj. 'up to, until, as far as' defining the temporal or local limit.
  It appears as *oþþe, oþþæt*, and *oð ðone fyrst ðe* 'up to the time at which' (a good example of how *þe* can turn a phrase into a conj.).

Note
oþ can be used alone as a conj.; see §168.

tō + dat., inst.
  Conj. 'to this end, that' introducing clauses of purpose with subj. and of result with ind.
tō + gen.
  Conj. 'to the extent that, so that'.
wiþ + dat., inst.
  Conj. lit. 'against this, that'. It can be translated 'so that', 'provided that', or 'on condition that'.

An Exercise in Analysis

§172 Now you are in a position to 'try your strength' by analysing and translating the following sentences *before* consulting the key given below:

A. Ond for ðon ic ðe bebiode ðæt ðu do swæ ic geliefe ðæt ðu wille, ðæt ðu ðe ðissa woruldðinga to ðæm geæmetige, swæ ðu oftost mæge, ðæt ðu ðone wisdom ðe ðe God sealde ðær ðær ðu hiene befæstan mæge, befæste.

B. Forðy me ðyncð betre, gif iow swæ ðyncð, ðæt we eac sume bec, ða ðe niedbeðearfosta sien eallum monnum to wiotonne, ðæt we ða on ðæt geðiode wenden ðe we ealle gecnawan mægen, ond gedon, swæ we swiðe eaðe magon mid Godes fultume, gif we ða stilnesse habbað, ðætte eall sio gioguð ðe nu is on Angelcynne friora monna, ðara ðe ða speda hæbben ðæt hie ðæm befeolan mægen, sien to liornunga oðfæste, ða hwile ðe hie to nanre oðerre note ne mægen, oð ðone first ðe hie wel cunnen Englisc gewrit arædan.

In A, we have

1   three noun clauses introduced by *ðæt* – one the object of *bebīode*, one the object of *gelīefe*, and one which is perhaps most simply explained as being in explanatory apposition to the clause *ðæt ðū dō*.

2   an adjective clause introduced by *ðe*.

3   two prepositional formulae –
for ðon adverb used alone 'therefore' and
tō ðæm . . . ðæt used as a divided prepositional conjunction.

4   two *swā* clauses, one of comparison (*swā ic gelīefe*) and the other of time (*swā ðū oftost mæge*).

5   an adverb clause of place introduced by *ðær ðær*.

In B, we have

1   two noun clauses –
the *ðæt* clause subject of *ðyncð* 'seems', which begins after *ðyncð* and has *ðæt*, the subject, and the object, repeated after *wiotonne*. It has two verbs – *wenden* and *gedōn*;
the *ðætte* clause object of *gedōn*.

2   four adjective clauses –
the *ðā ðe* clause, where the relative pronoun does not clearly tell us its case (see §163.1);
two *ðe* clauses, excluding that mentioned in 7;
the *ðāra ðe* clause.

3   two conditional clauses introduced by *gif*.

4   a *swā* clause of comparison.

5   a clause of purpose or result introduced by *ðæt* (following *hæbben*).

6   a clause of time introduced by *ðā hwīle ðe*. Here we must understand *oðfæste wesan*.

7   two prepositional formulae –
for ðȳ adverb 'therefore';
the temporal conjunction *oð ðone first ðe*, where *ðe* can be described as a relative pronoun 'until the time at which'.

These and similarly complicated sentences in Alfred's Preface to the *Cura Pastoralis* show the problems which faced the first men to write in English prose about difficult and complicated subjects. But they and later writers overcame them, often triumphantly.

Clauses of Place

§173   The main conjunctions are:

1   *þǣr* 'where', 'whither', *þider* 'whither', and *þanon* 'whence'. These may introduce definite and indefinite clauses.

2   *swā hwǣr swā* 'wherever' and *swā hwider swā* 'wherever, whithersoever'.

The prevailing mood is the indicative. In examples like *Beowulf* l. 1394 *ga þær he wille*, the subjunctive reflects the subjunctive in the principal clause, the indefiniteness of the adverb clause, and probably also the fact that the whole expression means 'no matter where he goes' and therefore has a concessive force. For other examples see *Genesis* ll. 2723–4 and a passage from Gregory's *Dialogues* where MS C reads *Far þu þider þe þu wille* and MS H *Far þu nu swa hwider swa þu wille* 'Go wherever you wish'.

Clauses of Time

§174   1   Conjunctions whose primary meaning is 'when' or 'while' are: *þā, þonne, mid þām (þe), þā hwīle (þe), þenden*, and *swā lange swā*.

2   Conjunctions whose primary meaning is 'after' are: *siððan* and *þæs þe*. *Æfter* is not used alone as a conjunction in OE.

3   'Before' is rendered by *ǣr* either alone or introducing a prepositional formula.

4   Conjunctions whose primary meaning is 'until' are: *oð, oð þe, oð þæt*, and *hwonne*; on the last, see §159 n. 2.

All these conjunctions usually take the indicative with the exception of *ǣr*, which prefers the subjunctive, and *hwonne*, which always seems to take the subjunctive (except in *Exodus* l. 251, which is therefore suspect).

Note
Doubtless the fact that both *ǣr* and *hwonne* clauses refer to a time AFTER the action of the verb of the main clause has something to do with the subjunctive, but the same is true of *oð þæt* which prefers the indicative. The interrogative origin of *hwonne* is also relevant. There are other factors too, but when they have all been investigated, we have to fall back on 'the attitude of the speaker' to explain some variations in mood.

The conjunctions which prefer the indicative may take the subjunctive if circumstances demand. Thus cf. *Beowulf* l. 1374 and l. 1485, in both of which *þonne*, while frequentative and/or indefinite and referring to the future, has the indicative after an indicative principal clause, with *Luke* 14: 13 *Ac þonne þu gebeorscype do, clypa þearfan* 'When you make a feast, call the poor', where the imperative *clypa* imparts to the sentence a further element of wishing and uncertainty which is reflected in the subjunctive *dō*. Again, while *þonne* frequentative in the past is followed by the preterite indicative, e.g. *Beowulf* ll. 1580 ff., it has the subjunctive when the time reference was to the future at the time of speaking. (We may call this the 'future-in-the-past'.) In these circumstances, the reference may be to a single act, e.g. *þa bæd he hine þæt he him þæs arwyrþan treos hwylcne hwego dæl brohte, þonne he eft ham come* 'he asked him to bring a little bit of that precious tree when he came home again' – *þonne*, the conjunction appropriate to a single act in the future, is retained for the future-in-the-past – or to a series of acts, e.g. *He þa ... geworhte anes fearres anlicnesse of are, to ðon, þonne hit hat wære, 7 mon þa earman men oninnan don wolde, hu se hlynn mæst wære þonne hie þæt susl þæron þrowiende wæron* 'He then made the likeness of a boar in brass with the object [of showing] how, when it was hot and the wretches had been put inside it, the noise would be greatest when they were undergoing the torture'.

Clauses of Purpose and Result

§175   Since a result is often a fulfilled purpose and a purpose a yet-to-be-completed result, these two have much in common. Both can be introduced by the following conjunctions: *þæt, þætte, swā þæt*, and *swā ... þæt*, though the last two are rare in purpose clauses. *þæs ... þæt* and *tō þæs ... þæt* occasionally introduce result clauses, more commonly in the poetry than in the prose. *þȳ læs (þe)* 'lest' is found only in negative clauses of purpose.

It is generally agreed that purpose clauses take the subjunctive, result clauses the indicative. This proposition cannot be proved, for it is only by classifying all clauses with the subjunctive as purpose and all clauses with the indicative as result that we can deduce the rule. This is clearly a circular argument. But it seems likely enough when we think of MnE usage.

Note

Much time has been spent on arguing whether a clause with the indicative can be purpose. This seems a pointless terminological controversy. A much-discussed example is *Elene* ll. 930 ff., where the indicative *wiðsæcest* is used of an event which has yet to take place. Some describe the *þæt* clause as purpose, some as result. The indicative clearly reflects the speaker's belief that a future event is sure to take place. In one sense it is therefore a probable result regarded by the speaker as certain. But it does not seem to have taken place. So in another sense it is an unfulfilled purpose which someone once thought certain to be fulfilled. Hence the indicative reflects the certainty of the speaker, when he spoke, that the event would take place. And that seems all that we can usefully say. Cf. *Husband's Message* ll. 26 ff.

The subjunctive occurs in result clauses under much the same conditions as in adjective clauses (see §165). They are:

1   When the principal clause contains an imperative or a subjunctive expressing a wish, e.g. *alswa litel þu gewurþe þet þu nawiht gewurþe* 'may you

become so small, that you become nothing'. Here the result is expressed as a tendency. A more difficult example is

> ... ne huru on weg aber   þone halgan gast,
> þæt he me færinga   fremde wyrðe

'... nor take away thy Holy Spirit so that he quickly becomes a stranger to me'. Here the result has not actually taken place. It is a possible future result of an action not yet performed. It is not the purpose or wish of the speaker that the Holy Spirit should depart from him. His purpose would require a *þæt ... ne* or *þý læs* 'lest' clause. It may be a purpose attributed by the speaker to God. But from the speaker's point of view it is a result he is anxious to avoid.

Sometimes it is impossible to decide whether a clause with a subjunctive after an imperative should be classified as purpose or result, e.g. *Andreas* ll. 1182–3 and *Andreas* ll. 1332–3

> Gað fromlice,
> ðæt ge guðfrecan   gylp forbegan

'Go quickly to humble the warrior's pride'. But this is probably a distinction without a difference; cf. *Elene* ll. 930 ff. discussed above.

2   When the principal clause contains a negative which implies that the content of the result clause is doubtful or unreal, e.g. *Beowulf* ll. 1366–7, where the poet means that no human being could possibly know. This should be compared with *Beowulf* ll. 1520–1 and *Maldon* ll. 117–19, where we have examples of litotes in which the negatives refer only to the verbs immediately following them. Hence 'He did not withhold the blow' means 'He gave him a very severe blow'. Thus a result which has actually taken place will not be put into the subjunctive under the influence of a negative in the principal clause.

3   When the principal clause contains a rhetorical question, e.g. *Andreas* ll. 1372–3

> Hwylc is þæs mihtig   ofer middangeard,
> þæt he þe alyse ...

'Who is there on earth so powerful that he can free you?' or '... powerful enough to be able to free you?' This of course means 'There is no-one ...'; cf. §165.3.

Causal Clauses

§176   The main causal conjunctions are the *for* formulae, *nū*, and *þæs* (*þe*). *þe*, *þȳ*, and *þȳ þe*, are sometimes found.

When the true cause is given, the causal clause has an indicative verb. The subjunctive is regularly used for a rejected reason, e.g. *Ne cwæþ he þæt na forþon þe him wære ænig gemynd þearfendra manna, ah he wæs gitsere* ... 'He said that, not because he cared at all about needy men, but because he was a miser . . .'.

Clauses of Comparison

§177   1   Comparisons involving 'than' are expressed in OE by *þonne* or (occasionally and only after a negative principal clause) *þon mā þe*. There is a strong tendency for the *þonne* clause to have the subjunctive when the principal clause is positive, e.g. *Ic Ælfric munuc and mæssepreost, swa þeah wæc-cre þonne swilcum hadum gebyrige, wearþ asend* . . . 'I Ælfric, monk and mass-priest, though weaker than is fitting for such orders, was sent . . .', and the indicative when the principal clause is negative, e.g. *Beowulf* ll. 247–9. How-ever, exceptions are not uncommon.

2   Comparisons involving 'as' may be expressed by
(*a*) *swā* 'as' or *swā swā* 'just as';
(*b*) *swā . . . swā* 'so . . . as, as . . . so';
(*c*) *swā* + superlative;
(*d*) *swylce* 'such as';
(*e*) *swylce . . . swā* 'such . . . as';
(*f*) *þæs* (*þe*), e.g. *Beowulf* l. 1341 and (with a superlative) *Beowulf* l. 1350.

For further details, see the appropriate word in §168. The prevailing mood in these clauses is the indicative.

3   Comparisons involving 'the . . . the' are expressed by *þy . . . þy*, e.g. *Maldon* ll. 312–13. The verbs are in the indicative.

4   Comparisons involving hypothesis are expressed by *swā* or *swilce* 'as if' followed by the subjunctive. When the time reference is to the past, the preterite subjunctive is found in the 'as if' clause, e.g. *Wanderer* l. 96 and *Finnsburh* l. 36. When it is to the present, we find the present subjunctive in the 'as if' clause, e.g. *Christ* ll. 179–81 and ll. 1376–7. The preterite subjunc-tive is not used of the present as it is in OE type 3 Conditions (see §179.4) or in MnE 'He runs as if he were tired'; the MnE equivalent of the OE idiom would be 'He runs as if he be tired'.

Clauses of Concession

§178   1   Simple concessive clauses are usually introduced by *þēah* (*þe*) 'though'. The prevailing mood is the subjunctive, whether the concession is one of fact or hypothesis.

Note
Sometimes we have *þēah . . . eall*, as in *Beowulf* l. 680 *þeah ic eal mæge*. Here *eall* is an adverb, perhaps with the sense 'easily'. But this probably represents a stage in the development of 'although'; see *OED* s.v. *all* C adv. II 10, and note that in such ME

examples as *The Pardoner's Tale* lines 371, 449, and 451 (line references to Skeat's edition), *al* is still an adverb and the concession is expressed by the word-order V.S.

2 Disjunctive concessions are expressed by *sam . . . sam* 'whether . . . or'. In such clauses, the subjunctive is the rule, e.g. *sam hit sy sumor sam winter* 'whether it is summer or winter'.

3 As in MnE, an element of concession is often present in indefinite adjective clauses (e.g. *Beowulf* ll. 942 ff. and ll. 142–3) or in indefinite adverb clauses of place (e.g. *Genesis* ll. 2723 ff.) or time (e.g. *Genesis* ll. 1832 ff.). On the possibility that there was a special OE idiom expressing indefinite concession, see Klaeber's note on *Beowulf* l. 968.

4 Concession can sometimes be expressed by putting the verb first without any conjunction. The two most common types are *swelte ic, libbe ic* 'whether I live or die' and *hycge swa he wille* 'let him think as he will', 'no matter what he thinks'. The first type often occurs in the form *wylle ic, nylle ic* 'willy nilly'.

Clauses of Condition

§179 1 In earlier versions of this *Guide*, I classified conditional clauses according to a system traditionally used for Latin and Greek. I have abandoned this because it does not really fit OE..I now distinguish these three types:

(1) (a) conceded and (b) denied conditions, e.g. (a) 'If you think that [and you have said that you do], you are wrong', and (b) 'Seek if you dare [but you do not]'.

(2) open conditions, e.g. 'If you think that [and I do not know whether you do or not], you are wrong', 'If you thought that [and you might], you would be wrong', and 'Seek if you dare [and you may or may not]'.

(3) rejected or imaginary conditions, e.g. 'If you believed this [but you do not], you would be wrong', 'If you had believed this [but you did not], you would have been wrong', and 'If [= Imagine that] you saw a mouse ruling over men, you would think it strange'.

In OE, conditions of all three types may be introduced by *gif* 'if'. *þær* 'if' sometimes introduces type 3 conditions.

2 Conditions of types 1 and 2 fall into two main groups – those in which both clauses have the indicative, e.g. *Maldon* ll. 34–5 and ll. 36–41, and those in which the verb of the principal clause is imperative or expresses a wish in the subjunctive. In these latter sentences, the 'if' clause usually has the subjunctive, e.g. *sec, gif þu dyrre* 'seek if you dare'. This point is well illustrated by the two almost parallel *gif* clauses in *Beowulf* ll. 445–53.

3 It is not always immediately clear whether a condition belongs to type 1 or 2, e.g. *Fed ðonne min sceap gif ðu me lufige* (cf. *John* 21: 15–17) – here Peter

says that he does love Christ and ultimately proves that he does – and *sec, gif þu dyrre* (quoted above from *Beowulf* l. 1379) – here Beowulf does dare when the time comes.

4 Type 3 conditions regularly have the preterite subjunctive in both clauses, e.g. *ac hit wære to hrædlic, gif he ða on cild-cradole acweald wurde* . . . 'it would have been too early if He (Christ) had been killed in His cradle . . .' and perhaps (with *þær* and in dependent speech)

> and þæt wiste eac   weroda Drihten,
> þæt sceolde unc Adame   yfele gewurðan
> ymb þæt heofonrice,   þær ic ahte minra handa geweald

'and the Lord of Hosts also knew that things would turn out badly between Adam and me about that heavenly kingdom, if I had control of my hands'.

Note
The use of 'perhaps' here is important. In MnE we can distinguish unreality in the past, present, and future, by means of the verb alone, e.g.

> If he had been here, it wouldn't have happened.
> If he were here, it wouldn't be happening.
> If he were coming, it wouldn't happen.

But (as is pointed out in more detail in §§195–198) the OE verb was not as flexible an instrument as the MnE verb. Hence an Anglo-Saxon had to use the preterite subjunctive in all these examples. In other words, he could say that a thing was unreal or impossible, but he was unable to say when it could not happen unless he used an adverb or some other device.

Thus both the OE examples cited in this section have the preterite subjunctive. But the first refers to something which did not happen in the past, while the second might refer to something which is impossible at the time when Satan spoke – the implication being 'if only I had control of my hands now, but I haven't'. But it could also be translated 'God knew that trouble would arise between Adam and me if I were to have control of my hands'.

This raises a further difficulty and explains the 'perhaps'. Does this interpretation mean that there was a possibility that Satan might have control of his hands (type 2 condition) or that such a thing was impossible when God spoke? The issue here is complicated by questions of God's foreknowledge, though perhaps our own knowledge of the story enables us to dismiss the latter possibility. But enough has been said to make it clear that the Anglo-Saxon 'rule' that 'unreality is timeless' is not without its advantages.

A clearer example is *Beowulf* ll. 960–1, discussed in §198.

5 *Būtan* and *nympe, nemne, nefne* both have two meanings – 'unless' and 'except that'. Meaning 'unless', both usually take the subjunctive, e.g. *Beowulf* l. 966 and l. 1056. Meaning 'except that', both usually take the indicative, e.g. *Beowulf* l. 1560 and l. 1353.

6 'On condition that' may be expressed by *gif* or by the *wiþ* formula (see §171).

7 Conditions expressed by the word-order V.S. without a conjunction – e.g. 'Had I plenty of money, I would be lying in the sun in Bermuda' – occasionally occur in OE prose, e.g. *eaðe mihte þes cwyde beon læwedum mannum bediglod, nære seo gastlice getacning* 'this saying could easily be concealed from laymen were it not [for] its spiritual meaning'. The only certain example in the poetry is *Genesis* ll. 368–70; here it is arguable whether a line is missing or whether the poet deliberately left the *þonne* clause unfinished to obtain a dramatic effect.

8 On comparisons involving hypothesis, see §177.4.

Adverb Clauses Expressing Other Relationships

§180 The divisions outlined above are for convenience only and are far from being watertight, for one relationship often involves another. Thus, while clauses of time with *oþ* (*þæt*) often shade into result, and *þæt* after verbs of motion can often be translated 'until', other temporal clauses may contain elements of cause or of condition. Similarly, indefinite adjective clauses are often the equivalent of conditional clauses, e.g. *Beowulf* ll. 1387–8. See also §178.3.

Note
This latter relationship is very clearly seen in some ME sentences which contain an adjective clause which must be rendered by a conditional clause in MnE, e.g. Hall *Selections from Early Middle English*, p. 54 l. 11 and l. 21 (cf. p. 54 l. 16) and *Sir Gawain and the Green Knight* l. 1112.

Other Ways of Expressing Adverbial Relationships

§181   1   Parataxis; examples will be found in §§182–186.
2   Participles; see §204.
3   Infinitives; see §205.
4   Prepositional phrases, e.g. *mid* expressing condition *mid Godes fultume* 'with God's help, if God helps us'; *þurh* expressing cause *þurh þæs cyninges bebod* 'by command of the king'; and *þurh* expressing time *þurh swefn* 'in a dream, while he dreamt'.

VI   PARATAXIS

Introduction

§182 The Anglo-Saxons were far from primitive. At the time of the Norman Conquest, England – although she no longer led Western Europe in monastic learning, as she had in the eighth century – was fruitful ground for new forms of devotion, was famous for her craftsmen, and had a well-developed economy and the most advanced administration north of the

Alps. It is of special interest here that her language was far more developed for the expression of both prose and poetry than any other contemporary European vernacular and that authors using it sometimes rose to very great heights. Look for example at the poem *The Dream of the Rood* and at the magnificent passage beginning *Ne forseah Crist his geongan cempan* in Ælfric's Homily on the Nativity of the Innocents.

Some of the reasons for the belief that Old English was a primitive language have been discussed in §§148–152. Another is the frequent use of parataxis. Some writers, steeped in the periodic structure of Latin and Greek, seem unable or unwilling to believe that parataxis can be anything but a clumsy tool used by people who did not know any better. Certainly, S. O. Andrew (in *Syntax and Style in Old English*) does well to draw our attention to inconsistencies in the editorial punctuation of Old English texts. But he allows himself to be swayed too much by his conviction that good writing must necessarily be periodic. Today, when the long and complicated sentence is losing favour in English, we will perhaps be more in sympathy with the constructions described in the following paragraphs, more able to appreciate the effect they produced, and less likely to believe that the juxtaposition of two simple sentences was necessarily less dramatic or effective than one complex sentence. During his journey to the Underworld in search of Eurydice, Orpheus met the Parcae. *Ða ongon he biddan heora miltse; ða ongunnon hi wepan mid him*, the story continues. Here the word-order supports the view that the two sentences are independent (see §151), and suggests that the writer is giving equal prominence to the two ideas. The effect he was after can perhaps be achieved by the translation 'Then he asked for their pity and they wept with him'. At the end of the same story, the final disappearance of Eurydice is related thus: *Ða he forð on ðæt leoht com, ða beseah he hine under bæc wið ðæs wifes; ða losade hio him sona* 'When he came into the light, he looked back towards his wife. Straightway she disappeared from his sight'. Here a powerful dramatic effect would be lost if we took only one of the clauses with *þā* + V.S. as principal.

§183 The term 'parataxis', with its adjective 'paratactic', has been abandoned by some writers because of its ambiguity. Here it is used in a purely formal sense to mean a construction in which sentences are not formally subordinated one to the other. 'Asyndetic' and 'syndetic' mean respectively without and with conjunctions such as *ond* and *ac*. The term 'co-ordinating' (often used for the MnE equivalents 'and', 'but', and so on) is avoided here because in OE *ond* and *ac* are frequently followed by the order S. . . . V. (see §145), which is basically a subordinate order. The opposite of 'parataxis' is 'hypotaxis', which implies the use of one or more of the conjunctions discussed in §§154–180. Examples follow.

Hypotaxis: When I came, I saw. When I saw, I conquered.
Asyndetic Parataxis: I came. I saw. I conquered.
Syndetic Parataxis: I came and I saw and I conquered.

List of Conjunctions and Adverbs Commonly Used

§184 On word-order after these words, see §§144 and 145.

1 Those meaning 'and', 'both ... and', etc. (traditionally called 'cumulative'):

> *and, ond* 'and' (see below);
> *æ̇ghwæþer* (*ġe*) ... *ġe* ... (*ġe*) '(both) ... and ... (and)';
> (*æ̇gþer*) (*ġe*) ... *ġe* ... (*ġe*) '(both) ... and ... (and)';
> *ēac* 'also, and'; *ġe* 'and'; *ġe* ... *ġe, æ̇gþer* ... *and* 'both ... and'.

The *ond* clause can of course imply more than mere continuity and is often the equivalent of an adverb clause. Thus *ofer Eastron gefor Æþered cyning; ond he ricsode V gear* could be translated 'During Easter Æthered died after ruling five years'. This of course often happens today, especially in conversation.

2 Those meaning 'but', 'however', etc. (traditionally called 'adversative'):

> *ac* 'but, on the contrary'; *furþum* 'also, even';
> *hūru* 'however, indeed', etc.;
> *hwæþere* 'however, yet'; *swāþēah* 'however, yet';
> *þēah* 'however, yet' (see also §178);
> *þēahhwæþere* 'however, yet'.

3 Those meaning 'either ... or' (traditionally called 'alternative'):

> *hwīlum* ... *hwīlum* 'at one time ... at another time';
> (*æ̇gþer*) *oþþe* ... *oþþe*; *swa* ... *swā*; *þe* ... *þe*.

4 Those involving a negative:

> *nā, ne, nō* 'not';
> (*nāhwæðer ne*) ... *ne* ... (*ne*) 'neither ... nor ... (nor)';
> *nalles, nealles* 'not at all, not';
> (*nāðor ne*) ... *ne* ... (*ne*) '(neither) ... nor ... (nor)';
> *næfre* 'never'; *næs* 'not' (a short form of *nalles*).

An example of 'not only ... but also' will be found in *na þæt an þæt he wolde mann beon for us, ðaða he God wæs, ac eac swylce he wolde beon þearfa for us, ðaða he rice wæs* 'not only was He willing to become man for us when He was God, but He was also willing to become poor for us when He was rich'.

The following points should be noted:

(*a*) The OE verb is normally negated by *ne* immediately preceding it. But if the negative is stressed, as in *Wanderer* l. 96 and *Seafarer* l. 66, *nā* (= *ne* + *ā*) or *nō* (= *ne* + *ō*) is used. In *Phoenix* l. 72 the MS *no* is unstressed and should probably be emended to *ne* as a scribal anticipation of *o*.

(*b*) The arrangement seen in *Ne com se here* — *Ne* + V.S. – is common in negative principal clauses; see §146.4.

(c) Contraction of the negative *ne* with a following word beginning with a vowel, *h*, or *w*, produces *nis* from *ne is*, *næfde* from *ne hæfde*, *noldon* from *ne woldon*, and so on.

(d) *Ne* not before a finite verb is a conjunction, e.g. *ne tunge ne handa* 'neither tongue nor hands', *ne leornian ne tæcan* 'neither to learn nor to teach'.

(e) *Nā* and *nō* are used to negate words other than finite verbs, e.g. *He wæs Godes bydel ond na God* 'He was God's messenger and not God'.

(f) One negative does not cancel out another, as it does in formal MnE. The OE use is similar to that seen in such non-standard sentences as 'I didn't do nothing to nobody'; cf. *on nanum men nyton nane are* '[they] show mercy to no-one'. This could be added to the list of things which make some people think of OE as a primitive language; see §182.

(g) On a 'semi-subordinating' use of *ne*, see §185.2.

5   Those meaning 'for' (traditionally called 'illative'). A useful article by T. B. Haber on MnE 'for' (*American Speech* 30 (1955), 151) states: 'The only practical conclusion is that the conjunction has two uses, subordinating and co-ordinating, and that punctuation is of no significance in identifying either.' In other words, MnE 'for' can sometimes be replaced by 'because'. In OE, the situation is even more complicated, for *forþon* can mean, not only 'for' and 'because', but also 'therefore'. No rule can be laid down for distinguishing these uses; see §§169–70.

Parataxis without Conjunctions

§185   Two main types of asyndetic parataxis may be distinguished.

1   Here the two sentences are of equal status, as in the well-known *Veni. Vidi. Vici.* Examples are especially common in the poetry, e.g. *Beowulf* ll. 1422–4 and *Maldon* ll. 301–6.

2   Examples of the second type occur in *Eadmund cyning awearp his wæpnu, wolde geæfenlæcan Cristes gebysnungum* and *þa comon þeofas eahta, woldon stelan þa maðmas*, where the clauses beginning with *wolde* and *woldon* respectively could be translated 'wishing to imitate Christ's example' and 'intending to steal the treasures'. Note

(a) These clauses do not themselves contain a grammatically-expressed subject.

(b) They are actually, though not formally, subordinate to the clause which precedes them; for this reason they are sometimes said to be in 'semi-subordination'.

(c) They explain the motive for the action of the principal clause and are the equivalent of an adverb clause of purpose or cause.

This idiom occurs with verbs other than *willan*, e.g. *he sæt on ðæm muntum, weop ond hearpode* which can conveniently be translated 'he sat on the mountains, weeping and harping'. Similar examples occur with an initial negative, e.g. *Beowulf* ll. 1441–2 'Beowulf arrayed himself in princely armour without (or 'not') worrying about his life'.

Some Special Idioms

§186 1 . . . *wæs gehāten* '. . . was called' is frequently used independently of the rest of the sentence, e.g. *mid heora cyningum, Rædgota ond Eallerica wæron hatne* 'with their kings, [who/they] were called R. and E.' (note the change from the dative to the nominative case) and *þa wæs sum consul, þæt we heretoha hataþ, Boetius wæs gehaten* 'there was a certain consul – we use the word *heretoha* – [who/he] was called B.'. Cf., with the verb 'to be' only, . . . *gefor Ælfred, wæs æt Baðum gerefa*, 'A., [who/he] was reeve at Bath, died'.

2 For '*swā* + negative + indicative', see §168 s.v. *swā* 2(*d*).

VII CONCORD

§187 The main rules of agreement in OE are set out below. They will present little difficulty to any reader with a knowledge of an inflected language.

1. Nouns, Pronouns and their Modifiers

(*a*) They agree in number, gender, and case, e.g. *se Ælmihtiga Hælend* 'the Almighty Saviour', *ðæs eadigan apostoles* 'of the blessed apostle', and *and þe cwicne gebindaþ* 'and will bind you alive'.

Note
The masc. ending -*e* in nom. acc. pl. of adjectives is often used for fem. and neut., especially in later texts.

(*b*) The participle in a participial phrase usually shows similar agreement, e.g. *Hinguar and Hubba, ge-anlæhte þurh deofol* 'H. and H., united by the devil'. But it need not, e.g. *Abraham geseah þær anne ramm betwux þam bremelum be þam hornum gehæft* 'A. saw there a ram caught among the brambles by his horns'.

(*c*) *Gehāten* 'called' with a noun usually has the nominative irrespective of the case of the word with which it is in apposition, e.g. *into anre byrig, Gaza gehaten* 'into a city called Gaza'; cf. *for ðy hit man hæt Wislemuða* 'therefore we call (lit. 'one calls') it W.' where the nominative *Wislemuða* is the equivalent of the modern italics or inverted commas, and the second example in §186.1.

(*d*) After *wesan* and *weorþan* the participle often agrees with the subject, e.g. *hie wurdon ofslægene* 'they were slain' and *þe mid him ofslægene wæron* 'who were killed with them'. But it need not, e.g. *þa wurdon hiora wif swa sarige on hiora mode ond swa swiðlice gedrefed* ... 'then their wives became so sorrowful and so greatly distressed in mind ...'. See further §§201–203. So too with adjectives.

(*e*) After *habban*, the participle may agree with the object or may remain uninflected; see §200.

2. Pronouns and their Antecedents

(*a*) They agree in number and gender, e.g. *to þæm cyninge* ... *he* ... *his feores* 'to the king ... he ... for his life'; *anne flotan* ... *se* 'a pirate ... he (lit. 'that')'; and *se hearpere* ... *ðæs nama* 'the harper, whose name'.

(*b*) The main exceptions arise from the conflict between natural and grammatical gender, e.g. *ðæs hearperes wif* (neut.) ... *hire sawle* 'the harper's wife ... her soul' and *an swiðe ænlic wif, sio wæs haten Eurydice* 'a most excellent wife, who was called E.'. Similarly, in a passage from the Preface to the *Cura Pastoralis* (selection 5, end of first paragraph) we find *ðone wīsdōm* followed first by the grammatically right masculine *hiene* and then by the neuter *hit* which seems appropriate to us. Thus there are already signs that the feeling for grammatical gender is weakening.

Note
Agreement in case between pronoun and antecedent is a matter of chance, not principle, despite Quirk and Wrenn *An Old English Grammar* §121(*c*). In the examples they cite, *rōde* and *hēo* do not agree in case and the relative *ðāra þe* would have to be replaced by the acc. pl. *þā* of the declined relative *se*, i.e. *ðāra* has the case of the principal clause; see §163.1.

(*c*) Special uses of *hit, þæt, hwæt*, and the like, in which these neuter pronouns are used without regard to the number and gender of the noun to which they refer, should be noted, e.g. *þæt wæron eall Finnas* 'they were all Lapps' and *Hwæt syndon ge* ... ? 'Who are you ... ?' See further §168 s.v. *þæs* ... *þæt*, note 1.

3. Subject and Verb

(*a*) Subject and verb agree in number and person. Dual pronouns are followed by plural verbs.

(*b*) Collective nouns and indefinite pronouns cause much the same problems as they do today, e.g. *an mægð* ... *hi magon cyle gewyrcan* 'a tribe ... they can make cold' and *þonne rideð ælc, and hit motan habban* 'then each man rides, and [they] can have it'.

(*c*) With *ond þæs ymb XIIII niht gefeaht Æþered cyning ond Ælfred his broður*, where *gefeaht* is singular, cf. 'Here comes Tom, and Jack, and all the boys'.

(*d*) When the relative pronoun *þāra þe* means 'of those who', the verb of the adjective clause can be singular or plural.

VIII THE USES OF THE CASES

These will not present much difficulty to those familiar with an inflected language. On the cases used after prepositions, see §§213–214.

Nominative

§188 The case of the subject, of the complement, and of address, e.g. *Gehyrst þu, sælida?* 'Do you hear, seaman?' See also §187.1(*c*).

Accusative

§189 1 The case of the direct object.

2 It also expresses duration of time, e.g. *ealne dæg* 'all day', and extent of space, e.g. *fleon fotes trym* 'to flee one foot's pace'.

Note

It is important to realize that already in OE the nominative and accusative are frequently the same. In the plural they are always the same except in the 1st and 2nd pers. pron. In the singular, many nouns have the same form in the nominative and accusative, and the distinction depends on the form of any demonstrative or possessive adjective, or on that of any adjective, which may qualify the noun. See further §140.

Genitive

§190 1 The case of possession, e.g. *Hæstenes wif* 'Hæsten's wife'.

2 The subjective genitive – *þæs cyninges bebod* 'the king's command', i.e. 'the king commanded' – differs in function from the objective genitive – *metodes ege* 'fear of the Lord', i.e. 'we fear the Lord'.

3 The genitive may describe or define, e.g. *swete hunig and wynsumes swæcces* 'honey sweet and of pleasant taste', *ðreora daga fæsten* 'a fast of three days', and *an lamb anes geares* 'a one-year-old lamb'.

4 The partitive genitive is common, e.g. *an hiora* 'one of them' and *þreora sum* 'one of three'. See also §194.

5 The genitive is used adverbially, e.g. *dæges ond nihtes* 'by day and night', *micles to beald* 'much too bold', *upweardes* 'upwards', *þæs* 'therefore, so, after that'.

6 The genitive occurs after some adjectives, e.g. *þæs gefeohtes georn* 'eager for the fight', and after some verbs, e.g. *fanda min* 'try me' and *hie þæs fægnodon* 'they rejoiced at that'. The glossary gives you this information when you need it.

Dative

§191   1   The case of the indirect object, e.g. *ond he hi him eft ageaf* 'and he afterwards gave them back to him'.

2   It may express possession, e.g. *him on heafod* 'on his head'.

3   It may express time, e.g. *hwilum* 'at times' and *ðære ylcan nihte* 'in the same night'. Other adverbial uses include *flocmælum* 'in (armed) bands' and *gearmælum* 'year by year'.

4   The dative absolute is used in imitation of the Latin ablative absolute, e.g. *gewunnenum sige* 'victory having been gained'.

5   The dative occurs after some adjectives, e.g. *ise gelicost* 'most like to ice', sometimes after comparatives, e.g. *sunnan beorhtra* 'brighter than the sun', and after some verbs, e.g. *þæt he him miltsian sceolde* 'that he should have mercy on him'. Here too the glossary will help you.

Instrumental

§192   Where there is no special instrumental form (and sometimes when there is), the dative serves.

1   The instrumental expresses means or manner, e.g. *þone ilcan we hataþ oþre naman æfensteorra* 'we call the same by another name – evening star', *fægere ende his lif betynde* 'closed his life with a fair end' (but cf. the dative in *geendode yflum deaþe* 'ended with an evil death'), and *hlutre mode* 'with a pure mind'.

2   It expresses accompaniment, e.g. *lytle werode* 'with a small band'.

3   It expresses time, e.g. *þy ilcan geare* 'in the same year'.

IX ARTICLES, PRONOUNS, AND NUMERALS

Articles and Pronouns

§193   1   There are no 'articles' as such in OE. The demonstrative *se* does duty for 'the' and 'that', the demonstrative *þes* means 'this', e.g. *Her on þysum geare for se micla here, þe we gefyrn ymbe spræcon* . . . 'In this year the great army which we spoke about before went . . .'. Sometimes, however, *se* can be translated 'this', e.g. *anne æþeling se wæs Cyneheard haten — 7 se Cyneheard wæs þæs Sigebryhtes broþur* 'a princeling who was called C. and this C. was the brother of the S. already mentioned'.

2   The demonstrative is frequently not used in OE where we would use it today, e.g. *wælstowe gewald* 'command of the battlefield', and, from the poetry (where its absence is even more common), *fram beaduwe* 'from the battle' and *Oddan bearn* 'the sons of Odda'. But the reverse is sometimes true, e.g. *sio lar* 'learning'.

3   In examples like *Æþered cyning* we have either absence of a demonstrative pronoun 'Æthered the King' or (more likely in view of *Iohannes se godspellere* 'John the Evangelist') a different arrangement of appositional elements 'King Æthered'. Hence *Æþelwulf aldormon* might be the equivalent of 'General Smith'.

4   The indefinite article is even rarer; thus we find *holtes on ende* 'at the edge of a wood', *to wæfersyne* 'as a spectacle', and *on beorg* 'onto a mountain'. *Ān* is sometimes used, e.g. *to anum treowe* 'to a tree' and *an wulf* 'a wolf'. But usually *ān* and *sum* mean something more, e.g. *an mægð* 'a certain tribe' and *sum mon* 'a certain man'. Sometimes these words have an even stronger sense, e.g. *þæt wæs an cyning* 'that was a peerless King', 'that wás a King', and *eower sum* 'a particular one among you', 'your leader'. In this sense, and as the numeral 'one', *ān* is strong. Meaning 'alone', it is usually weak, e.g. *he ana*, but may be strong, e.g. *ðone naman anne* 'the name alone'.

5   *Se* is also used as a relative pronoun; see §162.3. Sometimes, as in *Beowulf* l. 1296, it may be either demonstrative or relative. But the difficulty is of little practical consequence.

6   The third person pronoun is sometimes used ambiguously, so that we cannot readily tell to whom it is referring. A well-known series of examples is found in the story of Cynewulf and Cyneheard (selection 6, third paragraph). But this is rather the result of inexperience in handling the language than of defects in the language itself, for later in its development, OE managed to make the meaning clear with no more pronouns at its disposal. The same is, of course, true of MnE.

7   A pronoun subject is frequently not expressed. Often the subject not expressed is the same as that of the preceding clause. But the absence of a subject does not certify that it has not changed; see, e.g. *Maldon* ll. 17–21, where the subject changes twice in l. 20 without any pronoun. A pronoun object may be similarly unexpressed, e.g. the sentence quoted in §167.6. Sometimes, however, *sē* is used instead of *hē* to make clear that a subject has changed, e.g. *Maldon* ll. 150 and 227. This avoids the ambiguity which could arise from a repeated or an absent *hē*, e.g. *Maldon* l. 286 and *Beowulf* l. 57.

Numerals

§194   The cardinal numerals can be used

1   as adjectives agreeing with a noun, e.g. *þrim gearum ær he forþferde* 'three years before he died' and *mid XXXgum cyningum* 'with thirty kings';

2   as nouns followed by a partitive genitive, e.g. *to anre þara burga* 'to one of the cities' and *þritig cyninga* 'thirty kings'.

X VERBS

On the detailed uses of the indicative and subjunctive in subordinate clauses, see the discussions on the appropriate clause.

The Uses of the Present and Preterite Tenses

§195   As we have seen in §89, the OE verb distinguished only two tenses in conjugation – the present and the preterite. Hence, despite the fact that the beginnings of the MnE resolved tenses are found in OE (see below), the two simple tenses are often used to express complicated temporal relationships. This is one of the things which made Professor Tolkien once say in a lecture that most people read OE poetry much more quickly than did the Anglo-Saxon minstrel, reciting or reading aloud as he was to an audience which needed time to pick up the implications of what he was saying. And this would apply, not only to the subject-matter, especially to the hints and allusions which frequently had great significance, but also to the relationships between paratactic sentences such as those discussed in §§182–185 and to the actual relationship in time between two actions both of which were described by a simple tense of a verb. Thus it is important for us to understand what these simple tenses could imply.

§196   The present expresses, not only a continuing state as in *Wlitig is se wong* 'The plain is beautiful', and *ðeos woruld nealæcð þam ende* 'this world is drawing near to its end', but also the passing moment, the actual 'now' for which MnE often uses a continuous tense, e.g. *hwæt þis folc segeð* 'what this people are saying, say now'. It is also used for the future, e.g. *þas flotmenn cumaþ* 'these seamen will come', and (as in equivalent examples in MnE) for the future perfect, e.g. *seþe þæt gelæsteð, bið him lean gearo* 'a reward will be ready for him who does (shall have done) that', and (with a subjunctive *gefeohte* as explained in §179.2) *gif hwa gefeohte on cyninges huse, sie he scyldig ealles his ierfes* 'if anyone fight (shall have fought) in the king's house, let him forfeit all his property'.

In the principal clause in the last sentence, the subjunctive *sie* expresses a command and could be translated 'he shall forfeit'. The present subjunctive can also express a wish, e.g. *abreoðe his angin* 'may his enterprise fail', or a prayer, e.g. *God þe sie milde* 'May God be merciful to you'.

The only verb which has a special future form is the verb 'to be', where *bið* and its forms are used for the future, e.g. *bið him lean gearo* above, and for the statement of an eternal truth (a use sometimes called 'gnomic'), e.g. *wyrd bið ful aræd* 'Fate is quite inexorable' and *þonne bið heofena rice gelic þæm tyn fæmnum* 'Then the Kingdom of Heaven is like unto (the) ten virgins'. But *is* may do the same job, e.g. *Heofena rice is gelic þæm hiredes ealdre* 'The Kingdom of Heaven is like unto a man that is an householder'.

The historic present rarely, if ever, occurs.

§197 The preterite indicative is used

1 of a single completed act in the past;

2 of an act continuing in the past. Both of these are exemplified in *soðlice þa ða men slepon, þa com his feonda sum* 'truly, while men were sleeping, one of his enemies came';

3 for the perfect, e.g. *ic mid ealre heortan þe gewilnode* 'I have wished for Thee with all my heart';

4 for the pluperfect, e.g. *sona swa hie comon* 'as soon as they had come' and (with a strengthening *ær*) *and his swura wæs gehalod þe ær wæs forslægen* 'and his neck, which had been cut through, was healed'. (Cf. the use of *ærur* in *Dream of the Rood* l. 108.)

§198 The preterite subjunctive may refer to the past, e.g. *ond ge wiðsocon þæt in Bethleme bearn cenned wære* 'and you denied that a child was born in Bethlehem', or to the future-in-the-past, e.g. the two sentences quoted at the end of §174.

It has already been pointed out in §179.4 that unreality is timeless in OE. An interestingly ambiguous example of this is seen in *Beowulf* ll. 960–1

> Uþe ic swiþor
> þæt ðu hine selfne   geseon moste . . . !

Here Beowulf might be saying to Hrothgar either

'I could wish that you could see Grendel now'; in other words 'I wish that he hadn't got away'

or 'I could wish that you could have seen Grendel yesterday'; in other words 'I wish that you had been at the fight and had seen how badly wounded he was'

or 'I could wish that you could see Grendel tomorrow'; in other words 'I wish that we could find his body and so know that he is dead'.

But the context strongly suggests the second.

The Resolved Tenses
Introduction

§199 This term is used to mean tenses made up from a participle (present or past) or an infinitive together with the verb 'to be', the verb 'to have', or one of the 'modal' verbs (see §206), e.g. MnE 'He is coming', 'He is come', 'He has come', 'He will come'. The beginnings of these forms are seen in OE, with one important difference which throws light on their origin. A MnE example will explain this. In *Ephesians* 6: 14, the Revised Version reads 'Stand therefore, having girded your loins with truth'. If we parsed 'having girded', we would perhaps call it the perfect participle of the verb 'to gird', with 'your loins' its object; at any rate, we would say that it was part of the verb 'to gird'. But the Authorized Version reads 'Stand therefore having your loins girt about with truth'. Here 'your loins' is the object of the participle 'having' and 'girt about with truth' is a phrase describing 'your loins'; hence 'girt' is adjectival rather than verbal. That this was its original function in such phrases in OE becomes clear when we study the agreement of some of the examples cited below; to make this point, it will be convenient if we take first the ancestor of the MnE perfect tense with 'have'.

The Verb 'to have' as an Auxiliary

§200   Examples in which the participle is adjectival are *he us hafað þæs leohtes bescyrede* 'he has us deprived of that light' (where the present tense of *habban* is followed by *bescyrede* a past participle acc. pl. strong, agreeing with *ūs*) and *ac hi hæfdon þa heora stemn gesetenne and hiora mete genotudne* 'but then they had their term of service finished and their food used up' (where a past tense of *habban* is followed by two participles both of which are declined acc. sg. masc. strong, agreeing with *stemn* and *mete*, the objects of *hæfdon*). These are clearly the ancestors of the MnE perfect and pluperfect respectively.

But examples also occur in which there is no such declining of the past participle to agree with the object, e.g. *Eastengle hæfdon Ælfrede cyninge aþas geseald* 'The East Anglians had oaths given to King Alfred' and *Hæfde se cyning his fierd on tu tonumen* 'The king had his army divided in two'; cf. §187.1(*b*). This was, of course, a necessary stage in the development of the MnE perfect and pluperfect tenses. The modern arrangement in which the participle precedes the object instead of having final position is found in such examples as *Nu ðu hæfst ongiten ða wanclan truwa þæs blindan lustes* 'Now you have realized the fickle loyalty of blind pleasure'.

The Verb 'to be' as an Auxiliary of Tense

§201   1   It is found with the present participle as the ancestor of the MnE continuous tenses. But here too the participle was originally adjectival rather than verbal. It should also be noted that the OE combination is not the exact equivalent of the modern usage. Often it means the same as the corresponding simple tense, e.g. *þa wæs se cyning openlice andettende þam biscope* 'Then the king openly confessed to the bishop', though it may give greater vividness. (This construction is now agreed to be of native rather than of Latin origin.) But sometimes it implies that an action continued for some time, e.g. *ond hie þa . . . feohtende wæron* 'and then they kept on fighting' and *ða ða se apostol þas lare sprecende wæs* 'while the apostle was explaining this teaching'. In these examples, it comes close to the modern use.

2 The verb 'to be' is also found with the past participle forming the perfect and pluperfect of intransitive verbs, e.g. *Swæ clæne hio* [= *lar*] *wæs oðfeallenu on Angelcynne* 'So completely was learning fallen away in England' (where the participle is declined nom. sg. fem. strong, agreeing with the subject) and *hu sio lar Lædengeðiodes ær ðissum afeallen wæs* 'how the learning of Latin was fallen away before this' (where the participle is not declined). Here too the participle was originally adjectival rather than verbal.

The Passive

§202 Only one OE verb had a synthetic passive, viz. *hātte* 'is called', 'was called', e.g. *se munuc hatte Abbo* 'the monk was called A.'. Otherwise the idea was expressed by the impersonal *man* 'one' with the active voice, e.g. *Her mon mæg giet gesion hiora swæð* 'Here one can still see their track', or by the verbs 'to be' or 'to become' with the past participle, e.g. *to bysmore synd getawode þas earman landleoda* 'the miserable people of this land are (have been) shamefully ill-treated', *Æfter þæm þe Romeburg getimbred wæs* 'After Rome was (had been) built', and *æfter minum leofum þegnum þe on heora bedde wurdon mid bearnum and wifum færlice ofslægene* 'after my beloved thanes who became (have been) suddenly killed in their beds with their wives and children'. The inflexions in the first and third of these examples show that here too the participle is adjectival rather than verbal. But again the participle was not always declined, e.g. *hie beoð ahafen from eorðan* 'they are raised from the earth'. (Can we definitely say it is not declined in the example about Rome?)

§203 The difference between the forms with *wesan* and those with *weorðan* is not well-defined. The former sometimes seem to emphasize the state arising from the action, e.g. *he eall wæs beset mid heora scotungum* 'he was completely covered with their missiles' and (showing the continuing state by the use of *bið*) *ne bið ðær nænig ealo gebrowen* 'nor is any ale brewed there', and the latter the action itself, e.g. *þær wearþ se cyning Bagsecg ofslægen* 'there King B. was killed' (lit. 'became slain'). But this does not always hold; cf. e.g. *on þæm wæron eac þa men ofslægene* 'on it too the men were slain'. Such fluctuations are natural in a developing language. The fact that the *weorðan* form of the idiom disappeared suggests that the language found other ways of making the distinction when it was necessary, e.g. *þær se cyning ofslægen læg* 'where the king lay slain'; it was, claims J. M. Wattie, 'the only false start' in the development of the MnE verb.

Other Uses of the Present and Past Participles

§204 1 Present and past participles are found as nouns, e.g. *brimliþendra* 'of the seamen' and *He is se frumcenneda* 'He is the first-born', and as adjectives, e.g. *þinne ancennedan sunu* 'your only son'.

2 They also introduce phrases which may be the equivalent of adjective clauses, e.g. the sentences quoted in §187.1(*b*), or which may express various adverbial relationships, such as time, e.g. *þæt man his hlaford of lande lifigendne drife* 'that one should drive his lord from the land while he still lives', or cause, e.g. *me þearfendre* 'to me in my need'. (What sex is the last speaker?)

3 Together with a noun or a pronoun, a participle may be inflected in the dative case in imitation of a Latin ablative absolute; see §191.4.

4 Sometimes the exact grammatical status of such a phrase is not certain. Thus the first two words in *astrehtum handum to Gode clypode* 'with outstretched hands called to God' are taken by some as an absolute and by others as a dative of 'attendant circumstances'. Perhaps they are both. At any rate, such ambiguities are merely terminological.

The Uses of the Infinitives

§205 This section sets out the normal uses of the OE uninflected and inflected infinitives. Exceptional uses of the one in the functions here allotted to the other, however, do occur.

1 The uninflected infinitive is usual after the auxiliaries mentioned in §206 and after *uton* 'let us', *þurfan* 'need', and *durran 'dare'. The infinitive of a verb of motion is frequently not expressed in such circumstances, e.g. *ær he in wille* 'before he will go in'.

As in MnE, there are circumstances in which either the infinitive without *tō* or a present participle can be used, e.g. *Ic geseah ða englas dreorige wepan and ða sceoccan blissigende on eowerum forwyrde* 'I saw the angels weep bitterly and the demons rejoicing at your destruction'.

On the accusative and infinitive, see §161.

2 The inflected infinitive with *tō* is common in the following functions:

(*a*) To express purpose, e.g. *an wulf wearð asend to bewerigenne þæt heafod* 'a wolf was sent to guard the head' and, with a passive sense, *bindað sceafmælum to forbærnenne* 'bind them in sheaves for burning, to be burnt'. But the simple infinitive also occurs, e.g. *ut eode ahyrian wyrhtan* 'went out to hire workers'.

(*b*) With the verb 'to be' to express necessity or obligation, e.g. *Is eac to witanne* 'It must also be noted'.

(*c*) To complete the sense of a verb, e.g. *and begunnon ða to wyrcenne* 'and then [they] began to work'. But cf. *ða ongan ic ða boc wendan on Englisc* 'then I began to translate the book into English', where the infinitive without *tō* occurs.

(*d*) To complete the sense of a noun, e.g. *anweald to ofsleanne and to edcucigenne* 'power to kill and to restore to life', or of an adjective, e.g. *wæron æþelingas . . . fuse to farenne* 'the nobles were eager to depart'.

(*e*) As the subject, or as the complement, of a sentence, e.g. *to sittanne on mine swyðran healfe. . . nys me inc to syllanne* 'to sit on my right hand is not for me to give to you two'.

The 'Modal' Auxiliaries

Introduction

§206 Some forms of the OE verbs *cunnan*, *willan*, *sculan, *magan*, and *mōtan, still survive as auxiliaries today, viz. 'can', 'will', 'would', 'shall', 'should', 'may', 'might', and 'must'. As in OE, they are followed by the infinitive without 'to'. Their semantic history is a complicated one and even today the uses of some, especially 'shall' and 'will' and 'should' and 'would', cause great confusion to very many foreign speakers of English. Readers of OE too will find difficulties with them, but of a different sort, for the range of meanings they had in OE was wider than it is now.

Magan

§207 In *eorðe mæg wið ealra wihta gehwilce* 'earth prevails against every creature', *magan* means 'to prevail against' and has the full force of an independent verb; cf. Hopkins's 'I can no more'. In *þæt he ealle þa tid mihte ge sprecan ge gangan* 'so that all the time he could speak and walk', it means 'to be able', while in *Luke* 16: 2 *ne miht þu leng tunscire bewitan* 'you can no longer hold the stewardship', it means 'to be permitted to'. In these senses, it expresses a shade of meaning which the subjunctive of a simple verb could hardly do. The same is true in *Dream of the Rood* ll. 37–8, where we have a statement of fact 'I could have destroyed all his foes' and not of possibility 'I might have destroyed all his foes'. But this last use – the MnE one – does occur in OE. A striking example is found in *Andreas* ll. 544 ff.

> Nænig manna is . . .
> ðætte areccan mæg oððe rim wite . . .

'There is no man . . . [of such a sort] that he may relate or know the number'. The proper mood in such clauses is the subjunctive (see §175.2); hence *wite*. But parallel to it is *āreccan mæg* 'may relate, may tell'.

Note
K. R. Brooks, the latest editor of *Andreas*, follows Grein in emending to *mæge*. Though possible, this does not seem essential.

Thus *magan* has shades of meaning which cannot always be accurately distinguished. Does *Genesis B* ll. 436–7 mean 'what we can win by our own strength' or 'what God will allow us to win'? Consider too *ðu miht* in *Dream of the Rood* l. 78.

When it means 'to be permitted to' *magan* is a rival of **mōtan* 'to be allowed to'; cf. *Luke* 16: 2 quoted above with *Matthew* 20: 15 *ne mot ic don þæt ic wylle?* where the Authorized Version has 'Is it not lawful for me to do what I will?', and *Maldon* ll. 14 and 235 with *Maldon* ll. 83 and 95.

But in the sense of 'to be able to' it frequently comes close to *cunnan*; cf. Cædmon's statement (in the second paragraph of selection 9) *Ne con ic noht singan* 'I do not know how to sing anything' with the angel's reply *Hwæðre þu meaht me singan*[1] 'Yet you can sing to me'. Here, as the Latin original *nescio cantare* suggests, *cunnan* may have its full sense of 'to know how to'. But it comes close to the modern sense of 'to be able to'.

**Mōtan*

§208   The preterite of **mōtan* 'to be allowed to' is *mōste*, the ancestor of MnE 'must'. In *Maldon* l. 30 the present tense *þū mōst* comes close to meaning 'you must'. But it may be a very formal and ceremonious extension of the permissive use, perhaps with ironical overtones: 'The Danes bid me say that they are graciously pleased to allow you to send tribute in exchange for protection'. The sense of 'to be allowed to, may' seems to be the prevailing one for **mōtan* in OE.

Cunnan

§209   For an example of *cunnan* 'to know how to' shading into 'to be able, can' (its MnE sense), see §207 above.

**Sculan*

§210   The most important function of **sculan* is to express necessity or obligation. Thus it must be translated 'must' in *Se byrdesta sceall gyldan* 'The wealthiest must pay', expressing a general obligation, and 'has had to' in *Wanderer* l. 3, where *sceolde* has no future reference at all. In *Maldon* l. 60 too, *sceal* means 'must', but here the reference is more clearly to one specific act which must take place in the future.

Whether **sculan* ever represents the simple future is a matter of some dispute. Cædmon's reply to the comment of the angel quoted at the end of §207 was *Hwæt sceal ic singan?* Some of you may be tempted to translate this 'What shall I sing?' But the Latin has *Quid debeo cantare?* which demands the translation 'What must I (ought I to) sing?' Here then **sculan* clearly does not represent a simple future. And on the whole it will be safer for you to assume that it always has an idea of obligation, except in examples like those

---

[1] So some MSS. MS T lacks *me*; so some read *þu me aht singan* 'you must sing to me'. But here (i) we might expect an infl. inf. after *aht*; (ii) that *aht* could mean 'must' is uncertain.

discussed in the next two paragraphs. When Ælfric in his grammar equates *lecturus sum cras* with *ic sceal rædan tomerigen*, it might seem a clear case of 'I shall read tomorrow'. But it probably means 'I must read tomorrow', for elsewhere Ælfric equates *osculaturus* with *se ðe wyle oððe sceal cyssan*. This does not mean that *wyle* and *sceal* mean the same thing, but that *osculaturus* has two possible meanings for Ælfric – futurity 'He is going to kiss' (see §211) and obligation 'He has to kiss'. So the OE version of *Matthew* 20: 10 *And þa þe þær ærest comon wendon þæt hi sceoldon mare onfon*, which represents the Latin *Venientes autem et primi, arbitrati sunt quod plus essent accepturi*, is perhaps best translated 'And those who had come there first thought that they ought to receive more'.

* *Sculan* can also express what is customary, e.g. *And ealle þa hwile þæt lic bið inne, þær sceal beon gedrync and plega* 'And all the time the body is within, there shall be drinking and playing'.

In *ðæs nama sceolde bion Caron* 'whose name is said to be C.', *sceolde* shows that the reporter does not believe the statement or does not vouch for its truth. You will probably meet other examples of this.

Willan

§211 The original function of *willan* seems to have been the expression of wish or intention, e.g. *ic wille sellan* 'I wish to give', *þe þær beon noldon* 'who did not wish to be there', and *he wolde adræfan anne æþeling* 'he wished to expel a princeling'. In these (with the possible exception of the second), there is some future reference. How far *willan* had gone along the road to simple futurity is difficult to determine, but examples like *Hi willað eow to gafole garas syllan* 'They wish to (will) give you spears as tribute',

> æghwylc gecwæð,
> þæt him heardra nan hrinan wolde

'everyone said that no hard thing would touch him', and *þa Darius geseah, þæt he oferwunnen beon wolde* 'When D. saw that he would be conquered' (note the passive infinitive), come pretty close to it.

Willan, like MnE 'will', is sometimes found 'expressing natural disposition to do something, and hence habitual action' (*OED* s.v. 'will' 8), e.g. *He wolde æfter uhtsange oftost hine gebiddan* 'He would most often pray after matins'.

On paratactic *wolde*, see §185.2 and cf. the *þæt* clause with *willan* in

> Geseah ic þa frean mancynnes
> efstan elne mycle þæt he me wolde on gestigan

'I saw the Lord of mankind hasten with great zeal in His wish to climb on to me'.

Impersonal Verbs

§212 These are more common in OE than in MnE, but should not cause you much trouble if you notice that the subject 'it' is often not expressed, e.g. *me ðyncð betre* 'it seems better to me' and *hine nanes ðinges ne lyste* lit. 'it pleased him in respect of nothing'. But *hit* does appear, e.g. *hit gelamp* 'it happened'.

XI PREPOSITIONS

§213 The most important prepositions, with their meanings and the cases they govern, are set out below in alphabetical order. For their use in prepositional conjunctions, see §171.

Those marked with a dagger † govern both accusative and dative, the distinction usually being accusative of motion, e.g. *and heo hine in þæt mynster onfeng* 'and she received him into the monastery', and dative of rest, e.g. *on þam huse* 'in that house'. However, this distinction is not always observed.

Prepositions often follow the word they govern, e.g. *him to* 'against them' and *him biforan* 'before him'.

Sometimes words which often occur as prepositions are used without a noun or pronoun, e.g. *þa foron hie to* 'then they went thither' and *het þa in beran segn* 'then [he] ordered [them] to carry in the banner'. Here we have something very similar to the separable prefixes of modern German.

List of Prepositions

§214 (Note: Some prepositions may be followed by the dative or the instrumental. As there is no significance in this variation, the instrumental has not been included in the list.)

æfter		dat. (acc.) 'after, along, according to'
ær		dat. (acc.) 'before'
æt		dat. 'at, from, by'; (acc. 'as far as, until')
be		dat. (acc.) 'by, along, alongside, about'
beforan		dat. acc. 'before, in front of'
betweox		dat. acc. 'among, between'
binnan	†	'within, into'
bufan	†	'above, upon'
būtan		dat. acc. 'except, outside, without'
ēac		dat. 'besides, in addition to'
for		dat. acc. 'before (of place), in front of, because of'
fram		dat. 'from, by (of agent)'
ġeond		acc. (dat.) 'throughout'

in	†	'in, into'
innan	†	'in, within'; (occasionally gen.)
mid		dat. acc. 'among, with, by means of'
of		dat. 'from, of'
ofer	†	'above, over, on'
on	†	'in, into, on'
on-ġēan		dat. acc. 'against, towards'
oþ		acc. (dat.) 'up to, until'
tō		gen. 'at, for, to such an extent, so'
		dat. 'towards, to, at, near'
		dat. 'as', in the idiom seen in *to frofre* 'as a consolation' and *to menniscum men* 'as a human being'
		(acc. 'towards')
tō-ġēanes		dat. 'against, towards'
þurh		acc. (dat. gen.) 'through, throughout, by means of'
under	†	'under, beneath'
wiþ		acc. gen. dat. 'towards, opposite, against, along, in exchange for'
ymb(e)		acc. (dat.) 'after, about or concerning'

6

An Introduction to Anglo-Saxon Studies

I SOME SIGNIFICANT DATES

§215 If the Anglo-Saxon period is taken as beginning in 449 and ending in 1066, it lasted for 617 years. It may help you to put this in perspective if you realize that this is roughly the same period of time as that which separates the death of Edward III from the present day, or, to put it in literary terms, the birth of Chaucer from the death of Dylan Thomas.

Note
Where possible, the dates in §216 are taken from *Handbook of British Chronology*, ed. F. M. Powicke and E. B. Fryde (London, Royal Historical Society, 2nd ed., 1961).

§216 See pp. 120–123.

II HISTORY

§217 The Germanic settlements in Britain, which (recent archaeological finds suggest) may have begun at least half a century earlier than the traditional A.D. 449, did not result in the immediate subjugation of the whole island under one Germanic king. Indeed, there is much evidence to suggest a vigorous revival of British fortunes, culminating about the time of the victory of Mons Badonicus (*c.* 490–517), which led to a renewed British predominance in some western and south-midland areas formerly overrun by the invaders. Only with the battles that the Chronicle associates with the West-Saxon leaders Ceawlin, Cuthwulf, Cutha, and Cuthwine (especially Biedcanford 571 and Dyrham 577), was Saxon control re-established in the Chilterns and Cotswolds. Romano-British elements, of course, still survived extensively in the population of Anglo-Saxon England.

The invading English, therefore, lived in independent kingdoms – there were ten south of the Humber in 600 – cut off from one another by geographical barriers and by hostile British. It is in such conditions of isolation that sound-changes flourish, and hence peculiarities which were originally individual or tribal and which would have been eliminated in a larger community flourished unchecked. Thus by *c.* 700, the date of the earliest linguistic records, the four dialects mentioned in §2 – Northumbrian,

Mercian, West-Saxon, and Kentish – can be distinguished in a language which at the time of the invasions appears to have been spoken in much the same way by all those who came to England.

The two hundred or so years after the English victory at the unidentified Biedcanford are not well-documented and the history of the period is often obscure. There was certainly much fighting between the various kingdoms, with now one, now another, temporarily 'top-dog' under some powerful warrior-king, though there was a period of comparative peace during the late seventh and the eighth centuries in which the Northern civilization which produced Bede, Alcuin, and the like, flourished. By 800, however, four great kingdoms survived – Northumbria, Mercia, Wessex, and East Anglia.

Then came the Danes. First they made what might be called 'smash-and-grab' raids in the summer, taking their booty back home with them. In 851 they are recorded as wintering on the Isle of Thanet. In 865 they ravaged Kent. In 867 they moved from East Anglia to York. Over the next few years there was intense activity. One by one, the kingdoms of Northumbria, East Anglia, and Mercia, ceased to exist as independent kingdoms and in 878 Wessex too was nearly extinguished, for in that year King Alfred was taking refuge in Æthelney 'with a small band' while the Danes plundered his kingdom. But Alfred was equal to the challenge. His grasp of the principles of war as revealed by a study of his campaigns against the Danes, and his activities in education, learning, and administration, over the next twenty years until his death in 899, are such that, for some people at any rate, his only rival for the title 'The greatest Englishman of all' is Sir Winston Churchill. The Anglo-Saxon Chronicle has two simple, but revealing, phrases in its account of this period. In 878, it says, the whole of Wessex surrendered to the Danes *buton þam cyninge Ælfrede* 'except King Alfred'. He escaped and rallied his forces. Men flocked to his banner *and his gefægene wærun* 'and were glad of him'.

By 880, then, only Wessex remained of the four kingdoms existing in 800. The subsequent years were a period of uneasy peace in which the Danes settled and ploughed and in which the boundaries of Danelaw were established. The arrival of another great army from France in 892 led to more bitter fighting in which the invaders were helped by those in Northumbria and East Anglia. But gradually Wessex, under Alfred and his successors, won back land from the settled Danes and reconciled them to English rule. In 954 the Scandinavian kingdom of York ceased to exist and the permanent unification of England as one kingdom began. As a result England was able to enjoy a period of comparative peace in the second half of the tenth century in which the great revival of Benedictine monasticism took place, and in which England began to achieve nationhood – a short passage in *The Battle of Maldon* (ll. 51–54) may perhaps contain the beginnings of a sense of patriotism. Nevertheless, in the Laws of Canute we still find a threefold

§216 TABLE OF DATES

Date	Lay	Religious	Literary
449	Traditional date of coming of Angles, Saxons, and Jutes.		The legend of Arthur may rest on a British leader who resisted the invaders.
			c. 547 Gildas writes *De Excidio Britanniae.*
560–616	Æthelbert King of Kent.		
c. 563		St. Columba brings Celtic Christianity to Iona.	
597		St. Augustine brings Roman Christianity to Kent.	
616–632	Edwin King of Northumbria.		
c. 625	Earliest possible date for Sutton Hoo ship burial.		
627		Edwin converted to Christianity.	
632	Edwin killed by heathen King Penda of Mercia.		
635		Aidan settles in Lindisfarne, bringing Celtic Christianity.	
635		King Cynegils of Wessex converted.	
641	Oswald King of Northumbria killed by Penda.		
654	Penda killed by Oswy King of Northumbria.		
664		Synod of Whitby establishes supremacy of Roman Christianity.	

Date		
664		
657–680	St. Chad becomes bishop. Hild Abbess of Whitby.	Cædmon uses Germanic alliterative verse for religious subjects during this period.
c. 678	English missions to the continent begin.	
680		Approximate earliest date for composition of *Beowulf*. Date of first linguistic records.
c. 700		
709	Death of Aldhelm, Bishop of Sherborne.	
731		Bede completes *Historia Ecclesiastica Gentis Anglorum*.
735	Death of Bede. Birth of Alcuin.	
757–796	Offa King of Mercia.	
782	Alcuin settles at Charlemagne's court.	
793	Sacking of Lindisfarne. Viking raids begin.	*fl.* 796 Nennius, author or reviser of *Historia Britonum*.
800	Four great kingdoms remain – Northumbria, Mercia, East Anglia, Wessex.	
780–850		Cynewulf probably flourishes some time in this period.
804	Death of Alcuin.	
851	Danes first winter in England.	
865	Great Danish Army lands in East Anglia.	

§216 TABLE OF DATES (cont.)

Date	Lay	Religious	Literary
867	Battle of York. End of Northumbria as a political power.		
870	King Edmund of East Anglia killed by Danes. East Anglia overrun.		
871	Alfred becomes King of Wessex.		
874	Danes settle in Yorkshire.		
877	Danes settle in East Mercia.		
880	Guthrum and his men settle in East Anglia. Only Wessex remains of the four Kingdoms.		
?886	Boundaries of Danelaw agreed with Guthrum. Alfred occupies London.		The period of the Alfredian translations and the beginning of the Anglo-Saxon Chronicle.
892	Further Danish invasion.		
896	Alfred builds a fleet.		
899	Death of King Alfred.		
899–954	The creation of the English Kingdom.		
c. 909		Birth of Dunstan.	
937	Battle of Brunanburh.		Poem commemorates the battle.
954	The extinction of the Scandinavian kingdom of York.		
959–975	Edgar reigns.		
960		Dunstan Archbishop of Canterbury. The period of the Monastic Revival.	

Date	Event	Literary work
c. 971		*The Blickling Homilies*
978 or 979	Murder of King Edward.	
950–1000		Approximate dates of the poetry codices – Junius MS, Vercelli Book, Exeter Book, and *Beowulf* MS.
978 or 979 –1016	Ethelred the Unready reigns.	
988	Death of Dunstan.	
991	Battle of Maldon.	Poem commemorates the battle.
990–992		Ælfric's *Catholic Homilies*.
993–998		Ælfric's *Lives of the Saints*.
1003–1023	Wulfstan Archbishop of York.	
c. 1014		*Sermo Lupi ad Anglos*.
1005–	Ælfric Abbot of Eynsham.	
c. 1012		
1013	Sweyn acknowledged as King of England.	
1014	Sweyn dies.	
1016	Edmund Ironside dies.	
1016–1042	Canute and his sons reign.	
1042–1066	Edward the Confessor.	
1066	Harold King. Battle of Stamford Bridge. Battle of Hastings. William I King.	

division into Wessex, Mercia, and Danelaw, which reflects the divisions of the earlier period.

The subsequent history of Anglo-Saxon England is well-known – the reigns of Ethelred the Unready, of the Danish dynasty, and of Edward the Confessor, were followed by Harold's victory at Stamford Bridge and his defeat at Hastings.

§218   The fortunes of Christianity fluctuated in Anglo-Saxon England, and students of its literature must grasp the implications of this fact, which are discussed in §§243–245. The Christianity of Roman Britain was not accepted by the pagan invaders, who brought with them the Germanic heroic code, which was in many ways no ignoble way of life. St. Columba and his followers brought Celtic Christianity to the north, while St. Augustine and his followers from Rome spread their teaching from the south until in 664 the Synod of Whitby established the supremacy of Rome. But heathenism was never very far away. King Edwin of Northumbria was killed by the pagan Penda, King of Mercia, in 632. Throughout the Anglo-Saxon period, preachers inveighed against paganism. Alcuin asked his famous question 'What has Ingeld to do with Christ?' in 797, in a letter condemning the recitation of heathen poetry to monks. The invading Danes brought their paganism with them. Both King Alfred and King Ethelred stood sponsor at the baptism of some of their foes, and in 1012, during the lifetime of Ælfric and Wulfstan, Ælfeah Archbishop of Canterbury was murdered by drunken Danes. It is therefore possible that any Christian poet writing in Old English between 680 and 850, when most of the extant poetry was probably written, could have been a convert from paganism or the son of a pagan. If he was not either of these, he lived in a society where the battle between the pagan Germanic religions and Christianity had not been finally resolved. Early Christian poetry adapts pagan symbolism to its own use. This crucial ambivalence is seen in the Benty Grange helmet (§244) and in the Sutton Hoo ship burial, which could be a memorial either to the pagan King Rædwald or to one of his early Christian successors.

III   ARCHAEOLOGY

Introduction

§219   The belief that Anglo-Saxon civilization was decadent before the Norman Conquest dies hard, despite recent attempts to refute it. But it is without foundation. By 1066, English missionaries had preached Christianity in Scandinavia and, despite two centuries of Danish attacks, political unity had been achieved. The idea of nationhood had developed among the people; in its account of the dispute between Earl Godwine and Edward the Confessor over Count Eustace, the Chronicle observes that 'it was hateful to almost all of them to fight against men of their own race, for there were very few on either side who were worth much, apart from Englishmen. Moreover, they did not wish to put this country at the mercy of foreigners by fighting each other' (MS D, 1052). Despite the wars and rumours of wars of this period, England in 1066 possessed (according to R. W. Chambers)

a civilization based upon Alfred's English prose as the national official and literary language. English jewellery, metal-work, tapestry and carving were famed throughout Western Europe. English illumination was unrivalled, and so national that the merest novice can identify the work of the Winchester school. Even in stone-carving, those who are competent to judge speak of the superiority of the native English carver over his Norman supplanter. In building upon a large scale England was behind Normandy. But what little is left to us of Eleventh Century Anglo-Saxon architecture shows an astonishing variety. Its mark is 'greater cosmopolitanism, as compared to the more competent, but equally more restricted and traditional architecture of the Normans'.

Unfortunately, space does not permit a full treatment of these points; all that can be done is to provide you with the means of testing for yourself the truth of R. W. Chambers's vividly expressed view that it seems as if 'Eleventh-Century England was getting into the Fifteenth; as if England was escaping from the Dark Ages without passing through the later Middle Ages at all.' A short Bibliography is given first. This is followed by a list of topics accompanied by brief comments and references to the books cited.

Note
The quotations given above are from R. W. Chambers *On the Continuity of English Prose from Alfred to More and his School* (Early English Text Society).

List of Abbreviated Titles

§220 For convenience, each book is given a brief title which is used in the sections which follow.

The Anglo-Saxons
D. M. Wilson *The Anglo-Saxons* (3rd ed., Penguin, 1981). This includes thirty-eight figures and seventy-nine monochrome illustrations, covering all the topics listed below.

A-S England
P. Hunter Blair *An Introduction to Anglo-Saxon England* (2nd ed., Cambridge, 1977)

Archaeology
The Archaeology of Anglo-Saxon England, ed. David M. Wilson (Methuen, 1976), now available in paperback (Cambridge, 1981)

Note
These three books may profitably be consulted on most of the topics discussed below. All contain useful Bibliographies. See also §258.

Architecture
  E. A. Fisher *An Introduction to Anglo-Saxon Architecture and Sculpture* (Faber
       and Faber, 1959)
Art
  C. R. Dodwell *Anglo-Saxon Art. A New Perspective* (Manchester, 1982)

Note
David M. Wilson *Anglo-Saxon Art from the Seventh Century to the Norman Conquest* with 285 illustrations, 73 in colour (Thames and Hudson, 1984), can be recommended as an alternative. But it is perhaps less conveniently arranged for the beginner. Its chapter headings are 1. Taste, personalities and survival; 2. The seventh-century explosion; 3. The eighth and ninth centuries; 4. Influences; 5. From Alfred to the Conquest. The Index does not contain main entries under the headings architecture, buildings, carving, dress, embroidery, jewellery, metalwork, sculpture, or weapons.

Beowulf Arch.
  Rosemary J. Cramp '*Beowulf* and Archaeology', *Medieval Archaeology* 1
       (1957), 57–77
Beowulf Introduction
  R. W. Chambers *Beowulf An Introduction with a Supplement by C. L. Wrenn*
       (3rd ed., Cambridge, 1959)
Everyday Life
  R. I. Page *Life in Anglo-Saxon England* (London and New York, 1970)
How They Lived
  G. A. Lester *The Anglo-Saxons How They Lived and Worked* (David and
       Charles, 1976)
Jewellery
  R. Jessup *Anglo-Saxon Jewellery* (Faber and Faber, 1950)
Bayeux Tapestry
  Reproductions of this will be found in
  E. Maclagan *The Bayeux Tapestry* (King Penguin, 1949)
  Douglas and Greenaway *English Historical Documents Volume II 1042–1189*
       (Eyre and Spottiswoode, 1953)
  F. Stenton and others *The Bayeux Tapestry* (London, 1957)

The sections on archaeology are inevitably out of date in some places because many discoveries are not written up until years after they are made. One case in point is the timber material; knowledge of which has expanded enormously in recent years. New information can be found in the Introduction to *The Anglo-Saxons*, in the works listed in §258, in *Anglo-Saxon England*, published annually by Cambridge University Press, and in *Medieval Archaeology*, which each year offers an account of new finds under the heading *Medieval Britain in 19***. Colour slides of manuscripts, jewellery, and so on, are available from The Colour Centre, Farnham Royal, Slough, Berkshire.

Weapons and Warfare

§221　See *The Anglo-Saxons*, chapter IV.

It may be of interest to note here how archaeological finds prove the accuracy of the *Beowulf* poet's descriptions of swords, coats-of-mail, helmets, and the like. Thus his mention in ll. 1448–54 of a helmet with chain-mail is confirmed by the discovery in York of the Coppergate helmet, a magnificent piece of Anglo-Saxon craftsmanship in iron and brass with a curtain of mail protecting the neck of the wearer, while the helmet described in ll. 1030–4 can be identified as a Romanesque helmet with a solid comb and not the ribbed helmet seen in the Bayeux Tapestry. See further *Beowulf Arch.*, pp. 57–67, and *The Coppergate Helmet* by Dominic Tweddle (York, 1984).

Other points worthy of study are the Danish strategy in the last decade of the ninth century and Alfred's methods of countering it, and the careful way in which the young Beowulf leads his 'platoon' during his journey to Denmark and his stay there. When reading *The Battle of Maldon* you should ask whether Byrhtnoth's decision to let the Danes cross the causeway unmolested was tactically right or the result of *ofermod* (a characteristic attributed only to Byrhtnoth and Satan). (It can scarcely be a misguided expression of the English sense of 'fair play'.)

Life and Dress

§222　Some knowledge of how the Anglo-Saxons dressed, lived, ate, and drank, will help you to realize more clearly that the writers and scribes whose work you read, and the warriors, priests, statesmen, and others, whose lives you study, were human beings like yourself, subject to weariness and pain, and prey to the same emotions as you are. This knowledge can be acquired from *The Anglo-Saxons*, chapter III, or from *Everyday Life*, which give a reconstruction of life in Anglo-Saxon times. *How They Lived* also gives some valuable insights into the way our ancestors lived, thought, and felt. The Bayeux Tapestry can be studied with profit. Works in Anglo-Saxon which throw light on the more personal and intimate sides of life include the *Leechdoms*, the *Charms*, and the *Riddles*. Ælfric's *Colloquy* (ed. G. N. Garmonsway, 2nd ed., Methuen, 1947) gives a picture of the life and activities of the middle and lower classes of whom we hear little elsewhere. But now and then those who are on the watch will catch momentary glimpses. Thus in the Chronicle for 897 (Parker MS), we find the names of three Frisian sailors killed in a sea-battle. The death of these men, who had been teaching the Anglo-Saxons the art of sea-fighting, is given poignancy by a few lines from the *Maxims* or *Gnomes* of the Exeter Book:

> Welcome is her beloved to the Frisian wife when the ship lies at anchor. His ship has returned and her husband, her own bread-winner, is at home. She welcomes him in, washes his sea-stained garments, gives him new clothes, and grants him on his return what his love demands.

Here are three Frisians whose garments will need no washing and who will be looked for in vain.

Architecture and Buildings

§223   Monochrome plates I and II in *Jewellery* illustrate timber huts and buildings. *Everyday Life* discusses timber huts and halls with illustrations – and supplements the remarks which follow – in chapter IX 'King's Hall, Peasant's Cottage, Town House'. See also *The Anglo-Saxons*, chapter III.

Aerial photographs taken in 1949 led to excavations at Old Yeavering, Northumberland, which revealed an Anglo-Saxon township. A large timber fort dated from the second half of the sixth century. A township outside the fort appeared to have developed in the seventh century. It included a massive timber hall with other smaller halls (one of which may have been a pagan temple later converted to Christian use) and a large timber grandstand for outdoor meetings. The large hall was replaced by an even more ambitious one and the grandstand was enlarged in the reign of King Edwin. The whole township was then destroyed by fire, probably by Cadwallon after Edwin's death in 632. The township was then rebuilt, still in timber, in what may have been Celtic style, and a Christian church was built, around which there grew a large cemetery. This township too was destroyed by fire – perhaps by Penda in 651. The great hall, two smaller halls, and the church, were rebuilt. But towards the end of the seventh century, Yeavering was abandoned in favour of a new site called Melmin, a few miles away.

At Cheddar in Somerset, another Saxon royal residence was excavated in 1960–2. In King Alfred's time, it consisted of a two-storey hall and three smaller buildings, the largest of which was probably a *bur*; see *Beowulf* ll. 140 and 1310. Later kings carried out additions and reconstructions.

The discoveries at Yeavering throw light on the hall in *Beowulf* (see *Beowulf Arch.*, pp. 68–77) and help to fill out the picture given by the poet. Those at Cheddar may serve to illustrate two interesting stories in the Chronicle – the death of King Cynewulf after being trapped in a *bur* which, like that at Cheddar, was separate from the hall, not part of it (selection 6; see note to line 11) and the escape of Archbishop Dunstan, who was left standing alone on a beam when the upper floor of a hall collapsed at Calne, Wiltshire (Laud MS, 978).

On these excavations, see Philip Rahtz *The Saxon and Medieval Palaces at Cheddar* (Oxford, 1979) and B. Hope-Taylor *Yeavering — An Anglo-British centre of early Northumbria* (HMSO, 1977).

Excavations on Cowdery's Down, Basingstoke, Hampshire, in 1978–81 revealed an ancient habitation-site re-used by the Anglo-Saxons but abandoned *c.* 800, and provided well-preserved and detailed evidence for timber architecture of the sixth and seventh centuries A.D.; see *The Archaeological Journal* 140 (1983), 192–261.

§224 Stone was used mainly for churches. But excavations in Northampton in 1981–2 revealed a rectangular stone hall *c.* 37.5 × 11.5 metres, with two rooms subsequently added to the west of the building, increasing its length by 6 metres. Tentatively dated early in the eighth century, it seems to have directly replaced a seventh-century timber hall and possibly decayed or was demolished during the Danish occupation of Northampton in the late ninth and early tenth centuries. See *Current Archaeology* 85 (1982), 38–41. *Architecture* contains a useful introduction to the study of Anglo-Saxon churches and crypts, with plans, photographs, and a bibliography. See also *The Anglo-Saxons*, pp. 50 ff. There are a large number of Saxon churches worth visiting. One which for some reason has proved particularly memorable is that of St. Peter at Bradwell-iuxta-Mare in Essex, which is built mostly of masonry from the nearby Roman fort. A visit to this, to the site of the battle of Maldon on a farm on the R. Blackwater, and to the new nuclear power-station, would make quite an interesting day!

However, wood was used for churches when stone was not readily available. The church at Greenstead, Essex, where (tradition relates) the body of King Edmund of East Anglia rested in 1013 on its way from London to Bury St. Edmunds, is a surviving example of the kind, though its timbers may not date back to Anglo-Saxon times.

Sculpture and Carving

§225 *Architecture* gives an interesting introduction, with illustrations, to works in stone. Survivals include crosses such as those at Ruthwell and Bewcastle, sundials like that at Kirkdale, sepulchral slabs, fonts, and figures like the angels in the Church of St. Lawrence at Bradford-on-Avon. The different types of ornamentation show influences from different countries and civilizations – Celtic, Mediterranean, Northern, and even Eastern.

The carved oak coffin of St. Cuthbert (late seventh-century) and the Franks Casket of whalebone carved with historical and legendary scenes framed with runes (early eighth-century) survive to show that Anglo-Saxon artists worked in media other than stone.

See further *The Anglo-Saxons*, pp. 53 ff., 152 ff., and 158 ff., and *Art*, chapter IV.

Jewellery and Metalwork

§226   A fascinating and well-illustrated account which tells where the jewels can be seen will be found in *Jewellery*. The author writes:

> Side by side with its interest for the archaeologist and the historian, Anglo-Saxon jewellery has a foremost appeal to the artist and the crafts-man of today, who find in a contemplation of its design and technique the exercise of something more than a bare academic interest. To the practis-ing jeweller especially its excellence needs no commendation, and to him it has often yielded an inspiration far from that of unalloyed sentiment.

See also *The Anglo-Saxons*, pp. 137 ff. and 161 ff., and *Art*, chapter VII.

To test the truth of this claim, those in a position to do so should view what Anglo-Saxon jewellery they can, especially the Kingston Brooch and the jewels of the Sutton Hoo Treasure in the British Museum (see §230) and the Alfred and Minster Lovell Jewels in the Ashmolean Museum, Oxford. Some of these are shown in colour in *Jewellery*. Other well-known treasures include the Pectoral Cross of St. Cuthbert (in the Cathedral Library, Durham), finger-rings which belonged to King Æthelwulf and to Queen Æthelswith, King Alfred's sister (both in the British Museum), and neck-laces of amethyst, gold, or other material. *Jewellery*, *The Anglo-Saxons*, and *Art*, offer monochrome illustrations. *Art* has colour plates of an ivory crucifix and a chalice.

By viewing these beautiful objects, we are able to see that the love of beauty and craftsmanship we observe in *Beowulf* is no mere artistic pose, but an accurate reflection of the attitude of the people of his time. Like so many of their descendants, they could combine fierceness in battle with love of the beautiful.

Embroidery

§227   'The tapestries', sings the *Beowulf* poet, 'shone gold-embroidered along the walls, many wondrous sights for those among men who gaze upon such things.' Unfortunately, none of these survive. The only remains of Anglo-Saxon embroidery of any consequence are the early tenth-century vestments now among the relics of St. Cuthbert at Durham, which were made to the order of Queen Ælfflæd, King Æthelstan's queen. These include St. Cuthbert's stole, illustrated in colour in *Art*.

Strictly speaking, as Sir Eric Maclagan points out, the Bayeux Tapestry is 'no tapestry at all, the design being embroidered upon the material and not woven into it'. It is very possible that it was made in England within twenty years of the Conquest by English needlewomen working to the order of Bishop Odo of Bayeux.

See further *Art*, chapters V and VI.

Coins

§228 See *Archaeology*, pp. 349–372.

Manuscripts and Runic Inscriptions

§229 On illuminations and decorations, see *The Anglo-Saxons*, pp. 148 ff. and 156 ff., and *Art*, chapter IV and the relevant colour plates.

On the contents and whereabouts of manuscripts, see

N. R. Ker *Catalogue of Manuscripts containing Anglo-Saxon* (Clarendon Press, 1957).

On handwriting, see (in addition to the above)

N. Denholm-Young *Handwriting in England and Wales* (2nd ed., Cardiff, 1964).

On runes, see

R. I. Page *An Introduction to English Runes* (Methuen, 1973).

The Sutton Hoo Ship-Burial

§230 In 1939, the excavation of a barrow at Sutton Hoo, Suffolk, revealed the ship-cenotaph of an East Anglian King. R. L. S. Bruce-Mitford *The Sutton Hoo Ship Burial* (London, 1968) gives a useful summary of the finds and contains four colour plates, including one of the great gold buckle (5.2 inches long weighing 14.6 ounces) which is portrayed on the cover of this *Guide*. The importance of this find for students of *Beowulf* has been discussed by Professor Wrenn in *Beowulf Introduction*, pp. 508–523. He summarizes his conclusions thus:

> The Sutton Hoo discoveries, then, have furnished new evidence bearing on the date and genesis of *Beowulf*, clearing away obstacles to the early dating of the poem and affording a possible explanation of why so much Scandinavian subject-matter should appear in an English poem. They have further clarified the blend of Christian and pagan elements in a yet homogeneous work. They have shown that the highly aesthetic approach to treasures in gold and gems and craftsmanship, which appears in *Beowulf* at first sight to be anachronistic, is paralleled at Sutton Hoo: that that joy in such treasures and the power to appreciate them which seemed a sophistication in *Beowulf* shared by its poet with his audience,

had already been demonstrated by the craftsmen of East Anglian Rendlesham in the ship-burial of Sutton Hoo. Much light too has been thrown by comparison of the Sutton Hoo objects on the nature of some of the weapons and armour mentioned in *Beowulf*, as well as on the type of harp which must have accompanied its recitation.

Another article on the same subject by the same author will be found in *Mélanges de Linguistique et de Philologie* (Fernand Mossé in Memoriam) (Paris, 1959). It is reproduced in *An Anthology of Beowulf Criticism*, ed. by Lewis E. Nicholson (University of Notre Dame Press, 1963). On Music and Harps, see this and the relevant passages in *Everyday Life*.

IV LANGUAGE

See first Preliminary Remarks on the Language (§§1–4).

Changes in English

§231   It has already been pointed out in §140 that Old English was in process of changing from an inflected to an uninflected language. It has also been shown in the discussions on syntax that the distinction between subject and object – originally made by the contrast between nominative and accusative endings – was increasingly brought out by word-order and that prepositions more and more took over the function of the oblique cases as the inflexional endings became reduced. These changes in accidence and syntax, and in the pronunciation of unstressed vowels, affected the English language far more fundamentally than the later changes in spelling and in the pronunciation of vowels in stressed syllables.

The primitive Germanic languages developed a stress accent on the first syllable of words in place of the shifting stress of the original IE language which is seen, for example, in classical Greek and which has already been mentioned in §§90 and 105–106. As a result, differences in the pronunciation of unstressed syllables which had been important for making distinctions of meaning gradually disappeared. An important example in the endings of verbs has already been mentioned in §113.3, and there are occasional spellings which suggest that the nom. pl. ending *-as* and the gen. sg. ending *-es* of strong masc. and neut. nouns were not always clearly distinguished in late OE.

Before the case endings finally disappeared, we can see the same job being done twice. In *he ofsloh ge þone cyning ge ða cwene* 'he slew both the king and the queen', we see subject and object distinguished by word-order and case-ending. In *mid ealre þære fierde* 'with the whole army', a preposition is followed by an oblique case. This stage was necessary before one of the two devices doing the same job could disappear. But once they existed together, the disappearance of one of them became very likely, for few human beings like doing the same job twice. The increasing use of, and finally complete reliance on, word-order and prepositions made possible the ultimate disappearance of noun inflexions, apart from the genitive ending -s and the distinction between singular and plural. Similarly, new ways were found of distinguishing tense and mood in the verb; see the article by J. M. Wattie mentioned in §256.

The Danish Invasions

§232   These tendencies were already apparent in OE before the influence of the dialects spoken by the Danish invaders of the ninth century could have made itself felt and may well have been more advanced in colloquial OE than in the more conservative forms of the language recorded in the manuscripts. But the Danish invasions and settlements must in fact have hastened the process and perhaps caused it to be more complete than it might otherwise have been. OHG (the ancestor of Modern German) and OE were very similar in their grammatical structure. Yet today, while German has many inflexions and retains the three word-orders S.V., V.S., and S. . . . V., and other typically Germanic grammatical devices such as the distinction between strong and weak forms of the adjective, English has dispensed with them. Why? The Norman Conquest used to be blamed. As we shall see below, it was certainly not without effect here, although its influence on the language was felt more powerfully elsewhere. But the language of the invading Danes was, like Old English, a Germanic language. The roots of many words were similar, but the inflexional endings differed. When a Dane married an Anglo-Saxon woman, it must have been very confusing for their offspring to hear the one say *segls, segli*, where the other said *segles, segle*, or to find that one said *nema nemir nemi* for the present subjunctive singular forms of the verb 'to take' while the other used *nime* for all persons. Some confusion of endings was inevitable as a result of the fixing of the main stress (already mentioned in §231) in all Germanic languages, but this confusion must have been greater in bilingual communities of Danes and Anglo-Saxons.

The Norman Conquest

§233   Since King Ethelred had married a Norman wife in 1002, the influence of French began before the Conquest. But with the Conquest, and its subsequent use as the language of the court and of administration, Norman French became more important. Certain developments already under way in English may have been reinforced by similar tendencies in Norman French and also in Central French, which began to influence English after the accession of the Angevin Henry II in 1154. These are the standardization of word-order as S.V.O. and the loss of inflexions, which resulted in the development of the simple case system of Modern English. The commencement of parallel trends is attested in continental French of the twelfth century, although their completion was long drawn out and varied from region to region. Again, the fact that many French words had plurals in *-s* must have helped the native *-s* ending of *stanas* to oust its rival, the *-n* ending of *naman*, and to become the plural ending of Modern English nouns. But perhaps the most important influences of French were on vocabulary (see §234), on spelling, and on English prose. The French scribes abandoned the conservative English spelling, which often made distinctions which no longer existed, and introduced their own system. As a result it appears that sound-changes which had occurred gradually over the centuries had happened all at once. A similar situation might arise today if English were to be respelt phonetically by Russian scribes who used their own alphabet with the addition of a few English letters. After the Conquest, English prose gradually ceased to be used for official purposes and for history, but was still used for sermons and other religious works. Further reading on this topic is suggested in §259.

Vocabulary

§234   The vocabulary of OE was basically Germanic and the language was less hospitable to borrowings than it is today, frequently preferring to make its own compounds rather than admit foreign words; see §137. But some were admitted. Up to the time of the Norman Conquest, the following groups can be distinguished:

1   Latin
     (*a*) words borrowed in Pr. Gmc. times;
     (*b*) pre-650 borrowings in Britain;
     (*c*) post-650 borrowings in Britain.
2   Greek
     (*a*) direct borrowings, mostly by the Goths;
     (*b*) borrowings through Latin.
3   Celtic.
4   Scandinavian.
5   French.

References to books which deal with this subject will be found in §261. If you do study them, you will find it interesting to note how the words borrowed from the different languages reflect the relationships which existed between the two peoples concerned and so throw light on the history of the period.

Some Questions

§235 If, while studying OE, you consciously note the differences between OE and MnE, you will make your task easier and more interesting. Questions you might like to answer with the help of one of the histories of the language mentioned in §253 are.

1 Where did the -*s* plural of MnE come from? Did French have any influence here? (This has already been touched on in §233.)

2 Where did the -*s* of the MnE genitive singular come from?

3 How did 'of' become a sign of possession, as in 'The mast of the ship'?

4 When did -*eth* disappear as the ending of 3rd sg. pres. ind.?

5 Why do we find in Chaucer the ending -*en* for the pres. ind. pl. when OE has -*að*? Where did this -*en* ending come from?

V LITERATURE

Introduction

§236 As has been pointed out in §218, the Germanic tribes who settled in England in the fifth century brought with them the Germanic heroic code. What we learn of it from Old English literature generally confirms the observations of Tacitus in his *Germania*. The salient points are these. The Germanic warrior was a member of a *comitatus*, a warrior-band. Life was a struggle against insuperable odds, against the inevitable doom decreed by a meaningless fate – *Wyrd*, which originally meant 'what happens'. There is no evidence in their literature that the pagan Anglo-Saxons believed in a life after death like that of Valhalla, the hall in Scandinavian mythology reserved for dead heroes, though there are references to the worship of heathen gods such as Woden, and the practice of placing coins, weapons, and other goods, with the bodies of the dead in both inhumation and cremation burials, suggests a belief in some kind of after-life where they could be used. On this see *The Anglo-Saxons*, pp. 35–6. It is, however, a different kind of immortality which is stressed in their literature. This was *lof*, which was won by bravery in battle and consisted of glory among men, the praise of those still living. These two ideas of *wyrd* and *lof* acquired Christian overtones; see §§244–245. So the reference of passages like those from *Beowulf* which follow is unlikely to be entirely pagan:

Swa sceal man don,
þonne he æt guðe   gegan þenceð
longsumne lof;   na ymb his lif cearað

'So must a man do when he thinks to win enduring fame in battle; he will show no concern for his life' and

Wyrd oft nereð
unfægne eorl,   þonne his ellen deah!

'Fate often spares an undoomed man when his courage is good'.

§237   A pagan warrior brought up in this tradition would show a reckless disregard for his life. Whether he was doomed or not, courage was best, for the brave man could win *lof* while the coward might die before his time. This is the spirit which inspired the code of the *comitatus*. While his lord lived, the warrior owed him loyalty unto death. If his lord were killed, the warrior had to avenge him or die in the attempt. The lord in his turn had the duty of protecting his warriors. He had to be a great fighter to attract men, a man of noble character and a generous giver of feasts and treasures to hold them. So we read in *The Battle of Finnsburh*

Ne gefrægn ic næfre wurþlicor   æt wera hilde
sixtig sigebeorna   sel gebæran,
ne nefre swanas hwitne medo   sel forgyldan
ðonne Hnæfe guldan   his hægstealdas

'I have never heard it said that sixty conquering warriors bore themselves better or more worthily in mortal combat, or that any retainers repaid the shining mead better than Hnæf's retainers repaid him'.

The whole code receives one of its last and finest expressions in *The Battle of Maldon*, especially in the oft-quoted lines spoken by the old warrior Byrhtwold:

Hige sceal þe heardra,   heorte þe cenre,
mod sceal þe mare,   þe ure mægen lytlað

'Courage must be the firmer, heart the bolder, spirit the greater, the more our strength wanes' (or 'our force diminishes'). Here we see a noble manifestation of 'man's unconquerable mind'.

§238   Sometimes a conflict arose between loyalty to *comitatus* and loyalty to kin. The annal for 755 in the Parker MS of the Chronicle tells us of warriors who, in reply to offers of safe-conduct and money from kinsmen in a hostile force, said 'that no kinsman was dearer to them than their lord, and they would never follow his slayer'. This seems to have been the proper attitude. But, as Miss Whitelock points out, the fact that the Laws of Alfred allow a man to fight in defence of a wronged kinsman only if it did not involve fighting against his lord suggests that the claims of kin sometimes overrode the duty to a lord.

§239   A woman given in marriage as a *freoðuwebbe* 'a peace-weaver' to patch up a blood feud was often involved in such a conflict between loyalty to her lord, her husband, on the one hand, and to her family on the other. Freawaru was in this position, Hildeburh may have been; both feature in *Beowulf*. Sigemund's sister Signy was also involved in such a conflict of loyalties, although in her case the feud arose after the marriage. Thus the 'eternal triangle' of Anglo-Saxon literature is based on loyalty rather than on sexual love (though such poems as *The Wife's Lament* and *The Husband's Message* show that such love existed – if we need any assuring on the point). No woman inspired the hero Beowulf, as far as we know. The great love of heroic literature is that of man for man in the noblest sense, the loyalty of warrior to warrior and of warrior to lord. This is not peculiar to the Anglo-Saxons. In the *Chanson de Roland*, Roland's betrothed Aude receives passing mention – even that is perhaps unusual – but Roland's great love is for Oliver. Just before his last battle, Roland cries to Oliver:

> For his liege lord a man ought to suffer all hardship and endure great heat and great cold and give both his body and his blood. Lay on with thy lance, and I will smite with Durendal, my good sword which the King gave me. If I die here, may he to whom it shall fall say 'This was the sword of a goodly vassal'.

Again, in his book *Island of the Dragon's Blood*, Douglas Botting tells the story of a sixteenth-century battle between the Portuguese and Arabs on the island of Socotra. The Portuguese leader, Tristan da Cunha, offered the Arabs terms. The story goes on:

> But the Arabs replied that they were much obliged to the worthy chief captain for wishing to spare their lives but that, in telling them of their captain's death, he had given them a sufficient reason for declining to receive the favour, for the Fartaquins [Mahri Arabs] were not accustomed to return alive to their land and leave their captain dead on the field, especially as he was the son of their King. Therefore he might do as he pleased for they were not going to yield.

But it is important to grasp that this loyalty is fundamental to much Old English poetry. Of course, the time was not far distant when the interest of writers switched from the 'heroic' love of man for man to the 'romantic' love of man for woman. C. S. Lewis characterizes the change which then came over European literature as a revolution compared to which 'the Renaissance is a mere ripple on the surface of literature'.

§240   Among the members of the *comitatus*, there was an insistence on decorum and etiquette – *cuþe he duguðe þeaw* 'he knew the usages of noble warriors' observes the *Beowulf* poet at one point – a respect for well-tried weapons, a love of precious jewels and beautiful things, joy in ships and in warriors marching, in horse races and beer, and in feasting and music in the hall. There was too a pride in being a well-governed people. The hall was an oasis of comradeship, order, warmth, and happiness, in sharp contrast to the threatening and chaotic world of discomfort and danger which lay outside. Old English poetry is not made up entirely of gloomy moments. Sometimes there is laughter and mirth.

§241   But there is also a great awareness of the transitoriness of life – *þis læne lif* 'this transitory life' sings the poet. Some critics of Old English literature sometimes talk as if this were an idea peculiar to Germanic or Anglo-Saxon paganism. But other peoples have grasped the idea that life is transitory. Numerous passages could be cited from Latin and Greek authors. Rider Haggard quotes a Zulu saying that life is 'as the breath of oxen in winter, as the quick star that runs along the sky, as the little shadow that loses itself at sunset'. A famous passage in *The Wisdom of Solomon*, chapter V, compares the passing of the things of this earth to the passage of a shadow, of a ship in the waves, and of a bird or an arrow through the air. In *James*, chapter IV, we read that life is 'a vapour that appeareth for a little time, and then vanisheth away'. You should therefore view with suspicion any comment on such poems as *The Wanderer* and *The Seafarer* which draws unreal distinctions between pagan and Christian elements as a result of failure to realize that the transience of life is a perpetual human theme peculiar to no civilization, age, or culture.

This theme of transience receives frequent expression in Old English poetry. Three fine examples are *The Wanderer* ll. 92–110, *The Seafarer* ll. 80–93, and a passage from the less-known *Solomon and Saturn*:

> Lytle hwile   leaf beoð grene;
> ðonne hie eft fealewiað,   feallað on eorðan
> and forweorniað,   weorðað to duste

'For a little while the leaves are green. Then they turn yellow, fall to the earth and perish, turning to dust.' But while the theme is universal, the response is often different. In both *The Wanderer* and *The Dream of the Rood*, the passing of friends is lamented. But whereas in *The Wanderer* the thought provokes the famous response 'Where are they now?', the dreamer who has gazed upon the Cross affirms triumphantly that they live now in Heaven with the King of Glory.

§242   The transitoriness of all joys was brought home with special force to the man without a lord, always a figure of misery in Old English literature. He may have survived his lord because he was a coward who ran away from battle, like the sons of Odda in *The Battle of Maldon*, or by the fortune of war which decreed that he was badly wounded, but not killed, like the two survivors of the fights in the already-mentioned annal for 755. He may even have betrayed his lord, like Ceolwulf, the foolish thane who ruled Mercia as a Danish puppet for a few years after 874. Because of this uncertainty, a lordless man was suspect wherever he went. We can perhaps to some extent conceive his misery if we ponder the state of mind of people who find themselves in one of the following situations today – a trade-unionist expelled from his union and unable to earn money by his only skill; an army officer or an administrator suddenly expelled without compensation from a former colonial territory where he had made his career; a citizen of the West deserting to the East (or vice versa) for ideological reasons; a discharged convict unable to get a job; or a lonely refugee from behind the Iron Curtain who has left dear ones behind him and now exists without hope in a camp for 'displaced persons'.

§243 What joy and hope the coming of Christianity in the sixth century must have brought to such a man! And not to him alone, but also to those safely within a *comitatus*. For even they had little, if any, belief in a personal after-life, and no awareness of what Professor Southern has called 'the personal and secret tie between man and God'. Surrounded by few of the material comforts we take for granted today, liable to sudden attack and without any real hope for the future, they too must have found in Christianity the peace which passeth understanding. Doubtless, it was still true that

> Forðon sceall gar wesan
> monig morgenceald   mundum bewunden,
> hæfen on handa,   nalles hearpan sweg
> wigend weccean,   ac se wonna hrefn

'For many a spear, cold with the chill of morning, must be grasped with the palms, lifted by the hand. No sound of harp shall wake the warriors, but the dark raven.' But now the warriors could lie down under the protection of the Almighty and could rise with the name of Christ upon their lips.

§244 To be sure, conversion was neither universal nor immediate. But those who experienced it must have been a strange blend of pagan and Christian, combining as they did the fierce courage and pride of paganism with the new hope derived from Christianity – a blend strikingly seen on the Benty Grange helmet which bears both the pagan boar and the Christian Cross. Something of the same (but perhaps in reverse) must, one imagines, be part of the make-up of those elderly Russians of today who were brought up Christians but who have consciously or unconsciously been influenced by the teachings of Marx. In 1961 Mr. Khrushchev was reported as saying that the Soviet Union possessed a 100-megaton bomb 'which, God grant it, we may never have to explode'. Whether this invocation of God was deliberately cynical, the accidental result of thought-habits formed in youth, or proof that he really was a Christian at heart, one cannot say. But the fact that he could call on God will help us to understand why the *Beowulf* poet could say in the same poem both

> Wyrd oft nereð
> unfægne eorl,   þonne his ellen deah!

'Fate often spares an undoomed man, when his courage is good' and

> Swa mæg unfæge   eaðe gedigan
> wean ond wræcsið   se ðe Waldendes
> hyldo gehealdeþ!

'Thus may an undoomed man whom the grace of the Almighty protects easily survive misery and banishment.'

From this it follows that a poem which contains apparently pagan and apparently Christian ideas (as opposed to one which deals with themes common to both, such as the transience of life) need not be a Christian reworking of a pagan poem. Its author may have been a converted pagan, or, like some elderly Russians today, a man who, because he had lived with survivors of a past civilization, could grasp its values imaginatively and appreciate them even while he himself belonged to a new age.[1]

§245 We have heard recently of Roman Catholic missionaries in Africa singing the Mass to the rhythms of a Congo war-chant and of the weaving of native songs and dances into the same church's baptismal ceremony in New Guinea. Missionaries in Anglo-Saxon England similarly 'baptized' pagan institutions, methods, and concepts. The Yeavering excavations give evidence of a pagan temple converted to Christian use. Bede's account of the poet Cædmon tells how, between 657 and 680, Cædmon sang his famous *Hymn* and so used heroic alliterative verse for Christian purposes – a development of great importance for Old English literature. And in *The Seafarer* and other poems, we find the pagan idea of *lof* Christianized – it now consists of praise on earth and life in Heaven and is to be won by fighting against the Devil and by doing good.

If we bear all this in mind, the incongruities to which our attention is so often drawn by critics of Old English poetry will trouble us less. After all, we can today 'thank our lucky stars' and say 'By Jove!' without believing that the stars really influence our lives or that Jupiter will protect us in battle. Similarly, if we find that our own interpretation of *Beowulf* commits us to the view that its author was a passionate believer in Christianity, we need not be deterred by the fact that he speaks of the power of *wyrd*; see §218 and note that the influence of Latin and Christian thought and means of expression is apparent (in varying degrees) in most of the texts in Part Two of this book.

§246 These problems loom large in Old English literature because we know very little about the genesis of most poems. *Cædmon's Hymn* is attributed to Cædmon and four poems – *Fates of the Apostles, Elene, Juliana*, and *Christ B* – bear Cynewulf's 'signature' in runes. But this does not give us much help, for Cynewulf is little more than a name. The unfortunate fact is that we just do not know for whom, by whom, when, where, or with what aim, most of the poems were written. This inevitably creates difficulties for us when we try to elucidate them and may lead us to criticize a poem for not having a structure which appeals to us or for not being the poem we think it ought to be.

---

[1] But see D.Whitelock *The Audience of Beowulf* (Oxford, 1951), esp. pp. 22–28.

Poetry

§247 In *An Introduction to Old English Metre*, Alan Bliss makes three points which need stressing here. The first is that 'OE poetry is not at all primitive; on the contrary, it is very highly artificial and sophisticated'. The second is that 'the vocabulary of OE poetry differs widely from that of prose'. The third is that 'OE poetry varies from most other types of poetry in that the metrical patterns are . . . selected from among the patterns which occur most commonly in natural speech'. The metrical unit is the half-line. Two half-lines alliterating together form the alliterative line which survived into ME and had a glorious flowering in the fourteenth century with such works as *Sir Gawain and the Green Knight* and *Piers Plowman*. See further §267.

§248 Apart from *The Metres of Boethius* and the Metrical Version of the Psalms found in the Paris Psalter, the bulk of Old English poetry is to be found in four manuscripts, all of which date approximately from the second half of the tenth century. They are the Junius MS, the Vercelli Book, the Exeter Book, and the *Beowulf* MS. Further description of these manuscripts here would be superfluous, but you may find it interesting to answer the following questions:

Why was the Junius MS so-called? And why did some people call it the Cædmon MS? Has it any connexion with Milton?
How did the Vercelli Book become associated with Italy?
Why is the *Beowulf* MS known as Cotton Vitellius A.xv? What happened to it in 1731?
Where can the Exeter Book be seen? How did it get there?

There are, of course, poems which are not found in these four manuscripts. They have been collected in a volume known as *The Anglo-Saxon Minor Poems*, which is referred to in §264.

§249 The extant poems can be roughly classified according to subject matter.

1. Poems treating Heroic Subjects
Beowulf. Deor. The Battle of Finnsburh. Waldere. Widsith.

2. Historic Poems
The Battle of Brunanburh. The Battle of Maldon.

3. Biblical Paraphrases and Reworkings of Biblical Subjects
The Metrical Psalms. The poems of the Junius MS; note especially *Genesis B* and *Exodus. Christ. Judith.*

4. Lives of the Saints
Andreas. Elene. Guthlac. Juliana.

5. Other Religious Poems
Note especially *The Dream of the Rood* and the allegorical poems – *The Phoenix, The Panther*, and *The Whale*.

6. Short Elegies and Lyrics

The Wife's Lament. The Husband's Message. The Ruin. The Wanderer. The Seafarer. Wulf and Eadwacer. Deor might be included here as well as under 1 above.

7. Riddles and Gnomic Verse

8. Miscellaneous

Charms. The Runic Poem. The Riming Poem.

Note

Four poems – *The Fates of the Apostles, Elene, Christ B*, and *Juliana* – contain Cynewulf's 'signature' in runes.

Prose

§250   As has already been pointed out in §182, English prose was far from being a primitive vehicle of expression at the time of the Norman Conquest. You will be able to watch it developing in the Chronicle and elsewhere. One interesting question you may try to answer for yourself is 'Whose prose do you prefer – that of Alfred or Ælfric?'

§251   Old English prose may be said to fall into the seven main divisions set out below.

1. The Anglo-Saxon Chronicle

The surviving manuscripts – lettered A to H – are discussed in *The Anglo-Saxon Chronicle*, ed. Dorothy Whitelock (Eyre and Spottiswoode, 1961), pp. xi–xviii. MS E (The Laud Chronicle) continues until the death of Stephen in 1154. This is, to all intents and purposes, the end of historical writing in English prose until the fifteenth century.

Miss Whitelock observes that 'the confident attribution of the work to Alfred's instigation cannot be upheld'.

2. The Translations of Alfred and his Circle

King Alfred explained his educational policy in his famous Preface to the *Cura Pastoralis*. This is perhaps the first of his translations. He also translated the *De Consolatione Philosophiae* of Boethius and the *Soliloquia* of St. Augustine, and was responsible for a legal code.

Bishop Wærferth of Worcester translated the *Dialogues* of Gregory the Great at Alfred's request. The OE version of Bede's *Ecclesiastical History* has long been attributed to Alfred. Miss Whitelock, in her British Academy Lecture in 1962, finds no evidence for this, but says that it remains a probability that the work was undertaken at Alfred's instigation. The same is true of the OE version of the *Historia adversus Paganos* of Orosius, which incorporates the story of the voyages of Ohthere and Wulfstan.

3. Homiletic Writings

The most important of these are

(*a*) *The Blickling Homilies*, 971.
(*b*) Ælfric's *Catholic Homilies*, 990–2, and *Lives of the Saints*, 993–8.
(*c*) *The Homilies* of Wulfstan, who died in 1023.

4. Other Religious Prose

This includes translations of portions of both the Old and New Testaments, and a version of the Benedictine Office.

5. Prose Fiction

Here we find the story of *Apollonius of Tyre*, *Alexander's Letter to Aristotle*, and *The Wonders of the East*. It has been said that these show 'that long before the Conquest the Anglo-Saxons found entertainment in the exotic romanticism of the East'.

6. Scientific and Medical Writings

7. Laws, Charters, and Wills

7
Select Bibliography

A separate Bibliography is provided for each chapter of Part One; details of the arrangement will be found in the Contents.

For convenience of reference, each section of the Bibliography has been given its own number and the section-numbers of the discussions to which the books relate have been placed in brackets after each heading in the Bibliography.

GENERAL

§252 A useful guide is

Fred C. Robinson *Old English Literature. A Select Bibliography* (Toronto, 1970).

For fuller details see

Stanley B. Greenfield and Fred C. Robinson *A Bibliography of Publications on Old English Literature to the end of 1972* (Toronto, 1980).

Two publications which appear each year deserve mention:

Anglo-Saxon England (Cambridge University Press)
Old English Newsletter (Center for Medieval and Early Renaissance Studies, State University of New York at Binghamton).

Their value will be apparent on inspection. Both offer annual bibliographies.

CHAPTER I
PRELIMINARY REMARKS ON THE LANGUAGE (§§1–4)

§253 An excellent Introduction to Old English will be found in §§1–22 of A. Campbell's *Old English Grammar* (Clarendon Press, 1959, reprinted with corrections 1962).

On the history of the English language generally, the following books can be recommended:

Albert C. Baugh and Thomas Cable *History of the English Language* (3rd ed., Prentice Hall, 1978)

Otto Jespersen *Growth and Structure of the English Language* (10th ed., Basil Blackwell, 1983).

You will not need a dictionary initially, as a Glossary is supplied in this volume. If you are curious, however, you should begin by using

J. R. Clark Hall *A Concise Anglo-Saxon Dictionary* (4th ed., with Supplement by H. D. Meritt, Cambridge, 1960).

The most complete dictionary is that known as *Bosworth-Toller*. It is published by the Oxford University Press, and consists of a Dictionary and Supplements. The original Dictionary was very deficient in the letters A–G. Here, in particular, you will have to consult both Dictionary and Supplements.

Some have found

J. F. Madden and F. P. Magoun Jr. *A Grouped Frequency Word-List of Anglo-Saxon Poetry* (The Harvard Old English Series, 1967)

a very helpful guide to learning vocabulary. This lists the words which occur in OE poetry, starting with those which are used most frequently. Most of the first 300 words at least are very common in prose texts.

CHAPTER 2
ORTHOGRAPHY AND PRONUNCIATION (§§5–9)
AND CHAPTER 3
INFLEXIONS (§§10–135)

§254 Although A. Campbell's *Old English Grammar* (see §253 above) is too detailed for you to use by itself in your first few months, it may be safely consulted when you are in difficulty. By looking at the Contents (pp. vii–xi) or the Index, you will be able to find full paradigms, lists of examples of strong verbs or anything else you want, and lucid explanations of any difficulty you may encounter.

CHAPTER 4
WORD FORMATION (§§136–138)

§255 Very helpful discussions and lists will be found in chapter IV of Quirk and Wrenn *An Old English Grammar* and in pp. 39–43 of N. Davis *Sweet's Anglo-Saxon Primer*, which are mentioned in §256.

CHAPTER 5
SYNTAX (§§139–214)

§256 The standard work at present is Bruce Mitchell *Old English Syntax* (2 vols., Clarendon Press, 1985). There are plenty of monographs, but many of them are in German and most of those in English are too complicated for the beginner. One which may prove useful is J. M. Wattie's article called 'Tense' in *Essays and Studies* XVI (1930); this deals with the topics discussed in §§195–211.

Short but helpful treatments of the syntax will be found in:

N. Davis *Sweet's Anglo-Saxon Primer* (Clarendon Press, 1953 or later)
P. S. Ardern *First Readings in Old English* (New Zealand University Press, 1948)
R. Quirk and C. L. Wrenn *An Old English Grammar* (Methuen, 1955 or later)
G. L. Brook *An Introduction to Old English* (Manchester University Press, 1955).

CHAPTER 6
INTRODUCTION TO ANGLO-SAXON STUDIES (§§215–251)

History (§§215–218)

§257 The following are recommended:

P. Hunter Blair *An Introduction to Anglo-Saxon England* (2nd ed., Cambridge, 1977)
P. Hunter Blair *Roman Britain and Early England 55 BC—AD 871* (Nelson, 1963)
F. M. Stenton *Anglo-Saxon England* (3rd ed., Oxford, 1971)
Dorothy Whitelock (ed.) *English Historical Documents* Volume 1 *c*. 500–1042 (2nd ed., London, 1979)
David Hill *An Atlas of Anglo-Saxon England 700—1066* (Basil Blackwell, 1981)
James Campbell (ed.) *The Anglo-Saxons* (Oxford, 1982)
Christine Fell *Women in Anglo-Saxon England* (London, 1984), now available in paperback (Basil Blackwell, 1986).

Archaeology (§§219–230)

§258 See §220, the section in which each topic is discussed, and

Richard N. Bailey *Viking Age Sculpture in Northern England* (London, 1980)
Rupert Bruce-Mitford, *The Sutton Hoo Ship Burial*
Vol. 1 *Excavations, background, the ship, dating and inventory* (London, 1975)

Vol. 2 *Arms, armour and regalia* (London, 1978)

Vol. 3 *Late Roman and Byzantine silver, hanging-bowls, drinking vessels, cauldrons and other containers, textiles, the lyre, pottery bottle and other items* (Parts I and II, London, 1983)

Rosemary J. Cramp *Early Northumbrian Sculpture* (Jarrow, 1965)

David A. Hinton *A Catalogue of the Anglo-Saxon Ornamental Metalwork 700– 1100 in the Department of Antiquities Ashmolean Museum* (Oxford, 1974)

H. M. Taylor and Joan Taylor *Anglo-Saxon Architecture* (3 vols., Cambridge, 1965–78)

David M. Wilson *Anglo-Saxon Ornamental Metalwork 700–1100 in the British Museum* (London, 1964).

Language (§§231–235)

History of English Prose

§259 On the topics mentioned in §233, see

R. W. Chambers *On the Continuity of English Prose from Alfred to More and his School* (Early English Text Society).[1]

Some of the points he raises are discussed in

N. Davis 'Styles in English Prose of the Late Middle and Early Modern Period' in *Les Congrès et Colloques de l'Université de Liège*, Volume 21 (1961), pp. 165–184.

See also

R. M. Wilson 'English and French in England 1100–1300', *History* 28 (1943), 37–60.

Vocabulary

Word Formation

See §255.

Changes of Meaning

§260 This is a difficult subject. Chapter VII of Simeon Potter *Modern Linguistics* (Andre Deutsch, 1957) is a useful and helpful introduction. See §4.

---

[1] But his suggestion (p. lxxxvi) that the line between OE and ME can be drawn between the Peterborough annals for 1131 and 1132 is not now accepted; see *The Peterborough Chronicle 1070–1154*, ed. Cecily Clark (2nd ed., Oxford, 1970), pp. lii–lxiii.

Borrowings

§261   See

M. S. Serjeantson *A History of Foreign Words in English* (Routledge and Kegan
   Paul, 1935)
A. Campbell *Old English Grammar* (see §253 above), chapter X.

Literature (§§236–251)

Topics raised in §§236–246

§262   On the transition from Epic to Romance, see

R. W. Southern *The Making of the Middle Ages* (Hutchinson, 1953), chapter V.

On the heroic way of, and attitude to, life, see

D. Whitelock *The Beginnings of English Society* (Penguin, 1952)
J. R. R. Tolkien *Beowulf: The Monsters and the Critics* (British Academy
   Lecture, 1936)
D. Whitelock *The Audience of Beowulf* (Oxford, 1951).

General Criticism

§263   W. P. Ker *Medieval English Literature* (Oxford, 1912) can still be
recommended, though its views on *Beowulf* are now generally out of favour.
More recent studies of Old English literature include:

E. G. Stanley (ed.) *Continuations and Beginnings* (London, 1966)
Stanley B. Greenfield and Daniel G. Calder *A New Critical History of Old
   English Literature*. With a survey of the Anglo-Latin background by
   Michael Lapidge (New York and London, 1986).

Poetry Texts

§264   Good reading editions include those in the Methuen and Man-
chester series. The standard edition of *Beowulf* remains that of Fr. Klaeber
Beowulf and the Fight at Finnsburg (D. C. Heath and Company, 3rd ed., 1950).
Virtually the entire corpus of Old English poetry is available in *The Anglo-
Saxon Poetic Records*, published by Columbia University Press and Routledge
and Kegan Paul. The volumes are

   I   Junius MS
   II   Vercelli Book
   III Exeter Book

IV   Beowulf and Judith
V   The Paris Psalter and the Meters of Boethius
VI   Anglo-Saxon Minor Poems.

These volumes contain no glossaries and are for the use of scholars rather than of beginners. *A Concordance to the Anglo-Saxon Poetic Records*, edited by Jess B. Bessinger, Jr. and programmed by Philip H. Smith, Jr., was published by Cornell University Press in 1978.

Other editions of poems to appear since Robinson's *Bibliography* (see §252 above) include

The Dream of the Rood edited by M. Swanton (Manchester, 1970)

A Choice of Anglo-Saxon Verse selected with an introduction by Richard Hamer (Faber, 1970)

Daniel and Azarias edited by R. T. Farrell (Methuen, 1974)

Finnsburh Fragment and Episode edited by D. K. Fry (Methuen, 1974)

T. A. Shippey *Poems of Wisdom and Learning in Old English* (Cambridge and Totowa, N.J., 1976)

The Battle of Maldon edited by E. V. Gordon with a supplement by D. G. Scragg (Manchester, 1976)

Exodus edited by P. J. Lucas (Methuen, 1977)

The Old English Riddles of the Exeter Book edited by Craig Williamson (Chapel Hill, 1977)

Christ and Satan: A Critical Edition by R. E. Finnegan (Waterloo, 1977)

Genesis A: A New Edition by A. N. Doane (Madison, 1978)

Resignation edited by Lars Malmberg (Durham, 1979)

The Guthlac Poems of the Exeter Book edited by Jane Roberts (Oxford, 1979)

The Old English Rune Poem: A Critical Edition by Maureen Halsall (Toronto, 1981)

The Battle of Maldon edited by D. G. Scragg (Manchester, 1981)

J. R. R. Tolkien *The Old English Exodus: Text Translation and Commentary* edited by Joan Turville-Petre (Oxford, 1981)

The Old English Riming Poem edited by O. D. Macrae-Gibson (Cambridge, 1983)

Old English Minor Heroic Poems edited by Joyce Hill (Durham, 1983).

Appreciation of the Poetry

§265   See §137 and

Alan Bliss 'v. The Appreciation of Old English Poetry' in *An Introduction to Old English Metre* (Basil Blackwell, 1962)

T. A. Shippey *Old English Verse* (Hutchinson, 1972).

The Use of Oral Formulae

§266 The oral nature of Old English poetry has been much discussed of late. But one needs to beware of the notion sometimes advanced that formulaic poetry is necessarily 'oral' and that all poems must be either strictly 'oral' or strictly 'literary'. Lettered or 'literary' poets certainly carried on the techniques of their 'oral' predecessors, and there seems no real reason why one man should not combine the two techniques. On this topic see initially

L. D. Benson 'The Literary Character of Anglo-Saxon Formulaic Poetry',
    Publications of the Modern Languages Association 81 (1966), 334–341
Jeff Opland *Anglo-Saxon Oral Poetry: A Study of the Traditions* (New Haven and
    London, 1980).

Metre

§267 Very helpful discussions on Old English metre will be found in C. S. Lewis *Rehabilitations and Other Essays* (London, 1939), pp. 117–32 – this has often been reprinted – and in John C. Pope *Seven Old English Poems* (W. W. Norton, new edition, 1981).

In the early stages you may find the following mnemonic helpful. It refers to the six types of half-line in the Sievers system as described by Professor Pope. In the doggerel (a University of Melbourne *macédoine*), each half-line conforms metrically to the basic pattern of one of the types and alliterates on the stressed syllables with the letter by which that type is known.

A.	Anna angry	$\acute{-} \times \acute{-} \times$	falling-falling
B.	And Byrhtnoth bold	$\times \acute{-} \times \acute{-}$	rising-rising
C.	In keen conflict	$\times \acute{-} \acute{-} \times$	clashing
Da.	Ding down strongly	$\acute{-} \acute{-} \grave{-} \times$	falling by stages
Db.	Deal death to all	$\acute{-} \acute{-} \times \grave{-}$	broken fall
E.	Each one with edge	$\acute{-} \grave{-} \times \acute{-}$	fall and rise

The late Grahame Johnston kindly supplied this series of half-lines from Old English poetry which illustrate the five types with the correct initial letter:

A.	*ān æfter ānum*	(*Beowulf* 2461)
B.	*wæs þæt beorhte bold*	(*Beowulf* 997)
C.	*of carcerne*	(*Andreas* 57)
Da.	*deorc dēapscua*	(*Beowulf* 160)
Db.	*dēop dēada wæg*	(*Maxims* I. 78, MS)
E.	*egsode eorl*	(*Beowulf* 6, MS).

Prose Texts

§268 Editions and translations of most of the prose texts are available. Important works which have appeared since Robinson's *Bibliography* (see §252 above) include

Ælfric's Catholic Homilies: The Second Series Text edited by Malcolm Godden (Early English Text Society, 1979)
The Old English Orosius edited by Janet Bately (Early English Text Society, 1980)
Vercelli Homilies IX—XXIII edited by Paul E. Szarmach (Toronto, 1981)
The Prose Solomon and Saturn and *Adrian and Ritheus* edited by James E. Cross and Thomas D. Hill (Toronto, 1982)
Eleven Old English Rogationtide Homilies edited by Joyce Bazire and James E. Cross (Toronto, 1982)
The Old English Herbarium and Medicina de Quadrupedibus edited by Hubert Jan de Vriend (Early English Text Society, 1984)
The Old English Life of Machutus edited by David Yerkes (Toronto, 1984).

Sources

§269 See

G. N. Garmonsway and Jacqueline Simpson *'Beowulf' and its Analogues* (London, 1968), now available in paperback (New York, 1971)
D. G. Calder and M. J. B. Allen *Sources and Analogues of Old English Poetry. The Major Latin Texts in Translation* (Cambridge and Totowa, 1976)
Daniel G. Calder, Robert E. Bjork, Patrick R. Ford and Daniel F. Melia *Sources and Analogues of Old English Poetry II. The Major Germanic and Celtic Texts in Translation* (Cambridge and Totowa, 1983).

APPENDIX A

Strong Verbs

This Appendix, which contains some of the more common strong verbs, is intended to illustrate §§90–109 and 131–134.

As is pointed out in §92, the 3rd pers. sg. pres. ind. is not part of the gradation series. For this reason, these forms are printed in italics in this Appendix.

You will find here further examples of the simplification of endings referred to in §112.2; note

and

$$drīehþ < drēogan \text{ (class II)}$$
$$cwiþþ < cweþan \text{ (class V)}$$
$$wierþ < weorþan \text{ (class III)}.$$

From *bindan* (class III) we find 2nd and 3rd pers. sg. pres. ind. *bintst* and *bint*.

Verbs in which Verner's Law forms occur (see §§105–107) are marked †.

Verbs without Verner's Law forms where they might be expected (see §108) are marked ‡.

When the forms of a verb rhyme with those of the verb before it in the list, the principal parts have been left for you to fill in.[1]

The Appendix is not a complete list of Old English strong verbs. You may find it useful to note down in the appropriate place any new verbs you come across in your reading.

APPENDIX A.1

Class I

Inf.	3rd Sg. Pres. Ind.	1st Pret.	2nd Pret.	Past Ptc.
bītan 'bite'	*bītt*	bāt	biton	biten
flītan 'contend'				
slītan 'tear'				
wītan 'blame'				
ġewītan 'go'				

---

[1] The principle of 'rhyme association' is an important one. Thus most verbs borrowed into English are made weak. But the French borrowing 'strive' became strong through association with verbs like 'drive'. Similarly the Old English weak verb 'wear' became strong through association with the strong verbs 'bear' and 'tear'.

Inf.	3rd Sg. Pres. Ind.	1st Pret.	2nd Pret.	Past Ptc.
wlītan 'behold'				
wrītan 'write'				
bīdan 'await'	*bītt*	bād	bidon	biden
glīdan 'glide'				
rīdan 'ride'				
slīdan 'slide'				
blīcan 'shine'	*blīcþ*	blāc	blicon	blicen
swīcan 'fail'				
drīfan 'drive'	*drīfþ*	drāf	drifon	drifen
belīfan 'remain'				
grīpan 'seize'	*grīpþ*	grāp	gripon	gripen
hrīnan 'touch'	*hrīnþ*	hrān	hrinon	hrinen
scīnan 'shine'				
stīgan 'ascend'	*stīgþ, stīhþ*	stāg[1]	stigon	stigen
hnīgan 'bow to'				
† līþan 'go'	*līþþ*	lāþ	lidon	liden
† scrīþan 'go'				see §108
† snīþan 'cut'				
‡ mīþan 'conceal'	*mīþþ*	māþ	miþon	miþen
‡ rīsan 'rise'	*rīst*	rās	rison	risen

Contracted Verbs (see §103.3)

	3rd Sg. Pres. Ind.	1st Pret.	2nd Pret.	Past Ptc.
† lēon 'lend'	*līehþ*	lāh	ligon	ligen
† tēon 'accuse'				
† þēon 'prosper'[2]				
† wrēon 'cover'				

Note

The following weak verbs are found with *ī* in the infinitive:

    cīdan 'chide', *cwīþan* 'lament', *ġedīgan* 'survive', and *līxan* 'gleam'.

APPENDIX A.2

Class II

Inf.	3rd Sg. Pres. Ind.	1st Pret.	2nd Pret.	Past Ptc.
bēodan 'command'	*bīett*	bēad	budon	boden
brēotan 'break'	*brīett*	brēat	bruton	broten
flēotan 'float'				

---

[1] The form *stāh* sometimes occurs as a result of unvoicing of *g*.

[2] Historically a verb of class III. See A. Campbell *Old English Grammar* §739.

Inf.	3rd Sg. Pres. Ind.	1st Pret.	2nd Pret.	Past Ptc.
ġēotan 'pour'				
scēotan 'shoot'				
† ċēosan 'choose'	*ċīest*	ċēas	curon	coren
† drēosan 'fall'				
† frēosan 'freeze'				
† hrēosan 'fall'				
† lēosan 'lose'				
crēopan 'creep'	*crīepþ*	crēap	crupon	cropen
drēogan 'endure'	*drīehþ*	drēag	drugon	drogen
flēogan 'fly'				
lēogan 'tell lies'				
hrēowan 'rue'	*hrīewþ*	hrēaw	hruwon	hrowen
† sēoþan 'boil'	*sīeþþ*	sēaþ	sudon	soden
brūcan 'enjoy'	*brȳcþ*	brēac	brucon	brocen
lūcan 'lock'				
būgan 'bow'	*bȳhþ*	bēag	bugon	bogen
dūfan 'dive'	*dȳfþ*	dēaf	dufon	dofen
scūfan 'shove'				

Contracted Verbs (see §103.4)

† flēon 'flee'	*flīehþ*	flēah	flugon	flogen
† tēon 'draw'				

Note

The following weak verbs are found with *ēo* in the infinitive:
frēogan 'love', *nēosan* (*nēosian*) 'seek out', and *sēowan* (*sēowian*) 'sew'.

APPENDIX A.3
Class III

Inf.	3rd Sg. Pres. Ind.	1st Pret.	2nd Pret.	Past Ptc.
(a) See §95.				
breġdan 'pull'[1]	*britt*[2]	bræġd	brugdon	brogden
streġdan 'strew'				
berstan 'burst'[3]	*birst*	bærst	burston	borsten
(b) see §§96–98.				
beorgan 'protect'	*bierhþ*	bearg	burgon	borgen

[1] This verb has been taken as the basic paradigm of class III (see §95) to make explanation easier. Originally it belonged elsewhere; see A. Campbell *Old English Grammar* §736 (b).

[2] Regular forms of 3rd sg. pres. ind. do not seem to be recorded.   [3] See §95 fn. 1.

Inf.	3rd Sg. Pres. Ind.	1st Pret.	2nd Pret.	Past Ptc.
ċeorfan 'cut'	*ċierfþ*	ċearf	curfon	corfen
hweorfan 'go'				
sweorcan 'grow dark'	*swiercþ*	swearc	swurcon	sworcen
weorpan 'throw'	*wierpþ*	wearp	wurpon	worpen
† weorþan 'become'	*wierþ*	wearþ	wurdon	worden
feohtan 'fight'	*fieht*	feaht	fuhton	fohten
† fēolan 'press on'[1]		fealh	fulgon	folgen

(*c*) see §§96–97 and 99.

delfan 'dig'	*dilfþ*	dealf	dulfon	dolfen
helpan 'help'	*hilpþ*	healp	hulpon	holpen
belgan 'be angry'	*bilhþ*	bealg	bulgon	bolgen
swelgan 'swallow'				
meltan 'melt'	*milt*	mealt	multon	molten
sweltan 'die'				

(*d*) see §100.

ġieldan 'pay'	*ġielt*	ġeald	guldon	golden
ġiellan 'yell'	*ġielþ*	ġeal	gullon	gollen
ġielpan 'boast'	*ġielpþ*	ġealp	gulpon	golpen

(*e*) see §101.

grimman 'rage'	*grimþ*	gramm	grummon	grummen
swimman 'swim'				
ġelimpan 'happen'	*ġelimpþ*	ġelamp	ġelumpon	ġelumpen
bindan 'bind'	*bint*	band	bundon	bunden
findan 'find'[2]				
grindan 'grind'				
windan 'wind'				
drincan 'drink'	*drincþ*	dranc	druncon	druncen
scrincan 'shrink'				
swincan 'toil'				
onġinnan 'begin'	*onġinþ*	ongann	ongunnon	ongunnen
winnan 'fight'				
singan 'sing'	*singþ*	sang	sungon	sungen
springan 'spring'				
swingan 'flog'				
þringan 'crowd'				
wringan 'wring'				
birnan 'burn'[3]	*birnþ*	barn	burnon	burnen
irnan 'run'[3]				

---

[1] See §133.2. Forms of 3rd sg. pres. ind. do not seem to be recorded.
[2] In the 1st pret. *funde* is found alongside *fand*; see §109.
[3] Originally *brinnan, rinnan*. But metathesis occurred; see §95 fn. 1.

Inf.	3rd Sg. Pres. Ind.	1st Pret.	2nd Pret.	Past Ptc.
(*f*) Exceptional				
friġnan 'ask'	*friġneþ*	fræġn	frugnon	frugnen
murnan 'mourn'	*myrnþ*	mearn	murnon	

Note
The following verbs are weak:
  hringan 'ring' and *ġeþingan* 'determine'.
On *bringan* see §123.2.

APPENDIX A.4

Class IV
(See §94 fn. 1)

Inf.	3rd Sg. Pres. Ind.	1st Pret.	2nd Pret.	Past Ptc.
beran 'bear'	*birþ*	bær	bǣron	boren
teran 'tear'				
brecan 'break'	*bricþ*	bræc	brǣcon	brocen
cwelan 'die'	*cwilþ*	cwæl	cwǣlon	cwolen
helan 'hide'				
stelan 'steal'				
scieran 'cut'[1]	*scierþ*	scear	scēaron	scoren
niman 'take'[2]	*nimþ*	nam, nōm	nōmon, nāmon	numen
cuman 'come'[2]	*cymþ*	cōm	cōmon	cumen

APPENDIX A.5

Class V
(See §94 fn. 2)

Inf.	3rd Sg. Pres. Ind.	1st Pret.	2nd Pret.	Past Ptc.
† cweþan 'say'	*cwiþþ*	cwæþ	cwǣdon	cweden
etan 'eat'	*itt*	ǣt[3]	ǣton	eten
fretan 'devour'				
metan 'measure'	*met*[4]	mæt	mǣton	meten
‡ ġenesan 'survive'	*ġeneseþ*[4]	ġenæs	ġenǣson	ġenesen
sprecan 'speak'	*spricþ*	spræc	sprǣcon	sprecen
specan 'speak'				
wrecan 'avenge'				
tredan 'tread'	*tritt*	træd	trǣdon	treden

[1] See §103.1.   [2] See §§103.2 and 109.
[3] See §109.   [4] Regular forms do not seem to be recorded.

Inf.	*3rd Sg.* *Pres. Ind.*	*1st Pret.*	*2nd Pret.*	*Past Ptc.*
wefan 'weave'	*wifþ*	wæf	wæfon	wefen
ġiefan 'give'[1]	*ġiefþ*	ġeaf	ġēafon	ġiefen
onġietan 'perceive'[1]	*onġiet*	onġeat	onġēaton	onġieten

Weak Presents (see §116)

biddan 'ask'	*bitt*	bæd	bædon	beden
licgan 'lie'	*liġeþ, liþ*	læġ	læġon	leġen
† þicgan 'partake'	*þiġeþ*	þeah[2]	þægon	þeġen
sittan 'sit'	*sitt*	sæt	sæton	seten

Contracted Verb (see §103.3)

† sēon 'see'	*siehþ*	seah[2]	sāwon	sewen

APPENDIX A.6

Class VI

Inf.	*3rd Sg.* *Pres. Ind.*	*1st Pret.*	*2nd Pret.*	*Past Ptc.*
dragan 'draw'	*dræhþ*	drōg	drōgon	dragen
faran 'go'	*færþ*	fōr	fōron	faren
galan 'sing'	*gælþ*	gōl	gōlon	galen
hladan 'load'	*hladeþ*[3]	hlōd	hlōdon	hladen
wadan 'go'	*wadeþ*[3]			
sacan 'quarrel'	*sæcþ*	sōc	sōcon	sacen
scacan 'shake'				
standan 'stand'[4]	*stent*	stōd	stōdon	standen

Weak Presents (see §116)

hebban 'lift'	*hefeþ*	hōf	hōfon	hafen
swerian 'swear'	*swereþ*	swōr	swōron	sworen
scieppan 'create'[5]	*sciepþ*	scōp	scōpon	scapen

Contracted Verbs (see §§103.3 and 108)

† lēan 'blame'	*liehþ*	lōh, lōg[6]	lōgon	lagen
† slēan 'strike'				slagen, slæġen

---

[1] See §103.1.   [2] See §97.
[3] Regular forms do not seem to be recorded.
[4] See §94 fn. 3.   [5] See §103.1.   [6] See §108.

APPENDIX A.7

Class VII
(See §104)

Inf.	3rd Sg. Pres. Ind.	1st Pret.	2nd Pret.	Past Ptc.
(a)				
bannan 'summon'	*benþ*	bēonn	bēonnon	bannen
spannan 'span'				
blāwan 'blow'	*blǣwþ*	blēow	blēowon	blāwen
cnāwan 'know'				
māwan 'mow'				
sāwan 'sow'				
flōwan 'flow'	*flēwþ*	flēow	flēowon	flōwen
grōwan 'grow'				
rōwan 'row'				
spōwan 'succeed'				
fealdan 'fold'	*fielt*	fēold	fēoldon	fealden
healdan 'hold'				
wealdan 'rule'				
feallan 'fall'	*fielþ*	fēoll	fēollon	feallen
weallan 'boil'				
weaxan 'grow'	*wiext*	wēox	wēoxon	weaxen
bēatan 'beat'	*bīett*	bēot	bēoton	bēaten
hēawan 'hew'	*hīewþ*	hēow	hēowon	hēawen
hlēapan 'leap'	*hlīepþ*	hlēop	hlēopon	hlēapen
	Weak Present (see §116)			
wēpan 'weep'	*wēpeþ*	wēop	wēopon	wōpen
(b)				
hātan 'call'	*hǣtt*	hēt	hēton	hāten
ondrǣdan 'fear'	*ondrǣtt*	ondrēd	ondrēdon	ondrǣden
rǣdan 'advise'[1]				
lǣtan 'let'	*lǣtt*	lēt	lēton	lǣten
slǣpan 'sleep'	*slǣpþ*	slēp	slēpon	slǣpen
	Contracted Verbs (see §108)			
† fōn 'seize'	*fēhþ*	fēng	fēngon	fangen
† hōn 'hang'				

---

[1] A weak preterite *rǣdde* is also found.

APPENDIX B

Some Effects of *i*-Mutation

The principle of *i*-mutation set forth in §§52–57 explains the relationship among a number of OE (and Modern English) words which otherwise may be unapparent or puzzling. Thus the *e* of the comparative and superlative forms of *old* (i.e. e*lder*, e*ldest*) is explained by the fact that the comparative and superlative suffixes in this adjective were originally *-ira* and *-ist*, the *i* of which caused mutation of the vowel. (See §75 for OE adjectives which follow this pattern.) Similarly, the OE suffix *-þ(o)*, *-þ(u)*, mentioned in §138 as the element that makes feminine abstract nouns out of adjectives, frequently had *i* in the suffix in pre-OE times (*-iþu*) and hence we see the effects of *i*-mutation in nouns formed from these adjectives:

fūl (*foul*) + -iþ(u), by *i*-mutation and subsequent loss of *i* = fȳlþ (*filth*)
hāl (*whole, hale*) + -iþ(u) = hǣlþ (*health*)
lang (*long*) + -iþ(u) = lengþ (*length*)
slāw (*slow*) + -iþ(u) = slǣwþ (*sloth*)
strang (*strong*) + -iþ(u) = strengþ (*strength*)
wrāþ (*wroth, angry*) + -iþ(u) = wrǣþþo (*wrath*)

Most pervasive, perhaps, is the *i*-mutation in Class I weak verbs explained in §117 *Note*. Weak I verbs are derived from nouns, adjectives, or from corresponding strong verbs. The following are derived from the nouns indicated:

cuss (*kiss*) + jan, by *i*-mutation and subsequent loss of *j* = cyssan (*to kiss*)
dōm (*judgment*) + jan = dēman (*to judge*)
drēam (*joy*) + jan = drīeman (*to rejoice*)
fær (*journey*) + jan = ferian (*to carry*)
flēam (*flight*) + jan = (ge)flīeman (*to put to flight*)
fōda (*food*) + jan = fēdan (*to feed*)
frōfor (*comfort*) + jan = frēfran (*to comfort*)
gelēafa (*belief*) + jan = gelīefan (*to believe*)
heorte (*heart*) + jan = hiertan (*to hearten*)
lāf (*leaving*) + jan = lǣfan (*to leave*)
lār (*lore*) + jan = lǣran (*to teach*)
lēoht (*light*) + jan = līehtan (*to shine*)
lust (*pleasure*) + jan = lystan (*to list, desire*)
nama (*name*) + jan = nemnan (*to name*)

sāl (*rope*) + jan = sǣlan (*to fasten*)
scrūd (*clothing*) + jan = scrȳdan (*to clothe*)
searu (*skill*) + jan = sierwan (*to plot*)
talu (*tale*) + jan = tellan (*to tell*)
þurst (*thirst*) + jan = þyrstan (*to thirst after*)
weorc (*work*) + jan = wyrċan (*to work*)

The following are derived from the adjectives indicated:

beald (*bold*) + jan = bieldan (*to embolden*)
brād (*broad*) + jan = brǣdan (*to spread*)
cōl (*cool*) + jan = cēlan (*to cool*)
cūþ (*known*) + jan = cȳþan (*to make known*)
eald (*old*) + jan = ieldan (*to delay*)
feorr (*far*) + jan = fierran (*to remove*)
full (*full*) + jan = fyllan (*to fill*)
fūs (*ready*) + jan = fȳsan (*to prepare*)
ġeorn (*eager*) + jan = ġiernan (*to be eager, yearn*)
hāl (*whole, hale*) + jan = hǣlan (*to heal*)
rūm (*roomy*) + jan = rȳman (*to make room*)
scearp (*sharp*) + jan = scierpan (*to sharpen*)
trum (*strong*) + jan = trymman (*to strengthen*)
wōd (*mad*) + jan = wēdan (*to be mad*)

The following are derived from strong verbs, imparting to the meaning of the strong verb a causative sense or a transitive function. The vowel of the weak verb is derived from the vowel of the preterite singular or 1st preterite (see §92) of the corresponding strong verb:

cwæl (pret. of cwelan, *to die*) + jan = cwellan (*to kill*)
dranc (pret. of drincan, *to drink*) + jan = drenċan (*to drench*)
fēoll (pret. of feallan, *to fall*) + jan = fiellan (*to fell*)
fōr (pret. of faran, *to go*) + jan = fēran (*to go, lead*)
hwearf (pret. of hweorfan, *to turn*) + jan = hwierfan (*to move about*)
læg (pret. of licgan, *to lie*) + jan = lecgan (*to lay*)
rās (pret. of rīsan, *to rise*) + jan = rǣran (*to rear, raise*) (Verner's Law §§105–108)
sang (pret. of singan, *to sing*) + jan = senġan (*to singe*)
sæt (pret. of sittan, *to sit*) + jan = settan (*to set*)
sprang (pret. of springan, *to spring*) + jan = sprenġan (*to break*)
swæf (pret. of swefan, *to sleep*) + jan = swebban (*to put to sleep, kill*)
swanc (pret. of swincan, *to toil*) + jan = swenċan (*to press hard*)
wand (pret. of windan, *to wind*) + jan = wendan (*to turn around, wend*)
wearp (pret. of weorpan, *to throw*) + jan = wierpan (*to recover*)

Part Two
Prose and Verse Texts

NOTE

The texts are arranged in order of increasing difficulty. The first three selections are normalized throughout, and palatal $\dot{c}$ and $\dot{g}$ are distinguished from velar c and g. The fourth selection is not normalized, but a few peculiarities have been removed to ease transition to the unnormalized texts in the remainder of the readings.

I

Practice Sentences

A. Although sometimes pronounced differently from their MnE descendants, many OE words have the same form and the same basic meaning as their MnE counterparts: e.g. *bliss*, *colt*, *dung*, *elm*, *finger*, *fox*, *handle*, *him*, *land*, *mist*, *nest*, *of*, *on*, *rest*, *sprang*, *winter*, *writ*. Indeed, entire sentences can have essentially the same appearance in OE and MnE, although it must be conceded that such sentences can be composed only through a rather artificial selection of words from the OE lexicon:

> Harold is swift. His hand is strong and his word grim. Late in
> līfe hē went tō his wīfe in Rōme.
> Is his inn open? His cornbin is full and his song is writen.
> Grind his corn for him and sing mē his song.
> Hē is dēad. His bed is under him. His lamb is dēaf and blind.
> Hē sang for mē.
> Hē swam west in storm and wind and frost.
> Bring ūs gold. Stand ūp and find wīse men.

B. Many other OE words appear strange at first glance, but when pronounced according to the rules set out in §§5–9 they become immediately recognizable as MnE words in earlier dress: e.g. *bæc*, *biscop*, *ċinn*, *diċ*, *disc*, *ecg*, *feðer*, *hecg*, *hwelp*, *lifer*, *piċ*, *ræfter*, *scort*, *þæċ*, *þing*, *þiðer*, *þrescold*, *wecg*, *wofen*. Among the following sentences set out for practice in pronunciation are a number of words which will become recognizable when pronounced correctly.

> Is his þeġn hēr ġīet?
> His līnen socc fēoll ofer bord in þæt wæter and scranc.
> Hwǣr is his cȳþþ and cynn?
> His hring is gold, his disc glæs, and his belt leðer.
> Se fisc swam under þæt scip and ofer þone sciellfisc.
> His ċicen ran from his horsweġe, ofer his pæð, and in his
> ġeard.
> Se horn sang hlūde: hlysten wē!
> Se cniht is on þǣre brycge.

5

10　Sēo cwēn went fram þǣre ċiriċe.

Hēo siteþ on þǣre benċe.

God is gōd.

þis trēow is æsc, ac þæt trēow is āc.

Hē wolde begān wiċċecræft, and hē began swā tō dōnne.

15　Fuhton ġē manlīċe oþþe mānlīċe?

His smið;ðe is þām smiðe lēof.

C.　After studying key paradigms 1, 2, and 4 (p. 4), you should find most of the grammatical relationships in the following sentences readily understandable:

Iċ bræc þone stān.

Se stān is miċel.

Ðæs stānes miċelnes is wundorliċ.

20　þes stānwyrhta ġeaf þǣm stāne hīw.

Hē slōh þone mann þȳ stāne.

Sēo sunne is swīðe miċel.

þǣr hēo scīnþ, þǣr biþ dæġ.

Niht is þǣre eorðan sceadu betwēonan þǣre sunnan and

25　　mancynne.

þis līf is lǣne, and þēos woruld drēoseþ and fealleþ.

Sing þisne song!

Hīe scufon ūt hira scipu and siġldon tō þǣre sǣ.

On þissum dæġe cwealdon wē þone fēond þisses folces.

30　Iċ ġeman þā naman þāra folca and þissa folca.

His wīfes nama wæs Elizabeþ.

þēos ġiefu is for ūs, and hēo līcaþ ūs.

Se dēaþ is þisses līfes ende, ac sēo sāwol is undēadliċ.

Hīe hine ne dorston þā þing āscian.

35　Hwæt þyncþ ēow be Crīste? Hwæs sunu is hē?

Hwæs sunu eart þū? And hwæs dohtor eart þū?

Hwȳ ġeworhte God þā yfelan nǣdran?

2

Two Old Testament Pieces

The Bible and its translations have had a profound influence on the English language and on English literature. Among early experiments in rendering Scripture into the vernacular is that of Ælfric, a dedicated scholar and gifted prose stylist who served as Abbot of Eynsham from 1005 until his death. He had serious reservations about the wisdom of translating the Old Testament (see selection 4 below), but on request he did so, rendering the Latin Vulgate version into relatively clean prose marred only occasionally by un-English, Latinate constructions. Readers can compare his work with that of the great King James translation, corresponding excerpts of which are provided on the facing page along with the Latin version for those who might like to compare the Old English with its approximate source. Since the King James translators worked from Greek and Hebrew originals rather than from the Vulgate, the correspondence between the two English versions is inexact.

The text is basically that of Bodleian Library, Oxford, MS Laud Misc. 509, but it has been normalized throughout.

The Fall of Man (Genesis 3: 1–19)

Old English Version

Ēac swelċe sēo nǣdre wæs ġēappre þonne ealle þā ōðre nīetenu þe God ġeworhte ofer eorðan; and sēo nǣdre cwæð tō þām wīfe: 'Hwȳ forbēad God ēow þæt ġē ne ǣten of ǣlcum trēowe binnan Para-dīsum?' þæt wīf andwyrde: 'Of þāra trēowa wæstme þe sind on
5 Paradīsum wē etað: and of þæs trēowes wæstme, þe is onmiddan neorxenawange, God bebēad ūs þæt wē ne ǣten, ne wē þæt trēow ne hrepoden þȳ lǣs þe wē swulten.' þā cwæð sēo nǣdre eft tō þām wīfe: 'Ne bēo ġē nāteshwōn dēade, þēah þe ġē of þām trēowe eten. Ac God wāt sōðlīċe þæt ēowre ēagan bēoð ġeopenode on swā
10 hwelċum dæġe swā ġē etað of þām trēowe; and ġē bēoð þonne englum ġelīċe, witende ǣġðer ġe gōd ġe yfel.' þā ġeseah þæt wīf þæt þæt trēow wæs gōd tō etanne, be þām þe hire þūhte, and wlitiġ on ēagum and lustbǣre on ġesihðe; and ġenam þā of þæs trēowes wæstme and ġeæt, and sealde hire were: hē æt þā. And hira bēġra
15 ēagan wurdon ġeopenode: hīe oncnēowon þā þæt hīe nacode wǣron, and sīwodon him fīclēaf and worhton him wǣdbrēċ.

Eft þā þā God cōm and hīe ġehīerdon his stefne, þǣr hē ēode on neorxenawange ofer middæġ, þā behȳdde Adam hine, and his wīf ēac swā dyde, fram Godes ġesihðe onmiddan þām trēowe neorxen-
20 awanges. God clipode þā Adam, and cwæð: 'Adam, hwǣr eart þū?'

---

3 forbēad ... þæt ġē ne ǣten Since OE uses multiple negation for emphasis (§184.4*f*), the negative sense of 'forbade' is here merely reinforced by *ne*. Translate either 'forbade ... that you should eat' or 'commanded ... that you should not eat'.

5 wē etað literally, 'we eat', but translate 'we do eat'.

6–7 ne wē þæt trēow ne hrepoden þȳ lǣs þe 'nor might we touch that tree lest ...'. As in l. 3, the double negative *ne* conj. (§184.4*d*) ... *ne* adv. (§184.4*a*) is for emphasis and should not be translated as double negative in Modern English.

8 Ne bēo ġē 'You will not be.' For the form and meaning of *bēo* see §§111 and 196. Cf. the form of *bēoð* in l. 10.

12 gōd tō etanne 'good to eat'. For this use of the inflected infinitive see §205.2*d*.

be þām þe 'as'. See glossary under *se, þæt, sēo* and §169.

hire þūhte 'it seemed to her'. Impersonal verb (§212).

14 The object of the verbs *ġeæt, sealde*, and *æt* (i.e. 'fruit') is understood (§193.7). hē æt þā 'he ate then'.

16 him ... him Both occurrences mean 'for themselves'. Cf. note to l. 18.

17–18 þā þā ... þā 'when ... then'. See §151.

18 hine 'himself'. In OE the personal pronouns also serve as reflexive pronouns: cf. the second *mē* 'myself' in l. 22.

King James Version

Now the serpent was more subtil than any beast of the field which the Lord God had made. And he said unto the woman, Yea, hath God said, Ye shall not eat of every tree of the garden?

2 And the woman said unto the serpent, We may eat of the fruit of the trees of the garden:

3 But of the fruit of the tree which *is* in the midst of the garden, God hath said, Ye shall not eat of it, neither shall ye touch it, lest ye die.

4 And the serpent said unto the woman, Ye shall not surely die:

5 For God doth know that in the day ye eat thereof, then your eyes shall be opened, and ye shall be as gods, knowing good and evil.

6 And when the woman saw that the tree *was* good for food, and that it *was* pleasant to the eyes, and a tree to be desired to make *one* wise, she took of the fruit thereof, and did eat, and gave also unto her husband with her, and he did eat.

7 And the eyes of them both were opened, and they knew that they *were* naked; and they sewed fig leaves together, and made themselves aprons.

8 And they heard the voice of the Lord God walking in the garden in the cool of the day: and Adam and his wife hid themselves from the presence of the Lord God amongst the trees of the garden.

9 And the Lord God called unto Adam, and said unto him, Where *art* thou?

Latin Vulgate Version

Sed et serpens erat callidior cunctis animantibus terrae, quae fecerat Dominus Deus. Qui dixit ad mulierem: Cur praecepit vobis Deus ut non comederetis de omni ligno paradisi? ²Cui respondit mulier: De fructu lignorum, quae sunt in paradiso, vescimur; ³de fructu vero ligni, quod est in medio paradisi, praecepit nobis Deus ne comederemus et ne tangeremus illud, ne forte moriamur. ⁴Dixit autem serpens ad mulierem: Nequaquam morte moriemini. ⁵Scit enim Deus quod in quocumque die comederitis ex eo, aperientur oculi vestri, et eritis sicut dii scientes bonum et malum. ⁶Vidit igitur mulier quod bonum esset lignum ad vescendum et pulchrum oculis aspectuque delectabile, et tulit de fructu illius et comedit deditque viro suo, qui comedit. ⁷Et aperti sunt oculi amborum. Cumque cognovissent se esse nudos, consuerunt folia ficus et fecerunt sibi perizomata.

⁸Et, cum audissent vocem Domini Dei deambulantis in paradiso ad auram post meridiem, abscondit se Adam et uxor eius a facie Domini Dei in medio ligni paradisi. ⁹Vocavitque Dominus Deus Adam et dixit ei: Ubi

Hē cwæð: 'þīne stefne iċ ġehīerde, lēof, on neorxenawange, and iċ
ondrēd mē, for þām þe iċ eom nacod, and iċ behȳdde mē.' God
cwæð: 'Hwā sæġde þē þæt þū nacod wære, ġif þū ne æte of þām
trēowe þe iċ þē bebēad þæt þū of ne æte?' Adam cwæð: 'þæt wīf
25 þæt þū mē forġēafe tō ġefēran, sealde mē of þām trēowe, and iċ æt.'
God cwæð tō þām wīfe: 'Hwȳ dydest þū þæt?' Hēo cwæð: 'Sēo
nædre bepæhte mē and iċ æt.'

God cwæð tō þære nædran: 'For þām þe þū þis dydest, þū bist
āwierġed betweox eallum nīetenum and wilddēorum. þū gæst on
30 þīnum brēoste and etst þā eorðan eallum dagum þīnes līfes. Iċ sette
fēondrædene betweox þē and þām wīfe and þīnum ofspringe and
hire ofspringe; hēo tōbrȳt þīn hēafod and þū sierwst onġēan hire hō.'

Tō þām wīfe cwæð God ēac swelċe: 'Iċ ġemaniġfealde þīne
iermða and þīne ġeēacnunga; on sārnesse þū ācenst ċild and þū
35 bist under weres onwealde and hē ġewielt þē.' Tō Adame hē cwæð:
'For þām þe þū ġehīerdest þīnes wīfes stefne and þū æte of þæm
trēowe, þe iċ þē bebēad þæt þū ne æte, is sēo eorðe āwierġed on
þīnum weorce; on ġeswincum þū etst of þære eorðan eallum
dagum þīnes līfes. þornas and brēmelas hēo āspryt þē, and þū etst
40 þære eorðan wyrta. On swāte þīnes andwlitan þū brȳcst þīnes
hlāfes, oð þæt þū ġewende tō eorðan, of þære þe þū ġenumen
wære, for þām þe þū eart dūst and tō dūste wierþst.'

<hr />

21–2 iċ ondrēd mē 'I was afraid.' The *mē* is reflexive and need not be translated
in Modern English. (But cf. early Modern English 'fear *thee* not'.)

22 For þām þe 'Because' (§§169–170). So also in ll. 28, 36, and 41–2.

29–32 gæst . . . etst . . . sette . . . tōbrȳt . . . sierwst present tense used with future
meaning (§196). Several present-tense verbs in the following paragraph (e.g.
ġemaniġfealde, *ācenst*, *ġewielt*, *etst*, *āspryt*, *brȳcst*) should also be translated as future.

32 tōbrȳt The verb ending -*eþ* has disappeared through syncope and assimilation. (See §112.2.) So also in *ġewielt*, *āspryt* in the following paragraph.

39 hēo is fem. nom. sg. agreeing in gender with its antecedent, *sēo eorðe*.

40–1 þīnes hlāfes The verb *brūcan* takes a genitive object here. See §190.6.

41 þære þe 'which'. þe combines with *þære* to form a compound rel. pron. See
§162.4.

10 And he said, I heard thy voice in the garden, and I was afraid, because I *was* naked; and I hid myself.

11 And he said, Who told thee that thou *wast* naked? Hast thou eaten of the tree, whereof I commanded thee that thou shouldest not eat?

12 And the man said, The woman whom thou gavest *to be* with me, she gave me of the tree, and I did eat.

13 And the Lord God said unto the woman, What *is* this *that* thou hast done? And the woman said, The serpent beguiled me, and I did eat.

14 And the Lord God said unto the serpent, Because thou hast done this, thou *art* cursed above all cattle, and above every beast of the field; upon thy belly shalt thou go, and dust shalt thou eat all the days of thy life:

15 And I will put enmity between thee and the woman, and between thy seed and her seed; it shall bruise thy head, and thou shalt bruise his heel.

16 Unto the woman he said, I will greatly multiply thy sorrow and thy conception; in sorrow thou shalt bring forth children; and thy desire *shall be* to thy husband, and he shall rule over thee.

17 And unto Adam he said, Because thou hast hearkened unto the voice of thy wife, and hast eaten of the tree, of which I commanded thee, saying, Thou shalt not eat of it: cursed *is* the ground for thy sake; in sorrow shalt thou eat *of* it all the days of thy life;

18 Thorns also and thistles shall it bring forth to thee; and thou shalt eat the herb of the field;

19 In the sweat of thy face shalt thou eat bread, till thou return unto the ground; for out of it wast thou taken: for dust thou *art*, and unto dust shalt thou return.

es? [10]Qui ait: Vocem tuam audivi in paradiso et timui eo quod nudus essem et abscondi me. [11]Cui dixit: Quis enim indicavit tibi quod nudus esses, nisi quod ex ligno, de quo praeceperam tibi ne comederes, comedisti? [12]Dixitque Adam: Mulier, quam dedisti mihi sociam, dedit mihi de ligno, et comedi. [13]Et dixit Dominus Deus ad mulierem: Quare hoc fecisti? Quae respondit: Serpens decepit me, et comedi.

[14]Et ait Dominus Deus ad serpentem: Quia fecisti hoc, maledictus es inter omnia animantia et bestias terrae: super pectus tuum gradieris et terram comedes cunctis diebus vitae tuae. [15]Inimicitias ponam inter te et mulierem, et semen tuum et semen illius; ipsa conteret caput tuum, et tu insidiaberis calcaneo eius. [16]Mulieri quoque dixit: Multiplicabo aerumnas tuas et conceptus tuos: in dolore paries filios et sub viri potestate eris et ipse dominabitur tui. [17]Adae vero dixit: Quia audisti vocem uxoris tuae et comedisti de ligno, ex quo praeceperam tibi ne comederes, maledicta terra in opere tuo: in laboribus comedes ex ea cunctis diebus vitae tuae. [18]Spinas et tribulos germinabit tibi, et comedes herbam terrae. [19]In sudore vultus tui vesceris pane, donec revertaris in terram, de qua sumptus es; quia pulvis es, et in pulverem reverteris.

Abraham and Isaac (Genesis 22: 1–19)

Old English Version

God wolde þā fandian Abrahames ġehīersumnesse, and clipode his
naman, and cwæð him þus tō: 'Nim þīnne āncennedan sunu Īsaac,
45 þe þū lufast, and far tō þām lande *Visionis* hraðe, and ġeoffra hine
þǣr uppan ānre dūne.' Abraham þā ārās on þǣre ilcan nihte, and
fērde mid twām cnapum tō þām fierlenan lande, and Īsaac samod,
on assum rīdende. þā on þām þriddan dæġe, þā hīe þā dūne ġe-
sāwon þǣr þǣr hīe tō scoldon tō ofslēanne Īsaac, þā cwæð Abra-
50 ham tō þām twām cnapum þus: 'Anbīdiað ēow hēr mid þām assum
sume hwīle. Iċ and þæt ċild gāð unc tō ġebiddenne, and wē siððan
cumað sōna eft tō ēow.' Abraham þā hēt Īsaac beran þone wudu tō
þǣre stōwe, and hē self bær his sweord and fȳr. Īsaac þā āscode
Abraham his fæder: 'Fæder mīn, iċ āscie hwǣr sēo offrung sīe; hēr
55 is wudu and fȳr.' Him andwyrde sē fæder, 'God foresċēawað, mīn
sunu, him self þā offrunge.' Hīe cōmon þā tō þǣre stōwe þe him
ġesweotolode God, and hē þǣr wēofod ārǣrde on þā ealdan wīsan,
and þone wudu ġelōgode swā swā hē hit wolde habban tō his suna
bærnette siððan hē ofslæġen wurde. Hē ġeband þā his sunu, and

---

44 **cwæð him þus tō** 'spoke to him thus'. In OE the preposition can sometimes
follow the object (§213).

45 **þām lande *Visionis*** 'the land of Moriah'. The Hebrew name *Moriah* was
taken by Biblical commentators to mean 'vision' etymologically, and both the
Vulgate and the OE translator preserve this sacral etymology, substituting the Latin
word *visionis* for the name itself. For the peculiar use of name-meanings by OE
writers, see *Anglia* 86 (1968), 14–58.

48–9 **þā dūne ... þǣr þǣr hīe tō scoldon tō ofslēanne** 'the mountain where
they must (go) to slay'. The verb of motion following *scoldon* is understood (§205.1).
For *þǣr þǣr* 'where' see §168, *þǣr* 3.

50 **ēow** reflexive. OE *anbīdian* takes a reflexive object, but modern 'wait' does
not. Therefore ignore *ēow* in translation.

51 **unc** The reflexive pronoun need not be translated.

54 **sīe** 'is, may be'. The present subjunctive form of the verb 'to be' is used here
because there is no offering present. Cf. the contrasting use of the indicative in 'hēr
is wudu and fȳr'. See §156.

55 **foresċēawað** pres. tense with future meaning.

57 **on þā ealdan wīsan** 'in the ancient manner'. The OE translator is concerned
to emphasize that human sacrifice, although seemingly condoned by the Old Testament, is no longer an acceptable practice.

59 **ofslæġen wurde** 'had been slain'. For pret. subj. expressing future-in-the-
past see §174.

King James Version

AND it came to pass after these things, that God did tempt Abraham, and said unto him, Abraham: and he said, Behold, *here* I *am*.

2 And he said, Take now thy son, thine only *son* Isaac, whom thou lovest, and get thee into the land of Mōrīah; and offer him there for a burnt offering upon one of the mountains which I will tell thee of.

3 And Abraham rose up early in the morning, and saddled his ass, and took two of his young men with him, and Isaac his son, and clave the wood for the burnt offering, and rose up, and went unto the place of which God had told him.

4 Then on the third day Abraham lifted up his eyes, and saw the place afar off.

5 And Abraham said unto his young men, Abide ye here with the ass; and I and the lad will go yonder and worship, and come again to you.

6 And Abraham took the wood of the burnt offering, and laid *it* upon Isaac his son; and he took the fire in his hand, and a knife, and they went both of them together.

7 And Isaac spake unto Abraham his father, and said, My father: and he said, Here *am* I, my son. And he said, Behold the fire and the wood: but where *is* the lamb for a burnt offering?

8 And Abraham said, My son, God will provide himself a lamb for a burnt offering: so they went both of them together.

9 And they came to the place which God had told him of; and Abraham built an altar there, and laid the wood in order, and bound Isaac his son, and laid him on the altar upon the wood.

Latin Vulgate Version

Quae postquam gesta sunt, tentavit Deus Abraham et dixit ad eum: Abraham, Abraham. At ille respondit: Adsum. [2]Ait illi: Tolle filium tuum unigenitum, quem diligis, Isaac, et vade in terram visionis, atque ibi offeres eum in holocaustum super unum montium, quem monstravero tibi. [3]Igitur Abraham de nocte consurgens stravit asinum suum ducens secum duos iuvenes et Isaac filium suum; cumque concidisset ligna in holocaustum, abiit ad locum, quem praeceperat ei Deus. [4]Die autem tertio, elevatis oculis, vidit locum procul, [5]dixitque ad pueros suos: Exspectate hic cum asino: ego et puer illuc usque properantes, postquam adoraverimus, revertemur ad vos. [6]Tulit quoque ligna holocausti et imposuit super Isaac filium suum; ipse vero portabat in manibus ignem et gladium. Cumque duo pergerent simul, [7]dixit Isaac patri suo: Pater mi. At ille respondit: Quid vis, fili? Ecce, inquit, ignis et ligna; ubi est victima holocausti? [8]Dixit autem Abraham: Deus providebit sibi victimam holocausti, fili mi. Pergebant ergo pariter: [9]et venerunt ad locum, quem ostenderat ei Deus in quo aedificavit altare, et desuper ligna composuit. Cumque alligasset Isaac filium suum, posuit eum in altare super struem lignorum [10]extenditque

60 his sweord ātēah, þæt hē hine ġeoffrode on þā ealdan wīsan. Mid
    þām þe hē wolde þæt weorc beġinnan, þā clipode Godes engel
    arodlīċe of heofonum, 'Abraham!' Hē andwyrde sōna. Sē engel him
    cwæð þā tō: 'Ne ācwele þū þæt ċild, ne þīne hand ne āstreċe ofer
    his swēoran! Nū iċ oncnēow sōðlīċe þæt þū swīðe ondrǣtst God,
65 nū þū þīnne āncennedan sunu ofslēan woldest for him.'

        þā beseah Abraham sōna underbæc and ġeseah þǣr ānne ramm
    betweox þām brēmelum be þām hornum ġehæft, and hē āhefde
    þone ramm tō þǣre offrunge and hine þǣr ofsnāð Gode tō lāce for
    his sunu Īsaac. Hē hēt þā þā stōwe *Dominus videt*, þæt is 'God ġe-
70 siehð', and ġīet is ġesæġd swā, *In monte Dominus videbit*, þæt is 'God
    ġesiehð on dūne.' Eft clipode se engel Abraham and cwæð, 'Iċ
    swerie þurh mē selfne, sæġde se Ælmihtiga, nū þū noldest ārian
    þīnum āncennedan suna, ac þē wæs mīn eġe māre þonne his līf, iċ
    þē nū bletsie and þīnne ofspring ġemaniġfealde swā swā steorran
75 on heofonum and swā swā sandċeosol on sǣ. þīn ofspring sceal
    āgan hira fēonda gatu, and on þīnum sǣde bēoð ealle þēoda
    ġebletsode for þām þe þū ġehīersumodest mīnre hǣse þus.'

        Abraham þā ġeċierde sōna tō his cnapum and fērdon him hām
    swā mid heofonlīċre bletsunge.

---

60 ġeoffrode pret. subj. 'might offer'.
Mid þām þe 'when' (§171).
63 tō see note to l. 44.
64–5 Nū iċ oncnēow . . . nū þū 'Now I perceive . . . now that thou'. *Nū . . . nū . . .*
are correlative conjunctions. See §§150–153.
64 ondrǣtst For this form instead of *ondrǣdest*, see §112.2.
67 ġehæft see §187(*b*).
69–70 *Dominus videt* 'The Lord sees.' In monte *Dominus videbit* 'on the
mountain the Lord will see'.

10 And Abraham stretched forth his hand, and took the knife to slay his son.

11 And the angel of the LORD called unto him out of heaven, and said, Abraham, Abraham: and he said, Here *am* I.

12 And he said, Lay not thine hand upon the lad, neither do thou any thing unto him: for now I know that thou fearest God, seeing thou hast not withheld thy son, thine only *son* from me.

13 And Abraham lifted up his eyes, and looked, and behold behind *him* a ram caught in a thicket by his horns: and Abraham went and took the ram, and offered him up for a burnt offering in the stead of his son.

14 And Abraham called the name of that place Jehōvahjīreh: as it is said *to* this day, In the mount of the LORD it shall be seen.

15 And the angel of the LORD called unto Abraham out of heaven the second time,

16 And said, By myself have I sworn, saith the LORD, for because thou hast done this thing, and hast not withheld thy son, thine only *son*:

17 That in blessing I will bless thee, and in multiplying I will multiply thy seed as the stars of the heaven, and as the sand which *is* upon the sea shore; and thy seed shall possess the gate of his enemies;

18 And in thy seed shall all the nations of the earth be blessed; because thou hast obeyed my voice.

19 So Abraham returned unto his young men, and they rose up and went together to Beershēba; and Abraham dwelt at Beershēba.

manum et arripuit gladium, ut immolaret filium suum. ¹¹Et ecce angelus Domini de caelo clamavit dicens: Abraham, Abraham. Qui respondit: Adsum. ¹²Dixitque ei: Non extendas manum tuam super puerum, neque facias illi quidquam: nunc cognovi quod times Deum, et non pepercisti unigenito filio tuo propter me. ¹³Levavit Abraham oculos suos viditque post tergum arietem inter vepres haerentem cornibus, quem adsumens obtulit holocaustum pro filio. ¹⁴Appellavitque nomen loci illius Dominus videt. Unde usque hodie dicitur: In monte Dominus videbit.

¹⁵Vocavit autem angelus Domini Abraham secundo de caelo dicens: ¹⁶Per memetipsum iuravi, dicit Dominus: quia fecisti hanc rem et non pepercisti filio tuo unigenito propter me, ¹⁷benedicam tibi et multiplicabo semen tuum sicut stellas caeli et velut harenam, quae est in litore maris; possidebit semen tuum portas inimicorum suorum: ¹⁸et benedicentur in semine tuo omnes gentes terrae quia oboedisti voci meae. ¹⁹Reversusque est Abraham ad pueros suos, abieruntque Bersabee simul, et habitavit ibi.

3

A Colloquy on the Occupations

Teachers of Latin in the Middle Ages sometimes composed dialogues or colloquies for their pupils to memorize, the assumption being that one learns a foreign language best by actually speaking it. Ælfric, who had already written a Latin *Grammar*, composed a *Colloquy* as a companion piece. He improved on the traditional form considerably, touching his characters with life and giving the exercise dramatic interest. His *Colloquy* is of particular value to modern readers because it offers an informal glimpse of Anglo-Saxon social structure, with representatives of various occupations explaining their function in the society in which they lived. Ælfric provides a series of questions for the Latin teacher to ask, and pupils assuming the roles of the various craftsmen then recite the assigned responses. By rotating pupils in the various roles, the teacher could be sure that each would learn a full range of vocabulary and syntactical structures.

Some time after Ælfric composed his Latin exercise, another Anglo-Saxon translated it into Old English. The charm of Ælfric's work is not wholly lost in this rendering, but as it stands the translation is inappropriate for modern students of Old English to use in learning the language, since it slavishly follows the Latin constructions of the source text, thus producing unnatural, distorted syntax and phrasing. But in 1897 Henry Sweet, one of the greatest modern scholars of Old English, revised the translation into idiomatic prose. The text below is an adaptation and abbreviation of Sweet's version, which was published in his *First Steps in Anglo-Saxon* (Oxford, 1897), pp. 28–38. The text is normalized throughout.

The Monk

Hwelċne cræft canst þū?
Iċ eom munuc.
Hwæt cunnon þās þīne ġefēran?
Sume sind ierþlingas, sume sċēaphierdas, sume oxanhierdas,
5 sume huntan, sume fisceras, sume fugleras, sume ċīepemenn, sume
sċōwyrhtan, sume sealteras, sume bæceras.

The Ploughman

Hwæt seġst þū, ierþling? Hū begǣst þū þīnne cræft?

Lā lēof, þearle iċ swince! Ǣlċe dæġe iċ sceal on dæġrǣd ūtgān. þonne sceal iċ þā oxan tō felda drīfan and tō þǣre sylh ġeocian. Nis
10 nān winter swā stearc þæt iċ dyrre æt hām lūtian: ne dearr iċ for mīnes hlāfordes eġe. Ac þonne iċ þā oxan ġeġcocod hæbbe, and þæt scear and þone culter on þǣre sylh ġefæstnod hæbbe, þonne sceal iċ fulne æcer erian oþþe māre.

Hæfst þū ænigne ġefēran?

15 Ġiese, iċ hæbbe cnapan: sē sceal þā oxan mid gāde þȳwan. Sē is nū hās for ċiele and hrēame.

Hwæt māre dēst þū? Hæfst þū ġīet māre tō dōnne?

Ġiese lēof, miċel iċ hæbbe tō dōnne! Iċ sceal þāra oxena binne mid hīeġe āfyllan, and hīe wæterian, and hira steall feormian.

20 Ēalā, þæt is miċel ġedeorf!

Ġiese lēof, hit is miċel ġedeorf, for þǣm þe iċ neom frēo.

The Shepherd

Hwæt seġst þū, scēaphierde? Hæfst þū æniġ ġedeorf?

Ġiese lēof, iċ hæbbe miċel ġedeorf! On ærnemerġen iċ drīfe mīn scēap tō lǣswe. Siþþan stande iċ ofer hīe mid hundum, þȳ lǣs þe
25 wulfas hīe forswelgen. þonne lǣde iċ hīe on ǣfen onġēan tō hira locum. Iċ hīe melce tuwa on dæġe. Iċ macie buteran and ċīese. And iċ eom mīnum hlāforde ġetrīewe.

The Oxherd

Ēalā oxanhierde, hwæt dēst þū?

Lā lēof, iċ swince þearle! þonne se ierþling þā oxan onġeocaþ,
30 þonne lǣde iċ hīe tō lǣswe; and ealle niht iċ stande ofer hīe, waciende for þēofum; and þæs on morgenne iċ hīe betǣċe eft þǣm ierþlinge, wel ġefylde and ġewæterode.

The Hunter

Is þes mann ān of þīnum ġefērum?
Ġiese.

10–11 for mīnes hlāfordes eġe 'for fear of my lord'. See §190.2.

11–12 þonne … þonne 'when … then'. See §§151–152.

15 sē 'he'. See §§15 and 193.7. When demonstrative se is used in place of personal pronoun, it is stressed and the vowel is long.

31 þæs 'afterwards'. A frequent idiomatic meaning of the gen. sg. of *þæt*. See §168 *þæs* 1.

35 Canst þū ǣniġ þing?

Ānne cræft iċ cann.

Hwelċne cræft canst þū?

Iċ eom hunta.

Hwæs hunta eart þū?

40 Iċ eom þæs cyninges hunta.

Hū begǣst þū þīnne cræft?

Iċ breġde mē nett, and āsette hīe on ġehǣpre stōwe. þonne ġetyhte iċ mīne hundas þæt hīe þāra wilddēora ēhten, oþ þæt hīe unwǣrlīċe on þā nett becumen. þonne hīe þus ġelǣht sind, þonne

45 cume iċ tō, and hīe on þǣm nettum ofslēa.

Ne canst þū būtan nettum huntian?

Ġiese, iċ cann būtan nettum huntian.

Hū?

Iċ fō þā wilddēor mid swiftum hundum.

50 Hwelċ wilddēor ġefēhst þū swīþost?

Iċ ġefō heorotas, and rān, and bāras, and hwīlum haran.

Wǣre þū tōdæġ on huntoþe?

Nese, for þǣm hit is sunnandæġ; ac ġiestrandæġ iċ wæs on huntoþe.

55 Hwæt ġefēnge þū?

Iċ ġefēng twēġen heorotas and ānne bār.

Hū ġefēnge þū hīe?

þā heorotas on nettum iċ ġefēng, and þone bār iċ ofsticode.

Hū wǣre þū swā ġedyrstiġ þæt þū bār ofsticodest?

60 þā hundas hine bedrifon tō mē, and iċ þǣr fæstlīċe onġēanstōd, and hine fǣrlīċe mid spere ofsticode.

Swīþe ġedyrstiġ wǣre þū þā!

Ne sceal hunta forhtmōd bēon, for þǣm missenlicu wilddēor wuniaþ on wudum.

65 Hwæt dēst þū ymb þīnne huntoþ?

Iċ selle þǣm cyninge swā hwæt swā iċ ġefō, for þǣm iċ eom his hunta.

Hwæt selþ hē þē?

Hē scrȳtt mē wel and fētt, and hwīlum hē mē hors selþ oþþe

70 bēag, þæt iċ þȳ ġeornor mīnne cræft begā.

---

42 **Iċ breġde mē nett** 'I weave nets for myself.' Compare modern colloquial English 'I bought me a hat.'

45 **cume iċ tō** 'I come up'. *Tō* here is the adverb.

69 **scrȳtt ... fētt** 'clothes ... feeds'. For the form of the verbs, see §112.2.

70 **þȳ ġeornor** 'the more eagerly'. This use of the instr. *þȳ* is the source of modern phrases like 'the bigger the better' or 'the more the merrier'. See §168 *þȳ*.

The Fisherman

Hwelċne cræft canst þū?

Iċ eom fiscere.

Hwæt beġietst þū of þīnum cræfte?

Bīleofan iċ mē beġiete, and scrūd, and feoh.

75 Hū ġefēhst þū þā fiscas?

Iċ gā on mīnne bāt, and rōwe ūt on þā ēa, and weorpe mīn nett on þā ēa. Hwīlum iċ weorpe angel ūt mid æse, oþþe spyrtan; and swā hwæt swā hīe ġehæftaþ iċ nime.

Hwæt dēst þū gif hit unclǣne fiscas bēoþ?

80 Iċ weorpe þā unclǣnan ūt, and nime þā clǣnan mē tō mete.

Hwǣr ċīepst þū þīne fiscas?

On þǣre ċeastre.

Hwā byġþ hīe?

þā ċeasterware. Ne mæġ iċ hira swā fela ġefōn swā iċ sellan

85 mæġe.

Hwelċe fiscas ġefēhst þū?

Ǣlas, and hacodas, and scēotan, and ealle ōþre fiscas þe on þǣm ēam swimmaþ.

For hwȳ ne fiscast þū on sǣ?

90 Hwīlum iċ dō swā, ac seldon; for þǣm hit is mē miċel rēwett tō þǣre sǣ.

Hwæt ġefēhst þū on þǣre sǣ?

Hæringas, and leaxas, and styrian, and loppestran, and crabban, and fela ōþerra fisca.

95 Wilt þū hwæl fōn?

Niċ!

For hwȳ?

For þǣm miċel pleoh is þæt man hwæl ġefō. Lǣsse pleoh mē biþ þæt iċ tō þǣre ēa gā mid mīnum bāte þonne iċ mid manigum

100 scipum on hwælhuntoþ fare.

For hwȳ swā?

For þǣm mē is lēofre þæt iċ fisc ġefō þe iċ ofslēan mæġ þonne iċ fisc ġefō þe nealles þæt ān mē selfne ac ēac swelċe mīne ġefēran mid ānum sleġe besenċan mæġ oþþe ofslēan.

---

74 mē See note to l. 42 above.

79 unclǣne fiscas Cf. Deuteronomy 14: 10: 'whatsoever [fish] hath not fins and scales ye may not eat; it is unclean unto you'. Some Anglo-Saxons scrupulously observed many of the Mosaic dietary laws.

80 mē tō mete 'for my food'. See §191.2.

84 hira . . . fela See §190.4.

102 mē is lēofre '(it) is more agreeable to me', i.e. 'I prefer'.

103 nealles þæt ān . . . ac ēac swelċe 'not only . . . but also'.

105 And þēah maniġe ġefōþ hwalas, and þǣm frēċennessum
ætberstaþ, and miċelne sceatt þanon beġietaþ.

Sōþ þū seġst; ac iċ ne dearr for þǣm iċ eom forhtmōd.

The Fowler

Hwæt seġst þū, fuglere? Hū beswīcst þū þā fuglas?

Iċ hīe on maniġfealde wīsan beswīce: hwīlum mid nettum,
110 hwīlum mid grīnum, hwīlum mid træppum, hwīlum mid līme,
hwīlum mid hwistlunge, hwīlum mid hafoce.

Hæfst þū hafocas?

Ġiese.

Canst þū temman hafocas?

115 Ġiese, iċ cann: hū scolden hīe mē nytte bēon, būtan iċ hīe
temman cūþe?

Sele mē hafoc!

Iċ þē selle lustlīċe, ġif þū mē selst swiftne hund. Hwelċne hafoc
wilt þū habban, þone māran hwæþer þe þone lǣssan?

120 Sele mē þone māran! Hū āfētst þū þīne hafocas?

Hīe hīe selfe fēdaþ on wintra ġe ēac swelċe mē, and on lenċtene
iċ hīe lǣte tō wuda ætflēogan; and iċ mē nime briddas on hærfest
and hīe ġetemme.

For hwȳ lǣtst þū þā ġetemedan hafocas þē ætflēogan?

125 For þǣm iċ nyle hīe on sumera fēdan, for þǣm þe hīe þearle
etaþ.

Ac maniġe fēdaþ þā ġetemedan ofer sumor, þæt hīe hīe eft
ġearwe hæbben.

Ġiese, hīe dōþ swā. Ac iċ nyle on swelċum ġeswince mid him
130 bēon, for þǣm iċ cann ōþre ġefōn – nealles ānne, ac maniġe.

The Merchant

Hwæt seġst þū, mangere?

Iċ secge þæt iċ eom swīþe nytt þǣm cyninge, and þǣm
ealdormannum, and þǣm weligum, and eallum folce.

Hū?

135 Iċ āstīge on mīn scip mid mīnum hlæstum, and fare ofer sǣ, and
selle mīn þing, and bycge dēorwierþu þing þe on þissum lande

---

115 būtan 'unless'. (So *cūðe* is subjunctive: see §179.5.)

118 Iċ þē selle The direct object (*hafoc*) is understood. See note to 2/14.

121 Hīe hīe selfe fēdaþ 'They feed themselves.' The first *hīe* is nom., the
second acc. (used reflexively).

122 mē 'for myself'. Cf. note to l. 42 above.

ācenned ne bēoþ; and iċ hit lǣde tō ēow hider ofer sǣ mid miċlum
plēo; and hwīlum iċ þolie forlidennesse, swā þæt mē losiaþ eall mīn
þing, and iċ self unēaþe cwic ætberste.

140   Hwelċ þing lǣtst þū ūs hider ofer sǣ?

Pællas, seoloc, seldcūþ rēaf, wyrtġemang, wīn, ele, elpendbān,
dēorwierþe ġimmas, gold, tin, mæstling, ār, seolfor, glæs, and fela
ōþerra þinga.

Wilt þū þīn þing hēr on lande sellan wiþ þǣm ilcan weorþe þe
145   þū hīe þǣr ūte mid ġebohtest?

Niċ; hwæt fremede mē þonne mīn ġedeorf? Ac iċ wile hīe wiþ
māran weorþe hēr sellan þonne iċ hīe þǣr mid ġebohte, þæt iċ
mǣge mē sum ġestrēon beġietan, þe iċ mē mid āfēdan mǣge and
mīn wīf and mīn bearn.

The Shoemaker

150   þū scōwyrhta, hwæt wyrċst þū ūs tō nytte?

Mīn cræft is ēow swīþe nytt and swīþe nīedbehēfe. Iċ bycge hȳda
and fell, and hīe ġearcie mid mīnum cræfte, and wyrċe þǣrof
missenliċes cynnes ġescȳ leþerhosa, þwangas, ġerǣdu, flascan, and
fǣtelsas; and ne mæġ ēower nān ofer winter wunian būtan mīnum
155   cræfte.

The Salter

Ēalā þū sealtere, hwæt fremeþ ūs þīn cræft?

Mīn cræft fremeþ ēow eallum þearle. Ne mæġ ēower nān
flǣscmetta brūcan būtan mīnum cræfte. Hwelċ mann mæġ
swētmetta brūcan būtan sealtes swæcce? Hwā ġefylþ his cleofan
160   and hēdærn būtan mīnum cræfte? Ēowru butere eall ēow losaþ and
ēower ċīese būtan iċ hīe mid mīnum cræfte ġehealde. Ne ġē ne
magon furþum ēowerra wyrta brūcan būtan mē.

The Baker

Hwæt seġst þū, bæcere? Hwǣm fremeþ þīn cræft?

Būtan mīnum cræfte ǣlċ bēod biþ ǣmettiġ ġeþūht, and būtan

138–9 **mē losiaþ eall mīn þing** 'all my things are lost to me', i.e. 'I lose
everything'.

148 **þe ... mid** 'with which'. See §163.3.

150 **ūs tō nytte** 'of use to us'.

154 **ēower nān** 'none of you'.

164 **biþ ... ġeþūht** 'will seem'.

165 hlāfe ǣlċ mete biþ tō wlǣttan ġehwierfed. Iċ ġestrangie manna
heortan: iċ eom wera mæġen; ġe furþum þā lȳtlingas nyllaþ mē
forþolian.

The Cook

Hwæt secge wē be þǣm cōce? Beþurfon wē his cræftes tō
āwihte?

170 Ġif ġē mē of ēowrum ġefērscipe ūtādrīfaþ, ġē etaþ ēowre wyrta
grēne and ēowre flǣscmettas hrēawe; ne magon ġē furþum fǣtt
broþ habban būtan mīnum cræfte.

Ne reċċe wē be þīnum cræfte: nis hē ūs nā nīedbehēfe, for þǣm
wē magon selfe sēoþan þā þing þe tō sēoþanne sind, and brǣdan þā
175 þing þe tō brǣdanne sind.

Ġif ġē mē ūtādrīfaþ and þus dōþ, þonne bēo ġē ealle þēowas,
and nān ēower ne biþ hlāford; and þēah hwæþre ġē ne magon etan
būtan mīnum cræfte.

Critique of the Occupations

Ēalā munuc, iċ ġesēo þē habban gōde ġefēran and swīþe nytte;
180 hæfst þū ōþre ēac him?

Iċ hæbbe īsensmiþas, goldsmiþas, seolforsmiþas, trēowwyrhtan,
and maniġe ōþre.

Hæfst þū wīsne ġeþeahtere?

Ġewisslīċe iċ hæbbe: hū mæġ ūre ġefērscipe bēon ġewissod
185 būtan ġeþeahtere?

Ēalā þū wīsa ġeþeahtere, hwæt seġst þū? Hwelċ þissa cræfta is
þē fyrmest ġeþūht?

Iċ þē secge, Godes þēowdōm is mē fyrmest ġeþūht betweox
þissum cræftum, swā swā Crīst on his godspelle cwæþ 'Fyrmest
190 sēċaþ Godes rīċe, and þās þing eall ēow bēoþ tōġeīeċed'.

And hwelċ woruldcræft is þē fyrmest ġeþūht?

Eorþtilþ; for þǣm se ierþling fētt ūs ealle.

(Se smiþ seġþ:) Hwanon hæfþ se ierþling scear oþþe culter,
oþþe furþum gāde, būtan of mīnum cræfte? Hwanon hæfþ se
195 fiscere angel, oþþe se scōwyrhta āwel, oþþe se sēamere nǣdle
būtan of mīnum ġeweorce?

---

168   secge wē See §111.
173   hē The masculine pronoun agrees with the gender of its antecedent *cræfte*.
174–5   tō sēoþanne ... tō brǣdanne 'to be boiled ... to be roasted'.
179   iċ ġesēo þē habban 'I see you to have', i.e. 'I see that you have'.
186–7   is þē ... ġeþūht 'seems to you'.
189–90   Luke 12:31 'But rather seek ye the kingdom of God; and all these things
shall be added unto you.'

(Se ġeþeahtere andswaraþ:) Sōþ þū seġst; ac ūs eallum lēofre is
mid þǣm ierþlinge tō wīcianne þonne mid þē: for þǣm se ierþling
selþ ūs hlāf and drynce; ac þū, hwæt selst þū ūs on þīnre smiþþan
200 būtan īsene spearcan, and bēatendra slecga swēġ and blāwendra
bielga?

(Se treowwyrhta seġþ:) Hwelċ ēower ne notaþ mīnes cræftes,
þonne iċ ēow eallum hūs wyrċe and scipu and missenlicu fatu?

(Se smiþ andswaraþ:) Ēalā trēowwyrhta, for hwȳ spriċst þū swā,
205 þonne furþum ān þȳrel þū ne miht dōn būtan mīnum cræfte?

(Se ġeþeahterc seġþ:) Ēalā ġefēran and gōde wyrhtan, uton
hrædlīċe ġesēman þās ġeflitu, and sīe sibb and ġeþwǣrnes betweox
ēow, and fremme ǣlċ ōþrum on his cræfte! And uton weorþian
þone ierþling, of þǣm wē beġietaþ ūs selfum bīleofan and fōdor
210 ūrum horsum! And iċ ġelǣre eallum wyrhtum þisne rǣd: þæt ānra
ġehwelċ his cræft ġeornlīċe begā. For þǣm sē þe his cræft forlǣtt,
sē biþ fram þǣm cræfte forlǣten. Swā hwelċ swā þū sīe, swā
mæsseprēost, swā munuc, swā ċeorl, swā cempa, begā ġeornlīċe
þīnne cræft! And bēo þæt þæt þū eart! For þǣm hit is miċel demm
215 and miċel scand ġif man nyle bēon þæt þæt hē is and þæt þæt hē
bēon sceal.

---

207 sīe 'let there be'. Pres. subj. of *bēon* (§127).
209 of þǣm 'from whom' (§162.3).
212–13 Swā hwelċ swā ... swā ... swā 'whatsoever ... whether ... whether'.
215 þæt þæt 'that which'.

4

Ælfric's Preface to Genesis

When a medieval scholar like Ælfric read the Bible, he saw behind the literal sense of the words a host of allegorical and typological meanings which had been discerned by biblical commentators from early Christian times to his own day. These meanings make up the 'spiritual sense' (*þæt gāstlice andgit*) as opposed to the literal meaning (*sēo nacede gerecednis*) of the Bible and are one of the means by which medieval Christians reconciled the sometimes bizarre and violent events of the Old Testament with the doctrine of the New. It is therefore understandable that when Ælfric's patron Æthelweard asked him to make the Old Testament available to the laity through translation, the devout scholar was apprehensive. What would the average Christian make of polygamy, human sacrifice, and other Old Testament practices when he read of them without a priest at hand to explain the 'real', spiritual sense of these things? In the Preface below, Ælfric explains these matters in a letter to Æthelweard, giving us a revealing example of how a medieval Christian scholar in Anglo-Saxon England analysed Scripture and applied it to his system of belief. He also makes it clear that he is at heart opposed to translation of the Old Testament (and elsewhere he even has misgivings about translating the New).

Although the prose of Ælfric's Preface is simple and straightforward and therefore seems appropriate as an early reading selection, some students may find the subject-matter unfamiliar and perplexing. Such students may prefer to read selection 7 before selection 4.

The text is that of Bodleian Library MS Laud Misc. 509, except that a few spellings have been normalized to ease transition into the unnormalized texts in the remainder of the reader.

Incipit prefatio Genesis Anglice

Ælfrīc munuc grēt Æðelwærd ealdormann ēadmōdlīce. þū bæde mē, lēof, þæt ic sceolde ðē āwendan of Lædene on Englisc þā bōc Genesis. Ðā þūhte mē hefigtīme þē tō tīðienne þæs, and þū cwæde
5   þā þæt ic ne þorfte nā māre āwendan þære bēc būton tō Isaace, Abrahames suna, for þām þe sum ōðer man þē hæfde āwend fram Isaace þā bōc oþ ende. Nū þincð mē, lēof, þæt þæt weorc is swīðe plēolic mē oððe ænigum men tō underbeginnenne, for þan þe ic ondræde, gif sum dysig man þās bōc ræt oððe rædan gehȳrð, þæt
10   hē wille wēnan þæt hē mōte lybban nū on þære nīwan ǣ swā swā þā ealdan fæderas leofodon þā on þære tīde ær þan þe sēo ealde ǣ gesett wære, oþþe swā swā men leofodon under Moyses ǣ. Hwīlum ic wiste þæt sum mæsseprēost, se þe mīn magister wæs on þām tīman, hæfde þā bōc Genesis, and hē cūðe be dæle Læden
15   understandan; þā cwæð hē be þām hēahfædere Iācōbe, þæt hē hæfde fēower wīf – twā geswustra and heora twā þīnena. Ful sōð hē sæde, ac hē nyste, ne ic þā gīt, hū micel tōdāl ys betweox þære ealdan ǣ and þære nīwan. On anginne þisere worulde nam se brōðer hys swuster tō wīfe, and hwīlum ēac se fæder tȳmde be his
20   āgenre dehter, and manega hæfdon mā wīfa tō folces ēacan, and man ne mihte þā æt fruman wīfian būton on his siblingum. Gyf hwā wyle nū swā lybban æfter Crīstes tōcyme swā swā men leofodon ær Moises ǣ oþþe under Moises ǣ, ne byð se man nā Crīsten, ne hē furþum wyrðe ne byð þæt him ænig Crīsten man mid ete.
25   þā ungelæredan prēostas, gif hī hwæt lītles understandað of þām

---

1   Incipit . . . Anglice 'Here begins the preface to Genesis in English.'
2   grēt For assimilation of the pres. tense ending -(e)þ both here and elsewhere (e.g. rǣt, stynt below) see §112.2. Writers of letters in OE frequently begin in the third person, as here, and then shift to the first person.
   Æðelwærd was a secular patron of Ælfric, a descendant of the house of King Alfred the Great, and the author of a Latin historical work, the *Chronicon Æthel-weardi.*
4   þūhte Impersonal verb with subject 'it' understood. See also þincð in the next sentence; cf. §212.
10   on þære nīwan ǣ 'in (the time of) the new law' (i.e. the New Testament).
10–11   þā ealdan fæderas 'the patriarchs' (of the Old Testament).
11   þā 'then'.
12   wære Subj. follows ǣr þan þe (§174.4).
14   be dæle 'in part'.
15–16   hē hæfde fēower wīf See Genesis 29: 16–30: 13.
17   sæde Originally sǣgde (§126), but between a front vowel and *d, n,* or *ð* OE *ġ* tends to disappear and the preceding vowel is lengthened. Cf. *foresǣde,* l. 97 below.
20   mā wīfa 'more wives (than one)'.
21   on 'from among'.
   hwā 'someone' (§20).
25   prēostas . . . hī The repetition of subject is otiose: see §148 and cf. *hē* (l. 78).
   hwæt lītles 'something of a little', i.e. 'a little something'.

Lædenbōcum, þonne þincð him sōna þæt hī magon mǣre lārēowas
bēon; ac hī ne cunnon swā þēah þæt gāstlice andgit þǣrtō, and hū
sēo ealde ǣ wæs getācnung tōweardra þinga, oþþe hū sēo nīwe
gecȳþnis æfter Crīstes menniscnisse wæs gefillednys ealra þǣra
30 þinga þe sēo ealde gecȳðnis getācnode tōwearde be Crīste and be
hys gecorenum. Hī cweþaþ ēac oft be Pētre, hwī hī ne mōton
habban wīf swā swā Pētrus se apostol hæfde, and hī nellað gehīran
ne witan þæt se ēadiga Pētrus leofede æfter Moises ǣ oþ þæt Crīst,
þe on þām tīman tō mannum cōm and began tō bodienne his hālige
35 godspel and gecēas Pētrum ǣrest him tō gefēran: þā forlēt Pētrus
þǣrrihte his wīf, and ealle þā twelf apostolas, þā þe wīf hæfdon,
forlēton ǣgþer ge wīf ge ǣhta, and folgodon Crīstes lāre tō þǣre
nīwan ǣ and clǣnnisse þe hē self þā ārǣrde. Prēostas sindon
gesette tō lārēowum þām lǣwedum folce. Nū gedafnode him þæt
40 hig cūðen þā ealdan ǣ gāstlīce understandan and hwæt Crīst self
tǣhte and his apostolas on þǣre nīwan gecȳðnisse, þæt hig mihton
þām folce wel wissian tō Godes gelēafan and wel bīsnian tō gōdum
weorcum.

We secgað ēac foran tō þæt sēo bōc is swīþe dēop gāstlīce tō
45 understandenne, and wē ne wrītað nā māre būton þā nacedan
gerecednisse. þonne þincþ þām ungelǣredum þæt eall þæt andgit
bēo belocen on þǣre ānfealdan gerecednisse; ac hit ys swīðe feor
þām. Sēo bōc ys gehāten Genesis, þæt ys 'gecyndbōc' for þām þe
hēo ys firmest bōca and spricþ be ælcum gecinde (ac hēo ne spricð
50 nā be þǣra engla gesceapenisse). Hēo onginð þus: *In principio creauit
deus celum et terram*, þæt ys on Englisc, 'On anginne gescēop God
heofenan and eorðan.' Hit wæs sōðlīce swā gedōn, þæt God
ælmihtig geworhte on anginne, þā þā hē wolde, gesceafta. Ac swā
þēah æfter gāstlicum andgite þæt anginn ys Crīst, swā swā hē self
55 cwæþ tō þām Iūdēiscum: 'Ic eom angin, þe tō ēow sprece.' þurh þis
angin worhte God Fæder heofenan and eorþan, for þan þe hē

---

27 þǣrtō '(pertaining) thereto'.
31 hwī '(asking) why'.
35 him tō gefēran 'for his companion' (§191.2).
39 gedafnode '(it) would befit' (pret. subj.).
40 hig An alternate spelling of *hī*, *hie* 'they'. Since OE *ig* sometimes becomes *ī*,
the sound *ī* was sometimes spelled *ig*.
47–8 feor þām 'far from that'.
48 gecynd, like Latin *genus*, means 'origin' and 'species'.
49–50 hēo . . . hēo . . . Hēo The pronoun agrees with the gender of its antecedent *bōc* (§187.2a).
50 *In principio* . . . 'In the beginning God created Heaven and earth.' Genesis
1:1.
55 Ic eom angin, etc. Revelation 1:8, 21:6, 22:13.

gesceōp ealle gesceafta þurh þone Sunu, se þe wæs æfre of him
ācenned, wīsdōm of þām wīsan Fæder.

Eft stynt on þǣre bēc on þām forman ferse, *Et spiritus dei ferebatur*
60   *super aquas*, þæt is on Englisc, 'And Godes Gāst wæs geferod ofer
wæteru.' Godes Gāst ys se Hālga Gāst, þurh þone gelīffæste se
Fæder ealle þā gesceafta þe hē gesceōp þurh þone sunu, and se
Hālga Gāst færð geond manna heortan and silð ūs synna forgifenisse, ǣrest þurh wæter on þām fulluhte, and siþþan þurh
65   dǣdbōte; and gif hwā forsihð þā forgifenisse þe se Hālga Gāst sylð,
þonne bið his synn æfre unmyltsiendlic on ēcnysse. Eft ys sēo
hālige þrīnnys geswutelod on þisre bēc, swā swā ys on þām worde
þe God cwæð: 'Uton wircean mannan tō ūre ānlīcnisse.' Mid þām
þe hē cwæð, 'Uton wircean,' ys sēo þrinnis gebīcnod; mid þām þe
70   hē cwæð, 'tō ūre ānlīcnisse,' ys sēo sōðe ānnis geswutelod; hē ne
cwæð nā menifealdlīce tō ūrum ānlīcnissum, ac ānfealdlīce tō ūre
ānlīcnisse. Eft cōmon þrī englas tō Abrahame and hē sprǣc tō him
eallum þrīm swā swā tō ānum. Hū clipode Abēles blōd tō Gode
būton swā swā ælces mannes misdǣda wrēgað hine tō Gode būtan
75   wordum? Be þisum lītlum man mæg understandan hū dēop sēo bōc
ys on gāstlicum andgite, þēah þe hēo mid lēohtlicum wordum
āwriten sig. Eft Iōsēp, þe wæs geseald tō Ēgipta lande and hē
āhredde þæt folc wið þone miclan hunger, hæfde Crīstes getācnunge þe wæs geseald for ūs tō cwale and ūs āhredde fram þām
80   ēcan hungre helle sūsle.

þæt micele geteld þe Moises worhte mid wunderlicum cræfte on
þām wēstene, swā swā him God self gedihte, hæfde getācnunge
Godes gelaðunge þe hē self āstealde þurh his apostolas mid menigfealdum frætewum and fægerum þēawum. Tō þām geweorce
85   brōhte þæt folc gold and seolfor and dēorwirðe gimstānas and
menigfealde mǣrða; sume ēac brōhton gātehǣr, swā swā God
bebēad. þæt gold getācnode ūrne gelēafan and ūre gōde ingehygd

---

58   wīsdōm i.e. Christ, the Logos.
Fæder see §60.2.
59–60   *Et spiritus* ... 'And the spirit of God was carried over the waters.'
Genesis 1:2.
61   þurh þone 'through which' (§162.3).
67   ys '(it) is' (§193.7).
68   Uton ... ānlīcnisse Genesis 1:26. In what follows, Ælfric (who was a
grammarian) concentrates on the significance of grammatical number in the scriptural passage.
72   Eft cōmon þrī englas, etc. Genesis 18:1–5.
73   Hū clipode Abēles blōd, etc. Genesis 4:10.
77   sig = *sī*, *sīe* 'may be'. See note to l. 40 above.
79   þe The antecedent is *Crīstes*. See §163.4.
81ff.   geteld The tabernacle is described in Exodus, chapters 35–9.

þe wē Gode offrian sceolon; þæt seolfor getācnode Godes sprǣca
and þā hālgan lāra þe wē habban sceolon tō Godes weorcum; þā
90 gimstānas getācnodon mislice fægernissa on Godes mannum; þæt
gātehǣr getācnode þā stīðan dǣdbōte þǣra manna þe heora sinna
behrēowsiað. Man offrode ēac fela cinna orf Gode tō lāce binnan
þām getelde, be þām ys swīðe menigfeald getācnung; and wæs
beboden þæt sē tægel sceolde bēon gehāl ǣfre on þām nȳtene æt
95 þǣre offrunge for þǣre getācnunge þæt God wile þæt wē simle wel
dōn oð ende ūres līfes: þonne bið se tægel geoffrod on ūrum
weorcum. Nū ys sēo foresǣde bōc on manegum stōwum swīðe
nearolīce gesett, and þēah swīðe dēoplīce on þām gāstlicum
andgite, and hēo is swā geendebyrd swā swā God self hig gedihte
100 þām wrītere Moise, and wē durron nā māre āwrītan on Englisc
þonne þæt Lǣden hæfð, ne þā endebirdnisse āwendan būton þām
ānum þæt þæt Lǣden and þæt Englisc nabbað nā āne wīsan on
þǣre sprǣce fadunge. Ǣfre se þe āwent oððe se þe tǣcð of Lǣdene
on Englisc, ǣfre hē sceal gefadian hit swā þæt Englisc hæbbe his
105 āgene wīsan, elles hit bið swīðe gedwolsum tō rǣdenne þām þe þæs
Lǣdenes wīsan ne can. Is ēac tō witanne þæt sume gedwolmen
wǣron þe woldon āwurpan þā ealdan ǣ, and sume woldon habban
þā ealdan and āwurpan þā nīwan, swā swā þā Iūdēiscan dōð. Ac
Crīst self and his apostolas ūs tǣhton ǣgðer tō healdenne þā ealdan
110 gāstlīce and þā nīwan sōðlīce mid weorcum. God gesceōp ūs twā
ēagan and twā ēaran, twā nosþirlu and twēgen weleras, twā handa
and twēgen fēt, and hē wolde ēac habban twā gecȳðnissa on þissere
worulde geset, þā ealdan and þā nīwan, for þām þe hē dēð swā swā
hine selfne gewyrð, and hē nǣnne rǣdboran nǣfð, ne nān man
115 þearf him cweðan tō: 'Hwī dēst þū swā?' Wē sceolon āwendan ūrne
willan tō his gesetnissum and wē ne magon gebīgean his gesetnissa
tō ūrum lustum.

Ic cweðe nū þæt ic ne dearr ne ic nelle nāne bōc æfter þissere of
Lǣdene on Englisc āwendan, and ic bidde þē, lēof ealdorman, þæt

---

92 ff. **fela cinna orf** 'cattle of many kinds'. Leviticus 3:9 specifies that the 'whole
rump' of the sacrificial animal must be offered, but Ælfric's spiritual interpretation
of the injunction is not in the Bible.

93   **be þām** 'concerning which' (§162.3).

93–4   **wæs beboden** '(it) was commanded' (§212).

101–2   **būton þām ānum þæt** 'except for the one [reason, namely] that'.

102–3   **āne wīsan on . . . fadunge** 'one manner in the disposition of language', i.e.
a common word order and idiom. (*Fadunge* 'disposition' is adopted here from one of
the other manuscripts of the Preface since the Laud manuscript's *fandunge* 'testing'
makes little sense.)

103   **āwent** See note to 2/32 above.

106   **Is** '(It) is'.

106–7   **sume gedwolmen wǣron** 'there were some heretics'.

114   **gewyrð** '(it) pleases' (§212).

120 þū mē þæs nā leng ne bidde þī læs þe ic bēo þē ungehīrsum oððe
lēas gif ic dō. God þē sig milde ā on ēcnisse. Ic bidde nū on Godes
naman, gif hwā þās bōc āwrītan wylle, þæt hē hig gerihte wel be
þære bȳsne, for þan þe ic nāh geweald, þēah þe hig hwā tō wōge
bringe þurh lēase wrīteras, and hit byð þonne his pleoh nā mīn:
125 mycel yfel dēð se unwrītere, gif hē nele hys wōh gerihtan.

---

120 þæs gen. obj. of *bidde*: 'ask me for that'.
123–4 þēah þe ... wrīteras 'although someone might bring it (the book) to error
through false scribes'.

5

Alfred the Great's Preface to his Translation of Gregory's *Pastoral Care*

Among the achievements of King Alfred the Great (sketched briefly in §§217 and 251 above), one of the most remarkable was the cultural renaissance he initiated in his realm even while he was leading his nation in a fight for survival against Scandinavian invaders. To save a people militarily without also restoring them culturally was apparently unthinkable to Alfred, and so he conceived and implemented a far-sighted plan for teaching all free Anglo-Saxons literacy in the vernacular and for translating the more important books of the period into English for all to read. In his letter to Bishop Wærferth, which serves as a preface to the King's translation of Pope Gregory the Great's *Cura Pastoralis* (*Pastoral Care*), the first of the important books to be translated, the elements of the programme for cultural revival are set forth, following a moving lament over the decay of learning which Alfred saw in England when he ascended the throne in 871. The prose has the intensity of deep conviction, but its pace is leisurely and aristocratic, its tone rich with nostalgia for the era of England's intellectual pre-eminence during the lifetime of Bede (673–735).

The text here is based upon that in Hatton MS 20 in the Bodleian Library, although a few unusual spellings (mainly in grammatical endings) have been replaced with more usual spellings from other manuscripts of the preface.

Ælfred kyning hāteð grētan Wærferð biscep his wordum luflīce ond frēondlīce; ond ðē cȳðan hāte ðæt mē cōm swīðe oft on gemynd, hwelce wiotan iū wæron giond Angelcynn, ægðer ge

---

1 hāteð grētan Wærferð biscep 'commands Bishop Wærferth to be greeted' (§161). For the use of the third person, see note to 4/2 above.

2 ond Before nasal consonants *a* often appears as *o* (§103.2). See below such spellings as *lond* (l. 12), *understondan* (l. 15), *mon* (l. 62).

ðē cȳðan hāte '(I) command you to be informed' (§161).

cōm '(it) has come'.

2–3 mē ... on gemynd 'into my mind' (§191.2).

godcundra hāda ge woruldcundra; ond hū gesæliglica tīda ðā
5 wǣron giond Angelcynn; ond hū ðā kyningas ðe ðone onwald
hæfdon ðæs folces Gode ond his ǣrendwrecum hīersumedon; ond
hīe ǣgðer ge hiora sibbe ge hiora siodu ge hiora onweald
innanbordes gehīoldon, ond ēac ūt hiora ēðel rȳmdon; ond hū him
ðā spēow ǣgðer ge mid wīge ge mid wīsdōme; ond ēac ðā
10 godcundan hādas, hū giorne hīe wǣron ǣgðer ge ymb lāre ge ymb
liornunga, ge ymb ealle ðā ðīowotdōmas ðe hīe Gode dōn scoldon;
ond hū man ūtanbordes wīsdōm ond lāre hieder on lond sōhte; ond
hū wē hīe nū sceoldon ūte begietan, gif wē hīe habban sceoldon.
Swǣ clǣne hīo wæs oðfeallenu on Angelcynne ðæt swīðe fēawa
15 wǣron behionan Humbre ðe hiora ðēninga cūðen understondan
on Englisc oððe furðum ān ǣrendgewrit of Lǣdene on Englisc
āreccean; ond ic wēne ðætte nōht monige begiondan Humbre
nǣren. Swǣ fēawa hiora wǣron ðæt ic furðum ānne ānlēpne ne
mæg geðencean be sūðan Temese ðā ðā ic tō rīce fēng. Gode
20 ælmihtegum sīe ðonc ðætte wē nū ǣnigne onstal habbað lāreowa.
Ond for ðon ic ðē bebīode ðæt ðū dō swǣ ic gelīefe ðæt ðū wille,
ðæt ðū ðē ðissa woruldðinga tō ðǣm geǣmetige, swǣ ðū oftost
mæge, ðæt ðū ðone wīsdōm ðe ðē God sealde ðǣr ðǣr ðū hiene
befæstan mæge, befæste. Geðenc hwelc wītu ūs ðā becōmon for
25 ðisse worulde, ðā ðā wē hit nōhwæðer ne selfe ne lufodon, ne ēac
ōðrum monnum ne lēfdon; ðone naman ǣnne wē lufodon ðætte wē
Crīstne wǣren, ond swīðe fēawa ðā ðēawas.
    Ðā ic ðā ðis eall gemunde, ðā gemunde ic ēac hū ic geseah, ǣr
ðǣm ðe hit eall forhergod wǣre ond forbærned, hū ðā ciricean

8–9 him ðā spēow 'they were successful then' (literally, 'it was successful to
them then'; see §212).

10 hādas, hū giorne hīe wǣron See note to 4/25.

14 oðfeallenu See §201.2.

17 ðætte See §155.

19 tō rīce fēng 'succeeded to the kingdom'.

22–4 ðæt ðū ðē ... befæste 'that you free yourself, as often as you can, from
worldly affairs to the end that you apply the wisdom that God gave you wherever you
can apply it'. See §172.A.

24 wītu The 'punishments' to which King Alfred refers are the Scandinavian
invasions: see §217.

25 hit The antecedent is *wīsdōm*. See §187.2, and compare *sīo lār ... hit* below
(ll. 45–6), where natural gender has again displaced grammatical gender.

26 lēfdon 'bequeathed, passed on' (taking this to be a non-West-Saxon spelling
of *lǣfdon* (l. 35) from *lǣfan* rather than from *līefan* 'allow', as previous editors have
assumed). The negligent Christians neither cherished learning themselves nor
bothered transmitting it to later generations.

26–7 ðone naman ǣnne ... ðā ðēawas 'we loved only the name that we were
Christians, and very few (of us loved) the (Christian) practices'.

29 forhergod ... ond forbærned 'ravaged ... and burned', i.e. by the Scandinavian invaders (§217).

30 giond eall Angelcynn stōdon māðma ond bōca gefylda, ond ēac
    micel mengeo Godes ðīowa; ond ðā swīðe lȳtle fiorme ðāra bōca
    wiston, for ðǣm ðe hīe hiora nānwuht ongietan ne meahton, for
    ðǣm ðe hīe nǣron on hiora āgen geðīode āwritene. Swelce hīe
    cwǣden: 'Ūre ieldran, ðā ðe ðās stōwa ǣr hīoldon, hīe lufodon
35 wīsdōm, ond ðurh ðone hīe begēaton welan ond ūs lǣfdon. Hēr
    mon mæg gīet gesīon hiora swæð, ac wē him ne cunnon æfter
    spyrigean. Ond for ðǣm wē habbað nū ǣgðer forlǣten ge ðone
    welan ge ðone wīsdōm, for ðǣm ðe wē noldon tō ðǣm spore mid
    ūre mōde onlūtan.'

40   Ðā ic ðā ðis eall gemunde, ðā wundrade ic swīðe swīðe ðāra
    gōdena wiotena ðe giū wǣron giond Angelcynn, ond ðā bēc ealla be
    fullan geliornod hæfdon, ðæt hīe hiora ðā nǣnne dǣl noldon on
    hiora āgen geðīode wendan. Ac ic ðā sōna eft mē selfum andwyrde,
    ond cwæð: 'Hīe ne wēndon ðætte ǣfre menn sceolden swæ
45 reccelēase weorðan ond sīo lār swæ oðfeallan: for ðǣre wilnunga
    hīe hit forlēton, ond woldon ðæt hēr ðȳ māra wīsdōm on londe
    wǣre ðȳ wē mā geðēoda cūðon.'

        Ðā gemunde ic hū sīo ǣ wæs ǣrest on Ebriscgeðīode funden,
    ond eft, ðā hīe Crēacas geliornodon, ðā wendon hīe hīe on heora
50 āgen geðīode ealle, ond ēac ealle ōðre bēc. Ond eft Lǣdenware
    swǣ same, siððan hīe hīe geliornodon, hīe hīe wendon ealla ðurh
    wīse wealhstodas on hiora āgen geðīode. Ond ēac ealla ōðra
    Crīstna ðīoda sumne dǣl hiora on hiora āgen geðīode wendon.

---

30 stōdon māðma ond bōca gefylda 'were full of books and of treasures'.
31–2 ðā swīðe lȳtle ... wiston 'they had very little benefit from the books'
(literally, 'they knew very little use of the books').
33–4 Swelce hīe cwǣden '(It is) as if they had said'. See §177.4 for the meaning
of *swelce*.
36 him ... æfter See §213.
38–9 mid ūre mōde 'with our mind(s)'.
40 wundrade Both the gen. pl. *wiotena* and the clause *ðæt hīe ... wendan* are
objects of the verb *wundrade*.
45 for ðǣre wilnunga 'on purpose, deliberately'.
46–7 ðȳ ... ðȳ See §167.7*a*.
48 ǣ The Old Testament, or perhaps only the Hexateuch ('the Law'), is meant.
49 hīe acc. sg. fem. The antecedent is *ǣ* (l. 48).
49–50 hīe hīe ... ealle ... ealle The first *ealle* is acc. sg. fem. modifying the
second of the two preceding *hīe*s, whose antecedent is again *ǣ* (l. 48); the second
ealle is acc. pl. fem. modifying *bēc*. Presumably *ealle ōðre bēc* refers to the remaining
books of the Bible.
    ðā wendon ... ealle The first *hīe* is nom. pl. referring to *Crēacas*; the second *hīe* is
acc. fem. sg. referring to *ǣ* (l. 48). *Ealle* is acc. fem. sg. modifying the second *hīe*.
51 siððan hīe hīe geliornodon, hīe hīe wendon ealla 'after they (*Lǣdenware*)
had learned them (*bēc*), they translated them all'. On the repetition of the subject
(*Lǣdenware ... hīe*), see §148.

Forðÿ mē ðyncð betre, gif īow swæ ðyncð, ðæt wē ēac sume bēc, ðā
55 ðe nīedbeðearfosta sīen eallum monnum tō wiotonne, ðæt wē ðā on
ðæt geðīode wenden ðe wē ealle gecnāwan mægen, ond gedōn, swæ
wē swīðe ēaðe magon mid Godes fultume, gif wē ðā stilnesse
habbað, ðætte eall sīo gioguð ðe nū is on Angelcynne frīora monna,
ðāra ðe ðā spēda hæbben ðæt hīe ðæm befēolan mægen, sīen tō
60 liornunga oðfæste, ðā hwīle ðe hīe tō nānre oðerre note ne mægen,
oð ðone first ðe hīe wel cunnen Englisc gewrit ārædan. Lære mon
siððan furður on Lædengeðīode ðā ðe mon furðor læran wille ond
tō hīerran hāde dōn wille.

Ðā ic ðā gemunde hū sīo lār Lædengeðīodes ær ðissum āfeallen
65 wæs giond Angelcynn, ond ðēah monige cūðon Englisc gewrit
ārædan, ðā ongan ic ongemang ōðrum mislicum ond manig-
fealdum bisgum ðisses kynerīces ðā bōc wendan on Englisc ðe is
genemned on Læden *Pastoralis*, ond on Englisc 'Hierdebōc',
hwīlum word be worde, hwīlum andgit of andgiete, swæ swæ ic hīe
70 geliornode æt Plegmunde mīnum ærcebiscepe, ond æt Assere
mīnum biscepe, ond æt Grimbolde mīnum mæsseprīoste, ond æt
Iōhanne mīnum mæsseprēoste. Siððan ic hīe ðā geliornod hæfde,
swæ swæ ic hīe forstōd, ond swæ ic hīe andgitfullīcost āreccean
meahte, ic hīe on Englisc āwende; ond tō ælcum biscepstōle on
75 mīnum rīce wille āne onsendan; ond on ælcre bið ān æstel, se bið
on fiftegum mancessa. Ond ic bebīode on Godes naman ðæt nān
mon ðone æstel from ðære bēc ne dō, ne ðā bōc from ðæm mynstre
– uncūð hū longe ðær swæ gelærede biscepas sīen, swæ swæ nū,
Gode ðonc, welhwær siendon. Forðÿ ic wolde ðætte hīe ealneg æt
80 ðære stōwe wæren, būton se biscep hīe mid him habban wille, oððe
hīo hwær tō læne sīe, oððe hwā ōðre bī wrīte.

54–61   Forðÿ ... ārædan See §172.B for a detailed analysis of this sentence.
55   ðæt wē Otiose restatement of *ðæt wē* in l. 54. See §148.
60   ðā hwīle ðe ... ne mægen 'as long as they are competent for no other
employment'.
69   hīe acc. sg. fem. The antecedent is *Hierdebōc*.
70–2   Plegmunde ... Assere ... Grimbolde ... Iōhanne These are scholars
whom King Alfred brought in from outside Wessex to help implement the cultural
revival he sought for his people. Plegmund was a Mercian who became Archbishop
of Canterbury in 890. Asser, a Welshman, became bishop of Sherborne and wrote a
Latin biography of King Alfred. Grimbold was a Frankish priest who was ultimately
canonized, and John (*Iōhannes*) a continental Saxon whom King Alfred established
as abbot of a new monastery at Athelney in Somerset.
75–6   se bið on fiftegum mancessa 'it will be worth fifty mancuses'. This use of
on is an idiom. for the gen. pl. *mancessa*, see §194.2.
78   uncūð '(it is) unknown'.
79–81   Forðÿ ic ... bī wrīte 'Therefore I have desired that they (the book and the
æstel) always remain at that place, unless the bishop wants to have them (or it, i.e.
the book) with him, or it (the book) is on loan somewhere, or someone is making a
copy (from it).'

6

Cynewulf and Cyneheard

This account appears in the Anglo-Saxon Chronicle, a year-by-year record of important events in the kingdom. (See the next selection for details.) The entry for the year 755 contains a narrative which exemplifies one of the cardinal virtues of Germanic society in the heroic age: unswerving loyalty to one's sworn leader, even when that loyalty is in conflict with claims of kinship. (See §§236–240.) For a contemporary audience, the violence and tragedy of the feud between Cynewulf and Cyneheard would have been transcended by the reassuring fact that the ideal prevailed: on both sides men made the heroic choice, and they chose right. The narration is so swift and breathless, the selection of detail so adroit, that some scholars have felt that the chronicler was recording a saga refined by many retellings in oral tradition. Supporting this view (and complicating the modern reader's task in following the narrative) is the tale's spontaneous syntax and free word-order, which require close attention to grammatical endings if the sentences are to be construed accurately. Readers should also be wary of the unusual spellings of some verb endings (*wǣron*, *-un*, *-an*; *locude* for *locode*; and the subjunctives *ūþon* and *ēodon* in lines 29 and 33, where we would expect *-en* for *-on*). See §113.3 for such spelling variations.

The text is that of Corpus Christi College, Cambridge, MS 173 except in line 29, where we adopt *cȳþde*, the reading of most manuscripts, for *cȳðdon* of our manuscript. For historical information about persons and places mentioned and chronological disturbances, see Whitelock's work cited in §251.1.

755.   Hēr Cynewulf benam Sigebryht his rīces ond Westseaxna wiotan for unryhtum dǣdum, būton Hamtūnscīre; ond hē hæfde þā

---

1 Hēr i.e. 'in this year': the chronicler uses an adverb of place rather than of time because he is referring to the dated slot in the manuscript where he is making his entry.

Sigebryht King of the West Saxons before Cynewulf, his kinsman, deposed him.

1–2 Cynewulf ... ond Westseaxna wiotan is the compound subject of the sentence. The verb benam is singular because in OE verbs normally agree only with that part of a compound subject which precedes them: see §§149.1 and 187.3c.

oþ hē ofslōg þone aldormon þe him lengest wunode. Ond hiene þā
Cynewulf on Andred ādrǣfde, ond hē þǣr wunade oþ þæt hiene ān
5   swān ofstang æt Pryfetes flōdan; ond hē wræc þone aldormon
Cumbran. Ond se Cynewulf oft miclum gefeohtum feaht uuiþ Bretwālum. Ond ymb xxxı wintra þæs þe hē rīce hæfde, hē wolde
ādrǣfan ānne æþeling se was Cyneheard hāten; ond se Cyneheard
wæs þæs Sigebryhtes brōþur. Ond þā geāscode hē þone cyning
10   lȳtle werode on wīfcȳþþe on Merantūne, ond hine þǣr berād ond
þone būr ūtan beēode ǣr hine þā men onfunden þe mid þām
kyninge wǣrun.

Ond þā ongeat se cyning þæt, ond hē on þā duru ēode ond þā
unhēanlīce hine werede oþ hē on þone æþeling lōcude, ond þā ūt
15   rǣsde on hine ond hine miclum gewundode; ond hīe alle on þone
cyning wǣrun feohtende oþ þæt hīe hine ofslægenne hæfdon. Ond
þā on þæs wīfes gebǣrum onfundon þæs cyninges þegnas þā
unstilnesse, ond þā þider urnon swā hwelc swā þonne gearo wearþ
ond radost. Ond hiera se æþeling gehwelcum feoh ond feorh

---

3   þā acc. sg. fem., agreeing in gender with its antecedent *Hamtūnscīre*.
þe him lengest wunode 'who had dwelt with him longest', i.e. who had remained
faithful to him longer than the rest.
4   Andred A large forest which extended from Kent into Hampshire (the area
now called the Weald).
5   Pryfetes flōdan 'the stream at Privett' (in Hampshire).
5–6   þone aldormon Cumbran This is the loyal *aldormon* slain by Sigebryht
(l. 3).
6–7   Bretwālum Britons (probably Cornishmen) descended from the original
inhabitants of England before the Anglo-Saxon invasion (§217).
7   Ond ymb xxxı wintra þæs þe ... literally 'And after 31 winters from that in
which ...'.
wintra i.e. 'years'. The Anglo-Saxons reckoned years in terms of winters. For the
case of *wintra* see §194.2; cf. §190.4. The passage of many years in the course of this
'annal' shows that this is not a normal chronicle entry (which would record only the
events of the year just ended) but rather is an independent tale which the chronicler
has interpolated into his sequence of yearly reports. The *Chronicle* records the death
of Cynewulf in the annal dated 784: apparently XXXI is an error for XXIX. The 784
entry reads as follows: *Hēr Cyneheard ofslōg Cynewulf cyning, ond hē þǣr wearþ ofslægen
ond lxxxiiii monna mid him.*
10   lȳtle werode See §192.2.
on wīfcȳþþe on Merantūne i.e. visiting a mistress in Merton.
11   būr i.e. the apartment where the lady receives the King. The *būr* stands
inside the stronghold (*burh*) but is separate from the main hall, where the King's
retinue is housed. The entire compound is surrounded by a wall and is entered
through *gatu* (ll. 27, 36) in the wall. The *būr* is entered through a *duru* (l. 13).
14   æþeling i.e. Cyneheard.
17   on þæs wīfes gebǣrum 'from the woman's outcries'.
18–19   urnon ... ond radost literally, 'they ran, whoever became ready and
quickest', i.e. each ran to the King as quickly as he could get ready.
19   hiera ... gehwelcum 'to each of them (i.e. the King's men)'.

20 gebēad, ond hiera nǣnig hit geþicgean nolde; ac hīe simle
feohtende wǣran oþ hīe alle lǣgon būtan ānum Bryttiscum gīsle,
ond sē swīþe gewundad wæs.

þā on morgenne gehīerdun þæt þæs cyninges þegnas þe him
beæftan wǣrun, þæt se cyning ofslǣgen wæs. þā ridon hīe þider,
25 ond his aldormon Ōsrīc, ond Wīferþ his þegn, ond þā men þe hē
beæftan him lǣfde ǣr, ond þone æþeling on þǣre byrig mētton þǣr
se cyning ofslǣgen læg (ond þā gatu him tō belocen hæfdon) ond þā
þǣrto ēodon. Ond þā gebēad hē him hiera āgenne dōm fēos ond
londes, gif hīe him þæs rīces ūþon, ond him cȳþde þæt hiera mǣgas
30 him mid wǣron, þā þe him from noldon. Ond þā cuǣdon hīe þæt
him nǣnig mǣg lēofra nǣre þonne hiera hlāford, ond hīe nǣfre his
banan folgian noldon. Ond þā budon hīe hiera mǣgum þæt hīe
gesunde from ēodon. Ond hīe cuǣdon þæt tæt ilce hiera gefērum
geboden wǣre þe ǣr mid þām cyninge wǣrun. þā cuǣdon hīe þæt
35 hīe hīe þæs ne onmunden 'þon mā þe ēowre gefēran þe mid þām
cyninge ofslǣgene wǣrun.' Ond hīe þā ymb þā gatu feohtende

20–1 **simle feohtende wǣran** i.e. 'kept on fighting'.

21 **gīsle** Presumably the hostage was taken in the course of Cynewulf's wars
with the Britons (ll. 6–7).

26 **ǣr** Here as elsewhere *ǣr* combined with pret. tense signals the pluperfect
(§197.4): 'and the men that he had left behind him'.

27 **þā gatu . . . hæfdon** Cyneheard's men 'had locked the gates (leading in) to
them', i.e. had locked themselves in the compound. Or, alternatively, one could
read, 'had locked the gates against them (King Cynewulf's men)'.

28 **hiera āgenne dōm** Cyneheard offers to let King Cynewulf's men name their
own price for allowing him to assume the kingship. (Giving enemies 'their own
judgment of compensation' is a common Germanic idiom and practice.)

30 **þā þe him from noldon** 'who did not want (to go) from him' (§205.1).

30 **cuǣdon hīe** 'they (Cynewulf's men) said'.

32 **Ond þā budon hīe** 'And then they (Cynewulf's men) offered'.

33 **ēodon** subj. 'might go'.

33–4 **Ond hīe cuǣdon . . . geboden wǣre** 'And they (Cyneheard's men) said
that the same (thing) had been offered to their (Cynewulf's men's) comrades'.

34–5 **þā cuǣdon . . . onmunden** 'Then they (Cyneheard's men) said that they
would not pay attention to that (offer of safe passage).' *Onmunan* with refl. pron.
(*hīe*) takes a gen. obj. (*þæs*).

35 **þon mā þe** '(any) more than (did)'. The mid-sentence shift into direct
discourse is characteristic of vivid oral narrative.

C. T. Onions, in earlier editions of Henry Sweet's *Anglo-Saxon Reader*, provided
the following dialogue to clarify the rapid shifts of speaker in the foregoing passage:

> *Cyneheard*. I offer you your own choice of money and land if you will grant
> me the kingship; and there are kinsmen of yours with us who will not leave me
> (us). *Osric*. No kinsman of ours is dearer to us than our liege lord, and we will
> never follow his slayer. We offer a safe exit to those of them who come out.
> *Cyneheard*. The same offer was made to your comrades who were with the king
> before. We pay no more regard to the offer than your comrades did who were
> killed along with the king.

36 **Ond hīe** 'And they (i.e. Cynewulf's men and Cyneheard's men)'.

wǣron oþ þæt hīe þǣrinne fulgon ond þone æþeling ofslōgon ond
þā men þe him mid wǣrun, alle būtan ānum, se wæs þæs aldormonnes godsunu; ond hē his feorh generede, ond þēah hē wæs oft
40 gewundad.

Ond se Cynewulf rīcsode xxxi wintra and his līc līþ æt Wintanceastre, ond þæs æþelinges æt Ascanmynster; ond hiera ryhtfæderencyn gǣþ tō Cerdice.

37 oþ þæt hīe 'until they (i.e. Cynewulf's men)'.
38–9 þæs aldormonnes presumably Osric, mentioned in l. 25.
39 ond hē his feorh generede The *hē* refers to the godson.
43 **Cerdice** the putative founder of the kingdom and royal line of the West
Saxons.

7

Selections from the Anglo-Saxon Chronicle

Around A.D. 890, during the reign of King Alfred the Great, Anglo-Saxon scholars compiled a year-by-year record of important events from antiquity to their own day. Copies of this Chronicle were distributed throughout the realm, and the annual record of happenings in England was continued by various hands in various places, sometimes only a short while after the events occurred. This annalistic activity at times approaches genuine historical writing and constitutes an important stage in the development of a narrative prose independent of Latin models. The following selections suggest the nature both of the Chronicle's prose style and of the events it portrays at one dark period in England's history. Norsemen were waging a war of conquest in the land, and the English King, Ethelred the Unready, adopted the disastrous policy of paying the invaders Danegeld rather than rallying his troops for defence, as King Alfred had done in an earlier time of trial (see §217). The leading men of the realm, moreover, were often untrustworthy, and the nation was demoralized. One Anglo-Saxon leader named Brihtnoth, whose death is noted briefly in the entry for 991, rejected the prevailing pusillanimity of his times and made a desperate stand against the invaders rather than pay Danegeld. His valour and that of his men is extolled in a moving heroic poem, *The Battle of Maldon*, which appears below as selection 12.

The entries are drawn from several manuscripts of the Chronicle, and some have been abbreviated. The words *tobrocon* (l. 39), *gefeordon* (l. 50), *se* (l. 52), and *beodon* (l. 74) have been normalized to *tōbrocen*, *gefērdon*, *sēo*, and *bēodan*.

980. Hēr on þȳs gēare wæs Æþelgār abbod tō bisceope gehālgod on vi nōnas Mai tō þām bisceopstōle æt Sēolesigge. And on þām

1 Hēr See 6/1n.
2 vi nōnas Mai i.e. May 2nd. (Latin terms are used by some chroniclers in reckoning time.)

ylcan gēare wæs Sūðhamtūn forhergod fram scipherige, and sēo
burhwaru mǣst ofslegen and gehæft. And þȳ ilcan gēare wæs
5   Tenetland gehergod; and þȳ ilcan gēare wæs Lēgeceasterscīr
gehergod fram norðscipherige.

981. Hēr on þīs gēare wæs Sancte Petroces stōw forhergod, and
þȳ ilcan gēare wæs micel hearm gedōn gehwǣr be þām sǣriman
ǣgþer ge on Defenum ge on Wēalum.

10   982. Hēr on þȳs gēare cōmon ūpp on Dorsǣtum iii scypu
wīcinga and hergodon on Portlande. þȳ ilcan gēare forbarn
Lundenbyrig. And on þām ylcan gēare forðfērdon twēgen ealdormenn, Æþelmǣr on Hamtūnscīre and Ēadwine on Sūðseaxum.

. . . . .

988.   Hēr wæs Wecedport geheregod, and Goda, se Defenisca
15   þegen, ofslagen, and mycel wæl mid him. Hēr gefōr Dūnstān
arcebisceop, and Æðelgār bisceop fēng æfter him tō arcestōle, and
hē lȳtle hwīle æfter þǣm lyfode – būtan i gēare and iii mōnþas.

. . . . .

990. Hēr Sigerīc wæs gehālgod tō arcebisceope, and Ēadwine
abbod forðfērde, and Wulfgār abbod fēng tō þām rīce.

20   991. Hēr wæs Gypeswīc gehergod, and æfter þām swīðe raðe
wæs Brihtnōð ealdorman ofslægen æt Mǣldūne. And on þām gēare
man gerǣdde þæt man geald ǣrest gafol Deniscan mannum for
þām mycclan brōgan þe hī worhtan be þām sǣriman. þæt wæs
ǣrest x þūsend punda. þǣne rǣd gerǣdde Sīrīc arcebisceop.

25   992. Hēr Ōswald se ēadiga arcebisceop forlēt þis līf and gefērde
þæt heofonlice, and Æðelwine ealdorman gefōr on þām ilcan
gēare. Ðā gerǣdde se cyng and ealle his witan þæt man gegaderode
þā scipu þe āhtes wǣron tō Lundenbyrig. And se cyng þā betǣhte
þā fyrde tō lǣdene Ealfrīce ealdorman and þorode eorl and
30   Ælfstāne bisceop and Æscwīge bisceop, and sceoldan cunnian gif
hī muhton þone here āhwǣr ūtene betræppen. Ðā sende se

---

12   Lundenbyrig nom. sg. Since burg is declined like bōc (§58), the normal nom.
sg. form is -burg, not -byrig. But in the Chronicle and elsewhere the form with i-
mutation occasionally appears as a nominative singular.

16   fēng . . . tō arcestōle 'succeeded to the archiepiscopal see after him'.

19   fēng tō þām rīce 'succeeded to the office (of abbot)'.

22   man gerǣdde . . . gafol 'advice was given so that tribute was first paid'.

Deniscan A late spelling of Deniscum (§65). The Anglo-Saxons used Denisc
loosely to refer to any and all of the Scandinavian peoples who were invading them.
The Vikings at Maldon seem to have been mainly Norwegians.

28   āhtes 'of any value' (gen. sg. of āwiht).

29   tō lǣdene Properly, tō lǣdenne 'for leading' i.e. 'as leaders'.

29–30   Ealfrīce ealdorman . . . Æscwīge bisceop The names of these leaders
are, correctly, in the dative case, but their titles are uninflected.

ealdorman Ælfríc and hēt warnian þone here, and þā on þēre nihte
ðe hī on ðone dæi tōgædere cumon sceoldon, ðā sceōc hē on niht
fram þǣre fyrde, him sylfum tō mycclum bismore. And se here þā
35 ætbærst, būton ān scip þǣr man ofslōh. And þā gemǣtte se here ðā
scipu of Ēastenglum and of Lunden, and hī ðǣr ofslōgon mycel
wæl and þæt scip genāmon eall gewǣpnod and gewǣdod, þe se
ealdorman on wæs.

993. Hēr on ðissum gēare wæs Bæbbanburh tōbrocen and mycel
40 herehūðe þǣr genumen; and æfter þām cōm tō Humbran mūðe se
here and þǣr mycel yfel gewrohtan ægðer ge on Lindesīge ge on
Norðhymbran. Þā gegaderode man swīðe mycele fyrde, and þā hī
tōgædere gān sceoldan, þā onstealdon þā heretogan ǣrest þone
flēam – þæt wæs Frǣna and Godwine and Friðegist. On þysum
45 ilcan gēare hēt se cyng āblendan Ælfgār Ælfrīces sunu ealdormannes.

994. Hēr on þisum gēare cōm Anlāf and Swegen tō Lundenbyrig
on Nativitas sancte Marie mid iiii and hundnigontigum scipum,
and hī ðā on ðā burh festlīce feohtende wǣron, and ēac hī mid fyre
50 ontendan woldon. Ac hī þǣr gefērdon māran hearm and yfel þonne
hī ǣfre wēndon þæt heom ǣnig burhwaru gedōn sceolde. Ac sēo
hālige Godes mōdor on ðām dæge hire mildheortnisse þǣre
burhware gecȳðde and hī āhredde wið heora fēondum. And hī
þanon fērdon, and wrohton þæt mǣste yfel þe ǣfre ǣnig here dōn
55 mihte on bærnette and hergunge and on manslihtum ægðer be ðām
sǣriman on Ēastseaxum and on Centlande and on Sūðseaxum and

32 **Ælfríc** This treacherous Ælfric (whose name is spelled *Ealfríce* in l. 29) was
ealdorman of Hampshire. He has no connection with Abbot Ælfric, author of the
Colloquy, Biblical translations, and other works.
hēt warnian (§161).
32–3 **on þēre nihte ðe hī on ðone dæi** 'in the night before the day on which
they'. (A day was regarded as going with the previous night.)
35 **ān scip … ofslōh** literally 'one ship where one destroyed', i.e. 'one ship
which was destroyed'.
36 **hī** The antecedent of *hī* is the collective noun *here* (l. 35).
41 **gewrohtan** A late spelling of *gewrohton*. The Chronicler first thinks of *here* as
a unit (*cōm*) and then pluralizes (*gewrohtan*) as he thinks of it as many men. See
§187.3*b*, and cf. ll. 61–2 below (*cōm… nāmon*).
45 **hēt … āblendan Ælfgār** (§161) This blinding of the son was presumably in
retribution for Ælfric's treachery.
47 **Anlāf and Swegen** Since it precedes the compound subject, *cōm* is singular.
(Anlāf is King Olaf Tryggvason of Norway, who ultimately converted his countrymen to Christianity; Swegen is Sweyn Forkbeard, King of Denmark and conqueror
of England in 1013. His son Canute was King of England and Denmark 1016–35.)
48 **Nativitas sancte Marie** '(the day of) the Nativity of Saint Mary', i.e.
September 8th.
49 **hī** (preceding *mid*) acc. sg. fem. (antecedent is *burh*).

on Hamtūnscīre. And æt nȳxtan nāman heom hors and ridon swā
wīde swā hī woldon and unāsecgendlice yfel wircende wǣron. Þā
gerǣdde se cyng and his witan þæt him man tō sende and him gafol
60 behēte and metsunge wið þon þe hī þǣre hergunge geswicon. And
hī þā þet underfēngon, and cōm þā eall se here tō Hamtūne and
þǣr wintersetle nāmon. And hī man þǣr fǣdde geond eall
Westscaxna rīce, and him man geald fēos xvi þūsend punda
· · · · ·

1011. Hēr on þissum gēare sende se cyning and his witan tō ðām
65 here, and gyrndon friðes, and him gafol and metsunge behēton wið
þām ðe hī hiora hergunge geswicon. Hī hæfdon þā ofergān (i) Ēastengle and (ii) Ēastsexe and (iii) Middelsexe and (iiii) Oxenafordscīre and (v) Grantabricscīre and (vi) Heortfordscīre and (vii)
Buccingahamscīre and (viii) Bedefordscīre and (ix) healfe
70 Huntadūnscīre and micel (x) on Hāmtūnscīre, and be sūþan
Temese ealle Kentingas and Sūðsexe and Hæstingas and Sūðrige
and Bearrocscīre and Hamtūnscīre and micel on Wiltūnscīre.
  Ealle þās ungesǣlða ūs gelumpon þuruh unrǣdas, þæt man
nolde him ā tīman gafol bēodan oþþe wið gefeohtan; ac þonne hī
75 mǣst tō yfele gedōn hæfdon, þonne nam mon frið and grið wið hī.
And nā þē lǣs for eallum þissum griðe and gafole hī fērdon
ǣghweder flocmǣlum, and heregodon ūre earme folc, and hī
rȳpton and slōgon.

---

57   nāman heom Late spellings of *nāmon him*. For the function of the pronoun
see note to 3/42.
58   unāsecgendlice a late form of acc. pl. neut. *-licu*.
73   þæt 'in that'.
74   him i.e. the Danes.
   ā tīman 'in time'.
75   mǣst tō yfele 'the most for harm', i.e. 'the most to (our) injury'.

8

Bede's Account of the Conversion of King Edwin

Saint Bede the Venerable – scientist, historian, philologist, and one of the Church Fathers – lived in the north of England from *c.* 673 to 735. His important work as a theologian earned him a place in the fourth heaven of Dante's *Paradiso*, but it is his work as a historian that has established his reputation among modern readers. At a time when most 'historical' writing was a mish-mash of fact and fiction, Bede's *Ecclesiastical History of the English People* (written, like virtually all his works, in Latin) maintained a high standard of accuracy, order, and verification of sources. It is also well written and has sustained the interest of readers both during and after the Middle Ages.

Sometime in the reign of King Alfred the Great (871–899), Bede's *History* was translated into Old English. The translation is vigorous and at times even eloquent, but one can also detect in it the struggle of a vernacular artist trying (not always successfully) to free himself from the alien syntax of his source text and to establish a native English prose style. All these features are present in the following excerpt from the Old English Bede, which recounts how Christianity was brought to the pagan Anglo-Saxons of Northumbria in 625. The first missionary work took place in 597 in Kent, and it is from there that Bishop Paulinus travelled to the court of King Edwin of Northumbria in hopes of persuading the ruler and his *witan* to renounce their pagan beliefs and accept Christianity. At the point where our excerpt begins, Paulinus has just succeeded in converting Edwin, but the King explains that he must put the matter before his *witan* before he can commit his subjects to the new faith. The deliberations of his advisers, which Bede records with deft and unobtrusive art, give us a remarkable glimpse of that pivotal moment in history when the warrior society of Anglo-Saxon England began to abandon Germanic paganism for the religion newly brought from Rome.

The text is basically that of Corpus Christi College, Oxford, MS 279 up to -*bedo* on l. 47 and of Bodleian Library MS Tanner 10 for

the rest, but we have occasionally adopted a simpler reading from
another manuscript when the base text is problematic, and in l. 56
we read *þā þe* for the various and conflicting readings of the manuscripts.

þa se cyning þā þäs word gehȳrde, þā andswarode hē him and
cwæð, þæt hē æghwæþer ge wolde ge sceolde þām geleafan onfōn
þe hē lærde; cwæð hwæþere, þæt hē wolde mid his freondum and
mid his wytum gesprec and geþeaht habban, þæt gif hī mid hine
5 þæt geþafian woldan, þæt hī ealle ætsomne on līfes willan Crīste
gehālgade wæran. þā dyde se cyning swā swā hē cwæð, and se
bisceop þæt geþafade.

þā hæfde hē gesprec and geþeaht mid his witum and syndriglīce
wæs fram him eallum frignende hwylc him þūhte and gesawen
10 wære þeos nīwe lār and þære godcundnesse bīgong þe þær læred
wæs. Him þā andswarode his ealdorbisceop, Cefi wæs hāten:
'Geseoh þū, cyning, hwelc þeos lār sīe þe ūs nū bodad is. Ic þē
sōðlīce andette þæt ic cūðlīce geleornad hæbbe, þæt eallinga
nāwiht mægenes ne nyttnesse hafað sīo æfæstnes þe wē oð ðis
15 hæfdon and beeodon, for ðon nænig þīnra þegna neodlicor ne
gelustfullīcor hine sylfne underþeodde tō ūra goda bīgange þonne
ic, and nōht þon læs monige syndon þā þe māran gefe and fremsumnesse æt þē onfēngon þonne ic, and in eallum þingum māran
gesynto hæfdon. Hwæt, ic wāt, gif ūre godo ænige mihte hæfdon,
20 þonne woldan hīe mē mā fultumian, for þon ic him geornlīcor
þeodde ond hȳrde. For þon mē þynceð wīslic, gif þū geseo þā þing
beteran and strangran þe ūs nīwan bodad syndon, þæt wē þām
onfōn.'

þæs wordum ōþer cyninges wita and ealdormann geþafunge

---

1   him i.e. Bishop Paulinus, who has just explained to the King his obligation to
accept Christianity.

5   woldan Here and elsewhere the scribe (who made this copy in the eleventh
century) uses -*an* instead of -*en* for the subj. pl. ending: cf. *wæran* (l. 6) and *woldan*
(l. 20). He also uses -*an* for -*on*: *spræcan* (l. 38), *beeodan* (l. 43). These spellings are
characteristic of the late Old English period.

9–10   hwylc him ... wære literally 'how seemed to them and was seen (by
them)'. The Latin word *videretur* 'seemed' is translated with two roughly synony-
mous expressions (*þūhte* and *gesawen wære*). This practice is common in the Old
English Bede and is symptomatic of the translator's awkwardness in dealing with
his Latin source. Cf. *hæfdon and beeodon* (l. 15) and *sōhte ond āhsode* (l. 53).

11   Cefi wæs hāten See §186.1. (Cefi's title *ealdorbisceop* means he was a *pagan*
high priest.)

19   godo = *godu* nom. pl. neut. Pagan gods are neuter, while the Christian God is
masculine.

24   þæs wordum ... wita 'To that one's words another counsellor of the King'.

25 sealde, and tō þǣre sprǣce fēng and þus cwǣð: 'þyslīc mē is
gesewen, þū cyning, þis andwearde līf manna on eorðan tō
wiðmetenesse þǣre tīde þe ūs uncūð is: swylc swā þū æt swǣsen-
dum sitte mid þīnum ealdormannum and þegnum on wintertīde,
and sīe fȳr onǣlæd and þīn heall gewyrmed, and hit rīne and snīwe
30 and styrme ūte; cume ān spearwa and hrǣdlīce þæt hūs þurhflēo,
cume þurh ōþre duru in, þurh ōþre ūt gewīte. Hwæt, hē on þā tīd
þe hē inne bið ne bið hrinen mid þȳ storme þæs wintres; ac þæt bið
ān ēagan bryhtm and þæt lǣsste fæc, ac hē sōna of wintra on þone
winter eft cymeð. Swā þonne þis monna līf tō medmiclum fæce
35 ætȳweð; hwæt þǣr foregange, oððe hwæt þǣr æfterfylige, wē ne
cunnun. For ðon gif þēos nīwe lār ōwiht cūðlicre ond gerisenlicre
brenge, þæs weorþe is þæt wē þǣre fȳlgen.' Þeossum wordum
gelīcum ōðre aldormen and ðæs cyninges geþeahteras sprǣcan.

Þā gēn tōætȳhte Cēfi and cwæð, þæt hē wolde Paulīnus þone
40 bisceop geornlīcor gehȳran be þām Gode sprecende þām þe hē
bodade. Þā hēt se cyning swā dōn. Þā hē þā his word gehȳrde, þā
clypode hē and þus cwæð: 'Geare ic þæt ongeat, þæt ðæt nōwiht
wæs þæt wē beēodan; for þon swā micle swā ic geornlīcor on þām
bīgange þæt sylfe sōð sōhte, swā ic hit lǣs mētte. Nū þonne ic
45 openlīce ondette, þæt on þysse lāre þæt sylfe sōð scīneð þæt ūs
mæg þā gyfe syllan ēcre ēadignesse and ēces līfes hǣlo. For þon ic
þonne nū lǣre, cyning, þæt þæt templ and þā wīgbedo, þā ðe wē
būton wæstmum ǣnigre nytnisse hālgodon, þæt wē þā hraþe
forlēosen ond fȳre forbærnen.' Ono hwæt, hē þā se cyning openlīce
50 ondette þām biscope ond him eallum, þæt hē wolde fæstlīce þām
dēofolgildum wiðsacan ond Crīstes gelēafan onfōn.

Mid þȳ þe hē þā se cyning from þǣm foresprecenan biscope
sōhte ond āhsode heora hālignesse þe hēo ǣr biēodon, hwā ðā

25 tō þǣre sprǣce fēng 'took up the discussion', i.e. 'took the floor'.
25–6 mē is gesewen 'seems to me' (literally 'is seen by me').
27 swylc swā (more usually *swylce swā*) + subj. means 'as if'. The poignant
simile introduced here is the subject of Wordsworth's sixteenth Ecclesiastical
Sonnet, but the poet misconstrues the terms of the comparison. The anonymous
counsellor compares the flight of a sparrow through a hall with the life of men on
earth (*þis andwearde līf manna on eorðan*). Wordsworth thinks the comparison is with
'the human Soul . . . / While in the Body lodged, her warm abode'.
37 þæs weorþe is þæt wē 'it is worthy of that, (namely) that we . . .'. The
pleonastic *þæs* anticipates the following clause (§148).
37–8 þeossum wordum gelīcum 'in words like these'.
41 hē i.e. Cefi.
43–4 swā micle swā ic geornlīcor . . . swā ic . . . lǣs 'the more eagerly I . . . the
less I', literally 'by so much as I more eagerly . . . so I less'.
48 þæt wē þā *þæt* conj. repeats the first *þæt* in l. 47; *þā* is a recapitulatory
pronoun (§148).
52–3 biscope . . . heora hālignesse 'high priest . . . of their religion' (i.e. Cefi).
53 hēo nom. pl. refers to Edwin's pagan subjects.

wīgbed ond þā hergas þāra dēofolgilda mid heora hegum þe hēo
55 ymbsette wǣron, hēo ǣrest āīdligan ond tōweorpan scolde, þā
ondsworede hē: 'Efne ic. Hwā mæg þā nū, þā þe ic longe mid
dysignesse beēode, tō bysene ōðerra monna gerisenlecor tōweorpan, þonne ic seolfa þurh þā snytro þe ic from þǣm sōðan Gode
onfēng?' Ond hē ðā sōna from him āwearp þā īdlan dysignesse þe
60 hē ǣr beēode, ond þone cyning bæd þæt hē him wǣpen sealde ond
stōdhors þæt hē meahte on cuman ond dēofolgyld tōweorpan, for
þon þām biscope heora hālignesse ne wæs ālȳfed þæt hē mōste
wǣpen wegan ne elcor būton on mȳran rīdan. þā sealde se cyning
him sweord þæt hē hine mid gyrde ond nom his spere on hond ond
65 hlēop on þæs cyninges stēdan ond tō þǣm dēofulgeldum fērde. þā
ðæt folc hine þā geseah swā gescyrpedne, þā wēndon hēo þæt hē
teola ne wiste, ac þæt hē wēdde. Sōna þæs þe hē nēalēhte tō þǣm
herige, þā scēat hē mid þȳ spere þæt hit sticode fæste on þǣm
herige, ond wæs swīðe gefēonde þǣre ongytenesse þæs sōðan
70 Godes bīgonges. Ond hē ðā hēht his gefēran tōweorpan ealne þone
herig ond þā getimbro, ond forbærnan. Is sēo stōw gȳt ætēawed gū
þāra dēofulgilda nōht feor ēast from Eoforwīcceastre begeondan
Deorwentan þǣre ēa, ond gēn tō dæge is nemned Gōdmundingahām, þǣr se biscop þurh ðæs sōðan Godes inbryrdnesse tōwearp
75 ond fordyde þā wīgbed þe hē seolfa ǣr gehālgode.
   Ðā onfēng Ēadwine cyning mid eallum þǣm æðelingum his
þēode ond mid micle folce Crīstes gelēafan ond fulwihte bæðe þȳ
endlyftan gēare his rīces.

55   hēo recapitulatory pronoun (§148).
56   þā ... þā þe 'those (pagan things) ... which'.
57   ōðerra monna gen. pl. Translate 'for other men'.
67   teola ne wiste 'did not perceive well', i.e. 'was not in his right mind'.
   Sōna þæs þe 'Immediately after', i.e. 'As soon as'. For þæs þe, see §168 þæs (þe)
and §174.2.
   71–2   Is sēo stōw ... dēofulgilda 'The place formerly of the idols is still pointed
out.'

Bede's Account of the Poet Cædmon

Cædmon is the first English poet whose name is known to us. Yet, to say that English poetry begins with him would be misleading, for when Cædmon's Anglo-Saxon forebears migrated from the Continent to the British Isles, they brought with them a well-developed poetic tradition shaped by centuries of oral improvisation in the Germanic north. Not only was this tradition rich with legends and characters, but it also included a highly formalized poetic diction and an intricate system of versification. In the normal course of Christianization this tradition would have been displaced by new subjects and new styles derived from Christian Latin poetry, for medieval missionaries were usually anxious and intolerant in the presence of established pagan traditions. But the ancient Germanic style survived in England, for it was demonstrated soon after the conversion that the old heroic tradition of poetry could be put in the service of Christian themes. The result of this wedding of Christian matter with pagan Germanic style is that unique blend of Christian and heroic elements which characterizes so much Old English poetry, such as *The Dream of the Rood*, *Andreas*, *Exodus*, and *The Fates of the Apostles*.

Bede's account in his *Ecclesiastical History* of how the illiterate cattle-herd Cædmon suddenly began singing of Christian subjects in the old heroic measure seems to capture that moment in history when two cultures began to merge. To the Anglo-Saxons, Cædmon's miracle was his instantaneous acquisition of the power of poetic composition through the agency of a divinely inspired dream. Modern readers familiar with the widely documented folk-motif of men suddenly acquiring poetic powers through a dream may dismiss Bede's story as essentially fabulous, but the nine-line *Hymn* itself attests to a minor miracle of literary history that cannot be denied: in these polished verses Cædmon demonstrated that the ancient heroic style was not incompatible with Christian doctrine and hence was worthy of preservation. The old Germanic poets had hailed Woden with such terms as 'Father of Armies' (cf. Old Norse *Herja-faðir* in the *Edda*) and Cædmon skilfully adapts the formula to make it reflect the Christian term for God, 'Father of

Glory' (Ephesians 1:17): *Wuldorfæder*. Kings were referred to as 'guardians of the realm' in traditional Anglo-Saxon poetry (cf. *Brytenrīces weard* and *rīces weard* in other Old English poems) and Cædmon appropriates the term for Christian poetry by altering it to *heofonrīces Weard*. The metre and the dignity of the phrases remain intact; only the spiritual quality has been changed. Through such expedients as these the ancient style was saved from disrepute and extinction, so that even poets who wished to treat subjects not specifically Christian (such as the poets of *Finnsburg*, *Maldon*, or *The Battle of Brunanburh*) were free to do so without reproach from the Christian establishment. And monastic scribes did not hesitate to preserve poems written in the old measure, thus making it possible for us to read today specimens of the earliest English poetry which would otherwise have been lost forever.

The text of the Old English Bede presented here is that of the Bodleian Library MS Tanner 10, although we have occasionally adopted a reading from one of the other manuscripts when these seemed preferable to Tanner, most notably in lines 32, 35, 36, 47, and 69.

In ðeosse abbudissan mynstre wæs sum brōðor syndriglīce mid godcundre gife gemǣred ond geweorðad, for þon hē gewunade gerisenlice lēoð wyrcan, þā ðe tō æfæstnisse ond tō ārfæstnisse belumpen, swa ðætte, swā hwæt swā hē of godcundum stafum þurh
5 bōceras geleornode, þæt hē æfter medmiclum fæce in scopgereorde mid þā mǣstan swētnisse ond inbryrdnisse geglǣngde ond in Engliscgereorde wel geworht forþbrōhte. Ond for his lēoþsongum monigra monna mōd oft tō worulde forhogdnisse ond tō geþēodnisse þæs heofonlican līfes onbærnde
10 wǣron. Ond ēac swelce monige ōðre æfter him in Ongelþēode ongunnon æfæste lēoð wyrcan; ac nǣnig hwæðre him þæt gelīce dōn meahte, for þon hē nales from monnum ne þurh mon gelǣred wæs, þæt hē þone lēoðcræft leornade, ac hē wæs godcundlīce gefultumed ond þurh Godes gife þone songcræft onfēng. Ond hē
15 for ðon nǣfre nōht lēasunge ne īdles lēoþes wyrcan meahte, ac efne þā ān þā ðe tō æfæstnesse belumpon, ond his þā æfestan tungan gedafenode singan.

9 geþēodnisse 'joining' of the heavenly life. This very awkward sense is probably the result of confusion (by the translator or a scribe) between Latin *appetitum* 'longing' (which is what Bede wrote in the Latin version) and *appictum*, past participle of *appingo* 'join'. 'Longing for the heavenly life' is what Bede intended.

16–17 his þā æfestan ... singan '(it) befitted that pious tongue of his to sing' (§212).

Wæs hē se mon in weoruldhāde geseted oð þā tīde þe hē wæs
gelȳfdre ylde, ond hē næfre nænig lēoð geleornade. Ond hē for þon
20 oft in gebēorscipe, þonne þær wæs blisse intinga gedēmed, þæt hēo
ealle sceolden þurh endebyrdnesse be hearpan singan, þonne hē
geseah þā hearpan him nēalēcan, þonne ārās hē for scome from
þǣm symble ond hām ēode tō his hūse. þā hē þæt þā sumre tīde
dyde, þæt hē forlēt þæt hūs þæs gebēorscipes ond ūt wæs gongende
25 tō nēata scipene, þāra heord him wæs þǣre neahte beboden, þā hē
ðā þǣr in gelimplicre tīde his leomu on reste gesette ond onslēpte,
þā stōd him sum mon æt þurh swefn ond hine hālette ond grētte
ond hine be his noman nemnde: 'Cedmon, sing mē hwæthwugu.'
þā ondswarede hē ond cwæð: 'Ne con ic nōht singan; ond ic for
30 þon of þeossum gebēorscipe ūt ēode, ond hider gewāt, for þon ic
nāht singan ne cūðe.' Eft hē cwæð, se ðe mid hine sprecende wæs:
'Hwæðre þū meaht mē singan.' þā cwæð hē: 'Hwæt sceal ic
singan?' Cwæð hē: 'Sing mē frumsceaft.' þā hē ðā þās andsware
onfēng, þā ongon hē sōna singan in herenesse Godes Scyppendes
35 þā fers ond þā word þe hē næfre gehȳrde, þāra endebyrdnes þis is:

> Nū wē sculon herigean heofonrīces Weard,
> Meotodes meahte ond his mōdgeþanc,
> weorc Wuldorfæder, swā hē wundra gehwæs,
> ēce Drihten, ōr onstealde.
> 40 Hē ǣrest sceōp eorðan bearnum
> heofon tō hrōfe, hālig Scyppend.
> þā middangeard monncynnes Weard,
> ēce Drihten, æfter tēode
> fīrum foldan, Frēa ælmihtig.

45 þā ārās hē from þǣm slǣpe, ond eal þā þe hē slǣpende song
fæste in gemynde hæfde, ond þǣm wordum sōna monig word in
þæt ilce gemet Gode wyrðes songes tōgeþēodde. þā cōm hē on

19–28 Ond hē ... nemnde See §153. For the semantic distinction between
þonne and *þā*, see §168 *þonne* 2.

20 þonne þær ... gedēmed, þæt 'whenever it was deemed (that there was)
cause for merriment there, (namely) that ...'. The sense of the Latin is different:
'whenever it would be decided, for the sake of merriment, that ...'. The Old English
translator mistook the Latin ablative *causā* for a nominative, thus arriving at his
version.

25 þāra heord 'the care of which'.

32 þū meaht mē singan 'thou canst sing to me'. See §207 and fn.

45 eal þā þe 'all those (things) which'.

47 Gode wyrðes songes 'of song dear to God'. Since this sentence tells us that
Cædmon immediately added more verses to the nine lines he composed in his
dream (and presumably sang this completed version to the Abbess and her
scholars), we should regard the text which we now call 'Cædmon's Hymn' as only a
fragment, the opening lines of a much longer poem in praise of the Creator.

morgenne tō þǣm tūngerēfan, þe his ealdormon wæs; sægde him
hwylce gife hē onfēng. Ond hē hine sōna tō þǣre abbudissan
gelǣdde ond hire þā cȳðde ond sægde. þā hēht hēo gesomnian
ealle þā gelǣredestan men ond þā leorneras, ond him ondweardum
hēt secgan þæt swefn ond þæt lēoð singan, þæt ealra heora dōme
gecoren wǣre, hwæt oððe hwonon þæt cuman wǣre. þā wæs him
eallum gesegen, swā swā hit wæs, þæt him wǣre from Drihtne
sylfum heofonlic gifu forgifen. þā rehton hēo him ond sægdon sum
hālig spell ond godcundre lāre word; bebudon him þā, gif hē
meahte, þæt hē in swinsunge lēoþsonges þæt gehwyrfde. þā hē ðā
hæfde þā wīsan onfongne, þā ēode hē hām tō his hūse, and cwōm
eft on morgenne, ond þȳ betstan lēoðe geglenged him āsong ond
āgeaf þæt him beboden wæs.

Ðā ongan sēo abbudisse clyppan ond lufigean þā Godes gife in
þǣm men; ond hēo hine þā monade ond lǣrde þæt hē woruldhād
ānforlēte ond munuchād onfēnge; ond hē þæt wel þafode. Ond hēo
hine in þæt mynster onfēng mid his gōdum, ond hine geþēodde tō
gesomnunge þāra Godes þēowa, ond hēht hine lǣran þæt getæl
þæs hālgan stǣres ond spelles. Ond hē eal þā hē in gehȳrnesse
geleornian meahte mid hine gemyndgade, ond swā swā clǣne nēten
eodorcende in þæt swēteste lēoð gehwerfde. Ond his song ond his
lēoð wǣron swā wynsumu tō gehȳranne þætte þā seolfan his
lārēowas æt his mūðe wreoton ond leornodon. Song hē ǣrest be
middangeardes gesceape ond bī fruman moncynnes ond eal þæt
stǣr Genesis (þæt is sēo ǣreste Moyses booc); ond eft bī ūtgonge
Israhēla folces of Ægypta londe ond bī ingonge þæs gehātlandes
ond bī ōðrum monegum spellum þæs hālgan gewrites canōnes
bōca, ond bī Crīstes menniscnesse ond bī his þrōwunge ond bī his
ūpāstīgnesse in heofonas ond bī þæs Hālgan Gāstes cyme ond þāra
apostola lāre; ond eft bī þǣm dæge þæs tōweardan dōmes ond bī
fyrhtu þæs tintreglican wiites ond bī swētnesse þæs heofonlecan
rīces hē monig lēoð geworhte. Ond swelce ēac ōðer monig be þǣm
godcundan fremsumnessum ond dōmum hē geworhte. In eallum

51 **him ondweardum** 'with them present', i.e. 'in their presence'.
52–3 **þæt ealra ... cuman wǣre** 'so that it might be determined by the judgement of them all what (that poetic skill was) or whence it had come'. The Old
English is awkward and unidiomatic because the translator is following his Latin
source too slavishly.
55 **hēo** 'they'. The same spelling of nom. pl. occurs below in ll. 101, 104, 106, 107,
and 114.
59–60 **ond þȳ ... wæs** 'and sang and gave back to them what had been dictated
to him, adorned with the best poetry'.
66 **eal þā** 'all those things which'.
67 **mid hine gemyndgade** 'remembered within himself', i.e. 'mulled over'.
69–70 **þā seolfan his lārēowas** 'the same ones his teachers', i.e. 'his very
teachers'.

þǣm hē geornlīce gēmde þæt hē men ātuge from synna lufan ond
māndǣda, ond tō lufan ond tō geornfulnesse āwehte gōdra dǣda;
for þon hē wæs se mon swīþe ǣfæst ond regollecum þēodscipum
ēaðmōdlīce underþēoded. Ond wið þǣm þā ðe in ōðre wīsan dōn
85   woldon, hē wæs mid welme micelre ellenwōdnisse onbærned; ond
hē for ðon fægre ænde his līf betȳnde ond geendade.

For þon þā ðǣre tīde nēalǣcte his gewitenesse ond forðfōre, þā
wæs hē, fēowertȳnum dagum ǣr, þæt hē wæs līchomlicre untrymnesse þrycced ond hefgad, hwæðre tō þon gemetlīce þæt hē ealle
90   þā tīd meahte ge sprecan ge gongan. Wæs þǣr in nēaweste
untrumra monna hūs, in þǣm heora þēaw wæs þæt hēo þā untrumran ond þā ðe æt forðfōre wǣron inlǣdan sceoldon, ond him þǣr
ætsomne þegnian. þā bæd hē his þegn on ǣfenne þǣre neahte þe
hē of worulde gongende wæs þæt hē in þǣm hūse him stōwe
95   gegearwode þæt hē gerestan meahte. þā wundrode se þegn for
hwon hē ðæs bǣde, for þon him þūhte þæt his forðfōr swā nēah ne
wǣre; dyde hwæðre swā swā hē cwæð ond bibēad. Ond mid þȳ hē
ðā þǣr on reste ēode, ond hē gefēonde mōde sumu þing mid him
sprecende ætgædere ond glēowiende wæs, þe þǣr ǣr inne wǣron,
100 þā wæs ofer middeneaht þæt hē frægn hwæðer hēo ǣnig hūsl inne
hæfdon. þā ondswarodon hēo ond cwǣdon: 'Hwylc þearf is ðē
hūsles? Ne þīnre forþfōre swā nēah is, nū þū þus rōtlīce ond þus
glædlīce tō ūs sprecende eart.' Cwæð hē eft: 'Bera'ð mē hūsl tō.' þā
hē hit þā on honda hæfde, þā frægn hē hwæþer hēo ealle smolt mōd
105 ond būton eallum incan blīðe tō him hæfdon. þā ondswaredon hȳ
ealle ond cwǣdon þæt hēo nǣnigne incan tō him wiston, ac hēo
ealle him swīðe blīðemōde wǣron; ond hēo wrixendlīce hine
bǣdon þæt hē him eallum blīðe wǣre. þā ondswarade hē ond
cwæð: 'Mīne brōðor, mīne þā lēofan, ic eom swīðe blīðemōd tō
110 ēow ond tō eallum Godes monnum.' Ond swā wæs hine getrym-
mende mid þȳ heofonlecan wegneste ond him ōðres līfes ingong
gegearwode. þā gȳt hē frægn, hū nēah þǣre tīde wǣre þætte þā
brōðor ārīsan scolden ond Godes lof rǣran ond heora ūhtsong
singan. þā ondswaredon hēo: 'Nis hit feor tō þon.' Cwæð hē:

87   nēalǣcte '(it) drew near' (§212).
88   þæt hē wæs In a clumsy effort to control the sentence the translator
introduces these three redundant words (§148). Ignore them when rendering into
modern English.
89   tō þon gemetlīce þæt 'to that (extent) moderately that', i.e. 'sufficiently
moderately that'.
92   æt forðfōre 'at (the point of) death'.
99   þe The antecedent is *him* in l. 98. See §163.4.
104–5   smolt mōd . . . hæfdon 'had a serene and friendly spirit without any
rancour toward him'.
106   nǣnigne incan . . . wiston 'felt no rancour toward him'.

115 'Teala: wuton wē wel þǣre tīde bīdan.' Ond þā him gebæd ond
hine gesegnode mid Crīstes rōdetācne, ond his hēafod onhylde tō
þām bolstre, ond medmicel fæc onslēpte, ond swā mid stilnesse his
līf geendade. Ond swā wæs geworden þætte swā swā hē hlūttre
mōde ond bilwitre ond smyltre wilsumnesse Drihtne þēode, þæt hē
120 ēac swylce swā smylte dēaðe middangeard wæs forlǣtende, ond tō
his gesihðe becwōm. Ond sēo tunge, þe swā monig halwende word
in þæs Scyppendes lof gesette, hē ðā swelce ēac þā ȳtmæstan word
in his herenisse, hine seolfne segniende ond his gāst in his honda
bebēodende, betȳnde. Ēac swelce þæt is gesegen þæt hē wære
125 gewis his seolfes forðfōre, of þǣm wē nū secgan hȳrdon.

121–4 Ond sēo tunge . . . betȳnde The awkward change of subject from *sēo tunge*
to *hē* is the result of a mistranslation, the Latin ablative *illáque linguá* having been
mistaken for a nominative. The Anglo-Saxon translator ought to have written *mid
þǣre tungan*: 'And with the tongue that had composed so many salutary words . . . he
then concluded his last words', etc.

124–5   is gesegen . . . of þǣm wē 'it is seen from what we'.

The Goths and Boethius: Prose and Verse from the Introduction to King Alfred's Boethius Translation

Among the works which King Alfred the Great translated into Old English as part of his educational programme (see selection 5 above and §251.2) was the philosophical treatise *De consolatione philosophiae* by the Roman consul Boethius. One of the most popular writings of the entire Middle Ages, the *Consolation* was composed after its author had been falsely accused of treason and imprisoned by Theodoric, King of the Ostrogoths and ruler in Rome. The injustice which occasioned Boethius's search for consolation and the pathos of his subsequent murder give the work a special force and immediacy, and so it is not surprising that King Alfred prefaced his translation with an account of the historical background of Boethius's fate: the invasion of Rome by the Goths, Theodoric's rise to power, and the imprisonment and execution of the philosopher. Nor is it surprising that this prefatory material should be recounted first in prose and then in poetry, for much of the Latin *Consolatio* itself is written in verse, and the Old English translator has left both prose and poetic renditions of each verse passage. The existence of these dual versions of the same material affords the modern student an excellent means of becoming acquainted with the form and style of Old English poetry. In the selection which follows (containing King Alfred's preface to his translation) one sees some of the most prominent features which differentiate the language of Old English poetry from that of Old English prose: the fondness for apposition, complicated syntax, colourful compounds like *sinc-geofa* and *wēalāf*, and a wealth of poetic synonyms for concepts like warrior and war.

The text for the prose (*a*) is from Bodleian Library MS 180 (except that *mið* [l. 2], *and* [l. 3], *gelæst* [l. 9], and *arwyrða wæs on* [l. 26] have been changed to *mid*, *hī þā*, *gelæste*, and *ārwyrða on*). The text for the verse (*b*) is from Bodleian Library MS Junius 12, except that *Gotene* [l. 5], *ealla* [l. 12], *Godena* [l. 38], *weorðmynða* [l. 51], and *hererine* [l. 71] have been changed to *Gotena*, *ealle*, *Gotena*, *weorðmynda*, and *hererinc*.

(*a*)

On ðǣre tīde ðe Gotan of Sciððiu mægðe wið Rōmāna rīce gewin ūp āhōfon and mid heora cyningum, Rǣdgōta and Eallerīca wǣron hātne, Rōmāne burig ābrǣcon, hī þā eall Ītālia rīce þæt is betwux þām muntum and Sicilia þām ēalonde in anwald gerehton; and þā
5   æfter þām foresprecenan cyningum þēodrīc fēng tō þām ilcan rīce. Se þēodrīc wæs Amulinga. Hē wæs Crīsten, þēah hē on þām Arriāniscan gedwolan þurhwunode. Hē gehēt Rōmanum his frēondscipe, swā þæt hī mōstan heora ealdrihta wyrðe bēon, ac hē þā gehāt swīðe yfele gelǣste, and swīðe wrāðe geendode mid
10 manegum māne. þæt wæs, tō ēacan ōðrum unārīmedum yflum, þæt hē Iōhannes þone pāpan hēt ofslēan.

þā wæs sum consul, þæt wē heretoha hātað, Bōētius wæs gehāten, se wæs in bōccræftum and on woruldþēawum se rihtwīsesta. Sē þā ongeat þā manigfealdan yfel þe se cyning
15 Ðeodrīc wið þǣm crīstenandōme and wið þām Rōmaniscum witum dyde. Hē þā gemunde þāra ēðnessa and þāra ealdrihta þe hī under þām cāserum hæfdon, heora ealdhlāfordum. þā ongan hē smēagan and leornigan on him selfum hū hē þæt rīce þām unriht-wīsan cyninge āferran mihte and on ryhtgelēaffulra and on
20 rihtwīsra anwealde gebringan. Sende þā dīgellīce ǣrendgewritu tō

2–3   **Rǣdgōta . . . hātne** '(who) were called Rædgota and Alaric'. See §186. The Anglo-Saxon writer is here telescoping (and confusing) actual events. The heathen Goth Radagaesius (*Rǣdgota*) was killed in battle five years before Alaric led his troops into Rome.

4   **in anwald gerehton** 'subjugated'.

4–5   The Anglo-Saxon writer here skips over many years and several reigns. Theodoric did not become King of Italy until A.D. 493 – more than eighty years after the death of Alaric.

5   **foresprecenan** The ending *-an* stands here for dat. pl. *-um*; see §65; cf. *gesceappēotan* 11(g)/4.

8   **heora ealdrihta wyrðe bēon** 'be in possession of their ancient rights', i.e. 'regain their ancient rights'.

11   **Iōhannes . . . ofslēan** In 525 Theodoric had Pope John I cast into prison, where he languished and soon died.

12–13   **Bōētius wæs gehāten** '(who) was named Boethius'.

14   **Sē þā ongeat** 'he then perceived'.

16–17   **hī under . . . ealdhlāfordum** *cāserum* and *ealdhlāfordum* are in apposition: 'they had under the emperors, their ancient lords'.

17–19   **þā ongan hē . . . āferran mihte** 'then he began to study and take thought within himself as to how he might remove the kingdom from the unrighteous king'. Actually Boethius denied that he had betrayed the King in this way, but his enemies claimed that he had written treasonous letters to the eastern emperor Justin I.

þām kāsere tō Constentinopolim, þǣr is Crēca hēahburg and heora
cynestōl, forþām se kāsere wæs heora ealdhlāfordcynnes. Bǣdon
hine þæt hē him tō heora crīstendōme and tō heora ealdrihtum
gefultumede. þā þæt ongeat se wælhrēowa cyning Ðēodrīc, þā hēt
25 hē hine gebringan on carcerne and þǣrinne belūcan. þā hit ðā
gelomp þæt se ārwyrða on swā micelre nearanessa becōm, þā wæs
hē swā micle swīðor on his mōde gedrēfed swā his mōd ǣr swīðor
tō þām woruldsǣlþum gewunod wæs; and hē þā nānre frōfre
beinnan þām carcerne ne gemunde, ac hē gefēoll niwol ofdūne on
30 þā flōr, and hine āstrehte swīðe unrōt, and ormōd hine selfne ongan
wēpan and þus singend cwæð.

(b)

Hit wæs gēara iū,   ðætte Gotan ēastan
of Sciððia   sceldas lǣddon,
þrēate geþrungon   þēodlond monig;
setton sūðweardes   sigeþēoda twā.
5 Gotena rīce   gēarmǣlum wēox.
Hæfdan him gecynde   cyningas twēgen,
Rǣdgōd and Alerīc;   rīce geþungon.
þā wæs ofer Muntgīop   monig ātyhted
Gota gylpes full,   gūðe gelysted,
10 folcgewinnes;   fana hwearfode
scīr on sceafte;   scēotend þōhton
Ītālia   ealle gegongan,
lindwīgende.   Hī gelǣstan swuā
efne from Muntgīop   oð þone mǣran wearoð,
15 þǣr Sīcilia   sǣstrēamum in
ēglond micel,   ēðel mǣrsað.
Ðā wæs Rōmāna   rīce gewunnen,
ābrocen burga cyst;   beadurincum wæs
Rōm gerȳmed;   Rǣdgōt and Alerīc
20 fōron on ðæt fæsten;   flēah cāsere
mid þām æþelingum   ūt on Crēcas.

(a) 22–4 **Bǣdon hine þæt ... gefultumede** 'bade him that he should assist them
(to return) to their Christianity and their ancient laws'. 'Their Christianity' is the
orthodox Christianity that the Romans were practising when the Arian Christian,
Theodoric, conquered them. Late in his reign he began to persecute them.

24–5 **hēt hē hine ... belūcan** Active infinitives to be translated as passive: 'he
commanded him to be brought to prison and to be locked up therein'. See §161.

26–8 **wæs hē swā micle swīðor ... gewunod wæs** 'he was so much the more
troubled in his mind in as much as his mind had previously been accustomed to
earthly blessings'.

Ne meahte þā sēo wēalāf   wīge forstandan
Gotan mid gūðe;   gīomonna gestrīon;
sealdon unwillum   eþelweardas,
25   hālige āðas.   Wæs gehwæðeres waa.
þēah wæs magorinca   mōd mid Crēcum,
gif hī lēodfruman   læstan dorsten.
Stōd þrāge on ðam;   þēod wæs gewunnen
wintra mænigo,   oðþæt wyrd gescrāf
30   þæt þe þēodrīce   þegnas and eorlas
hēran sceoldan.   Wæs se heretēma
Crīste gecnōden;   cyning selfa onfēng
fulluhtþēawum.   Fægnodon ealle
Rōmwara bearn   and him recene tō
35   friðes wilnedon.   Hē him fæste gehēt,
þæt hȳ ealdrihta   ælces mōsten
wyrðe gewunigen   on þære welegan byrig,
ðenden God wuolde,   þæt hē Gotena geweald
āgan mōste.   Hē þæt eall ālēag.
40   Wæs þæm æþelinge   Arriānes
gedwola lēofre   þonne Drihtnes ǣ.
Hēt Iōhannes,   gōdne pāpan,
hēafde behēawan;   næs ðæt hærlic dæd!
Ēac þā wæs unrīm   ōðres mānes,
45   þæt se Gota fremede   gōdra gehwilcum.
Ðā wæs rīcra sum   on Rōme byrig
āhefen heretoga,   hlāforde lēof,
þenden cynestōle   Crēacas wīoldon.
þæt wæs rihtwīs rinc;   næs mid Rōmwarum
50   sincgeofa sēlla   siððan longe;
hē wæs for weorulde wīs,   weorðmynda georn,
beorn bōca glēaw.   Bōītius

25 **Wæs gehwæðeres waa** 'It was an affliction (to the Romans) in both respects';
(to have to give both their wealth and their sacred oaths to the conquerors).

26–7 **þēah wæs ... dorsten** The conquered Romans looked to the Greeks in
the Eastern Empire (in Constantinople) for rescue from their Gothic invaders.
Under duress they had given 'holy vows' for allegiance to the Goths (l. 25a), 'Yet the
heart of the (Roman) warriors was with the Greeks if they would dare to help the
leader of the people (i.e. the exiled Roman emperor).'

28 **Stōd þrāge on ðām** 'it remained thus for a time'.

31–2 **Wæs ... Crīste gecnōden** 'was imputed to Christ', i.e. 'bore the Christian
name'.

34–5 **and him ... wilnedon** 'and soon petitioned for peace from him'.

48 **þenden ... wīoldon** 'while the Greeks controlled the throne'. Theodoric's
predecessor, Odowacer, had acknowledged the overlordship of the eastern emperor
in Constantinople, as had Theodoric when he became king, but Theodoric's
relations with the Greek emperor became strained in the closing years of his reign.

se hǣle hātte;   sē þone hlīsan geþāh.
Wæs him on gemynde   mǣla gehwilce
55 yfel and edwit,   þæt him elðēodge
kyningas cȳðdon;   wæs on Crēacas hold,
gemunde þāra āra   and ealdrihta,
þe his eldran mid him   āhton longe,
lufan and lissa.   Angan þā listum ymbe
60 ðencean þearflīce,   hū hē ðider meahte
Crēcas oncerran,   þæt se cāsere eft
anwald ofer hī   āgan mōste.
Sende ǣrendgewrit   ealdhlāfordum
dēgelīce,   and hī for Drihtne bæd
65 ealdum trēowum,   ðæt hī æft tō him
cōmen on þā ceastre,   lēte Crēca witan
rǣdan Rōmwarum,   rihtes wyrðe
lēte þone lēodscipe.   Ðā þā lāre ongeat
Ðēodrīc Amuling   and þone þegn oferfēng,
70 hēht fæstlīce   folcgesīðas
healdon þone hererinc;   wæs him hrēoh sefa,
ege from ðām eorle.   Hē hine inne hēht
on carcerne   clūstre belūcan.
þā wæs mōdsefa   miclum gedrēfed
75 Bōētius.   Brēac longe ǣr
wlencea under wolcnum;   hē þȳ wyrs meahte
þolian þā þrāge,   þā hīo swā þearl becōm.
Wæs þā ormōd eorl,   āre ne wēnde,
ne on þām fæstene   frōfre gemunde;
80 ac hē neowol āstreaht   niðer ofdūne
fēol on þā flōre;   fela worda spræc
forþōht ðearle;   ne wēnde þonan ǣfre
cuman of ðǣm clammum.   Cleopode tō Drihtne
gēomran stemne,   gyddode þus.

58   þe his eldran ... longe 'that his elders long had among themselves'.
64–5   hī for Drihtne ... trēowum 'asked them for the sake of God, (and because of their) ancient beliefs'.
66–8   lēte Crēca ... lēodscipe 'let Greek senators worthy of rule, let that nation have control over the Romans'.
71–2   'his (Boethius') mind was troubled, (in him was) fear of the leader (Theodoric)'.
72–3   Hē hine ... belūcan 'He commanded him to be locked in a prison, in a cell.' *Hine* is the object of *belūcan*. See §161.
76–7   hē þȳ wyrs ... becōm 'the worse he was able to endure so harsh a time when it befell'.
84   The lament which follows is the first of the Latin metres of Boethius, translated into OE.

Riddles

Riddles are popular in most cultures, and their presence in the Bible (e.g. Judges 14:14) and in Greek tragedy reminds us that they are more than a children's game. In the Old English period scholars like Aldhelm and Symphosius composed verse riddles in polished Latin hexameters, and the anonymous vernacular riddles presented here are sometimes based upon Latin originals. Indeed, since the Latin riddles are accompanied by their solutions (as the Old English are not), this correspondence between Latin and vernacular riddles has sometimes helped scholars to solve some knottier enigmas among the latter.

The Old English verse riddles fall into two basic types. In one type the riddler speaks in his own voice (*Ic seah, Wiga is*) describing the subject of the riddle and asking the reader to guess the answer. The description is in vague, metaphorical, deliberately misleading language with much anthropomorphizing of animals and inanimate objects. In the second type, which is equally mystifying and indirect in expression, the subject of the riddle describes itself (*Ic eom, Ic wæs*) and asks to be identified. The idea of inanimate objects speaking about themselves was not unfamiliar to Anglo-Saxons, for when they inscribed a weapon or piece of jewellery to mark possession, they often put the statement in the first person singular, as if the object itself were speaking. Thus the inscription on the King Alfred Jewel says, 'Ælfred mec het gewyrcan' ('Alfred had me made'), while another says, 'Ædred mec ah, Eanred mec agrof' ('Ædred owns me, Eanred engraved me'). This habit of mind culminates in one of the grandest achievements of Old English poetry, *The Dream of the Rood* (selection 14 below), in which the cross on which Christ died recounts with agony and awe the grim details of the crucifixion. Indeed, two of the riddles printed below (texts *n* and *o*) appear to have 'cross' as their solution and so may be seen as seed stages of *The Dream of the Rood*.

The subjects of the riddles presented here are various: farm implements, weapons, animals and insects, items of food or drink, the Bible, the natural world. Casual and intimate, they are brief meditations on familiar objects. They are often light but rarely humorous, and sometimes the riddlers seem to forget their primary purpose of creating a puzzle as they become absorbed in the curiosities and quaint perplexities which become apparent in the objects around us when we reflect on them. They explore paradoxes both in the object described and in the language describing the objects. Thoughtful probings of both the milieu and the language, the riddles reveal quirks and moods of the Anglo-Saxons quite unlike anything we find in their other poetry.

The riddles presented here have been selected from the Exeter Book, a tenth-century manuscript which contains some of the best poetry left by the Anglo-Saxons. It is a rich poetic miscellany containing nearly a hundred verse riddles and more than thirty different poems including *The Wife's Lament*, *The Wanderer*, and *The Seafarer*, all three of which appear below (selections 15, 16, and 17).

(a)

Wer sæt æt wīne   mid his wīfum twām
ond his twēgen suno   ond his twā dohtor,
swāse gesweostor,   ond hyra suno twēgen,
frēolico frumbearn;   fæder wæs þǣr inne
5   þāra æþelinga   ǣghwæðres mid,
ēam ond nefa.   Ealra wǣron fife
eorla ond idesa   insittendra.

(b)

Wiht cwōm gongan   þǣr weras sǣton
monige on mæðle,   mōde snottre;
hæfde ān ēage   ond ēaran twā,
ond twēgen fēt,   twelf hund hēafda,
5   hrycg ond wombe   ond honda twā,
earmas ond eaxle,   ānne swēoran
ond sīdan twā.   Saga hwæt ic hātte.

Riddle a The solution is 'Lot and his offspring'. Genesis 19:30–8 tells how Lot's two daughters, after an incestuous union with their father, each gave birth to a son. The riddle explores the complicated, overlapping kinship relations which resulted. Emendations: *Wer* for MS *wær* (l. 1), *hyra* for *hyre* (l. 3).

6 ēam ond nefa This refers to the sons in relation to each other. Since Lot is the father both of the daughters and their two sons, his four offspring are siblings. Therefore each son is both uncle and nephew to the other.

Riddle b The solution is 'one-eyed garlic pedlar'. Emendation: *hrycg* for MS *hryc* (l. 5).

(*c*)

Moððe word fræt.　Mē þæt þūhte
wrǣtlicu wyrd,　þā ic þæt wundor gefrægn,
þæt se wyrm forswealg　wera gied sumes,
þēof in þȳstro,　þrymfæstne cwide
5　ond þæs strangan staþol.　Stǣlgiest ne wæs
wihte þȳ glēawra,　þe hē þām wordum swealg.

(*d*)

Hrægl mīn swīgað,　þonne īc hrūsan trede,
oþþe þā wīc būge,　oþþe wado drēfe.
Hwīlum mec āhebbað　ofer hæleþa byht
hyrste mīne　ond þēos hēa lyft,
5　ond mec þonne wīde　wolcna strengu
ofer folc byreð.　Frætwe mīne
swōgað hlūde　ond swinsiað,
torhte singað,　þonne ic getenge ne bēom
flōde ond foldan,　fērende gæst.

Riddle c　Since the first word identifies the subject of the poem, this is not a riddle so much as an exploration of a paradox: the insect devours learning but is none the wiser for it. The whimsical meditation is enhanced by delicate puns on words like (*for*)*swelgan* (which can mean 'understand' as well as 'consume') and *cwide* (which can mean 'morsel' as well as 'statement').

5　þæs strangan staþol 'the (very) foundation of that mighty (utterance)', i.e. the vellum on which the *cwide* is written. *Staþol* could also refer to the intellectual content of the statement (cf. *staþolung* 'ordinance').

5–6　ne . . . swealg 'was not a whit the wiser in that he had swallowed (comprehended) those words'. For the þȳ . . . þe construction, see §167(*a*) and §177.3.

Riddle d　The solution is 'swan'. The Anglo-Saxons believed that when the swan was aloft the feathers in its wings produced music. In typical riddling fashion the poet refers to the swan's feathers with vague, metaphorical words like *hrægl* 'raiment', *hyrst* 'equipment', and *frætwe* 'trappings'.

5　wolcna strengu 'The strength of the skies' is the wind.

(e)

Nis mīn sele swīge,   ne ic sylfa hlūd
ymb dryhtsele;   unc dryhten scōp
sīþ ætsomne.   Ic eom swiftra þonne hē,
þrāgum strengra,   hē þreohtigra.
5 Hwīlum ic mē reste;   hē sceal rinnan forð.
Ic him in wunige   ā þenden ic lifge;
gif wit unc gedǣlað,   mē bið dēað witod.

(f)

Ic eom weorð werum,   wīde funden,
brungen of bearwum   ond of bēorghleoþum,
of denum ond of dūnum.   Dæges mec wǣgun
feþre on lifte,   feredon mid liste
5 under hrōfes hlēo.   Hæleð mec siþþan
baþedan in bydene.   Nū ic eom bindere
ond swingere,   sōna weorpe
esne tō eorþan,   hwīlum ealdne ceorl.
Sōna þæt onfindeð,   se þe mec fēhð ongēan
10 ond wið mægenþisan   mīnre genǣsteð,
þæt hē hrycge sceal   hrūsan sēcan,
gif hē unrǣdes   ǣr ne geswīceð.
Strengo bistolen,   strong on sprǣce,
mægene binumen,   nāh his mōdes geweald,
15 fōta ne folma.   Frige hwæt ic hātte,
ðe on eorþan swā   esnas binde,
dole æfter dyntum   be dæges lēohte.

Riddle e The solution is 'fish in the river'. The poet delights in the paradox of the silent, versatile fish in the rushing stream, which, though seemingly insubstantial, is essential to the fish's life and will survive its death. Emendations: *ymb dryhtsele*; *unc dryhten scōp* for MS *ymb unc . . . dryht scop* (l. 2), *swiftra* for *swistre* (l. 3), *rinnan* for *yrnan* (l. 5).

1 *Eom* is understood before *ic*.

Riddle f The solution is 'mead', an alcoholic beverage made from honey. Emendations: *bēorghleoþum* (l. 2) for MS *burghleoþum*, *weorpe* for *weorpere* (l. 7), *esne* for *efne* (l. 8).

3 **Dæges** 'by day'. See §190.5.

4 **feþre** The wings of the bees who gather the honey from which mead is made and bring it to the hive (*under hrōfes hlēo*).

17 **be dæges lēohte** i.e. the morning after.

(g)

Ic þā wiht geseah   wǣpnedcynnes.
Geoguðmyrþe grǣdig   him on gafol forlēt
ferðfriþende   fēower wellan
scīre scēotan   on gesceapþēotan.

5   Mon maþelade,   se þe mē gesǣgde:
'Sēo wiht, gif hīo gedȳgeð,   dūna briceð;
gif hē tōbirsteð,   bindeð cwice.'

(h)

Agob is mīn noma   eft onhwyrfed;
ic eom wrǣtlic wiht   on gewin sceapen.
þonne ic onbūge,   ond mē on bōsme fareð
ǣtren onga,   ic bēom eallgearo

5   þæt ic mē þæt feorhbealo   feor āswāpe.
Siþþan mē se waldend,   se mē þæt wite gescōp,
leoþo forlǣteð,   ic bēo lengre þonne ǣr,
oþþæt ic spǣte   spilde geblonden
ealfelo āttor   þæt ic ǣr gegēap.

10   Ne tōgongeð þæs   gumena hwylcum,
ǣnigum ēaþe   þæt ic þēr ymb sprice,
gif hine hrīneð   þæt mē of hrife flēogeð,
þæt þone māndrinc   mægne gecēapaþ,
fullwer fæste   fēore sīne.

15   Nelle ic unbunden   ǣnigum hȳran
nymþe searosǣled.   Saga hwæt ic hātte.

Riddle g   The solution is 'bull calf' or 'young ox'. In related contemporary Latin riddles, the poets make much of the calf's drinking milk from the 'four fountains' of the mother. Emendation: *Geoguðmyrþe* for MS *geoguð myrwe* (l. 2).

2   **him on gafol** 'as a gift to himself'.

6–7   i.e. while alive the bull will break the ground by pulling a plough through it, while the dead bull's hide will provide leather thongs that can tie people up. The shift from the grammatical gender of *wiht* in l. 6 to the logical gender of a bull in l. 7 may be intentionally mystifying.

Riddle h   The solution 'bow' is spelled backwards in the first word in the riddle. (This reverse spelling of *boga* was corrupted to *agof* by an inattentive scribe.) The riddler speaks first of the arrow as it passes into the bosom of the arched bow as the bowman takes aim (ll. 2–5) and then of the arrow's flight to its target after it is released (ll. 6–9). Emendations besides *Agob* are *on* for MS *of* (l. 3), *gegēap* for *geap* (l. 9), and *fullwer* for *full wer* (l. 14).

2   **on gewin sceapen** A characteristic riddler's double meaning: the bow is created in the toil and strife of the arrowsmith's shop; it is also given its (arched) shape in the course of battle when the bowman bends it.

5   **þæt ic mē . . . āswāpe** 'that I may remove that mortal danger (the arrow) far from me'.

6   **se mē . . . gescōp** 'who caused me that pain' (i.e. by bending the bow).

11   The noun clause *þæt ic . . . sprice* is the subject of the verb *tōgongeð*.

(j)

Ic wæs wǣpen, wiga. Nū mec wlonc þeceð
geong hagostealdmon golde ond sylfore,
wōum wīrbogum. Hwīlum weras cyssað;
hwīlum ic tō hilde hlēoþre bonne
5 wilgehlēþan; hwīlum wycg byreþ
mec ofer mearce; hwīlum merehengest
fereð ofer flōdas frætwum beorhtne;
hwīlum mægða sum mīnne gefylleð
bōsm bēaghroden; hwīlum ic on bordum sceal,
10 heard, hēafodlēas, behlȳþed licgan;
hwīlum hongige hyrstum frætwed,
wlitig on wāge, þǣr weras drincað,
frēolic fyrdsceorp. Hwīlum folcwigan
on wicge wegað, þonne ic winde sceal
15 sincfāg swelgan of sumes bōsme;
hwīlum ic gereordum rincas laðige
wlonce tō wīne; hwīlum wrāþum sceal
stefne mīnre forstolen hreddan,
flȳman fēondsceaþan. Frige hwæt ic hātte.

Riddle j The subject of the riddle, a horn, is described variously as a weapon and
fighter (while still growing on the animal's head), as an ornamented drinking horn,
and as a wind instrument (used to summon warriors to battle or to the wine-
drinking, or to sound the alarm after a robbery). Emendations: *on* supplied in ll. 9
and 14; *wrāþum* for MS *wraþþum* (l. 17).

3 **Hwīlum weras cyssað** Supply *mec*. Men kiss the horn when they put their lips
to it either to blow it or drink from it.

6–7 **hwīlum ... beorhtne** Again, *mec* is understood.

9–10 **hwīlum ... licgan** 'at times I must lie on the tables, hard, headless,
plundered' – presumably plundered of its contents (mead) after its lid ('head') has
been removed.

13–14 **Hwīlum ... wegað** *Mec* is understood.

(*k*)

Mec on þissum dagum   dēadne ofgēafon
fæder ond mōdor;   ne wæs mē feorh þā gēn,
ealdor in innan.   þā mec ān ongon,
welhold mēge,   wēdum þeccan,
5   hēold ond freoþode,   hlēosceorpe wrāh
swā ārlīce   swā hire āgen bearn,
oþþæt ic under scēate,   swā mīn gesceapu wæron,
ungesibbum wearð   ēacen gæste.
Mec sēo friþemæg   fēdde siþþan,
10   oþþæt ic āwēox,   wīddor meahte
sīþas āsettan.   Hēo hæfde swæsra þȳ læs
suna ond dohtra,   þȳ hēo swā dyde.

Riddle k   The cuckoo leaves its egg in the nest of other birds and flies away, leaving
the foster mother to hatch and feed the fledgling along with her own brood. As the
young cuckoo gains strength, it often evicts the fledglings who were hatched with it.
The subject of this riddle became a legendary example of ingratitude, as in the
Fool's observation in *King Lear* I. iv. 235: 'The Hedgesparrow fed The Cuckoo so
long that it had it head bit off by it young.' Emendations: *ofgēafon* for MS *ofgeafum*
(l. 1), *ān* supplied in l. 3, *þeccan* for *weccan* (l. 4), *swā ārlīce* for *nearlice* (l. 6).

1   on þissum dagum 'in these days', i.e. 'recently'.
dēadne The egg is only apparently dead, of course.
7   swā mīn gesceapu wæron 'as was my destiny'.
8   ungesibbum ... gæste 'among (nestlings) unrelated to me I became great
with life'.
11–12   Hēo hæfde swæsra þȳ læs ... þȳ hēo swā dyde A correlative use of the
instrumental *þȳ*: '*by so much* as she did so ... she had *so much* the fewer of her own
dear ones'. This idiom survives in MnE 'the bigger they come, the harder they fall'
and 'the more the merrier'. The word *the* in these constructions is a survival of OE
þȳ. Cf. 12/312–13.

(*l*)

　　Ic seah wrǣtlice　　wuhte fēower
　　samed sīþian;　　swearte wǣran lāstas,
　　swaþu swīþe blacu.　　Swift wæs on fōre,
　　fuglum framra;　　flēag on lyfte,
5　　dēaf under ȳþe.　　Drēag unstille
　　winnende wiga　　se him wegas tǣcneþ
　　ofer fǣted gold　　fēower eallum.

(*m*)

　　Wiga is on eorþan　　wundrum ācenned
　　dryhtum tō nytte,　　of dumbum twām
　　torht ātyhted,　　þone on tēon wigeð
　　fēond his fēonde.　　Forstrangne oft
5　　wīf hine wrīð;　　hē him wel hēreð,
　　þēowaþ him geþwǣre,　　gif him þegniað
　　mægeð ond mæcgas　　mid gemete ryhte,
　　fēdað hine fægre;　　hē him fremum stēpeð
　　līfe on lissum.　　Lēanað grimme
10　　þām þe hine wloncne　　weorþan lǣteð.

Riddle l The solution is two fingers and a thumb writing with a quill pen. Emendations: *flēag on* for *fleotgan* (l. 4) and *wegas* for *wægas* (l. 6).

4 **fuglum framra** 'more swift among the birds', i.e. swifter *in the air* (when the hand darts from the writing surface to the inkwell and back again) than it is when moving across the vellum page, writing. Perhaps also with a glance back at the time when the quill was a feather in the wing of a living bird flying through the air. See §191.5.

5 **under ȳþe** i.e. into the ink.　**Drēag** 'persevered'.

7 **fǣted gold** 'ornamented gold' (of the illuminated manuscript page).

Riddle m The solution is 'fire'. Emendations: *forstrangne* for MS *fer strangne* (l. 4), and *þām* supplied in l. 10.

3–4 **þone on ... fēonde** 'which foe bears against foe to his injury'. A reference, apparently, to the use of fire in warfare.

5–7 **hē him wel ... mæcgas** 'he obeys them well, compliant, he serves them, if women and men serve him ...'.

(*n*)

Ic seah in healle,   þǣr hæleð druncon,
on flet beran   fēower cynna,
wrǣtlic wudutrēow   ond wunden gold,
sinc searobunden,   ond seolfres dǣl
5   ond rōde tācn,   þæs ūs tō roderum ūp
hlǣdre rǣrde,   ǣr hē helwara
burg ābrǣce.   Ic þæs bēames mæg
ēaþe for eorlum   æþelu secgan;
þǣr wæs hlin ond āc   ond se hearda īw
10   ond se fealwa holen: frēan sindon ealle
nyt ætgǣdre;   naman habbað ānne,
wulfhēafedtrēo;   þæt oft wǣpen abǣd
his mondryhtne,   māðm in healle,
goldhilted sweord.   Nū mē þisses gieddes
15   ondsware ȳwe,   se hine on mēde
wordum secgan   hū se wudu hātte.

Riddle n The solution appears to be 'cross', although some details of the riddle remain obscure. In early Christian tradition the cross was thought to have been made from four different kinds of wood, the specific kinds varying from one authority to another. (See W. O. Stevens *The Cross in the Life and Literature of the Anglo-Saxons* Yale Studies in English 22 (New Haven, 1904), p. 10; reprinted in *The Anglo-Saxon Cross* with a new preface by Thomas D. Hill (New Haven, 1977), pp. 14–15.) Ceremonial crosses were ornamented with gold, silver, and jewels. See *The Dream of the Rood* below. Emendations: *healle* for MS *heall* (l. 1), *āc* for *acc* (l. 9).

2–3   fēower ... wudutrēow 'wondrous forest-wood of four different kinds'.

5–6   rōde tācn ... rǣrde 'the sign of the cross of the One (who) raised for us a ladder to the heavens'. Following *þæs* the relative *þe* is either understood or has been omitted by a scribe.

6–7   ǣr hē ... ābrǣce i.e. the harrowing of Hell.

12   wulfhēafedtrēo 'outlaw-tree', i.e. 'gallows'. The Anglo-Saxons regularly referred to the cross as gallows.

12–14   þæt oft ... sweord 'that often wards off from his lord (owner) a weapon ...'. An obscure sentence referring perhaps to the cross's power of protecting the believer from hostile attack.

15   se hine on mēde 'he who takes it upon himself' or 'he who presumes'.

(o)

Ic eom lēgbysig,   lāce mid winde,
bewunden mid wuldre,   wedre gesomnad,
fūs forðweges   fȳre gebysgad,
bearu blōwende,   byrnende glēd.
5 Ful oft mec gesīþas   sendað æfter hondum,
þæt mec weras ond wīf   wlonce cyssað.
þonne ic mec onhæbbe,   hī onhnīgaþ tō mē
monige mid miltse;   þǣr ic monnum sceal
ȳcan ūpcyme   ēadignesse.

(p)

Ic wæs fǣmne geong,   feaxhār cwene,
ond ǣnlic rinc   on āne tīd;
flēah mid fuglum   ond on flōde swom,
dēaf under ȳþe   dēad mid fiscum,
5 ond on foldan stōp;   hæfde ferð cwicu.

Riddle o This too is conjectured to be a riddle about the cross, or more specifically about *ān bēam*, the Old English words which can mean 'a cross', 'a tree', and 'a log'. Emendation: *hī onhnīgaþ* for MS *ond hi on hin gaþ* (l. 7).

2 **bewunden mid wuldre** 'girded with splendour' (probably with reference to foliage).

3 **fūs forðweges** 'ready for the way hence'. Usually this phrasing means 'ready for death', and this is the log's fate when afflicted by fire.

5 **sendað æfter hondum** 'pass from hand to hand'.

8–9 **þǣr ic ... ēadignesse** 'there I shall increase the ascendancy of happiness among men'.

Riddle p The solution is unknown. Scholars have suggested answers – 'cuttlefish', 'swan', 'water', 'siren', 'writing', 'ship's figurehead', etc. – but none satisfies all the conditions set forth in the poem. Emendation: *ferð* for MS *forð* (l. 5).

2 **on āne tīd** 'at the same time', 'all at once'.

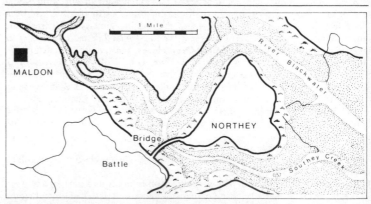

Plan of the Battle of Maldon in 991. From David Hill *An Atlas of Anglo-Saxon England* (Basil Blackwell, 1981), p. 64.

The Battle of Maldon

In August of the year 991 marauding Vikings sailed up the river Blackwater (then called 'Pante') and beached their ships on an island not far from the town of Maldon. The English ealdorman, Byrhtnoth, called out the local levy and, combining with this force the warriors from his own personal retinue, marched to the river-bank across from the island and confronted the Viking army. The ensuing battle (which is reported in the Anglo-Saxon Chronicle entry for 991 printed above on p. 197) is the subject of the poem which we are about to read.

The Battle of Maldon is the story of a military disaster suffered by the English in the course of their long and losing struggle against Scandinavian invaders. (Since 980 the Viking fleets had been raiding Southampton, Thanet, and elsewhere, and in the second decade of the eleventh century they seized the English throne.) The Anglo-Saxon king who presided over this prolonged humiliation of the English was Æthelræd (dubbed by later chroniclers 'the Unready'[1]), whose reign seems to have been characterized by demoralization in the military and, if a famous sermon by Archbishop Wulfstan is to be believed, in the populace as a whole. It is against this unhappy background that the battle of Maldon is fought by the Englishmen and celebrated by the poet. The poem is about how men bear up when things go wrong. The fighting men at Maldon, no less than those at Balaklava and Dunkirk, triumph in this test of character in a manner of which Englishmen have always been especially proud. The Anglo-Saxons who fight to the bitter end are portrayed by the poet as glorious in defeat, and their valour redeems the honour of their country. The poet of course idealizes the actual battle; his verses are poetry, not history.

To understand the action of the poem, and especially the action in ll. 62–99, one must have some idea of the geography of the battle. (See map on p. 224, which shows the site which most scholars agree to be the likeliest location of the battle.) The Vikings occupy the

---

[1] The name *Æðelræd* means 'noble counsel'. The sobriquet *unræd* means 'no counsel', i.e. 'folly'. 'Unready' is an inaccurate modernization of *unræd*.

island now called Northey, and Byrhtnoth's Anglo-Saxons array themselves across the water along the river-bank. At high tide the island is completely surrounded by water, but when the tide recedes (l. 71), an elevated road or causeway (called a *bricg* in ll. 74 and 78) is exposed, thus providing access to the island from the mainland. When the two armies first confront each other, the tide is in and the causeway is submerged (ll. 64–71). When the tide goes out, the Vikings begin to file across the causeway to the mainland, but the Anglo-Saxons block their progress from the narrow passageway to the shore (ll. 72–83). Seeing that they are at a serious disadvantage, the Vikings ask Byrhtnoth to order his troops to stand back and allow the invaders free passage to the shore (ll. 84–8). Byrhtnoth rashly agrees to give the enemy this advantage (ll. 89–95), and the battle begins.

Many of the English participants in the battle are named in the poem. (The poet seems to know nothing of the individual identities of the Vikings.) Extant documents from the period allow us to identify some of those mentioned, and it is to be assumed that all were actual Englishmen who were known to the poet's audience. Modern readers need not concern themselves with all the various names. It is important to remember the hero of the poem, Byrhtnoth (about whom a great deal is known), and his king, Æthelræd the Unready. We should also bear in mind the names of the cowardly sons of Odda: Godric, Godwig, and Godwine. Any other persons named in the poem can be assumed to be members of the Anglo-Saxon defending force – most likely members of Byrhtnoth's personal retinue, since the *fyrd*-men are generally left anonymous.

The Old English manuscript leaves containing *The Battle of Maldon* were destroyed by fire in 1731. Fortunately, a man named David Casley made a copy of the poem a few years before the fire and this copy is the basis for the present edition, except that modern conventions of punctuation, capitalization, word-division, verse-lineation, and long-vowel marking are introduced, and the following emendations are adopted: *tō hige* for MS *t hige* (l. 4), *þā* for *þ* (l. 5), *þām* for *þætam* (l. 10), *wīge* for *w . . . . ge* (l. 10), *randas* for *randan* (l. 20), *hilde* for *. . ulde* (l. 33), *wē* for *þe* (l. 61), *feohte* for *fohte* (l. 103), *grimme gegrundene* for *gegrundene* (l. 109), *wearð* for *weard* (l. 113), *wearð* for *wærd* (l. 116), *gestandan* for *ge stundan* (l. 171), *Geþancie* for *ge þance* (l. 173), *wearð* for *wurdon* (l. 186), *mearh* for *mear* (l. 188), *ærndon* for *ærdon* (l. 191), *Godwine* for *godrine* (l. 192), *þearfe* for *þære* (l. 201), *forlætan* for *for lætun* (l. 208), *ægðer* for *ægder* (l. 224), *wræce* for *wrece* (l. 257), *læge* for *lege* (l. 279), *crincgan* for *crintgan* (l. 292), *Forð þā* for *forða* (l. 297), *sunu* for *suna*

(l. 298), *geþrange* for *geþrang* (l. 299), *oðþæt* for *od þæt* (l. 324), *gūðe* for *gude* (l. 325).

brocen wurde.
Hēt þā hyssa hwæne   hors forlǽtan,
feor āfȳsan,   and forð gangan,
hicgan tō handum   and tō hige gōdum.
5   þā þæt Offan mæg   ǽrest onfunde,
þæt se eorl nolde   yrhðo geþolian,
hē lēt him þā of handon   lēofne flēogan
hafoc wið þæs holtes,   and tō þǽre hilde stōp;
be þām man mihte oncnāwan   þæt se cniht nolde
10   wācian æt þām wīge,   þā hē tō wǽpnum fēng.
Ēac him wolde Ēadrīc   his ealdre gelǽstan,
frēan tō gefeohte,   ongan þā forð beran
gār tō gūþe.   Hē hæfde gōd geþanc
þā hwīle þe hē mid handum   healdan mihte
15   bord and brād swurd;   bēot hē gelǽste
þā hē ætforan his frēan   feohtan sceolde.
   Ðā þǽr Byrhtnōð ongan   beornas trymian,
rād and rǽdde,   rincum tǽhte
hū hī sceoldon standan   and þone stede healdan,
20   and bæd þæt hyra randas   rihte hēoldon
fæste mid folman,   and ne forhtedon nā.
þā hē hæfde þæt folc   fǽgere getrymmed,
hē līhte þā mid lēodon   þǽr him lēofost wæs,

1   The opening lines of the poem are lost. They must have told how the Anglo-Saxon leader Byrhtnoth heard of the Vikings' arrival, gathered his troops, and led them to the river shore where they could challenge the invaders.
2   The subject of *Hēt* is Byrhtnoth, referred to as *se eorl* in l. 6. Cf. §161.
4   hicgan . . . gōdum 'to give thought to their hands and to virtuous courage', i.e. to think about courage and about the handiwork through which they can display that courage.
5–6   For the anticipatory *þæt* see §148.
7   handon = *handum*. *-on* for *-um* appears again in l. 23 (*lēodon*), l. 129 (*Denon*), l. 270 (*hwīlon*), 306 (*wordon*), etc. This is a feature of late Old English.
14   þā hwīle þe 'while, as long as' (so also in ll. 83, 235, and 272).
17–24   In ll. 17–21 Byrhtnoth gives elementary instructions to the members of the *fyrd* (ll. 140, 221), the home guard consisting of civilians who answer the call to arms when the local leader summons them in an emergency. In ll. 24–4 Byrhtnoth dismounts among his personal retinue of professional fighting men (*heorðwerod*), 'where it was most agreeable to him' (*þār him lēofost wæs*).
20   hēoldon = *hēolden* The subjunctive plural ending of verbs is invariably spelled *-on* in this poem rather than *-en*: e.g. *forgyldon* (l. 32), *dǣlon* (l. 33), *gangon* (l. 56), *syllon* (l. 61), *ēodon* (l. 229). This coalescence in spelling is characteristic of late Old English.

þǣr hē his heorðwerod   holdost wiste.

25 þā stōd on stæðe,   stīðlīce clypode
wīcinga ār,   wordum mǣlde,
se on bēot ābēad   brimlīþendra
ǣrǣnde tō þām eorle,   þǣr hē on ōfre stōd:
'Mē sendon tō þē   sǣmen snelle,

30 hēton ðē secgan   þæt þū mōst sendan raðe
bēagas wið gebeorge;   and ēow betere is
þæt gē þisne gārrǣs   mid gafole forgyldon,
þon wē swā hearde   hilde dǣlon.
Ne þurfe wē ūs spillan,   gif gē spēdaþ tō þām;

35 wē willað wið þam golde   grið fǣstnian.
Gyf þū þat gerǣdest,   þe hēr rīcost eart,
þæt þū þīne lēoda   lȳsan wille,
syllan sǣmannum   on hyra sylfra dōm
feoh wið frēode,   and niman frið æt ūs,

40 wē willaþ mid þām sceattum   ūs tō scype gangan,
on flot fēran,   and ēow friþes healdan.'
Byrhtnōð maþelode,   bord hafenode,
wand wācne æsc,   wordum mǣlde,
yrre and ānrǣd   āgēaf him andsware:

45 'Gehȳrst þū, sǣlida,   hwæt þis folc segeð?
Hī willað ēow tō gafole   gāras syllan,
ǣttrynne ord   and ealde swurd,
þā heregeatu   þe ēow æt hilde ne dēah.
Brimmanna boda,   ābēod eft ongēan,

50 sege þīnum lēodum   miccle lāþre spell,
þæt hēr stynt unforcūð   eorl mid his werode,
þe wile gealgean   ēþel þysne,
Æþelrēdes eard,   ealdres mīnes,
folc and foldan.   Feallan sceolon

55 hǣþene æt hilde.   Tō hēanlic mē þinceð
þæt gē mid ūrum sceattum   tō scype gangon
unbefohtene,   nū gē þus feor hider
on ūrne eard   in becōmon.
Ne sceole gē swā sōfte   sinc gegangan;

---

30 **hēton ðē secgan** Cf. 5/1, 10(*a*)/72–3, etc., and ll. 62 and 101 below. Cf. §161.
31 **wið** 'in exchange for'. Cf. ll. 35, 39.
31–3 **betere . . . þon** . . . See §168 *þonne*3(*c*). (*þon* = *þonne*.)
34 **gif gē . . . tō þām** 'If you are sufficiently rich for that (i.e. for the purpose of paying us off).'
38 **on hyra . . . dōm** 'according to their own stipulation'. Cf. 6/28.
50 **miccle lāþre spell** 'a much more unpleasant report (than they expect)'.

60 ūs sceal ord and ecg   ær gesēman,
grim gūðplega,   ær wē gofol syllon.'
    Hēt þā bord beran,   beornas gangan,
þæt hī on þām ēasteðe   ealle stōdon.
Ne mihte þær for wætere   werod tō þām ōðrum;
65 þær cōm flōwende   flōd æfter ebban,
lucon lagustrēamas.   Tō lang hit him þūhte,
hwænne hī tōgædere   gāras bēron.
Hī þær Pantan strēam   mid prasse bestōdon,
Ēastseaxena ord   and se æschere.
70 Ne mihte hyra ænig   ōþrum derian,
būton hwā þurh flānes flyht   fyl genāme.
Se flōd ūt gewāt;   þā flotan stōdon gearowe,
wīcinga fela,   wīges georne.
    Hēt þā hæleða hlēo   healdan þā bricge
75 wigan wīgheardne,   se wæs hāten Wulfstān,
cāfne mid his cynne,   þæt wæs Cēolan sunu,
þe ðone forman man   mid his francan ofscēat
þe þær baldlīcost   on þā bricge stōp.
þær stōdon mid Wulfstāne   wigan unforhte,
80 Ælfere and Maccus,   mōdige twēgen,
þā noldon æt þām forda   flēam gewyrcan,
ac hī fæstlīce   wið ðā fȳnd weredon,
þā hwīle þe hī wæpna   wealdan mōston.
þā hī þæt ongēaton   and georne gesāwon
85 þæt hī þær bricgweardas   bitere fundon,
ongunnon lytegian þā   lāðe gystas,
bædon þæt hī ūpgangan   āgan mōston,
ofer þone ford faran,   fēþan lædan.
    Ðā se eorl ongan   for his ofermōde
90 ālȳfan landes tō fela   lāþere ðēode.
Ongan ceallian þā   ofer cald wæter

60–1 **ær … ær …** 'first … before …'.
66 **lucon lagustrēamas** i.e. the rising tide submerges the causeway, completely encircling the island.
67 **hwænne** 'when, until'. See §159, note 2.
71 **hwā** 'someone'. Cf. 5/81.
81 **flēam gewyrcan** 'flee, yield'.
89–90 **ofermōde** 'pride' The national pride and manly defiance which Byrhtnoth has expressed so eloquently in his answer to the Viking messenger (ll. 45–61) has been carefully noted by the invaders, who play on Byrhtnoth's *ofermōd* to persuade him to grant them free access to 'too much land' (*landes tō fela*). The poet acknowledges that Byrhtnoth makes a tactical error here, but at a time when many Anglo-Saxons are seen as cowardly, he probably half admires this display of rash pride.

Byrhtelmes bearn   (beornas gehlyston):
'Nū ēow is gerȳmed,   gāð ricene tō ūs,
guman tō gūþe;   God āna wāt

95   hwā þǣre wælstōwe   wealdan mōte.'
Wōdon þā wælwulfas   (for wætere ne murnon),
wīcinga werod,   west ofer Pantan,
ofer scīr wæter   scyldas wēgon,
lidmen tō lande   linde bǣron.

100 þǣr ongēan gramum   gearowe stōdon
Byrhtnōð mid beornum;   hē mid bordum hēt
wyrcan þone wīhagan,   and þæt werod healdan
fæste wið fēondum.   þā wæs feohte nēh,
tīr æt getohte.   Wæs sēo tīd cumen

105 þæt þǣr fǣge men   feallan sceoldon.
þǣr wearð hrēam āhafen,   hremmas wundon,
earn ǣses georn;   wæs on eorþan cyrm.
Hī lēton þā of folman   fēolhearde speru,
grimme gegrundene   gāras flēogan;

110 bogan wǣron bysige,   bord ord onfēng.
    Biter wæs se beadurǣs,   beornas fēollon
on gehwæðere hand,   hyssas lāgon.
Wund wearð Wulfmǣr,   wælrǣste gecēas,
Byrhtnōðes mǣg;   hē mid billum wearð,

115 his swustersunu,   swīðe forhēawen.
þǣr wearð wīcingum   wiþerlēan āgyfen.
Gehȳrde ic þæt Ēadweard   ānne slōge
swīðe mid his swurde,   swenges ne wyrnde,
þæt him æt fōtum fēoll   fǣge cempa;

120 þæs him his ðēoden   þanc gesǣde,
þām būrþēne,   þā hē byre hæfde.
Swā stemnetton   stīðhicgende
hysas æt hilde,   hogodon georne
hwā þǣr mid orde   ǣrost mihte

125 on fǣgean men   feorh gewinnan,
wigan mid wǣpnum;   wæl fēol on eorðan.
Stōdon stædefæste;   stihte hī Byrhtnōð,
bæd þæt hyssa gehwylc   hogode tō wīge
þe on Denon wolde   dōm gefeohtan.

---

92 **Byrhtelmes bearn** i.e. Byrhtnoth.

115 **swustersunu** The relationship between a man and his sister's son was peculiarly close in Germanic society (Tacitus comments on it in *Germania*), and so this opening scene of killing and vengeance reveals the Anglo-Saxons' adherence to ancient traditions of loyalty, both familial and military. Note that it is Byrhtnoth's personal chamberlain (*būrþegn*) who instantly avenges his leader's heavy loss.

130   Wōd þā wīges heard,   wǣpen ūp āhōf,
        bord tō gebeorge,   and wið þæs beornes stōp.
        Ēode swā ānrǣd   eorl tō þām ceorle,
        ægþer hyra ōðrum   yfeles hogode.
        Sende ðā se særinc   sūþerne gār,
135   þæt gewundod wearð   wigena hlāford;
        hē scēaf þā mid ðām scylde,   þæt se sceaft tōbærst,
        and þæt spere sprengde,   þæt hit sprang ongēan.
        Gegremod wearð se gūðrinc;   hē mid gāre stang
        wlancne wīcing,   þe him þā wunde forgeaf.
140   Frōd wæs se fyrdrinc;   hē lēt his francan wadan
        þurh ðæs hysses hals,   hand wīsode
        þæt hē on þām fǣrsceaðan   feorh gerǣhte.
        Ðā hē ōþerne   ofstlīce scēat,
        þæt sēo byrne tōbærst;   hē wæs on brēostum wund
145   þurh ðā hringlocan,   him æt heortan stōd
        ǣtterne ord.   Se eorl wæs þē blīþra,
        hlōh þā, mōdi man,   sǣde Metode þanc
        ðæs dægweorces   þe him Drihten forgeaf.
            Forlēt þā drenga sum   daroð of handa,
150   flēogan of folman,   þæt sē tō forð gewāt
        þurh ðone æþelan   Æþelrēdes þegen.
        Him be healfe stōd   hyse unweaxen,
        cniht on gecampe,   se full cāflīce
        brǣd of þām beorne   blōdigne gār,
155   Wulfstānes bearn,   Wulfmǣr se geonga,
        forlēt forheardne   faran eft ongēan;
        ord in gewōd,   þæt sē on eorþan læg
        þe his þēoden ǣr   þearle gerǣhte.
        Ēode þā gesyrwed   secg tō þām eorle;

130   **wīges heard** evidently refers to some Viking, while *þæs beornes* (l. 131) refers to Byrhtnoth. The transition is so abrupt here that we might suspect the loss of a line or two introducing the Viking who is *wīges heard* 'bold in battle'.

134   **sūþerne gār** 'spear of southern make'. Vikings prized weapons produced in lands to the south of them, such as England and France.

135   **wigena hlāford** Byrhtnoth.

136-7   With a thrust of his shield Byrhtnoth knocks away the spear that the Viking had hurled into his body. Specifically, his shield breaks the spear-shaft in such a way that it 'forced out' (*sprengde*) the spear, which 'sprang back' (*sprang ongēan*) from the wound.

142   **feorh gerǣhte** 'reached the life'. That is, Byrhtnoth's hand guided the spear so that it reached (and thus extinguished) the life in the Viking. The phrase is strikingly Homeric. Cf. l. 226.

143   **Ðā hē . . . scēat** 'Then he (Byrhtnoth) swiftly pierced another (Viking).'

157   **sē** refers to the Viking who had wounded Byrhtnoth.

159   **gesyrwed secg** The 'armoured warrior' is yet another Viking.

160 hē wolde þæs beornes   bēagas gefecgan,
     rēaf and hringas   and gerēnod swurd.
     þā Byrhtnōð bræd   bill of scēðe,
     brād and brūneccg,   and on þā byrnan slōh.
     Tō raþe hine gelette   lidmanna sum,
165 þā hē þæs eorles   earm āmyrde.
     Fēoll þā tō foldan   fealohilte swurd;
     ne mihte hē gehealdan   heardne mēce,
     wæpnes wealdan.   þā gȳt þæt word gecwæð
     hār hilderinc,   hyssas bylde,
170 bæd gangan forð   gōde gefēran;
     ne mihte þā on fōtum leng   fæste gestandan.
     Hē tō heofenum wlāt:
     'Geþancie þē,   ðēoda Waldend,
     ealra þæra wynna   þe ic on worulde gebād.
175 Nū ic āh, milde Metod,   mæste þearfe
     þæt þū mīnum gāste   gōdes geunne,
     þæt mīn sāwul tō ðē   sīðian mōte
     on þīn geweald,   þēoden engla,
     mid friþe ferian.   Ic eom frymdi tō þē
180 þæt hī helscēaðan   hȳnan ne mōton.'
         Ðā hine hēowon   hæðene scealcas
     and bēgen þā beornas   þe him big stōdon,
     Ælfnōð and Wulmær   bēgen lāgon,
     ðā onemn hyra frēan   feorh gesealdon.
185 Hī bugon þā fram beaduwe   þe þær bēon noldon.
     þær wearð Oddan bearn   ærest on flēame,
     Godrīc fram gūþe,   and þone gōdan forlēt
     þe him mænigne oft   mēarh gesealde;
     hē gehlēop þone eoh   þe āhte his hlāford,
190 on þām gerædum   þe hit riht ne wæs,
     and his brōðru mid him   bēgen ærndon,
     Godwine and Godwīg,   gūþe ne gȳmdon,
     ac wendon fram þām wīge   and þone wudu sōhton,
     flugon on þæt fæsten   and hyra fēore burgon,

172 The second half of this line is missing. A few words may be lost, but since there are other metrical irregularities in the poem (e.g. in ll. 45, 75, 183, 271) it is also possible that this is a feature of the later, looser style of *The Battle of Maldon*.

173 Geþancie þē '(I) thank Thee.'

179 Ic eom frymdi tō þē 'I am suppliant to Thee', i.e. 'I beg Thee.'

180 hī acc. sg. fem. referring to *sāwul* (l. 177).

190 þe hit riht ne wæs Either 'as it was not right (to do)' (see §168 s.v. þe 6), or 'which was not right' (assuming þe hit to be a compound relative introducing an adjective clause). Or þe may be a scribal error for þēah or þēh 'although', but in that case one might expect the subjunctive.

195 and manna mā   þonne hit ænig mǣð wǣre,
      gyf hī þā geearnunga   ealle gemundon
      þe hē him tō duguþe   gedōn hæfde.
      Swā him Offa on dæg   ǣr āsǣde
      on þām meþelstede,   þā hē gemōt hæfde,
200 þæt þǣr mōdelīce   manega sprǣcon
      þe eft æt þearfe   þolian noldon.
        þā wearð āfeallen   þæs folces ealdor,
      Æþelrēdes eorl;   ealle gesāwon
      heorðgenēatas   þæt hyra heorra læg.
205 þā ðǣr wendon forð   wlance þegenas,
      unearge men   efston georne;
      hī woldon þā ealle   ōðer twēga,
      līf forlǣtan   oððe lēofne gewrecan.
      Swā hī bylde forð   bearn Ælfrīces,
210 wiga wintrum geong,   wordum mǣlde,
      Ælfwine þā cwæð,   hē on ellen spræc:
      'Gemunu þā mǣla   þe wē oft æt meodo sprǣcon,
      þonne wē on bence   bēot āhōfon,
      hæleð on healle,   ymbe heard gewinn;
215 nū mæg cunnian   hwā cēne sȳ.
      Ic wylle mīne æþelo   eallum gecȳþan,
      þæt ic wæs on Myrcon   miccles cynnes;
      wæs mīn ealda fæder   Ealhelm hāten,
      wīs ealdorman,   woruldgesǣlig.
220 Ne sceolon mē on þǣre þēode   þegenas ætwītan
      þæt ic of ðisse fyrde   fēran wille,
      eard gesēcan,   nū mīn ealdor ligeð
      forhēawen æt hilde.   Mē is þæt hearma mǣst;
      hē wæs ægðer mīn mæg   and mīn hlāford.'

198 **Swā him … āsǣde** 'Thus Offa had told him (earlier) in the day.' Evidently Byrhtnoth had called a meeting (*gemōt* l. 199) earlier that day to plan strategy with his *heorðwerod*, who had vowed to support him loyally in the field, as was their solemn obligation. See §237.

203–4 **ealle … heorðgenēatas** Byrhtnoth's personal retainers (*heorðgenēatas*), who would have been fighting close by him, could all see that their leader had fallen. Members of the *fyrd* fighting at a greater distance could not see this (ll. 239–42).

212 **Gemunu þā mǣla** '(I) remember the occasions.' Unexpressed subjects are entirely permissible in Old English when they can be readily inferred from the context (see §193.7), but their repeated use in direct discourse here (173, 212, 215) is probably a stylistic device aimed at suggesting the hurried speech of men talking to one another during the rush of battle.

215 **nū mæg … sȳ** 'now (one) can find out who is brave'. Cf. preceding note.

221 **fyrde** The aristocrat Ælfwine, kinsman of Byrhtnoth, identifies himself with the *fyrd*, the common militia. Distinctions between upper-class retainers and the levy are forgotten as aristocracy of rank is superseded by an aristocracy of courage.

225   þā hē forð ēode,   fǣhðe gemunde,
þæt hē mid orde   ānne gerǣhte
flotan on þām folce,   þæt sē on foldan læg
forwegen mid his wǣpne.   Ongan þā winas manian,
frȳnd and gefēran,   þæt hī forð ēodon.

230   Offa gemǣlde,   æscholt āscēoc:
'Hwæt þū, Ælfwine, hafast   ealle gemanode
þegenas tō þearfe,   nū ūre þēoden lið,
eorl on eorðan.   Ūs is eallum þearf
þæt ūre ǣghwylc   ōþerne bylde

235   wigan tō wīge,   þā hwīle þe hē wǣpen mæge
habban and healdan,   heardne mēce,
gār and gōd swurd.   Ūs Godrīc hæfð,
earh Oddan bearn,   ealle beswicene.
Wēnde þæs formoni man,   þā hē on mēare rād,

240   on wlancan þām wicge,   þæt wǣre hit ūre hlāford;
forþan wearð hēr on felda   folc tōtwǣmed,
scyldburh tōbrocen.   Ābrēoðe his angin,
þæt hē hēr swā manigne   man āflȳmde!'
    Lēofsunu gemǣlde   and his linde āhōf,

245   bord tō gebeorge;   hē þām beorne oncwæð:
'Ic þæt gehāte,   þæt ic heonon nelle
flēon fōtes trym,   ac wille furðor gān,
wrecan on gewinne   mīnne winedrihten.
Ne þurfon mē embe Stūrmere   stedefæste hælæð

250   wordum ætwītan,   nū mīn wine gecranc,
þæt ic hlāfordlēas   hām sīðie,
wende fram wīge,   ac mē sceal wǣpen niman,
ord and īren.'   Hē ful yrre wōd,
feaht fæstlīce,   flēam hē forhogode.

255   Dunnere þā cwæð,   daroð ācwehte,
unorne ceorl,   ofer eall clypode,
bæd þæt beorna gehwylc   Byrhtnōð wrǣce:
'Ne mæg nā wandian   se þe wrecan þenceð
frēan on folce,   ne for fēore murnan.'

260   þā hī forð ēodon,   fēores hī ne rōhton;
ongunnon þā hīredmen   heardlīce feohtan,
grame gārberend,   and God bǣdon

---

239 *þæs* gen. obj. of *wēnan* anticipating the *þæt* clause in l. 240. See §148.
242 **Ābrēoðe his angin** 'Damn his behaviour!'
255–9 The brief, simple speech of Dunnere befits his status as a 'simple churl' (*unorne ceorl*), and yet its mere appearance here puts him in the company of the noblest men in the region, all now united in common loyalty to the code of honour which requires that fighting men avenge their slain leader or die in the attempt.

þæt hī mōston gewrecan   hyra winedrihten
and on hyra fēondum   fyl gewyrcan.
265 Him se gȳsel ongan   geornlīce fylstan;
hē wæs on Norðhymbron   heardes cynnes,
Ecglāfes bearn,   him wæs Æscferð nama.
Hē ne wandode nā   æt þām wīgplegan,
ac hē fȳsde forð   flān genehe;
270 hwīlon hē on bord scēat,   hwīlon beorn tæsde,
æfre embe stunde   hē sealde sume wunde,
þā hwīle ðe hē wæpna   wealdan mōste.

þā gȳt on orde stōd   Ēadweard sc langa,
gearo and geornful,   gylpwordum spræc
275 þæt hē nolde flēogan   fōtmæl landes,
ofer bæc būgan,   þā his betera leg.
Hē bræc þone bordweall   and wið þā beornas feaht,
oðþæt hē his sincgyfan   on þām sæmannum
wurðlīce wrec,   ær hē on wæle læge.
280 Swā dyde Æþerīc,   æþele gefēra,
fūs and forðgeorn,   feaht eornoste.
Sībyrhtes brōðor   and swīðe mænig ōþer
clufon cellod bord,   cēne hī weredon;
bærst bordes lærig,   and sēo byrne sang
285 gryrelēoða sum.   þā æt gūðe slōh
Offa þone sælidan,   þæt hē on eorðan fēoll,
and ðær Gaddes mæg   grund gesōhte.
Raðe wearð æt hilde   Offa forhēawen;
hē hæfde ðēah geforþod   þæt hē his frēan gehēt,
290 swā hē bēotode ær   wið his bēahgifan
þæt hī sceoldon bēgen   on burh rīdan,
hāle tō hāme,   oððe on here crincgan,
on wælstōwe   wundum sweltan;
hē læg ðegenlīce   ðēodne gehende.

271 'Ever and anon he gave one (of the Vikings) a wound.' Since *st*- alliterates only with *st*- in the Germanic verse system, this line lacks alliteration altogether, but, like l. 282, it has rhyme to link the two half-lines. These lines anticipate the Middle English period, when rhyme displaces alliteration almost completely.

277 **Hē bræc þone bordweall** 'He penetrated the wall of shields.' Apparently Eadweard broke through the phalanx of the Vikings and fought individually with enemy warriors until he was overwhelmed and slain.

283 **cellod** occurs nowhere else, and its meaning is obscure. It is evidently an adjective describing the shield (*bord*).

285-6 **þā æt gūðe ... sælidan** 'Then Offa struck that Viking in the fight so that he fell to the earth.' What Viking? It has been reasonably suggested that a line or two has been lost between ll. 283 and 284, telling us who it was whose shield's rim was broken (l. 284), and this person would be *þone sælidan* of l. 286.

295   Ðā wearð borda gebræc.   Brimmen wōdon,
        gūðe gegremode;   gār oft þurhwōd
        fæges feorhhūs.   Forð þā ēode Wīstān,
        þurstānes sunu,   wið þās secgas feaht;
        hē wæs on geþrange   hyra þrēora bana,
300   ǣr him Wīgelines bearn   on þām wæle lǣge.
        þǣr wæs stīð gemōt;   stōdon fæste
        wigan on gewinne,   wīgend cruncon,
        wundum wērige.   Wæl fēol on eorþan.
        Ōswold and Ēadwold   ealle hwīle,
305   bēgen þā gebrōþru,   beornas trymedon
        hyra winemāgas   wordon bǣdon
        þæt hī þǣr æt ðearfe   þolian sceoldon,
        unwāclīce   wǣpna nēotan.
        Byrhtwold maþelode,   bord hafenode
310   (se wæs eald genēat),   æsc ācwehte;
        hē ful baldlīce   beornas lǣrde:
        'Hige sceal þē heardra,   heorte þē cēnre,
        mōd sceal þē māre,   þē ūre mægen lȳtlað.
        Hēr līð ūre ealdor   eall forhēawen,
315   gōd on grēote.   Ā mæg gnornian
        se ðe nū fram þīs wīgplegan   wendan þenceð.
        Ic eom frōd fēores;   fram ic ne wille,
        ac ic mē be healfe   mīnum hlāforde,
        be swā lēofan men,   licgan þence.'
320   Swā hī Æþelgāres bearn   ealle bylde,
        Godrīc tō gūþe.   Oft hē gār forlēt,
        wælspere windan   on þā wīcingas,
        swā hē on þām folce   fyrmest ēode,
        hēow and hȳnde,   oðþæt hē on hilde gecranc.
325   Næs þæt nā se Godrīc   þe ðā gūðe forbēah

                        *   *   *

300   'before the son of Wigelin lay down in the carnage'. (The same use of
reflexive pronoun with *licgan* appears in ll. 318–19 and need not be translated.)
Wīgelines bearn seems clearly to refer to Wistan, but how can he be the son both of
þurstān (l. 298) and *Wīgelin*? A metronymic would be very unusual – even in a poem
like *Maldon*, which seems to be addressed to an audience which knew the poem's
characters and their families. It has been conjectured that Wistan's father may have
been known by two different names, but it is also possible that lines introducing a
new character have been lost.
312–13   'Our resolve must be so much the firmer, our hearts so much the bolder,
our courage so much the greater, by so much as our (physical) strength diminishes.'
See §168 *þȳ* l.; cf. 11(*k*)/11–12 note.
325   The closing lines of the poem are lost. We know from other accounts of the
battle that the Vikings were victorious.

13

The Ruin

'Where are those who lived before us?' In every age and culture people have raised this haunting question, especially when prompted to such thoughts by an ancient ruin or some other relic of the past. In both their poetry and their prose the Anglo-Saxons were very given to reflection on former civilizations and the people who built them, so much so that their language had a special word for such meditation: *dūstscēawung* 'contemplation of the dust'. This theme occurs often as an incidental motif in longer works (e.g. *The Wanderer* ll. 73–110 and *Beowulf* ll. 2255–66), but *The Ruin* is an entire poem devoted to the depiction of an ancient ghost town and to the thoughts which the scene evokes.

The poet draws no explicit moral from his description of Roman ruins. He records rather the simple wonder with which the scene fills him: wonder at the ingenuity of the people who built the city, and wonder at the power of *wyrd* 'fate' which has laid it all waste. Although the poem is for the most part an admiring catalogue of artefacts and architecture, the objects described are all closely associated with the people who had made and used them. The poet marvels at how the builders conceived of such structures, he imagines how the inhabitants filled the city with life and joy, he muses over the fact that their eyes had fallen on the very objects he is studying, and he reflects on the powerful fate (*wyrd sēo swiþe*) that has swept them all into oblivion. Buildings and people alike have fallen (*crungon*, *gecrong*) and though the artefacts have survived their creators, their deteriorated state bears eloquent witness to the perishability of everything on earth. The transience of earthly things is emphasized by the repeated contrast between the ruins the poet sees and the city in its prime, which the poet re-creates with lively imagination. His details are so persuasive that some scholars have thought they could identify the city he describes as the Roman city of Bath, where thermal springs were skilfully channelled into stone baths much like those described in ll. 38–46. But other sites have also been suggested, and it could well be that the scene is a composite of various Roman ruins that the poet had seen.

The poem survives in the Exeter Book (see selection 11,

Riddles). Damage done to the later pages of the book have left *The Ruin* something of a ruin itself. Aside from a tentative reconstruction of l. 12, no effort is made to restore the damaged verses. Losses in the text are indicated by series of dots. Emendations include normalization of *þæs* to *þes* in ll. 9 and 30, deletion of *torras* (mechanically repeated from l. 3) in l. 4 following *hrīmgeat*, and the change of MS *geheapen* to *gehēawen* (l. 12), *secgrof* to *secgrōfra* (l. 26), *rof* to *hrōf* (l. 31), and *gefrætweð* to *gefrætwed* (l. 33).

> Wrǣtlic is þes wealstān;   wyrde gebrǣcon
> burgstede burston;   brosnað enta geweorc.
> Hrōfas sind gehrorene,   hrēorge torras,
> hrīmgeat berofen   hrīm on līme
> 5   scearde scūrbeorge   scorene, gedrorene,
> ældo undereotone.   Eorðgrāp hafað
> waldendwyrhtan,   forweorone, geleorene,
> heard gripe hrūsan,   oþ hund cnēa
> werþēoda gewitan.   Oft þes wāg gebād
> 10   rǣghār ond rēadfāh   rīce æfter ōþrum,
> ofstonden under stormum;   stēap gēap gedrēas.
> Wunað gīet se wealstān   wederum gehēawen
> fel on . . . .
> grimme gegrunden . . . .
> 15   . . . . scān   hēo . . . .
> . . . . g orþonc   ǣrsceaft . . . .
> . . . . g   lāmrindum bēag
> mōd mo . . . .   yne swiftne gebrægd
> hwǣtrēd in hringas,   hygerōf gebond
> 20   weallwalan wīrum   wundrum tōgædre.

1-2 **wyrde . . . burston** 'the fates broke, smashed the city'.

enta geweorc 'the work of giants'. The Anglo-Saxons used this expression to refer to the impressive stone buildings left by the Romans. Cf. *Wanderer* l. 87.

3-5 **Hrōfas sind . . . gedrorene** The verb *sind* should be carried over, in both singular and plural senses, in the ensuing verses: 'The roofs are fallen, the towers [are] in ruins, the frosty gate [is] despoiled. . . .'

6-7 **undereotone** and **forweorone** are past participles with *-on-* for *-en-*, a rare but attested spelling.

9 **gewitan** = *gewiton* '[shall] have passed away'. See §198.

9-11 **Oft þes wāg . . . stormum** 'Often this wall, red-stained and grey with lichen, unmoved beneath the storms, has survived kingdom after kingdom.'

11 **stēap . . . gedrēas** *stēap* and *gēap* modify *wāg* (cf. l. 9), the understood subject of *gedrēas*.

13-18 It is best to skip over the fragmentary words and phrases, of which little sense can be made. Resume in l. 18 with *swiftne gebrægd*.

18-20 **swiftne gebrægd . . . tōgædre** '. . . put together (*gebrægd*, past ptc.) a swift, quick plan in rings; one strong in intelligence (*hygerōf*) bound the wall-braces together marvellously with wires.'

Beorht wǣron burgrǣced,   burnsele monige,
hēah horngestrēon,   hereswēg micel,
meodoheall monig   mondrēama full,
oþþæt þæt onwende   wyrd sēo swīþe.
25 Crungon walo wīde,   cwōman wōldagas,
swylt eall fornōm   secgrōfra wera;
wurdon hyra wigsteal   wēsten staþolas,
brosnade burgsteall.   Bētend crungon
hergas tō hrūsan.   Forþon þās hofu drēorgiað,
30 ond þes tēaforgēapa   tigelum scēadeð
hrōstbēages hrōf.   Hryre wong gecrong
gebrocen tō beorgum,   þǣr iū beorn monig
glædmōd ond goldbeorht   gleoma gefrætwed,
wlonc ond wīngāl   wīghyrstum scān;
35 seah on sinc, on sylfor,   on searogimmas,
on ēad, on æht,   on eorcanstān,
on þās beorhtan burg   brādan rīces.
Stānhofu stōdan,   strēam hāte wearp
wīdan wylme;   weal eall befēng
40 beorhtan bōsme,   þǣr þā baþu wǣron,
hāt on hreþre.   þæt wæs hȳðelic.
Lēton þonne gēotan . . . .
ofer hārne stān   hāte strēamas
un . . . .
45 .þþæt hringmere   hāte . . . .
. . . .   þǣr þā baþu wǣron.
þonne is . . . .
. . . . re;   þæt is cynelic þing,
hūse . . . .   burg . . . . .

---

27 **wurdon . . . staþolas** 'their sanctuaries (place of idols) became waste places'.
Wigsteal could also mean 'war places', but a possible Biblical source in Amos 6:9
('and the sanctuaries of Israel shall be laid waste') has been suggested, and this
would support the meaning 'places of idols, sanctuaries'.

28–9 **Bētend . . . hrūsan** 'The tenders (i.e. repairmen), the armies fell to the
earth.' *Hergas* could also mean 'idols, temples', and reference could be to the
wigsteall of l. 27: 'The tenders, the idols, fell to the earth.'

30–1 **ond þes tēaforgēapa . . . hrōf** 'and this red-curved roof of the vault splits
from the tiles'.

32 **gebrocen tō beorgum** 'broken into rubble-heaps'.

34 **wīghyrstum scān** 'shone in his war-trappings'. (The subject is *beorn monig*
'many a warrior'.)

38–9 **strēam hāte . . . wylme** 'the flowing water threw out heat, a great billow'.

40 **beorhtan bōsme** 'within its bright bosom', i.e. in the interior of the encircling wall that holds the hot bath-water.

41 **hāt on hreþre** 'hot to the core', i.e. 'very hot'.

42–3 **Lēton þonne . . . strēamas** 'They let the hot streams gush over the grey
stone.' From here to the end the text is too fragmentary to translate, except for l. 48b.

The Dream of the Rood
or
A Vision of the Cross

This, the earliest dream-vision poem in the English language, is the central literary document for understanding that resolution of conflicting cultures which was the presiding concern of the Christian Anglo-Saxons. The Germanic heroic tradition which the Anglo-Saxons brought with them to England celebrated courage, mastery, and aggressive action. The Christian outlook which the Anglo-Saxons in due course adopted stressed virtues like loving kindness and self-sacrifice. (See §§218, 236–246.) Finding a proper adjustment of the two competing ideals was a constant spiritual struggle. The poet of *The Dream of the Rood* discovered in the central event of Christian history an opportunity for using his people's native poetic tradition to encompass and naturalize the alien ideals of the new faith. In so far as the crucifixion required great courage of the Saviour, it offered the poet ample opportunity for displaying how the heroic diction of Old English poetry could serve to extol Christ's passion, especially since early Christianity perceived Christ in more heroic terms than later Christianity was to do: he was a warrior-king doing battle with the Devil (as one can readily see by reading the sources and analogues of the poem in D. G. Calder and M. J. B. Allen's *Sources and Analogues of Old English Poetry* (Cambridge, 1976), pp. 53–8). But there is a gentle, passive side to the character of Christ that is absent from the pagan heroic ethos. Under provocation he turns the other cheek. He forgives his tormentors. He accepts physical defeat for the sake of spiritual victory. He allows his adversaries to kill him. The poet of *The Dream of the Rood* accommodates the intermingled passivity and heroism of Christ by his daring and imaginative device of giving human characteristics and the power of speech to the inanimate cross on which Christ died. Possibly this literal personification of the cross was suggested to him by the Old English verse riddles, where various inanimate objects are made to speak out and describe their essential qualities. (See especially riddles *n* and *o* above.) The example of the riddles would have been reinforced by

Classical rhetorical exercises in prosopopoeia, which were prescribed in the schools. Whatever the source of the device, the poet uses it to portray a cross which is the passive, plangent sufferer in the crucifixion while Christ is left to be active and heroic – a figure reminiscent of the awesome Byzantine mosaics of Christ the King and also of Germanic heroes like Beowulf.

On a literary level the poem resolves not only the pagan–Christian tensions within Anglo-Saxon culture but also current doctrinal discussions concerning the nature of Christ, who was both God and man, both human and divine. But throughout its imaginative poeticizing of theological issues, *The Dream of the Rood* remains a thoroughly Germanic poem with an exciting plot, vivid martial imagery which makes heroic all that happens, startling effects such as the gory, talking cross whose drops of blood surrealistically congeal into beautiful gems and then become blood again. The characterization of the cross is also quintessentially Germanic: it presents itself as a loyal retainer (all creatures on earth being members of God's retinue) who is forced by his very loyalty to become the instrument of his beloved Lord's execution.

That this poem gripped the imagination of its Anglo-Saxon audience is suggested by the fact that a large, ornamented Anglo-Saxon stone cross in the town of Ruthwell has been inscribed with excerpts from *The Dream of the Rood* written in the ancient runic alphabet of the Germanic peoples (§229). Each passage quoted is from portions of the poem spoken by the animate cross. One of the passages, quoted here in the Northumbrian dialect of the inscription (slightly restored), may be compared with ll. 44–5 of the poem:

> Ahof ic riicnæ kyninc
> heafunæs hlafard   hælda ic ni dorstæ

A silver reliquary cross in Brussels is also inscribed with verses which echo lines spoken by the cross in *The Dream of the Rood*.[1] The poem and the idea of a speaking cross evidently met with cordial responsiveness in the imaginations of the Anglo-Saxons.

Like virtually all Old English poems, *The Dream of the Rood* has no title in its original manuscript (The Vercelli Book), its present title being an invention of modern scholars. It has also been called *A Vision of the Cross*, which is perhaps more suitable. Following are emendations which have been adopted in the text which follows: *hwæt* for MS *hæt* (l. 2), *eaxl* for *eaxle* (l. 9), *geweorðod* for *geweorðode* (l. 15), *Wealdendes* for *wealdes* (l. 17), *sorgum* for *surgum* (l. 20),

---

[1] Rod is min nama; geo ic ricne cyning bær byfigynde, blode bestemed. Cf. ll. 44 and 48.

ǣnigum for *nǣnigum* (1. 47), *sorgum* supplied in 1. 59, *grēotende* for *reotende* (1. 70), *stefn* for *syððan* (1. 71), *holtwudu* for *holmwudu* (1. 91), *anforht* for *unforht* (1. 117), *þām* for *þan* (1. 122), *mē* for *he* (1. 142).

Hwæt, ic swefna cyst   secgan wylle,
hwæt mē gemǣtte   tō midre nihte,
syðþan reordberend   reste wunedon.
þūhte mē þæt ic gesāwe   syllicre trēow
5   on lyft lǣdan   lēohte bewunden,
bēama beorhtost.   Eall þæt bēacen wæs
begoten mid golde;   gimmas stōdon
fægere æt foldan scēatum,   swylce þǣr fīfe wǣron
uppe on þām eaxlgespanne.   Behēoldon þǣr engel dryhtnes ealle
10 fægere þurh forðgesceaft;   ne wæs ðǣr hūru fracodes gealga,
ac hine þǣr behēoldon   hālige gāstas,
men ofer moldan   and eall þēos mǣre gesceaft.
Syllic wæs se sigebēam,   and ic synnum fāh,
forwundod mid wommum.   Geseah ic wuldres trēow

1–2 **swefna cyst** in 1. 1 and the clause introduced by *hwæt* in 1. 2 are parallel objects of the verb *secgan*: 'to tell the best of dreams, (to tell) what . . .'. See §159.

2 **mē gemǣtte** 'came to me in a vision', i.e. 'I dreamed' *gemǣtan* (like *þūhte* in 1. 4) is an impersonal verb with dative of person. See §212.

4 **syllicre** is often said to be an absolute comparative ('exceedingly rare'), but some comparative meaning can also be implicit: 'a rarer tree (than all the others)'. Cf. ll. 90–4 below.

5 **on lyft lǣdan** 'lifted into the air'. The infinitive following *gesāwe* has a passive sense. See §161. So also *þenian* following *geseah* in 1. 52.

8 **foldan scēatum** Either 'at the surface of the earth' (i.e. at the foot of the cross) or 'at the corners of the earth', the cross being seen as extending across the sky to four points on the horizon. With this verse begins the first of several groups of hypermetric lines which appear periodically throughout this poem (in ll. 8–10, 20–3, 30–4, 39–43, 46–9, 59–69, 75, and 133) and occasionally in other poems as well (e.g. *The Wanderer*, ll. 111–15, *The Seafarer*, ll. 106–9). Obviously some special effect was achieved by shifting from normal to hypermetric verses, but we cannot be sure what that effect was. The hypermetric verses seem to be systematic variations on the regular verse-types, most of them being expanded A-verses. The effect of hypermetric verses was exclusively aural and not visual, since the Anglo-Saxons wrote poetry continuously across the page from margin to margin just like prose and did not lineate their poems into separate verses.

9–10 **Behēoldon . . . forðgesceaft** 'All those fair by eternal decree gazed on the angel of the Lord (i.e. Christ or possibly the cross) there.' 'Those fair by eternal decree' are the *hālige gāstas* of l. 11 – the loyal angels who were predestined to remain in Heaven. Line 9b is long even for a hypermetric line and therefore has often been emended. But since it makes sense as it stands and none of the emendations is entirely satisfactory, we retain the manuscript reading.

11 **hine** refers to the nearest masculine antecedent, *gealga* 'the cross'.

15   wædum geweorðod   wynnum scīnan,
gegyred mid golde;   gimmas hæfdon
bewrigen weorðlīce   Wealdendes trēow.
Hwæðre ic þurh þæt gold   ongytan meahte
earmra ærgewin,   þæt hit ærest ongan
20   swǣtan on þā swīðran healfe.   Eall ic wæs mid sorgum gedrēfed;
forht ic wæs for þǣre fægran gesyhðe;   geseah ic þæt fūse
bēacen
wendan wǣdum and blēom: hwīlum hit wæs mid wǣtan
bestēmed,
beswyled mid swātes gange,   hwīlum mid since gegyrwed.
Hwæðre ic þǣr licgende   lange hwīle
25   behēold hrēowcearig   Hǣlendes trēow,
oð ðæt ic gehȳrde   þæt hit hlēoðrode;
ongan þā word sprecan   wudu sēlesta:
'þæt wæs gēara iū   – ic þæt gȳta geman –
þæt ic wæs āhēawen   holtes on ende,
30   āstyred of stefne mīnum.   Genāman mē ðǣr strange fēondas,
geworhton him þǣr tō wæfersȳne,   hēton mē heora wergas
hebban;
bǣron mē þǣr beornas on eaxlum,   oð ðæt hīe mē on beorg
āsetton;
gefæstnodon mē þǣr fēondas genōge.   Geseah ic þā Frēan
mancynnes
efstan elne micle,   þæt hē mē wolde on gestīgan.
35   þǣr ic þā ne dorste   ofer Dryhtnes word
būgan oððe berstan,   þā ic bifian geseah
eorðan scēatas.   Ealle ic mihte
fēondas gefyllan,   hwæðre ic fæste stōd.

15   wǣdum geweorðod 'adorned with garments'. 'Garments' is a poetic reference to the gold and jewelled adornments. In l. 22 it refers to these and the blood covering the cross as well.

19   earmra ærgewin 'ancient hostility of wretched ones', i.e. those who crucified Christ. *Ærgewin* and the following *þæt* clause are parallel objects of *ongytan*.

20   on þā swīðran healfe 'on the right side'. According to Christian tradition, it was Christ's right side that the centurion pierced with a spear.

31   geworhton ... wæfersȳne 'they made (me) into a spectacle for themselves there'. This refers to the Romans' use of crosses for the public (and ignominious) execution of felons.

33   gefæstnodon ... genōge 'Enemies enough (i.e. many enemies) secured me there.'

34   þæt hē ... gestīgan '(in) that he wanted to ascend onto me', i.e. 'in his wish to ascend onto me'. See §211.

36–7   þā ic bifian ... scēatas 'when I saw the surface of the earth tremble'. Matthew 27:51 says that the earth trembled at the crucifixion.

37–8   Ealle ... gefyllan, hwæðre ... 'I was able to fell (i.e. could have felled) all the adversaries, but. . . '.

Ongyrede hine þā geong hæleð   – þæt wæs God ælmihtig! –

40 strang and stīðmōd;   gestāh hē on gealgan hēanne,

mōdig on manigra gesyhðe,   þā hē wolde mancyn lȳsan.

Bifode ic þā mē se beorn ymbclypte;   ne dorste ic hwæðre

būgan tō eorðan,

feallan tō foldan scēatum,   ac ic sceolde fæste standan.

Rōd wæs ic ārǣred;   āhōf ic rīcne Cyning,

45 heofona Hlāford;   hyldan mē ne dorste.

þurhdrifan hī mē mid deorcan næglum;   on mē syndon þā dolg

gesīene,

opene inwidhlemmas;   ne dorste ic hira ǣnigum sceððan.

Bysmeredon hīe unc būtū ætgædere;   eall ic wæs mid blōde

bestēmed,

begoten of þæs guman sīdan   siððan hē hæfde his gāst

onsended.

50   'Feala ic on þām beorge   gebiden hæbbe

wrāðra wyrda: geseah ic weruda God

þearle þenian.   þȳstro hæfdon

bewrigen mid wolcnum   Wealdendes hrǣw,

scīrne scīman;   sceadu forð ēode,

55   wann under wolcnum.   Wēop eal gesceaft,

cwīðdon Cyninges fyll: Crīst wæs on rōde.

Hwæðere þǣr fūse   feorran cwōman

tō þām Æðelinge;   ic þæt eall behēold.

Sāre ic wæs mid sorgum gedrēfed,   hnāg ic hwæðre þām secgum

tō handa

60 eaðmōd, elne mycle.   Genāmon hīe þǣr ælmihtigne God,

āhōfon hine of ðām hefian wīte;   forlēton mē þā hilderincas

standan stēame bedrifenne;   eall ic wæs mid strǣlum

forwundod.

Ālēdon hīe ðǣr limwērigne;   gestōdon him æt his līces hēafdum;

behēoldon hīe ðǣr heofenes Dryhten,   and hē hine ðǣr hwīle

reste,

65 mēðe æfter ðām miclan gewinne.   Ongunnon him þā moldern

wyrcan

beornas on banan gesyhðe,   curfon hīe ðæt of beorhtan stāne;

49 **begoten** 'drenched' modifies *ic* in l. 48.

51–2 See note to l. 5 above.

54 **scīrne scīman** 'the bright radiance' is in apposition with *wealdendes hrǣw*.

57 **fūse** 'eager ones'. In view of John 19: 38–9, the eager ones would appear to be Joseph of Arimathea and Nicodemus, who came to claim the body of Jesus.

59 **þām secgum tō handa** 'to the hands of the men'. Poss. dat. See §191.2.

62 **strǣlum** 'with arrows'. The cross is referring to the hostile nails of l. 46.

63 **gestōdon . . . hēafdum** 'they positioned themselves at his body's head'. Dat. pl. *hēafdum* with singular meaning is an Old English idiom. Cf. *brēostum* in l. 118.

66 **banan** 'of the slayer'. The cross refers to itself as Christ's slayer.

gesetton hīe ðǣron sigora Wealdend.   Ongunnon him þā
sorhlēoð galan
earme on þā ǣfentīde,   þā hīe woldon eft sīðian,
mēðe fram þām mǣran þēodne;   reste hē ðǣr mǣte weorode.

70   Hwæðere wē ðǣr grēotende   gōde hwīle
stōdon on staðole;   stefn up gewāt
hilderinca;   hrǣw cōlode,
fæger feorgbold.   þā ūs man fyllan ongan
ealle tō eorðan;   þæt wæs egeslic wyrd!

75   Bedealf ūs man on dēopan sēaþe;   hwæðre mē þǣr Dryhtnes
þegnas,
frēondas gefrūnon,
gyredon mē   golde and seolfre.
    'Nū ðū miht gehȳran,   hæleð mīn se lēofa,
þæt ic bealuwara weorc   gebiden hæbbe,

80   sārra sorga.   Is nū sǣl cumen
þæt mē weorðiað   wīde and sīde
menn ofer moldan   and eall þēos mǣre gesceaft,
gebiddaþ him tō þyssum bēacne.   On mē Bearn Godes
þrōwode hwīle;   for þan ic þrymfæst nū

85   hlīfige under heofenum,   and ic hǣlan mæg
ǣghwylcne ānra   þāra þe him bið egesa tō mē.
Iū ic wæs geworden   wīta heardost,
lēodum lāðost,   ǣr þan ic him līfes weg
rihtne gerȳmde,   reordberendum.

90   Hwæt, mē þā geweorþode   wuldres Ealdor
ofer holtwudu,   heofonrīces Weard,
swylce swā hē his mōdor ēac,   Marīan sylfe,
ælmihtig God   for ealle menn
geweorðode   ofer eall wīfa cynn.

95   'Nū ic þē hāte,   hæleð mīn se lēofa,
þæt ðū þās gesyhðe   secge mannum;
onwrēoh wordum   þæt hit is wuldres bēam,
se ðe ælmihtig God   on þrōwode

69   mǣte werode 'with little company'. Germanic understatement meaning
'alone'. So also in l. 124.

70   wē i.e. the three crosses.

76   The second half of this line is lost, but the sense is clear: the cross was
buried, and then many years later St. Helena recovered it and adorned it as a
precious relic.

79–80   þæt ic bealuwara ... sārra sorga 'that I have suffered distress from
dwellers in iniquity, from sore sorrows'. *Bealuwara* and *sorga* are parallel genitives
dependent on *weorc*.

86   þāra þe ... tō mē 'of those in whom is fear of me'. See §162.1 and 2.

92   swylce swā 'just as'.

98   se ðe ... þrōwode 'on which almighty God suffered'. See §163.1.

for mancynnes   manegum synnum
100 and Adomes   ealdgewyrhtum.
Dēað hē þǣr byrigde;   hwæðere eft Dryhten ārās
mid his miclan mihte   mannum tō helpe.
Hē ðā on heofenas āstāg.   Hider eft fundaþ
on þysne middangeard   mancynn sēcan
105 on dōmdæge   Dryhten sylfa,
ælmihtig God   and his englas mid,
þæt hē þonne wile dēman,   se āh dōmes geweald,
ānra gehwylcum,   swā hē him ǣrur hēr
on þyssum lǣnum   līfe geearnaþ.
110 Ne mæg þǣr ǣnig   unforht wesan
for þām worde   þe se Wealdend cwyð:
frīneð hē for þǣre mænige   hwǣr se man sīe,
se ðe for Dryhtnes naman   dēaðes wolde
biteres onbyrigan,   swā hē ǣr on ðām bēame dyde.
115 Ac hīe þonne forhtiað,   and fēa þencaþ
hwæt hīe tō Crīste   cweðan onginnen.
Ne þearf ðǣr þonne ǣnig   anforht wesan
þe him ǣr in brēostum bereð   bēacna sēlest;
ac ðurh ðā rōde sceal   rīce gesēcan
120 of eorðwege   ǣghwylc sāwl,
sēo þe mid Wealdende   wunian þenceð.'
    Gebæd ic mē þā tō þām bēame   blīðe mōde,
elne mycle,   þǣr ic āna wæs
mǣte werede.   Wæs mōdsefa
125 āfȳsed on forðwege,   feala ealra gebād
langunghwīla.   Is mē nū līfes hyht
þæt ic þone sigebēam   sēcan mōte
āna oftor   þonne ealle men,
well weorþian.   Mē is willa tō ðām
130 mycel on mōde,   and mīn mundbyrd is
geriht tō þǣre rōde.   Nāh ic rīcra feala
frēonda on foldan,   ac hīe forð heonon
gewiton of worulde drēamum,   sōhton him wuldres Cyning;

107–9 **þæt hē þonne ... geearnaþ** 'in that He who has power of judgement
wishes to pass judgement then on each of those even as he shall have earned for
himself (while) here in this transitory life'. *Ærur* with the present (with future
meaning) *geearnaþ* yields a future perfect in meaning. Similarly *ǣr... bereð* in l. 118.
124–6 **Wæs mōdsefa ... langunghwīla** '(My) mind was inspired with longing
(*āfȳsed*) for the way hence (to the next world), it has experienced in all (*ealra*) many
periods of longing (for the next life).'
129–30 **Mē is willa ... on mōde** 'The desire for that is intense in my heart.'
133   **him** This reflexive dative (with *sōhton*) need not be translated.

lifiaþ nū on heofenum   mid Hēahfædere,
135   wuniaþ on wuldre;   and ic wēne mē
daga gehwylce   hwænne mē Dryhtnes rōd,
þe ic hēr on eorðan   ǣr scēawode,
on þysson lǣnan   līfe gefetige,
and mē þonne gebringe   þǣr is blis mycel,
140   drēam on heofonum,   þǣr is Dryhtnes folc
geseted tō symle,   þǣr is singāl blis;
and mē þonne āsette   þǣr ic syþþan mōt
wunian on wuldre,   well mid þām hālgum
drēames brūcan.   Sī mē Dryhten frēond,
145   se ðe hēr on eorðan   ǣr þrōwode
on þām gealgtrēowe   for guman synnum;
hē ūs onlȳsde,   and ūs līf forgeaf,
heofonlicne hām.   Hiht wæs genīwad
mid blēdum and mid blisse,   þām þe þǣr bryne þolodan.
150   Se Sunu wæs sigorfæst   on þām sīðfate,
mihtig and spēdig,   þā hē mid manigeo cōm,
gāsta weorode,   on Godes rīce,
Anwealda ælmihtig,   englum tō blisse
and eallum ðām hālgum   þām þe in heofonum ǣr
155   wunedon on wuldre,   þā heora Wealdend cwōm,
ælmihtig God,   þǣr his ēðel wæs.

135–8   ic wēne mē ... gefetige 'I look forward each day to (the time) when the cross of the Lord ... will fetch me.' The *mē* in l. 135 is reflexive and need not be translated. On *hwænne* introducing a clause, see §159 note 2.

144   Sī mē Dryhten frēond 'May the Lord be a friend to me.' Cf. ll. 131–2.

146   for guman synnum 'for men's sins'. *Guman* is a late gen. pl. (for *gumena*).

148–9   Hiht wæs genīwad ... þolodan This sentence refers to Christ's harrowing of hell when, following the crucifixion, he descended to the nether regions and rescued from the burning fires all good people who had died since the creation.

150–6   These verses refer to Christ's ascension into heaven with all the souls he had rescued in the harrowing. The ascension actually takes place forty days later.

153   englum tō blisse 'to the delight of the angels'.

The Wife's Lament

The Wife's Lament is a woman's account of how she became
estranged from her young husband through the machinations of his
relatives. Forced to live alone in a settlement far away from him,
she suffers pitifully, yearning for him day and night. The details of
the plot are somewhat sketchy, the poet's main attention being on
the speaker's sadness and love-longing. It has been conjectured
that the woman speaking in the poem was a character known to the
audience from other narratives and that by knowing her story
beforehand they would have been better able to understand what is
going on in *The Wife's Lament*. It is true that we are told nothing
about why her husband originally had to leave her and make a sea
journey, about why and how his relatives persuaded him to reject
her, or about the identities of any of the principal characters. But
the general sequence of actions is fairly clear in the poem as it is
presented here. Her husband leaves, and the wife, smitten with
longing for him, joins him (ll. 6–10). His kinsmen, who want to
separate the couple from each other, get the husband to send her
back to his homeland where he orders her to live in a cave or hovel
in the midst of a forbidding grove of trees (ll. 11–32). (Sad
recollections of their former devotion to one another contrasted
with the husband's hostile state of mind at present intervene at
ll. 18–22.) Lines 32–41 are a poignant account of the abandoned
wife's longing and sorrow. The final section (ll. 42–53) seems to be
the wife's speculations as to the husband's present circumstances
and her assurances to herself that he must feel as sad as she when
he recalls their former life together. She closes with a gnomic
observation about the suffering of parted lovers.

Since thousands of lines of Old English poetry deal primarily
with women (e.g. *Elene*, *Judith*, *Juliana*), it is not surprising to find
in *The Wife's Lament* a concern with exploring the psychology of a
suffering woman. Yet some scholars have doubted that this is a
woman's monologue and try to interpret it as the lament of a man,
much like *The Wanderer*. Such interpretations have to begin by
altering or explaining away the grammatical endings in *gēomorre*
(l. 1) and *mīnre sylfre* (l. 2), which make it clear that the speaker is

feminine. Other interpretations have sought to introduce a love-triangle by suggesting that some of the speaker's references to her lord and lover are to one man (her husband) and others are to another (her lover). Yet other scholars have suggested that the monologue is spoken by the Heavenly Bride (i.e. the Church), who is commanded by Christ to remain in this world of sorrow until the Second Coming. Another suggests it is a voice from the grave. The narrative is sufficiently cryptic and the language of Old English poetry sufficiently flexible that a case can be made for a variety of different situations in the poem. As in much literary interpretation, the only available curb to ever more ingenious speculations about *The Wife's Lament* is common sense.

The text here is that of the Exeter Book, except that modern conventions of punctuation, capitalization, word-division, verse-lineation, and long-vowel marking are introduced, and the following emendations are adopted: *āwēox* for MS *weox* in l. 3, *hycgendne* for *hycgende* in l. 20, *nǣfre* for *no* in l. 24, *sceal* for *seal* in l. 25, and *sittan* for *sittam* in l. 37.

> Ic þis giedd wrece   bī mē ful gēomorre,
> mīnre sylfre sīð.   Ic þæt secgan mæg,
> hwæt ic yrmþa gebād,   siþþan ic ūp āwēox,
> nīwes oþþe ealdes,   nō mā þonne nū.
> 5 Ā ic wīte wonn   mīnra wræcsīþa.
> Ǣrest mīn hlāford gewāt   heonan of lēodum
> ofer ȳþa gelāc;   hæfde ic ūhtceare
> hwǣr mīn lēodfruma   londes wǣre.
> Ðā ic mē fēran gewāt   folgað sēcan,
> 10 winelēas wræcca,   for mīnre wēaþearfe.
> Ongunnon þæt þæs monnes   māgas hycgan
> þurh dyrne geþōht,   þæt hȳ tōdǣlden unc,
> þæt wit gewīdost   in woruldrīce
> lifdon lāðlicost,   ond mec longade.

2   sīð is acc. sing., parallel with *giedd*. 'I narrate this poem, . . . (narrate) my own experience.'

8   hwǣr . . . wǣre '(as to) where in the land my leader of men might be'. *Londes* (like *nīwes oþþe ealdes* in l. 4) is adverbial genitive (§190.5).

9–10   Ðā . . . wēaþearfe 'When, because of my woeful need, I set out, a friendless stranger, to visit the retinue'. Her husband, who has just been described as 'a leader of men' (*lēodfruma*, l. 8) is travelling with his retainers, and it is this group that she must seek out when she goes to visit him.

11–14   'The man's kinsmen began plotting that they would separate us, so that we two have lived most miserably, most far apart, and longing has afflicted me.'

15 Hēt mec hlāford mīn   herheard niman,
   āhte ic lēofra lӯt   on þissum londstede,
   holdra frēonda,   forþon is mīn hyge gēomor.
   Ðā ic mē ful gemæcne   monnan funde,
   heardsæligne,   hygegēomorne,
20 mōd mīþendne,   morþor hycgendne
   blīþe gebæro.   Ful oft wit bēotedan
   þæt unc̄ ne gedælde   nemne dēað āna
   ōwiht elles;   eft is þæt onhworfen,
   is nū swā hit   næfre wære,
25 frēondscipe uncer.   Sceal ic feor ge nēah
   mīnes felalēofan   fæhðu drēogan.
      Heht mec mon wunian   on wuda bearwe,
   under āctrēo   in þām eorðscræfe.
   Eald is þes eorðsele,   eal ic eom oflongad,
30 sindon dena dimme,   dūna ūphēa,
   bitre burgtūnas,   brērum beweaxne,
   wīc wynna lēas.   Ful oft mec hēr wrāþe begeat
   fromsīþ frēan.   Frӯnd sind on eorþan,
   lēofe lifgende,   leger weardiað,
35 þonne ic on ūhtan   āna gonge
   under āctrēo   geond þās eorðscrafu.
   þær ic sittan mōt   sumorlangne dæg;
   þær ic wēpan mæg   mīne wræcsīþas,
   earfoþa fela;   forþon ic æfre ne mæg
40 þære mōdceare   mīnre gerestan,
   ne ealles þæs longaþes   þe mec on þissum līfe begeat.
      Ā scyle geong mon   wesan gēomormōd,

15 OE *eard niman* means 'to take up an abode', so *herheard niman* means 'to take up (my) abode in a *herh*'. *Herh* (or *hearh*) refers either to a grove or a part of a pagan sanctuary or temple grounds. In view of l. 27b, it probably means 'grove' here.

18 'Then I found the man (who had been) very suitable to me. . . .'

22–3 ne . . . ōwiht 'naught, nothing': 'that naught but death alone should separate us'.

24 'it is now as if it had never been'.

27 Heht mec mon 'I was commanded (by my husband).'

32 mec hēr wrāþe begeat 'took hold of me cruelly here', i.e. 'caused me pain'.

34 leger weardiað 'occupy their bed', i.e. 'are in bed together'.

39–41 Forþon . . . longaþes 'Therefore I can never rest from that sorrow of mine nor from all that longing.'

42–52 Here the speaker seems to speculate over what might be the present state of her estranged spouse and to assure herself that whatever his circumstances he will certainly be sharing her sorrow over their separation.

42–3 Ā scyle . . . geþōht 'It may be that the young man must always be sorrowful (and) his heart's thought stern.' The subjunctive *scyle* suggests that she is only speculating about his state of mind, but the shift to indicative *sceal* indicates certainty ('at the same time he *must* have a cheerful demeanour along with his

heard heortan geþōht,   swylce habban sceal
blīþe gebǣro,   ēac þon brēostceare,
45   sinsorgna gedreag.   Sȳ æt him sylfum gelong
eal his worulde wyn,   sȳ ful wīde fāh
feorres folclondes,   þæt mīn frēond siteð
under stānhliþe   storme behrīmed,
wine werigmōd,   wætre beflōwen
50   on drēorsele,   drēogeð se mīn wine
micle mōdceare;   hē gemon tō oft
wynlicran wīc.   Wā bið þām þe sceal
of langoþe   lēofes ābīdan.

---

breast- cares'), since she has observed at first hand in ll. 20–1 that this is a characteristic of the young man.

45–7 Sȳ ... sȳ ... .The two subjunctives are used correlatively to introduce alternative speculations: 'Whether he is dependent (solely) upon himself for all his joy in the world, or whether he is outlawed far from his remote inheritance so that my dear one sits ....'

50–1 drēogeð ... mōdceare 'that lover of mine will experience great sorrow at heart'. This is the main clause upon which the preceding subordinate clauses depend.

The Wanderer

The Wanderer is one of several great meditative poems from the Exeter Book. It is a dramatic monologue briefly introduced by the Christian poet and briefly concluded by him with a terse exhortation to seek comfort in God the Father. The monologue itself is spoken by a heroic-age nobleman whose assessment of life's meaning shows no awareness of Christian enlightenment. The only outside forces of which he has knowledge are fate, the forces of nature, and a 'creator of men' (*ælda scyppend*, l. 85) whose only action in the poem is to lay waste all that men have made. The wanderer who speaks the monologue is in the worst possible circumstances for an Anglo-Saxon warrior in the heroic age: he is a retainer who has lost his lord and comrades and who therefore finds himself with no place in society, no identity in a hostile world. He is man *in extremis*, alone with his memories and naked to his enemies. This plight moves him to strenuous and painful reflection.

He begins by acknowledging the noble precept that a suffering man must bear up silently and, indeed, all that he says is spoken *on mōde* 'in his mind', i.e. 'silently to himself' (l. 111). He is *āna* (l. 8), and what we hear are his inmost thoughts. The depth of his feeling for his dead lord and lost comrades is dramatized by the unceasing sorrow that seems to attend his vain wanderings, and by his reveries of the past, which at times lead to hallucinatory illusions that his dead friends have returned and which leave him even deeper in sadness after his return to reality. At l. 58 he begins to move from his personal sorrow into a sense of the sorrowful state of the entire world, where all is transient and meaningless. Like the sparrow in Bede's story of the conversion of Edwin (8, ll. 24–38), men leave the hall at the end of life (l. 61) and pass into darkness and oblivion. With poetic imagination he evokes and laments a ruined city (ll. 75–110) and concludes with the hopeless observation that 'all the foundation of this earth will become empty'. He has summoned the full range of heroic-age wisdom to his meditation on existence, and the conclusion to which this wisdom brings him is that all is empty and without meaning. When his thoughts have run their course, the Christian poet returns and offers his terse comment: our only security lies with the Father in Heaven; we must seek consolation from Him.

Some modern readers have found a troubling imbalance in the monologue and authorial comment. The wanderer's hopeless situation and despairing scrutiny of the meaning of existence seem too briefly answered by the Christian poet's assertion that all our hope is in God the Father. But this assertion is in fact all that is needed since the wanderer's philosophizing – strong in feeling, high in dignity, and wisely reflective – demonstrates its own impotence before the transience and sorrow of the world. The poet can safely assume that if such an eloquent inquirer as the wanderer can find no more satisfying answer than 'eal þis eorþan gesteal idel weorþeð' (l. 110), then the Christian invitation to consolation requires no elaboration. This after all is the logic of the nameless nobleman who counselled King Edwin to accept Christianity: if our pagan faith offers nothing more than the meaninglessness of a sparrow's flight through a hall, then let us turn to the God whom Paulinus is proclaiming.

Later Christian poets have followed a similar course in presenting the superiority of Christianity to a noble but unavailing pagan alternative. Throughout the five books of *Troilus* Chaucer involves his readers in the beauties and disasters of love in the pagan Classical world, only to end with the brief but moving palinode exhorting his readers, 'Repeyreth hom fro worldly vanyte!' An even closer parallel is Samuel Johnson's *The Vanity of Human Wishes*, in which the poet gives eloquent expression throughout most of the poem to the Juvenalian commentator who surveys the world with stoic insight and learns from his survey nothing more than that helpless man must 'roll darkling down the torrent of his fate'. At this point the poet as Christian moralist interrupts with the command 'Enquirer cease!' and closes the poem with the solemn observation that only Christian faith offers hope and meaning to man. In all these poems it is the powerful and unavailing pagan perspective that moves the reader and makes the Christian's point, so that no Christian insistence is needed. And yet each poet leaves us permanently fascinated by the outlook he deftly rejects: Chaucer's Homeric milieu, Johnson's Roman stoicism, and the pre-Christian creed of the Anglo-Saxon wanderer.

The following emendations have been adopted: *healde* for MS *healdne* (l. 14), *minne* for *mine* (l. 22), *waþema* for *waþena* (l. 24), *freondlēasne* for *freond lease* (l. 28), *wenian* for *weman* (l. 29); *mōdsefa* for *mod sefan* (l. 59), *weorþan* for *wearþan* (l. 64), *ealre* for *ealle* (l. 74), *deorce* for *deornce* (l. 89), *hrūsan* for *hruse* (l. 102).

Facsimile of the opening page of *The Wanderer*, from the Exeter Book, folio 76b, lines 1–33a. Reproduced by kind permission of the Dean and Chapter of Exeter Cathedral.

Oft him ānhaga   āre gebīdeð,
metudes miltse,   þeah þe hē mōdcearig
geond lagulāde   longe sceolde
hrēran mid hondum   hrīmcealde sǣ,
5   wadan wræclāstas.   Wyrd bið ful ārǣd!
Swā cwæð eardstapa,   earfeþa gemyndig,
wrāþra wælsleahta,   winemǣga hryre:
'Oft ic sceolde āna   ūhtna gehwylce
mīne ceare cwīþan.   Nis nū cwicra nān
10   þe ic him mōdsefan   mīnne durre
sweotule āsecgan.   Ic tō sōþe wāt
þæt biþ in eorle   indryhten þēaw,
þæt hē his ferðlocan   fæste binde,
healde his hordcofan,   hycge swā hē wille.
15   Ne mæg wērig mōd   wyrde wiðstondan,
ne se hrēo hyge   helpe gefremman.
Forðon dōmgeorne   drēorigne oft
in hyra brēostcofan   bindað fæste;
swā ic mōdsefan   mīnne sceolde,
20   oft earmcearig,   ēðle bidǣled,
frēomǣgum feor   feterum sǣlan,
siþþan gēara iū   goldwine mīnne
hrūsan heolstre biwrāh,   ond ic hēan þonan
wōd wintercearig   ofer waþema gebind,
25   sōhte seledrēorig   sinces bryttan,
hwǣr ic feor oþþe nēah   findan meahte
þone þe in meoduhealle   mīne wisse,
oþþe mec frēondlēasne   frēfran wolde,

1–5   Oft him ānhaga . . . ful ārǣd! Because *gebīdeð* can mean both 'waits for' and 'experiences', this sentence has been variously interpreted. We suggest: 'The solitary man always waits for prosperity, for the favour of fate, although he, sad at heart, has long had to stir the ice-cold sea with his hands, traverse throughout the water-ways the paths of an exile. Fate is wholly inexorable!' *Oft* literally means 'often', but in poetry is frequently an understatement for 'always'. The pronoun *him* (l. 1) is dative of interest: 'for himself'.

7   winemǣga hryre (= hryra) 'of the deaths of kinsmen'. This is but one of several attempts by scholars to interpret the grammar of *hryre*.

9–11   Nis nū . . . āsecgan See §163.2.

11   tō sōþe 'for a truth', 'truly'.

14   hycge . . . wille 'think as he will', 'whatever he may want to think'.

17   drēorigne 'sorrowful (mind)', with *hyge* understood from l. 16.

22–3   siþþan gēara iū . . . biwrāh 'since years ago I concealed (i.e. buried) my lord in earth's darkness'. The subject of *biwrāh* is *ic*, understood from l. 19.

25   sōhte seledrēorig 'sad for the lack of a hall, I sought'.

27   mīne wisse 'might know of my own (i.e. my origins or people)'. Only if a lord has prior knowledge of the man's tribal affiliations will he be willing to accept the wanderer into his retinue.

wenian mid wynnum.   Wāt se þe cunnað,
30 hū slīþen bið   sorg tō gefēran,
þām þe him lӯt hafað   lēofra geholena:
warað hine wræclāst,   nales wunden gold,
ferðloca frēorig,   nalæs foldan blæd.
Gemon hē selesecgas   ond sincþege,
35 hū hine on geoguðe   his goldwine
wenede tō wiste.   Wyn eal gedrēas!
    Forþon wāt se þe sceal   his winedryhtnes
lēofes lārcwidum   longe forþolian:
ðonne sorg ond slæp   somod ætgædre
40 earmne ānhogan   oft gebindað,
þinceð him on mōde   þæt hē his mondryhten
clyppe ond cysse   ond on cnēo lecge
honda ond hēafod,   swā hē hwīlum ær
in gēardagum   giefstōlas brēac.
45 Ðonne onwæcneð eft   winelēas guma,
gesihð him biforan   fealwe wēgas,
baþian brimfuglas,   brædan feþra,
hrēosan hrīm ond snāw   hagle gemenged.
    þonne bēoð þӯ hefigran   heortan benne,
50 sāre æfter swæsne.   Sorg bið genīwad
þonne māga gemynd   mōd geondhweorfeð;
grēteð glīwstafum,   georne geondscēawað
secga geseldan;   swimmað oft on weg.

29–30 **Wāt se þe cunnað . . . gefēran** 'He who knows (at first hand) how cruel is
sorrow for a companion . . . understands.'

32 **warað hine wræclāst** 'the path of an exile claims him'.

37–44 **Forþon wāt . . . brēac** The long sentence in ll. 39–44 is the direct object
of *wāt* (l. 37): 'He who must long forgo his beloved lord's counsels knows (that)
when sorrow and sleep both together constrain the wretched solitary, it seems to
him . . .'.

43–4 **swā hē hwīlum . . . brēac** 'just as from time to time he used to make use of
the throne in days of old'. (*giefstōlas* is a late spelling of gen. sg. *giefstōles*.) 'Making
use of the throne' by embracing the lord, placing hand and head on his knees, etc. is
evidently a ritual confirming the close ties between the lord and his retainer.

46–7 **gesihð him biforan . . . brimfuglas** 'sees before him the fallow waves
(sees) the seabirds bathing', etc.

51–3 **þonne māga gemynd . . . geseldan** Either 'whenever the memory of
kinsmen passes through his mind, he greets joyfully (and) eagerly scrutinizes the
companions of men' or 'whenever the mind passes through the memory of kinsmen,
it greets joyfully (and) eagerly scrutinizes the companions of men'. *Secga geseldan*
(and the *flēotendra ferð* of l. 54) appear to refer both to the birds the wanderer sees
when he is awake and to the remembered kinsmen, whom he imagines he sees
before him in his dreams and reveries.

53 **swimmað oft on weg** 'they always drift away'. Just as in the next line *nō . . .
fela* means (by ironic understatement) 'none', here *oft* 'often' means 'always'. Cf. l. 1
above.

Flēotendra ferð   nō þǣr fela bringeð
55 cūðra cwidegiedda.   Cearo bið genīwad
þām þe sendan sceal   swīþe geneahhe
ofer waþema gebind   wērigne sefan.
    Forþon ic geþencan ne mæg   geond þās woruld
for hwan mōdsefa   mīn ne gesweorce
60 þonne ic eorla līf   eal geondþence,
hū hī fǣrlīce   flet ofgēafon,
mōdge maguþegnas.   Swā þes middangeard
ealra dōgra gehwām   drēoseð ond fealleþ;
forþon ne mæg weorþan wīs   wer, ǣr hē āge
65 wintra dǣl in woruldrīce.   Wita sceal geþyldig,
ne sceal nō tō hātheort   ne tō hrǣdwyrde,
ne tō wāc wiga   ne tō wanhȳdig,
ne tō forht ne tō fǣgen,   ne tō feohgīfre
ne nǣfre gielpes tō georn,   ǣr hē geare cunne.
70 Beorn sceal gebīdan,   þonne hē bēot spriceð,
oþþæt collenferð   cunne gearwe
hwider hreþra gehygd   hweorfan wille.
Ongietan sceal glēaw hæle   hū gǣstlic bið,
þonne ealre þisse worulde wela   wēste stondeð,
75 swā nū missenlīce   geond þisne middangeard
winde biwāune   weallas stondaþ,
hrīme bihrorene,   hrȳðge þā ederas.
Wōriað þā wīnsalo,   waldend licgað
drēame bidrorene,   duguþ eal gecrong,
80 wlonc bī wealle.   Sume wīg fornōm,

58–9 **Forþon ic geþencan ... gesweorce** 'Wherefore I cannot think for all this world why my mind does not grow dark.' The highly metaphorical *modsefa ... gesweorcan* 'mind darken' obviously means more than simply 'become sad', since the speaker has been sad ever since his wanderings began. Probably 'despair' or 'lose the light of reason' or something equally critical is intended.

61 **flet ofgēafon** lit. 'left the floor (of the meadhall)', i.e. 'died'.

66–9 **ne sceal ... geare cunne** 'must not be wrathful at all, nor precipitate of speech', etc. Although the literal sense is that a wise man 'must not be too wrathful, nor too precipitate in speech', etc., it is obvious that these are qualities to be avoided altogether. The use of *tō* 'too' here seems to be a rhetorical expression growing out of the Anglo-Saxons' predilection for understatement rather than absolute assertion. (An infinitive meaning 'be' should be understood following each *sceal*, this omission being characteristic of gnomic utterances in Old English.)

70–2 'Whenever he makes a vow, a stout-hearted warrior must wait until he knows precisely where the thoughts of his heart will tend.' Both here and in l. 69 the speaker is warning against rash vows (*gielp*, *bēot*) uttered in public, since a man would earn contempt if he failed to carry out what he boasted he would do.

73 **bið** 'it will be'.

80–4 **Sume wīg fornōm** 'War destroyed several' is followed by a description of the fate met by the corpses of individual members of the slain (*sumne* being acc. sg.

ferede in forðwege, sumne fugel oþbær
ofer hēanne holm, sumne se hāra wulf
dēaðe gedǣlde, sumne drēorighlēor
in eorðscræfe eorl gehȳdde.

85 Ȳþde swā þisne eardgeard ælda scyppend
oþþæt burgwara breahtma lēase
eald enta geweorc īdlu stōdon.

Se þonne þisne wealsteal wīse geþōhte
ond þis deorce līf dēope geondþenceð,

90 frōd in ferðe, feor oft gemon
wælsleahta worn, ond þās word ācwið:
"Hwǣr cwōm mearg? Hwǣr cwōm mago? Hwǣr cwōm
māþþumgyfa?
Hwǣr cwōm symbla gesetu? Hwǣr sindon seledrēamas?
Ēalā beorht bune! Ēalā byrnwiga!

95 Ēalā þēodnes þrym! Hū sēo þrāg gewāt,
genāp under nihthelm, swā hēo nō wǣre.
Stondeð nū on lāste lēofre duguþe
weal wundrum hēah, wyrmlīcum fāh.
Eorlas fornōman asca þrȳþe,

100 wǣpen wælgīfru, wyrd sēo mǣre,
ond þās stānhleoþu stormas cnyssað,
hrīð hrēosende hrūsan bindeð,
wintres wōma, þonne won cymeð,
nīpeð nihtscūa, norþan onsendeð

105 hrēo hæglfare hæleþum on andan."
Eall is earfoðlic eorþan rīce,
onwendeð wyrda gesceaft weoruld under heofonum.
Hēr bið feoh lǣne, hēr bið frēond lǣne,
hēr bið mon lǣne, hēr bið mǣg lǣne,

---

masc.). The bird of prey which carries off the body (piecemeal) and the wolf are a
familiar motif in Old English battle poetry. Cf. 12/106-7.

86-7 oþþæt burgwara ... stōdon 'until the ancient works of giants stood
empty, devoid of the revelry of their (erstwhile) inhabitants'.

87 enta geweorc Cf. 13/2 and note.

88 Se 'He who'. See §164.

92-3 Hwǣr cwōm 'where has gone'; loosely, 'what has become of'. This
haunting lament on the transience of earthly things may be based on *ubi sunt*
passages in Latin sermons, as has been suggested, but such a universal sentiment
hardly needs a specific source.

97 on lāste lēofre duguþe lit. 'in the track of the dear retinue', i.e. 'after (the
departure, i.e. death of) the dear retinue'.

99-100 Eorlas is acc. pl. masc.; þrȳþe, wǣpen, and wyrd are nom., parallel
subjects of *fornōman*.

107 onwendeð ... heofonum 'the operation of the fates changes the world
under the heavens'.

110   eal þis eorþan gesteal   īdel weorþeð!'
    Swā cwæð snottor on mōde,   gesæt him sundor æt rūne.
Til biþ se þe his trēowe gehealdeþ,   ne sceal næfre his
    torn tō rycene
beorn of his brēostum ācȳþan,   nemþe hē ǣr þā bōte
    cunne,
eorl mid elne gefremman.   Wel bið þām þe him āre sēceð,
115   frōfre tō Fæder on heofonum,   þǣr ūs eal sēo fæstnung
    stondeð.

114   **Wel bið ... sēceð** 'Well is it for the one who seeks mercy for himself.'

The Seafarer

Ever since the Anglo-Saxons migrated by ship from the Continent to the isle of Britain, Englishmen seem to have been more aware than most people of the importance and fascination of the sea and seafaring. One aspect of the seafaring life which has always captured the attention of people everywhere is the paradoxical state of mind called 'sea fever' – that irresistible call of the sea felt by experienced seamen who may on some occasions complain bitterly about the pains and trials of sea travel, but will sign on for another voyage when the opportunity presents itself. Poems and novels in many periods have treated this subject, but none has done so more convincingly than the Old English poetic monologue *The Seafarer*, which searches so deeply the thoughts and feelings of one Anglo-Saxon sailor that the poet Ezra Pound claims to have discovered in this work 'the English national chemical'.

But impressive as it is in its treatment of the physical and psychological rigours of seafaring life, the poem is about much more than that. Indeed, most of the latter half of the monologue does not mention the sea but rather is concerned with the impermanence of earthly riches and worldly fame and the importance of fixing one's attention on the world to come, where judgement will be severe and the rewards will be lasting. The juxtaposition of the seafarer's account of his involvement with the sea and his concerns for the future life is startling, but it is not incomprehensible. First he describes dramatically his sufferings at sea while men on land live in comfort, but he simultaneously expresses his disdain for the landlubber's life and his preference for the trials and challenges of seafaring. But then (ll. 64–6) his thoughts shift from considerations of sea voyages to his ultimate goal of union with the Lord in Heaven. To achieve this higher goal, one must forgo the pomps and joys of earthly existence and the fleeting benefits of gold and worldly goods at large. Just as the seafaring man is willing to deny himself the pleasures of life on land in order to take up the hard challenges of the sea, the devout Christian must be willing to renounce the pleasures of the flesh in order to arrive at his heavenly destination. Once this analogy is perceived, the vividness and force of the early description of the seafarer's lot take on in retrospect larger dimensions. The movingly expressed catalogue of pleasures that the seafarer renounces (ll. 44–7) seem on second thought like the determined exercise in self-abnegation that a Christian might practise on taking holy orders. The undefined cares which are hot in the seafarer's heart in l. 11 are echoed in ll. 64–6 when he speaks of the joys of the Lord being 'hotter' than transitory earthly existence. (And we may be reminded of Luke 24: 32: 'did not our heart burn within us, while he [the Lord] talked with us by the way . . . ?') Key words like *dryhten* and *lond* take on second meanings as the initial monologue of the seafarer is placed in juxtaposition with this broader conception of man's voyage through life to an ultimate destination. Scholars have detected artful symmetries and subtle allegories at work in *The Seafarer*, but perhaps the poet's strongest statement is the question implicit in the simple analogy he has established: if we can all accept the fact that seafaring men will forgo the pleasures of life on land for the obscure enticements of a dangerous ocean journey, is it unreasonable for Christianity to require renunciation of some earthly delights for the goal of eternal salvation?

As the notes below will indicate, *The Seafarer* presents some difficulties in syntax and thought transition, partly because of its strong feeling and sometimes passionate insistence. But its hard realism combined with lofty otherworldliness repays the effort required to read the poem. The following emendations have been adopted: *hleahtre* for MS *hleahtor* (l. 21), *ne ænig* for *nænig* (l. 25), *frēfran* for *feran* (l. 26), *gewītan* for *gewita* (l. 52), *sēftēadig* for *efteadig* (l. 56), *hwælweg* for *wælweg* (l. 63), *stondað* for *stondeð* (l. 67), *tīddege* for *tide ge* (l. 69), *bið* for *þæt* (l. 72), *fremum* for *fremman* (l. 75), *blæd* for *blæð* (l. 79), *nearon* for *næron* (l. 82), *mon* for *mod* (l. 109), *lufan* supplied in l. 112, *swiþre* for *swire* (l. 115), *wē* for *se* (l. 117).

> Mæg ic be mē sylfum   sōðgied wrecan,
> sīþas secgan,   hū ic geswincdagum
> earfoðhwīle   oft þrōwade,
> bitre brēostceare   gebiden hæbbe,
> 5   gecunnad in cēole   cearselda fela,
> atol ȳþa gewealc.   þær mec oft bigeat
> nearo nihtwaco   æt nacan stefnan,

2 geswincdagum 'in days of hardship'.
5 cearselda fela 'many a house of care'. The ship has often been a sorrowful abode for the seafarer.
6–7 mec oft bigeat . . . stefnan 'the anxious nightwatch often held me at the ship's prow'.

þonne hē be clifum cnossað.　Calde geþrungen
wǣron mīne fēt,　forste gebunden,
10 caldum clommum,　þǣr þā ceare seofedun
hāt'ymb heortan;　hungor innan slāt
merewērges mōd.　þæt se mon ne wāt
þe him on foldan　fægrost limpeð,
hū ic earmcearig　īscealdne sǣ
15 winter wunade　wrǣccan lāstum,
winemǣgum bidroren,
bihongen hrīmgicelum;　hægl scūrum flēag.
þǣr ic ne gehȳrde　būtan hlimman sǣ,
īscaldne wǣg.　Hwīlum ylfete song
20 dyde ic mē tō gomene,　ganetes hlēoþor
ond huilpan swēg　fore hleahtre wera,
mǣw singende　fore medodrince.
Stormas þǣr stānclifu bēotan,　þǣr him stearn oncwæð
īsigfeþera;　ful oft þæt earn bigeal,
25 ūrigfeþra;　ne ǣnig hlēomǣga
fēasceaftig ferð　frēfran meahte.

　　Forþon him gelȳfeð lȳt,　se þe āh līfes wyn
gebiden in burgum,　bealosīþa hwōn,
wlonc ond wingāl,　hū ic wērig oft
30 in brimlāde　bīdan sceolde.
Nāp nihtscūa,　norþan snīwde,
hrīm hrūsan bond,　hægl fēol on eorþan,

11　hāt' The correct nom. pl. fem. form (modifying *ceare*) is *hāte*, but here the *-e* is elided before the vowel of *ymb*.

12–14　þæt se mon ... hū ic ... 'The man whom it befalls most pleasantly on land does not know that, (namely) how I ...' etc. *þæt* anticipates the noun clause introduced by *hū*. See §148.

13　þe him. See §162.

15　winter 'in the winter' (adverbial acc.). The object of *wunade* is *sǣ* (l. 14).

16　A half-line appears to be missing, but the sense is unimpaired.

18　ic ne gehȳrde būtan 'I heard nought but'.

19–20　ylfete song ... tō gomene 'I made the song of the wild swan (serve) for my entertainment.'

23　him i.e. the storms.

24　þæt is object of *bigeal* and refers to the clamour of the storms and the tern (l. 23) according to most scholars, but the construction is odd. Alternatively, *þæt* could be explained as referring to the eagle, although *earn* is usually masc.

27　Forþon The usual meanings of *forþon* 'therefore', 'because' do not always serve well in *The Seafarer*, and it has been suggested that in this poem (as in a few other places) it may sometimes have the meaning 'indeed' or even 'and yet'.

27–9　him gelȳfeð lȳt ... hū ic ... 'he who has experienced joy of life in the cities (and) few baleful journeys little believes how I ...'. *Āh* in l. 27 is used as an auxiliary verb with past ptc. *gebiden*; *wyn* and *hwōn* are parallel objects of *āh gebiden*.

corna caldast.   Forþon cnyssað nū
heortan geþōhtas,   þæt ic hēan strēamas,
35 sealtȳþa gelāc   sylf cunnige;
monað mōdes lust   mæla gehwylce
ferð tō fēran,   þæt ic feor heonan
elþeodigra   eard gcsēce.
Forþon nis þæs mōdwlonc   mon ofer eorþan,
40 ne his gifena þæs gōd,   ne in geoguþe tō þæs hwæt,
ne in his dædum tō þæs dēor,   ne him his dryhten tō þæs
     hold,
þæt hē ā his sæfōre   sorge næbbe,
tō hwon hine dryhten   gedōn wille.
Ne biþ him tō hearpan hyge   ne tō hringþege,
45 ne tō wīfe wyn   ne tō worulde hyht,
ne ymbe ōwiht elles,   nefne ymb ȳða gewealc,
ac ā hafað longunge   se þe on lagu fundað.
Bearwas blōstmum nimað,   byrig fægriað,
wongas wlitigað,   woruld ōnetteð;
50 ealle þā gemoniað   mōdes fūsne

33–5 **Forþon cnyssað nū ... cunnige** 'And yet the thoughts of my heart are
pressing (me) now that I myself should explore the high seas, the tumult of the salt
waves.' But since the seafarer has already been to sea, some have argued that *sylf*
means 'alone'.

37 **ferð** is acc., direct object of *monað*.

38 **elþēodigra eard** 'land of foreigners', i.e. 'foreign lands'. Some have argued
that this could mean 'Heaven', *elþēodig* referring to those who are pilgrims on earth
and regard Heaven as their true home. See Hebrews 11: 13–16.

39 **nis þæs ... mon** 'there is no man so proud in spirit'. The repeated *þæs* (or *tō
þæs*) in ll. 40–1 means 'so' also. See §168 *þæs ... þæt* note 2.

40 **ne his ... gōd** 'nor so fortunate in his gifts'.

41–3 **dryhten ... dryhten** The first *dryhten* seems clearly to refer to the seafarer's earthly lord; the second one could have the same reference ('that he does not
always have concern as to what his lord might be willing to do for him [in return for
his services as a seafarer]'). But the sentence could also refer to what rewards on
earth or in the next life the Lord may have in store for him. The ambiguity is probably deliberate since this is where the poet begins to make his transition between the
seafarer's account of his experiences and Christian exhortation. Since Old English
scribes did not capitalize the first letter of terms for the Deity (as is regularly done in
Modern English), the play on the secular and religious meanings of *dryhten* was
easy.

44–6 **Ne biþ him ... gewealc** 'His thought is not for the harp nor for the ring-
taking, nor his pleasure in a woman nor his delight in the world, nor (is his thought)
about anything else but the rolling of the waves.' This description of how the seafarer willingly forgoes the delights of the land for a higher, harder goal establishes
the analogy between the self-abnegation of seamen and that required of Christians.

48–9 **Bearwas ... wlitigað** *Bearwas* 'groves' may be taken as the subject of
fægriað and *wlitigað* as well as of *nimað*. But since it is odd to say that *bearwas*
('groves', 'woods') beautify cities, some have preferred to take *fægriað* and *wlitigað*
as intransitive: 'the cities grow fair, the meadows become beautiful'.

50–1 **gemoniað ... tō sīþe** 'urge (the one) eager of spirit, (urge) the mind to the
journey'.

sefan tō sīþe   þām þe swā þenceð
on flōdwegas   feor gewītan.
Swylce gēac monað   gēomran reorde,
singeð sumeres weard,   sorge bēodeð
55 bitter in brēosthord.   þæt se beorn ne wāt,
sēftēadig secg,   hwæt þā sume drēogað
þe þā wræclāstas   wīdost lecgað.

Forþon nū mīn hyge hweorfeð   ofer hreþerlocan,
mīn mōdsefa   mid mereflōde
60 ofer hwæles ēþel   hweorfeð wīde,
eorþan scēatas,   cymeð eft tō mē
gīfre ond grǣdig,   gielleð ānfloga,
hweteð on hwælweg   hreþer unwearnum
ofer holma gelagu.   Forþon mē hātran sind
65 Dryhtnes drēamas   þonne þis dēade līf,
lǣne on londe.   Ic gelȳfe nō
þæt him eorðwelan   ēce stondað.
Simle þrēora sum   þinga gehwylce,
ǣr his tīddege   tō twēon weorþeð;
70 ādl oþþe yldo   oþþe ecghete
fǣgum fromweardum   feorh oðþringeð.
Forþon bið eorla gehwām   æftercweþendra
lof lifgendra   lāstworda betst,
þæt hē gewyrce,   ǣr hē on weg scyle,

---

51 þām þe swā þenceð 'by which (he [*mōdes fūs*]) intends': the *sepe* relative
(§162.4) with an unexpressed subject.

58 Forþon 'and yet'. (Alternatively, one can take this *Forþon* as correlative with
the *forþon* in l. 64: 'Indeed . . . because . . .'.) In this sentence the mind of the speaker
leaves his body and ranges like a bird over land and sea, locates his goal, and then
returns to urge him on to his destination.

58–61 hyge and mōdsefa are parallel subjects of *hweorfeð*; ēþel and scēatas are
parallel objects of *ofer*. ofer hreþerlocan 'beyond my breast'.

66 on londe Two senses are simultaneously operative here: 'land (as opposed to
sea)' and 'earth (as opposed to heaven)'.

67 þæt him . . . stondað 'that worldly goods will endure forever'. The *him* is
apparently reflexive and need not be translated.

68 þinga gehwylce 'in every circumstance', i.e. 'invariably'.

69 tō twēon weorþeð 'arises as an uncertainty', i.e. 'hangs in the balance'. Until
the end of his days (*ǣr his tīddege*) a man can never be sure when age, sickness, or
death might take his life from him.

72–80 Having mentioned the certainty of death, the poet seems at first to cite
the traditional Germanic-heroic view that earning fame after death through
valorous deeds in life is the best course for a man. But he Christianizes this admonition by specifying that the deeds should be in Christian action against the devil
and that the fame that counts is fame in Heaven, which will earn him the joy of
eternal life. Cf. Milton's *Lycidas*, ll. 78–84.

72–4 bið eorla . . . hē gewyrce 'for every man the best of reputations after death
(*lāstworda*) will be the praise of posterity (*æftercweþendra*), of the living, (will be) that
he should bring it about . . .'.

75   fremum on foldan   wið fēonda nīþ,
     dēorum dǽdum   dēofle tōgēanes,
     þæt hine ælda bearn   æfter hergen,
     ond his lof siþþan   lifge mid englum
     āwa tō ealdre,   ēcan līfes blǽd,
80   drēam mid dugeþum.

                         Dagas sind gewitene,
     ealle onmēdlan   eorþan rīces;
     nearon nū cyningas   ne cāseras
     ne goldgiefan   swylce iū wǽron,
     þonne hī mǽst mid him   mǽrþa gefremedon
85   ond on dryhtlīcestum   dōme lifdon.
     Gedroren is þēos duguð eal,   drēamas sind gewitene,
     wuniað þā wācran   ond þās woruld healdaþ,
     brūcað þurh bisgo.   Blǽd is gehnǽged,
     eorþan indryhto   ealdað ond sēarað,
90   swā nū monna gehwylc   geond middangeard.
     Yldo him on fareð,   onsȳn blācað,
     gomelfeax gnornað,   wāt his iūwine,
     æþelinga bearn,   eorþan forgiefene.
     Ne mǽg him þonne se flǽschoma,   þonne him þæt feorg
          losað,
95   ne swēte forswelgan   ne sār gefēlan,
     ne hond onhrēran   ne mid hyge þencan.
     þēah þe grǽf wille   golde strēgan
     brōþor his geborenum,   byrgan be dēadum,
     māþmum mislicum,   þæt hine mid wille,
100 ne mǽg þǽre sāwle   þe biþ synna ful
     gold tō gēoce   for Godes egsan,
     þonne hē hit ǽr hȳdeð   þenden hē hēr leofað.

80–100 This declaration of the demise of the past (heroic) age, though somewhat tinged with regret (e.g. ll. 85, 87–9), is concerned primarily to emphasize the
transience of worldly glory as contrasted with the eternal life in Heaven.

84   þonne hī . . . gefremedon 'when they performed the greatest of glorious
deeds among themselves'.

88   brūcað þurh bisgo 'live in (it) by toil'.

97–102 þēah þe grǽf . . . hēr leofað 'Although a brother may wish to strew the
grave with gold for his born (brother), bury (him) among the dead with various
treasures, which he wishes (to go) with him, gold, when he hides it here while he
lives on earth previously, cannot (be) of help before the terrible power of God to the
soul that is full of sin.' *þæt* (l. 99) is a neut. sg. relative pron. agreeing with *gold* (l. 97).
The familiar Christian admonition against hoarding gold and burying lavish
treasures with the dead is here introduced to stress that man is beyond earthly help
when he faces Judgement.

Micel biþ se Meotudes egsa,   for þon hī sēo molde
  oncyrreð;
se gestaþelade   stīþe grundas,
105 eorþan scēatas   ond ūprodor.
Dol biþ se þe him his Dryhten ne ondrǣdeþ;   cymeð him
  se dēað unþinged.
Ēadig bið se þe ēaþmōd leofaþ;   cymeð him sēo ār of
  heofonum,
Meotod him þæt mōd gestaþelað,   forþon hē in his
  meahte gelȳfeð.
Stīeran mon sceal strongum mōde,   ond þæt on staþelum
  healdan,
110 ond gewis wērum,   wīsum clǣne;
scyle monna gehwylc   mid gemete healdan
lufan wiþ lēofne   ond wið lāþne bealo,
þēah þe hē hine wille fȳres   fulne . . . .
oþþe on bǣle   forbærnedne
115 his geworhtne wine.   Wyrd biþ swīþre,
Meotud meahtigra   þonne ǣnges monnes gehygd.
Uton wē hycgan   hwǣr wē hām āgen,
ond þonne geþencan   hū wē þider cumen,
ond wē þonne ēac tilien,   þæt wē tō mōten
120 in þā ēcan   ēadignesse,
þǣr is līf gelong   in·lufan Dryhtnes,
hyht in heofonum.   þæs sȳ þām Halgan þonc,
þæt hē ūsic geweorþade,   wuldres Ealdor,
ēce Dryhten,   in ealle tīd.

Amen.

<hr>

103 **for þon hī sēo molde oncyrreð** 'before which the earth turns (itself) aside'.
Revelation 20: 11 'him . . . from whose face the earth and the heaven fled away' may
lie behind this.

108 'The Lord establishes that (good) spirit in him, because he believes in His
(the Lord's) power.'

110 **ond gewis . . . clǣne** 'and (keep it) steadfast in (its) pledges, pure in (its)
ways'.

111–12 'each man should hold in moderation his affection toward a friend and
his enmity toward a foe.'

113–15 **þēah þe hē . . . wine.** This seems to continue the sense of what precedes, but l. 113 is metrically defective, and the lines are probably corrupt: 'although
he may wish him (the *lāþne* of l. 112) full of fire (in hell?) or his friend (i.e. the friend
of the enemy?) consumed on a funeral pyre'.

117–18 These lines return the religious exhortation to the original seafaring
imagery.

119 **þæt wē tō mōten** 'that we may (proceed) thither'.

18

Beowulf

Beowulf is the first great English heroic poem, and yet its subject is not England but men and women from Germanic legend and history. It takes place in Northern Europe before Christianity had reached that part of the world. The poet, who wrote centuries later than the time of the poem's action, was a Christian and may even have been a churchman, but he claimed for his subject pre-Christian nations living in and around the lands from which the Anglo-Saxons had originally migrated to England. He admires the characters he describes, especially the hero Beowulf, but there is poignancy in his admiration, for he knows that these brave and eloquent people were ignorant of the revelation generally believed to be essential for Christian salvation.

The poem describes how a powerful warrior from the land of the Geats (a Scandinavian people dwelling in southern Sweden) travels to Denmark to do battle with a man-eating ogre who is killing King Hrothgar's thanes in a series of nocturnal attacks. Beowulf rids the Danes of their tormentor and returns to Geatland, where he puts his great strength at the service of his own people in their wars with hostile neighbours. Eventually, he becomes King of the Geats, and years later, when he is an old man, he gives his life in the course of slaying a dragon that had threatened to destroy the nation. His people bury him amid forebodings of disaster, for the Geats will not be able to withstand their enemies without Beowulf's strong supporting hand.

Beowulf is our most sustained demonstration of the power and range of Old English poetry. In the excerpts printed here readers will recognize several of the themes and strains encountered individually in the preceding poetic texts: appreciative descriptions of valour in battle, stirring speeches, elegiac reflections on man and his world, love of the past, and a keen sense of the transience of things.[1]

[1] The emendations and reconstructions required in these passages from *Beowulf* are extensive and so are relegated to this footnote. 'MS' refers to MS Cotton Vitellius A.XV in the British Museum; 'A' and 'B' refer to the two transcripts of the manuscript known as the Thorkelin transcripts. Textual details and complexities

(a) Beowulf's Fight with Grendel

For twelve years the monster Grendel has left his watery abode at
night and come to the royal hall Heorot to seize some of King
Hrothgar's warriors, whom he then eats. On the occasion described
in this selection the Geatish champion Beowulf and his fourteen
comrades are awaiting Grendel's attack. The monster stalks across
the moor, tears open the door to the hall and gobbles down one of
the Geatish warriors before Beowulf can do battle with him. The
two then fight, and after the fray the Danes and Geats follow
Grendel's tracks to the mere and then return to Heorot. Along the
way one of King Hrothgar's thanes celebrates Beowulf's courage
by reciting a poem about Sigemund, son of Wæls, Sigemund being
the ideal Germanic hero and a worthy figure with whom to
compare Beowulf.

> Cōm on wanre niht
> scrīðan sceadugenga.   Scēotend swæfon,
> þā þæt hornreced   healdan scoldon –
> 705   ealle būton ānum.   þæt wæs yldum cūþ,
> þæt hīe ne mōste,   þā metod nolde,
> se scynscaþa   under sceadu bregdan;

are avoided here. For a thorough description of the manuscript readings, see *The
Nowell Codex*, ed. Kemp Malone, Early English Manuscripts in Facsimile, vol. 12
(Copenhagen, 1963).

The emendations and reconstructions are as follows: *scynscaþa* for MS *synscaþa*
(l. 707), *æthrān* for MS *hran* (l. 722), *hē gebolgen* for MS ... *bolgen* (l. 723), *scēata* for
MS *sceat/ta* (l. 752), *wæs* for MS *he wæs* (l. 765), *betlīc* for MS *hetlic* (l. 780), *hrōf* for B
hr (l. 836), *Sigemundes* for MS *sige munde* (l. 875), *hwæþer* for MS *hwæþre* (l. 1314),
nægde for AB *hnægde* (l. 1318), *æþeling ǣrgōd* for MS *ærgod* (l. 1329), *nēodlaðum* for
MS *neod laðu* (l. 1320), *hwæder* for MS *hwæþer* (l. 1331), *gefægnod* for MS *ge frægnod*
(l. 1333), *onlīcnes* for MS *onlic næs* (l. 1351), *nemdon* for MS *nemdod* (l. 1354), *standeð*
for MS *standeð* (l. 1362), *hafelan beorgan* for MS *hafelan* (l. 1372), *sinnigne* for MS *fela
sinnigne* (l. 1379), *wundnum* for MS *wun/dini* (l. 1382), *mōstan* for MS *mæstan*
(l. 2247), *fȳra* for MS *fyrena* (l. 2250), *þāra* for MS *þana* (l. 2251), *þis līf ofgeaf* for MS
þis ofgeaf (l. 2251), *feormie* for MS *fe . r* ... (l. 2253), *scēoc* for MS *seoc* (l. 2254), *twelfe*
for MS *twelfa* (l. 3170), *ceare* for illegible space in MS (l. 3171), *ond cyning* for MS
cyning (l. 3171), *lǣded* for illegible space in MS (l. 3177), *wyruldcyninga* for MS
wyruldcyning (l. 3180).

702–3   Cōm ... scrīðan The threefold announcement of Grendel's approach to
Heorot is each time expressed using *cōm* plus an infinitive: *cōm ... scrīðan* 'came
gliding', *cōm ... gongan* 'came striding' (ll. 710–11), *Cōm ... sīðian* 'came stalking'
(l. 720).

703   sceadugenga 'walker in darkness', i.e. Grendel (who always attacks at
night).

706–7   þæt hīe ... bregdan 'that the demonic foe might not fling them beneath
the shades when the ruler did not wish (it)', i.e. Grendel could not kill them without
the consent of a higher power.

ac hē wæccende   wrāþum on andan
bād bolgenmōd   beadwa geþinges.
710   Ðā cōm of mōre   under misthleoþum
Grendel gongan;   Godes yrre bær;
mynte se mānscaða   manna cynnes
sumne besyrwan   in sele þām hēan.
Wōd under wolcnum   tō þæs þe hē wīnreced,
715   goldsele gumena   gearwost wisse
fǣttum fāhne.   Ne wæs þæt forma sīð,
þæt hē Hrōþgāres   hām gesōhte;
nǣfre hē on aldordagum   ǣr ne siþðan
heardran hǣle,   healðegnas fand!
720   Cōm þā tō recede   rinc sīðian
drēamum bedǣled.   Duru sōna onarn
fȳrbendum fæst,   syþðan hē hire folmum æthrān;
onbrǣd þā bealohȳdig,   ðā hē gebolgen wæs,
recedes mūþan.   Raþe æfter þon
725   on fāgne flōr   fēond treddode,
ēode yrremōd;   him of ēagum stōd
ligge gelīcost   lēoht unfǣger.
Geseah hē in recede   rinca manige,
swefan sibbegedriht   samod ætgædere,
730   magorinca hēap.   þā his mōd āhlōg:
mynte þæt hē gedǣlde,   ǣr þon dæg cwōme,
atol āglǣca   ānra gehwylces
līf wið līce,   þā him ālumpen wæs
wistfylle wēn.   Ne wæs þæt wyrd þā gēn,
735   þæt hē mā mōste   manna cynnes
ðicgean ofer þā niht.   þrȳðswȳð behēold
mǣg Higelāces   hū se mānscaða
under fǣrgripum   gefaran wolde.
Ne þæt se āglǣca   yldan þōhte,
740   ac hē gefēng hraðe   forman sīðe

708   hē i.e. Beowulf.
709   geþinges 'result, outcome' (object of *bād*, which takes gen.).
714   tō þæs þe 'to (the point) where, until'.
715   wisse 'knew', i.e. 'recognized'.
718–19   nǣfre hē ... fand! 'Never did he before nor after in the days of his life find hall-thanes (and) worse luck!'
722   hire i.e. the door (object of *æthrān*).
726   him of ēagum stōd 'from his eyes shone forth' (poss. dat.; see §191.2).
731   mynte þæt hē gedǣlde 'he intended to sever' (lit., 'he intended that he should sever').
734   Ne wæs ... gēn 'It was not by any means destined.'
738   under ... wolde 'would proceed with his sudden grips'.
740   forman sīðe 'at the first opportunity'.

slǣpendne rinc,   slāt unwearnum,
bāt bānlocan,   blōd ēdrum dranc,
synsnǣdum swealh;   sōna hæfde
unlyfigendes   eal gefeormod,
745 fēt ond folma.   Forð nēar ætstōp,
nam þā mid handa   higeþīhtigne
rinc on ræste,   rǣhte ongēan
fēond mid folme;   hē onfēng hraþe
inwitþancum   ond wið earm gesæt.
750 Sōna þæt onfunde   fyrena hyrde,
þæt hē ne mētte   middangeardes,
eorþan scēata   on elran men
mundgripe māran;   hē on mōde wearð
forht on ferhðe;   nō þȳ ǣr fram meahte.
755 Hyge wæs him hinfūs,   wolde on heolster flēon,
sēcan dēofla gedrǣg;   ne wæs his drohtoð þǣr
swylce hē on ealderdagum   ǣr gemētte.
Gemunde þā se gōda,   mǣg Higelāces,
ǣfensprǣce,   uplang āstōd
760 ond him fæste wiðfēng;   fingras burston;
eoten wæs ūtweard,   eorl furþur stōp.
Mynte se mǣra,   þǣr hē meahte swā,
wīdre gewindan   ond on weg þanon
flēon on fenhopu;   wiste his fingra geweald
765 on grames grāpum.   þæt wæs gēocor sīð,
þæt se hearmscaþa   tō Heorute ātēah.
Dryhtsele dynede;   Denum eallum wearð,
ceasterbūendum,   cēnra gehwylcum,
eorlum ealuscerwen.   Yrre wǣron bēgen,
770 rēþe renweardas.   Reced hlynsode.
þā wæs wundor micel,   þæt se winsele
wiðhæfde heaþodēorum,   þæt hē on hrūsan ne fēol,

745 **fēt ond folma** '(including) the feet and hands'.
748–9 **fēond** i.e. Grendel.   **hē onfēng ... gesæt** 'he (Beowulf) received (him, i.e. Grendel) quickly with hostile purpose and sat up against (Grendel's) arm'. Beowulf seizes Grendel in an arm-lock.
750 **fyrena hyrde** 'master of crimes', i.e. Grendel.
752–3 **on elran ... māran** 'a greater handgrip in (any) other man'.
754 **nō þȳ ... meahte** 'none the sooner could he (get) away', i.e. 'yet he could not (get) away'.
756–7 **ne wæs his ... gemētte** 'nor was his experience there such as (§168 *swelce* 2) he had ever before met with in the days of his life'.
760 **him** i.e. Grendel.
762 **se mǣra** i.e. Grendel.
þǣr hē meahte swā 'if he (Grendel) could (do) so'.
764 **wiste his ... geweald** 'he (Grendel) realized the control of his fingers (was)'.
769 **ealuscerwen** '?terror'. A mysterious word, recorded only here.

fæger foldbold;   ac hē þæs fæste wæs
innan ond ūtan   īrenbendum
775 searoþoncum besmiþod.   þǣr fram sylle ābēag
medubenc monig   mīne gefrǣge
golde geregnad,   þǣr þā graman wunnon.
þæs ne wēndon ǣr   witan Scyldinga,
þæt hit ā mid gemete   manna ǣnig
780 betlīc ond bānfāg   tōbrecan meahte,
listum tōlūcan,   nymþe līges fæþm
swulge on swaþule.   Swēg ūp āstāg
nīwe geneahhe: Norð-Denum stōd
atelīc egesa,   ānra gehwylcum
785 þāra þe of wealle   wōp gehȳrdon,
gryrelēoð galan   Godes andsacan,
sigelēasne sang,   sār wānigean
helle hæfton.   Hēold hine fæste
se þe manna wæs   mægene strengest
790 on þǣm dæge   þysses līfes.
    Nolde eorla hlēo   ǣnige þinga
þone cwealmcuman   cwicne forlǣtan,
ne his līfdagas   lēoda ǣnigum
nytte tealde.   þǣr genehost brægd
795 eorl Bēowulfes   ealde lāfe,
wolde frēadrihtnes   feorh ealgian,
mǣres þēodnes,   ðǣr hīe meahton swā.
Hīe þæt ne wiston,   þā hīe gewin drugon,
heardhicgende   hildemecgas,
800 ond on healfa gehwone   hēawan þōhton,
sāwle sēcan: þone synscaðan
ǣnig ofer eorþan   īrenna cyst,

773 hē i.e. the hall.
þæs 'so' (§168 *þæs* 2).
776 mīne gefrǣge 'as I have heard say'. Infrequently the poet enters the narrative in the first person.
778–9 þæs . . . þæt Anticipatory pronoun followed by noun clause (§148). *þæs* is object of *wēndon*, which takes gen.
786–8 Godes andsacan . . . helle hæfton i.e. Grendel. Cf. l. 711. The monster's screams of pain are described with grim irony as an unhappy song.
788 Hēold hine fæste '(Beowulf) held him (Grendel) firmly.'
791–2 Nolde eorla hlēo . . . forlǣtan 'The protector of men (Beowulf) did not want to let the murderous visitor go alive by any means.' But the monster does break away (ll. 819–21). It is important to notice that although he is 'the strongest of men in that day of his life' (ll. 789–90), Beowulf is subject to human limitations.
794–5 þǣr genehost . . . lāfe 'A warrior of Beowulf's in abundance brandished his ancient heirloom there', i.e. 'Many a warrior brandished his sword.'
800–1 ond on healfa . . . sēcan 'and intended to slash away on every side, to get (i.e. kill) the soul (of Grendel)'.

guðbilla nān   grētan nolde;
ac hē sigewæpnum   forsworen hæfde,
805 ecga gehwylcre.   Scolde his aldorgedāl
on ðæm dæge   þysses līfes
earmlic wurðan,   ond se ellorgāst
on fēonda geweald   feor sīðian.

Ðā þæt onfunde   se þe fela æror
810 mōdes myrðe   manna cynne,
fyrene gefremede   – hē fāg wið God –
þæt him se līchoma   læstan nolde,
ac hine se mōdega   mæg Hygelāces
hæfde be honda;   wæs gehwæþer ōðrum
815 lifigende lāð.   Līcsār gebād
atol æglæca;   him on eaxle wearð
syndolh sweotol,   seonowe onsprungon,
burston bānlocan.   Bēowulfe wearð
guðhrēð gyfeþe;   scolde Grendel þonan
820 feorhsēoc flēon   under fenhleoðu,
sēcean wynlēas wīc;   wiste þē geornor
þæt his aldres wæs   ende gegongen,
dōgera dægrīm.   Denum eallum wearð
æfter þām wælræse   willa gelumpen.
825 Hæfde þā gefælsod   se þe ær feorran cōm,
snotor ond swȳðferhð,   sele Hrōðgāres,
genered wið nīðe.   Nihtweorce gefeh,
ellenmærþum.   Hæfde Ēast-Denum
Gēatmecga lēod   gilp gelæsted,
830 swylce oncȳþðe   ealle gebētte,
inwidsorge,   þe hīe ær drugon
ond for þrēanȳdum   þolian scoldon,
torn unlȳtel.   þæt wæs tācen sweotol,
syþðan hildedēor   hond ālegde,
835 earm ond eaxle   – þær wæs eal geador
Grendles grāpe –   under gēapne hrōf.

801–5 Grendel's invulnerability to weapons seems to be explained here as the result of his having laid a spell on them, but the meaning of *forsworen* is uncertain.

805–8 **Scolde** 'had to' is to be construed with both *wurðan* and *sīðian*.

810–11 **mōdes myrðe ... gefremede** *myrðe* and *fyrene* are parallel gen. pl. nouns with -*e* for -*a* (cf. 16/7 note): 'had done to the race of men afflictions of spirit, crimes'.

811 **hē fāg wið God** 'he (who was) hostile towards God'. This phrase is parallel with and specifies *se þe* (l. 809).

817–18 **seonowe ... bānlocan** 'the sinews sprang asunder, the joints broke (apart)', that is, Grendel's arm was torn from his body.

822–3 **his aldres ... dægrīm** 'the number of his days, the end of his life, had run out'.

Ðā wæs on morgen   mīne gefrǣge
ymb þā gifhealle   gūðrinc monig;
fērdon folctogan   feorran ond nēan
840 geond wīdwegas   wundor scēawian,
lāþes lāstas.   Nō his līfgedāl
sarlīc þūhte   secga ǣnegum
þāra þe tīrlēases   trode scēawode,
hū hē wērigmōd   on weg þanon,
845 nīða ofercumen,   on nicera mere
fǣge ond geflȳmed   feorhlāstas bær.
Ðǣr wæs on blōde   brim weallende,
atol ȳða geswing   eal gemenged,
hāton heolfre,   heorodrēore wēol;
850 dēaðfǣge dēog,   siððan drēama lēas
in fenfreoðo   feorh ālegde,
hǣþene sāwle;   þǣr him hel onfēng.
þanon eft gewiton   ealdgesīðas
swylce geong manig   of gomenwāþe,
855 fram mere mōdge   mēarum rīdan,
beornas on blancum.   Ðǣr wæs Bēowulfes
mǣrðo mǣned;   monig oft gecwæð,
þætte sūð ne norð   be sǣm twēonum
ofer eormengrund   ōþer nǣnig
860 under swegles begong   sēlra nǣre
rondhæbbendra,   rīces wyrðra.
Nē hīe hūru winedrihten   wiht ne lōgon,
glǣdne Hrōðgār,   ac þæt wæs gōd cyning.
Hwīlum heaþorōfe   hlēapan lēton,
865 on geflit faran   fealwe mēaras,
ðǣr him foldwegas   fǣgere þūhton,
cystum cūðe.   Hwīlum cyninges þegn,
guma gilphlæden,   gidda gemyndig,
se ðe ealfela   ealdgesegena
870 worn gemunde,   word ōþer fand
sōðe gebunden;   secg eft ongan

837 mīne gefrǣge See l. 776 note.
847 Ðǣr wæs ... weallende 'There the water was surging with blood.' The men from far and near have followed Grendel's tracks back to the mere where he has his abode.
850 dēaðfǣge dēog 'the one doomed to death (i.e. Grendel) had been concealed'. The meaning of *dēog*, which occurs only here, is uncertain.
861 rīces wyrðra 'more worthy of a kingdom', i.e. 'more worthy of being a king'. This high praise leads naturally to the reassurance that they intended no dispraise of their own king (who had been unable to protect them from Grendel).
867 cystum cūðe 'known for their good qualities' refers to *foldwegas* nom. pl.
870–1 word ōþer ... gebunden '(the king's thane) found other words faithfully

sīð Bēowulfes   snyttrum styrian,
ond on spēd wrecan   spel gerāde,
wordum wrixlan;   wēlhwylc gecwæð,
875 þæt hē fram Sigemundes   secgan hȳrde
ellendǣdum,   uncūþes fela,
Wælsinges gewin,   wīde sīðas,
þāra þe gumena bearn   gearwe ne wiston,
fǣhðe ond fyrena,   būton Fitela mid hine,
880 þonne hē swulces hwæt   secgan wolde,
ēam his nefan,   swā hīe ā wǣron
æt nīða gehwām   nȳdgesteallan;
hæfdon ealfela   eotena cynnes
sweordum gesǣged.   Sigemunde gesprong
885 æfter dēaðdæge   dōm unlȳtel,
syþðan wīges heard   wyrm ācwealde,
hordes hyrde;   hē under hārne stān,
æþelinges bearn   āna genēðde
frēcne dǣde,   ne wæs him Fitela mid;
890 hwæþre him gesǣlde,   ðæt þæt swurd þurhwōd
wrǣtlicne wyrm,   þæt hit on wealle ætstōd,
dryhtlic īren;   draca morðre swealt.
Hæfde āglǣca   elne gegongen,
þæt hē bēahhordes   brūcan mōste
895 selfes dōme;   sǣbāt gehlēod,
bær on bearm scipes   beorhte frætwa,
Wælses eafera;   wyrm hāt gemealt.

---

bound together', 'other' meaning perhaps new words for this occasion. *Gebunden* seems to refer to the alliterative linking together of words in Old English verse.

872 **sīð ... styrian** 'to engage Beowulf's undertaking skilfully'. Some such sense as 'engage' is implied, because the thane does not narrate the hero's achievement but rather celebrates it by telling other heroic stories, exalting Beowulf's victory to the status of the greatest victories of Germanic legend, such as Sigemund's slaying of the dragon.

874–97   The first part of the thane's account of Sigemund's adventures describes his expeditions with his nephew Fitela (ll. 874–84). The details of this activity are to be found in the Old Norse *Volsungasaga*, chapters 3–8. Sigemund's dragon fight (ll. 884–97) is the event renowned in Germanic legend at large, only in other accounts the dragon is slain by Sigemund's son Siegfried. Indeed, it is possible that this passage says the same, since *wīges heard ... hē* (ll. 886–7) could refer to Siegfried. The Middle High German *Nibelungenlied* is the most famous of the accounts of Siegfried, but he is also prominent in Scandinavian literature.

879 **būton Fitela mid hine** 'except for Fitela (who was) with him'.

891 **þæt hit ... ætstōd** 'so that it (the sword) stuck into the wall'. The dragon is pinned to the wall.

893 **Hæfde ... gegongen** 'By his valour the combatant (i.e. Sigemund or Siegfried) had brought it about.'

895 **selfes dōme** 'according to (his own) judgement', i.e. 'to his heart's content'.

897 **wyrm hāt gemealt** 'the hot dragon was consumed (? in its own fire)'.

(b) *Beowulf Consoles Hrothgar for Æschere's Death*

The night after Beowulf's victory over Grendel, the Danes are surprised by another monstrous visitant: Grendel's mother comes to Heorot and slays Hrothgar's favourite thane, Æschere, in vengeance for her son's death. Beowulf, who has lodged in a separate building some distance from the royal hall, is brought to the King, and Hrothgar tells him of Æschere's death. He also describes to Beowulf the eerie lair where Grendel and his mother live, and this description (ll. 1357–79) is one of the most famous passages in all Old English literature. As if appalled by his own account of the monsters' dwelling place, he asks almost despairingly whether the hero will consider challenging this second monster. Beowulf's answer (ll. 1383–96) is the finest statement we have of the Germanic heroic ethos.

> þā wæs frōd cyning,
> hār hilderinc   on hrēon mōde,
> syðþan hē aldorþegn   unlyfigendne,
> þone dēorestan   dēadne wisse.
> 1310   Hraþe wæs tō būre   Bēowulf fetod,
> sigorēadig secg.   Samod ǣrdæge
> ēode eorla sum,   æþele cempa
> self mid gesīðum   þǣr se snotera bād
> hwæþer him alwalda   ǣfre wille
> 1315   æfter wēaspelle   wyrpe gefremman.
> Gang ðā æfter flōre   fyrdwyrðe man
> mid his handscale   – healwudu dynede –
> þæt hē þone wīsan   wordum nǣgde
> frēan Ingwina,   frægn gif him wǣre
> 1320   æfter nēodlaðum   niht getǣse.
>   Hrōðgār maþelode,   helm Scyldinga:
> 'Ne frīn þū æfter sǣlum!   Sorh is genīwod
> Denigea lēodum.   Dēad is Æschere,
> Yrmenlāfes   yldra brōþor,
> 1325   mīn rūnwita   ond mīn rǣdbora,
> eaxlgestealla,   ðonne wē on orlege
> hafelan weredon,   þonne hniton fēþan,

1309   þone dēorestan ... wisse 'knew the dearest one (to be) dead'.
1312   eorla sum 'a certain one of the warriors' or perhaps 'the important warrior' (i.e. Beowulf).
1313–14   bād hwæþer 'waited (to find out) whether'.

eoferas cnysedan.   Swylc scolde eorl wesan,
æþeling ǣrgōd,   swylc Æschere wæs!
1330 Wearð him on Heorote   tō handbanan
wælgǣst wǣfre;   ic ne wāt hwæder
atol ǣse wlanc   eftsīðas tēah,
fylle gefægnod.   Hēo þā fǣhðe wræc,
þe þū gӯstran niht   Grendel cwealdest
1335 þurh hǣstne hād   heardum clammum,
forþan hē tō lange   lēode mīne
wanode ond wyrde.   Hē æt wīge gecrang
ealdres scyldig,   ond nū ōþer cwōm
mihtig mānscaða,   wolde hyre mǣg wrecan,
1340 ge feor hafað   fǣhðe gestǣled,
þæs þe þincean mæg   þegne monegum,
se þe æfter sincgyfan   on sefan grēoteþ,
hreþerbealo hearde;   nū sēo hand ligeð,
se þe ēow wēlhwylcra   wilna dohte.
1345   Ic þæt londbūend,   lēode mīne,
selerǣdende   secgan hӯrde,
þæt hīe gesāwon   swylce twēgen
micle mearcstapan   mōras healdan,
ellorgǣstas.   Ðǣra ōðer wæs,
1350 þæs þe hīe gewislīcost   gewitan meahton,
idese onlīcnes;   ōðer earmsceapen
on weres wæstmum   wræclāstas træd,
nǣfne hē wæs māra   þonne ǣnig man ōðer;
þone on gēardagum   Grendel nemdon
1355 foldbūende;   nō hīe fæder cunnon,
hwæþer him ǣnig wæs   ǣr ācenned

1330 Wearð him . . . handbanan 'became his slayer in Heorot'.
1340 ge feor . . . gestǣled 'and has avenged the hostility far (i.e. thoroughly)'.
1341 þæs þe 'as'. See §177.2 (*f*).
1343 hreþerbealo hearde acc. sg., object of *hafað . . . gestǣled* (l. 1340).
1343-4   nū sēo hand . . . dohte 'now the hand lies low which did well by you as regards all good things'. Grammatically *sēo þe* rather than *se þe* (l. 1344) is required to agree with *sēo hand*, but the poet was no doubt thinking of the man rather than the feminine hand.
1347 swylce twēgen 'two such', i.e. Grendel and his mother.
1349-51 Ðǣra ōðer . . . ōðer 'One of them . . . the other.'
1350   þæs þe hīe gewislīcost 'as well as they'. See §177.2 (*f*).
1351-2   idese onlīcnes . . . on weres wæstmum 'the likeness of a woman (i.e. of a woman's shape) . . . in a man's shape'.
1353 nǣfne 'except that'. See §179.5.
1355-7   nō hīe fæder . . . gāsta 'they do not know whether they had any father born of mysterious demons'. Earlier in the poem the poet explains that the Grendelkin are the offspring of Cain, but the Danes, who know nothing of the Bible, are ignorant as to the monsters' parentage.

dyrnra gāsta. Hīe dȳgel lond
warigeað wulfhleoþu, windige næssas,
frēcne fengelād, ðǣr fyrgenstrēam
1360 under næssa genipu niþer gewīteð,
flōd under foldan. Nis þæt feor heonon
mīlgemearces, þæt se mere standeð;
ofer þǣm hongiað hrinde bearwas,
wudu wyrtum fæst wæter oferhelmað.
1365 þǣr mæg nihta gehwǣm nīðwundor sēon,
fȳr on flōde. Nō þæs frōd leofað
gumena bearna, þæt þone grund wite.
Ðēah þe hǣðstapa hundum geswenced,
heorot hornum trum holtwudu sēce,
1370 feorran geflȳmed, ǣr hē feorh seleð,
aldor on ōfre, ǣr hē in wille,
hafelan beorgan; nis þæt hēoru stōw!
þonon ȳðgeblond ūp āstīgeð
won tō wolcnum, þonne wind styreþ
1375 lāð gewidru, oð þæt lyft drysmaþ,
roderas rēotað. Nū is se rǣd gelang
eft æt þē ānum. Eard gīt ne const,
frēcne stōwe, ðǣr þū findan miht
sinnigne secg; sēc gif þū dyrre!
1380 Ic þē þā fǣhðe fēo lēanige,
ealdgestrēonum, swā ic ǣr dyde,
wundnum golde, gyf þū on weg cymest.'
    Bēowulf maþelode, bearn Ecgþēowes:
'Ne sorga, snotor guma! Sēlre bið ǣghwǣm,
1385 þæt hē his frēond wrece, þonne hē fela murne.
Ūre ǣghwylc sceal ende gebīdan

1357–76 The landscape described here is at once vivid and mysterious. There is a mere or pool surrounded by sheer cliffs with overhanging trees. A waterfall descends into the mere, and concealed behind this waterfall is a cave where Grendel and his mother live. The cave can be reached only by diving into the water and swimming under the waterfall. The Old Norse *Grettissaga*, which tells a story much like that of Beowulf's fight with the Grendelkin, describes the setting with precision.

1362 mīlgemearces 'in measurement by miles'. See §190.5.

1366 fȳr on flōde The fire in the water would be the fire burning in the cave of the Grendelkin (which Beowulf later sees), but to the Danes it is an inexplicable glimmering on the surface of the water.

1366–7 þæs . . . þæt See §168 þæs . . . þæt and note 1.

1370–1 ǣr hē feorh . . . wille 'he will sooner give up his life, his spirit, on the shore before he will (go) in'.

1376–7 Nū is se rǣd . . . ānum 'Now the remedy is again dependent upon you alone.'

worolde līfes,　wyrce se þe mōte
dōmes ǣr dēaþe;　þæt bið drihtguman
unlifgendum　æfter sēlest.

1390　Ārīs, rīces weard,　uton hraþe fēran,
Grendles māgan　gang scēawigan.
Ic hit þē gehāte:　nō hē on helm losaþ,
ne on foldan fæþm,　ne on fyrgenholt,
ne on gyfenes grund,　gā þǣr hē wille!

1395　Ðȳs dōgor þū　geþyld hafa
wēana gehwylces,　swā ic þē wēne tō.'
Āhlēop ðā se gomela,　gode þancode,
mihtigan drihtne,　þæs se man gesprǣc.

(c) The Lament of the Last Survivor

The last thousand lines of *Beowulf* describe the hero's final battle with a fire-breathing dragon. He is an old man and, having no progeny, the last of his line. The profoundly elegiac tone of this final section of the poem is established by the poet just after the section gets under way. He describes an unnamed man who is the sole survivor of his people, a people who lived in an earlier age long before the time of the poem's action. Since there is no one left to carry on the tribe's history, the heroic ideal of fame as the one means of survival beyond death is rendered meaningless. Having no other use for the treasures of his nation, he decides to bury them, and as there is no one to whom he can address his lament, he addresses it to the earth which is receiving the people's treasure. The speech prefigures the end of *Beowulf*, where the Geatish nation buries a treasure hoard with their slain king (selection 18(d) following). Compare selection 13.

'Heald þū nū, hrūse,　nū hæleð ne mōstan,
eorla ǣhte!　Hwæt, hyt ǣr on ðē
gōde begēaton.　Gūðdēað fornam,
2250　feorhbealo frēcne　fȳra gehwylcne

(b)　1387–8　wyrce...dēaþe 'let him who is able achieve fame before death'. This is the ruling ideal of the Germanic heroic ethos.

1392–4　hē...hē Grammatical gender: masc. *hē* agrees with the antecedent *māgan* (l. 1391).

1395–6　geþyld...gehwylces 'have patience in each of your afflictions'.

1397–8　gode þancode...gesprǣc. See §164.5.

(c)　2247　nū hæleð ne mōstan For *nū* see §168 *nū* 2.

leoda minra   þāra ðe þis līf ofgeaf,
gesāwon seledrēam.   Nāh, hwā sweord wege
oððe feormie   fæted wǣge,
dryncfæt dēore;   duguð ellor scēoc.
2255 Sceal se hearda helm   hyrstedgolde,
fǣtum befeallen;   feormynd swefað,
þā ðe beadogrīman   bȳwan sceoldon;
ge swylce sēo herepād,   sīo æt hilde gebād
ofer borda gebræc   bite īrena,
2260 brosnað æfter beorne.   Ne mæg byrnan hring
æfter wīgfruman   wīde fēran,
hæleðum be healfe.   Næs hearpan wyn,
gomen glēobēames,   ne gōd hafoc
geond sæl swingeð,   ne se swifta mearh
2265 burhstede bēateð.   Bealocwealm hafað
fela feorhcynna   forð onsended!'

(d) Beowulf's Funeral

The aged King Beowulf was successful in his fight with the dragon:
the creature that had threatened to destroy the Geatish nation was
himself destroyed by Beowulf's hand. But in the course of the fight
Beowulf received a mortal wound. The poet describes the hero's
suffering and death and records his speeches of farewell to his
people. The Geats cremate his body in an impressive pagan
ceremony, and then we are told in the present selection how they
bury his ashes and bid him farewell. The sadness of his funeral is
deepened by the people's awareness that with King Beowulf gone
the entire nation faces certain destruction by their surrounding
enemies, who had been kept at bay only by the protective power of
their king. With Beowulf's fall the nation will fall.

Geworhton ðā   Wedra lēode
hlǣw on hōe,   se wæs hēah ond brād,

(c) 2252 gesāwon seledrēam Assuming that the *ge*- prefix gave perfective meaning to the verb *sāwon* here, we can translate '(who) had seen the last of joys in the
hall'.

Nāh, hwā sweord wege 'I do not have anyone who can bear the sword.' Cf. 12/212
note.

2255–6 Sceal . . . befeallen 'Must (be) . . . deprived of'.

2258 ge swylce 'and likewise'.

2261 æfter wīgfruman 'along with the war-leader'. The corselet is personified
and described as a companion of the man.

2262 Næs (= *Ne ealles*) 'by no means (is there)'.

wægliðendum   wīde gesȳne,
ond betimbredon   on tȳn dagum
3160 beadurōfes bēcn,   bronda lāfe
wealle beworhton,   swā hyt weorðlīcost
foresnotre men   findan mihton.
Hī on beorg dydon   bēg ond siglu,
eall swylce hyrsta   swylce on horde ær
3165 nīðhēdige men   genumen hæfdon;
forlēton eorla gestrēon   eorðan healdan,
gold on grēote,   þær hit nū gēn lifað
eldum swā unnyt   swā hit æror wæs.
þā ymbe hlæw riodan   hildedēore,
3170 æþelinga bearn,   ealra twelfe,
woldon ceare cwīðan,   ond kyning mænan,
wordgyd wrecan,   ond ymb wer sprecan;
eahtodan eorlscipe   ond his ellenweorc
duguðum dēmdon,   swā hit gedēfe bið,
3175 þæt mon his winedryhten   wordum herge,
ferhðum frēoge,   þonne hē forð scile
of līchaman   læded weorðan.
Swā begnornodon   Gēata lēode
hlāfordes hryre,   heorðgenēatas;
3180 cwædon þæt hē wære   wyruldcyninga
mannum mildust   ond monðwærust,
lēodum līðost   ond lofgeornost.

3161–2 swā hyt ... mihton 'as splendidly as the very wise men were able to devise it'.
3164 eall swylce hyrsta 'all such treasures as'.
on horde 'from the hoard'.
3176 ferhðum frēoge 'cherish (him) in (his) heart'. For the dat. pl. *ferhðum* see 14/63 note.

A Note on the Punctuation of
Old English Poetry

One thing at least is certain about OE prosaists and poets, scribes and *scops*: they knew nothing of modern punctuation. Yet today modern punctuation is invariably used in OE texts presented to beginners and is probably the norm in scholarly editions. Why? The main reason appears to be the 'inadequacy' of the punctuation of OE manuscripts. This is less true of the prose, where some texts at any rate can be and have been presented with manuscript punctuation, than of the poetry where (as a glance at the facsimile of lines 1–33a of *The Wanderer* printed on page 254 will show) the punctuation can be almost non-existent. But there are good grounds for believing that the use of modern punctuation can distort both the syntax and the meaning of OE texts. The paragraphs which follow deal only with the poetry. But – *mutatis mutandis* – much that is said holds for the prose. Those interested can read further in *Review of English Studies* 31 (1980), 385–413.

A comparison of recordings of various great actors performing such passages as Hamlet's soliloquy 'To be, or not to be' or King Lear's outburst 'Ay, every inch a King' will reveal differences in stress, intonation, and timing, and in the arrangement of breath-groups and sense-groups. At least six contexts can be detected in which different interpretations were or may have been available to a *scop* performing an OE poem.

The first two are the result of the fact that *se* can be a demonstrative meaning 'that one, he', or a relative pronoun meaning 'who' (see §162.3) and that words such as *þa* and *þær* can be adverbs meaning 'then' and 'there' or conjunctions meaning 'when' and 'where' (see §168). The Anglo-Saxons would have distinguished these when speaking, but today we have no way of deciding which we have in any given context. Thus, in selection 12 we cannot be certain whether *þa* in line 5 means 'then' or 'when' or whether *be þam* in line 9 means 'by that' or 'by which'. So we do not know whether we have one sentence or two or three in lines 5–10, which are printed here with no punctuation apart from the initial capital and the final full stop:

> þa þæt Offan mæg   ærest onfunde
> þæt se eorl nolde   yrhðo geþolian
> he let him þa of handon   leofne fleogan
> hafoc wið þæs holtes   and to þære hilde stop
> be þam man mihte oncnawan   þæt se cniht nolde
> wacian æt þam wige   þa he to wæpnum feng.

With the text printed in this way, we can feel that lines 5–10 form a verse paragraph and can see that, if we do not translate, the grammatical questions posed above are not significant. But modern editors, using modern punctuation and thinking in terms of modern sentences rather than of OE verse paragraphs, have to make arbitrary decisions by putting either a comma or a semi-colon (or full stop) after *geþolian* in line 6 and *stop* in line 8. We could signal these ambiguities by using a double comma in these places.

The third of the six contexts referred to above can be illustrated from selection 18(*b*) from *Beowulf*, lines 1392–4:

> Ic hit þe gehate: no he on helm losaþ,
> ne on foldan fæþm,   ne on fyrgenholt,
> ne on gyfenes grund,   ga þær he wille!

There is a similarity between this and the first two contexts in that we cannot be sure whether *ga þær he wille* is independent of, or subordinate to, what goes before 'Let her go where she will' or '. . . no matter where she intends to go'; see §178.4. (For *he* 'she', see the note on the line.) This difficulty could be similarly resolved by using „ after *grund*.

We turn now to parentheses, which – it is increasingly being realized – play an important part in the construction of the OE verse paragraph. Space prevents a full exposition of this problem. But we may note that in selection 14 (*The Dream of the Rood*) line 39b *þæt* cannot be a relative pronoun referring to *geong hæleð* – that would require *se* – and that the line is therefore not an apologetic aside 'by the way, he was God Almighty' but a triumphant affirmation:

> – þæt wæs God ælmihtig! –

In the verse selections in this *Guide*, the problem of the possible parenthesis is perhaps best illustrated from selection 16 (*The Wanderer*), where both line 50b *sorg bið geniwad* and line 55b *cearo bið geniwad* have been taken as parenthetic. But the punctuation of this poem, especially lines 37–57, must be left for discussion in class or tutorial.

The fifth of our six contexts involves the *apo koinou* construction, seen in its most simple form in a sentence like 'I went out beagling is my favourite pastime', where *beagling* is a common element or *koinon* to two sentences 'I went out beagling' and 'Beagling is my favourite pastime.' Much of the magic and mystery of OE poetry will be lost to the reader insensitive to such constructions. The *koinon* can be a noun, an adjective, a verb, a phrase, or a principal or subordinate clause. Simple examples include two passages from selection 18, viz. 18(*a*)/753–4 *he on mode wearð // forht on ferhðe* (the *koinon* is *wearð forht*) and 18(*b*)/1357–8 *Hie dygel lond // warigeað wulfhleoþu* (*warigeað*). Rather more elaborate perhaps is *Andreas* 474:

> Ic wille þe,
> eorl unforcuð, anre nu gena
> bene biddan, þeah ic þe beaga lyt,
> sincweorðunga, syllan mihte,
> fætedsinces, wolde ic freondscipe,
> þeoden þrymfæst, þinne, gif ic mehte,
> begitan godne

'And now again, noble warrior, I wish to ask a favour of you, although I can give you few rings, few precious things, little beaten gold, I would (if I could) win your gracious friendship, O glorious prince', where the speaker's poverty makes him both reluctant to ask and fearful of a refusal. When you read lines 49–57 of selection 16, we would urge you to disregard the punctuation and to bear in mind the possibility of taking line 53a *secga geseldan apo koinou*. Similarly, when reading lines 162–8a of selection 12, you could ask yourself such questions as: When and how did the seaman hinder Byrhtnoth? What happened as a result of Byrhtnoth's injury? Why did it happen? If you do, you will see a relationship of time, cause, and effect, in a series of clauses which make a verse paragraph and of which only one – that in line 165 – need be taken as subordinate.

Finally, we turn to what for want of a better term can be called 'enjambment of sense' – the sort of separation seen in the *Andreas* passage quoted above, where the sequence *freondscipe ... þinne ... godne* gives dramatic emphasis: 'friendship ... your friendship ... your gracious friendship', and perhaps in line 151 of selection 12, *The Battle of Maldon*, where

þurh ðone æþelan Æþelredes þegen

can be translated 'through the noble thane of Æthelred', but is better rendered 'through that noble one, the thane of Æthelred'. After patient work with grammar and glossary, we may translate lines 7–8 of the passage from selection 12 printed in the third paragraph of this note thus: 'then he let the dear hawk fly from his hands towards the wood, and advanced to the battle.' But if we take it word by word, it reads: 'he let from him then from hands the dear one fly, the hawk towards the wood, and advanced to the battle.' This version restores to us what has been called 'the excitement of the momentary riddle' experienced by Anglo-Saxon hearers.

Much more could be said about OE poetry, with its technique of repetition with variation and advance, well demonstrated in lines 113–15 of selection 12, where the first half-line summarizes the contents of the three lines, with Wulfmær being identified in the next two first half-lines as a relation and then as a very close relation of Byrhtnoth, and the nature of his wound – fatal, with swords, cruelly cut down – being explained in the three second half-lines. But, as Chaucer said, *shortly for to maken is the best*.

Glossary

Abbreviations are the same as those on p. xiv except that within entries case, number, and gender are indicated with a single initial letter (nsm = nominative singular masculine, gpf = genitive plural feminine, isn = instrumental singular neuter, etc.) and verb classes are identified with a simple numeral, Roman for strong verbs and Arabic for weak, or else with *anom.* for anomalous verbs and *pret. pres.* for preterite present verbs. Thus if an entry word is followed by m. or f., this means it is a masculine noun or a feminine noun. If it is followed by II, this means it is a second-class strong verb, while a 2 would mean it was a second-class weak verb. In analysing verb forms we use an Arabic numeral to indicate person and s or p to indicate singular or plural (3p = third person plural). When verb forms are indicative, no mood is specified, but subjunctives and imperatives are marked subj and imp respectively. Where it seems helpful to do so, we indicate in parentheses the section in the *Guide* where the word or its general type is discussed. Following are abbreviations used in addition to, or instead of, those listed on p. xiv:

anom.	anomalous	pers. n.	personal name
compar.	comparative degree	p ptc	past participle
corr.	correlative	refl.	reflexive object
imp s	imperative singular	superl.	superlative degree
imp p	imperative plural	w.a.	with accusative object
interj.	interjection	w.d.	with dative object
interr.	interrogative	w.g.	with genitive object
MnE	Modern English	w.i.	with instrumental object
num.	numeral	w. refl.	with reflexive objective

The letter *æ* follows *a*, *þ/ð* follows *t*. The prefix *ge-* is ignored in alphabetizing words, so that *gemunan* appears under *m*. Occurrences of words are cited by text number and line: 3/25 refers to text number 3 (*A Colloquy on the Occupations*), line 25.

Probably the most difficult element of Old English vocabulary for the beginner is the considerable number of compound conjunctions like **mid þām þe** and **for þon**. Students will find it helpful to familiarize themselves with the list of conjunctions in §§168 and 171 before reading the texts or using the glossary.

This revised glossary was prepared in collaboration with Roy Michael Liuzza of Yale University.

ā adv. *forever, always* 4/121, 11(e)/6, 12/315, 15/5, 15/42, āwa 17/79, etc.; *ever* 18(a)/779 [archaic MnE aye]

ābǣdan 1 *repel, ward off* pres 3s ābǣd (= ābǣdeð) 11(n)/12

ābēag see ābūgan

Abēl pers. n. *Abel* gs Abēles 4/73

abbod m. *abbot* ns 7/1, 7/19

abbudisse f. *abbess* ns 9/61; gs abudissan 9/1; ds 9/49

ābēodan II *announce, deliver* (*a message*) imp s ābēod 12/49; pret 3s ābēad 12/27

ābīdan I *await* inf 15/53 [MnE abide]

āblendan 1 *blind* inf 7/45

Abraham pers. n. *Abraham* ns 2/46, 2/52; as 2/53, 2/71; gs Abrahames 2/43, 4/6

ābrecan IV *storm, sack* pret 3p ābrǣcon 10(a)/3; subj 3s ābrǣce 11(n)/7; p ptc ābrocen 10(b)/18

ābrēoðan II *fail, come to naught* pret subj 3s ābrēoðe 12/242 (see note)

ābūgan II *bend away, start* pret 3s ābēag 18(a)/775

ac conj. *but, however, but on the contrary* 1/13, 1/33, 2/9, 2/73, 3/11, etc.

āc f. *oak* ns 1/13, acc 11(n)/9

ācennan 1 *bring forth, give birth to, produce* pres 2s ācenst 2/34; p ptc ācenned 3/137, 4/58, 11(m)/1, 18(b)/1356

ācsian 2 *ask* pret 3s āhsode 8/53

āctrēo n. *oak tree* ds 15/28, 15/36

ācwealde see ācwellan

ācweccan 1 *shake, brandish* pret 3s ācwehte 12/255, 12/310 [MnE quake]

ācwellan 1 *kill* imp s ācwele 2/63; pret 3s ācwealde 18(a)/886

ācweðan V *utter* pres 3s ācwið 16/91

ācȳþan 1 *make known* inf 16/113

Adam pers. n. *Adam* ns 2/18, 2/20, 2/24; as 2/20; gs Adomes 14/100

ādl f. *sickness, disease* ns 17/70

ādrǣfan 1 *drive out, exile* inf 6/8; pret 3s ādrǣfde 6/4

āfeallan VII *fall off, fall (in death)* p ptc āfeallen *(decayed)* 5/64, 12/202

āfēdan 1 *feed* inf 3/148; pres 2s āfētst 3/120

āferran see āfierran

āfētst see āfēdan

āfierran 1 *remove* inf āferran 10(a)/19

āflȳman 1 *put to flight, cause to flee* pret 3s āflȳmde 12/243

āfyllan 1 *fill up* inf 3/19

āfȳsan 1 *impel* inf 12/3 *(drive away)*; p ptc āfȳsed 14/125

āgan pret. pres. *possess, own, have* inf 2/76, 10(b)/39, 10(b)/62, 12/87; pres 1s āh 12/175; 3s 14/107, 17/27; subj 3s āge 16/64; 1p āgen 17/117; pret 1s āhte 15/16; 3s 12/189; 3p āhton 10(b)/58. With negative: pres 1s nāh *do not have* 4/123, 14/131; 3s 11(f)/14

āġeaf see āġiefan

āgen see āgan

āgen adj. *own* asm āgenne 6/28; asn āgen 5/33, 11(k)/6; asf āgene 4/105; dsf āgenre 4/20

āġiefan V *give back* pret 3s āġeaf 9/60, 12/44; p ptc āgyfen 12/116.

āglǣca m. *combatant, belligerent* ns 18(a)/732, 18(a)/739, 18(a)/893; æglǣca 18(a)/816

agob see boga

āgyfen see āġiefan

āh see āgan

āhāfen see āhebban

āhēawan VII *cut down* p ptc āhēawen 14/29

āhebban VI, 1 *raise, lift up, wage (war)* pres 3p āhebbað 11(d)/3; pret 1s āhof 14/44; 3s āhefde 2/67, āhof 12/130, 12/244; 3p āhofon 10(a)/2, 12/213, 14/61; p ptc āhafen 12/106, āhefen 10(b)/47

āhlēapan VII *leap up* pret 3s āhlēop 18(b)/1397

āhlēop see āhlēapan

āhliehhan VI *laugh at, deride, exult* pret 3s āhlōg 18(a)/730

āhlōg see āhliehhan

āhof see āhebban

āhofon see āhebban

āhreddan 1 *rescue, save* pret 3s āhredde 4/79, 7/53

āhsode see ācsian

āhte see āgan

āhtes see āwiht

āhton see āgan

āhwǣr adv. *anywhere* 7/31

āīdliġan 2 *render useless, profane* inf 8/55

aldor see ealdor

aldordagum see ealdordæg

aldorman see ealdormann

aldorþeġn see ealdprþeġn

ālēag see ālēogan

ālecgan 1 *lay down* pret 3s ālegde 18(a)/834, 18(a)/851 *(give up)*, 3p āledon 14/63 (see note to 4/17)

ālēogan II *leave unfulfilled* pret 3s ālēag 10(b)/39

Alerīc see Eallerīca

ālimpan III *befall, come to pass* p ptc ālumpen 18(a)/733

alwalda m. *all-ruler, the Lord* ns 18(b)/1314

ālȳfan 1 *permit, allow* inf 12/90; p ptc ālȳfed 8/62

alle see eall

Amuling pers. n. *Amuling* ns 10(b)/69; gp Amulinga 10(a)/6

āmyrran 1 *wound* pret 3s āmyrde 12/165

ān adj. (§§83, 193.4, 194) *a, an, one, only* nsm 3/33, 11(b)/3, 11(k)/3, āna *alone* 12/94, 15/22, 15/35, 16/8; asm ānne 2/66, 3/36, 3/56, 5/18 (ānne ānlēpne *a single one*) ænne 5/26, etc.; dsm ānum 3/104, 4/74, 6/21, etc.; asn 3/205, 5/16; dsn ānum 4/103; asf āne 5/75, 11(p)/2; dsf ānre 2/46; apn ān 9/16; gp ānra (ānra gehwelc *each one*) 3/210, 14/108; as pron. asm ænne 12/117, 12/226

ānbīdian 2 *wait, abide* imp p ānbīdiað (w. refl. ēow) 2/50

āncenned adj. *only begotten* asm āncennedan 2/44, 2/65; dsm 2/73

and conj. *and* 1/2, 1/3, 1/5, 2/2, 2/5, etc.; ond 5/2, 5/4, etc.

anda m. *malice, hostility* ds andan 16/105, 18(a)/708

andettan 1 *confess* pres 1s andette 8/13, ondette 8/45; 3s 8/50

andġit n. *meaning, sense* ns 4/46; as 4/27; ds andgite 4/54, andgiete 5/69.

andġitfullīce adv. *clearly, intelligibly* superl. andgitfullīcost 5/73

andsaca m. *enemy, adversary* as ondsacan 18(a)/786

andswarian 2 *answer* pres 3s andswaraþ 3/197, 3/204; pret 3s andswarode 8/1, ondsworede 8/56, ondswarede 9/29, ondswarade 9/108; 3p ondswarodon 9/101, ondswaredon 9/114

andswaru f. *answer* as andsware 9/33, 12/44, ondsware 11(n)/15

andweard adj. *present* nsn andwearde 8/26

andwlita m. *face* gs andwlitan 2/40

andwyrdan 1 *answer* pret 1s andwyrde 5/43; 3s 2/4, 2/55, 2/62

ānfeald adj. *simple, onefold* dsf ānfealdan 4/47

ānfealdlīce adv. *in the singular* 4/71

ānfloga m. *solitary flier* ns 17/62

anforht adj. *very frightened, terrified* nsm 14/117

ānforlǣtan VII *abandon, renounce* pres subj 3s ānforlēte 9/63

angel m. *hook* as 3/77, 3/195 [MnE angle]

Angelcynn n. *the English people, England* as 5/3, 5/30; ds Angelcynne 5/14, 5/58

anġinn n. *beginning* ns angin 4/55, 12/242 (see note); ds anginne 4/18, 4/51

ānhaga m. *solitary one, one who dwells alone* ns 16/1

ānhoga m. *solitary one, one who contemplates alone* as ānhogan 16/40

Anlāf pers. n. *Olaf* ns 7/47

ānlēpe adj. *single* asn ānlēpne 5/18

ānlīcnes f. *image* ds ānlīcnisse 4/68, 4/70; dp ānlīcnissum 4/71. See onlīcnes

ānne see ān

ānnis f. *oneness, unity* ns 4/70

ānrǣd adj. *resolute* nsm 12/44, 12/132

ānre see ān

anwald see onweald

anwealda m. *ruler, Lord* ns 14/153

apostol m. *apostle* ns 4/32; np apostolas 4/36; gp apostola 9/78

ār n. *copper* as 3/142 [MnE ore]

ār m. *messenger* ns 12/26

ār f. *mercy, favour* ns 17/107; as āre 16/1, 16/114; gs 10(b)/78; gp āra 10(b)/57

ār f. *oar*

ārās see ārīsan

ārǣdan 1 *read* inf 5/61, 5/66; p ptc ārǣd *predetermined, inexorable* 16/5

ārǣran 1 *raise, erect, establish* pret 3s ārǣrde 2/57, 4/38; p ptc ārǣred 14/44

arċebiscop m. *archbishop* ns arcebisceop 7/16, 7/24, 7/25; ds ærcebiscepe 5/70, arcebisceope 7/18

arċestōl m. *archiepiscopal see* ds arcestōle 7/16

āreċċean 1 *translate, render* inf 5/17, 5/73

ārfæstnis f. *piety* ds ārfæstnisse 9/3

ārian 2 *spare* inf 2/72

ārīsan I *arise* inf 9/113; imp s ārīs 18(b)/1390; pret 3s ārās 2/46, 9/22, 9/45, 14/101

ārlīċe adv. *honourably, kindly* 11(k)/6

arodlīċe adv. *vigorously* 2/62

Arriān pers. n. *Arius* gs Arriānes 10(b)/40

Arriānisc adj. *Arian* dsm Arriāniscan 10(a)/7

ārwyrðe adj. *honourable* as noun nsm ārwyrða 10(a)/26

āsǣde see āsecgan

asca see æsc

Ascanmynster n. *Axminster* as 6/42

āsceacan VI *shake* pret 3s āsceoc 12/230

āsceoc see āsceacan

āscian 2 *ask* inf 1/34; pres 1s āscie 2/54; pret 3s āscode 2/54

ġeāscian 2 *learn by asking, learn of, discover* pret 3s geāscode 6/9

ġeāscode see ġeāscian

āsecgan 3 *say, tell* inf 16/11; pret 3s āsǣde 12/198

āsettan 1 *set, set up* inf 11(k)/11 (sīþas āsettan *to set out on journeys*); pres 1s āsette 3/42, subj 3s 14/142; pret 3p āsetton 14/32

āsingan III *sing, recite* pret 3s āsong 9/59

āsong see āsingan

āspryttan 1 *sprout, bring forth* pres 3s āspryt 2/39

assa m. *ass* dp assum 2/48, 2/50

āstāg see āstīgan

āstandan VI *stand up, get up* pret 3s āstōd 18(a)/759

āstealde see āstellan

āstellan 1 *establish* pret 3s āstealde 4/83

āstīgan I *proceed, ascend* pres 1s āstīge 3/135, 3s āstīgeð 18(b)/1373; pret 3s āstāg 14/103, 18(a)/782

āstōd see āstandan

āstreaht see āstreċċan

āstreċċan 1 *stretch out, extend* imp s āstreċe 2/63; pret 3s āstrehte (w. refl.) 10(a)/30; p ptc āstreaht 10(b)/80

āstyrian 1 *remove* p ptc āstyred 14/30 [MnE stir]

aswapan VII *sweep away, remove* pres 1s āswāpe 11(h)/5

ātēah see ātēon

ateliċ adj. *horrible, dreadful* ns 18(a)/784

ātēon II *draw, unsheathe* pret 3s ātēah 2/60, 18(a)/766 (sið . . . ātēah *took a journey*); subj 3s ātuge 9/81

atol adj. *terrible, hateful* nsm 18(a)/732, 18(a)/816, nsn 18(a)/848, 18(b)/1332, asn 17/6

attor n. *venom* as 11(h)/9

ātuge see ātēon

ātyhtan 1 *produce, entice* p ptc ātyhted 10(b)/8, 11(m)/3

āð m. *oath* ap āðas 10(b)/25

āwa see ā.

āwearp see āweorpan

āweaxan VII *grow up* pret 1s āweox 11(k)/10, 15/3.

āweċċan 1 *awaken, arouse* pret 3s āwehte 9/82

āwel m. *awl* as 3/195

āwendan 1 *translate, change, distort* inf 4/3, 4/5, 4/101 (*change*); pres 3s āwent 4/103; pret 1s āwende 5/74; p ptc āwend 4/6

āweorpan III *throw away, discard* inf āwurpan 4/108; pret 3s āwearp 8/59

āweox see āweaxan
āwierġan 1 *curse, damn* p ptc āwierġed 2/29, 2/37
āwiht n. *aught, anything* gs āhtes 7/28 (see note); ds 3/168 (to āwihte *at all*)
āwrītan I *write* inf 4/100; p ptc āwriten 4/77, np āwritene 5/33
āwurpan see āweorpan

ǣ f. *law, scripture* ns 4/12, 4/28, 5/48, 10(b)/41; as 4/40; ds 4/10, 4/12, 4/23
ǣcer m. *cultivated field* as 3/13 [MnE acre]
ǣdre f. *vein, stream* dp ēdrum 18(a)/742
ǣfǣst adj. *pious* nsm 9/83; asf ǣfǣstan 9/16; apn ǣfǣste 9/11
ǣfǣstnes f. *religion* ns 8/14; ds ǣfǣstnisse 9/3, ǣfǣstnesse 9/16
ǣfen m. *evening* as 3/25; ds ǣfenne 9/93
ǣfensprǣc f. *evening speech* as ǣfensprǣce 18(a)/759
ǣfentīd f. *evening-time* as ǣfentīde 14/68 [archaic MnE eventide]
ǣfre adv. *forever, always, ever* 4/57, 4/66, 5/44, 7/54, etc.
ǣft see eft
ǣfter adv. *afterwards* 9/43, 17/77
ǣfter prep. w.d. *after, according to* 4/22, 4/33, 4/54, 5/36, etc.
ǣftercweðende m. pl. (pres ptc) *those speaking after (a man's death)* gp ǣftercweðendra 17/72
ǣfterfylġan 1 *follow, come after* pres subj 3s ǣfterfylige 8/35
ǣġhwǣm see ǣġhwā
ǣġhwā pron. *every one, everything* dsm ǣġhwǣm 18(b)/1384
ǣġhwǣþer see ǣġðer
ǣġhwǣðres see ǣġðer
ǣġhweder adv. *in all directions* 7/77
ǣġhwylc pron. *each* nsm 12/234, 18(b)/1386, as ǣġhywlcne ānra *every one* 14/86; as adj. nsf 14/120
ǣglǣca see āglǣca
ǣġðer pron. *each, both* ns 12/133, 12/224; gs ǣġhwǣðres 11(a)/5; ǣġðer ġe ... ġe *both ... and* 2/11, 4/37, 5/37, 7/9, etc., ǣġhwǣþer ġe ... ġe 8/2 [MnE either]
Ǣgypta see Ēgipte
ǣht f. *possessions, property* as ǣhta 4/37, ǣht 13/36; ap ǣhte 18(c)/2248
ǣl m. *eel* ap ǣlas 3/87
ǣlċ pron., adj. *each, every* nsm 3/164; gsm ǣlces 4/74; dsm ǣlcum 5/74; dsn 2/3, 4/49; gsn ǣlces 10(b)/36; dsf ǣlcre 5/75; ism ǣlċe 3/8
ǣlde m. pl. *men* gp ǣlda 16/85, 17/77; dp yldum 18(a)/705, eldum 18(d)/3168
ǣldo see yldu

Ǣlfere pers. n. *Ǣlfere* ns 12/80
Ǣlfgār pers. n. *Ǣlfgar* as 7/45
Ǣlfnoð pers. n. *Ǣlfnoð* ns 12/183
Ǣlfred pers. n. *Ǣlfred* nsm 5/1
Ǣlfrīc see Ealfrīc
Ǣlfrīc pers. n. *Ǣlfric* gp Ǣlfrīces 12/209
Ǣlfstān pers. n. *Ǣlfstan* ds Ǣlfstāne 7/30
Ǣlfwine pers. n. *Ǣlfwine* ns 12/211, vs 12/231
ǣlmihtig adj. *almighty* nsm 4/53, 9/45, 14/39, 14/93, (se Ǣlmihtiga *the Almighty*) 2/72, 14/98, etc.; asm ǣlmihtigne 14/60; dsm ǣlmihtegum 5/20
ġeǣmetiġan 2 *free, empty, disengage* pres subj 2s geǣmetige 5/22
ǣmettig adj. *empty* nsm 3/164
ǣnde see ende
ǣniġ adj. *any* nsm 424, 7/54, etc.; asm ǣnigne 5/20; gsm ǣnges 17/116; dsm ǣniġum 11(h)/11, 11(h)/15, etc.; asn ǣnig 3/22, 3/35, 9/100, etc.; as pron., nsm 14/110, 14/117, 18(a)/779; hyra ǣnig *any of them* 12/70; ǣnige þinga *in any way, by any means* 18(a)/791; as noun 18(b)/1356
ǣnliċ adj. *unique, solitary, beautiful* nsm 11(p)/2
ǣnne see ān
ǣr adv. *before, previously* (§§168, 197.4) adv. 5/34, 6/26, 8/75, 9/88, 10(b)/75, 11(f)/12, 11(h)/7, etc.; compar: see ǣror; superl: see ǣrest; conj. *before* 6/11, 11(n)/6, 12/279, 12/300, etc.; w. subj. *rather than* 12/61, *before* 17/74; ǣr þan (or þǣm) ðe *before* 4/11, 5/28 [MnE ere]
ǣrende see ǣrende
ǣrċebiscop see ārċebiscop
ǣrdǣg m. *daybreak, early morning* ds ǣrdǣge 18(b)/1311
ǣrende n. *message* as ǣrǣnde 12/28 [MnE errand]
ǣrendġewrit n. *letter* as 5/16, 10(b)/63; ap ǣrendgewritu 10(a)/18 [MnE errand, writ]
ǣrendwreca m. *messenger, minister* dp ǣrendwrecum 5/6
ǣrest adj. *first* nsf ǣreste 9/72, 15/6 [archaic MnE erst, erst(while)]
ǣrest adv. *first* 4/35, 4/64, 5/48, 7/22, 9/40, etc., ǣrost 12/124, etc.
ǣrġewin n. *ancient hostility* as 14/19
ǣrgōd adj. *good from old times, very good* ns 18(b)/1329
ǣrnan 1 *run, gallop* pret 3p ǣrndon 12/191
ǣrnemerġen m. *early morning* ds 3/23
ǣror adv. *earlier* 14/108, 18(a)/809, 18(d)/3168
ǣrsceaft n. *ancient work* ns 13/16
ǣr þan þe, ǣr ðǣm ðe see ǣr
ǣs n. *bait, food* ds ǣse 3/77; *carrion* ds ǣse 18(b)/1332, gs ǣses 12/107

æsc m. *ash (tree)* ns 1/13; *ash (spear)* as 12/43, 12/310; gp asca 16/99
Æscferð pers. n. *Æscferth* ns 12/267
Æschere pers. n. *Æschere* ns 18(b)/1323, 18(b)/1329.
æschere m. *army in ships, Viking army* ns 12/69
æscholt n. *spear made of ash* as 12/230
Æscwīg pers. n. *Æscwig* ds Æscwīge 7/30
æstel iii. *pointer used to keep one's place as one reads* ns 5/75
æt prep. w.d.s. *at, from* 3/10, 4/21, 5/70, 9/27 (*to*), etc.
*ge*æt see *ge*etan
ætberstan III *escape* pres 1s ætberste 3/139; 3p ætberstaþ 3/105; pret 3s ætbærst 7/35
ætēawed see atȳwan
æten see etan
ætflēogan II *fly away* inf 3/122, 3/124
ætforan prep. w.d. *in front of, before* 12/16
ætgædere adv. *together* 9/99, 14/48, ætgædre 11(n)/11; somod ætgædre *together* 16/39, 18(a)/729
æthrīnan I w.g. or d. *touch* pret 3s æthrān 18(a)/722
ætsomne adv. *together* 8/5, 9/93, 11(e)/3
ætstandan VI *stand fixed, stop* pret 3s ætstōd 18(a)/891
ætsteppan VI *step forth* pret 3s ætstōp 18(a)/745
ætstōd see ætstandan
ætstōp see ætsteppan
ætren see ættryne
ætterne see ættryne
ættryne adj. *poisoned, fatal, deadly* nsm ætren 11(h)/4, ætterne 12/146; asm ættrynne 12/47
ætwītan 1 w.d. *reproach* inf 12/220, 12/250
ætȳwan *appear, show* pres 3s ætȳweð 8/35; p ptc ætēawed 8/71
æðele adj. *noble* nsm 12/280, 18(b)/1312; asm æðelan 12/151
Æþelgār pers. n. *Æthelgar* ns 7/1, 7/16; gs Æþelgāres 12/320
æþeling m. *prince, atheling* ns 6/19, 18(b)/1329; as 6/8, 6/14; gs æþelinges 6/42, 18(a)/888; ds æþelinge 10(b)/40, 14/58; gp æþelinga 11(a)/5, 17/93, 18(d)/3170; dp æðelingum 8/76, 10(b)/21
Æþelmǣr pers. n. *Æthelmær* ns 7/13 [MnE Elmer]
æþelo n. pl. *origin, descent, noble lineage* ap 12/216, æþelu 11(n)/8
Æþelred pers. n. *Æthelred* gs Æþelredes 12/53, 12/151, 12/203
Æþerič pers. n. *Ætheric* ns 12/280
Æðelwine pers. n. *Æthelwine* ns 7/26

*ge*bād see *ge*bīdan

baldlīce adv. *boldly* 12/311; superl. baldlīcost 12/78
bana m. *slayer* ns 12/299; as banan 14/66, ds 6/32 [MnE bane]
*ge*band see *ge*bindan
bānfāg adj. *adorned with bone* asn 18(a)/780
bānloca m. *joint, body* np bānlocan 18(a)/818, ap 18(a)/742
bār m. *wild boar* as 3/56, 3/58, 3/59; ap hāras 3/51
bāt m. *boat* as 3/76; ds bāte 3/99
bāt see bītan
baþian 2 *bathe* inf 16/47; pret 3p baþedan 1(f)/6
baþu see bæð
Bæbbanburh f. *Bamburgh* (*Northumberland*) ns 7/39
bæc n. *back* as 12/276 (ofer bæc *away, to the rear*)
bæcere m. *baker* ns 3/162; np bæceras 3/6
bæd see biddan
bæde see biddan
bæl n. *fire, funeral pyre* ds bæle 17/114
bær see beran
*ge*bǣre n. *outcry* dp gebǣrum 6/17
bærnett n. *burning* ds bærnette 2/58, 7/55
*ge*bǣro n. *demeanour* as 15/44; is 15/21
bæron see beran
bærst see berstan
bæð n. *bath* ds bæðe 8/77; np baþu 13/40, 13/46
be prep. w.d. *about, concerning* 1/35, 3/168, 3/173, 4/31, etc., bi 9/72, etc.; *near, by* 12/152, 12/318, 12/319, big 12/182; be þam *through that* 12/9; be þām þe *as, according as* 2/12; be sūðan see sūðan
bēacen n. *beacon, sign, portent, symbol* ns 14/6, as 14/21, as bēcn 18(d)/3160 (*monument*); ds bēacne 14/83; gp bēacna 14/118
*ge*bēad see *ge*bēodan
beadogrīma m. *war-mask, helmet* as beadogrīman 18(c)/2257
beadu m. *battle* ds beaduwe 12/185; gp beadwa 18(a)/709
beadurǣs m. *rush of battle, onslaught* ns 12/111
beadurinc m. *warrior* dp beadurincum 10(b)/18
beadurōf adj. *bold in battle* gsm beadurōfes 18(d)/3160
bēag see būgan
bēag m. *ring* (*of precious metal used for money or ornaments*) as 3/70, bēg (as plural) 18(d)/3163, ap bēagas 12/31, 12/160 [MnE (through Yiddish) bagel]
bēaggifa m. *ring-giver, lord* as bēahgifan 12/290
bēaghroden adj. *adorned with rings* nsf 11(j)/9

běahhord n. *ring-hoard, treasure* gs běah-hordes 18(a)/894

bealo n. *harm, injury, ruin* as (?) 17/112 [MnE bale]

bealocwealm m. *baleful death* ns 18(c)/2265

bealohȳdig adj. *intending evil, hostile* nsm 18(a)/723

bealosīþ m. *painful journey, bitter experience* gp bealosīþa 17/28

bealuware m. pl. *dwellers in iniquity, evildoers* gp bealuwara 14/79

běam m. *tree, log, cross* ns 14/97; gs běames 11(n)/7; ds běame 14/114, 14/122; gp běama 14/6 [MnE beam]

bearm m. *bosom, lap* on bearm scipes *in the hold of a ship* as 18(a)/896

bearn n. *child, son* ns 12/92, 12/155, 12/209, 12/186, 12/238, etc.; np 10(b)/34, 17/77; ap 3/148, 11(k)/6, 17/93; gp bearna 18(b)/1367; dp bearnum 9/40

Bearrocscīr f. *Berkshire* as Bearrocscīre 7/72

bearu m. *grove* ns 11(o)/4; ds bearwe 15/27; np bearwas 17/48, 18(b)/1363; dp bearwum 11(f)/2

běatan VII *beat, pound* pres ptc gpm běatendra 3/200; pres 3s běateð 18(c)/2265; pret 3p běotan 17/23

beæftan prep. w.d. *behind* 6/24

bebēad see bebēodan

bebēodan II *command, commend* pres ptc bebēodende 9/124; pres 1s bebīode 5/21, 5/76; pret 1s bebēad 2/24, 2/37; 3s 2/6, 4/87, bibēad 9/97; 3p bebudon 9/56; p ptc beboden 4/94, 9/25, 9/60

bebīode see bebēodan

beboden see bebēodan

bebudon see bebēodan

běċ see bōc

běcn see běacen

becōm see becuman

becuman IV *come* pres subj 3p becumen 3/44; pret 3s becwōm 9/121, becōm 10(a)/26, 10(b)/77 (*befell*); 3p becōmon 5/24 (*befell*), 12/58 [MnE become]

becwōm see becuman

bedǽlan I w.d. *deprive* p ptc bedǽled 18(a)/721

Bedefordscīr f. *Bedfordshire* as Bedefordscīre 7/69

bedelfan III *bury* pret 3s bedealf 14/75

bedrīfan I *drive, chase* pret 3p bedrifon 3/60; *cover over, sprinkle* p ptc asm bedrifenne 14/62

beēode see begān

befæstan I *apply, use* inf 5/24, pres subj 2s befæste 5/24

befeallan VII *fall* p ptc befeallen *deprived, bereft* 18(c)/2256

befēng see befōn

befēolan III (§133.2) w.d. *apply oneself* inf 5/59

beflōwan VII *flow around, surround by water* p ptc beflowen 15/49

befōn VII *enclose* pret 3s befēng 13/39

began see beginnan

begān anom. (§128) *practise, perform, surround* inf 1/14; imp s begā 3/213; pres 2s begæst 3/7, 3/41; subj 1s begā 3/70; 3s 3/211; pret 1s beēode 8/57, 3s 6/11, etc.; 1p beēodon 8/15, beēodan 8/43; 3p biēodon 8/53

begǽst see begān

beġeat see beġietan

beġēaton see beġietan

běġen m. (§84) *both* np 12/183, 12/191, 12/291, 12/305, 18(a)/769; ap 12/182; gp běgra 2/14

beġeondan prep. w.d. *beyond* 8/72, begiondan 5/17

beġēotan II *drench, cover* p ptc nsn begoten 14/7 (*covered*); nsm 14/49

beġietan V *get, gain, acquire, lay hold of* inf 3/148, 5/13; pres 1s begiete 3/74; 2s begietst 3/73; 1p begietaþ 3/209; pret 3s begeat 15/32, 15/41, bigeat 17/6; 3p begēaton 5/35, 18(c)/2249

beginnan III *begin* inf 2/61; pret 3s began 1/14, 4/34

beġiondan see beġeondan

begnornian 2 *lament, bemoan* pret 3p begnornodon 18(d)/3178

begong m. *circuit, compass, region* as 18(a)/860

beġoten see beġēotan

behātan VII *promise* pret 3p behēton 7/65; subj 3s behēte 7/60

behealdan VII *behold, gaze at, watch over* pret 1s behēold 14/25, 14/58, 3s 18(a)/736; 3p behēoldon 14/9, 14/11, 14/64

behēawan VII *cut off* inf behēawan 10(b)/43

behēte see behātan

behionan prep. w.d. *on this side of* 5/15

behlȳþan I *strip, despoil* p ptc behlȳþed 11(j)/10

behrēowsian 2 *repent* pres 3p behrēowsiað 4/92

behrīman I *cover with frost* p ptc behrīmed 15/48

behȳdan I *hide, conceal* pret 1s behȳdde 2/22; 3s 2/18

beinnan adv. *within* 10(a)/26

ġebelgan III *enrage* p ptc gebolgen 18(a)/723

belimpan III *pertain* pret 3p belumpen 9/4, belumpon 9/16

belocen see belucan

belt m. *belt* ns 1/4

belūcan II *contain, lock shut* inf 10(a)/25, 10(b)/73; p ptc belocen 4/47, 6/27

belumpen (= belumpon) see belimpan

benam see beniman

benċ f. *bench* ds bence 1/11, 12/213
beniman IV *deprive* pret 3s benam (w.a. of person and g. of thing) 6/1
benn f. *wound* np benne 16/49
bēo see bēon
bēod m. *table* ns 3/164
bēodan II *offer* inf 7/74; pres 3s bēodeð (*announce*) 17/54; pret 3p budon 6/32
ġebēodan II *offer* pret 3s gebēad 6/20, 6/28; p ptc geboden 6/34
bēon anom. (§127) *be* inf 3/63, 3/115, 3/130, etc., imp s bēo 3/214; pres 1s eom 2/22, 3/2, 3/40, etc., bēom 11(d)/8, 11(h)/4; 2s eart 1/36, 2/20, 2/42, 3/39, bist 2/28, 2/35; 3s is 1/1, 1/3, 1/4, 2/5, 2/37, 4/17 (ys), etc.; biþ 1/23, 3/98, 3/177, 4/66, etc.; byð 4/23; 2p bēoð 2/10, bēo 3/176; 3p sind 2/4, 3/44, sindon 4/38, siendon 5/79, syndon 8/17, bēoð 2/9, 2/76, 3/79, 3/137, 3/190; subj 2s sīe 3/212; 2p bēo 2/8; 3s sīe 2/54, 3/207, 5/20, 8/12, 8/29, etc., sȳ 12/215, bēo 4/47; 3p sīen 5/55; pret 1s wæs 3/53; 2s wǣre 2/42, 3/52, 3/59, 3/62; 3s wæs 1/31, 2/1, 2/12, 2/73, etc., was 6/8; 3p wǣron 2/16, 4/107, 5/18, 7/58, etc.; wǣrun 6/12, 6/16, 6/24, wǣran 11(1)/2; subj 2s wǣre 2/23; 3s 4/12, 5/29, 6/34, 8/10, 9/97, etc.; 3p wǣren 5/80, wǣran 8/6. With negative: pres 1s neom 3/21; 3s nis 3/9, 3/173, 9/114, 11(e)/1; 3p nearon 17/82; pret 3s næs 10(b)/43, 12/325; subj 3s nǣre 6/31; 3p nǣren 5/18, nǣron 5/33
ġebēorscipe m. *feast, beer party* gs gebēorscipes 9/24; ds gebēorscipe 9/20, 9/30
beorg m. *mound of stone* as 14/32 (*hill, mountain*), 18(d)/3163; ds beorge 14/50; dp beorgum 13/32
ġebeorg n. *defence* ds gebeorge (*peace*) 12/31, 12/131, 12/245
beorgan III w.d. *save, protect* inf 18(c)/1372; pret 3p burgon 12/194
beorghliþ n. *mountain-slope* dp beorghleoþum 11(f)/2
beorht adj. *bright* npn 13/21; nsf 16/94; asm beorhtne 11(j)/7; asf beorhtan 13/37; dsm 13/40, 14/66; apf beorhte 18(a)/896; superl. beorhtost 14/6
beorn m. *man, warrior* ns 10(b)/52, 13/32, 14/42, 16/70, 16/113, 17/55; as 12/270; gs beornes 12/131, 12/160; ds beorne 12/154, 12/245, etc.; np beornas 12/92, 12/111, 14/32, etc.; ap beornas 12/17, 12/62, 12/182, etc.; gp beorna 12/257; dp beornum 12/101
bēot n. *vow, boast, threat* as 12/15, 12/27 (on bēot *threateningly*) 12/213, 16/70
bēotan see bēatan
bēotian 2 *vow* pret 1p bēotedan 15/21; 3s bēotode 12/290

Bēowulf pers. n. *Bēowulf* ns 18(b)/1310, 18(b)/1383; gs Bēowulfes 18(a)/795, 18(a)/856, 18(a)/872; ds Bēowulfe 18(a)/818
bepǣċan 1 *deceive* pret 3s bepǣhte 2/27
berād see berīdan
beran IV *carry, bear, bring* inf 2/52, 11(n)/2, 12/12, 12/62; imp p berað 9/104; pres 3s bereð 14/118, byreð 11(d)/6, 11(j)/5; pret 3s bær 2/53, 18(a)/711, 18(a)/846, etc.; 3p bǣron 12/99, 14/32; subj 3p bēron 12/67
berēofan II *destroy, ravage* p ptc berofen 13/4
berīdan I *ride up to, overtake* pret 3s berād 6/11
berofen see berēofan
berstan III *burst, fall apart* inf 14/36; pret 3s bærst 12/284; 3p burston 13/2 (transitive: smashed, broke), 18(a)/760, 18(a)/818
beseah see besēon
besenċan 1 *cause to sink, drown* inf 3/104
besēon V *look* pret 3s beseah 2/66
besmiþian 2 *fasten* p ptc besmiþod 18(a)/775
bestandan VI *stand alongside* pret 3p bestōdon 12/68
bestēman 1 *make wet, drench* p ptc bestēmed nsm 14/48, nsn 14/22
beswīcan I *ensnare, deceive* pres 1s beswīce 3/109; 2s beswīcst 3/108; p ptc apm beswicene 12/238
beswillan 1 *drench, soak* p ptc beswyled nsn 14/23
besyrwan 1 *ensnare, entrap* inf 18(a)/713
ġebētan 1 *improve, remedy* pret 3s gebētte 18(a)/830
betǣċan 1 *entrust, deliver* pres 1s betǣċe 3/31; pret 3s betǣhte 7/28
betǣhte see betǣċan
bētend m. *rebuilder, restorer, keeper of a flame* (?) np 13/28
betera adj. (compar. of gōd; cf. §76) *better* ns betre 5/54, betera (as noun *the better* [*one*]) 12/276; nsn betere 12/31; apn beteran 8/22
betimbran 1 *build* pret 3p betimbredon 18(d)/3159
betliċ adj. *excellent, splendid* asn 18(a)/780
betræppan 1 *entrap* inf 7/31
betre see betera
betst adj. (superl. of gōd; cf. §76) *best* nsn 17/73 (as noun); isn betstan 9/59
betwēonan prep. w.d. *between* 1/24
betweox prep. w.d. *between, among* 2/29, 2/31, 2/67, 3/188, 3/207, 4/17, betwux 10(a)/3 [MnE betwixt]
betȳnan 1 *close, conclude* pret 3s betȳnde 9/86, 9/124
beþurfan pret. pres. w.g. *need* pres 1p beþurfon 3/168
beweaxan VII *grow over* p ptc npm beweaxne 15/31

bewindan III *wind around, envelop* p ptc
bewunden 11(0)/2, 14/5
beworhton see bewyrcan
bewrēon 1 *cover* pret 3s biwrāh 16/23; p ptc
bewrigen 14/17, 14/53
bewunden see bewindan
bewyrcan 1 *build around, surround* pret 3p
beworhton 18(d)/3161
bi see be
bibēad see bebēodan
ġebīcnian 2 *signify, indicate* p ptc gebīcnod
4/69
bīdan I *await* inf 9/115, 17/30 (*remain*); pret
3s bād 18(a)/709, 18(b)/1313 (*remain*) [MnE
bide]
ġebīdan I w.g. *await, experience* inf 16/70,
18(b)/1386; pres 3s gebīdeð 16/1; pret 1s
gebād 12/174, 14/125, 15/3; 3s 13/9, 18(a)/
815, 18(c)/2258; p ptc gebiden 14/50, 14/79,
17/4, 17/28
bidǣlan 1 *deprive* p ptc nsm bidǣled 16/20
biddan V *ask, bid* pres 1s bidde 4/121; subj 2s
4/120; pret 2s bǣde 4/2; 3s bæd 8/60,
10(b)/64, 12/20, 12/128, 12/170, 12/257; 3p
bǣdon 9/108, 10(a)/22, 12/87, 12/262, 12/
306; subj 3s bǣde (w.g.) 9/96 [MnE bid]
ġebiddan V *pray* infl inf (to) gebiddenne
2/51; pres 3p gebiddaþ (w. refl. d.) 14/83;
pret 3s gebæd (w. refl. d.) 9/115, 14/122
bidrēosan II *deprive* p ptc bidroren nsm 17/
16; npm bidrorene 16/79
bidroren see bidrēosan
bielg m. *bellows, leather bag* gp bielga 3/201
[MnE belly]
biēodon see begān
bifian 2 *shake, tremble* inf 14/36; pret 1s bifode
14/42
biforan prep. w.d. *in front of* 16/46 [MnE
before]
big see be
bigang see bigong
biġeal see biġiellan
ġebīgean 1 *bend* inf 4/116
biġeat see beġietan
biġiellan III *scream round about, yell against*
pret 3s biġeal 17/24
bigong m. *worship* ns 8/10; gs bīgonges 8/70;
ds bīgange 8/16, 8/44
bihōn VII *hang around* (*with*) p ptc w.i.
bihongen 17/17
bihongen see bihōn
bihrēosan II *cover* p ptc npm bihrorene 16/77
bīleofa m. *sustenance, food* as bīleofan 3/74,
3/209
bill n. *sword* as 12/162; dp billum 12/114
bilwit adj. *innocent* isn bilwitre 9/119
ġebind n. *binding, commingling* as 16/24, 16/57
bindan III *bind* pres 1s binde 11(f)/16; 3s

bindeð 11(g)/7, 16/102; 3p bindað 16/18;
subj 3s binde 16/13; pret 3s bond 17/32; p
ptc gebunden apn 18(a)/871
ġebindan III *bind, hold fast* pres 3p gebindað
16/40; pret 3s ġeband 2/59, gebond 13/19;
p ptc gebunden 17/9
bindere m. *binder* ns 11(f)/6
biniman IV *deprive* p ptc binumen 11(f)/14
binn f. *bin, manger* as binne 3/18
binnan prep. w.d. *within, in* 2/3, 4/92
binumen see biniman
biscepstōl m. *episcopal see* ds biscepstōle 5/74,
bisceopstōle 7/2
biscop m. *bishop, high priest* ns bisceop 7/16,
7/30 (see note), 8/7; as biscep 5/1, bisceop
8/40; ds biscepe 5/70, bisceope 7/1,
biscope 8/50, 8/52
bisgu f. *occupation, concern, care* as 17/88; dp
bisgum 5/67 [MnE busy]
bismor m. *disgrace* ds bismore 7/34
bīsnian 2 *set an example, instruct by example* inf
4/42
bistelan IV *deprive of* p ptc bistolen 11(f)/13
bītan I *bite* pret 3s bāt 18(a)/742
bite m. *bite, cut* as 18(c)/2259
biter adj. *bitter, grim, fierce* nsm 12/111; gsm
biteres 14/114; asf bitre 17/4, bitter 17/55;
npm bitre 15/31; apm bitere 12/85
biþ see bēon
biwāune see biwāwan
biwāwan VII *blow upon* p ptc npm biwāune
16/76
biwrāh see bewrēon
blāc adj. *black* npn blācu 11(1)/3
blācian 2 *grow pale* pres 3s blācað 17/91
blanca m. *white (or grey) horse* dp blancum
18(a)/856
ġeblandan VII *taint, infect, corrupt* p ptc
geblonden 11(h)/8
blāwan VII *blow* pres ptc gpm blāwendra
3/200
blǣd m. *glory* ns 16/33, 17/79, 17/88; dp
blēdum (*blessings*) 14/149
blēdum see blǣd
blēo n. *colour* dp blēom 14/22
bletsian 2 *bless* pres 1s bletsie 2/74; p ptc ge-
bletsode 2/77
bletsung f. *blessing* ds bletsunge 2/79
bliss f. *bliss, joy, happiness* ns blis 14/139, 14/
141; ds blisse 14/149, 14/153, gs 9/20 (*merriment*)
blīðe adj. *friendly, cheerful* asn 9/105, 15/44;
isn 14/122, 15/21; np 9/108; compar. blīðra
happier nsm 12/146 [MnE blithe]
blīðemōd adj. *friendly* nsm 9/109; np
blīðemōde 9/107
blōd n. *blood* ns 4/73, as 18(a)/742; ds blōde
14/48, on blōde *bloody* 18(a)/847

blōdiġ adj. *bloody* asm blōdigne 12/154
ġeblonden see ġeblandan
blōstma m. *blossom* dp blōstmum 17/48
blōwan VII *bloom* pres ptc nsm blowende
11(o)/4 [MnE blow 'blossom']
bōc f. *book* ns 4/44, booc 9/72; as 4/3; gs bēc
4/5; ds 4/67; ap 5/41, 5/50; gp bōca 4/49,
5/30, 9/78, 10(b)/52
bōccræft m. *literature, scholarship* dp bōccræftum 10(a)/13
bōcere m. *scholar* ap bōceras 9/5
boda m. *messenger* ns 12/49
bodian 2 *preach* infl inf (tō) bodienne 4/34;
pret 3s bodade 8/41, p ptc bodad 8/12, 8/22
[MnE bode]
boga m. *bow* nsm agob (reverse spelling)
11(h)/1; np bogan 12/110
ġebohte see ġebycgan
ġebohtest see ġebycgan
Boētius pers n. *Boethius* ns 10(a)/12, Boītius
10(b)/52; gs Boētius 10(b)/75
bolgenmōd adj. *enraged* ns 18(a)/709
bolster n. *pillow* ds bolstre 9/117 [MnE bol-
ster]
bond see bindan
ġebond see ġebindan
bonnan VII *summon* pres 1s bonne 11(j)/4
bord n. *board, side of a ship* as 1/2; *shield* ns 12/
110; as 12/15, 12/42, 12/131, etc.; ap 12/62,
12/283; gs bordes 12/284; gp borda 12/295,
18(c)/2259; dp bordum 11(j)/9 (*tables*), 12/
101
bordweall m. *shield-wall* as 12/277
ġeboren n. (p ptc) *one born in the same family,
brother* ds geborenum 17/98
bōsm m. *bosom* as 11(j)/9; ds bōsme 11(h)/3,
11(j)/15, 13/40
bōt f. *remedy* as bōte 16/113 [MnE boot
'compensation']
brād adj. *broad, wide, spacious* ns 18(d)/3157;
asn 12/15, 12/163; gsn brādan 13/37
bræc see brecan
ġebræc n. *crashing* ns 12/295, as 18(c)/2259
ġebræcon see ġebrecan
brǣd see breġdan
brǣdan 1 *roast, broil* inf 3/174; infl inf (tō)
brǣdanne 3/175
brǣdan 1 *spread* inf 16/47
ġebrǣgd see ġebreġdan
brēac see brūcan
breahtm m. *noise, revelry* gp breahtma 16/86
brecan IV *break* pres 3s briceð 11(g)/6; pret
1s bræc 1/17; 3s 12/277; p ptc brocen
12/1
ġebrecan V *shatter, smash* pret 3p gebrǣcon
13/1; p ptc gebrocen 13/32
breġdan III *weave, knit, braid* pres 1s breġde
3/42; *pull, drag, fling, draw* (*a sword*) inf

18(a)/707, pret 3s brǣd 12/154, 12/162,
brægd 18(a)/794
ġebreġdan III *weave together, conceive* pret 3s
gebrǣgd 13/18
brēmel m. *bramble, brier* ap brēmelas 2/39; dp
brēmelum 2/67
brenġan 1 *bring* pres subj 3s brenge 8/37
brēost n. *breast* ds brēoste 2/30; dp (w sg
meaning) brēostum 12/144, 14/118, 16/
113
brēostcearu f. *grief of heart* as brēostceare 15/
44, 17/4
brēostcofa m. *heart* ds brēostcofan 16/18
brēosthord n. *inmost feelings* as 17/55
brēr m. *brier* dp brērum 15/31
Bretwālas m. pl. *the Britons* dp Bretwālum
6/7
briceð see brecan
bricg f. *bridge, causeway* as bricge 12/74, 12/78;
ds brycge 1/9
bricgweard m. *guardian of the bridge* ap
bricgweardas 12/85
bridd m. *young bird* ap briddas 3/122
Brihtnōð pers. n. *Brihtnoth* ns 7/21. See also
Byrhtnōð
brim n. *sea, water* ns 18(a)/847
brimfugol m. *seabird* ap brimfuglas 16/47
brimlād f. *sea-way, path of ocean* ds brimlāde
17/30
brimliðend m. *seafarer, viking* gp
brimliðendra12/27
brimmann m. *seafarer, viking* np brimmen
12/295; gp brimmanna 12/49
bringan 1 *bring* pres 3s bringeð 16/54; subj 3s
bringe 4/124; pret 3s brōhte 4/85; 3p
brōhton 4/86; p ptc brungen 11(f)/2
ġebringan 1 *bring* inf 10(a)/20, 10(a)/25; pres
subj 3s gebringe 14/139
brocen see brecan
ġebrocen see ġebrecan
brōga m. *terror* ds brōgan 7/23
* brōhte see bringan
brond m. *burning, fire* gp bronda 18(d)/3160
[MnE brand]
brosnian 2 *decay* pres 3s brosnað 13/2, 18(c)/
2260; pret 3s brosnade 13/28
broþ n. *broth* as 3/172
ġebrōðru see brōðor
brōðor m. *brother* ns brōðor 12/282, 17/98,
18(b)/1324, brōðer 4/19, 9/1, brōþur 6/9;
npm 9/109, 9/113, brōðru 12/191, gebrōðru
12/305
brūcan II (w.g.) *enjoy, use, benefit from, eat* inf
3/158, 3/159, 3/162, 14/144, 18(a)/894; pres
2s brȳcst 2/40; 3p brūcað 17/88; pret 3s
brēac 10(b)/75, 16/44 [MnE brook]
brūneccg adj. *with shining blade* asn 12/163
brungen see bringan

brycge see bricg
brȳcst see brūcan
bryhtm m. *blink* ns 8/33
bryne m. *burning, fire* as 14/149
brytta m. *bestower, one who gives* as bryttan 16/25
Bryttisc adj. *British* ds Bryttiscum 6/21
būan 1 *inhabit, dwell* pres 1s būge 11(d)/2
Buccingahamscīr f. *Buckinghamshire* as Buccingahamscīre 7/69
budon see bēodan
būgan II *bend, bow, turn away* inf 12/276, 14/36, 14/42; pret 3s bēag 13/17; 3p bugon 12/185
būge see būan
ġebunden see ġebindan
bune f. *goblet, cup* ns 16/94
būr m. *chamber, cottage* as 6/11; ds būre 18(b)/1310 [MnE bower]
burg f. *stronghold, enclosure* as burh 7/49, 12/291, burig 10(a)/3, burg 11(n)/7, 13/37 (*city*); ds byrig 6/26, 10(b)/37, 10(b)/46; ap byrig 17/48; gp burga 10(b)/18; dp burgum 17/28 [MnE borough]
burgon see beorgan
burgrǣced n. *city building* np 13/21
burgsteall n. *city* ns 13/28
burgstede m. *city* as 13/2, burhstede 18(c)/2265 (*courtyard pavement*)
burgtūn m. *protecting hedge* np burgtūnas 15/31
burhwaru f. *citizenry, population* ns 7/4, 7/51; ds burhware 7/53; gp burgwara 16/86
buriġ see burg
burnsele m. *bathing hall* np 13/21
būrþēn m. *servant of the bower, chamberlain* ds būrþēne 12/121
burston see berstan
būtan prep. w.d. *without, except, but, only* 3/46, 3/47, 3/158, 3/160, būton 4/45, 4/75, 6/2, etc., 7/17 (w.a. *only*); conj (§179.5) w. ind. *except, only* 4/5, 4/21, w. subj. *unless* 3/115, 3/161, 12/71, etc.
butere f. *butter* ns 3/160; as buteran 3/26
būton see būtan
būtū n. dual *both* 14/48
bycgan 1 *buy* pres 1s bycge 3/136, 3/151; 3s bygþ 3/83
ġebycgan 1 *buy* pret 1s gebohte 3/147; 2s gebohtest 3/145
byden f. *tub* ds bydene 11(f)/6
byht n. *dwelling* ap 11(d)/3
byldan 1 *encourage, embolden* pret 3s bylde 12/169, 12/209, 12/320; pret subj 3s bylde 12/234
byre m. *opportunity* as 12/121
byreð see beran
byrġan 1 *bury* inf 17/98

Byrhtelm pers. n. *Byrhtelm* gs Byrhtelmes 12/92
Byrhtnōð pers. n. *Byrhtnoth* ns 12/17, 12/42, 12/101, etc.; as 12/257; gs Byrhtnōðes 12/114. See also Brihtnōð
Byrhtwold pers. n. *Byrhtwold* ns 12/309
byriġ see burg
byriġan 1 *taste* pret 3s byrigde 14/101
byrnan III *burn* pres ptc nsf byrnende 11(o)/4
byrne f. *corselet, coat of mail* ns 12/144, 12/284; as byrnan 12/163; gs 18(c)/2260 [MnE byrnie]
byrnwiga m. *mailed warrior* ns 16/94
bȳsen f. *exemplar, original, example* ds bȳsne 4/123, bȳsene 8/57
bysiġ adj. *busy* npm bysige 12/110
bysiġian 2 *afflict, occupy, trouble* p ptc gebysgad 11(o)/3 [MnE (to) busy]
bysmerian 2 *mock, revile* pret 3p bysmeredon 14/48
bȳwan 1 *polish, adorn, prepare* inf 18(c)/2257

cāf adj. *brave, quick, vigorous* asm cāfne 12/76
cāflīċe adv. *bravely, boldly* 12/153
cald n. (*the*) *cold* is calde 17/8
cald adj. *cold* asn 12/91, dp caldum 17/10; superl. caldast nsn 17/33
ġecamp m. *battle* ds gecampe 12/153
cann see cunnan
canōn m. *canon* gs canōnes 9/74
canst see cunnan
carcern n. *prison, dungeon* as carcerne 10(a)/25; ds 10(a)/29, 10(b)/73
care see cearo
cāsere m. *emperor* ns 10(b)/20, 10(b)/61, kāsere 10(a)/22; ds kāsere 10(a)/21; np cāseras 17/82; dp cāserum 10(a)/17 [MnE caesar]
ceallian 2 *call out, shout* inf 12/91
ġecēapian 2 *buy* pres 3p gecēapaþ 11(h)/13
cearo f. *care, trouble, sorrow* ns 16/55; as ceare 16/9, 18(d)/3171; np ceare 17/10
cearseld n. *abode of care* gp cearselda 17/5
ġecēas see ġecēosan
ċeaster f. *town* as ceastre 10(b)/66, ds 3/82 [MnE (Win)chester, (Man)chester, etc.]
ċeasterbūend m. *city-dweller* dp ceasterbūendum 18(a)/768
ċeasterware f. pl. *city-dwellers* np 3/84
Cedmon pers. n. *Cædmon* ns 9/28
Cēfi pers. n. *Cefi* ns 8/11, 8/39
cellod adj. see note to 12/283
cempa m. *warrior, champion* ns 3/213, 12/119, 18(b)/1312
cēne adj. *keen, brave* nsm 12/215, gpm cēnra 18(a)/768; compar. cēnre nsf 12/312
cēne adv. *boldly, bravely* 12/283
Centland n. *Kent* ds Centlande 7/56

cēol m. *keel, ship* ds ceole 17/5

Cēola pers. n. *Ceole* gs Cēolan 12/76

ceorfan III *carve, hew out* pret 3p curfon 14/66

ċeorl m. *peasant, yeoman, free man of the lowest rank* ns 3/213, 12/256; as 11(f)/8; ds ceorle 12/132 [MnE churl]

ġeċēosan II *choose* pret 3s gecēas 4/35, 12/113; p ptc gecoren 9/54, dpm gecorenum (*chosen ones, disciples*) 4/31

Cerdiċ pers. n. *Cerdic* ds Cerdice 6/43

ċicen n. *chicken* ns 1/6

ċiele m. *chill, cold* ds 3/16

ċīepan 1 *sell* pres 2s cīepst 3/81

ċīepemann m. *merchant* np cīepemenn 3/5

ġeċierran 1 *return* pret 3s gecierde 2/79

ċīese m. *cheese* ns 3/161; as 3/26

ċild n. *child* ns 2/51; as 2/63; ap 2/34

ġecinde see ġecynd

cinn see cynn

ċiriċe f. *church* ds 1/10; np ciricean 5/29

clammum see clomm

clǣne adj. *clean, pure* nsn 9/67; asn 17/110; apm clǣnan 3/80

clǣne adv. *utterly, entirely* 5/14 [MnE clean]

clǣnnis f. *purity, cleanness* ds clǣnnisse 4/38

cleofa m. *cellar, pantry* as cleofan 3/159

clēofan II *split, cleave* pret 3p clufon 12/283

cleopode see clipian

clif n. *cliff* ds clifum 17/8

clipian 2 *call, summon, cry out* pret 3s clipode 2/20, 2/43, 2/61, 2/71, 4/73, clypode 8/42, 12/25, 12/256, cleopode 10(b)/83 [archaic MnE clepe, yclept]

clomm m. *grip, fetter* dip clommom 17/10, clammum 10(b)/83, 18(b)/1335

clūstor n. *prison* ds clūstre 10(b)/73

clyppan 1 *embrace* inf 9/61; pres subj 3s clyppe 16/42 [MnE clip]

clypode see clipian

cnapa m. *servant, boy* as cnapan 3/15; dp cnapum 2/47, 2/50, 2/78

ġecnāwan VII *understand* inf 5/56 [MnE know]

cnēo n. *knee* as 16/42; *generation* gp cnēa 13/8

cniht m. *boy, youth, squire, servant* ns 1/9, 12/9, 12/153 [MnE knight]

cnōdan VII *impute, attribute* p ptc gecnōdon 10(b)/32

cnossian 2 *toss, dash, drive* pres 3s cnossað 17/8

cnyssan 1 *dash against, batter* pres 3p cnyssað 16/101, 17/33 (fig. *urge, press*); pret 3p cnysedan (*clashed*) 18(b)/1328

cōc m. *cook* ds cōce 3/167

cōlian 2 *cool* pret 3s cōlode 14/72

collenferð adj. *stout-hearted* nsm 16/71

cōm see cuman

cōmen see cuman

cōmon see cuman

con (= cann) see cunnan

const see cunnan

Constentinopolim f. *Constantinople* ds 10(a)/21

consul m. *consul* ns 10(a)/12

ġecoren see ċēosan

corn n. *kernel, grain* gp corna 17/33 [MnE corn]

crabba m. *crab* ap crabban 3/93

ġecranc see ġecringan

cræft m. *calling, trade, skill* ns 3/151, 3/163; as 3/1, 3/7, 3/41, etc.; gs cræftes 3/168; ds cræfte 3/73, 3/151, 3/155, 4/81 [MnE craft]

Crēacas m. pl. *the Greeks, Greece* npm 5/49, 10(b)/48; ap Crēacas 10(b)/56, Crēcas 10(b)/21, Crēcas 10(b)/61; gp Crēca 10(a)/21, 10(b)/66; dp Crēcum 10(b)/26

crincgan III *fall, perish* inf 12/292; pret 3p cruncon 12/302, crungon 13/25, 13/28 [MnE cringe]

ġecringan III *fall, perish* pret 3s gecranc 12/250, 12/324, gecrang 18(b)/1337, gecrong 13/31, 16/79

Crīst pers. n. *Christ* ns 4/33, 14/56; gs Crīstes 4/29, 8/77; ds Crīste 1/35, 4/30, 8/5, 10(b)/32, 14/116

Crīsten adj. *Christian* nsm 4/23, 10(a)/6; np Crīstne 5/27; npf Crīstna 5/53

crīstendōm m. *Christendom, Christianity* ds crīstendōme 10(a)/23, crīstenandōme 10(a)/15

ġecrong see ġecringan

crungon see crincgan

cuǣdon see cweðan

culter m. *coulter, a cutting blade on a plough* as 3/12, 3/193

cuman IV *come* inf 8/61, cumon 7/33, etc.; pres 1s cume 3/45; 2s cymest 18(b)/1382; 3s cymeð 8/34, 16/103, 17/61, etc.; 1p cumað 2/52; subj 3s cume 8/30; pret 3s cōm 2/17, 4/34, 7/40, etc., cwōm 9/58, 11(b)/1, etc.; 3p cōmon 2/56, 4/72, 7/10, cwōman 13/25, etc.; subj. 3s cwōme 18(a)/731; 3p cōmen 10(b)/66; p ptc cuman 9/53, cumen 12/104

Cumbra pers. n. *Cumbra* as Cumbran 6/6

cumon see cuman

cunnan pret. pres. *know, know how to, can* pres 1s cann, 3/36, 3/47, 3/115, 3/130, con 9/29; 2s canst 3/1, 3/35, 3/37, const 18(b)/1377, etc.; 3s can 4/106; 1p cunnon 5/36, cunnun 8/36; 3p cunnon 3/3, 4/27, etc.; subj 3s cunne 16/69 (*have knowledge*), 16/71, 16/113; 3p cunnen 5/61; pret 1s cūðe 9/31; 3s 4/14; 1p cūðon 5/47; 3p 5/65; subj 1s cūþe 3/116; 3p cūðen 4/40, 5/15 [MnE can]

cunnian 2 *try, find out* inf 7/30, 12/215; pres 3s cunnað 16/29 (*knows at first hand*); subj is

cunnian (*cont.*)
  cunnige 17/35; p ptc gecunnad 17/5 (*experienced, has come to know*)
curfon see ceorfan
cūð adj. *familiar, well known* ns 18(a)/705; npm cūðe 18(a)/867; gpn cūðra 16/55 [MnE (un)couth]
cūþe see cunnan
cūðlič adj. *certain* comp. as cūðlicre 8/36
cūðlīċe adv. *clearly* 8/13
cūðon see cunnan
cwǣde see cweðan
cwæð see cweðan
cwalu f. *death* ds cwale 4/79
cwealdon see cwellan
cwealmcuma m. *murderous visitor* as cwealmcuman 18(a)/792
cwellan 1 *kill* pret 2s cwealdest 18(b)/1334, 1p cwealdon 1/29 [MnE quell]
cwēn f. *woman, queen* ns 1/10.
cwene f. *woman* ns 11(p)/1
cweðan V *say* inf 14/116; pres 1s cweðe 4/118; 3s cwyþ 14/111; 3p cweþaþ 4/31; pret 1s cwæð 5/44; 2s cwǣde 4/4; 3s cwæð 2/2, 2/7, 2/20, 2/21, 2/44, 3/189, etc.; 3p cuǣdon 6/30, 6/34, cwǣdon 9/106 etc.; subj 3p cwǣden 5/34 [archaic MnE quoth]
ġecweðan V *speak, utter* pret 3s gecwæð 12/168, 18(a)/857, 18(a)/874
cwic adj. *alive* nsm 3/139; asm cwicne 18(a)/792; asn cwicu 11(p)/5; apm cwice 11(g)/7; gpm cwicra 16/9 [MnE quick]
cwide m. *statement, saying* as 11(c)/4
cwideġiedd n. *spoken utterance* gp cwidegiedda 16/55
cwīðan 1 *bewail, lament* inf 16/9, 18(d)/3171; pret 3p cwīðdon 14/56
cwōm see cuman
cyme m. *coming* ds 9/76
cymeð see cuman
ġecynd n. *species, kind, origin, lineage* ds gecinde 4/49
ġecyndbōc f. *book of origin*, i.e. *book of Genesis* ns 4/48
ġecynde adj. *proper, lawful* apm 10(b)/6 [MnE kind]
cyneliċ adj. *noble* nsn 13/48
cyneriċe n. *kingdom* gs kynerīces 5/67
cynestōl m. *royal seat, throne* ns 10(a)/22; ds cynestōle 10(b)/48
Cynewulf pers. n. *Cynewulf* ns 6/1, 6/4, 6/6, etc.
cyng see cyning
cyning m. *king* ns kyning 5/1, cyng 7/27, 7/45, cyning 8/1, 8/76, 10(a)/14, 10(a)/24, 18(a)/863, 18(b)/1306; as 6/10, 8/60, etc., kyning 18(d)/3171; gs cyninges 3/40, 6/17, etc.; ds cyninge 3/66, 3/132, 10(a)/19, kyninge

6/12; np cyningas 17/82, kyningas 5/5; ap cyningas 10(b)/6, kyningas 10(b)/56; dp cyningum 10(a)/2, etc.
cynn n. *kin, family, kind, race* ns 1/3; as 14/94; gs cynnes 3/153, 12/217, 12/266, 18(a)/712, 18(a)/735, etc.; ds cynne 12/76, 18(a)/810; gp cynna 11(n)/2, cinna 4/92
cyrm m. *cry, uproar* ns 12/107
cyssan 1 *kiss* pres 3p cyssað 11(j)/3, 11(o)/6; subj 3s cysse 16/42
cyst f. *best* ns 10(b)/18, 18(a)/802, as 14/1; dp cystum 18(a)/867 (*good quality, excellence*)
cȳðan 1 *reveal, make known, inform* inf 5/2; pret 3s cȳþde 6/29, 9/50; 3p cȳðdon (*declared*) 10(b)/56
ġecȳðan 1 *show, make known, declare* inf 12/216; pret 3s gecȳðde 7/53
ġecȳþnis f. *testament* ns 4/29; ds gecȳðnisse 4/41; ap gecȳðnissa 4/112
cȳþþ f. *kinfolk* ns 1/3 [MnE kith (and kin)]

ġedafenian 2 (impersonal verb (§212) w.d.) *befit* pret 3s gedafenode 9/17; subj gedafnode 4/39
dagas see dæġ
daroð m. *spear* as 12/149, 12/255
dǣd f. *deed* ns 10(b)/43; as dǣde 18(a)/889; gp dǣda 9/82; dp dǣdum 6/2, 17/41, 17/76
dǣdbōt f. *penitence, penance* as dǣdbōte 4/65
dæġ m. *day* ns 1/23, etc.; as dæg 12/198, 15/37, dæi 7/33; gs dæges 11(f)/3 (as adv.), 11(f)/17; ds dæge 1/29, 2/10, 2/48, 3/26, etc., tō dæge *today* 8/73; np dagas 17/80; gp daga 14/136; dp dagum 2/38, 11(k)/1, etc.
dæġrǣd n. *dawn* as 3/8
dæġrim n. *number of days* ns 18(a)/823
dæġweorc n. *day's work* gs dægweorces 12/148
dæi see dæġ
dǣl m. *part, portion* as 5/42, 5/53, 11(n)/4, 16/65; ds dǣle 4/14 [MnE deal]
dǣlan 1 *share* pret subj 3p dǣlon 12/33 [MnE deal]
ġedǣlan 1 *part, separate* pres 1p gedǣlað 11(e)/7; pret 3s gedǣlde (*shared*) 16/83; subj 3s 15/22, 18(a)/731
dēad adj. *dead* nsm 11(p)/4, 18(b)/1323; nsn dēade 17/65; asm dēadne 11(k)/1, 18(b)/1309; np dēade 2/8; dp (as noun) dēadum 17/98
dēaf see dūfan
dēagan VII *conceal, be concealed* pret 3s dēog 18(a)/850
dēah see dugan
dearr see durran
dēaþ m. *death* ns 1/33, 11(e)/7, 15/22, 17/106, as 14/101; gs dēaðes 14/113; ds dēaðe 9/120, 16/83, 18(b)/1388

dēaðdæġ m. *death-day* ds dēaðdæge 18(a)/885

dēaðfæġe adj. *fated to die, doomed* ns 18(a)/850

ġedēfe adj. *fitting, seemly* nsm 18(d)/3174

Defenas m. pl. *Devon, the people of Devon* dp Defenum 7/9

Defenisc adj. *Devonian, from Devon* nsm Defenisca 7/14

degelīċe see dēogollīċe

dehter see dohtor

dēman 1 *judge, deem* inf 14/107; pret 3p dēmdon 18(d)/3174 (*praised*); p ptc gedēmed 9/20

demm m. *misfortune, loss* ns 3/214

Dene m. pl. *Danes* dp Denum 12/129 (*vikings*), 18(a)/767, 18(a)/823; gp Denigea 18(b)/1323

Denisc adj. *Danish* dp Deniscan 7/22

denu f. *valley* np dena 15/30; dp denum 11(f)/3

dēofol m.n. *the devil* ds dēofle 17/76; gp dēofla 18(a)/756

dēofolġild n. *idol* as dēofolgyld 8/61; gp dēofolgilda 8/54; dp dēofolgildum 8/51, dēofulgeldum 8/65

dēog see dēagan

dēogol adj. *secret, hidden, mysterious* asn dȳgel 18(b)/1357

dēogollīċe adv. *secretly* dēgelīċe 10(b)/64, dīgellīċe 10(a)/20

dēop adj. *deep, profound* nsf 4/44, 4/75; dsm dēopan 14/75

dēope adv. *deeply, profoundly* 16/89

dēoplīċe adv. *profoundly, deeply* 4/98

dēor adj. *bold, brave* nsm 17/41; dip dēorum 17/76

deorc adj. *dark* asn deorce 16/89; dp deorcum 14/46

dēore adj. *dear, precious, beloved* asn 18(c)/2254; superl. asm dēorestan 18(b)/1309

ġedeorf n. *toil, hardship* ns 3/20, 3/21, 3/146; as 3/22, 3/23

Deorwente f. *the Derwent River* ds Deorwentan 8/73

dēorwierþe adj. *valuable, costly* apm 3/142, dēorwirðe 4/85; apn dēorwierþu 3/136 [archaic MnE dearworth]

derian 1 *harm* inf 12/70

dēst see dōn

dēð see dōn

dīgellīċe see dēogollīċe

ġedihtan 1 *direct* pret 3s gedihte 4/82

dim adj. *gloomy* npf dimme 15/30 [MnE dim]

disc m. *dish* ns 1/4

dō see dōn

dōgor n. *day* dis 18(b)/1395; gp dōgra 16/63, dōgera 18(a)/823

dohte see dugan

dohtor f. *daughter* ns 1/36, np 11(a)/2; ds dehter 4/20; gp dohtra 11(k)/12

dol adj. *foolish* nsm 17/106; apm dole 11(f)/17 (*dazed*)

dolg n. *wound* np 14/46

dōm m. *judgement* as 6/28, 12/38; gs dōmes 9/77, 14/107; dis dōme 9/52, 18(a)/895; dp dōmum 9/80; poet. *glory, reputation, fame* ns 18(a)/885, as 12/129; gs dōmes 18(b)/1388; ds dōme 17/85 [MnE doom]

dōmdæġ m. *day of judgment* ds dōmdæge 14/105 [MnE doom(s)day]

dōmgeorn adj. *eager for glory* npm dōmgeorne 16/17

dōn anom. (§128) *do, make, take* inf 3/205, 4/96, 5/63 (*promote*), etc.; infl inf (tō) dōnne 1/14, 3/17; pres 1s dō 3/90; 2s dēst 3/17, 3/28, 3/65, 3/79; 3s dēð 4/113; 2p dōþ 3/176; 3p 3/129, 4/108; subj 2s dō 5/21; 3s 5/77; pret 2s dydest 2/26, 2/28; 3s dyde 2/19, 8/6, 9/24, etc.; p ptc gedōn 4/52, 12/197

ġedōn anom. (§128) *do* inf 5/56, 7/51, 17/43

Dorsǣte m. pl. *Dorset, men of Dorset* dp Dorsǣtum 7/10

dorste see durran

dorston see durran

dōþ see dōn

draca m. *dragon* ns 18(a)/892 [archaic MnE drake]

ġedræg n. *bearing, concourse, (noisy) company* as 18(a)/756, gedreag 15/45 (*multitude*)

drēag see drēogan

ġedreag see ġedræg

drēam m. *joy, delight* ns 14/140, 17/80; gs drēames 14/144; ds drēame 16/79; np drēamas 17/65, 17/86; gp drēama 18(a)/850; dp drēamum 14/133, 18(a)/721 [MnE dream]

ġedrēas see ġedrēosan

drēfan 1 *stir up, disturb* pres 1s drēfe 11(d)/2

ġedrēfan 1 *trouble, afflict* p ptc gedrēfed nsm 10(a)/27, 10(b)/74, 14/20, 14/59

dreng m. (*viking*) *warrior* gp drenga 12/149

drēogan II *suffer, perform, be engaged in* inf 15/26; pres 3s drēogeð 15/50; 3p drēogað 17/56; pret 3s drēag 11(l)/5; 3p drugon 18(a)/798, 18(a)/831

drēorgian 2 *grow desolate* pres 3p drēorgiað 13/29

drēoriġ adj. *sad* asm drēorigne 16/17 [MnE dreary]

drēoriġhlēor adj. *sad-faced* nsm 16/83

drēorsele m. *desolate hall, hall of sorrow* ds 15/50

drēosan II *decline* pres 3s drēoseþ 1/26, 16/63

ġedrēosan II *collapse, perish* pret 3s gedrēas

*ġe*drēosan (*cont.*)
  13/11, 16/36 (*perish*); p ptc gedroren nsm 17/86; npf gedrorene 13/5
drīfan I *drive* inf 3/9; pres 1s drīfe 3/23
drihten m. *lord, the Lord* ns 9/39, 12/148, dryhten 11(e)/2, 14/101, etc.; gs Drihtnes 10(b)/41, dryhtnes 14/9, 14/35, 14/75, 17/65, 17/121; ds Drihtne 9/54, 9/119, 10(b)/64, 10(b)/83, 18(b)/1398
drincan III *drink* pres 3p drincað 11(j)/12; pret 3s dranc 18(a)/742 3p druncon 11(n)/1
drohtoð m. *course, way of life* ns 18(a)/756
*ġe*drorene see *ġe*drēosan
druncon see drincan
dryht f. *multitude, men* dp dryhtum 11(m)/2
dryhten see drihten
dryhtguma m. *retainer, warrior* ds drihtguman 18(b)/1388
dryhtliċ adj. *lordly, magnificent* nsn 18(a)/892; superl. dsm dryhtlicestum 17/85
dryhtsele m. *retainer's hall, splendid hall* ns 18(a)/767
drynce m. *drink* as 3/199
dryncfæt n. *drinking vessel, cup* as 18(c)/2254
drysmian 2 *become gloomy* pres 3s drysmaþ 18(b)/1375
dūfan II *dive* pret 3s dēaf 11(l)/5, 11(p)/4
dugan pret. pres. w.d. *be of use* pret 3s dēah 12/48, dohte 18(b)/1344
duguð f. *advantage, benefit* ds duguðe 12/197; dip duguðum 18(d)/3174 (*power, excellence, glory*)
duguð f. *troop of seasoned retainers, mature men* ns 16/79, 17/86, 18(c)/2254; ds duguþe 16/97; dp dugeþum (*heavenly host*) 17/80
dumb adj. *dumb* dpm dumbum 11(m)/2
dūn f. *hill, down, mountain* as dūne 2/48; ds 2/46, 2/71; np dūna 15/30; ap 11(g)/6; dp dūnum 11(f)/3
Dunnere pers. n. *Dunnere* ns 12/255
Dūnstān pers. n. *Dunstan* ns 7/15
durran pret. pres. *dare* pres 1s dearr 3/10, 3/107; 1p durron 4/100; subj 1s dyrre 3/10, durre 16/10, 2s dyrre 18(b)/1379; pret 1s dorste 14/35, 14/42, 14/45, etc.; 3p dorston 1/34; subj. dorsten 10(b)/27
duru f. *door* ns 18(a)/721, as 6/13, 8/31
dūst n. *dust* ns 2/42; ds dūste 2/42
*ġe*dwola m. *heresy* ns 10(b)/41; ds gedwolan 10(a)/7
*ġe*dwolmann m. *heretic* np gedwolmen 4/106
*ġe*dwolsum adj. *misleading* nsn 4/105
dyde see dōn
*ġe*dygan 1 *survive* pres 3s gedygeð 11(g)/6
dȳgel see dēogol
dynnan 1 *resound* pret 3s dynede 18(a)/767, 18(b)/1317
dynt m. *blow* dp dyntum 11(f)/17 [MnE dint]

dyrne adj. *secret* asm 15/12; gpm dyrnra 18(b)/1357
dyrre see durran
dyrre see durran
*ġe*dyrstiġ adj. *daring, bold* nsm 3/59, 3/62
dysiġ adj. *ignorant, foolish* nsm 4/9 [MnE dizzy]
dysiġnes f. *folly* as dysignesse 8/59; ds 8/57 [MnE dizziness]

ēa f. *river* as 3/76, 3/77; ds 3/99, 8/73; dp ēam 3/88
ēac adv. *also. and* 4/19, 4/31, 7/49, 14/92, etc.; prep. w.d.i. *in addition to, besides* 30180, 10(b)/44, 12/11; ēac swā *likewise, also* 2/19; ēac swelce (swā), swelce ēac *also, moreover* 2/1, 2/33, 3/103, 3/121, 9/79, ēac swylce 9/120; ēac þon *moreover, besides* 15/44; ne ēac *nor even* 5/25 [archaic MnE eke]
ēaca m. *increase* ds ēacan 4/20; tō ēacan *in addition to* 10(a)/10
ēacen adj. *increased, endowed, great* nsm 11(k)/8
*ġe*ēacnung f. *child-bearing, increase* ap ġeēacnunga 2/34
ēad n. *wealth* as 13/36
ēadiġ adj. *blessed* nsm 17/107, ēadiga 4/33, 7/25
ēadiġnes f. *blessedness, bliss* as ēadignesse 17/120, gs 8/46, 11(o)/9
ēadmōdlīċe adv. *humbly* 4/2
Ēadrīc pers. n. *Eadric* ns 12/11
Ēadweard pers. n. *Edward* ns 12/117, 12/273
Ēadwine pers. n. *Eadwine* ns 7/13, 7/18, 8/76 [MnE Edwin]
Ēadwold pers. n. *Eadwold* ns 12/304
eafora m. *offspring, son* ns eafera 18(a)/897
ēage n. *eye* as 11(b)/3; gs ēagan 8/33; np ēagan 2/9, 2/15; ap 4/111; dp ēagum 2/13, 18(a)/726
eahtian 2 *esteem, praise* pret 3p eahtodan 18(d)/3173
eal see eall
ēalā interj. *oh, lo* 3/20, 3/28, 3/156, 3/179, etc.
eald adj. *old, ancient* nsm 12/310, 15/29, ealda 12/218 (see fæder); asm ealdne 11(f)/8; nsf ealde 4/11, 4/28; asf ealdan 2/57, 2/60, 4/40, ealde 18(a)/795; npm ealdan 4/11 (see fæder); npn eald 16/87; apn ealde 12/47; ipm ealdum 10(b)/65; compar. yldra 18(b)/1324
ealdes adv. *long ago* 15/4
ealdġeseġen f. *old tradition* gp ealdgesegena 18(a)/869
ealdġesīð m. *old comrade or retainer* np ealdgesīþas 18(a)/853
ealdġestrēon n. *ancient treasure* dp ealdgestrēonum 18(b)/1381

ealdġewyrht n. or f. *deed of old, former action* dp
ealdgewyrhtum 14/100
ealdhlāford m. *lord from old times* dp ealdhlāfordum 10(a)/17, 10(b)/63
ealdhlāfordcynn n. *hereditary lordship, race of
ancient kings* gs ealdhlāfordcynnes 10(a)/22
ealdian 2 *grow old* pres 3s ealdað 17/89
ealdor m. *leader, prince* ns 12/202, 12/222, 12/
314, 14/90, 17/123; gs ealdres 12/53, ds
ealdre 12/11
ealdor n. *life, age* ns 11(k)/3; as aldor 18(b)/
1371; gs ealdres 18(b)/1338, aldres 18(a)/
822; ds ealdre 17/79 (āwa tō ealdre *for ever
and ever*)
ealdorbisceop m. *high-priest* ns 8/11
ealdordagas m. pl. *days of life* dp aldordagum
18(a)/718, ealdordagum 18(a)/757
ealdorġedǣl n. *separation from life, death* ns
aldorgedāl 18(a)/805
ealdorman m. *nobleman, ruler* ns 4/119, 7/21,
7/29 (see note), aldormon 6/25, etc.; as
ealdormann 4/2, aldormon 6/3, 6/6; gs
ealdormannes 7/45; np ealdormenn 7/12,
aldormen 8/38; dp ealdormannum 3/133,
8/28 [MnE alderman]
ealdorþeġn m. *chief thane* as aldorþegn 18(b)/
1308
ealdriht n. *ancient right* gp ealdrihta 10(a)/8,
10(a)/16, 10(b)/36, 10(b)/57; dp ealdrihtum
10(a)/23
ealfela adj. *very much, a great many* as 18(a)/
869, 18(a)/883
ealfelo adj. *entirely harmful, dire* asn 11(h)/9
Ealfrīc pers. n. *Ælfric* ns Ælfrīc 7/32; gs
Ælfrīces 7/45; ds Ealfrīce 7/29
ealgian 2 *defend* inf ealgian 12/52, 18(a)/796
Ealhelm pers. n. *Ealhelm* ns 12/218
eall adj. *all* nsm 7/61; asm ealne 8/70; gsm
ealles 15/41; nsn eall 14/6; asn 5/30, 14/58,
14/94; nsf 3/160, 14/12, 14/55, eal 15/46,
etc.; asf ealle 3/30, 5/50, 9/89, 10(b)/12;
npm ealle 3/176, 7/27, 11(n)/10, 14/128,
alle 6/15; apm 3/87, 3/192, 5/11, 7/71, 12/
320, 14/37, etc.; gpm ealra 11(a)/6; dpm
eallum 11(l)/7; npn ealle 2/1, eall 3/138,
3/190; apn eal 9/45; dpn eallum 2/29; gpn
ealra 4/29, 14/125; npf ealle 2/76; apf ealle
4/62, ealla 5/41; gpf ealra 12/174; as pron.
asn eall 13/26, 13/39; npm ealle 14/9
eall adv. *all, entirely, completely* 7/37, 12/314,
14/20, 14/82, eal 15/29
Eallerīca pers. n. *Alaric* ns Eallerīca 10(a)/2;
as Alerīc 10(b)/7
eallġearo adj. *entirely ready, eager* nsf 11(h)/4
eallinga adv. *utterly* 8/13
ealneġ adv. *always* 5/79
ēalond n. *island* ds ēalonde 10(a)/4
ealra see eall

ealuscerwen f. *dispensing of ale, distress, terror*
ns 18(a)/769 (see note)
ēam m. *uncle* ns 11(a)/6, 18(a)/881
eard m. *homeland, country* as 12/53, 12/58, 12/
222, 17/38, 18(b)/1377
eardġeard m. *city, dwelling place* as 16/85
eardstapa m. *wanderer* ns 16/6
ēare n. *ear* ap ēaran 4/111, 11(b)/3
carfcōc scc carfoð
earfoð n. *hardship* gp earfoða 15/39, earfeþa
16/6
earfoðhwīl f. *time of hardship* as earfoðhwīle
17/3
earfoðlic adj. *full of trouble, fraught with hardship* nsn 16/106
earh adj. *cowardly* nsn 12/238
earm m. *arm* as 12/165, 18(a)/749, 18(a)/835;
ap earmas 11(b)/6
earm adj. *poor, wretched* asm earmne 16/40;
asn earme 7/77; npm earme 14/68; as noun
gp earmra 14/19
earmceariġ adj. *wretched and troubled* nsm 16/
20, 17/14
earmlic adj. *miserable, pitiable* ns 18(a)/807
earmsceapen adj. *wretched, miserable* nsm
18(b)/1351
earn m. *eagle* ns 12/107, 17/24
ġeearnian 2 *earn, deserve* pres 3s geearnaþ 14/
109
ġeearnung f. *favour, act deserving gratitude* ap
geearnunga 12/196
eart see beon
ēast adv. *east* 8/72
ēastan adv. *from the east* 10(b)/1
Ēastdene m. pl. *the Danes* dp Ēastdenum
18(a)/828
Ēastengle m. pl. *East Anglia* ap 7/66; dp Ēastenglum 7/36
ēasteð n. *riverbank* ds ēasteðe 12/63
Ēastseaxe m. pl. *Essex, the East Saxons* ap Ēastsexe 7/67; dp Ēastseaxum 7/56; gp Ēastseaxena 12/69
ēaðe adv. *easily* 5/57, 11(h)/11, 11(n)/8
ēaðmōd adj. *humble* nsm 14/60, 17/107
ēaðmōdlīce adv. *humbly* 9/84
eaxl f. *shoulder* as eaxle 18(a)/835, ds 18(a)/
816; ap eaxle 11(b)/6; dp eaxlum 14/32
eaxlġespann n. *crossbeam, intersection* ds
eaxlgespanne 14/9
eaxlġestealla m. *shoulder-companion, comrade*
ns 18(b)/1326
ebbe m. *ebb-tide* ds ebban 12/65
Ebriscġeðiode n. *the Hebrew language* ds 5/48
ēċe adj. *eternal, everlasting* nsm 9/39, 17/124;
dsm ēcan 4/80; gsn ēces 8/46, ēcan 17/79;
asf ēcan 17/120; gsf ēcre 8/46; as adv. *eter-
nally* 17/67
ecg f. *edge, sword* ns 12/60; gp ecga 18(a)/805

ecghete m. *deadly hatred, violence* ns 17/70
Ecgláf pers. n. *Ecglaf* gp Ecgláfes 12/267
ēċnis f. *eternity* ds on ēcnysse *forever and ever* 4/66, ecnisse 4/121
Ecgþēow pers. n. *Ecgtheow* gs Ecgþēowes 18(b)/1383
ēċre see ēċe
edor m. *building* np ederas 16/77
ēdrum see ǣdre
edwīt n. *reproach, disgrace* ns 10(b)/55
efne adv. *even, only* 8/56, 9/15, 10(b)/14
efstan 1 *hasten* inf 14/34; pret 3p efston 12/206
eft adv. *again, afterwards, thereupon, back* 2/7, 2/17, 2/52, 2/71, 3/31, 3/126, 5/49, etc., æft 10(b)/65; eft ongean *in reply, back again* 12/49, 12/156; eft onhwyrfed *reversed, backwards* 11(h)/1
eftsīð m. *journey back, return* ap eftsīðas tēah *returned* 18(b)/1332
eġe m. *fear, terror* ns 2/73, 10(b)/72, ds 3/11
eġesa m. *awe, terror* ns 14/86, 18(a)/784, egsa 17/103; ds egsan 17/101
eġesliċ adj. *fearful, awesome, dreadful* nsf 14/73
Ēġipte m. pl. *Egyptians* gp Egipta 4/77, Ǣgypta 9/73
ēġlond n. *island* ns 10(b)/16
ēhtan 1 w.g. *chase, pursue* pres subj 3p ēhten 3/43
elcor adv. *otherwise* 8/63
eldran see ieldran
eldum see ælde
ele m. *oil* as 3/141
Elizabeþ pers. n. *Elizabeth* ns 1/31
ellen n. *courage, strength* as 12/211; ds elne 16/114, 18(a)/893, elne mycle *with great zeal* 14/34, 14/60, 14/123
ellendǣd f. *deed of valour* dp ellendǣdum 18(a)/876
ellenmǣrþu f. *fame for courage, heroic deed* dp ellenmǣrþum 18(a)/828
ellenweorc n. *valorous deed* ap 18(d)/3173
ellenwōdnis f. *zeal* gs ellenwōdnisse 9/85
elles adv. *otherwise, else* 4/105, 15/23, 17/46
ellor adv. *elsewhither* 18(c)/2254
ellorgǣst m. *spirit from elsewhere, alien spirit* ns ellorgāst 18(a)/807; ap ellorgǣstas 18(b)/1349
elne see ellen
elpendbān n. *ivory, elephant bone* as 3/141
elra adj. *another* dsm elran 18(a)/752
elþēodiġ adj. *alien, foreign* as noun: np elðēodge 10(b)/55; gp elþēodigra 17/38
embe see ymbe
ende m. *end, conclusion* ns 1/33, 18(a)/822; as 4/7, 4/96, 18(b)/1386; ds 14/29 (on ende *from the edge*) is ænde 9/86

endebyrdan 1 *arrange, dispose* p ptc geendebyrd 4/99
endebyrdnes f. *order, succession, sequence* ns 9/35; as endebirdnisse 4/101, endebyrdnesse 9/21
ġeendian 2 *end, complete* pret 3s geendade 9/86
endlyfta adj. *eleventh* isn endlyftan 8/78
engel m. *angel* ns 2/61, 2/71; as 14/9; np englas 4/72, 14/106; dp englum 2/11, 14/153, 17/78; gp engla 4/50, 12/178
Englisc adj., noun *English* ns 4/102; as 4/3, 4/51, 5/16, 5/61, etc.
Engliscġereord n. *the English language* ds Engliscgereorde 9/7
ent m. *giant* gp enta 13/2, 16/87
ēode see gān
ēodon see gān
eodorcan 1 *chew the cud* pres ptc eodorcende 9/68
eofor m. *boar, figure of a boar* ap eoferas 18(b)/1328
Eoforwīċċeaster f. *York* ds Eoforwicceastre 8/72
ēoh m. *horse* as 12/189
eom see bēon
eorcanstān m. *jewellery, precious stone* as 13/36
eorl m. *nobleman* ns 7/29, 10(b)/78, 12/6, 12/51, 12/89, etc.; gs eorles 12/165; ds eorle 10(b)/72, 12/28, 12/159, 16/12; np eorlas 10(b)/30; ap 16/99; gp eorla 11(a)/7, 16/60, 17/72, 18(b)/1312; dp eorlum 11(n)/8, 18(a)/769 [MnE earl]
eorlscipe m. *nobility* as 18(d)/3173
eormengrund m. *spacious ground, earth* as 18(a)/859
eornoste adv. *earnestly, determinedly* 12/281
eorðe f. *earth* as eorðan 2/30, 4/52, 4/56, 12/126, 12/286, 12/303, etc.; gs 1/24, 2/40, 9/40, 14/37, etc.; ds 2/2, 2/38, 2/40, etc.
eorþgrāp f. *grip of earth* ns 13/6
eorþscræf n. *cave* ds eorðscræfe 15/28, 16/84; ap eorðscrafu 15/36
eorþsele m. *cave, barrow* ns 15/29
eorþtilþ f. *farming, earth-tilling* ns 3/192
eorþweġ m. *earthly way* ds eorðwege 14/120
eorþwela m. pl. *worldly prosperity* np eorþwelan 17/67
eoten m. *giant* ns 18(a)/761; gp eotena 18(a)/883
ēow see ġē
ēower *of you* see ġē
ēower poss adj. *your* nsm 3/161; dsm ēowrum 3/170; nsf ēowru 3/160; npm ēowre 6/35; npn ēowre 2/9; apf ēowre 3/170; gpf ēowerra 3/162
erian 1 *plough* inf 3/13
esne m. *man* as 11(f)/8; ap esnas 11(f)/16

etan V *eat* infl inf (tō) etanne 2/12; pres 2s etst
2/30, 2/39; 1p etað 2/5; 2p 2/10, 3/170; 3p
3/126; subj 3s ete 4/24; eten 2/8; pret 1s æt
2/25, 2/27; 3s 2/14, 2s æte 2/36, subj 2s æte
2/23, 2/24, 2/37; 1p æten 2/6; 2p æten 2/3
ᵹeetan V *eat, devour* pret 3s ᵹeæt 2/14
ēþel m. *homeland, territory* ns 14/156; as 5/8,
10(b)/16, 12/52, 17/60; ds ēðle 16/20
eþclweard m. *defender of the homeland* np ēþel-
weardas 10(b)/24
ēðnis f. *ease, comfort* gp ēðnessa 10(a)/16

ᵹefadian 2 *arrange, phrase* inf 4/104
fadung f. *arrangement, order (of words)* ds
fadunge 4/103
fāh adj. *stained, guilty, outcast* nsm 14/13, 15/
46, 16/98 *(decorated)*, fāg 18(a)/811 *(in a state
of feud with)*; asm fāgne 18(a)/725, fāhne
18(a)/716
fana m. *banner* ns 10(b)/10 [MnE
(weather)vane]
fandian 2 w.g. *test* inf 2/43
faran VI *go, travel, advance* inf 12/88, 12/156,
18(a)/865; imp s far 2/45; pres 1s fare 3/135;
3s færð 4/63, fareð 11(h)/3, 17/91 *(him on
fareð overtakes him)*; subj 1s fare 3/100; pret
3p fōron 10(b)/20 [MnE fare]
ᵹefaran VI *proceed, act, die* inf 18(a)/738; pret
3s gefōr 7/15, 7/26
fatu see fæt
fæc n. *interval* ns 8/33; as 9/117; ds fæce 8/34,
9/5
fæder m. *father* ns 2/54, 2/55, 4/56, 11(a)/4,
11(k)/2, etc.; as 2/54, etc.; ds 4/58, 16/115;
np ealdan fæderas *patriarchs* 4/11; nsm
ealda fæder *grandfather* 12/218
fæᵹe adj. *fated, doomed to die* nsm 12/119,
18(a)/846; dsm fǣgean 12/125; npm fǣge
12/105; as noun gsm fǣges 12/297, dsm
fǣgum 17/71 [archaic MnE fey]
fæᵹen adj. *rejoicing, fawning, overly happy* nsm
16/68 [MnE fain]
fæᵹer adj. *beautiful, pleasant* nsm 14/73, nsn
18(a)/773; dsf fægran 14/21; ism fægre
9/86; npm fægere 14/8, 14/10, 18(a)/866,
dpm fægerum 4/84 [MnE fair]
fæᵹere adv. *pleasantly, well* fægre 11(m)/8;
properly, with care fægere 12/22
fæᵹernis f. *beauty, excellent feature* ap fægernissa 4/90 [MnE fairness]
fæᵹnian 2 *rejoice* pret 3p fægnodon 10(b)/33
ᵹefæᵹnian 2 *make glad* p ptc gefægnod 18(b)/
1333
fæᵹrian 2 *make or become beautiful, adorn* pres
3s fægriað 17/48
fæᵹrost adv. superl. *most happily, most
pleasantly* 17/13

fæhðo f. *feud, battle, enmity* as fæhðe 12/225,
fæhðe 18(a)/879, 18(b)/1333, 18(b)/1340,
18(b)/1380, fæhðu 15/26
fælsian 2 *cleanse, purge* p ptc gefælsod 18(a)/
825
fæmne f. *maiden, woman* ns 11(p)/1
færgripe m. *sudden grip, sudden attack* dp
færgripum 18(a)/738
fǣrlīce adv. *quickly, suddenly* 3/61, 16/61
færsceaða m. *sudden attacker, viking* ds
færsceaðan 12/142
færð see faran
fæst adj. *fast, firm, fixed* nsm 18(b)/1364, nsf
18(a)/722
fæste adv. *firmly, fast* 8/68, 9/46, 10(b)/35,
11(h)/14, 12/21, 12/103, etc.
fæsten n. *stronghold, fortress* as 10(b)/20, 12/
194; ds fæstene 10(b)/79
fæstlīce adv. *steadfastly, firmly, steadily* 3/
60, 8/50, 10(b)/70, 12/82, 12/254, festlīce
7/49
fæstnian 2 *fasten, establish (truce)* inf 12/35; p
ptc gefæstnod 3/12
ᵹefæstnian 2 *fasten* pret 3p gefæstnodon 14/
33
fæstnung f. *(place of) stability, permanence* ns
16/115
fæt n. *vessel, utensil* ap fatu 3/203 [MnE vat]
fæt n. *gold ornament, ornamental plate* dp fætum
18(c)/2256, fættum 18(a)/716
fæted adj. *ornamented, plated* asn 11(l)/7,
18(c)/2253
fætels m. *pouch, bag* ap fætelsas 3/154
fætt adj. *fat, rich* asn 3/171
fæðm m. *embrace* ns 18(a)/781, as 18(b)/1393
(interior) [MnE fathom]
fēa adv. *little* 14/115
feaht see feohtan
feala see fela
feallan VII *fall, fall in battle* inf 12/54, 12/105,
14/43; pres 3s fealleþ 1/26, 16/63; pret 3s
fēoll 1/2, 12/119, 12/166, 12/286, fēol
10(b)/81, 12/126, 12/303, etc.; 3p fēollon
12/111
ᵹefeallan VII *fall* pret 3s gefēoll 10(a)/27
fealohilte adj. *golden hilted* nsn 12/166
fealu adj. *tawny, dark* nsm fealwe 11(n)/10,
apm 16/46, 18(a)/865 [MnE fallow]
fēasceaftiᵹ adj. *wretched, desolate* asn 17/26
fēawe pl. adj. *few* np fēawa 5/14, 5/18, 5/27,
etc.
feaxhār adj. *grey-haired* nsf 11(p)/1
ᵹefecgan 2 *fetch, carry off* inf 12/160.
fēdan 1 *feed* inf 3/125; pres 3s fētt 3/69, 3/192;
3p fēdaþ 3/121, 3/127, 11(m)/8; pret 3s
fēdde 11(k)/9, fædde 7/62
ᵹefēhst see gefōn
fēhð see fōn

fela adj. (usually w.g.: see §190.4) *many* 3/84 (hira . . . fela *many of them*), 3/94, 3/142, etc.

felaléof adj. *dearly loved* gsm felaléofan 15/26

*ge*félan 1 *feel* inf 17/95

feld m. *field* ds felda 3/9, 12/241

fell n. *skin* ap 3/152

fenfreoðo f. *refuge in the fens* ds 18(a)/851

feng see fón

*ge*feng see *ge*fón

fenġelád n. *fen-path, tract of swamp* as 18(b)/ 1359

fenhli ð n. *fen slope, marshy tract* ap fenhleoþu 18(a)/820

fenhop n. *retreat in the fen* ap fenhopu 18(a)/ 764

feoh n. *money* ns 16/108; as 3/74, 6/19, 12/39; gs féos 6/28, 7/63; ds féo 18(b)/1380 [MnE fee]

feohgífre adj. *greedy, avaricious* nsm 16/68

*ge*feoht n. *battle, fight* ds gefeohte 12/12; dp gefeohtum 6/6

feohtan III *fight* inf 12/16, 12/261; pres ptc feohtende 6/16, 6/21, 7/49, etc.; pret 3s feaht 6/6, 12/254, 12/277, 12/281, etc.; 2p fuhton 1/15

*ge*feohtan III *fight, achieve by fighting* inf 7/74, 12/129

feohte f. *battle, fight* ns 12/103

feol see feallan

feolan III *penetrate* pret 3p fulgon 6/37

feolheard adj. *hard as a file* apn féolhearde 12/ 108

feoll see feallan

*ge*feoll see *ge*feallan

*ge*feon V *rejoice* pres ptc geféonde (w.g. or i. *rejoicing in*) 8/69, 9/98; pret 3s gefeh 18(a)/ 827

feond m. *enemy* ns 11(m)/4, 18(a)/725; as 1/28, 18(a)/748; ds féonde 11(m)/4; np féondas 14/30, 14/33; ap fýnd 12/82, féondas 14/38; gp féonda 2/77, 17/75, 18(a)/808; dp féondum 7/53, 12/103, 12/264 [MnE fiend]

feondrǣden f. *enmity* as féondrǣdene 2/31

feondsceaþa m. *enemy, robber* ap féond-sceaþan 11(j)/19

feor adj. *far* nsn 4/48 (w.d. *far from*), 8/72, 9/114, etc.; gsn feorres 15/47

feor adv. *far* 11(h)/5, 12/3, 12/57, 15/25, 16/ 21, 16/26, etc.

feore see feorh

feorg see feorh

feorgbold n. *life-house, dwelling of the soul, body* ns 14/73

feorh n. *life* ns 11(k)/2, feorg 17/94, as feorh 6/19, 6/39, 12/125, 12/142, 12/184, etc.; gs féores 12/260, 12/317; ds féore 12/194, 12/ 259; is 11(h)/14

feorhbealo n. *threat to life, deadly evil* ns 18(c)/ 2250, as 11(h)/5

feorhcynn n. *race of men* gp feorhcynna 18(c)/ 2266

feorhhūs n. *life-house, body* as 12/297

feorhlāst m. *bloody track* ap feorhlāstas 18(a)/ 846

feorhséoc adj. *mortally wounded* ns 18(a)/820

feormian 2 *clean* inf 3/19; pres subj 3s feormie 18(c)/2253

*ge*feormian 2 *consume, eat up* p ptc gefeormod 18(a)/744

feormynd m. *cleanser, polisher* np 18(c)/2256

feorran adv. *from afar* 14/57, 18(a)/825, 18(a)/ 839, 18(b)/1370

féos see feoh

féower num. *four* ap 4/16, 11(g)/3, 11(l)/1, 11(l)/7, 11(n)/2

féowertýne num. *fourteen* dpm féowertýnum 9/88

*ge*féra m. *companion, comrade* ns 12/280; as geféran 3/14, 8/70; ds 2/25, 4/35, 16/30; np 3/3, 3/206, 6/35; ap 3/103, 3/179, 12/170, 12/229; dp geférum 3/33, 6/33

féran 1 *set out, proceed, go* inf 12/41, 12/221, 15/9, 17/37, etc.; pres ptc nsm férende 11(d)/9; pret 3s férde 2/47, 8/65; 3p férdon 2/78 (w. refl. obj.), 7/54, 18(a)/839

*ge*féran 1 *reach by travel, attain, meet with* pret 3s geférde 7/25; 3p geférdon 7/50

feredon see ferian

férende see féran

ferhðe see ferð

ferian 1 *go* inf 12/179

ferian 2 *carry* pres 3s fereð 11(j)/7; pret 3s ferede 16/81; 3p feredon 11(f)/4; p ptc ge-ferod 4/60

fers n. *verse* ds ferse 4/59; ap fers 9/35

*ge*férscipe m. *fellowship, community* ns 3/184; ds 3/170

ferð n. *spirit, mind* ns 16/54; as 11(p)/5, 17/26, 17/37; ds ferðe 16/90, ferhðe 18(a)/754; dp (w. sg. meaning) ferhðum 18(d)/3176

ferðfriþende adj. *life-sustaining* apm 11(g)/3

ferðloca m. *breast, heart* ns 16/33; as ferðlocan 16/13

festlice see fæstlice

fét see fót

feter f. *fetter* dp feterum 16/21

fetian 2 *fetch* pres sub 3s gefetiġe 14/138; p ptc fetod 18(b)/1310

fétt see fédan

féða m. *foot-soldier, infantry* as féðan 12/88, np 18(b)/1327

feðer f. *feather* np feþre 11(f)/4; ap feþra 16/ 47

ficléaf m. *figleaf* ap 2/16

fierlan adj. *far off, distant* dsm fierlenan 2/47

fīf num. *five* npm fife 11(a)/6, 14/8

fīfteġ num. *fifty* dp fīftegum 5/76

ġefillednys f. *fulfilment* ns 4/29

findan III *find, meet* inf 16/26, 18(b)1378, 18(d)/3162 (*devise*); pret 1s funde 15/18; 3s fand 18(a)/719, 18(a)/870; 3p fundon 12/85; p ptc funden 5/48, 11(f)/1

finger m. *finger* np fingras 18(a)/760; gp fingra 18(a)/764

fiorm f. *use, benefit* as fiorme 5/31

fīras m. pl. *people, human beings* gp fȳra 18(c)/2250; dp fīrum 9/44

firmest see fyrmest

first m. *period of time, time* as 5/61

fīrum see fīras

fisc m. *fish* ns 1/5; as 3/102, 3/103; np fiscas 3/79; ap 3/75, 3/81, 3/86, 3/87; gp fisca 3/94; dp fiscum 11(p)/4

fiscere m. *fisherman* ns 3/72, 3/195; np fisceras 3/5

fiscian 2 *fish, catch fish* pres 2s fiscast 3/89

Fitela pers. n. *Fitela* ns 18(a)/879, 18(a)/889

flān m. *arrow, missile* as 12/269; gs flānes 12/71

flasce f. *flask, leather bottle* ap flascan 3/153

flǣschoma m. *covering of flesh, body* ns 17/94

flǣscmete m. *meat* ap flǣscmettas 3/171; gp flǣscmetta 3/158

flēag see flēogan

flēam m. *flight* as 7/44, 12/81, 12/254; ds flēame 12/186

flēogan II *fly* inf 12/7, 12/109, 12/150, 12/275 (*flee*); 3s flēogeð 11(h)/12; pret 1s flēah 11(p)/3; 3s flēag 11(l)/4, 17/17

flēon II *flee* inf 12/247, 18(a)/755, 18(a)/764, 18(a)/820; pret 3s flēah 10(b)/20; 3p flugon 12/194

flēotend m. *swimmer, seafarer* (*seabird*) gp flēotendra 16/54

flet n. *floor, hall* as 11(n)/2, 16/61

ġeflit n. *dispute, rivalry, contest* as 18(a)/865; ap geflitu 3/207

flocmǣlum adv. *in* (*armed*) *bands* 7/77 [archaic MnE flockmeal]

flōd m. *body of water, stream, tide* ns 12/65, 12/72, 18(b)/1361; ds flōde 11(d)/9, 11(p)/3, 18(b)/1366, flōdan 6/5; ap flōdas 11(j)/7 [MnE flood]

flōdwegas m. pl. *paths of the ocean* ap 17/52 [MnE floodways]

flōr m. *floor* as 18(a)/725; as flōr 10(a)/30, flōre 10(b)/81; ds 18(b)/1316

flot n. *sea* as 12/41

flota m. *seaman, viking* np flotan 12/72; as 12/227

flōwan VII *flow* pres ptc flōwende nsm 12/65

flugon see flēon

flyht m. *flight* as 12/71

flȳman 1 *put to flight* inf 11(j)/19; p ptc geflȳmed 18(a)/846, 18(b)/1370

fōdor n. *fodder, food* as 3/209

folc n. *folk, people, nation* ns 4/86, 8/66, 12/45, 12/241, 14/140; as 4/78, 7/77, 11(d)/6, 12/22, 12/54; gs folces 1/29, 4/20, etc.; ds folce 3/133, 4/39, 12/227, etc.; is 8/77; gp folca 1/30

folcġesīð m. *companion of the people, warrior* ap folcgesīðas 10(b)/70

folcġewinn n. *battle* gs folcgewinnes 10(b)/10

folclond n. *country* gs folclondes 15/47

folctoga m. *leader of the people, chief* np folctogan 18(a)/839

folcwiga m. *warrior* np folcwigan 11(j)/13

foldbold n. *building* 18(a)/773.

foldbūend m. *earth-dweller, man* np foldbūende 18(b)/1355

folde f. *earth, ground* as foldan 9/44, 12/54, 18(b)/1361; gs 14/8, 14/43, 16/33, 18(b)/1393; ds 11(p)/5, 12/166, 12/227, 14/132, 17/13, 17/75

foldweġ m. *way, path* np foldwegas 18(a)/866

folgað m. *retinue* as 15/9

folgian 2 w.d. *follow* inf 6/32; pret 3p folgodon 4/37

folme f. *hand* ds folme 18(a)/748; ds folman 12/21, 12/108, 12/150; dp folmum 18(a)/722; ap folma 18(a)/745; gp 11(f)/15

fōn VII *catch, seize* inf 3/95; pres 1s fō 3/49; 3s fēhð 11(f)/9 (fēhð ongean *struggles against*); fōn tō rīce *succeed to the kingdom* (or *the office,* etc.) pret 1s fēng 5/19; 3s 7/16, 8/25 (see note), 10(a)/5, 12/10

ġefōn VII *catch* inf 3/84, 3/130; pres 1s gefō 3/51, 3/66, 3/102, 3/103; 2s gefēhst 3/50, 3/75, 3/86, 3/92; 3p gefōþ 3/105; subj 3s gefō 3/98; pret 1s gefēng 3/56, 3/58; 2s gefēnge 3/55, 3/57; 3s gefēng 18(a)/740

for prep. w.d.a.i. *for, because of* 1/32, 2/65, 2/68, 3/10, 3/16, 7/76 (*in spite of*), 9/8, etc.; for hwon *why* 9/95–6; for hwȳ *why* 3/89, 3/101, 3/124; for þǣm *because* 3/53, 3/63, 3/66, 3/90, 3/98, 3/102, 3/107, 3/125; for þǣm þe *because* 2/22, 2/28, 2/36, 2/42, 2/77, 3/21, 3/125, 4/6; for ðon *therefore, because, and so* 5/21, 8/15, 8/61, 9/96; for ðȳ *therefore, because.* See §169

fōr f. *journey, course* ds fore 11(l)/3

ġefōr see ġefaran

foran to adv. *beforehand* 4/44

forbarn see forbeornan

forbǣrnan 1 *burn, burn up* inf 8/71; pres subj 1p forbǣrnen 8/49; p ptc forbǣrned 5/29, asm forbǣrnedne 17/114

forbēad see forbēodan

forbēah see forbūgan

forbēodan II *forbid* pret 3s forbēad 2/3

forbeornan III *burn down* pret 3s forbarn 7/11
forbūgan II *flee from* pret 3s forbēah 12/325
ford m. *ford* as 12/88; ds forda 12/81
fordōn anom. (§128) *destroy* pret 3s fordyde 8/75 [MnE fordo]
fore prep. w.d. *for, in place of* 17/21, 17/22
foregangen VII *precede* pres subj 3s foregange 8/35
foresċēawian 2 *provide* pres 3s foresceawað 2/55
foresecgan 3 *mention before* p ptc foresǣde (*aforementioned*) 4/97
foresnotor adj. *very wise, very clever* npm foresnotre 18(d)/3162
foresprecan V *say before* p ptc dsm foresprecenan (*aforementioned*) 8/52, dpm 10(a)/5
forġēafe see forġiefan
forġiefan V *give* pret 2s forġēafe 2/25; 3s forġēaf 12/139, 12/148, 14/147; p ptc forgifen 9/55, ap forgiefene 17/93 [MnE forgive]
forġifenis f. *forgiveness* as forgifenisse 4/65
forgyldan III *buy off* pret subj 3p forgyldon 12/32
forheard adj. exceedingly hard asm forheardne 12/156
forhēawan VII *cut down* p ptc forhēawen 12/115, 12/223, 12/288, 12/314
forherġian 2 *ravage* p ptc forhergod 5/29, 7/3, 7/7
forhicgan 2 *despise, scorn* pret 3s forhogode 12/254
forhogdnis f. *contempt* ds forhogdnisse 9/8
forht adj. *afraid* nsm 14/21, 16/68, 18(a)/754
forhtian 2 *fear* pres 3p forhtiað 14/115; pret subj 3p forhtedon 12/21
forhtmōd adj. *timorous* nsm 3/63, 3/107
for hwon see for
for hwȳ see for
forlǣtan VII *abandon, neglect, forsake, let (go)* inf 12/2, 12/208, 18(a)/792; pres ptc forlǣtende 9/120; pres 3s forlǣtt 3/211, forlǣteð 11(h)/7; pret 3s forlēt 4/35, 7/25, 9/24, 11(g)/2 (*gave*), 12/149, 12/156, 12/187, etc.; 3p forlēton 4/37, 5/46, 14/61, 18(d)/3166; p ptc forlǣten 3/212, 5/37
forlēosan II *destroy* pres subj 1p forlēosen 8/49 [MnE p ptc forlorn]
forlēt see forlǣtan
forlidennes f. *shipwreck* as forlidennesse 3/138
forma adj. *first* nsm 18(a)/716, asm forman 12/77; ds 4/59, 18(a)/740 [MnE form(er), forem(ost)]
formoni adj. *very many* (*a*) nsm 12/239
forniman IV *take away* pret 3s fornōm 13/26, 16/80, fornam 18(c)/2249; 3p fornōman 16/99

fornōm see forniman
fōron see faran
forsēon V *reject, despise* pres 3s forsihð 4/65
forsihð see forsēon
forst m. *frost* is forste 17/9
forstandan VI *understand, withstand* inf 10(b)/22; pret 1s forstōd 5/73
forstelan IV *rob, steal* p ptc asm forstolen 11(j)/18 (as noun: *that which has been stolen*)
forstōd see forstandan
forstrang adj. *very strong* asm forstrangne 11(m)/4
forswelgan III *devour, eat* inf 17/95; pret 3s forswealg 11(c)/3; pres subj 3p forswelgen 3/25
forswerian VI w.d. *make useless by a spell* p ptc forsworen 18(a)/804 [MnE forswear]
forð adv. *forth, forward* 11(e)/5, 12/3, 12/12, 12/170, etc.; to forð *too deeply, too successfully* 12/150
for þan þe see for
for þǣm see for
for þǣm þe see for
forþbringan 1 *produce, bring forth* pret 3s forþbrōhte 9/7
forðencan 1 *despair* p ptc forðōht *in despair* 10(b)/82
forðfēran 1 *die* pret 3s forðfērde 7/19; 3p forðfērdon 7/12
forðfōr f. *forth-faring, death* ns 9/96; gs forðfōre 9/88, 9/125; ds 9/92; forþfōre 9/102
forðġeorn adj. *eager to advance* nsm 12/281
forðġesceaft f. *eternal decree* as 14/10
forðian 2 *carry out, accomplish* p ptc geforðod 12/289
forðōht see forðencan
forþolian 2 *do without, dispense with* inf 3/167, 16/38
for þon see for
forðȳ adv. *therefore* 5/54, 5/79
forðweġ m. *the way forth, departure* gs forðweges 11(o)/3, ds forðwege 16/81, 14/125
forwegan V *carry off, kill* p ptc forwegen 12/228
forweorone see forweosan
forweosan I *perish* p ptc ap forweorone 13/7
forwundian 2 *wound sorely* p ptc forwundod 14/14, 14/62
fōt m. *foot* np fēt 17/9; ap 4/112, 11(b)/4, 18(a)/745; gs fōtes 12/247; dp fōtum 12/119, 12/171; gp fōta 11(f)/15
fōtmǣl n. *space of a foot* as 12/275
fracod adj. *vile, wicked* as noun gsm fracodes 14/10
fram prep w.d. *from, by* 1/10, 2/19, 3/212, 7/3, etc.

fram adv. see from

framra adj. see from

franca m. *spear* as francan 12/140; ds 12/77

ġefrǽġe n. *information through hearsay* is mīne gefrǽġe *as I have heard say* 18(a)/776, 18(a)/ 837

frǽgn see frignan

Frǽna pers. n. *Frǽna* ns 7/44

frǣt see fretan

frǽtwan I *ornament, adorn* p ptc frǽtwed 11(j)/11

ġefrǽtwan I *adorn* p ptc gefrǽtwed 13/33

frǽtwe f. pl. *ornaments* np 11(d)/6; ap frǽtwa 18(a)/896; dp frǽtewum 4/84; ip frǽtwum 11(j)/7

frēa m. *lord, master, the Lord* ns 9/44; as frēan 12/184, 12/259, 14/33, 18(b)/1319; gs 15/33; ds 11(n)/10, 12/12, 12/16, 12/289

frēadryhten m. *lord* gs frēadryhtnes 18(a)/ 796

frēċennes f. *danger, harm* dp frēċennessum 3/105

frēcne adj. *daring, dangerous, audacious* nsn 18(c)/2250, asn 18(b)/1359, asf 18(a)/889, 18(b)/1378

frēfran I *console, comfort* inf 16/28, 17/26

fremman I *accomplish, perpetrate, advance, benefit* pres 3s fremeþ 3/156, 3/163; subj 3s fremme 3/208; pret 3s fremede 10(b)/45; subj 3/146

ġefremman I *bring about, provide, do* inf 16/16, 16/114, 18(b)/1315; pret 3s gefremede 18(a)/811; 3p gefremedon 17/84

fremsumnes f. *benefit* ap fremsumnesse 8/17; dp fremsumnessum 9/80

fremu f. *beneficial action, good deed* dip fremum 11(m)/8, 17/75

frēo adj. *free* nsm 3/21; gpm frīora 5/58

frēod f. *friendship, peace* as frēode 12/39

frēogan 2 *love* pres subj 3s frēoge 18(d)/3176

frēoliċ adj. *free, noble, beautiful* nsn 11(j)/13; npn frēolico 11(a)/4

frēomǽġ m. *noble kinsman* dp frēomǽgum 16/ 21

frēond m. *friend, lover* ns 14/144, 15/47, 16/ 108; as 18(b)/1385; np frȳnd 15/33, frēondas 14/76; ap frȳnd 12/229; gp frēonda 14/132, 15/17; dp frēondum 8/3

frēondlēas adj. *friendless* asm frēondlēasne 16/28

frēondlīċe adv. *lovingly, in friendly fashion* 5/2

frēondscipe m. *friendship, love* ns 15/25; as 10(a)/8

frēoriġ adj. *frozen* nsm 16/33

freoþian 2 *care for, protect* pret 3s freoþode 11(k)/5

fretan V *eat up, devour* pret 3s frǣt 11(c)/1 [MnE fret]

frignan III *ask, inquire* pres ptc frignende 8/9; imp 2s frige 11(f)/15, 11(j)/19, frīn 18(b)/ 1322; pres 3s frīneð 14/112; pret 3s frǽgn 9/100, 9/104, etc.

ġefrignan III *find out, learn by asking* pret 1s gefrǽgn 11(c)/2; 3p gefrūnon 14/76

frīn see friġnan

frīneð see friġnan

frīora see frēo

frīð m. *peace* as 7/75, 12/39; gs friðes 7/65, 10(b)/35, 12/41; dp friðe 12/179

Friðeġist pers. n. *Frithegist* ns 7/44

friþemǽġ f. *protective woman* ns 11(k)/9

frōd adj. *old, wise, experienced* nsm 12/140, 12/ 317, 16/90, 18(b)/1306, etc.

frōfor f. *consolation, solace* as frōfre 16/115; gs 10(a)/28, 10(b)/79

from adj. *active, swift, strong* comp. nsm framra 11(l)/4

from adv. *away* 6/33, fram 12/317

from prep. see fram

fromsīþ m. *departure* ns 15/33

fromweard adj. *about to depart, passing away* dsm fromweardum 17/71

fruma m. *beginning* ds fruman 4/21, 9/71

frumbearn n. *first-born* np 11(a)/4

frumsceaft f. *first creation* as 9/33

ġefrunon see ġefrignan

frymdi adj. *desiring, requesting, entreating* ns 12/179 (ic eom frymdi tō þē *I beseech you*)

frȳnd see frēond

fuglere m. *fowler* ns 3/108; np fugleras 3/5

fugol m. *bird* ns fugel 16/81; ap fuglas 3/108; dp fuglum 11(l)/4, 11(p)/3 [MnE fowl]

fuhton see feohtan

ful adv. *very, completely* 11(o)/5, 12/253, 12/ 311, 15/1, 15/18, 15/21, etc., full 12/153

fulgon see fēolan

full adj. *full, entire, completed, filled* nsm 10(b)/9; nsf 13/23, 17/100; asm fulne 3/13, 17/113; asn ful 4/16; be fullan *completely* 5/42

fulluht see fulwiht

fulluhtþēaw m. *rite of baptism* dp fulluhtþēawum 10(b)/33

fullwēr m. *complete atonement* as 11(h)/14

fulne see full

fultum m. *help, support* ds fultume 5/57

fultumian 2 *help, support* inf 8/20; p ptc ge-fultumed 9/14

ġefultumian 2 *help* pret subj gefultumode 10(a)/24

fulwiht m. f. *baptism* gs fulwihte 8/77; ds fulluhte 4/64

funde see findan

funden see findan

fundian 2 *hurry, direct a course to* pres 3s fundaþ 14/103, 17/47

furþum adv. *even* 3/162, 3/166, 4/24, 5/16, etc.

furþur adv. *further* 5/62, 18(a)/761, furðor 5/62, 12/247

fūs adj. w.g. *eager, ready (for death or battle)* nsm 11(o)/3, 12/281; asm fūsne 17/50; asn fūse (*brilliant, shining*) 14/21; as noun npm fūse (*hastening ones*) 14/57

fyl m. *fall, death* as 12/71, 12/264, fyll 14/56

fylġan 1 w.d. *follow* pres subj 1p fylgen 8/37

fyllan 1 *fill, satisfy* p ptc gefylde 3/32

fyllan 1 *fell, cut down* inf 14/73

*ge*fyllan 1 *fill, replenish* pres 3s gefylleð 11(j)/8, gefylþ 3/159; p ptc npf gefylda 5/30

*ge*fyllan 1 *fell, kill, strike down* inf 14/38

fyllo f. *fill, plenty, feast* ds fylle 18(b)/1333

fylstan 1 w.d. *help* inf 12/265

fȳnd see fēond

fȳr n. *fire* ns 2/55, 8/29; as 2/53, 18(b)/1366; gs fȳres 17/113; ds fȳre 7/49; is 8/49, 11(o)/3

fȳra see firas

fȳrbend f. *band forged with fire* dp fȳrbendum 18(a)/722

fyrd f. *national army, the English levy* as fyrde 7/29, 7/42; ds 7/34, 12/221

fyrdrinc m. *warrior* ns 12/140

fyrdsceorp n. *war-ornament* ns 11(j)/13

fyrdwyrðe adj. *distinguished in war* nsm 18(b)/1316

fyren f. *crime, wickedness, sin* gp fyrena 18(a)/750, fyrene 18(a)/811; ap 18(a)/879

fyrgenholt n. *mountain-wood* as 18(b)/1393

fyrgenstrēam m. *mountain stream* ns 18(b)/1359

fyrmest adj. (superl. of forma) *foremost, first* nsm 3/187, 3/188, 3/191, 12/323; nsf firmest 4/49

fyrmest adv. *first of all* 3/189

fyrhtu f. *horror, fear* dsf 9/78 [MnE fright]

fȳsan 1 *send forth, shoot* pret 3s fȳsde 12/269

gād f. *goad* as gāde 3/194; ds 3/15

Gadd pers. n. *Gadd* gp gaddes 12/287

*ge*gaderian 2 *gather* pret 3s gegaderode 7/27, 7/42, etc.

gafol n. *tribute* as 7/22, 7/59, 7/65, 11(g)/2 (him on gafol *as a gift to himself*), gofol 12/61; ds gafole 7/76, 12/32, 12/46

galan VI *sing, sound* inf 14/67, 18(a)/786 [MnE (nightin)gale]

gamol adj. *old, aged, ancient* nsm gomela 18(b)/1397

gān anom. (§128) *go, walk* inf 7/43, 12/247; imp 2p gāð 12/93; pres 1s gā 3/76; 2s gǣst 2/29; 3s gǣþ 6/43; 1p gāð (w. refl. unc) 2/51; subj 1s gā 3/99; 3s 18(b)/1394; pret 1s ēode 9/30; 3s 2/17, 6/13, 9/23, etc.; 3p ēodon 6/28, etc.; subj 3p 6/33, 12/229

ganet m. *gannet* gs ganetes 17/20

gang m. *flow* ds gange 14/23; *track* as 18(b)/1391 [MnE gang, gang(ster)]

gangan see gongan

*ge*gangan see *ge*gongan

gār m. *spear* ns 12/296; as 12/13, 12/134, 12/154, etc.; ds gāre 12/138; ap gāras 12/46, 12/67, 12/109 [MnE gar(fish)]

gārberend m. *spear-bearer, warrior* np 12/262

gārrǣs m. *storm of spears, battle* as 12/32

gāst m. *spirit, soul, angel* ns 4/61, gǣst 11(d)/9; as 9/123, 14/49; gs Gāstes 9/76; ds gāste 12/176, gǣste 11(k)/8; np gāstas 14/11 (*souls, angels*); gp gāsta 14/152, 18(b)/1357 [MnE ghost]

gāstliċ adj. *spiritual* asn gāstlice 4/27; dsn gāstlicum 4/54 [MnE ghostly]

gāstlīċe adv. *spiritually, in the spiritual sense* 4/40, 4/44

gātehǣr n. *goat-hair* as 4/86

gatu see ġeat

gǣst see gān

gǣste see gāst

gǣstliċ adj. *spectral, terrifying* nsn 16/73

gǣþ see gān

ġe conj. *and* 3/121, 3/166; (ǣġðer) ġe . . . ġe *both . . . and* 2/11, 5/37, etc.

ġē pron. (§21) *ye, you* np 1/15, 2/3, 2/8, 2/10, 3/161, 3/170, etc.; gp ēower 3/154, 3/177, 3/202; dp ēow 1/35, 2/3, 2/50 (refl.), 2/52, 3/137, 3/157, 3/190, īow 5/54

ġeac m. *cuckoo* ns 17/53

ġeador adv. *together* 18(a)/835

ġeaf see ġiefan

ġeald see ġieldan

gealga m. *gallows, cross* ns 14/10; as gealgan 14/40

*ge*ealgean see ealgian

gealgtrēo n. *gallows-tree, cross* ds gealgtreowe 14/146

*ge*ġeap see *ge*ġeopan

ġēap adj. *deceitful* comp ns ġēappre 2/1

ġēap adj. *spacious, wide* nsm 13/11; asm ġēapne 18(a)/836

ġēar n. *year* as 7/17; ds geare 7/21, 7/47, 7/64, etc.; is 7/1, 7/7, 7/10, 8/78

ġēara adv. *long ago* 10(b)/1, 14/28 (geara iu *years ago, very long ago*), 16/22 [archaic MnE (days of) yore]

ġearcian 2 *prepare* pres 1s gearcie 3/152

ġeard m. *yard, enclosure* as 1/6

ġēardagas m. pl. *days gone by* dp gēardagum 16/44, 18(b)/1354

ġeare adv. *readily* 8/42; *clearly* 16/69, gearwe 16/71; gearwe ne . . . *not at all* 18(a)/878; superl. gearwost nsm 18(a)/715

ġēarmǣlum adv. *year by year* 10(b)/5

ġearo adj. *ready, prepared* nsm 6/18, 12/274; npm gearowe 12/72, 12/100; apm gearwe 3/128

ġearwe see ġearo

ġeġearwian 2 *prepare* pret subj 2s gegearwode 9/95

ġeat n. *gate* ap gatu 2/76, 6/27, 6/36

Ġēatas m. pl. *the Geats* gp Ġēata 18(d)/ 3178

Ġēatmæcgas m. pl. *men of the Geats* gp Ġēatmecga 18(a)/829

ġefe see ġiefu

ġēman 1 *take heed* pret 3s gēmde 9/81

ġēn adv. *yet* 8/39, 11(k)/2, 18(a)/734, 18(d)/ 3167

ġēo adv. *formerly, of old* iū 5/3, 10(b)/1, 13/32, 14/28 (see ġeara), 14/87, giū 5/41, gū 8/71, etc.

ġēoc f. *help* ds gēoce 17/101

ġeocian 2 *yoke* inf 3/9; p ptc gegeoced 3/11

ġēocor adj. *grievous, sad* nsm 18(a)/765

ġeofon m. or n. *sea, ocean* gs gyfenes 18(b)/ 1394

ġeoguðe see gioguð

ġeoguðmyrþ f. *delight of the young (i.e. milk)* gs geoguðmyrþe 11(g)/2

ġēomor adj. *sad* nsm 15/17; dsf gēomorre 15/1, gēomran 17/53; dsm gēomran 10(b)/ 84

ġēomormōd adj. *sad-minded, serious* nsm 15/ 42

ġeond prep. w.a. *through, throughout* 4/63, 7/62, 15/36, 16/3, giond 5/3, 5/30, etc. [MnE (be)yond]

ġeondhweorfan III *pervade, visit every part* pres 3s geondhweorfeð 16/51

ġeondscēawian 2 *survey, examine every part* pres 3s geondscēawað 16/52

ġeondþenċean 1 *meditate on, ponder every part* pres 1s geondþence 16/60; geondþenceð 16/89

ġeong adj. *young* nsm 11(j)/2, 12/210, 14/39, 15/42, etc.; nsf 11(p)/1; as noun nsm geonga 12/155

ġeġēopan II *take to oneself, receive, swallow* pret 1s gegēap 11(h)/9

ġeorn adj. w.g. *eager* nsm 10(b)/51, 12/107, 16/69; npm georne 12/73, giorne 5/10

ġeorne adv. *eagerly, zealously, readily* 12/123, 12/206, 12/84, 16/52; compar. geornor 3/70, 18(a)/821

ġeornful adj. *eager* nsm 12/274

ġeornfulnes f. *desire* ds geornfulnesse 9/82 [MnE yearnfulness]

ġeornlīċe adv. *eagerly, zealously* 3/211, 9/81, 12/265; comp geornlicor 8/20, 8/40, 8/43

ġēotan II *pour* inf 13/42

ġidda see ġiedd

ġiedd n. *word, speech, riddle* as 15/1, gied 11(c)/3; gs gieddes 11(n)/14; gp gidda 18(a)/868

ġieddian 2 *sing, recite* pret 3s gyddode 10(b)/ 84

ġiefan V *give* pret 3s geaf 1/20

ġiefstōl m. *throne* gs giefstolas 16/44

ġiefu f. *gift* ns 1/32, gifu 9/55; as gyfe 8/46, gife 9/14, 9/49, etc.; ds 9/2; ap gefe 8/17; gp gifena 17/40 (see note)

ġieldan III *pay, render* pret 3s geald 7/22, 7/63 [MnE yield]

ġiellan III *cry out* pres 3s gielleð 17/62 [MnE yell]

ġielpes see ġylp

ġielphladen adj. *covered with glory, proud* nsm 18(a)/868

ġiernan 1 *entreat, beg for* pret 3p gyrndon (w.g.) 7/65 [MnE yearn]

ġiese adv. *yes* 3/15, 3/18, 3/21, 3/113, etc.

ġiestrandæġ m. *yesterday* ns 3/53

ġiet adv. *yet, still* 1/1, 2/70, git 4/17, gȳt 8/71, etc.; þā gȳt *still* 12/168, etc.

ġif conj. *if* 2/23, 3/79, 3/118, 3/170, 4/9, gyf 4/21, etc.

ġife see ġiefu

ġifeðe adj. *given, granted by fate* nsm gyfeþe 18(a)/819

ġifhealle f. *gift-hall* as gifhealle 18(a)/838

ġifre adj. *greedy, ravenous* nsm 17/62

ġilp see ġylp

ġimm m. *gem* gimmas np 14/7, 14/16; ap 3/142

ġimstān m. *jewel* ap gimstanas 4/85 [MnE gemstone]

ġioguð f. *young people, youth* ns 5/58; ds geoguðe 16/35, 17/40

ġīomonn n. *men of yore* gp gīomonna 10(b)/ 23

ġiond see ġeond

ġiorne see ġeorn

ġīsl m. *hostage* ns gȳsel 12/265; ds gīsle 6/21

ġit see ġiet

ġiū see ġēo

glæd adj. *kind, gracious* asm glædne 18(a)/863 [MnE glad]

glædlīċe adv. *joyfully* 9/103 [MnE gladly]

glædmōd adj. *joyous* nsm 13/33

ġeglængde see glengan

glæs n. *glass* ns 1/4, as 3/142

glēaw adj. *wise, clear-sighted* nsm 10(b)/52, 16/73; comp nsm glēawra 11(c)/6

glēd f. *ember, burning coal* ns 11(o)/4 [MnE gleed]

glengan 1 *adorn* p ptc geglængde 9/7, geglenged 9/59

glēobēam m. *harp* gs glēobēames 18(c)/2263

gleomu f. *splendour* ds gleoma 13/33

glēowian 2 *make merry, joke* pres ptc glēo-wiende 9/99

glīwstafum adv. *joy,..lly* 16/52

gnornian 2 *mourn, feel sorrow* inf 12/315; pres 3s gnornað 17/92

gōd adj. *good* nsm 1/12, 17/40, gōda 18(a)/758 (as noun); asm gōdne 10(b)/42, gōdan 12/187 (as noun); asn gōd 12/13; asf gōde 4/89, 14/70 (gōde hwīle *a long while*); npm 3/206; apm 3/179; gpm gōdena 5/41, gōdra 10(b)/45; dsm gōdum 12/4; gpf gōdra 9/82; dpn gōdum 4/42

God m. *God* ns 1/12, 1/37, 2/2, 2/3, 2/55, 4/52, etc.; as 2/64, etc.; gs Godes 2/19, 2/61, 3/188, etc.; ds Gode 2/68, 5/11, etc.

god n. (*pagan*) *god* np godo 8/19; gp goda 8/16

gōd n. *good, goodness, goods* as 2/11; gs gōdes 12/176; dp gōdum 9/64

Goda pers. n. *Goda* ns 7/14

godcund adj. *divine, religious* gsf godcundre 9/56; dsf 9/2; npm godcundan 5/10; gpm godcundra 5/4; dpm godcundum 9/4; dpf godcundan 9/80

godcundlīce adv. *divinely* 9/13

godcundnes f. *divinity, Godhead* gs godcund-nesse 8/10

Gōdmundingahām m. *Goodmanham* (*Yorkshire*) ns 8/73

Godrīc pers. n. *Godric* ns 12/187, 12/237, 12/321, 12/325

godspell n. *gospel* as godspel 4/35; ds god-spelle 3/189

godsunu m. *godson* ns 6/39

Godwig pers. n. *Godwig* ns 12/192

Godwine pers. n. *Godwin* ns 7/44; 12/192

gofol see **gafol**

gold n. *gold* ns 1/4, 16/32, 17/101; as 3/142, 4/87, 11(l)/7, 11(n)/3, 14/18; ds golde 12/35, 14/7, 14/16, 14/77, 17/97, etc.; is 11(j)/2

goldbeorht adj. *bright with gold* nsm 13/33

goldġiefa m. *gold-giver, lord* np goldgiefan 17/83

goldhilted adj. *gold-hilted* asn 11(n)/14

goldsele m. *gold-hall* as 18(a)/715

goldsmiþ m. *goldsmith* ap goldsmiþas 3/181

goldwine m. *generous lord* ns 16/35; as 16/22

gomela see **gamol**

gomelfeax adj. *hoary-haired* as noun nsm 17/92

gomen n. *entertainment, pastime, sport, mirth* ns 18(c)/2263; ds gomene 17/20

gomenwāþ f. *joyous journey* ds gomenwāþe 18(a)/854

gongan VII *go, walk* inf 9/90, 11(b)/1, 18(a)/711, gangan 12/3, 12/40, 12/62, 12/170; pres ptc gongende 9/24, 9/94; pres 1s gonge 15/35; pret 3s gang 18(b)/1316, subj 3p gangon 12/56

ġegongan VII *get, obtain, overrun* inf 10(b)/12, gegangan 12/59; p ptc gegongen 18(a)/822, 18(a)/893

Gota m. *Goth* ns 10(b)/9, 10(b)/45; np Gotan 10(a)/1, 10(b)/1; ap 10(b)/23; gp Gotena 10(b)/5, 10(b)/38

gram adj. *fierce, hostile* npm grame 12/262; gsm grames 18(a)/765; npm graman 18(a)/777; as noun dpm gramum 12/100

Grantabriċscir f. *Cambridgeshire* as Granta-bricscire 7/68

grāpe f. *grasp, claw* ns grāpe 18(a)/836; dp grāpum 18(a)/765

grǣdiġ adj. *greedy* nsm 17/62, nsf 11(g)/2

græf n. *grave* as 17/97

gremian 2 *enrage* p ptc nsm gegremod 12/138; npm gegremode 12/296

Grendel pers. n. *Grendel* ns 18(a)/711, 18(a)/819; as 18(b)/1334, 18(b)/1354; gs Grendles 18(a)/836, 18(b)/1391

grēne adj. *green, raw* apf 3/171

grēot n. *dirt, dust* ds grēote 12/315, 18(d)/3167

grēotan II *weep* pres ptc grēotende np 14/70; pres 3s grēoteþ 18(b)/1342

grēt see **grētan**

grētan 1 *greet, approach, touch* inf 5/1, 18(a)/803 (*harm*); pres 3s grēt 4/2, grēteð 16/52; pret 3s grētte 9/27

grim adj. *fierce* nsm 12/61

grimme adv. *grimly, fiercely* 11(m)/9, 12/109, 13/14

grīn n. *snare* dp grīnum 3/110

grindan III *grind, sharpen* p ptc gegrunden 13/14; apm gegrundene 12/109

gripe m. *grasp* ns 13/8

grið n. *truce* as 7/75, 12/35, ds griðe 7/76

grund m. *ground, earth* as 12/287, 18(b)/1367, 18(b)/1394; ap grundas 17/104

ġegrundene see **grindan**

gryrelēoð n. *song of terror, terrible song* as 18(a)/786; gp gryrelēoða 12/285

ġū see **ġeō**

guma m. *man* ns 16/45, 18(a)/868, 18(b)/1384; gs guman 14/49; np 12/94; gp gumena 11(h)/10, 18(a)/715, 18(a)/878, 18(b)/1367, guman 14/46 (see note)

gūð f. *war, battle* as gūðe 12/325, gs 10(b)/9, 12/192; ds 10(b)/23, 12/13, 12/94, 12/187, etc.

gūðbill n. *war-sword* gp gūðbilla ns 18(a)/803

gūðdēað m. *death in battle* ns 18(c)/2249

gūðhrēð n. *glory in battle* ns 18(a)/819

gūðplega m. *the game of battle, conflict* ns 12/61

gūðrinc m. *warrior* ns 12/138, 18(a)/838

ġyddode see **ġieddian**

ġyf see **ġif**

ġyfe see **ġiefu**

ġyfenes see **ġeofon**

ġyfeþa see ġifeþa

ġylp m. *boasting, pride* as gilp 18(a)/829; gs gylpes 10(b)/9, gielpes 16/69 [MnE yelp]

ġylpword n. *boasting word* dp gylpwordum 12/274

ġȳman 1 w.g. *care about or for* pret 3p gȳmdon 12/192

Ġypeswīċ m. *Ipswich* ns 7/20

gyrdan 1 *gird* pret 3s gyrde 8/64

gyrndon see ġiernan

gyrwan 1 *adorn, prepare, dress* pret 3p gyredon 14/77; p ptc gegyred 14/16, gegyrwed 14/23

ġȳsel see ġīsl

gyst m. *stranger* np gystas 12/86 [MnE guest]

ġystran adv. *yesterday* 18(b)/1334

ġyt see ġiet

habban 3 *have, hold* inf 2/58, 3/119, 3/172, 4/112 (*keep*); pres 1s hæbbe 3/11, 3/12, 3/15, 3/23, 8/13; 2s hæfst 3/14, 3/17, 3/22, 3/112, 3/180, hafast 12/231; 3s hæfþ 3/193, 4/101, etc., hafað 8/14, 13/6; 1p habbað 5/37, etc.; subj 3s hæbbe 4/104; 3p hæbben 3/128, 5/59; pret 3s hæfde 4/6, 4/14, 6/7, 8/8, etc.; 1p hæfdon 8/15; 3p 4/20, 4/36, 6/16, etc., hæfdan 10(b)/6; subj 8/19, 9/101. With negative: pres 3s næfð 4/114; 3p nabbað 4/102

hacod m. *pike* ap hacodas 3/87 [MnE haked]

hād m. *office, order* as 18(b)/1335 (*manner*); ds hāde 5/63; np hādas 5/10; gp hāda 5/4 [MnE (mother)hood, (child)hood]

hafast see habban

hafela m. *head* as hafelan 18(b)/1327, ds 18(b)/1372

hafenian 2 *raise aloft* pret 3s hafenode 12/42, 12/309

hafoc m. *hawk* ns 18(c)/2263; as 3/117, 3/118, 12/8; ds hafoce 3/111; ap hafocas 3/112, 3/114, 3/120, 3/124

hagle see hæġl

hagostealdmon m. *bachelor, warrior* ns 11(j)/2

hāl adj. *safe, unhurt* npm hāle 12/292 [MnE hale, whole]

ġehāl adj. *whole, intact* ns 4/94

hālettan 1 *hail* pret 3s hālette 9/27

hālgian 2 *consecrate* pret 1p hālgodon 8/48; p ptc gehālgod 7/1, gehālgade 8/6, gehālgode 8/75 [MnE hallow]

hāliġ adj. *holy* nsm 9/41, Hālga 4/63; asn hālige 4/34, hālig 9/56; gsn hālgan 9/66, 9/74; nsf hālige 7/52; npm 14/11; apm 10(b)/25; apf hālgan 4/89; as noun ds Hālgan (*God*) 17/122; gpm hālgum (*the Saints*) 14/143, 14/154

hāliġnes f. *religion* gs hālignesse 8/53, 8/62 [MnE holiness]

hals m. *neck* as 12/141

hālwende adj. *salutary, salvific* apn 9/121

hām adv. *homewards, home* 2/78, 9/23, 12/251

hām m. *home* as 14/148, 17/117, 18(a)/717, ds (or locative) hām 3/10, hāme 12/292

Hamtūn m. *Southampton* ds Hamtūne 7/61

Hamtūnscīr f. *Hampshire* as Hamtūnscīre 7/72; ds 6/2, 7/13, 7/57

Hāmtūnscīr f. *Northamptonshire* ds Hāmtūnscīre 7/70

hand f. *hand* ns 12/141, 18(b)/1343; as 2/63, 12/112, hond 8/64, 17/96, 18(a)/834; ds handa 12/149, 14/59, 18(a)/746, honda 9/104, 9/123, 18(a)/814; ap handa 4/111, honda 11(b)/5, 16/43; dp handum 12/4, 12/14, hondum 11(o)/5, 16/4, handon 12/7

handbona m. *slayer with the hand* ds handbanan 18(b)/1330

handscalu f. *hand-troop, companions* ds handscale 18(b)/1317

hār adj. *hoary, grey, grey-haired* nsm 12/169, 18(b)/1307, hāra 16/82; asm hārne 13/43, 18(a)/887

hara m. *hare* ap haran 3/51

hās adj. *hoarse* nsm 3/16

hāt n. *heat* ds hāte 13/38 (see note)

hāt adj. *hot* dsm hāton 18(a)/849; npm hāt 18(a)/897; npn 13/41; npf 17/11; npm hāte 13/43, 13/45; compar. hātra npm hātran 17/64

ġehāt n. *promise* ap 10(a)/9

hātan VII *command, order, call, name* pres 1s hāte 5/2, 14/95; 3s hāteð 5/1; 1p hātað 10(a)/12; pass. hātte 1s 11(f)/15, 11(h)/16, 11(j)/19 (hwæt ic hātte *what I am called*); 3s 10(b)/53, 11(b)/7, 11(n)/16; pret 3s hēt 2/52, 2/69 (*named*), 7/32, 9/52, etc., hēht 8/70, 9/50, 9/65, 10(b)/70, etc.; 3p hēton 14/31; p ptc gehāten 4/48, 10(a)/13, hāten 6/8, 12/75, 12/218, np hātne 10(a)/3 [archaic MnE hight]

ġehātan VII *promise, vow* pres 1s gehāte 18(b)/1392; pret 1s gehāte 12/246; 3s gehēt 10(a)/7, 10(b)/35, 12/289

hātheort adj. *angry, impulsive* nsm 16/66 [MnE hotheart(ed)]

ġehātland n. *promised land* gs gehātlandes 9/73

hātte see hātan

hæbbe see habban

hæfde see habban

hæfdon see habban

hæfst see habban

hæft m. *captive* asm hæfton 18(a)/788

ġehæft adj. *caught* asm gehæft 2/67

ġehæftan 1 *catch, hold captive* pres 3p gehæftaþ 3/78; p ptc gehæft 7/4

hæfþ see habban

hægl m. *hail* ns 17/17, 17/32; ds hagle 16/48

hæglfaru f. *hailstorm* as hæglfare 16/105

hǣlan 1 *heal, save* inf 14/85

hæle m. *warrior, man* ns 10(b)/53, 16/73

hǣlend m. *Saviour (lit. Healer)* gs Hǣlendes 14/25

hæleþ m. *hero, warrior* ns 14/39, 14/78, 14/95; np 11(f)/5, 11(n)/1, 12/214, 18(c)/2247, hælæð 12/249; gp hæleða 11(d)/3, 12/74; dp hæleþum 16/105, 18(c)/2262

hǣlo n. *prosperity, luck* as hæle 18(a)/719

hǣlo f. *salvation* gs 8/46 [obs. MnE heal]

ɡehǣp adj. *suitable* dsf gehæpre 3/42 [MnE hap(py)]

hærfest m. *autumn* as 3/122 [MnE harvest]

hæring m. *herring* ap hæringas 3/93

hærliċ adj. *noble* nsf 10(b)/43

hæs f. *behest, command* gs hæse 2/77

hæste adj. *violent* asm hæstne 18(b)/1335

Hæstingas m. pl. *Hastings (Sussex)* ap 7/71

hæþen adj. *heathen* npm hæðene 12/181; asf hæþene 18(a)/852; as noun npm 12/55

hæþstapa m. *heath-stalker, stag* ns 18(b)/1368

hē, hēo, hit pron (§18) *he, she, it* pl. *they* nsm hē (*he*) 1/14, 1/21, 1/35, 2/14, etc.; asm hine (*him*) 1/34, 2/18 (refl.), 2/45, 3/60, 3/61, 6/14 (refl.), etc., hiene 5/23, 6/3, etc.; gsm his 1/1, 1/2, 1/3, 1/31, etc.; dsm him 2/55, 2/56, 2/62, etc.; nsn hit (*it*) 3/21, 3/53, etc.; asn 2/58, etc.; nsf hēo (*she*) 1/11, 1/23, 1/32, 2/26, 2/32, hīo 5/81; asf hīe 5/49, 5/80, etc.; gsf hire (*her*) 2/14, 2/32, 7/52, etc.; dsf 2/12, 9/50, etc.; np hīe (*they*) 1/28, 1/34, 2/15, 2/17, 2/48, 2/49, 2/56, 3/42, 3/43, 3/121, hī 4/26, 7/49, hig 4/40, 4/41, hēo 9/55, 9/104, 9/106, etc.; ap hīe (*them*) 3/19, 3/25, 3/26, 3/30, 3/121 (refl.), 3/123, 3/161, hī 7/53; gp hira (*their*) 1/28, 2/14, 2/76, 3/84, hiora 5/7, 5/18, 7/66, hiera 6/19, hyra 11(a)/3; dp him (*them*) 2/16, 3/180, 5/36, heom 7/57, etc.

hēa see hēah

hēafod n. *head* as 2/32, 9/116, 16/43; ds hēafde 10(b)/43; dp hēafdum 14/63 (w. ds meaning: see note); gp hēafda 11(b)/4

hēafodlēas adj. *headless* nsm 11(j)/10

hēah adj. *high* nsm 16/98, 18(d)/3157, nsn 13/22; nsf hēa 11(d)/4; asm hēanne 14/40, 16/82; dsm hēan 18(a)/713; apm hēan 17/34; compar. hīerra (§75) dsm hīerran 5/63

hēahburg f. *chief city* ns 10(a)/21

hēahfæder m. *patriarch* ds hēahfædere 4/15; 14/134 (*God the father*)

healdan VII *keep, observe, hold, stand firm* inf 12/14, 12/19, 12/41 (w.d. of person and g. of thing), 12/74, etc., healdon 10(b)/71; infl inf (tō) healdenne 4/109; pres 3p healdaþ 17/87; subj 3s healde 16/14; pret 3s hēold

11(k)/5 (*foster, cherish*), 18(a)/788; 3p hīoldon 5/34 (*occupied*); subj 3p hēoldon 12/20

ɡehealdan VII *hold, maintain, preserve* inf 12/167; pres 3s gehealdeþ 16/112, subj 1s gehealde 3/161; pret 3p gehīoldon 5/8

healf adj. *half* asf healfe 7/69

healf f. *side* (w.d. of person) ds healfe 12/152, 12/318, 18(c)/2262, as 14/20; gp healfa 18(a)/800

heall f. *hall* ns 8/29; ds healle 11(n)/1, 11(n)/13, 12/214

healðegn m. *hall-thane* ap healðegnas 18(a)/719

healwudu m. *wood of a hall* ns 18(b)/1317

hēan adj. *wretched* nsm 16/23

hēanliċ adj. *humiliating, shameful* nsn 12/55

hēanne see hēah

hēap m. *band, troop, company* as 18(a)/730 [MnE heap]

heard adj. *hard, resolute, bitter, fierce, brave* nsm 11(j)/10, 12/130, 13/8, 15/43, 18(a)/886, hearda 11(n)/9, 18(c)/2255; nsn hearde 18(b)/1343; asn 12/214; asm heardne 12/167, 12/236; asf hearde 12/33; gsn heardes 12/266; dpm heardum 18(b)/1335; compar. heardra nsm 12/312, heardran asf 18(a)/719; superl. heardost nsn 14/87

heardhicgende adj. *brave-minded* npm 18(a)/799

heardlīċe adv. *fiercely* 12/261 [MnE hardly]

heardsǣliġ adj. *unfortunate, unhappy, ill-fated* asm heardsǣligne 15/19

hearm m. *damage, harm, grief, sorrow* ns 7/8, as 7/50; gp hearma 12/223

hearmscaþa m. *pernicious enemy* ns 18(a)/766

hearpe f. *harp* as hearpan 9/22, gs 18(c)/2262, ds 9/21, 17/44

heaþodēor adj. *brave in battle* dpm heaþodēorum 18(a)/772

heaþorōf adj. *brave in battle* npm heaþorōfe 18(a)/864

hēawan VII *hew, cut down, kill* inf 18(a)/800; pret 3s hēow 12/324; 3p hēowon 12/181

ɡehēawan VII *gash* p ptc gehēawen 13/12

hebban VI *raise up, lift* inf 14/31 [MnE heave]

hēdærn n. *storeroom* as 3/160

hefian see hefiġ

hefiġ adj. *heavy, oppressive* dsn hefian 14/61; compar. npf hefigran 16/49

hefiġan 2 *weigh down, burden* p ptc hefgad 9/89

hefiġtīme adj. *burdensome, troublesome* nsn 4/4

heġe m. *fence, enclosure* dp hegum 8/54

hēht see hātan

helsceaða m. *thief from hell, devil* np helsceaðan 12/180

hell f. *hell* ns hel 18(a)/852; gs helle 4/80, 18(a)/788

helm m. *protection, cover, helmet* ns 18(b)/1321 (*lord*), 18(c)/2255, as 18(b)/1392

help f. *help* as helpe 16/16, 14/102

helwaru f. pl. *inhabitants of hell* gp helwara 11(n)/6

ġehende prep. w.d. *near to* 12/294

hēo see hē

heofon m. *heaven* as 9/41, heofenan 4/52, 4/56; gs heofenes 14/64; ap heofonas 9/76, 14/103; gp heofona 14/45; dp heofonum 2/62, 2/75, 12/172, 14/85, 14/134, etc.

heofonliċe adj. *heavenly* asm heofonlicne 14/148; asn heofonlice 7/26; gsn heofonlican 9/9, heofonlecan 9/78; isn heofonlecan 9/111; nsf heofonlic 9/55; dsf heofonlicre 2/79

heofonrīċe n. *kingdom of heaven* gs heofonrīces 9/36, 14/91

heold see healdan

heolfor m. or n. *blood, gore* ds heolfre 18(a)/849

heolstor m. *darkness, hiding-place* as 18(a)/755, ds heolstre 16/23 [MnE holster]

heom (= him) see hē

heonon adv. *hence, from here* 12/246, 14/132, 15/6, 17/37, 18(b)/1361

heora see hē

heord f. *care, custody* ns 9/25 [MnE herd]

hēore adj. *safe, pleasant, good* nsf hēoru 18(b)/1372

heorodrēor m. *battle-blood* ds heorodrēore 18(a)/849

heorot m. *deer, stag* ns 18(b)/1369; ap heorotas 3/51, 3/56, 3/58 [MnE hart]

Heorot m. *Heorot* ds Heorute 18(a)/766, Heorote 18(b)/1330

heorra m. *lord* ns 12/204

heorte f. *heart* ns 12/312; as heortan 17/11; ds 12/145; gs 15/43, 16/49, 17/34; ap 3/166, 4/63

Heortfordscīr f. *Hertfordshire* as Heortfordscīre 7/68

heorðġenēat m. *hearth-companion, retainer* np heorðġenēatas 12/204, 18(d)/3179

heorðwerod n. *body of household retainers* as 12/24

hēow see hēawan

hēr adv. *here* 1/1, 2/50, 2/54, 3/144, etc.

hēran see hīeran

here m. *invading army* ns 7/34, 7/41; as 7/31; ds 12/292

hereġeatu f. *heriot, war-equipment* as 12/48

herehūð f. *booty, plunder* as herehūðe 7/40

herenes f. *praise* ds herenesse 9/34, herenisse 9/123

herepād f. *coat of mail* ns 18(c)/2258

hererinc m. *soldier, hero* as 10(b)/71

hereswēg m. *noise of an army, martial sound* ns 13/22

heretēma m. *ruler* ns 10(b)/31

heretoga m. *military leader, commander* ns 10(b)/47, heretoha 10(a)/12; np heretogan 7/43

hēreð see hīeran

herġas see heriġ

herġen see heriġean

herġian 2 *ravage* pret 3p hergodon 7/11, heregodon 7/77; p ptc gehergod 7/5, 7/20, geheregod 7/14 [MnE harry]

herġung f. *ravaging, harrying* ds hergunge 7/55, 7/60

heriġ m. *pagan sanctuary, fane* as 8/71; ds herige 8/68; np hergas 13/29; ap 8/54

herheard m. *abode in a grove* as 15/15

heriġean 1 *praise* inf 9/36; pres subj 3s herge 18(d)/3175, 3p hergen 17/77

hēt see hātan

hī see hē

hicgan 3 *think, plan, be intent upon* inf 12/4 (see note), hycgan 15/11, 17/117; pres ptc asm hycgendne 15/20; pres subj 3s hycge 16/14

hider adv. *hither* 3/137, 3/140, 12/57, 14/103, hieder 5/12

hīe see hē

hieder see hider

hīeg n. *hay* ds hīege 3/19

hiene (= hine) see hē

hiera see hē

hīeran 1 (w.d.) *obey, hearken to, hear* inf hēran 10(b)/31, hȳran 11(h)/15; 3s hēreð 11(m)/5; pret 1s hȳrde 8/21, 18(b)/1346; 1p hȳrdon 9/125; 3s hȳrde 18(a)/875

ġehīeran 1 *hear* inf gehīran 4/32, gehȳran 8/40, 14/78; infl inf (tō) gehȳranne 9/69; pres 2s gehȳrst 12/45; 3s gehȳrð 4/9; pret 1s gehīerde 2/21, gehȳrde 12/117, 14/26, 17/18; 2s gehīerdest 2/36; 3s gehȳrde 8/1, 8/41, etc.; 3p gehīerdon 2/17, gehīerdun 6/23, gehȳrdon 18(a)/785

hierdebōc f. *shepherd book* as 5/68

hīerran see hēah

hīersumian 2 *be obedient, obey* pret 3p hīersumedon 5/6

ġehīersumian 2 *obey* pret 2s gehīersumodest (w.g.) 2/77

ġehīersumnes f. *obedience* gs gehīersumnesse 2/43

hig (= hīe) see hē

hige m. *mind, heart, courage, thought* ns 12/312, hyge 15/17, 16/16, 17/44, 17/58, 18(a)/755; ds 12/4, 17/96

Higelāc see Hyġelāc

higeþīhtig adj. *strong-hearted, determined* asm higeþīhtigne 18(a)/746 hiht see hyht

hild f. *battle* as hilde 12/33; ds 11(j)/4, 12/8, 12/48, 12/55, 12/123, etc.

hildedēor adj. *brave in battle* nsm 18(a)/834; npm hildedēore 18(d)/3169

hildemecg m. *warrior* np hildemecgas 18(a)/799

hilderinc m. *warrior* ns 12/169, 18(b)/1307; np hilderincas 14/61; gp hilderinca 14/72

hine see hē

hinfūs adj. *eager to get away* nsm 18(a)/755

hīo (= hīe) see hē

ġehioldon see ġehealdan

hiora see hē

hira see hē

ġehīran see ġehīeran

hire see hē

hīredmann m. *retainer, warrior* np hīredmen 12/261

his see hē

hit see hē

hīw n. *shape, form* as 1/20 [MnE hue]

ġehladan VI *load* pret 3s gehleōd 18(a)/895

hlāf m. *bread* as 3/199; gs hlāfes 2/41; ds hlāfe 3/165 [MnE loaf]

hlāford m. *lord, master* ns 3/177, 6/31, 12/135, 12/189, etc.; as 14/45; gs hlāfordes 3/11, 18(d)/3179; ds hlāforde 3/27, 10(b)/47, 12/318

hlāfordlēas adj. *lordless, without a lord* nsm 12/251

hlǣder f. *ladder* as hlǣdre 11(n)/6

hlǣst m. *load, freight* dp hlǣstum 3/135

hlǣw m. *mound, barrow, cave* as 18(d)/3157, 18(d)/3169

hleahtor m. *laughter* ds hleahtre 17/21

hlēapan VII *leap, gallop* inf 18(a)/864; pret 3s hlēop 8/65

ġehlēapan VII *leap upon, mount* pret 3s gehlēop 12/189

hlēo n. *protection, shelter, protector* ns 12/74, 18(a)/791; as 11(f)/5

hlēomǣg m. *protecting kinsman* gp hlēomǣga 17/25

hlēop see hlēapan

hlēosceorp n. *protecting garment* ds hlēosceorpe 11(k)/5

hlēoðor n. *sound, cry, voice* as 17/20; is hlēoþre 11(j)/4

hlēoðrian 2 *make a noise, speak* pret 3s hlēoðrode 14/26

hliehhan VI *laugh, exult* pret 3s hlōh 12/147

hlīfian 2 *tower, rise up* pres 1s hlīfige 14/85

hlimman III *roar, resound* inf 17/18

hlin m. *maple* ns 11(n)/9

hlīsa m. *fame, reputation* as hlisan 10(b)/53

hlōh see hliehhan

hlūd adj. *loud* nsm 11(e)/1

hlūde adv. *loud, loudly* 1/8, 11(d)/7

hlūttor adj. *pure* isn hlūttre 9/118

hlynsian 2 *resound* pret 3s hlinsode 18(a)/770

hlystan 1 *listen* pres subj 1p hlysten 1/8

ġehlystan 1 *listen* pret 3p gehlyston 12/92

hnāg see hnīgan

hnǣgan 1 *bring low, humble* p ptc gehnǣged 17/88

hnīgan I *bow down* pret 1s hnāg 14/59

hnītan I *strike, clash together* pret 3p hniton 18(b)/1327

hof n. *building* np hofu 13/29

hogian 2 *think, give thought, intend* pret 3s hogode 12/133; 3p hogodon 12/123; subj 3s hogode 12/128

hōh m. *heel* ds hō 2/32; *promontory* ds hōe 18(d)/3157

ġehola m. *confidant, close friend* gp geholena 16/31

hold adj. *loyal, friendly, gracious* nsm 10(b)/56, 17/41; gpm holdra 15/17; superl. holdost asn 12/24

holen m. *holly* ns 11(n)/10

holm m. *sea* as 16/82; gp holma 17/64

holt n. *wood, forest* gs holtes 12/8, 14/29

holtwudu m. *tree of the forest, forest* as 14/91, 18(b)/1369

hond see hand

hongian 2 *hang* pres 1s hongige 11(j)/11; 3p hongiað 18(b)/1363

hord n. *hoard, treasure* gs hordes 18(a)/887; ds horde 18(d)/3164

hordcofa m. *heart* as hordcofan 16/14

horn m. *horn* ns 1/8; dp hornum 2/67, 18(c)/1369

horngestrēon n. *abundance of gables* ns 13/22

hornreced adj. *gabled house* as 18(a)/704

hors n. *horse* as 3/69, 12/2; dp horsum 3/210

horsweġ m. *bridle path, horseway* ds horsweġe 1/6

hraðe adv. *quickly, soon* 2/45, 8/48, raðe 7/20, 12/30, 12/164, 12/288, etc. [MnE rath(er), archaic MnE rathe]

hrædlīċe adv. *forthwith, swiftly* 3/207, 8/30

hrædwyrde adj. *hasty of speech* nsm 16/66

hræġl n. *dress, garment* ns 11(d)/1 [archaic MnE rail]

hrǣw n. *corpse* ns 14/72, as 14/53

hrēam m. *shouting* ns 12/106; ds hrēame 3/16

hrēaw adj. *raw* apm hrēawe 3/171

hreddan 1 *save, rescue* inf 11(j)/18

hremm m. *raven* np hremmas 12/106

hreoh adj. *troubled* nsm hreoh 10(b)/71, hrēo 16/16; asf 16/105 (*fierce*); dsn hrēon 18(b)/1307

hrēoriġ adj. *ruinous* npm hrēorge 13/3

hrēosan II *fall* inf 16/48; pres ptc nsf hrēosende 16/102; p ptc npm gehrorene 13/3

hrēowcearig adj. *sorrowful, troubled* nsm 14/25
hrepian 2 *touch* pret subj 1p hrepoden 2/7
hrēran 1 *set in motion, stir* inf 16/4
hreþer n. *heart* as 17/63; ds hreþre 13/41; gp hreþra 16/72
hreðerbealo n. *distress* ns 18(b)/1343
hreðerloca m. *enclosure of the heart, breast* as hreðerlocan 17/58
hrif n. *belly, womb* ds hrife 11(h)/12
hrīm m. *frost* ns 13/4, 17/32; as 16/48; is hrīme 16/77 [archaic MnE rime]
hrīmceald adj. *ice-cold* asf hrīmcealde 16/4
hrīmġeat n. *frosty gate* ns 13/4
hrīmġicel m. *icicle* dp hrīmgicelum 17/17
hrīnan 1 *touch* 3s hrīneð 11(h)/12; p ptc hrinen 8/32
hrinde adj. *covered with frost* nsm 18(b)/1363
hring m. *ring* ns 1/4, 18(c)/2260 (*ring-mail, armour*); ap hringas 12/161, 13/19
hringloca m. *ring-mail shirt, corselet* ap hringlocan 12/145
hringmere m. *circular pool* as 13/45
hringþegu f. *receiving of rings (by a retainer from his lord)* ds hringþege 17/44
hrīð f. *snowstorm* ns 16/102
hrōf m. *roof* ns 13/31, as 18(a)/836; gs hrōfes 11(f)/5; ds hrōfe 9/41; np hrōfas 13/3
hrōstbēag m. *circle formed by inner roofwork, ceiling-vault* gs hrōstbēages 13/31
ġehrorene see hrēosan
Hrōðgār pers. n. *Hrothgar* ns 18(b)/1321; as 18(a)/863; gs Hrōðgāres 18(a)/717, 18(a)/826 [MnE Roger]
hrūse f. *earth* ns 18(c)/2247; as hrūsan 11(d)/1, 11(f)/11, 13/29, 16/102, 17/32, 18(a)/772; gs 13/8, 16/23
hrycg m. *back* as 11(b)/5, is hrycge 11(f)/11 [MnE ridge]
hryre m. *ruin, fall* ns 13/31, as 18(d)/3179; gp 16/7 (see note)
hrȳðig adj. *snow-swept, exposed to storms* npm hrȳðge 16/77
hū adv. *how* 3/7, 3/41, 3/48, 3/57, 3/75, etc.; conj. 16/30, 16/35, 16/61, etc.
huilpe f. *curlew* gs huilpan 17/21 [dialectal MnE whaup]
Humbre f. *the Humber River* gs Humbran 7/40; ds Humbre 5/15
hund m. *dog* as 3/118; ap hundas 3/43; dp hundum 3/24, 3/49, 18(b)/1368 [MnE hound]
hund num. *hundred* ns 11(b)/4, 13/8
hundnigontiġ num. *ninety* dp hundnigontigum 7/48
hunger m. *hunger, famine* ns hungor 17/11; as hunger 4/78; ds hungre 4/80
hunta m. *huntsman* ns 3/38, 3/39, 3/40, etc.; np huntan 3/5

Huntadunscīr f. *Huntingdonshire* as Huntadunscīre 7/70
huntian 2 *hunt* inf 3/46, 3/47
huntoþ m. *hunting, game* as 3/65 (*game*); ds (on) huntoþe (*on a*) *hunt* 3/52, 3/54
hūru adv. *certainly* 14/10
hūs n. *house* ns 9/91; as 3/202, 8/30, 9/24; ds hūse 9/23, 9/94
hūsl n. *Eucharist, the consecrated bread and wine for Holy Communion* as 9/100, 9/103; gs hūsles 9/102
hwā, hwæt pron. (§20) *who, what, someone, something* ns hwā 2/23, 3/83, 3/159, 4/21 (*someone*), 4/65 (*someone*), 8/56, etc.; as hwænne 12/2 (*each one*); gs hwæs 1/36, 3/39; nsn hwæt 1/35, 8/35; asn 3/3, 3/7, 3/17, 3/22, 3/28, 3/55, 3/65, 3/66 (see swā), 3/73, 3/78 (see swā), 3/92, 4/25 (*something*), 4/40, etc.; dsn hwǣm 3/163; isn hwon 9/96 (see for), 17/43 (to hwon *to what, as to what*); hwȳ *why* 1/37, 2/2, 2/26, hwī 4/31, for hwȳ (see for)
ġehwā pron. *each* gsn gehwæs 9/38; dsm gehwam 16/63, 17/72
hwanon adv. *whence* 3/193, 3/194, hwonon 9/53
hwæder see hwider
hwæl m. *whale* as 3/95, 3/98; gs hwæles 17/60; ap hwalas 3/105
hwælhuntoþ m. *whale-hunt* as 3/100
hwælweg m. *path of the whale, the sea* as 17/63
hwænne pron. see hwā
hwænne conj. *until the time when* 12/67, 14/136
hwǣr adv. *where* 1/3, 2/20, 3/81, 5/81 (*somewhere*), etc.; conj. 2/54, 15/8, 16/26
ġehwǣr adv. *everywhere* 7/8
hwæs see hwā
ġehwæs see ġehwā
hwæt interj. *lo!* 8/19, 8/31, 12/231, 14/1, 18(c)/2248
hwæt pron. see hwā
hwæt adj. *vigorous, quick, active* nsm 17/40
hwætrēd m. *ingenuity, quick design* as 13/19
hwætwugu pron. *something* as 9/28
hwæðer adj. *whether* 9/100, 18(b)/1314, 18(b)/1356, hwæþer 9/104. See hwæþer þe
ġehwæðer indef. adj. *either* nsm 18(a)/814, asf gehwæðere 12/112
hwæþere adv., conj. *however, nevertheless, yet, but* 8/3, hwæðre 9/32, 9/89, 14/18, 14/38, 14/42, etc.
ġehwæðeres adv. *in both respects* 10(b)/25
hwæþer þe conj. *or* 3/119
hwæþre see hwæþere
hwearfian 2 *wave* pret 3s hwearfode 10(b)/10
hwelċ interrogative pron. and adj. *which, what, what kind of* nsm 3/186, 3/212 (swa

hwelċ (*cont.*)

hwelc swa *whatsoever*); asm hwelcne 3/1, 3/37, 3/71, 3/118; dsm hwelcum (see swa) 2/10; dsm hwylcum 11(h)/10 (each, any); swā hwelc(um) (... swā) swā *whoever* see swā; nsf hwylc 8/9 (*of what sort*), hwelc 8/12, hwylc 9/101; asf hwylce 9/49; npn hwelc 5/24; apn 3/50, 3/140

ġehwelċ pron., adj., *each* nsm 3/211 (ānra gehwelc *each one*), gehwylc 12/128, 12/257; dsm gehwelcum 6/19, gehwilcum 10(b)/45, gehwylcum 14/108; ism gehwylce 14/136, 16/8, 17/36

hweorfan III *turn, go* inf 16/72; pres 3s hweorfeð 17/58, 17/60

ġehwerfde see ġehwierfan

hwettan 1 *whet, incite* pres 3s hweteð 17/63

hwī see hwā

hwider adv. *whither, in which direction* 16/72, hwæder 18(b)/1331

hwierfan 1 *turn, change* p ptc gehwierfed 3/165

ġehwierfan 1 *turn* pret 3s gehwyrfde 9/57, gehwerfde 9/68

hwīl f. *time, while* as hwīle 2/51, 7/17, etc.; dp hwīlum *sometimes* 3/51, 3/69, 3/77, 3/90, 3/109, 3/110, 3/111, 4/12 (*once, at one time*), 4/19, etc.; ðā hwīle ðe conj. *while, as long as* 5/60, 12/14, 12/83, 12/235, etc.

hwīlum see hwīl [archaic MnE whilom]

hwistlung f. *whistling* ds hwistlunge 3/111

hwon see hwā

hwōn adj. (as noun) *little, few* as (w.g.) 17/28

hwonon see hwanon

hwȳ see hwā

hwylc see hwelc

hwylce see hwelc

ġehwyrfde see ġehwierfan

hycgan see hicgan

hycgendne see hicgan

hȳd f. *hide, skin* ap hȳda 3/151

hȳdan 1 *hide, hoard* pres 3s hȳdeð 17/102

ġehȳdan 1 *conceal* pret 3s gehȳdde 16/84

ġehygd f. *thought, intention* ns 16/72, 17/116

hyge see hige

hygegēomor adj. *sad at heart* asm hygegēomorne 15/19

Hygelāc pers. n. *Hygelac* gs Higelāces 18(a)/737, 18(a)/758, Hygelāces 18(a)/813

hygerōf adj. *resolute* as noun nsm 13/19

hyht m. *hopeful joy, bliss* ns 14/126, 17/45, 17/122, hiht 14/148

hyldan 1 *bow, bend* inf 14/45 (w. refl.)

hȳnan 1 *injure, lay low, kill* inf 12/180; pret 3s hȳnde 12/324

hȳra see hē

hȳran see hīeran

ġehȳran see ġehīeran

hȳrde see hīeran

hyrde m. *guardian, keeper* ns 18(a)/750, as 18(a)/887 [MnE (cow)herd, (shep)herd]

ġehȳrd see ġehīeran

ġehȳrde see ġehīeran

ġehȳrnes f. *hearing* ds gehȳrnesse 9/66

hyrst f. *ornament, trapping* np hyrste 11(d)/4; ap hyrsta 18(d)/3164; ip hyrstum 11(j)/11

hyrstedgold n. *fairly-wrought gold* ds hyrstedgolde 18(c)/2255

ġehȳrð see ġehīeran

hys (= his) see hē

hyse m. *warrior, youth* ns 12/152; gs hysses 12/141; np hyssas 12/112, hysas 12/123; ap hyssas 12/169; gp hyssa 12/2, 12/128

hȳþelic adj. *convenient* nsn 13/41

Iācōb pers. n. *Jacob* ds Iācōbe 4/15

iċ pron. (§21) *I* ns 1/17, 1/30, 2/21, 2/22, 3/2, 3/23, etc.; as mē 2/25, 2/72, 3/103, mec 16/28, 17/6; gs mīn (*of me*) 2/73; ds mē 2/25, 2/27, 3/74 (*for myself*), 3/80, 3/122

īdel adj. *idle, worthless, vain* nsm 16/110; gs īdles 9/15; asf īdlan 8/59; npn īdlu 16/87

ides f. *woman* gs idese 18(b)/1351; gp idesa 11(a)/7

ieldran m. pl. (§75) *elders, ancestors* npm 5/34, eldran 10(b)/58

iermðu f. *misery* ap iermða 2/34

ierþling m. *ploughman, farmer* ns 3/7, 3/29, 3/192; as 3/209; ds ierþlinge 3/32, 3/198; np ierþlingas 3/4 [MnE earthling]

īewan 1 *disclose, show* pres subj 3s ȳwe 11(n)/15

ilca adj., pron. *same, the same* asn ilce 6/33, 9/47; dsn ilcan 3/144, 7/26, 7/45, 10(a)/5, ylcan 7/3, 7/12; isn ilcan 7/4, 7/8; dsf 2/46 [MnE ilk]

in prep. w.d. *in*, w.a. *into* (§213) w.d. 9/5, 9/7, 9/34, 9/61, 9/90, etc.; w.a. 1/2, 9/10, 9/46, 9/64, 9/76, etc.

in adv. *in, inside* 12/58, 12/157, 18(b)/1371

inbryrdnes f. *inspiration* as inbryrdnesse 8/74, inbryrdnisse 9/6

inca m. *rancour* as incan 9/106; ds 9/105

indryhten adj. *very noble, aristocratic* nsm 16/12

indryhto f. *nobility* ns 17/89

inġehygd f. *intention, conscience* as 4/87

ingong m. *immigration, entry* as 9/111; ds ingonge 9/73

Ingwine m. pl. *The Danes* gp Ingwina 18(b)/1319

inlǣdan 1 *bring in* inf 9/92

innan adv. *from within* 17/11, 18(a)/774; in *innan inside* 11(k)/3

innanbordes adv. *at home, within the nation* 5/8

inne adv. *inside, within* 8/32, 9/99, 11(a)/4, 10(b)/72
insittende adj. *sitting within* as noun: gpm insittendra 11(a)/7
intinga m. *cause* ns 9/20
inwidhlemm m. *malicious wound* np inwidhlemmas 14/47
inwidsorh f. *evil care or sorrow* as inwidsorge 18(a)/831
inwiþþanc m. *hostile purpose* dp inwitþancum 18(a)/749
Iōhannes pers. n. *John* as 10(a)/11, 10(b)/42
Iōsēp pers. n. *Joseph* ns 4/77
īow (= ēow) see ġē
īren n. (*iron*) *sword* ns 12/253, 18(a)/892; gp īrenna 18(a)/802, īrena 18(c)/2259
īrenbend f. *iron band* dp īrenbendum 18(a)/774
irnan III *run* inf rinnan (*hasten, flow*) 11(e)/5; pret 3s ran 1/6; 3p urnon 6/18
is see bēon
Īsaac pers. n. *Isaac* ns 2/47, 2/53; as 2/44, 2/52, 2/69; ds Īsaace 4/5
īsceald adj. *ice-cold* asn īscealdne 17/-14, īscaldne 17/19
īsen adj. *iron* ap īsene 3/200
īsensmiþ m. *blacksmith* ap īsensmiþas 3/181
īsigfeþera adj. *having icy feathers* nsm 17/24
Israhēlas m. pl. *Israelites* gp Israhēla 9/73
Ītālia m. pl. *the Italians, Italy* ap 10(b)/12; gp 10(a)/3
iū see ġēo
Iūdēiscan adj. pl. *Jewish* (*people*), *the Jews* np 4/108; dp Iūdēiscum 4/55
iūwine m. *friend* (*or lord*) *of former days* ap 17/92
īw m. *yew* ns 11(n)/9

kāsere see cāsere
Kentingas m. pl. *Kent* ap 7/71
kynerīċes see cynerīċe
kyning see cyning

lā interj. *lo! oh!* 3/8, 3/29
lāc n. *sacrifice, offering* ds lāce 2/68, 4/92
ġelāc n. *rolling, tumult* as 15/7, 17/35
lācan VII *sport, contend, fight* pres 1s lāce 11(o)/1
lāf f. *heirloom, inheritance* as lāfe 18(a)/795, 18(d)/3160
lāgon see licgan
lagu m. *sea, water* as 17/47
ġelagu n. pl. *expanse* (*of ocean*) ap 17/64
lagulād f. *sea-way* ap lagulāde 16/3
lagustrēam m. *water, river* np lagustrēamas 12/66
lāmrind f. *crust of mud* dp lāmrindum 13/17
land n. *land, country* as lond 5/12, 18(b)/1357;

gs londes 6/29, 15/8, landes 12/90, 12/275; ds lande 2/45, 2/47, 3/136, 4/77, etc.
landbüend m. pl. *earth-dweller, inhabitant* ap londbūend 18(b)/1345
lang adj. *long, tall* nsm langa 12/273; asf lange 14/24 (lange hwīle *a long time*); tō lang *too long* (*a time*) 12/66; compar. nsf lengre 11(h)/7
ġelang see ġelong
lange adv. *long, for a long time* longe 5/78, 8/56, 10(b)/50, 10(b)/58, etc., lange 18(b)/1336; compar. leng *longer* 4/120, 12/171; superl. lengest 6/3
langoþ m. *longing* gs longaþes 15/41; ds langoþes 15/53
langung f. *longing, yearning* as longunge 17/47
langunghwīl f. *time of longing, time of spiritual desire* gp langunghwīle 14/126
lār f. *teaching, doctrine* ns 5/45, 5/64, 8/10; as lāre 5/10, 10(b)/68; gs 9/56; ds 4/37, 9/77; ap lāra 4/89 [MnE lore]
lārcwide m. *counsel* dp lārcwidum 16/38
lārēow m. *teacher* ap lārēowas 4/26, 9/70; gp lārēowa 5/20; dp lārēowum 4/39
lāst m. *track* np lāstas 11(l)/2; ap 18(a)/841; ds on lāste (see note) 16/97; dp lastum 17/15
lāstword n. *reputation left behind* gp lāstworda 17/73
lāð adj. *hateful* nsm 18(a)/815; gsm lāþes 18(a)/841; dsf lāðere 12/90; npm lāðe 12/86; apm lāð 18(b)/1375; as noun asm lāþne 17/112; compar. lāðre asn 12/50; superl. lāðost nsm 14/88 [MnE loathe(some)]
laðian 2 *invite, summon* pres 1s laðige 11(j)/16
ġelaðung f. *church, congregation* gs gelaðunge 4/83
lāðlicost adv. (superl. of lāðlice) *in most wretched fashion* 15/14
lāðost see lāð
lāðre see lāð
læċċan 1 *capture, catch* p ptc gelæht 3/44 [colloquial MnE latch (onto)]
lædan 1 *lead, bring, lift* inf 12/88, 14/5 (see note); infl inf (tō) lædene 7/29 (see note); pres 1s læde 3/25, 3/30, 3/137; 2s lætst 3/140; pret 3p læddon 10(b)/2; p ptc læded nsm 18(d)/3177
ġelædan 1 *lead* pret 3s gelædde 9/50
Læden n. *Latin* ns 4/101, 4/102; as 4/14, 5/68; gs Lædenes 4/106; ds Lædene 4/3, 5/16
Lædenbōc f. *Latin book* dp Lædenbōcum 4/26
Lædengeðīode n. *the Latin language* as 5/62; gs Lædengeðīodes 5/64
Lædenware m. pl. *the Romans* npm 5/50
læfan 1 *leave, bequeath* pret 3s læfde 6/26; 3p lēfdon 5/26, læfdon 5/35
lægon see licgan

*ġe*læht see læċċan

læn n. *loan* ds læne 5/81

læne adj. *temporary, transitory* nsm 16/108, 16/
109 (twice); nsn 1/26, 16/108, 17/66; dsn
lænan 14/109, 14/138

læran 1 *teach, advise* inf 5/62, 9/65; pres 1s
lære 8/47; subj 3s lære 5/61; pret 3s lærde
8/3, 9/62, 12/311; p ptc læred 8/10

*ġe*læran 1 *teach, advise, urge* pres 1s gelære
3/210; p ptc npm gelærede 5/78, gelæred
9/12; superl apm gelæredestan *most learned*
9/51

*ġe*læredestan see *ġe*læran

lærig m. *rim of a shield* ns 12/284

læs adv. *less* 8/44, 11(k)/11; nōht þon læs
nevertheless 8/17; þȳ læs þe *lest* 2/7, 3/24,
4/120

læs f. *pasture* ds læswe 3/24, 3/30

læssa adj. (compar. of lȳtel; cf. §76) *less,
smaller* asm læssan 3/119; nsn læsse 3/98

læsst adj. (superl. of lȳtel; cf §76) adj. *least,
smallest* nsn læsste 8/33

læstan 1 w.d. *follow* inf 10(b)/27, 18(a)/812 (*do
service, avail*) [MnE last]

*ġe*læstan 1 *perform, carry out, continue* inf 12/
11; pret 3s gelæste 10(a)/9, 12/15; 3p
gelæstan 10(b)/13; p ptc gelæsted 18(a)/829

læswe see læs

lætan VII *let, allow* pres 1s læte 3/122; 2s lætst
3/124; 3s læteð 11(m)/10; pret 3s lēt (*cause,
w. verb of motion*) 12/7, 12/140; 3p lēton
12/108, 13/42, 18(a)/864; subj 3s lēte 10(b)/
66, 10(b)/68

lætst see lædan

læwede adj. *unlearned, lay* dsn læwedum 4/39
[MnE lewd]

*ġe*lēafa m. *belief, faith* as gelēafan 4/87; ds
4/42, 8/2, 8/77

lēan VI *blame, find fault with* pret 3p lōgon
18(a)/862

lēanian 2 w.d. *repay, reward* pres 1s lēanige
18(b)/1380, 3s lēanað 11(m)/9

lēas adj. (w.g.) *devoid of, without* nsm 18(a)/
850; nsn 15/32; npf lease 16/86 [MnE
(home)less, (bottom)less, etc.]

lēas adj. *false* nsm 4/121

lēasung f. *lying, fable, fiction* gs lēasunge 9/15

leax m. *salmon* ap leaxas 3/93 [MnE (through
Yiddish) lox]

lecgan 1 *lay* pres 3p lecgað 17/57; subj 3s
lecge 16/42

lēfdon see læfan

lēgbysig see līgbysig

Lēġeċeasterscir f. *Cheshire* ns 7/5

leġer n. *bed* ap 15/34

lencten m. *spring* ds lenctene 3/121 [MnE
lent]

leng see lange

lengest see lange

lengre see lange

lēod m. *man, member of a tribe or nation, prince*
ns 18(a)/829

lēode f. or m. pl. *people* np 18(d)/3156, 18(d)/
3178; ap lēoda 12/37, lēode 18(b)/1336,
18(b)/1345; gp lēoda 18(a)/793; dp lēodum
12/23, 12/50, 14/88, 15/6, 18(b)/1323,
18(d)/3182

lēodfruma m. *leader, lord* ns 15/8; ds lēodfruman 10(b)/27

lēodscipe m. *nation* as 10(b)/68

lēof adj. *beloved, dear, pleasant, agreeable* (*in
direct address*) *sir, sire* ns 2/21, 3/8, 3/18,
3/21, 3/23, 3/29, 4/3, lēofa 14/78, etc.; asm
lēofne 12/7, 12/208, 17/112 (as noun); gsm
lēofes 15/53 (as noun), 16/38; dsm lēofan
12/319; dsf lēofre 16/97; npm lēofan 9/109,
lēofe 15/34 (as noun); gpm lēofra 15/16 (as
noun), 16/31; compar. lēofre *more agreeable,
preferable* 3/102, 3/197, 10(b)/41; nsm lēofra
dearer 6/31; superl. lēofost *most pleasing,
most agreeable* nsm 12/23 [archaic MnE lief]

leofað see libban

leofede see libban

leofodon see libban

Lēofsunu pers. n. *Leofsunu* ns 12/244

lēoht n. *light* ns 18(a)/727; ds lēohte 11(f)/17,
14/5

lēohtliċ adj. *apparently easy, unimportant* dpn
lēohtlicum 4/76

leomu see lim

*ġe*lēoran IV *pass away* p ptc npm geleorene
13/7

leornere m. *scholar* ap leorneras 9/51 [MnE
learner]

leornian 2 *learn, study* inf leornigan 10(a)/18;
pret 3s leornade 9/13; 3p leornodon 9/70

*ġe*leornian 2 *learn* inf 9/67; pret 1s geliornode
5/70; 3s geleornode 9/5, geleornade 9/19;
3p geliornodon 5/49; p ptc geliornod 5/42,
geleornad 8/13

lēoð n. *song, poem, poetry* ns 9/69; as 9/19,
9/52, etc.; gs lēoþes 9/15; isn lēoðe 9/59; ap
lēoð 9/3, 9/11, 9/79

lēoðcræft m. *poetic art* as 9/13

leoþo see liþ

lēoþsong m. *song, poem, poetry* gs lēoþsonges
9/57; dp lēoþsongum 9/8

lēt see lætan

lēte see lætan

lēton see lætan

*ġe*lettan 1 *hinder, prevent* pret 3s gelette 12/
164

leðer m. *leather* ns 1/4

leþerhose f. *leather gaiter* ap leþerhosa
(*leggings*) 3/153

libban 3 *live* inf lybban 4/10, 4/22; pres ptc

npm lifgende 15/34, lifigende 18(a)/815, gp lifgendra 17/73; pres 3s lifað 18(d)/3167, leofað 18(b)/1366; 3p lifiaþ 14/134, leofað 17/102, 17/107; subj 1s lifge 11(e)/6; 3s 17/78; pret 3s leofede 4/33, lyfode 7/17; 1p lifdon 15/14; 3p leofodon 4/11, 4/22, lifdon 17/85

līc n. *body* ns 6/41; gs līces 14/63; ds līce 18(a)/733

ge līc adj. w.d. *like* np gelīce 2/11; dp gelīcum 8/38

ge līce adv. *like, similar to* 9/11; superl. gelīcost *just like, most like unto* nsn 18(a)/727

licgan V *lie, lie dead* inf 11(j)/10, 12/319; pres ptc licgende nsm 14/24; pres 3s līþ 6/41, 12/232, 12/314, ligeð 12/222, 18(b)/1343; 3p licgað 16/78; pret 3s læg 6/27, 12/157, 12/204, 12/227, leg 12/276, etc.; 3p lægon 6/21, lāgon 12/112, 12/183; subj 3s læge 12/279, 12/300

līchoma m. *body* ns 18(a)/812; ds līchaman 18(d)/3177

līchomlīc adj. *bodily* ds līchomlicre 9/88

līcian 2 *please* pres 3s līcaþ 1/32 [MnE like]

līcsār n. *bodily pain, wound* as 18(a)/815

lidmann m. *sailor, viking* np lidmen 12/99; gp lidmanna 12/164

ge līefan 1 *believe, trust in* pres 1s gelīefe 5/21, gelýfe 17/66; 3s gelýfeð (w. refl. d.) 17/27, 17/108

līf n. *life* ns 1/26, 2/73, 8/26, 8/34, etc.; as 7/25, 9/86, 9/118, etc.; gs lifes 1/33, 2/30, 2/39, 8/5, etc.; ds līfe 11(m)/9, 14/109, 14/138, 15/41

līfdagas m. pl. *life-days, life* ap 18(a)/793

lifdon see libban

ge līffæstan 1 *bring to life* pret 3s gelīffæste 4/61

lifge see libban

līfgedæl n. *parting from life, death* ns 18(a)/841

lifgende see libban

lifiaþ see libban

lifte see lyft

līg m. *flame, fire* gs līges 18(a)/781; ds ligge 18(a)/727

līgbysig adj. *beset by flames, flammable* nsm lēgbysig 11(o)/1

ligeð see licgan

līhtan 1 *alight, dismount* pret 3s līhte 12/23

lim n. *limb* ap leomu 9/26

līm m. *sticky material, birdlime* ds līme 3/110, 13/4 (*cement*)

limpan III (impers. w.d.) *befall, happen* pres 3s limpeð 17/13

ge limpan III *befall* pret 3s gelomp 10(a)/26; 3p gelumpon 7/73; p ptc gelumpen 18(a)/824

ge limplīc adj. *suitable* is gelimplicre 9/26

limwērig adj. *weary of limb, exhausted* asm limwērigne 14/63

lind f. *shield (of linden-wood)* as linde 12/244; ap 12/99

Lindesīg f. *Lindsey* ds Lindesīge 7/41

lindwīgend m. *warrior* np lindwigende 10(b)/13

līnen adj. *linen, made of flax* nsn 1/2

ge liornod see ge leornian

liornung f. *learning* as liornunga 5/11; ds 5/60

liss f. *kindness, joy* gp lissa 10(b)/59; dp lissum 11(m)/9

list f. *art, skill, cunning* ds liste 11(f)/4; dp listum 10(b)/59, 18(a)/781

lītel see lýtel

līþ see licgan

liþ n. *limb* ap leoþo 11(h)/7

līþe adj. *gentle, kind* superl līðost 18(d)/3182 [MnE lithe]

loc n. *enclosure, sheepfold* dp locum 3/26 [MnE lock]

lōcian 2 *look* pret 3s lōcude 6/14

lōcude see lōcian

lof n. *praise* ns 17/73, 17/78; as 9/122

lofgeorn adj. *eager for praise, eager for fame* superl lofgeornost nsm 18(d)/3182

ge lōgian 2 *place, put, arrange* pret 3s gelōgode 2/58

lōgon see lēan

ge lomp see ge limpan

lond see land

londbūend see landbūend

londstede m. *country* ds 15/16

ge long adj. *belonging to, dependent on* nsn 17/121, nsf 15/45, nsm gelang 18(a)/1376

longaþes see langoþ

longe see lange

longian 2 impers. w.a. *afflict with longing* pret 3s longade 15/14

longunge see langung

loppestre f. *lobster* ap loppestran 3/93

losian 2 *escape, be lost, perish* pres 3s losaþ 3/160 (*spoil, go bad*), 17/94, 18(b)/1392; 3p losiaþ 3/138 [MnE lose]

lūcan II *lock, join, enclose* pret 3p lucon 12/66

lufian 2 *love* inf lufigean 9/61; pres 2s lufast 2/45; pret 1p lufodon 5/25, 5/26

luflīce adv. *affectionately* 5/1 [obs MnE lovely]

lufu f. *love* ds lufan 9/81, 17/121; gp 10(b)/59

ge lumpon see ge limpan

Lunden f. *London* ds 7/36

Lundenbyriġ f. *London* ns 7/12 (see note); ds 7/28, 7/47

lust m. *desire* ns 17/36; dp lustum 4/117 [MnE lust]

lustbǣre adj. *desirable, pleasant* nsn 2/13

*ġe*lustfullīċe adv. *willingly* compar. gelustfullīcor 8/16
lustlīċe adv. *gladly, willingly* 3/118 [MnE
lust(i)ly]
lūtian 2 *skulk, lurk* inf 3/10
lybban see libban
*ġe*lȳfed adj. *advanced* gsf gelȳfdre 9/19
*ġe*lȳfeð see *ġe*līefan
lyfode see libban
lyft f. *air, sky* ns 11(d)/4, 18(b)/1375; ds lyfte
11(l)/4, lifte 11(f)/4; on lyft *in the air, aloft*
14/5
lȳsan 1 *release, redeem, ransom* inf 12/37, 14/41
*ġe*lysted adj. *desirous of* nsm 10(b)/9
lȳt adj. indecl. w.g. *few, little* 15/16, 16/31; as
adv. 17/27
lytegian 2 *use guile, deceive* inf 12/86
lȳtel adj. *little* as lȳtle 7/17; gs lītles 4/25; is
lȳtle 6/10; dp lītlum 4/75 (used substan-
tively: *little things*)
lȳtlian 2 *diminish, grow less* pres 3s lȳtlað 12/
313
lȳtling m. *child* np lȳtlingas 3/165 [MnE
dialect littling]

mā adj., noun, adv. *more* as (indeclinable
noun) 5/47, 18(a)/735; np 12/195; ap 4/20;
adv. 8/20, 15/4, þon mā þe *any more than*
6/35 [archaic MnE mo]
macian 2 *make* pres 1s macie 3/26
Maccus pers. n. *Maccus* ns 12/80
magan pret. pres. *be able, can, be competent*
pres 1s mæg 3/84, 3/102, etc.; 2s miht
3/205; 3s mæg 3/104, 3/154, 3/184, 4/75,
etc.; 1p magon 3/174, 5/57; 2p 3/162, 3/171;
3p 4/26; subj 1s mæge 3/85, 3/148; 2s 5/23;
1p mægen 5/56; 3p 5/60; pret 1s meahte
5/74, 14/18, mihte 14/37; 3s meahte 9/12,
9/15, etc., mihte 4/21, 7/55, etc.; 3p mihton
4/41, meahton 5/32, etc.; subj 3s meahte
9/57; 3p muhton 7/31 [MnE may]
māge f. *kinswoman* ns mēge 11(k)/4; gs māgan
18(b)/1391
magister m. *teacher* ns 4/13 [MnE master]
mago m. *young man, youth* ns 16/92
magon see magan
magorinc m. *warrior* gp magorinca 10(b)/26,
18(a)/730
maguþegn m. *young retainer* np maguþegnas
16/62
man see mann
man indefinite pron. *one, they* ns 3/98, 3/215,
4/21, 4/75, mon 5/61, etc.
*ġe*man see *ġe*munan
mān n. *crime* gs mānes 10(b)/44; ds māne
10(a)/10
mancess m. *mancus (a gold coin worth 30 silver
pence)* gp mancessa 5/76

mancynn n. *mankind* as 14/104, mancyn 14/
41; gs mancynnes 14/33, 14/99, monncynnes 9/42; ds mancynne 1/25
māndǣd f. *evil deed* gp māndǣda 9/82
māndrinc m. *evil drink, poison, deadly drink* as
11(h)/13
manega see maniġ
mangere m. *merchant* ns 3/131 [MnE
(fish)monger]
manian 2 *exhort, urge, admonish* inf 12/228;
pres 3s monað 17/36, 17/53; pret 3s
monade 9/62
*ġe*manian 2 *exhort, urge, remind* pres 3p
gemoniað 17/50; p ptc gemanode 12/231
maniġ adj., pron. *many, many a* (w.sg. noun)
nsm mænig 12/282; asm mænigne 12/188,
manigne 12/243; asn monig 10(b)/3; dsn
manegum 10(a)/10; np manega 4/20, 12/
200, manige 3/127, monige 5/17, 8/17,
11(b)/2, etc.; ap manige 3/130, 3/182; apn
monig 9/46, 9/79, mænigo 10(b)/29; gp
monigra 9/8; dpn manigum 3/99; dpf
manegum 14/99; gp manigra 14/41
maniġeo see menigu
maniġfeald adj. *manifold, various* nsf menigfeald 4/93; apf manigfealde 3/109, menigfealde 4/86; apm manigfealdan 10(a)/14;
dpm menigfealdum 4/83; dpf manig-
fealdum 5/66
*ġe*maniġfealdan 1 *multiply, increase* pres 1s
gemanigfealde 2/33, 2/74
manlīċe adv. *manfully, nobly* 1/15
mānlīċe adv. *wickedly* 1/15
mann m. *person, man* ns 3/33, 3/158, mon
5/77, etc.; as mann 1/21, mannan 4/68,
mon 9/12, monnan 15/18; gs mannes 4/74;
ds men 4/8, 9/62; np 4/22, 6/25, menn
5/44; ap men 9/81; gp manna 3/165, 4/63,
8/26, monna 5/58, 8/34, etc.; dp mannum
4/34, monnum 5/26, 9/12, 11(o)/8, etc.
mānscaða m. *wicked ravager, evil-doer* ns
18(a)/712, 18(a)/737, 18(b)/1339
mansliht m. *manslaughter, slaying* dp manslihtum 7/55
māra adj. (compar. of micel §76) *more, larger*
asm māran 3/119, 3/120, 7/50, 18(a)/753;
asn māre 2/73, 3/13, 3/17, 4/5, 4/45; dsn
māran 3/147; asf māran 8/17, 8/18
Maria pers. n. *Mary* as Marian 14/92
maðelian 2 *speak, make a speech* pret 3s
maðelode 12/42, 12/309, 18(b)/1321, 18(b)/
1383, maþelade 11(g)/5
māðm m. *treasure* as 11(n)/13; gp māðma
5/30; dp māðmum 17/99
māþþumgyfa m. *giver of treasure* ns 16/92
*ġe*mǣc adj. *suitable* asm gemæcne 15/18
mæcg m. *man* np mæcgas 11(m)/7
mæg m. *kinsman* ns 6/31, 12/5, 12/114, 12/

224, 12/287, 16/109, etc.; as 18(b)/1339; np
mǣgas 6/29, māgas 15/11; gp māga 16/51;
dp mǣgum 6/32

mǣg see magan

mǣgen n. *strength, power* ns 3/166, 12/313; gs
mǣgenes 8/14; ds mǣgene 11(f)/14, 18(a)/
789; is mǣgne 11(h)/13 [MnE (might and)
main]

mǣgenþise f. *force, violence* ds mǣgenþisan
11(f)/10

mǣgð f. *tribe, nation* ds mǣgðe 10(a)/1

mǣgð f. *maiden, woman* np mǣgeð 11(m)/7;
gp mǣgða 11(j)/8

mǣl n. *time, occasion* ap mǣla 12/212; gp
10(b)/54, 17/36

mǣlan 1 *speak* pret 3s mǣlde 12/26, 12/43,
12/210 [MnE (black)mail]

*ge*mǣlan 1 *speak* pret 3s gemǣlde 12/230, 12/
244

Mǣldūn m. *Maldon* ds Mǣldūne 7/21

mǣnan 1 *speak of, relate, bemoan* inf 18(d)/
3171; p ptc mǣned 18(a)/857

mǣnig see manig

mǣnige see menigu

mǣran 1 *make famous* p ptc gemǣred 9/2

mǣre adj. *famous, illustrious, glorious, notorious*
nsm 18(a)/762 (as noun), nsf 14/12, 14/82,
16/100; asm mǣran 10(b)/14; gsm mǣres
18(a)/797; np mǣre 4/26

mǣrsian 2 *proclaim, mark out* pres 3s mǣrsað
10(b)/16

mǣrðu f. *glorious thing, fame, glory* ns mǣrðo
18(a)/857; ap mǣrða 4/86; gp mǣrþa 17/84

mǣssepreost m. *mass-priest* ns 3/213, 4/13;
ds mǣsseprioste 5/71

mǣst adj. *most, greatest* asn mǣste 7/54; asf
mǣstan 9/6, mǣste 12/175

mǣst adv. *mostly* 7/4

mǣst n. *most, greatest* ns 12/223; as 7/75, 17/84

mǣstling m. *brass* as 3/142

*ge*mǣtan 1 (impers. w.d. of person) *dream*
pret 3s gemǣtte 14/2

mǣte adj. *small, limited* isn 14/69 (see note),
14/124

*ge*mǣtte see *ge*mētan

mǣð f. *propriety, fitness* ns 12/195

mǣðel n. *assembly* ds mǣðle 11(b)/2

mǣw m. *mew, seagull* as 17/22

mē see ič

meahte (n.) see miht

meahte (v.) see magan

meahtigra see mihtig

mearc f. *boundary, region, border* ap mearce
11(j)/6

mearcstapa m. *wanderer in the wasteland,
border-haunter* ap mearcstapan 18(b)/1348

mearg see mearh

mearh m. *horse* ns 18(c)/2264, mearg 16/92;

as mearh 12/188; ds mēare 12/239; ap
mēaras 18(a)/865; dp mēarum 18(a)/855
[MnE mare]

mec see ič

mēce m. *sword* as 12/167, 12/236

mēdan 1 *presume* (?) pres subj 3s mēde 11(n)/
15

medmičel adj. *moderate, brief* asn 9/117; ds
medmiclum 8/34, 9/5

medobenč f. *mead-bench* ns medubenc 18(a)/
776

medodrinc m. *mead* ds medodrince 17/22

mēge see māge

*ge*mealtan III *melt* pret 3s gemealt 18(a)/897

melcan III *milk* pres 1s melce 3/26

*ge*mengan 1 *mingle* p ptc gemenged 16/48,
18(a)/848

mengeo see menigu

menifealdlīce adv. *in the plural* 4/71 [MnE
manifoldly]

menigfeald see manigfeald

menigu f. *multitude* ns mengeo 5/31; ds
mǣnige 14/112, manigeo 14/151

menn see mann

menniscnis f. *incarnation* ds menniscnisse
4/29, menniscnesse 9/75 [MnE mannish-
ness]

meodo m. *mead* ds 12/212

meodoheall f. *mead-hall* ns 13/23; ds meoduhealle 16/27

meotod m. *creator* ns 17/108, meotud 17/116,
metod 18(a)/706, 12/175; gs Meotodes
9/37, metudes 16/2, meotudes 17/103; ds
metode 12/147

Merantūn m. *Merton* ds Merantūne 6/10

mere m. *pool, lake* ns 18(b)/1362; as 18(a)/845;
ds 18(a)/855 [MnE mer(maid)]

mereflōd m. *sea-tide, ocean* ds mereflōde 17/
59

merehengest m. *sea-horse* (*ship*) ns 11(j)/6

merewēriġ adj. *sea-weary* gs merewērges 17/
12 (as noun)

*ge*met n. *measure, metre* as 9/47; mid gemete
with moderation, in proper measure 11(m)/7,
17/111, 18(a)/779 (*in any wise*)

mētan 1 *meet, encounter* pret 1s mētte 8/44; 3s
18(a)/751; 3p mētton 6/26

*ge*mētan 1 *meet* pret 3s gemētte 18(a)/757,
gemǣtte 7/35

mete m. *food* ns 3/165; ds 3/80 [MnE meat]

*ge*metlīce adv. *moderately* 9/89

metod see meotod

metsung f. *provisions* as metsunge 7/60, 7/65

mētte see mētan

mētton see mētan

mēðe adj. *weary, tired* nsm 14/65, npm 14/69

meðelstede m. *meeting-place, assembly* ds
meþelstede 12/199

miccle adv. *much* 12/50

miċel adj. *great, large, much* nsm 1/18, 3/214; asm micelne 3/106, miclan 4/78; gsm miccles 12/217; dsm mycclum 7/34; ism micle 8/77, 14/34 (elne micle *with great zeal*), etc.; nsn 3/20, 3/21, 3/98, 4/17, etc.; asn 3/23, mycel 7/15, 7/36, 7/39, etc.; dsn miclum 3/137; isn micle 8/43; nsf 1/22, 3/214; asf 15/51; gsf micelre 9/85; dpn miclum 6/6 [MnE dialect mickel]. See *miccle, miclum*

miċel n. *much, a great part* as 3/18, 7/70, 7/72

miċelnes f. *size* ns 1/19

miclum adv. *greatly, severely* 6/15, 10(b)/74

mid prep. w.d.a.i. *with, amid, by means of* 2/47, 2/50, 2/79, 3/15, 4/24, etc.; as adv. *in attendance, at the same time* 14/106; mid þām þe *when* 2/60, 4/69; mid þȳ (þe) *when* 8/52, 9/97

midd adj. *middle, mid* dsf midre 14/2

middanġeard m. *world, middle earth* ns 16/62; as 9/42, 9/120, 14/104, 16/75, 17/90; gs middangeardes 9/71, 18(a)/751

middæġ m. *midday, noon* as 2/18

Middelseaxe m. pl. *Middlesex* ap Middelsexe 7/67

middeneaht f. *midnight* as 9/100

mid þām see mid

mid þȳ see mid

miht f. *power, might* as mihte 8/19, meahte 9/37, 17/108; ds mihte 14/102

miht (v.) see magan

mihte (n.) see miht

mihte (v.) see magan

mihtiġ adj. *mighty, powerful* nsm 14/151, 18(b)/1339; dsm mihtigan 18(b)/1398; compar. meahtigra nsm 17/116

mihton see magan

milde adj. *merciful, kind* nsm 4/121; nsm 12/175; superl. mildust nsm 18(d)/3181 [MnE mild]

mildheortnes f. *mercy, pity* as mildheortnisse 7/52

mil̇ġemearc n. *measure by miles* gs mīlgemearces 18(b)/1362

milts f. *mercy, favour, reverent joy* as miltse 16/2; ds 11(o)/8

min poss. adj. *my, mine* nsm 2/54, 2/55; asm mīnne 3/70, 3/76, etc.; gsm mīnes 3/11; dsm mīnum 3/27, 3/172; isn mīne gefræge *as I have heard tell* 18(a)/776, 18(a)/837; asn mīn 3/76, 3/135; nsf mīn 14/130; gsf mīnre 2/77; dsf 11(j)/18; npm mīne 9/109; apm 3/43, 3/103; dpm mīnum 3/135; npn mīn 3/138; apn 3/23, 3/135, 3/149

min (pron.) see iċ

mine 16/27 see note

misdæd f. *misdeed* np misdæda 4/74

misliċ adj. *various* ap mislice 4/90; dpf mislicum 5/66, 17/99

missenliċ adj. *various, manifold* gsn missenlices 3/153; npn missenlicu 3/63; apn 3/203

missenlīċe adv. *in various places* 16/75

misthliþ n. *misty hill, cover of darkness* dp misthleoþum 18(a)/710

mīþan 1 *conceal* pres ptc asm mīþendne 15/20

mōd n. *spirit, courage, mind* ns 10(b)/26, 12/313, 13/18, 16/15, 16/51, 18(a)/730; as 9/104, 15/20, 17/12, 17/108; gs mōdes 11(f)/14, 17/36, 17/50, 18(a)/810; ds mōde 5/39, 10(a)/27, 11(b)/2, 14/130, 16/41, 16/111, 17/109, 18(a)/753, 18(b)/1307; is 9/98, 9/119, 14/122; np 9/8 [MnE mood]

mōdceariġ adj. *troubled in thought* nsm 16/2

mōdcearu f. *grief of heart* as mōdceare 15/51; gs 15/40

mōdġeþanc m. *conception, purpose* as 9/37

mōdiġ adj. *brave, courageous* nsm 14/41, mōdi 12/147, mōdega 18(a)/813; npm mōdige 12/80, mōdge 16/62, 18(a)/855

mōdiġlīċe adv. *boldly, bravely* mōdelice 12/200 [MnE moodily]

mōdor f. *mother* ns 7/52, 11(k)/2; as 14/92

mōdsefa m. *heart, spirit* ns 10(b)/74, 14/124, 16/59, 17/59; as mōdsefan 16/10, 16/19

mōdwlonc adj. *proud of heart, spirited* nsm 17/39

molde f. *earth* ns 17/103; as moldan 14/12, 14/82

moldern n. *earth-house, sepulchre* as 14/65

ġemon see ġemunan

monade see manian

monaðˈ see manian

mōnað m. *month* ap mōnþas 7/17

mondrēam m. *joy of men, revelry, festivity* gp mondrēama 13/23

mondryhten m. *liege lord* as 16/41; ds mondryhtne 11(n)/13

ġemoniað see ġemanian

moniġ see maniġ

monn see mann

monnan see mann

monncynnes see manncynn

monðˈwǣre adj. *gentle, kind* superl. monðˈwǣrust nsm 18(d)/3181

mōr m. *moor, marsh, wasteland* ds mōre 18(a)/710; ap mōras 18(b)/1348

morgen m. *morning* as 18(a)/837; ds morgenne 3/31, 6/23, 9/48, 9/59 [MnE morn]

morþor n. *crime, murder* as 15/20; ds morðˈre 18(a)/892

mōste see mōtan

ġemōt n. *meeting, council, encounter* ns 12/301; as 12/199

mōtan pret. pres. *may, be allowed to* pres 2s mōst 12/30; subj 3s mōte 4/10, 12/95, 12/

177; 3p mōton 4/31; subj 3p mōten 17/119; mōton 12/180; pret 3s mōste 8/62, 18(a)/706, 18(a)/735; 3p mōston 12/83, 12/87; subj 3s mōste 10(b)/39, 10(b)/62; 3p mōstan 10(a)/8, mōsten 10(b)/36

moððe f. *moth* ns 11(c)/1

Moyses pers. n. *Moses* gs 4/12, 9/72, Moises 4/23

muhton see magan

ġemunan pret. pres. *remember* pres 1s geman 1/30, 14/28, gemunu 12/212; 3s gemon 15/51, 16/34, 16/90; pret 1s gemunde 5/28, 5/40, 12/225; 3s 10(a)/15, 10(a)/29, 10(b)/57, 10(b)/79, 18(a)/758, 18(a)/870; 3p gemundon 12/196

mundbyrd f. *protection, hope of protection* ns 14/130

mundgripe m. *hand-grip* as 18(a)/753

munt m. *mountain* dp muntum 10(a)/4 [MnE mount]

Muntġiop m. *the Alps* as 10(b)/8; ds 10(b)/14

munuc m. *monk* ns 3/179, 3/213, 4/2

munuchād m. *monastic orders* as 9/63 [MnE monkhood]

murnan III *mourn, care about* inf 12/259; pres subj. 3s murne 18(b)/1385; pret 3p murnon 12/96

mūð m. *mouth* as mūþan 18(a)/724; ds mūðe 7/40, 9/70

mycclan see miċel

myċel see miċel

ġemynd n. *mind, remembrance* as 5/3, 16/51; ds gemynde 9/46, 10(b)/54

ġemyndgian 2 *remember* pret 3s gemyndgade 9/67

ġemyndgian 2 adj. w.g. *mindful* nsm 16/6, 18(a)/868

mynster n. *church, monastery* as 9/64; ds mynstre 5/77, 9/1 [MnE (West)minster]

myntan 1 *intend, think* pret 3s mynte 18(a)/712, 18(a)/731, 18(a)/762

Myrce m. pl. *the Mercians* dp Myrcum 12/217

myre f. *mare* ds myran 8/63

myrðu f. *disturbance, trouble, affliction* gp myrðe 18(a)/810

nā adv. *no, by no means, not at all, never* 3/173, 4/5, 4/23, etc., nō 15/4, 16/54, etc.; nā þē læs *nevertheless* 7/76

nabbað see habban

naca m. *boat, ship* gs nacan 17/7

nacod adj. *naked* nsm 2/22, 2/23; asf nacedan (*bare, literal*) 4/45; np nacode 2/15

nāh see āgan

nāht see nānwuht

nalæs see nealles

nales see nealles

nam see niman

ġenam see ġeniman

nama m. *name* ns 1/31, 12/267, noma 11(h)/1; as naman 2/44, 11(n)/11; ds 4/122, 5/76, 14/113 (see note), noman 9/28; ap naman 1/30

ġenamon see ġeniman

nān (= ne ān) pron., adj. *none, not one, not any, no* nsm 3/10, 3/154, 3/177, etc.; asm nænne 4/114, 5/42; nsn nan 18(a)/803; asf nane 4/118; gsf nānre 10(a)/28

nānwuht pron. *nothing* as 5/32, nōht 9/15, 9/29, nāht 9/31

nāp see nīpan

nāteshwōn adv. *not at all* 2/8

nāwiht n. *nothing* ns nōwiht 8/42; as 8/14 [MnE naught]

nædl f. *needle* as nædle 3/195

nædre f. *snake, serpent* ns 2/1, 2/2, 2/27; ds nædran 2/28; as nædran 1/36 [MnE (a)n adder]

næfne see nefne

næfre adv. *never* 6/31, 9/15, 9/19, 9/35, etc.

næfð see habban

nægan 1 *accost, address* pret 3s nægde 18(b)/1318

nægl m. *nail* dp næglum 14/46

nænig pron. *none, no one* ns 6/20, 6/31, 8/15, 9/11, etc.; as 9/19

nænne see nān

næren (= ne wæren) see bēon

næs (= ne wæs) see bēon

næs adv. *by no means* 18(c)/2262

næss m. *headland, bluff* ap næssas 18(b)/1358; gp næssa 18(b)/1360

ġenæstan 1 *contend, grapple* pres 3s genæsteð 11(f)/10

ne adv., conj. *not, nor* 1/34, 2/3, 3/63, 3/84, 3/161 (ne . . . ne *nor*), 4/23, 4/24, etc.

nēah adv. *near, imminent* 9/96, 9/112, 15/25, 16/26, 18(a)/745, nēh 12/103 [MnE nigh]

ġeneahhe adv. *often, very, frequently* 16/56, 18(a)/783, genehe 12/269; superl. genehost 18(a)/794

neahte see niht

nēalēcan 1 *draw near* inf 9/22; pret 3s nēalēhte 8/67, nēalæcte 9/87

nealles adv. *not at all* nales 9/12, 16/32, nalæs 16/33, nealles (þæt) ān . . . ac *not only . . . but* 3/103, 3/130

nēan adv. *from near, near* 18(a)/839

nearo adj. *narrow, close, anxious* nsf 17/7

nearolīċe adv. *densely* 4/98 [MnE narrowly]

nearones f. *distress, strait* ds nearanessa 10(a)/26 [MnE narrowness]

nearon see bēon

nēat n. *cattle, neat* gp nēata 9/25

ġenēat m. *mounted retainer, follower* ns 12/310

nēawest f. *neighbourhood* ds nēaweste 9/90

nefa m. *nephew* ns 11(a)/6; ds nefan 18(a)/881
nefne conj. *except, but* 17/46, næfne 18(b)/
1353. See nemne
nēh see nēah
*ge*nehe see *ge*neahhe
*ge*nehost see *ge*neahhe
nele (= ne wile) see willan
nellað (= ne willað) see willan
nemnan 1 *call, name* pret 3s nemnde 9/28; 3p
nemdon 18(b)/1354; p ptc genemned 5/68,
nemned 8/73
nemne conj. *except* 15/22. See næfne
nemðe see nymþe
nēodlaðu f. *desire* dp nēodlaðum 18(b)/1320
nēodlīċe adv. *diligently* compar. nēodlīcor
8/15
neom (= ne eom) see bēon
neorxenawang m. *Paradise* gs neorxena-
wanges 2/19; ds neorxenawange 2/6, 2/18,
2/21
nēotan II w.g. *use, make use of* inf 12/308
neowol adj. *prostrate* nsm 10(b)/80, niwol
10(a)/29
*ge*nerian 1 *save, protect* pret 3s generede 6/39;
p ptc genered 18(a)/827
nese adv. *no* 3/53
nēten see nīeten
nett n. *net* as 3/76; ap 3/42, 3/44; dp nettum
3/45, 3/46, 3/109, etc.
*ge*nēþan 1 *venture (on)* pret 3s genēðde 18(a)/
888
niċ adv. *no, not I* 3/96, 3/146
nicor m. *sea-monster* gp nicera 18(a)/845
nīedbehēfe adj. *necessary* nsm 3/151, 3/173
nīedbeðearf adj. *necessary, essential* superl. npf
nīedbeðearfosta 5/55
nīehst adv. *next, last* æt nyxtan *at last, at length*
7/57
nīeten n. *beast, cattle* ns nēten 9/67; np
nietenu 2/1; ds nytene 4/94
niht f. *night* ns 1/24, 18(b)/1320; as 3/30, 7/33
(on niht *by night*), 18(a)/736; gs neahte 9/93;
ds nihte 2/46, 7/32, 14/2, neahte 9/25, niht
18(a)/702, 18(b)/1334; gp nihta 18(b)/1365
nihthelm m. *cover of night* as 16/96
nihtscūa m. *shadow of night* ns 16/104, 17/31
nihtwaco f. *night-watch* ns 17/7
nihtweorc n. *night-work* ds nihtweorce 18(a)/
827
niman IV *take* inf 12/39, 12/252, 15/15; imp s
nim 2/44; pres 1s nime 3/78, 3/80, 3/122; 3p
nimað 17/48; pret 3s nam 4/18, 7/75, nom
8/64, etc.; 3p naman 7/57, namon 7/62; p
ptc genumen 2/41, 7/40
*ge*niman IV *take, seize* pret 3s genam 2/13; 3p
genamon 7/37, 14/30, 14/60; subj 3s
gename 12/71; p ptc genumen nsm 18(d)/
3165

*ge*nip n. *darkness, mist* ap genipu 18(b)/1360
nīpan I *grow dark* pres 3s nīpeð 16/104; pret 3s
nāp 17/31
*ge*nīpan I *grow dark* pret 3s genāp 16/96
nis (= ne is) see bēon
nīþ m. *hatred, malice, trouble, affliction* as 17/75;
ds nīðe 18(a)/827; gp nīða 18(a)/845, 18(a)/
882
niþer adv. *downwards* 10(b)/80, 18(b)/1360
[MnE nether]
nīðhedig adj. *hostile* npm nīðhedige 18(d)/
3165
nīðwundor n. *fearful wonder, portent* as 18(b)/
1365
*ge*nīwad see nīwian
nīwan adv. *newly* 8/22
nīwe adj. *new* nsm 18(a)/783, nsf 4/28, 8/10;
dsf nīwan 4/10, 4/18
nīwes adv. *recently* 15/4
nīwian 2 *restore, renew* p ptc genīwad nsm 14/
148, 16/50, 16/55, genīwod 18(b)/1322
niwol see neowol
nō see nā
*ge*nōg adj. *enough* npm genōge 14/33 (*many*)
nōht adv. *not, not at all* 5/17, 8/72, nāwiht
8/14; nōht þon læs *nevertheless* 8/17
nōht see nānwuht
nōhwæðer conj. *neither* 5/25 (nōhwæðer ne
. . . ne *neither . . . nor*)
nolde (= ne wolde) see willan
noldest (= ne woldest) see willan
noldon (= ne woldon) see willan
nom see niman
noman see nama
norð adv. *northwards* 18(a)/858
norðan adv. *from the north* 16/104, 17/31
Norðdene m. pl. *the Danes* dp Norðdenum
18(a)/783
Norðhymbre m. pl. *Northumbria* dp
Norðhymbran 7/42, Norðhymbron 12/266
norðsciphere m. *northern fleet, attack fleet of the
Northmen* ds norðscipherige 7/6
nosþyrl n. *nostril* ap nosþirlu 4/111
notian 2 w.g. *use, enjoy* pres 3s notaþ 3/202
notu f. *employment* ds note 5/60
nōwiht see nāwiht
nū adv., conj. *now that, now* adv. 2/64, 2/74,
etc.; conj. 2/64 (nū . . . nū *now . . . now that*),
2/72, 12/57, etc.
*ge*numen see niman
nȳdgestealla m. *comrade in battle* np nȳdgesteallan 18(a)/882
nyle (= ne wyle) see willan
nymþe conj. *unless, except* 11(h)/16, 18(a)/781,
nemþe 16/113
nyste (= ne wyste) see witan
nytene see nieten
nytnisse see nyttnes

nytt adj. *useful* nsm 3/132, 3/151; npm nytte 3/115; apm 3/179, 18(a)/794; npn nyt 11(n)/11

nytt f. *use, utility* ds nytte 3/150, 11(m)/2

nyttnes f. *usefulness, benefit* gs nyttnesse 8/14, nytnisse 8/48

nȳxtan see nīehst

Odda pers. n. *Odda* rs Oddan 12/186, 12/198
of prep. w.d. *from* 2/3, 2/14, 2/25, 3/33 (*of*), 4/3, etc.

ofdūne adv. *down* 10(a)/27, 10(b)/80

ofer prep. w.d.a. *over, after* 1/2, 1/5, 2/2, 2/18, 2/64, 3/24, etc.; ofer bæc see bæc

ōfer m. *bank of a river* ds ōfre 12/28, 18(b)/1371

ofercuman IV *overcome* p ptc ofercumen 18(a)/845

oferfēng see oferfōn

oferfōn VII *seize* pret 3s oferfēng 10(b)/69

ofergān anom. (§128) *overrun* p ptc ofergān 7/66 [MnE overgo]

oferhelmian 2 *overhang, overshadow* pres 3s oferhelmað 18(b)/1364

ofermōd n. *pride, arrogance, overconfidence* ds ofermōde 12/89

Offa pers. n. *Offa* ns 12/198, 12/230, 12/286, 12/288; gs Offan 12/5

offrian 2 *offer* inf 4/89; pret 3s offrode 4/93

ġeoffrian 2 *sacrifice, offer up* pret subj 3s geoffrode 2/60; p ptc geoffrod 4/97

offrung f. *offering, sacrifice* ns 2/54; as offrunge 2/56; ds 2/69

ofġiefan V *abandon* pret 3s ofgeaf 18(c)/2251; 3p ofgēafon 16/61; p ptc ofġēafon 11(k)/1

oflongian 2 *seize with longing* p ptc oflongad 15/29

ofscēotan II *shoot, kill with a missile* pret 3s ofscēat 12/77

ofslæġen see ofslēan

ofslēan VI *slay, destroy* inf 2/65, 3/102, 10(a)/10; infl inf (tō) ofslēanne 2/49; pres 1s ofslēa 3/45, pret 3s ofslōg 6/3, ofslōh 7/35; 3p ofslōgon 6/37, 7/36; p ptc ofslagen 2/59, 7/15, ofslæġen 6/24, 6/27, 7/21, ofslegen 7/4, asm ofslægenne 6/16

ofslegen see ofslēan

ofslōg see ofslēan

ofsnāð see ofsnīðan

ofsnīðan I *slaughter* pret 3s ofsnāð 2/68

ofspring m. *offspring* ns 2/75; as 2/74; ds ofspringe 2/31

ofstang see ofstingan

ofstician 2 *stab to death* pret 1s ofsticode 3/58, 3/61; 2s ofsticodost 3/59

ofstingan III *stab to death* pret 3s ofstang 6/5

ofstlīċe adv. *quickly* 12/143

ofstondan VI *remain standing* p ptc ofstonden 13/11

oft adv. *often* 5/2, 6/6, etc.; compar. oftor 14/128; superl. oftost 5/22

on adv. *on, onward* 8/61

on prep. w.d.a. *on, onto, upon, in, into* w.d. (*on, in*) 1/9, 1/11, 1/29, 2/4, 2/9, 2/17, 2/21, 3/26 (*during*), 6/17 (*from*), etc.; w.a. (*onto, upon, into*) 3/44, 3/76, 3/122, 6/15 (*against*), etc.

onarn see onirnan

onblēan 1 *kindle* p ptc onblōud 8/29 [archaic MnE anneal]

onbærnan 1 *kindle, inspire* p ptc onbærnde 9/9, onbærned 9/85

onbreġdan III *swing open* pret 3s onbræd 18(a)/723

onbūgan II *bend* pres 1s onbuge 11(h)/3

onbyrigan 1 w.g. *taste* inf 14/114

oncierran 1 *turn* inf oncerran 10(b)/61; pres 3s oncyrreð (w. refl.: *change direction, turn aside*) 17/103

oncnāwan VII *recognize, perceive, acknowledge* inf 12/9; pret 1s oncnēow 2/64; 3p oncnēowon 2/15

oncnēow see oncnāwan

oncnēowon see oncnāwan

oncweðan V. w.d. *answer* pret 3s oncwæð 12/245, 17/23

oncyrreð see oncierran

oncȳðð f. *grief, distress* as oncȳþðe 18(a)/830

ond see and

ondette see andettan

ondrǣdan VII *be afraid, dread* pres 1s ondrǣde 4/9; 2s ondrǣtst 2/64; 3s ondrǣdeþ 17/106; pret 1s ondrēd (w. refl.) 2/22

ondrēd see ondrǣdan

ondswarodon see andswarian

ondsworede see andswarian

ondweard adj. *present* dp ondweardum 9/51

onemn prep. w.d.a. *alongside* 12/184

ōnettan 1 *hasten on, be active* pres 3s ōnetteð 17/49

onfēng see onfōn

onfēngon see onfōn

onfindan III *discover, realize* pres 3s onfindeð 11(f)/9; pret 3s onfunde 12/5, 18(a)/750, 18(a)/809; 3p onfundon 6/17; subj 3p onfunden 6/11

onfōn VII w.d.a. *receive, accept, take up* inf 8/2, 8/51; pres subj pl 8/23; pret 1s onfēng 8/59; 3s 8/76, 9/14, etc.; 3p onfēngon 8/18; subj 3s onfēnge 9/63; p ptc onfongne 9/58

onga m. *arrow, dart* ns 11(h)/4

ongan see onġinnan

onġēan adv., prep. w.d. *again, against* 2/32, 3/25, 11(f)/9, 12/49, 12/100, 12/137, 12/156, 18(a)/747

ongēanstandan VI *stand opposite, withstand* pret 1s ongēanstōd 3/60 onġeat see onġietan

Ongelþēod f. *the English people, England* ds Ongelþēode 9/10

onġemang prep. w.d. *among* 5/66

onġeocian 2 *unyoke* pres 3s ongeocaþ 3/29

onġietan V *understand, perceive* inf 5/32, 16/73, ongytan 14/18; pret 1s ongeat 8/42; 3s 6/13, 10(a)/14, 10(a)/24, 10(b)/68; 3p ongēaton 12/84

onġinnan III *begin* pres 3p onginð 4/50; subj 3p onginnen 14/116; pret 1s ongan 5/66; 3s 9/61, 10(a)/17, 10(a)/30, 12/12, 12/17, 12/89, 12/91, ongon 11(k)/3, angan 10(b)/59, etc.; 3p ongunnon 9/11, 12/86, 12/261, 14/65, 14/67, 15/11

ongon see onġinnan

ongunnon see onġinnan

ongyrwan 1 *unclothe, strip* pret 3s ongyrede 14/39

onġytan see onġietan

onġytenes f. *knowledge* gs ongytenesse 8/69

onhæbbe see onhebban

onhebban VI *raise up, exalt* pres 1s (w. refl.) onhæbbe 11(o)/7

onhnīgan I *bend, bow down* pres 3p onhnīgað 11(o)/7

onhrēran 1 *stir, move* inf 17/96

onhweorfan II, 3 *change* p ptc onhworfen 15/23; eft onhwyrfed *turned around, backwards* 11(h)/1

onhworfen see onhweorfan

onhwyrfed see onhweorfan

onhyldan 1 *lower, incline* pret 3s onhylde 9/116

onirnan III *give way, spring open* pret 3s onarn 18(a)/721

onlīcnes f. *image* ns onlīcnes 18(b)/1351. See ānlīcnes

onlūtan II *bow, incline, bend down* inf 5/39

onlȳsan 1 *liberate, redeem* pret 3s onlȳsde 14/147

onmēdla m. *pomp, magnificence* np onmēdlan 17/81

onmiddan prep. w.d. *in the middle of* 2/5, 2/19 [MnE amid]

onmunan pret. pres. w.g. *pay attention to* pret subj 3p onmunden 6/35

onmunden see onmunan

ono hwæt interj. *lo and behold!* 8/49

onsendan 1 *send, send forth* inf 5/75; pres 3s onsendeð 16/104; p ptc onsended 14/49, 18(c)/2266

onslēpan 1 *fall asleep* pret 3s onslēpte 9/26, 9/117

onspringan III *spring asunder* pret 3p onsprungon 18(a)/817

onstal m. *supply* as 5/20

onstellan 1 *institute, set the example for, estab-*

lish pret 3s onstealde 9/39; 3p onstealdon 7/43

onsȳn f. *appearance, face* ns 17/91

ontendan 1 *kindle, burn* inf 7/50

onwæcnan VI *awaken* pres 3s onwæcneð 16/45

onweald m. *authority, power, jurisdiction, command* as onwald 5/5, anwald 10(a)/4, 10(b)/62; ds onwealde 2/35, anwealde 10(a)/20

onweġ adv. *away* 16/53

onwendan 1 *change* pres 3s onwendeð 16/107; pret 3s onwende 13/24

onwrēon 1 *reveal, disclose* imper. 2s onwrēoh 14/97

open adj. *open* npm opene 14/47

openian 2 *open* p ptc npn geopenode 2/15

openlīċe adv. *openly* 8/45, 8/49

ġe openode see openian

ōr n. *beginning* as 9/39

ord m. *point, spear, vanguard* ns 12/60, 12/69, 12/146, 12/157, etc.; as 12/47, 12/110; ds orde 12/124, 12/226, 12/273

orf n. *cattle, livestock* as 4/92

orlege n. *war, battle, strife* ds orlege 18(b)/1326

ormōd adj. *despondent, sad* nsm 10(a)/30, 10(b)/78

orþonc m. *skill, intelligence* ns 13/16

Ōsrīċ pers. n. *Osric* ns 6/25

Ōswold pers. n. *Oswold* ns 12/304

oð prep. w.a. *up to, as far as, until* 4/7, 4/96, 5/61, etc.; conj. *until* 6/3, oþ þæt *until* 3/43, 4/33, etc.

oðberan IV *carry away* pret 3s oþbær 16/81

ōðer adj., pron. *other, another, next* nsm 4/6, etc.; asm ōþerne 12/143; dsm ōþrum 3/208, 12/133, 18(a)/814; dsn 13/10; gsn ōðres 9/111; asf ōðre 9/84; ōþre . . . ōþre *one . . . the other* 8/31; apm ōþre 3/87, 3/130, 3/180; gpm ōþerra 3/94, 8/57; dpm ōðrum 5/26; npn ōðre 2/1; apn ōðer 9/79; gpn ōþerra 3/143; dpn ōðrum 10(a)/10; npf ōðra 5/52; apf ōðre 5/50; ōðer twēga *one of two things* 12/207

oðfæstan 1 *set (to a task)* p ptc np oðfæste 5/60

oðfeallan VII *fall away, decline* p ptc oðfeallan 5/45; nsf oðfeallenu 5/14

ōðre see ōðer

oþþe conj. *or* 1/15, 3/13, 3/69, 3/77, 3/104, 4/9, etc.

oðþringan III *wrest away* pres 3s oðþringeð 17/71

ōwiht pron. *anything* nsn 15/23; as 8/36, 17/46

oxa m. *ox* ap oxan 3/9, 3/11, 3/29; gp oxena 3/18

oxanhierde m. *oxherd* ns 3/28; np oxanhierdas 3/4

Oxenafordscīr f. *Oxfordshire* as Oxenafordscīre 7/67

pāpa m. *pope* as pāpan 10(a)/11, 10(b)/42
Pante f. *the river Blackwater in Essex* as Pantan 12/68, 12/97
Paradīsus m. *Paradise* as Paradīsum 2/3, 2/5
Paulīnus pers. n. *Paulinus* as 8/39
pæll m. *purple garment, silk robe* ap pællas 3/141 [MnE pall]
pæð m. *path* as 1/6
Petroces stōw f. *Padstow (Cornwall)* ns 7/7
Pētrus pers. n. *Peter* ns 4/32, 4/33; as Pētrum 4/35; ds Pētre 4/31
pleoh n. *danger, risk* ns 3/98, 4/124; ds plēo 3/138
plēolič adj. *dangerous* nsn 4/8
Portland n. *Portland (Dorset)* ds Portlande 7/11
prasse m. *array, military force* ds prasse 12/68
prēost m. *priest* np prēostas 4/25, 4/38
pund n. *pound* gp punda 7/24, 7/63

rā m. *roebuck* ap rān 3/51 [MnE roe]
rād see rīdan
ġerād adj. *skilful, apt* asn gerāde 18(a)/873
ramm m. *ram* as 2/66
ran see irnan
rān see rā
rand m. *shield-boss, shield* ap randas 12/20
randhæbbend m. *shield-bearer, warrior* gp rondhæbbendra 18(a)/861
raðe see hraðe
ræčan 1 *reach (out)* pret 3s ræhte 18(a)/747
ġeræčan 1 *touch, reach, wound* pret 3s geræhte 12/142, 12/158, 12/226
ræd m. *advice* ns 18(b)/1376; as 3/210, 7/24
rædan 1 *read* inf 4/9; infl inf (tō) rædenne 4/105; pres 3s ræt 4/9; *instruct, give council, rule* inf 10(b)/67; pret 3p rædde 12/18
ġerædan 1 *advise* pres 2s gerædest 12/36; pret 3s gerædde 7/22, 7/24, 7/27, 7/59
rædbora m. *advisor* ns 18(b)/1325; as rædboran 4/114
Rædgōd pers. n. *Radagaisus* ns Rædgōt 10(b)/19, Rædgōta 10(a)/2; as 10(b)/7
ġerædu n. pl. *harness, trappings* ap 3/153; dp gerædum 12/190
ræghār adj. *grey with lichen* nsm 13/10
ræhte see ræčan
ġeræhte see ġeræčan
ræran 1 *lift up, offer up* inf 9/113; pret 3s rærde 11(n)/6 *(raised)* [MnE rear]
ræsan 1 *rush* pret 3s ræsde 6/15
ræste see rest
ræt see rædan
rēadfāh adj. *stained with red* nsm 13/10
rēaf n. *garment, raiment* as 3/141, 12/161 *(armour)*
reččan 1 *care about, care* pres 1p recce 3/173; pret 3p rōhton 12/260 [archaic MnE reck]

reččan 1 *explain, relate* pret 3p rehton 9/55
ġereččan 1 *wield, control* 3p gerehton 10(a)/4
reččelēas adj. *negligent, careless* npm reccelēase 5/45 [MnE reckless]
reced m. *building, hall* ns 18(a)/770; gs recedes 18(a)/724; ds recede 18(a)/720, 18(a)/728
ġerecednis f. *narrative* as gerecednisse 4/46; ds 4/47
recene adv. *quickly* 10(b)/34, rīcene 12/93, rycene 16/112
ġereġnad adj. *ornamented, decorated* nsm 18(a)/777; asn gerēnod 12/161
regollic adj. *regular, according to (monastic) rule* dpm regollecum 9/83
rehton see reččan
ġerēnod see ġereġnad
renweard m. *guardian of the house* np renweardas 18(a)/770
reord f. *voice* ds reorde 17/53
ġereord n. *speech, voice* dp gereordum 11(j)/16
reordberend m. *speech-bearer, man* np 14/3; dp reordberendum 14/89
rēotan II *weep* pres 3p rēotað 18(b)/1376
rest f. *rest, resting place* as reste 9/98, 14/3; ds 9/26, ræste 18(a)/747
restan 1 *rest, lie, remain* pres 1s reste (w. refl.) 11(e)/5; pret 3s reste 14/64 (w. refl.), 14/69
ġerestan 1 *rest* inf 9/95, 15/40
rēþe adj. *fierce, cruel, furious* npm 18(a)/770
rēwett n. *rowing* ns 3/90
rīce n. *kingdom, reign* ns 10(b)/5; as 3/190, 6/7, 7/63, 10(a)/3, 10(a)/18, 13/10, 14/119, etc.; gs rīces 6/1, 6/29, 8/78, 13/37, 17/81, 18(a)/861, 18(b)/1390; ds rīce 5/19, 5/75, 10(a)/1, 10(a)/5, 10(b)/7, 16/106 [MnE (bishop)ric, German Reich]
rīce adj. *powerful, great* asm rīcne 14/44; gp rīcra 10(b)/46 (as noun), 14/131; superl. rīcost *most powerful, noblest, richest* nsm 12/36
ricene see recene
rīcost see rīce
ricsian 2 *reign* pret 3s rīcsode 6/41
rīdan I *ride* inf 8/63, 12/291, 18(a)/855; pres ptc rīdende 2/48; pret 3p rād 12/18, 12/239; 3p ridon 6/24, 7/57, riodan 18(d)/3169
rīdende see rīdan
ridon see rīdan
riht adj. *fitting, right* nsn 12/190; asm rihtne 14/89; dsn ryhte 11(m)/7
riht n. *justice, right* gsm rihtes 10(b)/67
ġerihtan 1 *correct* inf 4/126; pres subj 3s gerihte 4/122; p ptc geriht nsf 14/131 *(directed)* [MnE right]
rihte adv. *properly, correctly* 12/20
rihtġelēaffull adj. *orthodox* gpm ryhtgelēaffulra 10(a)/19
rihtwīs adj. *righteous, upright* nsm 10(b)/49;

rihtwīs (*cont.*)
  gpm rihtwīsra 10(a)/19; superl. rihtwīsesta 10(a)/14
rīnan 1 *rain* pres subj 3s rīne 8/29
rinc m. *man, warrior* ns 10(b)/49, 11(p)/2, 18(a)/720; as 18(a)/741, 18(a)/747; ap rincas 11(j)/16; gp rinca 18(a)/728; dp rincum 12/18
rinnan see irnan
riodan see rīdan
*ge*risenlič adj. *suitable, proper, honourable* apn gerisenlice 9/3; compar. as gerisenlicre 8/36
*ge*risenlīče adv. *fittingly* compar. gerisenlecor 8/57
rōd f. *rood, cross* ns 14/44, 14/136; as rōde 14/119; gs 11(n)/5; ds 14/56, 14/131 [MnE rood]
rōdetācn n. *sign of the cross* ds rōdetācne 9/116 [MnE rood token]
rodor m. *sky, heaven* np roderas 18(b)/1376; dp roderum 11(n)/5
rōhton see reččan
Rōm f. *Rome* ns 10(b)/19; ds Rōme 10(b)/46
Rōmana pl. *Romans* gp 10(a)/1, 10(b)/17, Rōmane 10(a)/3; dp Rōmanum 10(a)/7
Rōmanisc adj. *Roman* dp Rōmaniscum 10(a)/15
Rōmwara pl. *Romans* gp 10(b)/34; dp Rōmwarum 10(b)/49, 10(b)/67
rondhæbbendra see randhæbbend
rōtlīče adv. *cheerfully* 9/102
rōwan VII *row* pres 1s rōwe 3/76
rūn f. *consultation, secret meditation* ds rūne 16/111
rūnwita m. *confident, trusted counsellor* ns 18(b)/1325
rycene see recene
ryhte see riht
ryhtfæderencyn n. *direct paternal ancestry* ns 6/42
rȳman 1 *extend* pret 3p rȳmdon 5/8
*ge*rȳman 1 *open (a way)* pret 1s gerȳmde 14/89; p ptc gerȳmed 10(b)/19, 12/93 (ēow is gerȳmed *passage is granted to you*)
rȳpan 1 *plunder* pret 3p rȳpton 7/78

saga see secgan
same see swā
samed see samod
samod adv. *too, at the same time* 2/47, 18(a)/729, samed 11(l)/2, somod 16/39; prep w.d. *simultaneously with* 18(b)/1311
sanct m. *saint* gs sancte 7/7, 7/48
sandčēosol m. *sand, grains of sand* as 2/75
sang see singan
sang see song

sār n. *pain, wound* as 17/95, 18(a)/787
sār adj. *sore, painful, grievous* npf sāre 16/50; gp sārra 14/80
sāre adv. *sorely, grievously* 14/59
sārlič adj. *painful, sad* nsn 18(a)/842
sārnes f. *pain* ds sārnesse 2/34 [MnE soreness]
*ge*sawen see *ge*sēon
sāwol f. *soul* ns 1/33, sāwul 12/177, sāwl 14/120; as sāwle 18(a)/801, 18(a)/852; ds 17/100
sǣ f. and m. *sea* as 16/4, 17/14, 17/18; ds 1/28, 2/75, 3/89, 3/91; dp sǣm 18(a)/858
sǣbāt m. *sea-boat, ship* as 18(a)/895
sǣd n. *seed, offspring* ds sǣde 2/76
sǣde see secgan
sǣfōr f. *sea-voyage* ds sǣfōre 17/42
sǣgan 1 *lay low, slay* p ptc gesǣged 18(a)/884
*ge*sǣgd see secgan
sǣgde see secgan
*ge*sǣġde see secgan
sǣl m. or f. *time, occasion* ns 14/80; *happiness, joy* dp sǣlum 18(b)/1322
sǣl n. *hall* as 18(c)/2264
sǣlan 1 *bind, fasten* inf 16/21
*ge*sǣlan 1 *befall, chance, turn out favourably* pret 3s gesǣlde 18(a)/890
sǣlida m. *sailor, viking* ns 12/45; as sǣlidan 12/286
*ge*sǣliġlič adj. *blessed, happy* npf gesǣliglica 5/4
sǣmann m. *sailor, viking* np sǣmen 12/29; dp sǣmannum 12/38, 12/278
sǣrima m. *coast* ds sǣriman 7/8, 7/23, 7/56 [MnE sea rim]
sǣrinc m. *sea-going warrior, viking* ns 12/134
sǣstrēam m. *ocean current* dp sǣstrēamum 10(b)/15
sǣt see sittan
scān see scīnan
scand f. *shame, disgrace* ns 3/215
sceacan VI *flee, hasten away* pret 3s scēoc 7/33, 18(c)/2254 [MnE shake]
scead n. *shade* ap sceadu 18(a)/707
scēadan VII *part* pres 3s scēadeð 13/30
sceadu f. *shadow, shade, darkness* ns 1/24, 14/54
sceadugenga m. *walker in darkness* ns 18(a)/703
scēaf see scūfan
sceaft m. *staff, shaft* ns 12/136; ds sceafte (*staff*) 10(b)/11
*ge*sceaft f. *creation, creature* ns 14/12, 14/55, 14/82, 16/107 (wyrda gesceaft *ordained course of events*); as gesceafta 4/54; ap 4/63
sceal see sculan
scealc m. *man, warrior* np scealcas 12/181
scēap n. *sheep* ap 3/24
*ge*sceap n. *creation* ds gesceape 9/71; np gesceapu 11(k)/7 (*destiny, fate*)

*ġe*sceapþēote f. *appointed channel* dp gesceapþēotan 11(g)/4
sceapen see scieppan
*ġe*sceapenis f. *creation* ds gesceapenisse 4/50
scēaphierde m. *shepherd* ns 3/22; np scēaphierdas 3/4
scear n. *ploughshare* as 3/12, 3/193
sceard adj. *cut, mutilated, chipped* npf scearde 13/5
sceat m. *surface, region* ap scēatas 14/37, 17/61, 17/105; ds scēate 11(k)/7 (*fold, bosom*); gp scēata 18(a)/752; dp scēatum 14/8, 14/43
scēat see scēotan
sceatt m. *money, payment* as 3/106; dp sceattum 12/40, 12/56 [MnE (through Old Norse) scot(free)]
scēawian 2 *see, behold, look at* inf 18(a)/840, scēawigan 18(b)/1391; pret 1s scēawode 14/137; 3s 18(a)/843
sceld see scield
scēoc see sceacan
sceolde see sculan
sceole see sculan
scēop see scieppan
scēotan II *thrust, shoot, throw* inf 11(g)/4; pret 3s scēat 8/68, 12/143, 12/270 [MnE shoot]
scēote f. *trout* ap scēotan 3/87 [MnE shoat]
scēotend m. *warrior, bowman* np 10(b)/11, 18(a)/703
scēð f. *sheath* ds scēðe 12/162
sceððan VI *injure* inf 14/47 [MnE (through Old Norse) scathe]
scield m. *shield* ds scylde 12/136; ap sceldas 10(b)/2, scyldas 12/98
sciellfisc m. *shellfish* as 1/5
scieppan VI *create* pret 3s scēop 9/40, scōp 11(e)/2; p ptc sceapen 11(h)/2 [MnE shape]
*ġe*scieppan VI *create* pret 3s gescēop 4/51, 4/110, gescōp 11(h)/6
scieppend m. *creator* ns Scyppend 9/42, 16/85; gs Scyppendes 9/34, 9/122
scieran IV *rend, tear* p ptc npf scorene 13/5 [MnE shear]
scile see sculan
scīma m. *light, radiance* as scīman 14/54
scīnan I *shine* inf 14/15; pres 3s scīnþ 1/23, scīneð 8/45; pret 3s scān 13/15, 13/34
scinþ see scīnan
scip n. *ship* as 1/5, 3/135, 7/37; gs scipes 18(a)/896; ds scype 12/40, 12/56; np scypu 7/10; ap scipu 1/28, 3/203, 7/28; dp scipum 3/100, 7/48
scipen n. *shed* ds scipene 9/25
sciphere m. *fleet, attack squadron* ds scipherige 7/3
scīr adj. *gleaming, resplendent* nsm 10(b)/11,

asn 12/98; asm scīrne 14/54; apm scīre 11(g)/4 [MnE sheer]
Sciððia f. *Scythia* ds Sciððiu 10(a)/1, Sciððia 10(b)/2
scoldon see sculan
scomu f. *shame* ds scome 9/22
scōp see scieppan
*ġe*scōp see *ġe*scieppan
scopgereord n. *poetic language* ds scopgereorde 9/6
scorene see scieran
scōwyrhta m. *shoemaker* ns 3/150, 3/195; np scōwyrhtan 3/6
*ġe*scrāf see *ġe*scrīfan
scranc see scrincan
*ġe*scrīfan I *ordain* pret 3s gescrāf 10(b)/29 [MnE shrive]
scrincan III *shrink* pret 3s scranc 1/2
scrīpan I *glide, move, wander* inf 18(a)/703
scrūd n. *clothing* as 3/74 [MnE shroud]
scrȳdan 1 *clothe* pres 3s scrȳtt 3/69
scrȳtt see scrȳdan
scūfan II *shove, push* pret 3s scēaf 12/136, 3p scufon 1/28
sculan pret. pres. *must, have to, ought to* pres 1s sceal 3/8, 3/9, 3/13; 3s sceal 3/15, 3/63, 3/216, etc.; 1p sculon 9/36; 2p sceole 12/59; 3p sceolon 12/54, 12/220; subj 3s scyle 15/42, 17/111, 17/74 (on weg scyle *must depart*), scile 18(d)/3176; pret 1s sceolde 4/3, 17/30; 3s 8/2, 12/16, etc.; 3p sceoldon 2/49 (*had to* [*go*]), sceoldon 12/19, 12/105, 12/291, etc; subj 3s sceolde 7/51; 3p scolden 3/115, 9/113, sceoldan 5/13, sceoldan 7/30 (*ought to have*), sceoldon 7/33, etc.; sceolden 9/21 [MnE shall]
scūr m. *shower, storm* dp scūrum 17/17
scūrbeorg f. *protection from storms* (*i.e. buildings*) np scūrbeorge 13/5
*ġe*scȳ n. pl. *shoes, footwear* ap 3/153
scyld see scield
scyldiġ adj. w.g. *guilty* ns ealdres scyldig *having forfeited his life* 18(b)/1338
Scyldingas m. pl. *descendants of Scyld, i.e. the Danes* gp Scyldinga 18(a)/778, 18(b)/1321
scyle see sculan
scyldburh f. *wall of shields* ns 12/242
scynscaþa m. *demonic foe, hostile demon* ns 18(a)/707
scyppend see scieppend
scyp see scip
scypu see scip
*ġe*scyrpan 1 *accoutre, equip* p ptc gescyrpedne 8/66
se, þæt, sēo dem. pron., def. art. (§16) m. n. f. *that, the, he, she, it, who, which* (§162.3) nsm se 1/5, 1/8, 1/9, 1/18, 1/33, 2/55, 3/15 (*he*), etc.; asm þone 1/5, 1/17, 1/29, 2/52, 3/12,

se, þæt, sēo (*cont.*)
þæne 7/24; gsm þæs 1/19, 3/40, etc.; dsm þǣm 1/20, 3/66; ism þȳ 8/32; nsn þæt 2/4, 2/11, tæt 6/33, etc.; asn 1/2, 1/5, 1/13, 2/6, þet 7/61, etc.; gsn þæs 2/5, 4/105, 6/29, *after, afterward* 3/31, 6/7, etc.; dsn þām 2/2, 2/10, 2/12 (be þām þe *as*), 4/39, 4/101; isn þȳ 2/7 (þȳ lǣs þe *lest*), 3/24, 3/70 (see note), 9/60, þon 6/35 (see note), 9/114, etc., þē (w. compar.) *the, by that* 12/146, 12/312, 12/313; nsf sēo 1/10, 1/33, 2/1, 2/2, 2/26, sīo 5/45; asf þā 2/30, 2/56, 3/76, 6/3; gsf þǣre 1/24, etc.; dsf 1/9, 1/11, 1/24, 1/28, 2/41 (þǣre þe *which*), 3/9, þēre 7/32; np þā 3/60, 3/166, etc.; ap 1/30, 3/9, 3/11, 3/29, 3/44, 3/49, 3/58, 3/75, 3/80, 3/108, etc.; gp þāra 1/30, 2/4, 3/18, 3/43, þǣra 4/29, etc.; dp þām 2/67, þǣm 3/87, 3/105, etc.

seah see sēon
*ge*seah see *ge*sēon
sealde see sellan
sealt n. *salt* gs sealtes 3/159
sealtere m. *salter, salt-maker* ns 3/156; np sealteras 3/6
sealtȳþ f. *salt seawave, ocean wave* gp sealtȳþa 17/35
sēamere m. *tailor* ns 3/195
sēarian 2 *grow sere, wither, fade* pres 3p sēarað 17/89
searobunden adj. *cunningly fastened* asn 11(n)/4
searogim m. *precious stone* ap searogimmas 13/35
searosǣled adj. *skilfully bound* nsf 11(h)/16
searoþonc m. *ingenuity, skill* dp searoþoncum 18(a)/775
sēaþ m. *pit* ds sēaþe 14/75
sēcan 1 *seek, search for, visit* inf 11(f)/11, 14/104, 14/127 (*resort to*), 15/9, 18(a)/756, 18(a)/801, sēcean 18(a)/821; imp s sēc 18(b)/1379; imp p sēcaþ 3/190; pres 3s sēceð 16/114; subj 3s sēce 18(b)/1369; pret 1s sōhte 8/44, 16/25; 3s 5/12, 8/53; 3p sōhton 12/193, 14/133
*ge*sēcan 1 *seek* inf 12/222, 14/119; pres subj 1s gesēce 17/38; pret 3s gesōhte 12/287, 18(a)/717
secg m. *man, warrior* ns 12/159, 17/56, 18(a)/871, 18(b)/1311; as 18(b)/1379; ap secgas 12/298; gp secga 16/53, 18(a)/842; dp secgum 14/59
secgan 3 *say, tell* inf 9/52, 11(n)/8, 11(n)/16, 12/30, 14/1, 15/2, 17/2, 18(a)/875, etc.; imp s saga 11(b)/7, 11(h)/16, sege 12/50; pres 1s secge 3/132; 2s segst 3/7, 3/22, 3/107, 3/108, 3/197; 3s segþ 3/193, segeð 12/45; 1p secge 3/168, secgað 4/44; subj 2s secge 14/96; pret 3s sægde 2/23, 2/72, sǣde 4/17, 12/

147, etc.; 3p sægdon 9/55; p ptc gesægd 2/70
*ge*secgan 3 *say* pret 3s gesægde 11(g)/5, gesǣde (þanc gesǣde *gave thanks*)12/120
secgrōf adj. *sword-valiant, brave* gpm secgrōfra 13/26
sefa m. *heart* ns 10(b)/71; as sefan 16/57, 17/51; ds 18(b)/1342
sēftēadig adj. *blessed with comfort* ns 17/56
*ge*seġen see *ge*sēon
seġnian 2 *bless, cross* (*oneself*) prs ptc segniende 9/123
*ge*seġnian 2 *bless, cross* (*oneself*) pret 3s gesegnode (w. refl.) 9/116
segst see secgan
segþ see secgan
*ge*selda m. *companion* ap geseldan 16/53
seldcūþ adj. *rare* asn 3/141
seldon adv. *seldom* 3/90
sele m. *hall, house* ns 11(e)/1; as 18(a)/826; ds 18(a)/713
seledrēam m. *revelry in the hall* as 18(c)/2252; np seledrēamas 16/93
seledrēorig adj. *sad at the loss of a hall* nsm 16/25
selerǣdend m. *counsellor in the hall* ap selerǣdende 18(b)/1346
selesecg m. *retainer* ap selesecgas 16/34
sēlest adj. (superl. of gōd; cf. §76) *best* nsm sēlesta 14/27; asm w.g. sēlest 14/118; nsn 18(b)/1389
self pron., adj. *self, himself, herself, etc., same, very* nsm 2/3, 2/56, 4/38, 4/83, seolfa 8/58, 8/75, sylfa 11(e)/1; asm selfne 2/72, 3/103 (*myself*), sylfne 8/16, seolfne 9/123; gsm seolfes 9/125; dsm selfum 5/43, sylfum 7/34, 9/55, 17/1; gsf sylfre 15/2; nsn sylfe 8/45; asn 8/44; npm selfe 3/174 (*ourselves*), 5/25 (*ourselves*), seolfan 9/69; apm selfe 3/121; gpm sylfra 12/38
sēlla see sēlra
sellan 1 *give, sell* inf 3/84, 3/144, syllan 8/46, 12/38, 12/46; imp s sele 3/117, 3/120; pres 1s selle 3/66, 3/118, 3/136; 2s selst 3/118, 3/199; 3s selþ 3/68, 3/69, 3/199, silð 4/63, sylð 4/65, seleð 18(b)/1370 (*give up*); subj 3p syllon 12/61; pret 3s sealde 2/14, 2/25, 5/23, 8/63, etc.; 3p sealdon 10(b)/24; subj 3s sealde 8/60; p ptc geseald 4/77
*ge*sellan 1 *give, give up* pret 3s gesealde 12/188; pret 3p gesealdon 12/184
sēlra adj. (compar. of gōd; cf. §76) *better* nsm 18(a)/860, sēlla 10(b)/50; nsn sēlre 18(b)/1384
selþ see sellan
*ge*sēman 1 *reconcile, settle* (*a dispute*) inf 3/207, 12/60
sendan 1 *send* inf 12/30, 16/56; pres 3p

sendað 11(o)/5; pret 3s sende 7/31, 10(a)/
20, 10(b)/63, 12/134; 3p sendon 12/29; subj
3s sende 7/59

sēo see se

ġesēo see ġesēon

seofian 2 *lament, sigh* pret 3p seofedun 17/10

Sēolesīġ f. *Selsey (Sussex)* ds Sēolesigge 7/2

seolfa see self

scolfne see self

seolfor n. *silver* as 3/142, 4/85, sylfor 13/35; gs
seolfres 11(n)/4; is seolfre 14/77, sylfore
11(j)/2

seolforsmiþ m. *silversmith* ap seolforsmiþas
3/181

seoloc m. *silk* as 3/141

sēon V *look, see* inf 18(b)/1365; pret 1s seah
11(l)/1, 11(n)/1, 3s 13/35

ġesēon V *see* inf gesion 5/36; imp s geseoh
8/12; pres 1s gesēo 3/179; 3s gesiehð 2/69,
2/71, gesihð 16/46; subj 2s gesēo 8/21; pret
1s geseah 5/28, 11(g)/1, 14/14, 14/21, 14/33,
etc.; 3s 2/11, 2/66, 8/66, etc.; 3p gesāwon
2/48, 12/84, 12/203; subj 1s gesāwe 14/4;
p ptc gesawen 8/9, gesewen 8/26, gesegen
9/54, 9/124

seonu f. *sinew* np seonowe 18(a)/817

sēoþan II *boil* inf 3/174; infl inf (tō) sēoþanne
3/174 [MnE seethe]

ġeset n. *dwelling* ap gesetu 16/93

ġesetnis f. *law, decree* ap gesetnissa 4/116; dp
gesetnissum 4/116

ġesett see settan

settan 1 *set, put, establish, set out, go, set down,
compose* pres 1s sette 2/30; pret 3p setton
10(b)/4; p ptc gesett 4/12, 4/98, geset 4/113,
geseted 9/18, 14/141; npm gesette 4/39

ġesettan 1 *set, put, compose* pret 3s gesette 9/26,
9/122; 3p gesetton 14/67

ġesewen see ġesēon

sibb f. *peace, concord* ns 3/207; as sibbe 5/7

sibbeġedriht f. *band of kinsmen* as 18(a)/729

sibling m. *kinsman, sibling* dp siblingum 4/21

Sībyrht pers. n. *Sibyrht* gs Sībyrhtes 12/282

Siċilia f. *Sicily* ns 10(b)/15; ds 10(a)/4

sīde f. *side* ds sīdan 14/49, ap 11(b)/7

sīde adv. *widely* 14/81 (wīde and sīde *far and
wide*)

sīe see bēon

ġesiehð see ġesēon

sīen see bēon

siendon see bēon

ġesiene adj. *visible* nsn gesyne 18(d)/3158;
npn gesiene 14/46

sierwan 1 *contrive, plot* pres 2s sierwst 2/32

siġ (= sīe) see bēon

siġebēam m. *tree of victory, cross* ns 14/13; as
14/127

Siġebryht pers. n. *Sigebryht* as 6/1

siġelēas adj. *without victory, in defeat* asm
sigelēasne 18(a)/787

Siġemund pers. n. *Sigmund* gs Sigemundes
18(a)/875; ds Sigemunde 18(a)/884

Siġerīċ pers. n. *Sigeric* ns 7/18, Sīrīc 7/24

siġeþēod f. *victorious nation* np sigeþēoda
10(b)/4

siġewǣpen n. *weapon of victory* dp sigewǣp-
num 18(a)/804

siġlan 1 *sail* pret 3p sigldon 1/28

siġle n. *jewel, brooch, necklace* ap siglu 18(d)/
3163

sigor m. *victory* gp sigora 14/67

sigorēadig adj. *victorious* nsm 18(b)/1311

sigorfæst adj. *triumphant, victorious* nsm 14/
150

ġesihð f. *sight, vision, presence* ds gesihðe 2/13,
2/19, 9/121, gesyhðe 14/21, 14/41, 14/66, as
14/96

silð see sellan

simle adv. *always* 4/95, 6/20, 17/68

sīn poss. pron. *his, her, its* isn sīne 11(h)/14

sinc n. *treasure* as 11(n)/4, 12/59, 13/35; gs
sinces 16/25; ds since 14/23

sincfāg adj. *decorated with treasure, richly
adorned* nsm 11(j)/15

sincġeofa see sincġyfa

sincġyfa m. *one who gives treasure, lord* ns sinc-
geofa 10(b)/50; as sincgyfan 12/278; ds
18(b)/1342; as 12/278

sincþegu f. *receiving of treasure* as sincþege 16/
34

sind see bēon

sindon see bēon

singāl adj. *perpetual, everlasting* nsf 14/141

singan III *sing, resound* inf 9/17, 9/21, etc.;
pres ptc singend nsm 10(a)/31; asm
singende 17/22; imp s sing 1/27, 9/28; pres
3s singeþ 17/54, 3p singað 11(d)/8; pret 3s
sang 1/8, song 9/45, 9/70, etc.

sinnig adj. *sinful* asn sinnigne 18(b)/1379

sinsorg f. *constant sorrow* gp sinsorgna 15/45

sīo see se

siodu m. *morality* as 5/7

ġesīon see ġesēon

Sīrīc see Siġerīċ

siteþ see sittan

sittan V *sit* inf 15/37; pres 3s siteþ 1/11, 15/
47; subj 2s sitte 8/28; pret 3s sæt 11(a)/1, 3p
sǣton 11(b)/1

ġesittan V. *sit* pret 3s gesæt 16/111, 18(a)/749
(*sat up*)

sīð m. *journey, fate, lot* ns 18(a)/765, 18(a)/716
(*time, occasion*); as 11(e)/3, 15/2, 18(a)/872;
ds sīþe 17/51, 18(a)/740 (*time*); ap sīþas
11(k)/11, 17/2, 18(a)/877

ġesīþ m. *companion* np gesīþas 11(o)/5; dp
gesīþum 18(b)/1313

sīðfæt m. *journey, expedition* ds sīðfate 14/150

sīðian 2 *travel* inf 11(l)/2, 12/177, 14/68, 18(a)/720, 18(a)/808; pres subj 1s sīðie 12/251

sīððan adv. *afterwards, later* 2/51, 3/24, 4/64, 5/62, etc.; conj. *after, since, when* 2/59, 15/3, syðþan 14/3, etc.

sīwian 2 *sew, stitch together* pret 3p sīwodon 2/16

slāt see slītan

slǣp m. *sleep* ns 16/39; ds slǣpe 9/45

slǣpan VII *sleep* pres ptc slǣpende 9/45; asm slǣpendne 18(a)/741

slēan VI *strike, beat* pret 3s slōh 1/21, 12/163, 12/285; 3p slōgon 7/78; subj 3s slōge 12/117 [MnE slay]

slecg m. *sledge-hammer* gp slecga 3/200

sleġe m. *blow, stroke* ds 3/104

slītan I *tear, rend* pret 3s slāt 17/11, 18(a)/741 [MnE slit]

slīðen adj. *cruel* nsf 16/30

slōgon see slēan

slōh see slēan

smēagan 1 *contrive, reflect, investigate* inf 10(a)/17

smiþ m. *blacksmith* ns 3/193, 3/204; ds smiðe 1/16

smiððe f. *smithy* ns 1/16; ds smiþþan 3/199

smolt adj. *peaceful, serene* asn 9/104

smylte adj. *serene* ism 9/120; dsf smyltre 9/119

snāw m. *snow* as 16/48

snell adj. *keen, bold* np snelle 12/29

snīwan 1 *snow* pres subj 3s snīwe 8/29; pret 3s snīwde 17/31

snottor adj. *wise* nsm 16/111, snotor 18(a)/826, 18(b)/1384, snotera 18(b)/1313; npm snottre 11(b)/2

snytro f. *wisdom* as 8/58; dp snyttrum 18(a)/872

socc m. *sock* ns 1/2

softe adv. *easily* 12/59

sōhte see sēcan

ġesomnian 2 *gather, assemble* inf 9/50; p ptc gesomnad 11(o)/2

ġesomnung f. *community* ds gesomnunge 9/65

somod see samod

sōna adv. *immediately* 2/52, 2/62, 2/78, 4/26, etc. [MnE soon]

song m. *song, cry* ns song 9/68; as song 1/27, 17/19, sang 18(a)/787

songcræft m. *poetic art* as 9/14

sorg f. *sorrow, grief, trouble* ns 16/30, 16/39, 16/50, sorh 18(b)/1322; as sorge 17/42, 17/54; gp sorga 14/80; dp sorgum 14/20, 14/59

sorgian 2 *sorrow, grieve, care* imp s sorga 18(b)/1384

sorh see sorg

sorhlēoþ n. *song of sorrow, dirge* as 14/67

sōþ adj. *true* gsm sōðan 8/69; dsm 8/58 [archaic MnE sooth]

sōþ n. *truth* as 3/107, 3/197, 4/16, etc.; tō sōþe *as a fact* 16/11 [archaic MnE (for)sooth]

sōðe adv. *truly, faithfully* 18(a)/871

sōðgied m. *lay of truth, story about actual events* as 17/1

sōðlīċe adv. *truly* 2/9, 2/64, 4/52, etc. [archaic MnE soothly]

spǣtan 1 *spit* pres 1s spǣte 11(h)/8

spearca m. *spark* ap spearcan 3/200

spearwa m. *sparrow* ns 8/30

spēd f. *means, opportunity, wherewithal* as on spēd *successfully* 18(a)/873; ap speda 5/59

spēdan 1 *be prosperous, be wealthy* pres 2p spēdað 12/34

spēdiġ adj. *successful* nsm 14/151

spell n. *story, message* as 9/56, 12/50, spel 18(a)/873; gs spelles 9/66; dp spellum 9/74

spēow see spōwan

spere n. *spear* as 8/64, 12/137; ds 3/61; is 8/68; ap speru 12/108

spild m. *destruction* ds spilde 11(h)/8

spillan 1 *destroy* inf 12/34

spor n. *track, trail* ds spore 5/38 [MnE spoor]

spōwan VII *succeed* (impersonal, w.d.) pret 3s spēow 5/9

sprǣċ f. *utterance, speech, language* gs sprǣċe 4/104; ds 8/25, 11(f)/13; ap sprǣca 4/88

sprǣcan (= sprǣcon) see sprecan

ġesprec n. *conference, discussion* as 8/4

sprecan V *speak, say* inf 9/90, 14/27, 18(d)/3172; pres ptc sprecende 8/40, 9/31, 9/99, etc.; pres 1s sprece 4/55, sprice 11(h)/11; 2s spricst 3/204; 3s spricð 4/49, spriceð 16/70; pret 3s spræc 4/72, 10(b)/81, 12/211, 12/274; 3p sprǣcan 8/38, sprǣcon 12/200, 12/212

ġesprecan pret 3s gespræc 18(b)/1398

sprengan 1 *break, cause to spring or quiver* pret 3s sprengde 12/137

spricst see sprecan

springan III *spring (away)* pret 3s sprang 12/137

ġespringan III *spring forth, arise* pret 3s gesprong 18(a)/884

spyriġean 1 *follow, follow in the footsteps of* inf 5/37

spyrte f. *basket, eel basket* as spyrtan 3/77

stafum see stæf

stān m. *stone* ns 1/18; as 1/17, 13/43, 18(a)/887; gs stānes 1/19; ds stāne 1/20, 14/66; is 1/21

stānclif n. *rocky cliff, crag* ap stānclifu 17/23

standan VI *stand, remain* inf 12/19, 14/43, 14/

62; pres is stande 3/24, 3/30; 3s stynt 4/59, 12/51, standeð 18(b)/1362, stondeð 16/74, 16/97, 16/115; 3p stondaþ 16/76, 17/67; pret is stōd 14/38; 3s 10(b)/28, 12/25, 12/28, 12/145, etc., stōd him . . . æt *appeared to him* 9/27; 1p stōdon 14/71, 3p 5/30, 12/63, 12/72, 12/79, 12/100, etc.

ġestandan VI *stand up* inf 12/171; pret 3p ġestōdon 14/63 (w. refl., see note)

stang see stingan

stānhliþ n. *cliff* ds stānhliþe 15/48; ap stānhleoþu 16/101

stānhof n. *stone building* np stānhofu 13/38

stānwyrhta m. *stone-mason* ns 1/20

ġestaðelian 2 *establish, make steadfast* pres 3s gestaþelað 17/108; pret 3s gestaþelade 17/104

staðol m. *fixed position* as 11(c)/5 (*foundation*); ds staðole 14/71; dp staðelum 17/109

stædefæste see stedefæst

stæf m. *letter* dpm stafum 9/4

stǣlan 1 *avenge* p ptc gestǣled 18(b)/1340

stælgiest m. *thievish guest, thieving stranger* ns 11(c)/5

stǣr n. *history* as 9/72; gs stǣres 9/66

stæð n. *bank, shore* ds stæðe 12/25

ġesteal m. *foundation* ns 16/110

steall m. *stall* as 3/19

stēam m. *moisture* ds stēame 14/62 [MnE steam]

stēap adj. *high* nsm 13/11 [MnE steep]

stearc adj. *severe* nsm 3/10 [MnE stark]

stearn m. *tern* ns 17/23

stēda m. *stallion* as stēdan 8/65 [MnE steed]

stede m. *place, position* as 12/19 [MnE stead]

stedefæst adj. *steadfast, unyielding* npm stedefæste 12/249; stædefæste 12/127

stefn m. *trunk, stem, root* ds stefne 14/30; *prow or stern of a ship* ds stefnan 17/7

stefn f. *voice* ns 14/71; as stefne 2/17, 2/21, 2/36, is 11(j)/18

stemn f. *voice* is stemne 10(b)/84

stemnettan 1 *stand firm* pret 3p stemnetton 12/122

steorra m. *star* ap steorran 2/74

stēpan 1 w.d. *exalt* pres 3s stēpeð 11(m)/8

steppan VI *step, advance* pret is stōp 11(p)/5; 3s 12/8, 12/78, 12/131, 18(a)/761

stician 2 *stick* pret 3s sticode 8/68

stīeran 1 w.d. *steer, control* inf 17/109

ġestīgan I *climb up, mount, ascend* inf 14/34; pret 3s gestāh 14/40

stihtan 1 *direct, command, exhort* pret 3p stihte 12/127

stilnes f. *peace* as stilnesse 5/57; ds 9/117 [MnE stillness]

stingan III *stab, pierce* pret 3p stang 12/138 [MnE sting]

stið adj. *stern* nsn 12/301; as stīðan 4/91; apm stiþe 17/104

stiðhicgende adj. *firm of purpose, resolute* npm 12/122

stiðlīċe adv. *sternly, loudly* 12/25

stiðmōd adj. *resolute, brave* nsm 14/40

stōd see standan

stōdhors n. *stallion* as 8/61 [MnF. studhorse]

stōdon see standan

stondaþ see standan

stōp see steppan

storm m. *storm* ds storme 15/48, is 8/32; np stormas 16/101, 17/23; dp stormum 13/11

stōw f. *place* ns 8/71, 18(b)/1372; as stōwe 2/69, 18(b)/1378; ds stōwe 2/53, 2/56, 3/42, etc.; ap stōwa 5/34; dp stōwum 4/97

strang adj. *strong* nsm 14/40, strong 11(f)/13; gsm strangan 11(c)/5; dsm strongum 17/109; npm strange 14/30; compar. nsm strengra 11(e)/4; apn strangran 8/22; superl. strengest nsm 18(a)/789

ġestrangian 2 *strengthen* pres is gestrangie 3/165

strǣl m. or f. *arrow* dp strǣlum 14/62

strēam m. *river* ns 13/38; as 12/68; ap strēamas 13/43, 17/34 (*sea*)

strēgan 1 *strew, spread* inf 17/97

strengra see strang

strengu f. *strength, power* ns 11(d)/5; ds strengo 11(f)/13

ġestrēon n. *wealth, profit, treasure* as 3/148, 18(d)/3166, gestrīon 10(b)/23

strong see strang

stund f. *time, short while* as stunde 12/271

Stūrmere m. *village of Sturmer (Essex)* as 12/249

stynt see standan

styria m. *sturgeon* ap styrian 3/93

styrian 1 *stir up* inf 18(a)/872 (*treat of, engage*); pres 3s styreþ 18(b)/1374

styrman 1 *storm* pres subj 3s styrme 8/30

sulh f. *plough* ds sylh 3/9, 3/12

sum pron., adj. (§193.4) *a certain, some* nsm 4/6, 9/1, 10(a)/12, 10(b)/46, 12/149, 12/164, etc.; asm sumne 5/53, 16/81, 16/82, etc.; gsm sumes 11(c)/3, 11(j)/15; asn sum 3/148, 9/55, 12/285, sume 2/50; nsf sum 11(j)/8; asf sume 12/271; dsf sumre 9/23; npm sume 3/4, 3/5, 3/6, 17/56 (þā sume *those particular ones*); apm 16/80; apf 5/54

sumor m. *summer* as 3/127; gs sumeres 17/54; ds sumera 3/125

sumorlang adj. *long as in summer* asm sumorlangne 15/37

ġesund adj. *unharmed* npm gesunde 6/33 [MnE (safe and) sound]

sundor adv. *apart* 16/111 [MnE (a)sunder]

sunnandæġ m. *Sunday* ns 3/53

sunne f. *sun* ns 1/22; ds sunnan 1/24

sunu m. *son* ns 1/35, 1/36, 12/76, 12/298, 14/ 150; as 2/44, 2/59, 2/65, 2/69, 4/57, 7/45; gs suna 2/58; ds 2/73, 4/6; np suno 11(a)/2, 11(a)/3; gp suna 11(k)/12

sūsl f. *torment* gs sūsle 4/80

sūð adv. *south* (*wards*) 18(a)/858

sūðan adv. *from the south* be sūðan *south of* 5/19, 7/70

sūðerne adj. *southern, of southern design* asm 12/134

Sūðhamtūn m. *Southampton* ns 7/3

Sūðriġe pl. *Surrey* ap 7/71

Sūðseaxe m. pl. *Sussex, the South Saxons* ap Sūðsexe 7/71; dp Sūðseaxum 7/13, 7/56

sūðweardes adv. *southwards* 10(b)/4

swā adv. (§168 s. v. swā) *thus, so* 1/14, 2/70, 3/10, 3/59, 3/101, swǣ 5/14, 5/78 (*such*); swǣ *same likewise, similarly* 5/51; conj. *as* 3/84 (swā fela . . . swa *as many as*), 15/24 (w. subj. *as if*), 7/58 (swā wīde swā *as far as*); ēac swā *likewise, also* 2/19; swā hwæt swā *whatsoever* 3/66, 3/77, 9/4; swā hwelc swā *whoever* nsm 6/18; swā hwelc swā . . . swā . . . swā *whatsoever* . . . *whether* . . . *or* 3/212; swā hwelcum . . . swā *whatsoever* 2/9; swā swā *just as* 2/58, 2/75, 3/189, 4/10, 4/22; swā þēah *however* 4/27

swam see swimman

swān m. *swineherd* ns 6/5

swāse see swǣs

swāt m. *sweat* gs swātes (*blood*) 14/23; ds swāte 2/40

swaþu see swæð

swaþul m. or n. *flame, heat* ds swaþule 18(a)/ 782

swæ see swā

swæcc m. *taste, flavour* ds swæcce 3/159

swæs adj. *beloved* asm swæsne 16/50; npf swāse 11(a)/3; gpm swæsra 11(k)/11

swæsendu n. pl. *banquet* dp swæsendum 8/27

swætan 1 *bleed* inf 14/20

swæð n. *track, swath* as 5/36; np swaþu 11(l)/3

swealg see swelgan

sweart adj. *dark, black* npm swearte 11(l)/2 [MnE swart]

swefan V *sleep, sleep in death* inf 18(a)/729; pres 3p swefað 18(c)/2256; pret 3p swæfon 18(a)/703

swefn n. *dream* as 9/27, 9/52; gp swefna 14/1

swēġ m. *sound, din* ns 18(a)/782; as 3/200, 17/ 21

Sweġen pers. n. *Swein* ns 7/47

sweġl n. *sky, heaven* gs swegles 18(a)/860

swelċe adj. *likewise, such* swylce 14/8, 15/43; dsn swelcum 3/128; swylce swā *just as* 14/ 92; adv. ēac swelce, swelce ēac *also, likewise* 2/1, 2/33, 9/79, 3/103, 3/121; conj. *as if*

5/33; swylc . . . swylc . . . *such* . . . (*just*) *as* 18(b)/1328–9; pron. *such* gsn swulces 18(a)/ 880

swelgan III w.d. *swallow, imbibe* inf 11(j)/15; pret 3s swealg 11(c)/6, swealh 18(a)/743; sub 3s swulge 18(a)/782

sweltan III *die, perish* inf 12/293; pret 3s swealt 18(a)/892; subj 1p swulten 2/7

swencan 1 *press hard, harass, afflict* p ptc geswenced 18(b)/1368

sweng m. *blow, stroke* gs swenges 12/118

swēora m. *neck* as swēoran 2/64, 11(b)/6

ġesweorcan III *grow dark, become obscured* pres subj 3s gesweorce 16/59

sweord n. *sword* ns swurd 12/166, 18(a)/890; as sweord 2/53, 2/59, 8/64, 11(n)/14, swurd 12/15, 12/161, etc.; ds swurde 12/118; ap swurd 12/47; dp sweordum 18(a)/884

sweostor f. *sister* as swuster 4/19; np gesweostor 11(a)/3 (see §138 Prefixes, ġe-); ap geswustra 4/16

sweostersunu m. *sister's son* ns swustersunu 12/115

sweotol adj. *clear, manifest* nsn 18(a)/817, 18(a)/833

ġesweotolian 2 *reveal, show* pret 3s gesweoto-lode 2/56; p ptc geswutelod 4/67, 4/70

sweotule adv. *openly* 16/11

swerian VI *swear* pres 1s swerie 2/72

swēte adj. *sweet* asn 17/95 (as noun); superl. asn swēteste 9/68

swētmete m. *sweetmeat* gp swētmetta 3/159

swētnis f. *sweetness* as swētnisse 9/6; ds swēt-nesse 9/78

ġeswīcan 1 *cease, desist* pres 3s geswiceð 11(f)/ 12; pret subj 3p geswicon 7/60, 7/66

swift adj. *swift* nsm 11(l)/3, swifta 18(c)/2264; asm swiftne 3/118, 13/18; dpm swiftum 3/49; compar. nsf swiftre 11(e)/3

swiġe adj. *silent, still* nsm 11(e)/1

swīgian 2 *be quiet, fall silent* pres 3s swigað 11(d)/1

swimman III *swim* pres 3p swimmaþ 3/88, 16/53; pret 1s swom 11(p)/3, 3s swam 1/5

ġeswinc n. *toil, hardship* ds geswince 3/129; dp geswincum 2/38

swincan III *labour, toil, struggle* pres 1s swince 3/8, 3/29

ġeswincdagas m. pl. *days of toil* gp geswinc-dagum 17/2

ġeswing n. *vibration, swirl, surf* ns 18(a)/848

swingan III *fly* pres 3s swingeð 18(c)/2264

swingere m. *beater, scourger* ns 11(f)/7

swinsian 2 *sing, sound melodiously* pres 3p swinsiað 11(d)/7

swinsung f. *melody* ds swinsunge 9/57

swīþe adj. *mighty* nsf 13/24; compar. swīþre nsm 17/115; asf swīðran 14/20 swīðe adv. *very, exceedingly* 1/22, 3/62, 3/151, 3/179, 4/7, 11(l)/3, 12/115 (*cruelly*), etc.; swīðe swīðe *very much* 5/40; superl. swīþost 3/50 (*especially*)

swīðferhð adj. *strong-minded, brave* nsm 18(a)/ 826

swīðran see swīðe

swōgan VII *resound, make a noise* pres 3p swōgað 11(d)/7 [MnE sough]

swom see swimman

swuā see swā

swulten see sweltan

swurd see sweord

swuster see sweostor

swustersunu see sweostersunu

*ġe*swustra see sweostor

*ġe*swutelod see *ġe*sweotolian

swylce see swelce

swylt m. *death* ns 13/26

sȳ (= sīe) see bēon

*ġe*syhðe see *ġe*sihð

sylf see self

sylfor see seolfor

sylh see sulh

syll f. *sill, floor* ds sylle 18(a)/775

syllan see sellan

syllic adj. *marvellous, wondrous* nsm 14/13; compar. syllicre asn 14/4 (see note)

symbel n. *feast* ds symble 9/23, symle 14/141; gp symbla 16/93

syndolh n. *very great wound* ns 18(a)/817

syndon see bēon

syndriġlīċe adv. *individually, separately, especially* 8/8, 9/1 [archaic MnE sundrily]

*ġe*syne see *ġe*siene

synn f. *sin* gp synna 4/63, 9/81, 17/100; dp synnum 14/13, 14/99, 14/146

synscaða m. *malefactor, miscreant* as synscaðan 18(a)/801

synsnǣd f. *huge morsel* or *sinful gobbet* dp synsnǣdum 18(a)/743

*ġe*syntu f. *prosperity* as gesynto 8/19

*ġe*syrwed adj. *armed* nsm 12/159

tācn n. *sign, token* ns tācen 18(a)/833; as tācn 11(n)/5

*ġe*tācnian 2 *prefigure, betoken* pret 3s getācnode 4/30, 4/87, 4/88

*ġe*tācnung f. *prefiguration, signification, type* ns 4/28; as getācnunge 4/78 [MnE tokening]

tǣċan 1 *teach, show, direct* pres 3s tǣcð 4/103; pret 3s tǣhte 4/41, 12/18; 3p tǣhton 4/109

tǣcnan 1 *point out, signify, direct* pret 3s tǣcneð 11(l)/6

tæġel m. *tail* ns 4/94

tǣhte see tǣċan

*ġe*tæl n. *account, sequence* as 9/65

tǣsan 1 *lacerate, tear apart* pret 3s tǣsde 12/ 270 [MnE tease]

*ġe*tǣse adj. *agreeable* nsf 18(b)/1320

tæt (= þæt) see sē

tēaforgēap adj. *red curved* nsm tēaforgēapa 13/30

tēah see tēon

teala adv., interj. *well* 9/115, teola 8/67

*ġe*teld n. *tabernacle* ns 4/81; ds getelde 4/93

tellan 1 *account, reckon, consider* pret 3s tealde 18(a)/794 [MnE tell]

Temese f. *the Thames* ds 5/19, 7/71

temman 1 *tame* inf 3/114, 3/116; p ptc apm getemedan 3/124, 3/127

*ġe*temman 1 *tame* pres 1s getemme 3/123

templ n. *temple* as 8/47

Tenetland n. *Thanet* ns 7/5

*ġe*tenge adj. w.d. *near to, resting on* nsm 11(d)/8

teola see teala

tēon n. *injury, harm* as 11(m)/3

tēon 1 *adorn* pret 3s tēode 9/43

tēon II *go* (*on a journey*) pret 3s tēah 18(b)/ 1332

tīd f. *time* ns 12/104; as 8/31, 9/90, 11(p)/2 (on āne tīd *at the same time*), 17/124, tīde 9/18; gs tīde 8/27; ds 4/11, 9/23, 9/87, 9/112; np tīda 5/4 [MnE tide]

tīddeg m. *span of life, final hour* ds tīddege 17/ 69

tiġel f. *tile* dp tigelum 13/30

til adj. *good* nsm 16/112

tilian 2 *strive, endeavour* pres subj 1p tilien 17/ 119

tīma m. *time* ds tīman 4/14, 4/34, 7/74

*ġe*timbre n. *building, structure* ap getimbro 8/71

tin n. *tin* as 3/142

tintreġlić adj. *tormenting* gsn tintreglican 9/78

tīr m. *glory* ns 12/104

tīrlēas adj. *inglorious, vanquished* gsm tīrlēases 18(a)/843

tīðian 2 (w.d. of person and g. of thing) *grant* infl inf (tō) tīðienne 4/4

tō prep. w.d. *to, into, for, as a* 1/28, 2/2, 2/7, 2/25, 2/68, 3/9, 3/150 (tō nytte *of use*), 4/5, 4/92 (tō lace *as an offering*), 7/1, 8/34, 12/10 (fōn tō *take up*), etc.; adv. cume . . . tō *arrive* 3/45; with the infl inf (§205.2), 2/12 (tō etanne *for eating, to eat*), 2/49, 2/51, 3/17, etc.

tō adv. *too* 12/55, 12/66, 12/90, etc.

tōætȳcan 1 *add* pret 3s tōætȳhte 8/39

tōætȳhte see tōætȳcan

tōberstan III *break apart, shatter* pres 3s tōbirsteð 11(g)/7; pret 3s tōbærst 12/136, 12/144

tōbrecan IV *destroy, break open, shatter* inf 18(a)/780; p ptc tōbrocen 7/39, 12/242

tōbrȳtan 1 *crush* pres 3s tōbrȳt 2/32
tōcyme m. *coming, advent* ds 4/22
tōdāl n. *distinction, difference* ns 4/17
tōdæġ adv. *today* 3/52
tōdǣlan 1 *part, separate* pret 3p subj tōdǣlden
  15/12
tōgǣdere adv. *together* 7/33, 7/43, 12/67,
  tōgædre 13/20
tōġēanes prep. w.d. *against* 17/76
tōġeþēodan 1 *add* pret 3s tōgeþēodde 9/47
tōġeiecan 1 *increase, add to* p ptc tōgeieced
  3/190
tōgongan VII w.g. *pass away* (impers.) pres 3s
  tōgongeð 11(h)/10
*ġe*toht n. *battle* ds getohte 12/104
tōlūcan II *pull asunder, destroy* inf 18(a)/781
torht adj. *bright, splendid* nsm 11(m)/3
torhte adv. *brightly, splendidly* 11(d)/8
torn n. *resentment, grief, affliction* as 16/112,
  18(a)/833
torr m. *tower* np torras 13/3
tōtwǣman 1 *divide, break up* p ptc tōtwǣmed
  nsn 12/241
tōweard adj. *coming, future* gsm tōweardan
  9/77; gpn tōweardra 4/28 [MnE toward]
tōwearde adv. *beforehand, in advance* 4/30
tōwearp see tōweorpan
tōweorpan III *throw down, demolish* inf 8/55,
  8/57, 8/61, 8/70; pret 3s tōwearp 8/74
træppe f. *trap* træppum 3/110
tredan V *tread on, trample* pres 1s trede
  11(d)/1; pret 3s træd 18(b)/1352
treddian 2 *step, go* pret 3s treddode 18(a)/725
trēow n. *tree* ns 1/13, 2/12; as 2/6, 14/4, 14/14,
  14/17, 14/25, etc.; gs trēowes 2/5; ds trēowe
  2/3, 2/8, 2/10, etc.; gp trēowa 2/4
trēow f. *faith, trust* as trēowe 16/112; dp
  trēowum 10(b)/65 (*beliefs*)
trēowwyrhta m. *carpenter* ns 3/202; ap trēowwyrhtan 3/181
*ġe*triewe adj. *faithful* nsm 3/27 [MnE true]
trodu f. *track, footprint* ap trode 18(a)/843
trum adj. *strong* nsm 18(b)/1369
trym n. *step, pace* as 12/247
trymedon see trymian
trymian 2 *array, draw up, encourage* inf 12/17;
  pret 3p trymedon 12/305; p ptc getrymmed
  asn 12/22
*ġe*trymman 1 *strengthen* pres ptc getrym-
  mende 9/110 [MnE trim]
*ġe*trymmed see trymian
tunge f. *tongue* ns 9/121; as tungan 9/16
tūnġerēfa m. *town reeve, overseer of an estate* ds
  tūngerēfan 9/48
tuwa adv. *twice* 3/26
twā see twēġen
twām see twēġen
twēġen num. (§84) *two* npm 7/12, 11(a)/2,

11(a)/3, 12/80; apm 3/56, 10(b)/6, 11(b)/4,
  18(b)/1347; dpm twām 2/47, 2/50, 11(m)/2;
  dpn 11(a)/1; gpn twēga 12/207; npf twā
  10(b)/4, 11(a)/2; apf 4/16, 11(b)/3, 11(b)/5,
  11(b)/7 [archaic MnE twain]
twelf num. *twelve* npm 4/36, 11(b)/4, twelfe
  18(d)/3170
twēo m. *doubt, uncertainty* ds twēon 17/69 (tō
  twēon weorþeð *becomes an occasion for uncertainty*)
twēone num. *two* dp be sǣm twēonum
  between the seas, on earth 18(a)/858
*ġe*tyhtan 1 *train, urge on, incite* pres 1s getyhte
  3/43
tȳman 1 *propagate, beget* pret 3s tȳmde 4/19
  [MnE teem]
tȳn num. *ten* dpm 18(d)/3159

þā adv. *then* (§151 and §168 s. v. þonne) 2/7,
  2/11, 2/13, 2/15, 2/20, 2/46, 2/49, 2/56,
  2/59, 2/61, 4/4, etc.; conj. *when* 8/66, 15/9,
  þā þā *when* 2/17; þā . . . þā *then . . . when*
  2/48, *when . . . then* 5/28, 5/40, 8/1, 9/23,
  9/33, 9/57, etc.; þā gȳt *still* 12/168, 12/273
þā pron. see se
þafian 2 *consent to* pret 3s þafode 9/63
*ġe*þafian 2 *consent to, approve* inf 8/5; pret 3s
  geþafade 8/7
*ġe*þafung f. *assent* as geþafunge 8/24
*ġe*þah see *ġe*þicgan
þanc see þonc
*ġe*þanc n. *thought, purpose* as 12/13
*ġe*þancie see *ġe*þoncian
þancode see þoncian
þanon adv. *thence, therefrom* 3/106, 7/54,
  18(a)/763, 18(a)/844, 18(a)/853, þonan
  10(b)/82, 16/23, 18(a)/819, 18(b)/1373
þār see þǣr
þās see þes
þǣm, þām see se
þǣne (= þone) see se
þǣr adv., conj. (§152, §168) *there* 2/46,
  2/57, 3/60, 3/145, etc.; conj. *where* 2/17,
  6/26, etc.; þǣr . . . þǣr *where . . . there* 1/23;
  þǣr þǣr *there where, where* 2/49, *wherever*
  5/23
þǣra see se
þǣre see se
þǣrfe see þearfe
þǣrinne adv. *therein* 6/37, 10(a)/25
þǣrof adv. *thereof, from that* ðætte 3/152
þǣron adv. *therein* 14/67
þǣrrihte adv. *immediately* 4/36
þǣrtō adv. *thereto* 4/27, 6/28
þæs adv. (g. s. of þæt) *afterwards* 3/31 (þæs on
  morgenne *next morning*), 6/7 (þæs þe *after*)
þæs pron. see se
þæt conj. *that, so that* 2/3, 2/6, 2/9, 2/23, 2/37,

2/60, 2/64, 3/43, 3/59, 8/68, 10(b)/30 (þæt
þe), etc.
þæt pron. see **se**
þætte (= þæt þe) conj. (§155) *that* ðætte 5/17,
5/26, etc.
þe indeclinable relative particle (§162) *which,
who, that* 2/1, 2/4, 2/5, 2/22, 2/36, 2/45
(whom), 2/56, 3/87, etc.; *as* 12/313; sē þe *he
who* 3/211; þc him *to whom* 17/13
þē see **þū**
þē (= þȳ, isn of se) see **se**
þēah adv. *though, yet, however, nevertheless*
3/105, 4/98, 6/39, etc.; swā þēah *however*
4/27; conj. þēah (þe) *although* 2/8
þēah hwæþre adv. *moreover, nevertheless* 3/177
geþeaht n. *council, deliberation* as 8/4
geþeahtere m. *counsellor, adviser, manager* ns
3/185, 3/197; as 3/183; np geþeahteras
8/38
þearf f. *need, stress, danger* ns 9/101, 12/233; as
þearfe 12/175, ds 12/232, 12/307, þærfe 12/
201
þearf see **þurfan**
þearflīce adv. *profitably, with good effect* 10(b)/
60
þearl adj. *severe* nsf 10(b)/77
þearle adv. *severely, exceedingly* 3/8, 3/29,
3/125 (*ravenously*), 3/157 (*greatly*), 10(b)/82,
12/158, 14/52 (*violently*)
þēaw m. *custom, practice* ns 9/91, 16/12; ap
ðēawas 5/27; dp þēawum 4/84
þeċċan I *cover* inf 11(k)/4; pres 3s þeceð
11(j)/1
þegen see **þcġn**
þeġenlice adv. *loyally, nobly* 12/294
þeġn m. *nobleman, thane, retainer, warrior* ns
1/1, 6/25, 18(a)/867, þegen 7/15; as þegn
9/93, 10(b)/69, þegen 12/151; ds þegne
18(b)/1341; np þegnas 6/17, 10(b)/30, 14/75
(*disciples*), þegenas 12/205, 12/220, ap 12/
232; gp þegna 8/15; dp þegnum 8/28
þeġnian 2 *serve* inf 9/93; pres 3p þegniað
11(m)/6
geþencan see **geþenċean**
þenċean I *think, intend* inf 10(b)/60, þencan
17/96; pres 1s þence 12/319; 3s þenceð 12/
258, 12/316, 14/121, 17/51; 3p þencaþ 14/
115; pret 2s þōhte 18(a)/739; 3p þōhton
10(b)/11, 18(a)/800
geþenċean I *think, ponder, consider* inf 5/19,
geþencan 16/58, 17/118; imp s. geðenc
5/24; pret 3s geþōhte 16/88
þenden conj. *while* 10(b)/38, 10(b)/48,
11(e)/6, 17/102
þenian I *stretch out* inf 14/52 (see note) [MnE
thin]
ðēning f. *divine service* ap ðēninga 5/15
þēod f. *people, nation* ns 10(b)/28; gs þēode

8/77; ds þēode 12/90, 12/220; np þēoda
2/76, ðīoda 5/53, gp þēoda 12/173
geþēodan I *join* pret 3s geþēodde 9/64
þēodde see **þēowan**
geþēode n. *language* as geðīode 5/33, 5/52,
etc.; gp geðēoda 5/47
þēoden m. *prince, lord* ns 12/120, 12/232, 12/
178; as 12/158; gs þēodnes 16/95, 18(a)/797;
ds þēodne 12/294, 14/69
þēodland n. *nation* as þēodlond 10(b)/3
geþēodnis f. *joining* ds geþēodnisse 9/9
þēodrīċ pers. n. *Theodoric* ns 10(a)/5, 10(a)/
15, 10(a)/24, 10(b)/69; ds þēodrīce 10(b)/30
þēodscipe m. *discipline* dp þēodscipum 9/83
þēof m. *thief* ns 11(c)/4; dp þēofum 3/31
geþēon III *flourish* pret 3p geþungon 10(b)/7
þēos see **þes**
ðeosse (= ðisse) see **þes**
þeossum (= þissum) see **þes**
þēow m. *slave, servant* np þēowas 3/176; gp
ðīowa 5/31, þēowa 9/65
þēowan I *serve* pret 1s þēodde 8/21, 3s þēode
9/119
þēowdōm m. *service* ns 3/188
þēowian 2 w.d. *serve* pres 3s þēowaþ 11(m)/6
þēre (= þ̄re) see **se**
þes m., **þēos** f., **þis** n. dem. pron. *this* þās pl.
these (§17) nsm þes 1/20, 3/33; asm þisne
1/27, 3/210, þysne 12/52; dsm þissum 1/29;
nsn þis 1/13; asn 2/28, 4/55, etc.; gsn þisses
1/29, 1/32; dsn þissum 3/136, 5/64, þisum
7/47; isn þȳs 7/1, þis 7/7; gsf þisere 4/18,
þisre 4/67, ðeosse 9/1; nsf þēos 1/32; asf
þas 4/9; dsf þissere 4/112; ðisse 5/25, þysse
8/45; gsf þisse 16/74; np þās 3/3, 7/73; ap
16/91, 16/101; gp þissa 1/30, 3/186, 5/22;
dp þisum 4/75, þeossum 8/37
þet (= þæt) see **se**
þicgan V *receive, take, partake of* inf ðicgean
18(a)/736
geþicgan V *prosper, thrive* pret 3s geþāh 10(b)/
53
geþicgean V *accept* inf 6/20
þider adv. *thither* 6/18, 10(b)/61, 17/118
þīn poss. adj. *thy, thine* asm þinne 2/44, 2/65,
2/74, 3/7, 3/41, 3/65; gsm þines 2/40; dsm
þīnum 2/31, 3/73; asn þīn 2/32; gsn þīnes
2/30, 2/36, 2/39; dsn þīnum 2/30, 2/73; asf
þīne 2/21, 2/63; npm þīne 3/3; apm 3/81,
3/120; gpm þīnra 8/15; dpm þīnum 3/33;
apn þīn 3/144; apf þīne 2/33
þinċeð see **þynċan**
þīnen f. *handmaid* ap þīnena 4/16
þing n. *thing* ns 13/48; as 3/35; np 3/139,
3/190; ap 1/34, 3/136, 3/139, 8/21, 9/98; gp
þinga 3/143, 4/30, 17/68 (þinga gehwylce *in
all circumstances*), 18(a)/791 (ǣnige þinga *in
any way, by any means*); dp þingum 8/18

*ge*þinge n. *result, issue* gs geþinges 18(a)/709
ðīod see þēod
*ge*þīode see *ge*þēode
þīow see þēow
þīowotdōm m. *service* ap ðīowotdōmas 5/11
þis see þes
þisere see þes
þissa see þes
þisse see þes
*ge*þōht m. *thought* ns 15/43, as 15/12, np geþōhtas 17/34
*ge*þōhte see *ge*þencean
þōhton see þencean
þolian 2 *suffer, endure* inf 10(b)/77, 12/201, 12/307, 18(a)/832; pres 1s þolie 3/138; pret 3p þolodan 14/149
*ge*þolian 2 *endure, tolerate* inf 12/6
þon adv. *than* 12/33
þon i. s. of þæt (see se) *the* (used with comparatives) 8/17; for þon see for; wið þon þe see wiþ
þonan see þanon
þonc m. w.d. of person and g. of cause *thanks* (*for*) ns 5/20, 5/79, 17/122; as þanc 12/120, 12/147
þoncian 2 *thank* pret 3s þancode 18(b)/1397
*ge*þoncian 2 w.d. of person and g. of cause *thank, give thanks to* pres 1s geþancie 12/173
þone see se
þonne adv. *then* (§§151–152, 168 s.v. þonne) 2/10, 3/9, 3/12, 3/25, 3/30, 3/42, 3/44, 3/146, etc.; conj. *when, whenever* 3/11, 3/30, 3/44, 3/205, etc.; conj. w. compar. (§177) *than* 2/1, 2/73, 3/99, 3/146, 3/198, 8/18, 11(h)/7, 12/195, etc.
þorfte see þurfan
þorn m. *thorn* ap þornas 2/39
þorod pers. n. *Thorod* ds þorode 7/29
þrāg f. *time, interval* ns 16/95; as þrāge 10(b)/77; ds þrāge *for a time* 10(b)/28; dp þrāgum *sometimes, at times* 11(e)/4
*ge*þrang n. *throng, crowd* ds geþrange 12/299
þrēanȳd f. *distress, sad necessity* dp þrēanȳdum 18(a)/832
þrēat m. *host, troop* is þrēate 10(b)/3 [MnE threat]
þreohtig adj. *enduring* compar. nsm þreohtigra 11(e)/4
þridda num. *third* dsm þriddan 2/48
þrīe num. *three* gp þrēora 12/299, 17/68 (þrēora sum *one of three things*); dp þrīm 4/73
þrīm see þrīe
*ge*þringan III *oppress, pinch, constrict* pret 3p geþrungon 10(b)/3; p ptc geþrungen npm 17/8
þrīnnys f. *trinity* ns 4/67 [archaic MnE threeness]

þrōwian 2 *suffer* pret 1s þrōwode 17/3; 3s 14/84, 14/98, 14/145
þrōwung f. *passion, suffering* ds þrōwunge 9/75
*ge*þrungen see *ge*þringan
þrycċan 1 *oppress* p ptc þrycced 9/89
þrym m. *majesty, glory* ns 16/95
þrymfæst adj. *glorious* nsm 14/84; asm þrymfæstne 11(c)/4
þrȳðe f. pl. *multitude* 16/99
þrȳðswȳð adj. *strong, mighty* nsm 18(a)/736
þū pron. *thou, you* ns 1/36, 2/20, 2/23, 2/24, 2/26, 2/40, 3/1, 3/7, etc.; as þē 2/35, 2/74, 3/179; ds þē 2/23, 2/24, 2/31, 2/37, 2/39, 2/74, 3/68, 3/124 (*from you*), 4/4 (*for you*)
*ge*þūht see þynċan
þūhte see þynċan
*ge*þungon see *ge*þēon
þurfan pret. pres. *need* pres 3s þearf 4/115, 14/117; 1p þurfe 12/34; 3p þurfon 12/249; pret 1s þorfte 4/5
þurh prep. *through, by, by means of* 2/72, 4/64, etc., þuruh 7/73, 9/21 (*in*), 9/27 (*in*)
þurhdrīfan I *pierce, drive through* pret 3p þurhdrifan 14/46
þurhflēon II *fly through* pres subj 3s þurhflēo 8/30
þurhwadan VI *pierce, pass through* pret 3s þurhwōd 12/296, 18(a)/890
þurhwunian 2 *persist* pret 3s þurhwunode 10(a)/7
þurstān pers. n. *Thurston* gs þurstānes 12/298
þuruh see þurh
þus adv. *thus, in this way, as follows* 2/44, 2/50, 2/77, 3/44, 3/176, etc.
þūsend num. *thousand* ns 7/24, 7/63
þwang m. *thong, strap* ap þwangas 3/153
*ge*þwǣre adv. *gently, obediently* 11(m)/6
*ge*þwǣrnes f. *concord, tranquillity* ns 3/207
þȳ see se
þȳ lǣs þe see lǣs
*ge*þyld f. *patience* as 18(b)/1395
*ge*þyldiġ adj. *patient* nsm 16/65
þynċan 1 (impersonal verb [§212] w.d.) *seem* inf þincean 18(b)/1341; pres 3s þyncþ 1/35, þincð 4/7, 4/26, þynceð 8/21, þinceð 12/55, 16/41; pret 3s þūhte 2/12, 4/4, 9/96, 11(c)/1, 12/66, 14/4, 18(a)/842; 3p þūhton 18(a)/866; p ptc geþūht 3/164 (biþ geþūht *will seem*), 3/187 (is geþūht *seems*), 3/191 [archaic MnE (me)thinks]
þȳrel n. *hole* as 3/205 [MnE (nos)tril]
þyslīċ pron. *such* ns 8/25
þȳstro n. *darkness* ds 11(c)/4, np 14/52
þȳwan 1 *drive, urge, goad* inf 3/15

ūhta m. or f. *period just before dawn* ds ūhtan 15/35; gp ūhtna 16/8

ūhtcearu f. *grief before dawn* as ūhtceare 15/7
ūhtsong m. *matins* as 9/113
unārīmed adj. *countless* dp unārīmedum 10(a)/10
unāsecgendlič adj. *unspeakable* ap unāsecgendlice 7/58
unbefohten adj. *unopposed, without a fight* npm unbefohtene 12/57
unbindan III *unbind, loosen* p ptc unbunden 11(h)/15
unc see wit
unclǣne adj. *unclean* npm 3/79; apm unclǣnan 3/80
uncūð adj. *unknown, strange* ns 5/78, 8/27; gsn uncūðes 18(a)/876 [MnE uncouth]
undēadlič adj. *immortal* nsf 1/33 [archaic MnE undeadly]
under prep. w.d.a. *under* 1/5, 2/35, 4/12, etc.
underbæc adv. *behind, back* 2/66
underbeğinnan III *undertake* infl inf (tō) underbeginnenne 4/8
underetan V *eat under, undermine* p ptc npf undereotone 13/6
underfēngon see underfōn
underfōn VII *accept* pret 3p underfēngon 7/61
understandan VI *understand* inf 4/15, 4/40, 4/75; infl inf (tō) understandenne 4/45; pres 3p understandað 4/25
underþēodan I *subject, devote* pret 3s underþēodde 8/16; p ptc underþēoded 9/84
unearh adj. *undaunted, not cowardly* npm unearge 12/206
unēaþe adv. *with difficulty, hardly* 3/139
unfæğer adj. *horrible* nsn 18(a)/727
unforcūð adj. *noble, of unblemished reputation* nsm 12/51
unforht adj. *unafraid* nsm 14/110; npm unforhte 12/79
unğehīrsum adj. *disobedient* nsm 4/120
unğelǣred adj. *unlearned, ignorant* np unğelǣredan 4/25; dp unğelǣredum 4/46
unğesǣlþ f. *misfortune* np unğesǣlða 7/73
unğesibb adj. *unrelated* dsm unğesibbum 11(k)/8
unhēanlīče adv. *not ignobly, valiantly* 6/14
unlifğende adj. *not living, dead* gsm unlyfiğendes 18(a)/744; asm unlyfiğendne 18(b)/1308; dsm unlifğendum 18(b)/1389
unlȳtel adj. *great, not little* nsm 18(a)/885; asn 18(a)/833
unmyltsiendlič adj. *unforgivable* ns 4/66
unnan pret. pres. w.d. of person and g. of thing *grant, allow* pret subj 3p ūþon 6/29
ğeunnan pret. pres. w.g. *grant* pres subj 3s geunne 12/176
unnyt adj. *useless* nsn 18(d)/3168

unorn adj. *simple, humble* nsm 12/256
unrǣd m. *ill advice, foolish policy* gs unrǣdes 11(f)/12; ap unrǣdas 7/73
unrihtwīs adj. *unjust, wicked* dsm unrihtwīsan 10(a)/18
unrīm n. *countless number* ns 10(b)/44
unrōt adj. *sad, despondent* nsm 10(a)/30
unryht adj. *unjust, wrongful* dp unryhtum 6/2 [MnE unright]
unstille adv. *not still, restlessly* 11(l)/5
unstilnes f. *disturbance* as unstilnesse 6/18 [MnE unstillness]
untrum adj. *infirm, sick* gp untrumra 9/91; compar. ap untrumran 9/91
untrymnes f. *infirmity* ds untrymnesse 9/88
unþinged adj. *unprepared for, unexpected* nsm 17/106
unwāclīče adv. *not weakly, bravely* 12/308
unwǣrlīče adv. *unawares* 3/44 [MnE unwar(i)ly]
unwearnum adv. *irresistibly* 17/63, 18(a)/741 (*eagerly, greedily*)
unweaxen adj. *not fully grown* nsm 12/152
unwillum adv. *unwillingly* 10(b)/24
unwrītere m. *inaccurate scribe* ns 4/125
ūp see ūpp
ūpāstīğnes f. *ascension* ds ūpāstīğnesse 9/76
ūpcyme m. *up-springing, ascendancy* as 11(o)/9
ūpgang m. *landing, passage to land* as 12/87
ūphēah adj. *lofty* npf ūphēa 15/30
ūplang adj. *upright* nsm 18(a)/759
ūpp adv. *up* 7/10, ūp 10(a)/2, 11(n)/5, 12/130, 14/71, 15/3, etc.
uppe adv. *up, above* 14/9
uppan prep. w.d. *upon, on* 2/46
ūprodor m. *the heavens above* as 17/105
ūre poss. adj. *our* nsm 3/184, 12/232, etc.; asm ūrne 4/87; asn 7/77; asf ūre 4/87; dsf 4/68; dpm ūrum 12/56; npm ūre 5/34; npn 8/19; gpn ūra 8/16; dpn ūrum 3/210; dpf 4/71
ūrigfeþra adj. *dewy-feathered* nsm 17/25
urnon see irnan
ūs see wē
ūsic see wē
ūt adv. *out* 1/28, 3/76, 3/77, 3/80, 5/8 (*outward*), etc.
ūtādrīfan I *drive out, expel* pres 2p ūtādrīfaþ 3/170, 3/176
ūtan adv. *from without, on the outside* 6/11, 18(a)/774, ūtene 7/31
ūtanbordes adv. *from abroad* 5/12
ūte adv. *outside, abroad* 3/145, 5/13, etc.
ūtene see ūtan
ūtgān anom. (§128) *go out* inf 3/8
ūtgong m. *exodus, emigration* ds ūtgonge 9/72
uton, wuton (1st pers. pl. subj. of wītan used w. inf) *let us* 3/206, 3/208, 4/68, 4/69, 17/117, 18(b)/1390, wuton 9/115

ūtweard adj. *turning outward, striving to escape* nsm 18(a)/761

ūþon see unnan

uuiþ see wiþ

Visionis see note to 2/45

wā m. *woe, affliction* ns waa 10(b)/25; as interj. 15/52; cf. wēa

wāc adj. *slender* asm wācne 12/43; *weak* nsm 16/67; compar. npm wācran (as noun) 17/87

wācian 2 *weaken, turn coward* inf 12/10

wacian 2 *watch, keep awake* pres ptc waciende 3/31 [MnE wake]

wadan VI *go, advance* inf 12/140, 16/5 (*travel*); pret 3s wōd 12/130, 12/253, 16/24, 18(a)/714; pret 3p wōdon 12/96, 12/295 [MnE wade]

ġewadan VI *pass, penetrate* pret 3p gewōd 12/157

wado see wæd

wāg m. *wall of a building* ns 13/9, ds wāge 11(j)/12

waldend see wealdend

waldendwyrhta m. *master builder, the king's builder* ap waldendwyrhtan 13/7

walo see wæl

wand see windan

wandian 2 *flinch, draw back* inf 12/258; pret 3p wandode 12/268

wanhygdig adj. *foolhardy, reckless* nsm 16/67

wanian 2 *diminish, lessen* pret 3s wanode 18(b)/1337

wāniġean 2 *bewail* inf 18(a)/787

wann adj. *dark, black* nsm won 16/103; nsn 18(b)/1374; nsf wann 14/55; dsf wanre 18(a)/702 [MnE wan]

warian 2 *attend, hold* pres 3s warað 16/32; 3p warigeað 18(b)/1358 (*guard, occupy, inhabit*)

warnian 2 *warn* inf 7/32

wāt see witan

ġewāt see ġewītan

waðum m. *wave* gp waðema 16/24, 16/57

wæċċan 2 *keep awake, watch* pres ptc wæccende 18(a)/708. See wacian

wæd n. *water, sea* ap wado 11(d)/2

wæd f. *clothing, covering* dp wēdum 11(k)/4, wǣdum 14/15, 14/22 [MnE (widow's) weeds]

wǣdbrēċ f. pl. *breeches* ap 2/16

wǣdian 2 *equip* p ptc gewǣdod 7/37

wǣfersȳn f. *spectacle* ds wǣfersȳne 14/31

wǣfre adj. *wandering* nsm 18(b)/1331

wǣg m. *wave* as 17/19; ap wēgas 16/46

wǣge n. *cup, flagon* as 18(c)/2253

wǣglīðend m. *seafarer* dp wǣglīðendum 18(d)/3158

wǣgun see wegan

wæl n. *slaughter, carnage* ns 7/15, 12/126, 12/303; as 7/37; ds wæle 12/279, 12/300 (*field of slaughter, battlefield*); np walo 13/25 (*slaughtered men, the slain*)

wælgǣst m. *murderous spirit* ns 18(b)/1331

wælgīfre adj. *greedy for slaughter* npn wælgīfru 16/100

wælhrēow adj. *fierce, cruel* nsm wælhrēowa 10(a)/24

wælrǣs m. *murderous conflict* ds wælrǣs 18(a)/824

wælrǣst f. *bed of death, death in battle* as wælrǣste 12/113

Wæls pers. n. *Wæls* gs Wælses 18(a)/897

Wælsing pers. n. *son of Wæls, i.e. Sigemund* gs Wælsinges 18(a)/877

wælsleaht m. *battle, slaughter* gp wælsleahta 16/7, 16/91

wælspere n. *deadly spear* as 12/322

wælstōw f. *place of slaughter, battlefield* gs wælstōwe 12/95, ds 12/293

wælwulf m. *wolf of slaughter* (*viking*) np wælwulfas np 12/96

wǣpen n. *weapon* ns 11(j)/1, 12/252; as 8/60, 8/63, 11(n)/12, 12/130, 12/235; gs wǣpnes 12/168; ds wǣpne 12/228; np wǣpen 16/100; gp wǣpna 12/83, 12/272, 12/308; dp wǣpnum 12/10 (tō wǣpnum fēng *took up arms*), 12/126

wǣpnedcynn n. *the male sex* gs wǣpnedcynnes 11(g)/1

wǣpnian 2 *arm* p ptc gewǣpnod 7/37

wǣre see bēon

wǣron see bēon

wǣrun (= wǣron) see bēon

wæs see bēon

wæstm m. *fruit, result* ds wæstme 2/4, 2/5; dp wæstmum 8/48, 18(b)/1352 (*growth, stature, form*)

wǣta m. *moisture, blood* ds wǣtan 14/22

wæter n. *water* as 1/2, 4/64, 12/91, 12/98, 18(b)/1364; ds wætere 12/64, 12/96, wætre 15/49; ap wæteru 4/61

wæterian 2 *water, give water to* inf 3/19; p ptc gewæterode 3/32

wē pron. *we* np 1/29, 2/5, 2/6, 4/45, etc.; ap ūsic *us* 17/123; dp ūs 1/32, 2/6, 3/140, 3/173, 3/197, etc.

wēa m. *woe, misery* gp wēana 18(b)/1396

weal m. *wall* ns 13/39, 16/98; ds wealle 16/80, 18(a)/785, 18(a)/891, 18(d)/3161; np weallas 16/76

wēalāf f. *survivors, woeful remnant* ns 10(b)/22

Wēalas m. pl. *Cornwall, Cornishmen* dp Wēalum 7/9

ġewealc n. *rolling, tossing* as 17/6, 17/46

ġeweald n. *control, dominion, power* as 4/123,

10(b)/38, 11(f)/14, 12/178, 14/107, 18(a)/
764, 18(a)/808

wealdan VII w.g. *wield, control* inf 12/83, 12/
95, 12/168, 12/272; pret 3p wīoldon 10(b)/
48 [MnE wield]

ġe**wealdan**VII *rule, control* pres 3s gewielt
2/35

wealdend m. *ruler, the Lord* ns 14/111, 14/155,
waldend 11(h)/6, Waldend 12/173; as 14/
67; gs wealdendes 14/17, 14/53; ds wealdende 14/121; np waldend 16/78

wealhstod m. *translator* ap wealhstodas 5/52

weallan VII *well, surge, boil* p ptc weallende
18(a)/847; pret 3s weol 18(a)/849

weallwala m. *wall-brace* ap weallwalan 13/20

wealstān m. *masonry* ns 13/1

wealsteal m. *foundation* as 16/88

weard m. *guardian* ns 9/42, 14/91, 17/54,
18(b)/1390; as 9/36 [MnE ward]

weardiġan 2 *occupy* pres 3p weardiað 15/34

wearoð m. *shore* as 10(b)/14

wearp see weorpan

wearþ see weorðan

wēaspel n. *tidings of woe* ds wēaspelle 18(b)/
1315

wēaþearf f. *grievous need* ds wēaþearfe 15/10

weaxan VII *grow* pret 3s wēox 10(b)/5 [MnE
wax]

Weċedport m. *Watchet (Somerset)* ns 7/14

wēdan 1 *be insane, rave* pret 3s wēdde 8/67

weder n. *wind, storm, (bad) weather* is wedre
11(o)/2

Wederas m. pl. *the Geats* gp Wedra 18(d)/
3156

wēdum see wǣd

weġ m. *way, path, road* as 14/88, 17/74, 18(a)/
763, 18(a)/844, 18(b)/1382; ap wegas 11(l)/6

wēgas see wǣg

wegan V *carry* inf 8/63; pres 3s wigeð
11(m)/3; 3p wegað 11(j)/14; subj 3s wege
18(c)/2252; pret 3p wǣgun 11(f)/3, wēgon
12/98 [MnE weigh]

weġnest n. *viaticum, provisions for a journey* isn
wegneste 9/111

wel adv. *well* 3/32, 3/69, 4/42, 9/63 *(readily)*,
well 14/129, etc.

wela m. *prosperity, riches* ns 16/74; as welan
5/35 [MnE weal]

weler m. *lip* ap weleras 4/111

welhold adj. *very kind* nsf 11(k)/4

welhwǣr adv. *well-nigh everywhere* 5/79

welhwylc pron., adj. *every (one)* gpm
welhwylcra 18(b)/1344; as noun asn
welhwylc *everything* 18(a)/874

weliġ adj. *rich, well-to-do* dsf welegan 10(b)/
37; dp weligum 3/133

wellan see willa

welm m. *fervour* ds welme 9/85

wēn f. *expectation* ns 18(a)/734

wēnan 1 *think, expect* inf 4/10; pres 1s wēne
5/17, 14/135 (ic wēne mē *I look forward to*),
18(b)/1396; pret 3s wēnde 10(b)/78, 10(b)/
82, 12/239; 3p wēndon 5/44, 7/51, 8/66,
18(a)/778 [archaic MnE ween]

wendan 1 *wend one's way, go, turn, translate* inf
5/43, 5/67, 12/316, 14/22; pres 1s went
(goes) 1/10; subj 1s wende 12/252; pret 3p
wendon 5/49, 12/193, 12/205

ġe**wendan** 1 *return* pres subj 2s gewende 2/41

wēndon see wēnan

wenian 1 *accustom* inf 16/29 *(entertain)*; pret 3s
wenede 16/36

went see wendan

wēofod n. *altar* as 2/57

wēop see wēpan

weorc n. *work, task, deed* ns 4/7; as 2/61,
9/38, 14/79; ds weorce 2/38; dp weorcum
4/43

ġe**weorc** n. *labour, workmanship, handiwork* ns
13/2; ds geweorce 3/196, 4/84; np geweorc
16/87

weorode see werod

weorpan III *throw, cast* pres 1s weorpe 3/76,
3/77, 3/80, 11(f)/7; pret 3s wearp 13/38
[MnE warp]

weorþ n. *worth, price* ds weorþe 3/144, 3/147

weorðan III *become* inf 5/45, 11(m)/10, 16/64,
wurðan 18(a)/807; pres 3s wierþst *(wilt
return)* 2/42; 3s weorþeð 16/110, 17/69; pret
3s wearþ 6/18, 11(k)/8, 12/186 (wearð . . .
on fleame *took to flight*), 12/295; 3p wurdon
13/27; w. p ptc forming passive (§202) inf
18(d)/3177; 3s wearð 12/106, 12/113, 12/
114, 12/116, 12/135, 12/138, etc.; 3p wurdon
2/15; subj 3s wurde 2/59, 12/1; p ptc
geworden 9/118, 14/87

ġe**weorðan** III *please* pres 3s gewyrð (impersonal: *it pleases*) 4/114

weorðe adj. *worthy, dear, valuable, in possession
of* nsm wyrðe 4/24, weorð 11(f)/1; gsn
wyrðes 9/47, 10(b)/67; nsf weorðe 8/37; np
wyrðe 10(a)/8, 10(b)/37; compar. nsm
wyrðra 18(a)/861

weorþian 2 *respect, honour* inf 3/208, 14/129;
pres 3p weorðiað 14/81

ġe**weorþian** 2 *honour, exalt* pret 3s
geweorðode 14/90, 14/94, geweorþade 17/
123; p ptc geweorðad 9/2, asm geweorðod
14/15

weorþlice adv. *splendidly, magnificently* 14/17;
superl. weorðlicost 18(d)/3161 [MnE
worthily]

weorðmynd f. *honour, dignity* gp weorðmynda
10(b)/51

weoruld see woruld

weoruldhāde see woruldhād

wēpan VII *weep* inf 10(a)/31, 15/38; pret 3s wēop 14/55

wer m. *man, husband* ns 11(a)/1, 16/64; as 18(d)/3172; gs weres 2/35, 18(b)/1352; ds were 2/14; np weras 11(b)/1, 11(j)/3, 11(j)/12, 11(o)/6; gp wera 3/166, 11(c)/3, 13/26, 17/21; dp werum 11(f)/1 [MnE were(wolf)]

wēr f. *covenant, pledge* dp wērum 17/110

werg m. *criminal* ap wergas 14/31

werian 1 *defend, protect* pret 3s werede 6/14; 1p weredon 18(b)/1327; 3p 12/82, 12/283

wēriġ adj. *weary, exhausted* nsm 17/29, nsn 16/15; asm wērigne 16/57; npm wērige 12/303

wēriġmōd adj. *disconsolate* nsm 15/49, 18(a)/844

werod n. *troop, company* ns 12/64, 12/97; as 12/102; ds werode 12/51, weorode 14/152; is werode 6/10, 14/69, werede 14/124; gp weruda 14/51

werþēod f. *people* gp werþēoda 13/9

weruda see werod

wesan anom. *be* inf 14/110, 14/117, 15/42, 18(b)/1328. See bēon

west adv. *west* 12/97

wēste adj. *deserted* nsm 16/74

wēsten n. *desert, wasteland* ds wēstene 4/82

wēstenstaþol m. *deserted place* ap wēsten-staþolas 13/27

Westseaxe m. pl. (§46) *West Saxons* gp West-seaxna 6/1, 7/63

wīc n. *abode* ns 15/32; ap 11(d)/2, 15/52, 18(a)/821

wiċċecræft m. *witchcraft* as 1/14

wicg n. *horse* ns wycg 11(j)/5, ds wicge 11(j)/14, 12/240

wīcian 2 *dwell* infl inf (tō) wīcianne 3/198

wīcing m. *viking* as 12/139; ap wīcingas 12/322; gp wīcinga 7/11, 12/26, 12/73, 12/97; dp wīcingum 12/116

wīd adj. *broad* apm wīdan 13/39; apm wīde 18(a)/877; compar. wīdre asm 18(a)/763

wīddor see wīde

wīde adv. *far, far and wide* 11(d)/5, 11(f)/1, 13/25, 14/81, 15/46, etc.; swā wīde swā *as far as* 7/57; compar. wīddor 11(k)/10; superl. wīdost *farthest, most widely* 17/57 [MnE wide]

ġewīdost adv. superl. *as far apart as possible* 15/13

ġewidre n. *weather, storm* ap gewidru 18(b)/1375

wīdwegas m. pl. *distant regions* ap 18(a)/840

wierþst see weorðan

wīf n. *woman, wife* ns 2/4, 2/11, 2/18, 2/24, 11(m)/5; as 3/149; gs wīfes 1/31, 2/36, 6/17; ds wīfe 2/2, 2/8, 2/31, 4/19, 17/45; np wif 11(o)/6; ap 4/16, 4/32; gp wīfa 4/20, 14/94; dp wīfum 11(a)/1

wīfcȳþþu f. *company or intimacy with a woman* ds wīfcȳþþe 6/10

Wīferþ pers. n. *Wiferth* ns 6/25

wīfian 2 *take a wife, marry* inf 4/21

wīġ n. *war, battle* ns 16/80; gs wīges 12/73, 12/130, 18(a)/886; ds wīge 5/9, 12/10, 12/128, 12/193, 12/235, 12/252, 18(b)/1337; is 10(b)/22

wīġa m. *warrior* ns 11(j)/1, 11(l)/6, 11(m)/1, 12/210, 16/67; as wīgan 12/75, 12/235; np 12/79, 12/126, 12/302; gp wīgena 12/135

wīġbed n. *altar* ap wīgbedo 8/47, wīgbed 8/54, 8/75

Wīgelin pers. n. *Wigelin* gs Wīgelines 12/300

wīġend m. *warrior* np 12/302

wigeð see wegan

wīġfruma m. *war-chief* ds wīgfruman 18(c)/2261

wīġhaga m. *battle-wall, wall of shields* as wīhagan 12/102

wīġheard adj. *hard in war, fierce* asm wīgheardne 12/75

wīġhyrst f. *war trappings* dp wīghyrstum 13/34

wīġplega m. *battle-play, fighting* ds wīgplegan 12/268, 12/316

wīġsteal n. *place of war, place of idols* (?) np 13/27

wīhagan see wīġhaga

wiht f. and n. *creature, being* ns 11(b)/1, 11(g)/6, 11(h)/2; as 11(g)/1; ap wuhte 11(l)/1 [archaic MnE wight]

wihte adv. *at all* 11(c)/6, wiht 18(a)/862 [MnE whit]

wiites see wīte

wilddēor n. *wild beast* np 3/63; ap 3/49, 3/50; gp wilddēora 3/43; dp wilddēorum 2/29

wile see willan

wilġehlēþ m. *familiar companion, comrade* ap wilgehlēþan 11(j)/5

willa m. *will, desire, pleasure, delight* ns 14/129, 18(a)/824; as willan 4/116; gp wilna 18(b)/1344

willan anom. *wish, desire, will* pres 1s wile 3/146, wille 12/221, 12/247, wylle 12/216, etc.; 2s wilt 3/95, 3/119, 3/144, wille 12/37; 3s wille 4/10, wile 12/52, wyle 4/22, etc.; 1p willað 12/35, 12/40; 3p 12/46; subj 2s wille 5/21; 3s 5/62; pret 2s woldest 2/65; 3s wolde 1/14, 2/43, 2/58, 2/61, etc.; 3p woldon 4/107, 7/50, 9/85; subj 3s wolde 16/28; 3p woldan 8/5. With negative: nyllan *be unwilling, will not* pres 1s nyle 3/125, 3/129, nelle 4/118, 11(h)/15, 12/246; 3s nyle 3/215, nille 17/99, nele 4/125; 3p nyllaþ 3/166, nellað 4/32, pret 2s noldest 2/72; 3s nolde 6/20, 7/74, 12/6, etc.; 1p noldon 5/38; 3p 12/81, 12/185, 12/201 wille f. *fountain* ds willan 8/5; ap wellan 11(g)/3 [MnE well]

wilnian 2 w.g. *desire, petition for* pret 3p wilnedon 10(b)/35

wilnung f. *desire* ds wilnunga 5/45

wilsumnes f. *devotion* ds wilsumnesse 9/119

wilt see willan

Wiltūnscīr f. *Wiltshire* ds Wiltūnscīre 7/72

wīn n. *wine* as 3/141; ds wīne 11(a)/1, 11(j)/17

ġewin see ġewinn

wind m. *wind* ns 18(b)/1374; ds winde 11(j)/14, 11(o)/1, 16/76

windan III *fly, wave, circle in the air* inf 12/322; pret 3s 12/43; pret 3p wundon 12/106

ġewindan III *go, turn* inf wīdre gewindan *reach a more remote place by flight* 18(a)/763

windiġ adj. *windy* apm windige 18(b)/1358

wine m. *friend, lord* ns 12/250, 15/49, 15/50; as 17/115; ap winas 12/228

winedryhten m. *beloved lord* as 12/248, 12/263, 18(d)/3175, wīnedrihten 18(a)/862; gs winedryhtnes 16/37

winelēas adj. *friendless* ns 15/10, 16/45

winemǣg m. *beloved kinsman* ap winemagas 12/306; gp winemǣga 16/7; dp winemagum 17/16

wīngāl adj. *flushed with wine* nsm 13/34, 17/29

ġewinn n. *war, strife* as gewinn 12/214, gewin 10(a)/1, 11(h)/2, 18(a)/798, 18(a)/877; ds gewinne 12/248, 12/302, 14/65 (*agony*)

winnan III *suffer, struggle, fight* pres ptc nsm winnende 11(l)/6; pret 1s wonn 15/5; 3p wunnon 18(a)/777 [MnE win]

ġewinnan III *conquer, win* inf 12/125; p ptc gewunnen 10(b)/17, 10(b)/28

winnende see winnan

wīnreced n. *wine hall* as 18(a)/714

wīnsǣl n. *hall* np wīnsalo 16/78

wīnsele m. *hall* ns 18(a)/771

Wintanċeaster f. *Winchester* as Wintanceastre 6/41

winter m. *winter, year* ns 3/10; as 3/154, 8/34, 17/15; gs wintres 8/32, 16/103; ds wintra 3/121, 8/33; gp wintra 6/7, 6/41, 10(b)/29, 16/65; ip wintrum 12/210

wintercearig adj. *desolate as winter* nsm wisa 16/24

wintersetl n. *winter quarters* as wintersetle 7/62

wintertīd f. *wintertime* ds wintertīde 8/28 [MnE wintertide]

wioldon see wealdan

wiotan see wita

wiotonne see witan

wīr m. *wire, metal rod* dp wīrum 13/20

wīrboga m. *twisted ornamental wire* ip wīrbogum 11(j)/3

wirċean see wyrċan

wīs adj. *wise* nsm wisa 3/186, 10(b)/51, 12/219, 16/64; asm wīsne 3/183, wīsan 18(b)/1318; dsm wīsan 4/58; apm wīse 5/52

ġewis adj. *aware* nsm 9/125; *trustworthy, unfailing* asn 17/110

wīsdōm m. *wisdom* ns 4/58; as 5/12, 5/23, etc.; ds wisdōme 5/9

wīse f. *way, manner, wise* as wisan 2/57, 2/60, 4/102, 4/105 (*idiom*), 9/58 (*subject-matter*), 9/85; ap 3/109; dp wīsum 17/110

wīse adv. *wisely, prudently* 16/88

wīsian 2 *guide* pret 3s wīsode 12/141

wīslīċ adj. *wise* nsn 8/21

ġewislīcost see ġewisslīċe

wisse see witan

wissian 2 *guide, instruct* inf 4/42; p ptc gewissod 3/184

ġewisslīċe adv. *certainly* 3/184; superl. gewislīcost 18(b)/1350

wist f. *feasting* ds wiste 16/36

Wīstān pers. n. *Wistan* ns 12/297

wiste see witan

wistfyllo f. *fill of feasting* gs wistfylle 18(a)/734

wit dual pron. *we two* n 11(e)/7, 15/13, 15/21; a unc 11(e)/2, 11(e)/7, 14/48, 15/12, 15/22; d unc (refl.) 2/51; g uncer 15/25

wita m. *wise man, counsellor*, pl. *the witan* ns 8/24, 16/65; np witan 7/27, 7/59, 10(b)/66, 18(a)/778, wiotan 5/3, 6/2; gp wiotena 5/41; dp wytum 8/4, witum 8/8, 10(a)/15

witan pret. pres. *know* inf 4/33; infl inf (tō) witanne 4/106, (tō) wiotonne 5/55; pres ptc np witende 2/11; pres 1s wāt 8/19, 16/11, 18(b)/1331; 3s 2/9, 12/94, 16/29, 16/37, etc.; subj. wite 18(b)/1367; pret 1s wiste 4/13; 3s 8/67, 12/24, 18(a)/764, 18(a)/821; 3p wiston 5/32, 9/106 (see note), etc.; subj. 3s wisse 16/27 (see note), 18(a)/715, 18(b)/1309. With negative: pret 3s nyste (*did not know*) 4/17

ġewitan pret. pres. *know, ascertain* inf 18(b)/1350

ġewītan I *depart* inf 17/52; pres 3s gewīteð 18(b)/1360; subj. 3s gewīte 8/31; pret 1s gewāt 9/30, 15/9; 3s 12/72, 12/150, 14/71, 15/6, 16/95; 3p gewitan 13/9, gewiton 14/133, 18(a)/853; p ptc npm gewitene 17/80, 17/86

wīte n. *punishment, torment* as 11(h)/6, 15/5; ds wīte 14/61; gs wiites 9/78; np wītu 5/24; gp wīta 14/87

ġewitenes f. *departure, death* gs gewitenesse 9/87

witod adj. *appointed, decreed, ordained* nsm 11(e)/7

wiþ prep. w.a.d. *against, in return for, from*

wiþ *(cont.)*
3/144, 3/146, 4/78, uuiþ 6/7, 7/53, 7/74, etc.; w.g. 12/8; wið þon (þām) þe *provided that* 7/60, 7/65

wiðerlēan n. *requital* ns 12/116

wiðfōn VII *lay hold on* pret 3s wiðfēng 18(a)/760

wiðhabban 3 w.d. *withstand, hold out against* pret 3s wiðhæfde 18(a)/772

wiðmetenes f. *comparison* ds tō wiðmetenesse w.g. *in comparison with* 8/27

wiðsacan VI w.d. *renounce, forsake* inf 8/51

wiðstondan VI *withstand* inf 16/15

wlanc adj. *proud, splendid* nsm wlonc 11(j)/1, 13/34, 17/29, wlanc 18(b)/1332; asm wlancne 12/139, wloncne 11(m)/10; dsn wlancan 12/240; nsf wlonc 16/80; npm wlance 12/205, wlonce 11(o)/6; apm wlonce 11(j)/17

wlætta m. *nauseating substance* ds wlættan 3/165

wlenco f. *prosperity, riches* gp wlencea 10(b)/76

wlītan I *look* pret 3s wlāt 12/172

wlitiġ adj. *beautiful* nsm 11(j)/12; nsn 2/12

wlitiġian 2 *brighten, make beautiful* pres 3p wlitigiað 17/49

wlonc see wlanc

wōd see wadan

wōdon see wadan

wōg n. *error* as wōh 4/125; ds wōge 4/123

wōh see wōg

wōh adj. *curved, bent, twisted* ipm wōum 11(j)/3

wolcen m. or n. *cloud, sky* gp wolcna 11(d)/5; dp wolcnum 10(b)/76, 14/53, 14/55, 18(a)/714, 18(b)/1374 [archaic MnE welkin]

wōldæg m. *day of pestilence* np wōldagas 13/25

wolde see willan

wom m. *sin, iniquity* dp wommum 14/14

wōma m. *tumult* ns 16/103

womb f. *womb, belly* as wombe 11(b)/5

won see wann

wong m. *ground* as 13/31; ap wongas 17/49 (*fields, meadows*)

wonn see winnan

wōp n. *weeping, lamentation* as 18(a)/785

word n. *word* as 12/168, 14/35; ds worde 14/111; ap word 8/1, 8/41, 9/35, 9/46, 9/56, 11(c)/1, etc.; gp worda 10(b)/81; dp wordum 4/75, 5/1, 8/24, etc.

wordġyd n. *lay, elegy* as 18(d)/3172

ġeworhte see ġewyrċan

wōrian 2 *decay, moulder* pres 3s wōrað 13/12, wōriað 16/78

worn m. *large number* as 16/91, 18(a)/870

woruld f. *world* ns 17/49; as 16/58, weoruld 16/107, 17/87; gs worulde 4/18, 9/8, 15/46, 16/74, worolde 18(b)/1387; ds worulde

4/113, 5/25, 9/94, 12/174, 14/133, etc., weorulde 10(b)/51

woruldcræft m. *secular occupation* ns 3/191

woruldcund adj. *secular* gpm woruldcundra 5/4

woruldcyning m. *earthly king* gp wyruldcyninga 18(d)/3180

woruldġesǣliġ adj. *prosperous, happy* nsm 12/219

woruldhād m. *secular life* as 9/62; ds weoruldhāde 9/18

woruldrīċe n. *kingdom of the world, the whole world* ds 15/13, 16/65

woruldsǣlþa f. pl. *worldly prosperity* dp woruldsǣlþum 10(a)/28

woruldþēaw m. *worldly custom* dp woruldþēawum 10(a)/13

woruldþing n. *worldly affair* gp woruldðinga 5/22

wōum see wōh

wrāh see wrēon

wrāð adj. *hostile, cruel, angry* dsm wrāþum 18(a)/708; gp wrāðra 14/51, 16/7; dpm wrāþum 11(j)/17

wrāðe adv. *cruelly, fiercely* 10(a)/9, 15/32 [MnE wroth]

wræce m. *wanderer, exile* ns 15/10; gs wræccan 17/15

wræclāst m. *path of exile* ns 16/32; ap wræclāstas 16/5, 17/57, 18(b)/1352

wræcsīð m. *misery* ap wræcsīðas 15/38; gp wræcsīða 15/5

wrǣtliċ adj. *wondrous, strange, splendid* nsm 11(h)/2, 13/1; asm wrǣtlicne 18(a)/891; asn wrǣtlic 11(n)/3; nsf wrǣtlicu 11(c)/2; asf wrǣtlice 11(l)/1

wrecan V *utter* inf 17/1, 18(a)/873, 18(d)/3172; pres 1s wrece 15/1

wrecan V *avenge* inf 12/248, 12/258, 18(b)/1339; pres subj. 3s wrece 18(b)/1385; pret 3s wræc 6/5, 18(b)/1333, wrec 12/279; subj. 3s wrǣce 12/257 [MnE wreak]

ġewrecan V *avenge* inf 12/208, 12/263

wrēgan I *accuse* pres 3p wrēgað 4/74

wrēon I *cover, wrap* pres 3s wrīð 11(m)/5; pret 3s wrāh 11(k)/5

wreotan see wrītan

ġewrit n. *writing, writ* as 5/61, 5/65; gs gewrites 9/74

wrītan I *write* 1p wrītað 4/45; pret 3p wreoton 9/70

writere m. *writer* ds 4/100

wrīð see wrēon

wrixendlīċe adv. *in turn* 9/107

wrixlan 1 w.d. *change, exchange, vary* inf 18(a)/874

ġewrohtan see ġewyrċan

wudu m. *wood, forest, tree* ns 2/55, 11(n)/16,

14/27, 18(b)/1364; as 2/52, 2/58, 12/193; ds wuda 3/122; dp wudum 3/64; gp wuda 15/27

wudutrēow n. *forest tree* as 11(n)/3

wuhte see **wiht**

wuldor n. *glory* gp wuldres 14/14, 14/90, 14/97, 14/133, 17/123; ds wuldre 11(o)/2, 14/135, 14/143, 14/155

Wuldorfœder m. *Father of Glory, God* gs 9/38

wulf m. *wolf* ns 16/82; np wulfas 3/25

Wulfgār pers. n. *Wulfgar* ns 7/19

wulfheafedtrēo n. *gallows, cross* as 11(n)/12

wulfhliþ n. *wolf-slope, retreat of wolves* ap wulfhleoþu 18(b)/1358

Wulfmǣr pers. n. *Wulfmær* ns 12/113, 12/155; as Wulmær 12/183

Wulfstān pers. n. *Wulfstan* ns 12/75; gs Wulfstānes 12/155; ds Wulfstāne 12/79

wund f. *wound* as wunde 12/139, 12/271; dp wundum 12/293, 12/303

wund adj. *wounded* nsm 12/113, 12/144

wunden adj. *twisted* nsn 16/32; asn 11(n)/3; dsn wundnum 18(b)/1382

*ġe*wundian 2 *wound* pret 3s gewundode 6/15; p ptc gewundad 6/22, 6/40, gewundod 12/135

wundon see **windan**

wundor n. *wonder* ns 18(a)/771; as 11(c)/2, 18(a)/840; gp wundra 9/38; dp wundrum as adv. *astonishingly, wonderfully* 11(m)/1, 13/20, 16/98

wundorliċ adj. *remarkable, wonderful* nsf 1/19; dsm wunderlicum 4/81

wundrian 2 *wonder, marvel at* pret 1s wundrade 5/40; 3s wundrode 9/95

wundrum see **wundor**

wunian 2 *dwell, subsist, occupy* inf 3/154, 14/121, 14/143, 15/27; pres 1s wunige 11(e)/6; 3p wuniaþ 3/64, 14/135, 17/87; pret 1s wunade 17/15; 3s wunode 6/3, wunade 6/4; 3p wunedon 14/3, 14/155

*ġe*wunian 2 *remain, be accustomed to* inf gewunigan 10(b)/37; pret 3s gewunade (*was accustomed to*) 9/2; p ptc gewunod 10(a)/28

wuniġe see **wunian**

wuolde (= wolde) see **willan**

wurdon see **weorðan**

wurðan see **weorðan**

wurðlīċe adv. *worthily, honourably* 12/279

wuton see **uton**

wycg see **wicg**

wyle see **willan**

wylm m. *surge* ds wylme 13/39

wyn see **wynn**

wynlēas adj. *joyless* apn 18(a)/821

wynliċ adj. *delightful* compar. apn wynlicran 15/52

wynn f. *benefit, joy* ns wyn 15/46, 16/36, 17/45,

18(c)/2262; as wyn 17/27; gp wynna 12/174, 15/32; dp wynnum 14/15 (as adv. *beautifully*), 16/29

wynsum adj. *delightful* npm wynsumu 9/69 [MnE winsome]

wyrċan 1 *make, form, produce* inf 9/3, 9/11, etc., wircean 4/69; pres ptc wircende 7/58; pres 1s wyrce 3/152, 3/203; 2s wyrcst 3/150; subj. 3s wyrce 18(b)/1387; pret 3s worhte 4/56; 3p worhton 2/16, worhtan 7/23, wrohton 7/54 [MnE work, wrought]

*ġe*wyrċan 1 *make, form* inf 12/81, 12/264; pres subj. 3s gewyrce 17/74 (*accomplish*); pret 3s geworhte 1/37, 2/2, 4/53, 9/80; 3p geworhton 14/31, 18(d)/3156, gewrohtan 7/41; p ptc geworht 9/7, asm geworhtne 17/115 (his geworhtne wine *the friend he has made*)

wyrd f. *fate, events* ns 10(b)/29, 11(c)/2, 13/24, 14/74, 16/5, 16/100, 17/115, 18(a)/734; ds wyrde 16/15; np wyrde 13/1; gp wyrda 14/51, 16/107 [MnE weird]

wyrdan 1 *injure, destroy* pret 3s wyrde 18(b)/1337

wyrhta m. *workman* np wyrhtan 3/206; dp wyrhtum 3/210 [MnE wright]

wyruldcyninga see **woruldcyning**

wyrm m. *worm, serpent, dragon* ns 11(c)/3, 18(a)/897; as 18(a)/886, 18(a)/891

wyrman 1 *warm* p ptc gewyrmed 8/29

wyrmliċ n. *serpent shape, serpentine pattern* dp wyrmlicum 16/98

wyrnan 1 w.g. *withhold* pret 3s wyrnde 12/118

wyrp f. *change (for the better)* as wyrpe 18(b)/1315

wyrs adv. (compar. of yfele) *worse* þȳ wyrs (*by so much*) the worse 10(b)/76

wyrt f. *herb, plant, vegetable* ap wyrta 2/40, 3/170; gp 3/162; dp wyrtum 18(b)/1364 [MnE wort]

wyrtġemang n. *mixture of herbs and spices, unguent* as 3/141

*ġe*wyrð see *ġe*weorðan

wyrðe see **weorðe**

wytum see **wita**

ȳcan 1 *increase, cause to grow* inf 11(o)/9 [MnE eke (out)]

yfel adj. *evil* gs yfeles 12/133; asf yfelan 1/37

yfel n. *evil, harm* ns 10(b)/55; as 2/11, 4/125, 7/41, etc.; ap 7/58, 10(a)/14; dp yflum 10(a)/10

yfele adv. *ill, badly* 10(a)/9

ylcan see **ilca**

yldan 1 *delay* inf 18(a)/739

yldu f. *age, old age* ns yldo 17/70, 17/91; gs ylde 9/19; ds ældo 13/6

yldum see **ælde**

ylfetu f. (*wild*) *swan* gs ylfete 17/19

ymb prep. w.a. *about, concerning, with regard to, after* 3/65, 5/10, 6/7, 6/36, embe 12/249, 12/271, etc.

ymbclyppan 1 *embrace* pret 3s ymbclypte 14/42

ymbsettan 1 *surround* p ptc ymbsette 8/55

yrhðo f. *cowardice* as 12/6

Yrmenlāf pers. n. *Yrmenlaf* gs Yrmenlāfes 18(b)/1324

yrmþu f. *hardship* gp yrmþa 15/3

yrnan see irnan

yrre n. *anger* as 18(a)/711

yrre adj. *angry* nsm 12/44, 12/253; npm 18(a)/769

yrremōd adj. *angry* nsm 18(a)/726

ys (= is) see bēon

ȳtmæst adj. *last* ap ȳtmæstan 9/122 [MnE utmost]

ȳþ f. *wave* as ȳþe 11(l)/5, 11(p)/4; gp ȳþa 15/7, 17/6, 17/46, 18(a)/848

ȳþan 1 *lay waste, destroy* pret 3s ȳþde 16/85

ȳþġeblond n. *commingling of the waves, surge* ns 18(b)/1373

ȳwe see īewan

Indexes to Part One

INDEX OF WORDS

The references are to the numbered sections.
The letters LV mean that the word in question will be found in 'Learning the Vocabulary' in the section 'How to Use this Guide'.
The abbreviations n. and fn. stand for 'Note' and 'Footnote' respectively.

æ follows *a*, *þ* follows *t*.
ċ is to be found under *c*, *ġ* under *g*, and *ð* under *þ*.
ġe- is ignored, so that *ġemunan* appears under *m*.

Nouns, adjectives, and pronouns, will be found under the nominative singular, and verbs under the infinitive. Verbs discussed in Appendices A and B only are excluded.

You may find it useful to remember that lists of conjunctions used in adverb clauses are given in §168 (non-prepositional) and §171 (prepositional).